THE CAMBRIDGE
ANCIENT HISTORY

VOLUME IX

THE CAMBRIDGE ANCIENT HISTORY

SECOND EDITION

VOLUME IX

The Last Age of the Roman Republic, 146–43 B.C.

edited by

J. A. CROOK

Fellow of St John's College and
Emeritus Professor of Ancient History, Cambridge

ANDREW LINTOTT

Fellow and Tutor in Ancient History,
Worcester College, Oxford

The late ELIZABETH RAWSON

Formerly Fellow and Tutor in Ancient History,
Corpus Christi College, Oxford

CAMBRIDGE
UNIVERSITY PRESS

Published by the Press Syndicate of the University of Cambridge
The Pitt Building, Trumpington Street, Cambridge CB2 1RP
40 West 20th Street, New York, NY 10011-4211, USA
10 Stamford Road, Oakleigh, Melbourne 3166, Australia

First published 1994

Printed in Great Britain at the University Press, Cambridge

A catalogue record for this book is available from the British Library

Library of Congress Catalogue card number: 75-85719

ISBN 0 521 25603 8 hardback

SE

CONTENTS

List of maps *page* xi

List of text-figures xi

Preface xiii

PART I

1 The crisis of the Republic: sources and source-problems 1
by ANDREW LINTOTT
I Ancient theories about the late Republic 6
II Modern interpretations of the late Republic 10

2 The Roman empire and its problems in the late second century 16
by ANDREW LINTOTT
I Spain 20
II Gaul 23
III Sicily 25
IV Africa 27
V Macedonia and Greece 31
VI Asia 33
VII Military strength and the empire 36

3 Political history, 146–95 B.C. 40
by ANDREW LINTOTT
I The Roman constitution in the second century B.C. 40
II The agrarian problem and the economy 53
III Politics after the fall of Carthage 59
IV Tiberius Gracchus 62
V Caius Gracchus 77
VI The aristocracy and Marius 86
VII Marius and the *equites* 90
VIII Generals and tribunes 92

4 Rome and Italy: the Social War 104
by E. GABBA, *Istituto di Storia Antica, Università degli Studi, Pavia*

5 Mithridates 129
by JOHN G. F. HIND, *Lecturer in Ancient History, School of History, University of Leeds*
I The dynasty 130
II The kingdom 133
III Mithridates' Black Sea empire 137
IV Kings and Romans in western Anatolia, 108–89 B.C. 140
V Threats and bluffs 143
VI Mithridates' conquest of Asia, 89–88 B.C. 144
VII Overreach 149
VIII Athens, Delos and Achaea 150
IX The sieges of Athens and Piraeus 153
X The battles in Boeotia 154
XI Reaction in Asia, 86 B.C. 159
XII The Treaty of Dardanus, the fate of Asia and the felicity of Sulla 161

6 Sulla 165
by ROBIN SEAGER, *Reader in Classics and Ancient History, University of Liverpool*
I Sulla, Sulpicius and Marius, 88 B.C. 165
II *Cinnanum tempus*, 87–84 B.C. 173
III The civil war, 83–81 B.C. 187
IV Sulla's dictatorship and its aftermath, 82–78 B.C. 197

7 The rise of Pompey 208
by ROBIN SEAGER
I The revolt of Lepidus, 78–77 B.C. 208
II Politics at Rome, 77–71 B.C. 210
III The wars against Sertorius and Spartacus, 79–71 B.C. 215
IV The first consulship of Pompey and Crassus, 70 B.C. 223

8*a* Lucullus, Pompey and the East 229
by A. N. SHERWIN-WHITE, *Formerly Reader in Ancient History, University of Oxford*
I Preliminary operations: Murena and Servilius 229
II The opening of the Third War 233
III The campaign in Pontus 237
IV Lucullus in Armenia 239
V Lucullus and the cities 244
VI Pompey in the East 248
VII The end of Mithridates 254
VIII The Caucasian campaigns 255
IX The organization of gains and the annexation of Syria 258
X Pompey in Judaea and Nabatene 260
XI Parthia and Rome 262
XII The eastern settlement of Pompey 265
XIII Gabinius and the aftermath of Pompey 271

8b The Jews under Hasmonean rule 274
by TESSA RAJAK, *Reader in Classics, University of Reading*
I The period 274
II The sources 277
III The emergence of Judaea as a Hellenistic state 280
IV Territorial expansion 287
V Conquest and Judaization 291
VI Hellenization and the image of the Hasmonean ruler 296
VII Divisions in Jewish thought and society 299

8c Egypt, 146–31 B.C. 310
by DOROTHY J. THOMPSON, *Fellow and Lecturer in Ancient History, Girton College, Cambridge*
I The later Ptolemies 310
II Egypt: society and economy 322

9 The Senate and the *populares*, 69–60 B.C. 327
by T. P. WISEMAN, *Professor of Classics, University of Exeter*
I *Lustrum* 327
II The tribunes 329
III Pompey's absence 338
IV The peasants' revolt and the bankrupts' plot 346
V Return of the hero 358

10 Caesar, Pompey and Rome, 59–50 B.C. 368
by T. P. WISEMAN
I Caesar and Clodius 368
II The conquest of Gaul 381
III Egypt and Parthia 391
IV *Fin de siècle* 403
V The reconquest of Gaul 408
VI The final crisis 417

11 Caesar: civil war and dictatorship 424
by the late ELIZABETH RAWSON
I The civil war 424
II The dictatorship 438

12 The aftermath of the Ides 468
by the late ELIZABETH RAWSON

PART II

13 The constitution and public criminal law 491
by DUNCAN CLOUD, *Associate Senior Lecturer in the School of Archaeological Studies, University of Leicester*
I The Roman constitution 491

II *Ius publicum* 498
III *Quaestiones perpetuae* 505

14 The development of Roman private law 531
by J. A. CROOK

15 The administration of the empire 564
by JOHN RICHARDSON, *Professor of Classics, University of Edinburgh*
I Provinces and *provinciae*: the origins of the system 564
II The basis and limits of the governor's power 572
III The governor at work 580
IV Taxation 585
V Jurisdiction 589
VI The *provinciae* and the provincials 591
VII *Provinciae*, provinces and empire: the beginnings of a change in perceptions 593

16 Economy and society, 133–43 B.C. 599
by C. NICOLET, *Professor at the Sorbonne (Paris I)*
I Context: geography and demography 600
II Italian agriculture 609
III Industry and manufacture 623
IV Commerce and money 627
V Economy and society 640

17 The city of Rome and the *plebs urbana* in the late Republic 644
by NICHOLAS PURCELL, *Fellow and Tutor in Ancient History, St John's College, Oxford*

18 The intellectual developments of the Ciceronian age 689
by MIRIAM GRIFFIN, *Fellow and Tutor in Ancient History, Somerville College, Oxford*
I Education 690
II Social setting 692
III Hellenization 696
IV Scholarship and science 701
V Pythagoreanism 707
VI The new poetry 710
VII History and related studies 711
VIII Cicero's theoretical works 715
IX Cicero and Roman philosophy 721

19 Religion 729
by MARY BEARD, *Lecturer in Ancient History, and Fellow of Newnham College, Cambridge*
I The constants 729
II Sources of evidence and the problems of comparison 734

III Political and religious disruption 739
IV Neglect and adaptation 742
V Competition, opposition and the religion of the *populares* 745
VI Political dominance and deification: the divine status of Caesar and its antecedents 749
VII The differentiation of religion 755
VIII Roman religion and the outside world 763

Epilogue 769
by J. A. CROOK, ANDREW LINTOTT and ELIZABETH RAWSON

Stemmata 777

Chronological table 780

BIBLIOGRAPHY

Abbreviations *page* 799

A General studies 807
B Sources 811
 a. Literary sources 811
 b. Epigraphy and numismatics 816
 c. Archaeology 821
C Political history 824
 a. 146–70 B.C. 824
 b. 70–43 B.C. 829
D The East 835
 a. Mithridatica 835
 b. The Jews 838
 c. Egypt 842
 d. Other eastern matters 845
E The West 847
F The law 849
 a. Public law and criminal law 849
 b. Private law 855
G Economy and society 861
H Religion and ideas 871

Index 878

NOTE ON THE BIBLIOGRAPHY

The bibliography is arranged in sections dealing with specific topics, which sometimes correspond to individual chapters but more often combine the contents of several chapters. References in the footnotes are to these sections (which are distinguished by capital letters) and within these sections each book or article has assigned to it a number which is quoted in the footnotes. In these, so as to provide a quick indication of the nature of the work referred to, the author's name and the date of publication are also included in each reference. Thus 'Syme 1952 (A 118) 100' signifies 'R. Syme, *The Roman Revolution*, 2nd edn, Oxford, 1952, p. 100', to be found in Section A of the bibliography as item 118.

MAPS

1	The Roman world about 118 B.C.	*page* 18
2	Italy and Sicily	42
3	Central Italy	117
4	The Pontic area	134
5	Asia Minor	138
6	Central Greece	152
7	Latium	188
8	Spain	216
9	The East	230
10	Judaea	276
11	Egypt	312
12	Gaul	382
13	Italy	426
14	The Roman world in 50 B.C.	566

TEXT-FIGURES

1	Rome in the last two centuries of the Republic	71
2	The centre of Rome in the late Republic	370

PREFACE

Historical divisions are arbitrary, and beginnings and endings necessary but misleading. The present volume has for its main theme the process commonly known as the 'Fall of the Roman Republic', and there are good reasons for beginning the narrative of that process with the tribunate of Tiberius Gracchus in 133 B.C. But the traumas of the Republic that then began had an intelligible background, and we have explored it, as was foreshadowed in the preface to Vol. VIII², by beginning our analysis at 146 B.C., the year of the destruction of Carthage and Corinth, which the Romans regarded as the apogee of their fortunes. Indeed, especially in the chapter on Roman private law, which, beyond the Twelve Tables, has not been dealt with in any earlier volume, we have harked back unashamedly as far as seemed needful. As for an end-point, the death of Cicero on 7 December 43 B.C. was chosen in preference to the Ides of March 44, partly because symbols are as important as events, and Cicero's death symbolizes, now as it did then, the demise of the Republic, and partly because the greatest of all the pieces of luck that launched the young C. Iulius Caesar ('Octavian') on his course to domination was the death of both the consuls of 43 B.C. in the action against Antony: Octavian's usurping entry into the consulship on 19 August 43 is the second most symbolic date in the funeral annals of the Republic.

In accordance with a trend that it is now well-nigh banal to cite, somewhat less space and weight are devoted in this volume than in Vol. IX of the original *CAH* to close narrative of political and military events, and somewhat more to 'synchronic' analyses of society, institutions and ideas; but we have not banished 'l'histoire événementielle', for it would have been absurd to do so. In the first place, narrative is an entirely valid historical genre in its own right, giving its own particular satisfaction to the reader, and, in the second, a work of this character will be expected to furnish a reliable account of public events. Finally, though the time has unquestionably come to make generally available some of the fruits of the past fifty years of scholarly cultivation of the terrain of socio-economic and intellectual history, we have seen it as our task here to assist in building some bridges between that terrain and the political history of Rome. For a very important question, to say the least, about the last century of the Republic is how its social, economic, legal, intellectual, religious and even architectural changes or resistances to change were related to the story of political change or failure to change, and so of civil strife, dictatorship and collapse – whether helping to determine that process or responding and corresponding to it. If it is thought that by dividing our volume, accordingly, into two parts we have deepened the chasm rather than created any bridge, we plead that we have given readers the best construction-kit we could, on both sides, for building their own.

A brief survey of the narratives in Part I may help the reader to appreciate its intended structure. Andrew Lintott sets the scene in chapter 1, which has two themes. The first is a critical sketch of the evidence for the period – not an exhaustive 'conspectus of sources', which would have taken too much space and of whose likely helpfulness we were sceptical. The second is about theories: theorizing about the 'Crisis of the Roman Republic' began contemporaneously with the events, and has been done ever since, sometimes by the most eminent of political philosophers and historians; and because history is an argumentative and philosophical subject the search for underlying principles, structures and explanations is renewed in each generation, and readers may expect to learn something about the answers given in previous generations before they read on and begin to make up their own minds. Lintott continues in chapter 2 with a survey of Rome's overseas empire and its problems in the years from 146 onward: settlement and acquisition of land abroad by Roman citizens; Spain and Gaul and the rapid penetration of the West by Roman ways of dealing with things; Sicily and social unrest; the province of Africa and its relationship to the kingdom of Numidia, leading to the story of the Jugurthine War; the new province of Macedonia and the partial integration of mainland Greece with it; the beginnings of the province of Asia out of the bequeathed kingdom of Pergamum, its attempt under Aristonicus to reject the Roman yoke and its influx of Romans and Italians 'on the make'; and, finally, the nature and strength of the Roman army and the demands made on it.

Chapter 3, again by Lintott, begins the main narrative with the internal political history of Rome in the fifty years 146 to 95 B.C., prefaced by analysis of that elusive entity the 'Roman Constitution' (really the traditions on which politics normally worked) and of the nature of Roman political life – how far it was a game played only by teams of leading families, and so on. (It is here that the reader will learn why 'faction' is to play less of a role in what follows than historians have given it in the recent past.) Then comes the agrarian crisis of Italy and all that led up to the Gracchi, including the tribunician legislation of the years following 146; and that is followed by the central narrative of the Gracchi, Marius, and Saturninus and Glaucia. In chapter 4, E. Gabba narrates the origins of the demand of Rome's Italian *socii* for admission to Roman citizenship and the 'Social War' of 91–89 B.C. by which, in the end, they achieved their demand, after which Rome was no longer a 'city state' and its citizen population was more widespread and differently constituted – events whose consequences were, arguably, the real 'Roman Revolution'. (In fact, the integration of Italy, a theme of the first importance embracing the early Principate as well as the late Republic, will receive appropriate treatment in the new edition of Volume x.)

Chapter 5 is an account by John G. F. Hind of the principal subplot to the drama of the late Republic, one such as no human dramatist could have contrived more satisfactorily to entwine with the central political tale: the story of the last larger-than-life-sized Hellenistic monarch, Mithridates VI Eupator of Pontus, and his conflicts with Rome; this chapter takes the story down to the end of the first episode in the conflict, the Peace of Dardanus in 85 B.C.

Chapters 6 and 7 revert to internal political narrative, told by Robin Seager: in chapter 6 the rise and dictatorship of Sulla, who attempted to shore up the traditional political order but by his own precedent hastened its downfall, and in chapter 7 the rise of Pompey down to his first consulship with Crassus in 70 B.C.

In the first part of chapter 8, A. N. Sherwin-White tells the later part of the saga of Mithridates and Rome, relating the campaigns of Lucullus and his efforts to relieve the economic distress of the province of Asia, followed by the triumphant eastern progress of Pompey, which hugely extended Roman power in the East and involved Rome for the first time with Parthia and Judaea. That is the cue for Tessa Rajak to give, in the second part of the chapter, an account of the Maccabees and the Hellenization of Judaea under their rule. The third part is devoted to a final eastern subplot, told by Dorothy J. Thompson: the politics, society and culture of Egypt in the time of the later Ptolemies, now in the shadow of Rome, their story culminating in that other grandly doomed Hellenistic monarch, Cleopatra VII Thea Philopator.

The two decades of Roman internal political débâcle are consigned to T.P. Wiseman: chapter 9 the sixties B.C. and chapter 10 the fifties, that period of great complexity because there is, for once, abundant evidence, with all the politics that led to the civil war between Pompey and Julius Caesar. Caesar, from the Rubicon to the Ides of March, is taken over in chapter 11 by Elizabeth Rawson, and she continues the story in chapter 12 to the death of Cicero.

Part II comprises seven chapters and an epilogue. The chapters work outwards, as it were, from the political story: law and administration, economy and the rise of the great conurbation of the city of Rome, and then ideas and their background, and finally religion. In accordance with the overall policy of the new *CAH*, no express account is here attempted of the *belles-lettres* of the last century of the Republic, important though the Roman achievement in literature undoubtedly is to a rounded understanding of the period: Volume II of the *Cambridge History of Classical Literature* now claims that domain. Nor will any attempt be found here to assess the intellectual and spiritual life of the non-Roman peoples of the age: the editors have sadly to report that A. Momigliano was to have contributed a final chapter that would have added substance to that aspect of the period as well as distinction to the volume. His death having deprived us of the chapter at a fairly late stage, we decided that nothing by any other hand could, or ought to, replace it.

Duncan Cloud, then, in chapter 13, handles two themes of Roman public law. The first concerns developments in the 'Roman Constitution' in the last age of the Republic, a subject about which there is, in fact, rather less to say than the reader might expect. The second theme, however, is the rapid development, from minimal beginnings, of a major system of criminal law courts, one of the striking achievements of the age, and only too appropriate to a period of such vertiginous change in political and social behaviour. In chapter 14, J. A. Crook attempts, first, to sketch the rules of law that to some degree framed and structured Roman society in the late Republic, and then to characterize the developments the law underwent and the part played by such factors as Greek philosophy in influencing those developments. Cloud and Crook have sought to evaluate and criticize Roman law as well as describe it, because its strengths and weaknesses, successes and limitations are closely relevant to many aspects of economy, society, ideas and even politics.

John Richardson begins chapter 15 by showing how administration of a territorial empire was not within the thought-world of the Romans in the earlier Republic: they thought, rather, in terms of tasks distributed amongst officials – mostly, in fact, military commands. Administration was something the Romans learnt the hard way, and the late Republic was their schooling period. The chapter continues with analysis of the powers and duties of Roman administrators and of the mechanisms set up by the Romans to meet overseas responsibilities that they only came to recognize *post hoc*: one of the links between law and politics is that the machinery set up to curb excessive power and corruption of officials could all too easily be used as the forum for the pursuit of political enmities.

Natural transition joins C. Nicolet (chapter 16), whose theme is the expanding economy of Rome and Italy and its impact on the economies of Rome's subject states, to Nicholas Purcell, who in chapter 17 puts into the dossier the city of Rome itself, already huge in population and constituting of itself a major economic influence; and in that case, too, we come back to politics, for the Roman plebs, less and less entitled to claim itself to be the essential community of Roman citizens but more and more coherent as a new force in politics, is a crucial part of the story of the Republic's last years.

Miriam Griffin, in chapter 18, progresses from the social setting of Roman intellectual life, education, patronage, libraries and so forth, to some of its characteristic products, particularly philosophy, and then back to the social dimension, with a discussion of how much such activities meant to the Roman elite who took them up with such relish. Finally, Mary Beard, in chapter 19, intertwines the spheres of religion and politics as the Romans themselves did, replacing the stereotype of 'decline of religion in the late Republic' by a new perception of how religious and political changes belong together in a single story of change and response to change.

The brief epilogue is the joint work of all three editors.

As concerns references to evidence the contributors have followed the policy requested of them by the editors, following, in their turn, the general policy laid down for the new *CAH*: that is to say, they have not given footnotes for uncontroversial matter derived from standard sources but have indicated anything that is heterodox or in need of particular justification in their accounts. The editors have, however, seen no need to be doctrinaire, and subjects have been allowed, within reason, to determine their own treatment.

Responsibility for this preface belongs to only two of the three editors, J. A. Crook and Andrew Lintott; for their beloved colleague Elizabeth Rawson died on 10 December 1988. Fortunately for readers, that lamentable event occurred relatively late in the preparation of the volume: our colleague had shared all the planning with us, had written and revised her own contributions, edited her share of those of others, and worked on the bibliography. Insight, care, enthusiasm, scholarship and wisdom: such were the qualities of the late Martin Frederiksen referred to by his fellow-editors in the preface to Volume VIII; those, and in no lesser measure, were the qualities also of Elizabeth Rawson, and of the editorial contribution to the present volume it would be wrong to attribute no more than a third part to her.

Not as an editor, but as a collaborator after the death of Elizabeth Rawson, we have had the exceptional good fortune to secure the help of Ursula Hall. She is not to be saddled with any responsibility for defects of structure or content, for all such matters were settled long before she joined us; but in all the technical stages of turning the material into a book she has borne a major part, and by her close reading and wise and learned advice has deserved well indeed of the editors and of those who may read the volume.

Chapter 4 was translated by M. H. Crawford, to whom we express our grateful thanks, chapter 16 by J. A. Crook. The maps were drawn by Reg Piggott, the index compiled by Barbara Hird. Glennis Foote was our acute and vigilant sub-editor; and all the staff of the Press co-operated in the making of this book with their customary patience and dedication.

J. A. C.
A. L.

CHAPTER 1

THE CRISIS OF THE REPUBLIC: SOURCES AND SOURCE-PROBLEMS

ANDREW LINTOTT

By the end of the second century before Christ the Romans faced a crisis as a result of their mastery of the Mediterranean, which was made sharper by an increased political awareness resulting from their wider experience and the intellectual contacts made during the acquisition of empire. What Florus[1] regarded as the robust maturity of Rome, which was doomed to collapse into the senility of the Principate, is made a more complex and more rewarding study by Roman self-consciousness. The most penetrating assessment of the Roman rise to power before 150 B.C. was made by Polybius – a Greek familiar with Rome but still an outsider. The Roman histories which had begun to be written from *c.* 200 B.C. onwards are lost to us but for a few citations and quotations, but, even if they were to be recovered, it is doubtful if we would find anything to compare with Polybius' analysis. Before the second century had ended, however, not only had the sheer bulk of Roman historical writing increased but the material had become diversified. Sempronius Asellio, who lived in the period of the Gracchi, drew a distinction between writing mere annals, the traditional Roman narrative of events in a strict chronological framework, and histories, which interpreted by seeking causation and motive. In practice this meant that Romans no longer always wrote omnibus narratives stretching from Aeneas, or the wolf and twins, to their own day, but produced monographs on specific topics from the past or present, biographies and autobiographies. Moreover, the development of Roman intellectual life led to other forms of writing in prose – treatises, especially on oratory and law, and letters. Meanwhile, Greek interest in Rome did not cease, and one of the most influential sources for later writers whose native language was Greek was the Stoic philosopher Posidonius, who in addition to works on geography and ethnography wrote a full-scale Roman history which picked up the story where Polybius left it.[2]

The works of the Roman annalists culminated under the emperor Augustus with the work of Livy, 120 of whose 142 books dealt with

1 Florus I, intro. 7–8. On the implicit theory see Griffin 1976 (A 42) 194ff.

2 See *HRR*; Badian 1966 (H 4); Malitz 1983 (B 69).

history down to the death of Cicero. However, the only products actually of the Republican period to survive are two monographs and some substantial fragments of a history by Sallust, one short biography by Cornelius Nepos and the military commentaries of Caesar. Nor have we complete books of Livy on the period after 167 B.C. The accounts of the late Republic in Livy and his predecessors, and equally the important contribution of Posidonius, can only be partially pieced together from fragments, epitomes and later derivatives. The most valuable later sources are Greek historians of the Principate. Appian, honoured with the status of procurator of the emperor in the second century A.D., wrote an account of the expansion of Roman power subdivided according to theatres of war and included a history of the civil wars and their political background. Half a century later Cassius Dio, a senator and twice consul under the Severi, compiled a gigantic annalistic history of Rome from its origins to his own time, interspersed with Thucydidean generalizations and interpretations. (We have more or less intact the section dealing with 69 B.C. onwards.) To these we must add the biographer Plutarch, who in about A.D. 100 illustrated political and moral virtue by comparing eminent Greeks with Romans of the Republic in his *Parallel Lives*. On such works is much of the narrative thread of late Republican history based.

However, by far the most important sources we possess are the works of Cicero who, although he never wrote the history of Rome his friends expected of him, has provided through his correspondence a direct insight into politics and upper-class Roman society between 67 and 43 B.C., and in his published speeches and theoretical treatises tells much of his own lifetime and the age that preceded it. This means that for the period in which he was active as a lawyer and politician, 81–43 B.C., we are in direct contact with Roman public life, while for the fifty odd years before this his works tell us of events which he either lived through or learnt of from those with first-hand experience.

There are of course problems in using Ciceronian material. In his letters to Atticus Cicero tells the truth, as he sees it, and that view may change from week to week. His own letters to other acquaintances and those of his correspondents may on occasion be dishonest, disingenuous or deliberately obscure. In speeches he sometimes risks the lie direct about a point of fact, more often he suppresses or wilfully misinterprets events to suit his case. Extreme examples are his assertions that Clodius plotted to kill Milo in 52 and that Catiline had actually concocted a preliminary conspiracy in 66, over two years before the one which he himself suppressed. His veracity at many points can, however, be checked against his other works or against the secondary sources, and modern scholars relish the occasions when his falsehoods can be detected. But caution is in order: we should not suppose that the material in Plutarch, Appian and Dio is sober, mainstream and value-free, providing automatically a corrective to the tendentiousness in Cicero. The writers under the Principate were as much at the mercy of their primary sources as we are, and these included both encomiastic biographies of men like Pompey, Caesar, Cato and Cicero himself, and by contrast published harangues or written invectives. Even the history of Asinius Pollio, a younger contemporary of Cicero and Caesar, whose account of the civil wars lies behind much of Appian and Plutarch and probably influences Dio as well, is likely to have been contaminated by his own support for Caesar and highly critical attitude to Cicero.[3]

There are further important shortcomings in our source-material on the late Republic. First, the evidence in inscriptions is small compared with that available for the Principate and with the contemporary literary evidence. In particular we have few public documents relating to the period between the dictatorships of Sulla and Caesar. Moreover, although we know much from archaeology about the city of Rome itself, our knowledge of urban developments in Italy and the provinces is patchy. As for rural archaeology, much is being done currently to illuminate land-tenure and the nature of agricultural establishments in Italy, but much more remains to be done. In one field the historian is well supplied. The Roman coinage of the Republic is immensely rich and it has been exhaustively analysed, not only in order to establish chronology and to interpret legends and iconography, but also to draw more general conclusions about the size and likely causes of issues. There have also been important studies of the coinages of Rome's allies.[4]

The sheer bulk of the historical tradition, even if elements in it conflict, allows us to form a clear picture of what was happening from about 70 B.C. onwards. Interpretation remains difficult. Contemporaries were arguably too close to events to see their significance; writers under Augustus, on the other hand, were too concerned with explaining and justifying the new dispensation as a reincarnation of the old and thus preferred to seek individual scapegoats rather than probe the defects of Roman society and government as a whole. I shall return to this problem. On the other hand, study of the period from the destruction of Carthage to 70 B.C. suffers from the comparative paucity of Ciceronian evidence and the fact that we cannot extract a good continuous narrative from what remains of the writers under the Principate who digested Republican sources. The decade from 80 to 70 B.C. is so thinly covered

3 Gabba 1956 (B 38); 1957 (B 39).

4 Crawford 1974 (B 144); 1985 (B 145); cf. e.g. M. Thompson, *The New-style Silver Coinage of Athens* (New York, 1961); A. Giovannini, *Rome et la circulation monétaire en Grèce au IIe siècle avant Jésus Christ* (Basle, 1978).

that even a one-line fragment of Sallust's *Histories* is precious. The preceding decade which embraces the Social, Mithridatic and first civil wars, ending in Sulla's dictatorship (a period originally described by contemporaries like Sisenna, Lucullus, Lucceius and Sulla himself) is better documented from the military point of view, but the politics are tantalizingly unclear. As for the period that began the crisis of the late Republic, some great issues – the land-problem, the relations between Rome and Italy and between the Senate and the equestrian order – stand out; so do the figures of the Gracchi and that of the new man who was Rome's military saviour, C. Marius. But we know less of politics year to year than we do where the books of Livy survive and where we have rich Ciceronian evidence. In consequence vital background knowledge is lacking and the historian is liable to become too dependent on the presentation of events in the surviving source-material. He frequently finds himself served with a neatly packaged briefing, which raises more questions than it answers.

As always, Roman writing about the politics of this time is highly tendentious, but the problem is not simply one of bias. Two of the reformers who resorted to violence, L. Appuleius Saturninus and C. Servilius Glaucia, are damned by a uniformly hostile tradition, as are the political activities of Marius. On the other hand, both favourable and unfavourable accounts of the Gracchi survive. More important is the fact that the power struggle between the demagogic politicians and the bulk of the Senate is made to overshadow everything else by the sources. The merits and demerits of particular reforms are obscured in the attempt to make a moral assessment of those who subverted or defended the *status quo*. It is not easy to detect the thinking of men contemporary with the events in our secondary sources – an exception are the speeches attributed to Tiberius Gracchus by Plutarch and Appian which seem ultimately to derive from C. Gracchus' biography of his brother. Fragments of oratory (for example those of C. Gracchus and Scipio Aemilianus) preserved by the antiquarians and grammarians of the Principate are valuable.[5] Further interesting contemporary or near-contemporary comments on the late Republic may be detected in histories dealing with a different period. The senate's disavowal of the treaty made with the Spaniards in 137 (to which there is also contemporary reference in the coinage) has affected the tradition about the treaty or *sponsio* supposed to have been made by the consuls of 321. Ti. Gracchus' attitude in his conflict with his fellow-tribune Octavius received oblique comment in the annalistic accounts of the actions of his father when tribune in 187. Even the arguments about late Republican agrarian policy were transposed into early Republican history by Dionysius of

[5] *ORF.*

Halicarnassus, so that we find denunciation of small allotments and advocacy of large farms rented out by the state in a speech ascribed to the consul of 495 B.C.[6]

A vital check on our literary evidence is provided by epigraphic documents and archaeology. A disturbing fact about the inscriptions is that the official acts that they record are ignored or obscured by our literary sources, so that we are quite unprepared for the material that they contain. On one side of the so-called 'Tabula Bembina' (bronze fragments which once belonged to Cardinal Bembo, now known to have been first owned by the dukes of Urbino) there is a *lex de repetundis*, that is a law about the recovery of property improperly seized by Romans in authority, which must be a part of the legislation of C. Gracchus. Our literary sources do indeed tell us that he changed the juries in this court, but they give us no idea of the massive reform of procedure shown on the fragments and the change in the ethos of the court that this implies. Another example is the law of 101–100 B.C. about the praetorian provinces and the administration of Rome's affairs in the East, once only known from a partial text at Delphi but now further illuminated by an inscription at Cnidus containing new material. This is totally ignored by our sources on Saturninus and Glaucia, and yet it must be a measure with which they were involved and one which gives their politics a new dimension.[7] The reverse of the bronze fragments engraved with the *lex de repetundis* has an agrarian law of 111 B.C. This law was mentioned by Appian in a brief sentence, but the text itself and its implications about earlier legislation show the inadequacies of the apparently careful account of this legislation in Appian. Two parts of this law dealt with land in North Africa and at Corinth. No other source tells us that the Romans were planning land-division at Corinth at this point. As for Africa, the extent of Roman settlement there (including the colony which literary sources tell us that C. Gracchus tried to found) cannot be appreciated without the study of this inscription together with the archaeological evidence for Roman land-division largely deriving from French air-photography.[8]

Archaeology cannot solve the problems caused by the inadequacy of literary sources, but it can at least remind us where they are inadequate. The revolt in 125 B.C. of the Latin colony on the Samnite border, Fregellae (near modern Ceprano), is dealt with by our surviving texts in a few sentences. The cause remains obscure, but current excavation has provided testimony to the prosperity of the town and the brutality of the

[6] Dion. Hal. *Ant. Rom.* VIII.73; cf. Gabba 1964 (B 41). Livy IX.1–7: cf. Crawford 1974 (B 144) no. 234; 1973 (F 39). Livy XXXVIII.56; XXXIX.5: cf. Richard, 1972 (C 122).

[7] Lintott 1983 (B 192); Sherwin-White 1982 (C 133); Hassall, Crawford and Reynolds 1974 (B 170).

[8] Chevallier 1958 (E 3); Piganiol 1954 (E 22).

repression. Seven years later the Romans founded their first colony in southern Gaul, Narbo Martius (Narbonne). Cicero at least indicates to us that the measure was controversial, but the colony might be dismissed as a mere military outpost, had it not become clear from excavation that the site was important commercially, perhaps even before the founding of the colony.[9]

The problem, then, in the period from the Gracchan reforms to the Sullan reaction is that the relative lack of source-material makes it difficult to redress the selective and tendentious formulation of issues and events in the accounts which we possess. Some fundamental aspects of this bias will be considered in the next chapter. The corrective required from the historian is not merely to be counter-suggestible in face of the tradition, but to realize that the accounts of political conflicts, though they reflect disputes which genuinely occurred, mask a great deal of agreement in the governing class about how the city, Italy and the overseas empire should be managed. This may be summed up as a more controlled and thoroughgoing exploitation of the resources of the Mediterranean. Some politicians maintained a more or less high-minded conservatism about such exploitation. On the whole, however, the competitive nature of the Roman aristocracy meant that politicians would fiercely resist the plans of rivals, when these were alive, but subsequently would not hesitate to endorse these measures and enjoy their products.

I. ANCIENT THEORIES ABOUT THE LATE REPUBLIC

Polybius in his encomium of the Roman constitution in Book VI also portended its subsequent decay. It was not immune from the process of growth and decay according to nature, which was common to all constitutions and was in form cyclic since it started with primitive monarchy and returned to tyranny. Although the Roman Republic was stabilized by a balance between the monarchic, oligarchic and democratic elements, which prevented any part rapidly getting the upper hand, in the long run it would succumb to the luxury and ambition arising from its unchallenged empire. The greed of rich men would oppress the people and the ambition of others would exploit this discontent. Then the people would no longer wish to obey their leaders or share power with them, but seek to dominate everything of importance. The resulting freedom or democracy would be in truth mob-rule and a clear beginning of the decline to tyranny. If this was written before 146 B.C., it was a theoretical analysis which turned out to be prophetic. (Polybius had made a similar judgement on C. Flaminius, the radical tribune of 232

[9] Crawford and Keppie 1984 (B 284); Clemente 1974 (E 6) 61ff.

who went on to be consul and censor.) However, it may have resulted from Polybius revising his work during the Gracchan period. To judge from the surviving fragments of Diodorus – in particular his characterization of C. Gracchus' ambitions according to the classic model of the demagogue and his denunciation of the greed of the equestrian order – Polybius' interpretation was followed by Posidonius. It also seems to have influenced greatly subsequent Roman accounts.[10]

Roman writers after the fall of the Republic were happy to claim that this fall was inevitable. Rome was unable to bear the burden of its own weight; the moral corruption arising from greed, luxury and ambition had no external check, especially once the threat of Carthage had been completely uprooted. Constitutional change was not seen as significant in itself – largely, no doubt, because the Romans did not think that the constitution had changed. However, for the poet Lucan and the historian Florus there was a nexus linking wealth to poverty and both of these to desires which only demagogy and ultimately civil war could satisfy. Such explanations derived not just from Polybius and any other historian who followed him but from warnings uttered by statesmen at the time. According to Posidonius, Scipio Nasica opposed the destruction of Carthage on the ground that its existence forced the Romans to rule their empire justly and honourably, while its destruction would bring civil strife to Rome and weaken the foundations of the empire as Roman magistrates could oppress their subjects without fear. Although there is controversy about the ascription of these beliefs to Nasica, there is no doubt that such ideas were in circulation in the middle of the second century.

We cannot rehearse here the question, whether the destruction of Carthage was such a critical event in the history of the Roman empire. A more ruthless attitude abroad was already to be discerned earlier in the century. Civil strife certainly became important after 146 B.C. when Rome's power was at a new height. As for luxury, greed and ambition there was no question that these abounded in the second century. Sallust schematically placed their onset after the fall of Carthage, but they were denounced before this in the works of Cato the Censor, which Sallust knew well, and in Polybius, as well as by the annalist L. Piso, a contemporary of the Gracchi. Cato inveighed against slack and high-handed magistrates, corpulence and expensive imports of pickled fish from the Black Sea. Piso pilloried the decline of sexual chastity and the acquisition of luxury furniture – sideboards and one-legged tables – corruption which began with the triumph of Manlius Vulso in 186. At the same time the psaltery- and sambuca-players had arrived with their

[10] Polyb. VI.8.1–8; 9.10–14; 57.5–9; II.21.8; Diod. XXXIV/XXXV.27–9; Walbank 1972 (B 123) 130ff; Malitz 1983 (B 69) 375.

Asiatic dances. About 130 Scipio Aemilianus deplored mixed dancing-classes and the sexual licence which they were held to stimulate, in a speech against the legislation of Ti. Gracchus. This neatly illustrates how a connexion was made between general morality and political radicalism.[11]

Of course, greed for wealth and power were not vices suddenly discovered by the Romans in 146 or indeed in the second century. There is enough evidence from earlier times to suggest that the type of Roman idealized by later ages, the Curius and Cincinnatus – a fighting farmer of stern scruples, dedicated to the simple life and the work ethic – was, if not a myth, at least not totally representative. Yet it would indeed be a paradox to say that these vices had nothing to do with the crisis in the late Republic. Appetites expanded with the Roman empire and the strains produced by competition among the aristocracy are clearly in evidence from the early second century onwards, not least in laws against bribery (first in 181) and conspicuous extravagance in giving dinners (first in 182). One cannot completely discount the Romans' own feeling about what was wrong.

Nevertheless it is, and was, hard to explain the problems of the late Republic simply in terms of aristocratic moral failings. Was the difference to be found not so much among the men who sat in the Senate as among the legionaries? It is interesting that Sallust himself, while he talks of the greed for wealth and power in the introduction to the *Catiline*, later in that work and in his subsequent monograph, the *Jugurtha*, links the acquisition of wealth with the creation of poverty among others, as Polybius had suggested, in particular with the expulsion of peasant families from their ancestral landholdings. The sufferings of the rural population were a theme in the oratory of Tiberius Gracchus himself, probably recorded for posterity in his brother's memoir of him. The expansion of the estates of the rich and the resentment of the plebs are stated by Lucan and Florus to have been fundamental reasons for civil strife: 'hence might became the measure of right and domination of one's fatherland by force of arms respectable'. The agrarian problem also dominates the early chapters of Appian's *Civil Wars*, although here the author links it directly with the conflicts over the reforming tribunes, rather than with the civil war that eventually followed. It is only in his account of the civil wars after Caesar's murder that the desire of the soldiers to improve their economic condition through fighting is stressed.[12]

The poverty caused by the greed of the wealthy was thus accepted by a

11 Sall. *Cat.* 10–11; *Iug.* 41; *H.* I.11–12M; Piso, fr. 34, cf. Livy XXXIX.6.7–8; Scipio Aemilianus, *ORF* no. 21, fr. 30 = Macrob. *Sat.* III.14.6–7. See Lintott 1972 (A 63).

12 Lucan I.160–82; Florus I.47.7–13; II.1.1–2; App. *BCiv.* I.7–27; V.17.

number of Roman writers as a cause of civil conflict in the Forum and ultimately of civil war, though this was sometimes seen more in moral than socio-economic terms. The poor, it was held, fought not so much because they were poor, but because poverty had embittered them and made them violent and greedy themselves. Moreover, the griefs of the poor were not thought to excuse their aristocratic leaders for clashes with fellow-aristocrats. In spite of his appreciation of the miseries of the plebs Sallust both in the *Catiline* and the *Histories* declared that the claim of its leaders to be defending plebeian rights was fraudulent: like the leaders of the Senate, they were using honourable pretexts to seek personal power – a judgement deriving from Thucydides' account of civil strife at Corcyra in 427 B.C. Florus writes in the same vein, when assessing the Gracchi. Their measures appeared just, but they damaged the wealth of the state and the interest of the possessing classes (themselves part of the people): in reality they and other tribunes sought domination for their office rather than protection for the rights of the people.

An exception to the general hostility of historians to the demagogic tribunes is the friendly treatment of the Gracchi to be found in both Plutarch and Appian. One explanation offered for this is that C. Gracchus' own account of his brother and himself was their ultimate source. However, apart from this the talents and romantic aura of the Gracchi (deriving from their illustrious background and their tragic deaths) made them the favourite demagogues of those in principle opposed to demagogy. Cicero cleverly exploits their names both to disparage other demagogues by comparison and to assert his own adherence to popular principles. This privileged status was not shared by men like Saturninus, Glaucia or P. Sulpicius. Perhaps only one source shows obliquely the case that might be made for radical tribunes – the *Ad Herennium*, an oratorical handbook which seems to have been written in the eighties and quotes powerful examples of popular rhetoric denouncing enemies of the plebs.[13] As for its conservative opponents, whatever historians believed about the corruption of the aristocracy, the most obstinate defenders of the *status quo* – men like L. Opimius, Metellus Numidicus and Cato Uticensis – were revered for this adherence to principle, in the same way that the hard men of the early Republic, the Appii Claudii, Papirius Cursor and Manlius Torquatus, were awesome figures in the annals of that period.

The military leaders who undertook civil war were bitterly criticized by their contemporaries and not surprisingly much of this survives in later sources. Sulla was remembered for his proscriptions (the emperor

[13] *Rhet. Her.* IV.31, 48, 68, cf. Cic. *Verr.* V.163; *Leg. Agr.* II.10, 31; *Rab. Perd.* 14; *Har. Resp.* 41–3; *Clu.* 151; *Font.* 39; *Brut.* 125–6; *De Or.* I.38.

Septimius Severus was unusual in openly praising them in contrast to Caesar's clemency) and Sallust also indicted him for beginning the corruption of troops through slack discipline in order to secure loyal adherents in civil war. Marius' reputation never really recovered from its handling by his political opponents, not least Sulla. Pompey was treated mildly by writers under Augustus as the man who in theory represented law and order, but the pointed attacks made on him in the late Republic were not forgotten and for Lucan, Seneca and Tacitus he is as blameworthy as Caesar. As the Principate progressed, writers became less obsessed with naming the guilty men. Cassius Dio is particularly remarkable for refraining from denunciation of individuals, though he has much to say about corruption in general. However, by that time the death of the Republic seemed so remote and so natural an event that post-mortem analysis had become truly academic.

II. MODERN INTERPRETATIONS OF THE LATE REPUBLIC

Historiography since the Renaissance has been reluctant to accept the Roman aristocracy's explanation of why it was overthrown, though it has selectively exploited specific items in that explanation. Machiavelli in his *Discorsi sopra la prima deca di T. Livio*, although he adopted Polybius' view that Rome's mixed constitution was a virtue, believed the violent conflicts between Senate and plebs that shook early Rome to have been a blessing because they created freedom. As for the conflicts that began with the Gracchi, these certainly led to a destruction of liberty, but they were an inevitable consequence of Rome's greatness. For they could only have been avoided if the Romans had renounced using the plebs in war or admitting foreigners to citizenship, and in that case Rome would never have had the power to obtain her empire. Thus militarism and multiracialism were at the root of the Republic's decline. A further awkward consequence of the extension of empire was the prolongation of military commands, which led the citizen to forget the Senate and recognize the leadership only of its own commanders. The Republic would have lasted longer if Rome had solved this problem and also that of 'la legge agraria', which, Machiavelli recognized, produced strife fatal to the Republic.[14]

Machiavelli's position is intriguingly provocative: he has in fact turned Polybius upside down. The virtue of the Roman constitution is not the stability that consists in tightly interlocked parts but the balance which comes from free play in a tumultuous conflict. Moreover, he has distanced himself from the aristocratic view of Polybius and Roman

[14] *Discorsi* (ed. A. Oxilia (London, 1955). Trans. L. J. Walker. London, 1970) I.2, 4, 5, 6, 37; III.24.

writers. The tumults are not to be blamed on the plebs and its leaders. Rather, the Romans should not have allowed conflicts to get out of hand and they should have exercised greater control over their armies. It should be stressed that Machiavelli regarded the strife between 'i grandi' and 'la plebe' as genuine, not factitious: indeed the hostility between the two bodies transcended any specific issue.

Machiavelli had the benefit of writing at a time when the social and political organization of cities bore some resemblance to that of Republican Rome. If anything, he makes Rome look less sophisticated than it was. A little over two centuries later, similar themes are found in Montesquieu's *Considérations sur la grandeur et décadence des romains*. It is the soldiers' attachment to generals entrusted with great commands by the tribunes which in his view overthrew the Republic, while the turbulence of the city is ascribed to the increase in citizenship, which created a divided community where all did not share the old Roman values. Nevertheless he regards the urban violence in general as a necessary accompaniment to imperial success, since a brave and warlike people would not be submissive in domestic affairs.[15]

When Mommsen came to write in the nineteenth century his fundamental *Römische Geschichte*, he did not apply the standards of the German people at the time but those of contemporary British parliamentary democracy. In his analysis of politics at the time of the Gracchi he discounted the democratic element in the Roman constitution, on the ground that their assemblies were not, like a parliament, representative of the people as a whole. Moreover, he treated the conflict between the supporters of senatorial dominance, whom the Romans called *optimates*, and the *populares*, who in fact acted through the assemblies in the popular interest, as something carried on in the Roman Senate, similar to the party conflicts between Liberals and Conservatives in the British parliament. He therefore found it easy to accept Sallust's view that Roman politics was simply an unscrupulous struggle for power between members of the aristocracy, on the ground that the elections, which gave Romans office and thereby in due course a seat in the Senate, were not contested on programmes and political principles but on personality. He clearly thought that the British parliamentary system in his day was truly representative of popular feeling. If he had written after Namier, he might have been disposed to compare the Senate to the British parliament of the eighteenth century.[16]

The Roman tradition about moral corruption and the disruption of the constitution by power-seeking demagogues was therefore quite

[15] *Considérations* (*Œuvres complètes* VII, ed. R. Caillois. Paris, 1949), chs. 8, 9.

[16] Mommsen 1854–6 (A 76) vol. IV, ch. 2; L. Namier, *The Structure of Politics at the Accession of George III*, 2nd edn, (London, 1968).

acceptable to Mommsen, except that he believed that the political system deserved to be overthrown – both because of the oppression of peasant farmers in Italy by the rich through the monopolization of the land and the extensive use of slaves and because of inefficiency and corruption in managing the empire. He believed that there ought to have been a political struggle against the nobility and the capitalist landowners but there was not in fact, or only accidentally through the medium of the demagogues. These were too preoccupied with the *status quo* or their own aspirations within the system to make effective reforms, but they pointed the way to a revolution by their monarchic ambitions, if only they had based these on the people as a whole and not on the city-mob. In his view the Roman empire under the Republic was managed by a corrupt clique of incompetent men, whom the people were powerless to control constitutionally. This regime merited and eventually underwent a complete revolution through military force, which subjected it to a monarch, who did represent the people of the empire – Caesar.

For Mommsen the collapse of the Republic ceases to be a problem. It was simply a matter of waiting for the one perennially successful department of the *res publica*, the army, to take over. Yet this view is an outsider's view with a vengeance: in disdaining to judge the Romans in context and by standards which they themselves might have endorsed, it contrasts not only with the ancient sources but with the sympathetic views of Machiavelli and Montesquieu. The analysis is still fundamental to much historical scholarship of today, though Mommsen's successors have tried to view events more from inside and forborne to make his sweeping judgements. Their attitudes to the Republic have been tempered by the fact that even Mommsen himself came to realize that his enthusiasm for the monarchy of the Caesars was misplaced.

Mommsen's followers have tended to accept that the late Republic was a fundamentally aristocratic state, in which the democratic element was bogus – an appeal to a corrupt city-mob. They have differed in their view of the monarchic ambitions of those who tried to dominate the political process. In particular Eduard Meyer argued that, while Caesar sought to be an absolute monarch, Pompey aspired to a principate, a monarchy within the existing oligarchy, which was a precedent for Augustus. Mommsen's modernizing view of the political struggle has also been rejected. The nature of aristocratic politics was above all analysed by Gelzer and Münzer. Gelzer showed the way that the aristocracy tended to monopolize office and power through family connexions and clients. Furthermore, he explained the meaning of the terms *optimates* and *populares*: the former described the majority, sometimes even the whole, of the governing class, who defended the authority of the Senate and the *status quo*; the latter were individuals or small groups with little or no organization or coherence over a period, who chose to work politically through the assemblies rather than to submit to majority opinion in the Senate. This view fitted the evidence better than Mommsen's parliamentary model and accounted for the monarchic style and aspirations of leading *populares*.[17]

Münzer went further in arguing on the basis of his prosopographical inquiries that the true parties in the aristocracy were small factions based on family, which struggled for supremacy with any weapon that lay to hand – manipulation of clients, demagogy and ultimately violence and civil war. Whereas Mommsen had applied Sallust's bleak judgement on the speciousness of the values of *optimates* and *populares* mainly to the *populares* and saw them as the chief aspirants to tyrannical power, Münzer believed that the *optimates* also each sought dominance for their group in a narrow oligarchy. This approach found its most eloquent expression in Syme's *The Roman Revolution*, which applied this doctrine to the last decades of the Republic and the civil wars – a period when the prevalence of force over law makes it most plausible. Politics after 49 B.C. became patently a power struggle and that conflict was to some extent foreshadowed in the non-military conflicts of the previous twenty years. Münzer's approach has also greatly influenced the work of Badian, although he takes factional conflict to have been based on much more flexible groupings than a rigid interpretation of Münzer's work would suggest.

On the other hand historians influenced more by Gelzer, for example Strasburger and L. R. Taylor, have argued that the confrontation between *optimates* and *populares* was not entirely unprincipled or devoid of ideology: what distinguished the two groups was attitudes to political method rather than political programmes. Christian Meier in his major study, *Res Publica Amissa*, suggested that the aristocracy only used the plebs to secure its own interests or to benefit small interest-groups that were unrepresentative of the people as a whole. There was a *popularis* ideology, but it was obsolescent, since the assemblies were not the people and major issues of liberty, especially the right of *provocatio* which safeguarded the citizens from arbitrary arrest and execution, were no longer in question. Such views tend to deny any important conflict within the aristocratic political system and stress its stability. Meier indeed holds that the complexity and impermanence of political groupings in conjunction with the multiplicity of ties of dependence completely rule out the clear-cut factional struggle presupposed by Münzer and to some extent by Badian. He even suggests that the patron–client relationships of the aristocracy imported a genuinely representative element into senatorial practice. The system was brought down by

[17] Meyer 1922 (C 227); Gelzer 1912 (A 40); Münzer 1920 (A 79).

factors which the aristocracy failed to assimilate properly, the wealthy men outside the Senate in the equestrian order and the professional armies under long-serving commanders.[18]

A still more flattering view of the late Republic has been propounded by Erich Gruen in *The Last Generation of the Roman Republic*. While accepting the thesis that the essence of politics was the struggle of family factions, he argues that they were on the whole carried out within certain limits, conventionally understood rather than constitutional, since a modicum of violence was acceptable. Only civil war endangered this system and this was the product of exceptional circumstances. From the opposite point of view the author of this chapter has argued in *Violence in Republican Rome* that it was precisely because the aristocracy tolerated a modicum of violence that the genuine conflicts between the popular leaders and the rest of the aristocracy became unmanageable and spiralled upwards into civil war.

Other historians, for example Brunt and de Martino, have returned to the theme of struggle between class-interests as the unbalancing factor. However, unlike Mommsen and his followers, they believe that this was reflected in the conflict between *optimates* and *populares*. They concede that Gelzer rightly interpreted these terms and that the men did not form organized political parties, but believe that this does not exclude the representation by the *populares* of the class-interests of the common people. The motives of the demagogic leaders are irrelevant: what matters is that they could only gain influence by satisfying genuine popular discontent. Yet to an extent these historians are at one with Mommsen in believing that the only way the discontent of the poor could effectively express itself was through civil war.[19]

Most modern interpretations share the same appreciation of what actually happened and of the legal and social background against which it happened. Historians are in agreement also that political groupings were not parties in the modern sense, even if there is no sharply defined unanimity about what they really were. There is uncertainty, however, as to how far *popularis* activity can be subsumed in the aristocratic political game or should be treated as something subversive of aristocratic dominance: what in fact did *popularis* leaders think they were doing? It has at least been rightly stressed that not only Cicero but even Sallust on occasion states that the optimate and *popularis* views of politics were genuinely opposed and irreconcilable.[20] The most unanswerable questions concern the degree of plebeian self-consciousness. It is

[18] Syme 1952 (A 118); Badian 1985 (A 1); Taylor 1949 (A 120); Strasburger 1939 (A 116); Meier 1966 (A 72).

[19] Gruen 1974 (C 209); Lintott 1968 (A 62); Brunt 1971 (A 17), 1988 (A 19); de Martino 1973 (A 71).

[20] Perelli 1982 (A 90) 25–69.

difficult to talk of class-consciousness or a broadly agreed community of interests among the poor. We may still wonder whether the plebeians did articulate grievances and demands, whether they were generally conscious of their rights and liberties as something achieved by earlier plebeian struggles and not gifts from above: might some of them even have viewed civil wars as revolutionary activities or at least deliberate blows against their oppressors?

CHAPTER 2

THE ROMAN EMPIRE AND ITS PROBLEMS IN THE LATE SECOND CENTURY

ANDREW LINTOTT

Traditionally, foreign affairs come first in histories of the middle Republic, domestic politics in those of the late Republic. Yet, although developments in Rome and Italy came to overshadow all else in the fifty years after the destruction of Carthage, it is wrong to write as if the Romans, as it were, changed trains in 146 B.C. In fact Rome's expansion abroad, because of the power and wealth it created for both the *res publica* and individuals and because of the accompanying problems, continued to be the main stimulus for political changes.

Polybius claimed in passages probably written between 167 and 146 that the Romans had become masters of the world with which his history dealt. This did not mean that they administered the whole area or even that they were interested in what was happening in every part, but that ultimately they expected their will to be obeyed in matters affecting their interests here.[1] It was a hegemony that even after 146 was looser than those of the great Hellenistic powers had been in their smaller spheres of influence, but as stern or sterner when Roman power was concentrated on a particular trouble spot. The methods by which this hegemony was exercised have been discussed in the previous volume. There was fighting almost every year in one part of the Mediterranean or another, but more often than not the Romans exerted power without direct recourse to arms. In the territories administered by Rome in the West the focus was the Roman magistrate or pro-magistrate in whose province the territory was. No Roman magistrates were regularly based east of the Adriatic before 148: embassies were here the chief channel of Roman control. Foreign envoys came to winter in Rome bringing complaints from the injured and self-justification from the suspect; in the spring Roman embassies left for foreign parts to investigate problems, reconcile allies and, where necessary, to coerce.

Their effectiveness was mixed. The Romans failed to save Orophernes of Cappadocia in 157 or Prusias of Bithynia in 149; they failed to obtain for Ptolemy Euergetes II the possession of Cyprus as well as Cyrene during the reign of his brother. On the other hand, though their methods

[1] Derow 1979 (B 26); Brunt 1978 (A 18); Lintott 1981 (A 64).

were far from attractive, they kept the kingdom of Syria weak – by burning its fleet and hamstringing its elephants after the death of Antiochus IV and later by using a pretender to harass Demetrius I, who contrary to their intentions had become Antiochus' successor. Where they believed a serious threat to their security and hegemony existed, they acted ruthlessly. Carthage and Macedonia fell victim within a few years to a resumption of serious military activity, while the Achaeans, more a nuisance than a threat, paid the penalty of defiance when in too close proximity to a Roman army. Carthage was destroyed in order to eliminate a stronghold of anti-Roman feeling and a power base which could rival Rome. So too was Corinth, not so much through fear but as a deliberate act of frightfulness to mark the beginning of a new era in Greece.[2]

In consequence, the area of direct Roman administration was increased, with Punic Africa, Macedonia and parts of Greece now directly subjected to Roman magistrates. Nevertheless, it does not seem at first sight that the pattern has changed. The embassies sent by the Romans to settle the dispute in Numidia between Jugurtha and his brothers from 116 onwards resemble those sent forty years before to stop the war between Pergamum and Bithynia. In the Roman law of 101–100 engraved at Delphi and Cnidus the senior consul is instructed, as part of a campaign to put down piracy, to write to the kings in Syria, Egypt, Cyprus and Cyrene and to give a special audience to the Rhodians.[3] Yet Jugurtha died in the Mamertine prison after Roman military intervention, while the pirates were directly attacked by Roman forces in their homeland. This intervention can be explained by asserting that Roman interests were more directly involved than, for example, in Asia Minor before 150, but this increased involvement itself requires explanation.

The spread of Roman administration to Africa in 146 and to Asia in 133 onwards (to which we will return) is clearly relevant. So too is the presence of Romans and Italians as private individuals in these areas. There is solid evidence for the settlement of Romans and Italians in Sicily and Spain; the evidence for their presence in other regions of the Mediterranean is more scattered but equally important. The family of the Rammii, for example, is now attested in Thessaly in the middle of the third century and it was surely a Roman who about 200 set up the genealogy of Romulus and Remus on Chios. Perhaps the most exotic piece of evidence is an Egyptian papyrus, dated to *c.* 200–150, recording a maritime loan for a voyage to the 'Scent-Producing Land' of the Horn of Africa. Most of those involved are Greek Egyptians, but one of the

[2] *Off.* 1.35 has Cicero's verdict on Corinth. See in general Sherwin-White 1984 (D 291) ch. 2; *id.* 1977 (D 75); Accame 1946 (D 250).

[3] Hassall, Crawford and Reynolds 1974 (B 170) 202–3; cf. Sall. *Jug.* 15; 21; 25.

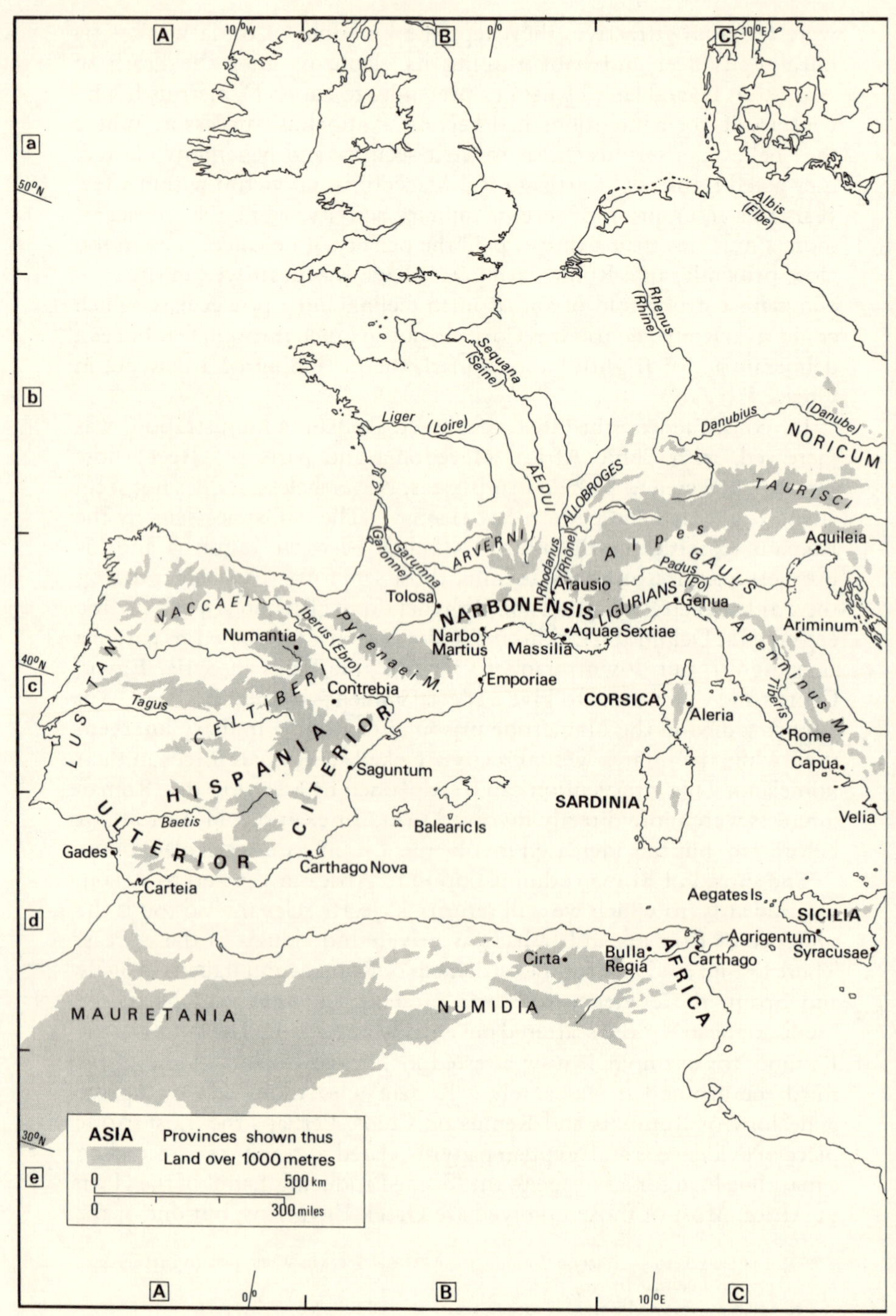

1 The Roman world about 118 B.C.

SARMATIANS
BASTARNAE
Borysthenes (Dnieper)
DACIANS
GETAE
TAURI
SCORDISCI
Dravus
Savus
Pontus Euxinus (Black Sea)
ILLYRIANS
LIBURNIA
Danubis
THRACIANS
Hebrus
Sinope
PONTUS
BITHYNIA
Halys
Byzantium
Nicomedia
GALATIA
Dyrrachium
MACEDONIA
Thessalonica
Cyzicus
MYSIA
PHRYGIA
Brundisium
Pella
Apollonia
Tarentum
Pergamum
CAPPADOCIA
EPIRUS
THESSALY
Aegaeum Mare
ASIA
Taurus M.
Corcyra
Delphi
Chios
Ephesus
Tarsus
CILICIA
Athens
Aphrodisias
SYRIA
Rhegium
Dyme
Corinth
CARIA
PELOPONNESE
Argos
Delos
LYCIA
Olympia
Cos
Apamea
Sparta
Rhodus
Salamis
Cnossus
Cyprus
Creta
Jerusalem
Cyrene
Alexandria
CYRENAICA
AEGYPTUS
Nilus
Sinus Arabicus

traders is from Marseilles (Massilia), the guarantors include another Massiliot, a Carthaginian and a man from Velia in Italy, while the go-between is called Cnaeus.[4]

After 150 B.C. the evidence for the dispersion of Romans and Italians increases but the problem of quantification remains. The number of adult male Romans of Roman or Italian descent resident in Spain in 50 B.C. has been put as low as 30,000. The figures given for the massacres of Romans or Italians by Mithridates in 88 B.C. – 80,000–150,000 in Asia and 20,000 on Delos and the other Aegean islands – are likely to have been grossly inflated by pro-Roman sources (conceivably they include the slaves of Italian households). The evidence from Roman and Italian names inscribed in Greece, mainly at Delos, is sounder, but its implications uncertain. It is clear that, after Delos was assigned to Athens for administration and made a free port by Rome in 166, a number of Italians with their freedmen and slaves made Delos one of their bases for business activities or retirement. They associated in *collegia* (lodges), which maintained cults of the Lares Compitales, Mercury, Apollo and Hercules and dedicated shrines and *fora* to them. However, Delos was arguably exceptional because of its importance as a trading centre, especially for slaves. A very plausible case has been made that the Forum of the Italians – a large unpaved court with two narrow access passages, which was surrounded by small rooms and whose cult-statue had a grille to protect it – was in fact a slave-market.[5] However, even if we must renounce any attempt to measure the numbers of Roman and Italian emigrants abroad, there are two significant features of this movement, the acquisition of land abroad by Romans and Italians, particularly by men of substance, and the settlement by the community of veteran soldiers overseas, both in formal colonies and on individual plots. These will be analysed in greater detail in the regional surveys that follow.

I. SPAIN

Spain had been one of the spoils of the Second Punic War, sufficiently important for the Romans to have increased the number of praetors to six in 197 B.C. in order to provide regular magistrates for two provinces, Citerior (Nearer) and Ulterior (Further). The two commands were separated at a point west of Carthago Nova by a boundary, which must have become more theoretical the more it extended into the partially subdued interior. Much fighting had taken place up to and including the governorship of Tiberius Gracchus (cos. 177) in 179–178. His settlement

[4] *Sammelbuch* III (1926) no. 7169.

[5] Brunt 1971 (A 16) 224–33. Cf. Val. Max. IX.2 ext. 3; Memnon, *FGrH* 434 F 22; Plut. *Sulla* 24.4; Strab. X.5.3 (486); XV.5.2 (664). Coarelli 1982 (B 276).

of the province produced a lull until 155, when fighting was resumed against the so-called 'autonomous Lusitanians' in the west of the peninsula and spread, partly through unprovoked Roman aggression, partly through co-operation between the Spanish peoples under the leadership of Viriathus, to the Vaccaei and ultimately to the Numantines in the north. These wars, which were characterized by Roman repudiation of agreements made with the Spaniards by Fabius Aemilianus, Q. Pompeius and C. Hostilius Mancinus, ended with the siege and destruction of Numantia at the hands of Scipio Aemilianus as consul in 134. (A full account of operations up to this point is to be found in Vol. VIII, pp. 118–42.) All the Iberian peninsula except the far north-west was now subject to the Romans, at least formally. We have references to later fighting in Spain between 114 and 111 (the proconsul L. Piso Frugi being killed then), in 104–102 against the Lusitanians and from 98 to 93 against the Arevaci and Celtiberi under T. Didius (cos. 98). This last war was notorious for Didius' treacherous massacre of the whole population of Colenda, a settlement founded by his predecessor. It is significant that, as Appian remarked, these wars were not begun at times when the Romans were preoccupied in Gaul and Italy with the threat of the northern tribes.[6]

The value of Spain to the Romans, as to the Carthaginians before them, lay in its provision of auxiliary soldiers, especially cavalry and light-armed troops, grain and above all base and precious metals. Polybius stated that within a circuit of 20 stades (4 kilometres) round New Carthage there were 40,000 workers in the silver-mines, whose product was worth 25,000 denarii a day. According to Diodorus, some individual prospectors extracted a Euboic talent (6,000 denarii) in three days, and he refers to Italians who employed slave-labour and introduced more technology into the workings with elaborate underground tunnels drained by Archimedian screws. Interesting in this context is the first appearance of what we may call a Roman provincial coinage, the Iberian denarius. These are silver coins with local types and legends, but struck to the Roman denarius standard (just under 4g) and bearing the denarius sign (X). They come from northern Spain, especially Osca near the Ebro and are believed to have been current from *c.* 200–150 B.C. down to Sertorius' time. It is most probable that their function was to be a convenient means for the Spaniards to pay their taxes and the Romans to pay for Spanish goods and services in return.[7] Rome had imposed general levies in goods and money on the Spaniards from 197, although

[6] App. *Hisp.* 99.428–100.437. See Lopez Melero 1984 (B 193) and Richardson 1986 (E 25) 199ff for a recently discovered inscription from Alcantara recording a surrender (*deditio*) in 104.

[7] *ILS* 8888; Polyb. XXXIV.9.8–11; Strab. III.2.10 (148); Diod. V.36–8; Richardson 1976 (E 24); Crawford 1985 (B 145) 84ff; Knapp, 1977 (B 179).

the exactions originally would not have fallen uniformly on all subject Spaniards but only on the peoples within reach of the current Roman officials. A regular tribute was probably laid down by Ti. Gracchus (cos. 177) during his governorship in 179, but it was disregarded by some peoples and there was a reassessment in Celtiberia by M. Marcellus in 152 (the total tribute paid there was to be 3,600,000 denarii). The Spaniards were, as far as we know, the first provincials to complain about Roman injustice in these exactions (in 171): the charges included the use of military prefects to collect money, corruption in commuting grain-contributions into money and corruption in farming out a 5 per cent tax (probably a levy on sales or transit).[8]

We know little of the administration of Spain. Apart from the initial division of powers in 197, it is likely that there was a long process of giving legal recognition to Spanish communities and assigning them territory, in which the governorships of M. Cato (195), Ti. Gracchus (179–178) and M. Marcellus (152–151) were high points. We hear later of ten-man senatorial commissions assisting Scipio Aemilianus in 134 and T. Didius in the nineties. Two important linked features of the administration were Romano-Italian immigration and the creation of towns. Italica, the later birthplace of the emperors Trajan and Hadrian, was settled with Roman veterans by Scipio Africanus in 206; in 171 Carteia was founded as a Latin colony for the offspring of Roman fathers and Spanish mothers (who were not by Roman law full Roman citizens). Corduba, the creation of M. Marcellus, was probably another Latin colony, as were Palma and Pollentia, established in 123 by Q. Metellus in the Balearic islands for 3,000 Romans from Spain. Apart from full Roman citizens living in Spain, there must have been many of mixed Romano-Hispanic descent like the settlers at Carteia and the bandit-chiefs, Curius and Apuleius, who took part in the Viriathic War. Some of these were granted full Roman citizenship (perhaps after military service or a magistracy in a Latin community) and thus we find later Roman senators like Q. Varius Hybrida and L. Fabius Hispaniensis. Communities were also created for Spaniards without Roman or Latin status. About 190 L. Aemilius Paulus granted the *servi* of the Hastenses living in the *turris Lascutana* their liberty and land to occupy; Gracchus founded Gracchurris near the Ebro and later Iliturgi in Baetica; D. Brutus (cos. 138) created Valentia for Spaniards who had fought under Viriathus and also Brutobriga (see Vol. VIII², pp. 118–42).

The extent to which the demarcation of communities and the foundation or confirmation of local administrations had proceeded within fifty years of the fall of Numantia is shown by a remarkable document, which has recently come to light at Contrebia in Celtiberian

[8] App. *Hisp.* 43.179–44.183; Strab. III.4.13 (162–3); Livy XLIII.2.12.

territory. A bronze inscription records a judicial decision by the governor, C. Valerius Flaccus, in 87 B.C. regarding a dispute over the purchase of land and water-rights involving three villages. The governor behaves like a Roman praetor in a private lawsuit, laying down a series of formulae according to which the judges, in this case the senate of Contrebia, are to judge the case. All the judges are Spanish. Yet the document is in Latin and the procedure used is a uniquely Roman one. This unparalleled piece of evidence gives a fascinating glimpse of the extent to which Roman ideas and methods were coming to prevail in Spain.[9]

II GAUL

The southern part of Transalpine Gaul was the land-link between Italy and Spain. The Roman connexion with this area went back to their first alliance with Massilia (Marseilles), said to have been made *c.* 400 B.C. This alliance had been reinforced through co-operation during the Second Punic War, but in spite of considerable expansion in Cisalpine Gaul (Vol. VIII², pp. 107–18) – as far as Genua in the west (linked with Cremona by the Via Postumia in 148) and Aquileia in the east – there had been little Roman intervention on the far side of the Alps. In 155/4 the Massilians had asked for help against the Ligurians living in the region of Antibes and Monaco, and a Roman land-expedition led by Q. Opimius from Cisalpina secured their renewed subjection to Massilia. Excavation at native Celtic or Celto-Iberic sites on or near the south coast of France has revealed a great deal of black-glaze Campanian ware and Italian amphorae of wine and oil imported during the second century B.C. The area was thus well known to traders from Italy, though there is no sure evidence of Italians settling. The evidence of direct Roman political influence consists of two highly controversial texts: Polybius' remarks about the measuring of the later Via Domitia from Gades to the Alps may be a late addition and need not refer to events before 125 B.C., while Cicero's statement about the Roman veto on the planting of vines and olives among the Transalpine tribes comes among other assertions that have an element of folklore.[10]

Massilia's cultural influence was strong. The education she provided for leading Gauls led to their using Greek letters to write Celtic and the Greek language itself for legal purposes. She may even have purveyed agricultural and military technology. Yet her military power was by now

9 Richardson 1983 (B 227); Birks, Rodger and Richardson 1984 (B 133). On the growth of Roman influence in Spain see Richardson 1986 (E 25) 172ff.

10 *ILLRP* 452; Polyb. XXXIII.9–10; III.39.8; Strab. IV.1.5 (180–1); 6.3 (203); Cic. *Rep.* III.16 (accepted by Goudineau in Nicolet 1978 (A 83) II.685–9); Clemente 1974 (E 6) 19.

relatively weak. Thus in 125 B.C. an attack on her by the Salluvii gave the Romans a reason for intervention. Fulvius Flaccus (cos. 125) and Sextius Calvinus (cos. 124) successively defeated the Ligurians, Salluvii and Vocontii and succeeded in opening a corridor of communication about a mile wide between Cisalpina and Massiliot territory, where Sextius planted a garrison at Aquae Sextiae (Aix-en-Provence) below the Celtic citadel of Entremont. Under Cn. Domitius Ahenobarbus (cos. 122) and Q. Fabius Maximus (cos. 121) these operations were extended into a conquest of southern Transalpine Gaul. The Allobroges, north of the Isère, were attacked on the ground that they were harbouring a Salluvian chief and had made war on the Aedui, who were friends of Rome. The Arverni from the Cevennes were also drawn into this conflict, no doubt because their chief Bituitus claimed supremacy over the other tribes in the area. The Gauls were comprehensively defeated at the confluence of the Rhône and the Isère (according to Roman sources, with enormous casualties) and Domitius eventually celebrated his success by riding through the new province on an elephant.[11]

As a result the Gauls as far as Toulouse were subjected to tribute; a Roman road was built along the old route from Emporiae to the Rhône; further, in 118 Domitius Ahenobarbus joined with a young orator, L. Licinius Crassus, in legislating for the foundation of the colony Narbo Martius (Narbonne), south of the Celtic settlement of Montlaurès. The subjected peoples did not rebel against Roman administration, but within a few years Roman armies suffered serious defeats by tribes from outside the province – L. Cassius by a section of the Helvetii who had migrated to Aquitania (107), M. Silanus (109), Q. Caepio and Cn. Mallius (105) at the hands of the Cimbri from beyond the Rhine at Arausio (Orange). During his campaign Caepio seized 15 million denarii-worth of uncoined silver and gold from the Celtic sacred treasuries near Tolosa (Toulouse). The area then became the base for C. Marius' defence of the empire against the Germanic tribes in 104–102, which led to the defeat of the Teutones and Ambrones near Aquae Sextiae. A by-product was the construction of the Rhône canal, whose transit-dues Marius assigned to the Massiliots as a reward for their services against the Germans.

The initial invasion could be justified by the need to protect Massilia, but the subsequent operations seem to reproduce the familiar Roman pattern of the pursuit of military glory for its own sake, while political support for the establishment of Roman power may have been furnished by Romans who had realized the economic potential of the region and wished to be able to buy land there. Fifty years after its foundation the province abounded with Roman citizens, especially businessmen. Ear-

[11] See also Livy *Per.* LXI; Val. Max. IX.6.3; Strab. IV.1.11 (185); 2.3 (191); Posidonius, Jac. *FGrH* 87 F 18; App. *Celt.* 1.7; 12.

lier, before 85 B.C. at least, Cicero's client C. Quinctius formed a partnership there with Sex. Naevius to undertake both ranching and agriculture or arboriculture. The partnership also acquired slaves to sell in Italy, possibly in exchange for wine. There is also epigraphic and numismatic evidence for Roman immigration and influence on commerce.[12]

III. SICILY

Agricultural exploitation is central to the history of the next province to be considered – Sicily (about events and organization in Corsica and Sardinia we have too little evidence for a worthwhile discussion). After Syracuse's defection and recapture in the Second Punic War there was no rival in Sicily to Roman administration. Though three cities had treaties with Rome and five had been declared free cities, immune from tribute, the rest paid tithes on agricultural produce according to a system once created by Hiero II of Syracuse. Some land had been confiscated – notably the rich *ager Leontinus* – and was rented out to Romans, Italians or Sicilians by the censors. We know of a colony being settled at Agrigentum (?197), presumably of ex-soldiers. Further early evidence of Italian immigration is a dedication by the 'Italicei' at the free city of Halaesa. Nevertheless the Greek part of the island was still firmly Greek, as an inscription recording the itinerary of *theoroi*, religious envoys from Delphi, shows.[13]

In our period Sicily was convulsed by two slave revolts (138/7–132 and 104–101) which are important not only in themselves but also because of the social and economic conditions that are said to have produced them. According to Posidonius,[14] the first revolt was caused by one Damophilus, a Greek owner of a large estate devoted to ranching at Henna, who provoked his slaves into killing his wife and himself as the beginning of a general uprising. The first leader was Eunus, a Syrian from Apamea with a reputation for magic and miracle-working, who assumed the royal name of Syria, Antiochus. In the south-west of Sicily near Agrigentum another leader arose, a Cilician called Cleon. Enormous numbers are ascribed to the rebels by our sources – 20,000 rising to 200,000 – though Posidonius merely puts Eunus' original force at 6,000 and Cleon's at 5,000. The slaves are said to have been partly herdsmen

[12] Road – *ILLRP* 466a. Treasure – Strab. IV.1.13 (188); Pos., *FGrH* 87 F 33. Cic. *Quinct.* 11–12. Cf. on wine A. Tchernia, 'Italian wine in Gaul at the end of the Republic', in Garnsey 1983 (G 101) 87–104; on 'monnaies à la croix' Clemente 1974 (E 6) 80–1; on inscriptions Rolland 1955 (B 235).

[13] Cic. II *Verr.* 3.13–14; 5.56; 4.123; *Phil.* II.101; *Leg.Agr.* II.57; *ILLRP* 320; Manganaro 1964 (B 197).

[14] *FGrH* 87 F 108 = Diod. XXXIV/V.2.2ff. Cf. Florus II.7.4ff. Vogt 1974 (A 123) 39–92. Second revolt – Diod. XXXVI.3ff; Florus II.7.10ff.

and partly agricultural slaves working in chain-gangs. They received some support from the local free population, which was delighted to see the sufferings of the rich, and it was more destructive than the slaves, in that it looted and plundered recklessly, whereas the slaves did not fire or ravage the farms they hoped to use themselves. Eight commanders were involved in fighting the revolt before M. Perperna and P. Rupilius brought it to an end by recapturing Henna and Tauromenium, killing Cleon and capturing Eunus alive.

In 104 the pattern was repeated. The occasion was the attempt by the governor to implement a *senatus consultum* urging the release of citizens of allied communities, who had been forced into service as slaves in the provinces. Eight hundred men were quickly released, but Nerva then abandoned his task under pressure from the local nobility. After some sporadic outbreaks a major uprising of 2,000–6,000 men occurred at Heraclea, led by a flute-player called Salvius, who played at orgiastic religious ceremonies for women and had a reputation for divination. He was given the rank of king and the name Tryphon (held by a previous Syrian king). In the territory of Segesta and Lilybaeum the herdsmen rebelled under a Cilician shepherd, Athenion, who took a silver sceptre and purple robe and was crowned as king. As before, the free poor joined in the revolt, and their destructiveness contrasted with Athenion's care for what he thought to be his own property. Although on this occasion the towns remained secure, the slaves there were suspected of being ready to join the rebels. The praetor who succeeded Nerva in 103, L. Lucullus, defeated Tryphon and Athenion in the field, but Athenion escaped to maintain the struggle for another two years until he was killed and his supporters slowly eliminated by M'. Aquillius.

Posidonius' introduction to the first revolt has a strong moralizing tone and is carefully harmonized with his general view of decadence after the fall of Carthage deriving from the greed and lawlessness of Romans in the provinces. The rich landowners in Sicily are said to have been mostly Roman knights, who are anachronistically credited with control of the lawcourts. They neglected to clothe or feed properly the vast numbers of slaves they possessed and so turned them into brigands. In fact we do not hear specifically of any Roman slave-owners in the first revolt, although in the second revolt P. Clonius, Vettius and the Varii brothers are mentioned. Furthermore, Posidonius' picture of society in Sicily is distorted in that it neglects the Greek landowners and in particular the less wealthy proprietors who were the core of the citizen body in the Greek cities. However, it would be wrong to abandon Posidonius' view entirely and argue that these were Sicilian nationalist revolts. The oriental origins and royal aspirations of the leaders confirm what is in any case probable, that many of the slaves involved had been imported from the East (or their ancestors had been). Syrians were regarded as stupid, submissive and physically strong – ideal for certain agricultural tasks. Although poor Sicilians became involved, their activities were marginal and indeed contrary to the aims of the leaders of the rebels. Moreover, we have the unimpeachable evidence of a contemporary inscription, in which a magistrate operating in Italy and Sicily at the end of the first revolt claims to have rounded up and returned to their masters 917 runaway slaves of Italian owners. The success of the slaves in Sicily would have been a magnet for those working with herds or on the land in south Italy.[15]

In Sicily we see a province in which the Romans were already well established, and in which they and the rich Sicilians themselves had begun to run large estates with slave-labour both for agriculture and stock-raising. This had not eliminated traditional Greek society, but it was contributing to the tension between rich and poor, which had for centuries been a feature of Greek life, and had led to social unrest among the slaves which could spread to Italy itself.

IV. AFRICA

After the defeat of Carthage, Scipio Aemilianus annexed to Rome what survived of Punic territory after Numidian claims had been satisfied – the land within the so-called 'royal' or 'Phoenician' trenches – while formally assigning the remaining territory to the children of king Massinissa, i.e. king Micipsa, his brothers and descendants. A ten-man commission established by a Lex Livia then arrived, and with their aid Scipio punished Rome's enemies and rewarded her friends. Carthage and other Punic cities which had remained loyal to her were destroyed, and the site of Carthage was formally consecrated; cities which had defected to Rome were granted their liberty, among them Utica, which also received additions to its territory stretching from modern Bizerta to near Carthage itself and became the residence of the Roman governor. The commission imposed tribute on all men and women who remained within Rome's new province, outside the free cities.[16] The Carthaginians, who did not flee across the border into Numidia, as some clearly did, or become members of the free cities, were apparently expected to live in villages or on individual farms.

French aerial surveys have shown that there is a gigantic system of centuriation (the characteristic orthogonal Roman land-division) with one axis running roughly north-west to south-east from near Bizerta to

[15] *ILLRP* 454. For the theory of nationalist revolts Verbrugghe 1972 (E 30) and 1974 (E 31).

[16] Pliny *HN* v.25; App. *Pun.* 54.235–6; 135.639–41; Eumachos of Naples, *FGrH* 178 F 2; lex agraria (*Bruns* no. 11), lines 79, 81.

near Sidi-bou-Ali, which would have been entirely within the royal trenches. This is differently oriented to another which begins just south of it and includes land first annexed in 46 B.C. The former grid is therefore of Republican date and must have been the basis of the land-distribution carried out under the Lex Rubria devised by C. Gracchus and in subsequent years. It is, however, a vast scheme, whose main axis is almost 160 km. long, and the possibility should be considered that it may in part even antedate the Lex Rubria and show that the Romans assigned land to citizens or allies in this area immediately after 146, either through sale or lease by the censors, as is attested later in the Lex agraria of 111.[17] In 125 a plague of locusts caused devastation and depopulation in Africa. Two years later C. Gracchus, perhaps seeing in this disaster the opportunity for a new settlement policy, proposed through the Lex Rubria the foundation of a colony on the site of Carthage with land-assignations in the hinterland. Six thousand men were eventually enrolled, probably more than the law envisaged. The maximum allotment was 200 *iugera* (about 50 hectares), that is, a complete Roman *centuria*. Various portents were announced and alleged to show that the refoundation of Carthage was unlucky. As a result, the Lex Rubria was repealed in 121 after street-fighting and the deaths of C. Gracchus and Fulvius Flaccus. Nevertheless, a land-commission continued to operate there, allotting land to the former colonists, resettling those who had been improperly deprived of land and supervising the execution of the sales of land carried out at Rome and the leases of the censors. How many emigrants, as opposed to absentee landlords, actually received land in Africa, we cannot tell. We know nothing of any urbanization or even the creation of *fora* as meeting-places in this period: probably many immigrants resided in the free cities. Nevertheless, from then onwards the Roman presence in Africa was much more than the small Roman administration.[18]

There were also Romans and Italians in the neighbouring kingdom of Numidia. Micipsa, who had succeeded Massinissa in 148 B.C., developed a new capital at Cirta (usually identified with Constantine), at which Carthaginians, Greeks, Romans and Italians congregated, leaving Thugga to be the city of Massinissa's temple. An additional reason for the kingdom's prosperity was the exploitation of the land in the Bagradas valley and the area of Mactar, taken from Carthage by Roman arbitration in the years preceding her final struggle (Micipsa was able to send grain to C. Gracchus when he was quaestor in Sardinia in 125–124 in spite of the locust-plague). On Micipsa's death, however, *c.* 118 a crisis arose which was to become the subject of one of Sallust's historical

[17] Lex agraria, 70ff, 82–3, 85–9; Chevallier 1958 (E 3); Piganiol 1954 (E 22) Tab.I.

[18] Oros. v.11.2–5; App. *BCiv.* 1.24.102–4; *Pun.* 136.644–5; lex agraria 52ff, esp. 60–1; *ILLRP* 475.

monographs. Micipsa was survived by two sons of his own, Adherbal and Hiempsal, and an older adopted son fathered by his dead brother Mastarnabal, Jugurtha. Mastarnabal, like Micipsa, had been reputed for his Greek culture (he had won a chariot-victory at the Panathenaia); his son was handsome, athletic and personable and had gained a good name for himself when leading a contingent of Numidian cavalry, which Micipsa had supplied to help Scipio Aemilianus at Numantia.[19] The princes found it impossible to co-operate: Jugurtha had Hiempsal murdered and drove Adherbal out of the kingdom. Adherbal appealed to the Senate, declaring, according to Sallust, that he ruled his kingdom merely as a bailiff for the Romans. In 116 a senatorial commission of ten divided Numidia, assigning the western sector, adjoining Mauretania, to Jugurtha and the more civilized sector, including the ex-Punic territory, to Adherbal. Jugurtha exploited this division to mount a new war against Adherbal, eventually defeating him and shutting him up in his capital in 112. Adherbal sent successive appeals to Rome for help. An embassy of three young men was not permitted by Jugurtha to interview him; an embassy of three senior senators summoned Jugurtha to Utica but had no more success in stopping the siege. Finally, Adherbal surrendered on the recommendation of the Italians who were helping to defend him, but both he and they were killed by Jugurtha.

These developments led to a popular outcry and the Senate resorted to war in 111 in order to enforce Jugurtha's submission to Roman power. (Jugurtha may have anticipated that this attack would come anyhow and so his actions may not have seemed to him foolishly provocative.) After some fighting, Jugurtha came to terms with the consul Bestia: he formally surrendered himself and his kingdom to Rome, but was allowed to retain his crown at the cost of a small indemnity. Suspected of having bribed the consul and his officers, he was brought to Rome under safe conduct to testify, but this was thwarted by a tribune's veto. He then contrived the murder of Massiva, son of Micipsa's brother Gulussa, whom the Senate were considering as a rival claimant to the Numidian throne. So all dealings with him were abandoned and he was allowed to return to Africa, but the Senate accepted the necessity of a military solution. Meanwhile, Jugurtha's methods and the collusion of a number of senators with him created a political crisis at Rome (ch. 3. pp. 88ff).

Sp. Albinus, the consul who resumed the war in 110, failed to get to grips with his enemy, while his brother, whom he left in charge as a legate in the succeeding winter, was trapped by Jugurtha after an assault on his camp and was forced to make a treaty. This treaty was disowned by the Senate – a procedure now familiar from Spanish precedents. In

[19] Strab. XVII.3.13 (832); Diod. XXXIV/V.35.1; Plut. *C. Gracch.* 2.3; Sall. *Jug.* 6, 7, 21, 26; Livy *Per.* L.

109 the war was continued with increased vigour under Q. Metellus after new recruitment and intensified military training. These were also the main features of C. Marius' programme, when he obtained from the people the command in 107. While the Romans soon came to control eastern Numidia – the area immediately west and south of the province, they found it difficult in country ideal for cavalry to reduce a highly mobile enemy, who preferred ambushes and harassment to pitched battles. Marius managed to destroy a number of Numidian strongholds in operations extending to near the Mauretanian border, but his problems were compounded when Jugurtha forged an alliance with Bocchus, king of Mauretania, at the price, according to Sallust, of a third of Numidia (this allowed Bocchus to fight for the territory as his own). The war was ended by diplomacy, especially that of L. Sulla, who in 105 persuaded Bocchus to renew his old friendship with Rome and betray Jugurtha. The Romans made no territorial acquisitions: Bocchus was confirmed in his kingdom and Jugurtha's brother, Gauda, was granted Numidia, bolstered by Marius through the settlement of Gaetulian cavalry from his army in the Bagradas valley. (This is the best explanation of the fact that Uchi Maius and Thuburnica later recorded Marius as their founder; the province was not extended along the valley as the later presence of Hiarbas at Bulla Regia shows.)[20] Roman veterans were settled in the surveyed portion of the province itself and on the island of Kerkenna after a law of Saturninus in 103.[21]

The Romans had been reluctant to embroil themselves in a Numidian War but in the end they would settle for nothing short of Jugurtha's unconditional surrender and death, because they did not trust him to conform with Roman policy. Sallust ascribed the apparent feebleness and indecision in Roman behaviour down to 110 to the corruption of leading senators by Jugurtha's bribes. Modern scholars have argued that on the contrary the Romans were following a rational policy: a war in Numidia was difficult and expensive; Roman interests were best served by a strong ruler friendly to Rome and any closer involvement in Numidian affairs was counter-productive; thus it was largely popular agitation, swelled by the complaints of businessmen like those previously killed at Cirta, which led Rome into an unnecessary conflict.[22] Although there is no reason to question the fact that Jugurtha used bribery, one cannot necessarily infer from the bribe-taking that the senators' political judgement was wrong. The Romans had no forces of their own originally stationed in Africa (indeed the protection of the province depended on Numidian military support); they had little

[20] Brunt 1971 (A 16) 577–80; cf. Gascou 1969 (B 157) 555–68. Old view Quoniam 1969 (B 222); Broughton 1929 (E 2) 19, 32. [21] *De Vir. Ill.* 73.1; *Inscr. Ital.* XIII.3 no. 7.

[22] De Sanctis 1932 (A 104) 187ff; Syme 1964 (B 116) 174ff.

knowledge of the remoter parts of the kingdom; their forces were ill-suited to the type of campaigning required. However, the kingdom was a dependency from which they expected obedience, and Jugurtha had humiliated Roman diplomacy more seriously than Attalus and Prusias had done in Asia Minor nearly forty years before. Above all, Roman and Italian lives and property were at stake, not merely in Cirta but in the province itself where thousands of settlers had recently acquired land. The provisions of the *lex agraria* of 111 to consolidate land-assignments in Africa into a permanent pattern coincide with the beginning of military operations against Jugurtha. Money from rents and purchases was due to the treasury; credit depended on confidence that the western frontier of the province was secure. There were clearly Romans in Africa eager to draw profits from Numidia: apart from the businessmen massacred at Cirta, we may suspect the knights in the Roman army, who were friends of Marius, of having this object in view. However, new economic exploitation was not the motive of the Roman government: the war was rather the assertion of authority and the protection of investment.

V. MACEDONIA AND GREECE

After half a century of trying to control at arm's length events on the far side of the Adriatic, the Romans began to maintain there permanently a magistrate and troops. The story of the defeat of Andriscus and the Achaean League has been told elsewhere (Vol. VIII², pp. 319–23). Its sequel was the establishment of a new province in Macedonia in 148/7 and the addition to it of a considerable part of Greece in 146/5. Macedonia had already been made subject to tribute in 167, when it was organized as four independent republics. These regions (*merides*) were still the basis of Roman administration under the Principate, while the cities themselves were supervised now, as under the Macedonian kings, by boards of *politarchai*.[23] The border of Macedonia was extended to the river Hebrus, and this became the terminus of the Via Egnatia, which ran from two starting-points on the Adriatic, Apollonia and Dyrrachium, across the mountains to Pella and Thessalonica and then eastwards towards the Hellespont. Its construction, no doubt following the track of earlier royal routes, was undertaken sufficiently early in the province's history to be known to Polybius and a milestone of a Cn. Egnatius C. f. has been recently found near Thessalonica (conclusively disproving the odd theories about the origin of the name of the road to be found in standard reference works).[24]

23 Livy XLV.18.6–7; 29.5–10; 30.1; Acts 16:12; Cormack 1977 (B 143); Koukouli-Chrysanthaki 1981 (B 180).

24 Polyb. XXXIV.12.2a–8; Strab. VII.7.4 (322–3); fr. 48; *AE* (1973) no. 492; Walbank 1985 (B 254).

One revolt by a pseudo-Philip was suppressed by a quaestor *c.* 140. Much of the efforts of the governors was devoted to fighting the Thracians to the north and east of the province and extending Roman influence in these areas. M. Cosconius fought a war *c.* 135 and received an embassy from the city of Cyzicus in Asia requesting protection. Q. Pompeius was killed fighting Gauls, probably Scordisci, in 119, but his quaestor T. Annius successfully protected the province against invasion. C. Cato was defeated in 114, but this was compensated by the victories of M. Livius Drusus (cos. 112) and M. Minucius Rufus (cos. 110). Then in 102–101 T. Didius won further victories against the Thracians, and the Cnidus fragments of the Roman law about the provinces show that a new territory, the Caenic Chersonese, east of the Hebrus had been formally annexed to the province.[25] This shows the tendency of Roman power here to expand towards the Hellespont, like that of the former Macedonian kings.

The Achaean League had revolted in 147 in reaction to Roman instructions that Sparta, Corinth, Argos and Orchomenus should be separated from it. Sympathy and support had come from Thebes and Chalcis. The settlement imposed by L. Mummius after the rebellion had been crushed was in part a reprisal, in part an effort to ensure that there should be no further uprisings. Cicero states that Mummius destroyed Corinth and subjected many cities of Achaea and Boeotia to the *imperium Romanum*. According to Pausanias, Boeotia had to pay an indemnity to Heraclea and Euboea, as did the Achaeans to Sparta. Moreover, the league councils of the Achaeans, Boeotians and Phocians were dissolved, tribute was demanded and oligarchic governments imposed.[26] Greece did not have a governor of its own until the Principate, but it is clear that in the late Republic regions of Greece were administered and taxed by the Romans. A fragment of an inscription with a proconsul's letter addressed to the Guild of Dionysiac Artists refers to a province and another area 'which they rule'. These are plausibly restored as Macedonia and Greece respectively.[27] On a newly discovered stone there are instructions by L. Mummius and Q. Fabius Maximus relating to the Dionysiac Artists in Macedonia, Boeotia and the Peloponnese.

The territory of Corinth became Roman *ager publicus* and was being surveyed with a view to sale or settlement at the time of the Lex agraria of 111. The same thing is probably true of the land of Chalcis and Thebes, cities also destroyed by Mummius. A *senatus consultum* of 78 B.C. rewarding Greek sea-captains refers to the leasing by the censors of Euboea and here in 85 Sulla gave 10,000 *iugera* as a reward to the

[25] *MRR* I, years 143, 135, 119, 112, 110, 101; Hassall, Crawford and Reynolds 1974 (B 170) 204.
[26] Paus. VII.16.9–10; Cic. II *Verr.* 1.55; Accame 1946 (D 250) 16ff.
[27] Sherk 1984 (B 239) 44, cf. Dittenberger, *SIG* 683, lines 64–5.

Mithridatic general, Archelaus. Oropus too seems to have been leased by the censors before Sulla's time. Epigraphic evidence also confirms the installation of oligarchies. In the documents of Peloponnesian cities under the new order we no longer have references to the council (*boule*) and popular assembly (*demos*) but to the magistrates and *sunedroi*. In one city, Dyme in Achaea, there was a rising against the newly appointed oligarchic government during the governorship of Fabius Maximus. The rebels had burnt the town hall with its records and proposed laws 'in defiance of the constitution given by Rome to the Achaeans' – perhaps including the cancellation of debts.[28]

After a short while the Romans abolished the indemnities and restored both the councils of the leagues and the rights of Greeks to hold land in other cities. This is perhaps attested in the epigraph of an honorific statue at Olympia set up to their commander by Achaean cavalrymen who had served under a Domitius Ahenobarbus (probably in the conquest of southern Gaul). Civic administration continued both in the regions annexed by Rome and the cities like Athens and those of the Thessalian League which were free from Roman burdens. However, intervention by the Roman governor occurred in matters affecting the free as well as the subject cities, for example in the long-running dispute over the privileges of branches of the Guild of Dionysiac Artists. The mixture of dependence and independence is well illustrated by the way that Attic tetradrachms and Macedonian tetradrachms adapted by the Romans from a type used by Philip V and Perseus became standard coinages.[29]

VI. ASIA

In 146 between Greece and the Parthian empire centred on Iran there lay kings, cities and peoples, who were to a great extent nominally friends and allies of the Roman people, without necessarily being friends of each other. In 133 the situation changed sharply, when Attalus III of Pergamum died while still comparatively young and without an obvious natural successor and his will in favour of the Roman people came into force. The Pergamene side to the story has been told already (Vol. VIII², pp. 373–80); its implications for Roman domestic politics will be tackled in the next chapter (pp. 68, 79). Our present concern is its contribution to Roman empire-building. It is first important to notice that Tiberius Gracchus' proposal about the cities and the revenues of the kingdom implies an expectation that the windfall would be accepted (if it had not been accepted already). Through the will the royal lands became

[28] Lex agraria 96–7; Cic. *Leg. Agr.* 1.5; S.C. de Asclepiade (*Bruns* no. 41) 6, 23; Plut. *Sulla* 23.4–5; *SIG* 683, 15; 735–6, *passim*; Sherk 1984 (B 239) 43 (now probably to be dated to 145 B.C.).

[29] *SEG* 15 (1958) no. 254; Sherk 1984 (B 239); *SIG* 704–5; 729; Crawford 1985 (B 145) 115ff, 152ff.

the public property of the Roman people, while the cities were made autonomous, freed from tribute and indeed assigned territory for revenue. A decree of Pergamum, passed before the ratification of the will was known, shows the city distributing its citizenship rapidly to soldiers, subject peoples and foreigners in the town and its associated territory, in order to forestall any protest that this provision in the will was being ignored. It seems unlikely that at the time the Pergamenes knew that Gracchus planned to legislate about the cities. In the event in spite of Gracchus' murder the will was adopted and there was a nationalist reaction under Aristonicus, a bastard son of Eumenes II.[30]

Aristonicus received support from some cities, who presumably had not profited sufficiently from the will, and from slaves, for whom he is said to have created a new city or citizenship as members of the City of the Sun (Vol. VIII², p. 379). He was resisted by the forces of neighbouring kings, including Nicomedes II of Bithynia and Mithridates V of Pontus, and the remaining cities. A Roman commission of five, sent out to settle the kingdom, was replaced by consular commanders with armies. P. Crassus (cos. 131) was defeated and died. His successor, M. Perperna, was victorious and captured Aristonicus, but he too died and the settlement of Asia fell to M'. Aquillius (cos. 129) and a senatorial commission of ten. It was a slow process, involving the reduction of a number of rebellious cities and strongholds (an inscription shows fighting in Mysia Abbaitis and probably in Caria) and the building of roads. Aquillius eventually triumphed at Rome in November 126, having become the recipient of a religious cult with a priesthood at Pergamum.[31]

The nature of his settlement is not so clear, nor was it immediately ratified, since it was still the subject of debate and legislation about the time of C. Gracchus' tribunates (124–122). Much of Greater Phrygia was originally conceded to Mithridates V of Pontus; Nicomedes II of Bithynia also hoped for concessions. The Lycian League remained autonomous allies of Rome, as did many cities in Caria and in the Pergamene kingdom proper, e.g. Pergamum, Ephesus, Laodicea-on-Lycus, Aphrodisias. Over the revenues extracted from the province there is unsolved controversy. On the one hand it is certain that Rome drew rents from the leases of the public (once royal) land, leases which may have in part been taken up by Roman citizens. For the rest it is alleged in a speech attributed by Appian to M. Antonius in 42–41 B.C.

30 Strab. XIV.1.38 (646–8); Plut. *Ti. Gracch.* 14.1–2; *OGIS* 338; other sources in *Greenidge–Clay* 11–12, 17–18; Robinson 1954 (B 234); Vogt 1974 (A 123) 93–102.

31 *IGRR* IV.292; *ILLRP* 455–6; Holleaux 1938 (B 174), cf. *Bull.ep.* (1963) no 220; (1984) 349–52, 384; Dakaris 1987 (B 147) 16–17 – dedication by three Cassopeans who served in war-chariots under Perperna. J. and L. Robert, *Claros* I, *Les décrets hellénistiques* (Paris, 1989).

that the Romans had rescinded the taxes which they paid to Attalus, until demagogues arose at Rome and with them the need for tribute. This is apparently confirmed by the fragment of the speech of C. Gracchus against the Lex Aufeia, a law which seems to have been enacting Aquillius' settlement, since in this speech Gracchus claims to be increasing Rome's revenues and defending the welfare of the Roman people. Against this, an inscription partially preserving a *senatus consultum* relating to disputes in Pergamene territory refers to the farming out of the revenues of Asia and to the decision of a magistrate about land in a dispute probably involving tax-collectors (*publicani*). A consul, M'. Aquillius, is mentioned in the decree. If he is the consul of 129, then we have evidence for the collection of revenues near Pergamum before C. Gracchus, but, if he is the consul of 101, the argument collapses. It is likely in view of their general practice that from 129 the Romans at least drew revenues from transit-dues (*portoria*) in Asia and imposed an indemnity or tribute on the cities that had sided with Aristonicus, in addition to the rents on public land.[32] Then C. Gracchus enacted that the collection of direct and indirect taxes in Asia should be farmed out to *societates* of *publicani* at an auction in Rome, and it seems probable to the present writer that this formed part of a general overhaul of Asiatic taxation in the interest of increased income. The desire to extract the maximum profit from Asia was not, however, confined to so-called demagogues. When Mithridates V died, the Romans reannexed Phrygia at the expense of his son.

In the years that followed a great number of Romans and Italians migrated into Asia, even if we discount the more exaggerated figures given for those massacred on Mithridates VI's orders. Not surprisingly, there were arguments over taxation. Apart from the issue at Pergamum (mentioned above) we have epigraphic evidence of a long-running dispute between Priene and the Roman tax-collectors over the exploitation of salt-pans. Businessmen spread into neighbouring kingdoms. Nicomedes III of Bithynia complained, when asked by Marius for military aid in 104, that Romans had taken his subjects as slaves. This in turn led to greater public involvement in politics and strategy in Asia Minor. The Delphi–Cnidus law about the provinces of 101–100 was concerned not only with the elimination of piracy but with the consolidation of Roman rule in the East. The province of Asia now extended to include Lycaonia and there is a reference too to Pamphylia. Cilicia had been made a praetorian province, presumably as the centre of

32 *IGRR* IV.1692; *ILLRP* 174–7; Reynolds 1982 (B 226) 6ff; App. *BCiv.* V.4.17; *ORF* no. 48, fr. 44; Sherk 1984 (B 239) 12; Mattingly 1972 (B 200). An inscription from Ephesus of Nero's reign shows how the Romans adapted the Attalid system of taxation, especially in relation to *portoria*, Engelmann and Knibbe 1989 (B 150).

campaigning against the pirates. Meanwhile Didius' operations in Thrace had led to the province of Macedonia almost stretching to Byzantium.[33] Roman physical power surrounded the Aegean and was penetrating further into Asia Minor than at any previous time, further than in the aftermath of the defeat of Antiochus III at Magnesia in 190. The irony was that the submissive Seleucid and Egyptian kingdoms – the basis of Rome's indirect rule in the East – were at this time insecure, while beyond the Halys and the Euphrates new challengers to the Roman empire, Mithridates VI and the Parthians, were building up their power.

VII. MILITARY STRENGTH AND THE EMPIRE

The foregoing survey has largely been concerned with what was from the Roman point of view the credit side of the empire – territorial expansion and public and private advantages that accrued from it. The consequent problems in Rome and Italy will be the subject of the next chapter. However, it is appropriate to consider here one particular item on the debit side of the balance sheet, the demands made on the Roman army.

Immediately after the Third Macedonian War the Romans did not have to maintain as many men under arms as in the preceding period of conquest, but this changed from 149 onwards and requirements reached a new peak in the last decade of the century with the coincidence of the Jugurthine War, the great invasions of the northern tribes and some campaigning in the East. Up to her defeat at Arausio in 105 Rome needed at least eight legions and in 101 at least twelve were probably in service, as many as at any time since the Second Punic War. The burden fell in theory on those with property (*assidui*). Those below the minimum property qualification – the *proletarii* or *capite censi* – were not normally liable for service in the legions, though they could serve in the fleet and in an emergency (*tumultus*), when the city of Rome's own safety was at stake, they had since the time of the war with Pyrrhus been drafted and armed as legionaries. Some may have gone with Scipio Aemilianus to Numantia in 134. Marius is known to have enrolled volunteers from the *capite censi*, when reinforcing the African legions in 107. He would have been doing nothing abnormal, if he had continued to recruit *capite censi* in the crisis caused by the German threat in 104 onwards, and not only volunteers but conscripts.[34]

Difficulty in recruiting soldiers is directly attested by resistance to levies for the Third Macedonian War in 171 and later and for Spanish

[33] *IPriene*, no. 111; Diod. XXXVI.3; Hassall, Crawford and Reynolds 1974 (B 170) 201–4.
[34] Brunt 1971 (A 17) 394–415, 430–1; Gabba 1976 (C 55) 2–19.

Wars from 151 onwards. It is also indirectly attested by the reduction of the minimum property qualification from the 10,000–11,000 *asses* – attributed to the system of Servius Tullius, but in fact deriving from the Second Punic War – to the 4,000 *asses* known to Polybius. (Rich has raised serious doubts about whether the figure of 1,500 *asses* attributed to the Servian constitution in Cicero's *De Republica* can in fact be taken as the property qualification current in 129.) Scipio Aemilianus was forced to seek volunteers for his Numantine campaign in 134. C. Gracchus legislated to prevent the enlistment of under-age soldiers. In 109 the Senate felt it necessary to annul previous legislation which, it held, damaged Rome's war-effort by limiting conscription. It is not certain how far the problem arose from the numerical shortage of *assidui*: the problem was at least compounded by the reluctance to serve of those available and fit to fight.[35]

However, the recruitment problem was not all: the record of the army in the field was not beyond reproach. The early débâcles against Jugurtha may be put down to corruption and poor leadership. Yet there were a series of disasters and near-disasters in the fighting on the northern frontier – Sex. Pompeius in Macedonia in 119, C. Cato in Thrace in 114, Cn. Carbo in Norican territory in 113, M. Silanus in the Rhône valley in 109, L. Cassius on the west coast of Gaul in 107, Q. Caepio and Cn. Mallius at Arausio in 105. These failures and the patchy record of the army in Spain in the Viriathic War earlier cast doubt not only on the quality of the generals and their troops but on the tactical effectiveness of the Roman army. Apart from the change in recruitment, our sources ascribe to Marius some limited changes in military practice. The eagle became for the first time the chief legionary standard; light-armed troops ceased to use *parmulae* (small round shields); the *pilum* (a throwing spear) was fitted with a weak rivet, so that the shaft drooped from the head on impact, thus hampering the man hit and preventing the weapon from being immediately reused; soldiers were expected to carry more of their own equipment over their shoulders on a special fork-shaped carrier. No one mentions a major change in tactical organization. Yet the form of the Roman army did change fundamentally between the middle Republic, for which we have detailed evidence from Polybius and to some extent from Livy, and the time of Caesar's Gallic War, when Caesar himself provided authoritative descriptions of the army's operations. Modern scholars have tended to ascribe the decisive change to Marius, partly on account of his reputation as an innovator and of the challenge of the Germanic invasions, partly because what are on our

35 Livy I.43.8; Dion. Hal. *Ant. Rom.* IV.17–18; Polyb. VI.19.2; Gell. *NA* XVI.10.10; Cic. *Rep.* II.40; Plut. *C. Gracch.* 5; Asc. 68C; Rich 1983 (C 121); Hopkins 1978 (A 53) 35ff for calculations of the proportion of young adults that were required for conscription.

evidence the last traces of the old system can be found in Sallust's *Jugurtha*.[36]

The legion known to Polybius was already a complex military machine, as sophisticated as the Hellenistic formations it defeated, and far removed from the majority of the hoplite phalanxes of the classical Greek world. It was subdivided into three ranks, which each contained ten maniples; a maniple had two centurions and 100–200 men, depending on the rank to which it belonged. The first two ranks, the *hastati* and *principes*, were equipped with body-armour and one-metre-high convex shields (*scuta*), throwing-spears (*pila*) and Spanish swords (*gladii*). The third rank of *triarii*, the heavy infantry, who were only half in number of each of the first two ranks, had the heavy thrusting-spear (*hasta*) in place of the *pilum* but were otherwise equipped in the same way. Each rank had 400 light-armed troops (*velites*) assigned to it, who had no body-armour but a helmet and carried a sword, javelins and a light shield. The youngest recruits were made *velites*; then the ranks of *hastati*, *principes* and *triarii* were filled in ascending order of age. The most experienced, the *triarii*, were understood to be the last line of defence. At the beginning of the levy 300 cavalry were recruited from Roman citizens to be associated with each legion. There was thus variation in equipment between and even within ranks, and considerable flexibility and mobility, which appeared to best advantage in hilly country and over rough ground. Furthermore the small divisions of the army made it well suited for attacks over a small front or flank-attacks. In these respects Polybius judged the legion superior to the Macedonian phalanx, which was invincible in the right position on suitable terrain but cumbersome and vulnerable from the flank and rear.[37]

By Caesar's time the system of separate ranks differentiated by age and arms had disappeared, though the names (e.g. *hastatus*) were still used to distinguish centurions. Romans were no longer recruited as light-armed troops into legions: this function was performed by allied auxiliaries organized in separate units. Similarly Roman cavalry had been entirely replaced by the allied cavalry, mainly from Gaul, Spain or Numidia, which Rome had been using since the Second Punic War. Within the legion itself the tactical unit was the cohort of about 400–500 men, which was also used independently in minor operations. It is easy to understand why the Romans substituted more effective allied cavalry and light infantry for their own, especially if they were short of manpower. The changes in the heavy infantry are a greater problem. In fact we find cohorts attested in Polybius' and Livy's accounts of Spanish campaigns before 190 and such units were used, according to Frontinus, in Spain

36 Kromayer and Veith 1928 (A 59) 299ff, 376ff; Marquadt and Wissowa 1881–5 (A 69) II.432ff.

37 Polyb. VI.19ff; XVIII.27–32; Livy VIII.18.3ff; Rawson 1971 (B 93) 13–31.

later in the second century. Yet camps outside Numantia were still organized in manipular sections. The last positive evidence for the *hastati*, *principes* and *triarii* functioning as separate ranks is in Sallust's account of Metellus' battle against Jugurtha at the river Muthul, but shortly after this passage we find both Metellus and Marius using cohorts as their tactical unit. *Velites* still appear in this war and indeed are said by Frontinus to have been used by Sulla at Orchomenus in 86.[38]

It has been argued that the evidence suggests a more gradual introduction of the cohort, and that this can be explained in part by the requirements of campaigning in Spain, where a number of self-sufficient detachments were required, in part by the need to have a more solid basic unit in pitched battles when confronting the concentrated charges of Celts or Iberians; the process was then completed by Marius in order to create a suitable defence against the Cimbri. This is more convincing than simply to explain the change as a sudden response to the German threat, but perhaps is itself not quite sufficient. In one sense the formation of the legion becomes less complex and sophisticated. The challenge of the great Hellenistic armies was absent after Pydna. Meanwhile the army suffered a shortage of recruits and, more important – to judge from Marius' efforts in 107 – a shortage of experienced men re-enlisting. Instead men formerly *capite censi* were pressed into legionary service. The grading of ranks by age would in these circumstances have become inappropriate and the specialization of the *triarii* in the use of the *hasta* a luxury. The soldiers may well have become man for man poorer soldiers through lack of battle experience and this in turn may have made the maniple too small to be secure as a unit. Marius still deserves credit as a reformer, but as one who brought to a close a period of evolution, which was as much a decline in Roman fighting-power as a response to new challenges. Faced with an army which was becoming less differentiated, skilled and disciplined, Marius made a virtue of uniformity by training every legionary properly in one repertoire of skills.

[38] Sall. *Jug.* 46.7; 49.6; 54.3; 55.4; 56.4; 100.4; 105.2; Frontin. *Str.* II.3.17; Keppie 1984 (A 57) 46–50, 63ff; Bell 1965 (C 22); Schulten 1927 (B 316) III.134ff.

CHAPTER 3

POLITICAL HISTORY, 146–95 B.C.

ANDREW LINTOTT

Roman morality and political harmony were at their height, wrote Sallust, between the Second and Third Punic Wars. After this came the evils that accompany prosperity – strife, greed, ambition and the pursuit of ascendancy by powerful men.[1] The inadequacies of this kind of explanation and of the precise dividing line drawn here by Sallust were discussed in chapter 1 (pp. 7–9). In spite of this there is no doubt that the razing of Carthage introduced an era of political crisis, whose antagonisms recalled the dimly remembered struggles of the early Republic and brought into question the stability of the constitution which Polybius admired.

Polybius thought that the common people were wronged through the greed of some men and given a false sense of importance through the ambitions of others. These exploited the truculence and recklessness of the poor in order to dominate the constitution and created what was in name democracy but was in fact mob-rule. Modern scholars are in general reluctant to recognize so dramatic a change, at least in Polybius' lifetime. The present writer has argued in an earlier book that the violence of the late Republic should not be regarded as the result of a sudden reversal of Roman values but the re-emergence of long-standing attitudes and conflicts, which had been temporarily suppressed by political prudence and the profits from success abroad. On the other hand, it is not excessively superficial to look to the personalities of men like the Gracchi and see in their imagination and resolve the initial moment of a new political process. However, this can only be done when we have discerned how much of the late Republic was already present in that middle period renowned in Sallust's eyes for its moderation.

I. THE ROMAN CONSTITUTION IN THE SECOND CENTURY B.C.

Aristotle would have treated the Roman constitution either as a mixture of the basic forms of constitution (monarchy, oligarchy and democracy), as Polybius did later, or else as one of the more moderate forms of

[1] Sall. *H.* I.11M.

democracy, close to the ill-defined border he drew between this and moderate oligarchy. The Roman body politic was not completely in the power of either rich or poor; all citizens to some extent participated in politics, but the law was sovereign, and the few offices were only available to those with a property qualification. The social basis of the constitution was in theory a class of farmers, rather than the manual workers and tradesmen in the city.[2]

In its early years the Republic was a broad oligarchy, whose hereditary aristocracy sought to justify its dominance of office and policy by appealing to assemblies of men who formed its supreme military arm – the heavily armed soldiers of the *classis*, that is, the Roman equivalent of the hoplite phalanx. The struggle of the plebeians with the patricians led not only to a change of balance in the relationships of the primitive constitution, but introduced a new element which, in spite of clever grafting, was never fully reconciled with the ethos of the dominant class. The aristocracy was opened to outsiders; the importance of the assemblies as the source of authority and of rewards and penalties was more strongly asserted; indeed the written laws passed by assemblies came to supersede aristocratic traditions even in such reserved fields as religion. All this lay within the framework of the original constitution. However, the poor also acquired their own spokesmen and magistrates (the tribunes and aediles of the plebs) and their own assembly (the *concilium plebis*). Moreover, through collective physical action and the guarantees of support that they gave to their tribunes, they achieved protection against arbitrary treatment by magistrates. This protection against summary physical punishment through execution and flogging, called *provocatio*, became enshrined in law (the first law was probably of 300 B.C.). Similarly, the existence and functions of the tribunes themselves became accepted as a constitutional fact from the time of the Twelve Tables onwards. This process culminated in the Lex Hortensia of 287 B.C., by which *plebiscita* were given the force of laws without further ratification. The tribunes thus achieved the right to legislate and prosecute in their own assemblies, and their physical inviolability (sacrosanctity), which the plebs had originally sworn to uphold, allowed them not only to defend the persons of individual citizens (*auxilium*) but to impede actions by other magistrates (*intercessio*) and so veto their taking effect.[3]

Such was the process of natural growth, which produced Rome's mixed constitution. This constitution, however, in Polybius' view, was still dominated at the time of the Second Punic War by its aristocratic element, the Senate – by contrast with Carthage, which had already passed its zenith and allowed the common people too much influence in

[2] Arist. *Pol.* 1291b–1293b; 1266a; 1279b.

[3] Bleicken 1955 (F 24); Lintott 1972 (F 102).

2 Italy and Sicily

deliberation.[4] In fact, not only the oligarchic element in the Senate, but the monarchic element in the magistracies played an enormous part. Rome's executive in the second century B.C. was to be found in eight annually elected senior magistrates (two consuls, six praetors) supported by those ex-consuls and ex-praetors whose annual term had been prolonged in service abroad. Among junior officials, the aediles looked after the fabric of Rome itself and the administration of life there. Quaestors were assistants to senior magistrates or in some cases had independent, mainly financial, functions. There were also elected boards to administer the mint, city police-work and from time to time the distribution of land. The censors every five years reviewed the size and class-structure of the citizen body and regulated certain aspects of state income and expenditure.

The senior magistrates were granted immense discretion in the fighting of wars and the government of subject peoples, limited only by the possibility of prosecution once they left office – a real threat, but one which could be frustrated, as is shown by Servius Galba's escape from charges of brutality in 149 and the acquittals between 138 and 123 in the first four cases known to us *de repetundis* (concerning the recovery of money illegally extracted from allies).[5] The authority exercised by Roman magistrates abroad is exemplified by the fact that it was Scipio Aemilianus himself as proconsul, who after the defeat of Carthage in 146 drew the line which was to separate Roman territory from that assigned to the descendants of Massinissa (p. 27). Although senior magistrates did not have such arbitrary powers in the domestic field on account of the potential opposition of tribunes, the legal framework of political activity and the tradition of consulting the advice of the Senate, it required the initiative of a senior magistrate or a tribune to set in motion legislation or a policy in administration. The Senate could not meet without being convened by a consul, praetor or tribune, nor could the formal and informal meetings of the people required for legislation.

Voting in assemblies decided who should hold office and what laws should bind the *populus Romanus*, but this democratic sovereignty was so heavily nuanced in practice that historians have tended to react excessively and completely underrate the popular element in the constitution. The organization of the military assembly (*comitia centuriata*), which elected consuls and praetors, has been described in Vol. VIII², pp. 198–204, 337–8, 440–3). In its revised form, dating from the late third century, the knights (*equites*) and the wealthiest of the five other classes had a disproportionate influence, to the extent that in a closely contested consular election with three front-running candidates for two places the result would probably have been decided early in the returns of the third

[4] Polyb. VI.9.10–12; 10.12–14; 51.3–8. [5] Lintott, 1981 (F 104) 166–7, 173–5, 209.

class, the fourth and fifth being effectively disfranchised. The divisions within the classes by tribes (the regional voting-districts used to form the centuries whose decisions were the component blocks in the election) favoured those with a country domicile against those from the city of Rome itself. There were thirty-one rural tribes to four urban. (The votes of freedmen were confined by 146 B.C. to the urban tribes, though this restriction had been removed for a period in the early second century.) However, this imbalance was modified to some extent by the fact that seventeen of the rural tribes had territory within a day's journey from Rome. Moreover, migration to Rome would have already entailed that many of those living there were registered in a rural tribe. The tribal assemblies – the *comitia tributa* and the *concilium plebis* – voted simply with the thirty-five tribes as their component blocks. Thus in these assemblies, where the greater part of legislation took place, there was no clear bias towards the wealthy.[6]

Nevertheless, assemblies might be unrepresentative for a more circumstantial reason – the scanty attendance of men from distant voting-districts, perhaps two-thirds of the total Roman citizen body at the time. Attendance from such areas was expected and indeed organized by politicians, in whose interest it was, for major and predictable events, like the consular elections, or an important bill. For instance, C. Marius solicited support from the country areas as well as the town before his election in 108. Votes on legislation occurring at irregular intervals during the year, however, could not be expected to command consistent support, especially as they might clash with local preoccupations. Ti. Gracchus got countrymen to come and vote for his agrarian bill, but was unable to mobilize them again to vote for his re-election to the tribunate, because it was harvest-time.[7] Politicians canvassed before elections – traditionally over three market-days (*nundinae*). Similarly they presented bills to informal gatherings (*contiones*) before formal legislation in a duly convened assembly (in 98 it was laid down that the publication of a bill must extend over at least three market-days prior to legislation). However, *contiones* were not occasions for general debate. They must have resembled rather a public meeting held by a candidate for election in contemporary democratic countries. Citizens who were not magistrates had a right to speak, but no doubt these were members of the governing class. The audience would have been usually small (*contiones* often met in the Comitium – a small open-air auditorium outside the senate-house) and there were on occasion competing *contiones* in the Forum.

Nevertheless, in the second century B.C. the assemblies decided not only on alterations in public and private law but on major policies over a

[6] Taylor 1960 (F 156); 1966 (F 157). [7] Sall. *Iug.* 73.6; App. *BCiv.* 1.14.58–9.

wide range of issues. Such issues were citizenship, colonization and public land, finance (including taxation, coinage and interest-rates), religion, social matters, for example the restraint of conspicuous luxury in sumptuary laws, and in foreign policy the making of war, peace and treaties. Assemblies were also used to conduct political prosecutions, especially by tribunes and aediles, though the procedure was cumbersome and in capital cases according to a law of the Twelve Tables the final vote had to be held in the *comitia centuriata*. However, the *populus Romanus* did not on the whole concern itself with the details of administration, especially of war and foreign policy, and in this it differed widely from the assembly of classical Athens.

As we have noticed in chapter 1, scholars since Mommsen have been inclined to treat the assemblies as institutions manipulated by the aristocracy or at least by individual aristocrats. Of course, even the Athenian assembly fell under the sway of its leading politicians, and once it is granted that a Roman assembly had a choice between following a Fabius and following a Cornelius Scipio or between a Scipio and the rest of the aristocracy, then it has a genuine power of decision. There was, however, one particular way in which a Roman voter was subject to pressure from the aristocracy until the beginning of this historical period. The Lex Gabinia of 139 introduced for the first time secret ballot into elections; there followed a series of laws extending this right – the Lex Cassia of 137 about non-capital prosecutions, the Lex Papiria of 131 about legislation and the Lex Coelia of 107 about capital prosecutions. A notorious passage of Cicero argues that previously open voting had allowed the authority of the 'best men' to have its greatest effect. The presiding magistrate and his polling officers (*rogatores*) would have been especially well placed to exploit this, but pressure and intimidation from other quarters was possible and in fact continued after the introduction of secret voting.[8]

In the middle Republic the *fasti* show many instances of the succession of one member of a family by another in the consulship, for example the Postumii and Popillii Laenates in the years 174–172, and there are texts attesting the importance of the presidency of electoral assemblies. Yet the presiding magistrate did not always have his way, or else he had to resort to extreme measures for success. Appius Claudius (cos. 185) was alleged to have used force to get his brother elected for 184. By contrast, the pursuit of popular favour (*ambitio*) by new men led to the creation of a special judicial process for electoral bribery (*ambitus*) and made the results of elections less predictable.[9] The whole issue of patron–client

[8] Cic. *Leg.* III.34; Lintott 1968 (A 62) 69–73.

[9] Livy XXXIX.32.10–14; cf. XXXV.10.9; XXXVIII.3.5; XL.17.8; XL.19; *Per.* XLVII; Plaut. *Amph.* 62ff; *Poen.* 36ff, Rilinger 1976 (F 131).

relationships, which have been thought to have determined the voting of the lower classes, will be considered below in the context of the working of the aristocracy. Here it is sufficient to remark that the influence of presiding magistrates and the growth of *ambitus* both contradict the notion that the votes of humble men were securely tied to the wishes of existing patrons. More generally, though popular feeling frequently expressed itself in the support of one prominent aristocratic politician or another, there was an autonomy in this, which went beyond the machinations of the politicians themselves. Scipio Aemilianus received his first consulship in 147, before the normal time, through popular demand. Those who supported Ti. Gracchus in 133 did so largely because they favoured his measures. Similarly, the humble men, who voted for ballot laws like the Lex Gabinia or earlier for Cato's *lex de provocatione*, would have done so for the most part not through personal connexions with the legislators and their backers but because the measure itself secured their allegiance. It is significant that the Leges Porciae and the Lex Cassia were both celebrated by coins bearing the type of Libertas.[10]

The extent of popular influence on politics in Rome must also be judged by reference to the power of the aristocracy, in particular the workings of the Senate. After the regular admission of plebeians to curule magistracies and the Senate in the fourth century B.C., access to high office was limited *de facto*, if not *de iure*, by a property qualification. Only those whose families came from the senatorial order, the equestrian order or perhaps the obscure order of *tribuni aerarii* (who probably had to possess the same financial status as *equites*) were in a position to apply. On late third-century figures this amounted to about 8 per cent of the total adult male citizen population. After one hundred years this proportion may well have risen through the influx of wealth from overseas. The minimum property qualification of *equites* in the late Republic, 400,000 sesterces, was modest compared with the average wealth of senators. The membership of the Senate was determined by the censors every five years. By the late second century any man who had held at least the curule aedileship had the right to become a member, unless he was in some way morally disreputable, and this privilege was extended to ex-tribunes by a Lex Atinia.

The feature of this aristocracy, which immediately catches the eye, is the core of families who maintained themselves at the centre of politics with their members regularly in high office, some patrician, like the Fabian and Cornelian *gentes*, some plebeian like the Caecilii Metelli and branches of the *gens Sempronia*. A small number of plebeian *gentes*, still

[10] Crawford 1974 (B 144) nos. 266, 270. On the democratic element in Roman politics in general see Millar 1986 (C 113); Lintott 1987 (A 65).

important in the last years of the Republic, could boast consulships attained by their members in the late fourth or early third century (in addition to those above, examples are the Claudii Marcelli, Domitii and Licinii). In fact about half the consuls in the late third and second centuries B.C. came from ten *gentes*, though within these there were often many different branches. However, this does not mean that the Roman aristocracy was a closed group – like the mediaeval Venetian aristocracy, for example. Sallust complained that the nobility passed the consulship from hand to hand and thought that a new man sullied the dignity of the office. Yet one third of those who reached the consulship between the Second Punic War and the end of the Republic were from families with no consular members in the last three generations and of these only about 10 per cent probably had praetorian antecedents. Only one third of these consulars without consular ancestry had a consular son, whereas the sons of those with consular ancestry were more likely to maintain consular standing in their generation, especially about the time of the Second Punic War. Thus outside the leading families in the aristocracy there were many gains and losses of the status that went with high office, and it is also likely that at the fringe of the Senate its composition by families was fluid even before the admission of new recruits into Sulla's enlarged Senate from enfranchised Italian communities.[11]

The Senate was the meeting-place of the governing class and the only official location where genuine debate about politics could take place. As such, it settled matters which otherwise would have led to controversy between magistrates and between them and the rest of the governing class, such as the allocation of provinces, troops and money. Moreover, it was the only body which could be expected to make authoritative policy recommendations to magistrates, whether these were matters for executive action or to be formulated into legislative proposals before an assembly. Its decrees, though technically never more than advice to magistrates, had in Italy and elsewhere among Rome's allies the effect of mass-edicts by Roman magistrates, although the majority of the senators were not in office at the time. Indeed, these decrees were treated as more authoritative than a magistrate's decision.[12] They also were privileged, in so far as the Senate, unlike the magistrates who executed the decrees, could not be held to account for taking arbitrary decisions, even if these were contrary to the will of the *populus Romanus*.

The essence of procedure in the Senate was that the convening magistrate (consul, praetor or tribune) put forward a subject for discussion and then asked the opinion of members in order of seniority. When these had either delivered opinions at length or indicated their

[11] Sall. *Iug.* 73.6–7; Hopkins and Burton 1983 (A 54) 55ff.

[12] Polyb. VI.13.4–5; *Bruns* nos. 36ff; Sherk 1984 (B 239) esp. no. 9, lines 63ff.

assent to a previous speaker, he selected a motion or motions for a vote from among the opinions put forward. The consequent resolution might be vetoed by tribunes, so becoming a *senatus auctoritas*, which had not the claim to obedience of an uncontested decree, *senatus consultum*. The *senatus consulta* were recorded permanently in writing in the treasury, like laws. (*Auctoritates* by contrast might also be drafted but would not be engraved on bronze.) Generally, the authority of the senior senators, the ex-consuls called to speak first, would have been decisive in debates, though there was to be one famous occasion on 5 December 63 B.C. when the fate of the Catilinarian conspirators hung on the opinions of a praetor-elect and a tribune-elect, Caesar and Cato. On many items of business a consensus would have prevailed. Yet on occasions – for example over the treatment of Carthage in 152 and in 133 over Ti. Gracchus' agrarian bill and later his attempt to get re-elected – there was major controversy between leading members.[13] It is still not clear on our evidence, however, how policy was normally formed in the Senate, or whether, as has been suggested, there was an inner ruling group which was effectively the government of Rome.

According to Sallust, the tradition of politics, factions and every kind of malpractice had arisen, when the era of concord had ended with the destruction of Carthage. He talks of two *partes*, the nobility and the *populus* or plebs – the 'few' and the 'many' of the Greek world. Although both sides are criticized for tearing the Republic apart, it is the few powerful men (the Latin *potentes* is the equivalent of Greek *dunatoi*, that is, the governing class), who take effective decisions about foreign and domestic policy, official postings, war and finance, and so reap the profits, while the poor die through war or poverty, expelled from the land by more powerful men. The nobility prevail through *factio* – a word which in its original sense is not equivalent to faction in English, but means rather the power and influence associated with wealth. Elsewhere in Sallust *factio* is said to be the depraved form of friendship, what might be termed a cabal or conspiracy, or else it is the term for the dominant class, like the English word 'establishment'. Cicero similarly uses the word for an oligarchic ruling group or junta.[14] Sometimes Sallust portrays Roman politics as a struggle between a largely coherent aristocracy in the Senate and a mass of poor men assisted by a few popular heroes. However, in his treatment of the late Republic he adopts the cynicism expressed by Thucydides in the digression on civil strife at Corcyra: politicians, although they might adopt honest-sounding programmes of defending the rights of the people or the authority of the Senate, under the pretext of the public interest strove for their own power. How far this description was fair, it would be premature to

[13] Astin 1967 (C 2); Badian, 1972 (C 16) 706ff.

[14] Seager 1972 (A 109).

decide at this point. It is, however, relevant to point out that such corrupt politics would have derived their specious appeal from the existence of genuine traditions of defending the status of the aristocracy or the rights of the people.

These traditions are frequently alluded to in Cicero's speeches and philosophical works. It is the function of the so-called good men (*boni* or *optimates*) to maintain tranquillity and respect for rank (*otium cum dignitate*). This was the preservation of the *status quo* through deference for the authority of the Senate, which in turn rested on the dignity of its members, who had been elected to high office by the people. This dignity depended in theory on merit (*virtus*), but Cicero makes it plain that wealth, which in practice gave its possessors the greatest status in the community, was also a *sine qua non*. The monopolization of the adjectives denoting virtue by the wealthy governing class of Rome – a characteristic earlier of Greek aristocracies – is first attested in the eighties B.C., but probably goes back to the second century and reflects the influence of Greek political thought on Rome. The basic ideology, however, was fundamental to the aristocracy since the early Republic. There were on the other hand dissenters, those who wanted their actions and words to be agreeable to the *populus* and legislated in the interest of the masses, the *populares*. Though Cicero was sceptical about the pretensions of such political opponents of his in his own day, he conceded that in the past at least men had genuinely sought to serve the will of the common people.[15]

It is easy to see how Mommsen was misled into likening the *optimates* and *populares* to Conservatives and Liberals in the British parliament. His successors and critics, however, were able to show that this was simply not the way Roman politics worked, chiefly by appealing to Cicero's less philosophical utterances. There were in fact no political parties in the modern sense with organizations and formulated policies. The *optimates* might embrace at some periods the whole governing class at Rome, while the *populares* were essentially individuals who might on occasion combine with or imitate others of their kind, but at bottom lacked coherence and continuity on the political scene. It is hard to link *popularis* politicians on the basis of a common programme and, although they did share a *modus operandi* – that of direct appeal to the assembly bypassing the Senate, this tactic was sometimes adopted by those of conservative outlook. Men did not usually stand for elections by appealing to policies. (Cicero, if we take as genuine the letter from his brother on canvassing, was advised to avoid political commitments.) Indeed men entered politics to fulfil personal expectations, either of maintaining their due place in Roman society or of achieving a new rank commensurate with their worth, and to assist their relatives and friends. Their *virtus* was to

[15] Ferrary 1982 (A 29); Perelli 1982 (A 90) 25ff; Balsdon 1960 (F 14).

find expression in the offices they held and the glory they derived from their service to the state, especially in war.[16]

On what basis, then, were political alliances made among senators? In Cicero's day these were essentially viewed as personal connexions, based on kinship and friendship (*amicitia*) and cemented by exchange of political and private services (*beneficia* or *officia*). The latter was summed up in the word *gratia*, which meant both the thanks due to someone for his help and the consequent influence of the donor. Ideally political allies were intellectually and temperamentally congenial with mutual liking for one another; in practice more utilitarian relationships were to be found. There is a resemblance to British politics in the eighteenth century and many statements made about this period can be illuminatingly transferred to the politics of Rome. Charles James Fox's remark, 'Is it possible to be happy in acting with people of whom one has the worst opinions, and being on a cold footing (which must be the case) with all those whom one loves best, and with whom one passes one's life?', could have been taken straight from Cicero's treatise *On Friendship*. The late Republic and the British political scene in the eighteenth century were both worlds of small political groups constructed out of families and friendships, which could swiftly break and reform, and whose members frequently had conflicting allegiances.[17]

There are, however, important differences. Although both British and Roman politicians sought office and its rewards for themselves and their friends, there was constitutionally no 'government' by a political group in Rome. Rather, the Senate relied on a persistent consensus and the co-operation of leading magistrates for stability in policy. Nor were there at Rome the factors that promoted coherence out of the loose and shifting interplay of politicians in Britain – the basic mould of government and opposition and the large resources of patronage available to government. The nearest parallel to the latter at Rome are the posts of legates, tribunes and prefects at the disposal of great commanders, notably those available to Caesar and Pompey. The granting of these posts and advocacy in the courts were probably the two most important ways of winning friends by performing services.

On the evidence of the regular assistance afforded by friends and kinsfolk at elections and during political prosecutions and their less frequent association in political policies, Münzer and his followers have argued that, rather than large ideological parties, small family factions determined the course of Roman politics: these sought by investing their members with magistracies, commands and prestige to become *de facto* the government at Rome and to dominate the state in their own interest.

[16] Earl 1961 (B 31) ch. 3; Strasburger 1939 (A 116); Meier 1966 (A 72) 116ff; Wiseman 1985 (A 132) 1–43.

[17] R. Pares, *King George III and the Politicians* (Oxford, 1953) 75.

There are several problems with this thesis. The first is the sheer lack of evidence from the period for which we have the most detailed information (that covered by Cicero's letters) of factions of this kind. Certainly, everyone, not least Cicero, strove to acquire as many personal connexions as possible with influential men and with associations like tribes, guilds (*collegia*) and clubs (*sodalitates*), but in this they were not limited to men with whom they regularly associated. An important text from the very end of the Republic, when a cleavage had developed between the supporters of Caesar and of Pompey, contrasts party-sentiment with personal connexions. The reference to party-sentiment is itself unparalleled, and this is contrasted with the connexions (*necessitudines*) which we know from Cicero's writings to have been regarded as the important factor in other elections.[18] Secondly, even if we assume that factions of the kind presupposed by Münzer existed, though concealed by our sources, it is not plain how they would have regularly mobilized the votes needed to get members of the group into office and the measures they favoured into effect. Scipio Aemilianus was dismayed in 142, when Q. Pompeius, whom he believed to be his supporter, broke away and campaigned on his own account for the consulship against Scipio's favoured candidate, C. Laelius. Scipio and Ti. Gracchus, who were not only cousins but connected by marriage through Gracchus' sister, were at odds politically and further divided by Gracchus' marriage to the daughter of an opponent of Scipio's, Appius Claudius.

The links produced by marriages and adoptions produced such a complex network that it becomes difficult to isolate a stable unit between the microcosm of the individual politician and his intimates and the macrocosm of the *potentes* (the leading senators) viewed as a whole. An election like that of 54 B.C. could create bewildering uncertainty about allegiances. As for the belief that the type of faction envisaged could rely on a block of supporters through *clientelae*,[19] as we have seen earlier, this is not supported by the evidence about the early second century. This does not mean that patron–client relationships were unimportant. A contemporary document, the *lex de repetundis* inscribed on bronze (see p. 5) proves the contrary. This disqualifies as *patroni* (advocates) of the accuser and witnesses for the prosecution those who are in any patron–client relationship (*fides*) with the accused. It is of course on occasions when a man's political existence, if not his continued membership of the community, was at stake, that he could expect the support of friends and connexions, whatever their political views (the best example of this is the roll-call of incompatibles who supported M. Scaurus in 54).[20] However,

[18] Cic. *Comment. Pet.* 16–19, 30; *Fam.* VIII.14.1; Meier 1966 (A 72).

[19] See most recently Rouland 1979 (A 99), and for a critique of such views Brunt 1988 (A 19) 382ff.

[20] Gruen 1974 (C 209) 332–7.

an important feature of the clauses in the *lex de repetundis* is that they refer to both present and past patron–client relationships, demonstrating both their impermanence and on the other hand the residual effect that was believed to survive a break in such a connexion. In this light such links seem less rigid and more likely to conflict with one another. The very growth of bribery is testimony to a weakening rather than a strengthening of control by the aristocracy. We may be inclined to apply what Namier wrote about Britain, contrasting aristocratic bullying with the demand for benefits from below: 'Corruption was not a shower-bath from above . . . but a waterspout springing from the rock of freedom to meet the demands of the People'.[21]

One way of meeting such arguments is to accept that groups were not rigid and their ascendancies on the whole not very effective, but to regard the faction thesis as an ideal model of the Roman political game. Even then theoretical difficulties remain. Münzer's statement, 'Every political party strives for power and a dominant position in the state',[22] is for us today a self-evident truth: it might indeed be taken as an analytic statement defining the word 'party' and distinguishing it from other political associations and pressure-groups. Yet one should not call a Roman political group a party and endow it with the characteristics implied by that word now. Roman groups did strive for office for their members, but this did not correspond to placing itself in government, as it did in eighteenth-century Britain. In order to prove that, one would have to show that voting in the Senate was regularly on group lines; and this was not even true of the last twelve months of the Republic, when battle-lines were already being drawn between Caesarian and Pompeian supporters, still less can it be asserted about the Senate's conduct in 133.

As for *optimates* and *populares*, even though they came from the same social class with its framework of individual and family connexions, this is no reason to deny the divergence of ideology highlighted by Cicero. There were standard *popularis* themes – the physical welfare of the *populus*, to be maintained by land-distribution and later that of corn; the preservation of liberty through the laws about *provocatio*, secret ballot, criminal courts and other limitations on the aristocracy. There was also in Cicero's day a recognized canon of *popularis* leaders, stretching back to C. Flaminius, tribune and author of an agrarian law in 232. On the other side men talked of the defence of law and order and of the treasury.[23] Of course, those with one ideology did on occasion borrow the political clothes of the other. An optimate like M. Livius Drusus (tribune, 91) or Cato Uticensis might pass a bill in the popular interest about grain or

[21] L. Namier, *The Structure of Politics at the Accession of George III*, 2nd edn (London, 1968) 104. On electoral bribery at Rome see Lintott 1990 (A 66).

[22] Münzer 1920 (A 79) 1.

[23] Cic. *Acad.* II.13; *Sest.*98; Sall. *Iug.* 31; *H.* I.55; III.48M.

land for reasons of expediency, or else, like Cicero, pose as a *popularis* in order to make his political mark. The extent to which *popularis* politicians pursued their own interests more than those of the men they claimed to represent may be judged from the history that follows, but the mere possession of personal ambition does not disqualify a man from advancing the interests of others.

It is hard to pick on specific destabilizing forces in Roman politics after the Third Punic War. Conflicts between senatorial authority and the will of assemblies were not new. The tension latent between the *imperium* of the consul and senatorial *auctoritas* on one side and tribunician obstruction on the other was embedded in the constitution. Although the Romans tended to equate 'new things' with revolution, their constitution was continually altering through statutes and precedents creating new traditions, which were acceptable, if they could be reconciled with the basic ethos of society. Nevertheless, the existence of two distinct political traditions was a potential source of conflict. To this we must add an external political influence (apart from the social and economic problems to which we shall shortly turn). Just as the Romans had become self-conscious about their history under Greek influence, so they were becoming self-conscious about their constitution through Greek philosophy. Even before Polybius' history was published, Romans were discussing their politics in Greek terms. Regular contact with Greek thinkers is attested for Scipio Aemilianus, his nephew Q. Tubero, C. Laelius and Ti. Gracchus. Theoretical study may have stiffened both oligarchic and democratic sympathies in Roman politicians and made them more reluctant to compromise. More concretely, some of the political measures of the period before Sulla appear to reflect the political methods and legal procedures of Athenian democracy.[24]

II. THE AGRARIAN PROBLEM AND THE ECONOMY

Even our ancient sources, preoccupied as they are with constitutional change and moral decline, do not neglect the economic and social conditions of the second century. Appian and Plutarch provide a generally consistent picture of the agrarian problem which was the target of Ti. Gracchus' legislation, and this account has been the core of the lengthier explanations of modern scholars. According to Appian, the Romans had exploited the territory seized during their conquest of Italy in order to reward and strengthen the farming people from whom they drew their military manpower. On cultivated land they either founded new cities, that is colonies, or they assigned, sold or rented allotments to

[24] Plut. *Aem.* 6.8–10; *Ti. Gracch.* 8.6; Cic. *Tusc.* IV.4–5; Hassall, Crawford and Reynolds 1974 (B 170) 219; Nicolet 1972 (F 124) 212ff.

individuals; land, which had become unworked through war, they allowed to be cultivated without formal distribution by anyone who wished, in return for a rent based on produce – 10 per cent on crops, 20 per cent on fruits – or an appropriate tax on head of cattle. It should be stressed that this last category of land was still the public property of the Roman people (*ager publicus*), as indeed was rented land and even some of the land sold (the *trientabula* granted to rich men as partial repayment for loans during the Second Punic War). Our sources tell us that in practice the rich had come to monopolize the public land occupied at will, acquiring holdings by persuasion or force and farming these with the aid of chattel-slaves, rather than the free men who might be taken away for military service. Hence the rich became richer, slaves more numerous and the poor not only poorer but fewer. A law had been passed limiting holdings of public land to 500 *iugera* (125 hectares or about 300 acres), but this was disregarded. Hence Gracchus deplored not only the injustice which was being done to those who fought for Rome but the danger of replacing potential warriors with slaves, who could not be used for military service but might on the contrary rebel.[25]

Historians in this century from Tenney Frank and Rostovtzeff to Toynbee and Brunt[26] have seen the accumulation of *ager publicus* by the wealthy as but one feature of a more general change in the nature of Roman agriculture, the growth of large-scale 'capitalist' exploitation, which affected both public land and that owned by private citizens. The wealth deriving from empire through booty, commerce and the private profits of public enterprises (such as tax-contracts and the supply of the army overseas) was concentrated in the hands of the upper classes. They sought to perpetuate and increase this wealth by investment in the agriculture likely to produce the most satisfactory returns. Their guides in this were the Hellenistic writers on agriculture, especially the Carthaginian writer Mago, whose work was translated into Latin by D. Silanus, and Cato the Censor, who had written an original notebook on agriculture in Latin. Their works detailed how land could be best used to produce wine and oil for sale and to rear cattle on a large scale, primarily through employing slaves. The peasant or modest landholder, who used the labour of his family and whose farming might be disrupted by military service, was unable to compete with this large-scale and economically rational agriculture. Thus the poor man, who was dispossessed of his land, was afflicted not only by injustice and violence but, worse still, the harsh facts of economic life.

Other ancient sources tend to confirm the basic reliability of Appian's account of the condition of public land, whose ultimate sources were

[25] App. *BCiv.* 1.7.26–10.40; Plut. *Ti. Gracch.* 8; *Greenidge – Clay* 1–4; Tibiletti 1948 (C 142); 1950 (C 143). [26] Frank 1920 (A 34); Rostovtzeff 1926 (A 97); Toynbee 1965 (A 121); Brunt 1971 (A 16).

probably the contemporary memoir of C. Gracchus on his brother's work and (with an opposite bias) the histories of C. Fannius. The existence of a law, irksome to senators, which restricted holdings of *ager publicus* to 500 *iugera* and limited grazing, is attested by a speech of Cato in 167, and in the view of many scholars it is to a legislator of this period rather than, as Varro thought, C. Licinius Stolo in the fourth century that we should attribute the limits specified. Excessive grazing on public land had led to prosecutions by aediles, while the growth of large-scale ranches in south Italy is demonstrated by the revolts of herdsmen and other slaves. The Romans would have acquired large amounts of public land there through confiscations after the Second Punic War, including areas in towns and villages. In 173 the consul L. Postumius had been sent to restrict encroachment on public land in the *ager Campanus*. Here any large-scale farming would have probably embraced the cultivation of vines, olives and cereals, perhaps with slave-gangs, as in Sicily.[27]

It is also significant that the interdicts, legal injunctions used to guarantee possession or the recovery of possession, especially when it had been lost through violence, developed in this period (the fundamental interdict, 'uti possidetis', dates from before 161). Equally there is no doubt about the availability of slaves. For example L. Aemilius Paulus, Scipio Aemilianus' father, had enslaved 150,000 men in Epirus in 168/7 and the father of Ti. Gracchus a proverbially large number from Sardinia, when consul in 177. The great slave revolts in Sicily, the first contemporary with the tribunate of Ti. Gracchus himself, have already been discussed in their provincial context (pp. 25–7). A magistrate who helped to suppress the first of these claimed to have restored 917 slaves to Italian owners. In fact there were at the same time outbreaks of rebellion by slaves in Italy itself, including one involving 4,000 slaves at Minturnae. Gracchus is said by his brother to have been inspired to propose his legislation by seeing chain-gangs of slaves in Etruria, while he was on a journey from Rome to Pisa.[28] What no ancient source tells us are the general scale and any regional variations in the growth of landholdings at the expense of the poor. Nevertheless, the pattern of events outlined by Appian seems consistent with the other evidence.

It is much more difficult to develop plausible hypotheses about the general state of Italian agriculture and its social implications. Cato's jottings are fundamental, but cannot sustain an excessive superstructure of theory. The money which flowed into private hands from Rome's conquests and the spread of Italian commerce had to be placed somewhere. Some, as we have seen, was invested in property abroad (ch.

[27] *ORF* fr. 167; Livy XLII.1–8; Tibiletti 1948 (C 142) 191ff.

[28] Lintott 1968 (A 62), 126; Polyb. XXX.15; Livy XLI.28.8; *De Vir. Ill.* 57.2; *ILLRP* 454; Oros. V.9.4f; Obseq. 27–27b; Plut. *Ti. Gracch.* 8.9.

2, *passim*), some in silver and luxury-goods, but the bulk would have been used to buy land in Italy. Cato's work gave advice on how this should be done, not necessarily in such a way as to maximize profit, but rather so that the investment should not be squandered: if deployed rationally, it would create both material rewards and reputation for the owner. Cato's four first choices were vineyard, watered garden, osier-bed and olive-yard in that order. Grazing and cereal land follow. He does not think in vast units: 100 *iugera* of vineyard, 120 or 240 *iugera* of olives are the modules for which the optimum personnel and equipment are calculated. The economics of pasturage are not really discussed in what survives of his writings, nor the appropriate balance in making a mixed farm, though it is assumed that the owner will use the manure from his animals to fertilize his crops and fruit.[29]

In itself the idea of mixed farming is as old as Homer, and even Rostovtzeff was forced to admit that there is no real evidence for technological improvements in agriculture during the Hellenistic age. (An exception to this in Italy is the olive-mill.) What Romans would have learnt from agricultural writers was more concerned with the allocation of money and labour. Nor did this necessarily require a very large investment: the 'villa' system of farming recommended by Cato could be practised on holdings of 100–200 *iugera*, the size of allotments made in colonies such as that founded by C. Gracchus in Africa. However, a rich man could certainly have owned a number of farms of this size, large by peasant standards but small in comparison with later estates, and the evidence of the Ciceronian period suggests that this was common practice. Furthermore, heavy investment in grazing would have required much greater tracts of territory (especially since transhumance between winter and summer pastures was common) and may have been the main reason for the monopolization of *ager publicus* by the rich.[30]

At this point the very incomplete archaeological evidence provides a partial check on hypothesis. We have the remains of the 'villas' (Cato's term), which were the centre of rich men's estates. These contained wine-presses, oil-mills, storage-vats and slave-quarters, as well as reception-rooms, porticoes and peristyles for the owner. Added to this is the evidence from shipwrecks and deposits on shore of the export of wine, one of Cato's favoured crops, to the western Mediterranean. Most Republican villas are dated to the first century B.C., but a second-century origin is attested for some in Latium, Campania, the *ager Cosanus* and perhaps Samnium. However, the existence of such farms did not entail the eclipse of the smallholders in the second century. Their existence is

[29] Cato *Agr.* 1.7; 3.5; 10–11; cf. 3.2.

[30] Brunt 1971 (A 16) 371–5; Gabba and Pasquinucci 1979 (G 95).

archaeologically attested in the *ager Cosanus*, eastern Samnium, the *ager Falernus* and Campania, and perhaps in southern Etruria (though the evidence here has come under question) and should be inferred elsewhere, given the need for the villas to recruit free labour at harvest-time. They would have also provided some local market for the villa to supplement its outlets further afield. In short, there are no good grounds for inferring a general decline of the small independent farmer in the second century, apart from what our sources tell us about the condition of the *ager publicus*. We can, however, see the beginnings of a system of agriculture, which was to lead to an immense concentration of land in a few hands by the early Principate – the *latifundia* of the elder Pliny.[31]

It is equally difficult to give more precision to Appian's statements about social conditions in Italy. We have no reason to doubt that poor farmers who lived on *ager publicus* were either landless or under pressure from great landowners, especially those whose business was cattle-raising. The problem is the extent of this phenomenon and its effect on the military might of Rome. The heads of adult males (*capita*) counted by the censors gradually declined from 337,022 in 164/3 B.C. to 317,933 in 136/5 at a time when losses of soldiers on campaign cannot have been so serious as during the preceding sixty years. The view that these figures represent only those who had sufficient property to be enrolled in the *classes* of the *comitia centuriata* is without support in the sources and is rebutted by the very fact that those below the *classes* were called *capite censi*. More probably it was the total adult male population that was counted, or at least those who performed their civic duty in registering (economic depression may well have led to a failure to register). When the considerable, though unquantifiable amount of manumission in the second century is taken into account – which should have led to an increase in the census total, if birth and survival rates of existing citizens remained stable – then it seems that a decline in population or a decline in registration had occurred. The implications for Rome's military strength, however, depend on assumptions about how many of these were *assidui*, listed in the *classes* and regularly liable for legionary service. In fact the total number of citizens counted in the middle of the second century was greater than the corresponding number before the Second Punic War. Estimates of the quantity of *assidui c.* 130 B.C. vary from 75,000 to 200,000 men. In the latter case there was no fundamental shortage of citizens for the army, in the former there was.[32] In this uncertainty it is tempting to put one's faith in Ti. Gracchus and say that

[31] Giardina and Schiavone 1981 (G 104); Rathbone 1983 (G 208); 1981 (G 207); Frederiksen, 1970–1 (B 292) (but cf. Liverani 1984 (B 308)); Garnsey 1979 (G 97); Celuzza and Regoli 1982 (B 270); Cotton 1979 (B 280).

[32] Brunt 1971 (A 16) 22–5, 75–7; Astin 1967 (C 2) 337; Rich 1983 (C 121) 294–5; cf. the table of census figures on p. 603.

the crisis must have been grave, were it not for the probability that his view of the situation was impressionistic, based on his seeing fewer free citizens in the fields and knowing the difficulty of recruitment. It would be imprudent to envisage him doing careful calculations like a modern civil servant, especially when what we know of him suggests a man guided by a moral vision of what society in Italy should be.

Some scholars have sought to add to the agrarian crisis a crisis in Rome itself, caused by the increase in population and lack of employment there. However, the evidential foundation for this is weak. Issues of silver coin did not in fact decline in the period following the revaluing of the denarius from ten to sixteen *asses c.* 140 B.C., and indeed the higher value given to silver coinage increased the amount of money in circulation. Nor was there a significant decline in public building activity after 138. However, although there is nothing to show urban unemployment in these years, the problem of feeding the city was considerable. A recently discovered document from Thessaly shows a Q. Metellus buying grain there as aedile. The quantity was about 450,000 *modii* of wheat, which would have been about two and a half months' supply for the plebs at Rome in the late Republic but at this date should have sufficed for nearly double that time. The purchase seems to have been made in the period of spring to mid-summer before the new harvests in the West, when the price of grain was at its height. It seems more likely to be a crisis measure to deal with a sudden scarcity. Such conditions might have been created by the Sicilian slave revolt *c.* 135 B.C. or the plague of locusts which devastated Africa in 125.[33] The price of grain varied dramatically by season and region, apart from any special pressures through sudden scarcity. According to Polybius the famine-price in Italy during 211 B.C. was ten *sestertii* a *modius*, whereas strikingly low prices were to be found locally in Lusitania and Cisalpine Gaul about the middle of the second century of one *sestertius* a *modius* and about one *as* a *modius* respectively. Livy records prices of four *asses* and two *asses* for special distributions *c.* 200 B.C. These prices are low compared with those attested in the Hellenistic world about this time, which do not fall below one denarius (= four *sestertii* = ten *asses*) for an equivalent amount. What regular prices at Rome were by the middle of the second century can only be conjectured – perhaps not as much as one denarius a *modius*. Nor is it clear what effect, if any, the revaluing of the denarius had on the price of grain. The only pointer is the price C. Gracchus chose for his corn distributions – $6\frac{1}{3}$ *asses* a *modius*.[34] This is in almost the same proportion to 4 *asses* as the rise in the value of the denarius, and perhaps indicates that

[33] Crawford 1974 (B 144) II.640ff; Coarelli 1977 (G 42) 17–18; Garnsey, Gallant and Rathbone 1984 (B 156). Cf. Cic. II *Verr.* 3.72; Oros. V.11.2–5.

[34] *Schol. Bob.* 135 St.; Asc. *Pis.* 8C; cf. *Rhet. Her.* I.21. Garnsey and Rathbone, 1985 (C 60).

the cost of everyday items paid for in bronze *asses* had tended to increase in proportion to the rise in the value of silver.

It is appropriate to end this survey by returning to the social and economic factor to which the ancient sources gave most weight – the sheer wealth of the upper classes, symbolized by the probably inaccurate but paradigmatic figure which Cicero assigned to P. Licinius Crassus Mucianus (cos. 131), surnamed 'the rich', that of 25 million denarii. Such wealth provided immense opportunities for acquiring political support. The first law against bribery (*ambitus*) was passed in 181, the year after the Lex Orchia, the first sumptuary law which limited the expenditure on guests invited to dinner. The Lex Fannia followed in 161 and in 143 its provisions were extended to all Romans in Italy by the Lex Didia – a demonstration that conspicuous expenditure was not confined to the governing class.[35] The purchasing power of the rich drew to Italy slaves and luxury goods. One likely reason for the revaluing of the denarius and *sestertius* is increasing demand and a higher market price for silver through its use in cutlery, plate and other items of house-furnishing. The expenditure of the wealthy would have stimulated economic life in the cities and created employment among the free poor as well as slaves, especially in the building and retail trades. However, the price to be paid was the concentration of economic power and appetites among the few. Denunciation of extravagance and praise of old-fashioned frugality was a theme common to Cato the Censor, Scipio Aemilianus and L. Calpurnius Piso, historian and consul in 133. Such men realized the political implications of the increase of wealth, though none of them had any remedies for these that were more than palliatives.

III. POLITICS AFTER THE FALL OF CARTHAGE

In the years immediately following the destruction of Carthage there were two conspicuous features of political life – vigorous tribunician activity and a tendency among leading men in the Republic to be 'accident-prone'.[36] In 145 a bill was proposed by C. Licinius Crassus that priesthoods should be assigned by election rather than co-option – a proposal that was rendered more attractive to the people by the tribune's turning to address the Forum at large rather than the more select gathering in the Comitium. C. Laelius, the friend of Scipio Aemilianus and praetor in that year, successfully opposed it by an appeal to tradition.

[35] Cic. *Rep.* III.17; Shatzman 1975 (A 112); Lintott 1972 (A 63) 631–2.

[36] In general source-references to the following narrative may be found in *MRR* and *Greenidge–Clay*. Those given in footnotes are selected for emphasis or because they are difficult to locate. The political history of 146–133 B.C. is well described in Astin 1967 (C 2) 97–136, 175–89. See also *CAH* VIII[2] 191–6.

The following year there was the sumptuary law, the Lex Didia (see p. 59), which extended the legal limit on expenditure on banquets throughout Italy. Then in 142 Scipio conducted an especially rigorous censorship, during which he orated on the solemnity of his office. However, in the elections for the consulships of 141, his favoured candidate Laelius was defeated, after Q. Pompeius, who as a friend of Scipio's was expected to support Laelius, deserted him and canvassed on his own account. Moreover, Scipio himself was charged before the people in 140 by the tribune Ti. Claudius Asellus on account of misconduct in his censorship. For Asellus had been humiliated by Scipio through demotion from his rank in the knights. However, Asellus was unsuccessful in this, as he was in his attempt to prevent the consul Q. Servilius Caepio from setting out for his Spanish province, probably as a result of a dispute over the levy of troops. We also hear of a resolution in the Senate, promoted by the consular Appius Claudius (later Ti. Gracchus' father-in-law) that there should be only one levy a year. The same year Laelius, who had now reached the consulship, proposed an agrarian bill to deal with the monopolization of the public land by the rich, only to withdraw it in face of opposition from those whose interests he was damaging.

In 139 a tribune achieved real success. A. Gabinius passed the first law about secret ballot, establishing its use in elections. We know nothing about the circumstances in which this bill was enacted. No doubt it was presented as a blow struck for the *libertas* of the people – which indeed it was – but it may also have been argued to be a blow against corruption, since those who bribed could no longer check who voted for them, and thus it would have been acceptable to those who were afraid of demagogic canvassing, such as practised by Q. Pompeius. The year following two energetic tribunes, C. Curiatius and Sex. Licinius, created a precedent by imprisoning the consuls, because they would not allow tribunes to secure the exemption of men from conscription. Curiatius also pressed the consuls to propose special purchases of corn, similar to those made by Q. Metellus according to the document from Thessaly (p. 58). While resisting this suggestion at a public meeting, Scipio Nasica secured silence from the *contio* by saying: 'Be quiet please, citizens: I know more about the public interest than you.' Whether purchases were made or not, is unclear. The famine, however, brought the poor out on to the streets, and one of the tribunes who died in office was given a funeral by the people. There were also notable acquittals. Two ex-governors charged with taking money illegally from provincials (*de repetundis*) escaped in spite, or because, of their enmity with Scipio and perhaps with the help of bribery. Moreover, a group of state contractors (*publicani*), who had leased the pitch-works in the Silva Sila in Calabria, were eventually freed of charges relating to murders perpetrated by their slave-gangs. Meanwhile, on the other side of the straits of Messina the first Sicilian slave revolt was perhaps already in its early stages.

A second law about secret ballot, the Lex Cassia, relating to trials before assemblies (on non-capital charges), was passed in 137, after Scipio Aemilianus had dissuaded the tribune Antius Briso from vetoing it. It is possible that the exception for capital cases was introduced by the tribune to meet initial objections to the bill, the subject of which was more sensitive for the aristocracy than elections in that it involved their potential ruin. However, the year was more famous for the scandal over the treaty that C. Hostilius Mancinus and his quaestor Ti. Gracchus had negotiated when surrounded by the Numantines in Spain. In 140 Q. Pompeius had himself disowned an inglorious treaty he had made with the same people under less desperate circumstances. On this occasion nothing was done until Mancinus and his quaestor had returned to Rome, where both Pompeius' and Mancinus' behaviour was investigated by a tribunal presided over by a consul of 136, Furius Philus, with Scipio Aemilianus and Laelius among his advisers. Their decision, accepted by Mancinus, was to repudiate his treaty and to surrender Mancinus naked and in bonds to the Spaniards as expiation of the religious offence arising from the breach of his promise. The assembly accepted this proposal. Gracchus was not to be surrendered, in spite of the fact that he had been instrumental in making the treaty through the influence with the Spaniards he had inherited from his father. The decisions were controversial, and may have led to the deliberate rewriting of the history of the agreement made with the Samnites at the Caudine Forks in 321, which was recalled on contemporary denarii issued by Ti. Veturius, though the treatment of a praetor of Sardinia in 236 provided a more recent precedent. Scipio was suspected of favouring his relative, but Gracchus was anyhow popular with the army which he had helped to escape. He for his part was indignant that his own reputation for good faith (*fides*) among the Spaniards had been destroyed, and in Cicero's view this, combined with the fright he received from the senatorial investigation, explained his defection from the optimate cause.[37]

Meanwhile in Spain the proconsul Lepidus began a war contrary to instructions from the Senate, was ineffective and so both deprived of his command and fined when prosecuted later at Rome. As a result of the failures in Spain and the simultaneous threat of the Sicilian slave revolt Scipio was exempted in 135 from the current law forbidding re-election to the consulship by a plebiscite passed on the advice of the Senate. Nevertheless, when he became consul in 134 and was assigned Spain as

[37] Crawford 1974 (B 144) I no. 234; Crawford 1973 (F 39); Cic. *Har. Resp.* 43.

his province, he was refused permission to conscript new troops by the Senate and granted no immediate cash. Instead he took a troop of clients and friends from Italy and contingents sent by cities and foreign kings. Among them were Ti. Gracchus' younger brother Caius, C. Marius, a man of equestrian rank from Arpinum, and the Numidian prince Jugurtha.

IV. TIBERIUS GRACCHUS

The decade which preceded Ti. Gracchus' tribunate showed considerable ambivalence in the attitudes both of the Senate and the assemblies. On the one hand, the Senate was still the body that had presided over the defeats of Carthage, Syria and Macedon, conscious of Rome's military reputation and reluctant to appear soft; on the other hand there was a perception that Rome's resources were not unlimited and some members were prepared to admit that all was not well at home. The assemblies for their part continued to love a great general, but the people were becoming more restive than they had been for some time under the hardships caused by military service, shortages of corn and the land problem. When Ti. Gracchus became tribune in December 134, he appears to have been already regarded as a friend of the people and he was encouraged by graffiti on public buildings and monuments to recover the public land which was being held in excess of the legal limit. The issue had come to life in Laelius' consulship; more might be expected of Gracchus as a man from the core of the nobility (his father had been consul twice and censor). The proposal that he made was generous in its treatment of offenders. Existing occupiers of public land, who had no formal lease, were to be guaranteed possession without rent of 500 *iugera* (125 hectares) with an additional 250 for each child. What remained was then to be distributed to the poor by a three-man commission in allotments which could not be sold. A possessor could thus easily maintain at least one villa-estate from what once had been entirely public land. The rub lay in the commission, because holdings were to be assigned at its discretion, and this meant that the commissioners could repossess on behalf of the public the best-developed land and that which had been used as security for debts and dowries. This point would have been emphasized, if Gracchus, as Plutarch states, was provoked by opposition into including a clause demanding immediate evacuation of all land held beyond the legal limit.[38]

Vital uncertainties remain about this apparently straightforward proposal. These are first, the legal status both of the land left to existing possessors and that to be newly assigned; secondly, eligibility for the

[38] App. *BCiv.* 1.9.37; 10.39; Plut. *Ti. Gracch.* 8.10; 10.4.

new allotments, especially whether allies could participate; thirdly, the size of the new allotments. Here the most important evidence is provided by the agrarian law of 111 B.C. engraved on one face of the so-called 'Tabula Bembina'. This law seems to have brought to an end the process of land-surveying and reallocation in Italy, which began in 133. The first ten lines, after listing various types of land and buildings which were public in 133 and since then had been in some way assigned, declare them all now to be private property and liable to be recorded in the census. They are later declared to be free of rent and tax. There is no suggestion in what survives of the text that the law is repeating an earlier provision, although it is obvious that the original public status of the land had been subject to considerable modification since 133. In particular it appears that before 111 B.C. both the prior possessors of public land, whose holding was not in excess of the legal limit, and the recipients of new allotments had been able to bequeath their property, and the rights of the new owners are recognized by the law.

Our literary sources tell us that Ti. Gracchus made the new allotments inalienable by sale in 133, though presumably they could be transmitted by inheritance, and that the right to sell them was first granted in a law passed a few years after C. Gracchus' death. C. Gracchus, moreover, had subjected the new allotments to rent. The holdings of prior possessors had also been subjected to rent after C. Gracchus' legislation by the tribune Sp. Thorius in a bill which allowed them to retain their present holdings in so far as this was legal.[39] Under Roman law public and private property are two mutually exclusive categories with no intermediate stage between them. Nevertheless the Gracchan legislation introduced categories of land with the characteristics of both public and private property, whose ultimate status raised problems of legal definition, which were only solved when the law of 111 enacted that the majority of allotments were to be private land. The present writer would conclude that no public land was made private by the land legislation before 111 (except when a straight exchange was made between public and private landholdings, as described in that text) and furthermore that no holdings of public land could properly contribute to a person's rating in the census before that date. If this is so, it excludes the interpretation of Ti. Gracchus' law as a move to increase the availability of military recruits by assigning the poor sufficient property to become *assidui* (see p. 57 above) – a policy which would in any case have been short-sighted, if his long-term aim was to promote viable family farms, which would lead to the breeding of children.

If Appian and Plutarch preserve the substance and indeed some of the phraseology of Ti. Gracchus' rhetoric, then the orator talked of the

[39] App. *BCiv.* 1.10.38; 27.122; Plut. *C. Gracch.* 9.4.

poverty and depopulation of Italy as a whole and not just of the countryside occupied by Romans. Latins and Italian allies almost certainly suffered from the bill as holders of excessive amounts of public land, but there is no clear-cut evidence apart from Gracchus' speeches that the poor Italians were among the beneficiaries. Indeed, according to Appian and Cicero the land commission was held to have disturbed the Latins and allies by breaking treaties in its work up to 129. The only Roman public land mentioned by the law of 111 as being in the hands of Latins or allies had either been leased by the censors or been granted *en bloc* to a community for exploitation or been given to allies who before the passage of the law were in some special category (the first two kinds of land were still Roman *ager publicus* after 111). We cannot suppose that grants by the commission to individual allies, whether new recipients or prior possessors, were mentioned in a lacuna in the first ten lines, since all the land discussed there was declared private under Roman law and liable to be registered in a Roman census. Moreover, there was a legal problem about the assignation of land to allies as a private property. Except for Latins, who had the right of *nexum* or *commercium* (which allowed them to acquire property at Rome), it would have been impossible for foreigners (*peregrini*) to own Roman land, unless they were granted this right or the land was ceded by Rome to their own community. Foreigners could enjoy the use of Roman public land as lessees or possessors, but could not receive it as property which could be disposed by inheritance or sale. It appears from the Lex agraria of 111 that there were no assignations on a large scale of Roman land to allies as their private property. Gracchus may have taken the view that, while he provided for Roman citizens, the Italian communities should follow his example in their own territories. More practically, short of actually enfranchising a mass of non-Romans (which one source alleges that he promised), he had two ways of making good his rhetoric: he might exempt some public land from assignation to Romans and then either lease it to poor allies or assign it to their communities on condition that they did the same. It is not evident that he did either of these things, but it is possible that the clausula in the law of 111, referring to land exempted by C. Gracchus from distribution, deals with territory reserved for occupation by allies.[40]

A prior possessor, who had four children, was entitled to have up to 1,500 *iugera* of public land; the size of allotments to new recipients must have been on a different scale. A yardstick is provided by the law of 111 (line 14), which fixes 30 *iugera* as the maximum which can be made private by occupation and cultivation after the passage of that law. Such land

[40] Lex agraria (*Bruns* no. 11), lines 1, 3, 4, 6 and *passim*, cf. 21–2. For the view that land distribution was connected with enfranchisement, Richardson 1980 (C 123).

would have probably been uncultivated at the time and unlikely to be immediately productive. It may be noted that at 250 *sestertii* a *iugerum* (one quarter of the price given by Columella in the first century A.D.), a lot of 30 *iugera* would have probably put a man into the next to lowest class of the *comitia centuriata*. More probably, we should allow for variations in size depending on the quality of land (10 *iugera* were later considered adequate in the fertile *ager Campanus*). Nor would the allotments have been expected to provide all the resources required by a family. It was still possible to graze animals on public pasture-land and use public woods for activities such as feeding pigs, hunting and collecting plants and berries. Furthermore, smallholders and their families could earn extra money as temporary labour especially at harvest-time, while the women could produce textiles at home.

Although Gracchus' bill was proposed at a time when military weakness and the number of slaves seemed urgent political issues, it was not an emergency measure to deal with a crisis, but one which sought to improve the social and economic conditions of Italy in the long term. There can be no question either that Gracchus hoped to further his own prospects. The career of Scipio Aemilianus and the funeral of the tribune, who died in 138, showed in their different ways the extent to which popular support could be mobilized by an adventurous and charismatic figure. However, in a world where even traditional patron–client allegiances were shifting, such support could not be relied on without limit and it is unlikely that he expected to secure a lasting dominance of Roman politics for himself and his friends. It is more plausible to see, as Plutarch did, the motive of the Gracchi as the love of glory or the fear of anonymity. The fundamental preoccupation of the Roman nobility with fame is attested in this century in the epitaphs of the Scipiones and the language of Roman comedy as well as in historical narratives.[41] In spite of the Numantine treaty, Gracchus had not become a maverick apart from the Roman aristocracy and its values. Nor was he on his own. He had originally the support of one consul of 133, the jurist P. Mucius Scaevola, and also of his father-in-law Appius Claudius (cos. 143) and the chief *pontifex* P. Licinius Crassus Mucianus (cos. 131). We hear also of younger friends of Gracchus from the senatorial order, C. Carbo and C. Cato.

The bill of 133 was not the first controversial agrarian law to be proposed at Rome. The Lex Flaminia in 232, which divided the *ager Gallicus* on the Adriatic coast into allotments, was only passed after fierce resistance from the Senate. There had been opposition too to the laws limiting the use of public land. Gracchus was, however, the first man to propose redistribution of land already held – something bound to cause

[41] Plut. *Agis et Cleom.* 2.7; Earl 1967 (A 28) 25–35. Wiseman 1985 (A 132) 1–6.

fear among possessors, recalling the more revolutionary redistributions, which, though rare, had become a bogey in the Greek world. Both Cicero and Plutarch compared the Gracchi to the reforming kings of Sparta in the late third century, Agis IV and Cleomenes III, who sought to re-establish Spartan austerity and military might by cancelling debts and redistributing land and property according to the model of the old Lycurgan constitution. About 150 B.C. Polybius drew a parallel between the Roman and the Spartan constitution, and Romans had before this direct acquaintance with Spartan politics, especially with the tyrant Nabis, who to some extent had continued the policy of the reforming kings. The comparison between their policy and that of Gracchus was, therefore, probably in the mind of both the legislator and his opponents. Although the legislator had practical aims and his opponents practical objections, which stemmed from the damage to their own interests, the argument between them would have been conducted in part on ideological grounds. Cicero regarded land distribution as an offence against concord and equity because it infringed the principle of private property. Similar arguments were probably used in 133. Gracchus on his side took his stand also on justice, that the public land of the Roman people should belong to the Roman people and not a fraction of it.[42]

Gracchus' proposal brought him enormous public support. A contemporary historian, Sempronius Asellio, claimed that he was escorted by not less than 3,000–4,000 men; Posidonius described how men came flooding in from the countryside to support Gracchus. It is interesting that those who hoped to benefit from the bill still lived in rural Italy, presumably working as tenants or hired labourers or on inadequate holdings of their own. However, according to our chief sources, Appian and Plutarch, it was not only supporters of the bill but others, who were afraid for their land, who flocked to Rome, and this inevitably made the anticipation of the bill more tense. M. Octavius, a former friend of Gracchus and a colleague in the tribunate, was persuaded by those whose interests were threatened to veto the proposal when it was put to the assembly. Gracchus adjourned the assembly and put pressure on Octavius to give up his obstruction, in particular by threatening in an edict to veto any other public business himself and by sealing the treasury. A tribune had the power to veto anything he wanted, but it had not been the custom to veto bills in the plebian interest (for example, such obstruction had not, as far as we know, been used against Flaminius in 232). In 188 four tribunes had been dissuaded from blocking a bill granting citizenship to Fundi, Formiae and Arpinum by the argument that such privileges were essentially in the gift of the people. In 137 Scipio Aemilianus had discouraged M. Antius Briso from vetoing the

[42] Cic. *Off.* II.78–81; Plut. *Ti. Gracch.* 9.3; App. *BCiv.* I.10–11; Fraccaro 1914 (C 51) 86–9.

Lex Cassia. However, Octavius continued his obstruction in a further assembly and this almost led to violence (indeed Plutarch alleges that the rich seized the voting urns).[43]

Gracchus was then persuaded by two senior consulars to refer the matter to the Senate. There was no constitutional requirement to do so, but it was proposed as a well-established procedure for resolving differences without a struggle. In practice the Senate made no suggestion acceptable to Gracchus in spite of his eminent friends: so he resorted to promulgating in the assembly the abrogation of Octavius' magistracy on the ground that he was betraying his office. After appealing insistently to Octavius to abandon his stand, Gracchus took the vote and Octavius' deposition was approved by the first eighteen tribes of the thirty-five. He was consequently dragged from the tribunal by Gracchus' own freedman attendants, while his friends protected him from being lynched by the crowd. A new tribune was elected in his place and at last Gracchus' bill could become law without impediment.

While the disregard of the Senate was neither contrary to law nor tradition (however much men might prefer that Senate and assemblies should work in co-operation as in the heyday of the middle Republic), the deposition of a tribune was unprecedented and its legality debatable, to the extent that T. Annius (cos. 153) challenged Gracchus by a formal legal wager (*sponsio*) to show that he had not expelled from office a colleague who was sacrosanct. A convenient example of the deposition of a curule magistrate was that of the proconsul M. Lepidus in 136, but it is doubtful whether this is relevant. The debate in 133 was between the proposition of Gracchus that a tribune's office was conditional on his obeying the people's will – a view which is found in Polybius' analysis of the Roman constitution – and Annius' contention that the inviolability of the tribune, however disruptive his behaviour, was the essential feature of his office. Gracchus' answer to this was that, while a tribune must be allowed to do appalling acts like demolishing the temple of Jupiter Capitolinus and burning the newly constructed shipyards, what he could not do was to damage the sovereignty of the plebeian assembly. This debate did not end in 133 and we find echoes of it, probably deriving from late Republican annalists, in Livy's treatment of the actions of Gracchus' father, when tribune in 187.[44]

In accordance with the agrarian bill a three-man commission was elected to pass judgement on old holdings and to assign new holdings of public land, *IIIviri agris iudicandis adsignandis*. These were originally Tiberius himself, his father-in-law Appius Claudius and his brother C.

[43] Livy XXXVIII.36.7–8; Cic. *Brut.* 97; Badian 1972 (A 4) 694ff.

[44] Plut. *Ti. Gracch.* 15.2–3 (cf. Cic. *De Or.* 1.62); Livy XXXVIII.56; XXXIX.5; Richard 1972 (C 122). On *sponsio* see Crook 1976 (F 199).

Gracchus. In due course Ti. Gracchus was to be replaced by P. Crassus Mucianus, and then both Crassus and Appius Claudius by M. Fulvius Flaccus and C. Papirius Carbo (their names are commemorated on a number of boundary stones which survive today). However, the Senate frustrated Tiberius by refusing to give his commission tents and other equipment from public resources and granting an expense allowance of a mere six *sestertii* a day – this on the proposal of Scipio Nasica, alleged to have been the holder of a huge amount of public land. The commission needed surveyors and transport-animals, and there was also precedent for giving cash to new settlers for their initial expenses.[45] At this point the windfall of the legacy of the Pergamene kingdom (pp. 33–5 above) allowed Tiberius to propose the seizure of money immediately available from the royal treasury in order, it seems, to fund the distribution of land. He declared, furthermore, that he would produce proposals about the cities of the kingdom (which Attalus III had left free), presumably with the aim of extracting revenue for Rome. This provoked attacks on him in the Senate by Metellus Macedonicus and Q. Pompeius, in which the former denounced him for associating with the poorest criminal elements in the population and the latter suggested that the Pergamene envoy, who had called on Ti. Gracchus, had given him the purple robe and diadem from Pergamum as a future king. Thus Gracchus was already being portrayed as morally decadent and an incipient tyrant.

It was against this background that he stood for re-election to the tribunate. There was, according to Livy, an old law banning tenure of the same magistracy twice within ten years, to which exceptions had certainly been made allowing early second consulships. The most recent precedent we know for successive tribunates was that of Licinius Stolo and Sextius in the years of anarchy, which culminated in the opening of the consulship to plebeians in 367, but this story may owe something to late Republican historical elaboration. In 131 C. Carbo was to propose unsuccessfully that the plebs could elect the same man tribune as often as they wanted. If this bill had been passed, the resulting constitutional position would have been far more extreme than that arising from the single repeat of an annual magistracy, and it is hard to draw conclusions from this about the legitimacy of Ti. Gracchus' canvass. It should be remembered that there was considerable flexibility in arguments based on tradition at Rome. Recent tradition could be denounced as a corruption of the correct behaviour of remote antiquity; alternatively obedience to ancient precedents could be rejected as pedantic antiquarianism in comparison with the realistic practices of the recent past. Moreover, knowledge of the remote past depended on the biassed and insecurely founded reconstructions of recent annalists. The chief argu-

[45] Plut. *Ti. Gracch.* 13.2–3; Cic. *Leg. Agr.* II.32; Livy XL.38.6–7; App. *Syr.* 1.4.

ment that could be used in Gracchus' defence was the accepted independence of the plebian assembly in creating its own officials.

Gracchus is said to have hoped that repetition of his magistracy would protect him from his enemies: he would remain sacrosanct and have the opportunity to mobilize popular support on his behalf. He might have argued in self-justification that his own survival in political life was the best way to guarantee the execution of his legislation. On the other hand, if there is any truth in the accounts of his new proposals, he was not intending to stand pat on what he had done but to put more controversial proposals to the plebs. According to Appian, as the election took place at harvest-time, Gracchus' rural supporters were unable to come and help him and he therefore sought the support of the urban plebs. This would have made new proposals especially desirable. A number of ideas are attributed to him, which mostly relate to what was proposed or actually enacted by his brother Caius – reduction of military service, appeal to assemblies from the sentences of judges, a mixture of knights and senators on jury panels, even the promise of citizenship to Italian allies. If these proposals were actually mentioned in his speeches and do not merely derive from apocryphal ascription by his brother or later sources, they suggest an attitude more aggressive than defensive, one which sought to exploit the powers of the tribunate and assembly even further.

There were early warnings of the violence that occurred at the election. Plutarch claims that there were conspiracies among the rich from the time of the agrarian bill. The circumstances of the deposition of Octavius would have sharpened feelings more. On the first day of the election, after two tribes had voted for Ti. Gracchus, pressure was brought on Rubrius, the presiding tribune, that Gracchus should not be accepted as a candidate. Rubrius withdrew and was replaced by Mummius, the man chosen as tribune instead of Octavius. That evening Gracchus put on mourning and commended the safety of his own son and mother to his supporters. Before dawn the following day he and his men occupied the slopes of the Capitoline hill and the centre of the Forum in preparation for the assembly. His opponents forced their way in and tried to impede the election but, according to Appian, they were driven out of the Forum with sticks and clubs. Meanwhile a Senate meeting was held in the temple of Fides (by the stairway up the western cliff of the Capitol) to discuss Gracchus' imminent re-election. The presiding consul, P. Mucius Scaevola, was urged by Scipio Nasica to defend the public interest and kill the tyrant (a gesture by Gracchus in the assembly was interpreted as a request for a diadem), but he refused to use force or kill a citizen without trial. Nasica then claimed that the consul was betraying the Roman constitution and used the formula of a

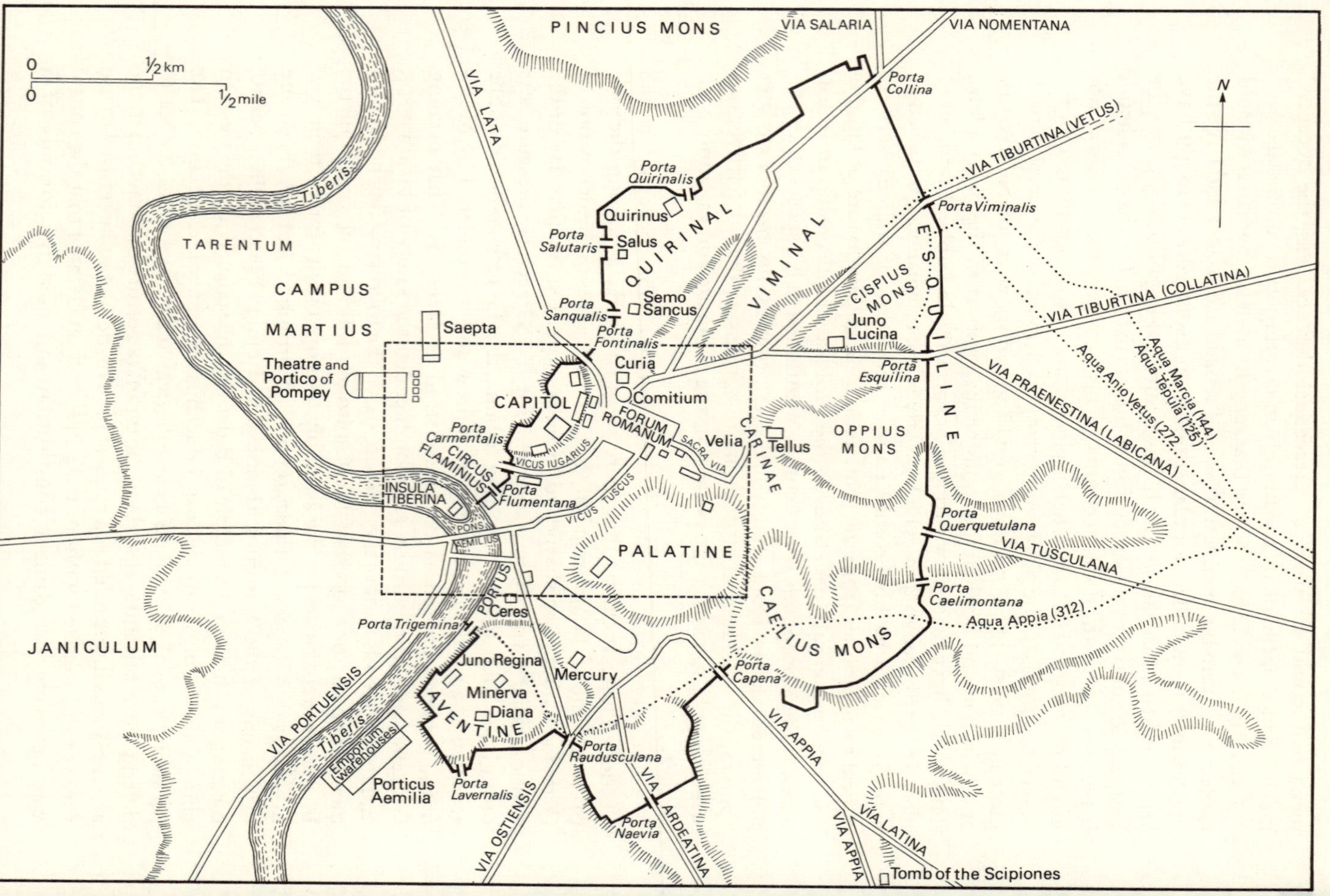

PINCIUS MONS
VIA SALARIA
VIA NOMENTANA
0
½ km
0
½ mile
VIA LATA
Porta Collina
N
VIA TIBURTINA (VETUS)
Porta Quirinalis
Quirinus
QUIRINAL
VIMINAL
Porta Viminalis
Porta Salutaris
Salus
TARENTUM
ESQUILINE
CISPIUS MONS
Semo Sancus
CAMPUS
MARTIUS
Porta Sanqualis
Juno Lucina
VIA TIBURTINA (COLLATINA)
Saepta
Porta Fontinalis
Aqua Marcia (144)
Aqua Tepula (125)
Aqua Anio Vetus (272)
Curia
Porta Esquilina
Theatre and Portico of Pompey
Comitium
VIA PRAENESTINA (LABICANA)
CAPITOL
FORUM ROMANUM
OPPIUS MONS
Porta Carmentalis
SACRA VIA
Velia
Tellus
CARINAE
CIRCUS FLAMINIUS
VICUS IUGARIUS
INSULA TIBERINA
Porta Flumentana
VICUS TUSCUS
Porta Querquetulana
PONS AEMILIUS
PALATINE
VIA TUSCULANA
PORTUS
Porta Caelimontana
Ceres
Aqua Appia (312)
Porta Trigemina
CAELIUS MONS
JANICULUM
Juno Regina
Mercury
Porta Capena
Minerva
Diana
VIA PORTUENSIS
AVENTINE
Tiberis
Emporium (warehouses)
Porta Raudusculana
VIA APPIA
Porticus Aemilia
Porta Lavernalis
VIA OSTIENSIS
VIA ARDEATINA
Porta Naevia
VIA LATINA
VIA APPIA
Tomb of the Scipiones

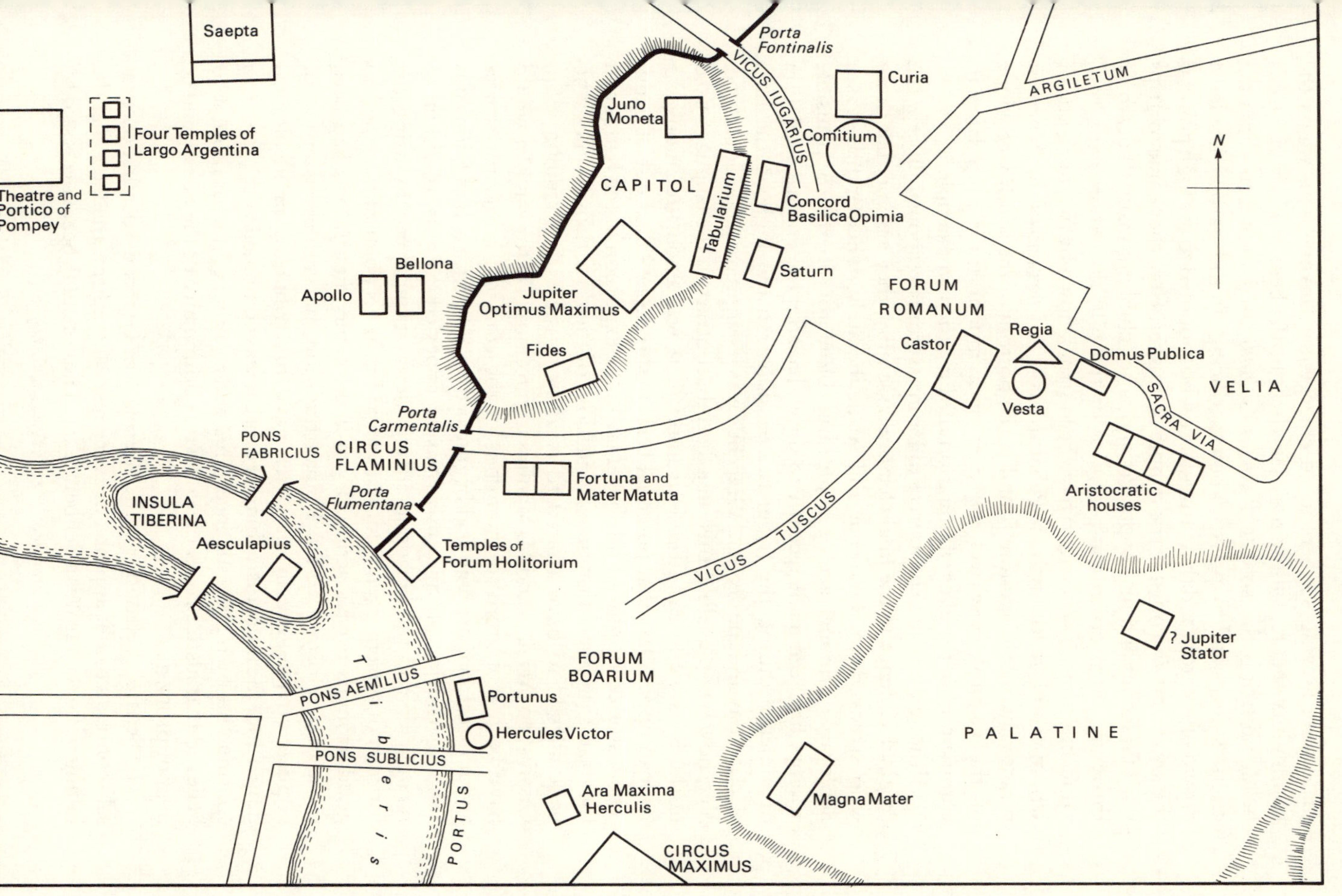

Fig. 1. Rome in the last two centuries of the Republic.

magistrate levying soldiers in an emergency: 'anyone who wants the community secure, follow me'. He also put the hem of his toga on his head, imitating the so-called *cinctus Gabinus* used by consuls in such circumstances and by priests when sacrificing. In this garb he headed a crowd of senators and their attendants who mounted to the high point of the *area Capitolina* outside the temple of Jupiter. Here they came to grips with Gracchus and his supporters and, after clubbing many to death or throwing them down the precipice of the hill, they routed the rest. Gracchus himself was said to have been struck down by two men, one of whom was his fellow-tribune P. Satureius. The fine head of the Athenian tyrant-slayer Aristogeiton, found at the bottom of the south-west slope of the Capitol, may well be part of a monument set up later to commemorate the alleged imitation of the Athenian example.[46]

Although our ancient sources differ in assigning responsibility for the original violence in the final electoral assembly, they assume that those who struck down Gracchus did so deliberately, whether this was a deplorable criminal act or a glorious blow for liberty. A plausible attempt has been made recently to show that after the gradual escalation of violence during the tribunate, passions ran too high on the final election day and the death of Gracchus was its unpremeditated outcome. Yet, however plausible, this runs directly contrary to the language used in the Senate and the attitude it implied. It was axiomatic among the Roman upper class that potential tyrants should be killed out of hand. The historical origins of this belief lay in the expulsion of the Kings and the deaths (by execution or assassination) of the three demagogues who were alleged to have aspired to tyranny in the early Republic – Sp. Cassius, Sp. Maelius and M. Manlius Capitolinus. These examples would have been reinforced in the minds of the educated by horror stories about Greek tyrants who had begun as demagogues, such as Dionysius and Agathocles of Syracuse. Nasica appealed to this tradition of tyrannicide and then made in effect a declaration of war by using the formula of the emergency military levy. From his point of view he had good grounds for his action. Even if Gracchus' first moves had been those of a reformer within Roman tradition, his ruthless assertion of popular sovereignty in all crises gave his tribunate an ideological dimension, the more disturbing because it was combined with a desire to continue his own pre-eminence. This was a capital crime for those who believed that justice lay in the collective dominance of the Senate and of men of property.

The Senate's behaviour in the aftermath of Gracchus' death, however self-contradictory it appears, in every respect confirms the view that the killing of Gracchus was a deliberate act. The consul P. Scaevola is said by

[46] Lintott 1968 (A 62) 183; Coarelli 1969 (C 43).

Cicero to have given *ex post facto* approval to the deed by virtue of the decrees which were then passed. The consuls of 132 were instructed to investigate and execute those who had conspired with Gracchus (C. Blossius of Cumae, a Stoic philosopher, was among those investigated and released but the rhetor Diophanes was not so lucky). When Scipio Aemilianus returned from his victory at Numantia, he was asked at a public meeting whether the killing was justified and replied that it was, if indeed Gracchus had planned to seize a tyranny. Earlier at Numantia he had quoted Homer, 'so I would have perish anyone who does such things'. However, Nasica himself was challenged in the Senate to defend his conduct with a wager (the same procedure that had been used against Gracchus by Annius) and, like Gracchus, he refused, rejecting Scaevola as an arbiter. Then, although *pontifex maximus*, he was sent as an ambassador to Pergamum, where he died.

Meanwhile the vacancy on the land commission was filled by the election of Crassus Mucianus (Scaevola's brother and C. Gracchus' father-in-law) and its work was allowed to go forward. It is unlikely that this was merely a sop to public feeling: rather it reflected the amount of support that the Lex Sempronia had in principle among the Senate, provided, no doubt, that the commissioners were thought to be sound men who would handle existing possessors of public land with care. Those who regarded its operations as fundamentally unjust would have remained disquieted. Scipio Aemilianus made a speech denouncing what is probably Gracchus' law earmarking funds from Asia for this work. In this he seems to have compared the financial exploitation of Asia with the importation of Asiatic luxury and sexual licence. There is an irony here, since Scipio had maintained good relations with Attalus III and had received presents of war-supplies from him at Numantia.[47] Boundary stones (*termini*) set up by the commissioners of 132 have been found in Campania, northern Lucania and in the *ager Gallicus* near Fanum, while those of the succeeding commission have appeared in southern Samnium near the Campanian border and recently in northern Apulia near Luceria. A tantalizing sidelight on their operations is the monument in the Val di Diano, which commemorates the achievements of a man who built a road from Rhegium to Capua, returned runaway slaves at the end of the Sicilian slave revolt (ch. 2, pp. 25–7) and, as he claimed, was the first to make herdsmen yield place to arable farmers on the public land. Although he is generally held to be Popillius Laenas, the consul of 132, a strong case has been made for identification with T. Annius, praetor *c.* 132, one of whose milestones has been found elsewhere on this road. This monument at the entrance to Lucania is in an area of centuriation near the find-spots of Gracchan *termini*. It seems that the man who

[47] *ORF* no. 21, fr. 30; Cic. *Deiot.* 19.

commemorated himself was competing with the land commission for glory as the saviour of rural Italy.[48]

We have no clear evidence of the success or failure of the commission's resettlement programme. Appian's gloom over the fate of the poor, when its operations finally ceased, is no argument against the viability of the original allotments. The increase recorded in the census figures between 131 and 125 of some 75,000 adult males is in the writer's view best explained by new registrations (ch. 2, pp. 36–7) and is testimony to the initial attractiveness of the land-grants. Moreover, although our sources from the Principate tend to anticipate the concentration of property which had occurred by the first century A.D., there is plenty of evidence for the survival of smallholdings in this period (pp. 56–7). Indeed this is implicit in the law of 111, whose legislator thought it worthwhile to confirm new allotments as private property and to encourage the formation of 30-*iugera* private holdings in the future through the occupation and cultivation of public land.

The major difficulties faced by the commission were those of discriminating between existing public and private land and of handling non-Roman occupiers of public land. Complaints came from the wealthy possessors about the lots which were eventually adjudged theirs, but jurisdiction in disputes lay in the hands of the commission. Italian landowners objected to this jurisdiction and in 130–129 found a champion in Scipio Aemilianus. Scipio secured by a decree of the Senate the transfer of jurisdiction in such cases to the consul, but the latter left for his province. We do not know what happened in the long run. Jurisdiction in matters arising from land distribution was assigned to any consul or praetor by the law of 111 and it may be that subsequent consuls heard the allies' cases. There is certainly no reason to suppose that the commission ceased to be active in other respects in spite of the understandable obstruction by possessors.

Shortly after this intervention Scipio died mysteriously at night. Although this seems to have been ascribed to natural causes in the funeral oration, his wife (who was Ti. Gracchus' sister), C. Carbo and C. Gracchus were all suspected of murdering him. This bears witness to his identification with the opposition to Ti. Gracchus and his political programme. Cicero's statement that the death of Ti. Gracchus divided the people into two halves is an over-simplification. Scipio had opponents in the Senate like Metellus Macedonicus, who probably had sympathy with the aims of Gracchan legislation (as censor in 131 he had spoken in favour of increasing the birth-rate) but none with his political methods. There were also opponents such as C. Carbo and C. Gracchus who, following the example of Ti. Gracchus, wanted to use the

[48] *ILLRP* 467–74; 454; 454a; Pani 1977 (B 216); Wiseman 1964 (B 259); 1969 (B 260).

assemblies under their own leadership to direct political policy. This attitude is illustrated by Carbo's successful bill requiring secret ballot in legislative assemblies and his unsuccessful bill, which was supported by C. Gracchus, that unlimited re-election to the tribunate should be allowed. If there was a consensus in practice about the agrarian problem, the way had been opened to future conflict about the balance of the constitution. A further proposal, which should be mentioned in this context, is one for the return of public horses mentioned by Cicero in *De Republica*. Scholars since the last century have assumed that the object of this proposal was to deprive senators of horses subsidized by the treasury and of membership of the centuries of knights in the *comitia centuriata*, but this is not stated in the text, nor is there confirmatory evidence elsewhere.[49] It seems more likely to be a proposal for the abolition of the public horse entirely, on the ground that there was no longer military justification for their existence, since Rome had come to depend on foreign cavalry. The bill would have abolished a class distinction, as Cicero complains, and also have saved the treasury money spent on payment for animals and fodder. Thus Cicero could suggest that the bill's authors were seeking a *largitio*, a hand-out of welfare for the people, from the money saved.

Meanwhile a spur to further radical reforms was provided by the exacerbation of some of Rome's long-standing difficulties. The Gracchan agrarian policy had already brought to the surface the problem of Rome's relations with her Italian allies (on which see Volume VIII², pp. 207–43). Fulvius Flaccus, one of the land commissioners, sought, when consul in 125, to remove the objections of the Italian upper classes to the redistribution of land by offering Roman citizenship to allies or, if they did not wish to lose their separate identities, physical protection against Roman magistrates in the form of *provocatio* – something which would have been especially desirable in view of the horrific stories about the behaviour of Romans in Italy, which were recounted by Cato the Censor and later by C. Gracchus in their speeches. The *lex de repetundis* on the 'Tabula Bembina' from Urbino (lines 78–9) made the same alternative offers to successful non-Roman prosecutors, but it seems to have excluded giving *provocatio* to magistrates in allied communities (it is not stated that these were only Latin, as Mommsen suggested). This has been linked with the possession of Roman citizenship by magistrates in Latin cities, attested as existing before the Social War of 90 B.C. However, if these men were already Roman citizens, this clause was irrelevant to them from the start. Nor is it certain that the allied magistrates were excluded from receiving *provocatio* because they possessed it already. As Gabba has argued in Vol. VIII² (pp. 241–2), the

49 Cic. *Rep.* IV.2; Mommsen 1887–8 (A 77) III.505–6.

legislator may have been reluctant to confer on the local magistrates the freedom from public duties which was a concomitant of the *provocatio* privilege. It is none the less conceivable that the concession of Roman citizenship to Latin magistrates was already effective in 123–122. However, the wholesale grant of Roman citizenship and *provocatio* proposed by Flaccus was a different matter. It is important to realize that if a community decided to assume the Roman citizenship, it lost its separate juridical identity and there was no way that an individual member could retain his old status as a foreigner combined with *provocatio*. The decision to choose *provocatio* rather than citizenship in response to Flaccus' offer would have had to be made by the community as a whole.

In 126, the year before Flaccus' consulship, a law of M. Iunius Pennus had excluded non-Romans from the city, either because there was a threat to public order from Italians gathering in the city to support Flaccus at the elections, or because it was suspected that Roman citizenship was being usurped. This measure cannot have lasted long. Nevertheless, Flaccus made no progress with his proposal before he left for his war against the Gauls (p. 24 above). It is tempting to connect with his failure the revolt in this year of Fregellae, a Latin colony on the border of Samnium, and, according to one source, the simultaneous revolt of Asculum, the Picene capital. Fregellae had been in 177 the focus for migration of Samnites and Paelignians. Excavation has revealed an apparently prosperous town with developed private architecture and drainage, flanked by a popular shrine dedicated to Aesculapius with an altar to Salus (Health), which specialized in curing diseases of the foot. There is, however, no evidence of spectacular monuments, such as the contemporary theatre and shrines of Samnite Pietrabbondante. We have no information about the cause of the revolt, and it may have been a response to harsh intervention by the Senate or Roman magistrates in a matter which concerned Fregellae alone. In the event Q. Numitorius Pullus betrayed his own city and it was conquered and flattened by L. Opimius, then praetor, much as Carthage had been, to the distress of the other Latins.[50]

The supply of grain to Italy had already been a problem in the previous decade (pp. 58, 60). When C. Gracchus was quaestor in Sardinia in 126, grain for his army was provided by king Micipsa of Numidia, which is remarkable in what was normally a grain-exporting province. The following year there was a plague of locusts in Africa. In the words of the poet Lucan later, 'a starving people knows not how to fear'. Apart from the misery that ensued from corn shortages for the poor, the possibility

50 Livy XLI.8.8; *De Vir. Ill.* 65.1; Cic. *Inv. Rhet.* II.105; *Fin.* V.62; Crawford, Keppie, Patterson and Vercnocke 1984 (B 284).

of riots was disturbing to the aristocracy.[51] Another cause for disquiet was the fact that the prognostications of the moralists about the results of the destruction of Carthage were being proved true, not only by luxury at Rome (there was yet another sumptuary law, a Lex Licinia, in 131 or later) but by the conduct of senators in Italy and the provinces. Wealth was still on a small scale by comparison with the late Republic, if we believe the story that Aemilius Lepidus was charged before the censors in 125–124 for renting a house for 6,000 *sestertii* a year. So probably was extortion. Yet after the introduction in 149 of a permanent tribunal to investigate illegal appropriations by Romans in authority to the detriment of allies, the *quaestio de repetundis*, in all the cases known to us the accused went free (a partial exception was M. Iunius Silanus, who committed suicide after being condemned by his father in a private family hearing). In particular the activities of M'. Aquillius, who had been made responsible for settling the new province of Asia after the war with Aristonicus (ch. 2. pp. 34–5) became a scandal, yet he was acquitted after his return in 126.

V. GAIUS GRACCHUS

While quaestor in Sardinia from 126 to 124 C. Gracchus tried to distance himself conspicuously from current trends in profiteering. Micipsa's gift of grain also added to his political stature. He returned to Rome early in 124 without apparently waiting for his replacement (he could have argued that he had been forced to neglect his other office of land commissioner for too long) and immediately had to defend himself against charges of misconduct on this count and complicity in the revolt of Fregellae. Canvass for the tribunate brought him election in fourth place. He was a less appealing man than his brother, but his powerful oratory and flamboyant deportment on the platform were later regarded as the beginning of a new era in demagoguery. Once elected, he revived memories of the catastrophe of Tiberius and his supporters, not only as a personal misfortune but as a failure by the plebeians to maintain their tradition of defending their tribunes. He proposed two bills with an element of reprisal. The first, banning from future office any magistrate deposed by the people and so threatening M. Octavius, was perhaps withdrawn (or a prosecution of Octavius for flouting the law was not pressed), allegedly after representations from Gracchus' mother Cornelia. The second was generally a reinforcement of the *provocatio* legislation, which sought to prevent proceedings like those under Popillius Laenas' tribunal in 132: no capital trial of a citizen was to be held without the sanction of the assembly; furthermore any magistrate who deprived a

[51] Plut. *C. Gracch.* 2.5 (cf. Livy XXXVI.2.13); Oros. V.11.2–5; Lucan III.58.

man of his citizen rights without trial, that is by execution or exile, as if he were an enemy, was himself to be tried before the people. Subsequently Gracchus prosecuted Popillius Laenas on this count and drove him into exile.[52]

The flood of new legislation which followed, although it was within existing *popularis* tradition in so far as its ultimate concern was the welfare of the people (*commoda populi*), created new precedents both in the sheer quantity and in the radical nature of the proposals. Our sources tend to conceive Gracchus' legislation as an elaborate plot against the authority of the Senate, and there is truth in this inasmuch as he was subjecting magistrates and senators to new controls. Yet he showed no sign of wanting to replace the Senate in its normal functions and it is surely a distortion to see his measures merely as instrumental, designed to create sufficient public favour for him to achieve this further end. It is equally unsound to treat his earlier measures as justifiable exercises in demagoguery on the ground that they were intended to prepare the ground for the enfranchisement of the Italians. The measures were important individually as attempts to solve political problems, but also collectively, because the means chosen often recalled the procedures of Greek democracy and the total effect was to use popular sovereignty to create an administration in the popular interest. The chronology of the legislation is impossible to reconstruct with certainty, except in so far as both the *lex de repetundis* and the Italian proposal probably belong to 122. The following treatment is therefore more schematic than sequential.[53]

Gracchus developed his brother's agrarian land legislation in a new bill which exempted an important section of public land from distribution – perhaps so that it could be rented by non-Romans – and which imposed a rent on new allotments, thus emphasizing that they were still public land. Linked with this and perhaps incorporated in it were schemes for colonies in Italy (Scyllacium, Tarentum and Capua are sites mentioned) and for the building of roads. The latter, apart from their obvious functions, would have contributed to the success of farmers on allotments deep in the countryside and to the growth of *vici*, villages where houses were assigned to those who maintained the roads.[54] Through a fellow-tribune named Rubrius he also enacted that some of the land Rome owned in North Africa should be used to settle a colony with a refounded Carthage (Iunonia) as its centre and generous allotments of up to 200 *iugera* – clearly a colony provided with an upper class from the start (ch. 2, p. 28).

To improve the corn supply he introduced a measure which by virtue

[52] Lintott 1968 (A 62) 163–4.

[53] On ancient views of C. Gracchus see Nicolet 1983 (C 116). On chronology Stockton 1979 (C 137) 226–39.

[54] Lex agraria (*Bruns* no. 11), lines 11–12.

of its intended permanence went beyond those of which we know in the Greek world. Corn was to be sold to citizens at a price of 6⅓ *asses* a *modius* (see above, p. 58), thus probably a little below the price fetched by wheat immediately after the harvest. This was made possible by the building of granaries at Rome where corn could be kept the year round after being bought when the price was low. By contrast, when he believed that corn had been improperly exacted by a praetor in Spain for despatch to Rome, he had the price of the corn sent back to the Spanish cities through a decree of the Senate. It is also possible that he proposed a limit on debt repayments as a further means of assisting the poor.[55]

It appears from an anecdote about L. Piso Frugi that the grain law was opposed because it shared out the property not of individuals but of the community as a whole: thus it was believed not unjust, as the agrarian bill of 133 had been, but rather recklessly prodigal. However, Gaius showed his concern with the revenues needed to pay for his operations by the introduction of new transit-dues and more significantly in the organization of the province of Asia. We know he spoke against a bill which would have confirmed the gift by Aquillius of part of Phrygia to Mithridates, claiming to do so in the name of the treasury and public welfare (chapter 2, p. 35). He himself passed what was probably a substitute bill about the administration of Asia, which included a new arrangement for collecting the direct taxes. These were to be farmed out to a company of tax-collectors (*societas publicanorum*) after an auction at Rome, and its representatives would collect the money in the province instead of the Roman magistrates. The *societates* had as their core a contractor (*manceps*) and partners (*socii*), who were non-senators, but these were backed by a number of guarantors and shareholders, among whom senators might have been found. The companies were unusual in being the only form of business association to which Roman law permitted a legal personality something like that of a modern company.[56] The Asian direct taxes would have been the plum contract for such companies and this probably had implications from the start throughout business circles in Rome, as it clearly did later in Cicero's day. Gaius' bill, therefore, affected the interests not only of the treasury and the common people who received benefits from it, but also of the moneyed classes, and the tax companies became the centres of important political pressure-groups.

A number of other constitutional and administrative reforms are briefly treated in our sources. By a law which was to remain valid down to 52 B.C. the Senate was required to settle the consular provinces before the election of the consuls concerned (in this epoch the elections were shortly before the end of the consular year). This would have diminished

[55] Brunt 1971 (A 17) 90. [56] Badian 1972 (A 4) 67–81. Nicolet 1971 (G 173); 1979 (G 175).

jobbery in the allocation, although occasionally, when a new military crisis arose, these provinces had to be changed – a procedure for which the law seems to have allowed. A proposal was made to mix centuries from different classes of the *comitia centuriata*, when allotting the order in which their returns of votes were to be made: this would not have affected greatly the fundamental bias towards the wealthy in the assembly, but would have ensured that, when there were three or four candidates with similar numerical support, the chances of those who drew their support from the poorer citizens would not be prejudiced. The cynic might say that Gaius was providing for his own future. We have no evidence that this bill was in fact passed. Terms of military service were also altered: no soldier less than seventeen years old was to be conscripted and there were to be no deductions from pay for clothing and equipment supplied. It is not stated, however, that C. Gracchus had reduced the period of compulsory military service, although this seems to have occurred by 109 B.C..

There are more complex problems about Gaius' policy of eliminating corruption and the dominance of the aristocracy in the courts. The Lex Sempronia about capital trials, discussed earlier (pp. 77–8), should not be forgotten in this context: it was to be a positive stimulus towards the establishment by legislation of permanent criminal courts as well as special tribunals. A measure, later incorporated in the Lex Cornelia de sicariis et veneficis (which dealt with banditry, poisoning and murder) provided that those who conspired to secure the condemnation of a person on a capital charge should themselves be liable to a capital prosecution. This does not seem to be a reaction to Popillius' tribunal of 132 but rather to misconduct in regular courts, such as that attested in 141, when Hostilius Tubulus, who had presided as praetor over an investigation into bandits, was accused of judicial corruption and a tribunal was set up through a bill passed by P. Scaevola, later the associate of Tiberius Gracchus.[57] However, the feature of Gaius' legislation that the majority of our ancient sources choose to emphasize, usually with hostile overtones, is his transfer of judicial competence to the equestrian order (pp. 90–91), which is said to have set them at odds with the Senate and cut down the Senate's power. Most of the accounts do not explain the measure in detail; Livy mentions a proposal to add 600 from the equestrian order to the Senate, Plutarch one to add 300 equestrians to the Senate, adding that the resulting 600 were to share all judicial duties. There is no evidence of an enlarged Senate later, but it is possible that we have here garbled evidence of a genuine reform, by which non-senators were generally admitted to judicial functions, which previously, according to Polybius, were monopolized by the Senate.[58]

[57] Cic. *Fin.* II.54; IV.77; *Nat. D.* III.74; Ewins 1960 (F 47).

[58] Livy *Per.* LX; Plut. *C. Gracch.* 5.2–4; Polyb. VI.17.7; Brunt 1988 (A 19) 194–204.

The clearest evidence of the nature of the reform that excited our literary authorities is provided by the fragments of a *lex de repetundis* (ch. 1, p. 5), which, though they contain no direct testimony to their author, can be shown to have belonged to Gaius' legislation.[59] This law not only prescribed the selection of jurors who had not been senators or minor magistrates, but inaugurated a new era of criminal procedure. It allowed Rome's allies, either in person or through delegated representatives, to prosecute Roman ex-magistrates, senators or their sons for the improper seizure of property. The jurors were to be fifty in number extracted by selection and rejection from an album of 450 men with no connexion with the Senate or the magistrates. Procedure was elaborately detailed and disobedience by members of the court was punished by fines. Successful prosecutors were also rewarded with citizenship or other privileges – *provocatio* and immunity from both conscription and public duties in their own communities (pp. 75–6). The political aspect of the law was not merely the granting of public duties as jurors to equestrians, but the granting of judicial power in cases where senators and their like were the defendants and the prosecution derived from embittered allies and subjects of Rome. This law in itself would explain the vaguer statements in our literary sources. The proposals mentioned by Livy and Plutarch, which brought together senators and equestrians, may have been Gaius' initial plans later abandoned or some more general measures affecting judges in other cases. According to Diodorus, who follows Posidonius, Gracchus regarded this judicial legislation as a sword threatening the Senate, and Cicero claims that Gracchus talked of throwing daggers into the Forum for citizens to fight duels.[60] We should not suppose from this that he planned to destroy the Senate but simply to break its monopoly of political influence. At the same time he sought to toughen public criminal procedure which in the past had been lenient to senatorial malefactors guilty of brutality and extortion in the empire. For prosecutions in the assembly and the creation of special tribunals by legislation might founder through obstruction by a tribune friendly to the defendant or appeals to the sympathy of the crowd, while the quasi-private procedure under the Lex Calpurnia de repetundis both was unsuited to complex cases and led merely to restitution for what had been lost, unlike the new law which provided that the damages should be double what had been taken.

It is a commonplace among modern authorities that the ensuing equestrian juries were venal and vindictive. This view is chiefly based on the case of P. Rutilius Rufus, condemned *c.* 92 B.C. after making the tax-collectors of Asia his enemies. However, it is worth noticing that Rutilius was condemned for receiving bribes (presumably from provin-

[59] Sherwin-White 1972 (B 240); 1982 (C 133); Lintott 1981 (A 64) 177–85.

[60] Cic. *Leg.* III.20; Diod. XXXVII.9.

cials), which was by then actionable under the *lex de repetundis*, and there is nothing to show that he was not technically guilty on that count. In general in this court the prosecution had to originate from complaints by allies. The statistics of *repetundae* cases from the time of Gaius' legislation onwards show that about 50 per cent of all prosecutions succeeded.[61] Although an improvement from the point of view of Rome's allies on what happened before, this was not an outstanding success rate. Yet the senatorial grievance against the jurors in this period was that they condemned, not that they acquitted unjustly. A fairer conclusion might be that the personal animus of jurors against senators on trial did no more than counterbalance the tendency of other jurors to acquit those with whom they had business and social connexions.

The passing of the *lex de repetundis* probably belongs to the beginning of Gaius' second tribunate, since the text of the inscription shows that the law was passed near the beginning of the calendar year. Gaius had achieved re-election in the midst of his legislation in circumstances which are far from clear. He did not canvass but, according to Plutarch, was chosen spontaneously by the tribes themselves and the presiding magistrate ratified his election. Arguably, this re-election did not suit his plans, since he was required in Africa to supervise the founding of the new colony at Carthage during 122. His colleague in the agrarian commission, Fulvius Flaccus, was also elected tribune, while a friend, C. Fannius, became consul. One other major bill was proposed by him (or by Flaccus with his support) this year – to improve the civil rights of Latins and Italians. It is evident from our sources that the Latins were offered full Roman citizenship, but other Italians were not. The latter are said to have been offered the right to vote. Modern scholars have assumed that this is a roundabout description of a grant of Latin status (which did include the right of all Latins present at an election to vote in one of the thirty-five tribes). However, the most important features of Latin status were the private rights of intermarriage, access to Roman courts on the same terms as Romans and acquisition of land and other major items of property owned by Romans.[62] Nor should we forget the religious cults which Rome shared with Latium. By virtue of these privileges Latins had become more assimilated to Romans than they had been by the suffrage and it would be odd if our sources had missed the point. It may be suggested, therefore, against current orthodoxy that what Gaius offered Italians was merely some form of voting rights in elections and legislation, which they could enjoy if present at Rome at the time. Gaius' proposal was, consequently, modest in that it sought

[61] Lintott 1981 (F 104) 194–5, 209–12.

[62] App. *BCiv.* 1.23.99; Plut. *C. Gracch.* 5.2; 8.3; *ORF* no. 32, fr. 1. On Latin rights see Sherwin-White 1973 (F 141) 108–16; on Gracchus' re-election see Stockton 1979 (C 137) 169ff.

only to absorb in the Roman citizen body those already closely linked by language, law and religion.

There was, however, strong opposition to the bill, in which two leading figures are named. One was the consul Fannius, who had been expected to be Gaius' supporter. The one surviving fragment of his famous speech on the subject runs, 'I suppose you imagine that, if you give citizenship to the Latins, you will still have a place in the assembly in which you are standing, and will participate in the games and festivals. Don't you realize that they will swamp everything?' The other was M. Livius Drusus, a fellow-tribune of Gaius, who is said to have sought to rival him in popular favour at the prompting of the Senate – by proposing twelve new colonies with 3,000 places each, the cancellation of the rents on the new allotments and the grant of freedom from flogging to Latins even on military service. Gaius' tribunate was apparently interrupted by his visit to the new colony in Africa, where the foundation of the town was overcast by evil omens. (It is not clear how he managed to justify his absence from the city, where as tribune he had a duty to remain: it may even be that this was sanctioned by a *senatus consultum*, which would have had the ulterior motive of removing him temporarily from the political scene.) We do not know whether the bill about the allies was abandoned, voted down or vetoed by Livius Drusus. It still seems to have been an open issue at the time of the consular elections, when Fannius expelled Latins and allies from Rome by an edict. Interestingly, Gaius produced an edict in reply, promising to use his protective powers as tribune of the plebs on behalf of those being expelled, in spite of the fact that they were not members of the Roman people, but in the event did not fulfil his promise. At all events the bill became moribund and L. Opimius, an enemy of Gracchus and previously responsible for destroying Fregellae, was elected consul. Gracchus himself was not re-elected tribune, although it is said that he had a majority of votes. This was probably because his votes were not considered until after those of ten other candidates, who had already been approved by a majority of the tribes.[63]

During 121 there was an attempt to repeal parts of his legislation. It is possible that modifications to his grain bill were proposed, but its repeal by a M. Octavius Cn. f. seems to belong to the last decade of the century, shortly before the law of Saturninus which revived the Gracchan provisions. In 121 may also fall the first post-Gracchan land law, which allowed the sale of some landholdings within the *ager publicus*, though not apparently new allotments, as most modern scholars believe (see below, pp. 86–7). Above all, the Lex Rubria about Africa was the focus

[63] Hall 1964 (F 74) at 295.

of an attack by a tribune, Minucius, which Gracchus and Fulvius Flaccus prepared to resist by mobilizing supporters.

While Gracchus and his entourage were watching the critical assembly from a newly built stoa on the Capitol, an attendant carrying entrails from a sacrifice jeered at them and was stabbed to death with styluses. The following day a meeting of the Senate was held, to which Gracchus and Flaccus were summoned but which they did not attend, fearing a repetition of the events of 133. The Senate then voted that Opimius should defend the *res publica* and see that it came to no harm; he was also urged to overthrow the tyrants. In reaction to this Flaccus and Gracchus armed their followers and seized the shrine of Diana on the Aventine hill. Opimius raised a militia from among the people of Rome, stiffening it with a force of Cretan archers, who happened to be available near the city. He declined to negotiate with his opponents, but ordered them to submit themselves in person to the judgement of the Senate. Then, after promising its weight in gold as a reward for Gracchus' head, he marched on the Aventine from the slope of the Velia. After a struggle Flaccus and his sons were killed, while Gracchus was either killed or committed suicide, when he had fled over the wooden Pons Sublicius to the far bank of the Tiber. Opimius went on to hold an inquiry into the supporters of C. Gracchus, similar to that of 132. Many were executed after a brief investigation without the formalities of trial.[64]

Opimius was later prosecuted before the people by a tribune, P. Decius Subulo, on the ground that he had executed Roman citizens who had not been legally condemned, that is, he had violated precisely Gracchus' Lex Sempronia, which had sought to prevent capital condemnations without the sanction of the people. Opimius' whole conduct in arming forces and bringing about the deaths of Gracchus and his companions was brought into question in the case. He successfully defended himself by appealing to the decree of the Senate which urged him to save the state and by claiming that his opponents did not deserve to be treated like Roman citizens. He was on better ground defending his military measures than the killing of captured Romans in cold blood, and so the broad-based attack of the prosecution may have been self-defeating. The case was important because, by contrast with 133, the deaths had not been the result of private violence – which, even if excused in the light of Roman tradition, was not strictly a constitutional precedent – but the calculated act of a magistrate who justified himself by the trust placed in him by the Senate. Constitutionally, the Senate could pass any decree it liked, it was the magistrate who was responsible for any illegal actions he undertook. Nevertheless, the decree urging the

[64] Stockton 1979 (C 137) 195ff; Lintott 1972 (F 102) 259ff. On the career of Fulvius Flaccus, who tends to become overshadowed by C. Gracchus, Hall 1977 (C 72).

defence of the public interest was valuable support, if he was charged with breaking the laws. Opimius' acquittal enabled the decree (usually known to modern historians as the *senatus consultum ultimum*, following an indignant phrase of Caesar's) to become an institution for emergencies, when the Senate believed that only the use of quasi-military force against citizens would save the situation. From a purely theoretical point of view there was much to be said for it. If there was violence and disorder in the city, a magistrate was unlikely to suppress it without breaching the personal immunities guaranteed by *provocatio*. However, the decree was vague and could be treated by magistrates as *carte blanche* for the most brutal reprisals. It was also clearly an instrument of class politics both then and on later occasions, in that the victims were those who had challenged the authority of the Senate by appealing to assemblies.[65]

Opimius' escape from punishment for his breach of the Lex Sempronia was complemented by the recall of Popillius Laenas from exile. The Senate's authority thus prevailed in the end, and the following period was to be denounced, in a speech attributed by Sallust to C. Memmius, the tribune of 111 B.C., as one in which the people were made a laughing-stock by the arrogant few.[66] On the other hand, the lesson that future *populares* might derive from the fate of the Gracchi was not that reverence for law and order was essential, but that they needed superior force and especially the support of magistrates with *imperium*. This was one respect in which the Gracchi influenced their successors from Saturninus to Clodius and the implications for the aristocracy were uncomfortable. It may be asked whether it was worthwhile for the Senate to purchase its renewed dominance at this price, especially as it could not erase what Gaius had done. It is true that the African bill was repealed, but many Gracchan settlers were left in Africa and other Romans were allowed to acquire territory by purchase there. Apart from the evidence of the agrarian law of 111 B.C. (p. 87), there is a boundary-stone of *c.* 120–119 from the territory of Carthage showing a new agrarian commission, including C. Carbo, who had reneged on his Gracchan affiliations by defending Opimius.[67] The Gracchan land and colony schemes in Italy were also modified and a bill about the Italians and Latins was not to be reintroduced for thirty years. Yet most of C. Gracchus' bills passed into the corpus of Roman legislation, often with far-reaching consequences. The aristocracy's reaction resembled that of a general dealing with a mutiny, who accedes to most of the demands but executes the ringleaders to preserve discipline.

As for C. Gracchus himself, he was more resourceful politically than

[65] Lintott 1968 (A 62) 149–74. [66] Sall. *Iug.* 31.2.
[67] *ILLRP* 475; Cic. *De Or.* II.106, 165, 170.

his brother but equally a man with a vision. Although the solutions he advanced for current problems assumed the continuance of the existing political framework, within this framework the balance of power was to be changed. Both major and minor reforms were to be introduced by legislation. He wanted senatorial administrators to be bound by rules laid down by assemblies, to be liable to prosecution by their inferiors and to condemnation by men from outside the senatorial milieu. It was impossible for him to introduce Greek democracy to Rome but, just as he recalled Greek demagogues in vaunting his incorruptible devotion to the people,[68] so he saw the people as the proper reference-point in the management and exploitation of Rome's ever-increasing imperial resources.

VI. THE ARISTOCRACY AND MARIUS

The judgement that Sallust put in the mouth of Memmius was not entirely fair. Apart from the survival of the majority of C. Gracchus' enactments, tribunician activity did not cease when he died. C. Marius, a man of equestrian family from Arpinum, who embarked on a senatorial career after his military service, passed in his tribunate of 119 a *lex tabellaria*, which sought to limit intimidation in voting assemblies by making narrower the wooden galleries which led from the waiting-enclosures to the voting-baskets. He is alleged by Plutarch also to have taken a diametrically opposed attitude by obstructing a grain bill. However, the probability is that any grain bill at this time was modifying C. Gracchus' provisions and that Plutarch has misunderstood an act whose aim was to uphold the integrity of the existing generous grain provision. The following year an important measure was carried in defiance of senatorial authority, the law proposing the foundation of a colony at Narbonne, which followed Gracchan precedent in creating a colony overseas in a position which was also of commercial importance (p. 24 above). It was vigorously supported by the young L. Licinius Crassus, later Cicero's mentor in oratory, who had also distinguished himself for successfully prosecuting C. Carbo – perhaps *de repetundis* under the procedure established by C. Gracchus. Another law which gave vent to popular feeling was the Lex Peducaea of 114 which set up a special tribunal to judge unchaste Vestal Virgins and their seducers, thus replacing the jurisdiction of the *pontifex maximus*.

The agrarian arrangements in Italy were, however, modified. One bill allowed the sale of land which had been granted from the public domain. Appian understood this to apply to the smallholdings of the new

[68] *ORF* no. 48, fr. 44.

assignees, but the implication of the *lex agraria* of 111 is that under the earlier law only the established *possessores* were allowed this privilege.[69] Later the Lex Thoria put an end to the operations of the land commission, allowing the retention of existing holdings of public land by *possessores*, but only those, as appears from the law of 111, which did not exceed the limit of the Leges Semproniae, and subjecting them to a rent. The proceeds were to be used towards distributions, possibly to provide initial finance for the new smallholders in Italy. The agrarian law preserved on bronze (passed some time between 1 March and the harvest of 111) abolished this rent for all legitimate possession of *ager publicus* by citizens, which did not depend on a lease, and this land was now made private.[70] Thus the *status quo* was formalized. Some land, nevertheless, was to remain public, including land given to villagers who maintained the roads, land leased out by the censors (including blocks granted to Italian communities), drove-roads (*calles*) and pasture-land. It was also provided that up to 30 *iugera* of public land could be made private by a possessor who rendered it cultivable. However, the implication of the law was that as much as could be done to redistribute Roman public land in Italy had now been done. Henceforward new enterprises of this kind were to take place abroad, as the sections of the law on Africa and Corinth illustrate: in the former land is shown to be still available for purchase or rent, in the latter surveying for centuriation was taking place with a view to future assignments. Appian viewed this law as a betrayal of the aims of the Gracchi. It may have seemed so to a writer in the early Principate, when estates were vastly expanding and the number of proprietors drastically contracting, but it does not follow that the new smallholdings were unviable or immediately abandoned (pp. 56–7). The pressure of the wealthy on the land was undeniable, but it seems more likely that the power of capital only became rampant in the dislocation which followed the social and civil wars in the decade 90–80 B.C.

Nevertheless, the decade following the death of C. Gracchus was sufficiently reactionary to evoke the bitter ripostes against the nobility at the time of the Jugurthine War. Indeed, it is this period above all which prompted Sallust to declare Roman politics to be ruled by *factio paucorum*, the established power of a small number of *nobiles*. The general truth of this statement and its implications have been discussed earlier (pp. 48–52), but it is appropriate here to mention a modern interpretation of the period, which has evolved from it, namely the predominance of a 'Metellan faction'.[71] Between 123 and 109 the consulship was held by six

[69] App. *BCiv.* 1.27.121; lex agr. 15–16 (no rights for buyers of new allotments before 111), cf. 16–17 (purchase from old *possessores* recognized).

[70] Badian 1964 (C 10); Gabba 1958 (B 40) 93–5; Johannsen 1971 (B 176).

[71] Badian 1957 (C 6), followed above all by Gruen 1968 (C 68) 106–35.

Caecilii Metelli, four sons of Q. Metellus Macedonicus (cos. 143) and two sons of L. Metellus Calvus (cos. 142). In addition P. Scipio Nasica (cos. 111) and M. Aemilius Scaurus (cos. 115 and now the *princeps senatus*), regarded by Sallust as a key figure in the domination of the nobility, were sons-in-law of Metelli. Other political associates have been detected in those who were colleagues in consulships with Metelli or were related to those who had been their colleagues, including L. Aurelius Cotta (cos. 119) and Q. Servilius Caepio (cos. 106). One may argue that this plethora of Metelli is a historical fluke caused by the reproductive capacity of the previous generation and an unusually high rate of survival of children. An already powerful family was thus bound to bulk even larger both politically and socially among the aristocracy. Yet this does not imply that the importance and the limitations of kinship links as political moments had changed. On the other hand, those who see family groupings as the driving forces in Roman politics can simply argue that the 'Metellan faction' presents in a particularly blatant form the kind of political association normally created by a much more subtle and complex network of relationships. After the doubts voiced earlier about explanations of politics in terms of a struggle between family factions, it is only necessary here to consider how far the concept of a 'Metellan faction' helps to elucidate the history of the post-Gracchan epoch. If we accept that for ten years or so the major figures were nobles hostile to Gracchan policies, whether these were consuls or senior members of the Senate, it is certainly possible that the Metellan family provided the political and social cement which made their dominance more coherent. However, in my view it does not follow that the Metelli themselves provided leadership or a political strategy, nor that those connected with them retained political cohesion in the following period, when traditional aristocratic politics were once again challenged. Sallust in the *Jugurtha* (16.2) attributed Opimius' influence in the Senate to his crushing of C. Gracchus and the plebs, not to friendship with Metelli.

The imperial aspects of the war with Jugurtha have been discussed earlier (ch. 2, pp. 28–31). Initially Jugurtha's bribes reinforced a not unreasonable reluctance to get deeply involved in Numidia, but his humiliation of Roman diplomacy and the potential threat he posed to the province of Africa led to a volte-face in Roman policy. This change came originally without any stimulus from *popularis* tribunes, but from 111 onwards, when Jugurtha's methods had become common knowledge, it was easy for the tribunes to exploit the theme of senatorial incompetence and corruption in a matter of national pride. C. Memmius, tribune in 111, passed a bill requiring a praetor, L. Cassius, to bring Jugurtha to Rome for questioning – a plan which was in the end frustrated when another tribune forbade him to give testimony. In 110 after Jugurtha had returned to Africa, there was further agitation by tribunes and two sought to be re-elected. The following year the consul Metellus was obstructed by tribunes, when he tried to take new forces to Africa after Albinus' defeat. Then C. Mamilius proposed that a special tribunal (*quaestio*) should be established to investigate those who had advised Jugurtha to disregard decrees of the Senate, who had received bribes, who had handed back his elephants and deserters and had made formal agreements about peace and war with enemies. The bill thus ostensibly sought to protect both the authority of the Senate and the ultimate discretion of the people in matters of peace and war. It threatened any member of the various embassies to Numidia as well as L. Bestia and Sp. Albinus, consuls in 111 and 110, together with their military advisers, especially M. Scaurus.

We are told that the guilty men tried to block the bill by intrigue, especially through Latins and allies.[72] Sallust's phraseology suggests that tribunes or other magistrates were bribed or blackmailed to use a veto or religious obstruction with allies acting as intermediaries. This, like the appeal of Italian possessors of public land in 129, illustrates the connexions which Italians had with the Roman aristocracy. In the event Scaurus managed to be chosen one of the presidents of the tribunal, but at least five eminent senators, including Bestia, Albinus and L. Opimius were condemned. Those who served on the tribunals are said to have been Gracchan judges, probably therefore taken from the album established by C. Gracchus' *lex de repetundis*. The political attitudes of wealthy men outside the senatorial order were becoming more obviously important in these years. It would not have been surprising if individuals of this standing had regularly an influence behind the scenes in the previous hundred years, one which only came to the fore in crises, such as the scandal of the fraudulent shippers in 212 or the argument over state contracts in 169. Military failure was bad news for those involved in finance and public contracts, even if their interests lay more at home than overseas, since the collapse of financial confidence (*fides*) was contagious. More particularly we know that Italian businessmen had suffered through involvement with Adherbal in Numidia, others were buying land in the African province, while Roman *equites* were active in the Numidian campaign as 'soldiers and businessmen'. It was their support that C. Marius, then a subordinate officer of Metellus, solicited in 108, when agitating against his commander's conduct of the war and seeking the consulship for himself.[73]

[72] Sall. *Iug.* 40.3.

[73] Livy xxv.3–4; xliii.16, Sall. *Iug.* 21.2; 26.1; 65.4; Vell. Pat. ii.11.

VII. MARIUS AND THE *EQUITES*

Before considering the implications of Marius' career a brief digression on the nature of the equestrian order, as it came to be understood politically, is not out of place. Fundamentally, the *equites Romani* were the men chosen by the censors, who were assigned horses at public expense with further allowances for fodder and who voted in eighteen special centuries in the *comitia centuriata.* Many of these were young men who would afterwards become senators, some were brothers or other close relatives of senators, others had no connexion with the Senate. They shared with senators the insignia of the gold ring. However, the term *equites* seems also to have been applied by writers from Polybius onwards to a far wider group who did military service on horseback. We hear of an equestrian property qualification (*census*), perhaps of 400,000 sesterces in the late Republic, whose possession did not automatically entail equestrian status. It is also stated that this status was *de facto* hereditary. Although it has been powerfully argued by Nicolet that the only proper reference of the phrase *equites Romani* is to the members of the eighteen centuries, the confused accounts of some of our sources suggest that in the late Republic an ambiguity had crept in, and it seems that one reason for that ambiguity was the application of the term *equites* to those non-senators who sat in the courts and were frequently tax-contractors, when their opposition to the Senate was being recounted.[74] If in the inscribed *lex de repetundis* of C. Gracchus the now lost positive qualification of its jurors was membership of the *equites Romani*, there would have been no ambiguity, but it is likely that this qualification was far more complex. When, therefore, following our ancient sources, we refer to a conflict between Senate and *equites*, we mean by the second term not the members of the equestrian centuries but those wealthy non-senators, who may for the most part have been members of the equestrian centuries but were not necessarily so (they may have had strictly a different status, for example that of *tribunus aerarii* which involved a similar property qualification). Those young *equites*, who were mainly sons of senators and would soon themselves become senators, should not be assumed to have had an equestrian loyalty in politics.

Although our sources derive the breach between Senate and *equites* from the judiciary legislation of C. Gracchus, the condemnations under the Lex Mamilia and the election of Marius to his first consulship in 107 are the first clear evidence of equestrian hostility to senatorial administration in this period. Marius was not only a valuable instrument of this reaction but he symbolized it. Of equestrian family by birth and a native of Arpinum like the Cicerones, he might have been content with municipal magistracies, military service and financial enterprise, perhaps

[74] Nicolet 1966 (A 80); Henderson 1963 (C 76); Wiseman 1970 (A 131).

in the service of the *res publica*. In fact one source alleges that he was involved in tax contracts. He also had a long and distinguished military career, including service under Scipio at Numantia, and became a tribune of the soldiers. However, about the time of C. Gracchus' ascendancy he embarked on politics at Rome, becoming quaestor, tribune (p. 86) and then, after surviving charges of bribery, praetor. He was regarded by Metellus in Numidia as under his patronage while on his staff. He had connexions also with the Herennii, one of whom was formally his patron, but it is not clear whence he had derived political backing in his previous career. Marius' success in reaching the consulship cannot be entirely dissociated from previous connexions (even if our sources say nothing about them in this context), but Sallust's insistence that it depended on a wide canvass, including farm workers and labourers in the city, cannot be discounted, nor can the fact that he was assisted by *equites* who were businessmen.[75] The votes of the latter in the equestrian centuries or the first class were vital and many must have disregarded prior allegiances to vote for Marius. Their justification was no doubt that in a crisis Rome needed the best man possible (the same argument had worked in favour of Scipiones in the more recent past and for new men like Fabricius Luscinus and Curius Dentatus in the almost legendary era of the war against Pyrrhus (vol. VIII^2, pp. 412–13, 447–9)). It is interesting that a Hortensius originally elected consul for 108 was condemned while in office and a suffect consul replaced him. Marius on the other hand was a man of old-fashioned severity and untainted by the most recent senatorial corruption. Sallust treats the election of a new man as an epoch-making blow against the nobility. In fact men with no known consular or praetorian connexions who had reached the consulship in the last twenty years were rare compared with those in other periods but still some 15 per cent of the total. When such a man was elected, this was regarded by his noble competitors as a personal humiliation, but it would not have been taken by the nobility as a vote of no confidence, in view of the ample precedents, unless the special circumstances of the election strongly suggested this.[76]

Once elected, Marius was assigned Africa as his province by a plebiscite which thus overruled the regular procedure laid down by C. Gracchus. The assignation of Africa to Scipio Aemilianus in 147 was a recent precedent for this (the appointment of Scipio Africanus to Spain in 211 had by contrast been made after the Senate had ceded its discretion to the assembly). In turn Marius' appointment was the forerunner of a series of major commands conferred by the people ending with the fateful allocations to Caesar, Pompey and Crassus in the fifties. The Senate allowed Marius to conscript, but he evaded the opposition that

[75] Sall. *Iug.* 65; 73; Carney 1962 (C 41); Passerini 1934 (C 117) 10–32.

[76] Frequency of 'new men', Hopkins and Burton 1983 (A 54) 55ff. Definition – Brunt 1982 (C 34).

Metellus had encountered in 109 by only recruiting volunteers, especially the time-served soldiers (*evocati*), promising them victory and booty. He also included in this levy the propertyless *capite censi* – a move criticized by later historians, on the ground that it filled the army with unprincipled men who were ideal material for aspirants to dictatorial power. This judgement was easy to make when the Republic had been destroyed, especially in the light of the period after Caesar's murder, when armies were bought and soldiers learnt to sell their services at the highest price. However, Marius showed no sign of realizing the potential for revolution in his action, nor may it have been apparent to most of his contemporaries. Critics at the time are more likely to have seized on the breach of a principle at the root of Roman society, one which it shared with classical Greek cities, whereby the defence of the community was entrusted normally to those with a considerable stake in it through property. Similarly, their commitment to the defence of Rome justified their dominance in the *comitia centuriata* which elected the highest magistrates. Thus Marius would have been charged with levying worthless men, who were more likely to damage Rome by desertion than subversion.[77]

If Marius and his contemporaries were short-sighted, they are not necessarily to be blamed. The proportion of propertyless men who were in fact recruited cannot be determined. The Romans continued to levy regularly by conscription rather than by asking for volunteers. The lure of military service is not self-evident, when an ordinary soldier was paid one denarius every three days, augmented, if he was lucky, by booty and donatives at triumphs. It is true that Marius was the first commander known to us to be closely connected with major distributions of land to his ex-soldiers. Yet at this stage land assignment was a process which required the co-operation of the Senate and other magistrates: it could not be demanded from a general. In fact Roman armies were only to be used for civil war after their scruples had been drowned in a blood-bath of fighting with their own Italian allies, and the Roman soldiers who served then were raised by wholesale conscription. It may as well be argued that civil war created the self-seeking unprincipled soldier as the converse.[78]

VIII. GENERALS AND TRIBUNES

While Marius was conducting his long campaign in Numidia, the story elsewhere was the increasingly familiar one of defeat and corruption followed by retribution in the courts at Rome. In 107, after the defeat of

[77] Sall. *Iug.* 84.2–5; 86.1–3; Plut. *Mar.* 9.1; Gell. *NA* XVI.10.11; Gabba 1976 (C 55) 16–33.
[78] Brunt 1962 (C 30) 75–9; = 1988 (A 19) 257–65.

L. Cassius by the Tigurini in Aquitania, C. Popillius saved the lives of the remaining soldiers at the price of a humiliating agreement. Before he was prosecuted on this count in an assembly, the tribune C. Coelius enacted that secret ballot should be used in capital trials before the people and in the event Popillius was condemned. (It should be remarked that condemnation on a capital charge in an assembly was rare – the other certain recent example was that of P. Popillius Laenas, charged by C. Gracchus in 123.) The following year the consul Q. Servilius Caepio passed a *lex de repetundis*, which provided that the jurors should be drawn from a mixed panel of senators and *equites*. It is not clear whether this was the first law of this kind since the work of C. Gracchus: this depends on whether the Lex Acilia referred to by Cicero is to be taken as part of the Gracchan legislation or a subsequent law. However, it seems clear that in any case the basic principles of Gracchus had been preserved until 106. Caepio's law may also have introduced the procedure called *divinatio*, whereby the jury selected the prosecutor from a number of applicants. L. Crassus is said to have supported the proposal with an impassioned plea to the people to save senators from the jaws of ravening beasts. This is normally taken to refer to the equestrian jurors, but it may also apply to the prosecutors, who were, as Cicero's *Brutus* shows, becoming a recognized class at this time.[79]

However, on 6 October the following year Caepio himself and Mallius, consul of that year, shared responsibility for the disastrous defeat by the Cimbri near Arausio (Orange) in the Rhône valley, while Caepio himself was alleged to have plundered gold from a sacred lake near Tolosa (Toulouse) belonging to Roman allies. Caepio was deprived of his *imperium* – perhaps at the instance of the tribune C. Norbanus, if his office began in December 105, as has been plausibly suggested. This would then have been the occasion when two tribunes, who tried to veto a bill of Norbanus, were driven by violence from the temple where the proposer stood, and the *princeps senatus*, Scaurus, was struck by a stone – the so-called *seditio Norbana*. Another tribune, L. Cassius, who was an enemy of Caepio, passed a law expelling from the Senate any man condemned in a trial before the people or deprived of his command by them. A special tribunal was later set up to investigate the matter of the gold taken from Toulouse. Caepio seems to have been condemned both by this tribunal and by the assembly. Certainly, he was thrown into prison because he had been condemned on a capital charge and only released through the intervention of the tribune L. Reginus in 104 or 103. Meanwhile another active tribune of 104, Cn. Domitius, unsuccessfully tried to prosecute M. Silanus for his earlier defeat by the Cimbri in 109. (Silanus, we are told, had wronged a Gallic client who had been a

[79] Lintott 1981 (F 104) 186–91.

family friend of Domitius' father, the conqueror of the Arverni.) Domitius, however, did secure the adoption of a bill which put an end to the co-option of the ordinary members of the colleges of priests, substituting election by a minority (i.e. seventeen) of the tribes. He thus evaded religious objections to election by the people *en masse* by a sophism.[80]

A further law which belongs to either 104 or 101 is the *lex de repetundis* of C. Servilius Glaucia. This not only restored to the equestrian order their former monopoly of judging these cases, but introduced new procedure and changed the scope of the law. Trials henceforth in this court were compulsorily divided into two parts (a procedure called *comperendinatio*) and the previous permission for adjournment, if more than a third of the jury was undecided, was abolished. A supplementary inquiry was instituted regarding money which had been passed on by the condemned man to other people. *Divinatio* to select the prosecutor was either retained or introduced (p. 93), and, probably for the first time, the selected prosecutor was given time to search for evidence in the region where the crimes had occurred (*inquisitio*). The financial penalty was augmented by loss of status. Moreover, the law began to take into account the acceptance of freely given bribes as well as exactions under physical or moral pressure. Although this very severe law made the prosecution of misconduct by Roman magistrates more comprehensive and effective, it was contrary to the spirit of C. Gracchus' legislation, in that through *divinatio* prosecutions would tend to be assigned to Romans, rather than the injured allies, thus providing material for aspiring politicians and the new breed of professional accusers. A fragment of bronze from Tarentum containing complex provisions for rewarding those who had contributed to a successful accusation and for demanding an oath of obedience to the law, may preserve the final section of Glaucia's law.[81]

Thus the political trend visible at the outset of the Jugurthine War continued. Military humiliation and the misconduct of commanders abroad rendered the aristocracy vulnerable to attacks by tribunes, and their success in exploiting these weaknesses encouraged further *popularis* activity. At the same time the German tribes, even though they had retired north with their spoils in 105, posed a serious threat to Italy itself and a further danger near home was presented by the new Sicilian slave revolt in 104 (ch. 2, p. 26). The military situation was to give C. Marius an even greater opportunity to advance his career, while popular unrest stimulated tribunes not only to harass the aristocracy with a sort of political guerilla warfare but to reassert the pre-eminence of the assembly in a revival of politics according to the Gracchan model.

[80] Ferrary 1979 (C 49) 92–101.

[81] Lintott 1981 (F 104) 189–97; 1982 (B 191); Ferrary 1979 (C 49) 101–34.

Thanks to the diplomacy of his legate Sulla, who persuaded king Bocchus of Mauretania to surrender Jugurtha, Marius had been able to complete his Numidian campaign by the time that the news of Arausio reached Rome. He was then elected consul for the second time in his absence. This may be simply ascribed to the wave of popular feeling that simultaneously overwhelmed Caepio, but we cannot exclude the possibility that both in 105 and 104 the Senate acquiesced in the dispensation of Marius from the law limiting re-election in order to placate the rest of the people. After his first major victory over the Teutones and Ambrones in 102 his re-election was said to have been by common consent. Moreover, there seem to have been no special political implications in his policy of recruitment and military training in 104, such as there had been in 107. *Capite censi* may well have been recruited, but this was the sort of crisis in which restrictions on recruitment and exemptions from military service were normally suspended – in Roman terminology a *tumultus*. In fact no more than six Roman legions may have been used to fight the Germans but these were supplemented by more than their equivalent in allies.[82]

Marius' absence from Rome kept him aloof from the bitterness caused by the prosecutions of 104. However, the following year he was associated with a tribune, L. Appuleius Saturninus, who secured for him the settlement of demobilized soldiers on land in Africa. When faced with an attempt by his colleague Baebius to veto the bill, Saturninus drove him away with a hail of stones, brutally cutting short any argument about the proprieties of Baebius' action. The principle of settlement in the provinces was already firmly established and the arguments used by Ti. Gracchus against Octavius (pp. 66–7) could have been applied with equal force to Baebius. He in turn might have argued that the allotments of 100 *iugera* were too generous (in spite of the precedent set by the Lex Rubria) and would have cost the treasury the rent or sale price which the land would otherwise have produced. In any event the bill was implemented and the father of Julius Caesar, who was Marius' brother-in-law, was among the land commissioners. The location of the settlements has been already discussed (ch. 2, p. 30). Another agrarian bill of the period, proposed by L. Marcius Philippus, was voted down – perhaps because it concerned Italy, where there were by now vested interests even among the poor – but left its mark by virtue of the comment by its proposer, that there were not 2,000 men at Rome who really possessed property.[83]

Saturninus joined in the harrying of incompetent magistrates. He not only prosecuted Mallius and drove him into exile but, probably in his first tribunate in 103, created a new permanent court to deal with those

[82] Brunt 1971 (A 16) 430–1, 685.

[83] Cic. *Off.* II.73. On Saturninus, Glaucia and Marius see Badian 1958 (A 1) 198–210; Ferrary 1977 (C 49).

who damaged the majesty of the Roman people (*quaestio de maiestate*). This vague phrase came to cover a multitude of sins, and it is impossible to be sure what the original legislator intended it to mean. It certainly could be applied to the cases of treason or military incompetence by a commander, such as had been recently prosecuted before assemblies. It is also likely that it was aimed at tribunes or other magistrates, who deliberately obstructed the people's will – for example Octavius in 133 and more recently Baebius and the tribunes who had protected Caepio. Ironically, it was later interpreted as a measure against tribunes who used violence. For C. Norbanus was himself accused in this court in 95. The jurors were *equites* and the procedure was probably modelled on that of the *quaestio de repetundis*. It is possible that we have part of the text of this law on a fragment of bronze from Bantia, but other identifications of the fragment have been proposed.[84]

In 102 Saturninus supported a L. Equitius, when he claimed to be the son of Ti. Gracchus at the censorship. The censor, Metellus Numidicus, the man from whose patronage Marius had broken away, refused to register Equitius where he wished (presumably in the rural tribe of the Sempronii, as opposed to an urban tribe, where freedmen and other humble men at Rome were enrolled). Metellus would have also expelled Saturninus and Glaucia from the Senate, if his colleague Metellus Caprarius had permitted this. One source tells of the censor being blockaded on the Capitol and rescued by *equites*. This personal clash and Saturninus' dismissal from his quaestorian post by the Senate a few years earlier are cited by our authorities as explanations for Saturninus' embittered violence. Saturninus was certainly a more abrasive personality than the Gracchi, but his violence cannot be simply explained in these terms. There is also an element of political calculation: he used force to surmount swiftly hurdles which his political opponents thrust in his path, assuming that fears of popular hostility would make his opponents reluctant to risk military action in Rome and that Marius would in the last resort support him.[85]

Marius' army meanwhile defeated the Teutones and Ambrones near the Roman fort of Aquae Sextiae (Aix-en-Provence). A more serious invasion of the Cimbri through the Alpine passes was eventually repelled the following year at Vercellae (Campi Raudii) in Cisalpine Gaul. M'. Aquillius, Marius' colleague in the consulship of 101, brought to an end the Sicilian slave-war. However, new theatres of war had opened in the East. Lycaonia was detached from Cappadocia by Rome. In 102 the

[84] Ferrary 1983 (C 50) (dating law to 100); on *Bruns* no. 9 (p. 53) see Tibiletti 1953 (F 160) 57–75; Lintott 1978 (B 190).

[85] App. *BCiv.* I.28.126–7; Val. Max. IX.7.2; *De Vir. Ill.* 73; Oros. V.17.3; Cic. *Har. Resp.* 43; *Sest.* 101; *Inscr. Ital.* XIII.3, no. 16; Badian 1962 (C 8) 218–19.

praetor M. Antonius was given as his province Cilicia and a campaign against the pirates. T. Didius made an expedition beyond the river Hebrus in Thrace and by 101 had added to the province of Macedonia an area known as the Caenic Chersonese (see below). There was also a foretaste of future trouble when an embassy from Mithridates VI of Pontus was suspected by Saturninus of trying to bribe senators and he treated them with such violence that he was afterwards charged with violating their diplomatic immunity (p. 142 below).

In 101 Glaucia, the author of the latest *lex de repetundis*, was tribune. After Marius' victory he presided over the tribunician elections, in which Saturninus was elected for the second time with the assistance of soldiers returned from the war, and a competitor A. Nunnius (or Ninnius) was killed. One somewhat confused source states that L. Equitius sought the tribunate unsuccessfully in the latter's place.[86] Marius himself was re-elected to a sixth consulship, allegedly after bribery (presumably he had distributed some of the Cimbric spoils to his soldiers, who were the electors). However, it is not clear how and on what grounds he was freed from legal restrictions on candidature this time. Glaucia himself became praetor immediately following his tribunate, something not illegal, since the tribunate was outside the normal *cursus* of offices, but distinctly unusual.

Important legislation in 100 is ascribed to Saturninus by our literary sources. However, a further item must be added either to the year 101 or 100, which reflects on his policies and the attitude of *populares* at this time. This is the law about the praetorian provinces (ch. 2, pp. 32, 35–6), now known to us from two overlapping groups of texts from Delphi and Cnidus, which has been traditionally termed the 'pirate law'. This law was a plebiscite passed after the election of Marius and L. Valerius Flaccus to the consulships of 100 but before the provincial arrangements for that year had been completed by the Senate (a task which the law claimed for itself). Most of the measures themselves are not particularly remarkable. New levies are not to be sent to Macedonia; the future governors of this province are to concern themselves with tribute-collecting and must visit the newly acquired Caenic Chersonese for at least sixty days; Cilicia is made a praetorian province and diplomacy is to be undertaken with Rhodes and the kings of the eastern Mediterranean to ensure a concerted campaign against the pirates; the governor of the province of Asia meanwhile is to secure Lycaonia and perhaps Pamphylia. However, there are also general provisions about a governor's conduct. He must not move outside his province except for the purpose of travelling to and from his tasks or for reasons of state (in this the law

[86] Livy *Per.* LXIX; App. *BCiv.* I.28.127–8; Val. Max. IX.7.1–3; *De Vir. Ill.* 73; Flor. II.4.1 (emphasizing Saturninus' own position as C. Gracchus' political heir).

repeated the provisions of a Lex Porcia passed apparently in the February of the same year). Any man appointed in the absence of a regular governor was to have the governor's full powers of jurisdiction until his return to Rome. The coda of the law is a series of enforcement clauses, requiring magistrates to obey the law and to swear oaths to that effect and threatening anyone who obstructs the performance of its provisions with a fine of 200,000 sesterces on each count – enough to drive many of them into exile. A special form of judicial procedure was established for the exaction of these fines.[87]

The apparently commonplace nature of the majority of its chapters should not hide from us the radical features of the law. This law and the preceding Lex Porcia are the first laws known to us to lay down general positive rules for provincial governors – something developed later in Julius Caesar's *lex de repetundis*, the legislation of Augustus and the edicts of later emperors. In this plebiscite, as in the bills of the Gracchi about Asia, a tribune deals with the details of imperial administration, which were normally left to the Senate, and directs the magistrates' activities. Finally, coercion and threats are used to enforce the law in a manner reminiscent of the Athenian democracy at the height of its power. The oaths themselves are not new. The agrarian law of 111 refers to earlier oaths required by legislators, and such requirements, in conjunction with penal clauses, exist on the bronze fragments from Bantia and Tarentum, but these fall short of the elaborate procedure we have here.[88] The law is thus radical in form and principle, if not apparently in content, in that it asserts the sovereignty of the assembly over the minutiae of Roman government. If the law belongs to early 100, it is difficult not to ascribe it to Saturninus or a friendly colleague of his; if it is a law of late 101, then the influence of Servilius Glaucia must be suspected. The law envisages the co-operation of C. Marius and it is likely that it had his blessing.

The legislation of Saturninus in 100 known to us from literary sources has a familiar appearance, recalling the Gracchi, though the land laws had the particular function of accommodating Marius' veterans. A grain law, which restored distributions to the plebs at Rome at the Gracchan price, was fiercely resisted by the younger Servilius Caepio, who was quaestor at the treasury that year. When Saturninus ignored the vetoes of tribunes, Caepio at the head of a gang broke up the apparatus required for voting. The law, however, seems eventually to have been passed and Caepio later in the year issued with a colleague coins celebrating the buying of corn according to a decree of the Senate. Saturninus' land

[87] Hassall, Crawford and Reynolds 1974 (B 170), cf. *Greenidge–Clay* 279–81 for the original Delphi text; Lintott 1976 (B 189); Ferrary 1977 (C 49).

[88] Tibiletti 1953 (F 160) 61ff; Passerini 1934 (C 117) 121ff.

legislation included projects for founding colonies in Sicily, Achaea and Macedonia – using the looted gold from Toulouse. We also hear of a colony founded by C. Marius in Corsica. Iunonia and Narbo Martius were precedents for colonization outside Italy, but the policy was not a prerogative of *populares*, as is shown by the settlements in the Balearic Islands and the foundation of Eporedia in Cisalpina this year. In fact, the centuriation of the land of Corinth, prior to some kind of settlement, had been ordered in the final section of the agrarian law of 111, and this may have been one of the sites chosen by Saturninus.[89]

A further land bill, however, became the focus of a struggle between Saturninus and his political opponents. This proposed the distribution into allotments of land in Cisalpine Gaul, which the Cimbri had taken from its previous inhabitants. We do not know the scale or the situation of these allotments. It is therefore impossible to establish if there could have been any valid objections to the bill, such as the hostility that it would have provoked among the local inhabitants. In principle, the measure was little different from earlier laws assigning land in Cisalpina or from Flaminius' plebiscite of 232. We are told that the bill was resisted by the urban plebs on the ground that the Italians were being excessively privileged. It was only passed in the assembly after violence in which countrymen, who had served under Marius and had been specially brought into the city by Saturninus, were victorious. Although there was clearly hostility among the urban plebs towards Roman citizens from rural Italy, who would have constituted the bulk of Marius' army and the majority of likely recipients under the law, this does not entirely explain the reference to Italians. Marius must have been providing land for allies as well. We know that in one of Saturninus' bills it was laid down that Marius could create three (so the Cicero manuscripts) new Roman citizens in each colony. This would have enabled him to reward Italian allies who had served him well and also make a political gesture of good will towards Italy, something which he had done on his own account, when he had enfranchised a cohort of Umbrian auxiliary troops on the field of battle.[90]

Saturninus forced through this agrarian bill in defiance of vetoes attempted by other tribunes and of demands to adjourn the assembly because thunder had occurred. He is said to have told his aristocratic opponents that it would hail on them, if they would not keep quiet. In fact this is the first known example of religious obstruction being used against a contentious tribunician bill. It is probable that there genuinely was thunder and his opponents seized on this as a means of resisting him.

[89] *Rhet. Her.* 1.21; Crawford (B 144) no. 330; *Greenidge–Clay* 107, 111; lex agr. 96ff.

[90] App. *BCiv.* 1.29.130–30.134; Cic. *Balb.* 46, 48; Val. Max. v.2.8; *De Vir. Ill.* 73.7; Badian 1958 (A 1) 207.

The formal, including the religious, requirements for legislation had been laid down in the Leges Aelia and Fufia before 133. Nevertheless, up to 100 B.C. a presiding magistrate was allowed considerable discretion about recognizing or ignoring reports of evil omens, although, if he chose to ignore them, he might be prosecuted later. As it happened, this controversial incident seems to have created a precedent: the reporting of genuine or fictitious portents became a common form of obstruction in the late Republic.[91] On this occasion, after the urban plebs had backed the obstructors, they were forced back by the demobilized soldiers loyal to Marius. When they resorted to using clubs, the Marians did the same and overcame them. So the responsibility for first using force rested with Saturninus' supporters, but that for first using weapons with his opponents.

After the passage of the bill the opposition found a new focus in the oath which all senators (not only the magistrates, as in the law about the praetorian provinces) were required to swear within five days on pain, according to Appian, of a fine of 500,000 sesterces and expulsion from the Senate. The old enemy of Marius and Saturninus, Metellus Numidicus, refused to swear this oath. Marius circumvented the resistance of other senators by suggesting that the obligation imposed by the oath was contingent on the validity of the law and oath-taking did not prejudge this issue. This manoeuvre seems to have been both well founded in law and politically adroit. Marius did not wish to lose a law in his own interest, but he preferred to avoid confrontation with his opponents. Saturninus tried to have Metellus removed from the Senate for refusing to swear, but other tribunes protected him. In response, Saturninus proposed a bill exiling Metellus, presumably on the ground that he was no longer obeying the laws as a citizen should (his argument would thus have been similar to that used to justify the killing of Gracchan supporters who were 'enemies'). In face of this Metellus withdrew into exile, in order, it is said, to prevent a civil war, and Saturninus had proclamation duly made by Marius that Metellus was forbidden fire and water.[92] The event brought odium on Marius among the aristocracy and among other opponents of Saturninus, which was to be exploited in due course in order to achieve Metellus' recall. In the longer term the story became a legend – initially because it was grist to the mill of historians hostile to Marius like Rutilius Rufus and Posidonius, later because perhaps of the parallels with the exile of Cicero, which the orator himself highlighted. As a result the affair overshadows the rest of Saturninus' actions in other accounts and has done much to obscure their true significance.[93]

[91] Astin 1964 (F 7).

[92] App. *BCiv.* 1.30.135–31.140; Plut. *Mar.* 29; *Greenidge–Clay* 106–7; Lintott 1972 (F 102) 245–6.

[93] Most obvious in Plut. *Mar.* 29; Malitz 1983 (B 69) 378–9.

At the time Saturninus must have appeared unstoppable: the legislation met with no challenge and both he and L. Equitius were elected tribunes for the following year. Then, probably towards the end of the year (even if Appian's chronology may not be secure), the consular elections were held. One candidate was M. Antonius, who was still outside the city with his soldiers waiting for a triumph, another was C. Memmius, formerly an active tribune in 111 but now feared by Saturninus, a third was Glaucia, who was seeking with Saturninus' support to become consul directly after being praetor, contrary to the *lex annalis*. On the day of the election Glaucia's candidature was not accepted, Memmius was clubbed to death by Saturninus' men and the assembly was adjourned in confusion. Saturninus gathered further support from the countryside and seized the Capitol. Meanwhile the Senate passed for the second time in Roman history the *senatus consultum ultimum*, requesting the consuls, with the co-operation of the other magistrates, to defend the public interest. Marius himself probably took the view that, if anyone was to take action against Saturninus and Glaucia, it was in all their interests that he should do so.

The consuls considered employing M. Antonius' army, but decided initially to avoid the dangerous precedent of bringing a regular Roman army into the civil sector of Rome, defined by the *pomoerium*, the sacred boundary of the city. Marius distributed arms and formed a militia, with which he besieged Saturninus' men on the Capitol. They surrendered and were imprisoned in the senate-house after receiving some kind of guarantee against summary execution from Marius. But this did them no good. They were attacked by a lynch-mob and either stoned to death in the senate-house or killed while seeking sanctuary elsewhere (the details in the sources are highly coloured and often inconsistent). The dead included Saturninus and Glaucia themselves, L. Equitius, M. Saufeius, currently quaestor, and Saturninus' brother, Cn. Cornelius Dolabella.[94]

Marius gained little advantage from his attempt to preside over a disciplined restoration of law and order. After he left office, relatives of Metellus Numidicus (especially his son, later surnamed Pius) dogged his path with the sombre and dishevelled appearance which indicated mourning, and pleaded for Metellus' restoration.[95] After obstruction by P. Furius, who was in the writer's view tribune in 99, this was enacted the following year, while Furius himself was torn to pieces by a mob, when he was prosecuted by two tribunes after leaving office. One of these, however, was himself later condemned, allegedly for openly praising Saturninus. Another victim was Sex. Titius, who as tribune in 99 had

[94] App. *BCiv.* 1.32.141–33.146; *Greenidge–Clay* 108–9. A different chronology in e.g., Badian 1984 (C 17) with references to earlier discussions. See also Passerini 1934 (C 117) 281ff.

[95] Diod. XXXVI.15; Cic. *Red. Sen.* 37; *Red. Pop.* 6; App. *BCiv.* 1.33.147–8. Cf. Lintott 1968 (A 62) 16–20 on the significance of mourning.

succeeded in passing an agrarian law, which perhaps had developed some of Saturninus' proposals. As for Saturninus' own legislation, Cicero tells us that, although not formally repealed, its validity remained in question and some of the colony foundations were simply not put into effect. However, the coin-evidence points towards the implementation of allotments in Cisalpina. In this way a clear decision on the controversy was avoided. Titius' success suggests that there was still support for radical measures and it would have been politically unwise to rescind Saturninus' acts directly. However, in 98 the consuls passed the Lex Caecilia Didia, which declared that infringements of the auspices caused by the neglect of evil omens rendered legislation invalid, entrusting decisions in such matters to the Senate. So preparations were made to frustrate the next *popularis* legislator.[96]

The political pendulum appeared to be swinging back towards senatorial dominance. After a prosecution of the younger Caepio for his violence in obstructing Saturninus had failed, C. Norbanus was also prosecuted, equally unsuccessfully, for sedition in his attacks on the elder Caepio a decade before – ironically under Saturninus' own law *de maiestate*. In 95 the consuls L. Licinius Crassus and Q. Mucius Scaevola risked the obvious offence to allied opinion by passing a law instituting trials for those who were illegally usurping Roman citizenship. This was to embitter leading Italians and bring to the fore once again the issue of granting Latins and Italians citizenship *en bloc*. There can be no doubt that there was a conflict between the 'good men', who were seeking to re-establish senatorial authority, and those loyal to Marius and the policies of Saturninus, but whether these formed two coherent 'factions', one Metellan and the other Marian, is questionable. The 'good men' themselves were divided by an especially bitter quarrel between M. Livius Drusus, the future tribune of 91, and the younger Caepio, which became a factor in the even graver division that was to result from the policies of Drusus in his tribunate.[97]

It was no coincidence that Glaucia's restoration of the *quaestio de repetundis* to equestrian jurors had not so far been challenged. *Equites* are reported to have protected Metellus Numidicus from Saturninus in 102 and to have shared in the repression of Saturninus in 100 (the members of the first group were conceivably all young aristocrats, but this does not seem to have been true of the second group). There was a precedent: according to Sallust *equites* had deserted the Gracchan cause. However interested they were in certain reforms, men of property and standing were reluctant to see the political fabric torn by sheer disorder, even if they could acquiesce in the profits of a more limited use of force, such as

[96] Lintott 1968 (A 62) 136ff; Crawford (B 145) 181–3.

[97] Badian 1957 (C 6); Gruen 1965 (C 66).

assisted the passage of the land legislation.[98] Nevertheless, when (*c.* 92 B.C.) Rutilius Rufus was condemned for taking bribes from Greeks to the detriment of Roman tax-collectors while legate to the governor of Asia, Q. Scaevola, this renewed the old fears of senators and provided another element in the political conflict which came near to disintegrating Roman and Italian society at the end of the decade.[99]

That story will be told in the following chapter. Meanwhile, this section is appropriately closed, in the Roman fashion, by an obituary on Saturninus and Glaucia. It is futile to attempt a revaluation of them by toning down the violence in their politics. No doubt there was more used on the other side than our sources record, but we cannot completely rewrite the vulgate. It is more important to recognize that their use of violence was a reasoned reaction to the defeat of the Gracchi by force. Saturninus and Glaucia counted on being backed by a friendly consul, but Marius in the end deserted them. They were seeking not merely to implement necessary reforms but, in the tradition of C. Gracchus, to direct policy from the assembly. Since most of their measures could not appeal to more than a section of the population, they faced continual political battles which they were determined to win at all costs. The denigration they suffered after their deaths is an unconscious compliment from their aristocratic political opponents. As for the plebs, it is significant that thirty-seven years afterwards Caesar and Labienus should have sought to win popular favour by prosecuting a man involved in the deaths of Glaucia and Saturninus.[100]

[98] Sall. *Iug.* 42.1; Brunt 1965 (C 31) 118; (A 17) 90ff.

[99] *Greenidge–Clay* 125–7.

[100] Cic. *Rab. Perd.*; Suet. *Iul.* 12; Dio XXXVII.26–8.

CHAPTER 4

ROME AND ITALY: THE SOCIAL WAR

E. GABBA

The relationship between Rome and the Italian allies reached a turning-point with the agrarian proposal of Ti. Gracchus in 133 B.C. For, as the historical tradition represented by Book I of the *Civil Wars* of Appian reveals with great clarity, it is at this moment that there emerged an 'allied problem' with political and institutional dimensions. The resumption by the Roman state of *ager publicus* which had been occupied more or less legally by Italian as well as by Roman *possessores* probably involved a breach of the treaties which bound Rome and the allied states. Even if it is not possible to say whether the resumption of *ager publicus* affected particularly lands occupied by Italian *possessores*, it is clear that the links between the upper classes of Italy and Rome, which had become ever closer in the course of the two generations which followed the Hannibalic War, were gravely compromised.

The serious economic and social consequences of the agrarian law for the upper classes of Italy were an implicit contradiction of a policy on the part of Rome which had up to that point set out to guarantee the supremacy, viability and acceptability of the ruling classes of the communities of Italy in the context of those communities, and hence their position as representatives of the communities *vis-à-vis* Rome. The intervention of Scipio Aemilianus (ch. 3, p. 74) only succeeded in part in healing the breach; and the diminution in the importance of the agrarian problem after C. Gracchus did not mean that trust once gone could be restored. It is disputed whether the *proletarii* of the Italian communities were eligible for the distribution of the *ager publicus* which had been resumed by the agrarian commission; whether they were or not, this would have had implications for the social tensions within the Italian, and indeed Latin, communities. We have no other evidence for these tensions, but we can be sure that they will have been no less serious than those within the Roman state and we may legitimately suspect that they will have been even more serious, for a variety of reasons, notably the continued existence of local taxation, long suspended at Rome; this is indeed the impression which the Italian perspective on the crisis given by

For Rome's relations with Italy in the second century B.C. see Gabba in *CAH* VIII², ch. 7, pp. 197–243.

Appian can and should suggest. The case of the revolt of the Latin colony of Fregellae in 125 B.C. is emblematic. The city had on various occasions been the representative of the Latin colonies at Rome; it had also undergone profound changes in the ethnic composition of the citizen body in the course of the preceding fifty years. At the moment of the violent breach with Rome, the city must simply have shattered in two; nor will it have been a question only of the 'betrayal' of the city to Rome by Q. Numitorius Pullus, i.e. by an aristocracy linked in one way or another to Rome. Every social, and indeed ethnic, group of the city must have been involved; for after the revolt it was possible to found nearby the Roman colony of Fabrateria Nova with those citizens of the Latin colony who had remained loyal.[1]

The various proposals for general grants of Roman citizenship made during the 120s B.C., to compensate for the economic loss caused by the agrarian law, were naturally directed above all at the Italian and Latin upper classes, who were the only ones who would have been able in practice to benefit from them. The proposals also contained clauses offering alternative and different benefits and privileges, also to be found in the extortion law of the Gracchan period as recognition and reward for successful prosecutors. All this is probably an indication that there did not yet exist a general awareness of the practical value of Roman citizenship as compared with the obviousness of economic loss and loss of prestige. Rome was probably also very reluctant to deprive the allied communities of their wealthy ruling classes; there was perhaps also an awareness of the difficulties which were likely to result from an extension of the functions of the Roman state consequent on an increase in the citizen body. So when the magistrates of Latin colonies were granted the right to acquire Roman citizenship, probably after 125, this was no doubt done in such a way as not to remove them from their communities.

In any case, perhaps partly as a result of the various Roman proposals for grants of citizenship,[2] but mostly as a result of the rapid deterioration in the general political situation, the allies became progressively more aware of the need to cease to be subjects and to share in the exercise of imperial power, hence to acquire Roman citizenship. On the other hand, those increased pressures ran up against growing Roman hostility to this kind of general grant. It was not simply a manifestation of proud and stubborn exclusiveness, though that of course existed and displayed itself in the unprecedented harshness of some Roman magistrates towards the allies;[3] rather it will have been the result of a not unreason-

[1] Numitorius: Cicero, *Inv. Rhet.* II.105; *Fin.* V.62; Fabrateria: Vell. Pat. I.15.4; Coarelli 1981 (B 275).

[2] App. *BCiv.* I.152. For all citations of Appian, I assume reference to my commentary, *Appiani Bellorum Civilium Liber I*, Gabba 1967 (B 40).

[3] C. Gracchus, *de legibus promulgatis*, *ORF* fr. 48, pp. 191–2 (Teanum Sidicinum, Cales, Ferentinum).

able fear that the whole political and institutional structure of the Roman state would collapse.

Furthermore, there were continually present at Rome, in unprecedented numbers, Italians of diverse social origin and often also different political tendencies; their participation in *contiones* aroused the xenophobic feelings of the urban plebs. That body was itself growing dangerously in size and taking up a position steadily more opposed to that of the rural plebs; its feelings could be only too readily invoked by crude and vigorous demagogy.[4] The Roman government resorted to measures to expel Italians and incurred substantial odium as a result (Vol. VIII^2, pp. 240–2).[5]

This complex political situation can be understood if it is seen as developing against a background of growing prosperity, affecting much of the centre and south of Italy from the middle of the second century onwards; naturally there were regional variations (the Greek cities of the deep south remained in pronounced decline) and great inequalities in the impact of the changes on different social classes.[6] This growing prosperity is not incompatible with the existence of a crisis for traditional patterns of Italian agriculture, which was being transformed in response to the development of the Italian economy as a whole. The crisis naturally had grave social consequences, in terms of the decline of the independent peasant proprietor, but the process was, and is, typical of periods of rapid change.

It is the archaeological evidence above all which reveals the scale of public (above all temple) building programmes, again with regional variations, and the extent to which Italy had been influenced by Greek artistic traditions.[7] The number of sanctuaries built or rebuilt reveals the political interest of the upper classes in precisely this form of activity; in some cases, the enormous economic resources of the temples were administered by local notables involved in one form or another of business activity and, as at Praeneste, with eastern connexions.[8] At the same time, a monetary economy was spreading even to the most remote areas of the peninsula, evidence both of the commercial activities of the upper classes and of their growing wealth. There will have been rewards for the lower classes also, if only as a result of the upsurge in public building programmes, pursued in Italy as at Rome with clear awareness of their implications.

The investment of the wealth acquired by the upper classes of Italy was naturally directed for the most part to agriculture, encouraging its

[4] C. Fannius, *ORF*, fr. 4, p. 144. [5] For Lucilius 1088, see Cichorius 1908 (B 16) 208–12.

[6] Crawford 1985 (B 145) 173–87; for the environment in Italy in general, see Giardina and Schiavone 1981 (G 104) I chs. 6–20. [7] In general, see *Hellenismus*.

[8] Bodei Giglioni 1977 (G 17) 59–76; F. Coarelli, in *Les Bourgeoisies* 217–40.

development in more modern and profitable directions, concentrating on production for the market; hence bitter hostility towards the Gracchan proposals, which for a time must have placed a question mark over the development just described. (It does not seem possible, however, to show that after the Gracchan period Rome actually increased Roman exploitation of *ager publicus* at the expense of the allies.)[9]

The widespread prosperity mentioned above derived, in the Italian communities and the Latin colonies, as at Rome, from increasing participation in the exploitation of the provinces and from the existence of the empire in general; for one practical result of this, as has been well shown, was a growth in exchange between Italy and the provinces.[10] There will have been various ways in which men participated in the process, not least what may have been an official practice of distributing booty to allied communities; the range of provenances of the dedicatory inscriptions of L. Mummius after his conquest of Greece in 146 may reflect a practice of this kind, and the existence in the Po valley of land belonging to communities in the centre and south could be interpreted as the result of grants made by the Roman state in return for services rendered.[11] Official distribution of the rewards of conquest is certainly likely, to make up for the fact that, while Roman citizens did not pay *tributum* after 167, the citizens of the allied communities did not enjoy any such privilege;[12] and the exemption from local taxation which the Roman government could grant to individual members of the allied communities in special circumstances could only have the effect of increasing the resentment of those who still had to pay.

Naturally, the principal source of riches for individual members of the allied communities was energetic participation in business activities in the provinces. It used to be held that Italians formed the dominant element among men of business in the East; that now seems less certain and careful and up-to-date analysis of the names of the traders on Delos would seem to suggest rather a predominance of Roman citizens;[13] if so, the term 'Romaioi', generally regarded as a blanket term for Romans, Latins and allies, will have been used with greater accuracy. This shift of emphasis, however, does not alter the fact of a substantial community of interest and of a shared mentality, unaffected by juridical differences. Conflicts have been alleged between men of business, whether Roman or Italian, and Roman *equites*, the latter involved above all in public building contracts and in military supply, in other words in large-scale economic and commercial activity, in the western provinces as well as

[9] Nagle 1973 (B 74). [10] Crawford 1985 (B 145) 339–40.

[11] *ILLRP* 327–30; Beloch 1926 (A 9) 624; an alternative hypothesis in Crawford 1985 (B 145) 339–40. [12] App. *BCiv.* 1.30.

[13] Wilson 1966 (A 128); Cassola 1971 (G 35); Solin 1982 (D 293).

elsewhere. However, although such conflicts have been held to be one of the possible causes of the Social War,[14] there is no evidence that they existed.

The 'unity' of the business class outside Italy is attested by such well-known episodes as the defence of Cirta in Numidia against Jugurtha by Italian men of business.[15] And the protection afforded by the Roman government was extended indifferently to Roman citizens, Latins and Italian (or overseas) allies, as emerges at various points in the Delphi and Cnidus versions of the law about provinces of 101 (ch. 3, pp. 97–8).[16] It is indeed perhaps in terms of the advantages and privileges which the Italian allies derived from the protection of the Roman government that one should explain the acquisition of the citizenship of cities in Magna Graecia by Greek and oriental men of business, a phenomenon attested for the end of the second and the beginning of the first centuries B.C.; these were men who had business relationships with the cities concerned; and one cannot exclude the possibility that their acquisition of citizenship there was seen as a first step towards Roman citizenship.[17]

The situation characteristic of the East was probably also largely true of Sicily,[18] and above all of Cisalpine Gaul; already in the second century B.C., alongside a programme of colonization which had involved for the most part the land south of the Po, there had occurred both spontaneous Roman and Italian immigration and large-scale investment in land by the upper classes, both north and south of the Po.[19]

The fact that the Latin and Italian business classes also formed the political groups in power in the allied states could only underline the gap which existed between allies and Roman citizens in Italy. Whereas, in the provinces, the juridical distinction was at the very least of no great practical importance, in Italy the allies were ever more visibly subject to Rome and wholly unable to influence the political decisions of the ruling power, which now closely affected the economic interests of the upper

[14] Salmon 1962 (C 127).

[15] Sall. *Iug.* 26.1 cf. 21.2; 26.3; 41.1; Gabba 1976 (C 55) 85–6; for Sall. *Iug.* 64.5; 65.4; Vell Pat. II.11.2, see Gabba 1972 (C 56) 776.

[16] Delphi copy, B6: *πολῖται Ῥωμαίων σύμμαχοί τε ἐκ τῆς Ἰταλίας Λατῖνοι*; Cnidus copy, col. II, lines 6–7; cf. col. III, lines 30–4; Hassall, Crawford and Reynolds 1974 (B 170) 201–2. The phrase seems to be a poor translation of the asyndeton 'cives Romani socii Italici nominis Latini', where, as in Livy XXI.55.4; XXXVIII.35.9 there figure allies as well as Latins; *contra*, Jones 1926 (B 177) 168–9, holding that the *socii Italici* were excluded.

[17] *IDélos* 1724 (106–93 B.C.); Mancinetti Santamaria 1982 (D 281); 1983 (G 151).

[18] Fraschetti (G 74), though the interpretation of the inscription from Polla, *CIL* I², 638 = *ILLRP* 454, does not seem acceptable.

[19] For the Sasernae, whose properties are perhaps to be localized in the neighbourhood of Dertona, see Kolendo 1973 (G 139); for Cornelius Nepos in Insubria, perhaps in the neighbourhood of Ticinum, see Gabba, in *Storia di Pavia* I, (Milan, 1984) 219; for the presence of *Italiotai* in Noricum, Polyb. XXXIV.10.13; Strab. IV.6.12.

classes among them. Traditional links between the Roman upper classes and Italian notables could not cope with the strain and will have seemed progressively more inadequate.[20] At the same time, the assimilation of the behaviour of the Italian elites to Roman norms, which had forged ahead at ever greater speed over the previous century, had gone beyond language and culture to affect the political systems and magistracies of the allied cities. (The most striking evidence of the process would be the Lex Osca Tabulae Bantinae, if we could be sure that it belonged to the turn of the second and first centuries, thus to before the Social War, even if only just.)[21] At the same time, this assimilation of the political structures of the allies to those of Rome will have prepared the way in general terms for the process of municipalization which followed the Social War.

Demand for Roman citizenship will have grown after 123, not least because of worries aroused by the clear decline in the standards of political behaviour at Rome. And it is precisely in this period that men from outside Rome acquired the right to plead in the courts there; what resulted was a growth of municipal and even Italian forensic rhetoric.[22] The development derived from the possibility under the extortion law of the Gracchan period for an ally, among others, to accuse a senator of extortion; and the new rhetoric was often identified with a *popularis* political position. It is this shift in the origins of accusers in the courts that explains both the emergence of a school of Latin rhetoric and its suppression in the 90s, in order to defend traditional avenues of social and political integration.[23]

On the other hand, the Germanic threat represented by the Cimbric invasion of the territory of the Veneti in the north-east will have revived feelings of Italian solidarity; these feelings will have extended both to the lower orders and to the Celtic and Ligurian peoples of the Po valley, like those attested by Polybius in the face of the Gallic threat a century earlier. As Caesar reveals, perhaps with some exaggeration, the Germanic threat was still felt as a real one fifty years later. The more or less legal grant of Roman citizenship by C. Marius to two cohorts of Camertes on the battlefield during the Cimbric War is a clear indication of the value by now attached to such a reward.[24] And in the closing years of the second century, during the tribunates of L. Appuleius Saturninus (103 and 100), the allied problem is represented in our tradition as inextricably linked to that of the Roman and Italian *proletarii* enrolled in the armies of Marius

[20] Wiseman 1971 (A 130). [21] *Bruns* no. 8.

[22] Cic. *Brut.* 167–72; cf. 180; 241–2; David 1983 (G 54).

[23] Gabba 1953 (C 54) 269–70; David 1979 (G 53).

[24] Cic. *Balb.* 46–7; Val. Max. v.2.8; Plut.*Mar.* 28.3.

and to the need to reward them with land, in accordance with the promises made in 107.[25]

The Lex Appuleia of 103 provided for the distribution of 100 *iugera* a head of land in Africa to the soldiers of Marius, whether Roman or allied, while the settlements of allied soldiers at least may be connected with the African cities of imperial date which called themselves Marian.[26] There followed in 100 B.C. a more complex agrarian law (if indeed there was only one); it provided for the assignation of land in Cisalpine Gaul and overseas,[27] and hence consciously avoided touching *ager publicus* in the centre and south of the peninsula. The same law is conventionally regarded as providing for the foundation (whether in Italy or not) of citizen colonies, to which, however, allies were also admitted; to three of these in each colony Marius was authorized to grant Roman citizenship. The practice is already attested in the first half of the second century, and we know of one case in our period, T. Matrinius of Spoletium, a Latin, who was later accused before the *quaestio* concerning illegal acquisition of citizenship (established by the Lex Licinia Mucia of 95) and acquitted as a result of the intervention of Marius himself.[28] There is explicit testimony that the allies, that is the allied soldiers recruited among the lower orders, were the beneficiaries of the law along with the rural plebs, arousing as a result the hostility of the urban plebs.[29] Even if the provisions of the Lex Appuleia of 100 were not in fact put into effect, large numbers of Italian allies must none the less have acquired Roman citizenship more or less legally in this period; for the censors of 95 felt it necessary to have a law passed, the Lex Licinia Mucia, specifically to exclude from the citizen body those who had entered it illegally.[30]

It seems very likely that this provision was designed in particular to deal with allies belonging to the upper classes, the *principes Italicorum populorum* who had succeeded somehow or other in acquiring citizenship; their feelings were now so aroused that the law was later regarded as one of the principal causes of the outbreak of the Social War.[31] The *quaestio* was characterized by Cicero as *acerrima*,[32] and it was said that the

[25] The sources reveal the origin of the soldiers of Marius for the most part in the rural proletariat, Gabba 1976 (C 55) 24: the tradition in Appian will have schematized the opposition between rural and urban plebs, which emerged in the Gracchan period and came to the fore in the course of 100 B.C., but not invented it; *contra*, Schneider 1982–3 (C 131).

[26] *De Vir. Ill.*73.1; *Inscr. Ital.* XIII, 3, no. 7 for Cerceina (but see Barnes 1971 (C 19) who suggests rather Mariana on Corsica); Brunt 1971 (A 16) 577–81.

[27] App. *BCiv.* I. 130; *De Vir. Ill.*73.5 (colonies in Sicily, Achaea, Macedonia).

[28] Cic. *Balb.* 48; Badian 1958 (A 1) 260–1; 1970–1 (C 15) 404.

[29] Gabba 1956 (B 38) 76–9.

[30] Cic. *Off.* III.47; *Balb.* 48 and 54; *Corn.*, fr. 10; Asc. 67–8C. The title of the law was 'de civibus redigundis' and no doubt referred to the reduction of those who had no right to the citizenship to their legal status as allies; there are no grounds for supposing, with *Schol.Bob.* 129, 11. 10–14 Stangl, that the law expelled anyone from Rome; or that it abolished the possibility of acquiring the citizenship *per migrationem et censum* (Cic. *Balb.* 54).

[31] Asc 68C.

[32] Cic. *Balb.* 48.

law evoked general disapproval, even in Cisalpine Gaul south of the Po,[33] presumably because of the *quaestio* instituted under it. It is, however, unclear whether the celebrated remark of Cicero that *metus iudiciorum* was one of the causes of the Social War is to be regarded as referring to this *quaestio*.[34]

It has been argued that the Lex Licinia Mucia was a reaction to the census of 97, supposedly conducted with a certain openness and generosity towards the allies,[35] and attempting to satisfy the aspirations of their upper classes. The hypothesis cannot be verified. Cicero recalls an episode in which a crowd which included allies prevented M. Aemilius Scaurus from speaking and as a result of which he suggested the law to the consuls; the anecdote has some value, though one need not necessarily accept the specific occasion on which Scaurus is alleged to have been interrupted.[36]

The political conflicts of the 90s, marked *inter alia* by great political trials, involved major issues such as the nature of Roman foreign policy in the East and, in particular, the 'allied question'. This was brought suddenly to the fore once again in 91, the year of the tribunate of M. Livius Drusus; the year marked virtually the end of the long historical process which had seen a constant increase in the insistence of the allied demand 'for the Roman citizenship, in order to be partners in empire instead of subjects'.[37] The demand was thus in the first instance of a political nature and, as we have seen, had emerged and grown within the upper classes of the allies, though even among them it was not universally supported.

The political programme of Livius Drusus, worked out in agreement with a large group within the senatorial class and vigorously supported by it almost to the end, seems reasonably clear both in its totality and in its ultimate goal.[38] That was to reinforce and restore the authority of the Senate, principally by means of a law on the composition of the juries in the *quaestiones perpetuae*; these were given to the senators, but after (apparently) the injection into the Senate of 300 *equites*. The proposal

[33] Whether one accepts the standard correction of Sallust, *Hist.* I.20, by Maurenbrecher, 'citra Padum omnibus lex ⟨in⟩ grata fuit', or whether one adopts the correction 'frustra' proposed by La Penna 1969 (B 63) 254: see Luraschi 1979 (F 105) 85–6 n.188.

[34] Cic. *Off.* II.75: 'tantum Italicum bellum propter iudiciorum metum excitatum'. One may infer from the context that Cicero is concerned to establish, in connection with the legislation of Drusus in 91, a link between the rebellion of the allies and the problem posed by the centrality of the extortion courts: Gabba 1976 (C 55) 70 and 88; *contra*, Badian 1969 (C 12) 489–90; 1970–1 (C 15) 407–8.

[35] Gabba 1976 (C 55) 179–80; Badian 1958 (A 1) 212–13; 1968 (A 3) 53; 1970–1 (C 15) 402–6; *contra*, Brunt 1965 (C 31) 106.

[36] Cic. *De Orat.* II.257; Bates 1986 (C 20) 272–3.

[37] App. *BCiv.* I.154–5; Vell. Pat. II.15.2; Just. XXXVIII.4.13.

[38] Gabba 1972 (C 56) 787–90. I here adopt the chronology of the legislation of Drusus there proposed, though this is not universally accepted: Gabba 1976 (C 55) 131–3; for the grounds on which the legislation was declared invalid, Lintott 1968 (A 62) 140–3.

could be seen as inimical to the interests of the *equites* as a whole and was opposed by them, although its intention was in fact an even-handed reconciliation of the two opposing positions. To this ultimate goal the entire legislative activity of Drusus was apparently directed; it included also an agrarian or colonial law and probably also, as the last stage, the grant of citizenship to the allies. According to the tradition represented in Appian, concerned principally with the problem of the allies, this last proposal was really the crowning measure of Drusus.[39] It is in any case certain that on it the group which supported Drusus was not in agreement.

In general terms and in the light of our knowledge of the politics of the period after 89, it is legitimate to argue that for the upper classes of Italy the acquisition of Roman citizenship meant the direct exercise of political power and that this process was seen, and rightly seen, by the group around Drusus as a further reinforcement of a moderate political position within a Roman governing class enlarged in this way. There will naturally have been an awareness of the widespread existence, perhaps mostly at the level of the lower classes among the allies, of deeply rooted anti-Roman feeling; but presumably it was supposed that it would be possible to control it easily.

Certainly the agrarian law of Drusus, which seems to have raised a question mark over the position of the *ager publicus* still in the hands of the allied upper classes aroused opposition among some allies; that, however, did not in fact weaken the excellent relations which Drusus maintained up to the moment of his death with the Italian leaders.[40] Their hopes remained pinned on his political initiative until his murder and it was this which was the signal for the outbreak of the revolt.

Not all the allies were in agreement with the proposals of Drusus as a whole; and, according to Appian, the consuls, of whom L. Marcius Philippus in particular was bitterly hostile to Drusus, were able to bring to Rome some Etruscans and Umbrians to manifest their opposition, presumably in the course of *contiones*.[41] This passage poses problems which cannot easily be resolved, not least because of our uncertainty over the chronology of Drusus' measures. If the episode is to be placed late in 91, the protests would seem to have been directed against the agrarian law, presumably already passed; and, in addition, there would seem to have been opposition to the citizenship law, still to be voted on. Wherever their opposition was directed, the attitude of the Etruscans

39 App. *BCiv.* 1.155 and 162.

40 Plut. *Cat. Min.* 2.1–2. Val. Max. III.1.2; Sen. *Brev. Vit* 6.1; *De Vir. Ill.* 80.1. The 'prophecy of Vegoia', preserved in the corpus of the Agrimensores, 350 Lachmann, is related to the agrarian law of Drusus by Heurgon 1959 (C 77); for a different date, Turcan 1976 (C 146).

41 App. *BCiv.* 1.163.

and Umbrians is described as diverging from that of other Italian allies; and it is hard not to see the whole affair as in any case a consequence of the peculiar situation of the Etruscan and Umbrian elites within the social and economic structures of their communities. For their lower classes were largely agricultural serfs, who would as a result of the citizenship law have achieved a quite intolerable degree of juridical and political equality with their masters.[42]

The exclusive attitude of part of the Roman governing class remained unchanged; it was indeed no doubt reinforced by resentment of the growing personal prestige of Drusus among the Italian allies, which would certainly have been translated into political power if they had succeeded in obtaining the citizenship as a result of his efforts. For oligarchies cannot tolerate the emergence of one of their members possessed of power too far beyond that of the rest. An extraordinary document, probably referred to by the consul Philippus in one of his speeches against Drusus, is preserved in a fragment of Diodorus: it is an oath of loyalty to Rome and a promise of unconditional support to Drusus, as the person through whom Roman citizenship had been obtained; it must have been sworn by the Italian leaders.[43] The text seems to document an awareness of the necessity of creating religious as well as other links with the new citizens-to-be, so as to overcome traditional local loyalties. It is significant that after the Social War the cult of Capitoline Jupiter was founded in many of the new *municipia*, whereas many sanctuaries in the centre and the south, which had been the centres of tribal political and religious activities, were closed.

Naturally, however, as we have seen, the most obviously negative aspect of the programme of Drusus for the oligarchy was the unacceptable personal power which he would have achieved and which the text we have been considering reveals in the clearest possible manner; hence the hardening of the opposition. Drusus lost at the beginning of September in 91 one of his most influential supporters in the Senate, L. Licinius Crassus; the consul Philippus then managed to persuade the assembly to repeal his laws, and, shortly after, towards the middle of October, Drusus was assassinated.[44]

The death of Drusus meant the end of allied hopes and was the

[42] Gabba 1972 (C 56) 788–9; there was a similar situation at Vicetia in Transpadana after 49 B.C.: Gabba 1983 (G 91) 42–4. Differences in the structure of property and in the nature of the agrarian economy, between Umbria and inland Etruria on the one hand and coastal Etruria on the other hand, are suggested by J. Heurgon, 'L'Ombrie à l'époque des Gracques et Sylla', in *Atti I Convegno Studi Umbri 1963* (Perugia, 1964) 124–5; *contra*, Gabba, in 1979 (G 95) 36–7. When Appian then says that the Etruscans welcomed the Lex Julia de civitate, *BCiv.* 1.213, he is to be understood as saying that it was welcome to the lower classes.

[43] Diod. XXXVII.11. The genuineness of the text was denied by Rose 1937 (C 124) 165–81, because of an alleged inconsistency with the normal Roman formula, but defended by Taylor 1949 (A 120) 46 and 198 (n. 67).

[44] App. *BCiv.* 1.164. *Inscr. Ital.* XIII, 3, no. 74: 'in magistratu occisus est'.

decisive factor behind the outbreak of armed revolt.[45] The allies began to plan, to exchange hostages among themselves and to form agreements for action,[46] precisely the behaviour which Rome had always managed to make impossible, by not creating any kind of confederation between her allies, but only unilateral treaties with each of them individually. Although the steps taken by the allies were secret, the Roman government soon got to hear of them, not least because in some cases they were already, towards the end of 91, organizing armed forays against Rome; one such was commanded by the Marsian leader, Q. Pompaedius (or Poppaedius) Silo, and was only by chance thwarted by a certain Caius Domitius (perhaps in fact the consul of 96, Cnaeus Domitius).[47] The Roman government entrusted the job of watching what was going on to magistrates or ex-magistrates with long-standing links with the different areas which were known to be disaffected; it may be that it was in that capacity that Domitius was able to act and it was certainly in that capacity that Q. (or C.) Servilius found himself in Picenum. When he discovered that an exchange of hostages was in progress at Asculum, he voiced threats which provoked his murder in 'an explosion of hatred against Rome', which engulfed all the many Romans in the city and immediately conferred an entirely new dimension on the revolt against Rome.[48] It was of course led by the local elites who were anxious for the Roman citizenship in order to be able to enter the Roman ruling class, but it had at the same time to deploy the anti-Roman feelings which were widespread among the masses and which, long repressed, were now given free rein.

In Rome, the outbreak of the revolt of the allies brought about a renewal of the link between the *equites* and the tribunes, which had been weakened by the events of 100, when Senate and *equites* had found themselves united in opposition to the projects of Appuleius Saturninus and his supporters. At the beginning of 90, a law of the tribune Q. Varius Hybrida set up a *quaestio extraordinaria* with *equites* as jurors, to inquire who was responsible for the events which had led to the revolt of the allies. Naturally, since it was the only *quaestio* which functioned during the war, it was also used without scruple for personal political ends;[49] not all of those condemned were friends or supporters of Drusus or his policy. Only a year later, in 89, was the nobility, encouraged by a turn for the better in the course of the war, able to get the composition of the

[45] App. *BCiv* I.169. For narratives of the war, see von Domaszewski 1924 (C 46); Haug 1947 (C 74); De Sanctis 1976 (C 129). [46] App. *BCiv*. I.170.

[47] Diod. XXXVII.13.1; Gabba 1976 (C 55) 261 n. 16. It would also be possible to date the event somewhat earlier, at the same time as the arrival of the Etruscans and Umbrians in Rome.

[48] Diod. XXXVII.13.2; cf. 12.1–3; App. *BCiv*. I.171–4; Laffi 1975 (B 303).

[49] Asc. 67–8C; Val.Max. VIII.6.4; App. *BCiv*. I.165 (wrongly dating the law before the uprising); Badian 1969 (C 12); Gabba 1976 (C 55) 133–4.

juries in the *quaestio* 'ex lege Varia' changed; this was done by means of a law of the tribune M. Plautius Silvanus, which introduced annual election by the tribes. Senators and 'quidam ex plebe' began to serve on the juries and the *equites* lost their monopoly. Q. Varius and his colleague in the tribunate, Cn. Pomponius, were immediately condemned under the law.[50]

Before the outbreak of open hostilities, but when the allies were already under arms, towards the end of 91, there was perhaps one last attempt by the Italians to arrive at a peaceful settlement of their differences with Rome; it was, however, rejected by the Senate.[51] War was now inevitable. It took its name, the Marsian War, from the people who were the first to take up arms; when its scale was fully understood, which did not take long, it came to be called the Italian and then the Social War. The greater part of the allied peoples living along the ridge of the central and southern Apennines took part: besides the people of Asculum and other groups in Picenum, there were the Marsi, the Paeligni, the Vestini, the Marrucini (all Sabellian), the Frentani, the Hirpini, the Lucani, the Samnites, the people of Pompeii and other cities of southern Campania (all Oscan), the people of Apulia and the citizens of Venusia.[52] Other peoples were more or less forcibly brought to side with the rebels during the first year of the war: Nola and perhaps Nuceria and some cities in Apulia.[53] On the other hand, the intervention of some Etruscans and Umbrians at the end of 90 must have been limited in duration. Finally, there is some evidence for the presence of Gallic troops among the rebel armies, which suggests that help arrived also from Gallia Cisalpina.[54] All the Latin colonies remained loyal, with the exception of Venusia, whose participation in the revolt is not easy to explain except on the supposition of a marked change in the composition of the population in the course of the second century B.C., as had happened at Fregellae. In the vast majority of cases, traditional ties with Rome were too strong and had always assured the Latins a privileged position among the allies; as a result, the local aristocracies, now themselves in large measure possessed of the Roman citizenship acquired *per magistratum*, presumably had no great difficulty in keeping their communities loyal to Rome.

Naturally, even in the communities listed above, not everyone joined the revolt. We know of individual cities which did not follow the lead of the ethnic group to which they belonged, for instance Pinna among the Vestini; we also know of often violent disagreements within single

[50] Asc. 79C; Gabba 1976 (C 55) 144–6; 1972 (C 56) 791. [51] App. *BCiv.* I.176.

[52] App. *BCiv.* I.175; Livy *Per.* 72; Oros. V.18.8; Eutropius V.3.1; on the rebel peoples, their leaders and their eventual distributions in the tribes, see Salmon 1958 (C 126).

[53] App. *BCiv.* I.185; 187; 190. [54] App. *BCiv.* I.219–20.

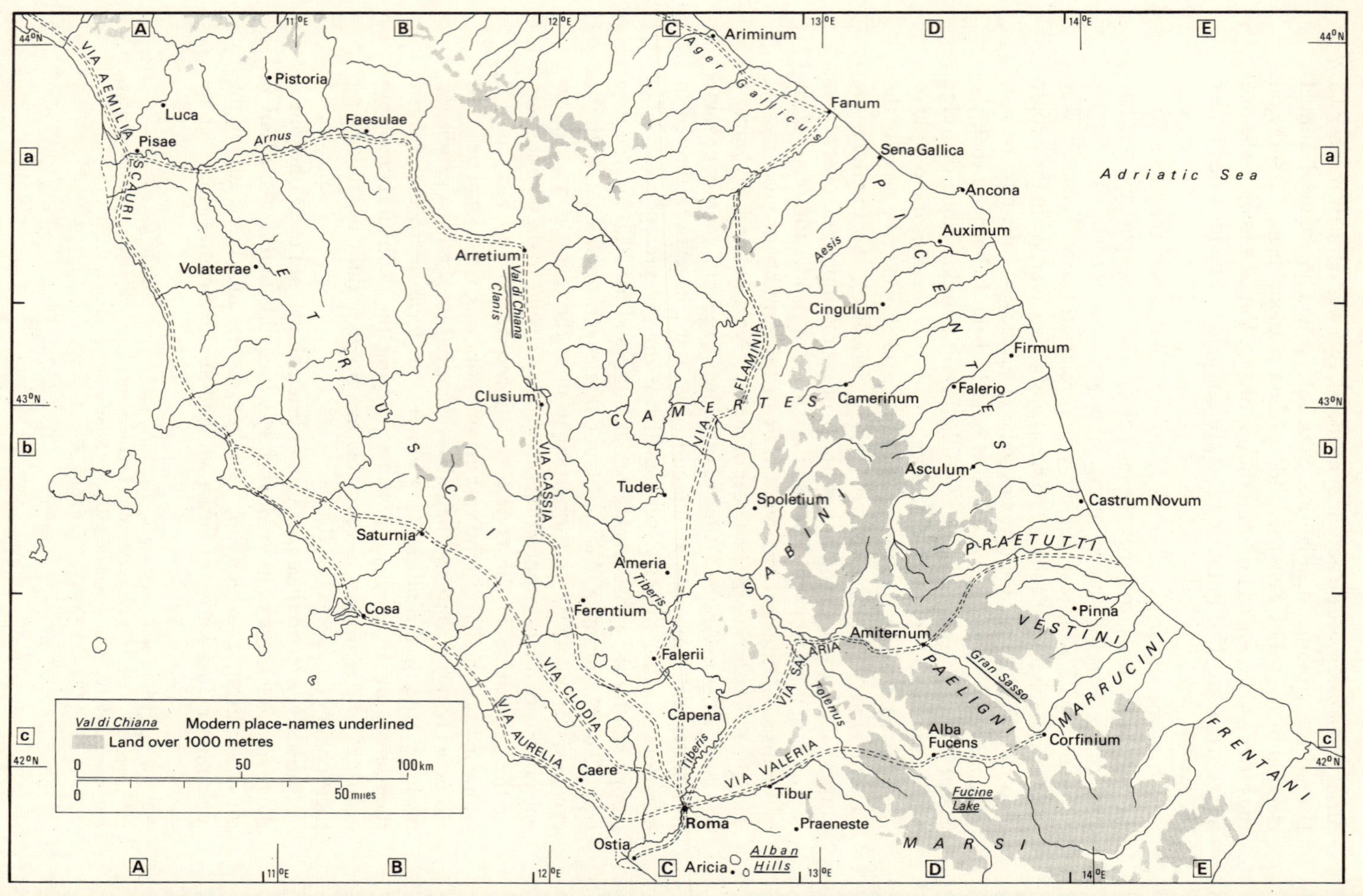
Adriatic Sea
Ariminum
Ager Gallicus
Fanum
Sena Gallica
Ancona
Auximum
Aesis
Cingulum
Firmum
Falerio
Camerinum
Asculum
Castrum Novum
P I C E N T E S
C A M E R T E S
S A B I N I
PRAETUTTI
VESTINI
MARRUCINI
FRENTANI
PAELIGNI
M A R S I
Pinna
Corfinium
Gran Sasso
Amiternum
Alba Fucens
Fucine Lake
Tolenus
Spoletium
Praeneste
Tibur
Alban Hills
Aricia
Roma
Ostia
Caere
Capena
Falerii
Tiberis
Ameria
Ferentium
Tuder
VIA FLAMINIA
VIA SALARIA
VIA VALERIA
VIA CASSIA
VIA CLODIA
VIA AURELIA
VIA AEMILIA SCAURI
Clusium
Val di Chiana
Clanis
Arretium
E T R U S C I
Saturnia
Cosa
Volaterrae
Faesulae
Pistoria
Arnus
Luca
Pisae
Val di Chiana Modern place-names underlined
Land over 1000 metres
0 50 100 km
0 50 miles
44°N
43°N
42°N
11°E
12°E
13°E
14°E

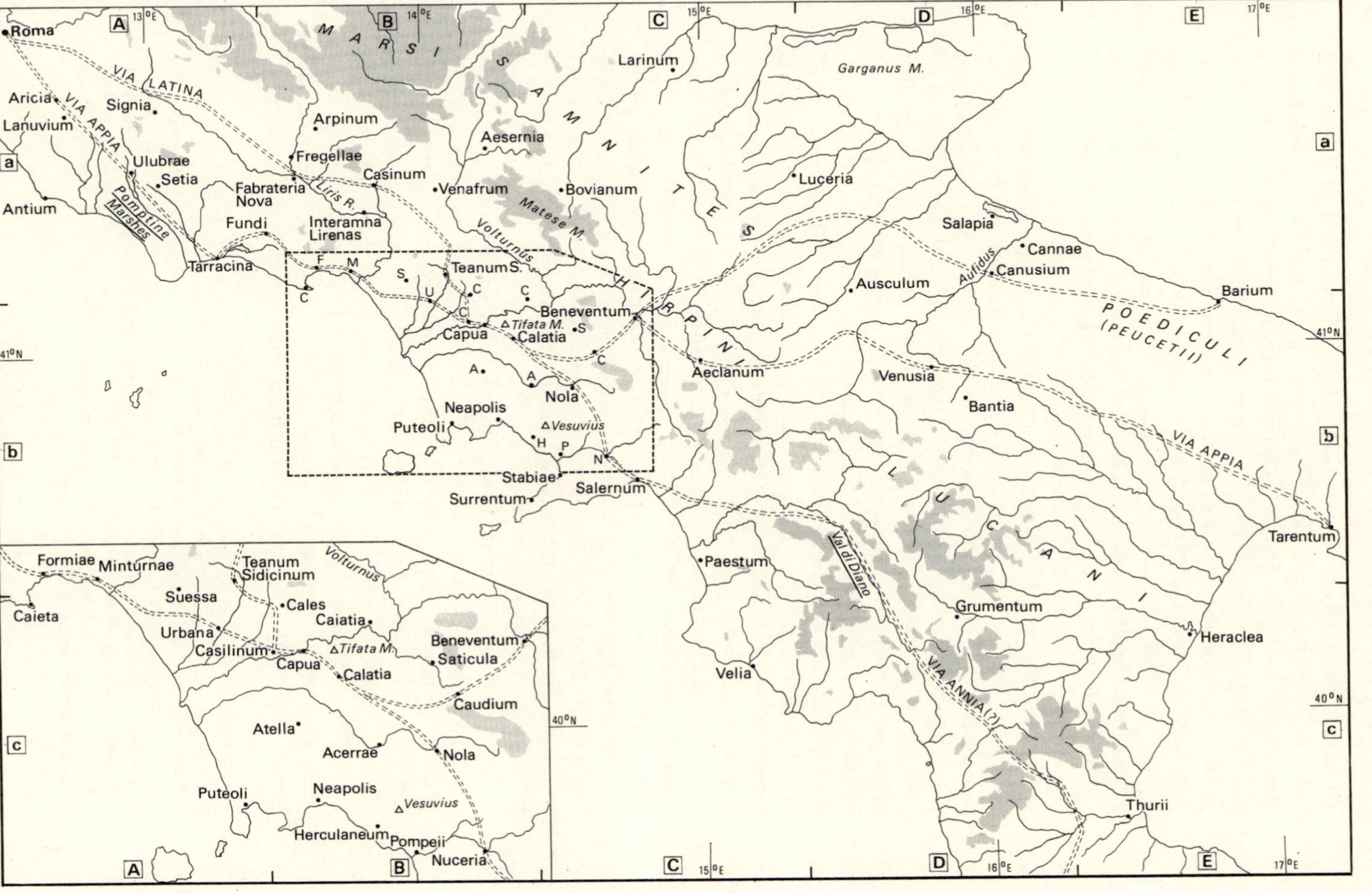

3 Central Italy

communities and even of positions overtly favourable to Rome. But even Velleius, writing under Tiberius and a descendant of a notable of Aeclanum among the Hirpini who had fought with Sulla, shows still a clear conviction that the allied cause had been fundamentally just.[55] In general, the populations most hostile to Rome, who continued to resist longest after the end of the war, were those of the Samnite and Lucanian group, mindful of their long rivalry with Rome. It is Velleius who records the threat of Pontius Telesinus on the eve of the battle of the Colline Gate in 82, that it was necessary to destroy the lair of the 'wolves' who were the *raptores Italicae libertatis*.[56]

Even though the rebels consisted of diverse groups, they were fully aware that their cause was one and that it was necessary in consequence to organize themselves into a single people. They renamed their capital at Corfinium as Italica, a name rich in symbolism,[57] but it would be to go too far to suppose that they had at that moment a truly Italian consciousness and that they founded a unitary state with an appropriate system of government. Unity was necessary for the conduct of the war. The choice of Corfinium, the chief town of the Paeligni, was based largely on strategic considerations, since it lay at a junction on the roads which linked Picenum with the rebel areas to the south. A federal assembly was instituted, consisting of a senate with 500 members, who were the representatives of the rebel communities; although these were grouped under the umbrella of the name Italia, as appears from their coinage,[58] they must have preserved all the traditional apparatus of self-government. It is not clear whether within the senate at Corfinium there was a smaller body responsible for the conduct of the war; in any case, following the known and tried Roman model, two consuls and twelve praetors were elected each year.[59]

In 90, the two supreme commanders, who were probably also re-elected for the following year, were the Marsian leader Poppaedius Silo and the Samnite C. Papius Mutilus; the former had been in touch with Drusus and had begun the rebellion, the family of the latter had already played a leading role in the wars against Rome in the fourth century B.C.[60] The two divided the war between them: Poppaedius Silo directed operations on the northern front, in the territory of the Piceni and the Marsi, Papius Mutilus on the southern front, in Samnium, Lucania,

[55] Vell. Pat. II.15.2; 16.2; cf. Ovid, *Am.* III.15.7–10: Gabba 1976 (C 55) 346–60.

[56] Vell. Pat. II.27.2.

[57] Strab. V.4.2; Vell.Pat. II.16.4; Diod. XXXVII.2.6–7.

[58] Sydenham 1952 (B 247) nos. 617–24 (Italia); 625–8 (Viteliu). Some coins bore the names of the two commanders Q. Silo and C. Papius Mutilus (*embratur* on nos. 640–1). On nos. 619–21 there is an oath-taking scene with eight or six soldiers, on no. 628 the Sabellian bull goring the Rome wolf.

[59] Diod. XXXVII.2.4; Strab. V.4.2; Sherwin-White 1973 (F 141) 147; Meyer 1958 (C 112) 74–9.

[60] Gabba 1958 (B 40) 132–4. For family continuity between the time of the Samnite Wars and the Social War, see de Sanctis 1909 (A 103) 207ff.

Apulia and Campania. Each had under his orders six commanders responsible for particular sectors. In total, the rebels were in a position to field an army of about 100,000 men, including cavalry and infantry, in addition to the troops which were necessary to guard the cities under their control and whose numbers cannot readily be calculated.[61] The whole military structure which the Italian allies had placed at the disposal of Rome was now mobilized in the cause of the rebellion. Their experience, their military skill, their knowledge of tactics, strategy, logistics, all these they owed to the wars fought alongside Rome.

The strategy of the rebels, which they had certainly planned beforehand, was to take the offensive on all fronts; its central aim was the elimination of the Latin colonies and in general the enclaves of Roman territory within the zone controlled by themselves; for only in this way could it become entirely self-contained. The routes which the Romans had followed as they penetrated into enemy territory in the course of the conquest of Italy thus acquired once again a military relevance which had seemed to have disappeared for ever; the difference was that in this case they could be used in the opposite direction also, against Rome, provided the rebels could overcome the obstacles represented by the fortified Latin colonies. Those ancient towns on the skirts of the Apennines thus recovered their traditional function. And while in the fourth and third centuries the Italian peoples had fought and lost, for the most part without ever uniting, the battle might seem now to be more equal, because the enemies of Rome were at one. But the forces of the ruling city were enormously superior.

The troops which Rome had at her disposal at the outset were at least equal to those of the rebels. Levies were also undertaken among Roman citizens in Gallia Cisalpina.[62] Many of the allies remained loyal; the fact that Rome controlled not only Capua, which had the Roman citizenship, but also central Campania as a whole, turned out to be crucial, not least for reasons of logistics and supply. The Romans could also count on forces supplied by allies outside Italy, such as Numidia and some eastern communities, and by the provinces, Spain, Sicily and Gallia Cisalpina.[63] It is clear that Rome's reserves, based on her position as an imperial power, were far superior to those of the rebels and that their effect would have been felt fairly rapidly, even if before long the war with Mithridates, which broke out at the end of 89, was to put an end to the arrival of reinforcements from the East. Still, the rebels could always attempt to conquer and maintain control over the whole of central and southern Italy and on this basis impose a compromise solution; it may even be that

[61] App. *BCiv.* I.177. [62] Appian. *BCiv.* I.177; Plutarch, *Sert.* 4.1.

[63] Cic. *Leg. Agr.* II.90; App. *BCiv.*I.188–9; 220; *ILS* 8888 (Spain); Cicero, *II Verr.* 2.5; 5.8 (Sicily); SC de Asclepiade (*RGDE* no. 22), I.7; Memnon *FGrH* 434 F 21 (the eastern provinces).

this was their aim. The fragment of a speech preserved in *Ad Herennium* IV.13, and perhaps delivered in a case arising out of the Lex Varia, is interesting in this context; the Roman politician concerned noted with some exaggeration the disparity of the forces in the field and the impossibility of an allied victory; and the only explanation he could find for the Italian attempt was to suppose the complicity of politicians in Rome.

The Roman consuls of 90, L. Iulius Caesar and P. Rutilius Lupus, probably only had at their disposal forces at the level normal for Roman magistrates; nor indeed at the moment of their election had the war been foreseeable. But they had access to *legati* of considerable experience, first and foremost C. Marius and L. Cornelius Sulla; other generals of distinction emerged in the course of the war, such as Cn. Pompeius Strabo, Q. Sertorius, Q. Caecilius Metellus Pius.[64]

Perhaps already at the end of 91 or, if not, at the beginning of 90, P. Vettius Scato, the praetor of the Paeligni, moved from the area of Corfinium to invest the Latin colony of Aesernia, where many Roman refugees from Apulia had taken shelter.[65] He succeeded in defeating the consul, L. Caesar, but not in capturing the colony; the rebels were forced to undertake a siege, which turned out to be lengthy. At about the same time, Marius Egnatius the Samnite succeeded in capturing Venafrum, a Roman *praefectura*, and thereby prevented the despatch of reinforcements from Campania to Aesernia.[66] In Lucania, M. Lamponius, the praetor of the Lucani, after a mixture of successes and reverses, captured Grumentum, perhaps also a Latin colony.[67] The colony of Alba Fucens was also attacked, but not captured, although P. Praesenteius, a Marsian, defeated P. Perperna as he attempted to move up to the relief of the city.[68]

But the rebels won their most important victories in Campania and in Picenum. Moving up from the south, Papius Mutilus seized Nola and without hesitation enlisted his Roman prisoners after killing their officers. Advancing along the coast, he captured Herculaneum, Stabiae, Surrentum and the citizen colony of Salernum, here also enlisting prisoners as well as slaves.[69] But although he gained control of the area around Nuceria, he was unable to take the fortress of Acerrae, which blocked the road to Capua, the principal Roman base on the southern front. Meanwhile, in the first few months of the year, in the vicinity of Falerio in Picenum, C. Vidacilius of Asculum, T. Lafrenius, the praetor of the Piceni, and P. Ventidius had managed to defeat Cn. Pompeius Strabo and force him to take refuge in the Latin colony of Firmum.[70] The

[64] For lists of the legates in 90 and 89, *MRR* II, 28 ff and 36 ff.

[65] App. *BCiv.* I.182; Livy *Per.* 72.

[66] App. *BCiv.* I.183; for the war in Samnium, see Salmon 1967 (A 101) 340–68.

[67] App. *BCiv.* I.184. [68] App. *BCiv.* I.183; Livy *Per.* 72. [69] App. *BCiv.* I.185–6.

[70] App. *BCiv.* I.204.

way was thus open for Vidacilius to make a swift move down into Apulia, where Canusium, the Latin colony of Venusia and other cities went over to him or were captured; he too enlisted Romans of the lower orders and slaves.[71] The Italian armies were coming to resemble the armies on one side in a civil war.

Aesernia and Acerrae continued to resist. The consul L. Caesar, perhaps from a base at Teanum and crossing the range of the Matese, attempted to relieve Aesernia, but was decisively defeated at the crossing of the Volturnus by the Samnite Marius Egnatius and had to fall back on Acerrae. Another attempt by Sulla to relieve Aesernia also failed, though it did succeed in re-supplying the city. Finally, however, even this Latin colony was forced to surrender.[72]

Before Acerrae, the armies of L. Caesar, reinforced by Gallic and Numidian auxiliaries, and of Papius Mutilus, in touch with Vidacilius in Apulia by means of the Via Appia past Aeclanum and Venusia, fought a series of indecisive engagements.[73] Acerrae was in fact the keystone of the Roman defence, since it ensured the maintenance of links between Capua and the great Latin colony of Beneventum, firmly in Roman hands. On this front, stalemate had been reached, which suggests that the rebel offensive in Campania had run out of steam, despite its initial successes.

There had also been fierce fighting on the central front against the Marsi, astride the Via Valeria, which linked Rome with the capital of the rebels at Italica-Corfinium. A measure of the importance of this area is the presence of C. Marius, along with the consul Rutilius. Alba continued to resist and on 11 June 90 a great battle was fought in the valley of the River Tolenus between the two Roman generals and Vettius Scato. Rutilius fell into an ambush at the crossing of the river and was killed, but Marius won a decisive victory and drove back the enemy with heavy losses.[74] Not long afterwards, towards July, Q. Servilius Caepio, who had succeeded Rutilius, along with some of his men, was the victim of a trick played by the enemy commander-in-chief himself, Q. Poppaedius Silo, who had pretended to surrender. Similar episodes were no doubt not infrequent.[75] Marius took over the command of the whole front and moved energetically forward. There was a major battle on hilly ground covered with vineyards, probably to the south of the Fucine Lake; L. Cornelius Sulla managed to turn the flank of the enemy and the Marsi were defeated. Among the dead was Herius Asinius, the

[71] App. *BCiv.* I.190.

[72] App. *BCiv.* I.199; Oros. V.18.16; Front. *Str.* I.5.17; Livy *Per.* 73. The dedication to Victory by two Samnite magistrates in the sanctuary at Pietrabbondante is no doubt to be related to these successes in Samnium, La Regina 1980 (B 307) 175.

[73] App. *BCiv.* I.188–9.

[74] App. *BCiv.* I.191–5; Ovid *Fast.* VI. 563; Oros. V.18.11–13; Livy *Per.* 73.

[75] App. *BCiv.* I.196–8.

praetor of the Marrucini.[76] Although the Marsi were by no means subdued, the Roman strategy of opening a route to the Adriatic to split the enemy in two was now apparent. Success came only in the following year; but in this area the initiative now lay with the Roman generals, who were in a position to mount offensives from the powerful bases under their control.

It was probably in the same general period that Sex. Iulius Caesar set off for the north to relieve Firmum, after a victory perhaps over the Paeligni.[77] As we have seen, Pompeius Strabo had retreated there, where he had then been blockaded by T. Lafrenius. The siege lasted for some considerable time; but a city so powerfully fortified and in such a naturally strong position was virtually impregnable. Towards the end of the year, perhaps in October, learning of the approach of Sex. Caesar, Pompeius Strabo mounted two sorties. The army of T. Lafrenius was caught between them and routed, Lafrenius himself was killed; the rebel army took refuge in Asculum, which was now in its turn besieged by Strabo.[78] The whole northern rebel front was in a state of collapse; towards December, T. Vidacilius returned from Apulia to bring help to his own city and succeeded in entering it before the siege lines were complete.[79] The siege was entrusted by the Romans to Sex. Caesar.

Just as the fortunes of war appeared to be turning in favour of the Romans, rebel movements began in some Etruscan and Umbrian communities, presumably not the same ones as had opposed Drusus the year before and taken the side of Philippus. Even if the disturbances were soon suppressed, there was for a moment the risk that a completely new front was about to be opened along the coast north of Rome.[80]

At the end to the first year of the war, the failure of the rebel cause was already clear. It was perhaps in a moment of desperation in this phase of the war that the Italians brought themselves to think the impossible and open negotiations with Mithridates VI of Pontus, whom some of their leaders will have got to know in the course of their business activities in the eastern provinces. The king was invited to come to Italy in support of the rebels; his reply was, not surprisingly, evasive.[81]

At Rome, on the other hand, it must have become clear to everyone, even the most rigid, that, whatever the outcome of the war in purely military terms, there was no alternative to granting the Roman citizenship to the allies, now that the Romans were faced with an armed demand for it. In the course of a parley, one of the allied leaders had repeated yet again that the rebels, or at any rate their leaders, were fighting in order to

[76] App. *BCiv.* I.201–3 (confused). [77] App. *BCiv.* I.210; 205.

[78] App. *BCiv.* I.205–6; Livy *Per.* 74; Laffi 1975 (B 303) xxii–xxxiii. [79] App. *BCiv.* I.207–8.

[80] Sisenna, frr. 94–5 *HRR*, App. *BCiv.* I.211; Livy *Per.* 74; Oros. V.18.17.

[81] Posidonius *FGrH* 87 F 36; Diod. XXXVII.2.11: Gabba 1976 (C 55) 88–9. Two of the coins of the rebels are normally related to these events: Sydenham 1952 (B 247) nos. 632 and 643.

be admitted to a share in the Roman citizenship, not to bring about its end.[82] In other words, even among the allies, it was realized that there was no other possible outcome to the war, even if they had boosted their morale by appeals to the notion of Italian independence. A complete parting of the ways certainly did not now seem possible, if indeed it ever had. The pointlessness of the war and the tragic role of the Roman conservatives in provoking it were now clear to everyone.

It was for reasons such as these, towards October 90, that the Roman Senate, encouraged by the shift of the war in their favour, took the initiative by granting Roman citizenship to those allies who had remained loyal, in the first instance the Latin colonies and the other Latin communities, and to those who had laid down their arms or were prepared to lay them down within a specified period; the time allowed was no doubt not long – Velleius uses the word 'maturius'; it may be that the condition was met principally by the Etruscans and Umbrians. Such were the terms of the Lex Iulia de civitate, proposed by the consul L. Iulius Caesar on the basis of a decree of the Senate.[83]

Late as this measure was, it none the less removed the principal *raison d'être* of the insurrection, even if it was unable to undo all the terrible effects of the foolish and exclusive attitude which had prevailed up to that point; in particular, it was impossible to put an end to the war which was now in full swing. The terms of the law were no doubt complex; in the first place, it provided that it was for the allied communities themselves freely to decide whether or not to accept the offer of Roman citizenship; we hear indeed of occasional hesitations, as in the case of Neapolis and of Heraclea in Lucania.[84] Further, the law laid down certain basic rules governing the incorporation of the new citizens in the Roman citizen body; at any rate for a time, they were to be placed in a number of tribes additional to the original thirty-five, perhaps eight in number. The plan was for these tribes to vote after the others so that their political influence would be limited.[85] The provision was probably regarded as transitional, until it might be possible to deal with the complex process of more or less tripling the size of the citizen body; for such a process was bound to have widespread implications at a local level as well as in the centre. And the Roman state was indeed to be transformed as a result of the process. Italy became the territory of the city of Rome as a result of

[82] Cic. *Phil.* XII.27.

[83] App. *BCiv.* I.212–14; Vell. Pat. II.16.4; Gabba 1976 (C 55) 89–96; Taylor 1960 (F 156) 101–3; Sherwin-White 1973 (F 141) 150–3; Galsterer 1976 (A 38) 187–204; Luraschi 1978 (C 102).

[84] Cic. *Balb.* 21.

[85] App. *BCiv.* I.214–15; Vell. Pat. II.20.2. It may even be that the Lex Iulia to which the decree of Pompeius Strabo refers (*ILS* 8888) is different from the Lex Iulia de civitate. It is hard to know what the relationship is between the Lex Iulia and the Lex Calpurnia mentioned by Sisenna, fr. 120 *HRR*, cf. fr. 17 *HRR*.

this law and its successors; but the political and administrative articulation of that territory involved a complete rethinking of the structure of the Roman state and of how it functioned. In the immediate crisis the passage of the law helped the Roman war effort, not least because it created divisions and hence weaknesses within the allied communities;[86] only the most intransigent elements could now wish the war to continue.

The rebellion in Etruria and Umbria mentioned above must have been planned in association with the Marsi. The latter, in ignorance of the speed with which the movement had been suppressed, set out in the depths of winter from the basin of the Fucine Lake across the wilds of Gran Sasso; it was probably in January of 89, in the consulship of Cn. Pompeius Strabo and L. Porcius Cato. The intention was no doubt to mount a massive combined operation, first to raise the siege of Asculum and then to descend into Umbria. The Marsi were led by Vettius Scato. But the strategy devised by the two consuls to meet the threat succeeded, perhaps by reason of their numerical superiority. Perhaps not far from Asculum Strabo defeated the Marsi, who were forced to undertake a disastrous retreat across the snow-covered mountains. Cato had meanwhile taken over the command from C. Marius (we do not know why he was excluded from the command in the second year of the war, since his age should have been outweighed by his experience). He attacked the Marsi in the area of the Fucine Lake and defeated them, dying however perhaps as a result of treachery.[87] In any case the victory of Strabo was decisive; the siege of Asculum could now take its course without any possibility of relief from outside and the Romans were finally in a position to attack the central nucleus of the rebels from the north. The Marsi were finally forced to surrender; Corfinium was captured and the seat of the Italici transferred to Bovianum; the Vestini submitted, having failed to force the people of Pinna to abandon their alliance with Rome; likewise the Marrucini, perhaps after a final attempt at resistance.[88]

Towards the end of the summer of 89 the rebellion in the northern and central areas was for all practical purposes over, from Picenum to the borders of Samnium; only Asculum still held out, urged on by the heroic energy of Vidacilius.

In the south also, in 89, the Romans moved over to the offensive, under the able leadership of Sulla. His army, with Cicero in its ranks, had been reinforced by a legion of loyal Hirpini, raised by Minatius Magius of Aeclanum; he was also supported by a fleet. While he was besieging Pompeii, L. Cluentius came to its relief and won a short-lived success before being defeated between Nola and Pompeii. The Roman siege of Nola was to continue for a long time still, while that of Pompeii now

[86] App. *BCiv.* I.213. [87] App. *BCiv.* I.216–17; Laffi 1975 (B 303) xxx–xxxii.
[88] App. *BCiv.* I.227; Diod XXXVII.2.9.

came rapidly to an end. Stabiae fell on 30 April and Herculaneum on 11 June.[89] Sulla was now in a position to move against the Hirpini and attack Aeclanum, where the anti-Roman party now evidently had the upper hand. Lucanian reinforcements under Lamponius and Ti. Cleppius were slow to arrive; the city, inadequately protected by a wooden palisade (stone walls were only built after the war), surrendered and the whole area of the Hirpini followed suit; it was let off lightly by Sulla,[90] who lost no time in attacking the heart of Samnium. He set off on a long circular march, which brought him into the north of the region, contrary to the expectations of Papius Mutilus, who was defeated not far from Aesernia, escaping thither with a few of his troops.[91] Sulla moved on to Bovianum, whither the rebel government had been transferred, and managed to take it after a short, but bitter, struggle. The capital was moved once again, this time to Aesernia. All these victories over the Samnites will have taken place between July and September of 89; towards October of that year, Sulla went to Rome to stand in the elections for the consulship, succeeding along with Q. Pompeius Rufus.[92]

A consequence of the victories of Pompeius Strabo over the peoples along the coast of the Adriatic was the defeat or submission of the peoples of Apulia. After a phase of the war which remains obscure to us, but which saw the defeat and death of the Samnite Marius Egnatius, operations were conducted for the Romans by C. Cosconius. He came down the coast from the north, took Salapia and Cannae and besieged Canusium; a first encounter with the Samnite Trebatius resulted in defeat; but soon after he won a victory on the River Aufidus and Trebatius took refuge in Canusium. The people of Larinum surrendered immediately, along with Ausculum, the Poediculi and then Venusia, this last to the praetor Q. Caecilius Metellus; Metellus then went on to complete the submission of Iapygia with a victory over Q. Poppaedius Silo, who had retreated to that area after the collapse of the northern front. The rebel leader died in the battle.[93]

A few minor strongholds still held out, along with Asculum, defended by Vidacilius. The uselessness of the struggle should have been apparent; but he took steps to bring about the deaths of his political enemies as an act of revenge and then committed suicide; the surrender of the city followed soon after, in November 89. The well-known decree of Pompeius Strabo granting the Roman citizenship to a troop of Spanish

[89] App. *BCiv.* i.227; Cic. *Div.* I.72; Plut. *Cic.* 3.2 (Cicero in the army of Sulla); Vell. Pat. II.16.2 (Minatius Magius); Pliny *HN* III.70 (Stabiae); Ovid *Fast.* VI.567–8 (Herculaneum).

[90] App. *BCiv.* I.222–3; Diod. XXXVII.2.11.

[91] App. *BCiv.* I.223–4.

[92] App. *BCiv.* I.223–5; La Regina 1966 (B 187); also in 1980 (B 307) 30–3.

[93] App. *BCiv.* I.227–30; Livy *Per.* 75.

horsemen is dated 17 November; his triumph fell on 25 December.[94] With the fall of Asculum, where the rebellion had begun two years earlier, the military failure of the allies was complete; but the victors had in fact had to recognize and accept precisely those demands of the allies for which they had fought and lost.

During 89, another law dealing with the citizenship had been passed, the Lex Plautia Papiria, in order to carry to completion the incorporation of the allies into the Roman state. It was proposed by the tribunes M. Plautius Silvanus, who had earlier succeeded in putting an end to the activities of the 'quaestio ex lege Varia', and C. Papirius Carbo. Much is uncertain, but it is likely that various references in our sources are to be ascribed to this law; they are located close to the end of the war and relate to the acceptance in general of the allies into the Roman citizenship, with a few particular exceptions, notably the Samnites and the Lucanians.[95] Only one clause is specifically attributed to the Lex Plautia Papiria (and some think that that is all it contained); it provided for the extension of Roman citizenship to those who were *adscripti* in an allied community, i.e. had received its citizenship in an honorary capacity, were domiciled in Italy at the moment of the passage of the law, and made application to the urban praetor within sixty days.[96] It is likely, however, that while this provision covered *adscripti* in allied communities domiciled in Italy and was cited by Cicero precisely in this context, other chapters dealt with a more general grant of citizenship, leaving out only the Samnites and Lucanians who were still intransigently under arms. (It is above all because of them that the Social War merged into the civil war that followed.) Meanwhile, the Lex Plautia Papiria probably left the detailed application of its provisions to be settled by decrees of the Senate, some of which are mentioned in the historical tradition; the reason was no doubt that that was the only way to organize the rapid acquisition of the right to vote by the new citizens.

Still within 89, an equally important law emanating from the consul Pompeius Strabo organized the incorporation of the allied communities north of the Po, and perhaps also of some Ligurian tribes south of the river. Some of the peoples involved had taken part in the Social War on one side or the other, as we have seen. All of them were granted the status of Latin colonies, without any introduction of colonists from outside; and they were all granted the right for their magistrates to acquire the Roman citizenship. The process by which local institutions were moulded into Roman ones was a long one and it was certainly not complete by 49, when all these communities received full Roman citizenship. It is possible that the Lex Pompeia also provided that some

[94] App. *BCiv.* I.209–10; *ILS* 8888; *Inscr. Ital.* XIII.I. pp. 85 and 563.

[95] App. *BCiv.* I.231; Vell. Pat. II.17.1 and 20.2; *Schol.Bob.* 175 st.

[96] Cic. *Arch.* 7.

of the less civilized tribes of the Alpine foothills should be attributed to the nearest cities of the plain. It is in any case clear that the Lex Pompeia set on foot in Transpadane Gaul a process of Romanization and urbanization which succeeded in grafting itself on to the existing structures of Celtic society.[97]

One problem demands particular attention. The extension of the Roman citizenship to the whole of Italy, from the straits of Messina to the Po, meant a complete transformation of the territorial organization of the Roman state, and its reorganization on the basis of the *municipia*, the internal subdivisions of the Roman state, into which the former Latin colonies and allied communities were now transformed. The Roman state in fact ceased to be a city state and became a state made up of numerous *municipia*, at any rate as far as the organization of its territory was concerned; political institutions remained for all practical purposes unchanged.

It is generally believed, probably rightly, that general rules were laid down for the government and administration of the new *municipia*, perhaps based on earlier constitutions prescribed for Latin colonies. For example, criteria for the inclusion of the new citizen-communities in the tribes, once their concentration in a number of supplementary tribes had been abandoned, will have been laid down, or at least indicated or suggested; those criteria will have been influenced by local political considerations. In many cases, the territories of the new *municipia* will also have been fixed; that will have been a complex process, since it is clear that in some cases existing tribal communities were split into more than one *municipium*, perhaps sometimes as a punishment; that process will have been particularly common in Transpadane Gaul. There will also have been general criteria for the selection of the urban seats of government of the *municipia*; and a process of urbanization will have begun even where it had not occurred or even begun before.[98] Paradoxically, the destruction wrought by the Social War will have favoured this development. In some cases, specially in Transpadane Gaul, the grant of Roman or Latin citizenship will have involved survey and division of the land, indispensable for the definition of the social structure of the new community.[99] We know that envoys of the Roman government were entrusted with the constitution of the new *municipia*;[100] they will often have been people who already had a local reputation and power base, though of course perceived as politically reliable by Rome; in some cases, in their capacity as envoys of Rome, they will have formed part of the

97 Asc. 2–3C; Pliny *HN* III.138; it seems to me that the episode at Milan recorded by Frontinus, *St.* I.9.3. is to be placed in the context of these activities of Strabo, Gabba 1984 (C 59).

98 Gabba 1983 (C 58) on Vit. I.4.11–12.

99 Gabba 1985 (G 94) 279–83

100 Note, for example, Caes. *BCiv.* 1.15.2, on Labienus at Cingulum.

first college of local magistrates, nominated by the central power or by its representatives, not elected.[101] In some cases, such envoys were authorized to modify, at their discretion and in the light of local conditions and without reference to Rome, the text of the municipal charter, based on the general rules laid down in measures passed through the Roman assemblies.[102]

It took a long time to incorporate everyone into the structure of the Roman state, from 89 to the age of Caesar; but the general outlines of the process to be followed must have been fixed immediately after the Social War; and it cannot be excluded that it was precisely the Lex Plautia Papiria (or some other law passed not long afterwards, perhaps under Sulla) which included the provisions relevant to the process, just as the earlier Lex Iulia had already included some provisions governing the actual exercise of the right to vote.[103]

[101] Cicero, *Clu.* 25; Lex municipii Tarentini 7–14 (*Bruns* no. 27).

[102] Tabula Heracleensis, 159–60 (*Bruns* no. 18); Gabba 1985 (G 94) 279–83. Similarities even between the fragmentary texts in our possession of municipal and colonial charters in the first century B.C. suggest common models at least for some elements.

[103] Galsterer 1976 (G 96) insists rather on the spontaneous aspects of the process.

CHAPTER 5

MITHRIDATES

JOHN G. F. HIND

Mithridates VI Eupator 'the Great' was to become a byword for his hatred of Rome and his atrocities in Asia. At the end of his life, in 63 B.C., rumour had it that he was still planning to march on Italy, like an eastern Hannibal, via Scythia, Thrace and the Illyrians. Many myths arose about him during his fifty-seven-year reign and his more than forty years of confrontation with Rome. By the end of the Roman Empire he was one of her few former enemies, alongside Pyrrhus, Hannibal and Cleopatra, to be canonized among the eighty notable ancient Romans.[1] As one who died aged sixty-nine (some said seventy or seventy-two), he almost qualified to be one of the 'Macrobioi', the 'long-lived', of the ancient world. During all but his first thirteen years of life he ruled a kingdom, Pontus, which took its name from the 'Deep Sea' itself. It lay almost beyond the world known to Rome, and had beneath its sway Thracians, Scythians, Sarmatians, the Cimmerian Bosporus and Colchis, the legendary land of gold, poisons and witchcraft. The king himself was immensely gifted as well as resourceful. He was said to speak twenty-two, twenty-five, fifty languages; and during his 'heroic' first seven years as king, as a fugitive in the interior of Pontus, he had trained his physique to great endurance and to a high resistance to poisons:

> He gathered all that springs to birth
> From the many-venomed earth;
> First a little, thence to more,
> He sampled all her killing store;
> . . .
> – I tell the tale that I heard told.
> Mithridates, he died old.[2]

He bore a noble Persian name, and his family claimed descent from either Darius himself or one of his associates in the rebellion against the Median

[1] *De Vir. Ill.* 76. See already Cic. *Mur.* 32 and a couple of generations later Vell. Pat. II.18, cf. 40 on his international standing.

[2] A. E. Housman, *A Shropshire Lad*, 62. Languages: Val. Max. VIII.7; Pliny *HN* VII.88; XXV.6; Gell. *NA* XVII.17; Poisons: Just. XXXVII.3; App. *Mith.* 111; Pliny *HN* XXV.2.5.

Magi. Small wonder that, in Persian-Parthian fashion, he claimed at the height of his success to be 'Great King' and 'King of Kings'.

The extant ancient sources for Mithridates and his kingdom are numerous, and varied in length and detail.[3] Some fifty ancient writers contribute, ranging from fragments of works by his courtiers and by contemporary scholars to late Roman *breviaria* and *vitae* which derive much of their material from the now lost books of Livy. Our fullest sources are works of the first and second centuries A.D. Plutarch's *Life of Sulla* and Appian's *Mithridatica* provide overlapping narratives in Greek, and Strabo's *Geography* and Memnon's local history of Heraclea on the Black Sea add circumstantial detail about Pontus and about events in the Mithridatic Wars. Latin sources offer less, though Justin's *Epitome of the World History of Pompeius Trogus* (first century B.C.) traces the rise of Pontus under Mithridates' father and the growth of tension in Asia between Mithridates and the Roman governors. But it was the speeches of Cicero – *pro Flacco*, *pro Murena*, *pro lege Manilia* – that moulded posterity's view of the monarch as the recidivist enemy of Rome and perpetrator of the Asiatic atrocities.

I. THE DYNASTY

Mithridates was reckoned sixteenth in descent from Darius (though the claim may have been manufactured in the first century B.C.).[4] The direct line can be traced only from the fourth century. A Mithridates inherited from his father Ariobarzanes (*c.* 362–337) a little fief at Cius, and perhaps Myrlea, to the west of Bithynia on the Propontis, as a dependency of Darius III, the last Achaemenid king of Persia. He lost, then recovered, his position, and eventually was 'liberated' by Alexander the Great. For a time he was a vassal of Antigonus Monophthalmus, but was killed by him for treating with Cassander in 302 B.C.[5]

The son of Mithridates of Cius, also a Mithridates, later surnamed Ktistes, 'founder', escaped eastwards. With six horsemen he entered Paphlagonia, first reaching Cimiata in the Amnias valley; later he moved further east to Amasia in Pontic Cappadocia. If this second move took place in 297 B.C. it would help to explain the era of Pontus, which dated from that year (though it may have been a court fiction of later Mithridatid date designed to give Pontus an era equal to that of Bithynia).[6] After the defeat and death of Lysimachus at Corupedium, in

[3] Sources chronologically arranged: *Greenidge–Clay*, 55f. Discussion of the sources: Reinach 1890 (D 55) 417–55; Sherwin-White 1984 (D 291) 116–18; McGing 1986 (D 35) 176–9. Footnote references are not given to the main narratives.

[4] Meyer 1878 (D 38) 31–8.

[5] For the dynasty at Cius: McGing 1986 (D 35) 13–15.

[6] Pontic era: Diehl 1938 (D 12) 1850; Robert 1937 (B 229) 231; Perl 1968 (D 53) 299; Bickermann 1980 (A 11) 72.

the wake of successes won by the northern states of Cius, Tium and Bithynia, this Mithridates warred against Seleucus I and secured his independence. In 281/0 B.C. he took the title 'King' of a state which comprised eastern Paphlagonia and northern Cappadocia,[7] and along with Nicomedes of Bithynia he settled Gaulish tribes in parts of eastern Phrygia, which came to be known as Galatia. In 279 Amastris, a coastal city on the western border of Paphlagonia, was acquired for him by his son from its ruler Eumenes. Mithridates' kingdom now reached to the river Sangarius in the west; well might he be called 'Founder' and be our choice as the first Mithridates of the dynasty which was to number six of that name, and eight kings overall, in 218 years down to the death of Eupator, 281–63 B.C.[8]

The next kings, Ariobarzanes (266–*c.* 250) and Mithridates (*c.* 250–189) had respectively a short and a very long reign, if the latter was not actually two kings (Mithridates II and III). The former added Amisus on the Black Sea to the kingdom; the latter formed a marriage alliance with Seleucus II by taking Seleucus' sister Laodice as his wife and receiving as her dowry Phrygia Maior. However he failed in an attempt to take Sinope by siege.

Pharnaces, king *c.* 189–*c.* 159, pressed upon the coastal cities and his neighbours to the west more ambitiously than his predecessors. He was successful in overmastering Sinope, *c.* 182 B.C., holding on to it even after a war with Eumenes of Pergamum and Ariarathes of Cappadocia, though he had to submit to the loss of some recent gains in Paphlagonia and Galatia; a Roman senatorial commission acted as 'honest broker' between the kings in these years after the Roman defeat of Antiochus III at Apamea. The commissioners were careful to rein back Pharnaces from western Asia Minor, barring him from the small city of Tium, but they were neglectful of the more remote Sinope. Pharnaces then took Cotyora and Cerasus (Pharnacia), former colonies of Sinope even further east, and he secured the overlordship of Armenia Minor, with its city of Trapezus, when the king, another Mithridates, handed it over to him.[9] His strengthened hold on his own coastline was matched by a vigorous policy embracing all the shores of the Black Sea: he had treaties with Odessus on the west (Bulgarian) coast and with Chersonesus in the south Crimea.[10] Towards the end of his life Pharnaces cemented a friendship

[7] Syncellus 523.5.

[8] Sources for Mithridates of Cius and Mithridates Ktistes probably go back to Hieronymus of Cardia (App. *Mith.* 8). Rostovtzeff thought Mithridates of Cius was the first of the Pontic dynasty, *CAH* IX[1] 217–18, but the prevailing view treats Ktistes as the first: Reinach, 1890 (D 55) 7–8; Molyev 1985 (D 43); McGing 1986 (D 35) 15–19; 1986 (D 34) 250–3; Molyev 1983 (D 42A).

[9] It reverted to independence later, but the pantomime of 'voluntary submission' was to be repeated under Mithridates the Great.

[10] Strab. XII.3.11, 16; Polyb. XXIII.9; XXIV.1.14; XXV.2; XXVII.17.

with the Seleucids by marrying Nysa, a daughter or granddaughter of Antiochus III. On his death, *c.* 159, Pontus was an important power in Asia Minor, though a combination of local kings could still counter it and it could not stand up to Roman diplomacy or threats of force.[11]

Under the successors of Pharnaces, Mithridates Philopator Philadelphus, perhaps his younger brother, and Mithridates Euergetes, probably his son, the kingdom prospered through calculated docility to Rome. The former is known from an inscription on the Capitol, where alliance with the Roman people is mentioned:[12] also a king Mithridates is said to have aided Attalus II of Pergamum against Prusias II of Bithynia in 155/4 B.C., and may well have been Philopator Philadelphus. There are also splendid portrait coins, whose reverses have legends in his own name and that of his sister Laodice, and show statues of Perseus and of Zeus and Hera, hinting at the dynasty's Persian origins and the elevated position of the brother–sister rulers.[13] On any reckoning Philopator's reign can only have been short (*c.* 159 to 151/0).

He was succeeded by Mithridates Euergetes, who had another Laodice as his queen, the mother of Mithridates the Great. He helped Rome in the Third Punic War, *c.* 149, and, after the death of Attalus III, helped Rome again during the revolt of Aristonicus (ch. 2, p. 34).[14] Rome dispensed bounty, in the form of other people's property, to her allies in the Asian war: to Mithridates were allowed the long-claimed lands of Phrygia Maior (a huge bribe having been paid, it was said, to the Roman commander, M'. Aquillius). Euergetes also secured, separately, Inner Paphlagonia, as heir of its king, Pylaemenes, and Galatia: both had been targets for the ambitions of Pharnaces. And when he married his daughter, yet another Laodice, to Ariarathes VI of Cappadocia he gained an interest there too, even 'invading it as though it were a foreign country' (although the circumstances are unclear).[15] During this time, some eleven years before his father's death, Mithridates Eupator was born, at Sinope.

Whether at the instance of some pro-Roman faction disturbed at his over-mighty role among his neighbours, or as a result of a palace plot, Euergetes was assassinated at Sinope.[16] Pontus thereupon, from *c.* 121/0,

[11] *IOSPE* I 402; Minns 1913 (D 39) no. 172; Sherk 1984 (B 239) 30; Kolobova 1949 (D 27); Molyev 1976 (D 41) 12–17; Burstein 1980 (D 256) 1–12; McGing 1986 (D 35) 24–34.

[12] *OGIS* 375; Mellor 1978 (B 202).

[13] Polyb. XXXIII.12; Habicht 1956 (D 269) 101–10; coins: Waddington 1925 (B 253) 13, no. 7; Seltman 1955 (B 237) Pl.LVI, 10 and LVII, 1; Kraay–Hirmer 1966 (B 182) 376–7 and Pl.210.

[14] App. *Mith.* 10 makes Euergetes the first king of Pontus to be a 'Friend of the Roman People': if he is not identical with Philopator Philadelphus that must be a mistake. It is just possible that they are identical and that Mithridates V was Chrestus, Eupator's brother (see below). For Euergetes: Reinach 1890 (D 55) 42–7; Geyer 1932 (D 16) no. 11; Magie 1950 (A 67) 194f; Thompson 1961 (B 249) 422f (but dating the Mithridates–Aristion coins too early).

[15] App. *Mith.* 10; Just. XXXVII.1.4; XXXVIII.5.4.

[16] Strab. X.4.10; Memnon *FGrH* 434 22.2F.

underwent a period of weakness, with Laodice ruling in the name of her two sons Eupator and Chrestus, both minors. She pursued a philo-Roman policy, but from a far weaker position than her husband. In 119 or 116 Rome withdrew Phrygia Maior from Laodice's Pontus, thus nullifying the fruits of the bribe to Aquillius and nurturing resentment among Pontic patriots for the future.[17] Soon it became clear that Laodice sided with her younger son, Chrestus: indeed, for a few years he may have been regarded as the reigning Mithridates, and Laodice may have ruled through him. Eupator is now said to have escaped from a suspicious riding accident; and the great romantic episode now follows (perhaps part of the later Mithridates-myth): he retired secretly to the mountains of eastern Pontus and Armenia Minor, moving ever on from day to day, building up his resistance to poisons and his physical endurance, and getting to know many of the peoples of Pontus and their languages. The period was said to have lasted seven years, though the figure may be conventional, even magical, and represent the ideal education of an Iranian prince.[18] Finally, *c.* 113 (according to the date most scholars have deduced from Appian and Justin: perhaps in fact a few years earlier) Eupator returned to Sinope and overturned affairs at the court, throwing Laodice into prison, but allowing his brother to continue as a colleague without the title of king[19] for some while, before in the end, at an unknown date (though after 115), he was put to death.

II. THE KINGDOM

The proper name of Mithridates Eupator's kingdom was 'Cappadocia by the Euxine' or 'Cappadocia by Pontus', in distinction to the inland region of 'Cappadocia by Taurus' or 'Greater Cappadocia'.[20] This coastal, northern region grew to be much the more prosperous, possessing fertile areas in the major river valleys behind the coast (Amnias, Iris, Lycus) while politically centred on the Greek cities of the southern shore of the Black Sea, first Amastris and then Amisus and Sinope.[21] To the west lay relatively minor states, Paphlagonia, Tium and the strong city state of Heraclea. Inland to the south-west were Phrygia Maior and Phrygia Epictetus and the three tribes of the Gauls. Directly south lay the related and extensive, but economically weak, kingdom of (Greater) Cappadocia. Eastward was Armenia Minor, and along the coast beyond Trapezus were the principalities of the Colchians; and around the further shores of the Black Sea were Greek cities struggling to maintain their independence against Thracians, Getae and Scythians.

17 *OGIS* 436. Date: Glew 1977 (D 18) 388f; Sherwin-White 1977 (D 75) 70; 1984 (D 291) 96.
18 Widengren 1960 (D 83). 19 *IDélos* 1560–1. 20 Polyb. v.43.1; Strab. XII.1.4.
21 Magie 1950 (A 67) 177–86; McGing 1986 (D 35) 2–10.

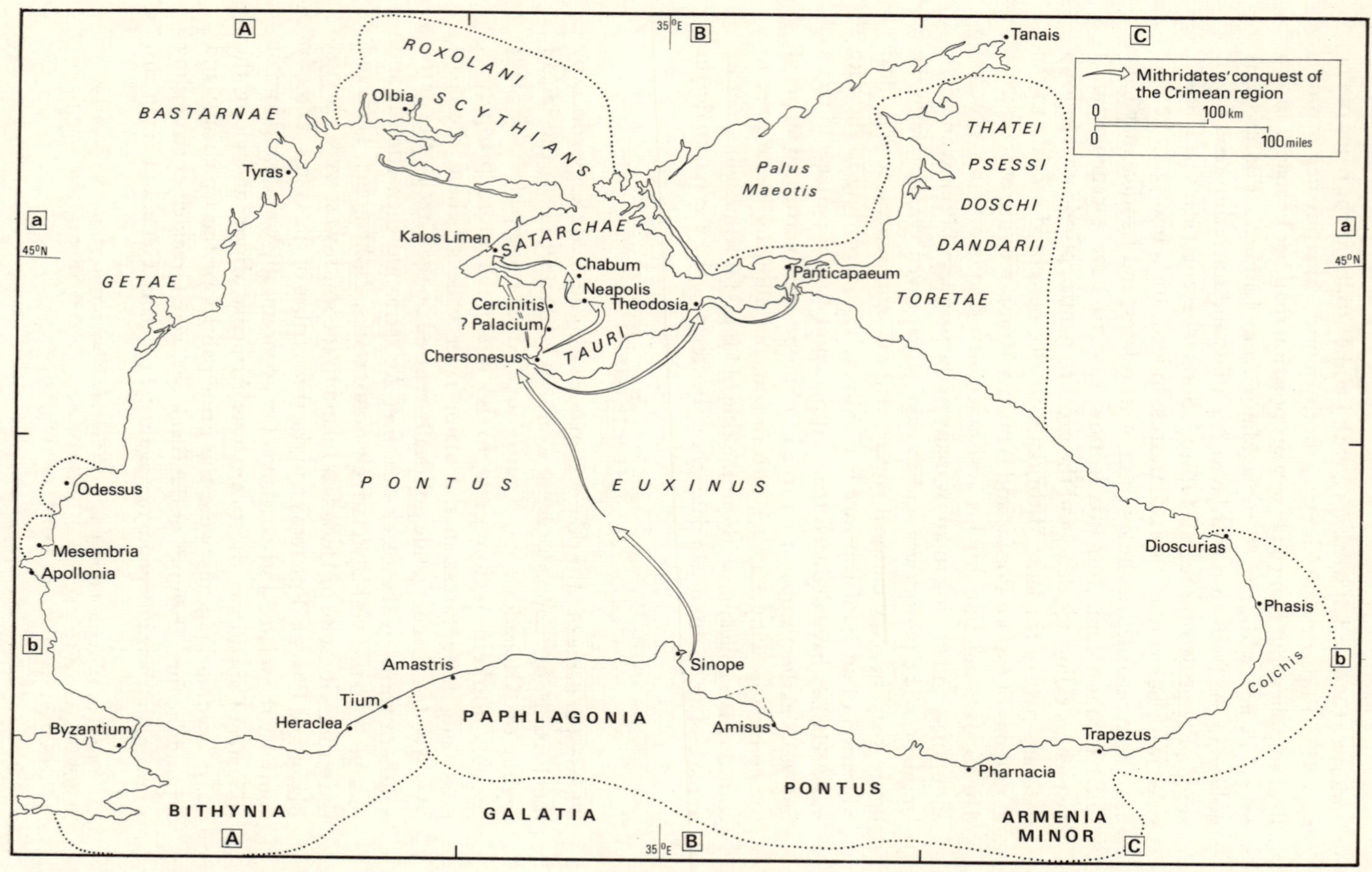

4 The Pontic Area

Only Armenia Maior, in the wider arc of Anatolia, might have been a rival to Pontus, and its period of greatness was still to come, under king Tigranes, *c.* 83–65 B.C.; this coincided with Mithridates Eupator's own collapse at the end of the first war with Rome and lasted until the end of their joint resistance in the third war. Since the Peace of Apamea Rome had been the 'Cloud in the West', which Hellenistic kings had to keep a weather eye on. It had loomed closer with the annexation of Pergamum as the 'province of Asia' after 129 and Rome's further intervention in the form of consular appointments to Cilicia and Lycaonia, certainly by 102 and possibly as early as 116.[22] Mithridates Euergetes had been very circumspect in his dealings with Rome, and so was Eupator, who waited twenty-three years before being pushed into war with Rome.

Mithridates' ancestral kingdom was not large, but had economic, military and naval potential.[23] Pontus is a land of east–west mountain ranges and river valleys. The latter, running parallel to the shore of the Black Sea at a distance of 110 to 160 kilometres, were the heartland of the kingdom; as for the mountains, south of Cotyora and Cerasus they reach 3,000 metres and further east toward Trabzon and Rize 4,000.[24] There was a north–south route from Amisus to Tarsus via Amasia and Zela in Pontus and Mazaca and Tyana in Cappadocia – an ancient route that linked the Black Sea with the Mediterranean, mentioned by Herodotus.[25] The only other real north–south route ran from Trapezus in Colchis south-west over the Zigana Pass and then south-eastwards into the valley of the river Acampsis: it was the path taken – in reverse – by Xenophon in the *Anabasis*.[26]

Pontus was rich in minerals. Iron and silver were mined near the coast south of Pharnacia, the fabled source of 'Chalybian steel'. Studies of the mineral resources of modern Turkey have stressed the concentration of metalworking in north-eastern Pontus. There are also copper, lead, zinc, arsenic, and ruddle (for painting ships), found especially inland of Sinope.[27]

The climate of the Pontic coast is much less harsh than that of inland Cappadocia, and it is the best-watered part of Asia Minor, the Pontine mountains in the east ensuring that more of the precipitation is deposited at that end of the coastal strip. The consequence is a splendid forest growth, ever denser towards the east – oaks, alders, beeches, chestnuts

[22] Syme 1939 (D 294); Sherwin-White 1976 (D 74); 1984 (D 291) 97–101.

[23] Geography: Ramsay 1890 (A 94); Anderson, Cumont and Grégoire 1910 (B 131); Maximova 1956 (D 37) 13–31, Weimert 1984 (D 82).

[24] G. Williams, *Eastern Turkey* (London, 1972); Calder and Bean 1958 (D 257).

[25] Hdt. I.72. [26] Other routes: Munro 1901 (D 45); Winfield 1977 (D 85).

[27] C. W. Ryan, *A Guide to the known Minerals of Turkey* (Ankara, 1960); P. de Jesus, *Prehistoric Mining and Metallurgy in Anatolia*, *BAR* S.74, 1980; R. F. Tylecote, 'Ironsands from the Black Sea', *AS* 31 (1981) 187–9.

and walnuts, with above them coniferous forests and below them many species of fruit tree, including the cherry, which takes its name from Cerasus, the plum, pear, apricot and apple. The region was famed for ship-timbers, and the fleet of classical Sinope, the very large Pontic fleet of the Mithridatids, and the later Roman Black Sea fleet based at Trapezus, all had a ready supply. Olive-growing produced a vigorous trade in Sinopian oil and a pottery industry making amphorae in which to export it. On some of the coastal plains, e.g. Themiscyra, and in the Iris–Lycus valleys horses were grazed in great numbers and sheep and cattle pastured.[28]

The organization of Pontus as observable under its last two kings, Mithridates the Great and his son Pharnaces II, reflects the geographical, climatic and ethnic facts and the historical traditions of the region. On the Black Sea coast the Greek cities had councils, assemblies and magistracies, some by long tradition, such as Sinope and Amisus, others as a result of re-foundation on the Greek pattern, such as Amastris (by Amastris the daughter of Oxyathres) in the late fourth century or Pharnacia (by Pharnaces I). Sinope and Amisus were chosen by Pharnaces I, Euergetes and Mithridates the Great to be their capitals and were adorned with public buildings accordingly: Sinope was also the site of the tombs of these later Mithridatids.[29] The major inland centres were much more Paphlagonian or Cappadocian in character, with an Iranian aristocracy going back three or four hundred years. The most important were in the fertile Iris–Lycus valleys. Amasia on the river Iris was the old capital from before the time of Pharnaces I and the resting-place of four earlier kings, with an uncompleted fifth tomb perhaps intended for Pharnaces.[30] The region to the west of Amasia was called Chiliocomum, 'The Thousand Villages', which gives a hint as to the source of the city's wealth. Strabo was proud of his Amasian origin.[31] But there were other rich areas: Phanaroea east of Amasia, on the river Lycus, Dazimonitis to the south on the upper Iris, and Phazimonitis north of Amasia between the Halys and the Iris. In the time of Mithridates Eupator Pontus was divided into eparchies, perhaps governed by *strategoi*, and there may have been subdivisions called hyparchies. Nobles of Iranian ancestry ruled some localities from their castles: the villages under their control could be very numerous for, while Chiliocomum's thousand is unlikely to have been literal, L. Murena, in his brief campaign into Pontus, is reported to have overrun four hundred 'villages'. The political centre of the economic heart of Pontus was clearly Amasia. Its central area was garrisoned under a *phrourarchos*, usually a eunuch, in charge of entry into

[28] Strab. XII.3.11–40.

[29] Rostovtzeff 1932 (D 61) 212–13; 219–20; Möll 1984 (D 44); Olshausen and Biller 1984 (D 51); Robinson 1906 (D 56); 1905 (B 233).

[30] Rostovtzeff 1932 (D 61) 218.

[31] Strab. XII.3.39–41; Lomouri 1979 (D 31).

the citadel:[32] there was a royal palace and a temple to Zeus Stratios, a Hellenized form of the Iranian Ahuramazda, chief protector of the dynasty.

In addition to the royal towns, forts and treasuries and the castles of the Pontic nobility, another major characteristic of inland Pontus, as of southern Cappadocia, was the temple estates, drawing revenue from huge areas. Ameria, near Cabira, was a 'comopolis', a 'village-city', dedicated to the divinity Mēn Pharnacou: near Pontic Comana was another temple-town dedicated to the goddess Ma; and to the south-west, near Zela, was a temple of the Iranian Anaitis. They were served by priests, temple slaves or serfs: many of the females were temple prostitutes. Comana channelled trade to and from Armenia: Strabo calls it an *emporion*, and it was bustling with soldiers and merchants, not the least of its attractions being the temple establishment of 6,000 sacred slaves.

The chief deities of Pontus all have a syncretistic (mixed) aspect to them. There were Paphlagonian (at Sinope) and Cappadocian (former Hittite?) native elements, overlaid by 'magian' and other Iranian elements dating from the Achaemenid Persian period. These had been reinterpreted in Greek guise and with Greek names during the period of formation of Pontus as a kingdom. Hence Ahuramazda (Persian 'Sun') was addressed as Zeus Stratios at Amasia. Mēn at Ameria, the great moon-god, was given the Iranian title Pharnacou. Ma of Comana was equated with Rhea/Cybele, the 'Great Mother'. In view of the important role played by the cults of Zeus Stratios and Mēn Pharnacou in the official ritual of the Pontic dynasty, it is not unreasonable to connect these sun and moon deities with the 'star and crescent' badge of Pontus and its ruling family.[33]

III. MITHRIDATES' BLACK SEA EMPIRE

With the accession of Mithridates Eupator a period of vigorous assertiveness began. He championed Hellenic and Iranian elements alike against a Roman influence which, even in the province of Asia, had roots only fifteen years deep; but his anti-Roman sentiment, fuelled by the retraction of the grant of Phrygia Maior, was probably not yet as overriding as his Iranian and Seleucid pride. His ambition was to achieve great things amongst his regal peers. Among his friends from childhood were an elite group of *syntrophoi*: for his wider ventures beyond Pontus he needed the help of such a trusted set, some of whom were Greeks from Sinope and Amisus.

Mithridates' first move, probably, was to accept a hegemony over

[32] *OGIS* 365; Anderson, Cumont and Grégoire 1910 (B 131) nos. 66; 94; 95a; 200; 228.

[33] Strab. XII.3.32–7; XII.3.31; App. *Mith.* 66, 70.

PONTUS EUXINUS
COLCHIS
Sinope
Amastris
Tium
Heraclea
Byzantium
Propontis
Samothrace
Cyzicus
Cius
Nicomedia
Bithynium
OLGASSYS
Amnias
PAPHLAGONIA
GAZELONITIS
Amisus
PHAZIMONITIS
DIACOPENE
Amasia
Pharnacia
(Cerasus)
Cotyora
Trapezus
Eupatoria
Cabeira
Comana
Mons Paryadres
PHANAROEA
Iris
Lycus
Gaziura
PONTUS
Zela
PIMOLISENE
Tavium
DAZIMONITIS
ARMENIA MINOR
ARMENIA MAJOR
Dardanus
Granicus
Ilium
Lemnos
Myrlea
BITHYNIA
Sangarius
Ancyra
PHRYGIA MINOR
MYSIA ABBAITIS
Rhyndacus
EPICTETUS
PHRYGIA MAIOR
GALATIA
Halys
Mytilene
Lesbos
Pergamum
Pitane
Thyateira
Magnesia ad S.
PHRYGIA
? Leontoncephalae
Chios
Erythrae
Smyrna
Sardis
Clazomenae
ASIA
Synnada
Mazaca (Eusebeia)
CAPPADOCIA
Colophon
Ephesus
Maeander
Apamea
LYCAONIA
Samos
Magnesia
Tralles
Laodicea
Aphrodisias
Tyana
Iasus
Tabae
CARIA
PISIDIA
Stratonicea
Termessus
PAMPHYLIA
Tarsus
Cos
PERAEA
Caunus
Cnidus
Telmessus
LYCIA
CILICIA
Patara
Rhodes
Euphrates
Crete
Land over 1000 metres
200 km
100 miles
Cyprus

5 Asia Minor

Armenia Minor from its king, Antipater, perhaps *c.* 115–114 B.C. (though some scholars think as late as 106): and the next gain will have been Colchis. Only Strabo and Memnon mention the annexation, and they give no date, Strabo merely linking it with Armenia Minor and Memnon making it fall to Mithridates early in his career of expansion: some date it before, and some after, the campaigns in the Crimea.[34] It was certainly subject to Mithridates by 89, for it was mentioned as one of his possessions in Pelopidas' speech on behalf of his master to the Roman generals at the start of the first Roman war. The land was a useful addition, with alluvial gold, honey, wax, flax, hemp and timber; it was also the western end of an important trade route to the Caspian, up the Phasis and down the Cyrus rivers, and a vital land and coastal sailing link with the Cimmerian Bosporus. Mithridates' domination of Colchis was the long-term end of the process of economic and cultural penetration of the eastern shore of the Black Sea achieved by Greek cities such as Sinope as early as the fifth century B.C.; and now those well-tried connexions, plus the growing reputation of Mithridates and his generals, attracted an appeal from Chersonesus, across the narrow waist of the Black Sea.

Chersonesus appealed, at some date between 114 and 110 B.C. (perhaps 113),[35] to Mithridates as its only source of aid. Sinope was now the capital of Pontus, while Heraclea, the mother-city of Chersonesus, was no longer equal to the task of sending troops against her colony's enemies, the Scythians and the Tauri of the steppeland and piedmont parts of the Crimea. The call was answered with an expedition of 6,000 Pontic troops under Mithridates' general Diophantus,[36] and subsequently with two further expeditions; after several major campaigns against the Scythians in the steppelands north of Chersonesus and the crushing of a rebellion by one Saumacus in Panticapaeum on the Bosporus, Mithridates was master of all the Crimean region. He later developed links in the north-west and west of the Black Sea, where we hear of military aid to Olbia and Apollonia. Thus, in a decade or so, Mithridates had converted the whole of the Sea (Pontus) into a lake dependent on the kingdom (Pontus), and had unified politically the complementary economic elements of the various shores, which had been tending towards a unity for 300 years.[37] Only the mountainous

34 Strab. XI.2.17,18; XII.3.1; Memnon *FGrH* 34 223F. Colchis before Crimea: most lately Molyev 1976 (D 41) 24–8; Shelov 1980 (D 71). First coins of Eupator from Dioscurias dated *c.* 105–90 B.C., Dundua and Lordkipanidze (D 14); Todua 1990 (D 77B) 48–59.

35 Date: Niese 1887 (D 48); Vinogradov (D 78) 644–5. Some prefer 111/10 B.C. Tauri and Scythians: Leskov 1965 (D 28); Savelya (D 66); Sheglov (D 68); Solomonnik 1952 (D 77A) 116–17; Schultz 1971 (D 67); Vysotskaya 1972 (D 80); 1975 (D 81).

36 The main sources for all these campaigns are Strab. VII.3.17; 4.3 and 7 the great 'Diophantus-Inscription', *IOSPE* I.352; *SEG* XXX, 963. See Minns 1913 (D 39) 582–91; Molyev 1976 (D 41) 28–43; *CAH* VI², ch. 11.

37 *IOSPE* I.226; *IGBulg* I².392; Shelov 1985 (D 72), and 1986 (D 73) 36–42; Vinogradov 1989 (D 78A) 257–62.

Caucasus coast, with its unruly piratical tribes, the Achaei, Heniochi and Zygi, remained outside Mithridates' bidding, but even they normally let him pass if he was on his way through with an army. Still independent, to the west and in the direction of the Roman province of Asia, were Heraclea Pontica and the kingdom of Bithynia, centred on the Propontis.

Prolific coinages are an index of the prosperity of Mithridates' kingdom at this time. The bronze coins are of a number of standard types, some referring to the dynasty, such as the head of Perseus, and most having on the obverse heads of the major Greek deities and their attributes. They were struck in some thirteen mint centres in Paphlagonia and Pontus, and one or two related types were struck also on the Bosporus between *c.* 110 and 70 B.C. They are frequently found on sites in Colchis and in the cities to the north of the Black Sea.[38] From 96/5 (the first dated issues, year 202) silver drachms and tetradrachms and gold staters were struck in the name of Mithridates Eupator. On the obverse his portrait is done in a realistic style with hair following the contours of the head: on the reverse Pegasus stoops to drink and the eight-rayed sun-star points to Persian ancestry. A few years later a more idealizing head of the king appears (*c.* 92–89), with wilder hair: perhaps an attempt to hint at him as the New Dionysus.[39]

IV. KINGS AND ROMANS IN WESTERN ANATOLIA, 108–89 B.C.

In the last decade of the second century B.C. Mithridates, still in his late twenties and early thirties, was compared by his court flatterers to Alexander and to Dionysus, though he had not won his northern empire in person but presided over it from his capital at Sinope. He had also studiously avoided confrontation with Rome; and the Romans at that time were disinclined to involve themselves beyond the province of Asia because the Jugurthan and Cimbric Wars and the raids by the Scordisci from the north-east kept them fully in play in Europe. Rome's attitude, however, gradually changed after Mithridates' acquisition of his Black Sea empire and after they had watched his interventions in states only just beyond the Roman province, during the years 114–101 B.C.[40]

Shortly after his Black Sea conquests, perhaps in 109/8 he travelled incognito through Bithynia and even into the province of Asia,

[38] Head 1911 (B 171); 502; 505; Imhoof-Blumer 1912 (B 175); Golenko 1965 (B 162); 1969 (B 163); Karyshovsky 1965 (B 178); Mattingly 1979 (D 283) 1513–15; McGing 1986 (D 35) 94–6; Golenko 1973 (B 164); Shelov 1983 (D 71B); 1982 (D 71A).

[39] Head 1911 (B 171) 501–2; Seltman 1955 (B 237) Pl. 57, 2 and 3; Kraay–Hirmer 1966 (B 182) Pl. 211; Price 1968 (B 221); McGing 1986 (D 35) 97–9.

[40] Just. XXXVII.3.4–5. Appian *Mith.* 13 makes Nicomedes' envoys play on Rome's fear of a powerful Asiatic king getting a foothold in Europe, just as in the case of Antiochus III.

gathering information; not surprisingly he was subsequently believed to have been spying out the land for his wars against Rome, though these were twenty years later.

In 108–107 Mithridates and Nicomedes of Bithynia saw a narrow window of opportunity and marched into Paphlagonia and partitioned it.[41] A Roman embassy ordered them to restore its freedom, but was fobbed off with royal speeches of justification, while Mithridates proceeded to occupy a piece of Galatia as well, which his father was supposed to have inherited from former rulers, and Nicomedes, far from restoring Paphlagonia to its king, installed his own son instead as a puppet ruler: the embassy, having no brief to deal with the veiled or open defiance of the kings, returned to Rome.[42]

Cappadocia is a longer tale. Mithridates had occupied himself with its affairs already, earlier, because his father had intervened there and his sister Laodice was still there as queen of Ariarathes VI, who had ruled since 130 B.C. Some time after 116 Ariarathes was murdered by a Cappadocian noble named Gordius (later, Mithridates was rumoured to have been behind the murder), and his two young sons succeeded to his throne under the tutelage of their mother: some fourteen years passed under that regime,[43] until in about 102 B.C. Nicomedes, no loyal partner in the annexation game, saw fit to send a garrison into Cappadocia and induce Laodice to marry him. Mithridates reacted sharply, expelled the garrisons, and handed the kingdom back to one of his nephews, Ariarathes VII Philometor. Soon, however, we hear that Mithridates was promoting the return of Gordius to Cappadocia and inciting him to add the son's murder to the father's. Ariarathes, warned of the plot, turned to all-out war against his erstwhile benefactor, levying a large Cappadocian army and adding troops from neighbouring kings. Mithridates is said to have invaded Cappadocia with 80,000 infantry, 10,000 cavalry and 600 scythed chariots – hugely exaggerated figures, no doubt, but in any case a battlefield parley and the assassination of the young king removed the need for an engagement (*c.* 101). Mithridates installed his own son as Ariarathes IX, and Gordius was made regent, for the boy was only eight.[44] This puppet regime seems to have lasted some four or five years.

About the time of the battle, or a little before, an embassy from Mithridates went to Rome, apparently attempting to bribe senators to ratify his presence in Paphlagonia and Galatia since 107/6 and to counter

[41] Waddington, Babelon and Reinach 1925 (B 253) 231 no. 40, dated year 190 of the Bithynian era; the palm on the reverse may refer to the victory in Paphlagonia. Paphlagonia: Liebmann-Frankfort 1968 (D 276) 160–3; Olshausen 1972 (D 49) 810–11. [42] Just. XXXVII.4; XXXVIII.7.

[43] Chronology of Cappadocian kings 130–85 B.C. and their regnal years on coins: Mørkholm 1979 (B 208); Coarelli 1982 (B 142). [44] Just. XXXVIII.1.

the more recent claims of Nicomedes and Laodice to joint control of Cappadocia. That is the occasion on which Appuleius Saturninus is said to have been rude to the Pontic envoys and to have been impeached – perhaps really for attacking the king's Roman patrons.[45] And soon C. Marius was to show a predatory interest in the region:[46] he travelled to Asia in 99 or 98, and, in the short way Roman statesmen adopted with foreign kings, is said to have admonished Mithridates 'either to be greater than the Romans or to obey them'.[47]

In about 97 the Cappadocians rebelled against the cruelty of Mithridates' proxy rulers, and called in the brother of the former king from the province of Asia, where he was being educated. Mithridates moved promptly, defeated him and chased him from the kingdom, and the young man died of an illness – at which point Nicomedes played another card in the game, taking up the claims of another young man, said to be a third brother. He sent this pretender, and his wife Laodice, Mithridates' sister, to Rome to testify that her former husband had recognized three legitimate sons. Mithridates counteracted by sending Gordius to Rome to claim that *his* Cappadocian king was a son of the earlier Ariarathes (V) who had aided Rome in the war against Aristonicus. The Senate found all this too tiresome to attempt to unravel, and reacted by ordering Mithridates out of Cappadocia and – perhaps more unexpectedly – Nicomedes out of Paphlagonia:[48] both peoples were to be 'autonomous' and free from taxation. Mithridates did withdraw (and perhaps stepped back from his portion of Paphlagonia at the same time – at least in 89 B.C. he claimed to have done so), and the Cappadocian nobility chose themselves a king, one Ariobarzanes. It was Sulla, the current governor of Cilicia who, on instructions from the Senate, went with a few troops from his province plus some Asiatic levies, and actually established Ariobarzanes in power.[49]

On the other hand, two major developments tipped the balance of power in Asia Minor in favour of Mithridates. In 96 or 95 Tigranes I, 'The Great', succeeded to the throne of Armenia and was happy to ally himself with Mithridates by marrying his daughter Cleopatra:[50] and in 94 Nicomedes of Bithynia died, leaving his kingdom to his son Nicomedes

[45] Diod. XXXVI.15; Badian 1958 (A 1) 287.

[46] Marius' designs: Luce 1970 (C 101). Badian dates them to 98 B.C. 1959 (D 3) 173; Sherwin-White to 99, 1984 (D 291) 108–9.

[47] Plut. *Mar.* 31.2–3.

[48] Aemilius Scaurus was accused of taking bribes, perhaps in connexion with this diplomacy in 97/6 B.C., Val. Max. III.7.8; Ascon. 21C; Badian 1956 (D 2) 120f; 1959 (D 3) 172–3; Marshall 1976 (D 282).

[49] Dated by scholars at 93/2 B.C., 97/6, 95/4. Vell. Pat. II.15.3, Val. Max. V.7 ext. 2, and the Cappadocian regnal years are the main sources. J. Rich, reviewing McGing 1986 (D 35), *JRS* 77 (1987) 244, warns against undue confidence in conclusions from the coinage.

[50] Tigranes' accession date only approximate: Badian 1964 (A 2) 167–8, 176 n. 49. Tigranes as overlord of kings: App. *Syr.* 48; Plut. *Luc.* 21.

IV. In 91/0, Rome being in any case distracted by the Social War, Mithridates urged his new son-in-law to walk into Cappadocia, again using Gordius as agent. At the first appearance of Tigranes' generals Ariobarzanes fled to Rome: Mithridates was rid of a hostile king on his borders without himself making a move. But then, much more provocatively, he expelled the young Nicomedes from Bithynia, after an initial assassination attempt had failed. When the Senate found time it ruled that both the exiled kings were to be restored, and M'. Aquillius, cos. 101, the son of the organizer of the province of Asia, was appointed to lead a commission, along with Manlius Maltinus,[51] to deal with the troublesome monarchs of Pontus and Armenia. So far, in Bithynia Mithridates claimed to be acting for a half-brother of Nicomedes called Socrates Chrestus – in which he probably had as much, or little, right as the older Nicomedes had had in Paphlagonia or he himself in Cappadocia:[52] but that gained him no credit at Rome, even though he still disclaimed direct aggression in Bithynia.

V. THREATS AND BLUFFS

Mithridates was at the height of his power, secure in his alliance with Armenia and in the friendship or even (so his ambassador Pelopidas claimed) alliance of the Arsacid king of Parthia, another 'Mithridates the Great'. With Tigranes he had a division-of-spoils compact: Pontus was to take any conquered cities or territory, Armenia all captives and movables. He called for contingents from his Black Sea dependants and – more hopefully than realistically – from the Cimbri, already a spent force in Gaul: certainly, also, from the nearer Gauls, the Galatians. Far beyond his normal range of activity, he sent to the kings of Syria and Egypt, perhaps rather to secure their friendly neutrality than their active aid. And Memnon says he approached the Medians and Iberians. Rome, by contrast, was still in trouble with the Italians and had to maintain large forces in the Alpine region, Macedonia, Gaul and Spain: no more than five legions could be made available against Mithridates, and then only after much delay.[53]

Yet, after all the impressive preparation, Mithridates again retired from Bithynia in response to Rome's demand: he even had his own Bithynian puppet-ruler, Socrates, put to death.[54] Further, when Aquillius and his colleagues directed a small force drawn from the troops of the province of Asia under Cassius, plus some others from Phrygia and Galatia, towards Armenian-occupied Cappadocia, Tigranes also retreated.

[51] Better, perhaps, Mancinus. There was a third, but his name is garbled, *MRR* II p. 39, n. 19.

[52] Just. XXXVII.4; XXXVIII.2. Bithynia under Nicomedes IV: Vitucci 1953 (D 79) 107–10.

[53] Sherwin-White 1984 (D 291) 126–8.

[54] Just. XXXVIII.5.

But now the Roman protégés in Bithynia and Cappadocia were faced with the bill to the Roman commissioners for their restoration and the repayment of their debts, and neither could do so. The commissioners, making Roman foreign policy on the spot, urged their protégés to recoup their losses and pay their debts by invading Mithridates' own kingdom. Ariobarzanes declined, knowing the vulnerability of his own kingdom to the power of Pontus, but Nicomedes reluctantly drove into Pontic territory as far as Amastris, and, as an economic measure, closed the exit of the Black Sea to ships from Pontus. That pressure put on their clients by the Roman commissioners was the disastrous and fatal miscalculation: they had misread the signs, and had made up their minds that Mithridates was a craven spirit, branded as such by twenty years of backing away from Rome.[55] Mithridates did retire into his own territory, but it was to be for the last time, before he struck back hard at the Roman province. He complained, through his general and envoy Pelopidas, about Nicomedes' action. Rebuffed, he sent his son Ariarathes, fast, into Cappadocia and drove Ariobarzanes out yet again. A second time Pelopidas was sent to the Roman commissioners, and proudly listed the peoples of Mithridates' empire and his allies, adding that even Rome's provinces of Asia, Achaea and Africa might be vulnerable.[56] Those words were taken by Aquillius and his colleagues as threat of war. They had Pelopidas put under close arrest and then sent him back to his master with orders not to return. The First Mithridatic War (or Mithridates' first Roman war) was under way – without, it must be said, the ratification of the Senate and People of Rome.

VI. MITHRIDATES' CONQUEST OF ASIA, 89–88 B.C.

Much of the action probably took place in the campaigning season of 89, Mithridates taking advantage of the war still raging between Rome and the *socii*.[57] Some of the *socii* appealed to him when he was at the height of his success and in control of Asia, but it was already too late for him to give effective aid. His victories in the field in western Pontus and Bithynia, and his occupation of Phrygia, Bithynia and some cities of Ionia, may be assigned to 89. His organization of the coast of Asia (Magnesia, Ephesus, Mytilene), the conquest of outlying areas to north and south (Paphlagonia, Caria, Lycia and Pamphylia), and the massacre

[55] Luce 1970 (C 101) 186f; *contra*, Sherwin-White 1984 (D 291) 119–20. Economic interests of Mancinus (if the name is right): Harris 1979 (A 47) 90; 98 n. 1; 100.

[56] Aristion (Athenion) is alleged to have claimed that Carthaginians were negotiating with Mithridates in 88 B.C. (Ath. V.214A), perhaps actually Numidians.

[57] Historians used to give 88 B.C., based on App. *Mith.* 17 (Olympic year 173); Cic. *De Imp. Cn. Pomp.* 7, for all down to the Asiatic massacre. But see Badian 1976 (D 4) 109–10; Sherwin-White 1977 (D 75) 74 n. 86; 1980 (D 77) 1979–95; 1984 (D 291) 112; 121–7; McGing 1986 (D 35) 108–9.

of the Italians, may reasonably be thought to belong to the spring and summer of 88; and in the autumn he was drawn into the unsuccessful siege of Rhodes, which he had to break off by the early winter. Appian's narrative at this point perhaps reflects the experiences of P. Rutilius Rufus who wrote a history in Greek, while in exile from Rome. During Mithridates' advance and occupation of Asia he fled from Mytilene to find safety with the Smyrnaeans.[58]

M'. Aquillius set about raising troops from Bithynia, exiled Cappadocians, Paphlagonians and Galatians. C. Cassius, the governor of Asia, had his own forces, and Q. Oppius, probably praetor in 89, had another army, mainly of allied troops, on the borders of Lycaonia. Each Roman contingent is said to have comprised 40,000 men.[59] In addition, Nicomedes had a national levy estimated at 50,000 infantry and 6,00 cavalry. The dispositions were defensive, guarding four routes from Pontus into Bithynia and Asia, though these bases, in a semicircle round Pontus and its puppet-regime of Cappadocia, might well turn into launching-points for offensives. Nicomedes was to be based in eastern Paphlagonia, that portion recently ceded by Mithridates; Cassius was to guard the boundary of Bithynia and Galatia; Aquillius stood on Mithridates' line of march into Bithynia, and Oppius was by the foothills of Cappadocia.[60] To strengthen further Nicomedes' hold on the key to the Black Sea, a fleet was posted at Byzantium under Minucius Felix and Popillius Laenas. Total numbers were 176,000 men, not counting the fleet. Against that, Mithridates is said to have had 250,000 infantry and 40,000 cavalry: Memnon says he left Amasia and entered Paphlagonia with an invasion force of 150,000. All the figures are suspicious multiples of 10,000, and undoubtedly exaggerated; Mithridates' fleet, however, did have the potential to dominate the eastern Mediterranean, for he had 300 decked ships plus 100 with two banks of oars; he also had a terror-weapon against enemy infantry in the shape of 130 scythed chariots.

Nicomedes made the first move in the war, from Bithynium (later Claudiopolis) through Paphlagonia into western Pontus, and the first battle took place on a plain by the river Amnias. The Pontic generals, Archelaus and Neoptolemus (brothers, who came perhaps from Sinope or Amisus) caused panic among Nicomedes' infantry with the scythed chariots, and Nicomedes' camp was captured and he fled to the Roman armies, while as yet Mithridates' main arm, the Pontic infantry phalanx, had not even been in action. After the battle Mithridates adopted a magnanimous stance, recalling that of Alexander, by dismissing

58 The end of App. *Mith.* 21 (see also *BCiv.* 1.55) probably marks the end of the campaigning season. Rutilius: Cic. *Rab. Post.* 27; Dio fr. 97.4; Athen. IV.66; Sherwin-White 1984 (D 291) 117–18.

59 There were only a few actual Roman citizens in these armies; *FGrH* 434 22.6 F Memnon; Just. XXXVIII.3.8.

60 Magie 1950 (A 67) II 1093 n. 57 and 1101 n. 26.

prisoners to their homes. It was a pose he was to hold on to on several occasions during the following months, and he could afford it, for in this one day he had destroyed the largest of the armies and the power of his main rival in Asia Minor.

Nicomedes joined M'. Aquillius, who guarded the line of approach from Paphlagonia into Bithynia. Mithridates' army crossed Mount Scorobas into eastern Bithynia; and when a mere 100 of Mithridates' allied Sarmatian cavalry met a regiment of 800 Bithynian horse, Nicomedes' men were again defeated, and he retreated further to join Cassius. The Pontic generals now came upon the nearest of the Roman-led armies, that of Aquillius, at a stronghold called Protopachium in eastern Bithynia. In the Roman defeat that followed Aquillius lost about a quarter of his alleged 40,000 men; 300, probably Asiatic Greeks, who were captured and led before Mithridates, were set free; Aquillius' camp was taken; and Aquillius fled by night back to Pergamum, the seat of the governor of Asia. Further south, Cassius had taken in Nicomedes, and perhaps had the other commissioners with him: they occupied a fortress in Phrygia called Leontoncephalae, thus falling back into the *provincia* too, if not so far. There they spent some time drilling their ill-assorted troops, but gave up in disgust and retreated even further, Nicomedes betaking himself to Pergamum, having given up hope of retaining Bithynia. Although Cassius still had his army he obviously had little faith in it, in spite of help from Chaeremon of Nysa; he fell back to the Aegean coast and crossed to Rhodes. The Roman fleet that was sealing the Bosporus straits dispersed after the news of Mithridates' victories, and the latter's 400 ships had free passage into the Propontis and the Aegean.

The king in person now made a progress through Bithynia, and moved on to occupy Phrygia, Mysia to the north of Pergamum, and the nearby Roman-administered areas. The take-over proceeded quietly and quickly: officers were despatched to receive the submission of outlying Lycia and Pamphylia, and of Ionia, where the chief Greek cities of Roman Asia lay. Caria, at least, offered more resistance. Oppius had fallen back into the city of Laodicea, where he had time to seek, and obtain, reinforcements from Aphrodisias;[61] so at Laodicea Mithridates met his first threat of organized resistance since entering the Roman province – which he met by proclaiming an amnesty to the citizens if they would surrender Oppius. The Laodiceans handed Oppius over in mock formality, preceded by his lictors, and Mithridates kept him in his entourage in some style as a captured Roman general and later set him free, whereupon Oppius made his way to Cos. Cassius was safe in Rhodes. Aquillius, the main culprit, suffered the worst fate. He, too, abandoned the mainland of Asia for Lesbos, but was handed over by the

[61] Chaeremon: *SIG* 741; Aphrodisias: Reynolds 1982 (B 226) 1–4; 11–20 nos. 2 and 3.

citizens of Mytilene. Mithridates had him tied to an ass and put him up to public ridicule, wearing a placard; and eventually, hauled back to Pergamum, he was to die through having molten gold poured down his throat, in mockery of the avarice that had brought on the war.[62]

Mithridates' campaign in Asia Minor had been totally successful. Four armies had either been defeated or had disintegrated. Rome's forty-year-old administration of Asia had collapsed. Many cities welcomed Mithridates, especially tax-paying communities and those where Roman and Italian money-lenders had been most active. Mithridates set about appointing satraps in western Asia, underlining his claims to a Persian heritage, and *episcopi*, 'overseers', in many cities. In a bid for popularity he remitted taxes for a five-year period and cancelled debts owed by states and private persons: being now in control of the wealth of Bithynia and the revenues of Asia he was able to make an early and impressive show of that *philanthropia* which was an important part of his programme and befitted the son of Euergetes.[63] One can understand the current of good will in certain cities, Delos, even Chios and Rhodes, on which he might hope to capitalize. On the other hand, cities that had privileged status in relation to Rome, such as Ilium, Chios, Rhodes and the Lycian cities, might be expected, in spite of all, to stick to Rome and their own interest. At Stratonicea near the coast of Caria Mithridates placed a garrison and imposed a fine, showing something of the iron fist he had so far kept hidden in Asia. His generals were delegated to deal with outlying areas, to the far south in Lycia and to the north in Mithridates' rear, where Pylaemenes may have been acting as a focus of resistance in his homeland of Paphlagonia. At Magnesia (probably the Carian one on the Maeander) resistance was offered, and Archelaus was wounded. Tabae in Caria and Patara and Telmessus in Lycia subsequently recorded their loyalty to Rome: Termessus also, remote on the western extremity of Pamphylia, stayed firm and some Pamphylian cities supplied ships to Lucullus in 86/5 B.C. Sanctuary was offered to Romans on Cos for a while, but soon Mithridates took that island over also. There he gained a hostage, in a son of Ptolemy Alexander, and Egyptian treasures, possibly including 800 talents raised by Jews for the Jerusalem Temple.[64]

Meanwhile, perhaps in the autumn of 89, news of Mithridates'

62 App. *Mith.* 21; Pliny *HN* XXXIII.48. But McGing 1980 (D 32) argues for confusion of father, cos. 129 B.C., with son. Gran. Lic. (XXXV. p. 27 Flemisch; *Greenidge–Clay* 187) describes Sulla asking for the return of Aquillius in 85 B.C.

63 Diod. XXXVII.26, Just. XXXVIII.3. *Philanthropia*: Glew 1977 (D 17); McGing 1986 (D 35) 109–10. Mithridates' letter: Welles 1934 (B 258) 295, nos. 73–4; his repair of earthquake damage at Apamea: Strabo XII.8.18.

64 Mithridates' Athenian supporters adorned Delos with a Heroön, Gross 1954 (D 21); Bruneau–Ducat 1965 (B 265) 140. See also *I Délos* 2039. Victories of Mithridates at Chios and Rhodes in equestrian games (not in person): Robert 1960 (B 231) 345, n. 4.

victories, and the collapse of Roman rule in Asia, reached Rome, still preoccupied with internal dissensions and the severe war against the allies. Senate and People declared war on Mithridates,[65] but steps to deal with the eastern crisis were implemented only slowly (ch. 6, pp. 166–73). When the command against Mithridates was given to L. Cornelius Sulla it took him some eighteen months to assemble five legions and to feel secure enough about the political situation he was leaving behind him in Rome (and he was, of course, wrong about that). And financially, Rome was in dire straits: the so-called 'Treasures of Numa' were in part sold off to support the coming war.

And now occurred the high point of horror, probably in the first half of 88: the 'Asiatic (or 'Ephesian') Vespers', in which 80,000 (less credibly 150,000) Roman and Italian expatriates were massacred in the cities of Asia.[66] Mithridates wrote secretly to all regional satraps and overseers of cities that, on the thirtieth day after the day of writing, they should have all Italian residents in their communities killed, along with their wives and children and any freedmen of Italian birth, and have their corpses cast out unburied. Mithridates offered freedom to slaves who killed or informed on their Italian masters, and relief of half their debt to any who dealt similarly with their creditors. His treasury would share the property of the victims half-and-half with their assassins or informers. The response from many Greek cities was enthusiastic, displaying as much their hatred of the Roman and Italian expatriates as their fear of Mithridates: Ephesus, temporarily his residence, Pergamum, Adramyttium, Tralles and Caunus were all the scene of atrocities. Mithridates' order was surely a calculated response to the news of Rome's declaration of war: besides exploiting the widespread unpopularity of the westerners, it ensured that no city that did his bidding now could ever hope to be received back into Roman allegiance. Many of the Asian cities were by now under 'tyrants', such as Philopoemen, *episcopus* at Ephesus; others are known at Adramyttium, Apollonis, Colophon and Tralles. The social divisions characteristic of the ancient city helped to produce these changes of local regime, to which Mithridates' present power in Asia was the spur. It was now the time for pro-Roman councillors and their sympathizers among the well-to-do to suffer for their real or perceived abuses; and Rome's own representatives, the governors and the *publicani*, were held responsible for the prevailing climate of

[65] Keaveney 1982 (C 87) 56–76; 1987 (C 94) 144. The last occasion on which the Roman assembly passed a vote for war? Rich 1976 (A 95) 14; 17; *contra*, Harris 1979 (A 47) 263.

[66] Sarikakis 1976 (D 65). Badian 1976 (D 4) 110–11, dates the massacre somewhat before the middle of 88, Sherwin-White 1980 (D 77) puts it in winter 89/88. The numbers probably exaggerated: Dio fr. 109.8, believed that the mutual pogroms of Marius and Sulla were far worse. Magie 1950 (A 67) I 216; Brunt 1971 (A 16) 224–7.

aggressive greed (*pleonexia*) and acquisitiveness (*philokerdia*), and for encouraging the evils of malicious litigation.[67]

Mithridates was now master of all western Asia Minor. He was hailed as the preserver of Asia, and a new era was proclaimed, upon the liberation of the cities from Rome, which lasted from 88 to 85 B.C. A short but splendid series of tetradrachms was issued from Pergamum,[68] and now, too, Mithridates could claim his Hellenistic and Iranian titles as overlord: *megas*, 'Great' and *basileus basileon*, 'King of Kings'. The latest holder of that Persian title, Mithridates II of Parthia, had died, and our Mithridates was now king over many vassals.[69]

VII. OVERREACH

It was tempting to push further into the Aegean and into Macedonia and Greece: it was also politic, and not obviously overreach, to strike into Europe before Rome collected a consular army under competent commanders: C. Sentius, the Roman commander in Macedonia, with only two legions, was kept fully occupied by Thracian tribes. Mithridates had large, victorious armies and command of the sea; all that was needed was an invitation to intervene, and that was to be forthcoming from anti-Roman parties at Athens, and to elicit first moral backing and then military support for pro-Mithridatic tyrants at Delos and Athens. But first he must deal with Rhodes, his only possible remaining challenger in the Aegean and the main remaining haven for Romans and Italians.[70]

In autumn 88, knowing what must come, the Rhodians strengthened their walls, constructed artillery against besiegers, and called in aid from the Lycians and the Telmessians. On Mithridates' approach they withdrew inside the harbour, closed their gates, and prepared to fight from the walls. Mithridates tried to enter the harbour but failed, and sat to await the arrival of his main-line infantry. When intervening skirmishes brought some advantage to them the Rhodians grew bolder: on two occasions sections of their fleet came off best, and then, when Mithridates' expected land forces set sail from Caunus they were scattered by a storm, and the Rhodians capitalized on the confusion to capture, ram and burn scattered ships and took 400 prisoners. Mithri-

67 *Orac. Sibyll.* III.350–5; Cic. *De Imp. Cn. Pomp.* 7; *Flac.* 60–1; Diod. XXXVII.5; Just. XXXVIII.7.8; App. *Mith.* 16; 21; 56. Dio fr. 101. Tyrants: Strab. XIII.1.66; XIV.1.42; App. *Mith.* 48: Plut. *Luc.* 3.4.

68 For coins dated by the new Asiatic era of Pergamum see Reinach 1888 (B 224) 195; Kraay–Hirmer 1966 (B 182) 377, no. 774.

69 Golenko and Karyszkovski 1972 (B 165) 29 n. 2; Karyshkovsky 1985 (D 25) 572–9; Yailenko 1985 (B 261) 617–19; Vinogradov, Molyev and Tolstikov 1985 (B 252) 596–9.

70 Diod. XXXVII.28; Reinach 1890 (D 55) 144–7; Magie 1950 (A 67) I 218–19.

dates, while preparing for another naval engagement, pressed on with the investment of the city. He had a structure built, on two ships fixed alongside, which served as a huge bridge fitted with catapults, to assist the scaling of the walls. It was nicknamed *sambuca*, probably after a triangular four-stringed instrument favoured by Rhodian musicians.[71] The huge device caused great alarm amongst the Rhodians, but in the event it collapsed under its own weight. Finally, Mithridates gave up the attempt to take the city and sailed off to the mainland, where he laid siege to Patara in Lycia, but failed to take that, either. Psychological warfare at once exploited the dent in his prestige resulting from the two failed sieges: religious propaganda began to be heard. The goddess Isis had been observed hurling fire from her temple upon the *sambuca*, and at Patara Mithridates had had a dream warning him not to cut down the sacred trees in the grove of Latona to make siege engines. He left Pelopidas to pursue the war against the Lycians, and applied himself to raising more troops in Asia Minor. He also conducted trials of people accused of plotting against him or considered to have pro-Roman sympathies – a further presage of the growth of opposition.

VIII. ATHENS, DELOS AND ACHAEA

Athens had not remained unaffected by the stirring events in Asia, and an envoy to Mithridates was found in the politician Aristion,[72] whose return was received with rejoicing at Athens by anti-Roman elements (in, perhaps, late spring, 88 B.C.). According to Athenaeus they were the 'mob' and according to Pausanias the 'turbulent element', but the apologia for Athens in Velleius and Plutarch, that the city was compelled by force to collaborate with Mithridates' generals, rings very hollow.[73] Aristion had himself elected *strategos epi ton hoplon*, 'magistrate in charge of the arms', and appointed colleagues and archons: some opposing aristocrats were killed and their property confiscated.[74] Philo, head of the Academy, escaped to Rome, with other important persons.[75]

A naval adventure was staged by this regime to try to seize Delos, the old possession of Athens, and install one Apellicon (another philosopher, said to be Peripatetic) as puppet-ruler in Aristion's interest, but it

[71] Marsden 1971 (A 70) 90–4; 1969 (A 70) 108–9.

[72] So named on the coins and in all literary sources except Athenaeus (from Posidonius), who calls him Athenion and makes him a Peripatetic. An old, unresolved crux.

[73] Strab. IX.1.20; Ath. V.212C; 213C; Paus. I.20.5; Vell. Pat. II.23; Plut. *Sulla* 12. Aristion coupled with Nabis and Catiline: Plut. *Mor.* 809C.

[74] But some upper-class support for Aristion: Dow 1947 (D 13); Laffranque 1962 (B 61).

[75] Cic. *Brut.* 306. Epicureans and Peripatetics may have hated the Athenian and the Roman establishment: Zeller 1923 (H 138) III 1, 386; Badian 1976 (D 4) 514–15; Candiloro 1965 (D 258) 158–71; Deininger 1971 (D 10) 245.

failed, because a Roman prefect, Orbius, with a few ships, plus the strong Italian merchant presence, was able to stiffen resolve there.[76] However, the naval fortress of the Piraeus, the ship-sheds with their space for hundreds of warships, and the actual navy of Athens, were on offer to Mithridates. Before long, the fleet of Mithridates' general Archelaus took Delos with overwhelming force and restored it and other strong points to Athens' control: there were put to death some 20,000 opponents of what was becoming known as the 'Cappadocian Faction' in the Aegean.[77] The sacred treasure of Delos was sent under guard to Athens to bolster the prestige of Aristion's regime, and 2,000 troops were sent to ensure its security.[78] The time of Archelaus' naval advance was probably late summer to autumn of 88. Part of his fleet made for Piraeus, but a contingent under Metrophanes split from it after Delos, destined for the ports of central Greece.

The states of southern and central Greece reacted variously. The Achaeans and the Spartans went over to Mithridates easily, as did Boeotia, except for Thespiae, which had to be besieged. Metrophanes' army had less success on Euboea, at the stronghold of Demetrias, and against the Magnesians, who resisted firmly. One reason for that was the presence of Bruttius Sura,[79] a legate of C. Sentius, the governor of Macedonia. He played a vital role in holding up the Pontic advance during the autumn and winter of 88/7, buying time for the arrival of Sulla's consular army, which eventually arrived in Greece in spring 87. With his small force Bruttius made naval raids on the island of Sciathus and perhaps on Piraeus itself. He ruthlessly crucified recaptured slaves and cut off the hands of the free-born, as an earnest of Rome's reaction to rebellious Greeks. He won a small naval victory, in which two Pontic ships were captured and their crews put to death; and receiving another 1,000 infantry and cavalry he fought a series of actions over three days near Chaeronea in which he came off on equal terms with the joint forces of Aristion and Archelaus – but his run of success was halted when Spartans and Achaeans turned up to their aid. Archelaus, whose forces were probably not yet as large as they were to become, pulled back to Athens and Piraeus, retaining Euboea as a safe base for his army and sheltering behind the protecting fleet. Bruttius Sura's reward for his services from Sulla's quaestor L. Lucullus, in the vanguard of the approaching army, was to be brusquely ordered back to Macedonia to join Sentius and leave the business of Mithridates to the new appointee.

[76] Strab. x.5.4; Ath. v.214D. The Pontic general Menophanes on Delos: Paus. III.23.5.

[77] The 'Kappadokizontes', App. *Mith.* 53 and 61. Mithridates was 'the Cappadocian', Cic. *Flac.* 61; Ath. v.215B.

[78] Coin hoards on Delos reflecting its fate at this time: Hackens and Lévy 1965 (B 295).

[79] Brettius in the Greek literary sources, Braitios in the inscriptions, *IG* IX.2.613; Plassart 1949 (B 219) 831.

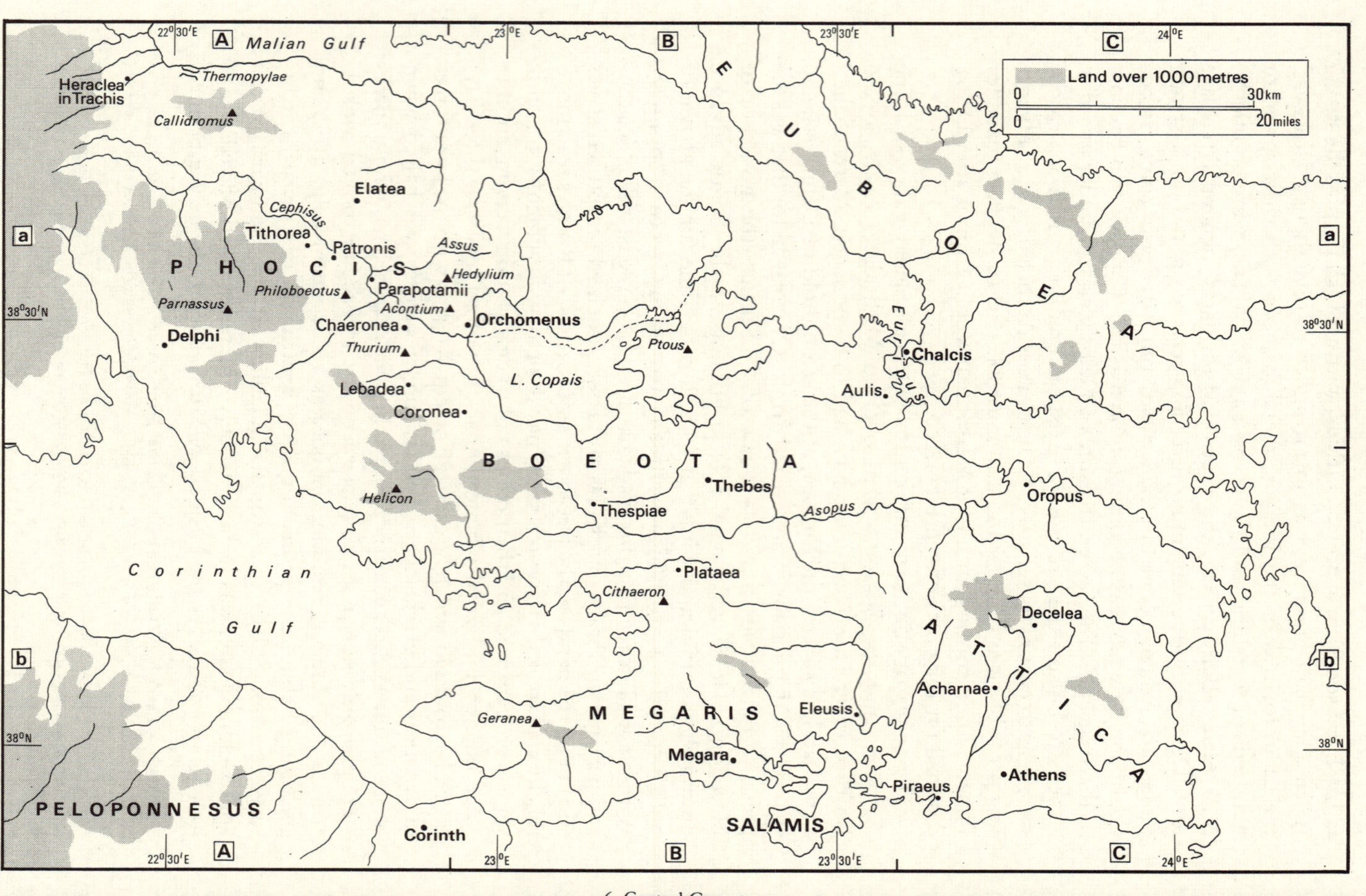

Land over 1000 metres
0 30 km
0 20 miles
22°30′E
23°E
23°30′E
24°E
38°30′N
38°N
A
B
C
a
b
Malian Gulf
Thermopylae
Heraclea in Trachis
Callidromus
Elatea
Cephisus
Tithorea
Patronis
Assus
PHOCIS
Hedylium
Philoboeotus
Parapotamii
Parnassus
Acontium
Delphi
Chaeronea
Orchomenus
Thurium
Ptous
L. Copais
Lebadea
Coronea
BOEOTIA
Thebes
Helicon
Thespiae
Asopus
Corinthian Gulf
Plataea
Cithaeron
Geranea
MEGARIS
Eleusis
Megara
PELOPONNESUS
Corinth
SALAMIS
Piraeus
Athens
Acharnae
Decelea
ATTICA
Oropus
Aulis
Chalcis
Euripus
EUBOEA

IX. THE SIEGES OF ATHENS AND PIRAEUS

Early in 87 B.C. Sulla with his five legions left Italy for Greece. He is first found in Thessaly, summoning provisions, reinforcements and money from Thessaly and Aetolia. He approached Attica through Boeotia, where most of the cities, headed by Thebes, returned to Roman allegiance; and on his arrival he was faced with conducting two sieges independently but simultaneously. Aristion and his supporters were shut up in the city of Athens from autumn 87 until 1 March 86, and in their redoubt on the Acropolis for several weeks after that. Separate from them, no longer linked to the city by the Long Walls,[80] was Piraeus, easily provisioned from the sea and so the obvious place for Archelaus to keep his garrison of Pontic troops. (The two main sources, Plutarch and Appian, oddly concentrate each on a different one of these related, but separate, sieges.) Sulla's greater effort and personal participation were directed against the strategically more important Piraeus. Twice he retired to Eleusis and Megara, largely because of lack of timber and other materials for siege engines: twice, unsuccessfully, Archelaus, himself closely beleaguered, tried to get supplies through to Athens city, where some of the defenders were reduced, it was said, to cannibalism. The Pontic troops in Piraeus were better off, because supplies, and reinforcements, arrived from Mithridates; but, to offset that, a Pontic army was defeated, with the loss of 1,500 men, by a northern detachment of Sulla's forces near Chalcis, just as Archelaus' intended aid to Athens was being cut off. The siege of Piraeus settled into a tough phase of building, mining, countermining and fighting in underground tunnels; the besieged kept Sulla at bay, and when he returned to Eleusis in the winter he had to protect his camp against cavalry raids.

Mithridates' command of the sea was still undisputed, and so was his ability to supply his strongpoints in Euboea and Piraeus. Sulla had no navy, to speak of, but he had control over north-west and central Greece, where it was in his interest to provoke a major land battle. The impasse lasted into the spring of 86. In an attempt to break it Sulla sent Lucullus, early in winter 87, to collect a fleet from naval powers as far away as Syria and Egypt, the Rhodians being in no position to help. For his part, Mithridates, contrariwise, determined to win land superiority in Greece, and sent a great army, under his son Arcathias, overland into Greece via Thrace and Macedonia. The small Roman army in Macedonia was overcome, and by spring 86 Arcathias' army, probably the largest ever sent by Mithridates even after it had left garrisons at Philippi and Amphipolis, was in Magnesia in north-east Greece. It was the trump

80 In ruins at this time and used to refurbish the fortifications of the city and the port, Livy XXXI.26; Paus. I.2.2.

card to win the war in Greece for Mithridates while Sulla's forces were divided between Athens, Piraeus and garrison duty opposite Euboea and in other towns in central Greece.

The besiegers of Athens city now had a lucky break. Indiscreet talk within informed them of a weak point in the defences, by the Heptachalcum between the western and Dipylon gates, and an attack was directed there. The Athenians were sapped also by dire famine, and the tyrant Aristion had become more and more unpopular and isolated. On 1 March they surrendered the main city to Sulla's troops: Aristion and his followers went up to the Acropolis, burning the Odeum in order to deny its materials to Sulla's forces. There was much destruction in the main city, though total burning was forbidden by Sulla in recognition of Athens' glorious past; and when the followers of Aristion finally gave up the Acropolis, many weeks later, at about the time of the battle of Chaeronea, they were summarily executed. Some forty pounds of gold and six hundred of silver fell into the hands of Sulla's legate, Curio.

Meanwhile, the siege of Piraeus was being pressed ever harder by Sulla: the groves of the Academy and Lyceum were cut for siege timbers and he took the temple treasures of Epidaurus, Delphi and Olympia.[81] Archelaus conducted a stout defence, but after losing 2,000 troops in a battle outside the *enceinte*, where he had ventured, he finally came to the decision to evacuate and, sailing off northwards, made contact with the northern army, flushed with successes in Thrace and Macedonia but commanded no longer by Arcathias, who had died of illness at Tisaeum in Magnesia; in fact, when the armies met at Thermopylae the overall command passed to Archelaus. Piraeus, abandoned, was destroyed by Sulla, and the arsenal of Philo burnt.

X. THE BATTLES IN BOEOTIA

The summer that followed the sieges of Athens and Piraeus saw two major battles, close to one another in both space and time. Our sources are Plutarch and Appian, with Plutarch, a native of Chaeronea, offering the fuller account of the battle in his city's territory. Both sources give only a brief sketch of the second battle, fought some weeks later at Orchomenus.[82] Chronology, strategy, numbers, tactics are all subject to doubts and variant interpretations. Chaeronea was fought in the early summer at about the same time as the surrender of the Acropolis, and Orchomenus in the high summer, before the autumn rains.[83] The total of

[81] H. A. Thompson 1934 (B 320) 394; 1937 (B 321) 223–4; D. B. Thompson 1937 (B 319) 411; Young 1951 (B 324) 155; 183; 262–3; Ervin 1958 (B 289). Temple treasures: Paus. IX.7.5.

[82] Sulla's memoirs were amongst the material available to Plutarch and Appian.

[83] Reinach 1890 (D 55) 168–76; Ormerod. *CAH* IX[1] 244–54; Sherwin-White 1984 (D 291) 139–40.

the original Pontic army is given by Appian as 120,000 men: Memnon is much more modest, saying 60,000, but the late writers Eutropius and Orosius agree with the higher estimate, and that some 110,000 were lost at Chaeronea.[84] Weeks later, with a new army of 80,000 incorporated into his surviving force, Archelaus lost almost the whole army at Orchomenus – a further 90,000 (i.e. he had no effective army left). Sulla's calculation, in 85 B.C., of Mithridates' total losses was 160,000, more modest than the implications of Plutarch and Appian. In any case, all the figures are exaggerated, because units were counted at their paper sizes – and casualties probably likewise reckoned by corps lost rather than corpses counted. Numbers on the Roman side were apparently minimized by Sulla: he seems to have reported that he had at Chaeronea only 15,000 infantry and 1,500 cavalry, of whom only fourteen or fifteen were missing, and two of those turned up by the evening! But others may have been engaged separately at Thurium and by the city of Chaeronea itself. It is usually believed that most of Sulla's five legions were at Chaeronea at least in the wider sense, which would make some 30,000 Romans, to which must be added some Macedonians and local Greeks: Appian says that the forces of Archelaus outnumbered the Romans by three to one, which would make Sulla's total army at Chaeronea about 40,000.[85]

One respect in which the Pontic forces most undoubtedly outnumbered the Roman was cavalry, and Archelaus' strategy was determined by the nature of his now very large army, whose cavalry contingent required plains, such as those of Macedonia and Thessaly, or, at the most southerly, those of Phocis and Boeotia. If he did lose control of the plains of central Greece he had in mind a retreat eastwards to Aulis and, from there, the crossing into Euboea, under the protection of the fleet. But at the time when the two armies were coming close to contact Archelaus was actually moving into Phocis, in a dangerous move to cut off an isolated Roman brigade to his north.

Sulla's strategy had taken him out of Attica. He was criticized in his own camp for transferring the war to central Greece, but in reality he had no option. He had an army which he believed could beat that of Pontus in the field, but the land of Attica was poor, and exhausted by his long presence there during the sieges: his troops needed the relative prosperity of Boeotia and Phocis for supplies. Most urgent of all was the need to link up with the brigade, of some 6,000 men, commanded by Hortensius, which was stranded in Thessaly and likely to be cut off by Archelaus. Hortensius did manage to join Sulla by crossing one of the passes unnoticed by the Pontic commanders, and met Sulla's main force at Patronis. It was a welcome addition: Hortensius was a vigorous and

[84] Eutropius v.6.3; Oros. vi.2.5.

[85] App. *Mith.* 41; *BCiv.* 1.79.

resourceful officer, and Sulla's men were spared the panic that might have been caused by the loss of their comrades in a separate engagement.

The first actions and counteractions of the two armies now took place on the plain of Elatea at Philoboeotus.[86] The Pontic generals offered battle, but Sulla declined several times because of their superiority in numbers, and kept his men digging earthworks. However, after the three days thus occupied, his troops besought him for something more interesting to do, so he set them the task of seizing an isolated steep hill, the acropolis of Parapotamii, to the south of Archelaus' camp. The successful Roman occupation of this strongpoint at once made Archelaus' position in the plain of Elatea impossible, so he struck camp and moved south-eastwards towards Chaeronea, in the direction of Aulis, Chalcis and the coast. The folk of Chaeronea begged for Roman help for their city, and Sulla sent his legate Gabinius with a legion, which reached the city even before the deputation got back. Sulla likewise moved south-eastwards across the river Assus and settled near Mt Hedylium, while Archelaus' position was between Mt Hedylium and Mt Acontium. Archelaus' move had in fact been a disastrous one: he was in an area that was rocky and cramped and gave no scope to his cavalry. It was the sign for Sulla now to work for a decisive engagement.

For one day Sulla waited, and then, leaving another legate, Murena, with a legion and two cohorts to face Archelaus, moved towards Chaeronea. Through Gabinius he got two citizens of Chaeronea to lead a small contingent of his men along a hill-track to a part of Thurium hill above the point where the Pontic detachment already stood; and then he drew up his own battle-line on the plain, with himself on the right and Murena on the left. Presently the men of Chaeronea and Sulla's detachment surmounted the track over Thurium and appeared above the Pontic troops: they caused great panic, and Archelaus' men rushed down the hill, badly upsetting the dispositions of the main force below. When Archelaus at last got his battle-line drawn up he sent into attack a cavalry force, which had little effect, and then the weapons of terror, the scythed chariots. But scythed chariots were only practically effective at a gallop or canter, and without momentum were easily neutralized. Sulla's men allowed the slowly lumbering things to pass through open lanes in the ranks; they jogged harmlessly by, to Roman jeers, and their crews were despatched by javelins from behind. When the main battle-lines joined, the Pontic phalanx yielded only slowly and there was much tactical movement; but ultimately the Romans pushed the phalanx back to the river Cephisus and towards Mt Acontium. Archelaus' troops were killed in huge numbers on the plain, and even more in the flight across the

[86] Hammond 1938 (D 23) with differences in detail from Kromayer 1907 (A 58) 353f, followed by Ormerod *CAH* IX[1] 249–52.

stony ground to their camp, because at first he excluded them, trying to rally them to fight, and only as a last resort admitted the survivors. Archelaus made off eastwards to the coast with, it was said, only 10,000 left of his great army.

Sulla was master of the field, even though he still had no means of finishing Archelaus off because of his continuing lack of a fleet: he had demonstrated his, and Rome's, superiority to the mightiest army Mithridates could assemble, led by a first-rate general. From the field he dashed with some light troops to the coast to try to deny Archelaus the crossing of the Euripus, but failed; so he marched back to central Greece to deal harshly with the Thebans, handing over half their territory to the sanctuaries to recompense the gods for the moneys he had taken himself for his sieges. In Athens, he took over from Curio the recent followers of Aristion; them he executed, Aristion he kept alive for the moment, and the Athenians in general were graciously allowed their liberty.[87] Meanwhile, Archelaus, from his base at Chalcis, was far from inactive: his fleet raided up and down the coasts of Greece, reaching Zacynthus, and destroyed some of the transports conveying the advance guard of the new Roman army under Flaccus sent by the government of Cinna.

From his base in southern Greece Sulla heard that Flaccus' army had landed and was on its way eastwards, nominally against the armies of Pontus but in fact to supersede him if he did not co-operate. He set off towards Thessaly to meet them, but, while at Melitaea in Phthiotis, heard that the lands behind him, Boeotia particularly, were being ravaged by a reassembled Mithridatic army – the rump of Archelaus' army plus a brigade of 80,000 led by Dorylaus, freshly arrived in Chalcis. So he turned south to fight his second great battle of the summer; and it was Archelaus who opted for a deciding battle on the same scale as at Chaeronea,[88] and chose the ground, by Orchomenus some 10 kilometres east of Chaeronea in the largest plain in Boeotia, eminently suited to his cavalry. Less favourably, however, the river Cephisus debouched into Lake Copais and its marshes and the short but navigable river Melas flowed by Orchomenus and also lost itself in the marshes.

Sulla accepted the challenge, a strategy that might at first have seemed an error. But he now put to good use the entrenching skills he had made the troops practise before Chaeronea. First, they dug a series of three-metre-wide ditches across the plain to contain the Pontic cavalry and hem Archelaus' troops in to the eastern, marshy end of the plain. The two armies drew their battle-lines quite close to each other. Archelaus' cavalry charged in force to sweep away the digging-parties, and nearly

[87] Gran. Lic. 24F (*Greenidge–Clay* p. 182); Paus. I.20.5: Strab. IX.I.20.

[88] Mommsen assigned Orchomenus to 85 B.C., but see Magie 1950 (A 67) II 1107 n. 47; Sherwin-White 1984 (D 291) 140 n. 32.

succeeded.[89] All depended, for Sulla, on containing those cavalry: he seized his sword (or a standard) and rallied his men on foot,[90] and two cohorts from the right wing, and his own escort, stabilized the danger area. After that turning-point the Romans won a decisive victory, even against a renewed cavalry attack. Meanwhile, Sulla's trenches had hemmed in Archelaus' main army so narrowly that in the closing phases of the action some Pontic archers had no room to draw bow and were reduced to stabbing with their arrows. Archelaus' men spent the night pent up in their fortifications together with the dead and wounded; and next day Sulla resumed the process of penning them in with entrenchments now no more than 200 metres from the camp. In a battle outside the camp to try to break this final investment the Pontic troops were defeated, and the camp fell. There followed total disaster for Archelaus' men: they were pursued and slaughtered, they lost their way in the marshes and were drowned. The commander himself hid in the marshes for two days, and then escaped in a boat, making his way to Chalcis.

All that Archelaus was able to collect from the wreckage of Mithridates' armies in Europe was a scattered detachment or two that had not been at Orchomenus. Sulla now turned to ravaging Boeotia, especially the coastal towns opposite Euboea, in revenge for their continual changes of sides: he then intended to turn once more northwards to Thessaly, to confront Flaccus. Before he left Boeotia, however, he learnt that Archelaus wanted an interview with him. Archelaus was treating from much the weaker position, to be sure, and although Mithridates had probably authorized these diplomatic moves his general could not be sure of their reception by the king. In the event Sulla and Archelaus reached a cordial agreement on terms, which were indeed then not fully acceptable to Mithridates, but which his deteriorating position in Asia over 86 and 85 B.C. was eventually to force him to underwrite. The terms were that Mithridates was to give up Asia and Paphlagonia and to hand back Bithynia to Nicomedes and Cappadocia to Ariobarzanes. He was to hand over seventy (or eighty) ships fully equipped to Sulla, plus a war indemnity of 2,000 (or 3,000) talents. In return Sulla would guarantee Mithridates his rule in Pontus and the rest of his territories, and secure for him the status of an ally of Rome. These terms remained on offer for some months, but Sulla did not waver in the demands he made. Meanwhile, Archelaus became his personal friend and stayed in his camp, was promised 2,500 hectares of land in Euboea, and was spoken of as a 'friend and ally of the Roman people' – a fate notably better than that of his personal enemy Aristion, who had now been executed by poison. Sulla marched north to Thessaly to winter, build ships, and await the arrival of Lucullus' fleet garnered from Cyprus, Phoenicia and Pamphy-

[89] Frontin. *Str.* II.3.17; Plut. *Sulla* 21.

[90] Frontin. *Str.* II.8.12; Amm. Marc. XVI.12.41.

lia: the seventy ships of Archelaus in Greece were detained as the first part of Sulla's demands or as the core of an invasion fleet if Mithridates should fail to accept the terms.

XI. REACTION IN ASIA, 86 B.C.

After Chaeronea, Mithridates met with increasing unrest amongst his new subject-allies of Asia. He had already harboured suspicions: sixty nobles from the cantons of Galatia had been lodged in Pergamum as hostages: now, they and their families were killed, some arrested by a stratagem and some slaughtered at an evening banquet. Three survivors fled to organize rebellion in Galatia. In Ionia, Mithridates resolved to deal finally with Chios, whose citizens he had suspected of disloyalty ever since some Chiots had collided with his flagship at the siege of Rhodes. What now followed was a warning to all the states of Asia of what would happen if Mithridates held them suspect. He had already demanded the confiscation of the property of Chiots who had fled to Sulla: now his general Zenobius seized the walls, disarmed the citizens and sent the children of the most prominent to Erythrae as hostages. In a bitter letter he listed his grievances against the Chiots and imposed a fine of 2,000 talents. They collected temple ornaments and the women's jewellery and paid up, but were accused of delivering short measure. They were led out of the theatre where they had been assembled, men, women and children, to be deported by ship to Mithridates' power base on the Black Sea. (This Achaemenid-style deportation was actually aborted by the people of Heraclea Pontica, who freed many of the Chiots when they reached the Black Sea.) The Ephesians then openly revolted, cancelling debts and taking other measures to maintain political unity, though they should have been a stronghold of the 'Cappadocian Faction', and other cities as far north as Smyrna and south as Tralles followed suit. Mithridates sent an army to reduce those in revolt – Colophon, Ephesus, Hypaepa, Metropolis, Sardis – and take terrible vengeance on those captured. In an attempt to stave off further desertions he proclaimed freedom for cities still loyal, cancellation of debts, citizenship for resident foreigners and freedom to slaves;[91] but defections continued. Four former supporters in Smyrna and on Lesbos formed a conspiracy, which one of them betrayed to Mithridates: the king himself is said to have overheard the final session at which the plot was hatched, hiding under a couch. The conspirators were tortured and executed. Further inquiries implicated another eighty

[91] Chiots: Ath. VI.266; revolt: App. *Mith.*48; Oros. VI.2.8. Ephesus: *SIG* 742. Mithridates is not likely to have sympathized with the lower orders beyond his political interest: de Ste Croix 1981 (A 100) 525; Magie 1950 (A 67) I 222–6; McGing 1986 (D 35) 126–30. Nor did the whole of the lower orders support him: Bernhardt 1985 (A 10) 33–64.

citizens of Pergamum, and denunciations spread into other cities. The total killed in this witch hunt for Roman sympathizers was 1,600. (On the other hand, the following year those who had sided with the 'Cappadocians' were killed, committed suicide, or fled to Mithridates in Pontus.) Some time late in 86 or early in 85 Cos and Cnidus defected from Mithridates, on the appearance of Lucullus with a fleet: Rhodes added its ships to those of Lucullus, and, sailing up the coast of Ionia, they drove the 'Cappadocian Faction' out of Colophon and Chios. Mithridates' cherished mastery of the sea was now under challenge.

The wild card in the Roman pack was the consular army of Flaccus, sent by Sulla's enemies in Rome. It had marched across Epirus and Macedonia and Thrace to Byzantium, but Flaccus had acquired a reputation for greed, harshness and unfairness, and there were desertions and indiscipline. C. Flavius Fimbria, usually thought to have been Flaccus' *legatus*,[92] seized the fasces and drove Flaccus off, with the support of the troops: the repulsed commander hid ignominiously in a house and then fled to Chalcedon and on to Nicomedia, where he found refuge within the walls, but Fimbria pursued him even there and had him dragged out of a well, where he was hiding, and beheaded. Fimbria appointed himself commander of the consul's army, and was in due time recognized as such by Cinna's regime in Rome: they needed a vigorous commander – and they had got one.

From such unpromising beginnings this Roman army, now under a competent, however literally 'self-made' general, began to have successes in Bithynia, though descending to the shocking despoliation of cities such as Nicomedia and Cyzicus as well. Fimbria's army fought several battles against Mithridates' generals, including a resounding one on the river Rhyndacus against a quartet of them. Mithridates' son escaped from that action to join him at Pergamum, but Fimbria's speed was such that the king himself had to leave in haste for the coast at Pitane. There, Fimbria almost encircled him with earthworks, leaving only the coastal side as an exit for him. Lucullus was off the coast with his fleet at the time, but refused to help corner Mithridates and hand the credit for completing the war to Sulla's adversaries; so Mithridates escaped by sea, later to attend his conference with Sulla. Fimbria rampaged through parts of Asia, punishing the 'Cappadocian Faction' and devastating the territory of any city that shut its gates to him. At Ilium, he treacherously burnt down the town and slaughtered its inhabitants, even though he had been admitted.

To Mithridates an agreement with Sulla, who now had a fleet to

[92] Plut. *Luc.* 2–3; Diod. XXXVIII.8; Livy *Per.* LXXX; Plut. *Mar.* 43; Magie 1950 (A 67) I 226–8; Bulst 1964 (C 35) 319–20. Fimbria's status: commonly said to have been *praefectus equitum* and *legatus*; according to Appian a *privatus* on Flaccus' staff; perhaps ex-quaestor, Lintott 1971 (C 100).

pursue him into Asia, was preferable to the humiliations he was now undergoing. There was a go-between of standing in Archelaus, and terms had been on the table for about a year, to get used to. The hostility of Fimbria's army to Sulla might yet be used as a bargaining counter; so might the still large Mithridatic fleet, and Sulla's starved financial situation.[93]

XII. THE TREATY OF DARDANUS, THE FATE OF ASIA AND THE FELICITY OF SULLA

The summit meeting between Sulla and Mithridates took place at Dardanus in the Troad, probably in autumn 85 B.C.[94] It opened with complaints by Mithridates about Roman dealings with him over western Asia Minor before 89; Sulla replied with a speech going back to his own dispositions in Cappadocia when he was commander in Cilicia, but concluding with the contemporary fact of the collapse of Mithridates' adventure in Greece with the loss of 160,000 men. Sulla insisted on the terms already adumbrated in his talks with Archelaus; Mithridates was compelled to consent, and Sulla welcomed him to the formal cessation of hostilities with a kiss of friendship. If he was to pay 2,000 talents indemnity,[95] it was after all only the sum demanded as reparations from Chios alone by his general Zenobius. He was to evacuate the part of Paphlagonia in dispute; the kings of Bithynia and Cappadocia were to get back their kingdoms, and Sulla's legate, Curio, was to see to that, once Fimbria had been eliminated. Prisoners were to receive their freedom and deserters to be handed over for punishment. Seventy ships and 500 archers were to be handed over. In return, Mithridates was confirmed as king in his own prosperous and untouched kingdom, and his Black Sea empire was intact. No king, not even Antiochus the Great, had emerged so little scathed after a full-scale war with Rome.

Mithridates sailed away through the Bosporus to his Pontic fastness with another twenty years of opposition to Rome ahead of him, for all that he was now an 'ally of the Roman people'. Fortunately for him, Rome's war with the allies in Italy had been superseded by civil war, and Sulla had western preoccupations: he was prepared to insist on his terms, but not to load them with provocations that might goad the king into further present resistance.[96] As for Fimbria, his legions submitted on Sulla's approach, and after an assassination attempt on Sulla had failed

93 For the speech given to Mithridates by Sallust: Raditsa 1969–70 (D 54).

94 Date: Reinach 1890 (D 55) 190–206; Ormerod *CAH* IX[1] 256; Magie 1950 (A 67) I 229–31; II 1110, n. 58; Liebmann-Frankfort 1968 (D 276) 183f; Sherwin-White 1984 (D 291) 143–8.

95 So Plut. *Sulla* 22. 5, but 3,000 Memnon *FGrH* 434 F 25.

96 Florus I.40; Badian 1970 (C 13) 19; Keaveney 1982 (C 87) 104–5; 122–7; 1987 (C 94) 117–61; Sherwin-White 1984 (D 291) 144–8; McGing 1986 (D 35) 130.

and a proffered conference had been declined, he committed suicide. His legions, in fact, were left behind in Asia to become its garrison under Murena.

The settlement of the cities of Asia – reparations, rewards, administrative and financial arrangements for the future – was set in hand. Sulla took his time over it, not leaving Ephesus until 84. Even then he dallied in Athens, being initiated into the Eleusinian Mysteries and appropriating the libraries of his tyrant opponents, before sailing to Italy with his by then enormous fleet of 1,200 ships and arriving in Rome in the spring of 83. The collaborating cities, and the 'Cappadocian Faction' in the others, were now to pay heavily.[97] Some eight or nine cities were rewarded with keeping their own government and with the title of 'Friend of the Roman People': Chios, Rhodes, the Carian cities Stratonicea, Aphrodisias and Tabae, some Lycian cities, Magnesia-on-the-Maeander, and Ilium far away to the north-west. All had resisted Mithridates. Rhodes even received back control of her Peraea, the mainland coast opposite the island, which she had forfeited in the aftermath of the Third Macedonian War.[98] Such exceptions made the reparations forced on the other cities all the more harsh. Sulla's troops were quartered on the errant cities over the winter: each legionary was to receive four tetradrachms a day, and centurions fifty drachmas. Slaves freed by Mithridates had to be returned to their masters. If cities resisted this harsh treatment, a massacre of free men and slaves followed. Communities were sold into slavery and city walls pulled down. Sulla called the representatives of the cities to Ephesus and delivered a harangue justifying Rome's policy towards them since the time of Antiochus III and the revolt of Aristonicus; he finished by reimposing the unpaid taxes of the last five years. The appalling total of 20,000 talents was to be paid (perhaps 8,000 indemnity and 2,400 arrears of tax annually since 89 B.C.): coming on the top of the billeting and the destruction of private and public fortunes, it was crippling, far into the future.[99] Loans had to be sought at high interest, theatres, gymnasia, harbours and city walls had to be mortgaged. Although Sulla's quaestor Lucullus is said to have been scrupulously honest, the communities of Asia were in a parlous state for years, and some of the arrangements were

[97] Memnon *FGrH* 434 F 25 says the cities that had supported Mithridates were given an 'amnesty', but it did not let them off the burdens. Most hardly treated were Adramyttium, Clazomenae, Ephesus, Miletus, Mytilene, Pergamum, Tralles and perhaps Phocaea, with Caunus suffering because of unwillingness to be subject to Rhodes, Keaveney 1982 (C 87) 110–12; 114–15.

[98] Chios: *SIG* 785; Rhodes: Strab. XIV.2.3; App. *Mith.* 61; *BCiv.* V.7; Stratonicea: *OGIS* 441; Tabae: *OGIS* 442; Aphrodisias: Reynolds 1982 (B 226) 1–4; Lycians: *ILLRP* 174–5; Magnesia: Strab. XIII.3.35: Ilium: App. *Mith.* 53.

[99] Asia was organized into forty-four regions, Cassiod. *Chron.* (*Greenidge–Clay* p. 191), perhaps for direct tax-gathering, the Asian *publicani* having been wiped out: Brunt 1956 (D 254).

being endorsed or revised by the Senate for some time afterwards.[100] Nor were all recalcitrancies immediately suppressed: as late as 81/80 Mytilene was still defiant and had to be eventually subdued by Minucius Thermus.[101]

The destruction of cities, the financial ruin of those that survived, the liberations of slaves and the proclamations requiring their re-enslavement, the removal of the fleets that had controlled the Aegean, first that of Mithridates, then that of Sulla, all led to a great increase in pirate activity. The pirate squadrons progressed from taking ships to assaulting forts, harbours and even cities, among which were the island of Samos, Clazomenae in Ionia and Iasus in Caria. They are said to have robbed the temple of the Cabiri on Samothrace of treasure worth 1,000 talents at a time when Sulla himself was on the island.[102] Even so, he may not have realized the scale of the monster he had helped to conjure up and the threat it was to pose throughout the Mediterranean down to 67 B.C.

Mithridates had been lucky to get the treaty he did and to win Sulla's support for his status as 'king and friend of Rome'. However, the outlook for him and for Pontus in the future was uncertain. At Rome, many thought the terms of the peace were not fair punishment for Mithridates' crimes: they had, after all, been granted by a political faction, that of Sulla, albeit the dominant one at the moment. There was nothing to prevent future Roman provocation designed to push Mithridates into another war in which he could be made to pay more adequately for the first one. The relative weakness of the Pontic field armies had been thoroughly exposed by Sulla's five legions, and even quite small forces like Bruttius Sura's, and renegade armies, like that of Fimbria, had been able to defeat Mithridates' generals. Those revelations made such a provocation all the more likely, and within two years Murena was invading Pontus in response to a call from Archelaus.[103] In the mean time, between 83 and 80, Mithridates was to be kept busy with revolts in his Black Sea empire, in Colchis, and among the tribes north and east of the Cimmerian Bosporus.

Sulla, by contrast, was everywhere victorious, having recovered all Mithridates' conquests in less than three years. Even his image and propaganda outdid Mithridates, though in terms more appropriate to the Republican than the Iranian tradition. His byname among the Greeks, after he had been induced to dedicate a double-headed axe to Aphrodite of Aphrodisias in Caria, was 'Epaphroditus', and a counter to Mithridates' identification with Dionysus. From the date of his triumph

[100] Magie 1950 (A 67) I 232–40; Brunt 1956 (D 254). Sherwin-White 1984 (D 291) 148; 244f.

[101] Mattingly 1979 (D 283) 1494 with n. 10.

[102] App. *Mith.* 63.

[103] He argued that the Peace of Dardanus had not been ratified: App. *Mith.* 64; Glew 1981 (D 19).

he took officially (he had had it unofficially for a long time) the *cognomen* 'Felix', 'The Fortunate', an answer to Mithridates' names of 'Megas' and 'Basileus Basileon'.[104] And if Mithridates had his 'historians in the service of, and writing to please, barbarian kings',[105] so did Sulla have his partisan writers, and his own *commentarii*, to influence contemporaries and posterity. *His* next business was with his enemies at Rome.

[104] Vell. Pat. II.24; App. *BCiv.* I.76; Balsdon 1951 (C 18). [105] Dion. Hal. *Ant. Rom.* I.4.3.

CHAPTER 6

SULLA

ROBIN SEAGER

I. SULLA, SULPICIUS AND MARIUS, 88 B.C.

As the year 89 drew to its close, the predominant feeling at Rome may well have been one of relief. The fall of Asculum meant that the Social War was to all intents and purposes won, though isolated pockets of resistance lingered. Yet even the most cursory essay in divination should have revealed grave causes for concern about the future. The war had been bitterly contested, and resentment was bound to simmer. Rome's concessions had been churlish and grudging. It seems that not all the Italians had yet been enfranchised, and the confinement of those who had within a minority of tribes made it clear that the Romans were determined to limit to the best of their ability the value of the prize that their allies had wrested from them. Thus the Italian question had by no means been settled: the struggle for even the most nominal equality still had much of its course to run, though the Italians could take comfort from the knowledge that there were still men at Rome who, for whatever motive, were prepared to champion their interests.

Nor did the manner in which the outbreak of war had been exploited in pursuit of private enmities give any grounds for hope that in internal affairs a spirit of conciliation would now prevail. The murder of Livius Drusus had gone unpunished, and the contentious operations of the *quaestio Variana* had inflicted wounds that were still unhealed. The war had enforced a temporary lull in political infighting, but now that it was over revival of the feuds of 90 could only exacerbate an already delicate situation and diminish further the always remote likelihood of a unified and statesmanlike approach to the problems of Italy. It could be safely predicted that the times would continue interesting and that the new citizens would have a large part to play.

The consulship of 88, to which Sulla was elected in the last weeks of 89, together with his friend Q. Pompeius Rufus, might have seemed no more than the just, if not inevitable, reward for his military achievements during the foregoing year. Yet it seems that he encountered competition from an unusual source: C. Iulius Caesar Strabo, aedile in 90, who had not held the praetorship, but nevertheless wanted to stand for the consulship. Unfortunately the date of Strabo's attempt cannot be regarded as absolutely certain: it is just possible that he tried to stand in 88 for 87. But the most natural reading of Cicero's accounts of the opposition to Strabo by the tribunes P. Sulpicius and P. Antistius suggests that it belongs to the beginning of their term of office, in December 89.[1] If this is correct, then it deserves to be stressed that Strabo would be standing in direct competition with Sulla: since both were patricians, both could not be elected. That fact may give a clue to one of Strabo's motives for seeking the consulship at this precise time. He had been on bad terms with Sulla for nearly a decade, and it would no doubt have pleased him to keep his enemy out.[2] But that was not the only attraction of a consulship in 88. To be singled out as a special case by securing exemption from the normal *cursus* would of course be a worthwhile achievement in any year – that seems to have been the only motive for the ill-judged attempt of Q. Lucretius Afella under Sulla.[3] But it may well already have been apparent that to hold the office in this particular year might bring a further prize: a command against Mithridates.

It has been said that Strabo could not have hoped for the command, even if he gained the consulship, because of his relative youth and lack of military experience.[4] That need not be the case. Custom still demanded that major military commands should be assigned to consuls: the means adopted to give Marius control in both the Jugurthine and Cimbric Wars bear witness to the strength of the practice. At this point it would hardly have been possible to predict such a drastic interference with tradition as Sulpicius was soon to essay. If therefore Strabo could obtain the consulship, he might indeed get the command as well, a golden opportunity for glory and profit. The prospect of the Mithridatic command also probably explains the interest of another unusual would-be candidate at the elections of 89: Cn. Pompeius Strabo, consul in that year, but eager to hold office again without a break.[5] However, it seems unlikely that either Strabo was allowed to stand.[6] At all events, Sulla and Pompeius Rufus were elected, and shortly afterwards Sulla's daughter was married to Pompeius' son. More attention was attracted by Sulla's own new marriage. He divorced his wife Cloelia on the grounds of her sterility and married Metella, widow of M. Scaurus. Some of the nobility are said to have disapproved of Sulla's presumption, but the Metelli were always ready to establish ties with men of talent who lacked other

[1] Cic. *Har. Resp.* 43; *Brut.* 226. Badian 1969 (C 12) 481ff; Katz 1977 (C 82); Keaveney 1979 (C 85); *contra*, Mitchell 1975 (C 114) 201; Lintott 1971 (C 99) 449ff.

[2] Keaveney 1979 (C 85) 454.

[3] For the form of the name see Badian *JRS* 1967, 227f.

[4] Luce 1970 (C 101) 191; Keaveney 1979 (C 85) 453; *contra*, Katz 1977 (C 82) 471ff.

[5] Vell. Pat. II.21.1, Katz 1976 (C 80) 329 n. 6; *contra*, Keaveney 1978 (C 84) 240.

[6] For Caesar, see Katz 1977 (C 82) 62; *contra*, Mitchell 1975 (C 114) 199.

advantages: Scaurus himself had been a case in point, and the young Pompey would one day be another.

It is chiefly the opposition of Sulpicius that lends importance to Caesar Strabo's ambitions. P. Sulpicius (he probably did not bear the *cognomen* Rufus)[7] was not only an orator of some distinction but already known as an associate of Livius Drusus, C. Cotta and Pompeius Rufus, apparently pledged to press on with the integration of the Italians into the Roman commonwealth which Drusus had tried to initiate in 91. By 88 that meant in practical terms the distribution of the new citizens throughout all the thirty-five tribes instead of trying to restrict the value of their votes by assigning them to only a limited number of tribes voting last, whether old or freshly created. It is reasonable to suppose that Sulpicius intended from the first to introduce a measure to that effect, and his stand against Strabo's request for a dispensation may be interpreted in that light. His action benefited Sulla more than anyone else, but also Sulla's running-mate Pompeius Rufus. Rufus was already a close friend of Sulpicius, and Sulla's political views may have been known to coincide at least in part with those of Livius Drusus.[8] Sulpicius will therefore have hoped to secure at worst the benevolent neutrality, if not the active support, of two consuls for whom his programme might have some attractions in itself and who were also in his debt for services rendered in the cause of their election.

More puzzling is Sulpicius' other recorded early action: the veto of a bill which recalled exiles on the ground that they had not been allowed to plead their case, even though he later introduced a law himself in favour of the same exiles. The identity of these exiles has been much discussed, and no solution is free from objections and difficulties. Perhaps the most likely suggestion is that they were the victims of the *quaestio Variana*.[9] If so, a further puzzle ensues: why should Sulpicius veto a measure which would have brought back to Rome the surviving supporters of Livius Drusus, men who were his friends and shared his political ideals, not least among them C. Cotta? Certainty is impossible, but it may be that once again Sulpicius was concerned to secure the good will of Sulla, who may have been opposed to such a move, particularly if the anonymous proposal against which Sulpicius interposed his veto had the backing of Marius.[10] Sulpicius might well have thought it worthwhile to leave his friends in exile a while longer if that sacrifice would help to win him Sulla's support for the fair distribution of the new citizens. Indeed, some at least of his friends might even have agreed with him.

But if Sulpicius' calculations had run along these lines, he was to be

[7] Mattingly 1975 (C 111). [8] Gabba 1973 (C 55) 383ff.

[9] Keaveney 1979 (C 85) 455ff; *contra*, Badian 1969 (C 12) 487ff, Lintott 1971 (C 99) 453.

[10] Porrà 1973 (C 118) 23f.

cruelly disappointed. Sulla may have shared Livius Drusus' views on the need to restore the authority of the Senate, but he had no commitment to the cause of the Italians. When Sulpicius introduced a bill to distribute both the new citizens and also freedmen throughout the thirty-five tribes, he met vigorous opposition not only from the old citizens but also from Sulla and even from Pompeius Rufus. From Sulpicius' standpoint this must have seemed an inexcusable betrayal, and the violence of his reaction is not hard to understand. If he was to have any hope of carrying out his programme now that Sulla and Rufus had let him down, he had urgent need of a fresh source of support. He did not have far to look. The command against Mithridates had been allotted to Sulla (which may mean that Rufus too had coveted it). But there was still one potential rival in the field: Marius, who was not only eager to have the command but might take particular pleasure in securing it at the expense of Sulla. That Marius and Sulpicius should be drawn together seems almost inevitable, though there is now no way of telling which took the initiative in forming their alliance. There can, however, be little doubt about its terms. Marius would lend all the support he could muster, much of it equestrian, to Sulpicius' proposal on the voting rights of the Italians, and in return Sulpicius would promulgate a bill depriving Sulla of the command against Mithridates and assigning it instead to Marius – constitutionally a much more dramatic step than Marius' acquisition of the command against Jugurtha, when he had been at least a consul in office. But for the moment this part of the bargain remained a closely guarded secret.

In addition to his distribution bill, Sulpicius also brought in other measures, one limiting the debts that senators might incur and one which, reversing his earlier attitude, provided for the recall of the exiles on the ground that they had been expelled by force. This may have been in part a favour to Marius, if Marius had indeed supported the previous proposal which Sulpicius had vetoed, but regardless of Marius' views on the subject Sulpicius must have felt that since his break with Sulla he no longer had any reason not to try to restore his friends. Surprisingly, he offered nothing to the urban plebs that might have made it more amenable to his Italian bill, and so it continued to resist him. Sulpicius' clash with Caesar Strabo had ended ominously in violence on the streets, and he showed no hesitation now. He is said to have surrounded himself with a private army 3,000-strong and a bodyguard of 600 *equites*, whom he called his 'anti-Senate'.[11] If this is true, he will surely have meant that they would serve to protect him against any such use of force by the Senate as had brought about the deaths of the Gracchi and Saturninus, not as an alternative council of state. The consuls must have feared that,

[11] Accepted: Keaveney 1983 (C 91) 54; *contra*, e.g. Badian 1969 (C 12) 485.

despite the widespread hostility to the bill, Sulpicius would succeed in intimidating the voters, and so they tried to block its passage by declaring a suspension of public business (*iustitium*) or a special holiday (*feriae imperativae*).[12]

The rioting worsened, and Sulpicius led a band of armed supporters into a meeting summoned by the consuls. He denounced the suspension of business as illegal and demanded its immediate withdrawal, so that voting on the bill could proceed. The consuls refused, Sulpicius threatened their lives, and fighting broke out, in which Rufus' son, who had been foolishly provocative, was one of numerous casualties. Rufus himself escaped, while Sulla was forced to take refuge in the house of Marius, though he later denied this humiliating fact in his memoirs. Clearly the two men must have come to some arrangement. Sulla was for the moment in a desperately weak position and must have agreed to lift the ban on public business and allow Sulpicius' legislation to go forward. Marius need have offered little in return: perhaps no more than a promise that Sulla's life would then be safe. It would be interesting to know whether Sulla expressed an intention of returning to the siege of Nola (unfinished business from the Social War on which he had been engaged until Sulpicius' activities had forced him to return to Rome) and whether Marius agreed to let him go. If the plan to deprive Sulla of the Mithridatic command had already been revealed, then Marius would surely have hesitated to allow him to rejoin his army, but it had not. So when Sulla left Rome, with Marius' blessing or not, he will have done so simply because he thought that Nola would be the safest place for him.

The ban on public business was duly raised, and Sulla withdrew to Campania. His headquarters were probably at Capua, which he visited on his way to Nola.[13] Sulpicius was now able to enact his laws without further effective opposition – the old citizens must have been cowed by the threat of fresh violence – and Sulla found out that Marius had tricked him, for the bill to transfer the Mithridatic command was now published and passed, though Sulla, unlike Pompeius Rufus, whose treachery in Sulpicius' eyes had been greater, was not stripped of his consulship.[14] So Sulla was presented with a choice. He could acknowledge the law as valid. To do so would mean total humiliation at the hands of his opponents, the end of his political career and perhaps even further danger to his life. Or he could attempt to reverse it and regain his command. He can hardly have been in any doubt. Like Caesar he was an outsider in politics, totally self-centred in pursuit of his ambitions, always ready to break the rules of the political game to achieve his objective. But unlike Caesar he had strong views, already well defined by

[12] Cf. Keaveney 1983 (C 91) 57.

[13] Keaveney 1983 (C 91) 59.

[14] But see Keaveney 1983 (C 91) 60f.

88, on what remedies were needed to set the Roman state to rights, and perhaps a belief that he was divinely appointed for the task. One of his basic constitutional convictions was that tribunician legislation in defiance of the Senate and the consuls should not be permitted. This coincidence of political principle and personal advantage was extremely convenient, but no less genuine for that. If Sulla hesitated it can only have been because he was not sure how his army would react. That the mass of senatorial and popular opinion would be wholly against him if he marched on Rome he must have known, but if his men were prepared to follow him the disapproval of others would be of no practical importance, and once he had succeeded he would then be able to impose his own interpretation on events.

He sounded out the army with some caution, complaining of the behaviour of Marius and Sulpicius towards him and implanting in the men the suspicion, surely false, that if Marius secured the command he would levy other troops and leave them behind, so that they would lose their share of the handsome profits of an easy war against effete orientals. Whether or not they believed this tale, the troops understood what was expected of them and urged him to lead them to Rome. Sulla's officers on the other hand, when they realized what was afoot, all returned to the city, with the exception of his quaestor, almost certainly L. Lucullus.[15] Sulla also had the support of Pompeius Rufus, whom he still treated as his colleague, though it is unclear whether Rufus joined him before he left Nola or at a later point on the march. When military tribunes sent by Marius to take over the army arrived in the camp, they were stoned to death by the troops. Any nagging hesitation that Sulla may have felt was eased by proofs of divine approval. These will have meant much to him, for there is no reason to doubt the depth and sincerity of his religious beliefs, even if some of the signs he recorded in his memoirs may be regarded with suspicion.[16] First the soothsayer Postumius promised him success, then a dream sent by the goddess Ma-Bellona revealed that he would strike down his enemies.

So the march on Rome began. Not only Sulpicius and Marius but the Senate and people as a whole were appalled at Sulla's action. It will have needed little pressure to persuade the Senate to send a series of embassies to try to halt the advance. But Sulla was confident now. When the first senatorial embassy asked him why he was marching against his fatherland, he boldly replied that he was coming to free it from tyrants. His soldiers went further, manhandling and insulting the envoys. Two further delegations were given a similar answer by Sulla, and he sent through them an invitation to the Senate, Sulpicius and Marius to meet him outside the city in the Campus Martius. It is true that Sulla promised

[15] Badian 1964 (A 2) 220; Levick 1982 (C 97). [16] Keaveney 1983 (H 68).

to abide by any agreement reached at such a meeting, but the implied estimate of his own importance in relation to the organs of the state is perhaps more revealing. A final embassy, inspired by Sulpicius and Marius in the hope of gaining time, asked Sulla not to come within five Roman miles of the city until the Senate had had time to deliberate further on the matter. Sulla and Rufus duly promised to make camp, but continued their march as soon as the envoys had left.

The result of the attack on Rome could never be in doubt, for the defenders had no regular troops at their disposal. What is striking is the fierceness of the resistance Sulla encountered. The people, though unarmed, pelted his soldiers from the roof-tops until he threatened to fire their houses, while his men almost broke when they were finally confronted by Marius' makeshift forces – only Sulla's personal daring shamed them into making a stand. But when Sulla summoned the detachment he had kept in reserve, Marius was driven back to the temple of Tellus, and after a proclamation offering freedom to any slave who would join his cause had failed to bear fruit he was forced to take to flight.

Sulla stationed troops all over the city, while he and Rufus remained vigilant throughout the night to ensure that no incidents disturbed the peace. On the following day he summoned the Senate and caused it to give official sanction to his private quarrel by declaring Marius, his son, Sulpicius and nine others who had fled with them to be enemies of the state on the grounds that they had stirred up sedition, fought against the consuls and offered freedom to slaves. The decree of the Senate was then reinforced by a law. For Sulla this unprecedented step had obvious advantages. It identified his cause, completely and instantly, with that of law and order and the *res publica* itself and retrospectively justified the march on Rome; it enabled him to condemn his enemies to death without delay in a situation where the *senatus consultum ultimum* would have been out of place; and by depriving them of their citizenship it appeared to rule out any subsequent complaint about the violation of their rights. But its constitutional implications were highly disquieting: it meant that men could be pronounced guilty of crimes against the state and sentenced to death without any semblance of trial. This fact may have weighed at least as much as their connexion by marriage with Q. Mucius Scaevola the augur, who flatly refused to admit that a man with Marius' record of service to the state could be called an enemy of Rome.[17] Of the twelve men outlawed, although the pursuit was keen, only Sulpicius was killed, betrayed by a slave. Marius, after a series of romantic adventures, made his way to safety in Africa, where he was joined by several others of the exiles, including his son.[18]

17 Val. Max. III.8.5; Bauman 1973 (C 21); Katz 1975 (C 79).

18 Carney 1961 (C 39) 112ff.

All the measures enacted by Sulpicius after the original suspension of public business by the consuls were now declared invalid because they had been passed by force. Thus Sulla was restored to the Mithridatic command and Pompeius to his consulship, and the distribution of the enfranchised Italians throughout all the tribes was annulled. Had Sulla had the wisdom and generosity to re-enact that law in his own name, much subsequent turmoil and bloodshed might have been avoided. Instead, he brought in laws of a very different nature. Only Appian records these constitutional measures and his account is far from clear, but there is no reason to dismiss the legislation of 88, shortlived as it was, as a mere retrojection of that of the dictatorship.[19] Sulla's overall objective at least is already clear: to prevent any magistrate, especially a tribune, from acting in concert with the people in disregard or defiance of the wishes of the Senate, and in general to strengthen the Senate and restore its predominance in the state, a task which was certainly urgent, as its poor showing when confronted first with Sulpicius, then with Sulla himself had made abundantly clear. Therefore Sulla enacted that no proposal should be brought before the people without the prior approval of the Senate, that the *comitia centuriata* should be restored to their 'Servian' form (see Vol. VII^2, pp. 199ff) by the removal of the tribal element from the voting procedure (this seems more likely than the alternative interpretation that Sulla abolished the legislative powers of the *comitia tributa*), so that, as Appian ingenuously puts it, voting would be controlled by the rich and wise, not by the poor and headstrong, and that 300 of the best men should be enrolled in the Senate.[20] Other measures, of which no details are unfortunately given, were taken to curtail the tribunician power; these may or may not have prefigured exactly those that were introduced in the dictatorship. Sulla was also aware of the financial crisis caused by the Social War and aggravated by the loss of Asia to Mithridates. He passed a law to remit a tenth of existing debts and fix interest rates for the future. Finally, he is said to have founded colonies, and, though no settlements appear in fact to have been made, he may well have intended to do so. Nobody knew better than he that it would be prudent to demobilize and disperse the armies of the Social War, and he may also have hoped to decrease the numbers of the urban plebs.

Though Sulla is not accused of passing these laws by force, the presence of his troops in the city must have done much to ensure that they were accepted without opposition, though it is also surely true that many senators, however much they disapproved of Sulla as an individual and of the march on Rome, will have found his legislation entirely acceptable. But it was vital to the credibility of his posture as liberator

[19] Keaveney 1983 (C 91) 81ff. [20] Gabba 1958 (B 40) 171f.

and champion of law and order that the army should remain no longer than was absolutely necessary. So, once his laws had been passed, he sent it back to Capua. But as soon as the threat had been removed opposition made itself felt. Friends of the exiles began to agitate on their behalf and there were rumours of plots against the lives of Sulla and Pompeius. Nevertheless, Sulla knew that it would destroy his image if he interfered too blatantly with the elections, and so he brought no improper pressure to bear. The results gave further proof of his unpopularity. His nephew, Sex. Nonius Sufenas, failed to gain the tribunate, and although Sulla was able to prevent the election of Q. Sertorius, he could not keep out the nephew of Marius, M. Marius Gratidianus. His candidate for the consulship, P. Servilius Vatia, was also rejected, though he had just obtained a triumph from his unknown praetorian province. The consuls elected, who may have been friends, were Cn. Octavius, who had no ties with Sulla but was thought to be opposed to reform, and L. Cornelius Cinna, whose success apparently gave hope to the friends of the exiles, though he had no connexion with Marius and at the time of his election there was nothing to suggest that he would take up the cause of the new citizens.[21] Perhaps before agreeing to announce the result of the election, Sulla had taken the curious step of binding both consuls designate by an oath to uphold his arrangements. He can hardly have hoped that this would prove an effective restraint, but it would at least serve to put Cinna in the wrong before gods and men if he tampered with Sulla's laws and give Sulla religious and moral grounds for any eventual reprisals he might feel moved to make.

By now considerations of his own security, his promises to his troops, and the requirements of the Mithridatic War all made it imperative that Sulla leave Italy without further delay. However, he was concerned for the safety of Pompeius Rufus. He therefore brought a measure before Senate and People to give his colleague Italy as his province with the troops at present commanded by Pompeius Strabo. An attempt to recall Strabo was frustrated by the veto of a tribune, C. Herennius,[22] but Rufus nevertheless went out to take over the army. Shortly after his arrival he was set upon and killed by the troops, who were almost certainly acting on Strabo's orders. Strabo rebuked them, but took no further disciplinary action, and no more attempts were made to relieve him of command.

II. *CINNANUM TEMPUS*, 87–84 B.C.

Cinna's first act, perhaps even before he took office, was to prompt a tribune of 87, M. Vergilius or Verginius, to institute a prosecution

[21] Katz 1976 (C 81) 505ff; Keaveney 1983 (C 91) 76ff.

[22] Sall. *H.* II.21, Badian 1955 (C 5) 107f; *contra*, Twyman 1979 (C 148) 187ff.

against Sulla. His aim will have been not to drive Sulla out of Italy – Sulla was going of his own accord – but to prevent his departure by stripping him of his *imperium* and securing his condemnation.[23] The ploy failed: no doubt men remembered only too well the last attempt to deprive Sulla of his command, and he was able to ignore the tribune's summons and depart for the Mithridatic War, leaving a detachment under Ap. Claudius to continue the siege of Nola. For what it was worth, Cinna had proved that Sulla's respect for law and order did not weigh against his own advantage, but now he turned to the more serious matter of an attack on those aspects of Sulla's legislation that seemed most vulnerable.

However, if Appian can be believed, it was the friends of the exiles who first encouraged the newly enfranchised Italians to renew their agitation for fair distribution throughout the thirty-five tribes, while a substantial bribe was needed to interest Cinna in their cause. Whatever the truth of that matter, once Cinna had declared himself in favour of the new citizens, matters rapidly came to a head. Octavius predictably took the opposite side, and both parties armed themselves with daggers. When Cinna promulgated bills providing for the distribution of the new citizens and freedmen and for the recall of the exiles, Octavius persuaded a majority of tribunes to veto.[24] This provoked the new citizens to riot against the tribunes, and it is possible that the *senatus consultum ultimum* was passed. Octavius led his supporters down the Via Sacra into the Forum and separated the two sides, though he kept out of Cinna's way. But then, allegedly on their own initiative, Octavius' men turned on the new citizens, many of whom were killed. The swiftness and vigour of Octavius' action had taken Cinna by surprise. He had expected that his superior numbers would carry the day. After an abortive offer of freedom to the slaves he left the city and at once began a tour of the neighbouring towns, among them Tibur and Praeneste, in order to acquire men and money for an attempt to recover his position by force of arms. He was joined by several of his leading supporters, among them Q. Sertorius and two tribunes, C. Milonius and Marius Gratidianus. Eventually he had with him no less than six of the tribunes of the year, though it is unclear exactly when individual sympathizers left the city: some tribunes may have disapproved of Cinna's treatment at the hands of the Senate more than they disliked his proposals, and so changed sides.

The Senate promptly took it upon itself first to deprive Cinna of his consulship, then to declare him a *hostis*, on the ground that in a state of emergency – which suggests that the *senatus consultum ultimum* was in

[23] Keaveney 1983 (C 91) 85f; *contra*, Bennett 1923 (C 24) 7.

[24] Accepted by Katz 1976 (C 81) 49f; *contra*, Gabba 1958 (B 40) 182.

force – he had, though consul, abandoned Rome and offered freedom to the slaves. In his place was elected L. Cornelius Merula, the *flamen Dialis*, though he later claimed that he had not wanted to stand. He had, perhaps significantly, no connexion with Sulla, while the taboos that surrounded his priestly office meant that in effect Octavius was left as virtual sole consul.[25] Though Merula was presumably elected by an assembly, the Senate's decree against Cinna was never confirmed by a law.[26]

Meanwhile Cinna had reached his destination, Nola, where the force left by Sulla was carrying on the siege. He bribed first the officers at Capua, then the troops, and made a dramatic appearance before them. He presented himself in his consular regalia, but then cast aside his fasces and, apparently treating the army as an assembly, addressed the men in true *popularis* fashion: his consulship had been their gift, for they, the people, had elected him, but now the Senate, by deposing him without the people's assent, had set the people's authority at naught and made a mockery of the institution of popular elections. His appeal soon had the desired effect. The soldiers raised him up, set him on his curule chair, restored his fasces and declared that he was still consul. They promised to follow wherever he led, and their officers took the oath of loyalty to Cinna before administering it to the men under their command. From Nola Cinna continued his visits to Italian towns, claiming that his sufferings had been the result of his efforts on their behalf. He succeeded in collecting a considerable sum of money and recruiting large numbers of men, while more supporters came from Rome to join him. Octavius and Merula began to fortify the city and tried to raise troops from those towns which remained loyal and from Cisalpine Gaul. They also summoned Pompeius Strabo, who still retained command of his army but had as yet taken no part in the events of 87, to come to the assistance of his country.

By this time news of the impending conflict had come to Marius in Africa, and he saw an opportunity to bring about his own return. Landing in Etruria, he offered his services to Cinna, who acknowledged him as proconsul and sent him the appropriate insignia. But Marius scrupulously refused to use them. He went from city to city, recalling his past achievements and promising to put through the distribution of the new citizens. By the time he reached Cinna's camp he had assembled 6,000 men, many of them slaves liberated from *ergastula*. Sertorius was allegedly reluctant to accept Marius as an ally, but when Cinna revealed that he had invited Marius to join them he gave way.

Strabo had encamped outside the Colline Gate, but he took no further action. His critics claimed that, if he had exerted himself, he could have nipped Cinna's enterprise in the bud. But Strabo's chief concern

[25] Cf. Katz 1979 (c 83). [26] Bennett 1923 (c 24) 8ff; Bauman 1973 (c 21) 286ff.

remained a second consulship, and he was not prepared to commit himself until he had sounded out both sides. Cinna divided his forces into three: the main body under himself and Cn. Papirius Carbo near the Colline Gate, a detachment under Sertorius on the left bank of the Tiber upriver from the city, and one downstream under Marius outside the Porta Ostiensis. His objective was to starve Rome into submission. Bridges were built across the Tiber both above and below the city to cut off the supply of food, while Marius, helped by the treachery of an officer of the garrison, Valerius, captured and sacked the port of Ostia. Cinna also sent a force north, probably commanded by Marius Gratidianus, which seized Ariminum to cut off any help that might come from Cisalpine Gaul. By now Strabo had failed to receive any suitable promises from Cinna and Marius, and so he at last took the field, fighting an indecisive engagement against Sertorius in the neighbourhood of the Janiculum. Desperate for support, the Senate now passed a decree granting citizenship to all those who had surrendered but not yet received enfranchisement. It was hoped that this belatedly opportunistic move would produce massive reinforcements, but though many men were promised, barely sixteen cohorts were raised. Octavius and Merula had only one more potential ally on whom they could call: Q. Caecilius Metellus Pius, praetor in 89, who was still in the field against the Samnites. They therefore instructed Pius to make peace with the Samnites on any terms that were consistent with the dignity of Rome and to come to the relief of the city. But the Samnites demanded citizenship not only for themselves but for all who had deserted to them, the return of all prisoners and deserters in Roman hands, and the return of all booty taken by the Romans, while refusing to surrender any booty they themselves had acquired. Metellus was reluctant to agree to such shameful terms and the Senate backed him up in his refusal. Marius and Cinna at once seized their opportunity, made all the concessions demanded by the Samnites and so secured their support.

Further treachery now gave the besiegers a chance to take the city. A military tribune, Ap. Claudius, opened the gates of the Janiculum to Marius, who let in Cinna and his men. However, the attackers were driven back across the Tiber by Octavius, who was reinforced by six cohorts from Strabo's army, and Milonius, Cinna's cavalry commander, was killed. The victory might well have been more conclusive, but Strabo prevented Octavius from following up his success. He did not want the war settled before the consular elections, for then his services would lose their market value. The arrival of Pius, a plausible candidate for a consulship of 86, had revived Strabo's interest in a possible deal with Cinna, with whom he renewed negotiations behind Octavius' back. However, Cinna may have responded with an attempt to suborn his army and arrange the murder of Strabo and his son, if a curious story in Plutarch has any basis in fact.[27] But the armies of Octavius and Strabo were now devastated by a plague, of which Strabo himself was the most distinguished victim. As he lay dying his tent was struck by lightning during a storm. The shock rendered Strabo unconscious, but when the Senate sent out C. Cassius, perhaps the consul of 96, to assume command of his army, the indignity briefly restored him to his senses. However, he died a few days later and his troops were eventually taken over by Octavius. Strabo had never been popular, and his recent conduct had aroused still greater dislike. There were serious disturbances at his funeral and his body was pulled from its bier and dragged through the mud, until the tribunes and some other senators intervened to rescue it from the fury of the mob.

The attackers now developed their plan of cutting off all Rome's potential sources of food. Marius set about gaining control of those towns in which corn was stored; he captured Antium, Aricia, Lanuvium and other places, some of which were betrayed to him. Then he and Cinna advanced along the Via Appia in the hope of forcing a decision before the defenders could find a fresh source of supply. They halted some 20 kilometres from Rome, probably in the neighbourhood of Aricia.[28] Octavius, Metellus and P. Licinius Crassus (probably the consul of 97 rather than his son) took up their position on the Alban Mount. Morale was becoming increasingly bad. Dissatisfied with Octavius' leadership, the troops had offered Metellus the command, and his refusal, though proper, had prompted numerous desertions. Of the generals, Crassus was still eager to fight, but the army's lack of enthusiasm led Metellus to try negotiations with Cinna, whom he agreed to acknowledge as consul, though Octavius on the one side and Marius on the other ensured that they came to nothing. Thereupon Metellus abandoned the resistance and withdrew to Africa. Cinna again offered freedom to slaves in the city who were prepared to join him, and this time there were many takers. The Senate, afraid that a famine would lead to riots, sent envoys to Cinna to negotiate for peace. Cinna's opening gambit was to ask whether they came to him as consul or as a private citizen. On this point, surprisingly perhaps, the legates had no instructions, and so they returned to the city, from which more and more deserters, free men as well as slaves, now came to join Cinna and Marius as they continued to advance, without waiting for the envoys to return, until they were encamped outside the walls.

The Senate thought it wrong that Merula should be deprived of his consulship when he had done no wrong, but Merula, perhaps in the hope of saving his life, insisted that he had never wanted office and abdicated

[27] Plut. *Pomp.* 3, see Keaveney 1982 (C 88) 112f. [28] Bennett 1923 (C 24) 20ff.

of his own accord, even offering to act as a mediator. Another embassy was sent to Cinna with orders to address him as consul, and it was as consul, on his tribunal, that Cinna received the envoys. All they asked was for him to swear that when he entered the city there would be no killing. Cinna, however, refused to take such an oath. He did give a promise that he would not willingly be the cause of any man's death, but disquietingly suggested that Octavius keep out of the way. Throughout these exchanges Marius stood beside Cinna's chair, grimly and ominously silent. Finally the envoys invited Cinna and Marius to enter the city, but Marius with a bitter smile refused, saying that as an exile he had no right to do so. So Cinna went in alone and promulgated a law, either on his own account or through the agency of the tribunes, recalling not only Marius but all the exiles, though it is said that Marius waited only until three or four tribes had voted before entering along with his personal bodyguard of freed slaves, the Bardyaei.

His friends advised Octavius to flee, but, mindful perhaps of the judgement he had passed on Cinna, he replied that while he was consul he would never leave the city and took his seat on his curule chair on the Janiculum. Attacked by a squadron of cavalry led by C. Marcius Censorinus, he still refused to run for it and so was killed there. His head was brought to Cinna and displayed before the rostra: he was the first consul to suffer such a fate. His death inaugurated a purge of opponents and personal enemies for which it is clear that Cinna was to blame as much as Marius.[29] Against most there was no pretence of legal proceedings: C. and L. Caesar, P. Crassus and his elder son, and M. Antonius were among those hunted down without ceremony, though Antonius' eloquence almost saved him at the last. In all this the particular vindictiveness of Marius is evidenced only twice, by his alleged eagerness to kill Antonius with his own hands and his refusal of clemency to Q. Ancharius. The unfortunate Merula and Marius' old rival Q. Lutatius Catulus received the semblance of a trial before the people: both committed suicide without waiting for the verdict. Merula was replaced as *flamen Dialis* by the young C. Iulius Caesar, who was to marry Cinna's daughter in 84. The appointment invites those with benefit of hindsight to fascinating if pointless speculation; however, it seems that he was never inaugurated. It is probable that there were few other victims apart from those whose names are recorded. We simply do not know why several of them were killed: opposition to Cinna or participation in the defence of Rome will presumably account for those who were not marked out by Marius as old enemies or false friends. None, significantly, can be certainly linked with Sulla in any way.[30] Other opponents, according to Appian, were removed from office. It was probably at this

[29] Bennett 1923 (C 24) 31.

[30] Bennett 1923 (C 24) 32; Keaveney 1984 (C 93) 115ff.

time that Ap. Claudius, commander of the troops at Nola who had restored Cinna to his consulship, was summoned by a tribune and, when he failed to appear, was deprived of his *imperium* and exiled, and, although there is no evidence, Metellus Pius must surely have been treated in similar fashion.

Comprehensive measures were taken against Sulla himself. He was declared a *hostis*,[31] and stripped of his priesthood (not an augurate, perhaps a pontificate),[32] his property was confiscated, his house destroyed and his legislation rescinded. His wife Metella and their children, however, escaped from the city to join Sulla in Greece. Meanwhile the freed slaves who had formed a significant element in the forces of Marius and Cinna, especially the Bardyaei, were exploiting the licence given them to plunder and kill. But eventually, after several warnings from Cinna, they were surrounded by Gallic troops, perhaps commanded by Sertorius, and wiped out. The roles assigned to Cinna and Sertorius in the taking and implementation of this decision and its placing before or after Marius' death depend on the readiness or reluctance of the sources to exculpate Cinna at Marius' expense and their attitude to Sertorius: to uncover the truth from behind these veils of prejudice is hardly possible.

Marius and Cinna became consuls for 86, so that Marius at last attained the seventh consulship, which, he claimed, had been foretold him. The procedure employed is unclear. Hostile sources say that there were no elections at all, either this year or in the subsequent years of Cinna's tenure of power. It is, however, more likely that elections were held at which only two candidates were allowed to present themselves.[33] The fulfilment of his destiny does not seem to have made the old and embittered Marius more amenable: on the first day of his consulship he caused one Sex. Lucilius or Licinius, tribune in 87, to be thrown from the Tarpeian Rock. He was looking forward to the Mithridatic command, but within a fortnight he was dead, perhaps of pneumonia. His funeral was enlivened by an attempt on the life of Q. Mucius Scaevola the *pontifex maximus*, made by Marius' quaestor, C. Flavius Fimbria.[34]

Thus began the so-called 'domination of Cinna', assessment of which is rendered painfully difficult by the way in which our scrappy sources are pervaded by the insidious influence of Sulla's own version of events, diffused without competition after his victory.[35] Detailed attempts have been made to determine the attitude of contemporaries to Cinna and his rule.[36] Certain general observations may be made here. From the first

[31] Bennett 1923 (C 24) 29; Bauman 1973 (C 21) 290ff; *contra*, Bulst 1964 (C 35) 319; Hackl 1982 (C 71) 236. [32] Badian 1968 (C 11) 38f; Keaveney 1982 (C 90).

[33] Bennett 1923 (C 24) 37, see *App BCiv.* 1.77.354 on 85.

[34] For Fimbria's office, cf. Lintott 1971 (C 100). [35] Badian 1964 (A 2) 206ff.

[36] Badian 1964 (A 2) 216ff. 1964 (B 2); Keaveney 1984 (C 93) 118ff.

many senators must have had mixed feelings about Sulla. Though they may have approved of the laws he passed when he got there, they viewed the march on Rome with unmitigated horror. The desire to avoid a repetition of the events of 88 and 87 will have inspired many to shun both extremes and to hope for a reconciliation. But to remain in Rome under Cinna's regime and even to hold office need indicate neither whole-hearted support for Cinna nor a special dislike or fear of Sulla. Those who did not feel personally threatened had no need to leave Rome, those who wished to attend the Senate or stand for office had to stay there, and the temptation to join Sulla at a time when his plans and prospects were still uncertain must have been slight. However, there must have been resentment among those whose ambition had kept them in the city at the promotion block caused by the repeated tenure of the consulship by Cinna and Carbo. There is certainly nothing to suggest that Sulla ever thought of treating all those who stayed at home as enemies, as the Pompeians were to do in 49. In 86 the *Sullani* were still in essence Sulla's officers. A certain number of refugees came to join him in Greece, but it was not yet known that Sulla would bring the Mithridatic War to a premature close and return to Italy in arms. Therefore not all of those who found it necessary to get out of Rome chose Sulla's camp as their refuge. The most noteworthy of those who went elsewhere were Metellus Pius, who found a haven in Africa thanks to the connexions of his father Numidicus, and the young M. Crassus, who secured shelter in Spain, where his family had ties.

Our knowledge of the events of these years is slight and hardly allows a coherent estimate of the policy of the regime, if indeed it had one.[37] Despite Cinna's attempt in 87 to revive Sulpicius' distribution bill he seems to have felt no urgency about putting it into practice: the number of citizens counted at the census of 86 was only 463,000, so the vast mass of enfranchised Italians cannot have been registered. The censors were L. Marcius Philippus and M. Perperna. Philippus achieved notoriety by excluding from the Senate his own uncle, the exiled Ap. Claudius. Other recorded measures were aimed at easing the economic crisis. In 86 the consul suffect L. Flaccus introduced a law, inevitably criticized by conservative sources, remitting three-quarters of existing debts, while either in this year or the next the praetors, supported by the tribunes, devised an edict to restore financial stability by reasserting the official rate of exchange between the denarius and the *as*, which had been subject to recent unofficial fluctuation.[38] One praetor, Marius Gratidianus, then anticipated his colleagues and the tribunes by publishing the measure and claiming the credit for it. His hope was to win sufficient popularity to bring him to the consulship, but in this he was disappointed, though he

[37] Cf. Bennett 1923 (C 24) 62ff. [38] Crawford 1968 (C 45).

did indeed become a popular hero and statues of him were erected throughout the city.

The young Pompey was also in the news in 86. His home had been sacked in the capture of Rome in 87 (perhaps a tribute to his father's unpopularity) and now he was brought to trial on an embezzlement charge in respect of items from the booty of Asculum which Strabo had diverted to his private use. But now that Strabo was dead, his son seemed worth cultivating, and Pompey was able to mobilize impressive support. He was defended by the censor L. Philippus, Cinna's associate Cn. Carbo and the rising orator Q. Hortensius, while the president of the court, P. Antistius, betrothed his daughter to the defendant during the proceedings. It is hardly surprising that the blame was shifted on to a freedman and Pompey triumphantly acquitted.

But the most important problem, for both Cinna and the Senate, was what to do about Sulla. L. Flaccus had succeeded Marius not only in the consulship but also in the Mithridatic command. Since Sulla had been declared a *hostis*, he could no longer be regarded as the representative of the Senate and People of Rome. Formally, therefore, Flaccus was being sent out, not to succeed Sulla, but to take over command of an army which for some time had had no legitimate commander. For Sulla, of course, the appointment of Flaccus was a straightforward attempt by his enemies to deprive him of his command, the validity of which remained in his eyes unimpaired, and no doubt he was right about the intentions of Cinna and Carbo. But the terms of reference of Flaccus' mission, as recorded by Memnon, show that there were already those at Rome – L. Valerius Flaccus, consul in 100, appointed *princeps senatus* by Philippus and Perperna, was to emerge as the most prominent – who felt that it was necessary, if not actually desirable, to come to some arrangement with Sulla. Flaccus had instructions to sound out Sulla in the hope that he would be prepared to co-operate or, failing that, at least agree to fight Mithridates first. It must surely follow from this that Flaccus had authority from the Senate to reinstate Sulla not only as a citizen but also as proconsul if he proved amenable.

It was unfortunate for Flaccus that he had inherited from Marius not only his command but his political aide Fimbria, as his quaestor. Fimbria assassinated him and brought this initiative to an abortive close, and it was not long before Fimbria himself lost his army to Sulla and was driven to suicide. However, in the meantime he had succeeded in blockading Mithridates himself at Pitane, with every hope of capturing the king had not Lucullus, who was in command of Sulla's fleet, refused to lend him any assistance. The ancient sources, saturated though they are in Sulla's own apologetics, condemn both Lucullus' unwillingness to help Fimbria and Sulla's peace with Mithridates at Dardanus as betrayals of Roman interests and opportunities, made because Sulla was more concerned to free his hands for a civil war against his enemies at Rome than with finishing off the most dangerous enemy of the state. This view was shared at the time by Sulla's own troops, despite the lengths to which he had always gone to secure their favour. Modern scholars have been inclined to make excuses for Lucullus and Sulla.[39] It is true that when the peace of Dardanus was made there was no prospect of an immediate successful conclusion to the war: Mithridates was still at large with considerable forces at his disposal, and, as subsequent events were to show, no Mithridatic war could be regarded as over as long as the king himself was on the loose. But if Lucullus had co-operated with Fimbria at Pitane, Mithridates would probably have been a prisoner. It is also true that Sulla was in no hurry, that he spent eighteen months arranging the affairs of Asia and Greece and cosseting his health before he invaded Italy. But that in itself is not enough to absolve him of the charge of being more concerned with revenge on opponents in Italy than with Mithridates. Precipitate haste would have been foolish in embarking upon so momentous an enterprise, and the months of administration in Asia and Greece were also a time of military, naval and financial preparation for the war to come.[40] The reorganization of the war-torn provinces was necessary and could hardly be neglected: if it had been, Sulla would have laid himself even more open to the accusation of neglecting Rome's interests in order to pursue a private feud. No doubt he thought of this, and he may also have reckoned that delay, punctuated by suitably phrased missives from himself, would help to spread dissension and despondency among his potential opponents at home.

As his colleague in the consulship of 85 Cinna had chosen Cn. Carbo. Once Sulla's actions had put it beyond doubt that he proposed to return to Italy in arms, the consuls wasted no time in beginning their military preparations and their propaganda campaign. They set about collecting money, troops and corn from all over Italy, courted the upper classes in the Italian towns, on whose attitude much would depend, and canvassed the support of the new citizens in general, claiming that the threat they now faced was the consequence of their devotion to the Italian cause. This had a certain plausibility, despite the fact that Sulpicius' proposal had still not been put into practice. For all the upheavals of subsequent years could be seen as stemming from the original clash in 88 between Sulpicius and Sulla, which had indeed arisen over the Italian question. No doubt the consuls also warned the Italians that, if Sulla gained control, they would certainly have no hope of fair distribution and might even lose their citizenship as well. That too, given Sulla's stand in 88,

[39] Bennett 1923 (C 24) 52; Sherwin-White 1984 (D 291) 142ff; *contra*, Badian 1964 (A 2) 225; 1970 (C 13) 19; Bulst 1964 (C 35) 321. [40] Pozzi 1913/14 (C 119) 644ff.

might well sound convincing. It would therefore be prudent for Sulla to try to persuade the Italians that they had nothing to fear, that he was not opposed to their legitimate aspirations, and of this Sulla proved well aware.

He had already written to the Senate, probably after the death of Fimbria. The contents of this letter are unknown, but the sending of it of course implied that Sulla considered himself to be a legitimate proconsul, not a public enemy. Probably late in 85 he wrote again. First he recited his achievements in the Jugurthine and Cimbric Wars, in Cilicia and in the Social War, in his consulship and most recently against Mithridates, and stressed that he had harboured the refugees driven out of Rome by Cinna. Then he complained of the treatment he had received from his enemies in return for these services, and promised that he would come to take vengeance on the perpetrators in the name of his murdered friends, his family and the whole city. But, he went on, he bore no grudge against the mass of citizens, old or new. The similarity of form and content between this letter and that written by Caesar at the outset of his civil war is immediately striking. The inclusion among his achievements of the acts of his consulship, the Mithridatic War, and his succour of the refugees implied the validity of those acts and of his standing as proconsul and the invalidity both of his proclamation as a *hostis* and of all the other measures taken against him. (This conviction that his position as proconsul was unimpaired by the acts of his mortal enemies and acceptable to the gods who showed their favour by granting him victories is also vigorously advertised on Sulla's coinage.)[41] The identification of his cause with that of the state, already implied by the point about the refugees, was reinforced by the terms in which he formulated his threat of vengeance. The final clause was nicely judged to create dissension between those who had played an active part in opposition to Sulla and support of Marius and Cinna and those who had merely acquiesced in what had gone on but might have feared that they would be judged guilty by association. It also constituted Sulla's first step towards undermining the potentially solid support of the new citizens for Cinna and Carbo in defence of their hard-won privileges.

The immediate response was all Sulla could have hoped for. The *princeps senatus* L. Flaccus took the lead in proposing that an embassy be sent to Sulla to try to reconcile him with his enemies and to encourage him, if he felt the need of guarantees of his safety, to write again to the Senate. This proposal clearly represents an effort, not merely to avoid a renewal of civil war, but, somewhat unrealistically, to assert the corporate authority of the Senate over any individual, whether Cinna and Carbo on the one hand or Sulla on the other. For the offer to provide

[41] Crawford 1964 (B 146) 148; Keaveney 1982 (C 87) 118f; 1982 (C 90) 154ff.

guarantees of Sulla's safety must, to be meaningful, imply that Sulla should disband his forces on reaching Italy like any other proconsul. It is unlikely that Cinna and Carbo opposed the motion, for such a course would have irrevocably branded them as the instigators of conflict. Nor were they strong enough to run the risk of offending C. Flaccus, brother of the suffect consul of 86, who was in command of an army in Gaul. There is thus no need to postpone Flaccus' proposal until after the elections and the consuls' departure from Rome.[42]

As an earnest of good will and a further attempt to establish its control the Senate instructed Cinna and Carbo to stop their preparations for war until a reply came from Sulla. The consuls agreed to do so, but in fact at once arranged their re-election for 84, so as not to have to return again to Rome for the elections, then went on with their recruiting drive. It was their intention to meet Sulla in Greece, whether on purely military grounds or to spare Italy the horrors of renewed civil war and deprive Sulla of the opportunity to put into practice his protestations of good will towards the new citizens. So they began to concentrate their forces at Ancona in order to ship them across to Liburnia. The first contingent was transported safely, but the second was hit by a storm, which caused the loss of several ships, and the survivors dispersed to their homes, saying that they did not want to fight against fellow-citizens. What followed is not entirely clear. According to Appian the troops still at Ancona, when they heard the news, refused to embark. Cinna called an assembly but was met with disobedience, and his efforts to impose discipline only caused an escalation of violence, which culminated in his death. Thus the mutiny and the assassination of Cinna arose entirely from the men's reluctance to fight and Cinna's attempt to force them to do so. Plutarch offers a story with a very different emphasis. He records that Pompey was in Cinna's camp, but, in fear of his life because of false accusations brought against him, secretly withdrew to a place of safety. His disappearance provoked a rumour that Cinna had had him done away with, and this inspired the mutiny which ended in Cinna's death. That Pompey should have appeared in Cinna's camp is hardly surprising, nor perhaps that, seeing which way the wind was blowing, he should quickly have decided to dissociate himself from Cinna, perhaps after tampering with the wavering loyalty of the troops. But it is hard to see why Cinna's men should be much concerned about Pompey's fate, and Plutarch's account of the outbreak of the mutiny must exaggerate his importance.[43]

Both the brevity and the partial nature of Cinna's 'domination' make it difficult to pass any confident judgement on him as a man or as a politician. He was aware of the potential of the appeal to an army that had

[42] As Gabba 1958 (B 40) 208.

[43] Bennett 1923 (C 24) 61; Keaveney 1982 (C 88) 116.

just been demonstrated by Sulla and showed some acuteness in exploiting a *popularis* line of argument when making his histrionic approach to the troops at Nola. But there is nothing in the evidence, such as it is, to suggest that he had any awareness of the political problems that confronted the Republic or any solutions to offer. His attitude to the major political issue of the day, the distribution of the new citizens, was clearly based entirely on self-interest: he took up their cause in order to gain support and once he was in power became decidedly lukewarm. We know little of the functioning of Senate, magistrates and courts. The Senate clearly met and discussed matters of moment. It was prepared to defy Cinna and Carbo and try to make them comply with its wishes, though equally Cinna and Carbo ignored the Senate's instructions when they felt so inclined. There are few traces of activity, corrupt or otherwise, in the courts, but, once the initial wave of killings and expulsions was over, there is equally little sign of extra-legal persecutions. Cinna appears, as far as we can tell, to have given no thought to his own position in the state, his only apparent aim to hold the consulship year after year, his only object in holding it the enjoyment of power for its own sake and for survival. From a purely senatorial point of view the killings of 87 were worse than anything that had gone before, though they pale into insignificance when compared with the slaughter that Sulla was soon to unleash.

After Cinna's death Carbo abandoned the plan of facing Sulla outside Italy and brought back the men who had already crossed to Liburnia. He was reluctant to return to Rome, but was forced to do so by the tribunes, who threatened to deprive him of his *imperium* unless he arranged for the election of a suffect consul. So Carbo visited the city, but the first day fixed for the election proved ill-omened and on the second lightning struck the temples of Luna and Ceres. The augurs decreed a further postponement, and eventually Carbo held office without a colleague till the end of the year.

Also some time after the death of Cinna envoys came from Sulla bearing his eagerly awaited reply to the Senate's overtures. Our sources differ as to its content and tone. Appian makes Sulla bluntly reject both the Senate's suggestions. To the appeal for reconciliation he replied that he himself could never be friends with those who had committed such crimes, but that he would not hold it against the state should it choose to grant them protection. As for the offer of guarantees, he pointed out that because of the loyalty of his army he had no need of such assurances and indeed was better placed to offer them not only to the refugees but to the Senate itself: in other words, he had no intention of disbanding his army. For himself he demanded the annulment of the *hostis* declaration and the restoration of his property, his priesthood and all his other honours. The

Epitome of Livy on the other hand offers a version much more favourable to Sulla: he promised to obey the Senate, provided only that the citizens expelled by Cinna who had taken refuge with him were restored, while nothing is said of any personal demands on his part. The version of Appian is surely to be preferred. Sulla's conception of himself as the equal of the state and his contempt for the Senate's efforts to cut him down to size seem wholly in character. The most he was prepared to do was to give the Senate the chance to repudiate his enemies and choose his side well in advance of the confrontation he was determined to force.

The Epitomator claims that the Senate was in favour of accepting Sulla's terms, but was prevented by Carbo and those who, like him, saw in war the only chance of their own survival. Appian says that the envoys returned from Brundisium to Sulla when they learned that Cinna was dead and that opinion at Rome was hostile to Sulla. This need not mean that they themselves never went to Rome to deliver their message to the Senate, a course of action which would clearly have put Sulla in the wrong. If Appian's words refer to their reception at Rome, this would be compatible with a division of opinion in the Senate, though if Appian's version of Sulla's letter is correct, Carbo may have had quite substantial support.[44]

The coinage of these years has as its principal themes not only peace and economic recovery but also the unity of Italy and the harmony of Italy and Rome.[45] But in reality Carbo was already worried about the loyalty of the Italians. Their patience had been sorely tried by Cinna's failure to keep his promise to distribute them through all the tribes and they might now be tempted by the guarantees offered by Sulla: the attitude of Cinna's troops at Ancona had been highly disquieting. So, after the rejection of Sulla's embassy, Carbo planned to take hostages from all the towns of Italy to make sure of their support. But the Senate, clearly eager to prove to Sulla that it was not committed to Carbo's cause, opposed this step, though Carbo seems to have tried to go ahead with the scheme regardless.[46] The Senate did pass a decree which at last provided for the distribution of the new citizens throughout the thirty-five tribes. Whether this was done at Carbo's instigation or to steal his thunder is unfortunately unclear. However, it was almost certainly Carbo who somewhat later proposed a second decree extending the same privilege to freedmen, as Sulpicius had originally intended. The Senate also voted that all armies should be disbanded. Carbo may well have supported this decree, which might serve to put Sulla in the wrong by branding him as the aggressor, but many of those who voted in favour

[44] Cf. Pozzi 1913/14 (C 119) 651; Ensslin 1926 (B 33) 446; Frier 1971 (C 53) 593f.

[45] Rowland 1966 (B 236); Crawford 1964 (B 146) 148.

[46] Cf. Val. Max. VI.2.10.

may still have cherished the futile hope that the Senate could even now assert its authority over the rival generals without a resort to force.

III. THE CIVIL WAR, 83–81 B.C.

In the spring of 83 Sulla crossed to Brundisium with an army that consisted in essence of the five legions with which he had fought the Mithridatic War, a force much smaller than that which his opponents could hope to muster, but experienced, used to working together and totally devoted to their general. Not surprisingly Brundisium welcomed the invaders and was rewarded in due course by exemption from customs duties. Once Sulla had committed himself, support began to arrive. M. Crassus is said to have joined him even before he crossed to Italy. When he heard the news of Cinna's death, Crassus had raised an army in Spain and made his way to Africa to link up with Metellus Pius, though the two men soon quarrelled. Pius had tried to secure control of Africa, but had been driven out by the governor, C. Fabius Hadrianus. He may then have taken refuge in Liguria before bringing his forces to Sulla soon after his landing. He still considered himself a proconsul and was acknowledged as such by Sulla: his accession brought Sulla considerable prestige. More dramatic was the arrival of Pompey. After Cinna's death he had remained on his estates in Picenum, but now he raised a legion from among his clients and set out to join Sulla. It is impossible to determine exactly when and where they met, but Sulla treated the young man with exceptional respect, laying on a guard of honour, rising to greet him and addressing him as *imperator*. Pompey was then sent back to Picenum to use his influence in the region in a further recruiting drive, while Crassus was sent to raise troops among the Marsi. Nor was it only exiles and other sympathizers who came to Sulla. Renegade supporters of Cinna and Carbo were to form an increasingly prominent element in his following.[47] The first to be mentioned is one of the most remarkable: P. Cornelius Cethegus, one of the twelve *hostes* of 88, who now threw himself on Sulla's mercy and offered his considerable, if dubious, talents to the cause. He was welcomed, as somewhat later was C. Verres, who had been Carbo's quaestor in 84 and was still serving under him, but went over to Sulla, bringing with him Carbo's military chest.

Feeling in Rome and Italy was predominantly hostile to Sulla. The memory of his march on Rome in 88 and his reputation as an implacable hater reinforced disapproval with fear. So, when the consuls L. Cornelius Scipio and C. Norbanus (representatives of the nobility on the one

[47] Keaveney 1984 (C 93) 142f.

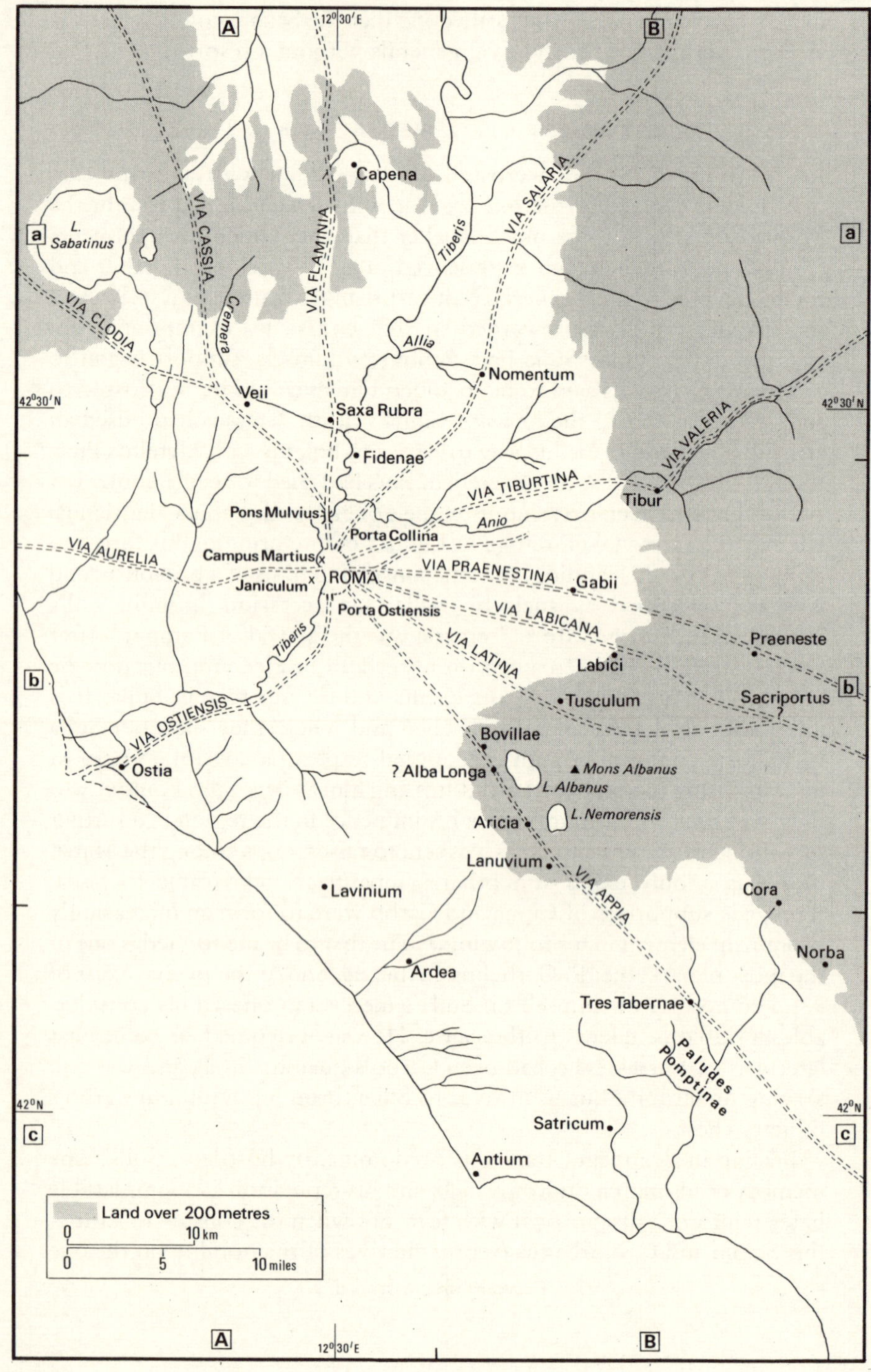

A
B
12°30′E
a
L. Sabatinus
VIA CASSIA
VIA FLAMINIA
Capena
Tiberis
VIA SALARIA
Cremera
VIA CLODIA
Allia
Nomentum
42°30′N
Veii
Saxa Rubra
Fidenae
VIA VALERIA
VIA TIBURTINA
Tibur
Pons Mulvius
Anio
Porta Collina
VIA AURELIA
Campus Martius
VIA PRAENESTINA
Janiculum
ROMA
Gabii
Porta Ostiensis
VIA LABICANA
Tiberis
VIA LATINA
Praeneste
Labici
b
Tusculum
Sacriportus ?
VIA OSTIENSIS
Bovillae
Ostia
? Alba Longa
Mons Albanus
L. Albanus
L. Nemorensis
Aricia
Lanuvium
VIA APPIA
Lavinium
Cora
Ardea
Norba
Tres Tabernae
Paludes Pomptinae
42°N
c
Satricum
Antium
Land over 200 metres
0 10 km
0 5 10 miles

7 Latium

hand, Italy on the other), strengthened by the passing of the *senatus consultum ultimum*, sent men all over Italy to collect troops, supplies and money, they received considerable support. It was clear that the first major theatre of war would be Campania, which may help to explain the proposal of a tribune, M. Iunius Brutus, to establish a colony at Capua.[48]

After the battle of Chaeronea the oracle of Trophonius at Lebadea had prophesied that Sulla would rout his enemies when he returned to Italy and, despite an unfavourable omen at Dyrrachium, he now received further signs of divine favour. The seer Postumius descried a promise of victory in a sacrifice made by Sulla at Tarentum, while on his march a slave, inspired by Ma-Bellona, also foretold his success, with a warning that, if he did not hurry, the Capitol would be destroyed by fire, as indeed it was on 6 July. At first Sulla was able to advance quickly. His generosity to his troops in Asia had been such that he was able not only to declare but to enforce a ban on looting. From Brundisium he followed the Via Appia, probably as far as Caudium. There he made a detour by way of Saticula and Calatia before heading for his first objective, Capua. Only now did he encounter opposition. The consuls had taken the dangerous step of dividing their forces to block his possible lines of advance, and Sulla found Norbanus stationed near Casilinum to defend the crossing of the Volturnus and the junction of the Viae Appia and Latina. Before resorting to battle Sulla tried negotiations, but his envoys were mistreated by Norbanus. No doubt Sulla's principal motives were to strengthen his image as a man of peace who had been driven to war by the intransigence of his enemies and, as always in his diplomatic manoeuvres, to undermine their precarious solidarity and spread dissension in their ranks. But if his offer had been accepted he would surely have been pleased. He might then have been able to gain control of Rome without having to fight for it, and it need not be supposed that he would have allowed himself to be cheated of his revenge on that account, even though he would have had to devise a somewhat different pretext. The armies clashed near the foot of Mount Tifata. Norbanus suffered heavy losses and was forced to withdraw to Capua.

Rather than waste time on a blockade, Sulla continued up the Via Latina towards Teanum Sidicinum, where the other consul Scipio was established. Morale in Scipio's army was already low and Sulla tried to undermine it further by again sending envoys to negotiate in the hope that battle would prove unnecessary. Unlike Norbanus, Scipio was prepared to listen. He may well have believed, however optimistically, that real advantages might accrue from a negotiated peace. Thousands of citizen lives would be saved, and although any agreement would leave Sulla master of Rome, he would have less excuse to indulge in violence

[48] Gabba 1973 (C 55) 151ff.

than if he came to the city as the victor in a long and bitter war, especially as he would find there more men who might try to restrain him than if his leading opponents were all already dead or in exile. So Scipio and Sulla met between Cales and Teanum and actually came to an agreement. Its contents are known only from Cicero's vague description in the *Twelfth Philippic*, which makes it clear at least that they were very wide-ranging: they covered the authority of the Senate, the votes of the people and the right of citizenship. That Sulla took it on himself to lay down the law on such matters demonstrates yet again his opinion of his own importance. It is likely that he agreed to stand by his recent acquiescence in the distribution of the Italians throughout all the tribes on condition that the measures he had passed in 88 to restore the predominance of the Senate and reform voting in the popular assemblies were acknowledged as valid. Scipio then sent a message to Norbanus at Capua to try to secure his assent. Unfortunately, from his point of view, he chose as his envoy Sertorius, who did not trust Sulla, had been against negotiating in the first place, and thought that there was greater hope of safety in carrying on the war. So on his way to Capua he turned aside and broke the truce arranged by Sulla and Scipio by seizing the town of Suessa, which had already gone over to Sulla. Sulla at once protested, and Scipio, despite his innocence, had no choice but to declare their agreement at an end and return Sulla's hostages.

For Sulla the collapse of the negotiations brought both diplomatic and practical advantages. His claim to be the champion of peace received a considerable boost and he could now maintain that his opponents had placed themselves wholly in the wrong. Indeed, he even used their continued resistance from this moment on as a formal justification for the blood-bath that followed the fighting. Moreover, Scipio's already unenthusiastic army had welcomed the prospect of peace and placed the blame on the consul when it receded. They made it clear that if Sulla approached their camp they would not resist but come over. So Sulla made as if to attack, but instead sent in his troops with orders to fraternize. This move was completely successful, and by the time Sulla himself entered the camp he found only the unfortunate Scipio and his son still there. He tried to persuade them too to change sides, but when they refused let them go. Sulla tried to repeat his trick by sending a second embassy to Norbanus, who was still at Capua, but the consul made no reply, so Sulla continued his advance, while Norbanus, it seems, abandoned Capua and retreated to Praeneste.

Meanwhile Carbo had based himself at Ariminum, the key to Cisalpine Gaul. He had already suffered a defeat in a cavalry engagement against Pompey in Picenum, where Pompey's attempts at recruiting had been much more successful than those of Carbo's emissaries: he had raised a further two legions. It was probably now, rather than when he first joined Sulla, that three enemy commanders attacked Pompey as he made his way back to Sulla: C. Carrinas, L. Iunius Brutus Damasippus, whom he routed, and a third whose identity is uncertain, perhaps C. Coelius Antipater.[49] Pompey also encountered the consul Scipio, who had acquired another army, but who now suffered the humiliation of seeing his troops desert for a second time. Later in the year Carbo visited Rome to hold the consular elections. While he was there he caused Metellus Pius and all other senators who were with Sulla to be declared *hostes*. The consuls elected were drawn from the hard core of the resistance to Sulla, the political heirs of Marius and Cinna, between whom and Sulla there was such a degree of mutual hatred that they had no choice but to fight to the last. Carbo himself was consul for the third time, and to try to exploit the magic of a name he took as his colleague C. Marius, son of the great man, who was only twenty-six.

Both sides devoted the remainder of 83 to recruiting and other preparations for the crucial campaign of 82. After his escapade at Suessa, Sertorius had raised a considerable force in the old Marian stronghold of Etruria, but he made himself unpopular at Rome by his criticisms of the inertia and incompetence that had marked the resistance to Sulla so far. He also disapproved of the choice of Marius as consul, perhaps because he had been hoping to be Carbo's colleague himself. So at the end of the year he left Italy to try to assume control of his praetorian province, Hispania Citerior. Sulla followed up his earlier assurances to the Italians by making a series of formal agreements with Italic peoples, in which he guaranteed that he would not deprive them of their citizenship nor interfere with their distribution throughout the tribes. It is probable, however, that no treaty was made with the Samnites, not because Sulla nursed an atavistic racial hatred or because he cherished any devious scheme to disguise a civil war fought to satisfy a private grudge as a struggle for national survival against Rome's oldest enemy, but because he denied the validity of the terms made by Marius and Cinna in 87 and so did not recognize the Samnites as Roman citizens.[50]

Bad weather had prevented any fighting in Italy over the winter, but the year began badly for Sulla's opponents in other theatres of war. The governor of Africa, Fabius Hadrianus, perished in a rising at Utica and the praetor Q. Antonius Balbus lost Sardinia and his life to L. Philippus, who had thrown in his lot with Sulla. When the campaign in Italy began in the spring, Sulla divided his forces. He himself continued his march towards Rome and Etruria, while Metellus headed north to tie Carbo down at Ariminum and try to gain control of Cisalpine Gaul. He enjoyed

[49] Tuplin 1979 (C 145); *contra*, Keaveney 1982 (C 88) 118f.

[50] Pozzi 1913/14 (C 119) 668, better than Salmon 1964 (C 128) 74ff.

an immediate success, defeating the praetor C. Carrinas in a battle on the Aesis. Carrinas suffered heavy casualties and withdrew, probably to Spoletium, while the whole region went over to Pius. Carbo now advanced in person against Metellus and contrived to surround him, but news soon came of a major defeat inflicted by Sulla on Marius, and so Carbo judged it prudent to return to Ariminum. On the way his rearguard suffered at the hands of Pompey, whom Sulla had sent to help Metellus.

Sulla had proceeded along the Via Latina and made contact with the consul Marius near Signia. The decisive battle took place at Sacriportus (the exact site is unknown, but it probably lay close to the junction of the Viae Latina and Labicana). Encouraged by yet another favourable dream, Sulla himself was at first eager to fight, but his men were exhausted, it was raining hard, and his officers at last persuaded him to make camp. Marius seized the opportunity to attack, but first his left wing began to give ground and then a substantial part of his force deserted. The remainder fled to Praeneste, with Sulla's men hot on their heels. Only the first arrivals got in safely before the gates were closed. Marius himself had to be hauled up on a rope. Sulla took many prisoners and put all the Samnites among them to death. According to Appian he announced as his reason that the Samnites had always been enemies of Rome. Whatever his exact words, the underlying implication must have been that Sulla did not acknowledge the Samnites as citizens. If he rejected, as he surely must have done, the validity of their agreement with Marius and Cinna, then logically they must have been for him still belligerents in the Social War – which may be what he actually said. This vindictive act was to have drastic consequences, for it provoked a massive rising in Sulla's rear which came close to depriving him of ultimate victory.

Sulla left another renegade, Q. Lucretius Afella, to besiege Praeneste, from which Marius sent a message to Rome instructing the urban praetor Brutus Damasippus to put to death any leading men whom he suspected of sympathy for Sulla. Damasippus summoned a meeting of the Senate, at which four men lost their lives. Pompey's father-in-law P. Antistius and C. Papirius Carbo Arvina were killed in the building, L. Domitius Ahenobarbus, consul in 94, and Q. Scaevola the *pontifex maximus*, the most distinguished of the victims, as they were trying to escape. The bodies were thrown into the Tiber.[51] Sulla sent detachments down all the roads to Rome – the Latina, Labicana and Praenestina – and it became clear that Damasippus' murders had done nothing to strengthen resistance, for the city at once opened its gates rather than face a

[51] After Sacriportus: Pozzi 1913/14 (C 119) 669; Keaveney 1982 (C 87) 138f; *contra*, Hackl 1982 (C 71) 251.

blockade. When Sulla himself arrived on the Campus Martius he found that all his opponents had fled. They were promptly declared *hostes* and their property was confiscated. Sulla probably did not enter the city – though the Senate would surely have granted him a dispensation – but summoned an assembly, to which he apologized for the present disturbances and promised that they would soon be brought to an end and the affairs of Rome put in order. Leaving a garrison of veterans behind, he set off without further delay to meet Carbo in Etruria.

Things had continued to go well for Sulla elsewhere.[52] Carbo had suffered a second defeat at the hands of Metellus, while Pompey had beaten Marcius Censorinus near Sena Gallica. But when news came of the siege of Praeneste Carbo's first priority inevitably became the relief of his colleague. With considerable skill he succeeded in withdrawing his forces from further confrontation with Metellus and established his base at Clusium. Norbanus was left at Ariminum to try to hold down Metellus. But Pius was able to ship his army to Ravenna and occupied the surrounding plain before making for Faventia, while Pompey now moved to rejoin Sulla. Meanwhile in the south Neapolis was betrayed to Sulla.

Sulla himself advanced along the Via Cassia towards Clusium, while another detachment took the Via Clodia to Saturnia. Both were successful: Sulla's cavalry defeated Carbo's on the Clanis, while the other force won a battle at Saturnia. A protracted clash between Sulla and Carbo before Clusium ended indecisively, but elsewhere his generals enjoyed consistent good fortune. Pompey and Crassus, who had occupied Tuder early in the year, defeated Carrinas near Spoletium and shut him up in the town. However, Carbo sent a force to relieve him and though Sulla inflicted some damage on it in an ambush it achieved its objective. But more important was the failure of a force of eight legions commanded by Censorinus, which Carbo sent to raise the siege of Praeneste. Pompey ambushed it in a defile and penned the survivors on a hill. Censorinus himself escaped and made his way back to Carbo, but his army blamed him for falling into Pompey's trap: the majority of the men dispersed to their homes, while one legion made its own way back to Ariminum.

But at this point help came for Praeneste from an unexpected quarter. Sulla's treatment of his Samnite prisoners after Sacriportus had provoked a rising of the Samnites, who were joined by the Lucanians, and a combined Samnite and Lucanian force, led by the Samnite C. Pontius Telesinus, the Lucanian M. Lamponius and the Capuan Gutta, set out for Praeneste. Sulla was in no doubt about the urgency of this threat. He at once left Carbo to his own devices at Clusium and hurried to protect

52 Pozzi 1913/14 (C 119) 670ff; Keaveney 1982 (C 88) 121ff.

Afella. It is impossible to determine from Appian's vague description exactly where or how Sulla disposed his forces, but he prevented the Italian army from making its way past Afella's position and effecting a junction with Carbo's forces to the north.[53] In alarm Marius made an attempt to break out, but this too failed.

In the north things went from bad to worse. Metellus had encamped at Faventia, where he was rashly attacked by Norbanus late in the day on extremely unsuitable ground. Norbanus was heavily defeated, and there followed the now familiar pattern of desertions and dispersals. Among those who went over to Metellus was a legion of Lucanians commanded by P. Albinovanus, another of the twelve *hostes* of 88. Albinovanus came to an arrangement with Pius to betray his fellow-commanders in exchange for an amnesty. He invited Norbanus and others to a banquet, at which all the guests were murdered. Norbanus had prudently stayed away and made his escape to Rhodes, where he later committed suicide when tracked down by Sulla's bounty-hunters. Albinovanus then surrendered Ariminum and the whole of Cisalpine Gaul went over to Pius, while M. Lucullus, who had been besieged by one Quinctius at Fidentia, made a successful sortie and defeated his opponent.[54]

Carbo sent a second force, this time of only two legions under Damasippus, to relieve Praeneste, but again Sulla blocked its path and it too could find no way past. At this and the collapse of resistance in the north Carbo seems suddenly to have lost his nerve. He abandoned his army at Clusium, intending to withdraw to Africa. A serious defeat at the hands of Pompey produced further dispersals, but Carrinas, Censorinus and Damasippus made a last effort to relieve Praeneste from the north, in conjunction with the Samnites who were trying once more to break through from the south. This attempt too failed, and so it was decided to try a diversion by marching on Rome itself, which now lay almost empty of both men and supplies, in the hope of drawing Sulla out of his impregnable position. By the early morning of 1 November the Italian force had reached a point just over a Roman mile from the Colline Gate. But although Telesinus may have made a speech urging his men to destroy the wolf in its lair, he made no attempt to take the city. No doubt, whatever his ultimate intentions may have been, he realized that it would be not only pointless but dangerous to allow his men to be distracted by the delights of sacking Rome while Sulla was still in the field. So the Samnites and their allies waited for Sulla to appear.

Sulla had sent a squadron of cavalry ahead while he himself hurried in full force down the Via Praenestina. About noon he encamped near the temple of Venus Erycina. The battle began in late afternoon, against the advice of some of Sulla's officers, who thought that the men were too

[53] Lewis 1971 (C 98). [54] Gabba 1958 (B 40) 244f.

tired. The right wing, commanded by Crassus, won an easy victory, but the left, under Sulla's own command, broke. Sulla risked his life in trying to rally his forces but they fled, despite his despairing prayers to Apollo, towards the city. Sulla was forced to take refuge in his camp, and some of his men rode for Praeneste to tell Afella to abandon the siege, though Afella refused to panic. But when Sulla's fleeing troops reached the gates of Rome the veterans dropped the portcullis, compelling them to stand and fight. The battle continued well into the night, as slowly but surely Sulla's men gained the upper hand, until finally they captured the Samnite camp. Telesinus himself was found among the dead, but Lamponius, Censorinus and Carrinas escaped. Later still messengers came from Crassus, who had pursued the enemy as far as Antemnae, and Sulla learned for the first time of his success.[55] Censorinus and Carrinas were soon captured and killed, and their heads were sent by Sulla to Afella at Praeneste, along with those of Telesinus, Damasippus, who had also fallen in the battle, and Marius Gratidianus, who was tortured and killed by L. Catilina at the tomb of Catulus, whom he had prosecuted after Cinna's capture of Rome. To all intents and purposes the civil war in Italy was over, though Praeneste had not yet fallen and a few other towns still held out – Norba fell early in 81, but Nola not until 80, Aesernia and Volaterrae only in 79 – and Sulla's enemies still held Sicily, Africa and Spain.[56]

When he learned of Crassus' success, Sulla went at once to Antemnae. There 3,000 of the survivors offered to surrender, and Sulla promised them safe-conduct if they killed those in the town who still favoured resistance. They did so, but when they emerged they were brought to Rome and penned in the Villa Publica along with the prisoners taken at the Colline Gate. There all were massacred by Sulla's troops, within earshot of the Senate, which Sulla had summoned in the temple of Bellona nearby to receive his report on the Mithridatic War. After his speech in the Senate Sulla addressed the people. He promised that things would change for the better if men obeyed him, but also made it clear that he would take revenge on any man of the rank of military tribune or above who had aided his enemies in any way since the day that L. Scipio had broken the truce.

Then Sulla set out for Praeneste. There Afella's display of the heads taken at the Colline Gate had proved that further resistance was useless, and the city surrendered. Confusion reigns in the sources as to the fate of Marius: either he was captured and killed while trying to escape, or he committed suicide, whether alone or in a pact with Telesinus' younger brother. His head was sent by Afella to Sulla. Some prisoners of senatorial rank were put to death at once by Afella, but the bulk of the

[55] Keaveney 1982 (C 87) 144ff.

[56] Aesernia: Keaveney–Strachan 1981 (B 52).

men taken was reserved to await the judgement of Sulla. His solution was to divide the prisoners into three groups: Romans, Praenestines and Samnites. The Romans were pardoned, the Samnites slaughtered, the Praenestines, apart from a few that Sulla felt had served his cause, met the same fate.[57]

To recover the vital corn-producing provinces of Sicily and Africa Sulla chose Pompey. The young man had already received one reward: a marriage alliance with Sulla.[58] The bride was Sulla's stepdaughter Aemilia, daughter of M. Scaurus. She was already married to M'. Acilius Glabrio and pregnant, but Glabrio was persuaded to divorce her while Pompey divorced the luckless Antistia. Yet the scheme came to nothing, for Aemilia shortly died in labour. Pompey's position was for the first time placed on a legal footing: he was granted praetorian *imperium* by the Senate. After his initial flight to Africa Carbo had decided to join forces with the governor of Sicily, M. Perperna. He established himself on the island of Cossyra and sent M. Brutus, praetor in 88, on a reconnaissance to Lilybaeum. Brutus, however, was surrounded by Pompey's fleet and committed suicide. Carbo himself then tried to land in Sicily, but found that Perperna had already left the island. He tried to escape to Egypt, but was captured at Cossyra and brought to Pompey, who had him put to death. The description of Carbo as still consul at the time of his death, whether legally accurate or not, places it before the end of 82. Pompey was later accused of ingratitude, since Carbo had defended him in 86, but Carbo's name had figured on the first proscription list, so although the proscriptions had not yet been legalized Pompey had little choice. Their previous connexion would merely have made it more essential for Pompey to give this proof of loyalty to Sulla. With his legate and brother-in-law C. Memmius, Pompey then devoted himself to the reorganization of the island and seized the opportunity to form numerous *clientelae*, his most noteworthy protégé being Sthenius of Himera.

In Sicily Pompey received a letter from Sulla to inform him that a further decree of the Senate had empowered him to proceed to Africa, where another refugee, Cn. Domitius Ahenobarbus, had secured the support of Hiarbas of Numidia. Leaving Memmius in charge of Sicily, Pompey invaded Africa and according to Plutarch took only forty days to capture Domitius and his camp, put Hiarbas to death and replace him with the more reliable Hiempsal, achievements for which he was saluted as *imperator*. Domitius too was executed: again his proscription provided the justification, but again there were repercussions later. In Sulla's eyes Pompey had now served his purpose. He wrote again, ordering Pompey to disband his army except for one legion, with which he should wait till

57 Keaveney 1982 (C 87) 149.

58 Plut. *Pomp.* 9.1ff; *Sulla* 33.3; though cf. Keaveney 1982 (C 88) 132.

his successor arrived. But Pompey wanted a triumph, and although he was in no position to offer a serious military challenge to Sulla, he calculated that he could afford to risk being awkward. His troops, no doubt suitably primed, refused to go home unless Pompey came with them, and so he brought them back to Italy in person. Once he realized that Pompey was not in revolt, Sulla stifled his resentment and even made a point of addressing him as Magnus, a name just given him by his troops in Africa. But now Pompey demanded his triumph. Sulla, angry at his presumption, refused on a technicality: Pompey was not yet a senator. Pompey persisted, impudently warning Sulla that more men worshipped the rising than the setting sun. Sulla gave way, and on 12 March 81 Pompey achieved the first great landmark of his extraordinary career: a triumph at the age of twenty-four while he was still an *eques*.[59]

IV. SULLA'S DICTATORSHIP AND ITS AFTERMATH, 82–78 B.C.

Sulla's treatment of his prisoners, savage though it was, was at least governed by rational considerations of a kind. But from the moment of his capture of Rome his supporters had run riot not only in the city but all over Italy, killing for profit, pleasure or personal vengeance anyone they pleased. Indeed the proscriptions, Sulla's most notorious legacy to Rome, were instituted as a response to protests against the arbitrary nature of these killings, though the details of the exchanges between Sulla and his critics remain uncertain. Even so loyal and distinguished an adherent of Sulla as Q. Catulus is said to have enquired whether anyone was to be left alive, but the first list was issued by Sulla after a plea that, if he would not reveal whom he proposed to spare, he would at least make known whom he had decided to punish, though it is not clear whether this request was made in spontaneous anger by a young and not easily identified C. Metellus or in prearrangement with Sulla by one Fursidius or Fufidius.

Those named on the lists were condemned to death without trial, their property was confiscated, and their descendants were barred from standing for office for two generations, though they were still liable to the duties of their station. Rewards were promised to those who killed the proscribed or gave information which led to their capture, penalties imposed on anyone who concealed or otherwise helped them. The first list was published before the fall of Praeneste, perhaps on the day after that meeting of the Senate which had been shocked by the slaughter of the prisoners. Its length is a matter of dispute: Appian speaks of 40 senators and some 1,600 *equites*, though the latter figure may represent the eventual total, while Plutarch and Orosius agree that the first list

[59] Badian 1955 (C 5); Seager 1979 (C 258) 12 n. 46; *contra*, Twyman 1979 (C 148).

contained 80 names. It was swiftly followed by two more, each containing some 220 names according to Plutarch. At first there was no indication of how long the lists would remain open; only later did Sulla announce that no names would be added after 1 June 81. Two consuls and two consulars were named on the first list: Carbo, Marius, Norbanus and L. Scipio, who had taken refuge at Massilia; so too was Sertorius. It seems that Scipio was deprived of his augurate and the vacant position in the college filled by Sulla himself.[60] Also proscribed, though somewhat later, was the young Julius Caesar, who refused to divorce Cinna's daughter when ordered to do so by Sulla. In consequence he lost his position as *flamen Dialis* designate, but was eventually pardoned by Sulla on the intercession of Mam. Lepidus, C. Cotta and the Vestal Virgins. Nor was the witch hunt confined to Rome. Agents both Roman and Italian visited every region, and in the towns of Italy just as in Rome itself the proscriptions were exploited by unscrupulous men to gain wealth and get rid of their political adversaries. Crassus is said to have earned Sulla's lasting displeasure by proscribing a man in Bruttium solely in order to secure his estate, while the activities of Oppianicus at Larinum and the Roscii at Ameria (of which later speeches by Cicero inform us) are no doubt typical of what went on all over the country.

If Sulla seriously intended the institution of the proscriptions to clarify and stabilize a totally confused situation, he failed completely, but it is hard to believe that he cared. The published lists were frequently tampered with, while in the carrying out of executions and the claiming of rewards, cases of mistaken and falsified identity were not uncommon. The criteria of guilt were never properly applied. Despite his disapproval of some who enriched themselves, Sulla himself seems to have been easily persuaded by his satellites to add names to the lists to satisfy personal grudges or greed for rich men's property and auctioned off confiscated goods to his favourites at prices well below the market value. Many such abuses must also have taken place without his knowledge; Cicero's insistence that Sulla had no part in his freedman Chrysogonus' machinations against Roscius is probably true. It was in any case inevitable that the rich should be the principal victims. Sulla was not concerned with pursuing the rank and file who had fought against him but only those who, thanks to their wealth or social standing, had played a more conspicuous part in the resistance, that is members of the senatorial and equestrian orders. However, the fact that the number of *equites* proscribed was twenty times greater than the total of senators was not a consequence of any special hatred of the order on Sulla's part, but a simple reflection of the relative numbers of senators and *equites* involved in the conflict.

[60] Badian 1968 (C 11) 38.

Even the dead had not escaped Sulla's vengeance: he had ordered the remains of the great Marius to be disinterred and scattered. But with his thirst for revenge eased if not yet slaked he took thought for his own position in the state. In November 82 the Senate decreed that all his acts, both as consul and proconsul, should be ratified. It also voted him a gilt equestrian statue, to be set before the rostra, the first time such an honour had been vouchsafed to a Roman citizen. The inscription read, according to Appian, 'Cornelio Sullae Imperatori Felici'; however, it may be that the last two words should be reversed. If so, this suggests that this decree of the Senate was the same that conferred on him officially the *agnomen* Felix, the formal assumption of which should probably be placed after the fall of Praeneste rather than after his triumph.[61] His adoption of the Greek surname Epaphroditos, which he had used during the Mithridatic War and after, was also perhaps approved at this time.

Sulla knew perfectly well what he wanted, the obsolete office of the dictatorship; but he proposed to make use of it in an unprecedented way which, by accident or design, had more in common with the functions of the *Xviri*, who were believed to have drawn up the Twelve Tables (Vol. VII², pp. 113ff), than with those of any previous dictator.[62] First he instructed the Senate to appoint an *interrex*, for both consuls had been proscribed and both were now dead. The Senate's choice fell on its *princeps*, L. Flaccus, though it is hard to believe that many were so sanguine as to hope, as Appian suggests, that he would arrange for consular elections to be held. Next Sulla wrote putting his own views to Flaccus: he thought that in the present situation the appointment of a dictator would be beneficial, not for the traditional brief fixed period but until stable government had been restored throughout the empire, and that he himself would be an eminently suitable candidate. So Flaccus promulgated a law. By its terms Sulla was to be made dictator indefinitely to put the state in order and draft laws. Any measure he might take was ratified in advance; whether or not he submitted his proposals to the people for formal validation was entirely up to him. In particular he was to have the right to condemn citizens to death without trial. The people had no choice and the law was duly passed. Flaccus nominated Sulla as dictator, and Sulla in turn named Flaccus as his *magister equitum*.[63] It perhaps needs to be emphasized that Sulla was not appointed dictator for life. The definition of his mission, broad though it was, constituted in itself a kind of time-limit, albeit an inevitably vague one. It was taken for granted that when Sulla had completed that mission according to his lights he would lay down his dictatorship, and there is

[61] Balsdon 1951 (C 18) 4f; Gabba 1958 (B 40) 263; *contra*, Keaveney 1983 (H 68) 45 n. 6.

[62] Bellen 1975 (C 23) 560ff; Keaveney 1982 (C 87) 162.

[63] Cic. *Att.* IX.15.2; Gabba 1958 (B 40) 341f.

nothing but the anachronistic surprise of later sources to suggest that Sulla himself considered for a moment the possibility of trying to retain his power for life. A minor puzzle concerns the number of his lictors. It is said that he had twenty-four and that this was unprecedented. The figure need not be doubted, but the comment may well be incorrect.[64]

Sulla promptly held elections for the consulships of 81. M. Tullius Decula and Cn. Cornelius Dolabella were elected. It is unfortunately unclear whether it was at these elections that Q. Lucretius Afella tried to stand, although he had held no previous public office, basing his claim on his services to Sulla at Praeneste. It is perhaps more likely that Afella stood now, while his success at Praeneste was still fresh in men's minds and before Sulla's law on observance of the regular *cursus* had been passed, than that he tried in deliberate defiance of Sulla's rules to stand against the formidable combination of Sulla himself and Metellus Pius for the consulship of 80.[65] But even now Sulla would not allow such irregularity. He warned Afella to withdraw, but when he persisted had him killed and made it clear to the people that no protests would be tolerated. Then on 27 and 28 January 81 Sulla celebrated his triumph over Mithridates. On the second day the treasures taken by Marius from Rome to Praeneste were exhibited, while the restored exiles marched in the procession, saluting Sulla as their saviour and father. The implication is clear: those Romans who had fought against Sulla were traitors who had by so doing given aid to the national enemy Mithridates. In view of Sulla's own dealings with Mithridates the irony could hardly be bettered.

But even before this Sulla may have begun on the great work of reform. His first law was probably that which, retrospectively and till 1 June, authorized the proscriptions. On a more constructive level his aim, broadly speaking, was to restore the predominance of the Senate, which since 133 had been subjected to intermittent challenge and gradual erosion. But to do this he had to reconstruct the Senate itself, which had been depleted to about half its normal strength of 300 first by the Social and civil wars, then by Sulla's own proscriptions. Sulla began by bringing the numbers up to 300, probably using the traditional criterion of distinguished service in war, which might explain the hostile tradition that he put common soldiers in the Senate, then he enrolled some 300 further members. (It is possible that each tribe was allowed to nominate eight or nine.)[66] These came from the equestrian order; the obvious and only other qualification will have been loyalty to Sulla. It has been claimed that Sulla was hostile to the *equites* and wanted to leave the order weak and leaderless by creaming off its best men into the Senate. There is

[64] Livy *Per.* LXXXIX; Marino 1973–4 (C 104) 420f; Keaveney 1983 (C 92) 193 n. 58.

[65] *Contra*, Gabba 1958 (B 40) 276f; Keaveney 1982 (C 87) 198f.

[66] Gabba 1958 (B 40) 343ff; 1973 (C 55) 159ff, 409ff.

no warrant for this. The structure of Roman society was simply such that the equestrian order was the only conceivable source of new senators on such a large scale. To keep the Senate up to strength in future Sulla increased the number of quaestors elected each year from eight to twenty and enacted that they should automatically enter the Senate at the end of their year of office instead of waiting for enrolment at the next census. There is, however, no evidence that Sulla was hostile to the censorship as an institution, wanted to abolish it, or sought to weaken it by this measure.

Sulla also acted to suppress those forces which had undermined the authority of the Senate over the previous fifty years. Outstanding among these had been the tribunate, and Sulla set out to render it politically harmless. The tribunes were deprived of the power to introduce legislation.[67] The right of veto remained, without restriction, if Caesar is to be believed, as he probably should be.[68] To ensure that the tribunate became, as Velleius puts it, a shadow without substance, Sulla also enacted that any man who held it should be debarred from tenure of any further public office. Thus, he hoped, men of talent and ambition would shun the tribunate, so that any future agitation for the restoration of its powers would prove ineffective. He also wished to establish the Senate's control over other magistrates, indeed over all individuals. To this end he revived the *lex annalis*, enforcing the proper order of the *cursus* – quaestorship, praetorship, consulship – and laying down minimum ages for election to each office: probably twenty-nine for the quaestorship, thirty-nine for the praetorship and forty-two for the consulship.[69] To prevent such inordinate accumulations of power and *auctoritas* as had recently been achieved, most dramatically by Marius but also to a lesser extent by Cinna and Carbo, Sulla resurrected another old rule, which required an interval of ten years before the iteration of any office.

But it was clear that in the future the greatest threat to senatorial control must come from a contumacious proconsul backed by an army, like Sulla's more loyal to its commander than to the state. Sulla understood the problem and did his best. He certainly did not lay down that consuls or praetors must remain in Rome until the end of their year of office.[70] Nor is it likely that the increase in the number of praetorships to eight was intended to make it possible to replace all provincial governors at the end of each year. There might quite often be cogent military or administrative grounds for prorogation, but even when no such grounds existed governors often remained in their provinces for

[67] Keaveney 1982 (C 87) 186 n. 3; *contra*, Gabba 1958 (B 40) 273f.

[68] Caes. *BCiv*. 1.5.1; 7.3; see Lintott 1978 (B 190) 127.

[69] Fraccaro 1956–7 (A 33) II 225ff; Gabba 1958 (B 40) 342f.

[70] Balsdon 1939 (C 167) 58ff; Giovannini 1983 (F 62) 75ff, 91ff.

two years or longer. In any case such a system could work only if every magistrate were compelled by law to take a province at the end of his year of office, but in fact there was no compulsion, nor even indeed any pressure. What Sulla did do, through the medium of his law of *maiestas*, was to limit strictly the action which a governor could take without authority from the Senate or People. He could not on his own initiative leave his province, lead his army outside it, enter a foreign kingdom or make war, and he must leave his province within thirty days of his successor's arrival. Of these provisions only the last was perhaps new, and it is clear that they were meant to be interpreted in the light of common sense, not in a fashion so literal as to make effective frontier defence impossible. But such legal safeguards would be of use only as long as the Senate was in reality stronger than any individual governor. Once a commander came upon the scene with the ambition to seize supreme power for himself and the military strength to give him a fair chance of success, then the fear of prosecution if he failed would no longer restrain him. Indeed the threat of political extinction in the courts might even help to drive him into open revolt.

But if the seeds of such a revolt had been sown in the eighties, when the young Caesar learned, like Sulla, to despise the Senate as it then was, it must be said that Sulla's new Senate was to show itself no more deserving of respect. Its members lacked the individual authority, the practical experience, the public spirit and above all the moral self-confidence to make a success of the mammoth task of social and political regeneration that lay before them. Many can have felt little commitment to the preservation of Sulla's work. The *Sullani* had come from various backgrounds and had joined Sulla for differing reasons. Both the extent of their personal loyalty to Sulla and the degree to which they shared his political views must have varied enormously. Essentially they had had only two things in common: an enemy and a leader. When both these factors ceased to operate, their natural diversity reasserted itself. A small core of aristocrats – Catulus, Hortensius, the Luculli and others – remained totally dedicated to Sulla's ideals, but the gulf between them and the mass of senators grew progressively wider, while all alike, haunted by the fear of a new Sulla, were trapped in a sterile conformism which exalted mediocrity and looked on talent with resentful suspicion.[71]

The Senate had also been weakened by its contest with the equestrian order for control of the *quaestiones*, especially the extortion court. Sulla's views on this subject were predictable: the juries were from now on to be drawn entirely from the Senate. In addition he revised and extended the whole system of standing courts in a reform which was to prove the most

[71] Meier 1966 (A 72) 243, 257, 265; Badian 1970 (C 13) 29ff, Keaveney 1984 (C 93) 146ff.

durable aspect of his work, surviving into the early Principate (ch. 13, pp. 512–30).

In dealing with the popular assemblies and the people in general, apart from abolishing tribunician legislation, Sulla stood by his promise to uphold the citizenship and voting rights of the new citizens, though freedmen were again confined to the four urban tribes. He enfranchised many of the slaves of his victims, allegedly more than 10,000 in number. Since Appian stresses that they were picked for their youth and strength, they were presumably intended not only to vote themselves but to exercise persuasion on their fellow-voters. However, they are never heard of again and there is nothing to suggest that they were ever called upon to fulfil their corporate function. Clearly no man inherited their loyalty after Sulla's death. Like any good Roman conservative Sulla saw the distribution of cheap corn to the people as a demoralizing drain on the treasury, and so distributions were abolished. He also deprived the people of the share in the choice of priests given to it by the Lex Domitia of 104. He restored the old system of co-option and increased the membership of the major priestly colleges to fifteen. The Sibylline books had been destroyed when the Capitol was burned in 83 and Sulla gave orders that the collection should be reconstructed.

He also passed various sumptuary restrictions. Gambling was prohibited except for bets on certain kinds of athletic contest. Price controls were imposed on exotic foods and limits placed on permitted expenditure for everyday meals, festive banquets, funerals and monuments to the dead, though these were much higher than those permitted by the Lex Licinia of the late second century. Such measures were always fashionable with reformers and always futile. Indeed Sulla himself was accused of breaking his own laws with his spending on public feasts and on Metella's funeral.

Sulla's treatment of Italy was guided by two considerations: the need to find land for his veterans – Appian says as many as twenty-three legions were settled – and the attitude of the Italian peoples in the recent war.[72] Some areas, such as Apulia, Calabria and Picenum, had largely favoured Sulla from the first. But the greater part had been hostile: Campania, Latium, and especially Etruria and Umbria. But even in regions that were predominantly hostile some communities will have been well disposed to Sulla, while within individual communities the allegiance of the leading families will not always have been unanimous. It is possible that a few of the towns where Sulla settled his men were not being punished for resistance but simply revived after the ravages of war, but the vast majority had been hostile and received colonists or other settlers to punish their recent indiscretions and secure their future

[72] Keaveney 1982 (C 89) 511ff.

loyalty. The penal element is particularly clear in places where the older community was reduced to an inferior status, as for instance at Clusium, Nola, Pompeii and Faesulae. Essentially three modes of settlement were employed: viritane allotments in existing colonies and *municipia*, the addition of a colony to an already existing *municipium*, and the establishment of a colony accompanied by the downgrading of the original inhabitants. The method chosen in individual cases perhaps reflected the degree of guilt of the community concerned. The exact number of Sulla's colonies cannot be determined, nor can it be said with confidence of several of the towns where Sullan settlements are known whether or not these had colonial status. However, Praeneste, Faesulae, Clusium, Arretium, Nola, Pompeii and Urbana may be regarded as certain, together with Sulla's one colony outside Italy, Aleria in Corsica. In at least two cases, Volaterrae and Arretium, Sulla not only confiscated land (though some of it at least was never settled, so that the former owners remained in illegal occupation until formally restored by Caesar in 59) but also deprived the people of their citizenship. However, even before Sulla's death the courts refused to uphold the latter measure.

Some areas which had been hostile were physically and economically unsuited to the development of urban communities, for instance Bruttium, Lucania and some parts of Samnium. Here, and elsewhere too, Sulla's supporters were allowed to amass large estates. Apart from such grants, would-be latifundists were often able to acquire land illegally from the veterans, though their allotments were supposed to be inalienable. Not all of them had an interest in farming, some were cheated when land was distributed, some inevitably received bad land, others were put off by the climate of ill will that must have greeted them in many areas. Some will have preferred to rejoin the army, for which there was ample opportunity in the next decade, for even those who had been longest in Sulla's service had got used to a life of luxury in Asia and may have found the prospect of hard work unappealing. For the dispossessed, on the other hand, there were few opportunities. Some made their way to Spain to join Sertorius, some remained on the land as tenants or labourers, some drifted to the towns, some took to brigandage. In a sense Sulla's arrangements stabilized the tenure of land in Italy for a generation, simply because they were so far-reaching that any serious attempt to overturn them, however well intentioned, would have engendered total confusion, and so such attempts were always resisted even by men like Cicero, who had no love of Sullan *possessores*. But the settlement of the veterans, though meant to bring security and guard against a *coup d'état*, created widespread friction and unrest which increased the likelihood of an attempted *coup*. Sulla was only very recently dead when trouble between the colonists and the dispossessed gave Lepidus his opportunity (ch. 7, pp. 208–10), while by the time of Catiline (ch. 9, pp. 346–60) the colonists themselves were ripe for trouble.

To commemorate his victories Sulla instituted games in 81, the *ludi Victoriae Sullanae*, which ran from 26 October to 1 November, the anniversary of the battle of the Colline Gate. To coincide with this first celebration he dedicated a tenth of his booty to Hercules and feasted the Roman people on a lavish scale. At some point he also extended the *pomoerium* (the sacral boundary of Rome); his justification was an adjustment of the boundary between Italy and Cisalpine Gaul. But during the games his wife Metella fell ill. Sulla was by now an augur, and to avoid pollution he had her removed from his house before she died and also divorced her.

The consular elections of 81 may have taken place in July, as became the custom after Sulla, so that the consuls designate came to play a leading part in senatorial debates in the second half of the year. Sulla himself stood and was elected, together with his most distinguished supporter, Metellus Pius. His candidature may perhaps have contravened his own *lex annalis*, since he had been consul less than ten years previously. However, we do not know when the law was passed and no doubt the Senate would have granted him a dispensation in case of need. Before entering office as consul he resigned the dictatorship, though the exact date remains controversial. It would probably be generally agreed that he laid it down at the end of 81.[73] It is, however, possible that he resigned somewhat earlier. The famous occasion when he dismissed his lictors and walked about the Forum as a private citizen, challenging anyone who wanted to call him to account, must surely be the day on which he gave up supreme power, not merely the last day of his consulship in 80. But if Sulla did this on the last day of 81, when he and everyone else knew perfectly well that on the next morning he would once more hold *imperium* and be attended by lictors, the challenge would be curiously hollow. It is therefore tempting to believe that Sulla, who understood the theatre, gave up his dictatorship long enough before the end of 81 for his gesture to have at least some dramatic force.

Whenever precisely it occurred, Sulla's resignation of the dictatorship and his appearance as consul with Pius might be read as indications that the crisis was over and that political and social life should now return to normal. In this year the trial of Sex. Roscius of Ameria gave the young Cicero the chance to preach an eloquent sermon on this text.[74] He was critical of the lawlessness and violence that had been rife immediately after Sulla's victory, but his real concern was for the future. It was not

73 Badian 1970 (C 14) 8ff; Keaveney 1980 (C 86) 158; *contra*, Twyman 1976 (B 117) 77ff, 271ff (mid-80).

74 Buchheit 1975 (B 7); Seager 1982 (B 106); *contra*, Kinsey 1980 (B 56); 1982 (B 57) 39f.

only men like Sulla's freedman Chrysogonus who had taken advantage of the troubled times to increase their fortunes by dubious means; too many of the nobility had been tempted to do the same. Cicero had probably been briefed by Roscius' noble patrons, but he exploited the freedom of speech enjoyed by a new man to lecture the nobles on their social and political duties: unless they devoted themselves to the restoration of traditional values and took up once more their inherited burden of public service, Sulla's victory would not have been worth winning. Cicero was taking no serious risk: neither Sulla nor any self-respecting noble could do other than agree with virtually every word he said. But his closing diatribe highlights the political and moral expectations that decent men might entertain of those whom Sulla had cast as the leading figures in his republic, expectations that were all too soon to be proved vain.

In 80 Sulla married again for the last time. His new wife Valeria, a relative of the orator Hortensius, had picked him up at a gladiatorial show. It was also probably in this year that a wife to replace Aemilia was found for Pompey. Again she was drawn from the circle of the Metelli: Mucia, half-sister of Q. Metellus Celer, consul in 60, and Q. Metellus Nepos, consul in 57. Both the consuls of 80 were allocated provinces. Pius received Hispania Ulterior, which had fallen into the hands of Sertorius. After his original flight from Italy Sertorius had been driven out of Spain by C. Annius Luscus. But in 80, after various adventures in Africa, he was invited to return by the Lusitani and lead them in revolt, and he soon inflicted a defeat on L. Fufidius, the governor of Ulterior. This one last pocket of external resistance clearly needed to be nipped in the bud, and so Pius was sent to regain control of the country. Sulla's province was Cisalpine Gaul, but he preferred not to take it. Instead he moved to a villa near Puteoli, spending his time in hunting, fishing, drinking with old friends from the world of the theatre and writing his memoirs.

The consular elections for 79 had brought to office loyal friends of Sulla, P. Servilius Vatia and Ap. Claudius Pulcher, who thus received compensation for his sufferings under Cinna. But the elections for 78 were a different matter, and the course of events makes clear what perhaps needs emphasis, that Sulla's resignation of absolute power did not betoken a total loss of interest in politics. He was still prepared to intervene in matters on which he had strong views, though now he could no longer be sure of getting his way. Of the consular candidates for 78 he supported the claims of Q. Catulus and perhaps Mam. Lepidus, but looked with disfavour on M. Lepidus, a renegade Marian who had enriched himself in the proscriptions and narrowly escaped prosecution for extortion after his governorship of Sicily in 80. Catulus safely secured election, but Mamercus failed, while M. Lepidus came top of the poll, thanks in part to the support of Pompey, with whom Sulla quarrelled fiercely, cutting the young man out of his will. It is unlikely that Pompey had any specific end in mind beyond the possibility that Lepidus, if elected, might create some kind of disturbance. Any emergency might give Pompey a chance to further his extraordinary career, whereas for him stability could only mean stagnation.

If such was Pompey's hope it was amply fulfilled, though it is unclear when Lepidus started to agitate for the repeal of some of Sulla's measures. The fullest source is the speech put into his mouth by Sallust, in which Lepidus is already consul, yet speaks as if Sulla were not only alive but still retained supreme power. Yet Lepidus had not long been in office when Sulla died. While dealing with a dispute in the affairs of Puteoli he suffered a massive haemorrhage, probably brought on by acute liver failure, the result of a lifetime of hard drinking, and he died the next day.[75]

The consuls had quarrelled constantly ever since taking office, but the question of Sulla's funeral divided them still more bitterly. Catulus was in favour of the unprecedented honour of a state funeral, Lepidus argued against. On this issue Pompey supported Catulus, and the partisans of Sulla carried the day. Sulla's body was brought to Rome on a golden bier with an ever-growing escort of veterans and others. At the ceremony farewell tributes were paid by the priestly colleges, the Senate and magistrates, the equestrian order, the veterans and the people. The funeral oration was probably delivered by Hortensius, or perhaps by L. Philippus – Sulla's son Faustus was too young – and the body was cremated. Even in death Sulla was lucky: the rain which had threatened all day held off until all was over. He himself had asked for burial, according to the custom of the Cornelii, but Philippus had judged it prudent to ignore his wishes, for fear that if he were buried his remains might one day suffer the same fate as he had meted out to those of Marius. On his tomb in the Campus Martius was inscribed the epitaph he had composed for himself: no friend ever outstripped him in doing good, no enemy in doing harm.

[75] Keaveney–Madden 1982 (C 95) 94f.

CHAPTER 7

THE RISE OF POMPEY

ROBIN SEAGER

I. THE REVOLT OF LEPIDUS, 78–77 B.C.

Catulus and Lepidus quarrelled again as they left Sulla's funeral, and Lepidus soon stepped up his agitation. He promised to rescind Sulla's acts, to recall those who had been driven into exile and to restore their lands to those who had been dispossessed to make way for Sulla's veterans. He may also have succeeded in passing a law reviving distributions of cheap corn. Another issue promptly raised and constantly debated in the years that followed was the tribunate. It seems, though the text of Licinianus is uncertain, that the tribunes of 78 asked the consuls to restore the tribunician power, but that Lepidus was the first to refuse and surprisingly convinced a majority of those present that such a measure would serve no useful purpose. If so, then he later changed his mind and championed the tribunate, allegedly in the interests of concord.

These squabbles may have been enough to inspire the consul Catulus to introduce his law against public violence, though it may equally have been a response to the more serious disturbances that soon arose.[1] The simmering discontent created by Sulla's expropriations in many parts of the Italian countryside boiled over in one of the worst-hit areas, Etruria. The Sullan colonists at Faesulae were attacked by men who had lost their land and in some cases their citizen rights as well. The Senate was sufficiently alarmed to send both consuls to suppress the rising. What happened next is obscure, but Lepidus seems to have put himself at the head of the insurgents and clashed with Catulus, who was prepared to use force to resist him. But instead of giving Catulus firm backing the Senate imposed an oath to keep the peace on both consuls and, to placate Lepidus and get him out of Italy, took the dangerous step of assigning him Transalpine Gaul, perhaps with Cisalpina too, since we find that the latter province was occupied in 77 by Lepidus' legate M. Iunius Brutus. No doubt many senators could not face the prospect of another civil war that might culminate in another capture of Rome and the loss of their

[1] Lintott 1968 (A 62) 111ff.

newly restored authority. But then, feeling that it had humoured Lepidus enough, the Senate summoned him to Rome to hold the consular elections. Instead Lepidus marched on the city at the head of the insurgents and issued a demand for an immediate second consulship. As a would-be new Sulla he was not impressive. It was true that he had hereditary ties in Cisalpine Gaul and needed to be suppressed before he could gain control there and perhaps establish a link with Sertorius, but the actual task of suppression should not have seemed forbidding: his makeshift forces, though numerous, presented no serious threat. Yet so haunted was the Senate by the spectre of civil war that despite his contumacy and his military weakness some senators were still in favour of coming to terms.

There were no consuls to give the Senate a lead, for though the year had turned the elections had still not been held. It was left to L. Philippus to rally opinion and propose the *senatus consultum ultimum*, under which Catulus as proconsul was charged with putting down his erstwhile colleague. The Senate also appointed a second commander to help Catulus in this task: Pompey, whose probable calculation of his own advantage was thus proved correct. His exact position is uncertain. His *imperium* was once more praetorian, but whether he was officially Catulus' legate or formally independent cannot be decided.[2]

As Lepidus continued his march on Rome, Catulus and Pompey occupied the Mulvian Bridge and the Janiculum, a battle was fought, and Lepidus retreated. Only at this late stage was he declared a *hostis*, a further proof of the Senate's conciliatory mood and perhaps of its reluctance to resort to the devices that had been so abused in the previous decade. Lepidus made his way to Etruria, pursued by Catulus, while Pompey headed for Cisalpine Gaul, where he besieged M. Brutus at Mutina. Brutus, perhaps deserted by his troops, surrendered and was shortly afterwards put to death. The exact circumstances are obscure: the version most charitable to Pompey was that Brutus was killed while trying to escape. As in the cases of Carbo and Domitius there may have been formal justification: it is not unlikely that Brutus had been declared a *hostis* at the same time as Lepidus. But this killing too was remembered against the 'adulescentulus carnifex', to use the phrase of the orator from Formiae, Helvius Mancia. After the execution of Brutus Pompey drove the remnants of his forces as far as Liguria, where Lepidus' son Scipio was captured and killed at Alba Pompeia. He then returned to Etruria in time to join Catulus in the final battle against Lepidus at Cosa. Defeated once more, Lepidus sought refuge in Sardinia, where he shortly afterwards fell ill and died. Those of his men who did not disperse were taken to Spain by Perperna.

[2] Seager 1979 (C 258) 15f; Helvius Mancia: Val. Max. VI.2.8.

Now that the rising was safely subdued Catulus ordered Pompey to disband his troops, but Pompey refused. The object of his contumacy was limited and specific. He was not threatening civil war to make himself dictator, he merely wanted to be sent to Spain, where for two years Metellus Pius had been making little headway against Sertorius. It is probable that Pius had already asked for support; the only question was who should be sent to assist him. Consuls had at last been elected for 77: Mam. Lepidus, in whose favour another loyal Sullan, C. Scribonius Curio, had stood down, and D. Brutus. Both, however, had declared their unwillingness to go to Spain. This refusal should not be taken as a sign of sympathy for Lepidus or Sertorius himself; they simply had no wish to undertake a difficult, dangerous and unrewarding war.[3] But it put the Senate in a quandary, for several other potential commanders were already engaged elsewhere: Servilius Vatia in Cilicia against the pirates, Ap. Claudius in Macedonia and C. Cosconius in Illyricum. As Pompey no doubt knew, there was no candidate more likely than himself, indeed there was none at all. It was his old protector L. Philippus who took the lead in pointing out to the Senate that it had no choice and proposed that Pompey be sent to Spain 'non pro consule' as he put it 'sed pro consulibus'.

II. POLITICS AT ROME, 77–71 B.C.

The young Caesar had returned to Rome from service in Cilicia under Servilius Vatia as soon as he heard of Sulla's death. Unlike his brother-in-law L. Cinna, who was one of those forced to take refuge with Sertorius, he had prudently avoided involvement with Lepidus. But in 77 he prosecuted Cn. Cornelius Dolabella, consul in 81 under Sulla's dictatorship, who had returned from his province of Macedonia to celebrate a triumph. Dolabella could command distinguished advocates – Hortensius and C. Cotta, Caesar's uncle by marriage – and Caesar not surprisingly failed to win his case. But his efforts put him in the public eye and gained him the good will of the Greeks, who turned to him again in the following year for help against another Sullan exploiter, C. Antonius. The case was heard by M. Lucullus, the peregrine praetor, who found in favour of the Greeks, though Antonius escaped by summoning the tribunes to his aid. Lucullus' edict (concerning the delicts that he would permit to be prosecuted before him) bears witness to the disturbed conditions still prevalent in the Italian countryside, for he found it necessary to include an action against crimes committed by armed bands of slaves.

The dominant political theme of the decade was to be the campaign to

[3] Seager 1979 (C 258) 17.

restore the tribunician power. After the abortive approach made by the tribunes of 78 to Lepidus and Catulus, nothing is heard of any agitation in 77, when the upheaval caused by Lepidus may have pushed the matter into the background. But in 76 a tribune, Cn. or L. Sicinius, raised the question of tribunician rights again. However, he had to face vigorous opposition from one of the consuls of the year, C. Curio, who more than made up for the notorious inertia of his colleague Cn. Octavius. What happened to Sicinius is far from clear: in the words put by Sallust into the mouth of Licinius Macer, Curio hounded him to destruction, whatever that may mean. Q. Opimius, a tribune of 75, somehow offended against Sulla's ordinances in the exercise of his veto and, perhaps more importantly, uttered sentiments unwelcome to distinguished men. On laying down his office he was prosecuted by Catulus and Hortensius and suffered a ruinous fine.

The consuls of 75 were L. Octavius, as lifeless as his namesake in the previous year, and C. Cotta, the former friend of Livius Drusus, an ambitious man with a brother standing for the consulship of 74, who was ready not only to spend money but also to pass laws that had popular appeal in order to win support. It was perhaps this motive, rather than fear, as Sallust makes Macer claim, that led Cotta to betray his position at the heart of the oligarchy and introduce a law, strongly disapproved of by the rest of the nobility, which once again allowed holders of the tribunate to stand for higher office. Cicero tried in 65 for reasons of his own to minimize the importance of the step, suggesting that it gave the tribunes a little dignity but no more power. Strictly speaking this was true, but it was plain that the removal of the ban would encourage men of talent to stand for the tribunate, so that the pressure for the restoration of its legislative powers would increase until it finally achieved its object.

Cotta also had other pressing matters to think about. There was a shortage of corn and prices were high. At one point an angry mob attacked the consuls, who were escorting Q. Metellus, later consul in 69 and now a candidate for the praetorship, down the Via Sacra, and forced them to take refuge in Octavius' house, which was fortunately close at hand. It is worth noting that Metellus failed to gain election.[4] In a speech put into his mouth by Sallust Cotta admitted his desire for popularity and insisted on his devotion to the people which had recalled him from exile. He also catalogued the problems that faced the Republic. In Spain both Pompey and Pius were clamouring for reinforcements, supplies and money, while on the other side of the Roman world armies were needed not only in Macedonia but also, because of the growing threat from Mithridates, in Cilicia and Asia, and Rome's economic difficulties meant

[4] Seager 1970 (B 103); 1972 (B 104). For the consuls exercising censorial functions and letting contracts, Cic. II *Verr.* 3.18; Engelmann and Knibbe 1989 (B 150) 25, line 73.

that she was less able than before to police the seas and guard the corn supply against enemies and pirates. This gloomy picture is largely justified. Servilius celebrated a triumph in 75, but despite his considerable achievement piracy was still a menace, while the problems of Sertorius and Mithridates remained unsolved.

The gravity of the situation in Spain was underlined by a letter of complaint from Pompey, which probably reached Rome at the beginning of 74. Sallust preserves a version. Pompey claimed that despite his repeated appeals his army had been reduced to starvation by lack of support from home. Spain and Gaul had been bled dry and his personal resources of cash and credit were exhausted. The letter ended with an oracular warning: unless help was forthcoming from the Senate, his army and with it the whole Spanish War would shift to Italy. This should not be taken as a veiled threat to join forces with Sertorius and invade Italy, but rather as a hint that he might be driven out of Spain and chased home by Sertorius. Of this there was no real possibility. Despite the relative lack of success enjoyed so far by Pius and Pompey, Sertorius was never in a position to mount an invasion of Italy even if he wanted to. Nevertheless, the letter produced the desired effect. New efforts were made to supply the men and materials needed for Spain; the consuls L. Lucullus and M. Cotta were prominent among those who exerted themselves. There is, however, no reason to assume that until now Pompey had been deliberately starved of supplies and reinforcements by men who resented his premature and irregular rise to prominence. However disquietingly abnormal his career, he was pursuing it at this time in the service of Sulla's Senate against Sulla's and the Senate's enemies, and not only he but the irreproachable Metellus had complained about the problems they had encountered in Spain. Nor can Lucullus and Cotta have been afraid that Pompey would come back from Spain to stake a claim to the command in any war against Mithridates that might be imminent. If he had just proved unable to cope with Sertorius, he would hardly seem a plausible candidate for immediate re-employment on an even more difficult mission. Lucullus and Cotta will simply have wanted to improve the situation in Spain and leave themselves free to exploit developments in the East.[5]

It is unfortunately unclear just when in 74 the consuls saw the chance to secure for themselves commands against Mithridates. The king had probably always intended to make a fresh attempt to drive the Romans out of Asia Minor. The conduct of Murena, Sulla's reaction to it and Rome's refusal to ratify the Peace of Dardanus will have given him in his own eyes at least ample excuse, and he may well have believed, rightly or wrongly, that Servilius' operations in Cilicia were directed as much

[5] Seager 1979 (C 258) 19.

against himself as against the pirates (see ch. 8, p. 232). In 75 C. Cotta had received Cisalpine Gaul as his province, Octavius Cilicia. Lucullus too was allocated Cisalpine Gaul; we do not know what province was originally assigned to M. Cotta. But when Octavius died early in 74 Lucullus resorted to sordid intrigue with the mysteriously influential P. Cethegus and his mistress Praecia to secure Cilicia for himself. Then something happened to cause a further dramatic revision of provincial appointments. Lucullus was given Asia as well as Cilicia and M. Cotta's province, whatever it was, was changed to Bithynia, whose king Nicomedes had died during 75. Moreover, a third important command was created for the praetor M. Antonius to deal with piracy. (Pirates had recently even captured Caesar, though he soon made them pay for their presumption.)[6] Antonius' appointment was to last for three years and to cover the whole coastline of the Mediterranean and its islands up to a distance of eighty kilometres from the sea; his *imperium* was to be equal with that of any governor with whom he might come into contact. However, his detractors were to say that Antonius caused greater devastation than the pirates.

The stimulus for these developments cannot have been Mithridates' invasion of Bithynia, which did not take place until spring 73, though the king may have made some ominous moves in 74. The most important factor was probably news of his pact with Sertorius, which is likely to have been concluded in summer 74.[7] Both Mithridates and Sertorius had already received assistance from the pirates, and their agreement must have made it seem at Rome as if all her major enemies were now combining to pose a single unified threat that spanned the Mediterranean. The Roman response, if viewed as a whole, reflects this reaction: a stepping-up of the war effort in Spain, a drive against piracy not merely in one isolated centre but over the whole Mediterranean, and action to protect Rome's most valuable province, Asia, and the obvious prime target for invasion, Bithynia, against any new initiative by Mithridates.

The tribunician power was again a cause of agitation in 74, but in this year it became somewhat fortuitously linked with another matter of which nothing had yet been heard since Sulla's legislation on the subject – senatorial control of the courts. The cause of the tribunes was taken up by L. Quinctius, but like Sicinius before him he found consular opposition too effective to be broken. Lucullus for the moment gained the upper hand and put a stop to Quinctius' efforts, though the tribune never forgave his adversary and was able to secure revenge some years later. But Quinctius was also exercised by another issue: bribery in the courts, as exemplified at the prosecution by Cluentius of Oppianicus for attempted murder, one of the high spots of that lurid tale of the

[6] Ward 1977 (C 151). [7] McGing 1984 (D 33) 17f; Sherwin-White 1984 (D 291) 162ff.

traditional rustic virtues so deviously narrated in Cicero's *pro Cluentio.* Quinctius defended Oppianicus, who was nevertheless condemned. The tribune decided that his client must therefore be the innocent victim of bribery – in fact it seems highly likely that substantial sums had been expended by both parties – and mounted a violent campaign against the president of the court, C. Iunius, and corrupt senatorial courts in general. From this point on the themes of the tribunate and the courts seem to have been linked in the public mind, though at this stage Quinctius' involvement was all that they had in common.

In 73 another tribune carried on the work of agitation, C. Licinius Macer, orator and historian. The speech ascribed to him by Sallust contains predictable complaints against domineering consuls and exhortations to the people to stand up for its rights. More importantly, for the first time the name of Pompey is brought into conjunction with the question of the tribunate. Macer allegedly made two claims. First, he said that those who wished to keep the tribunes powerless were putting forward the implausible excuse for delay that they could not come to any decision until Pompey returned. If this argument was really being used as a delaying tactic it must have caused a great deal of exasperation, since to claim that the Senate could not pronounce on the matter in the absence of one young man who was not even a senator was patently absurd. But Macer also claimed to know that when he did come home Pompey would use such influence as he had in favour of the restoration of tribunician power. It is hard to know whether Macer was telling the truth. It is not impossible that Pompey had already decided the line he was going to take on this issue and had made his views known to Macer with permission to publish, but there is no evidence now or later for any political link between the two men. It is therefore perhaps more likely that this was a cunning move by Macer made on his own initiative. By taking Pompey's name in vain, he could create in the people expectations of Pompey's support which Pompey, whatever his wishes, could not then disappoint without running the risk of a loss of popularity.

The year 73 also provided evidence of continuing problems with the corn supply. The governor of Sicily, C. Verres, was instructed first by a decree of the Senate, then by a law passed by the consuls, M. Lucullus and C. Cassius Longinus, to buy corn at a fair price in Sicily, over and above the regular annual tribute, for shipment to Italy. The law also provided for the sale of corn at a moderate fixed price (such provision had been abolished by Sulla). The model was a law of C. Gracchus, but the provenance of the present measure made it possible for the popular tribune Macer to attack it as a miserly sop designed only to lull the plebs into acceptance of its servitude.

It was the conduct of Verres in Sicily that brought to the attention of the Senate in 72 another of the subjects that was to come to the fore in 70, the misbehaviour of provincial governors. One of Verres' many victims was Sthenius of Himera (Thermae), who had secured the patronage of Pompey in 82 and had other protectors at Rome. Though the whole story of Verres makes it painfully clear that Roman patrons did as little for their provincial clients as was humanly possible,[8] Sthenius' case was taken up by the consuls of the year, L. Gellius Publicola and Cn. Cornelius Lentulus Clodianus. Both of these men appear to have been well disposed towards Pompey: they legislated to empower Pompey and Pius to make grants of Roman citizenship in Spain as a reward for services rendered. The best-known beneficiary of this measure was L. Cornelius Balbus of Gades. Lentulus also passed a law, consistent with his stance as censor two years later, demanding full payment to the treasury by those who had bought up confiscated property, many of whom had been granted remissions by Sulla of all or part of the price.

Sthenius' case was raised again by a tribune of 71, M. Lollius Palicanus, who may with some plausibility be regarded as an adherent of Pompey. He came from Picenum, Pompey's home territory, his sister or daughter married A. Gabinius, and his candidature for the consulship in 67 was ruthlessly blocked by the consul C. Calpurnius Piso, a committed opponent of Pompey. Palicanus also spoke on the subject of the tribunician power, while evidence that is unfortunately not reliable names him as the originator of the tripartite division of the juries that was brought in by L. Cotta in the following year. Whatever the truth of this last matter, it can at least be said that by the time of Pompey's return from Spain the restoration of the tribunician power, the composition of juries and the conduct of provincial governors had all emerged as issues on which action was needed and which for various reasons were closely linked in men's minds.

III. THE WARS AGAINST SERTORIUS AND SPARTACUS, 79–71 B.C.

Sertorius' defeat of Fufidius in 80 (ch. 6, p. 206) made it clear that he deserved to be taken seriously. Hispania Ulterior was assigned to Sulla's colleague in the consulship of 80, Metellus Pius; the governor of Citerior was M. Domitius Calvinus. Pius' plan seems to have been to crush Sertorius between himself and Calvinus, but Sertorius sent a force under L. Hirtuleius to prevent Calvinus' approach, and the proconsul was defeated and killed. Hirtuleius is described as quaestor of Sertorius; perhaps he had been legitimately appointed in 83, or perhaps Sertorius had already begun the practice of bestowing Roman titles on his

[8] Brunt 1980 (C 33).

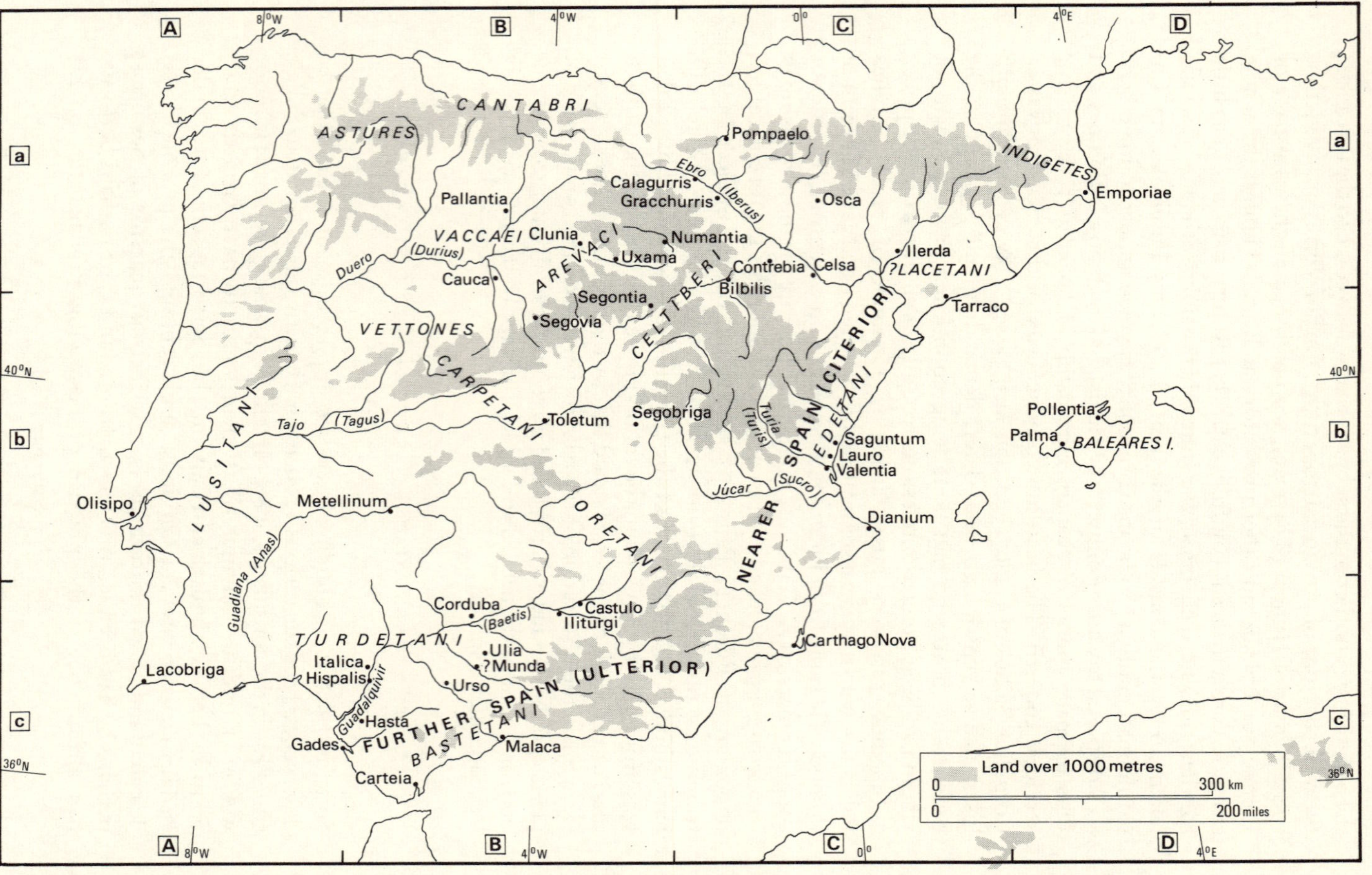
CANTABRI
ASTURES
Pompaelo
Ebro
(Iberus)
Calagurris
Gracchurris
Osca
INDIGETES
Emporiae
Pallantia
VACCAEI
Clunia
AREVACI
Numantia
Uxama
Duero
(Durius)
Cauca
Contrebia
Celsa
Ilerda
?LACETANI
Bilbilis
Tarraco
Segontia
Segovia
CELTIBERI
VETTONES
CARPETANI
SPAIN (CITERIOR)
EDETANI
Toletum
Segobriga
Turia
(Turis)
Pollentia
Palma
BALEARES I.
Tajo
(Tagus)
LUSITANI
Saguntum
Lauro
Valentia
Júcar
(Sucro)
NEARER
Olisipo
Metellinum
Dianium
ORETANI
Guadiana (Anas)
Corduba
(Baetis)
Castulo
Iliturgi
TURDETANI
Carthago Nova
Italica
Hispalis
Ulia
?Munda
Lacobriga
Urso
SPAIN (ULTERIOR)
Guadalquivir
Hasta
FURTHER
BASTETANI
Gades
Malaca
Carteia
Land over 1000 metres
0 300 km
0 200 miles

8 Spain

subordinates. The campaign was fought in southern Lusitania, between the Guadiana and the Tagus, towards and beyond which Metellus advanced from his base at Metellinum on the Guadiana. But the only other conspicuous success of the year belonged to Sertorius, who defeated and killed Pius' legate L. Thorius Balbus in the neighbourhood of Consabura. It is probable that the earliest negotiations between Sertorius and Mithridates belong to 79, though for the moment nothing came of them.[9]

For 78 Pius chose a different line of advance, operating to the west and south-west and besieging Lacobriga. He summoned assistance from the governor of Transalpine Gaul, L. Manlius, but Hirtuleius was again equal to his task of protecting Sertorius' rear: Manlius was defeated and forced to return to Gaul. This second year of failure led Pius to ask for reinforcement. In 77 Sertorius and Hirtuleius changed positions. Hirtuleius was deputed to defend Lusitania and keep Metellus contained, while Sertorius mounted an invasion of Citerior, advancing along a line from Consabura to Bilbilis by way of Segobriga, Caraca and Segontia. In the Ebro basin, in addition to his capital Osca, Sertorius controlled the strategic centres of Calagurris and Ilerda. This campaign brought him to the height of his power: only the south remained outside his domain. He had also in the course of the year received considerable reinforcements led by M. Perperna, who had escaped from the collapse of Lepidus' rising first to Sardinia and then to Spain, bringing with him a substantial number of troops. It is said that on his arrival Perperna wanted to maintain his independence and refused to join Sertorius until his men compelled him to do so. On the other side Metellus' request for help produced a result that he can hardly have expected, though there is nothing to suggest that he was displeased at the outcome. The consuls of 77 had no desire to go to Spain, whereas Pompey was eager for further employment and, thanks to the backing of L. Philippus in the Senate, secured a proconsular command to assist Metellus. But Pompey had to deal with rebellious tribes in Gaul and was forced to winter at Narbo, arriving in Spain only in the spring of 76.[10]

To oppose him Sertorius sent Perperna to cover the coastal region between Saguntum and Tarraco. Hirtuleius was again instructed to tie Metellus down in Lusitania and prevent his moving to meet Pompey, while Sertorius kept himself in reserve on the upper Ebro to intervene as developments might dictate. Pompey enjoyed some initial success, winning over the Indigetes and Lacetani, then advancing southwards. His aim was to gain control of the east coast as a springboard for expansion inland. Once Perperna had failed to stop him from crossing

[9] Scardigli 1971 (C 130) 252ff; Glew 1981 (D 19) 126; *contra*, Sherwin-White 1984 (D 291) 161.

[10] Gelzer 1949 (C 200) 47; Gabba 1958 (B 40) 301; *contra*, Grispo 1952 (E 18) 202 (autumn 77).

the Ebro, it was inevitable that action would be concentrated around Valentia, the next major obstacle for Pompey, since Saguntum and Lauro just to the north were hostile to Sertorius. This determined Sertorius' next move: an attempt to seize Lauro in order to block Pompey's route to Valentia. It brought him a brilliant success. Pompey lost 10,000 men, including his legate D. Laelius, and had to endure the humiliation of watching while Sertorius sacked and destroyed the city. This victory was, however, offset shortly afterwards when Metellus inflicted a crushing defeat on Hirtuleius at Italica. It is not clear whether in abandoning his original course of avoiding a pitched battle Hirtuleius acted on his own initiative or on instructions from Sertorius. Possibly Metellus had shown signs of marching east to assist Pompey and Hirtuleius had felt desperate measures were called for to prevent him. But though Pius' victory left him free to do so, instead he headed further north to Catalonia. After the débâcle at Lauro Pompey had withdrawn beyond the Ebro, so that Sertorius and Perperna were free to move to Lusitania to try to repair the situation there, while C. Herennius was left to guard Valentia.

After an incursion into Celtiberia during the winter of 76/5 Pompey again set out to subdue the east coast, drawing Sertorius and Perperna to confront him, while Pius marched against Hirtuleius, who remained in Lusitania. Despite his experience of the previous year, and probably despite clear orders from Sertorius, Hirtuleius came to meet him and a battle was fought at Segovia. The result was catastrophic for Sertorius. Though Pius himself was wounded, Hirtuleius and his brother were killed and the rebel forces overwhelmingly defeated. Again Pius, as in the previous year, was free to make for the east coast. There Pompey had scored an initial success, defeating Perperna and Herennius, who was killed, outside Valentia and taking the city. Over-confidence and the desire to beat Sertorius without waiting for Pius to arrive made him then attack the enemy leader near the Sucro. The result of the battle was inconclusive, though Pompey himself was lucky to escape with his life. Before further action was possible, Metellus appeared with news of the death of Hirtuleius. Despite the fact that both his opponents were now arrayed against him Sertorius felt the need to fight again to restore morale. The battle took place near Segontia.[11] Again it was indecisive: Sertorius himself defeated Pompey, whose brother-in-law C. Memmius was killed, but Perperna failed yet again, this time against Pius. Sertorius withdrew to Clunia, where he was blockaded for a time, though not without inflicting some losses on the besiegers. Then his opponents withdrew for the winter, Pius to Gaul, Pompey north of the Ebro, where he once again mounted an expedition into the hinterland.

[11] App. *BCiv.* 1.110.515 with Gabba *ad loc.*

Over the winter of 75/4 both sides engaged in negotiations of one kind and another. Both Pompey and Pius had already complained more than once in letters to Rome that they needed more men, more money and more supplies, but during the winter Pompey wrote again in terms alarming enough to galvanize the consuls into action. It is also probably to this winter that the renewal of Sertorius' dealings with Mithridates should be assigned, with agreement being reached in the summer of 74. The pact itself has nothing surprising about it. More than once in Rome's recent civil wars the participants had sought the aid of foreigners: Marius and Cinna that of the Samnites in 87, Sulla that of Mithridates in 85, Domitius that of Hiarbas in 81. Ancient and modern authorities alike differ vehemently over one point alone: whether Sertorius was prepared to concede to Mithridates not only Bithynia and Cappadocia but also the Roman province of Asia.[12] The conflicting traditions about Sertorius are so tendentious that we cannot now be certain whether or not he would have thought such a concession compatible with the dignity of Rome or his own. But it need not be supposed that Mithridates would have insisted on the cession of Asia before agreeing to a treaty. From his point of view Sertorius' function was to keep the Romans busy well away from Asia Minor. If his own enterprises there were successful he would have no need to abide by any agreement with Sertorius, whatever might have happened in Spain in the mean time. It is noteworthy that the king also sent an envoy to Pompey, though what he hoped to gain is by no means clear.

Mithridates agreed to send ships and money in exchange for military advisers, but by the time they arrived in 73 it was too late, for already in 74 the tide had begun to turn. Pompey and Metellus changed their tactics, abandoning the attempt to bring the enemy to battle in favour of a policy of reducing his strongholds. Both generals operated in Celtiberia: Pompey was forced by Sertorius to raise the siege of Pallantia but took Cauca, while Pius secured Bilbilis and Segobriga. At the end of the season they combined against Calagurris, but without success. In 73 Pompey operated again in Celtiberia, this time alone. By now the falling-away of Sertorius' Spanish support was even more marked, and he responded with harsh reprisals. By the end of the year almost all the towns of Celtiberia, the Ebro valley and the eastern seaboard had gone over: only Ilerda, Osca, Calagurris, Tarraco and Sertorius' port of Dianium remained loyal.

But it was his Roman officers who finally hastened Sertorius' inevitable end. The motives of the conspirators headed by Perperna are hard to disentangle from the moralizing and propaganda of our sources, but it seems likely that the setting of a price on Sertorius' head by Pius may

[12] Cf. Berve 1929 (C 26) 203ff; Gelzer 1962–4 (A 41) II, 139ff.

have encouraged his assassins to hope at least for amnesty if not rewards. Sertorius' murder marked the virtual end of resistance. A few towns held out to the bitter end: in Celtiberia Uxama and Clunia, in the Ebro basin Calagurris and Osca, and on the coast Valentia. But almost nobody was ready to fight for Perperna, who was quickly defeated by Pompey and put to death, despite his attempt to buy his life with Sertorius' papers, which Pompey wisely destroyed unread in the interests of concord.

Both in antiquity and in more recent times Sertorius has provoked the most disparate reactions.[13] In consequence nothing can be said with confidence and any statement about his character and intentions must be regarded as conjectural. Like others who escaped from the collapse of the resistance to Sulla in Italy, he tried to carry on the struggle elsewhere by exploiting local backing. He brought with him to Spain relatively few Roman and Italian supporters, though he acquired more with the arrival of Perperna, and he seems to have made no great appeal to Romans and Italians settled in the peninsula. From first to last the backbone of his following was formed by the native tribesmen who had invited him to lead them. Their goal must surely have been to liberate themselves from Roman domination, not merely to contribute to a change of government at Rome in the highly speculative hope that Sertorius and any other surviving opponents of Sulla might prove less ruthless in the exploitation of the provinces than the *Sullani*. Yet the liberation of Spain from the Roman yoke cannot have been any part of Sertorius' plans. It must therefore be true in some degree that, whatever his ultimate purpose, Sertorius was cheating his Spanish followers and using them for selfish ends. What that ultimate purpose was remains obscure. Sertorius appointed his officers to magistracies with Roman titles, he provided for the education in Roman style of the Spanish princelings he gathered as hostages at his capital of Osca, and he established, probably after the arrival of Perperna, a body which he called the senate, in which Mithridates' demand for the surrender of Asia was debated. These facts in themselves are hardly surprising. Sertorius, like the Italians in the Social War, knew only the Roman political and military system. It was natural, if not inevitable, that he should take it as his model when trying to impose some order on the situation in which he found himself. It is possible, though this is far less certain, that Sertorius conceived of his entourage as a genuine alternative to Rome, a Rome-in-exile. But even if that is so, it is still impossible to discover what Sertorius conceived of as the ultimate solution to this schism. Despite certain alarmist rumours put about at Rome he cannot have hoped to emulate Hannibal and mount an invasion of Italy. For that his forces were never strong enough, and his Spanish troops would not have followed him in an

13 Cf. Schulten 1926 (C 131A); Treves 1932 (C 144); Gabba 1973 (C 55) 287ff, 427ff.

enterprise which, regardless of its prospects of success, was completely irrelevant to their own aspirations. It may well be that for some time before the end the war had become for Sertorius an end in itself, beyond which he no longer looked. It was perhaps the realization of this, more than jealousy and Sertorius' increasingly cantankerous behaviour, that finally turned his officers against him. As for the Spaniards, once they understood that he had never had anything to offer them as a politician and now had nothing more to offer as a leader, most of them abandoned both him and the struggle. Those who carried on were fighting, not for anything that Sertorius had ever stood for, but for the freedom which had inspired them to rebel in the first place.

No details are known of Pompey's settlement of Spain, but it seems to have been characterized by the same shrewd blend of humanity and self-interest as he had shown already in Sicily and was to display in 67 when dealing with the pirates. Caesar attests that he acquired many clients in Citerior and bound the cities and tribes to him by his benefactions. Some of Sertorius' men were relocated in Aquitania at Lugdunum Convenarum, and Pompey may also have founded one city in Spain itself, Pompaelo. High in the Pyrenees he set up a trophy, on which he did not mention Sertorius but claimed to have reduced 876 towns from the Alps to the boundaries of Hispania Ulterior.[14]

It was fortunate for Rome that Pompey and Metellus got the upper hand in Spain so decisively in 73, for that year saw the outbreak of a serious upheaval in Italy itself, the slave insurrection led by Spartacus. The origins of the rising must have seemed trivial enough: a mere seventy-four gladiators escaped from a school in Capua under the leadership of the Thracian Spartacus, a former Roman auxiliary, and two Gauls, Crixus and Oenomaus, and occupied a position on Vesuvius. They must have quickly gained considerable support, for though at first only makeshift forces were sent against them, Spartacus and Crixus were able to deal with them with ease. The first victim was a praetor, C. Claudius Glaber, who tried to blockade the slaves on Vesuvius. They broke out, took him in the rear, stormed his camp and put his army to flight. It may have been in this engagement that Oenomaus was killed. Two more praetors, L. Cossinius and P. Varinius, Varinius' legate Furius and his quaestor C. Thoranius also suffered defeats. The numbers of the insurgents increased with alarming speed, swollen by both slaves and free herdsmen, until Spartacus is reported to have had 70,000 men, for whom he was keen to provide proper weapons and armour. At this point dissension arose as to what they should do. Spartacus saw that the best and ultimately the only useful course was to head north out of Italy before Rome mustered a serious force against them and then to disperse

14 Pliny *HN* III.18; VII.96; Strab. III.4.10 (161); IV.2.1 (190).

and seek freedom in their various homelands. But the German and Gallic element led by Crixus was seduced by the prospect of plunder and carried the day. Hence the latter part of 73 and the beginning of 72 were spent in spreading devastation all over southern Italy.[15]

Inevitably the growth of the insurrection provoked a reaction at Rome. Both consuls of 72, L. Publicola and Lentulus Clodianus, took the field with two legions each. The sources disagree as to whether the year's one success, the destruction of Crixus and his entire force near Mount Garganus, was won by Gellius or the praetor Q. Arrius. Since both men were defeated together by Spartacus, who had already inflicted a reverse on Clodianus, it may be that they should also share the credit for Crixus' annihilation. Spartacus had been pursuing his original plan and heading north, with Lentulus trying to block his path and Gellius pursuing him. He got as far as Cisalpine Gaul, where he defeated the proconsul C. Cassius Longinus, but for some reason he turned back and headed for Rome. Both consuls faced him in Picenum and were again defeated. However, Spartacus thought better of an attempt on Rome itself and instead occupied Thurii, in the far south. He then inflicted yet another defeat on a Roman commander, perhaps the praetor Cn. Manlius.

The consuls were now relieved of their command by a decree of the Senate, and a special command with proconsular *imperium* was conferred on M. Crassus, the victor of the Colline Gate, who had held the praetorship in the previous year.[16] Crassus took over the consuls' forces and recruited six new legions. His legate Mummius joined battle with Spartacus in defiance of Crassus' orders and was heavily defeated. To restore discipline Crassus revived the obsolete punishment of decimation (the execution of every tenth man), then he himself inflicted a first defeat on Spartacus and drove him southwards through Bruttium till he reached the sea. Spartacus hoped to cross to Sicily, but the pirates who had promised to provide him with transport let him down and a second attempt using boats and rafts which the slaves had built for themselves was thwarted either by Verres or the current in the straits. Over the winter Crassus cut off his enemy with a triple barrier of ditch, wall and stockade, probably on the promontory of Scyllaeum.[17] Twice Spartacus tried to break out, but both times he was thrown back with heavy losses.

Despite these successes a decision was taken at Rome (whether by the Senate alone or by the People is uncertain) to summon not only Pompey from Spain but also M. Lucullus, who had been campaigning in Thrace, to lend assistance to Crassus. It is unlikely, despite Plutarch's assertion to the contrary, that Crassus himself had asked for them to be recalled: he

[15] Gabba 1967 (B 40) 321.
[16] Marshall 1976 (C 226) 26ff; Ward 1977 (C 280) 83ff.
[17] Ward 1977 (C 280) 89 n. 20.

seems to have been eager to finish the war unaided. Spartacus tried to negotiate but Crassus of course refused, so Spartacus tried for a third time to break the blockade. This time he was successful and made for Brundisium with Crassus in pursuit. While his legate L. Quinctius held off Spartacus, Crassus twice defeated a breakaway group under Cannicus and Castus. On learning that M. Lucullus had arrived at Brundisium, Spartacus turned back into Bruttium and defeated Quinctius and the quaestor Cn. Tremellius Scrofa at Petelia. Then came the final confrontation with Crassus, in which Spartacus was killed, though his body was never found. Crassus ruthlessly pursued the survivors into the hills and eventually lined the Via Appia from Capua to Rome with 6,000 crucified prisoners. Five thousand fugitives from the battle who were trying to escape northwards fell in with the returning Pompey and were annihilated, an incident which prompted Pompey to write to the Senate that, although Crassus had defeated the slaves in a battle, it was he who had finally brought the war to an end.

IV. THE FIRST CONSULSHIP OF POMPEY AND CRASSUS, 70 B.C.

Both Pompey and Crassus now looked for their rewards. The war against Sertorius had been declared a *bellum externum*; thus Pompey and Pius could legitimately lay claim to triumphs. Crassus too coveted a triumph, but the suppression of a slave revolt merited only an ovation. However, Crassus' achievement was signalled by the special distinction of a laurel wreath instead of the customary myrtle. This honour was as much as he had a right to expect, but nevertheless he was jealous of Pompey's Spanish triumph. The unfriendly rivalry between the two men, which should not be underestimated,[18] probably went back to the time of Sulla, when Pompey, at least until the quarrel over Lepidus' election, had been shown every sign of favour, whereas Crassus, despite his services, had been disregarded. Yet it is said that Crassus sought Pompey's support when both men decided to stand for the consulship of 70. Though both had conspicuous military success on which to base their claims, their positions were in every other respect quite different. Crassus was of the proper age and had fulfilled all formal requirements, Pompey was still far too young and had held no public office. Nevertheless the Senate passed a decree which exempted him from the provisions of the *lex annalis*. It may seem that, apart from his personal dislike of Pompey, Crassus had no need to canvass his support since his own election could be seen as inevitable. However, he may have calculated that one consulship was bound to go to Pompey once his dispensation

[18] Ward 1977 (C 280) 97ff; *contra*, Marshall 1977 (C 226) 34ff.

had been granted and decided that there was no harm in a gesture to make doubly sure that he himself secured the other place.

There is no reason to suppose that either Crassus or Pompey extorted their consulships by the threat of force from a reluctant Senate or people. The summons to lend assistance against Spartacus had of course meant that Pompey had had every right to retain his army instead of disbanding it as soon as he set foot in Italy, as Metellus very properly did when he returned to celebrate his own triumph, probably shortly after Pompey's. It is true that Pompey kept his men together until his triumph, which was held on 29 December 71, saying that he was waiting for Pius, and that Crassus used Pompey's behaviour as an excuse to do likewise. So both men still had troops at their disposal when Pompey was given the right to stand and when the elections were held. But neither will have needed to resort to the threat of violence. Crassus had a strong and legitimate claim, and a consulship, however irregular, must have seemed not only to the mass of the people but to many senators no more than a just reward for Pompey's achievements. Even those to whom so drastic a breach of Sulla's regulations seemed distasteful or even positively dangerous will have realized that no lesser acknowledgment of Pompey's services to the state was practicable. A man who had commanded a proconsular army for the past seven years and was about to triumph for the second time could hardly be invited to stand for the quaestorship or even the praetorship. They might at least draw comfort from the reflection that, although Pompey had made his meteoric rise in defiance of Sulla's enactments, he had at least done so in defending Sulla's Senate against the last of Sulla's enemies. It is plausible that even within the Senate Pompey's consulship and its inevitability inspired general agreement and even fairly widespread approval.

Pompey's inexperience of public office was underlined when he asked his friend the learned M. Varro, who had served under him in Spain, to write him a short handbook on senatorial procedure. Nevertheless it was clear that he would not be inactive as consul. In his first public speech as consul designate he promised to restore the tribunician power and to take measures to check abuses in provincial government and the corruption of the courts.

The tribunate was dealt with first. It was the only matter in which Pompey and Crassus co-operated during their year of office, passing a joint law to restore the tribunes' legislative powers.[19] Both men will no doubt have hoped to profit in the future from laws introduced by tribunes, and neither will have been prepared to stand by and see the other gain all the popular favour that the introduction of the bill would bring to its author. There appears to have been no opposition: the

[19] Seager 1979 (C 258) 24 n. 91; *contra*, McDermott 1977 (C 103).

change must have appeared inevitable. However, the experience of some of the tribunes of the sixties makes it clear that certain prominent senators would rather have seen Sulla's curbs on the tribunate maintained and were prepared to show their resentment when the chance arose.[20] Apart from this single instance, where their separate interests dictated a brief collaboration, Pompey and Crassus continued on bad terms throughout the year. At his triumph Pompey had vowed lavish games in celebration of his victories, perhaps in a spirit of rivalry with the *ludi Victoriae Sullanae*. Crassus, not to be outdone, imitated another piece of Sullan ostentation: he dedicated a tithe of his property to Hercules, entertained the people at a gigantic banquet and distributed a three-month supply of corn.

For the first time since 86 censors were elected. The successful candidates were the consuls of 72, L. Gellius and Lentulus Clodianus, despite their failures in the war against Spartacus. They showed themselves enthusiastic supporters of the fashionable drive against corruption, expelling from the Senate no less than sixty-four of its members, including a consul of the previous year, Lentulus Sura, and C. Antonius, Cicero's eventual colleague in the consulship of 63, while among those who received the stigma of a censorial *nota* were some of the jurors at the trial of Oppianicus in 74. They counted 910,000 citizens, almost double the number recorded at the previous census: the long struggle of the Italians for equal rights was, in theory at least, over at last. They also pandered to Pompey's vanity by reviving the obsolete ceremony of the *transvectio equitum*, a review of the cavalry, in the course of which Pompey was able to boast that he had not merely performed the military service required of him by law, but had performed it under his own command.

Despite the concern expressed by Pompey before he took office, no legislative measures were taken to combat extortion in the provinces, while he clearly found reform of the courts a much less urgent matter than restoring the tribunician power. He took no direct action on the jury question and it was not until the autumn that a praetor, L. Cotta, brother of the consuls of 75 and 74, brought in a law to divide the juries into three equal groups: senators, *equites* and *tribuni aerarii*. (This last, whatever its origins, was by now a purely honorific title, whose holders possessed wealth similar to that of *equites*.) The language of Plutarch suggests that Pompey gave the bill no active support. By the time Cotta passed his law the case of C. Verres had been heard. Cicero more than once suggests that Verres' trial was the Senate's last chance to retain control of the courts, for an honest verdict by a senatorial jury might stave off otherwise inevitable legislation. That is highly unlikely, nor

[20] Seager 1969 (C 257). See below, ch. 9.

indeed is it probable that the condemnation of Verres mollified the critics of senatorial juries enough to prevent total transfer to the *equites*. Cicero several times speaks in the *Verrines* as if that were the prospect which faced the Senate, and no doubt there was talk along those lines in the spring and summer of 70. But whether there was ever a formal proposal for transfer, which was subsequently moderated, is extremely doubtful; Cicero may for rhetorical effect have deliberately misrepresented and exaggerated the effects of the Lex Aurelia in its final form, as if its provisions were tantamount to total transfer, as certain later sources do through sheer incompetence.[21] Despite our sources' tendency to treat the two non-senatorial orders as one, such records as survive of the voting of the three groups of jurors show no evidence of the *equites* and *tribuni aerarii* acting as a solid block in opposition to the senators. Indeed Cotta's solution seems to have worked very well. Control of the courts, which had been a bone of contention since the time of C. Gracchus, ceased to be an issue in the remaining decades of the Republic. Plainly most of those concerned found the Lex Aurelia acceptable, perhaps because the changes brought about by the upheavals of the Social and civil wars and Sulla's reconstruction of the Senate had created a community of background and outlook between the orders that would have been politically and socially out of the question before Sulla. Once again, however, some die-hards in the Senate would have preferred to see Sulla's arrangements upheld and in consequence harboured a grudge against Cotta.[22]

The trial of Verres itself has sometimes been seen as a confrontation between Pompey and the Metelli. This view cannot be maintained.[23] Cicero never lists the prosecution of Verres among his services to Pompey, and he had cogent enough reasons of his own for taking the case. He had made friends in Sicily during his quaestorship and, as at the trial of Roscius, the apathy of more distinguished patrons gave him a golden opportunity to show off his talents. To the pleasure of display was added the challenge of a direct contest with Hortensius, with a reward, if Cicero was successful, of Verres' praetorian standing in the Senate. The degree of Pompey's interest in the trial is debatable. He should have been concerned to protect his Sicilian clients, if only to preserve his credibility as a patron, and he had publicly condemned corruption in provincial government. But he certainly played no active part in the proceedings. It is not unreasonable to suppose that he was pleased by the outcome of the trial, but even more pleased that it had come about without potentially invidious effort on his own part.

The Metelli and their friends did their best for Verres. Hortensius,

[21] Seager 1979 (C 258) 25; Brunt 1980 (C 33) 286; *contra*, Bruhns 1976 (C 28) 266.

[22] Seager 1969 (C 257) 682ff.

[23] Seager 1979 (C 258) 25f; Brunt 1980 (C 33) 280ff.

who was probably an accessory after the fact of Verres' extortions, undertook the defence assisted by L. Sisenna. L. Metellus, Verres' successor in Sicily, did his best to hinder Cicero's investigations, bullied and threatened his witnesses, tried to suppress damning evidence and wrote to Pompey and Crassus on Verres' behalf. Every effort was made, first to substitute for Cicero a collusive prosecutor, Q. Caecilius Niger, then to put off the trial till 69, when Hortensius would be consul with Q. Metellus and the third brother, M. Metellus, would be praetor and assigned by happy chance to the presidency of the extortion court. Indeed, when C. Curio, the consul of 76, heard the results of the elections, he congratulated Verres on his acquittal! Yet it is hard to believe that, apart from the blow to Hortensius' professional pride, Verres' distinguished friends were greatly distressed by the verdict. Their motive for supporting Verres in the first place must have been financial: with three brothers all in line for office in rapid succession, even the Metelli must have felt the strain on their resources. They felt obliged to try to save him, but once the attempt had been made and failed they probably reflected that his disappearance from the scene was no great loss.

The spirit of conciliation which Pompey had shown in Spain at the end of the Sertorian War was further evidenced during 70 when a tribune, Plautius or Plotius, probably with Pompey's blessing, passed a law granting amnesty to the supporters of Lepidus, including those who had gone to Spain to join Sertorius.[24] Perhaps the only failure of the year, from Pompey's point of view, was his failure to obtain grants of land for his veterans. The same tribune proposed a bill to provide allotments for the men who had served in Spain under Pompey and Pius, but if the bill was passed it was never put into effect, and it may have been dropped on the ground that the treasury could not bear the expense.

It has been claimed that the restoration of tribunician power and the reform of the courts did not undermine the Sullan settlement to any great degree.[25] As far as the courts are concerned that is probably true, but the tribunate is another matter. Sulla had seen it as a major disruptive force, and both the bitter resistance to its restoration before 70 and the persistence of resentment afterwards indicate that leading men still shared this view. Nor were they mistaken. The fabric of the state might be merely shaken by a Gracchus, a Sulpicius or in time to come a Clodius. But the exploitation of the tribunate by Pompey, Caesar and Crassus was to do much to further that excessive growth of individual power which the oligarchy saw, with some justification, as the greatest threat to its collective predominance.

For the future Pompey himself could look forward to the dignity that

[24] Date: Taylor 1941 (C 140) 121 n. 32. [25] Gruen 1974 (C 209) 23ff.

every consular enjoyed, but perhaps to less power than a number of his peers. The very speed of his rise and its exclusively military nature had meant that he had had neither time nor opportunity to develop the intricate web of relationships that a man who had reached the consulship by more conventional paths would have built up over the years. In Spain Pompey had acquired some useful supporters: M. Varro, the military man L. Afranius, who was probably praetor in 71, and C. Cornelius. But he had also had some ill fortune: D. Laelius was killed at Lauro, though his son preserved the connexion, and Pompey's brother-in-law C. Memmius died at the Turia. Lollius Palicanus gained a praetorship for 69, but otherwise no known friends of Pompey appear in the *fasti*. For the moment he could only bide his time. He had declared that he had no intention of taking a province, and Crassus had followed suit. An ordinary governorship would merely have detracted from his glory – he seems already to have established as his guiding principle that nothing about his career must be ordinary. Only when circumstances created the chance of another major command would Pompey return to the stage. The ground had been prepared by the restoration of the tribunician power, and Pompey could afford to be patient till the time was ripe to use it. At the end of 70 he allowed himself the gesture of a public reconciliation with Crassus, after Crassus had taken the initiative with flattering words, whose double edge will have been apparent to others, though it may have been turned by the shield of Pompey's conceit.

CHAPTER 8*a*

LUCULLUS, POMPEY AND THE EAST

A. N. SHERWIN-WHITE

I. PRELIMINARY OPERATIONS: MURENA AND SERVILIUS

Mithridates might have accepted what the Peace of Dardanus seemed to offer – the recognition of his independence within his kingdom and freedom of action to the north and west, in the regions of his Crimean, Sarmatian and sub-Caucasian territories. The Peace required his withdrawal from the Roman dependencies south and west of the Halys in Bithynia, Paphlagonia, Galatia and Cappadocia, though he retained the coastal zone of Paphlagonia that his father Euergetes had acquired. So too a century earlier the Seleucids were left free by the Peace of Apamea in their activities 'beyond Taurus'. But in 83–82 B.C. Licinius Murena, left by Sulla to re-establish the Roman province of Asia, intervened against Mithridates, first in Cappadocia, where the king was attempting to restrict the territorial recovery of the restored Ariobarzanes, and then in western Pontus, where Murena carried out two extensive raids on the pretext that the military preparations of Mithridates for the recovery of the rebellious Greek cities of the Crimea were in fact aimed against Rome. After suffering the devastations of two great raids without resistance, when Murena appeared for the third time despite the intervention of a Roman arbiter who gave ambiguous advice, Mithri-

The principal sources for the campaigns and other activities of Lucullus and Pompey in the East are the *Mithridatica* of the historian Appian, the *Historia Romana* of Cassius Dio, and Plutarch's biographies of the two proconsuls. The local historian Memnon provides an independent account of the campaigns of Lucullus, including a lengthy internal history of the misfortunes of Heraclea and Sinope. All are relatively late works, written between the late first and early third centuries A.D., and except for Memnon derived ultimately, so far as can be judged, from the now fragmentary *Histories* III–V of Sallust, the lost books 93–102 of Livy, and the little-known histories of Pompey written by his contemporaries Posidonius and Theophanes. Much particular information about Mithridates and Tigranes is preserved by the geographer Strabo, who devoted about half of his twelfth book to the kingdom of Pontus, and also related the fortunes of many Greek cities of the Anatolian region, which are independently illuminated by a number of lengthy epigraphical documents. Of various brief epitomators Velleius Paterculus alone provides an independent survey of events, dating from *c.* A.D. 14. Finally the actions of Pompey and Gabinius in southern Syria are recounted mainly in the *Jewish Antiquities* and the *Jewish War* of Josephus, written in the Flavian period. Thus apart from civic inscriptions and sporadic information in speeches of Cicero, notably his *De Imperio Cn. Pompeii*, the surviving sources were written in the Principate. For the first decade they are collected in *Greenidge–Clay*.

SARMATIA
BASTARNAE
M. Palus
(Sea of Azov)
Phanagorea
Nymphaion
Theodosia
Taman Str.
Chersonesus
SCORDISCI
Danubius
Pontus Euxinus
(Black Sea)
PAIONES
Sinope
Amastris
Heraclea
PAPHLAGONIA
PONTUS
Amisus
Bosporus
Byzantium
Chalcedon
Amphipolis
MACEDONIA
Thasos
Propontis
Nicaea
Nicomedia
Halys
Amasia
Iris
EPIRUS
Cyzicus
Prusa
Lampsacus
Lemnos
Magnesia
Demetrias
Alexandria Troas
Tenedos
BITHYNIA
Sangarius
Zela
THESSALY
Sciathos
Rhyndacus
Pessinus
Megalopolis
Melitaea
COLOPENE
AETOLIA
EUBOEA
Pergamum
PHRYGIA
GALATIA
Chaeronea
Chios
Clazomenae
Philomelium
Mazaca
CAPPADOC
ACHAEA
Athens
Samos
Ephesus
ASIA
Apamea
Pappa
LYCAONIA
Iconium
Cybistra
Zacynthos
Tralles
Aphrodisias
ORONDEIS
M.
Priene
Miletus
Alabanda
L.Caralis
Isaura
Taurus
Cilician Gates
Delos
COM
PAMPHYLIA
Adana
Phaselis
Side
Soli
Cnidus
LYCIA
Olympus
Mallus
Epiphania
Amanus M.
Myra
CILICIA
Rhodes
Coracesium
Antioch
Cnossus
SYR
CRETE
Salamis
CYPRUS
Paphos
Emesa
Mediterraneum Mare
(Mediterranean Sea)
Byblos
Berytus
PHOENICIA
Antilibanus M.
Tyre
Damascus
Alexandrion
Joppa
Philadelphia
Jericho
CYRENAICA
JUDAEA
Jerusalem
Alexandria
Gaza
Pelusium
Petra
EGYPT
Nilus
Bitlis Modern place-names underlined
Land over 1000 metres
0 500 km
0 300 miles

9 The East

D
E
F
40°E
45°E
50°E
a
b
c
d
e
45°N
40°N
35°N
30°N
AORSI
Mare
Caspium
(Caspian
Sea)
Caucasus
M.
Dioscurias
COLCHIS
Phasis
IBERIA
Tiflis
Abas
ALBANIA
Cyrus
L.Sevan
Trapezus
TIBARENI
Cabira
CHALDAEI
Acampsis
Lycus
Nicopolis
LESSER ARMENIA
ARMENIA
Artaxata
Mt Ararat
Araxes
MELITENE
Arsanias
Antitaurus M.
SOPHENE
L.Gölcük
Tomisa
Amida
Bitlis
ATROPATENE
GORDYENE
MAGENE
OSRHOENE
Nisibis
Tigranocerta
Zeugma
Balik
Carrhae
Hierapolis
Beroia
IA
ADIABENE
Arbela
HYRCANIA
MEDIA
MESOPOTAMIA
Seleucia
Tigris
PARTHIA
BABYLONIA
Euphrates
PERSIS
NABATENE

dates led his army out and inflicted a series of defeats on Murena's forces, which he pursued through northern Galatia to the borders of Phrygia. An emissary of Sulla himself now arrived who put an end to the fighting and secured the evacuation of Cappadocian territory by Mithridates. Murena withdrew to hold an unearned triumphal celebration in Rome.

This affair reveals the existence of contrary policies at Rome. While Sulla was determined to maintain no more than the former protectorates beyond the borders of Asia in Cappadocia, Galatia and Bithynia, and to recognize Mithridates as a Roman vassal, his own man was bent on renewing war with Mithridates, and after Sulla's death a majority within the Senate connived at a refusal to ratify the Peace of Dardanus, of which Murena had denied the very existence on the grounds that it was not formulated in a written text. Yet Mithridates tried hard through his emissaries to secure the ratification of the Peace. When his agents failed to secure a hearing by the Senate in 78 he realized that powerful men were keen to renew a war that offered the prospect of vast enrichment. But he respected the Peace for the long period, in a king's reign, of eight years after his troubles with Murena.

After the withdrawal of Murena it was decided at Rome to restore Roman control over Pamphylia, Pisidia and Lycaonia, which had seen no Roman proconsul since 89 B.C. A permanent province was now established in the southern region, which was still known as 'Cilicia', though it contained no Cilician territory, because the suppression of pirates, known to have Cilicia as their main base, fell to the proconsuls. But the first enemy was Zenocoetes, who held maritime strongholds on the Lycian coast to the west of Pamphylia such as Olympus, Phaselis and their mountainous hinterland. The first effective proconsul was the consular P. Servilius, who operated with a considerable fleet of unknown composition and a force of five legions. In his first two years (78–77) he drove the light vessels of the pirates out of Pamphylian waters after a considerable but unlocated naval battle, and captured the strongholds of Zenocoetes by a series of land assaults.[1] He then set about the reconquest of mountainous Pisidia and the adjacent region of Isauria, which lies between the westernmost chain of Taurus and the open plateau of Lycaonia.

Through Pisidia and Isauria there passed the sole useful route for wheeled transport from Pamphylia to Iconium in western Lycaonia, on the main route from Apamea to Cappadocia. After the laborious capture of the central strongholds of Isaura Vetus and Isaura Nova, and the subjection of the Orondeis people around Misthion and Pappa to the north, beyond Lake Caralis, Servilius completed his conquest by

[1] Land assaults, cf. Strab. XIV.5.7 (671) with Cic. II *Verr.* 1.56, 4.21, *Leg. Agr.* 1.5, 2.50, Sall. *H.* II fr. 81–4, Florus I.41.5.

constructing a military highway along his main route, to be identified with the imperial road known from the late *Itineraries* which led from Side in Pamphylia by Pappa to Iconium. He thus opened for the first time, as the sources record, the direct route from the military region of Pamphylia to the confines of Cappadocia. There is no evidence whatever that his campaign into Isauria was conducted from the north, as has been supposed, through southern Phrygia, which was in the province of Asia, by Apamea and Philomelium. This campaign had nothing to do with the suppression of piracy: it opened up a new approach to Pontus from the south through Lycaonia and Cappadocia.[2] The threat of Mithridates mattered more to the Romans than the activities of pirates in the eastern Mediterranean, against whom a naval command was eventually established in 74 at the praetorian level. Mithridates was now faced by a dual threat from the Roman commanders in Asia and Cilicia. When war seemed likely in 74 the consul L. Lucullus secured the province of Cilicia rather than Bithynia, which was now available, because it was regarded as the centre of action against Mithridates, who rightly claimed that 'the Romans were awaiting an opportunity to attack him again'.[3]

II. THE OPENING OF THE THIRD WAR

Mithridates did not propose to fight his third war with Rome single-handed. He rebuilt his fleet, shattered by the surrender of 70 major vessels to Sulla: some 150 warships can be traced in the operations against Lucullus, out of an alleged strength of 400 ships of all types. He also made an agreement with the Cilician pirates, whose power had not yet been broken, and secured their active assistance in the first two years of the war. Further, before the war began he secured the advice of a military commission from the Roman forces that were maintaining themselves under C. Sertorius in Spain against the central Roman government (ch. 7, pp. 213 and 219). With this help he reorganized some part of the Pontic infantry on the Roman legionary pattern, armed with the heavy Roman spear and stabbing sword, and secured the aid of Roman military commanders in the field.

The immediate cause of the war was the Roman annexation of Bithynia. Nicomedes at his death, probably late in 75, having no legitimate heirs, left his kingdom to Rome, following the pattern of Attalus III in Asia and Ptolemy Apion in Cyrenaica. The Senate accepted the inheritance after rejecting the claims of a bastard son of Nicomedes to

[2] Strab. XII.6.2 (568), Oros. V.23.22; on Isaura Nova, Sall. *H.* II fr. 87 with Cic. *Leg. Agr.* 1.5, 2.50, and the inscription commemorating Servilius' payment of his vow (*AE* 1977 n. 816). Festus *Brev.* 11 improbably links the Isauri with Cilician pirates (*ibid.* 12.3). Military road, cf. Oros. V.23.22 with Eutropius VI.3, Festus *Brev.* 11. Cf. Ormerod 1924 (A 88) 214ff; Magie 1950 (A 67) II. 1169–74 nn. 21–5.

[3] App. *Mith.* 70.

the kingdom, and instructed the propraetor of Asia to take over the new province. In the early summer of 74 the news arrived of the death of the proconsul of Cilicia, who had recently arrived in succession to P. Servilius. In the following months there was a remarkable rearrangement of the consular commands for 74–73, originally made the previous year under the provisions of the Sullan Lex Cornelia. L. Licinius Lucullus gained Cilicia together with Asia in the place of Gallia Cisalpina, previously assigned to him, in expectation of war with Mithridates, and his colleague M. Aurelius Cotta secured Bithynia (ch. 7, p. 213). At this moment Mithridates had made no hostile move: Cotta had to argue during the senatorial debate on the new commands that the war with Mithridates had not ended in 82 but had merely been interrupted. Later in 74 the consuls were commissioned for war. Lucullus was instructed to take command of the legions in Asia and Cilicia, together with a legion from Italy, and in the words of Cicero 'to pursue Mithridates'. Cotta was left to hold the naval command in Bithynia, using the existing provincial flotillas, together with an unspecified military force, against the threat of the Pontic fleet.[4]

What action of Mithridates prompted these decisions is not clear. It is likely that he mobilized the great forces that he used in the first campaign during the summer of 74, and gave the Senate grounds for the despatch of the consuls, and it is also possible that Mithridates established advanced forces in eastern Paphlagonia before his westward march. The ambiguities of the principal historical sources have led to much debate about the moment when the consuls left Italy and when the war began, about whether they departed in the late summer of 74 and were immediately involved in the battle of Chalcedon and the siege of Cyzicus, or whether these campaigns took place in 73. But the neglected evidence of a passage in Cicero's speech *pro Cluentio*, the earliest of all relevant documents, solves the problem. Lucullus was present in Rome as consul late in November 74, when he was involved in the aftermath of the affair known as the *causa Iuniana*, which the tribune Quinctius investigated about the end of the tribunician year. Hence Lucullus cannot have arrived in Asia and mobilized his forces much before the end of the first quarter of 73.[5] Appian, the principal source, places the advance of Mithridates into Bithynia 'in the beginning of spring'. Though he gives no indication of the year it can only be 73.[6]

At that time Lucullus, after a training programme, mustered his five

[4] Plut. *Luc.* 6.1, 5–6, Cic. *Mur.* 33; Sall. *H.*II.71, on whose chronology see Bloch 1961 (B 6) esp. 70.

[5] Cic. *Clu.* 90, 108, with 136–7. Lucullus operates straightaway from a base in Asia (Plut. *Luc.* 7.1); he never reached Cilicia. For the former controversy over the initial date see Magie 1950 (A 67) II.1127 n. 47, 1204 n. 5, and *MRR* II 106–8. Cf. Vell. Pat. II.33.1, 'ex consulatu sortitus Asiam', though *sortitus* is inaccurate.

[6] App. *Mith.* 70.

legions in northern Phrygia near the Sangarius river, for an invasion of Pontus, presumably through Galatia to the lower Halys, the route that he followed in the next year. Mithridates anticipated him by marching rapidly through Paphlagonia into Bithynia in nine days, met with his fleet and defeated Cotta in a naval battle off Chalcedon, destroying the Roman fleet and driving Cotta with whatever land forces he had behind the walls of the city. Thence Mithridates marched westwards with the intention of capturing Cyzicus, the great port on the northern coast of Asia in the Propontis. Lucullus abandoned his planned invasion and turned westwards to the relief of Cotta, meeting only the rearguard of Mithridates at Otryae in the Bithynian lowlands, between Nicaea and Prusa.[7] After a successful engagement Lucullus pressed on to Cyzicus, where he found Mithridates vigorously organizing the investment of the city. He required Cyzicus, with its double harbour on either side of the peninsula in which the city stands, as the supply base for the large army with which he intended to destroy the Roman forces in Asia, as he had done in the first war. The sources may exaggerate when they give figures of 12,000 to 16,000 cavalry and up to 150,000 infantry for the Pontic army, twice or thrice the number that fought against Sulla at Chaeronea. But there is no doubt that they greatly outnumbered the forces of Lucullus.[8]

While Mithridates invested Cyzicus by land and sea, Lucullus occupied a strong defensive position with his five legions on high ground from which he could threaten the enemy's communications, in a strategy of siege and countersiege. He avoided a general engagement, and in a telling phrase attributed to Lucullus by Plutarch, he 'stamped on the stomach of Mithridates'.[9] Though the king controlled the sea with his naval forces he lacked an adequate maritime base for the supply of his large army. Cyzicus under its civic leaders, aided by a small Roman force that managed to enter the city across the sea channel, courageously held out against all the efforts of Mithridates. The king used every device of siegecraft, with assaults by land and sea, by ships and machines, and by tunnels, to take the city. But he was eventually compelled by the approach of winter first to dismiss most of his cavalry eastwards through Bithynia, and later, as supply difficulties increased, to withdraw his infantry westwards to the small harbour of Lampsacus for evacuation by sea.

Lucullus, harrying both attempts at the river crossings, inflicted heavy losses, taking at the Rhyndacus river (it is said) some 6,000 horses and

[7] For Otryae or Otroia cf. Strab. XII.4.7 (566) and Plut. *Luc.* 8.6. who sufficiently clarify the location.

[8] Numbers: Strab. XII.8.11 (575), Plut. *Luc.*7.5, Memnon (*FGrH* 2 B 434) F 27. 2–3; App. *Mith.* 69.

[9] Plut. *Luc.* 11.2.

15,000 men, and inflicting losses of the same scale on the infantry at the Granicus crossing. Mithridates, supported by his fleet, withdrew the remnants of his forces to Nicomedia in eastern Bithynia. Lucullus meanwhile had taken command of the ships that he secured from the Asian cities after the destruction of the fleet of Cotta at Chalcedon. When the Pontic forces were withdrawn from Lampsacus he was able in the spring of 72 to destroy the squadrons left to block his passage through the Hellespont, off Lemnos. The legates Triarius and Barba, likewise provided with a flotilla from Asia, sailed through the Propontis and rapidly captured Apamea, Prusa and Nicaea. Mithridates promptly withdrew from Nicomedia and passed through the Bosporus to Sinope in Pontus, but paused at the free-state of Heraclea, where he left a force of some 4,000 men to delay the Roman advance.

In the previous summer forces had been sent by Mithridates into Lycaonia and southern Asia to stir up the troublesome Isaurians and Pisidians, but they were driven out by the active Galatian tetrarch Deiotarus. The two proconsuls were now able to gather their forces at Nicomedia, where they debated the new situation with their legates. Despite suggestions that a diplomatic settlement could be arranged, the decision was taken to advance into Pontus and to destroy the power of Mithridates, while Triarius was despatched with a fleet that now numbered seventy ships to deal with the last Pontic naval force that survived in the southern Aegean. Total victory, with the consequent extension of provincial rule, was the objective.

Lucullus had utterly defeated Mithridates in the campaign of Cyzicus without ever risking a pitched battle against his united forces. The contrast with the method of Sulla's double annihilation of the Pontic forces in Boeotia is remarkable. It suggests that the calculations of Mithridates about his advantages in warfare based on mainland Anatolia were not ill founded. Only an exceptional military genius could have foreseen the strategy of Lucullus, who entirely neglected the usual Roman preference for pitched battles and quick results. Mithridates' mistake lay not in the initial attempt to capture Cyzicus but in his persistence with the siege when the method of his enemy was revealed. But the only alternative to an advance into Asia was to remain on the defensive at Nicomedia in Bithynia, where he would not have been waging war against the heartland of Roman power in the East. If he took Cyzicus his land forces could combine with his naval power to exclude the Romans from the whole Propontic area. But sea-power had its limitations when the Roman legions were already established on the Asiatic mainland before the Pontic fleet passed through the straits of Bosporus.

III. THE CAMPAIGN IN PONTUS

In the summer of 72 B.C. Lucullus advanced with his main forces through Galatia, south of Paphlagonia, to western Pontus. Meanwhile the legate Triarius with his fleet of seventy vessels disposed of the last Pontic fleet off Tenedos, and the proconsul Cotta with the remnants of his original forces and Bithynian reinforcements neutralized the fortress of Heraclea, where the Pontic commander Connocorix was besieged for the duration of two years. With five legions of uncertain strength Lucullus reached the lower Halys and marched downstream to the coastal zone around Amisus unopposed. The gates of Amisus were closed against him, and the city withstood a leisurely siege through to the year 70. Early in 71, if not sooner, Lucullus marched with his main forces through the Iris and Lycus valleys into the heart of Pontus. There Mithridates had gathered near Cabira a new army numbering some 40,000 infantry (it is said) and 4,000 cavalry. Lucullus had delayed his advance deliberately, according to the version of Plutarch, to allow Mithridates to commit himself to a campaign in central Pontus. Aware of the extent of the Pontic empire he had no intention of allowing himself to be drawn into distant campaigns among the mountains of eastern Pontus and Lesser Armenia.[10]

The decisive operation took place in the summer of 71. To avoid the forays of the effective Pontic cavalry Lucullus established his legions in a defensive position on high ground opposite Cabira. His food supplies came, somewhat surprisingly, across southern Pontus from Cappadocia, where the aged Ariobarzanes still held his throne. Mithridates attacked the supply route with his cavalry, but his assaults were repelled with heavy losses. Having learned his lesson from Lucullus, Mithridates was unwilling to risk a general engagement, and now attempted to withdraw his forces eastwards into the mountains of Lesser Armenia, where his resources of gold and silver were said to be stored in seventy strongholds, and where he could hope for the support of his powerful but hitherto unhelpful ally Tigranes, ruler of Great Armenia and many adjacent principalities. The attempted retreat turned to total disaster, thanks to the previous destruction of the bulk of the Pontic cavalry. Organization and discipline broke down as soon as the evacuation of the encampments began. Lucullus was able to assault the retiring columns unopposed, and succeeded, it seems, though it is never clearly stated, in destroying the bulk of the Pontic army.[11] Mithridates fled south-east

[10] Dates: the clearest evidence is in Phlegon *Ol.* 12.4 (*FGrH*, 2 B 257), who indicates that in the course of 72–71 B.C. after initiating the siege of Amisus, Lucullus wintered near Cabira and then defeated Mithridates in the next year. Cf. Magie 1950 (A 67) II 1210 n. 24.

[11] Lucullus succeeds: *Mith.* 81–2, Plut. *Luc.* 17–18.1. Numbers slain; Livy *Per.* XCVII has 60,000, Eutropius VI.8, 30,000.

through Comana to Armenia, where he became an unwelcome guest of Tigranes, who left him a virtual prisoner in an isolated fortress for the next eighteen months, through the last part of 71 to the end of 70.

Lucullus was left free to complete the territorial conquest of Pontus. The royal residences of Cabira and Eupatoria were captured quickly, and the Greek cities of Sinope and Amisus were taken after lengthy sieges. Lesser Armenia was occupied, and in the zone to the north the remote Chaldaei submitted and the wild Tibareni were chastised. These successes led Machares, son and regent of Mithridates in the Crimean Bosporus, who had recently been supporting the resistance of Sinope with sea-borne supplies, to seek terms as an 'ally and friend' of Rome. Earlier, the great Greek families that provided much of the administrative personnel of the kingdom, including the kinsmen of the later geographer Strabo, had betrayed their master and brought armies and provincial districts over to the Romans. But to complete his conquest Lucullus required the king himself, in whose person the authority of the kingdom resided, just as a generation earlier Marius had sought the capture of the Numidian king Jugurtha. Hence he sent the young Appius Claudius to treat with Tigranes for the surrender of the king's person.

Tigranes had no previous connexion with Rome. For the past twelve years he had been the most powerful ruler of the lands beyond the middle Euphrates. He succeeded about 96 B.C. to the throne of northern Armenia as the vassal of the Parthian monarch Mithridates Megas. His kingdom at that time was apparently restricted to the basin of the upper Euphrates tributaries and the upper Araxes, to the north of the watershed of the Antitaurus massif, though he may have held some territory to the south of the Bitlis pass. The western sector of southern Armenia, known as Sophene, was held by Artanes, descendant of one Zariadris, who like Artaxias, the grandsire of Tigranes, originated as a military commander in the time of Antiochus III (the Great). Gordyene, the south-eastern sector in the mountains separating southern Armenia from Mesopotamia and Adiabene, was ruled by the independent prince Zarbienos. While the Parthian dynasty was being weakened by dynastic feuds Tigranes extended his power by the annexation of Sophene and the submission of Gordyene under its prince. After the death of Mithridates Megas he secured Mesopotamia proper, between the two rivers, and Adiabene beyond the middle Tigris in northern Iraq, while in the north-east he gained control of the enclosed region of Media Atropatene. Finally, in about 82, he expelled the much weakened Seleucid kings from northern Syria and lowland Cilicia, and took the title of King of Kings.[12]

[12] For the chronology of Tigranes' reign see Plut. *Luc* 21.6 and Just. *Epit.* XL.1.3–4, 2.3, with Will 1982 (A 127) II.457f.

When Appius Claudius finally reached Antioch in his quest for Tigranes he showed little respect for the king. In the absence of Tigranes, busy with the organization of Phoenicia, Appius intrigued with subject rulers present at Antioch, including Zarbienos of Gordyene. When Tigranes on his return received him with the ceremonial of an eastern court, Appius behaved in the crudest Roman fashion. After delivering a letter from Lucullus, of which the contents are not reported, he stated that he had come either to take Mithridates off for the triumph of Lucullus or to declare war on Tigranes. The king inevitably refused to surrender Mithridates and said that he would defend himself against any Roman attack. Appius barely preserved diplomatic decencies by accepting a single goblet from the many valuable gifts that Tigranes offered.

In the course of 70 B.C. Appius made his report to Lucullus, now busy at Ephesus with the reorganization of Asia. When rumours circulated about the king's preparations for war Lucullus expressed his astonishment that Tigranes should prepare to fight the Roman power 'with cold hopes' after failing to help Mithridates before his defeat.[13] Lucullus quickly left Asia for Pontus, where he made his arrangements for the invasion of Armenia. About this time he also secured the despatch of the usual commission of senators 'for the settlement of affairs in Pontus'. The commission arrived to find that the proconsul had departed to wage war in Armenia, and awaited his return.[14]

IV. LUCULLUS IN ARMENIA

Appius Claudius could provide Lucullus with an excuse but not a legitimate justification for making war on Tigranes. His actions at Antioch were not those of a legate commissioned by a senatorial decree. There is no evidence that Lucullus himself had any authority from Rome for his invasion of Armenia. It is unlikely that he could have secured a senatorial decree extending his zone of operations in the year 70, when the radical consuls Cn. Pompeius and M. Crassus were in control of the senatorial agenda throughout the year. Cicero, speaking in the interest of Pompey in the first weeks of 66, implied that Lucullus had no Roman authority for the invasion of Armenia, which he described as though it was a private affair: 'When Lucullus came into the kingdom of Tigranes with his army . . . fear fell on those tribes which the Roman People had never thought to provoke or to try out in war.' The tone echoes the remarks of the hostile praetor Quinctius who had alleged in 68 B.C. that Lucullus was 'making one war out of another . . . he has sacked the

[13] For the reported remarks of Appius, Tigranes and Lucullus see Plut. *Luc.* 21.6, 23.7.

[14] The report of victory to Rome and the arrival of the commission are mentioned retrospectively by Plut. *Luc.* 35.6.

capital of Tigranes as though he had been sent not to defeat the kings but to strip them of their kingdoms'.[15]

These critical remarks suggest that Lucullus found it hard to defend the invasion on legitimate grounds. Tigranes was known to have had some form of alliance with Mithridates, but, as Lucullus was well aware, he had never yet helped him in a Roman war. A passage of Appian suggests that Lucullus tried to distinguish between his enemy Tigranes and the king's subjects in Sophene, with whom the Romans had no quarrel: 'Lucullus asked the barbarians only for necessities . . . they expected to suffer no harm while Lucullus and Tigranes settled their differences.'[16] But by crossing the Euphrates Lucullus greatly extended the foreign commitments of Rome, by making war against an independent empire that hitherto had no connexions with the Roman state of any sort, and eventually by invading territory to which the Parthian monarch rather than Tigranes had the prior claim.

In the summer of 69 Lucullus selected the best of his troops for the invasion of Armenia, numbering some 12,000 Roman legionaries – the better part of three legions – with the unusually large force of 4,000 provincial cavalry and light-armed troops. He marched through Cappadocia to the Euphrates crossing at Tomisa and entered northern Sophene. Thence he crossed the Antitaurus by, presumably, the only easy passage of the massif east of Lake Gölcük, down to Amida in the plateau of the upper Tigris basin, which constitutes southern Sophene. The invasion was aimed at the southern sector of the Armenian kingdom around which clustered the new dependencies, Mesopotamia in the south, leading to northern Syria and coastal Cilicia, Gordyene and Adiabene in the east and south-east beyond the upper and middle Tigris. All these lands had fallen to Tigranes at the expense of the Seleucid and Parthian dynasties. So Lucullus and his army entered for the first time the lands beyond Taurus and the Euphrates river. Armenia and Parthia took the place of Pontus and the Seleucid kingdom in Syria as the limits of Roman intervention.

What Lucullus intended can be seen from his actions, which reveal a change of method from his system of warfare against Mithridates. He now sought a quick result from a great pitched battle by making for the southern capital of Tigranocerta, on the border of Mesopotamia, which Tigranes was busy completing to be the centre of his new empire. The exact location of Tigranocerta is still somewhat uncertain. All the early evidence from Strabo and his sources places the city in the frontier zone of southern Armenia and Mesopotamia, but the *Annals* of Tacitus set it some fifty kilometres from the well-known fortress-city of Nisibis.[17]

[15] Cic. *De Imp. Cn. Pomp.* 23, Plut. *Luc.* 35.5–6. [16] App. *Mith.* 84.

[17] Site of Tigranocerta, see Strab. XI.12.4 (572), Tac. *Ann.* XV.5.2. For the controversy see Dillemann 1962 (D 262) 247ff.

Tigranes departed to muster his main forces and returned, when Lucullus had invested the city, with a great army organized largely in the old oriental style with tribal contingents armed and armoured in their native fashion. The most formidable elements were the squadrons of cataphracts, heavy cavalry clad in chain-mail derived from a Sarmatian model and armed with long and massive spears. Tigranes was astounded (it is said) at the small scale of the Roman army, 'small for an army, large for an embassy'.[18] But in the engagement near Tigranocerta Lucullus led a charge of Roman cohorts against the flank of the advancing cataphracts, ordering his men to attack horses rather than riders. The cataphracts were driven back in confusion on to the main body, which broke into total disarray. There was an immense slaughter, variously reckoned at 10,000 to 100,000 men.

The Roman victory, the only formally arranged battle among the operations of Lucullus, took place late in the season on 7 October. Tigranes fled northwards to be strengthened by the arrival of a reserve force under the command of Mithridates, who had been in no hurry because in his experience Lucullus was not given to rapid action. The flexibility of Lucullus in assessing the strategic situation and in his management of the tactics of battle showed a high military quality. But it was too late in the year to pursue his advantage through the high mountains, and after some rearguard actions the kings were able to retire to northern Armenia. Lucullus busied himself in the milder southern region with the capture and destruction of Tigranocerta. But if Tigranes had eluded him, he made other political gains. The local rulers of Sophene came to terms, and various Arab princes with whom Appius Claudius had negotiated at Antioch, made their submission. Lucullus himself visited Gordyene, where the disloyal ruler Zarbienos had been executed and buried in dishonour. He gave the dead prince royal obsequies, and secured control of the treasures and supplies of the principality. Meanwhile he sought to put an end to the imperial claims of Tigranes by the dismemberment of the population of Tigranocerta. The inhabitants, drawn from Syria and Cilicia, were restored to their homelands, Greeks and native persons alike, the cost being met from the spoils of the city. In the extreme south the last Seleucid prince Antiochus was allowed to return to claim the Syrian throne at Antioch.

During the winter of 69/8 B.C. Lucullus became aware of the Parthian factor. Phraates III had recently emerged as the ruler of all the Parthian territories westwards to Babylonia, reunited after a lengthy period of domestic strife. Tigranes opened negotiations with him for military support, offering the surrender of Adiabene, Mesopotamia and the 'Great Valleys', adjacent (it seems) to Gordyene. But Phraates made

[18] Plut. *Luc.* 27.4.

contact with Lucullus. According to the most probable version Lucullus sent a mission of distinguished Greeks, and the Parthian was invited either to join the Romans or to remain neutral. Eventually it seems that he was unwilling to commit himself, and either maintained a watchful neutrality or, as Memnon has it, came to terms with both sides.[19]

In the summer of 68 Lucullus sought to finish with Tigranes. Marching through the Antitaurus passage into northern Armenia, his devastations brought into the field the Armenian forces, which had been trained by Mithridates in the past months in methods of warfare learned from Lucullus himself. The kings avoided pitched battles with the Roman infantry and used their own cavalry to check the movements of the small Roman army and to attack its supplies. The zone of operations is not defined by the sources until Lucullus moved deeper into northern Armenia, crossed the Arsanias, the southern tributary of the Euphrates, where he brushed the Armenian resistance aside in a considerable engagement, and marched across central Armenia towards Artaxata.[20] The northern capital, set in north-eastern Armenia, beyond Mt Ararat in the upper Araxes valley, sheltered the king's family, barely rescued the previous year from Tigranocerta. But it was late in the season, and the Roman troops, hampered by autumnal storms, protested against continuing their advance, having now endured, apart from their military engagements, a march of some 1,500 kilometres 'as the crow flies' from Cyzicus. Lucullus promptly turned south and marched across the breadth of Armenia through the Antitaurus, presumably by the Bitlis pass in the east, to the southern edge of the upper Tigris basin. There he invested Nisibis, a strongly fortified town with a famous double wall, on the Mesopotamian border, still held by the king's brother. Tigranes cautiously followed the path of Lucullus but did nothing to help Nisibis, which he believed to be impregnable. Lucullus, after delaying his assault in the hope of enticing Tigranes, captured the city by a night attack, and spent the winter there, while Tigranes recovered minor fortresses in southern Armenia. Scraps of somewhat contradictory evidence suggest that Lucullus now planned an abortive campaign against Adiabene, still under the suzerainty of Tigranes, for the spring of 67 from a base in Gordyene. This may be connected with a similar scheme to march 'up country' from Gordyene, placed by Plutarch at an earlier date. He suggests that legates were being summoned from Pontus to assist, allegedly against the Parthians.[21]

Lucullus thus sought in military terms to bring Tigranes to battle by

[19] Parthia: Plut. *Luc.* 30.1, Memnon F 38.8, App. *Mith.* 87, Dio XXXVI.1–3; see below, pp. 262–5.

[20] App. *Mith.* 87 and Dio XXXVI.5.1 explain the Armenian methods, ignored by Plut. *Luc.* 31.3, 5–9.

[21] Campaign from Gordyene in 69–68 'against the Parthians', Plut. *Luc.* 30.2–3, 31.1; in 68–67, *ibid.* 34.6, cf. Eutropius VI.9, 'against the Persians'.

aggressive campaigns or by threatening his cities when he refused to be drawn. Politically, as he learned about the nature of the Armenian empire, he set about dissolving it into its original kingdoms. He was hardly concerned about Parthia, which at this time seemed a secondary power that had been stripped by Tigranes of its western dependencies in Adiabene and Mesopotamia, and was separated from the Roman world by the broad gravel deserts between Syria and Babylonia.

Meanwhile, late in 68, events in Pontus turned against Lucullus. Mithridates, with a force at the reported strength of 8,000 men, marched westwards into Lesser Armenia and set about attacking the Roman troops dispersed through Pontus, amounting to a couple of undermanned legions with supporting Asian levies. The legate Fabius was defeated and besieged in Cabira, where he was relieved by the forces of Triarius, marching from Asia or Bithynia at the summons of Lucullus for his abortive last campaign.[22] During the winter the peoples of Pontus, alienated by a hostile administration, flocked to join Mithridates. In the early summer of 67 he succeeded in luring out the Roman troops, then concentrated at Gazioura, some eighty kilometres south of Cabira, by threatening their principal storehouse of war material and booty located in the neighbourhood of Zela. He caught them and inflicted a great defeat on the field of Zela: the Romans lost 7,000 men and more than their quota of officers, including 24 military tribunes. This was the greatest success of Mithridates against Roman forces. Though it prolonged his survival in Pontus for only another year, it provided a golden promotion for the ambitious Roman consular Pompey, who in that same year was conducting naval operations on a grand scale against the persistent plague of piracy throughout the Mediterranean area.

Lucullus in southern Armenia at the end of 68 suffered from the insubordination of his troops, particularly the Fimbrian legions, which had served in the East since 86. The sporadic fighting since the fall of Tigranocerta had brought them no substantial booty, despite the recent capture of Nisibis. In a series of disturbances the dissatisfied troops demanded an end to the war. The young P. Claudius Pulcher, later known as Clodius, brother of the legate Appius Claudius, began his stormy political career by quarrelling with his proconsul Lucullus. He incited the troops against their commander, invoking the name of Pompey, and contrasting their supposed poverty with the proconsul's wagon-loads of personal booty. But when the news arrived of the defeat of Fabius in Pontus discipline was temporarily restored. Lucullus withdrew from Armenia in the spring of 67, but arrived too late to prevent the disaster of Zela. The defeated remnants met him in south-

[22] Dio XXXVI. 10.1.

eastern Pontus. Lucullus, learning that Mithridates had withdrawn to the stronghold of Talaura in Armenia Minor, found the route blocked by Median cavalry. Then, ever aware of strategic advantages, he proposed to march south-eastwards against Tigranes, who was slowly advancing from southern Armenia by the Tomisa crossing. Lucullus' precise location is not given in the sources, but his base could have been the route centre later known as Megalopolis (*mod.* Sivas), where the routes to northern Pontus, Lesser Armenia, western Cappadocia, and the Euphrates transit at Tomisa, meet. However, the dissatisifed troops refused to co-operate and he retired westwards into Cappadocia.[23]

By this time it was known that Lucullus had been formally replaced in his command by two new consulars, who reached Roman Cilicia and Bithynia during the summer of 67 (see below, p. 249). Marcius Rex, instructed to eliminate the pirates from their Cilician bases, brought three new legions from Italy. Acilius Glabrio, consul in 67, was commissioned to take over the eastern command from Lucullus by a plebiscite of the tribune Gabinius, following his creation of the general piracy command for Pompey, before the disaster of Zela was known at Rome. Learning the true situation on his arrival Glabrio lingered in Bithynia while Lucullus withdrew his battered forces into Galatia. Mithridates recovered the whole of Pontus, and Tigranes entered Cappadocia, whence Ariobarzanes had once more fled. The campaigns of Lucullus, who had never suffered defeat in battle, appeared to have been waged in vain.

V. LUCULLUS AND THE CITIES

The Greek cities of the coastlands of Propontis and the Pontic zone, whether fighting on the side of Mithridates or for Rome, showed a remarkable determination to defend themselves and their overlords in the third war. Cyzicus, no longer a free-state after the first war, sent its considerable navy to support the Romans at Chalcedon. Despite the heavy losses suffered in the naval battle the city offered a desperate resistance when heavily attacked by Mithridates, and with minimal direct aid from the forces of Lucullus repulsed every assault until Mithridates withdrew. Cyzicus received its reward afterwards in a renewal of its former status of 'free city' and in a considerable grant of adjacent territory.[24]

The story of Heraclea is told at length by the local historian Memnon.

[23] Movements of Lucullus: winters 68–67 B.C. in Gordyene, Plut. *Luc.* 34.6: in summer 67 B.C. is in Pontus, Dio XXXVI.14.1–2; frustrated perhaps at Megalopolis, Plut. *Luc.* 35.3–4 with Dio XXXVI.14.1–2.

[24] Cyzicus: Plut. *Luc.* 9–11.1, App. *Mith.* 73–5. Rewards, Strab. XII.8.11 (576).

When after the annexation of Bithynia Roman *publicani* ignored the independence of Heraclea and set up tax-collection centres in the civic territory, the citizens yielded to the pressure of Mithridates, sent five ships to join the Pontic fleet, and committed themselves irrevocably by murdering the Roman tax-collectors. Mithridates, on his return from the disaster of Cyzicus, occupied the city with partisan assistance and left a large garrison to hold it against the Roman advance. For the next two years Aurelius Cotta ineffectively besieged Heraclea where the civic fleet played a notable role, until the king's men and their supporters betrayed the city in the absence of Cotta to the legate Triarius, while the populace, determined to maintain their liberty, tried to continue resistance. The garrison sailed off to safety, but the city was ruthlessly sacked: the proconsul returned to the scene belatedly to claim his share of the spoils.[25]

A similar story of dissension between a royal garrison and the local citizens is related in the course of the siege of Sinope, the former Greek colony that became the principal city of Pontus. Two garrison commanders, Cleochares and Seleucus, murdered their colleague Leonippus, the favourite of the city population, said to be in touch with Lucullus. They gained control of the city and sought to eliminate the popular faction. Their greatest success was an attack by the civic fleet on a Roman supply squadron. But when Lucullus intensified the siege, and the city's food supplies from the Crimea were cut off by the transition of the Bosporan ruler to the Roman side, the garrison and its partisans seized what plunder they could and sailed away, leaving Sinope to be taken by Lucullus. At a third city, Amisus, resistance was better unified. The city stood a long siege at the same time as Sinope, aided by the skill in siege works of the garrison commander Callimachus. But Lucullus eventually stormed the city by a night attack, and Callimachus sailed off with his forces under cover of firing the city walls.[26]

In these civic sieges the garrison commanders and the city leaders followed a policy of vigorous resistance until the position grew desperate, when they turned to collusion and abandonment. They disregarded the interest of the resident population, who persisted in their course, either out of a justifiable fear of Roman reprisals or out of a determined loyalty to their king. The effective action of the civic fleets at Heraclea and Sinope, by themselves or in conjunction with the king's ships, must reflect the independence and prosperity of the citizen bodies that provided the ships and their crews.[27]

These three great cities were in a state of desolation after their capture.

[25] Heraclea: Memnon F 27.29, 34–5.

[26] Sinope: Memnon F 37, Plut. *Luc.* 23.1–4. Amisus: Memnon F 30.3–4; Plut. *Luc.* 19.2–4.

[27] Fleets: Memnon F 34.7; 37.2–3, 7.

But Lucullus set a notable example for Roman victors in his treatment of Amisus and Sinope. At Amisus he not only tried to check the conflagration, wholesale plunder and massacre of citizens at its capture, but set about a restoration as if the city had been, in the Roman formula, not 'taken in war' but 'surrendered into trust'. He aided the rebuilding of the city, the recovery of fugitive citizens, and the settlement of new colonists on abandoned lands. Sinope was likewise restored, and both became autonomous Greek cities within the provincial system. Lucullus was establishing a generous attitude towards Greek cities, which despite hostile actions in the past were the only possible base of Roman power at this time. He cited the precedent of Sulla who authorized the preservation of Athens, however reluctantly, despite its flagrant support of Mithridates. (The royal town of Cabira in Pontus surrendered on terms that preserved its existence.) In complementary style after the destruction of Tigranocerta the colonial inhabitants, Greek and non-Greek alike, were not sold into slavery but sent back to the cities in Syria, Cilicia and Cappadocia, from which they had been drafted to found the new capital.[28]

The eventual restoration of Heraclea was not due to Lucullus, because at the time of its capture it was in the power of the independent proconsul Aurelius Cotta. But Lucullus was not the only senator with rational opinions about the treatment of conquered peoples. Certain distinguished exiles from Heraclea organized an appeal to the Senate at the time when the proconsul Cotta, after his return to Rome, was being prosecuted by a tribune for misappropriation of booty. The Senate, accepting the plea that the defection of Heraclea was due to the pressure of Pontic forces, granted freedom to the enslaved Heracleots and restored their lands and the status of the city, though only some 8,000 of the inhabitants could be recovered.[29]

In the province of Asia the problem was different. The wealthy classes and the civic revenues were still burdened by the impositions of Sulla for arrears of tribute and payment of indemnities for the first war, amounting to 20,000 talents. The sum was not unreasonable: Mithridates had imposed a fine of 2,000 talents on Chios alone during the war. But the Asian cities, whose annual dues were hardly less than 2,000 talents in all, were steadily drained of their reserves by the continued warfare and the later exactions of Mithridates. To meet the Roman demands after the war they turned to the Roman financiers who came back to Asia after the reconquest. Many of these *negotiatores* had lost large sums when they had fled from Asia to escape the massacres of 88. Italy itself had been weakened and devastated by years of civil war, which continued after the

[28] Cabira, cf. Memnon F 30.1; Plut. *Luc.* 18.1 with Strab. XII.3.30 (556). Tigranocerta, cf. Plut. *Luc.* 29.5. [29] Heraclea restored, cf. Memnon F 39–40.

death of Sulla. Hence there was a general shortage of liquid funds that enabled the returning *negotiatores* and *publicani* to impose exceptional rates of interest, and to enforce the most severe conditions, both upon the depleted civic treasuries and upon the individual tax-payers. The cities were reduced to selling or pledging their public buildings, art treasures and revenues to the *negotiatores*, while the agents of the Roman tax-collectors were occupying the lands of private citizens and imprisoning or maltreating the landowners, in the process of securing payment of their extreme demands. Hence it is said that general indebtedness increased sixfold by the year 70, when Lucullus turned from warfare to deal with the affairs of Asia.

Lucullus established a system that freed Asia from its servitudes by the time of his departure to Rome in 66. Interest was fixed at the normal rate of 12 per cent a year, accumulated debts of interest in excess of the original amount of a loan were nullified, and the exaction of compound interest was forbidden under the penalty of the total cancellation of the debt. Conditions being thus alleviated, debtors were required to pay off their debts at the rate of 25 per cent of their annual income. The system worked well, so that within four years the wealthy classes were freed from public debts and restored to relative prosperity.[30]

It seems that the landed gentry from small and moderate estates suffered most under the Sullan system. But there were a number of financial magnates whose wealth appears untouched amid the financial distress of the property-owning classes. Some of these helped the cities in the post-Sullan period, anticipating or supplementing the general reforms of Lucullus. A decree of Priene records how the wealthy Zosimus paid for the restoration of the civic festivals that had been in abeyance since the first war, and at Pergamum the citizen Diodorus Pasparos was honoured for securing from the Senate some diminution of a long list of financial exactions and abuses, excessive rates of interest, and confiscation of estates. Joint appeals to Rome were also successful in alleviation of burdens: the Council of the Hellenes of Asia, created in the early years of the province, sent a mission to Rome to protest about the treatment of the province by the tax-collecting agencies. A special part was played by two leading citizens of Aphrodisias, whom the Council honoured for finally securing 'good results for Asia'.[31] The great magnates possessed exceptional wealth based on the ownership of vast estates. The accumulation of great fortunes seems to be a somewhat new development in the economy of Asia. It possibly arose from the sharp

[30] Debts and reforms: Plut. *Luc.* 20.3–5, App. *Mith.* 83, cf. Cic. *Flac.* 32, *QFr.* I.I.33. Asian dues for the amount cf. Sherwin-White 1984 (D 291) 244 n. 21.

[31] Zosimus, see *IPriene* 113, 37–63; 114, 17–29. Diodorus Pasparos, cf. *IGRR* IV.292, now firmly dated to the period after Sulla by Jones 1974 (D 273). Hellenes of Asia, see Drew-Bear 1972 (D 265) 443ff, revised in Reynolds 1982 (B 226) no. 5.

exploitation by enterprising individuals of the disturbed conditions of the times at the expense of the less fortunate. Among these Hiero of Laodicea may be mentioned, who in this period left no less than 12 million drachmae from his estates to his city. Later Pythodorus of Tralles, an intimate of Pompey, was able to buy back his estates, confiscated by Caesar, for a similar great sum.

The changed conditions of the cities of Asia in these years is shown by a senatorial decree of 78 that lists the detailed privileges allowed to certain citizens from the provincial cities of Clazomenae and Miletus who had served as captains in the Roman fleets during the past twelve years. Their cities were required to free them from all local dues and liturgies, to withdraw any sentences passed against them by local courts, and to restore any property confiscated in that period. They were allowed in future to refuse the jurisdiction of their civic courts in favour of the tribunal of a free-state of proven loyalty to Rome, or else the jurisdiction of a Roman magistrate and a jury of Roman citizens. They were also freed from any obligation to contribute to the payment of their city's public debts. The Senate thus interfered with a heavy hand in the internal finances and the judicial rights of the civic courts in favour of their protégés, who were evidently on bad terms with their fellow citizens.[32]

Altogether in the late Republican period favoured or extremely wealthy individuals tended to gain the precedence in the cities, whether these were oligarchically or democratically organized communes. From this milieu there emerged in the triumviral period the civic dynasts who secured dictatorial control of their cities.

VI. POMPEY IN THE EAST

When the reports of Lucullus about the defeat and expulsion of Mithridates from Pontus and the great victory over Tigranes at Tigranocerta reached Rome, politicians led by the praetor L. Quinctius began to agitate that the Anatolian provinces, now freed from the threat of Mithridates, should be made available to the regular magistrates. Lucullus had held them long enough, and was said to be maintaining the war in his own interest. Hence some time in 68 Asia was restored to praetorian allocation, and Cilicia, where Lucullus had never operated, was assigned to the consul Marcius Rex, with three new legions and a naval force, for his proconsular year 67. The transfer of Asia, and possibly that of Cilicia, was effected by a law of the people.[33] The Cilician

[32] Hiero's estates, cf. Strab. XII.8.16 (578). Pythodorus, *ibid.* XIV.1.42 (649). Captains privileged, *FIRA* I^7, n. 35.

[33] Asia, cf. Dio XXXVI.2.2, App. *Mith.* 90. Cilicia, cf. Dio XXXVI.15.1, 17.2, with Sall. *H.*V fr.14. For the politics at Rome see ch. 9 below.

commander was commissioned to renew the warfare against the pirates of upper Cilicia that had been suspended after the operations of Servilius in 78–75 by the war with Mithridates. Naval operations had been initiated earlier, in 74, when the praetor M. Antonius was empowered to repress piracy throughout the Mediterranean area by means of a newly created fleet of considerable, though unrecorded, size. He operated with some success in the West, along the Spanish and Sicilian coasts, but when he turned east to deal with the pirate bases in Crete his fleet was defeated in 71 or 70 by the light flotillas of the pirates, which received support from the organized cities of Crete that had remained in free alliance with Rome down to this time.

The Senate assigned Crete to Q. Metellus, consul in 69 and issued an ultimatum to the Cretan cities that led to open war in 68. But the menace now extended far beyond the Cretan area. The coasts of Italy suffered a series of piratical raids in which two praetors and their retinue were captured travelling along the road to Brundisium, the eastern trade routes were endangered, and the corn supplies of Rome itself were interrupted. Early in 67 the tribune A. Gabinius with strong support from many quarters proposed a bill that overrode the assignation of provinces to Q. Metellus and Marcius Rex by creating a great naval command for Pompey, now without office after his notable consulship. He was commissioned with proconsular powers to eliminate piracy throughout the Mediterranean area, within a territorial limit of fifty Roman miles inland from the coasts, and with *imperium* (the power to command) equal to that of any proconsul within the area. To assist him he was given a staff of fifteen *legati* – later increased to twenty – each of whom held praetorian *imperium*, an exceptional development that enabled the legates to act independently in areas far removed from their proconsul, though still under his authority. These arrangements, extended in the next year by the Lex Manilia, transformed the scope of a proconsular command, though they did not subordinate other proconsuls in their provinces to Pompey.[34] Gabinius next proposed a second bill, before the news of Zela reached Rome, that transferred the provincial area of Bithynia and Pontus, with the legions of Lucullus and the remnants of the war with Tigranes, to the consul Acilius Glabrio. No fresh troops were assigned to Glabrio, who reached Bithynia after the disaster of Zela in the summer of 67, his consular year, to find an alarming situation with which he made no attempt to cope: Mithridates had reoccupied his kingdom, and Cappadocia, from which Ariobarzanes had fled, was open to the raids of Tigranes.

[34] Powers under the Lex Gabinia and Lex Manilia, cf. App. *Mith.* 94 and 97; Dio XXXVI.37.1–2, 42.4, with Plut. *Pomp.* 25.3–6; 30.1. Cf. Asc. *Corn.* 58C. The inscription of Cn. Cornelius Lentulus Marcellinus now confirms App. *Mith.* 94 on the power of Pompey's legates, cf. Reynolds 1962 (D 287) 97ff.

In the course of 67 Pompey and his legates cleared the seas of organized piracy in a brief campaign of three months. His method was to divide his great fleet into separate divisions under the command of his legates, and they patrolled the Mediterranean area section by section, while he himself set about the central strongholds of the Cilician coast. Resistance rapidly collapsed and – though no detailed accounts of any engagements survive – Pompey with a fleet of sixty ships defeated the main fleet of the Cilician sector off Coracesium. But in Crete, the main centre of piracy in the southern Aegean, the proconsul Q. Metellus, who had been active the previous year, refused to allow a Pompeian legate to operate: he drove the man and his forces out of the island and completed the subjection of Crete with his own legions. Exploiting against Pompey the careful wording of the Lex Gabinia, he would tolerate no interference with his own consular power by a praetorian legate.

By the late summer of 67 organized piracy was effectively eliminated. Pompey was preparing to interfere personally in Crete, where he had powers of making war technically equal to those of the proconsul, when early in 66 his friends at Rome, acting through the tribune C. Manilius, were able to capitalize on the disaster of Zela by proposing the transfer of the command against Tigranes and Mithridates to Pompey. This bill set aside the commands of Marcius and Acilius, who had been assigned the territorial provinces of Lucullus. Acilius was so slow to take up his authority under the second Lex Gabinia that Lucullus was still quartered in Galatia with his legions when Pompey arrived to take over his new command. Since the former proconsuls were legitimately deprived of their commands before the end of their normal tenure this was in no way a *coup d'état*. By the Lex Manilia Pompey was given powers extending what he had already secured through the Lex Gabinia to enable him to deal with what appeared to be a great military crisis. Men and money were assigned to him on an exceptional scale because normal arrangements had proved inadequate. Though Plutarch and Appian write loosely as if Pompey had control of the armies of the whole empire, his powers were limited to a provincial and military area that corresponded to the extreme limits of the Armenian empire that Lucullus had invaded. Allied 'kings and dynasts, tribes and cities' were required to assist him, as was normal in any provincial war. An innovation was the grant of the power of making peace and war and forming alliances, as Lucullus had done without specific authority (see above, pp. 239–43). The vast distance of the area of warfare from Rome made any consultation with Rome impracticable: the consuls of the previous century, operating in the Aegean zone, had regularly secured retrospective authorization of their arrangements.

The size of the army allocated to Pompey is never clearly indicated.

Plutarch's figure of a force of 120,000 men authorized by the Lex Gabinia – no less than the strength of twenty-four legions – is wildly out of scale for any army of the later Republican period before the last years of the second triumvirate, and in no way fits the grant of 6,000 talents for the expenses of three years. In the campaign of 66 against Mithridates Pompey used the remnants of the army of Lucullus, amounting at most to three weakened legions, and the three legions of Marcius Rex from Cilicia, together with whatever legionary forces he held in lowland Cilicia after the reduction of the pirate bases. Though no other figures are known, it can be calculated from the total sum of money that Pompey distributed to his troops at the end of his command in 62 that his army then numbered some 45,000 serving legionaries – if one counts by the scale of individual grants that Caesar made in 48 B.C. These would comprise the manpower of some nine or ten legions, the largest army that had yet served in Anatolia.[35]

The Lex Manilia that proposed this command was supported by the praetor M. Cicero in a speech of skilful misrepresentation. The province of Asia, with its public revenues and the private investments of Roman financiers, is said to be threatened with invasion by the old enemy Mithridates. Border villages of Bithynia have been burned, and the inadequacy of the proconsul Glabrio is noted. There is no mention of the five or six legions present in Galatia and Cilicia. Instead Cicero insists on the necessity of sending a great general to save the richest source of Roman revenue. There is no hint of a war of expansion that would reduce the whole Armenian empire to subject status and lead to the annexation of Syria as a province. Not a word is said about the vast treasures that still awaited collection in the royal strongholds or the extension of the system of imperial taxation to great new provinces that would enrich the revenue of Rome. Instead the avarice of previous proconsuls is contrasted with the restraint of Pompey. Even Lucullus is not spared: though his successes against Mithridates are fairly summarized, his achievements in Armenia are minimized, with a dark reference to the plunder of a shrine of great wealth.[36] Cicero, like Sulla, appears to lack interest in the expansion of the Roman empire. But he reveals the political strength of the economic class of the tax-farmers and bankers that supported the despatch of Pompey and equally the crude desire for vast enrichment that possessed many members of the magisterial class.

Pompey, hearing of his new appointment early in 66, set about preparations for land warfare, gathering his forces inside Asia and

[35] Legions: the financial argument depends on the comparison of Plut. *Pomp.* 45.4, App. *Mith.* 116, Pliny *HN* XXXVII. 16, with App. *BCiv.* II.102 (422), on the distribution scale of Caesar.

[36] Cic. *De Imp. Cn. Pomp.* 23.

Galatia for an invasion of Pontus. Having learnt of the negotiations of Lucullus with the Parthian monarch, he renewed contact with king Phraates and secured his assistance. Tigranes was consequently occupied by a Parthian invasion from Media aimed at Artaxata in the summer of 66, and Mithridates was denied any help from Armenia when Pompey made his attack. But first Pompey opened negotiations with Mithridates, who was prepared to parley, as he had done in the past. When formal submission was required, and the surrender of his organized bands of Roman deserters, Mithridates broke off these negotiations. Pompey was following normal Roman procedure: as recently as the Cretan War the enemy was offered terms that were severe but not outrageous before fighting began.[37] Throughout his eastern command Pompey was to secure as much by military diplomacy as by naked force: after the summer of 65 his only considerable military operation was the siege of the fortress at Jerusalem.

Mithridates concentrated his forces, reduced to a figure of some 30,000 infantry, predominantly bowmen, and 2,000 or 3,000 cavalry, at the head of the Lycus valley in Lesser Armenia, a land that had suffered little from the past campaigns and housed the royal treasure-stores. In this mountainous zone he occupied a strong position on the unidentified heights of Dasteira, where Pompey endeavoured to encircle him with a series of fixed positions. After some six weeks of evenly balanced fighting Mithridates extricated his forces and withdrew by night eastwards towards the borders of the Armenian kingdom. Pompey pursued, and managed to cut off the Pontic army in a defile, where a night battle was fought in which the Pontic resistance rapidly collapsed. Ten thousand casualties were said to have been inflicted, and Mithridates escaped with about two thousand men to Sinora, the most easterly of his treasure-houses in Lesser Armenia. This is the essence of the story that can be recovered from the somewhat contradictory narratives of Plutarch and Dio, a brief summary in Strabo, the earliest source, and the elusive account of Appian, who describes an unlocated final battle in different terms. The only firm evidence for the location of the campaign is that the final phase took place in the district where Pompey later established the memorial settlement of Nicopolis, and that the last battle was within the territory of Lesser Armenia.[38]

At Sinora Mithridates learned that Tigranes had turned against him. He disbanded most of his followers and made his way with an essential quantity of coined money through northern Armenia to the coast of northern Colchis. There he remained for the following winter in the

[37] Cretan terms, cf. Diod. XL.1.2–3, App. *Sik.* 6.

[38] Sources, cf. Strab. XII.3.28 (555), Plut. *Pomp.* 32.4, Dio XXXVI.48, Oros. VI.43. App. *Mith.* 99–100 has an unlocated battle description.

stronghold of Dioscurias, situated near Sorghum, where the outermost chain of the Caucasus mountains reaches the sea. Next spring he withdrew across the mountains through hostile tribes to the coastal steppes beyond, whence he made his way round the sea of Azov, to his last strongholds in the Crimea, held by his disloyal son Machares.

In the latter half of 66 Pompey quickly abandoned the pursuit of Mithridates to secure the submission of Tigranes, the second part of his task. Tigranes, harassed by the Parthians, whom he forced to withdraw by a defensive strategy, yielded straightway to the overwhelming power of Pompey. When the Roman legions, marching through the upper Euphrates and the Araxes valleys, approached Artaxata, the northern capital, Tigranes rode out in royal attire to meet Pompey. He set his diadem at the feet of the *imperator*, and made a traditional *proskunēsis* or obeisance to him, thereby recognizing him as his overlord. Pompey co-operated by bidding the king rise and replacing his diadem. Later Tigranes was told that he was to retain his inherited kingdom, but that all his gains since he became king were to pass under Roman control as lands won by the spear of Rome, with direct reference to the victory of Lucullus at Tigranocerta. The formulation was the normal phraseology of the Hellenistic world, avoiding the cruder Roman style of a demand for *deditio*, or unconditional surrender.[39]

This scene revealed the intentions of Pompey in the Roman 'Far East'. He claimed for Rome the sovereign control over all the provinces of Tigranes' former empire, but allowed the central kingdom to survive as a dependent state without any change of dynasty or of the king's person. Somewhat later the status of Tigranes was confirmed by recognition as a 'friend and ally of the Roman people', but all his conquests were taken from him. Even Sophene, his first acquisition, was handed over to his disloyal son, who had guided Pompey and his legions to Artaxata. Plutarch does not name Mesopotomia, Adiabene or Gordyene in his somewhat inaccurate list of the provinces that Tigranes lost, saying that he was to retain what he held 'down to Pompey'.[40] But Lucullus had occupied Gordyene and the northern district of Mesopotamia, by the capture of Nisibis, and Pompey acquired control of Iberia, Albania and Media Atropatene by direct action, which transferred their nominal allegiance to Rome. Hence Pompey undoubtedly confined Tigranes to the core of Armenia, and claimed direct suzerainty over the rest of his empire for Rome. But in the south the Parthian king was already reclaiming his family's rights in Adiabene and Mesopotamia, which Pompey eventually for the most part conceded.

[39] Plut. *Pomp.* 33.5, App. *Mith.* 106, *Syr.* 49, Dio XXXVI.53.2. For the Greek formula see *LSJ* s.v. ΔΟΡΥ and compounds. [40] Plut. *Pomp.* 33.5.

VII. THE END OF MITHRIDATES

After a hazardous journey through the Caucasus, beset by hostile tribesmen, and across the steppes bordering the sea of Azov, where he had friends and dependants, Mithridates reached the Crimean Bosporus some time in the summer of 65 B.C. There he set about restoring his power, despite the hostility of his family and many of his former subjects, and prepared to defend himself against the naval forces that Pompey had stationed at Phasis to control the approaches to the Bosporus. Mithridates garrisoned the mainland port of Phanagorea across the straits of Taman, and sent forces to hold the Crimean harbours – Chersonesus, Theodosia and Nymphaion – evidently in expectation of a sea-borne attack. This rational and modest plan was upset by the revolt of the harbour garrisons that enabled his son Pharnaces to stage a successful *coup* within the army, particularly through the support of the regiment of Roman deserters. Pharnaces was declared king in 63 B.C. and his father secured either a voluntary death or assassination – both versions are given credence – at the hands of a Celtic warrior.

This rational account, related at length with many details by Appian, displays Mithridates making a shrewd and practical use of his limited forces to defend the last bastion of his power until the inevitable counterplot destroyed him. But the story is confused in Appian with a very different version. In this Mithridates proposed to march with a well-found army of 36,000 men, organized in sixty regiments, by the coast of the Black Sea to the Danube delta, and thence to descend upon Italy through Alpine passes. When the Scythians in the Crimea refused to join this adventure, he is said to have turned to a mysterious horde of Celts in a distant land, 'who had long been his associates for this purpose'. This story, told at length by Appian, is repeated briefly in sources derived from Livy with other additions. Plutarch reveals its origin by remarking that Pompey was criticized for 'planning to attack the Nabatean Arabs at the very time that Mithridates, *as men said*, was about to invade Italy through the lands of the Scyths and Paionians'. The intrusion of Celts and Paionians into the story is instructive. Celts were the traditional enemy of Rome at all periods, latterly involved in the invasion of Gaul and Italy by Cimbri and Teutones, whom the ancient geographers regarded as Celtic peoples, and most recently identified with the persistent attacks of the Scordisci on Roman Macedonia, precisely through Paionia, in the past generation. This tale about Mithridates and the invasion of Italy is drawn from the history of rumour, as Plutarch implies, and was elaborated by the political enemies of Pompey at Rome. But it was unknown to Cicero when late in the year of Mithridates' death he spoke at length, in his defence of the consular election of Murena, about the fear that Mithridates inspired even when driven out of his kingdom, which was ended only by his death. Cicero's advocacy of Murena's consulship would have been even more effective if he could have added the hints about the invasion of Italy, evidently not yet concocted.[41]

VIII. THE CAUCASIAN CAMPAIGNS

After the submission of Tigranes Pompey set about the imposition of Roman authority upon the peoples of his empire. Legates were despatched to the southern regions of Mesopotamia, Gordyene and Adiabene, but he reserved for himself military action against the more formidable peoples of Iberia and Albania, who held the regions between the northern Armenian mountains and the Caucasus massif, where only the coastal zone of Colchis had been part of the Pontic kingdom. This was not merely an outburst of personal ambition, or a substitute for the capture of Mithridates, as many modern and ancient critics have held, but a deliberate extension of Roman power at the far end of Anatolia. Instead of wintering his legions in the fertile zone of Artaxata, which has been reckoned among the candidates for the Garden of Eden, Pompey marched them northwards through the mountain frontier of Armenia by the gorges of the upper Cyrus river into the Iberian highlands, and thence eastwards towards Albanian territory. There they were stationed in three separate camps on the southern bank of the Cyrus.[42]

The Iberians inhabited the highlands between the Caucasus ranges and the frontier mountains of Armenia. The region is drained by the Phasis river, flowing westward from the Tiflis area to the Black Sea, and by the middle sector of the Cyrus, which rises in northern Armenia and breaks through gorges to enter the Iberian highlands, whence it flows eastwards to pass through the Albanian lowlands to the Caspian Sea. The Iberians were a relatively civilized people with an agricultural economy, settled villages and townships. Their society was organized in a system of four functional castes – rulers, military leaders who were also judges, peasants who provided fighting men, and 'royal serfs'. The Albanians were more primitive, primarily a pastoral people with a rudimentary economy, and much less suited to provision the legions of Pompey than the Iberians. The core of their fighting men was formidable, armed with bows or javelins and lightly armoured with breastplates and shields, though the mass was ill armed and wore skins.[43]

41 The invention in App. *Mith.* 109, Plut. *Pomp.* 41.2, and Dio XXXVII.11.1, is defended by Havas 1968 (D 24).

42 App. *Mith.* 103, alone displaces the Caucasian campaigns, setting them before instead of after the subjection of Armenia; cf. Plut. *Pomp.* 34–5, Dio XXXVI.53–4, with Vell. Pat. II.37, Livy *Per.* CI.

43 Iberi, cf. Strab. XI.3.1–6 (499–501). Albani, cf. *ibid.* 4.1–6 (501–3), Pliny *HN* VI.29.

The direction of march and the site of the winter camps indicates that the prime objective of Pompey was to demonstrate Roman power in an area where no proconsul had ever operated. In his previous military career he had waged internal wars against the political enemies of a senatorial faction, and assisted in the last phase of the servile war in Italy, while his naval warfare against piracy, however well organized, carried only glory of a secondary sort. In his first foreign war against a great kingdom the power of the enemy had been substantially weakened by his predecessor Lucullus. Hence Pompey had good reason to select for his attention what was reckoned the most formidable element among the allies and subjects of Tigranes, and to force a conquest that was entirely his own achievement, but yet served to establish Roman power in the far east of the Roman world.

During the winter of 66/5 Oroises, the supreme chief of the Albanian peoples, mustered his forces and crossed the Cyrus river to attack the Roman encampments in three separate actions. Pompey and his legates mastered the onslaught and imposed a truce upon the Albanians without entering their country. In the following spring he moved westwards into Iberian territory. While negotiating with the Iberian king Artoces, Pompey is said to have found that he was preparing for war – as he well might – and struck the first blow. Vigorous fighting ended with a Roman victory in the highlands of central Iberia, when Artoces failed to hold the crossing of the Pelorus river. Pompey made a formal peace, guaranteed by the surrender of the king's sons as hostages, and marched down the Phasis valley into the coastal zone of Colchis, where there was no serious resistance. At the port of Phasis he was met by his naval legate Servilius, who had reached there with a detachment of the Roman fleet.

Belatedly Pompey now considered and dismissed the possibility of pursuing Mithridates either by land through the Caucasian mountains or by sea to the Crimean Bosporus. Leaving Servilius to control the sea routes he marched his army back to Armenia. His failure to eliminate Mithridates was much criticized at Rome, where his supporters in 63 maintained that the Bosporus was beyond the reach of a Roman army. The historical tradition that represents Livy unites in regarding the march through Iberia as aimed at the pursuit of Mithridates, which was unfortunately impeded by the resistance of the Iberians and Albanians.[44] This evidently echoes the defence that Pompey concocted when it was learned that Mithridates had escaped to the Crimea and was preparing to defend himself again. Pompey underestimated the relentless vigour and resources of the aged king, as is revealed by his incautious remark that he had left a worse enemy than a Roman army to deal with him – hunger.

[44] Defence of Pompey, cf. Cic. *Mur.* 34, Plut. *Pomp.* 34.1, 35.1, Dio XXXVII.3.1–3, Livy *Per.* CI.

For Mithridates was in one of the principal granaries of the Greek world.[45]

Pompey next led his army through the whole length of Armenia to open a campaign against the Albanian people, whom he had defeated in border warfare in the previous winter but not subdued. Since he did not disturb the peace of Iberia he probably took the direct route northward from Artaxata by Lake Sevan to the Albanian frontier. He certainly entered Albania through the barren district of Cambysene, the border land between Armenia, Iberia and Albania.[46] Thence he marched into the heart of the country until in the intense heat of late summer at the crossing of the Abas river he met the main forces of Oroises, reputed to number 60,000 infantry and 12,000 cavalry. He awaited their attack with his infantry immobile, and inflicted a crushing defeat. Victory was followed by the grant of peace and the submission of adjacent peoples. Pompey continued his march southwards through a harsh and barren land towards the Caspian coast, but withdrew when faced by intolerable physical conditions at three days' march from the sea. This was the pattern of conquest that Caesar followed later in his first years in Gaul, where his spectacular victories in major battles were followed by the general submission of large groups of peoples without a systematic reduction of their lands.

By the end of 65 Pompey had returned to bases in Lesser Armenia and Pontus. His Caucasian campaigns, the last of his active warfare in the East, apart from local operations in Syria and Judaea in 63, are the only major military actions in which he advanced beyond the scope of his predecessor Lucullus. Since in his first campaign he began operations in Pontus far to the east of the area in which Lucullus had defeated Mithridates, it is not surprising that he reached the eastern limits of the Armenian empire, and in Albania advanced somewhat further. These campaigns gained Rome valuable support in the East. Twenty years later the Iberians quickly yielded to a legate of Antonius, and afterwards in the first century of the imperial period they regularly assisted in the defence of the Armenian area against the Parthians.

Pompey showed a certain interest in the trade routes described by ancient geographers that linked the trading stations at the eastern end of the Black Sea with the far-eastern caravan routes through eastern Iran and Bactria to India. The main route led from Phasis city by the Phasis and Cyrus valleys across the Caspian sea to the Hyrcanian coast, where it linked with the route from Syria and Babylonia through Iran to Bactria. Pompey secured information about the route and the transit of 'Indian goods', and doubtless marched along a sector of the highway through Iberia to Colchis, where Strabo describes it as a paved road for a four

[45] Plut. *Pomp.* 39.1.

[46] Route, cf. Plut. *Pomp.* 35.2–3, Dio XXXVII.3.3–5.

days' journey between the upper Phasis and the Cyrus valleys. There is no reason to doubt that this route, first mentioned by Herodotus, was active at this time for the transport of oriental wares to the dynasts of Colchis and the Crimean area together with another route to the north of the Caucasus, operated profitably by the Aorsi in the fifties and forties B.C.[47] But there is no reason to connect the mention of this trade with the economic interests of the magnates of the Roman business world. Their activities were confined at this time to easily accessible areas – tax-collection and money-lending in the settled provinces and subordinate kingdoms of the pacified Roman world, and the wholesale trade in slaves through Asia by the mart of Delos to the Roman market. The numerous men of affairs for whom Cicero wrote his letters of recommendation to proconsuls in the next twenty years were mostly confined in their scope to the older provinces of Asia, Macedonia and Achaea. A few reached Bithynia, none travelled further.[48]

IX. THE ORGANIZATION OF GAINS AND THE ANNEXATION OF SYRIA

Little is known about the activites of Pompey between the end of the Albanian campaign in the autumn of 65 and his arrival in northern Syria late in 64. There is no report of any military action apart from the capture of certain isolated fortresses. The winter was spent in Aspis, an unidentified site in Lesser Armenia. Much time was taken in checking the contents of the numerous treasure-houses of Mithridates, notably that at Talaura, where thirty days were spent on the count. In all Pompey collected no less than 36,000 talents in gold and silver, mostly in coined money at 6,000 drachmae to a talent. All had to be counted and registered in their lists by the proconsular *scribae*. The quaestors of Pompey were in charge of the audit, and since such vast sums were at stake Pompey, who prided himself upon his honesty in public finances, must have made some check upon the accounts, for which he was ultimately responsible.[49]

The main task of this year was the reorganization of Pontus as a province and the appointment or renewal of tenure of kings and princes in the numerous subordinate kingdoms that Pompey recognized or re-established in Anatolia. But these were not tasks on which proconsuls spent a great deal of time, if one may judge by the settlement of Anatolia after the defeat of Antiochus III in 189, or the pacification of Asia by

[47] Trade and routes, cf. Strab. II.1.15 (73), XI.2.17 (498), 3.5 (500), 7.3 (509), with Pliny *HN* VI.52 and Hdt. I.104.1, 110.2, IV.37.1. Aorsi route Strab. XI.5.8 (506).

[48] Cf. Cic. *Fam*. XIII *passim*: Philomelium *ibid.* 43–5, Bithynia, *ibid.* 61.

[49] The chronology of Dio XXXVII.7.5 has been misunderstood as placing 'Aspis' near the Albanian border. Treasure-houses, App. *Mith.* 107, 115, Dio XXXVII.7.5.

Sulla in 85, who left the detailed work to his legates. More time may have been required by the initiation of the scheme for the creation or enlargement of eleven Greek cities charged with the internal administration of the core of Pontus. But how much of the municipal detail was devised or set on foot personally by Pompey is unknown. In the course of the year Pompey was also occupied with negotiations with the Parthian king: a mission was received and letters were despatched. The legates likewise were no longer occupied with warfare: their operations in Adiabene and Mesopotamia were completed by the winter or spring of 64. Hence it was being said at Rome, as Plutarch records, that Pompey was 'ordering provinces and handing out gifts while the enemy – Mithridates – was still active and uncaptured'.[50]

Late in 64 Pompey moved southwards through Cappadocia and Cilicia into northern Syria. There was no organized resistance except possibly in Commagene, the mountainous principality wedged between the Taurus watershed, Cappadocia and the Syrian foothills. Its ruler Antiochus had made himself an independent king after the end of Seleucid power, and as the enemy of Tigranes had opened negotiations with Lucullus. He now yielded to Pompey who recognized his kingship and awarded him an extension of territory into western Mesopotamia.[51]

Pompey had already decided to annex northern Syria as a Roman province before he met Antiochus Philadelphos at Antioch, late in 64. This prince, whose claim to the kingship of Egypt had been vainly advanced at Rome by his mother Selene before 70, had secured the Seleucid succession at Antioch after the withdrawal of the Armenian forces from Syria in 69–68, and held it for a year, though at variance with his kinsman Philip, who maintained himself in lowland Cilicia. Both princes turned for help to Arab dynasts, Sampsiceramus of Emesa and one Zizos, who plotted to murder their protégés and to seize the kingdom. The plots failed, and Philip secured the support of Marcius Rex, proconsul of Syria in 67, who sent P. Clodius to assist him at Antioch. His rival Antiochus meanwhile had escaped from the hands of Sampsiceramus. When Pompey reached Antioch in 64 it was Antiochus, not Philip, who came to claim the Seleucid throne. But he did not satisfy Pompey, who is reported as saying that he could not grant the diadem to a man who could not keep his kingdom and was unwelcome to his subjects, and added that he would not allow Syria to fall to the despoiling raids of Arabs and Jews.[52] This is a clear reference to the activities of such men as Sampsiceramus, Aretas of Petra, the overlord of Nabatene beyond Jordan, and the brigand Cynaras, who held much of the

50 Plut. *Pomp.* 38.2; cities, below, pp. 266–8.

51 Commagene, cf. App. *Mith.* 106, 117, Plut. *Pomp.* 45.5.

52 Cf. Just. *Epit.* XL.2.3–4; Cic. II. *Verr.* 4.61.

Phoenician coast from Byblos to Berytus until Pompey dispossessed him, while the Hasmonean princes of Judaea had acquired many Greek settlements in southern Syria. The collapse of the Seleucid power had sown disorder among the rival dynasts of an area that had no internal unity of race or culture.

There was no general resistance to Pompey in Syria, which he annexed for the same reason that had led to the provincialization of Asia and Bithynia, the lack of any effective and trustworthy ruler who could manage the whole country in the interest of Rome. It has been widely held that Pompey annexed Syria mainly to eliminate piracy from the Levantine coast. But piracy was anathema to the trading states of Syria, which are described by Strabo in his account of the age of piracy as hemmed in by the hostile powers of Egypt, Cyprus and even Rhodes, that refused them help against the menace of pirates. Only a single nest of pirates is named along the Syrian coast, south of Phoenicia, at Joppa. Brigandage, which was prevalent in Syria, was a land-based activity, operated from mountain fastnesses against the coastal cities or by the desert nomads, such as Zenodorus, who somewhat later raided the caravans of Damascus. Pompey destroyed the strongholds of Syrian brigandage, but he left Cyprus, a home of pirates in the recent past, in the hands of its ruler Ptolemy brother of the Egyptian king, Auletes (ch. 8*c*, p. 319).[53]

Another factor in the annexation of Syria, sometimes suggested as the principal reason, was the possibility of a renewal of the Parthian interest shown by Mithridates Megas and his predecessors, who had attempted the conquest of Seleucid Syria. Parthia, it is true, did not yet appear to offer any threat to Roman supremacy. But the existence of an organized military state beyond the middle Euphrates, even if reckoned a second-class power at this time was doubtless among the factors that led Pompey to annex Syria and to establish some four legions in Cilicia and northern Syria. If the Romans left Syria to itself the Parthians were likely to intervene just as Tigranes had done.[54]

XI. POMPEY IN JUDAEA AND NABATENE

The first intention of Pompey in southern Syria was to deal with the aggressive king Aretas of Nabatene. However, he was approached by emissaries from the rival claimants to the high priesthood and kingship of Judaea, Hyrcanus and Aristobulus. Aretas had extended his power northward through Transjordania to the neighbourhood of Damascus, which he held for some years, and recently he had intervened in Judaea

[53] Pirates, cf. Strab. XIV.5.2 (669), XVI.2. 28 (759). Brigands. *ibid.* XVI.2.8 (751), 18 (755), 20 (756), 37 (761). [54] Parthia, see below pp. 262–5.

on the side of Hyrcanus. His power threatened the peace of Syria, while the feud between the Judean princes was an internal affair that had raged intermittently since the death of the regent Alexandra in 69. Before the arrival of Pompey the legate Aemilius Scaurus had gone to Syria in 64, apparently without any armed forces, to investigate the situation. He met representatives of Hyrcanus and Aristobulus in Judaea at the time when Hyrcanus had the advantage through the military support of Aretas. Scaurus not surprisingly favoured Aristobulus, and required Aretas to withdraw from Judaea.

By the time that Pompey had reached Antioch in the autumn of 64 Aristobulus had the upper hand in Judaea and Aretas had retired to Philadelphia in Transjordan. Pompey required both parties to await a settlement after his proposed expedition against Aretas. But when he learned early in 63 that Aristobulus had upset the situation by mobilizing forces at Alexandrion, a fortress that dominated the road from Damascus to Jerusalem, he promptly marched instead against Aristobulus and confronted him.[55] After fruitless parleys Aristobulus withdrew to Jerusalem, where he renewed his evasive negotiations. Pompey lost patience and managed to capture the recalcitrant prince outside the city. The partisans of Hyrcanus opened the gates to Pompey, but the numerous priesthood, with the supporters of Aristobulus, held the strongly fortified temple area against the invader for a siege of three months' duration. The final storming was simplified by exploitation of the inactivity of the defenders on the Sabbath days, which enabled the Romans to complete the machinery of assault and to take the stronghold on the Day of Atonement towards the beginning of October.[56] The fighting, though claimed as the conquest of Judaea by Roman sources, was limited to the fortress in Jerusalem. After its capture Pompey treated Judaea no differently from other subject principalities. He established Hyrcanus as high priest and ethnarch rather than king of Judaea, to the satisfaction of the numerous Jews, particularly amongst the clergy, who objected to the secular kingship. The man was more likely to make a pliant ruler than the unreliable Aristobulus, who was despatched as a prisoner to Rome.

The Hellenized territories in the north and the coastal settlements such as Gaza and Joppa that the Maccabean kings had taken from Seleucid control were returned to the Syrian province. Judaea was confined to the lands of the Jewish people. Pompey did not renew his interrupted campaign against Aretas. News of the death of Mithridates

55 The prime source is Joseph. *AJ* XIV.2 (29)–4 (79), *BJ* I.6.2–7 (127–57). Little of use is added by Dio XXXVII.16–16.1 and Plut. *Pomp.* 39.3.

56 Joseph. *AJ.* XIV.4.3 (64–6), confirmed by Strab. XVI.2.40 (763); against the confusion of Dio XXXVII.16.2–4. Cf. Schürer 1973–87 (D 153) I².239 n. 23.

in the Crimean Bosporus, received before he reached Jerusalem, drew him back to Amisus in Pontus, when the siege ended, to settle affairs with Pharnaces, who took over the power of the king. Aretas was left to Aemilius Scaurus, whom Pompey placed in charge of Syria. Scaurus raided Nabatean territory but did not take Petra or defeat the main forces of Aretas, who made a nominal submission and paid a fine or bribe of 300 talents to Scaurus. But the kingdom survived in diminishing independence until the time of the emperor Trajan.

XI. PARTHIA AND ROME

It has been widely held that the Parthians, the paramount power that displaced the Seleucids in the Orient, had no western ambitions before the defeat of M. Crassus in 53. But Parthian enterprise in the West began in the time of Mithridates I, who after the defeat of the Seleucid king Demetrius II Nicator in Media, in 130–129 B.C., retained him as a diplomatic prisoner with the intention of restoring him to the throne at Antioch as a Parthian vassal. Ten years later Mithridates' successor Phraates I after defeating the invasion of Antiochus Sidetes planned a counter-attack on Syria that was forestalled when eastern Iran was invaded by a horde from Sacastan. Mithridates II Megas revived these plans by subduing the dependent ruler of the north Syrian Galilei, who owed fealty to Antiochus Eusebes, about 93–92 B.C., and somewhat later defeated the last effective Seleucid king, Demetrius III, at Beroia in northern Syria, in support of his rival Philip.

While Mithridates was preparing his plans against Syria the incident occurred on the Cappadocian frontier that introduced the Parthians to the existence of the Roman power. The propraetor Sulla, after expelling from Cappadocia the Armenian forces that had resisted the restoration of Ariobarzanes to the kingdom, encountered the Parthian envoy Orobazus and held a tripartite discussion with Ariobarzanes and the Parthian about the possibility of friendship and alliance between Rome and Parthia. Or so Sulla reported. This has been taken to mean the actual establishment of a treaty relationship between the two powers. But such arrangements at this date, and later, required the sanction of the Senate or the Senate and People of Rome, as Sulla was well aware. When in Numidia in 105, he had duly forwarded the request of the Mauretanian king for a treaty with Rome through his proconsul to the Senate.[57] No proposals were now referred to Rome, and the Parthian king ordered the execution of Orobazus for lowering the dignity of himself by dealing with a barbarian on equal terms.

After 90 B.C. the Parthian power was diminished by dynastic feuds

[57] Cf. Plut. *Sulla*, 5.8–9, with Sall. *Iug.* 104.

that enabled the king of Armenia, Tigranes, to establish his independence and, as has been seen, to take control of the Parthian territories between Babylonia and southern Armenia, with Media Atropatene in the north-east, and to annex northern Syria and coastal Cilicia in the south-west. The rise of Tigranes coincided with the collapse of Roman power in Anatolia in the eighties and the renewed challenge of Mithridates Eupator in the later seventies. Contact between Rome and Parthia was restored when Lucullus invaded southern Armenia. After his victory at Tigranocerta he opened lengthy negotiations with the recently established king, Phraates III. But the king came to distrust the Roman envoys and no definitive agreement was made.[58]

When Pompey took charge of the war in the East he immediately reopened negotiations with Phraates, offering the same terms as Tigranes and Mithridates Eupator, who were still seeking Parthian aid. This presumably meant the transfer of the three regions of Adiabene, Mesopotamia and Gordyene, which are later mentioned as what Phraates regained, or expected to gain, in return for his invasion of Armenia. After some hesitation Phraates carried out his agreement, urged on by the disloyal son of Tigranes, who hoped to oust his father, in the summer of 66. He invaded northern Armenia by the Araxes valley and besieged Tigranes in Artaxata. Tigranes managed to vacate the city with his main forces and the siege was unsuccessful, but Phraates had prevented Tigranes from giving any help to Mithridates in Pontus. By the end of 65 Phraates had occupied Adiabene and Gordyene, when he was alarmed by the report of the advance of the legate Gabinius, who had marched by the route of Lucullus to recover southern Armenia and might threaten Mesopotamia, which Phraates had not yet occupied. The king promptly sought the 'renewal and confirmation' of his agreement. Pompey retaliated by demanding the surrender of Gordyene. When Phraates objected he sent a second legate, Afranius, to seize the region and to install Tigranes as its ruler. The Parthians departed without resistance, and Afranius pursued them beyond the Tigris into Adiabene as far as Arbela. Thence in the winter of 65 he withdrew his forces through the dry steppes of Mesopotamia, where he suffered difficulties with supplies that were solved by the semi-Greek city of Carrhae, before he reached northern Syria.

Cassius Dio states that the operations of Afranius were contrary to the agreement with Phraates, who sent a second mission to Pompey, demanding that the Euphrates should form the boundary between the two powers.[59] This was the first time that the issue of the Euphrates

[58] See pp. 241–2 above. For a fuller account see *Cambridge History of Iran* III.1 (Cambridge, 1983).

[59] Afranius in Gordyene, Adiabene, Mesopotamia, cf. Plut. *Pomp.* 36.2, Dio XXXVII.5.2–5. Second Parthian mission, cf. Plut. *Pomp.* 33.8, Dio XXXVII.6.3.

boundary arose between Rome and Parthia. There is a vague statement in the late Epitomator Orosius that Licinius Crassus invaded Mesopotamia 'contrary to the terms accepted by Lucullus and Pompey', but, since Mesopotamia was held by Armenia down to 65, and no Roman forces entered northern Syria until 64, there was no earlier opportunity for a conflict over the Euphrates frontier. When Pompey replied evasively that he would reckon as the Roman frontier 'whatever was right', and withheld the title of King of Kings from Phraates, the king sought redress by attacking Tigranes in southern Armenia in the summer of 64. The conflict with Tigranes ended in a stalemate, and left Pompey with an excuse for making war on Phraates in defence of Tigranes, who had recently been recognized as a 'friend and ally' of Rome. Pompey eventually rejected the notion, which was encouraged by his staff, with the remark that he had no formal commission to fight the Parthians. He solved the crisis that he had created by an offer of arbitration between the two kings over Gordyene which they accepted. Three nameless Romans, despatched from Syria in 64–63, settled the issue in favour of Tigranes. While the Armenian regained Gordyene, Phraates retained Mesopotamia, except for the western district of Osrhoene, which under its ruler Akbar became a Roman dependency at this time. So Pompey did not concede the Parthian claim to the Euphrates frontier, but left Phraates free to assert his control over the rest of Mesopotamia, which nine years later was Parthian territory when Crassus invaded it.[60]

There is no contemporary evidence for the intentions of Pompey towards Parthia. But his refusal to recognize the title of King of Kings indicates that he meant to weaken the standing of Phraates, and he used the situation that he had engineered in Gordyene in the same way. Since Pompey preferred in general to work under the cover of legitimacy it is unlikely that he seriously considered the invasion of Parthian territory beyond the lands occupied by Tigranes, without a specific mandate, at a time when his political enemies in Rome were already criticizing him for permitting the escape of Mithridates. The Parthians were left to prove their military effectiveness at the expense of M. Crassus. Their armed strength, which the Romans had not yet tested, lay in the combination of heavily armoured cavalry and mounted archers, a totally different style from the Roman infantrymen. Pompey took account of them by leaving a strong force of Roman legions as the garrison of Syria and Cilicia. Two Syrian legions are documented immediately after the departure of Pompey by a chance mention in Josephus. The legions of Cilicia do not

[60] Dispute over Gordyene, cf. Dio XXXVII.5.3, 6.4–5, 7.3, with Plut. *Pomp.* 39.5; Strab. XII.1.24 (747), XI.14.15 (532), confusingly including Gordyene in Mesopotamia, cf. Dio XL.12.2; 13.1–2, 20.1.

appear until the province became a consular command in 57–56. But Cilicia contained many independent peoples in the highlands that no Roman had yet subdued (as Cicero later found) and could not dispense with a garrison. The two discontented legions that were on the verge of mutiny when Cicero arrived in 52, despite the demobilization of time-served men by his predecessor, had been in Cilicia for many years. Four legions in Cilicia and Syria could deal with any trouble that the Parthians were likely to create on their present form, and maintain order within the provincial area.

XII. THE EASTERN SETTLEMENT OF POMPEY

1. *Military Control*

From the arrangements that Pompey made for the control of eastern Anatolia it is clear that military defence was not in the forefront of his mind. The frontier regions of Anatolia remained in the hands of politically reliable dynasts. The long-suffering Ariobarzanes was reinstated once more in Cappadocia. His territory was extended to include the region of Cybistra in eastern Lycaonia, through which passed the essential highway from Apamea in Phrygia through the Cilician Gates in the Taurus range to the Cilician coast and to Syria. Likewise Tomisa, the Euphrates bridgehead between Melitene and Sophene, was restored to him. The Cappadocian king was thus in nominal control of the two routes linking the Roman power with the new zone of influence in southern Armenia and Mesopotamia. South of Cappadocia the Euphrates crossing at Samosata was left under the control of Antiochus, whose dynasty continued to rule the mountainous principality of Commagene, which lies between southern Cappadocia and the Euphrates gorges. The king was given additional territory east of the river that secured his hold on the crossing. The western approaches to northern Armenia lay through Lesser Armenia and the adjacent mountains largely inhabited by the ferocious Tibareni, who had given trouble to both Lucullus and Pompey. This region through to the Black Sea coast was entrusted – possibly by stages – to the reliable and effective Deiotarus, the Galatian tetrarch. In the far north the vigorous Pharnaces was left in control of the Crimean Bosporus after his elimination of Mithridates, though he was not allowed to hold Colchis, on the mainland, where a Roman nominee was installed.

Pompey thus maintained the system of indirect rule in the frontier zones beyond which lay the kingdom of Armenia, itself reduced to a calculated dependence, but likely to assert itself if opportunity arose. Roman military power was confined to the enlarged province of Cilicia, which now included the western sector of the Taurus mountains and the coastal plain beyond, terminating at the Amanus chain that separates Cilicia from Syria. Though not a frontier province in the strict sense, Cilicia was a military zone with a force of some two legions – though their presence is not testified immediately – stationed in the western region of north Cilicia. These were a mobile force, to be used as Cicero used them in 52–51 B.C., for the repression of rebellious or unconquered peoples of upper Cilicia, and when occasion arose for the defence of the whole region against any external threat from Armenia or Parthia. As for the eastern sector of the combined province of Bithynia and Pontus, there is no evidence that whatever forces were assigned to it – which earned their praetorian proconsul the title of *imperator* in *c.* 57 – amounted to a substantial group. In Syria the northern territory was separated from immediate contact with Parthian commanders not only by the Euphrates river but by the principality of Osrhoene beyond the river in western Mesopotamia, which preferred Roman to Parthian suzerainty. The two legions testified as the Syrian garrison after the departure of Pompey were stationed presumably in the neighbourhood of Antioch, as later, when not engaged in Judaea or Nabatene in the south.[61]

2. *Internal government*

In Anatolia Pompey extended direct provincial government only to the Cilician plain, which was added to the province, and to central and western Pontus, which he combined with Bithynia. The two regions were very different. Coastal Cilicia was a land of Hellenistic cities which had suffered greatly through the depredations of the pirate fleets in their heyday, and by the actions of Tigranes, who had removed the populations of 'twelve Hellenic cities', mostly in the Cilician zone, to establish his new metropolis at Tigranocerta and to strengthen other settlements in that region. Pompey enlarged the achievement of Lucullus, who paid for the return of these peoples to their native cities, by the resettlement of 'vacant cities and empty lands' in the plain of coastal Cilicia with the numerous former citizens who had been driven to enlist in the pirate fleets by the badness of the times. Appian specifies Mallus, Adana and Epiphania on this account, in addition to Soli, about which Strabo enlarges, and Dyme in Achaea: some 20,000 survivors were thus settled.[62]

In Bithynia the Hellenic cities were numerous, being either ancient settlements or creations of the kings, though they had been largely reduced to townships by the encroachment of the royal domains on their

[61] Legions, cf. Joseph. *AJ* XIV.4.5 (79), 5.2 (84), 6.2 (98).

[62] Settlements, cf. Strab. XIV.3.3 (665), 5.8 (671), App. *Mith.* 96, 115.

former civic territories. Pompey restored to them the control of districts of adjacent territory as municipal land, and refurbished their internal government by the same system that he introduced into Pontus. Only three old Hellenic cities existed in Pontus, situated in the coastal region: Amastris, Amisus and Sinope, which had become the royal capital. In the townships of the interior there were a number of great Hellenized families, of which the best known is that of Strabo of Amasia, the geographical writer, which provided Mithridates with a number of civil administrators and military leaders. But the mass of the population lived in villages and townships according to the Iranian and pre-Iranian life-pattern.

The territory was administered under Mithridates by a system of district governorships or 'eparchies'. It was necessary for Pompey to replace these by a method of decentralized civic government with which the Romans were familiar. He promoted eight of the larger townships together with the existing Greek cities, widely distributed through the land, to the status of self-governing municipalities with a Hellenic style of internal government. Most of the land of central and western Pontus became the civic territory of the eleven cities, which each received control of several of the former eparchies. So much appears from Strabo's incomplete account of the arrangements of Pompey. Thus Amisus and Amasia each received four or five eparchies, Zela secured 'many', and Megalopolis gained the extensive districts of Colopene and Cimiane adjacent to Armenia Minor and Cappadocia.[63]

How the cities were related to their terrains and to the rural population is not clear. There was possibly a franchise limited to the city dwellers and to magisterial families, while the bulk of the population was excluded from civil or civic rights. The reorganization of Pontus was based on the principle, familiar from the provincial system of Macedonia and Asia, that proconsular administration depended on a substratum of local self-government. The sole exception proves the rule: the temple-state of Comana was granted to the favoured Archelaus, son of Mithridates' general, with a great extension of territory, to rule as a dynast. Strabo writes of Zela, one of the eleven cities, that 'Pompey assigned many eparchies to it and called it a city ': this was not a process of colonization in the old Greek sense, with the establishment of a body of settlers in a new township, but a reorganization of the existing population into a new system.[64] Pompey founded a genuinely colonial settlement only at Nicopolis in Lesser Armenia, where he established a community of ex-soldiery and native elements.

The method of civic administration introduced by Pompey is partly revealed by certain citations of the content of the Lex Pompeia

[63] Cf. Strab. XII.3.1 (541).

[64] Comana, cf. Strab. XII.3.34 (558). Zela, cf. *ibid.* 37 (560).

'concerning the cities of Bithynia and Pontus' in the letters of Pliny the Younger, imperial legate to the emperor Trajan, written about A.D. 110–11.[65] These, together with civic inscriptions from imperial times, prove that the pattern of government was basically Hellenic, with the normal machinery of elected annual magistrates, civic councils and voting assemblies of citizens. But the democratic system normal in the Hellenistic world was characteristically modified by the conversion of the city councils from annually elected bodies to permanent corporations composed of aldermen. These were nominated by censors, modelled on the Roman quinquennial pattern, who picked the councillors from the ex-magistrates and other members of the upper classes, defined by age and wealth, and expelled unsuitable persons. These methods turned the councils into local senates that represented the predominance of wealth. Their composition was controlled only by the civic censors, drawn from the same social class, and the efficacy of the censorship was limited also by the rarity of the office. The oligarchical councils doubtless rapidly acquired the ascendancy over the popular assemblies that they held in the time of Trajan, because the initiative in the presentation of proposals lay with the councillors. The size of the councils remains unknown, though the proposal for the increase of the council of Prusa in Bithynia by a hundred members, made in *c.* A.D. 97, suggest that as elsewhere in the Hellenized provinces the councils of Bithynia might number several hundred persons. But whether the Hellenized classes in Pontus were so numerous remains uncertain.[66]

Cappadocia, to which Ariobarzanes was restored, was a land of oriental civilization in which the notables expected kingly government, and had demanded its restoration at the beginning of Ariobarzanes' career, when the Senate was minded to abolish it. The administration was divided between twelve 'generalships' on the pattern of Seleucid bureaucracy. Hellenism, introduced by Ariarathes Eusebes in the second century B.C., did not greatly flourish. Mazaca, the royal capital and the base of the royal army, had some form of internal government based on the Greek pattern and derived (it was said) from the code of the early lawgiver Charondas of Catane. There were a few townships called *politeumata*, which normally in Hellenistic usage refers to local settlements of privileged foreigners. Anisa, one of these, had internal self-government on the Greek pattern, but no territory outside the township. Otherwise strongholds prevailed, and temple-towns that acted as market centres. Hence Cappadocia continued to be ruled by kings even after the rise of

[65] Pliny *Ep.* X.43.1, 75–80, 110.1, 112–13.

[66] Initiative of Councils, cf. Pliny *Ep.* X.39.5, 81.1, 6, 110.1. Increase at Prusa, cf. Dio Chrys. *Or.* XLV.7. Cappadocia, see Strabo XII.1.4.

Parthian power increased its strategic importance in relation to Armenia, down to the time of Tiberius Caesar.

Though the whole of the Cilician region became a Roman province, dynastic rule was recognized in districts such as troublesome Isauria, where Antipater of Derbe had extensive power. Likewise Tarcondimotus gradually extended his control of northern Amanus, while the 'free Cilicians' of the southern Amanus were left undisturbed by the provincial regime until the proconsulship of M. Cicero in 52–51 B.C. But in the Cilician plain the numerous Greek cities, strengthened by restoration and resettlement, provided for local administration.

Galatia, within the barren zone of central Anatolia, where the three tribal groups of the Tolistobogii, Tectosagi and Trocmi retained their traditional Celtic system, though vastly reduced in power, was left to the rule of the so-called tetrarchs. The most notable was the faithful Deiotarus, who dominated the Tolistobogii of western Galatia, and eventually secured from Rome his recognition as king. He was also given, now or a few years later, the principality of Lesser Armenia, together with adjacent mountainous territories through to the Black Sea.

Pharnaces, the surviving son of Mithridates Eupator, in return for the elimination of his father and the surrender of many notable persons, was recognized as the ruler of the Crimean Bosporus, and as a 'friend and ally' of Rome, without any known financial exactions. The kingdom of Armenia, and eventually the principality of Nabatene beyond southern Syria and Judaea, were treated less favourably. But though they paid indemnities at their submission, and though southern Armenia was stripped of stored treasure, they were not required to pay annual tribute. Further afield peoples such as the Iberi and Albani in the sub-Caucasian region, who had been defeated in battle, and the Medes of Atropatene, who had submitted to military pressure, remained in effective independence.

3. Methods of Taxation

In the past century 'friends and allies' of the Roman People had not paid regular taxes to Rome. There is no evidence that tribute was now exacted from any of the loyal rulers who were restored or recognized by Pompey in Anatolia. Cicero, when proconsul of Cilicia, briefly mentions tax-collectors in his province, and has much to say about certain great Romans who were extracting the repayment of loans from the Cappadocian king, but he never suggests that the king or his subjects paid taxes to the Roman treasury. Instead, he approved an arrangement of the king's own revenues that enabled him to pay his personal debts to Roman financiers.[67] If the weak kingdom of Cappadocia was not required to pay tribute it is unlikely that taxation was imposed on the Galatian tetrarchs, who had shown equal loyalty in the past: later Caesar required a large sum as a gift, not as arrears of taxation, from his ex-enemy Deiotarus. But the principalities carved out of the kingdom of Pontus were another matter. It is likely that they were treated like the minor dynasts in the Syrian region, who were certainly required to pay tribute. It is probable that in these territories tribute was paid in a lump sum directly to the authorities of the nearest province, Cilicia, Syria or Pontus. The proconsul of Syria a few years later arranged the collection of taxes from Syrian dynasts, under the arrangements of Pompey, and from Judaea, where he initiated the system, to the exclusion of the Roman financiers.[68]

Roman *publicani* managed the collection of the land and pasture dues, which were the principal Roman impost, from the civic communities of each provincial area. But Pompey modified the system in certain ways to the benefit of tax-payers. In Asia the former method continued by which the tax-right was leased by the consuls or censors at Rome to organized groups or *societates* of Roman businessmen, who thereby secured a monopoly of the system. Something similar is indicated for the Bithynian sector of the new province of Bithynia and Pontus, because in 51–50 B.C. a single composite group of *publicani* administered the collection of the whole of Bithynia.[69] But the taxation leases of the reorganized or newly organized provinces of Cilicia and Syria were let by the proconsuls of the provinces to *publicani* at an auction within their provinces, not apparently in a single block but commune by commune. Though the collection remained in Roman hands the communes ceased to be the monopoly of a single group of *publicani*. A second change was in the method of collection. Instead of direct collection from producers at vintage or harvest the system of *pactiones*, already used as an alternative method in some districts of Asia, was made universal. By this the civic authorities were enabled to make an agreement or *pactio* with the *publicani* for the payment of a fixed sum by the whole community, which they then collected from their citizens by their own agents. Thus a system of local collection was interposed between the *publicani* and the individual tax-payers. Cicero briefly remarked that 'the tax agreements have been completed' before he even set foot in his province: henceforth he was able to concentrate on the control of the excesses of the great money-lenders in their dealings with provincial cities.[70]

67 Cic. *Att.* VI.1.3. 68 Cf. below, p. 273.

69 Cf. Cic. *Fam.* XIII.9.2 for Bithynian *societas*.

70 So much may be gathered from Cic. *Prov. Cons.* 9–10 for Syria, and from *Att.* V.14.1 for Cilicia. On *publicani* in general see Brunt 1990 (A 20) ch. 13.

XIII. GABINIUS AND THE AFTERMATH OF POMPEY

The situation around Syria remained quiescent for a few years after the departure of Pompey, though trouble persisted with the Nabatean Arabs. Aulus Gabinius, the former legate of Pompey in the Mesopotamian area, arrived in 57, after his consulship, with a military command on the pattern of the Lex Manilia. A tribunician bill gave him several legions and a considerable sum of money, though neither is precisely described, for a period of three years, and authority to deal with adjacent makers of trouble. But though Cicero talks of Babylon and Persia being subject to his exactions it is clear that he lacked the extensive powers given by the Lex Manilia to Pompey.[71] Affairs in Parthia, with which at this time the ill-defined agreement with Pompey survived, gave an excuse for indirect intervention. After the murder of the king Phraates his sons Mithridates and Orodes quarrelled about the succession. Eventually Mithridates, expelled from the viceroyalty of Great Media by his brother, who held the kingship, turned to Gabinius, who initiated a pattern of intervention that had a long history in the imperial period. Lengthy intrigue was required to secure internal support in Parthia, so that the plot was not set up until the first months of 55, when Gabinius entered Mesopotamia across the Euphrates. But the unexpected opportunity of intervention in wealthy Egypt caused his sudden withdrawal.[72]

Ptolemy Auletes, the bastard son of Ptolemy Soter, had reigned for some twenty years of insecurity after the death of his father in 81. Soter's unsuccessful rival Alexander I left a will on the basis of which, it has been argued from obscure evidence, the annexation of Egypt itself was claimed by the Senate in 87 or 86.[73] Some twenty years later M. Crassus as censor in 65 supported a tribunician bill that probably proposed the confiscation of the treasures of the Ptolemies on a discreditable pretext.[74] After this scheme was defeated by optimate opposition the resourceful Caesar, as consul in 59, with the support of Pompey, secured for Auletes a senatorial decree, confirmed by a law of the people, that recognized him as the 'ally and friend' of Rome, for which he is said to have agreed the payment of 6,000 talents. But a quarrel with his subjects in Alexandria forced him to fly to Rome, where in 57 he sought support

[71] Powers of Gabinius: Cic. *Sest.* 24, *Dom.* 23, 55, *Pis.* 49. Length of command, *ibid. Prov. Cons.* 17, *Pis.* 55, 88, with Asc. 1–2C; Dio XXXIX.60.4. Territorial limits, Cic. *Dom.* 23, *Rab. Post.* 20, *Pis.* 49, Strab. XII.3.34 (558), against Cicero's exaggeration in *Dom.* 60 – 'alteri Syriam Babylonem Persas . . . tradidisses'.

[72] Mesopotamian incursion: Joseph. *AJ* XIV.6.2 (98), *BJ* I.8.7 (175–6), App. *Syr.* 51, Dio XXXIX.56.3, with Cic. *Att.* IV.10.1, fix the date.

[73] The will of Alexander: see Cic. *Leg. Agr.* 1.1, 2.41, *Reg. Alex.* fr. 5, as elucidated by Badian 1967 (D 169). For an alternative view Braund 1983 (A 13) 24–8.

[74] Cic. *Reg. Alex.* fr. 6.6, suggesting the exaction of concessions through threats, is to be set against the proposal for direct subjugation in Plut. *Crass.* 13.2, Suet. *Iul.* 11.

for his restoration against the counter-claims of Alexandria in the name of his elder daughter Berenice. The consul Lentulus Spinther, then an associate of Pompey, secured a senatorial decree authorizing the restoration of Auletes by himself as proconsul of Cilicia in the following year. But the authority was disputed at Rome early in 56 by the henchmen of Pompey and Crassus, seeking the transfer of the mission, and by optimate opponents of both who invoked a Sibylline oracle barring the use of force. Hence nothing was done, and Auletes left Rome a disappointed man, unaware that the private reconciliation of Pompey and Crassus by Caesar at Luca in April 56 had solved his problem: he was to be restored to the throne of Egypt by the agency of Gabinius as proconsul of Syria.

The situation was complicated when Archelaus of Comana, until recently the henchmen of Gabinius, unaware of the compact of Luca, accepted the invitation of the controllers of Alexandria to marry Berenice, the nominal queen of Egypt, and to resist the restoration of Auletes. In the spring of 55 Auletes reached Syria with a letter from Pompey as consul requiring Gabinius to restore the king to his kingdom. Gabinius promptly complied. He invaded Egypt, eliminated Archelaus and Berenice, and set up Auletes as king with a small force of Roman troops as his personal guard. He left the equestrian man of affairs, Rabirius Postumus, as the financial minister or *dioiketes* of Egypt, to secure the repayment of the Roman bankers who had supported Auletes, and to extract a reward of 10,000 talents for his services. The role of Pompey is further revealed by a scene in his house in which Rabirius, before leaving Rome, arranged a financial agreement with the king's representatives. Auletes managed to retain his throne, and after him his daughter Cleopatra ruled Egypt until the aftermath of the battle of Actium.

Whatever the faults of Gabinius he gave his first and last attention to the maintenance of order within his province. He did not intervene in Parthian affairs until the third year of his command. The first two years were spent in suppressing a revolt in Judaea stirred up by the Maccabean prince Alexander, son of the troublesome Aristobulus, now a prisoner at Rome. Alexander raised a considerable force to reoccupy the strongholds in eastern Judaea from which Pompey had driven his father. Hardly had Gabinius marched southward with his legions and defeated Alexander when Aristobulus escaped from Rome and arrived in Judaea to renew the rebellion with the same result. These operations marked the first conquest of the people and territory of Judaea by Roman forces in widespread fighting, in contrast to the isolated if considerable action of Pompey at Jerusalem. They revealed the intransigence not only of the clerical faction at Jerusalem but of the Jewish people against Roman intervention. Gabinius had the backing at first of the supporters of the high priest Hyrcanus, but the defection of the influential Pitholaus and his forces to Aristobulus undermined his position in Jewish esteem. Aristobulus was sent back to Rome, but Alexander remained in Judaea thanks to his mother's influence, where he stirred up yet another unsuccessful rebellion in 55. Gabinius in his last months after his return from Egypt repressed both this and a hostile movement in Nabatene.

Gabinius had followed up his victories by an attempt at a peaceful settlement before his Egyptian adventure. The high priest having proved an ineffectual ruler, unable to control his powerful kinsmen, was restricted to the religious supervision of Jerusalem. His political role was transferred to five regional councils, or *synhedria*, based on townships in the four principal regions of Judaea – Galilee, Peraea across Jordan, Idumea in the south, and Judaea proper, which was apparently split between the councils of Jerusalem and Jericho. Nothing more is known about them, apart from a general resemblance to the regional federations in Macedonia, Asia and Achaea, like which they 'had their civic life' and 'were organized as members of the *synhedria*'. These seem to have survived as a substratum under the power of Antipater (Hyrcanus' vizier and a potent aide to Gabinius) when he later became the effective ruler of Judaea, after which they disappear from certain record.[75]

The financial arrangements of Gabinius for his province, which are known obscurely from the ferocious and allusive attack of his political enemy Cicero, are of special interest. Gabinius hampered or restricted the Roman *publicani* in their activities by rulings at his tribunal and by administrative action, including the direct collection of taxation by his own agents in certain cities and principalities. Amongst these was Judaea, for which Gabinius appears to have established the system of direct payment to the Roman quaestor at Sidon. Gabinius, like Pompey, enriched himself at the expense of kings, but aimed at the fair treatment of the tax-paying provincials. Josephus, the local historian, writes over a century later that Gabinius 'departed after performing great and famous deeds in his government'. But that did not save him from condemnation by the *quaestio repetundarum* at Rome, manned largely by the people that he had offended.[76]

[75] Civic leagues: Joseph. *AJ* XIV.5.4 (91), *BJ* I.8.4–5 (170). Cf. *AJ* XIV.9.2 (158), *BJ* I.10.4 (203).

[76] For the innovations of Gabinius in Syrian taxation see Cicero's hostile version in *Prov. Cons.* 9.10, with *Pis.* 41. For Judaean taxation cf. Dio XXXIX.56.6 with Joseph. *AJ* XIV.10.6 (203). Comment of Josephus, *AJ* XIV.6.4 (104).

CHAPTER 8*b*

THE JEWS UNDER HASMONEAN RULE

TESSA RAJAK

I. THE PERIOD

The Roman seizure of Jerusalem in the autumn of 63 B.C. brought to a close a formative period in Jewish history. The previous century had seen Judaea's emergence as a power to be reckoned with in the region of Palestine, one comparable in extent, even if not quite in distinction, with the kingdom of David. The impact of this national experience continued for the Jews through the classical period, and, indeed, far beyond.

From the military leadership of Judas Maccabaeus and his Hasmonean brothers came, in due course, permanent authority, a dynastic succession and a monarchy which eventually gained independence. Defensive wars merged into aggressive ones; there was expansion westwards to occupy most of the cities of the coast, east to the Jordan, south into Idumaea and north to Samaria and the Galilee. However, long-term stability was not secured. Geographical factors alone would always make Palestine vulnerable. Religion made it volatile; and this period was one of intense religious activity. Thus, elements within Jewish society found the hardening authority, the profane habits, the wealth and perhaps the Hellenizing style of the Hasmoneans wholly unacceptable. The ruling family itself also fell prey to a war of succession, so, at the time of Pompey's annexation of Syria, the door was wide open to a Roman intervention which had been long in the making. One of the rival Hasmoneans then remained in control of a reduced Jewish entity, and he was made subject to Roman taxation and to the Roman order. This was the political outcome, together with a divided population and substantial discontent. It would be left to the Idumaean Herod, in an inventive exploitation of the role of client king under Augustus, to reconstruct what the Hasmoneans had built, in the spirit of his own day and age.

There can be no doubt that the religious and social effects of these upheavals were lasting. Differing political reactions were reflected in division within the community and this division bore ample cultural and religious fruits, however painful it may have been. Already at the time of the struggle against Antiochus Epiphanes (Antiochus IV) we observe the existence of ideological groupings, with the promoters of Hellenism on the one hand, and the *ḥasidim* (the pious) who attached themselves to Judas but later left the cause, on the other. While these tendencies, like later ones, had a manifestly political dimension, disagreements came increasingly to be expressed in terms of divergent attitudes to the central interest of Judaism – the Torah and its interpretation. Thus, the status of the Oral Law, the application of purity regulations, the character of the Temple cult and the role of the priesthood all became points of difference. The best-known groups, Pharisees, Sadducees and Essenes, crystallized during our period (even if, as is possible, they originated somewhat earlier); and they were to be distinctive in Jewish life down to the destruction of the Temple in A.D. 70. How far this centrifugal pattern was reflected in a Diaspora which was already large, but of which we know all too little during these years, it is impossible to tell. The political circumstances which gave rise to that fragmentation will be the central concern of this section; the developed religious culture of Second Temple Judaism is portrayed in the next volume.[1]

It was a combination of internal forces with external circumstances that made the growth of the Jewish state possible. The decline in the strength of the Seleucid kingdom and then the collapse of that kingdom into continuous power struggles were the obvious background to this development, presenting the Hasmoneans first with increasingly distracted masters, and afterwards with the chance to meddle profitably among warring rivals. Around the turn of the century an Egyptian revival of interest in the Palestinian coastal region and beyond was hampered by similar trouble within the Ptolemaic royal line. Also to be taken as a factor in the rise of the Judaean state was the growing involvement of Rome in the Near East. That reached an ironical conclusion when, in 63 B.C., Pompey's occupation of Jerusalem announced the end of Judaean independence, very nearly one hundred years after the Senate had, we are told, first expressed support for Jewish aspirations in a friendly (if insubstantial) alliance with Judas Maccabaeus.[2] All this is plain enough. Without favourable circumstances the Jewish gains would scarcely have been possible; and, but for the changing fortunes of the great powers, what was won might have been retained. Nevertheless, it would be a mistake to look only to these external causes, or to take Seleucid withdrawal as a foregone conclusion. Decades of military and political enterprise in Judaea were also required, and the internal dynamic which could fuel that effort is ultimately the

[1] Vol. x², ch. 14d.

[2] 1 Macc. 8. Just. *Epit.* 36.1.10 and 3.9 also seem to allude to the treaty. It should be noted that Sherwin-White 1984 (D 291) 70–4, follows the older scepticism as to the historicity of this document of formal alliance associated with so early a date. But see Gruen 1984 (A 43) app. 2, 745–7.

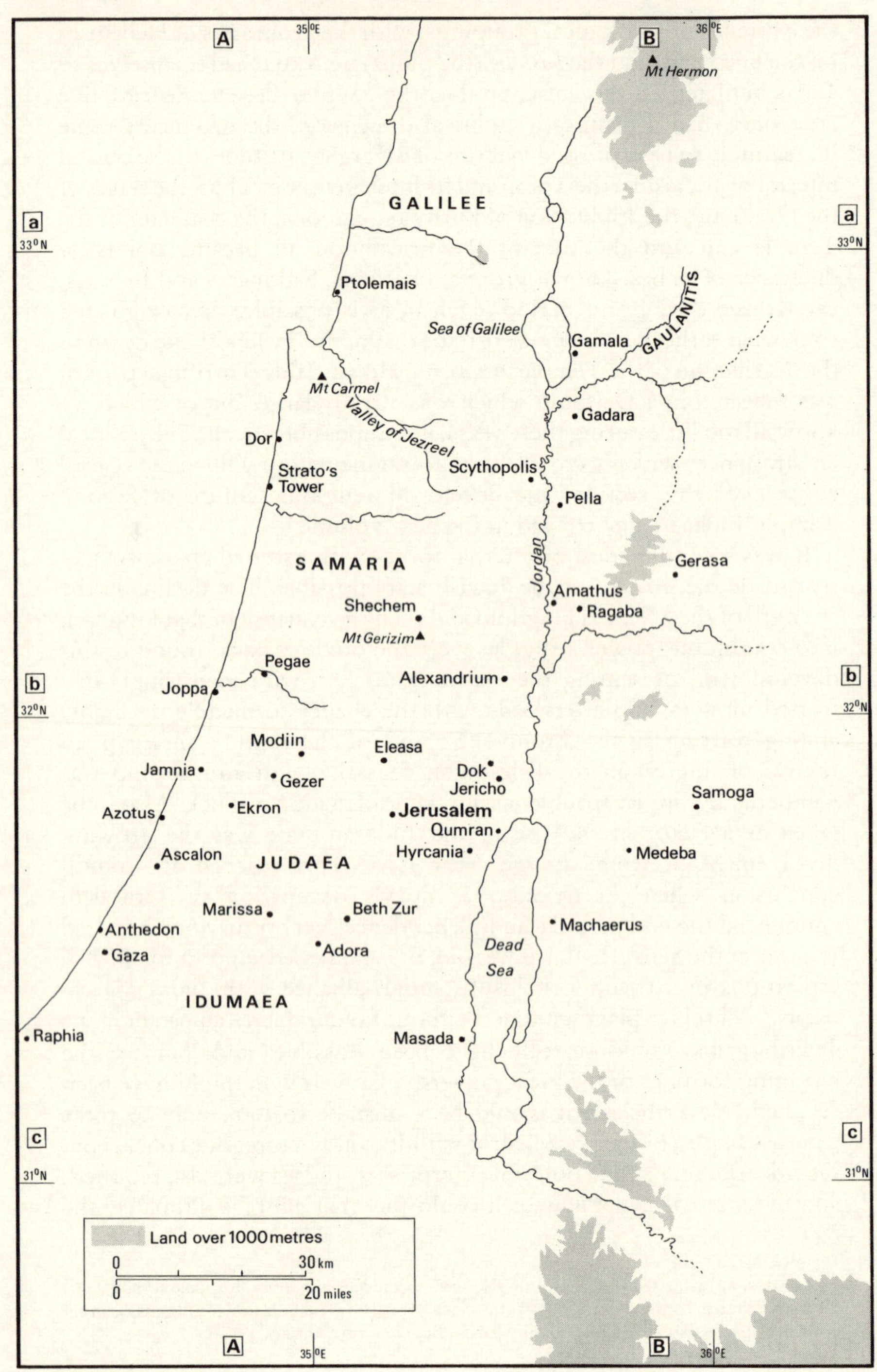
A
35°E
B
36°E
Mt Hermon
GALILEE
a
33°N
Ptolemais
GAULANITIS
Sea of Galilee
Gamala
Mt Carmel
Valley of Jezreel
Gadara
Dor
Strato's Tower
Scythopolis
Pella
Jordan
SAMARIA
Gerasa
Amathus
Ragaba
Shechem
Mt Gerizim
Pegae
Joppa
Alexandrium
b
32°N
Modiin
Eleasa
Jamnia
Gezer
Dok
Jericho
Samoga
Azotus
Ekron
Jerusalem
Qumran
Ascalon
Hyrcania
Medeba
JUDAEA
Marissa
Beth Zur
Machaerus
Anthedon
Gaza
Adora
Dead Sea
IDUMAEA
Raphia
Masada
c
31°N
Land over 1000 metres
0
30 km
0
20 miles

10 Judaea

most interesting part of the story. It has also been quite rightly remarked that what happened in Palestine had in itself an active role in bringing about the disintegration of the Seleucid empire, whether by military challenges (which were real enough), or as a result of political alliances, or even by example to others. For us what this means is that the relatively rich evidence for this period in Palestine apart from its intrinsic interest, is also an important resource for understanding the meaning of the shift in the East from Seleucid and Ptolemaic to Roman control.

II. THE SOURCES

The special nature of the evidence can be summed up simply by saying that there exists the rare phenomenon of an ample indigenous literature. In the first place, the modern interpreter benefits greatly from having continuous history written from a local perspective, yet under Greek influence; sometimes there are even two parallel accounts of the same events.

From our period, we have 1 and 2 Maccabees (the third and fourth books are of uncertain date and context). It is true that each is, in its own way, a highly tendentious work, favouring dynasty and Temple, but the value of both as coherent, detailed, almost contemporary descriptions hardly needs underlining. It is 1 Maccabees, composed, it would seem, in the late second century B.C., which covers the rule of the Hasmonean high priest Simon (143/2–135/4 B.C.) taking the story that had begun with Mattathias down to Simon's death.[3]

However, our ordered knowledge of the times comes above all from the writings of a prolific historian, Flavius Josephus, whose work mixes Greek reports on major events with fragments of local tradition. His later, long account, in the *Jewish Antiquities*, books XIII–XV (published in the 90s A.D.) draws upon a greater variety of Graeco-Roman writers than an earlier, condensed version which forms part of the introductory first book of the *Jewish War* (dating to between A.D. 75 and 79). Josephus seems to have been ready to exploit all available Jewish material, as is shown by his interesting paraphrase of the text of the first book of Maccabees (excluding only the last three chapters for reasons that are not entirely clear). We should expect no less of a highly educated priest, a

[3] For the dating of this work, see Nickelsburg 1981 (D 141) 159 and Momigliano 1980 (D 136). The formula at 1 Macc. 16:23–4 would seem to imply that John Hyrcanus (died 104 B.C.) was dead at the time of writing, but this is far from conclusive. Detailed commentaries: Abel 1949 (D 87); Goldstein 1976 (D 119). 2 Maccabees, a five-volume epitome of an earlier Greek history, while it does not cover the late Hasmonean period, is itself also a product of it. The first of two earlier letters contained in its opening chapters (1:1–9), from the Jews of Judaea to the Jews of Egypt, is dated to 188 of the Seleucid era, i.e. 124 B.C.: Attridge in Stone 1984 (D 161) 176–8; Habicht 1976 (D 121). On this letter, see below, p. 306. For translation and commentary to both books of Maccabees see Charlesworth 1985 (D 103).

man with Hasmonean royal blood, Pharisaic commitment and a political past in Jerusalem.[4] At the same time, the Jewish records had become somewhat patchy after the end of the biblical period (that of Chronicles, Ezra and Nehemiah), when prophecy was traditionally regarded as having come to an end; and Josephus was also willing to take advantage of what Gentiles had written. His principal continuous informant, Nicolaus of Damascus, was congenial enough to Josephus: apart from producing a Universal History in 144 books, and a biography of the emperor Augustus, Nicolaus had also been Herod's minister and a proponent of Jewish rights in the Greek cities of Asia Minor. Our enormous debt to this now largely lost writer for preserving the memory of the time between the late Hasmoneans and Herod's death is often forgotten. Josephus' contribution was, then, to integrate snippets of the Histories of Strabo, also now vanished (only the famous *Geography* survives), with what he read in Nicolaus.[5] He also knew Timagenes, Augustus' obstreperous historian, and he cites yet another writer of the Augustan age, Diodorus Siculus, who had taken his description of the dealings of Antiochus VII with Jerusalem from an earlier anti-Jewish source.[6]

Josephus, as well as narrating events, seeks at the same time to communicate to Greek readers something of the character of Jewish life and thought. It is in this spirit that he digresses, on more than one occasion, to explain the philosophical basis of the three leading Jewish *haireseis* (sects), and even those modern scholars who are disturbed by the extent to which Greek forms of thought and expression appear to have distorted the content of his digressions cannot avoid drawing heavily on Josephus for vital knowledge of the sects.[7] And now there exists another body of literature of a quite different kind to set against Josephus' remarks, at least on the Essenes. For modern scholarship, as much as for the lay public, the Dead Sea Scrolls found at and around Qumran, between, mainly, 1947 and 1956, were no less than a revelation. Their contributions to research are of many kinds as are the problems that they raise.[8] But few would deny that the documents (or at any rate those which have been so far published) illuminate one of Josephus' sects

[4] On Josephus, see also *CAH* Vol. x², ch. 14d. On Josephus' use of 1 Maccabees see Gafni 1989 (D 117). The impact of Josephus' Hasmonean ancestry on, especially, his *Antiquities* is studied by G. Fuks, 'Josephus and the Hasmoneans', *JJS* 41, 2 (1990) 166–76.

[5] For Nicolaus, Stern 1974 (D 158) no. 41, 227ff; Wacholder 1989 (D 168). The use of Strabo by Josephus: Stern 1974 (D 158) no. 42, 261ff.

[6] See below, p. 289.

[7] Moore 1929 (D 137) asserts a far-reaching Hellenization. But see now Beall 1988 (D 97) and the notes in Vermes and Goodman 1987 (D 167).

[8] One major text, the Damascus Document (CD), had been known since the end of the last century, when two manuscripts were discovered in the Cairo Genizah. For a conspectus of published texts, Schürer 1973–87 (D 153) III.1, 380–467. Translations in G. Vermes 1987 (D 166); Lohse 1971 (D 132). Introductions: Vermes 1982 (D 165); Knibb 1987 (D 127).

directly and brilliantly, giving us unmediated access to its thought-world, over an extended period of time – for it should be said straightaway that the identification of the Qumran sect with Josephus' Essenes is now generally accepted. The chronology of the sect's development, as cryptically reflected in its sectarian regulations and biblical interpretations (especially in their most characteristic form, the *pesher*) is still highly controversial. None the less, it will be seen below that a partial reconstruction can be made with an acceptable degree of probability.

Other Jewish texts among the Apocrypha and the Pseudepigrapha are likely to belong to this period, though their dating cannot be certain. Fragments of some of these have now, in fact, been found at Qumran, but from this finding we can infer no more than that members of the Qumran sect had an interest in reading them. Such texts as, for example, Jubilees and the Psalms of Solomon may sometimes embody cryptic responses to public matters, which can be both a basis for assigning a historical context to them and a source of interest for the historian; but the risk of circular argument is great.[9] There are also fragments (or alleged fragments) of Jewish texts written in Greek, some of them in Alexandria, which are likely to come from our era. These include the tragedian Ezekiel, the 'Jewish Homer' Sosates, the historian Eupolemus, who is plausibly though not certainly identified with Judas Maccabaeus' emissary of that name, and the additions to the book of Esther: their names and titles alone make it clear that from them we acquire a notion of the way in which some Jews were assimilating Greek culture. In this category, also, is the undamaged text of the *Letter of Aristeas* to Philocrates on the commissioning of the Septuagint version of the Bible, and this text can shed a little light on Judaea as well.[10]

One major development of the age (which some would regard as ultimately the most important of all for the Jewish religion) is shrouded in obscurity: the evolution of the orally transmitted interpretation of the Torah in terms of the Law (*halakhah*) and lore (*aggadah*) was proceeding apace, above all, no doubt, in Pharisaic circles. But the vast corpus of Rabbinic literature in which this interpretation is set out emerges only three centuries later, by which time there remained no more than garbled recollections of the sages and students of the period of the Second Temple. Rabbinic thought, for all its diversity, is notably lacking in historical concerns. Recollections purporting to be of pre-70 events and

[9] Translations and commentaries, Charlesworth 1985 (D 103) I. For an interpretation which ties the texts closely to historical events, see Mendels 1987 (D 134).

[10] Bibliography in Schürer 1973–87 (D 153) III, 470–694. Commentaries with translations in Charlesworth 1985 (D 103) II. See also ch. 3 (G. W. E. Nickelsburg) and ch. 4 (H. W. Attridge), in Stone 1984 (D 161). For an attempt to make a Hasmonean linkage, Collins 1980 (D 104).

debates are quite often to be found in this literature, for example, the anecdotes set in the court of Alexander Jannaeus. But such material tends to appear in works dating from late antiquity – the Talmudim of Jerusalem and of Babylon and the *Midrashim* (exegetical texts) – rather than in material compiled closer in time to the actual events, that is to say Mishnah and Tosefta (of *c.* A.D. 200). This and other considerations render the historical value of such anecdotes questionable, and they should play no more than a minor role in precise reconstruction of Second Temple Judaism. However, one document which should be singled out because it contains clear chronological reflections of Hasmonean achievements and may date to as early as the first century A.D., is *Megillath Taanith*, a list of dates on which fasting is forbidden.[11]

In singling out what is distinctive in the surviving evidence, we should not omit the major contributions made by archaeology, even if discoveries relating to our period have been at times overshadowed, once by the dominance of biblical discoveries, and latterly by the more visible attractions of the Herodian and Roman eras. For all that, architectural remains now bear witness to the Hasmonean dynasty's lifestyle and to something of its aspirations in urban expansion and in territorial defence. The coinage of the later Hasmoneans was less developed than their architecture, and indeed was for the most part artistically undistinguished; the full interpretation of this coinage still eludes us, and some would even doubt its political importance in its own day. Still, as evidence of the regime's image and ideology at certain moments, it is invaluable. The spade continues, of course, to produce new numismatic material.

III. THE EMERGENCE OF JUDAEA AS A HELLENISTIC STATE

The best way to understand the emergence of the Hasmoneans as powerful rulers in Judaea, is to look back to the beginning of the story. Judas Maccabaeus ('the Hammer?')[12] had emerged, on his father's death, as leader of the struggle against Antiochus IV's suppression of the Jewish cult (1 Macc. 3:1), but no official title is associated with him. The death-bed instructions ascribed to the old Mattathias have him declare Judas, in biblical style, to be the people's commander who would fight their battles for them. In fact, it is obvious that Judas' overall responsibility for the nation took on both military and political aspects: he appointed 'leaders of the people, commanders of thousands, of

[11] For a more positive evaluation of Talmudic evidence on the Hasmoneans, see Alon 1977 (D 89); also, with emphasis on the Jerusalem, rather than the Babylonian Talmud, Efron 1987 (D 114). On *Megillath Taanith*, see Lichtenstein 1931–32 (D 131) and bibliography in Schürer 1973–87 (D 153) I 114–15.

[12] No better etymology has yet been offered: Schürer 1973–87 (D 153) I, 158 n. 49.

hundreds, of fifties and of tens' (1 Macc. 3:55) and, after 164 B.C., he organized the priests to serve in the rededicated Temple service. Yet in the documents from 2 Maccabees which record the dealings of Lysias, Antiochus IV's viceroy, after the king's death (2 Macc. 11), there is no acknowledgement of Judas at all. Perhaps it was this very absence of formal position which led Josephus to the belief that Judas actually became high priest on the death of the Seleucid nominee, Alcimus (*AJ* XII. 414, 419 and 434). Yet this is not only unsupported by 1 Maccabees, where Alcimus is shown to have died *after* Judas (1 Macc. 9:54–6), but contradicts Josephus' own statement elsewhere that the high priesthood was vacant for seven years at the end of Alcimus' tenure (*AJ* XX.237; cf. *Vit.* 4). In any case, Judas himself was killed in battle about the autumn of 161, before any need arose for more precise definition of his position.[13]

Judas had been the third of Mattathias' five sons (1 Macc. 2:4–5); the survivors charged the youngest, Jonathan, with rescuing their fortunes after Judas' defeat and death at Eleasa in 160 B.C., and the destruction of his followers. Jonathan, now, was to be 'our ruler and commander and to fight our battles for us' (1 Macc. 9:30). The decision to continue the struggle, with the ultimate aim of ousting both the Seleucid general, Bacchides, and the Jewish Hellenizers who still held Jerusalem, was entirely in the spirit of Judas' activities since 164. The new element in the position of the leader was the registering of a popular vote in his favour. Jonathan, though tried and tested in war, was an instinctive politician just as Judas had been a natural general, and the younger brother may well have seen the value of securing a popular mandate by way of substitute for Judas' charisma.

But greater changes were to come. When Bacchides, making no headway, came to terms with Jonathan around 155 B.C., Jerusalem remained with the Hellenizers, yet Jonathan was not prevented from establishing himself at Michmash, a small place north of the city; there he 'began to judge the people'. This biblical archaism, characteristic of the idiom of 1 Maccabees, may well conceal an official grant and recognition by the Seleucid monarch Demetrius I of a local fiefdom.[14] Subsequent developments were startlingly rapid. Jonathan had fully grasped what opportunities the moment held for fishing in the troubled Seleucid waters to enhance his own position; out of Demetrius' conflict with his rival Alexander Balas, yet bigger privileges emerged for the Hasmonean leadership. The family's influence in Judaea was evidently now such that Jonathan could deliver better support than could the 'Hellenizers', and Demetrius was especially in need of troops. Once authorized to raise a proper army, Jonathan was able, in 152, to occupy and fortify Jerusalem,

[13] On the letter of Lysias in 2 Maccabees, Habicht 1976 (D 121) 178–85.

[14] Bickerman 1962 (D 99) 136–7.

though the Akra stronghold (which we should understand, therefore, to have been a sealed-off section of the city rather than a mere fort) was still in the hands of Hellenizers and Seleucids.[15]

It remained for Jonathan's dominant position in Jerusalem and in the country to be signalled with the high priesthood. The high priest was not necessarily the supreme figure in Jewish religious life, but the centrality of the Temple gave ready prominence among the people to those who managed it. The political significance of the high priest had perhaps originated in his role as a tax-collector for the Ptolemies. Then, from about 200 B.C. the holder's increasing cultic eminence is apparent, and in that period we see one high priestly line, that of Onias, gaining power and wealth through monopoly of the post. The bitter fighting over the high priesthood during the 160s had, no doubt, served permanently to fix its significance, so that for the late Seleucids, no less than for the Romans after them, it offered itself as the natural channel of control and influence. During the disturbances of the twenty years before Jonathan, there had been either Hellenizing high priests or none, and the appointment of one of the rebel Maccabee brothers was a momentous development. The change had been hastened by the ambitions of Alexander Balas: it was he who, asserting his right to rule and in effect outbidding Demetrius, had made Jonathan high priest. Demetrius then conjured up further offers to counter Alexander's. After the death of Demetrius, we find Jonathan appointed provincial governor (*meridarch*), and becoming one of the First Friends of Alexander Balas. From Demetrius II, exemption from tribute soon came, as well as what looks like a virtual licence to expand beyond the confines of Judaea, into Samaria. Then unfulfilled promises, or perhaps the waning fortunes of Demetrius II and the emergence of the pretender, Tryphon, led to fresh negotiations and to the renewal of Jonathan's high priesthood by the young Antiochus VI, together with the appointment of Jonathan's brother, Simon, as *strategos* of the whole coast. The standing and accoutrements of one of the king's Friends were once again added.

Thus the Maccabees, once the most unremitting of rebels, had become willing dependents of one Seleucid after another, governing Judaea by favour. The control that they were able to exercise lay principally in playing the various contenders off against one another. Jonathan was careful also to look further afield, sending ambassadors to Rome to renew the friendship and alliance between Jews and Romans originally negotiated through Judas' envoys.[16] Jonathan's ambassadors gave expression as well to Judaea's new self-consciousness as a Hellenistic state, by visiting (among other places) Sparta and securing letters that

[15] 1 Macc. 2:20ff, *AJ* XIII.42. On the location of the Akra, see below, n. 20.

[16] The dismissal of Jonathan's treaty as a fictitious doublet of the one made a few years later by Simon persists in some quarters: see Giovannini and Müller 1971 (D 118).

asserted kinship and ancient ties between the two peoples. The text of the letter from Jonathan which was handed to the Spartans alluded, apparently, to earlier contact between king Areius and Onias the high priest.[17] But Rome could not protect Jonathan within the world of intrigue in which he moved (far less, of course, could Sparta). That he should die by Tryphon's treachery, as he did in 143/2, seems in a sad way a fitting end to his career. The instability of the Seleucid kings brought perils to their friends; but there was no going back. The pattern of relationships had been set. As for the Hellenizers who remained in the Akra, they were becoming little more than a symbolic presence in Jerusalem and their day was almost done.

Within Jonathan's framework, there was room to push for ever greater freedom of action. In the year 142, as 1 Maccabees has it (13:41–2), 'the yoke of the Gentiles was taken away from Israel. And the people began to write on their records and their contracts, "in the first year of Simon, the great high priest, commander and leader of the Jews"'. Simon had taken over immediately from his younger brother and been drawn into a similar course of action, a show of strength, followed by well-judged diplomatic feelers. Determined military resistance had been necessary, even before his brother's death, to oust the now hostile Tryphon, who, tricking Jonathan, had invaded Palestine from the north-west. Negotiation with the usurping Tryphon's rival, Demetrius II, had been the next move. From him, it would appear, came by letter the offer of peace, immunity from tribute and remission of taxes or tax arrears (it is not clear which). Simon's high priesthood was implicitly recognized by Demetrius; it may or may not have been a Seleucid grant in the first place; either way, what mattered was the freedom from tribute, marking a new, autonomous status for Judaea, and possessing a symbolic meaning which was well captured in Josephus' accounts (*BJ* I.53; *AJ* XIII.211). The establishment of the new chronological era had the same significance, even if that does not seem to have survived as a lasting basis of reckoning.

At the same time, a degree of scepticism is perhaps called for, especially when we notice how both 1 Maccabees and Josephus wax lyrical about Simon's achievements ('his famous name became known all the way to the ends of the earth', 1 Macc. 14:9). It is worth remembering that the tradition that has reached us, channelled through 1 Maccabees, is dedicated to glorifying Judaea's Hasmonean rulers, and that Simon was the progenitor of the line. The first book of Maccabees was probably written under John Hyrcanus,[18] and Hyrcanus was Simon's son. A history of Hyrcanus' reign was known to the author of 1 Maccabees

[17] 1 Macc. 12:2; 12:5–23; 14:16–23; Joseph. *AJ* XIII.166–70. Bickerman 1988 (D 100) 184–5, proposes a Cyrenaic origin for the fictitious Spartan–Jewish relationship.

[18] And even if written soon afterwards, it was evidently dependent on Hyrcanus' memoirs.

(16:24), and it must have been a highly flattering record. It is likely to have opened with a retrospect over the achievements of Simon, and to have been responsible for fixing the picture of his rule. Moreover, this active image-making had been set in motion still earlier, for Simon himself was the dynasty's first and perhaps its best propagandist. He stamped his achievement on the public mind with festival and ceremony (but without for one moment, we may be sure, departing from the religious ban on making human images, which was strictly interpreted at the time).

The actual situation was not as clear-cut. Given the unsettled state of the Seleucid monarchy, Demetrius II's declaration did not guarantee the abandonment of future claims; and, in the event, it was not until the death of Antiochus VII Sidetes (in 129 B.C.) that Jerusalem would be left truly to her own devices. We may even doubt whether all the promises made to Simon in those years actually bore fruit, for the right to issue coins, granted to him in a letter from Antiochus VII, after Demetrius II's imprisonment in 140/39 (1 Macc. 15:6), seems never to have been exercised at all. There is a telling absence of any coinage of Simon's from the archaeological record.[19]

All this, however, is not to deny that Simon oversaw significant political developments. He imposed his authority on the whole country and he was the first Hasmonean to behave consistently as its ruler. His starting-point was Jerusalem, of whose psychological importance he showed full appreciation. An early move, made in 141 B.C., was therefore to bring about the surrender of the surviving garrison from the Akra, the city's Hellenistic base, which had been both fortress and separate urban centre and 'from which they had sallied forth and polluted the precinct of the Temple'. The location of the Akra is, strangely, still uncertain, though Jerusalem's western hill remains the most likely general area.[20] Jonathan had sealed off the zone with a wall, in an attempt to starve it out (1 Macc. 12:35–7), and there was little left for Simon to do but manage the expulsion, and to make the most of the transfer. Choruses, hymns and instruments as well as the traditional waving of palm branches accompanied the grand entry, and an annual festival was declared to commemorate the historic moment.[21] The Hellenists as a faction were never heard of again. The reconstruction and walling of the city, begun by Jonathan, could now be pushed on (1 Macc. 10:10–11; 13:10); and we should probably ascribe to Simon the inclusion, for the first time since

[19] Coins once attributed to Simon have been known for over a century to belong to the first Jewish revolt.

[20] In the absence of archaeological traces, an upper city site for the Akra has been favoured, in spite of Josephus, *AJ* XII.252: Avigad 1984 (D 93) 64–5. See also Tsafrir 1975 (D 163) proposing the south-eastern hill.

[21] 1 Macc. 14:51–2. This festival figures, under the date 23 Iyyar, in *Megillath Taanith* 6 (see n. 11).

the days of the first Temple, of the western hill as a living area within the city, and of much of the completed circumference of the so-called 'first wall'. Much of this wall's line can now be fairly securely traced and notable remains on the north and south-west sides have recently been uncovered, to add to those known on the south. The political meaning of walling Jerusalem needs no emphasis. We should not overlook the equally important general statement made by the planning of a spacious capital and its expansion over a difficult site.[22]

The year 140 saw another great public occasion, this one of an unprecedented constitutional character. The assembled people declared Simon high priest, commander and ethnarch – head of the nation – of the Jews, 'for ever, until a trustworthy prophet shall arise' (1 Macc. 14:41).[23] The amalgam of powers was not new, but the change lay in the manner of their conferment; they were now internally sanctioned and external approval was no longer regarded as necessary. This was a big step, even after Simon's previous advances. The Parthian invasion of Iran under Mithridates I will have emboldened him, and it is possible that by the time of the people's decree Demetrius II was already in Parthian captivity. Simon's powers were as monarchic as the purple robe and gold clasp which he was to wear, even though the name of king was avoided. His orders were not to be opposed, assemblies were not to be convened without his consent, all on pain of punishment; the unanimity of the popular decision was emphasized. On this Simon's position ultimately rested. It was endorsed by the new king Antiochus VII in a letter of 138 B.C., but not shaken by that king's rapid volte-face, his demands for either the return of the Jerusalem citadel and other towns, or else the payment of tribute on them, and his threat of war (1 Macc. 15:2–9; 26–35).

The form of rule set up by the decree for Simon drew on traditional Jewish conceptions. None the less, the people of Hasmonaean Jerusalem were sufficiently influenced by the style of the day in public affairs to have their declaration inscribed in bronze, just as a Greek city might do, and to display it in no less a place than the Temple precinct and also in its treasury. The new Jewish state was thus visibly Hellenistic in its public forms.

Once again, something of the spirit of the regime is encapsulated in the ruler's death. The aged Simon himself was murdered within five years of the decree, together with two of his sons, as he feasted and drank in a fortress near Jericho. The assassin was his son-in-law, the wealthy

22 Avigad 1984 (D 93) 65–74. The Hasmonean defences appear to have connected in several cases with elements of much earlier, Davidic construction.

23 This sentence is absent from Josephus' version, *AJ* XII.318: see Gafni 1989 (D 117) 118. The Hebrew title disguised in the unintelligible ἐν(α)σαραμελ of 1 Macc. 14:27, probably conceals *Sar ʾAm-El*, Prince of the People. Klausner in Schalit 1976 (D 152) 203.

and interestingly named Ptolemy son of Abubus (Aboub), who was commander of the plain of Jericho (1 Macc. 16:11), and had sought to involve other army officers in his conspiracy. This man does not appear to have been a Jew (*AJ* XIII.234–5); and, on the failure of his attempt to gain the support of Antiochus VII for a seizure of power, he fled to the court of a local dynast, Zeno Cotylas of the partly Hellenized city of Philadelphia (Amman).

John Hyrcanus, Simon's third son, who had already been governor of the important fortified town of Gezer, assumed the high priesthood on his father's death. This suggests that the latter post was designated as hereditary by the 'for ever' of Simon's investiture decree; and John was presumably already high priest when he sacrificed before setting out to attack Ptolemy. However, Josephus (*AJ* XIII.230) does not clarify the mechanism of succession, probably because it was of no interest to his source, a writer concerned, rather, with international affairs, on the one hand, or with domestic dramas, on the other.[24] It is clear, at any rate that a dynasty had been established, even if not yet a monarchy.

There would always be uneasiness and sometimes contention surrounding the definition of Hasmonean sovereignty. The Jews more often than not nursed doubts about the fitness of any man's holding power of a kingly type.[25] We may point to various ways in which Hyrcanus' rule was hedged about or challenged. Yet, in the first place, we should stress the impact of a thirty-one-year tenure (135–104 B.C.), followed by an accepted dynastic succession; John's rule (*arche*) is described in the pages of Josephus as both secular and religious (*BJ* I.68; *AJ* XIII.291; 299). With John too we see an independent coinage, albeit limited to bronze; these are the first coins, we may now be confident, to be minted by any Hasmonean.[26]

While Tyrian silver now became the principal major currency for the region, filling the gap left by the Seleucid withdrawal, everyday needs in Judaea were supplied by successive large issues of aniconic *perutot*, low denomination coins of which 336 made half a shekel. Their craftsmanship varied in quality. Economic prudence may have dictated the reluctance of John as well as that of his successors to launch forth into the minting of silver in a country without its own mines.[27] Whatever the reason for the lack of that kind of full declaration of autonomy, there was

[24] See Stern 1974 (D 158) 240 n. 251 for the argument that Nicolaus' material comes from a general Seleucid narrative, rather than one on the Jews.

[25] De Vaux 1965 (D 111) 98–9; a tendency which sought to promote monarchy is also, however, identifiable at times.

[26] The debate on the beginnings of Hasmonean coinage has centred on whether Yehonanan coins belong to John Hyrcanus I or to Hyrcanus II. The arguments of Meshorer 1982 (D 135) II.35–8, cannot stand up to the evidence of stratification from several sites: Barag and Qedar 1980 (D 95).

[27] Rappaport 1976 (D 150).

still considerable significance in the small coins that were produced, as can be seen from the care taken over the choice of title. Hyrcanus' coins carry two types of formula, both written in an archaic palaeo-Hebrew script which evoked the days of the first Temple. One group has 'Yeḥohanan the high priest and the council (or community) of the Jews' and another group has 'Yehonanan the high priest head of the council (or community) of the Jews'. We cannot date the change, and even the sequence of the two styles remains open to reassessment. But it may be reasonable to suggest that John was initially reluctant to take on any title beyond the traditional high priesthood, but that later a cautious formula was allowed to emerge, which still gave the assembled people a high visibility in its wording. The term for this entity, *ḥever*, may refer to a political body, like the later Sanhedrin. Equally, *ḥever* may have a more general connotation, signifying, in effect, the Jewish *demos*. Either way, the ruler shows extreme care not to separate himself from his people.[28] Even this caution, however, was not sufficient to curb the strictures of the more punctilious religious elements, as will be seen.

Simon's end in an army conspiracy, had revealed, among other things, how the military base of Maccabean authority, far from diminishing with the end of the struggle for survival, had become institutionalized. Almost to the end, the dynasty would remain a warrior dynasty. Peace was something to wonder at; but even then, it was the security born of victory that was spoken of. Under Simon, it was said, 'each man sat under his own vine and under his own fig tree. The enemies in those days left their land and the enemy kings were crushed' (1 Macc. 14:12–13). The dynasty's chronicler (as 1 Maccabees may fairly be dubbed) speaks with pride of the young men's appearance in their dazzling uniforms, and leaves us in no doubt that the regime's ideology contained a strong dose of militarism.

IV. TERRITORIAL EXPANSION

The largest territorial gains were to be made under Simon's successors. But a brief review of the Judaean state's expansion before the death of Simon will show that the map had already changed significantly by that date. The Jewish entity of the Persian and early Hellenistic period might be described as a small temple-state under a priesthood. Now, with a strong army and enlarged aspirations, it had outgrown that model. Defensive needs had shaded imperceptibly into aggressive or punitive policies.

From the beginning, the war against the Seleucids brought with it enmity with those Gentiles who lived locally, both inside and outside

[28] Meshorer 1982 (D 135) 47–8, with reference to U. Rappaport's paper in Hebrew.

Judaea. The culmination came after Jonathan's kidnapping, when the surrounding peoples are said to have been enchanted with the possibility of destroying Judaism root and branch (1 Macc. 12:53). The Maccabean Wars are seen at this point quite simply as a struggle against the heathen and it is impossible to distinguish, in the leaders' activities, between the vision of a holy and cleansing war, conceived of in biblical terms, and the real strategic need to weaken a threatening force. The archaic languages in which the reports are cast subordinates the practical to the ideological, and conceals a more nuanced situation: we know, at any rate, that not all the local tribes were unfriendly during this period, for the Nabatean Arabs across the Jordan gave the Maccabees useful information more than once.

Jonathan's campaigns show that he had on several occasions seized the strategic initiative in a manner which was wholly professional. He had tackled strategic coastal areas, in the name first of Alexander Balas and then of Tryphon. Cities that did not open their gates were assaulted, as were Azotus (Ashdod), Joppa and Gaza, though not Ascalon, which did. The Philistine town of Akron with its territory was acquired by way of reward. Other lasting results of his activities were the permanent garrisoning of Beth Zur, on Judaea's southern line, which was the Syrians' last remaining fortress apart from the Akra in Jerusalem; and, to the north, the gain by royal grants of three districts which had previously been reckoned as part of Samaria. Moreover, quite apart from acquisition, Jonathan's geographical and economic horizons were expanded by far-flung campaigns against Demetrius II, which took him through the northermost part of the Galilee and into the Lebanon.

It was left to Simon, as one of his first acts, permanently to settle Jews in Joppa, expelling the 'idolatrous' inhabitants (1 Macc. 13:11), or at any rate some part of them. This secured for his state an outlet to the sea, as was fully appreciated at (or near) the time (1 Macc. 12:43–8). Gezer (Gazara in Greek), strategically placed at the edge of the Judaean foothills and controlling Jerusalem's access to Joppa, was treated in the same way as the latter. Gezer's first excavator, Macalister, identified a 'Maccabaean castle', but this is now known to date from Solomon's time.[29] More recently, however, domestic architecture of the late second century has been revealed.[30] And now a suggestive possibility has been mooted, that an elaborate system of cisterns found within a complex of Hellenistic houses, are Jewish ritual bathing pools (*miqvaoth*), offering the necessary stopped channel between the pure and the impure water. They would then testify directly to occupation by 'those who obeyed the Law' of what previously had been ordinary Hellenistic living quarters.[31]

[29] Macalister 1911 (D 133) 209–23; Dever 1986 (D 113). [30] Seger 1971 (D 154).
[31] Reich and Geva 1981 (D 151).

Possible epigraphic testimony to the Maccabean occupation also exists, in the shape of half a dozen boundary markers, discovered at different times, bearing in Hebrew and Greek the words 'boundary of Gezer', sometimes with 'of Alkios' added. The conjecture that these represent limits within which freer movement and carrying could be permitted and that they attest Hasmonean observance is highly dubious.[32] But perhaps the most important archaeological information to emerge from this site, is that occupation was abandoned around 100 B.C. The same pattern was revealed with the excavation of Beth Zur, similarly a town fortified by the Seleucids and taken over by the Maccabees, where there are signs of vigorous growth under Jonathan and Simon, with settlement spreading outside the old walls, but soon afterwards coming to an end altogether. We may conclude that the urban development of this era was closely tied up with strategic needs, and that when these changed, in the later Maccabean period, the centres of population also shifted.

The territorial claims of Jonathan and Simon did not go untested. As soon as the new king Antiochus VII Sidetes had disposed of the usurper Tryphon, Simon's assistance became less important to him than the restoration of his lost revenues and his authority in Palestine. His general, Cendebaeus, was told to take possession of the coastal strip and to attack Judaea from Jamnia (1 Macc. 15:38–40). Josephus, who is here independent of 1 Maccabees, has the commander under instruction also to seize the Jewish leader in person (*AJ* XIII.225). Simon is said to have put 20,000 men into the field and to have held the day.

Hyrcanus had to deal with the consequences. Antiochus invaded and ravaged the country, and then laid Jerusalem under the strongest of blockades (*BJ* I.61; *AJ* XIII.236–46). Our information on this lengthy siege and on its outcome is somewhat obscured by the partisan character of our accounts: on the one hand, Josephus, in apologetic vein, highlights gestures made by Antiochus during and after the siege, gestures by which the monarch expressed special respect towards the piety of his adversaries; on the other, a fragment of a Greek account, surviving in Diodorus, appears to have used the story as a vehicle for an anti-Jewish outburst, focusing on advice given to the king after the conclusion of the siege, which urged him to extirpate the Jewish cult, there described in the most lurid terms. In any event, both accounts bring out the fact that Sidetes terminated the whole campaign in an unexpected and generous manner, with conduct very different from that of Epiphanes some thirty years earlier. No garrison was installed in Jerusalem; only a symbolic section of wall was taken down; and Joppa, Gezer and the other cities held by Simon were made subject to tribute,

32 Information on boundary stones collected in Schürer 1973–87 (D 153) I.191 n. 8. The inscription discovered by Macalister, *CIJ* I.1184, wishing a conflagration on the 'house of Simon', demands even greater caution from the interpreter.

but not removed from Jewish control.[33] Hyrcanus, who, according to Josephus' story in the *Jewish War*, had funded himself by rifling David's tomb, soon afterwards set off with his army to accompany Sidetes into Parthia, where he was treated with courtesy, if Josephus is to be believed. The collapse of this expedition, Sidetes' death in battle, the Seleucid abandonment of Iran and the renewal of wars within the dynasty finally left Hyrcanus a clear field. It is on record that the payment of general tribute now ceased permanently (*AJ* XIII.273).

So ended one dependence. We should not, however, conclude this discussion without observing that another was slowly growing. The puzzle of Sidetes' abrupt withdrawal from Jerusalem may well have its solution in a behind-the-scenes statement from the Roman Senate, who will at this point not have welcomed the threatened Seleucid revival. This interpretation depends upon a *senatus consultum* brought to us by Josephus as a tailpiece to his account of Hyrcanus' rule, but most appropriately associated with this stage in it, and with Antiochus VII (*AJ* XIII.257–64). The document records the report of a Jewish embassy to the Senate stating that Antiochus (we are not told which king of that name is meant) is holding various Jewish territories, including Joppa, Gezer and Pegae, in contravention of a previous senatorial decree. The embassy invokes a long-standing friendship and alliance between the Jewish and Roman peoples; and the body of the new decree reiterates that alliance without deciding on any immediate response. Such a restricted statement may well have been sufficient intimidation, and we cannot know what covert activity accompanied it.[34]

The history of Rome's alliances with the Jews was by now a well-established one, begun with Judas' famous treaty of 161 B.C., and reiterated and more widely publicized under Jonathan and then under Simon. Even if no more than token gestures, based upon a vague consciousness of her possible interests, had at first been intended on Rome's part, the situation had developed since those days. This is not the place to examine the wider perspectives.[35] But it is worth noting that the expulsion from Rome in 139 B.C. of the Jews residing there, which Valerius Maximus briefly reports, did not affect the diplomatic situation. The expulsion was evidently one of Rome's periodic reactions to foreign religions in the city, and not a general attack on Jews and their interests.[36]

[33] Rajak 1981 (D 147) against the view that Sidetes treated Jerusalem punitively.

[34] Sherwin-White 1984 (D 291) 77–8, for the context in Roman diplomacy.

[35] See *CAH* Vol. VIII² 382–7.

[36] Val. Max. I.3.2 (in epitome, with text uncertain). The Jews appear to be identified as worshippers of Jove Sabazios. This is the only clear evidence of the Jews in Rome at this time. Some regard the story as confused or apocryphal. See Lane 1979 (D 128) and Stern 1974 (D 158) no. 147, 357–60, on attempts to link the expulsion specifically with Simon's embassy.

V. CONQUEST AND JUDAIZATION

The rule of John Hyrcanus lasted for thirty-one years, from 135/4 B.C., until 104. His eldest son, Aristobulus, who succeeded him as high priest, lived for only one further year. There followed a regime nearly as long-lasting as that of Hyrcanus, for Alexander Jannaeus (Yannai), Aristobulus' brother, ruled for twenty-seven years as high priest; he also took the title of king. He was succeeded by his redoubtable widow, Salome Alexandra, who, it would seem, had previously been the widow of Aristobulus and, as such, had engineered Jannaeus' succession; and she occupied the throne between 76 and 67 B.C., the eve of Rome's arrival.[37]

The extension of Jewish territory continued throughout this period, and the dynasty's military capacity grew, especially after Hyrcanus introduced the practice of hiring mercenaries. None the less, it is important to point out that, of all the rulers, only Jannaeus pursued unequivocally aggressive policies. Hyrcanus, to be sure, paved the way; but his activities were restricted to carefully judged campaigns with limited targets, and there were long periods when he was not at war.[38]

Josephus gives a résumé of Hyrcanus's early wars, beginning in 129 B.C.: 'as soon as he had heard of the death of Antiochus [Sidetes], Hyrcanus marched out against the cities of Syria, expecting to find them devoid of soldiers and of anyone able to rescue them, which was indeed the case' (*AJ* XIII.254). This sweeping sentence heralds several important conquests: the capture of Medeba in Moab (southern Jordan), together with the neighbouring town of Samoga (or Samega); of the Samaritans' city of Shechem and of their shrine on Mount Gerizim; and, lastly, of the Idumaean cities of Adora[39] and Marissa, to the south of Judaea. The Idumaeans are said to have accepted circumcision and adopted the Jewish law, in order to retain their homeland.[40]

Towards the end of his life, Hyrcanus returned to the Samaritan region; this time two of his sons laid siege to the Hellenized city of Samaria (*AJ* XIII.275–83). The siege lasted a year, but neither the Samaritan population, nor Antiochus IX (Cyzicenus) who came to their aid, nor the two generals whom he later left behind there, nor even the troops supplied to Antiochus by Ptolemy Lathyrus could shake off

37 The marriages of Salome Alexandra: Sievers 1989 (D 155) 135–6. Putting the end of her rule in 67 B.C. is a consequence of accepting the best of the possible reconstructions of Hasmonean chronology: Schürer 1973–87 (D 153) I.200, n. 1.

38 Stern 1981 (D 159). For an assessment of the military capabilities of the later Hasmoneans, see now I. Shatzman, *The Armies of the Later Hasmoneans and Herod from Hellenistic to Roman Frameworks* (*Texte und Studien zum antiken Judentum* 25) (Tübingen, 1991).

39 Josephus also Hellenizes the name as Adoreon and Adoreus, as well as using the biblical form, Adoraim, in the parellel account, *BJ* I.63.

40 However, at *AJ* XIV.403, Josephus is still able to describe them as 'half-Jews'.

Hyrcanus. In the end, we hear, he effaced the whole settlement, by the method, if this can be believed, of undermining its foundations. Scythopolis, the Greek city situated at the key point where the valley of Jezreel meets the Jordan valley, was taken immediately afterwards. The *Jewish War (*1.66) says that it was razed to the ground and its inhabitants reduced to slavery, a rare case of enslavement being mentioned as a consequence of Hasmonean seizure.

The motivation behind these different campaigns is for the most part lost to us. To increase his resources may well have been a priority for Hyrcanus, given, on the one hand, the agriculturally unproductive character of his homeland, with, in addition, its lack of minerals of any kind, and on the other the demands of a new aristocracy in an enlarged city. Trading interests could go some way to explaining the conflict with the Nabateans, formerly a friendly people, since they had long operated by controlling the roads, and Medeba was situated on the King's Highway, the great trade route which skirted the desert and linked the Red Sea with Damascus.[41] The Samaritans had cut Judaea off on the north and the Idumaeans on the south; a cryptic remark in Josephus actually alludes to some connexion between those two zones, explaining the destruction of Samaria in terms of her interference with Marissa (*AJ* XIII.275). As for Hyrcanus' treatment of conquered territory, that followed for the most part the unremitting severity learned by his family through bitter necessity during their early struggles. Special vindictiveness was reserved for the Samaritans of Shechem, monotheists and once Jews, who, however, unlike the Jerusalemites, had accepted the transformation of their cult by Antiochus Epiphanes. Whatever its origins, the schism was now complete. The apocryphal book of Jubilees, thought by some to belong to this period, in its version of the biblical story of the rape of Dinah and of her brothers' brutal punishment of the Shechemites, omits to mention that the Shechemites had circumcised themselves before the assault, and this interpretation of the text may well have been meant to make more palatable Hyrcanus' treatment of Samaria/Shechem, by glossing over her connexion with Israel.[42]

We are not entitled to assume, as modern writers are inclined to do, that destruction and expulsion were the preordained lot of all those who, unlike the Idumaeans, would not convert; still less to imagine that Hyrcanus, and perhaps others of the later Hasmoneans, were seeking to ensure for every part of their holdings a purely Jewish occupation. That is to go well beyond our evidence; and such a total repopulation, with a

[41] On Nabatean–Jewish relations, Kasher 1988 (D 126) 6–24.

[42] For a summary of views on the Samaritan schism, see Purvis 1986 (D 143). On Samaria and Marissa, Egger 1986 (D 115) 102ff. For Jubilees, Mendels 1987 (D 134) 72–3, and also 104–5 on the Testament of Levi, another possible reflection of the treatment of Samaria.

complete reversion after Pompey's conquest to a pagan populace, is scarcely conceivable. What we know of the region's towns suggests that their inhabitants were for the most part ethnically and culturally mixed.

The Judaization of Edom must have had its own special story. In the light of indications in the ancient narratives that this transformation was at least partly voluntary and of the attachment of the Idumaeans to the Jewish cause at the time of the great revolt of A.D. 66–74,[43] a certain affinity between the Jews and a significant element within Idumaea seems probable. It is not unlikely that, in this area so close to Jerusalem, Jewish settlers had become thoroughly intermingled with the Semitic population. We know something of the inhabitants of Hellenistic Marissa from the names in the inscriptions of its remarkable rock-cut tombs, but they have not yielded a clear answer to this question.[44] Nor can we tell what caused the removal to Egypt of a community of persons with obvious Idumaean names who have been revealed to us in papyri.[45]

During his short period of rule, Aristobulus managed one enterprise. The outcome in this case too was the circumcision of at least a part of a defeated people. But Aristobulus looked northwards, to the upper Galilee, a choice perhaps determined by the presence of a Jewish population in this formally still Gentile territory. We learn from Josephus (*AJ* XIII.318) that some of the Ituraeans, who lived there and in the Hermon area, were ordered to convert or to leave. Regrettably, Josephus dependent as he is on his Greek informants, reduces the story to this single episode, leaving us, as so often, to deduce the wider context. It is remarkable that Strabo, the Greek writer whom Josephus actually cites at this point, so far from being critical of the questionable act, is prepared to praise Aristobulus for having served his nation well by its enlargement.[46]

The name of Alexander Jannaeus is not linked with any effective conversions, although we do hear that his troops wrecked the Transjordanian city of Pella because the inhabitants rejected the customs of the Jews (*AJ* XIII.397). That vague phrase may be taken as referring not to mass circumcision, with the threat of expulsion as alternative, but rather to a formal Judaization of the city's organs of government and the transference of political control to a Jewish element.

Apart from Pella, Jannaeus overran numerous towns in the course of a

43 On the conversion of Idumaea, see S. Schwartz, 'Israel and the nations roundabout: I Maccabees and the Hasmonean expansion', *JJS* 42, 2 (1991) 16–38. See also Goodman 1987 (D 120) 189–94.

44 For literature on Marisa, Schürer 1973–87 (D 153) II 4–5.

45 Rappaport 1977 (D 149).

46 From Strabo's lost Histories; he, in turn was, according to Josephus, citing Timagenes. Strabo's version is highly valued as a recognition of a new and wider concept of Jewish ethnicity by S. J. D. Cohen, 'Religion, ethnicity and "Hellenism" in the emergence of Jewish identity in Maccabean Palestine', *Religion and Religious Practice in the Seleucid Kingdom*, ed. P. Bilde, T. Engberg-Pedersen, L. Hannestad, J. Zahle (Aarhus, 1990) 204–24.

stormy career, with dramatic advances and equally dramatic setbacks. He has gone down in history as the destroyer of Greek cities, as a ruthless opponent of paganism and indeed of Hellenism. Yet the list of his conquests supplied by Josephus falls far short of warranting such a reputation. It will be noted that the places in question are described by Josephus not as Greek cities but merely as cities of 'Syrians, Idumaeans and Phoenicians'. What is involved is, simply, the achievement of Jewish control over the remaining parts of Palestine and over its surrounds: the coastal strip, Idumaea, Samaria, Carmel, the Peraea, Gaulanitis (the Golan) and Moab. Certainly, recalcitrant cities were not spared brutality: in the *Jewish War*, Josephus speaks of Jannaeus reducing Gaza, Raphia and Anthedon to servitude. But this brutality was matched by that of the other side, and seems to have been more a means of reducing opposition or punishing the obdurate than a bid to judaize whole populations by the sword. So, for example, Amathus in southern Jordan was demolished because its ruler, Theodorus, would not meet Jannaeus in combat. But there is good reason to believe also that allegations about the root and branch destruction of cities by Jannaeus are exaggerated, since many of those mentioned rapidly revived.[47] The context of those statements in Josephus shows that they originated in connexion with the subsequent refoundation of the cities by Pompey and Gabinius in the wake of the Roman occupation of 63 B.C.[48] They derive, in fact from the post-restoration propaganda, in which much had to be made of the achievements of the restorer. The same process has been noted in relation to Alexander the Great's activities at Gaza and at Tyre;[49] and Pompey, the new Alexander, was to arrive as the saviour of the 'Greeks' of Syria and of Palestine. The association of the cities with an image of Hellenism belongs more to the ideology of the Roman conqueror than to the mentality of the Jewish king, or, indeed, to the situation on the ground, where, at this time, the typical city of the region did not much resemble a Greek polis. The vacuum of recent years in international affairs had given scope to local tyrants, and it was to them that Jannaeus was most directly opposed. Both Zoilus, who ruled the coastal cities of Strato's Tower (later Caesarea) and of Dor, and Theodorus of Amathus (in southern Jordan) yielded to the Jewish king in the first decade of the first century B.C., after prolonged sieges. Archaeology suggests Zoilus' towns to have been massively constructed forts, rather than laid-out conurbations.[50]

[47] So Aryeh Kasher, in Hebrew and also *id., Jews and Hellenistic Cities in Eretz-Israel: Relations of the Jews in Eretz-Israel with the Hellenistic Cities during the Second Temple Period. (332 B.C.E.– 170 C.E.)* (*Texte und Studien zum antiken Judentum* 18) (Tübingen, 1990) 161–7. Against a view of the Hasmonean campaigns amongst the 'Greek' cities as a conflict of cultures, see already, Tcherikover 1966 (D 162) 247–8.

[48] Especially clear in the *Jewish War* version, *BJ* I.156.

[49] Jones 1937 (D 272) 237.

[50] Levine 1974 (D 130); Raban 1987 (D 145); Stern 1985 (D 157).

The wars of king Alexander Jannaeus seem dominated by pragmatic rather than by religious considerations. The coastal strip and the east bank of the Jordan, from Moab to the Golan, were now the central areas of attention. These were zones in which his predecessors had established a limited foothold. Now that Hyrcanus had dealt conclusively with the Idumaeans and the Samaritans, his closest neighbours, the main thrust of the campaigning was naturally carried further afield. Nevertheless, the target was even now not one of single-minded expansion; the power of the Jewish ruler was never sufficient for that. The main determining factor of the advance was a complex interaction, scarcely avoidable, with other rising powers in the region. With this came, perhaps, the lure of new commercial possibilities.

Thus, Jannaeus' opening venture was a major assault on the important port of Ptolemais (Akko). This went well, until it was cut short by the intervention from Cyprus of the deposed Egyptian king, Ptolemy Lathyrus. Jannaeus reached an accommodation with Lathyrus, which, in turn, was soon nullified by Jannaeus' own double-dealing: he was caught in secret negotiations with Lathyrus' mother, now ruling as Queen Cleopatra III (*AJ* XIII.324–37). Lathyrus went on to inflict two major defeats on Jannaeus, one in the lower Galilee and one in the Jordan valley, and then to invade Judaea. Only Cleopatra's military intervention halted his advance. In Josephus' narrative, Jannaeus' initial assault on Ptolemais remains unexplained; but it is not improbable that Lathyrus had already before nursed hopes of using the city as a springboard into Palestine and thence back to his own kingdom, while Jannaeus, for his part, had seen the advantages of gratifying Cleopatra by forestalling her son. Had Jannaeus merely been in search of a northern outlet to the sea, to serve the Galilee, which had probably become predominantly Jewish at the time of Aristobulus' conquest of the Ituraeans, he would hardly have moved so rapidly.[51] Rather, then, Egypt orientated politics seem at this stage to be the mainspring of action. The presence of two important Egyptian Jews, members of the Oniad clan, among Cleopatra's generals (*AJ* XIII.349) may go some way to explaining the role played by Jewish Palestine in the fortunes of the warring Ptolemies in these years. On the other hand, Jannaeus, unlike his predecessors, does not seem to have dealt with Rome, and there is no evidence of a renewal of their treaties.[52]

Lathyrus was eventually, though as it turned out temporarily, deflected by Cleopatra, and some time before her death in 101 B.C., she signed a treaty with Jannaeus at Scythopolis (*AJ* XIII.355). That observers were struck by the queen's subsequent disengagement from

51 For the probability that Aristobulus took most of the Galilee: Schürer 1973–86 (D 153) II.9.

52 On Ananias and Helkias, see Stern 1981 (D 159) 37. On Jannaeus and Rome, Rappaport 1968 (D 148).

the affairs of Palestine is revealed by the story in Josephus that Ananias, one of her Oniad generals, flatly refused to co-operate with her unless she undertook to leave the Jews alone. Whatever her real considerations, her decision was an invitation to Jannaeus to move in and onwards, and in the succeeding years he took not only the towns of the tyrants Zoilus and Theodorus but also notably, Gadara (south east of the Sea of Galilee) which was becoming a genuine centre of Greek culture, and Gaza.[53] The latter was the key to the southern sector of the coastal strip; it was also an established ally and outlet of the Nabateans. Their trade was threatened by Jannaeus, not only at Gaza, but also, and, perhaps, more so, by his activities across the Jordan. During some eight or nine years the Nabateans, with the help of the Seleucid monarch, Demetrius III, fought with unexpected tenacity to retain their sphere of influence and in battle they inflicted a serious defeat on the Hasmonean deep inside Judaea. But in the last years of his reign (83–76), Jannaeus was able to redress the balance, so that he finished master of most of what lay between the Golan (in the north) and Moab (in the south), including such places of importance as Gerasa and Gamala and, as already mentioned, Pella. The country was secured by a network of virtually impregnable fortresses, of which Josephus names three, Hyrcania, Alexandrium and Machaerus, all of them overlooking Transjordanian territory (*AJ* XIII.417). At Masada, Jannaeus' coins were found in abundance.

The new areas were an integral part of the kingdom which, on his death, the king bequeathed to his widow and successor, Salome Alexandra. The queen retained her husband's kingdom intact during her nine years of rule (76–67), and she substantially increased the army; but Judaea's power across the Jordan was to prove short-lived, and to be replaced almost immediately by a very different arrangement, the group of cities founded or refounded by Pompey which together became known as the Decapolis. The mixed character of these places had probably persisted throughout, and the enhanced Jewish presence of the Hasmonean period will have served in equal measure to hellenize the Jews and to judaize the region.[54]

VI. HELLENIZATION AND THE IMAGE OF THE HASMONEAN RULER

So far from being anti-Greek, the political style of the later Hasmoneans acquired a number of Hellenistic traits as time went on. Simon's accession, and the manner of his death had already shown something of this. The Maccabee brothers had had Semitic nicknames (1 Macc. 2:1–5);

[53] Kasher 1982 (D 125).

[54] For eastern aspects of the culture of Decapolis towns, Bowsher 1987 (D 101).

their successors took on Greek personal names which overshadowed their Hebrew ones. Aristobulus, also called Judas, even styled himself Philhellene, according to one interpretation of Josephus' words (*AJ* XIII.318). John Hyrcanus hired foreign mercenaries, and Jannaeus, and later even Salome Alexandra, followed suit: because the local populace was badly disposed, Cilicians and Pisidians (whom Josephus calls 'Greeks') were employed, together, perhaps with Thracians; and for the battle near Shechem against Demetrius figures of 20,000 Jews and 6,200 mercenaries or of 10,000 Jews and 9,000 mercenaries are given.[55] Jannaeus called himself king, as well as high priest, in a juxtaposition unsanctioned by Jewish tradition; and he feasted in public with his concubines in a manner perhaps not totally alien to David and Solomon but unacceptable in the Jewish high priesthood (*AJ* XIII.380). The testamentary choice of his widow, Salome Alexandra, as successor, in preference to either of his sons, also reveals Hellenistic influence.

Diplomatic ties and the social intercourse that went with them will have led the Hasmonean rulers, as also their wealthier subjects, to a share in the Graeco-oriental culture of their day. Contact with Jews from the established Diaspora centres in Alexandria and in Asia Minor, above all their regular presence in the capital, will have encouraged such developments. This is the period when the habit of pilgrimage on the three agricultural festivals probably took root; this both expressed the significance to Jews elsewhere of the Temple under its Hasmonean management and provided a framework for a participation more active than the mere contribution of the half-shekel for its upkeep. One of Alexandrian Jewry's most famous documents, the *Letter of Aristeas* to Philocrates, which is essentially the legend of Ptolemy II Philadelphus' commissioning of a Greek translation of the Bible by sages summoned from Jerusalem, may well have been written towards the end of the second century B.C., and sheds some light on Diaspora perceptions of Jerusalem at the time. The city is idealized and schematized and its scholars elevated, but little real knowledge of place or people emerges.[56] That the Oniads' cult at Leontopolis in the Egyptian Delta was enough of a rival to the Jerusalem Temple to explain the remoteness from Jerusalem expressed by the authors of this document, is a possibility which cannot be proved.

What little we know of Hasmonean architecture expresses the spirit of the age clearly enough. Paradoxically, such features emerge first, and most overtly, from a description, by none other than the militant author

[55] We may explain in terms of reactions to these Thracian mercenaries Jannaeus' nickname 'Thrakidas': Joseph. *AJ* XIII.383; Syncellus I (ed. Dindorf), p. 558: so, Stern 1981 (D 159) 31 n. 53.

[56] Collins 1983 (D 105) 81–6, with further bibliography on the *Letter of Aristeas*. On the unity of Jewry at this period, see A. Momigliano, *Alien Wisdom: The Limits of Hellenization* (Cambridge, 1975) 114–16.

of 1 Maccabees, of the tomb built by Simon for Jonathan in the ancestral town of Modiin, with its seven pyramids surmounted by columns bearing trophies of armour and carved ships, and its construction of polished stone (1 Macc. 13:25–30). Scarcely anything now survives of this great landmark, but the mixed idiom is one familiar to us in the architecture of the region, notably in the Nabatean rock-cut tombs of Petra. In Jerusalem, it is exemplified on a more intimate scale in the so-called tomb of Jason, a burial associated not directly with the dynasty, but, in all probability, with an aristocratic family of the time, over several generations. There the style, if the monument has been correctly reconstructed, has a pointed roof and a neat porch with Doric columns *in antis*. Surviving fragments reveal that the Corinthian order also made its appearance. Inside, graffiti appear to represent a naval battle, while an epitaph in Greek and Aramaic, quite well preserved, urges the enjoyment of life, of drink and of food. The naval battle recalls the ship motif on the tomb at Modiin, and may possibly be associated with the Hasmonean conquest of the coast.[57]

The description of the dynasty's mausoleum shows that its members had pretensions to be builders on a large scale at an early stage. Many of their projects were later lost in Herod's even more ambitious schemes, but in the case of the splendid winter palace in the Wadi Qelt (beside Jericho) Jannaeus' opulent edifice can still be seen as a separate unit. A colonnaded swimming-pool surrounded by a promenade, aqueducts to secure an ample water-supply and coloured frescoes within, bespeak Hellenistic influence, enthusiastically adopted.[58]

Jason's tomb is one proof, were proof needed, that at the very least some external aspects of a Hellenized lifestyle spread beyond the royal circle to the Jerusalem aristocracy. These new Hellenizers were not like those of the era of Antiochus IV's persecution, and there is no question of their compromising the integrity of Judaism's fundamental tenets. But there is no doubt that aspects of Hellenization were capable of offending significant elements in the population. We may deduce this by the great care, which we have already noted, taken by the later Hasmoneans over their self-presentation on their coinage. Hasmonean coins remained image-free to the very end, always replacing the customary ruler's portrait with a second symbol. After John Hyrcanus, the next to issue a major coinage was Alexander Jannaeus. Admittedly, and not unexpectedly, he was less conservative, using Greek and Aramaic, as well as Hebrew, and, on some types, openly advertising his kingship, either in words or with symbols of star and diadem. Yet the light weight of the coinage and the appearance of an undated lead issue at

[57] Jason's tomb: Rahmani 1967 (D 146), Avigad 1950–1 (D 91), and Benoit 1967 (D 98). Foerster 1978 (D 116); Peuch 1983 (D 142).

[58] Netzer 1975 (D 138); see also Bartlett 1982 (D 96) 116ff.

some point in his reign may point to difficulties in meeting the pressing demands of troop payments, and reminds us that the Jewish public was not the only target of the king's self-promotion. For the Jews, or the more traditional among them, he gave, on his Hebrew coins, his Hebrew name, Jonathan, rather than Alexander; and there were others on which he employed the old form of legend, devised by Hyrcanus, which referred simply to the high priesthood and the Jewish *ḥever*. Of two types of *bulla* or seal ascribed to Jannaeus, one names him (in palaeo-Hebrew script) as 'Jonathan high priest' and one as 'king'.[59] The chronological sequence of Jannaeus' numerous dies is not established. It is, none the less, tempting to associate with the major internal crisis of his middle years a group of puzzling overstruck coins, where 'Jonathan, the high priest and the *ḥever* of the Jews' has been made to obliterate the earlier text on the obverse.[60]

VII. DIVISIONS IN JEWISH THOUGHT AND SOCIETY

The Hasmoneans may have acted on behalf of the people, but this did not mean that their rule was acceptable to all. The shifting patterns of support and opposition to the ruling house are now in large part lost to us. We are, however, able, by combining with caution reports in Josephus, recollections in the Talmudic literature and allusions in the Qumran texts, to form some impression of the connexions between various groupings and political events. In a more general sense, the emergence of a military monarchy was bound to have large-scale social and religious repercussions in a tight-knit society, as that of Judaea had been. The formation of sects which dissociated themselves to a greater or a lesser extent from other Jews, begun under the impact of earlier pressures, was undoubtedly accelerated by the political changes of our period.

Even before the revolt of the Maccabees, the issue of Greek influence had brought about deep internal hostilities. It is worth remembering that the high priestly house which had dominated since the time of Alexander, that of Onias (descended from Zadok), had taken itself into Egyptian exile, during the 'Hellenistic reform' crisis. There, as has already been mentioned, they had gone so far as to construct with Ptolemaic consent, on land at Leontopolis, a temple which must in some sense have paralleled that of Jerusalem. This temple, although it can hardly have commanded the allegiance of Egyptian Jewry as a whole, lasted for several centuries and had sufficient importance for Vespasian

[59] Avigad 1975 (D 92).

[60] Meshorer 1982 (D 135) I.58, 79ff, 123ff; Ariel 1982 (D 90). On the internal crisis see below, pp. 306–7.

to find it necessary to destroy it in the aftermath of suppressing the Jewish revolt of A.D. 66–74.[61]

Throughout the period of the Maccabean revolt, a different party, that of the Hellenizing Jews, had remained loyal to the Seleucids and never found an accommodation with the Maccabean party. By 165 B.C. too, another highly characteristic reaction had manifested itself, one in which a select group isolated itself in the interests of piety or purity. A band of *ḥasidim* (righteous persons) is described as joining Judas; they allowed themselves to be slaughtered rather than desecrate the Sabbath by taking up arms. The survivors soon afterwards broke with Judas and were ill-advised enough to seek a reconcilation with the high priest Alcimus, the untrustworthy appointee of Antiochus V.[62] Thus, even pursuers of purity did not always avoid the political arena. As a group they then disappeared from history, but they are often regarded as the ideological progenitors of one of the major tendencies in Second Temple Judaism, sometimes of Pharisaism, or, more often of such circles as fostered eschatological speculation and authored apocalypses, among whom was the Qumran sect. An earlier, Mesopotamian origin, seems, however, more probable for the characteristic modes of thought of Jewish apocalypse.[63]

Be that as it may, the groupings which dominated the ensuing era are differently delineated by Josephus. It is in connexion with the rule of Jonathan that he first mentions the three major divisions, which he calls *haireseis* (sects) or 'philosophies', that were in existence 'at this time' – the Pharisees, the Sadducees and the Essenes; and he then offers a brief account of them (*AJ* XIII.171–3). We may take it, therefore, that Josephus' view, derived perhaps from tradition, was that these groupings had come into their own during the early Hasmonean period; and this is wholly plausible. It is a pity that Josephus then goes on to describe the bone of contention between them in terms which have nothing to do with the context from which they emerged. But this is because he has chosen at this point to focus on what might interest his Greek readers: contrasting opinions on fate and free will, and on the after-life (in which the Sadducees did not believe) would evoke for readers familiar debates in the philosophical schools. Josephus has it that the Sadducees regarded man as free to make his own choices, while the Essenes insisted on an all-powerful destiny and the Pharisees allowed for both fate and free will in

[61] Josephus, *BJ* I.31–3; VII.426–36; *AJ* XII.387–8; XIII.62–73, 285; XIV.131–2; XX.235–7; *Ap*. II.49–56. Josephus is inconsistent as to the foundation date. See Delcor 1968 (D 110); Hayward 1982 (D 122).

[62] On the *hasidim*, Hengel 1974 (D 123) ch. 6, esp. 175–80; but the three references in 1 and 2 Macc. (1 Macc. 2:42; 1 Macc. 7:12f; 2 Macc. 14:6) do not allow more than speculation as to the character of the grouping. For a radical denial that *hasidim* were a cohesive group at all, Davies 1977 (D 107).

[63] Stone 1982 (D 160) ch. 5, 37–4.

their system. This is, in fact, one of several doctrinal differences brought to the fore in his digressions.[64]

Many scholars believe that the evidence from Qumran bears witness to a more direct (though enigmatically expressed) response to contemporary affairs, on the part, at least, of the community who possessed the scrolls found in the caves near that site. In the present state of research there are few who would deny the identification of this community as a branch of the Essene sect. The specifically sectarian documents found in the Qumran library (which include, in fact, some of the best known of all the Dead Sea Scrolls) energetically castigate the sect's enemies and emphatically justify its members' withdrawal from the main body of the nation. None of the encoded allusions to persons, times or places is unequivocal. But in any case, even without a wholly secure chronology, this literature reveals much of the nature of religious dissension in the Jewish society of its time and of the range of sectarian attitudes to which this gave rise.

The documents reveal that 390 years after the exile to Babylon, they, a 'plant root', sprung from 'Aaron and Israel', made it their purpose to cast off the iniquity around them in what they perceived as an 'age of wrath'. After they had groped 'like blind men' for twenty years (the round number looks like a symbolic one), the drama began to unfold with the appearance of the 'Teacher of Righteousness', a certain priest, who made them understand the nature of the gulf between themselves and that 'congregation of traitors' which was firmly set in its unacceptable ways. By this time, the public evils had greatly increased, under the influence of a 'scoffer', who dealt in lies, abolished the moral boundaries and misled the people, by detaching them from the traditions of their forefathers, thus calling forth on them all the curses contained in the Covenant. His followers, 'seekers of smooth things', turned on the righteous few, persecuting and killing them.[65] If we are also to attach to the Teacher of Righteousness the psalms of thanksgiving from the somewhat damaged Hymns Scroll, then it emerges that his own former friends and companions had been among those who rebelled.[66] There was one powerful persecutor, a 'Wicked Priest', who, though 'called by the name of truth when he first arose', had betrayed God and defiled himself and the cult, out of greed and pride, so as to 'build a city of vanity with blood', and to rob the poor of their possessions. He had in the end been put to death by his enemies.[67] The elect saw themselves not only as

[64] On Josephus' sects, see p. 278, n. 7.

[65] This history underlies the Damascus Document (CD) 1–8. On the Teacher's priesthood: Commentaries on Psalms (4QPs), 37.2.19 and 3.15. For Qumran documents see Lohse 1971 (D 132) and Vermes 1987 (D 166).

[66] Hymns (Hodayoth, 1QH), 9 and 10.

[67] Commentary on Habakkuk (1QpHab), 7,10,12. For Qumran documents see Lohse 1971 (D 132) and Vermes 1987 (D 166).

guardians of the Law, but as priests, 'sons of Zadok', who were ultimately to protect the Temple from the utter defilement which those in charge had wrought in it. However, they had been driven for a period into exile, described, again, it would seem, symbolically, as located in Damascus. There they lived a life based upon the New Covenant, interpreting the Law punctiliously, in its ritual and its compassionate requirements. Living in perfect purity, they had to remain separate from the community and, especially, according to the Damascus Document, to avoid all contact with the Temple cult as it existed. They looked forward to the imminent punishment of the traitors and rebels and to their own salvation.[68]

It has been observed that the date of 390 years from the exile, even if we take it as an approximation accommodated to traditional reckonings, takes us to the beginning of the Hellenizing crisis, early in the second century. The withdrawal to 'Damascus' – that is to say, perhaps, to Qumran and similar places beside the Dead Sea[69] – would seem, then, to happen at about the time of the Hellenistic reform in Jerusalem. An identification of the Wicked Priest with Jonathan the Hasmonean, who did indeed die at the hands of his Gentile enemies, is plausible.[70] The archaeological evidence offered by the community's installations at Qumran cannot confirm this chronology but is consistent with it to the extent of revealing one stratum which precedes that of the Hyrcanus–Jannaeus era.[71] That there is no known historical personage with whom we can identify the Teacher of Righteousness is not wholly surprising: the bitter quarrels which were all-important to the history of the sect had no real claim to attention in the Hasmonean record; and both Teacher and followers had conveniently taken themselves out of sight of Jerusalem, probably without causing much disruption to public life. This should not, of course, stand in the way of our recognizing the historical importance of their action.

The sect's abhorrence of the ruling house did not come to an end with the withdrawal from Jerusalem; but when the Commentary on Nahum points the finger at a peculiarly cruel ruler, seemingly Jannaeus, who is dubbed 'the furious young lion', it is made clear that the lion's prey consisted not, now, of the Qumran sectaries, but, instead, of the 'seekers of smooth things', reasonably interpreted as the Pharisees.[72] Our

[68] Davies 1982 (D 108). That Essenes did, however, at times send offerings to Jerusalem is a contention made by Philip Callaway in *The History of the Qumran Community* (Sheffield 1988).

[689] Bar-Adon 1977 (D 94).

[70] D. Dimant in Stone 1984 (D 161) 542–7, explains in brief the identification and its consequences. See p. 542 n. 282, for its main supporters and note especially, Vermes 1987 (D 166) 137–62; *id.* 1981 (D 164). Attempts to shake the foundations of this methodology have not so far succeeded.

[71] Period 1a: De Vaux 1973 (D 112); Laperrousaz 1976 (D 129); Davies 1982 (D 109) 40ff.

[72] Commentary on Nahum (4QPNah) 2 and 3. For Qumran documents see Lohse 1971 (D 132) and Vermes 1987 (D 166).

damaged text seems to suggest that the crucifixion of the seekers by the king, by way of reprisal, shocked the sect, and added a new note of revulsion to their long-standing criticism of the Hasmoneans for the familiar vices of accumulating wealth, abusing power and polluting all that was holy. It is noteworthy that, even from their exile, these Essenes kept an eye on Jerusalem; indeed, the Nahum Commentary's public awareness extends to a unique reference to the doings of a king Antiochus (apparently Epiphanes) and a king Demetrius (most likely Jannaeus' adversary, Demetrius III). In this respect, the sectaries cannot be described as disengaged. Nor did the sad fate of the 'seekers of smooth things' under Jannaeus (if indeed he was the culprit) reduce any of the sectaries' animus against that group: the hatred continued.[73]

In 'exile' the Essenes formulated their own elaborate rules for a monastic lifestyle, based on a rigid hierarchy and a revised calendar, and centred upon purity and devotional practice.[74] Yet this did not entail their rejection of the central institutions of Jewish corporate life; they merely yearned for them to be faithfully administered according to the precepts of the Law. They interpreted that Law rigorously and with their own peculiar emphases; but the starting-point and general principles of that reading would probably have found a fair measure of agreement within Israel. It is a mark of this that the sect felt it worthwhile to explain and justify its self-separation. A document of extreme interest, not yet officially published, sets out points of difference in terms of *halakhah* (legal observance); and the emphasis, in the surviving part, falls on the Temple regime and on the purity of the entire Holy City.[75] The better known, and longer, Temple Scroll presents the Temple legislation from the Pentateuch with a number of additions, and within this context it finds room for a theory of Jewish kingship. Here a Bible-based reaction to the Hasmonean style of rule stands out plainly (the document is most usually dated, from its description of the Jewish monarch, to the period of Hyrcanus): the king must be Jewish; he must not have many horses; he must not make war in Egypt; he must not be polygamous; he must not acquire much silver and gold; his army must consist of God-fearers and is to protect him against foreigners; he must make all decisions in consultation with a council of twelve Israelites, twelve priests and twelve Levites; he must marry a Jewish wife; his conduct in war must follow certain set patterns and must be preceded by a consultation with the high priest of the Urim and Thummim. The conclusion is a resounding warning, whose contemporary meaning is undeniable: 'The king whose heart and eyes have gone astray from my commandments shall never

[73] On the Hasmoneans, cf. also the 'last priest' in the Habakkuk commentary (1QpHab), 9.4.7. A re-examination of this historical reconstruction in P. R. Callaway, *The History of the Qumran Community* (Sheffield, 1988). [74] Vermes 1987 (D 166) 87–115.

[75] Qimron and Strugnell 1985 (D 144).

have one to sit on the throne of his fathers, for I will cut off his posterity for ever so that it shall no more rule over Israel. But if he walk after my rules and keep my commandments and do that which is correct and good before me, no heir to the throne of the kingdom of Israel shall be cut off from among his sons for ever.'[76]

The Qumran texts shed direct light on the reactions of certain pious Jews to political change in Judaea, and, for all the continuing uncertainties, they cannot fail to claim a central position in any modern account of the Judaism of the second and first centuries B.C. They lend a new meaning to what we read of the Essenes in Josephus and other sources, not least by revealing how religious and political reactions might have combined in their origins. It is reasonable to suppose that sectarianism developed out of disagreements over political and social change, but that these disagreements were expressed largely in religious terms, and were then crystallized and sharpened through increasingly divergent interpretations of practice and belief.

From Philo and from Josephus, both of whom describe the Essene lifestyle in some detail,[77] we learn that it was possible to follow the sect's way of life without making for the wilderness. Communities were to be found in various towns of Judaea, or at any rate, close beside them. According to one statement of Josephus (who should have known, since he had for a time attached himself to the sect), there existed also some married Essenes. Still, whatever the mitigations, self-separation into a sealed environment, where every aspect of personal life was rigidly regulated, lay at the heart of the system. And this regulation did not diminish in intensity over time, even though variations in specific rules did occur and are reflected in the different Qumran Rules Documents.[78]

In the case of the Qumran Essenes, we may reasonably speak of a sect. The nature of the other major groupings within Judaism is in some ways even more elusive. The name of the Pharisees derives from a Hebrew word which means 'to separate', and there is Mishnaic evidence that the pursuit of ritual purity and strict tithing within enclosed table-fellowships (*ḥavuroth*) was a central part of their concerns.[79] Yet their activities had a political dimension at an early stage, as we have seen; and since, unlike the Essenes, they did not turn their backs on Jerusalem, to

[76] Temple Scroll (11QT), 56–9; Hengel, Charlesworth and Mendels 1986 (D 124) arguing for a date in the reign of Jannaeus. [77] *BJ* II.119ff; Philo, *Apol.* 1ff, *Quod omnis probus*, 76ff.

[78] A high level of overall consistency emerges from Beall's comparative material: 1988 (D 97).

[79] Pharisaic ascendancy: Joseph. *AJ* XIII.288; 298, with the possibility however, of anachronism or at least exaggeration, in a work written in the 90s A.D., when the successors of the Pharisees were certainly becoming dominant in Palestine. Oral law: *AJ* XIII.297, and see E. P. Sanders, *Jewish Law from Jesus to the Mishnah* (London and Philadelphia, 1990) 97–130. On the Pharisees generally, see Schürer 1973–87 (D 153) II 388–403. On table-fellowships: Neusner 1960 (D 139); *id.* 1973 (D 140) 64–71.

criticize from afar, it is not surprising that they were regularly involved in direct opposition to the rulers. It is perhaps also understandable, in the light of this opposition, that Pharisaic influence should have spread through society. Josephus claims that before A.D. 70 they had won wide popularity and that their interpretations, as embodied in an Oral Law supplementing the Torah, dominated public practice. Throughout the Hasmonean period, that influence was in the making.

The Sadducees, of whom we know the least, probably had already at this time the aristocratic character and links with the top echelons of the priesthood which were later their hallmark. Their name associated them with the lineage of Zadok the Priest. It is commonly held that they supported the ruling house and supplied many of its courtiers and agents. Even if this be true, there is no reason to suppose that, now or at a later date, all such individuals were in any sense Sadducees, or, on the other hand, to deny that there were certain more scholarly elements within Sadduceeism capable of interesting themselves in the questions of doctrine by which Josephus likes to define them and which Talmudic texts also ascribe to them.[80] We have no conception of the numbers involved in any of the groups at any period. Nor can we say to what extent the main groups either subsumed or coexisted with smaller sectarian units, as was certainly to be the case in the first century A.D.

The dynasty, whose authority would always depend on its beginnings as Israel's saviour, showed understandable reluctance to break irrevocably with those who stood for piety and purity. Hyrcanus was in his early days a pupil and favourite of the Pharisees (*AJ* XIII.289). His quarrel with them is couched in an anecdote which figures also in the Talmud. The core of this story is the Pharisaic demand, made, it is told, at a banquet given by the ruler, that Hyrcanus give up the high priesthood and retain the temporal leadership on its own.[81] The underlying reason for the demand could be that the two functions had traditionally been separated, or else that the Hasmonean house lacked the correct, Zadokite descent, or, again, that Hyrcanus' outward-looking activities were polluting the Temple. Josephus reports drastic results: Hyrcanus cancelled the Pharisees' religious ordinances (to which he had evidently accorded binding force), punished their followers, and took up with the

[80] Joseph. *AJ* XIII.282; association with high birth or wealth, *AJ* XIII.298; XVIII.17 (saying that they are few). See Schürer 1973–87 (D 153) II 404–14.

[81] *AJ* XIII.289–97; Babylonian Talmud, *Kiddushin* 66a, with a mistaken ascription to Jannaeus. On the Talmudic tradition, Derenbourg, *Essai sur l'histoire et la géographie de la Palestine*, (Paris, 1867) 79–80; on the legal interpretation, Klausner in Schalit 1976 (D 152) 270–4. For scepticism of Josephus' rupture story, see S. Mason, *Flavius Josephus on the Pharisees* (Leiden, 1991) 213–30. Hyrcanus' appearance in early rabbinic tradition as the instigator of certain reforms in tithing and sacrificial practice cannot either support or invalidate the rupture tradition: J. Sievers, *The Hasmoneans and their Supporters from Mattathias to the Death of John Hyrcanus I* (South Florida Studies in the History of Judaism 6) (Atlanta, 1990) 150–2.

Sadducees. Josephus, furthermore, believed that the breach was never healed. Yet the hazy recollections of this ruler in Talmudic literature are favourable, and Josephus himself proceeds to sum him up as a man both fortunate and charismatic. It may well be that the image of special spirituality was one adopted by Hyrcanus to counter Pharisaic disapproval, and that the historian reflects this projection when he says that Hyrcanus was honoured by God in three separate ways: with the leadership, with the high priesthood and with a prophet's power to make predictions (*BJ* I.68–9; *AJ* XIII.300). This last ability was exemplified in an episode which clearly gained widespread currency, for it is found in both Josephus and various Talmudic texts. It tells how Hyrcanus was busy about his high priestly duties when a voice from above (*bath-qol*) brought him the news of his sons' victory over Antiochus Cyzicenus. We observe that all three of Hyrcanus' roles are neatly united in this tale; but the religious capacity has pride of place.

Another hint of a religious division between ruler and people is perhaps to be detected in the letter which opens 2 Maccabees (see above, n. 3), where 'the brethren, the Jews in Jerusalem and throughout the land of Judaea' urge the Jews of Egypt to celebrate with vigour the festival commemorating the re-establishment of the Temple cult after the pollution by Jason, which had occurred in the month of Kislev over thirty years earlier. The ruler is not party to the letter, and the victor, Judas, the Maccabee, is not mentioned in it. But we have no basis for determining the nature of the anti-Hasmonean circles which may have produced the letter, and it must be remembered that these circles were not responsible for the historical work to which the letter was attached.

With Alexander Jannaeus, the conflicts intensified greatly and gave rise to mass slaughter. This time, not the Pharisees but the Jewish masses in general are given as the king's opponents, and the reconstruction which puts the Pharisees at the forefront of the reaction rests on no more than a plausible conjecture. To accept this, however, is not to accept the terms of a dichotomy created by modern scholarship, in which it is supposed that to follow Josephus is to relegate the Pharisees (and the Sadducees too) to being a political and not a religious 'party' and that, to avoid this unacceptable conclusion, Josephus' portrayal should be rejected. The Talmudic accounts of the flight of Simon ben Shetaḥ, one of the leading scholars of the era, may go some way to confirm that Jannaeus' quarrel was primarily with elements rigorous about the Law, both written and oral, as we know the Pharisees to have been, and to show that politics and religion were not distinguishable spheres of activity. At this time, objections seem, once again, to have been directed at the Hasmonean tenure of the high priesthood; in addition, since one popular outburst took the form of pelting of the king with the citrons carried at the Festival of Tabernacles, there would appear also to have been controversies about his holy-day observances.[82] For the rest, our evidence is too limited to allow us to understand how the slaughter of 6,000 citizens could follow from the pelting, or what could have been the character of the ensuing troubles in which, between about 90 and 85 B.C., 50,000 people perished, while their surviving associates had to seek the protection of King Demetrius III (Eukairos). A further 6,000 of his subjects apparently changed sides twice before Jannaeus took his most appalling revenge of all, crucifying 800 of them in public and massacring their wives and children while, it was said, he feasted openly with his concubines. That this act sent ripples even to Qumran is hardly surprising. Josephus' assurance that the king, having disposed of all the troublemakers, 'reigned thereafter in complete tranquillity' (*AJ* XIII.383), is scarcely believable, though he did recover somewhat from the military setbacks which, as we have described, also accompanied his middle years, and which, no doubt, had been partly a consequence of the uprising within his own borders.

There is no satisfactory way for us to check Josephus' version of these events, however much we may suspect him of exaggeration. Yet even the dreadful deeds he describes did not finally rupture the link between the Pharisees and the dynasty. Jannaeus, with striking pragmatism, concluded from his own extensive experience that the Pharisees were now a power in the land, without whose co-operation one could not govern securely. He allegedly left his widow and successor, the Queen Salome Alexandra, with the remarkable instructions to placate them instantly and to share power with them in the future. These concessions made them prepared, apparently, to go so far as honouring the corpse of Jannaeus.

Thus, during Alexandra's nine-year rule, Pharisees were thought to have come to dominate public life. Talmudic tradition remembered the reign with affection, valuing it especially as the heyday of Simon son of Shetaḥ. But the Pharisees became, in their turn, objects of public resentment. Elements hostile to them rallied to the side of Alexandra's younger son, Aristobulus, and during her last illness they organized themselves to take over the country. His supporters included much of the priesthood (*AJ* XIV.24), and it was that show of violence which persuaded the elder brother, Hyrcanus, formally to cede the throne to the younger shortly after the queen's death. However, under the impact

[82] Talmudic legends about Simon ben Shetah often make him Jannaeus' brother-in-law. Efron 1987 (D 114) 143–218, proposes a critical evaluation. On the pelting, Joseph. *AJ* XIII.372–3; *BJ* I.88.

of the Roman presence in the area and of his Idumaean adviser, Antipater (the father of Herod the Great), Hyrcanus' claim was soon revived and was eventually endorsed by Pompey when he arrived.

So it was that, in the latter years of the Hasmoneans, the most prominent of the divisions in Judaism, that between the Pharisees and the Sadducees, dominated Jerusalem and, if Josephus is to be believed, tore the state apart. Questions of power and of government were central to that dispute. There had been strong reactions to such issues from the early days, in the shape of the *ḥasidim* and of the Essenes and, in all probability, of similar groups about which we know nothing. But as the dynasty grew in worldliness and in ruthlessness, it aroused yet wider antagonisms. And in the end, perhaps under the influence of other Hellenistic monarchies, it fell prey itself to succession disputes. Under such pressures, the personal weaknesses of Hyrcanus and Aristobulus proved disastrous.

We cannot judge which sector of the population it was that presented itself to Pompey at Damascus, in the spring of 63 B.C., and requested the restoration of the traditional system of rule under a high priest (*AJ* XIV.41). Josephus describes this as the view of the 'nation', and it is worth remembering that much of the population may well not have been aligned with any of the major sects. Whatever the case, the sad day had arrived when these people preferred to deal with Rome than with either of their own aspiring rulers. Those hopes in a solution from the outside very rapidly faded, however, once Pompey had, after a month of siege, wrested the Temple Mount from the forces of Aristobulus, had marched into the Holy of Holies, had imposed Roman tribute and had taken many into slavery.

The Psalms of Solomon, preserved among the Apocrypha and Pseudepigrapha in the Christian Church, express the horror of the pious at that act of desecration. The psalms voice the feelings of those people who had been repelled, like the Qumran settlers, by the greed, lawlessness and arrogance of their own leaders. Here, too, we read of some who had even welcomed Pompey, the invader from the West, 'a man alien to our race'. But disillusion had soon left them with Messianism as their only refuge, when they had seen the conqueror do in Jerusalem 'all the things that the Gentiles do for the gods in their cities', and recoiled while 'Gentile foreigners went up to your place of sacrifice; they arrogantly trampled it with their sandals.'[83] The door had been opened to Pompey in equal measure by the feud between the princes, both of whom had courted him with gifts, and by the *naïveté* of the populace. Nevertheless,

[83] Psalm 2. Charlesworth 1985 (D 103) II.651–2. Efron's rejection (D 114 ch. 6) of the accepted association between the Psalms and Pompey, in favour of a Christian context, has not proved persuasive.

we may suggest that, even had the advancing Romans met with a united people, the outcome could, in the long run, hardly have been very different.

The Pompeian settlement of Palestine and the subsequent partition of Judaea by Gabinius are best described elsewhere, in the context of Rome's eastern policies.[84]

[84] See above, ch. 8*a*, pp. 260–2, 272–3.

CHAPTER 8c

EGYPT, 146–31 B.C.

DOROTHY J. THOMPSON

I. THE LATER PTOLEMIES

In Egypt 146 B.C., the year of the destruction of Corinth and Carthage, was the last full year in the life of Ptolemy VI Philometor, who died fighting in Syria in the following autumn. Apart from a brief period of joint reign (170–164 B.C.) when Egypt had been seriously threatened by Antiochus IV and when Rome, in July 168, first actively interfered in the affairs of the Ptolemies (Vol. VIII[2] 342–4), the two sons of Epiphanes (Philometor and Euergetes II) had conspicuously failed to co-operate. Similar tensions within the ruling house with all the resultant conflict, upheaval and lack of direction were to be a feature of the last century of Ptolemaic rule.

In 145 the younger son of Epiphanes was summoned by the people home from Cyrene where he had ruled in semi-exile. Returning via Cyprus, whence a well-timed amnesty decree[1] was aimed to strengthen his acceptability, Euergetes II now took his brother's widow as his wife. Supported only by the Jews and perhaps the intellectuals of the city, Cleopatra II had earlier pressed the claims of her son Ptolemy VII Neos Philopator. The boy was speedily liquidated by his uncle, in her arms on his mother's wedding-day according to one rhetorical account; Ptolemy VIII Euergetes II then claimed the succession and consummated his marriage. His traditional coronation at Memphis in 144 was timed to coincide with the birth of his new wife's child, suitably named Memphites. Two years later, together with his wife, Euergetes II voyaged south and on 10 September 142 consecrated the great Horus temple at Edfu.[2] The king who had earlier relied on the Alexandrian mob was apparently searching for wider support amongst the population of Egypt.

In looking beyond the Greek capital on the Mediterranean, in recognizing the importance of the ceremonial role of the king, and in presenting himself as traditional protector of the land of Egypt and its people, Euergetes II followed the examples of his father and of his elder

[1] *COrdPtol* 41–2. [2] Diod. XXXIII.13; Cauville and Devauchelle 1984 (D 178) 39.

brother. For the Egyptian population he sought the role of pharaoh. However, he was not respected by the Alexandrian Greeks or by visiting Romans who decried his monstrous paunch (he was disrespectfully known as Physcon, Pot-belly), his dress and lifestyle; his persecutions and his personal predilections resulted in a uniformly hostile reception by the classical commentators.[3] In *c.* 140 he took as a second wife his niece Cleopatra III, daughter of his first wife and of his late brother, Philometor. The jealous struggles of the two Cleopatras, mother and daughter, now began in earnest, and the attempted *coup* of Philometor's army officer Galaistes is but one sign of the simmering unrest.[4] The open persecution of the Greeks of Alexandria with the subsequent dispersal of the intelligentsia had probably started soon after his return to power. Such evil acts of individual rulers dominate the historiography of the period.[5] The evidence of the papyri, being scrappy and scattered in its survival, occasionally illuminates the scene but cannot supply the political framework which is missing from the record.

In 140/39 B.C. a Roman embassy headed by P. Cornelius Scipio Aemilianus, together with Spurius Mummius and L. Caecilius Metellus Calvus visited Alexandria on an eastern fact-finding mission. This may have been the occasion of Polybius' visit to the country. His unattractive picture of the divisions in Alexandria – ignoring the Jews of the city he divided the population there into Egyptians, unruly mercenaries and the Greek Alexandrians – may be matched by a Stoic account of the overweight and flimsily dressed ruler who needed Scipio's arm for support. The sumptuousness of the palace and of the royal entertainment did not make a favourable impression. Escorted upriver to Memphis on the regular tourist round, the Romans admired the natural resources of the kingdom which could be so great, if only rulers worthy of it could be found.[6]

The later Ptolemies did not provide such leadership. Towards the end of the decade, by November 132, Euergetes' personal problems came into the open with the outbreak of a bitter civil war between the king with his second wife Cleopatra III and her mother, his first wife, Cleopatra II.[7] In Egypt Cleopatra II took command of the troops and introduced a new system of dating and cult titles. Euergetes, who was still minting in Alexandria in late September 131,[8] now fled to Cyprus

3 Heinen 1983 (D 196) discusses the sources. 4 Diod. XXXIII.20, 22.

5 Polyb. XXXIV.14.6–8; Jac. *FGrH* 270 F 9, Menecles of Barca; Diod. XXXIII.6; Val. Max. IX.2.ext.5; Just. *Epit.* XXXVIII.8.2–4.

6 Polyb. XXXIV.14.1–5; Ath. XII.549d–e, probably Panaetius rather than Posidonius; Diod. XXXIII.28b.1–3.

7 The demotic Malcolm papyrus, *PLond* 10384 (11 Nov. 132 B.C.), had Cleopatra III without her mother in the dating formula (information from C. J. Martin, who is to publish this papyrus).

8 Mørkholm 1975 (B 207) 10–11; still in Egypt in October 131, *PLeid* 373 a + *UPZ* 128 (30 October 131 B.C.), in Lüddeckens 1960 (D 208) 93–5 Urk. 37.

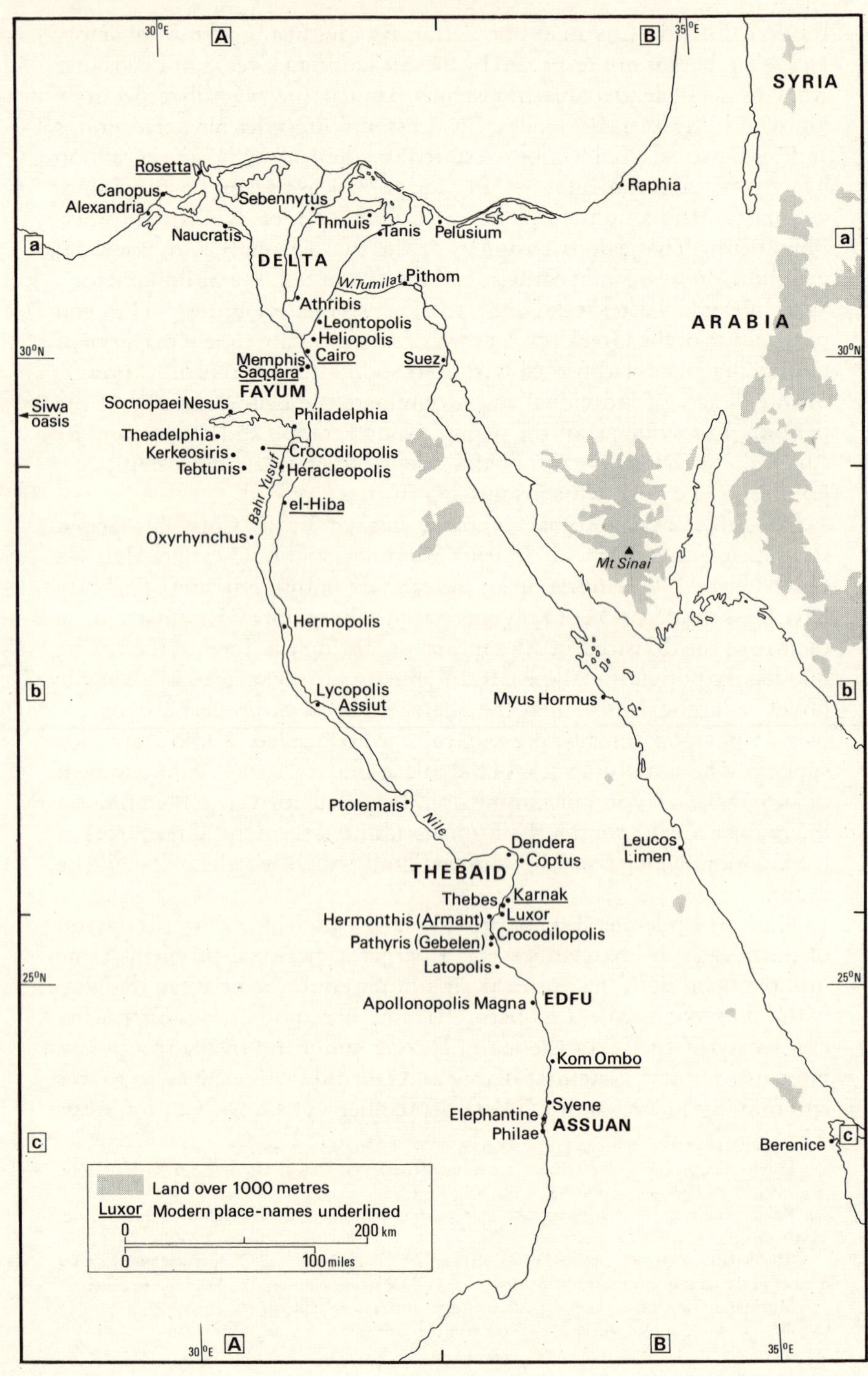

30°E
A
B
35°E
SYRIA
Rosetta
Canopus
Alexandria
Sebennytus
Thmuis
Tanis
Pelusium
Raphia
Naucratis
a
DELTA
W. Tumilat
Pithom
Athribis
Leontopolis
Heliopolis
ARABIA
30°N
Memphis
Cairo
Saqqara
Suez
FAYUM
Socnopaei Nesus
Siwa oasis
Philadelphia
Theadelphia
Kerkeosiris
Crocodilopolis
Tebtunis
Heracleopolis
Bahr Yusuf
el-Hiba
Oxyrhynchus
Mt Sinai
Hermopolis
b
Lycopolis
Assiut
Myus Hormus
Ptolemais
Nile
Dendera
Coptus
Leucos Limen
THEBAID
Thebes
Karnak
Hermonthis (Armant)
Luxor
Pathyris (Gebelen)
Crocodilopolis
Latopolis
25°N
Apollonopolis Magna
EDFU
Kom Ombo
Syene
Elephantine
Philae
ASSUAN
c
Berenice
Land over 1000 metres
Luxor Modern place-names underlined
0
200 km
0
100 miles

11 Egypt

where he had murdered Memphites, his son by Cleopatra II. These troubles (*ameixia*) are used as a key point in the later land surveys of Kerkeosiris in the South Fayum and in the Heracleopolite *nomos*; land grants were divided into those made up to Year 39 (132/1 B.C.) and those from Year 40 (131/30 B.C.).[9] In her husband's absence the papyri suggest that Cleopatra enjoyed some success even as far south as the Thebaid, but Euergetes II soon returned to reside in the old Egyptian capital of Memphis. With an Egyptian military leader, Paos, in the Thebaid, the king seems largely to have relied on native support. As so often when trouble broke out in Alexandria, elsewhere in Egypt the age-old rivalries surfaced in many forms. The conflicts which resulted from the instability of Ptolemaic rule might show racial, regional, religious and economic aspects. The breakaway tendency of Thebes and the south may be seen in the person of Harsiesis, a native ruler of short duration who profited from royal unrest to establish partial control in Thebes, the home of Amon.[10] 'The Potter's Oracle', an apocalyptic work in Greek most probably based on a demotic original, may date from these years. Following a period of assorted disasters – famine, murder, the collapse of the moral order, oppression and civil war – all would again be well with the Greek power finally destroyed. The Egyptian gods would be restored to Memphis; the city on the coast would be deserted.[11]

By April 129 Euergetes was once again sufficiently in control to begin to settle his Egyptian troops. In the forty-first year of his reign (130/29) the South Fayum village of Kerkeosiris received the first settlement there of Egyptian troops – eight cavalrymen (one with 30 *arourai* (7.5 hectares) and seven with 20 *arourai* (5 hectares)) and thirty infantrymen with 7 *arourai* (1.75 hectares). In close connexion with these military land grants 130 *arourai* of good cultivable land were dedicated to Soknebtunis (the local crocodile-god Souchos, lord of Tebtunis, a neighbouring town). Troops were thus rewarded, native cults encouraged and royal control upheld. This native settlement was made on land earlier belonging to substantial Greek cleruchs; immigrants were giving way to Egyptians.

Yet in the south the whole decade is marked by sporadic violence and banditry. The small-scale raids on the local dykes of Crocodilopolis by villagers from the neighbouring area of Hermonthis at the time of the Nile flood in September 123 typify this unrest. The priests of Souchos complained to a local official that the land has gone unsown; both their temple and the royal interest suffer.[12] How far such local disputes, the

[9] *PTebt* 60.67, 90; *BGU* 2441.119.

[10] Koenen 1959 (D 199).

[11] Koenen 1970 (D 201); Lloyd 1982 (D 206); cf Johnson 1984 (D 197) 116–21; Tait 1977 (D 234) 45–8 for a (later) demotic version.

[12] *WChrest* 11.

replay of age-old rivalries, derive directly from the political instability of the period is unknown. What is clear is that when political control from Alexandria was weak, all forms of abuse flourished. When on 28 April 118 the royal rulers, Euergetes II and his two queens, Cleopatras II and III, uneasily reconciled since 124, issued a decree of amnesty, its scope was far-reaching.[13] With the aim of restoring peace those who had fled were encouraged to return home. Royal generosity was coupled with an attempt to control the abuse of official power. Debts to the crown and all forms of arrears were remitted, whilst crown farmers, revenue-workers, beekeepers and textile-workers were protected in their professions. What had become the regular concessions were made to the temples and to their priests. The rights of military settlers (cleruchs) were increased. The summary arrest and imprisonment of individuals was limited and at all levels officials were restrained and controlled: no illegal levies at the customs-posts (or elsewhere), no bribes and requisitioning. Billeting was severely constrained and, following the troubles, the reconstruction of both temples and private housing was endorsed; planting and agriculture were encouraged. Such decrees of beneficence and bounty were well known in Egypt though this is the most comprehensive of all that survive. However practices prohibited in its provisions are likely to have continued and the extent of its coverage serves only to document the extent of the prevailing disorder.

The uneasy reconciliation of Euergetes II and his two wives was soon ended by his death in the summer of 116, in the fifty-fourth year of his reign. The succession was not clear and once again conflict in the ruling house, between the two Cleopatras, had economic repercussions. The state of agriculture in the years following Euergetes' death suggests the new rulers experienced some difficulty in establishing their control over the country. At Kerkeosiris in the South Fayum only 24 per cent of the cleruchic land of the military settlers was sown with wheat in 116/15 compared with 43 per cent in 119/18, and the derelict land rose from 24 per cent to 58 per cent of the area. By 113/12 however a noticeable improvement had taken place with only 34 per cent of this land registered as derelict and 34 per cent under wheat, the major crop of the country.[14] Such detailed records of change, preserved on waste papyrus used to wrap the sacred crocodiles, may of course simply reflect local conditions that are otherwise unknown, but often they can be shown to be the product of the political state of the country where lack of central control carried direct consequences for agriculture.

The actual succession following the death of Euergetes II is variously recorded; the different versions well illustrate the problem of sources for this period which lacks a coherent narrative. Of the classical authors the

[13] *PTebt* 5 = *COrdPtol.* 53 (118 B.C.) with Bingen 1984 (D 174) 926–32.

[14] *PTebt* I and IV.

main source for the alternating reigns of the two surviving sons of Euergetes II, Ptolemy IX Soter II and Ptolemy X Alexander, is Pausanias' guide to the monuments of Greece which comments on the statues of the Ptolemies at the entrance to the Odeum in Athens. For Pausanias, as for the later writers Justin and Eusebius, the story is one of jealousy and scandal, of plots and intrigues, of dastardly deeds of murder and the comings and goings of kings.[15] With a strong overlay of moral disapproval, classical authors ascribe full responsibility for the downfall of the Ptolemaic kingdom to these later kings and queens.[16] And following the death of Euergetes II, her uncle-husband, it is Cleopatra III who dominates the scene, scheming for the succession of the younger son Alexander. Egyptian sources however, especially the hieroglyphs on the temple walls at Edfu, have been seen as suggesting a somewhat different course of events. Contrary to the picture of the classical sources, Soter II and Alexander were perhaps only half-brothers, the sons respectively of the two wives of Euergetes II, Cleopatra II and her daughter Cleopatra III, and as competitors for the throne each was championed by his mother who, during her lifetime, ruled together with him.[17] All interpretations agree in stressing queenly power in these years; this reached an extreme in 105/4 when Cleopatra III replaced the regular male priest of the dynastic cult in Alexandria (*Sammelbuch* 10763). From a Pathyrite demotic contract (*PRyldem.* III 20) it is clear that at least for a brief period following the death of Euergetes II on 28 June 116 the two Cleopatras reigned together with Ptolemy IX Soter II; the queen who then shared the throne with Soter II was probably Cleopatra III. The king's younger brother Alexander was meanwhile based in Cyprus. By the end of October 107 Ptolemy X Alexander had supplanted his elder brother on the throne, whilst Soter II in turn sought refuge in Cyprus.[18] The joint reign of Cleopatra III and her son continued until her death in 101; she was now replaced on the throne by Alexander's wife Cleopatra Berenice, the daughter of Soter II. According to Pausanias, in a tale of murder and revenge, Alexander was personally responsible for his mother's death. Since her husband's death her position had not been altogether secure, and already in 103 it was perhaps a sense of insecurity that led her to send away to Cos her 'grandsons' (in fact two sons of Soter II and one of Alexander) accompanied by the royal treasure. The

[15] Paus. I.9.1–3; Just. *Epit.* XXXIX.3.1–2; 4.1–6; 5.1–3; Porph. *FGrH* 260 F 32 = Euseb. *Chron.* I.163–4 (Schoene).

[16] E.g. Ath. XII.550 b, Ptolemy X Alexander rivalled his father in obesity; his agility in after-dinner dancing was remarkable, whilst to relieve himself he needed two to support him.

[17] Cauville and Devauchelle 1984 (D 178) 47–50, disagreeing with Otto and Bengtson 1938 (D 216) 112–93, Volkmann 1959 (D 242) 1738–48 and Musti 1960 (D 214); in arguing that Cleopatra II continued as queen until 107 B.C. they fail to take account of contemporary Greek inscriptions, especially *OGIS* 739, and the cumulative evidence of demotic protocols, especially those from Thebes.

[18] For the date see Boswinkel and Pestman 1982 (D 177) 67–9.

alienation overseas of royal wealth was to become standard practice in the first century B.C.; on this first occasion the immediate beneficiary was Mithridates VI of Pontus who in 88 took both the island and the princes.[19]

With Soter II ruling in Cyprus as an independent king, the wealth and unity of the country were divided. Soon the division became tripartite when Soter II, retaining Cyprus alone, was replaced as king in Cyrene by Ptolemy Apion. Justin (XXXIX.5.2) tells that Apion, a bastard son of Euergetes II, received this inheritance from his father in 116 B.C. If so, inscriptions show his father's will was long ignored with Soter II ousted from Cyrene only after his loss of the Egyptian throne. Whether Rome had exercised influence on the will of Euergetes II cannot be known. The extent however of unofficial Roman penetration may be seen in two Latin graffiti from Philae in Upper Egypt that are contemporary with the king's death and dated by the consuls of that year. And when a member of the Senate visited in 112 official arrangements preceded his tour of the sights.[20] In any event, a further blow to Ptolemaic power was sustained when, as a recognized alternative to prolonging dynastic discord, on his death in 96 Ptolemy Apion left Cyrene to Rome. Rome's lack of immediate intervention is of less interest here than the act of legacy itself. Ptolemy X Alexander followed suit, leaving what remained of the Ptolemaic kingdom, both Cyprus and Egypt, to Rome.[21] Again Rome was to be slow in claiming her legacy but there is no clearer indication of her pre-eminence in Mediterranean politics than her recurrent nomination as territorial legatee.

Alexander survived on the Egyptian throne until 88 when the Alexandrians ejected him. Soter II now returned to take Alexandria, defeating Alexander in the countryside. The younger brother then fled to Myra in Lycia and from there towards Cyprus; the Edfu temple simply records a voyage to Punt, the archetypal 'foreign parts'. Caught at sea he was defeated and killed.[22] The elder brother, Soter II, in control of Alexandria still faced the problem of renewed revolt in the Thebaid. It took three years finally to crush the home of Amon and 'he did such damage that there was nothing left to remind the Thebans of their former prosperity'.[23]

This bare and somewhat confused outline of events may be supplemented by documents and inscriptions from Egypt. There had been

[19] App. *Mith.* 4.23.

[20] *SEG* XXVIII.1485; cf *PTebt* 33 = *WChrest* 3 (112 B.C.). Full discussion in van 't Dack 1980 (D 184) and 1983 (D 186).

[21] Badian 1967 (D 169) argues convincingly for this identification rather than with Alexander II.

[22] Euseb. *Chron* I.164 (Schoene) is the main source (cf Porph. *FGrH* 260 F 32.8–9). Using the numismatic evidence Mørkholm 1975 (B 207) 14–15 modifies the discussion of Samuel 1965 (D 230); see Zauzich 1977 (D 249) 193 for Year 26 = 29 of the king outside Egypt.

[23] Paus. I.9.3.

unrest in the Thebaid for some years. In 90 B.C. rebels had attacked the Latopolite and Pathyrite *nomoi*, and in the *stasis* of 88 Platon, as *epistrategos* of the Thebaid, had at least one native commander (Nechthyris) under him. A mosaic of local rivalries emerges with Pathyris supporting Platon, its priests loyal to Soter II against the neighbouring temples of Thebes; here it was Hathor opposing Amon.[24] Indeed during both phases of his reign Ptolemy IX Soter II, who through the name Lathyrus, Chick-pea, was made an object of ridicule to the Greeks, appears to have been well aware of Egyptian sensitivities and, especially, cults. Early in his reign, together with his mother he had made concessions to the priests of Chnoum at Elephantine[25] and, born in the same year as an Apis bull, he showed consistent concern for this particular cult. In contrast, under his brother Alexander sacred bulls tended to suffer. At Hermonthis in Upper Egypt the Buchis bull born in April 101 B.C., with Alexander on the throne, was not installed until April 82, after the restoration of Soter II; it survived only five years more. And in Memphis the Apis bull which had died in his brother's reign (sometime after June 96) was only given a proper burial in the eleventh year of its successor. This was in 87/6 when the Apis burial probably accompanied the second coronation of Soter II, now *wḥm-ḫ*ᶜ, 'repeating the diadem' in his celebration at Memphis of a thirty-year Sed-festival, a renewal of power in the old Egyptian style.[26] In his long-drawn-out struggle with Thebes Memphis had served as base for Soter II and the cults of Lower Egypt had supported this sovereign when faced with the defection of the south.

Internal dissension was only one of Egypt's problems; there was Rome too. At Edfu the great pylon had been started in 116 B.C. An inscription on the temple enclosure wall from around 88 records its decoration with inscriptions and all of the ritual scenes designed to repel strangers.[27] Yet it was in vain that the Egyptians sought for divine protection. In 87/6 whilst fighting was continuing in the Thebaid a group of Romans came to Alexandria. Sulla's quaestor L. Licinius Lucullus was looking for ships to build up a Sullan fleet. His encounter in Alexandria with the newly restored Ptolemy IX Soter II typifies the different modes of Rome and eastern kings. Met by the entire Egyptian fleet Lucullus was offered unprecedented hospitality within the royal palace. An entertainment allowance four times the norm was made and rich gifts offered him to the value of eighty talents; the statutory tourist visit upriver was arranged. Treated as an equal by an oriental king the

[24] *P Berl dem* 13.608 (90 B.C.); *Sammelbuch* 6300; 6644; *WChrest* 12 (88 B.C.). On the identification of those involved see Thomas 1975 (D 237) 117–19. [25] *OGIS* 168.

[26] Crawford 1980 (D 182) 12–14; Traunecker 1979 (D 241) 429–31.

[27] Cauville and Devauchelle 1984 (D 178) 43.

Roman quaestor was doubtless expected to reciprocate at some time in the future. As others were to learn, this was not the Roman way. Lucullus rejected both tour and gifts; he left without the ships he sought.[28]

From Lucullus Sulla will have received a firsthand report on the wealth of Egypt. So on the death of Soter late in 81, although to date Rome had taken no action on his younger brother's will, now that the Alexandrians lacked a king and Ptolemy X Alexander's widow was on the throne, Sulla sent out as king and consort the son of Ptolemy X, her stepson, Ptolemy XI Alexander II. Captured on Cos by Mithridates VI in 88, Alexander II had in 84 escaped from Pontus to Sulla and through him to Rome. Exiled from Egypt for the past twenty-three years, the new king did not care for his stepmother-wife whom he speedily had murdered. After only three weeks on the throne he in turn perished, at the hands of the Alexandrians who resented both the interference of Rome and the excesses of Sulla's nominee. These royal internecine conflicts, the people of Alexandria, and the power of Rome interacted to hasten the collapse of Ptolemaic Egypt.

For the moment Rome exercised restraint. The two sons of Soter II, sent like their cousin to safety on Cos in 103 and captured by Mithridates, now returned from Syria to their home. As Ptolemy XII Neos Dionysos the elder took the throne in Egypt, the younger brother made do with Cyprus for his rule. The (interrupted) thirty years of the reign of Ptolemy XII, more commonly called Auletes, the Fluteplayer, were fatal for the independence of the country. Popillius Laenas' ultimatum at Eleusis in 168 B.C. (Vol. VIII^2, pp. 344–5) and the testament of Ptolemy X Alexander were earlier stages in a process which was to culminate in the annexation of Egypt by Augustus. Under Auletes Egypt became subordinate to political issues and personalities in Rome as the king struggled to retain his control. His position at home was not unchallenged and in 75 two sons of Cleopatra Selene (by one of the Seleucid dynasty) came to Rome in quest of the Egyptian throne. They stayed just over a year before returning empty-handed, and the young Antiochus who returned via Sicily had bad experiences at the hands of its governor Verres. Meanwhile in Egypt Auletes hung on, cultivating good relations with the Egyptian hierarchy and sponsoring widespread temple-building. The great Horos temple at Edfu was finished in his reign and he built on to temples at Karnak, Deir el Medina and Medinet Habu in Thebes, Dendera, Kom Ombo, Philae, Dabod, Athribis, Medamud, Hermonthis and on Bigga Island. As always such gifts to the gods demanded some recognition in return and under Auletes there appears a significant development in the divinity of the king himself. Auletes was the first of

[28] Plut. *Luc.* 2.5–3.1.

the Ptolemies to call himself god, *theos*, without the use of his name, and in Memphis the high priest Psenptais was appointed his personal priest.[29]

To be pharaoh however was no longer sufficient and finally in 59 in return for 6,000 talents made over to Caesar and Pompey, the king was officially declared 'friend and ally' of the Roman people. Even before this, the independence of his kingdom was under threat. In 65 when M. Licinius Crassus as censor proposed making Egypt tributary to Rome he was vigorously opposed by his colleague Q. Lutatius Catulus. In 64/3 Pompey was in the East and extended Roman rule right up to the eastern border of Egypt. He did not, however, enter Egypt although the country was at variance with its king and the king himself invited him, sending him gifts, riches and clothing for his entire army. It was unclear, Appian records, whether he feared the strength of the kingdom which still enjoyed prosperity or the jealousy of his opponents, whether it was oracles which stopped him or some other reason. Strabo recorded a crown worth 4,000 gold pieces sent to Pompey in Damascus and the wealth of Egypt was becoming even better known at Rome.[30] When in 63 Cicero spoke out against the Rullan agrarian proposals (ch. 9 below, pp. 349–51) he stressed the prosperity of the country, the bounty of its fields.[31]

Soon after his recognition in Rome Auletes was driven from his kingdom by a populace enraged by his passivity. For Cyprus was being annexed by Rome and lost to Egypt. Probably with a view to paying for his new free corn distribution of 58, P. Clodius had proposed realizing the king's assets in Cyprus. M. Porcius Cato was sent out to put the proposal into effect and by 56 Cyprus was added to the province of Cilicia. As in 75/4 when Cyrene was at last settled by Rome and P. Lentulus Marcellinus successfully reorganized the royal lands which provided an income for Rome, so now Cyprus was to benefit the people of Rome, to the detriment of Egypt.[32] Ptolemy, the brother of Auletes, committed suicide rather than submit. Auletes himself, showing no opposition to the final dismemberment of his kingdom, was forced to flee to Rome where Pompey provided him with credit and temporary accommodation. In Egypt Auletes was replaced on the throne by his daughter Berenice IV, at first with her sister Cleopatra Tryphaena and later her new husband Archelaus, a son of Mithridates. Rome took notice. A counter-embassy from Alexandria appeared a threat to Auletes' safety in Rome and he again departed eastwards, to Ephesus

[29] Porter and Moss 1927- (D 221) for temple-building; *OGIS* 186.8–10 (14 May 62 B.C.) 'kyrios basileus Theos Neos Dionysos Philopator kai Philadelphos'; cf. the stele *BM* 886.4 'first prophet of the lord of two lands' (ed. Reymond 1981 (D 227) 147).

[30] App. *Mith.* 17.114; Strabo in Joseph. *AJ* XIV.35.

[31] Cic. *Leg. Agr.* II.43.

[32] Badian 1965 (C 162). For the Roman side of these events see ch. 10 below, p. 379.

where he found greater security living under the protection of Artemis within her temple. Egypt and the fate of the Egyptian king was now a Roman issue with Pompey and his opponents vying for an Egyptian command. In 57 the consul P. Lentulus Spinther was charged with the restoration of the Egyptian king, but the Sibylline books prevented the deployment of an army. Events however overtook political decisions and in the spring of 55 Aulus Gabinius, the proconsul in Syria, illegally left his province and escorted Auletes back to Alexandria. Cicero records Gabinius' fear of the fleet of Archelaus and the growing number of pirates in the Mediterranean.[33] The promises of 10,000 talents from the king cannot have been entirely unconnected. Mark Antony went to Alexandria as Gabinius' cavalry commander and in Gabinius' entourage was Antipater, the Idumaean councillor of Hyrcanus II, high priest of Jerusalem and father of Herod the Great. The Jews of Egypt might be a significant element in support of a particular sovereign and later, in 47, both Antipater and Hyrcanus were to be influential in gaining support for Caesar in the overthrow of Auletes' heirs. Many of the invading troops, the *Gabiniani*, who came to range themselves in support of the Ptolemaic dynasty, stayed on in Egypt – the first Roman troops of occupation.

Auletes celebrated his return with his daughter's death and other murders. His ability to fulfil his financial promises seems to have been somewhat limited. In Rome Gabinius was tried, fined the sum which had been promised him and went bankrupt. In Egypt Rabirius Postumus was appointed by the king to the chief financial post of the country, that of *dioiketes*, but in spite of abandoning his toga and adopting Greek dress he failed to recover the money owed to Pompey and other Romans; he was driven ignominiously from the country. The Alexandrians who earlier had shown 'all zeal in looking after those visiting from Italy, keen, in their fear, to give no cause for complaint or war' now had little time for Roman interference. Two sons of Bibulus, now governor of Syria, who in 50 were sent to recall the *Gabiniani* from the attractions of Alexandria in order to fight the Parthians were summarily put to death in the city.[34] Slaughter in the streets and in the gymnasium had become regular features of life in the capital city.

Auletes was not long to enjoy his position as king. He died in 51 leaving his kingdom to his elder son, Ptolemy XIII now aged ten, and to his daughter, Cleopatra VII aged seventeen; the news of his death reached Rome by the end of June.[35] The Roman people was named as witness to his will and a copy sent to Rome for deposit in the *aerarium* somehow ended up in Pompey's hands. Whatever the facts, the will of

[33] Cic. *Rab. Post.* 8.20. [34] Caes. *BCiv.* III.110; Val. Max. IV.1.15. [35] Cic. *Fam.* VIII.4.5.

Auletes made open recognition of the overriding power of Rome to control the future of Egypt. Any succession to the Egyptian throne now took place under Roman protection.

Cleopatra VII however was primarily an Egyptian queen, the first of her family to speak the language of the country she ruled.[36] Ignoring her brother she sought support within her kingdom. Barely a month after her accession she travelled upriver to Hermonthis to be present in person at the installation of the Buchis bull on 22 March 51; she was later to build a small birth-temple to the god at Hermonthis.[37] Likewise, when in the third year of her reign the Apis died, she herself met part of the cult expenses, endowing a table of offerings and providing daily rations for those involved in the rites of burial. Earlier Ptolemies had provided cash; the detail of Cleopatra's endowment is new and suggests some level of personal involvement in the bull cults of Egypt which had come to represent the essence of native religion. As the goddess Cleopatra the younger, *philopator*, 'father-loving', and *philopatris*, 'patriotic' (*BGU* 2376.1 (36/5 B.C.)), she was indeed queen of Egypt.

In Rome however civil war intervened and the uncertainty of the outcome can only have increased the dynastic tensions in Alexandria where, as regents, the eunuch Potheinus and general Achillas supported the cause of Ptolemy XIII against his elder sister. After Pharsalus Pompey fled in hope to Egypt where he was beheaded at Pelusium. The deed was not welcomed by Caesar when he reached Alexandria three days later. The Alexandrian War ensued, fought over the winter of 48/7. The rest of the story is well known (see below pp. 433–4). Re-established as queen by Caesar at first with Ptolemy XIII as her husband, and later in March 47 with her even younger brother Ptolemy XIV, Cleopatra VII used her scheming intelligence to the full. Cyprus was restored by Caesar to the crown of Egypt; it had served again as a haven for endangered Ptolemies when, together with his sister Arsinoe, the younger son of Auletes was sent there briefly before being summoned to the throne and marriage with his elder sister. Caesar dallied shortly, but then he left. Caesarion was born in 47, and in 46 Cleopatra and her son followed Caesar to Rome. She left in 44, soon after the Ides of March. In 41 Antony first formed a liaison with the queen, which he was to resume five years later. It lasted until after Actium and the capture of Alexandria by Octavian on 3 August 30 (Vol. x^2, ch. 1). Soon after, the queen died, a self-inflicted royal death at the bite of an asp, and Octavian was left to manage the inheritance of the Ptolemies.

[36] Plut. *Ant.* 27.3–4.

[37] Mond and Myers 1934 (D 213) II 12; Tarn 1936 (D 235) 187–9; Bloedow 1963 (D 175) 91–2; cf. Skeat 1954 (D 233) 40–1 for a more sceptical interpretation.

II. EGYPT: SOCIETY AND ECONOMY

What of the Egypt that Octavian was to inherit for Rome? The dynastic struggles of the last century of Ptolemaic control with constant changes of ruler, significant overseas expenditure by Auletes and, latterly, the absence of Cleopatra in Rome, had had their effect on the economy of Egypt. Normally Egypt was a rich country. In cash terms, even under the poor government of Auletes, Strabo (quoting Cicero) records that the annual income of the country was 12,500 talents. Auletes however had been extravagant in the alienation of this wealth: gifts, gold and provisions for Pompey in 63 B.C., 6,000 talents to Caesar and Pompey in 59 and 10,000 to Gabinius in 55; and the Alexandrian envoys opposing the king had equally brought their gold to Rome. The gold sarcophagus of Alexander the Great was even melted down to finance the king's expenditure and as *dioiketes* Rabirius had tried unsuccessfully to collect the debts owed to individual Romans.[38] On arrival in Alexandria in 48 Caesar was still owed almost 3,000 talents of which just over sixteen talents were paid towards his army costs; the rest was remitted.[39] Even Ptolemaic wealth was running low. The tetradrachm silver coinage which had maintained a high degree of fineness throughout the Ptolemaic period began to deteriorate under Auletes, dropping sharply in silver content in the years after his restoration.[40] This decline in the quality of the silver coinage is a more reliable reflection of the difficulties of Ptolemy XII and Cleopatra VII than the vagaries of the copper drachmae used as units of account within the written documents.[41]

Agriculture however – the *pulcherrimi agri*, the *agrorum bonitas* so envied in Rome – formed the constant basis of Egyptian wealth and well-being. And agriculture, besides needing regular supervision with a close control of the irrigation system, might suffer also from low Niles. The effects of both man-made and natural disaster on the cereal production of the country shows clearly in a group of Heracleopolite papyri now in Berlin.[42] The secession of Thebes and the south soon after the restoration of Soter II (pp. 316–17 above) figures also in Middle Egypt as a time of interruption of communications (*ameixia*) which in 84/3, in the Heracleopolite *nomos*, resulted in flight from the land and the loss of taxes to the state.[43] In the troubled middle years of the century unsettled conditions regularly interfered with corn-production and transport. Ship-contractors, *naukleroi*, might now be grouped in corporations and armed

[38] Strab. XVII.1.13; App. *Mith.* 17.114; Cic. *Rab. Post.* 3.6 with Suet. *Caes.* 54.3; Cic. *Pis.* 21.48–50; Plut. *Ant.* 3.2; Strab. XVII.1.8 for the sarcophagus, assuming Pareisactus, the son of Kokke, is Auletes; Dio XXXIX.13.2. [39] Plut. *Caes.* 48.4. [40] Walker 1976 (B 256) 150–2.

[41] Gara 1984 (D 193); on this hypothesis what is normally termed copper inflation (Reekmans 1951 (D 226)) is not a true inflation but reflects rather a change in accounting procedures.

[42] *BGU* VIII and XIV. [43] *BGU* 2370.37–42.

guards accompanied the corn-ships down the Nile.[44] The early years of Cleopatra's reign were particularly hard in the countryside as natural disaster combined with political problems. Instructions preserved for the collection of grain from the Heracleopolite *nomos* from 51/50 have an even more urgent tone than usual; in the same year, in Hiera Nesos, the local priests complain that the royal cult has suffered from the depletion of the local population.[45] A failure of the harvest is similarly suggested by a royal order issued on 27 October 50 which forbade, on pain of death, the transport of grain and pulses to any destination other than Alexandria; a loan contract of the same year foresees the possibility of corn reaching a vastly inflated price.[46] A shortage of water, *abrochia*, in Year 3 of Cleopatra VII (50/49 B.C.) led to the desertion of the village of Tinteris by all settlers in the area; the local farmers were unable to pay their taxes. And finally Pliny's notice of the lowest flood ever in the year of Pharsalus (48 B.C.) suggests not so much the anger of the gods as the culmination of a flood failure lasting over at least three years, and maybe more.[47] Peasants of course always complain and official papyrus archives in their nature preserve these complaints, but the accumulation of evidence does appear to add up to a picture of widespread disaster in these years. Another first-century papyrus preserves the tantalizing words 'greed' and 'Romans' in a sentence now incomplete.[48] Overseas debts would appear to have combined with natural catastrophe to oppress both the population of Egypt and the Ptolemaic state. The new trade with India was hardly sufficient to replace the income lost.[49] All of Cleopatra's powers were needed to counteract collapse; the kingdom she ruled was very down at heel.

To function, the Ptolemaic state depended on its administrative bureaucracy and on the army. Neither was particularly successful in these years. The last Ptolemaic decree to survive is an attempt to protect farmers in the Delta who originated in Alexandria from the illegal exactions and harassment of crown officials.[50] There is no reason to suppose that this decree was any more successful than its predecessors; undue pressure from officials would seem one unavoidable consequence of the unsalaried bureaucracy on which the Ptolemies relied. Central control was weak and government officials looked first to their own interests. Loyalty to the Ptolemies, reinforced through the dynastic cult, was not sufficient to counteract the pressures of personal interests.

The independence of Egypt depended on its military strength which by the late second century B.C. was both depleted and as much Egyptian as immigrant. Loyalty of the troops towards the state was variously

[44] *BGU* 1741–3 + 2368; 1742 (63 B.C.). Thompson (Crawford) 1983 (D 238) 66–9.
[45] *BGU* 1760; 1835.
[46] *COrdPtol* 73; *PSI* 1098.28–9.
[47] *BGU* 1842; Pliny *HN* V.58.
[48] *BGU* 2430.26.
[49] Strab. XVII.1.13.
[50] *COrdPtol* 75–6 (12 April 41 B.C.).

fostered though ultimately the ability to provide pay was the decisive factor. Since the early years of the dynasty soldiers had been settled on the land as cleruchs, and rights over this land, as over housing billets, were gradually extended over the years. In 60 B.C. a royal decree records the free testamentary disposition of such holdings and it is clear that by now even women might inherit cleruchic land.[51] (What in such cases happened to the military obligation is not clear.) Mercenaries too, from all over the Mediterranean, played an important part in the military protection of the country. In 58 Auletes was forced to flee his home because he had no mercenary troops;[52] the city garrison in Alexandria and household troops had presumably joined the other side. Since the reign of Philometor mercenary garrisons and their associated civilian communities had been regularly organized in *politeumata*, normally ethnic groupings with their own elected officers, the Idumaeans for example, the Boeotians or the Cretans; the activities of these groups were social and religious.[53] In a country where social groupings were traditional (the guilds for instance of the mummifiers and undertakers of pre-Ptolemaic Egypt), when times were unsettled the collective instinct grew more strong. Alongside the associations of goose-herds, donkey-drivers or ship-contractors, in their corporate dealings the mercenary *politeumata* too might protect the interests of their members in relation to the state.[54] And here too, as within the bureaucracy, the dynastic cult had a cohesive function; temples might be dedicated by representatives of these *politeumata* on behalf of the royal family, or influential officials praised for good will towards the ruling house.

A further role of the army should be mentioned. Both through garrisons and cleruchic settlement the Ptolemaic army was one of the more important forces for the integration of immigrants within Egyptian society. The family archive from 150 to 88 B.C. of Peteharsemtheus son of Panebkhounis or that of Dryton stationed in the garrison at Gebelen (Pathyris) show how easily such soldiers intermarried with Egyptian women; their children were bilingual often with both Greek and Egyptian names. Both languages might be used in legal documents and families who once came from Crete or Cyrene were thus assimilated into the society of Egypt.[55]

More generally however changes were taking place in the relations between Greeks and Egyptians in the administration, for instance, where those of Greek extraction would seem at first to have predominated within its upper echelons. From the late second century B.C.

[51] *COrdPtol* 71.12–15; *BGU* XIV Appendix 3.

[52] Dio XXXIX.12.2–3.

[53] Thompson (Crawford) 1984 (D 239).

[54] *IFay* 109 (37 B.C.); *WChrest* 440 (first cent. B.C.); *BGU* 1741–3 + 2368 (63 B.C.).

[55] Pestman 1965 (D 218) 47–105; Winnicki 1972 (D 245); Pestman 1978 (D 220) 30–7. For intermarriage and assimilation of Cyrenaeans in the Fayum earlier see *I Fay* 2 (224–221 B.C.).

however two governor-generals of the Thebaid and a series of *nomos* governors in the south are found with Egyptian names.[56] Whereas the apparent family succession to high administrative office found here may primarily reflect the breakaway tendency of the south, it also shows some change of emphasis and the opening up to Egyptians of the top levels of the administration. Similarly the increasingly frequent bi- or trilingual publication of royal decrees suggests some recognition by the ruling power of the importance of the Egyptian element in society. From Saqqara near Memphis a demotic archive with a few Greek documents shows that by the first century B.C. even those from the most traditional of Egyptian occupations, the mummifiers, had begun to adapt their ways to those of the ruling race. When in 99 Petesis, undertaker-in-chief of the Apis and Mnevis bulls, found himself and his property under attack he appealed to the king for protection. In answer to his request he was granted a wooden plaque with an official (but in the event ineffective) warning to trespassers, written in both Greek and Egyptian. When ten years later his son Chonouphis made a loan, the contract was in Greek; and when his granddaughter Thaues was also named Asklepias this was the first Greek name in a family recorded over ten generations.[57]

The process of reciprocal acculturation can be seen only sporadically. Whilst proceeding at different rates in different contexts it affected all levels of society. On the walls of the great temple at Edfu, Horos drags Seth around tied by his feet in a positively Homeric scene, and from the nearby cemetery of Hassaia come elaborate epitaphs in both Greek and hieroglyphs celebrating members of a family of senior military officers, who are also priests within the local cults, recorded with both Greek and Egyptian names; the same individuals are recorded in both Greek and Egyptian forms.[58] Both the culture of classical Greece expressed in epigrammatic form and the native culture of Egypt with all its religious overtones are there, in active intercommunication.

It was probably the gods and temples of Egypt which together remained the single most powerful force in the life of the Ptolemaic kingdom for Greek and Egyptians alike. Yet even this was a force diminished in strength. Greek cult continued for the Greeks, especially in Alexandria, yet increasingly behind Greek names Egyptian gods lurk in disguise. (Herakles Kallinikos for instance whose temple at Theadelphia was linked with that of Isis Eseremphthis may well have been Harsaphes or possibly Onouris.)[59] And for the Greeks too the religion of their adopted country proved strong and might be turned against

[56] De Meulenaere 1959 (D 211) and Shore 1979 (D 232); Thissen 1977 (D 236), Hermonthite.

[57] *UPZ* 106–9 (99–98 B.C.); 125 (89 B.C.); 118 (83 B.C.).

[58] Derchain 1974 (D 187) 15–19; Yoyotte 1969 (D 248); Clarysse 1985 (D 179) 62–4.

[59] *Sammelbuch* 6236 = *IFay* 114 (70 B.C.). Bonnet 1952 (D 176) 286–7.

foreign powers. Whilst Amon and the south were often in opposition to the powers of Lower Egypt, the high priesthood of Memphis remained consistently loyal to the Ptolemies and enjoyed strong personal relations with the ruling house. Ptolemies built Egyptian temples to the native gods and in return the gods of Egypt and their priesthood would support their rule. Concessions to the temples and their priests continued to form a regular element of Ptolemaic royal decrees. So in 100 B.C. when Ptolemy X Alexander I ruled with Cleopatra Berenice a royal decree was promulgated protecting sacred fish.[60] From the first century B.C. survives a series of decrees recording royal grants of asylum granted to village temples of Thracian, Greek and Egyptian gods, grants which recall those earlier made to the great Egyptian temples of Memphis or Bousiris, now in the troubled later years of Ptolemaic rule extended more widely.[61] Sometimes set up bilingually, these decrees may be seen to indicate an extension of violence in the countryside and the relative weakness of the local shrines. There are however two further respects in which they throw interesting light on the period. Firstly in these decrees, bound close to the local village cults, appears the dynastic cult of the Ptolemies, with cult images, sacrifices, libations, burnt offerings and sacred lights. Grants made to an Egyptian god like Isis Sachypsis or Isis Eseremphthis at Theadelphia might also benefit the royal gods. Secondly they illustrate the role of the army and the Greek military settlers in Egypt. These grants of asylum are regularly negotiated through senior army officers who now it seems were established as influential members of the local community. In these grants may be seen reflected the interlocking interests of priests, army and crown in the continuation and success of the Ptolemaic regime. Finally, however, through the troubled years of the first century B.C. not even the strength and power of the gods of Egypt could resist the force of Rome.[62]

[60] *PYale* 56.

[61] *Sammelbuch* 620 = *COrdPtol* 64 (96 B.C.); *IFay* 152 (95 B.C.); 112–13 (93 B.C.); 114 (70 B.C.); 135 (69 B.C.); 136 (69–68 B.C.); *COrdPtol* 70[2] (63 B.C.); *IFay* 116–18 (57 B.C.); *COrdPtol* 67 (46 B.C.); *BGU* 1212 (46 B.C.) with van 't Dack 1970 (D 183); Donadoni 1983 (D 188); *OGIS* 129 (47–30 B.C.) reaffirming an asylum grant for a synagogue made earlier by Euergetes II. My interpretation is at variance with that of Dunand 1979 (D 189).

[62] This chapter was last revised in 1986.

CHAPTER 9

THE SENATE AND THE *POPULARES*, 69–60 B.C.

T. P. WISEMAN

I. *LUSTRUM*

In 69 B.C. the Roman citizen body was ritually purified. The citizens assembled at dawn in the Campus Martius, each in the property-class and century to which he had been assigned. A bull, a ram and a boar were led solemnly three times round the assembled host and brought for sacrifice to the altar of Mars, where the censors stood in their purple togas, wreathed and anointed to pray for the gods' favour on a people cleansed.[1]

Sixteen years had passed since the last *lustrum*, more than three times the regular interval, and much had happened in the mean time to make the restoration of divine approval particularly urgent. There had been civil war, slave rebellion and natural disasters. Worst of all – for rule and empire were justified only by the moral superiority of the rulers – there was corruption in the political elite which cried out for a stern censorial purge.[2]

That duly took place. The censors had made full use of their arbitrary powers and amid popular applause expelled sixty-four senators, including the patrician consul of 71 B.C., P. Lentulus Sura.[3] It was a good moment for the eloquent and ambitious M. Cicero to publish his devastating exposure of another guilty man, C. Verres (ch. 7 above, pp. 214–15, 225–7).

It was also the essential moment for the dedication of the rebuilt temple of Jupiter Capitolinus, even though not completely finished (ch. 6, pp. 189, 203). Sulla had meant to dedicate it himself; instead of that name of ill omen, for the next 138 years the great architrave would immortalize Q. Lutatius Catulus, cos. 78.[4] And in the new temple the

[1] For the *lustrum* ritual, see for example Varro, *Ling.* VI.86–7 (quoting the *tabulae censoriae*), Livy I.44.1–2, Dion. Hal. *Ant. Rom.* IV.22.1–2, Polyb. VI.53.7 (togas), Ath. XIV.660C.

[2] Cic. *Div. Caec.* 8 ('censorium nomen . . . poscitur'). Ethical justification of empire: Posidonius ap. Sen. *Ep.* 90.4, Cic. *Rep.* III.36; cf. Livy XXII.13.11, Tac. *Ann.* XIII.56.1 ('melioribus parere').

[3] Livy *Per.* XCVIII ('censores asperam censuram egerunt'), Cic. *Clu.* 117–34 (130f for the applause), Plut. *Cic.* 17, Dio XXXVII.30.4.

[4] Cic. II *Verr.* 4.69, Val. Max. VI.9.5, Tac. *Hist.* III.72.3; Pliny *HN* VIII.138, Plut. *Poplicola* 15.2 (Sulla). Date: Phlegon *FGrH* 257F12.11, Cassiod. *Chron. ad ann.* 69, cf. Livy *Per.* XCVIII.

libri fatales were back in their stone chest, ready to give Rome oracular advice in any crisis. Sibylline prophecies had been sought out from every source by the *XVviri sacris faciundis*.[5]

The first name on the cleaned-up list of senators was that of Mam. Aemilius Lepidus, cos. 77; the *princeps senatus* had to be a patrician. But the true leader of the Senate was Catulus. His ancestral glory shone more brightly since the suppression of Marius' memory – his father's Cimbric trophies, now unrivalled, matched his ancestor's from the victory at the Aegates islands in the First Punic War – and his personal qualities of steadfast and ruthless determination gave him an authority none of his contemporaries could match.[6] The inscription on the Capitoline temple must have seemed a good omen for the restoration of the moral health of Rome.

Sertorius and Spartacus were dead; Mithridates had been defeated and driven from his kingdom; Lucullus' legions were invading Armenia; the pirates would be dealt with in the forthcoming Cretan campaign. At home, the long disputes over the jury-courts and the tribunes' powers had been settled at last; and the new citizens from allied Italy were presumably now enrolled in *classis* and *centuria*, full and equal members of the Roman *civitas*. And yet, in the very *lustrum* itself, a thoughtful observer might detect the elements of future crisis.

First, the sheer size of the citizen body. At the last *lustrum*, in 85, 463,000 *civium capita* were registered; at this one, 910,000. How was that going to affect elections? Increased competition was already built into the senatorial system, with twenty quaestors a year now starting the race and only two consulships as prizes for the winners, and now there would be many of the demoted senators adding to the queue as they sought to rebuild their careers.[7] The prizes were harder to get, and the means of getting them, from a vastly larger and untried electorate, were now much harder to control.

Second, the new citizens themselves. The incorporation of the Italian communities brought about, among other things, an increase in the number of wealthy citizens with financial interests overseas. One would like to know, when the censors were receiving the sworn statements of each citizen's property, how many now owned land in the provinces.[8]

[5] Dion. Hal. *Ant. Rom.* IV 62.5f, Fenestella fr. 18P, Lactant. *Div. Inst.* I.6.9. At least one of the censors may have been involved: *CIL* XIV.3573 (on the temple of Albunea, the Tiburtine Sibyl), with Coarelli 1987 (B 279) 103–10, 223–9.

[6] *Princeps senatus*: Val. Max. VII.7.6 (Mam. Lepidus); Cic. *Pis.* 6, Vell. Pat. II.43.4 (Catulus). Catulus' primacy: Cic. *Pis.* 6, *Off.* I.76, Dio XXXVI.30.4, Plut. *Mor.* 206A, 534D. His qualities: Cic. *Sest.* 101, *Att.* I.20.3, Sall. *H.* III.48.9M. Moral authority: Cic. I *Verr.* 44, *Phil.* II.12.

[7] Dio XXXVI.38.2 on their 'factions and cliques'.

[8] Known examples in Greek lands listed by Wilson 1966 (A 128) 159f. There had long been settlement in Africa and the West (*ibid.* 40, 50f).

Now that the subsidized grain system was re-established, a reliable market no doubt made provincial agriculture, in some areas, a good investment. Senators were probably not allowed to own land abroad, but as with other *negotia* – commercial or financial – they could keep the letter of the law by taking their profits vicariously through freedmen.[9] Like commerce and money-lending, agriculture too could profitably be carried on outside the areas where Rome ruled directly.[10]

Traditionally, the censor's prayer at the *lustrum* was for the gods to expand Rome's dominion.[11] There were many in the assembly who would echo that prayer, and in the last few years their wishes had been acted on; Isauria and Lycaonia added by P. Servilius, Cyrene and Bithynia organized under Roman rule, Pontus ready for annexation (or so it seemed), Egypt and Cyprus under serious consideration.[12]

So now there would be at least three more places where a Roman senator could be king for a year, dispensing judgement from the seat of a Ptolemy or a Nicomedes and receiving appropriate adulation in return. The Roman political elite had always been motivated by the competitive pursuit of glory, traditionally realized in the triumph; increasingly nowadays, glory (of a kind) might depend merely on the lot that allocated consular and praetorian provinces. The prizes for success in the elections – the newly competitive, newly unpredictable elections – were greater than they had ever been. It was not a recipe for political stability.

Three generations before, Polybius had predicted that the admirable 'mixed constitution' of the Roman Republic would eventually come to an end in competitive demagogy when rivalry for office became too fierce. That would bring about mob-rule, which by his theory of the cycle of constitutions led inevitably to monarchy.[13] By the time the next *lustrum* was performed – by the future emperor Augustus forty-one years later – the Romans could reflect that he had not been far wrong.

II. THE TRIBUNES

Two of the ingredients in the constitutional mixture Polybius admired had been removed by Sulla – the tribunes' rights to prosecute political criminals before the people, and to carry out the people's will by

[9] E.g. Cic. *Att.* VI.1.19, 5.2 (Cicero, Philotimus and the Chersonese). For the prohibition, see Rawson 1976 (G 209) 90f: (but contrast Nicolet (ch. 16, p. 618) and Lintott, (ch. 2, p. 20).

[10] E.g. Cic. *Leg. Agr.* II.42 on Alexandria and Egypt ('dicitur . . . demigraturos in illa loca nostros homines propter agrorum bonitatem et omnium rerum copiam').

[11] Val. Max. IV.1.10 ('ut populi Romani res meliores amplioresque facerent'). The change to 'ut perpetuo incolumes servent', falsely attributed by Valerius to Scipio Aemilianus (cf. Cic. *De Or.* II.268), may be late-Augustan.

[12] Pontus: Plut. *Luc.* 35.5, Dio XXXVI.43.2. Egypt (Cyprus was part of the same bequest): Cic. *Leg. Agr.* II.41f, cf. II *Verr.* 2.76 for the alternative (recognizing Ptolemy Auletes).

[13] Polyb. VI.57.5f, cf. 9.5–9.

legislation.[14] The element of 'democracy' was thus weakened, to the advantage of the elements of 'kingship' and 'aristocracy', the consuls and the Senate. Not that the three categories of Greek political theory meant much to the Romans: they saw a simple polarity between plebs and *patres*,[15] with the latter having the upper hand. What many thought of the Senate in the seventies B.C. may be seen from a phrase – 'your cess-pit of a senate-house' – that happens to survive from a contemporary satire on elections.[16]

Other fragments of Varro's *Menippean Satires* confirm Cicero and Sallust on the senatorial elite's abuse of its power – venal judgements by praetors in Rome and proconsuls in the provinces; profiteering from Rome's allies by usury, extortion and looting; the abuse of public funds for private profit; luxury villas built and furnished out of illegal plunder; *ad hoc* dispensations from the laws passed by a handful of conniving senators; and wholesale bribery of jurors if ever the law *was* invoked. 'The habit of corruption gripped the city like a plague.'[17]

One man untainted by it was Cn. Pompeius Magnus.[18] In restoring the power of the tribunes, as in seeing to the election of censors, Pompey had advertised a return to the ways of the old Republic. For the ideological argument was developed in historical rather than theoretical terms: thanks to Licinius Macer's new history of early Rome, the Sullan suspension of the tribunes' rights could be seen as equivalent to the selfish rule of the patricians in the fifth century, before the First Secession of the plebs.[19] Now as then, the people's tribunes were to be the guarantors of legality and justice.[20]

Wherever he went in the years immediately following his consulship, Pompey was escorted by large and enthusiastic crowds. He did not appear much in public, however, preferring to keep a dignified and impressive distance from the actual business of politics. It was not for a *princeps* to concern himself with details. He would await his country's call.[21]

[14] Polyb. VI.14.6, 15.10; 16.4–5. The tribunes' and other magistrates' right to initiate popular trials must have been restored in 70, with their other powers. Note Cicero's threat to prosecute Verres as aedile in 69 if the *quaestio* absolved him (I *Verr* 36–40; II *Verr*. I. 14; 5. 151 and 173). See Lintott 1968 (A 62) 26–7.

[15] Sall. *H*. IV.45M.

[16] Varro *Sat. Men*. 452B (from 'Serranus περὶ ἀρχαιρεσιῶν'): 'hunc vocasset e liquida vita in curiae vestrae faecem'.

[17] Varro *Sat. Men*. 264, 378, 498–9B; Cic. *Verr. passim*, *Leg. Man*. 37f, 64–6; Asc. 57–9C, 72–3C; Sall. *Cat*. 12f, *H*. IV.46M ('qui quidem mos ut tabes in urbem coniectus').

[18] For example Cic. *Leg. Man*. 13, 36, 40–2, 66f (on his *temperantia*, *continentia*, *innocentia*), Plut. *Pomp*. 1.3, 18.2.

[19] Cic. *Corn*. fr. 49P (cf. I *Verr*. 35f, II *Verr*. 5.175 'regia ista vestra dominatio'); Sall. *H*. I.11M (cf. I.12M, III.48M, *Cat*. 12f for the equivalent in the seventies).

[20] Sall. *H*. III.48M (*oratio Macri*), esp. 1, 5, 9, 13, 20, 22 on *ius* and *iniuria*. Cf. Cic. *Corn*. fr. 35P on the tribunes' care for public resources, squandered by 'they know who'.

[21] Plut. *Pomp*. 23.3f; Sall. *H*. III.48.23M (*princeps*).

At the first elections after the *lustrum*, the sovereign people gave praetorships to two of the fighting tribunes of the seventies, Lucullus' enemy L. Quinctius and C. Licinius Macer the historian of the plebs. It passed a law giving the whole newly elected college of tribunes responsibility for road and street repairs – an area of public spending where men like Verres had gained *gratia* and made corrupt profits[22] – and when the new tribunes entered office on 10 December it approved a sumptuary law proposed by one of them to curb private luxury. One of the clauses prevented magistrates and magistrates-elect from accepting dinner-invitations, and Antius Restio himself, the author of the bill, never dined out again in his life.[23] A new and puritanical regime was being announced.

It was aimed at men like the great orator Q. Hortensius, who banqueted on peacocks and watered his plane-trees with wine, and L. Lucullus, whose palatial villa on the coast at Baiae was now nearing completion; both were famous for their wickedly expensive fish-ponds.[24] Hortensius was consul in 69; he had been assigned the command in Crete, but gladly yielded it to his colleague Q. Metellus. News of the sack of Delos by a pirate fleet underlined the urgency of the crisis, and added to Lucullus' unpopularity. As proconsul of Asia, Lucullus should have protected Delos; but he was a thousand miles to the east, picking up the plunder of Mithridates' retreat. The wealthy province of Asia was removed from Lucullus' command by popular vote and given to one of the praetors.[25]

The following year the attack continued. Lucullus' reports to the Senate made out that Mithridates was totally defeated, and yet the war went on. His soldiers were near to mutiny, and L. Quinctius was able to harangue the populace on Lucullus' protraction of the war to fill his own coffers. The sovereign assembly removed Cilicia from Lucullus' command, and gave it to the consul Q. Marcius Rex.

Cilicia was particularly important at this moment, because along with Crete (where Q. Metellus was now bogged down besieging Cnossus) it was the main base for the pirates. Their successes were becoming intolerable: all coastal Italy was at their mercy; seaborne commerce was cut off, including the city's corn supply; and when two of Quinctius' colleagues were kidnapped, complete with lictors and praetorian insignia, the situation became a national scandal.[26]

The consulship was competed for in 68 with particular intensity: there was clearly the chance of a big command if the tribunes had their way.

[22] *ILLRP* 465a (for the date, see Syme 1979–88 (A 119) II 560–3), cf. Cic. II *Verr.* 1.154 (*avaritia*).

[23] Macrob. *Sat.* III.17.13 ('bono publico'), Gell. *NA* II.24.13; Syme 1979–88 (A 119) II 563.

[24] Varro *Rust.* III.6.6, Macrob. *Sat.* III.13.3; Badian 1973 (C 164) 131f on Varro *Rust.* III.17.9, Phaedrus II.5.20.

[25] Dio XXXVI.2.2; Phlegon *FGrH* 257F12.13 (Delos).

[26] Cf. Dio XXXVI.27.2–3 (Gabinius' speech) on σπουδαρχία.

Wealth and ambition had reacted swiftly to the challenge of the expanded electorate. Already organized agencies were in being for the mass distribution of bribes to the voters, and certain senators were real experts in the art.[27] In the new jury-courts, however, potentially sympathetic senators were now outnumbered by *equites* and *tribuni aerarii* who could afford to take a strict moral line. So when C. Piso was charged with bribery at the consular elections, he made sure the case did not come to court by first buying off the prosecution in a deal worth 3 million sesterces.[28]

The non-senatorial jurymen were another unpredictable factor to result from the *lustrum*. The two lists they were drawn from originated with the censors, who had selected them for the eighteen equestrian centuries or assessed their property at (probably) over the 400,000 sesterces mark.[29] Both classes included for the first time the wealthy local aristocrats of ex-allied Italy, to some extent ideologically opposed to their social equals in the senatorial elite, but unwilling to be submerged into a citizen body that resented them. As jurymen, and as voters in the centuriate assembly, their status was satisfactorily visible. But at the games, those annual corporate manifestations of the Quirites, only the senators had formal seats of honour. Something had to be done for the *dignitas* of the class.

One of the tribunes of 67 was L. Roscius Otho from the Latin town of Lanuvium, whose family was newly rich from the commercial exploitation of empire.[30] He succeeded in persuading the assembly to reserve the first fourteen rows of theatre seating for gentlemen of equestrian rank, perhaps as defined by the 400,000 sesterces property qualification (doubtless in some way invoking 'the custom of our ancestors').[31] Two years later, Cicero alleged that the Roman people had 'demanded' the Lex Roscia – but that was before a jury, and Roscius' subsequent unpopularity with the plebs tells a different story.[32] A third body, neither plebs nor *patres*, had been legally defined; the *patres*' monopoly of visible honour had been broken.

Two of Roscius' colleagues, A. Gabinius and C. Cornelius, were making the running against senatorial corruption and incompetence. Gabinius' first proposal was to demobilize part of Lucullus' army and transfer the *provincia* of Bithynia and Pontus to one of the consuls of 67 – not the intransigent C. Piso, but his more flexible colleague Manius

[27] Asc. 75C, Q. Cic. *Comment. Pet.* 19, Dio XXXVI.38.2. [28] Dio XXXVI.38.3, Sall. *H.* IV.81M.

[29] 400,000 was the figure under Augustus, and perhaps already, for the *census equester*.

[30] *ILLRP* 1262 (lead mines, Carthago Nova).

[31] Cf. Wiseman 1987 (A 133) 79f on the 'restoration' of the right (Vell. Pat. II.32.3, Cic. *Mur.* 40), and on the equestrian census as the qualification (for example, Hor. *Epist.* I.1.62–7). Linderski (*CPh.* 72, 1977, 55–60) and Rawson 1987 (C 250) think there was a further qualification, jury service or a minor magistracy. [32] Cic. *Corn.* fr. 53P ('efflagitavit'); Plut. *Cic.* 13.

Glabrio. Gabinius exhibited in the Forum a painting of Lucullus' luxurious villa;[33] the populace took the point, and passed the bill that effectively stripped Lucullus of his great command.

Meanwhile, Cornelius was attacking the (largely senatorial) practice of lending money to deputations from abroad – a way of exploiting the empire financially without ever leaving Rome.[34] The provinces, as the irate tribune told a public meeting, were being bled dry by the interest charged by Roman profiteers. A Lex Gabinia on the subject, attested many years later, suggests that Cornelius' colleague may have collaborated with him on getting a law passed despite the Senate's opposition.[35]

Cornelius himself now widened the range of his attack on the Senate with a bill restating the old principle that no individual should be exempted from the operation of the laws except by popular vote. That is, no more helpful decrees passed by a few conniving fellow-senators without even a pretence of confirmation by the people. One of Cornelius' tribunician colleagues, a certain P. Servilius Globulus, was persuaded to resist this proposal. The people assembled to vote; the crier began to read out the terms of the bill at the clerk's dictation; Globulus forbade both crier and clerk to speak. Cornelius himself then read the text. C. Piso, the consul, protested furiously that Globulus' right of tribunician veto had been improperly infringed, but the assembly knew which of its tribunes was doing the obstructing, and shouted him down. Some made as if to grab him; Piso ordered his lictor to arrest them; the crowd seized the lictor's fasces and smashed them; stones were thrown; Cornelius properly dismissed the assembly. A heated meeting of the Senate followed, at which Cornelius won a majority for a compromise: a quorum of 200 senators to be present for any vote on an 'exemption', and confirmation by the people to be required, but no veto to be allowed. An abuse had been checked, and the Senate retained something of its authority; but what mattered more than the result was the way it had been achieved.

Similar scenes attended Gabinius' proposal about the pirate menace. His bill envisaged a three-year command over all the Mediterranean and its hinterlands up to fifty Roman miles from the sea – with fifteen legates, a fleet of 200 ships, and the right to levy troops and draw on the public treasury as necessary – to be entrusted to whichever of the ex-consuls the people saw fit. The tribune did not mention Pompey's name. There was no need; the crowd in the Forum knew who it had to be.

So did the senators. To give such powers to one man would be tantamount to setting up a monarchy. Piso the consul declared in the

[33] Cic. *Sest.* 93; cf. Asc. 80C for the technique (Cn. Ahenobarbus in 104 B.C.).

[34] On Cornelius' tribunate see Griffin 1973 (C 207) convincingly defending Asconius' chronology against that of Dio.

[35] Asc. 57–8C; Cic. *Att.* V.21.12, VI.1.5, 2.7.

Senate that those who acted like Romulus must expect the fate of Romulus (in one version of his legend, he was torn to pieces as a tyrant).[36] Were the events of 133 B.C. going to be played out again, with Piso in the role of Nasica? Some senators did indeed attack Gabinius as if to kill him, but he got out in time, and the enraged populace invaded the senate-house.

Pompey himself kept out of the dispute. When invited to address the people, he urged them to choose someone else and listened with apparent reluctance as Gabinius appealed to him to heed his country's call. The purpose of this little comedy, typical of the disingenuous Pompey, was to emphasize how far he differed from the office-seekers of the senatorial elite.

When the time came for the bill to be voted on (Pompey was discreetly away at his Alban villa) his opponents tried once more to use the tribunate against itself, this time with L. Trebellius and L. Roscius (the author of the *lex theatralis*). Trebellius tried to speak, and when Gabinius would not give him leave, used his veto to stop the vote. Furious, Gabinius postponed it and proposed a new one, to depose Trebellius from the office of tribune as Ti. Gracchus had deposed Octavius in 133. Now, as then, the issue was popular sovereignty; should the tribune's veto be allowed to obstruct the people's will? The tribes were called. Seventeen of the thirty-five had voted for deposition before Trebellius yielded at last and withdrew the veto.[37] As for Roscius, unable to make himself heard, he indicated by a gesture that two men should be chosen, not Pompey alone. A deafening shout of anger disposed of that argument.

Gabinius now called Catulus to the rostra. No friend of Pompey, but a man of great authority and a patriot, Catulus did not share the unpopularity of Lucullus and Hortensius.[38] The assembly would at least give him a hearing, and it was possible that in the face of such unanimity he might withdraw his opposition for the sake of political harmony. He spoke in praise of Pompey, but insisted (rightly enough) that such powers for a single man were both dangerous and unconstitutional. Besides, suppose Pompey were to be killed; whom would they put in his place? 'You!' roared the crowd. Gabinius' proposal was voted into law.

Consciously modest, Pompey entered the city by night. At a renewed meeting the enthusiastic populace voted him even more in men and resources than Gabinius had proposed. The price of corn fell sharply as

[36] Plut. *Pomp.* 25.4 ('one of the consuls').

[37] Cic. *Corn.* fr. 31P ('neque . . . passus est plus unius collegae sui quam universae civitatis vocem valere et voluntatem'); cf. Plut. *Ti. Gracch.* 15.2.–3, App. *BCiv.* I.12.51, 53; Badian 1989 (C 166).

[38] See n. 6 above. His villa at Cumae was not that of a *piscinarius* (no mention at Varro *Rust.* III.3.10, Pliny *HN* IX.170–2, Macrob. *Sat.* III.15.6).

the dealers anticipated the resumption of regular supplies; and Pompey left Rome to organize his forces.

But would the Gabinian plebiscite be allowed to work? C. Piso used all the advantages of the consular *imperium* to frustrate it, interfering with Pompey's equipment programme and obstructing his recruiting officers. Ever more urgently, the issue demanded a solution: where, in the last resort, did sovereignty lie? Gabinius had no doubts about the matter, and prepared a bill for the people to deprive Piso of his elected office. A constitutional crisis was only avoided by the arrival of Pompey himself, on a flying visit between the Ligurian harbours and Brundisium, where his fleet was assembling for the great sweep eastwards. Huge crowds flooded out along the Via Aurelia to escort him into the city, and the tribunes immediately arranged a public meeting for him (no doubt in the Circus Flaminius, outside the *pomoerium*) where he calmed the situation with a conciliatory speech.[39] There was no need for rash action against the consul; everyone could see that Pompey had overwhelming support in all sections of the citizen body. So the great man went on his way, to achieve the most spectacular of all his victories.

Amid these excitements, and aided no doubt by the fact that he had once served under Pompey as quaestor,[40] C. Cornelius was pursuing his campaign against the abuse of senatorial authority. Now he wanted to prevent magistrates from exempting themselves from their own juridical edicts. The praetor's edict, at the start of his year of office, was supposed to lay down the procedural principles of his jurisdiction, but what if he simply ignored it? The Romans well remembered the urban praetorship of Verres, when what mattered was not the wording of his edict but the whim of his mistress Chelidon.[41]

And what praetors did in Rome, proconsuls did in the provinces. The concern Cornelius had already shown for Rome's provincial subjects was equally evident in this proposal to control magistrates' discretion in jurisdiction, and thus restrict their opportunities for bribe-taking.[42] No doubt his case was helped by the news from Africa, where the patrician L. Sergius Catilina (a man with an ugly past in the Sullan years) was busy extorting the maximum profit from his province. A deputation came to complain of the proconsul's depredations, which the Senate duly deplored.[43] In that climate, even the most ambitious senator could hardly

[39] Plut. *Pomp.* 27.1f, cf. Dio XXXVI.37.2.

[40] Asc. 57C (presumably in Spain).

[41] Cic. II *Verr.* 1.120f; cf. *Corn.* frr. 37–8P, with Lintott 1977 (C 224) 184–6, for other notorious cases. Cornelius' law was 'the beginning of the end of praetorian creativity in freely reshaping private law on an annual basis': Frier 1983 (F 204) 230f (though much of the edict was of course always tralatician). See pp. 548–9.

[42] Dio XXXVI.40.3–41.1 shows that Cornelius was concerned with corrupt proconsuls.

[43] Cic. *Tog. Cand.* fr. 3P ('nec senatum respexit, cum gravissimis vestris decretis absens notatus est'), Asc. 85C.

complain about Cornelius' proposal, and it was voted into law without opposition.[44]

Not so, however, his law on electoral bribery. Here too there was an urgent need for strong action, as the agents who undertook to deliver the vote of the unpredictable new centuriate assembly were driven to violence and murder as the time of the elections approached. This year, it mattered particularly that the choice of the Roman people should not be frustrated. One of the candidates was M. Lollius Palicanus, who as tribune in 71, probably with Pompey's approval, had urged the restoration of the *tribunicia potestas*. (His candidature was not going well, so the tribunes made an issue of it by challenging Piso to say what he would do if the centuries elected Palicanus. 'If that happens', said Piso, 'I will not declare the result.')[45] Cornelius therefore proposed a bribery law, including very severe penalties against agents as well as candidates.

The Senate, however, perhaps accepting the counter-argument that such penalties would deter juries from convicting, instructed the consuls to introduce a milder measure in their own name. Since this did not include penalties for agents, Cornelius and his colleagues insisted that it would prove ineffectual, and the continuing disturbances proved them right. Twice the praetorian elections had to be abandoned even after the centuries' votes had been announced.[46] Although legislation was not allowed in the period after the announcement of the elections, in this crisis the Senate voted a special dispensation to Piso to put forward a tougher version of his law, with penalties for agents reinstated. But when he came to propose it, hostile gangs chased him out of the Forum and he had to ask the Senate for a stronger bodyguard. (Glabrio, the other consul, had probably left for the East by now.)

The situation was full of ironies. Piso, who had bribed his way to the consulship the year before, was now sponsoring a bribery law which would deprive convicted men of all senatorial privileges, even the *ius imaginum*.[47] The consul who had had his fasces broken opposing Cornelius earlier in the year was now doing Cornelius' work for him. The defiant upholder of senatorial authority was now beset by gangs of men determined to corrupt the elections in the interest of ambitious senators. It was against them, not against a popular tribune and his supporters, that Piso now echoed the words of Nasica in 133 B.C., calling those who wished to save the Republic to come to vote for the bribery

44 Asc. 59C ('nemo repugnare ausus est, multis tamen invitis').

45 Val. Max. III.8.3. Gabinius was married to a Lollia (Suet. *Iul.* 50.1), perhaps Palicanus' daughter.

46 Cic. *Leg. Man.* 2; cf. *Att.* I.11.2 on the *iniquitates* of the praetorian elections.

47 Cic. *Sull.* 88; cf. *Mur.* 46 on the Lex Calpurnia, 'severissime scripta'.

bill.[48] The people did his bidding, and the Lex Calpurnia was passed – a moral victory for Cornelius.

When the elections were finally held, Lollius Palicanus did not win his consulship. The centuriate assembly preferred two worthy lightweights, Manius Lepidus and L. Volcacius Tullus. The latter result (Tullus came from a municipal family) evidently revealed the influence of the post-69 membership of the centuries of the *equites* and the *prima classis*.[49] So too did the success of M. Tullius Cicero of Arpinum, the first senator of his family but elected praetor at the top of the poll, to the embarrassment of his aristocratic competitors.[50] The Roman people might sneer at Cicero as an over-Hellenized intellectual,[51] but they knew him also as a brilliant forensic orator, and remembered his devastating attack on senatorial corruption in the Verres case. It was not only his wealthy equestrian friends whom Cicero had to thank for his election, and he made sure the Roman crowd knew he was grateful.[52] He probably never wavered, however, in his conservative conviction that the Senate should rule – in upright and conciliatory fashion, of course, and co-operating with the *equites* in defence of property and order.

After the elections, Cornelius kept up the pressure for reform, but without result.[53] The last few months of the year were always a dull period in Roman politics, as attention was concentrated on what might be expected from the incoming magistrates. Cornelius therefore handed over one of his pet projects to C. Manilius,[54] who would be entering his tribunate on 10 December. This was the restoration of P. Sulpicius' law (repealed by Sulla) allowing freedmen to vote in the tribe of their patron, rather than being confined to the four urban tribes. Since many freedmen were men of wealth,[55] that would alter the composition of the voting units in the centuries as well as the tribal assembly, with unpredictable results for the consular elections. There would certainly be fierce opposition, so it was better to leave the bill to a fresh tribune with his whole year of office before him.

For it was clear that the tribunes' political initiative would continue. The great news of Pompey's total success against the pirates seemed to

[48] Cic. *Corn.* fr. 46P ('at enim extremi et difficillimi temporis vocem illam, C. Corneli, consulem mittere coegisti: qui rem p. salvam esse vellent, ad legem accipiendam adessent'); cf. Val. Max. III.2.17, Vell. Pat. II.3.1, Plut. *Ti. Gracch.* 19.3.

[49] On the Volcacii see Wiseman 1971 (A 130) 276f (*contra*, Syme 1979–88 (A 119) II 603f on the *origo*); on Lepidus see Sumner 1964 (C 268) 87.

[50] Cic. *Tog. Cand.* frr. 5, 23P (C. Antonius); the others were L. Cassius Longinus and (probably) P. Sulpicius Galba.

[51] Plut. *Cic.* 5.2 (apparently referring to the seventies B.C.).

[52] Cic. *Leg. Man.* 71 ('me hoc honore praeditum, tantis vestris beneficiis adfectum'), cf. 2, 58, 69.

[53] Asc. 59C ('per quas contentiones totius tribunatus eius tempus peractum est').

[54] So at least it was alleged at his trial: Cic. *Corn.* fr. 10P.

[55] Dio LI.10.4, cf. App. *BCiv.* IV.34.146; examples in Treggiari 1969 (G 247) 239f.

confirm and ratify all that had been achieved in this *annus mirabilis* of the restored tribunician power. It may not have been coincidence that one of the tribunes just elected for 66 was the nephew and namesake of C. Memmius, scourge of the corrupt nobility forty-five years before.[56] The Sullan reaction had been effectively reversed.

But the Sullan oligarchy was powerful and tenacious, with an influence both inside and outside the Senate quite disproportionate to its small numbers. Piso had been a formidable opponent; if he had failed, that was mainly due to the talismanic presence of Pompeius Magnus, an advantage next year's tribunes would not enjoy. And Piso had been too openly the champion of indefensible privilege, too blatantly moved by anger and envy against Pompey.[57] If the oligarchs, however speciously, could regain the moral initiative, then all the hopes of the new *lustrum* would be dashed.

III. POMPEY'S ABSENCE

Manilius did everything wrong. When the tribunes entered office on 10 December, he tried to exploit the absence of consular opposition (Piso had no doubt left for his province) by pushing through the bill on freedmen's votes before the new consuls took office on 1 January. But he did it by not allowing the full statutory period to elapse between the promulgation of the law and the voting on it; and the day of the vote itself, at the end of the year, was the day announced by the praetor for the movable festival of the Compitalia, when no voting asssemblies should be held.[58] Not only that, but he used his enthusiastic crowd of supporters (slaves as well as freedmen, his enemies said) to block off access to the Forum, thus enabling one of the new quaestors to make a name for himself by charging through with a gang of his own, killing with impunity since the victims were in the wrong.[59] On the first day of the new year the Senate, with a clear conscience, declared the law invalid.

Popular frustration was made worse by the news from the East. Glabrio, sent by the Roman people to finish the war Lucullus was prolonging, had discovered that there was much more to do than just take the glory, and halted in Bithynia. Mithridates had taken full advantage, and it seemed the war was slipping out of Rome's control. Would Asia be threatened again? The financiers were getting anxious, and that meant dearer credit for the ordinary citizen.[60] Meanwhile, in

[56] Sall. *Iug.* 27.2, 30.3; stemma in Sumner 1973 (B 115) 87.

[57] Plut. *Pomp.* 27.1; cf. Dio XXXVI.26.1f (Pompey's speech), 33.3 (Catulus' speech).

[58] Cic. *Corn.* fr. 11P ('celeritas actionis'), Asc, 65C, Dio XXXVI.42.4f; Gell. *NA* X.24.3 (praetor), Varro *Ling.* VI.20 (no voting).

[59] Asc. 45C (L. Ahenobarbus, praised for *constantia*).

[60] Cf. Cic. *Leg. Man.* 18f ('non enim possunt una in civitate multi rem ac fortunas amittere, ut non plures secum in eandem trahant calamitatem').

Crete, Roman commanders were even fighting each other, as Metellus disputed the authority of Pompey's legates to operate in his province. (It is not clear whether Pompey's *imperium* had been defined as equal or superior to that of other proconsuls; if the latter, it was a new and ominous step.)[61]

The solution was obvious, and Manilius immediately proposed it. Lucullus should be recalled from Pontus, Glabrio from Bithynia, Marcius Rex from Cilicia; all the Roman forces in Asia Minor, and the whole conduct of the war, should be entrusted to Pompey. Lucullus' friends protested, but in vain. Catulus and Hortensius held out in determined opposition, as they had against Gabinius the year before; but this time, in the light of Pompey's brilliant success against the pirates, it was even harder to make their case. Four ex-consuls, including P. Servilius the conqueror of Isauria, supported the proposal;[62] so did the praetor M. Cicero, in his first ever speech from the rostra.

Cicero was polite about Lucullus, as he was also to Catulus and Hortensius (he would need at least their acquiescence when he came to stand for the consulship), but the main theme of his eloquence gave the thronging citizens in the Forum exactly what they wanted to hear. It was *their* empire and *their* revenues that were in danger; *they* had ended the pirate menace by putting Pompey in charge; magistrates and commanders were elected to do *their* bidding, not make private fortunes for themselves. Pompey, of couse, was not only a military genius but also a man who could keep his hands off other people's property, including their wives and children.[63] Manilius' law passed, without any of the strife that had attended the vote on the pirate command.

Pompey's enemies had hoped to get Gabinius before a jury, *pour décourager les autres*. That was now impossible (Gabinius left Rome and is next heard of east of the Euphrates),[64] but C. Cornelius was still available for prosecution. P. Cominius and his brother, men of equestrian rank from the former Latin colony of Spoletium, charged Cornelius before the treason court. On the day set for the trial, the praetor failed to appear, leaving the Cominii to face ugly threats against their lives if they did not drop the charge. The consuls, who had come to the Forum to support Cornelius, prevented murder being done, but the prosecutors were chased into some nearby premises. The following day the praetor appeared but the prosecutors did not. Some said the Cominii had been bribed to abandon the case. They had certainly been terrorized.[65]

The claims of the tribunes and their supporters to represent law and

61 Velleius (II.31, 2) calls it 'imperium aequum . . . cum pro consulibus'.

62 Cic. *Leg. Man.* 68; the others were C. Curio cos. 76, C. Cassius cos. 73, Cn. Lentulus cos. 72.

63 Cic. *Leg. Man.* 63f, 65f; see n. 18 above.

64 Dio XXXVII.5.2 (as a legate of Pompey).

65 Asc. 59–60C, Cic. *Corn.* frr. 13–17P.

justice suffered another setback when C. Licinius Macer – the ideologue, as it were, of the restored tribunate – was found guilty of extortion on return from the province which he governed after his praetorship of 68. Cicero was the presiding praetor. As he wrote to his friend Atticus, 'my handling of C. Macer's case has won popular approval to a quite extraordinary degree. Though I was favourably disposed to him, I gained far more from popular sentiment by his conviction than I could have gained from *his* gratitude if he had been acquitted.' Macer had let the Roman people down. When he heard the verdict, he killed himself.[66]

That juries and magistrates alike were taking a particularly strict line is suggested also by the extraordinary events at this year's consular elections. The successful candidates were P. Sulla and P. Autronius Paetus; Sulla was Pompey's brother-in-law, which no doubt outweighed his hated name.[67] But once again the campaign had been corrupt, and the two losers, L. Torquatus and L. Cotta, prosecuted Sulla and Autronius for bribery.[68] Violent disturbances broke out, but the juries defied the stone-throwers and condemned both the consuls-elect.[69]

The vote had to be held again, and this time there might be a new candidate. L. Catilina, who had just returned from Africa, still dogged by provincial embassies complaining about his depredations there, announced that he would be seeking election. A trial for extortion seemed certain – but who would prosecute? The Senate believed him guilty, and passed stern resolutions about it; but Catiline was tough and ruthless; it would take a brave man to make an enemy of him. Besides, he had the support of the deposed consuls-elect and their strong-arm men. If he were elected, or even allowed to stand, it would be a deplorable victory for corruption over the rule of law. Volcacius Tullus, the presiding consul, called his advisers and decided not to allow Catiline's candidature.[70] Cotta and Torquatus were duly declared elected.

There were other bribery trials that year; the 'struggle for office' (a phrase that was now more than a mere metaphor) was not confined to consular candidates. A certain L. Vargunteius was also found guilty, despite being defended by Hortensius.[71] The strictness of the juries

66 Cic. *Att.* I.4.2 (trans. Shackleton Bailey), Val. Max. IX.12.7, Plut. *Cic.* 9.1f.

67 According to Dio (XXXVI.44.3) he was the dictator's nephew; Cicero (*Off.* II.29) says merely 'propinquus'. The relationship with Pompey is inferred from a combination of Oros. V.23.12 and Cic. *QFr.* III.3.2.

68 It was Torquatus' son, later praetor 49, who prosecuted Sulla on his father's behalf (Cic. *Fin.* II.62).

69 Cic. *Sull.* 15 ('ille ambitus iudicium tollere ac disturbare primum conflato voluit gladiatorum ac fugitivorum tumultu, deinde, id quod vidimus omnes, lapidatione atque concursu') – blaming Autronius alone for forensic reasons.

70 Cic. *Tog. Cand.* fr. 16P, Asc. 89C, cf. Sall. *Cat.* 18.2f; Torquatus ap. Cic. *Sull.* 68 ('dixisti hunc, ut Catilinam consulem efficeret, contra patrem tuum operas et manum comparasse') – blaming Sulla alone for forensic reasons.

71 Cic. *Sull.* 6, cf. Sall. *Cat.* 28.1 and Linderski 1963 (C 219). For the *honoris certamen*,. Cic. *Sull.* 49.

reflected popular feeling, but the clean-up of public life had perilous consequences. It left dangerously ambitious men looking for a way – any way – to recover their position and recoup their wasted fortune, in a society where poverty and discontent offered easy opportunities to recruit armed bands for violent action.[72]

In the latter part of the year attention was concentrated on the return of Lucullus, which his enemies were eager to publicize as the deserved humiliation of an archetypal profiteer. Memmius the tribune had already prepared the way with a prosecution of Lucullus' brother Marcus for his acts as quaestor under Sulla in 83. Lucullus himself, a close friend of the dictator, had been guardian of his son Faustus Sulla (now of age), who was the most conspicuous of all the beneficiaries of the Sullan regime and from whom frequent attempts had already been made to recover the public moneys that had found their way into the family funds.[73] But Faustus' twin sister was married to Memmius.[74] So an unfriendly colleague was able simultaneously to win popular applause, embarrass Memmius, and take some of the pressure off Lucullus, by bringing an action against Faustus for embezzlement of public funds. Cicero, as praetor, gave it as his opinion that the principle was excellent but the time not ripe; the jury of the *quaestio de peculatu* took the view that the tribunician power gave too great an advantage to the prosecution, and did not allow the case to continue.[75]

It may have been for the same reason that M. Lucullus was acquitted, and that Memmius' threat to prosecute Lucullus himself came to nothing. Similarly, it seems that young P. Clodius, who was Lucullus' brother-in-law and the main agitator behind the mutiny in his army at Nisibis, had been threatening both the Luculli with prosecution, but to no effect.[76] Eager to stamp on real abuse, juries were evidently unwilling to act merely as the agents of private feuds. Lucullus knew the proper way to deal with Clodius; as soon as he reached home he divorced his wife in circumstances that brought the maximum discredit on her brother.[77]

What mattered most was the question of his triumph. This was a straightforward ideological issue between plebs and *patres*: a majority in the Senate was willing to give Lucullus his due, but the assembly, at

[72] See Brunt 1971 (A 16) 551–7 for the background. E.g. Cic. *Sull.* 15 (gladiators and *fugitivi*, 66), Suet. *Iul.* 10.2 (gladiators, 65), Cic. *Tog. Cand.* fr. 12P (*fugitivi*, 64), *Sull.* 54 (gladiators, 63), Sall. *Cat.* 56.5 (*fugitivi*, 63), Suet. *Aug.* 3.1 (*fugitivi*, 61).

[73] Plut. *Luc.* 4.4 (guardian), 38.1 (Memmius); Cic. *Leg. Agr.* 1.12, Asc. 73C ('res saepe erat agitata').

[74] Joseph. *BJ* 1.149, 154 (Faustus under Pompey in 63); Asc. 28C (Fausta).

[75] Cic. *Clu.* 94, *Corn.* fr. 34P, Asc. 73C; tribune not named, but 'non modo non seditiosus sed etiam seditiosis adversarius'.

[76] Memmius: Plut. *Cat. Min.* 29.3. Clodius: Cic. *Har. Resp.* 42 ('Romaeque recenti adventu suo cum propinquis suis decidit ne reos faceret').

[77] Cic. *Mil.* 73, cf. for example, Plut. *Luc.* 34.1, *Cic.* 29.3 (evidence of incest).

Memmius' urging against the man who had prolonged the war for his own enrichment, refused to allow it. The same treatment was given to Q. Metellus Creticus (as he now called himself), who had defied Pompey, and to Q. Marcius Rex as well.[78] The presence of these three nobles in the suburbs, tending their fading laurels and doubtless feeding as many of their loyal soldiers as might make a decent procession if ever their triumphs could be authorized, was a potent and humiliating symbol of the tribunes' power and the authority of the people.

Their friends were waiting for December, when Manilius' tribunate would come to an end and he would lose immunity from prosecution. The charge – extortion, possibly as quaestor[79] – was well chosen, calling Manilius to account not for his contentious tribunate, a matter that might divide a jury on political lines, but for misbehaviour in the provinces, on which they could be expected to take a unanimously severe view.[80] The prosecutors made their denunciation to Cicero, the praetor in charge of the *quaestio de repetundis*, on 27 December. Instead of allowing the usual ten days for the defence to seek legal advice, Cicero set the start of the trial for 29 December, the last day of his year of office. Summoned by the tribunes to explain himself before the indignant populace, Cicero protested that he had been trying to help Manilius; the praetor in charge next year might not be so sympathetic. Then Cicero assured the people, in a rousing attack on Pompey's enemies, that he would now be glad to appear in Manilius' defence.

The Forum was full of whispered rumours. Catiline was there, visibly armed. Some said, or said later, that Sulla and Autronius intended to murder the new consuls and appear in the Forum, complete with lictors, in the office they had lost in the courts.[81] That did not happen. Cotta and Torquatus duly entered on their consulship, but the rumours persisted, centred now on Catiline and a tough young aristocrat called Cn. Piso. A *coup d'état* was supposedly scheduled for 5 February. That did not happen either, but the Senate took it seriously enough to give the consuls a bodyguard. One of the tribunes vetoed a senatorial investigation. Piso, though only an ex-quaestor, was sent off to Spain with praetorian *imperium*.[82]

It was in this uneasy atmosphere that Manilius was brought to trial in

[78] Cic. *Acad.* II.3 (Lucullus), Sall. *Cat.* 30.4.

[79] Cic. *Corn.* fr. 8P; on Manilius' trial, see Phillips 1970 (C 236). Ramsey 1980 (C 239) thinks M. was prosecuted under the heading *quo ea pecunia*, in which case he need not have been a magistrate.

[80] Cf. Cic. *Clu.* 116: juries treated extortion like treason when assessing damages.

[81] Cic. *Cat.* I.15 (Catilina *cum telo*), *Sull.* 11, 68; cf. Suet. *Iul.* 9.1f, Sall. *Cat.* 18.5.

[82] Cic. *Tog. Cand.* fr. 22P (with Asc. 92C), *Mur.* 81; Dio XXXVI. 44.4f; Sall. *Cat.* 18.6–19.1 (giving the date); *ILLRP* 378. Later in the year, one of the consuls by appearing for Catiline at his trial indicated that he disbelieved the rumours (Cic. *Sull.* 81). Most modern scholars are also sceptical about this so-called 'First Catilinarian Conspiracy'; see esp. Seager 1964 (C 256).

January. Cicero, as promised, appeared for the defence. But Manilius' friends preferred more direct methods, and broke up the court by force.[83] The Senate instructed the consuls to guarantee security; the trial resumed; Manilius failed to appear, and was found guilty. The violence and rumours of violence in late 66 and early 65 were later to provide Cicero and others with ammunition to use against Catiline, and led to the stories of a preliminary Catilinarian conspiracy that never came to fruition.

What the sorry tale of recent events revealed was the fallibility of the people's champions. Twenty-five years later an experienced politician described the newly aggressive tribunate of the sixties as marking the start of a period when the protectors of the people's rights were as selfish and ambitious as the aristocratic 'establishment' which defended its own supremacy in the name of the Senate. Both sides were brutal and extreme; it was only Pompey's absence which gave the oligarchy the tactical advantage.[84] That was perhaps too schematically cynical; but certainly the loss of the moral initiative was a blow to popular confidence.

As a direct result of Manilius' débâcle, the prosecutors of Cornelius were emboldened to resume the case they had abandoned the previous year. Cornelius, once again facing the *quaestio de maiestate*, did not dare to have more than a few supporters with him for fear of giving his enemies the chance to allege a riot. Against him was ranged the full weight of senior senatorial authority – Catulus, Hortensius, Metellus Pius, M. Lucullus, the *princeps senatus* Mam. Lepidus – all prepared to testify that Cornelius two years before had read out the terms of his bill in defiance of a tribune's veto. *They* were now the defenders of the people's rights![85]

Even more conscious than usual of the crowd in the Forum surrounding the court, Cicero in his defending speech met the challenge head on: the *principes* were trying to exploit the effect of Manilius' behaviour, and the absence of Pompey, to humble the plebs and tarnish the whole concept of tribunician power. Manilius, he claimed, had been urged on by powerful and unscrupulous individuals like Catiline and Cn. Piso. But the great cause of the people's tribunes remained unsullied – and he took his audience through the whole heroic history of the tribunate, from the First Secession to their own time.[86] He was tactful but firm with the distinguished witnesses: was Cornelius to be sacrificed to the hostility of a few men of wealth and power, and their contemptible hangers-on? The jury must take thought for the liberty of Roman citizens, and for the man

[83] Cic. *Corn.* frr. 12, 19P; Asc. 60C.

[84] Sall. *Cat.* 38.1–39.1, describing the conflict in terms of plebs and *patres* (cf. n. 15 above).

[85] Asc. 60–1C ('etenim prope tollebatur intercessio, si id tribunis permitteretur').

[86] Cic. *Corn.* frr. 48, 19, 49–53P; the speech is reconstructed by Kumaniecki 1970 (B 60) 10–29.

who had called the people to the struggle against a cruel tyranny.[87] Cornelius, personally respectable and a protégé of Pompey's, was acquitted; the fact that all ten tribunes of the year supported him suggests that they really did see the tribunate itself as in danger.

Soon the plebs had something else to cheer. At the start of the first of the annual series of public festivals (*ludi Megalenses*, 4 April), the aediles' decorations of the city centre were seen to include gilded monuments to the victories of Marius, banned from public sight for seventeen years. This was the work of C. Julius Caesar, who was busy spending a fortune of his creditors' money on building a popular reputation. He was already well known for public-spirited generosity as curator of the Via Appia; now his aedilician games, and a gladiatorial show on his own account, were of a splendour that put his optimate colleague M. Bibulus wholly in the shade. Caesar had earlier caught public attention with his funeral speech for his aunt, Marius' widow, and he had gone out of his way to cultivate the inhabitants of the Transpadane region, where Marian veterans had been settled a generation before, and where the natives, and perhaps some early settlers of Italian origin, were aggrieved at not having full Roman citizenship.[88]

Catulus, whose *dignitas* suffered particularly as a result of the rehabilitation of Marius, accused Caesar in the Senate of bringing battering-rams to bear on the Republican constitution.[89] His words may seem unnecessarily portentous, but Rome was in a nervous and unsettled mood. Freak thunderstorms during the winter had done some damage on the Capitol, with lightning striking even a bronze image of the she-wolf. The *haruspices* consulted their volumes of Etruscan brontoscopy, and warned of fire, plague and destruction, the abolition of law (some bronze law texts had been struck by lightning) and civil disruption at the hands of 'men of noble birth'.[90] Catiline? P. Sulla? Cn. Piso? Caesar? Or perhaps P. Lentulus Sura, consul in 71, expelled by the censors and now rebuilding his career, who believed that the Sibyl's verses prophesied supreme power for three Cornelii – Cinna, Sulla and himself.[91] At the *haruspices'* suggestion, the consuls ordered a splendid new statue of Jupiter to be placed high on a column on the Capitol. They also announced that elections for the censorship would be held; the time was due for a new *lustrum*.

Meanwhile a tribune, C. Papius, put to the vote an 'aliens act' designed to expel from Rome (no doubt temporarily) non-citizens pretending that

[87] Cic. *Corn.* II frr. 1–4, 11–14P; Kumaniecki 1970 (B 60) 30–3.

[88] See Crawford 1985 (B 145) 183; Wiseman 1987 (A 133) 329–31. The Transpadanes were mostly Latins, which meant that their ex-magistrates had Roman citizenship; see pp. 75–6.

[89] Plut. *Caes.* 6.4; cf. n. 6 above. The law making Marius a public enemy was still technically valid.

[90] Cic. *Div.* I.20, *Cat.* III.19.

[91] Cic. *Cat.* III.9, 11; Sall. *Cat.* 47.2; Plut. *Cic.* 17.4.

they had the Roman franchise; and a new *quaestio* was set up to investigate this kind of fraud. Preventing the usurpation of citizenship, especially with elections approaching, could seem another blow against corruption. The bill may however have been chiefly aimed at the Transpadani, and thus at Caesar; an ambiguous passage of the historian Cassius Dio prevents us being sure of the object.[92]

One man who would not be standing in the elections was Catiline. His trial for extortion had finally been arranged, and his condemnation was confidently expected. But the prosecutor, young P. Clodius, was helpfully selective in the challenging of the jury, and the resulting panel looked as if they were quite willing to be impressed by Catiline's distinguished character witnesses – several *consulares* (Catulus was an old friend), and even one of this year's consuls, L. Torquatus, complete with curule chair and insignia of office. Seeing this, Cicero offered to appear for the defence; if Catiline was going to be acquitted, and therefore able to stand at next year's consular elections when Cicero himself would be a candidate, it would be worth having him under an obligation. But Catiline perhaps saw that too, and was confident of acquittal without Cicero's help.[93]

This year's elections passed off without incident. The consuls for 64 would be L. Caesar (a distant cousin of the aedile) and C. Marcius Figulus.[94] The censors, who entered office immediately on election, were Catulus and Crassus. It is a sign both of the inadequacy of our sources and of the unobtrusiveness of his political style that we hear practically nothing of Crassus between consulship and censorship. He had given his support to Manilius (who tried to blame him for the tactical fiasco of December 67); to Licinius Macer; and perhaps also to Catiline and Cn. Piso in the early months of 65.[95] But of where he stood on the great issues of the day, especially as they affected his old rival and enemy Pompey, we know nothing. All we can be sure of is that he was a man of great influence, whom nobody liked to cross.[96]

The censors did not agree on a programme. Crassus wanted the Transpadani included in the *lustrum* as Roman citizens. Catulus refused to consider it (it would have given Crassus and Caesar great *gratia*). Crassus wanted Ptolemy Alexander's testament recognized and Egypt

92 Dio XXXVII.9.5; cf. Gruen 1974 (C 209) 409–11.

93 Cic. *Att.* I.1.1, 2.1, with Phillips 1970 (B 86); *Har. Resp.* 42, *Pis.* 23 (Clodius as 'Catilinae praevaricator'); *Sull.* 81 (Torquatus), *Cael.* 13f (distinguished friends); cf. Oros. VI.3.1, Sall. *Cat.* 35 (Catulus).

94 Caesar. Sumner 1976 (C 270) for the relationship. Figulus: possibly identical with the (Minucius) Thermus of Cic. *Att.* I.1.2; see Shackleton Bailey *ad loc.*

95 Dio XXXVI.42.3; Plut. *Cic.* 9.1f; Cic. *de consiliis suis* (on which see Rawson 1982 (B 94)) ap. Asc. 85C, 92C, cf. Suet. *Iul.* 9.1f. He was also a juror in the Cornelius trial (Asc. 76C).

96 E.g. Plut. *Crass.* 7.9 (76 B.C.), Sall. *Cat.* 48.5 (63), Cic. *Att.* I.18.6 ('Crassus verbum nullum contra gratiam', 60).

and Alexandria annexed under direct Roman rule (see ch. 8*a*, p. 271; 8*c*, p. 319). Catulus strongly objected. The latter proposal was urged by the tribunes – great new revenues for the Roman people, and perhaps a new command for Pompey when he had finished with Mithridates. Crassus assured them that it would be a just war, like that against Jugurtha (remember Marius!), but his opponents successfully represented it as mere profiteering. 'Shall this be our imperial policy', demanded Cicero, who always deplored Crassus' greed, 'to make allies of those who give us money, and enemies of those who do not?'[97] Unwilling to prolong a political stalemate, the censors resigned.

Like Manilius' trial, the Alexandrian issue enabled the Senate to show itself as the champion of sound moral standards. Despite the encouragement of Cicero's splendid oratory in the speech *pro Cornelio*, the popular movement was in danger of losing its way – not just because its leaders were fallible, and its great symbolic champion far away, but also because the nature of its struggle was changing. The old polarities – plebs and *patres*, *libertas* and *dominatio* – seemed less applicable when the laws were being flouted by ruthlessly ambitious younger men with their fortunes still to make, whose anti-establishment rhetoric carried a specious attraction for the under-privileged of Rome. Among the consequences was Cicero's shift, not away from Pompey, but towards the Senate. He did not trust either Crassus or Caesar.

One symptom of the way things were going was the exploitation of district and trade associations (*collegia*) as a basis for electoral violence and bribery. No tribune could hope to get the assembly to ban the organizations around which most humble citizens' social life revolved. Effectively, the populace was now conniving in the corruption of public life which its tribunes had set out to curb five years earlier. The consuls of 64 had to rely on a *senatus consultum* to disband the *collegia*.[98] When they proposed a new and more severe bribery law, it was vetoed by a tribune.[99] And when they had censors elected – to carry out what Crassus and Catulus had failed to achieve, the moral cleansing of the Roman state in the eyes of the gods – the tribunes were afraid of expulsion from the Senate, and forced the censors' abdication. There would be no *lustrum*, no new start – and now it was the people's champions who prevented it.

IV. THE PEASANTS' REVOLT AND THE BANKRUPTS' PLOT

It may be ultimately to Licinius Macer's indignant pen that we owe a vignette from Rome's 'usable past': an episode attributed to the fifteenth

[97] Cic. *De Reg. Alex.* frr. 1–2, 6–7P, *Leg. Agr.* II.44; Plut. *Crass.* 13.1. Tribunes: Suet. *Iul.* 11.1 (alleging Caesar's involvement).

[98] Asc. 7C; cf. Lintott 1968 (A 62) 77–83, and Treggiari 1969 (G 247) 168–77.

[99] Cic. *Tog. Cand.* fr. 14P, Asc. 83C ('cum in dies licentia ambitus augeretur'): Q. Mucius Orestinus.

year of the Republic, portraying the misery of a gallant old soldier who had lost his land through no fault of his own, fallen into debt and been seized by a creditor, to be hauled off to a slave-prison and beaten.[100] For the sixties B.C., that was not just melodrama. A poor citizen farming far beyond the limit of the tribunes' *auxilium* at the first milestone might well have bitter experience of the *ergastulum* and the *carnificina* when bad harvests or bad health, his own misjudgements or rich neighbours' chicanery or violence, forced him to borrow or, if a tenant, fall behind with the rent. Many were old soldiers, even Sullan colonists; for the veterans of Sulla's legions must not be confused with the great profiteers of the proscriptions, whose estates covered whole territories.[101] Fifteen years on, some of the veteran settlers were as desperate as the peasants they had dispossessed, with the added resentment of disappointed hopes. All were equally at the mercy of the man who was both landowner and money-lender, with little chance of relief from the praetor's tribunal. Worst affected were the small farmers of Etruria, north-west Italy (Picenum and the *ager Gallicus*) and Apulia – all areas with a high concentration of Sullan colonies.[102]

Two other types of indebtedness combined with this rural crisis to bring about what the *haruspices* had foretold. One was the vicious circle of usury in the provinces – borrowing from Roman financiers to pay Rome's tribute and bribe her governors – which Cornelius had tried to control as tribune in 67. His opponent on that occasion, the consul C. Piso, had spent the last two years as proconsul of the two Gauls; now in 64 he was succeeded in Transalpina by L. Murena. Piso had been brutal in extortion; Murena was strict in enforcing repayments to Roman money-lenders, but turned a blind eye to the illegal profits of his own staff. The result was to drive to desperation the Allobroges of Transalpine Gaul, 'overwhelmed by public and private debt'.[103]

A very different type of debt problem was caused by the ruthlessly competitive ambition of certain senators, who borrowed hugely in order to bribe their way to the consulships and provincial commands that would make their fortunes, to cover their inevitably large legitimate political expenses, or to build grand palaces and villas and in other ways keep up with new standards of luxury. They were landowners, but what

100 Livy II.23.3–7, Dion. Hal. *Ant. Rom.* VI.26.1–2; cf. Sall. *H.* III.48.27M (Macer on flogging and imprisonment of *agrestes*).

101 E.g. Cic. *Leg. Agr.* III.8 on C. Quinctius Valgus and the *ager Hirpinus*; cf. *ILLRP* 523, 565, 598, 645–6. See Brunt 1971 (A 16) 300–12, 1988 (C 30) 250f.

102 Cic. *Cat.* II.6, *Sull.* 53, *Sest.* 9; Sall. *Cat.* 27.1, 30.2–5, 42.1, and esp. 28.4 for an analysis of the situation in Etruria. Sullan colonies (pp. 203–5 above): for Apulia, cf. Hor. *Sat.* I.6.73 (Venusia), *ILLRP* 592 (Ausculum).

103 Sall. *Cat.* 40.1. Piso: Sall. *Cat.* 49.2; Cic. *Att.* I.13.2 ('pacificatorem Allobrogum', surely ironical). Murena: Cic. *Mur.* 42, cf. 69 for the approval of the *societates*. Staff: Cic. *Har. Resp.* 42 on P. Clodius ('mortuorum testamenta conscripsit, pupillos necavit, nefarias cum multis scelerum pactiones societatesque conflavit').

they needed was ready cash in large sums; and they were not prepared to sell their estates (which provided the property-qualification on which their status depended) if their creditors insisted on repayment.[104] Two notorious examples – C. Antonius and L. Catilina – were among the candidates at the consular elections in 64. Not surprisingly they fought a very dirty campaign.[105]

Only three of the seven candidates – Antonius, Catiline, and Cicero – had a realistic chance of success, so the two nobles pooled their resources to defeat the 'new man'. Cicero fought back with a blistering attack on their moral credentials. One well-attested episode he emphasized particularly – the brutal murder of the popular hero M. Marius Gratidianus, whose severed head Catiline had supposedly brought through the streets of Rome to give to Sulla.[106]

The reminder came at an opportune time. For years now Sulla's executioners had enjoyed their rewards without fear of prosecution, sheltering behind an exemption clause in the Lex Cornelia, while many of his friends had directly acquired confiscated property, which should have been auctioned for the treasury's benefit. But this year the president of the *quaestio de sicariis* (which dealt with assassins, see ch. 13, pp. 521–3) was Caesar, whose own anti-Sullan record was unimpeachable, and the *quaestor urbanus* was M. Porcius Cato, who insisted on all debts to the public treasury being paid at once and in full. Cato, a man of optimate conviction but like his famous ancestor of rigid probity, demanded that the hit-men of the proscriptions should surrender their ill-gotten gains. Caesar, for his part, allowed charges of murder to be brought against them, and already two notoriously guilty men had been successfully prosecuted.[107]

Nothing could be more popular than this righting of an injustice that had rankled with Rome's citizens for nearly twenty years. Cicero too, with his speech for Pompey's command and the defence of Cornelius, had laid up a great fund of popular approval, which he could now draw on for his candidature. Catiline's supporters, on the other hand, seemed to be mainly dissolute young men with expensive tastes.[108] But Catiline was a patrician; he and Antonius (son of the famous orator and consul) insisted again and again on the traditional assumption that noble birth was a necessary qualification for the consulship, and that a 'new man' was unworthy of the honour. This prejudice, presented as *mos maiorum*, was their only legitimate advantage. But it was a potentially decisive one, for

104 See the detailed analysis by Frederiksen 1966 (G 78).

105 Q. Cic. *Comment. Pet.* 39, 54 ('fraudis atque insidiarum et perfidiae plena sunt omnia . . . multae insidiae, multa fallacia, multa in omni genere vitia'); *ibid.* 54–7 and Cic. *Tog. Cand.* fr. 1P on *largitio*.

106 Cic. *Tog. Cand.* frr. 9–10P, Q. Cic. *Comment. Pet.* 10, Asc. 84C.

107 Plut. *Cat. Min.* 17–18, Suet. *Iul.* 11, Asc. 90–1C (L. Luscius, L. Bellienus).

108 Sall. *Cat.* 14.5f, 17.6, Cic. *Cael.* 10, *Cat.* II.8.

it might enable the leaders of the senatorial establishment, and their hangers-on,[109] to vote with a clear conscience for two disreputable nobles against the man who had done so much to raise Pompey to that intolerable pinnacle of power.

In the end they did not do that. The evident unsuitability of Catiline, the diplomacy of Cicero and his friend Atticus (an *eques* with many noble friends),[110] and above all perhaps the prospect of having that marvellous oratorical gift under an obligation to them, finally swung their support behind the 'popular consul', who was duly elected by the vote of all the centuries.[111] Antonius just beat Catiline for second place. However, Catiline's luck had not completely deserted him. Prosecuted before Caesar's murder court later in the year, he was acquitted,[112] surviving to fight again for the consulship he had to win in order to avoid ruin.

As so often in recent years, the tribunician elections were hardly less important than the consular. The college of tribunes elected for 63 included a group with firm plans for reform. They met regularly that autumn, preparing their legislation. Chief among them was P. Servilius Rullus, who assumed the unkempt and bearded persona of a tribune from the days of the fifth-century secessions, one of Macer's heroes come back to life.[113] Crassus and Caesar are usually thought to have been behind him, as Cicero hints (one did not attack Crassus openly); if so, they were playing for the people's gratitude, and the co-operation of Pompey, who was too popular to be opposed, but could not be allowed too many chances to gain new influence.

On the agenda were debt and land, two fifth-century issues now urgent once again. There is said to have been an abortive proposal to abolish debts. The land issue was to be resolved by the radical use of public funds.[114] The war in the East was effectively over: Mithridates had fled to the ends of the earth; Pompey had turned south – to Syria, Judaea, Arabia, perhaps Egypt. Whatever the details of his settlement, there was going to be a huge gain for the public treasury, both immediately and in the long term, with booty and revenues from the conquered territories. What the Gracchi had done, turning the profits of empire to the direct benefit of the Roman citizen body, could now be done again on a grander scale.

A redistribution of land in Italy could be effected without the necessity

109 Cf. Cic. *Corn.* II fr. 3P ('adsentatores atque adseculae'), Asc. 61C ('familiares principum civitatis').

110 Q. Cic. *Comment. Pet.* 5, Cic. *Att.* I.2.2; for Atticus' friends among the *nobiles* (for example, *Att.* I.19.6), see Shackleton Bailey 1965–70 (B 108) I.6–12.

111 Cic. *Off.* II.59 ('cunctis suffragiis'), *Leg. Agr.* II.4 ('una vox universi populi Romani), I.23 ('consul veritate, non ostentatione, popularis').

112 Asc. 91C, Cic. *Att.* I.16.9, *Pis.* 95.

113 Cic. *Leg. Agr.* II.11–13.

114 Dio XXXVII.25.4 (χρεῶν ἀποκοπαί); Cic. *Leg. Agr.* II.10 ('largitio . . . quae . . . fieri nisi exhausto aerario nullo pacto potest'), cf. *Pis.* 4.

of confiscation: the treasury would buy from the present landowners, at generous terms which encouraged them to sell, and use the publicly owned *ager Campanus* and *ager Stellas*, the present revenues of which would not now be missed. Sullan confiscations were to be maintained, but some public land abroad sold off. New colonies could then be founded, offering a fresh start to the more desperate of the rural poor, a chance to tempt some of the urban plebs back to the land, and a ready-made scheme for the settlement of Pompey's veterans when they were discharged.[115] To administer this programme, a commission of ten would be elected, with praetorian *imperium* (to give them judicial authority) for a period of five years. Since all the tribunes at first supported the bill, and one or two at least (Labienus and Ampius Balbus?) are likely to have been Pompey's men, his friends must have approved the proposal.

The scheme also promised some incidental advantages for the Forum and the senate-house. The dangerous unrest in rural Italy had caused a sharp fall in land-values, with the result that ambitious senators, and other men of property who had borrowed for immediate expenses, were unable to turn their assets into cash when their creditors demanded repayment.[116] When the treasury was looking for land to buy, with plenty of money to spend, that problem would be solved overnight. And the post-70 political crisis, of thwarted ambition leading to bribery and violence in public life, would be eased by the election of *Xviri*. Ten men, at least, could hope for the *dignitas* (and the financial opportunities) of a five-year praetorian command with powers of jurisdiction throughout the whole empire.

Two men who perhaps hoped to be eligible were P. Sulla and P. Autronius Paetus. One of the new tribunes, Sulla's half-brother L. Caecilius Rufus, had a bill drafted for the reinstatement of Sulla and Autronius to citizen rights and membership of the Senate. Sulla was in Campania, allegedly collecting gladiators; Autronius was at Rome, surrounded by an aggressively demonstrative crowd of supporters. The atmosphere was tense, and not helped by the rumours of abolition of debts and redistribution of land, which had the effect of making credit tighter than ever.[117]

Cicero had not been invited to the planning sessions, and he was profoundly suspicious of those who were.[118] His ideal of a peaceful, law-abiding and harmonious republic had no room either for ruthless gamblers on the make or for lavish public spending and upheavals of the

[115] Cic. *Leg. Agr.* II, esp. 31 (Gracchan precedent), 67f (generous terms), 70 (urban plebs), 79 (*rustici*), 80–3 (Campanian and overseas *vectigalia*). See Sumner 1966 (C 269) for the political background and the probable relevance of Pompey's veterans.

[116] Val. Max. IV.8.3 ('propter tumultum pretiis possessionum deminutis'), Cic. *Leg. Agr.* II.68.

[117] Cic. *Sull.* 53–5 (P. Sulla), 62–4 (Caecilius), 66 (Autronius); *Leg. Agr.* II.8 ('sublata erat de foro fides').

[118] Cic. *Leg. Agr.* I.22 ('ei quos multo magis quam Rullum timetis'), II.12, 65.

property market. The tribunes were confident of the other consul's support, but Antonius had no stomach for a fight and allowed himself to be bought off by a deal over the consular provinces. In the lot, Cicero had drawn Macedonia and Antonius Cisalpine Gaul; now an exchange was publicly agreed. Antonius was the gainer (the hapless Greeks would give him more chance of restoring his shattered fortunes than the self-confident Latin colonists of the Transpadana), and this *beneficium* was his excuse for inactivity.[119]

On the first day of 63 B.C., the festival crowds escorting the new consuls to the meeting of the Senate on the Capitol were doubtless unusually anxious. After the routine religious business the first item on the agenda was the proposal about Autronius and Sulla. One of the praetors, on Sulla's behalf, announced that Sulla no longer wished his case to be brought to the people. Caecilius Rufus immediately withdrew his bill. He also (it is not clear why) abandoned his tribunician colleagues on the land and debt questions, supporting Cicero's attack and announcing that he would veto Rullus' land bill if it came to the vote.[120] Antonius kept quiet, and Cicero carried the Senate in opposition to the proposed legislation.

A few days later he carried the people too, appealing, in a speech of brilliant chicanery, to the 'true' popular tradition of liberty against tyranny – Rullus' board of ten would be ten kings, their colonies military garrisons. Partly because he convinced them that the glory of their hero Pompey was threatened, partly because the concessions Rullus had made to those occupying confiscated land looked like corrupt connivance with the hated Sullans (his own father-in-law was one), and partly because in the last resort the urban plebs had little interest in the problems of the countryside, Cicero succeeded in destroying the land bill and enhancing his own popularity at the same time.[121]

He needed all that popularity in the next few months, as he paid off the political debts of his election. He defended C. Piso at his trial for extortion in Gaul (Caesar was the prosecutor) and opened the gates at last for Lucullus to hold his long-delayed triumph.[122] Envious and ambitious men brooded bitterly on the power of the few. As Sallust makes Catiline say:

> It is they who own kings, tetrarchs, revenues; it is to them that peoples and nations pay tribute. All the rest of us, men of ability and character, high-born as well as low, have become a mere mob without influence or authority, subject to men who would live in fear of us if the Republic were in a healthy state.[123]

119 Cic. *Pis.* 5, *Sest.* 8, *Leg. Agr.* II.103, cf. Q. Cic. *Comment. Pet.* 9 ('Antonius umbram suam metuit'); see Allen 1952 (C 161) 233–4.

120 Cic. *Sull.* 65 ('improbis largitionibus restitit', cf. n. 114 above).

121 Cic. *Leg. Agr.* II and III.

122 Cic. *Flacc.* 98, Sall. *Cat.* 49.2; Cic. *Acad.* II.3, *Mur.* 37f, 69.

123 Sall. *Cat.* 20.7f.

And out in the countryside of Italy an even more dangerous resentment gathered force, now that Rullus' bill had failed.

On 3 May, perilously close to the Latin Festival, there was a total eclipse of the moon. Comets and meteors were seen. Augurs, *haruspices* and raving soothsayers all gave the same grim warning of civil war.[124]

In Rome, meanwhile, Cicero's control of the urban populace was still unshaken. When the *ludi Apollinares* opened on 6 July, the praetor L. Roscius Otho came in for some abusive whistles from those at the back of the theatre who resented the reservation of the first fourteen rows for the equestrian order, which he had introduced in 67. The knights applauded him, a riot broke out; Cicero summoned the people to the nearby temple of Bellona, and preached the harmony of good citizens to such effect that Otho was cheered by the whole audience when the show resumed.[125]

Cicero faced a stiffer challenge when a man who had participated in the lynching of Saturninus (ch. 3, p. 101) was brought to trial, pretty certainly as a warning to the Senate that the *senatus consultum ultimum* must not be abused, or even (as Cicero maintained the prosecutors were holding) that it could not in any circumstances justify putting citizens to death without full trial. The senator C. Rabirius, now an old man, was hounded by the tribune T. Labienus. The charge was *perduellio*, for which no standing jury-court existed, as it did for the related but more up-to-date charge of *maiestas*; senatorial and equestrian jurors would not have condemned Rabirius. An obsolete procedure was revived, and the praetor appointed two men to hear the case, C. Caesar and his cousin L. Caesar (cos. 64), who condemned Rabirius to the ancient penalty – to be tied to the stake and flogged to death in the Campus Martius. Rabirius appealed (Caesar was not an impartial judge), so the tribune prosecuted him before the popular assembly, in a deliberate re-creation of the conditions of the early Republic. The people itself would take vengeance on those who killed its champions. Cicero and Hortensius defended. Cicero argued that Labienus was no true representative of the people – the antique procedure was tyrannical, dating from the time of the Kings; he himself, though (he claimed) a true *consul popularis*, defended the right of the Senate to authorize action in a crisis. The trial was broken off by another anachronistic device. The warning stood, but it had not been formally endorsed by the people.[126]

In legislation too the tribunes were active, trying to demolish the remnants of the Sullan structure. Labienus succeeded in getting popular election of *pontifices* restored, but a proposal to abolish the restrictions on

[124] Cic. *Div.* I.18, 105, *Har. Resp.* 18; Pliny *HN* II.137.

[125] Plut. *Cic.* 13; the *ludi Apollinares* (given by the *praetor urbanus*, this year L. Valerius Flaccus) identified by the proximity of the Apollo and Bellona temples.

[126] Cic. *Rab. Perd.*, esp. 15 ('ex annalium monumentis atque ex regum commentariis'), 18 (hostile audience); Suet. *Iul.* 12 (appeal), Dio XXXVII.26f; Phillips 1974 (C 237).

the sons of the proscribed (ch. 6, pp. 197–8) was defeated by Cicero: the measure was just, but would cause political upheaval.[127] (This drove some of the men concerned into supporting Catiline and revolution.) The greatest popular success of the year, however, came not from the tribunes but from Caesar. Metellus Pius had recently died, and at the election for his successor as *pontifex maximus*, the thirty-seven-year-old Caesar defeated two senior *consulares*, one of them the leader of the senatorial establishment, Q. Catulus. It was a calculated gamble: he had borrowed so much to bribe the voters that failure would have meant ruin and exile.[128]

Catiline faced a similar crisis at the consular elections. He was confident of success, his following swollen by smallholders from Etruria and elsewhere who still had hope of debt relief and agrarian reform. Catiline boasted of his own debts, saying openly that only a poor man could faithfully defend the poor. But the poor did not decide elections in the *comitia centuriata*, so he spent what he borrowed on lavish bribery. When Cato threatened to prosecute, Catiline's counter-threat was of general destruction if anyone tried to stop him.[129]

Cato's brother-in-law D. Silanus was also a candidate; the other two were a distinguished and independent-minded jurist, Ser. Sulpicius Rufus, and L. Licinius Murena, Lucullus' legate. Sulpicius demanded a new and tougher bribery law. His friend Cicero obliged, and the assembly passed a Lex Tullia de ambitu with a penalty of ten years' exile. But the consul opposed Sulpicius' suggestion of a radical change in the structure of the centuriate assembly to make bribery more difficult. The effect would be to weaken its plutocratic bias – a popular suggestion, reminiscent of C. Gracchus and C. Manilius, which the Senate would not allow to go to the vote.[130]

Cicero postponed the election and challenged Catiline in the Senate about his intentions. Catiline was defiant. The mass of the Roman people was leaderless, like a mighty body with no head; he, Catiline, would be its head. That sort of talk lost him the support he needed, and when Cicero, with his bodyguard around him and a cuirass visible under his toga, went down to the Campus Martius to preside over the election, the centuries' votes were cast for Silanus and Murena.[131] For Catiline and his supporters, the last legal option had failed.

127 Dio XXXVII.37.1 (Sulla had repealed the Lex Domitia of 104 B.C.); Cic. *Pis.* 4 ('rei publicae statum convulsuri'), Quint. *Inst.* XI.1.85.

128 Plut. *Caes.* 7.1–3 (P. Isauricus the other candidate), Suet. *Iul.* 13. We do not know when precisely the elections were held (Dio XXXVII. 37 is likely to be wrong).

129 Cic. *Mur.* 49–51.

130 Cic. *Mur.* 46–7 (reference to Manilius textually corrupt), ps.-Sall. *ad Caes. sen.* II.8 (C. Gracchus).

131 Cic. *Mur.* 51f. One of the bodyguard was P. Clodius (Plut. *Cic.* 29.1), who was also much involved in the bribery (Cic. *Har. Resp.* 42), probably on Murena's behalf (Cic. *Dom.* 118, 134 for their *adfinitas*).

That was some time in late September.[132] On 18 October, in the evening, an unknown person handed in at Crassus' house a batch of letters. One was addressed to Crassus himself, and proved to be an anonymous warning to get out of Rome in secret: Catiline was planning a massacre. With two other senior senators, Crassus went straight to Cicero. Next morning the consul called the Senate and had the letters read; all had the same message, that there was a plan for simultaneous assassinations on 28 October. Meanwhile, news came from Faesulae in north Etruria that an armed revolt was being prepared, under the command of an ex-centurion, C. Manlius. Cicero, who had his own informants, announced in the Senate on 21 October that Manlius' army would be mobilized on 27 October. The Senate passed the *senatus consultum ultimum*, for the first time since the rebellion of Lepidus.[133]

Manlius' force appeared in arms on the stated day; rumours of similar risings came in from elsewhere in Italy. (Some ancient sources claim that these risings had been organized by Catiline, but there is no reason to think they were not spontaneous. The despair of the peasants will not have been confined to north Etruria.) Q. Marcius Rex, still in possession of *imperium* as he waited outside the city for permission to hold his triumph, was sent to Faesulae to deal with Manlius. Metellus Creticus, who had shared the humiliating three-year wait (recently prolonged by Cicero, who suspected the two men might prove useful), was to put down a reported slave revolt in Apulia. Cicero had allowed his own province of Cisalpine Gaul to go into the lot for the praetors. It had fallen to Q. Metellus Celer, who had served under Pompey in the East; that experienced soldier was to leave forthwith, going first to Picenum to keep control there. His colleague Q. Pompeius Rufus was to go to Capua.[134]

As Marcius Rex advanced up the Via Cassia, a deputation arrived from Manlius' makeshift army, pleading above all (according to Sallust) for relief from debt-bondage. Marcius Rex told them to lay down their arms, go to Rome to make their petition, and trust the traditional compassion and clemency of the Senate. But they had good reasons for no longer trusting that tradition.[135]

In Rome, Catiline and his friends, who included the praetor Lentulus Sura, had had to reconsider their strategy since the elections. Just as Autronius and Vargunteius had never resigned themselves to the verdict of the bribery court, so now Catiline would not acquiesce in the verdict of the voters. Lentulus still cherished his dream of being the third

[132] Suet. *Aug.* 5.1, 94.5 (C. Octavius was late for the meeting of the Senate on 23 September; his wife had just given birth to the future emperor Augustus).

[133] Plut. *Cic.* 15, *Crass.* 13.3 (from Cicero); Cic. *Cat.* 1.7. For the dates, see Hardy 1924 (C 211) 54–8.

[134] Sall. *Cat.* 30. Cisalpine Gaul: Cic. *Fam.* v.2.3, with Badian 1966 (C 163) 914–16.

[135] Sall. *Cat.* 33.

Cornelius to hold supreme power, and there were other malcontents and spendthrifts who hoped that a revolution might bring them out on top.[136] Cicero's informers reported secret meetings and the plotting of assassination and civil war. The massacre referred to in the mysterious letters had not happened, but on the morning of 7 November Vargunteius and an *eques* called Cornelius were turned away from Cicero's door because his information had named them as assassins.

The next day Cicero summoned the Senate to the temple of Jupiter Stator, which was easily defensible and close to his house. Even so, he was escorted by armed *equites* who picketed the temple while the meeting was going on.[137] The consul taunted Catiline with the discovery of his plans, but of course could not identify his informants (notably the dicer and spendthrift Q. Curius and his mistress). Catiline sat in sullen silence, then demanded that Cicero take a vote: if the Senate wished him to go into exile, he would go. Though the consul had been accused of exaggerating the danger to his own greater glory, the Senate gave no sign of support for Catiline. But such a vote would have been unprecedented, and Cicero could not press for it.

But that night Catiline left Rome. He was already facing prosecution in the *quaestio de vi*, and bankruptcy on 13 November when his creditors had to be paid, so it was entirely natural for an honourable man to go into voluntary exile – to Massilia, he said. He left a letter with Catulus, full of patrician resentment at the destruction of his career. 'I took up the cause of the oppressed because I was provoked by wrongs and insults, robbed of the reward of my work and effort, and unable to maintain a position of dignity.' Unworthy men were given the honour of high office, while he was ostracized because of a false suspicion. But if it ever had been a false suspicion, Catiline now made it true; he was travelling north up the Via Aurelia not to take ship for Massilia, but to put himself in command of Manlius' peasant army.[138] As soon as his arrival was reported, the Senate declared war on both him and Manlius, and put the consul Antonius in charge of the forces of the Republic to defeat them.[139]

In Rome at the time were two ambassadors from the Allobrogian Gauls, who had done what Marcius Rex advised Manlius' men to do – they had appealed to the traditional compassion and clemency of the Senate against ruinous usury and avaricious magistrates. Desperate at the Senate's refusal to help, they must have been sourly glad to see their recent proconsul, L. Murena, on trial for electoral bribery. Cato had brought the case 'in the interests of the Republic'; Cicero successfully

[136] Names (and motives) in Sall. *Cat.* 17, emphasizing discontented *nobiles*. See Gruen 1974 (C 209) 418–22.

[137] Cic. *Cat.* I.I, 21; Cicero's house was on the Carinae (Plut. *Cic.* 8.3; Cic. *QFr.* II.3.7). See Coarelli 1985 (B 277) 26–31 (Iuppiter Stator), 39f (Carinae).

[138] Sall. *Cat.* 35, cf. 31.4 (prosecution), Cic. *Cat.* I.14 (creditors).

[139] Sall. *Cat.* 36.2f.

defended Murena on the same grounds, insisting that Rome would need two consuls firmly in power in the new year to guard against continuing plots, not new elections with their potentiality for disorder. 'The Trojan horse is within, yes, within the walls!' The Allobroges now justified his portentous words, reporting that they had been approached to join a secret group led by the praetor Lentulus Sura. With the co-operation of the Gauls, Cicero captured letters – from Lentulus himself, a senator C. Cethegus and an *eques* L. Statilius – urging the Allobroges to rise in rebellion, and arrested a messenger, T. Volturcius of Croton, who carried a cryptic note from Lentulus to Catiline.[140]

At dawn on 3 December Cicero sent for the authors of the three letters, and for P. Gabinius, who had been one of the Allobroges' contacts; he despatched one of the praetors to seize a cache of weapons at Cethegus' house; and he summoned the Senate to the temple of Concord. Volturcius gave evidence, adding some more names (including Autronius and Vargunteius) and alleging that his verbal instructions from Lentulus had been to urge Catiline to recruit slaves and march on Rome, where the conspirators would create panic by arson and murder. The Allobroges gave evidence too, and incriminated L. Cassius, one of the praetors of the previous year. They confirmed the plan to fire the city, which they said had been fixed for 17 December, the Saturnalia. The letters were produced; Lentulus, Cethegus and Statilius acknowledged their seals; the tablets were opened and read, including the one Volturcius had been carrying from Lentulus to Catiline. All three men eventually confessed, as did Gabinius when he was brought in. The Senate voted that Lentulus should resign his praetorship; that he, Cethegus, Statilius and Gabinius should be held in custody; that Cassius, who had left Rome, should be arrested; and that four other men should be sought and detained – M. Caeparius of Tarracina, who was on his way to Apulia to stir up a slave revolt, P. Furius, a colonist from Faesulae, Q. Annius Chilo, a junior senator, and P. Umbrenus, the freedman who had first approached the Allobroges.[141]

Cicero's recent outspoken opposition to those who claimed to be the people's friends had earned him some unpopularity, orchestrated by two of the tribunes-elect.[142] But evidence of plans to burn the city, free slaves, and bring down savage Gauls on Italy changed the attitude of the urban plebs. When the Senate decreed a thanksgiving to the gods 'because the consul had delivered the city from fire, the citizens from slaughter, and Italy from war', on the very day that the new statue of Jupiter was being

[140] Cic. *Mur.* 78–85 (cf. n. 103 above), *Cat.* III.4–6, Sall. *Cat.* 40–6.

[141] Cic. *Cat.* III.6–14, Sall. *Cat.* 46–7.

[142] Cic. *Mur.* 83 (*seditio* and *discordia*), *Cat.* III.3 (*invidia*), IV.9 ('levitas contionatorum'); *Fam.* V.2.6 (Q. Metellus Nepos), Sall. *Cat.* 43.1 (L. Calpurnius Bestia).

erected on the Capitol to watch over Rome, Cicero had the Forum crowd eating out of his hand. For a moment, the whole citizen body, plebs and *patres*, was at one behind its consul.[143] That unanimity lasted just two days.

In an increasingly hysterical atmosphere, with attempts being made to incriminate leading politicians, notably Crassus and Caesar, and to rescue Lentulus and Cethegus from custody,[144] Cicero called on the Senate on 5 December – the 'Nones of December' – to consider the fate of the prisoners. Cicero knew what was at stake, but said he would prefer an immediate death penalty; it was for the Senate to decide. This was a position consistent with his words at the trial of Rabirius. After a tense debate, and despite a reasoned and courageous speech by Caesar as praetor-elect, proposing strict confinement as a punishment, the Senate was carried away by the force of Cato's denunciation of criminals taken in the act, and decided that the prisoners had forfeited their rights as Roman citizens; they should be put to death.[145] Cicero gave the orders immediately, and the five men (for Caeparius had been arrested and brought back) were summoned under guard to the Tullianum.

Cicero himself, with an escort of armed senior senators, brought Lentulus from his cousin's house on the Palatine, down the Via Sacra and through the crowded Forum. A patrician ex-consul from one of the greatest families in Rome, with a dignity of bearing that belied his vices, was being taken to his death. In Plutarch's words, 'the people shuddered in silence and did not interfere. For the young men especially, it was as if they were being initiated, with terror and amazement, into the ancient mysteries of some aristocratic regime.' Summary execution, without trial, for the intention to carry out what the Senate declared was treason; so some *populares* saw it. They no doubt remembered Sp. Maelius, the demagogue who had been killed by a senator four hundred years before on the suspicion of aiming at tyranny.[146]

The executions polarized political opinion. Cicero's supporters hailed him as the new founder of Rome, father of his country, worthy of the civic crown for saving the lives of citizens.[147] His opponents called him a tyrant, with the blood of Roman citizens on his hands.[148] On the last day of the year the new tribunes Q. Metellus Nepos and L. Bestia placed their bench in front of the rostra and forbade Cicero to address the people.

143 Cic. *Cat.* III, esp. 1f and 25 (fire), 15 (thanksgiving), 18–23 (gods); IV.14–7 (*consensio*).

144 Sall. *Cat.* 48 (Crassus), 49 (Caesar), 50.1f; Cic. *Cat.* IV.17.

145 The precise reconstruction of the debate is uncertain: Gelzer 1969 (C 198) 50ff.

146 Plut. *Cic.* 22.1; Sall. *Cat.* 47.4 (house of P. Lentulus Spinther), Cic. *Brut.* 235 (Lentulus' *formae dignitas*); Dion. Hal. *Ant. Rom.* XII.2 for a *popularis* version (Macer?) of the death of Sp. Maelius.

147 Cic. *Pis.* 6 (Q. Catulus, L. Gellius), Plut. *Cic.* 22.3, 23.3 (Cato).

148 Plut. *Cic.* 23.2 (δυναστεία), Cic. *Sull.* 21f (*regnum*), 30f (*iudices* approve, Forum crowd indignant).

One who had put others to death without a hearing had no right to be heard himself. He must take his required oath, that he had obeyed the laws, and say no more. To the cheers of his well-wishers, Cicero swore in ringing tones that the city and the Republic had been saved by him alone.[149]

The city, yes. But the Republic was still at war. With the lictors and fasces of an assumed *imperium*, Catiline was in command of two rebel legions – ill-armed, depleted by desertions after the news from Rome, but a disciplined and desperate force. Their standard was a silver eagle that Marius' army had carried against the Cimbri; their base was the Marian heartland of north Etruria.[150] The urban plot had been put down, but the peasants' revolt had not yet been defeated. (For the Allobroges, too, there was nothing left but rebellion.)

V. RETURN OF THE HERO

During the year 63 (perhaps to spoil Lucullus' triumph), two of the tribunes had got unheard-of honours voted to Pompey. He was permitted to wear a golden crown at all public games, with a *toga praetexta* in the theatre and the embroidered triumphal toga in the Circus. The *corona aurea* and *toga picta* were symbols of kingship, assumed by Tarquinius Priscus and his successors and denied to the great men of the Republic except on the one occasion of the triumph; for Pompey, the glory of the *triumphator* was to be renewed on every public holiday. (Cicero, anxious that the Senate too should be seen to honour Pompey, got it to vote him a lengthy thanksgiving.)[151]

Now, on the first day of 62 B.C., Caesar as praetor proposed a law transferring the reconstruction of the temple of Jupiter Optimus Maximus to Pompey. Catulus, he said, had been embezzling the public funds. The senior senators hurried down from the Capitol to the Forum in time to prevent the vote; but Caesar and the two tribunes had succeeded in re-creating the political atmosphere of ten years earlier, when it seemed that only the return of Pompey could vindicate the people against the avarice and cruelty of the dominant *patres*. Metellus Nepos, who had left Pompey's victorious army in order to hold the tribunate, kept up the pressure, denouncing the Senate, and Cicero in particular, for the unlawful execution of Lentulus and the others, and proposing to have Pompey elected consul *in absentia*. When the Senate overbore him, announcing immunity for those involved in the execu-

[149] Cic. *Fam.* v.2.7f ('qua iniuria nemo umquam in ullo magistratu improbissimus civis adfectus est'), *Pis.* 6. [150] Cic. *Cat.* II.13, Sall. *Cat.* 36.1, 59.3 (fasces, eagle).

[151] Vell. Pat. II.40.1 (T. Labienus, T. Ampius), Dio XXXVII.21.4 (Caesar in favour, Cato opposed); Dion. Hal. *Ant. Rom.* III.61–2.

tions (any prosecutor would be declared a public enemy), in the eyes of many citizens that no doubt merely confirmed the justice of his complaint.[152]

But Cato was also a tribune, the man whose hardline speech, in spite of his junior position, had won the day on the Nones. He now persuaded the Senate to relieve the poor and landless – not by radical debt- and property-reform but by extending the distribution of subsidized grain. His scheme more than doubled the treasury's financial commitment, but this time there were no cries of senatorial outrage.[153] Action on the economic front would alleviate the Senate's unpopularity, and weaken the appeal of Catiline's rebellion.

That rebellion was still the main issue of the day. Praetors had been sent to prevent sympathetic risings elsewhere in Italy,[154] but the main army was undefeated. What good were discredited men like Antonius and Marcius Rex against Catiline? Metellus Nepos proposed a bill for a special command: Pompey should return, with his army in being, to protect Rome. Cato delivered a fierce tirade in the Senate and swore that Pompey would never enter the city with soldiers while he was alive.

On the morning of the vote, Cato, with one fellow-tribune, Q. Minicius Thermus, pushed his way on to the platform and sat down on the tribunes' bench between Nepos and Caesar's curule chair. Amid the shouts and cheers, Nepos motioned to the clerk to read the bill. Cato ordered him to keep silent. Nepos stood up, took the document himself and began to read it. Cato snatched it from him. Nepos began to recite the bill from memory. Thermus stepped behind him and put his hand over his mouth. By now there was uproar. Cato was the target for volleys of stones, until he allowed himself to be led into the safety of a temple by the consul Murena. Nepos dismissed his armed supporters as soon as they had cleared the pro-Cato party out of the Forum, and prepared to have the bill voted on as if nothing had happened. But his opponents regrouped and came back with weapons. It was the turn of Nepos' supporters to scatter, and Cato emerged from the temple to reiterate his veto.

The Senate met that afternoon and passed the emergency decree. It was strongly urged that Nepos be stripped of his tribunate. But that would make him a martyr to senatorial tyranny, and Cato persuaded the *patres* to take no further action against him. In fact Nepos played into the Senate's hands. He called a public meeting, gave a furious harangue against the despotic behaviour of Cato and the Senate – they were all in a

152 Dio XXXVII.42.2f (Nepos), 44.1f (Caesar); Suet. *Iul.* 15, *Schol. Bob.* 134St; Cic. *Fam.* V.2.8–9 (clashes between Nepos and Cicero on 1 and 3 January); Plut. *Cat. Min.* 20.2 (Nepos as Pompey's agent).

153 Plut. *Cat. Min.* 26.1, *Caes.* 8.4; Rickman 1979 (G 212) 168–71.

154 Dio XXXVII.41.1, Oros. VI.6.7 (Q. Cicero to Bruttium, M. Bibulus to the Paeligni).

conspiracy against Pompey, but they would rue the day they had insulted so great a man! – and flung off headlong down the Via Appia to report.[155] (Pompey was at Rhodes, holding court among rhetoricians and philosophers; Nepos had to explain how, with much popular support, a favourable political climate, and the help of a troop of gladiators, he had succeeded only in making himself a laughing stock and Cato a hero. It must have given Pompey food for deep thought on who his friends should be.)

Caesar was a much better tactician. Suspended from his praetorship by the Senate for his part in the riot, he continued his judicial duties until it was clear that he would be prevented by force, then withdrew to his house. When a crowd gathered, noisily promising support, he calmed it down, and had the satisfaction of receiving a grateful delegation of senior senators who escorted him to the senate-house and reinstated him in office. His enemies now attacked him through the *quaestio de vi*, where Autronius, Vargunteius and other friends of Catiline had recently been condemned. A certain L. Vettius offered evidence that Caesar had been in treasonable correspondence with Catiline. Having got Cicero to attest that Caesar had given him valuable information against the conspirators, the praetor used his *coercitio* on the informer. Vettius' goods were seized, he was beaten and thrown into prison.[156]

In Etruria, meanwhile, Catiline had turned his rebel army northwards, hoping to escape across the Apennines. But Metellus Celer forestalled him. At Pistoria, therefore, Catiline turned again, to fight it out. Antonius left the battle to his legate M. Petreius, an experienced soldier. It was a bloody affair, for Catiline's troops were stiffened by elderly veterans. He and Manlius were killed with all their forces; they were desperate men who did not wish to survive their defeat.[157]

The end of Catiline, and of the threat (or hope) that he represented, calmed the political hysteria at Rome. And now official despatches came from Pompey, announcing the successful completion of all military and naval operations. He would soon be home, peace and prosperity were assured.[158] The consular elections were postponed to allow his legate M. Pupius Piso to compete; he was elected by a huge majority.[159]

But if the populace was confident, the *patres* were not. Pompey's whole career had consisted of special arrangements, exemptions, unprecedented powers, unexpected alliances. How was he going to fit back

155 Plut. *Cat. Min.* 26.2–29.2, Cic. *Sest.* 62, Dio XXXVII.43, Suet. *Iul.* 16; Cic. *Fam.* V.2.9 (with Shackleton Bailey *ad loc.*), *contra contionem Q. Metelli* fr. 1P.

156 Suet. *Iul.* 16–7; Cic. *Sull.* 6f, 71, *Cael.* 70 on the *quaestio de vi*.

157 Sall. *Cat.* 57–61, Dio XXXVII.39–40.

158 Cic. *Fam.* V.7.1 ('tantam enim spem oti ostendisti'), *Prov. Cons.* 27.

159 Dio XXXVII.44.3; Plut. *Pomp.* 44.1 (Cato objects to further postponement for Pompey himself to be present).

into Roman politics now that his glory was greater than ever? What line would he take on the newly polarized issue of senatorial authority versus popular liberty? Pompey, after all, had sent Metellus Nepos to be tribune; and he had replied very coolly to the enthusiastic account Cicero had sent of the events of 63. Cicero now wrote back:

> What I have done for the safety of the whole country stands approved in the judgement and testimony of the whole world. When you return, you will find that I have acted with a measure of policy and lack of self-regard which will make you content to have me as your political ally and private friend – a not much lesser Laelius to a far greater Africanus.

That proposal was made more in hope than in confidence.[160] But when, late in the year, Pompey finally landed at Brundisium, two things encouraged Cicero and the senatorial establishment to take heart. First, Pompey immediately demobilized his forces; and second, he divorced his wife, Metellus Nepos' half-sister Mucia.[161]

Pompey could not enter the city before his triumph, but he could install himself in his Alban villa and take part in whatever meetings of Senate or people might be called outside the *pomoerium*. He arrived in the vicinity of Rome in time for the entry into office in January 61 of his protégé M. Piso, whose job as consul would be to get the Senate to ratify Pompey's arrangements for the newly conquered lands of the East. That would not be easy, as they had been made without the assistance of the usual senatorial Commission of Ten, and without regard to Lucullus' intentions and decisions. But in any case Pompey found Piso otherwise occupied, at odds with his colleague (the patrician M. Messalla) over an apparently trivial matter that now threatened to divert attention from the great man's glorious return.

One of the new quaestors had been pursuing the wife of one of the outgoing praetors. The alleged adulterer was P. Clodius;[162] the lady was Pompeia, the wife of Caesar, at whose house the nocturnal rites of the Good Goddess, which no male was permitted to witness, were being held early in December when Clodius was discovered on the premises dressed as a woman. The matter was raised in the Senate, and referred to the *pontifices* and the Vestals for a ruling as to whether or not sacrilege had been committed. The college of *pontifices*, now chaired by Caesar himself (who immediately divorced his wife without admitting her guilt, so being able to retain his friendship with Clodius), included Catulus, M. Lucullus and Metellus Creticus, none of whom was likely to be sympathetic to the saboteur of Lucullus' Armenian campaign. The new

[160] Cic. *Fam.* v.7.3 (trans. Shackleton Bailey 1977 (B 110)); for Cicero's original letter 'de meis rebus gestis et de summa re publica', see Cic. *Sull.* 67, *Planc.* 85 (with *Schol. Bob.* 167St).

[161] Cic. *Att.* I.12.3 ('divortium Muciae vehementer probatur'); Plut. *Pomp.* 43, Dio XXXVII.20.6, Vell. Pat. II.40.2f.

[162] For his earlier career, see above, notes 76, 93, 103, 131.

consuls were in office when the priests reported that it was indeed sacrilege. Messalla, himself a *pontifex*, took a strong moral line; M. Piso was a friend of Clodius and tried to protect him.[163]

The Senate agreed with Messalla, and instructed the consuls to present a bill to the people setting up an *ad hoc* court to try Clodius for *incestum*, the jury to be selected by the praetor who would preside over the court. The familiar issue of senatorial authority was now involved, especially as Clodius and his raffish friends looked dangerously like the young dandies who had supported Catiline two years before. Not only that, but Clodius' enemies had been Pompey's enemies too (Catulus, Lucullus, Hortensius), and Clodius' friend the consul had been Pompey's nominee.[164]

Into this situation now walked Pompey himself. His first public speech had been eagerly awaited, but fell flat; studiously non-partisan, it had pleased nobody. Now, early in February, a tribune called a meeting in the Circus Flaminius (just outside the city gate) and asked Pompey what he thought of the Senate's proposal for a hand-picked jury. Piso had put him up to it, but cannot have liked the result. Pompey held forth like an elder statesman on the authority of the Senate; he considered it paramount on all subjects, and always had done. Encouraged by this, Messalla asked in the Senate a few hours later for the opinion of Pompey concerning the sacrilege and the bill the Senate had proposed. The same thing happened: Pompey went out of his way to approve *all* decrees of the Senate, including that one. 'And now', he remarked to his neighbour Cicero as he sat down, 'I think I've said enough about all that.'[165]

It was certainly enough for Cicero – approval not only of the hand-picked jury, but by implication also of the Senate's decision to execute the plotters. Pompey had shown his hand at last. (In fact he even tried to marry a niece of Cato's, but Cato declined the proposal; Cicero, convinced of the need to keep Pompey allied to the Senate, must have groaned.)

When the bill for setting up Clodius' trial came before the people, Piso and Clodius frustrated it by blatant ballot-rigging, which caused the assembly to be dismissed in disorder. The Senate instructed the consuls to urge the people to accept the bill; the majority was overwhelming (over 400 to about 15, Cicero says) but the tribune Q. Fufius vetoed the decree. Clodius' tactic was to present himself as a friend of the people victimized by the old senatorial clique. He was a patrician, but announced his desire to 'cross over' to the plebs and join the great

[163] *Pontifices*: Macrob. *Sat.* III.13.11 (Catulus), Cic. *Har. Resp.* 12. Piso and Clodius: Cic. *Att.* I.13.3.

[164] Cic. *Att.* I.14.5 ('ille grex Catilinae'), 16.11 ('comissatores coniurationis'), for example; 16.2 (Hortensius' *odium*).

[165] Cic. *Att.* I.14.1–4.

tradition of popular tribunes in opposition to senatorial domination.[166] Meanwhile, one of the present tribunes – Fufius, no doubt – was preparing a bill on the consular provinces, to give wealthy Syria (one of Pompey's recently conquered kingdoms) to the consul M. Piso, with Clodius as his quaestor.[167]

Fufius persisted in his veto until the Senate, at Hortensius' suggestion, backed down on the question of the hand-picked jury. He then put through a tribunician bill for the court to be set up, with the jury chosen by lot in the normal way, and in the spring the trial duly took place. Despite Cicero's misgivings about them, the jury seemed to be taking a severe view. Cicero himself braved the threats of Clodius' supporters to give evidence that the accused had been in Rome on the day in question; the *eques* Causinius Schola, who claimed for the defence that Clodius had been at his house at Interamna Lirenas, nearly 90 miles down the Via Latina, was therefore lying. The jury asked the Senate for a bodyguard. A 'guilty' verdict seemed inevitable.

Clodius had only two advantages – available money (no doubt the usurers knew that Syria was a rich province) and disreputable friends of both sexes. During the two nights of the trial period, we are told, one juror after another came to the house of a certain 'Calvus' (no doubt Licinius Calvus, Macer's son); some, it was said, received cash, some had their debts transferred to Clodius' creditors, some were won over by the promise of sexual favours. Clodius was acquitted by thirty-one votes to twenty-five. 'Is that why you wanted a guard', said Catulus bitterly; 'so your money shouldn't be stolen?' (It is the last we hear of the great man.)[168]

The Senate's authority had taken another knock. But the main loser was Cicero himself, who had committed himself against a dangerous enemy. His own position was very ambiguous. He had just spent 3,500,000 sesterces on a superb town house on the Palatine, once owned by Crassus; the money had been borrowed from P. Sulla, whom he had defended in 62 on a charge of being involved with Catiline, and from C. Antonius, now in Macedonia, who was paying, through a discreet lady go-between, for Cicero's help in preventing his supersession and Cicero's promised defence in the extortion trial that he would surely have to face.[169] That could be made to look like corruption; and the great house made it easy for any competent demagogue (and Clodius was

166 Cato's niece: Plut. *Cat. Min.* 30.2–4. Cic. *Att.* 1.14.5, 11.1.5, *in Clod. et Cur.* fr. 14P ('cum se ad plebem transire velle diceret').

167 Inferred from Cic. *Att.* 1.16.8 (with Balsdon 1962 (C 168) 140) and *in Clod. et Cur.* fr. 8P.

168 Cic. *Att.* 1.16.1–5 (reading 'Calvum ex νεανίαις'); Wiseman 1968 (C 284). 'Calvus', 'baldhead', is more traditionally supposed to be Crassus.

169 Sulla: Gell. *NA* XII.12.2f, ps.-Sall. *inv. in Cic.* 2. Antonius and 'Teucris': Cic. *Att.* 1.12.1 (with Shackleton Bailey *ad loc.*), *Fam.* V.5.2f, 6.2f.

certainly that) to class Cicero with Lucullus and Hortensius in the eyes of the Forum crowd. The executions still rankled – 'how long shall we endure this king?' – and for over a year it had been normal for Cicero to be whistled and jeered at by part of the Roman populace.[170]

But this year was different. The presence of Pompey, and his imminent triumph, mattered more to the Roman people than old resentments stirred up by Clodius. They saw Cicero as a friend of Pompey, and cheered him at the games. Perhaps they remembered the speech for Manilius' law. The people did not care much when Cicero attacked Clodius and M. Piso in the Senate, and got the allocation of Syria revoked. (Clodius had to get his province by sortition in the usual way, and the lot gave him Sicily.)[171]

Pompey still needed a friendly consul to get the ratification of his eastern settlement through the Senate against the opposition of Lucullus, Crassus and Cato.[172] He also still needed his veterans settled. M. Piso had let him down this year; one of next year's consuls was sure to be Q. Metellus Celer, half-brother of the wife Pompey had just pointedly divorced. L. Afranius, one of Pompey's old legates, was a reliable man, but a *novus homo* with no obvious credentials. Pompey set about sweetening the voters on Afranius' behalf; the Senate became indignant about bribery, and gave a tribune special dispensation to propose a *lex de ambitu* during the immediate pre-election period.[173] However, Afranius was elected with Celer for the year 60. Censors were elected too. Perhaps the return and triumph of Pompey would again, as ten years earlier, bring about a *lustrum* to cleanse the citizen body of its accumulated guilt.[174]

The triumph took place over two days at the end of September. It was, and it was meant to be, the greatest show Rome had ever seen.

Cn. Pompeius Magnus, *imperator*, having completed a thirty-year war, routed, scattered, slain or received the surrender of 12,183,000 people, sunk or taken 846 ships, received the capitulation of 1,538 towns and forts, subdued the lands from the Crimea to the Red Sea . . . having rescued the sea-coast from pirates and restored to the Roman people the command of the sea, celebrated a triumph over Asia, Pontus, Armenia, Paphlagonia, Cappadocia, Cilicia, Syria, the Scythians, the Jews, the Albanians, Iberia, the island of Crete, the Bastarnae, and in addition to these, over kings Mithridates and Tigranes.

As the placards in the procession boasted, every one of Pompey's soldiers had been given at least 6,000 sesterces; 20,000 talents in gold and

170 Cic. *Att.* I.16.10 ('quousque hunc regem feremus?'), 16.11 ('pastoricia fistula').

171 Cic. *Att.* I.16.8–11 ('missus est sanguis invidiae'); *in Clod. et Cur.* fr. 12P for the lot.

172 Plut. *Luc.* 42.5; for Crassus' continuing jealousy of Pompey, cf. Cic. *Att.* I.14.3.

173 Cic. *Att.* I 16.12f, with Badian's interpretation of the received text: 1984 (B 3). Celer and Mucia: Cic. *Fam.* V.2.4, Dio XXXVII.49.3. Afranius: Plut. *Mor.* 806B.

174 Dio XXXVII.46.4: probably C. Curio cos. 76 (Cic. *Off.* II.58); and L. Caesar cos. 64 (Nicolet 1980 (B 212) 112–25).

silver had been paid into the treasury; and the public revenues of the Roman people had been raised by Pompey's conquests from 50 million to 135 million denarii per annum.[175] Who could ever equal such an achievement? In the competitive world of Roman political ambition, that was more than just a rhetorical question. Pompey's golden crown was the symbol of a dangerous inflation in the price of glory.

By the time Afranius and Metellus Celer entered office, the main political issue was a quarrel between the Senate and the equestrian order. A proposed law on judicial corruption had failed to exempt equestrian jurors; and a society of *publicani*, finding they had bid too high at the censor's auction for the Asian tax contract (perhaps that of 65?), now wanted it renegotiated. Cicero knew the *equites* had a bad case on both issues, but supported them for the sake of the harmony he advocated between the two orders. The *lex de iudiciis* was dropped, but the request of the *publicani*, strongly supported by Crassus and equally strongly opposed by Cato, dragged on, paralysing the Senate's business.[176]

The tribunes of the new year (60 B.C.) included one who proposed a bill to transfer P. Clodius to the plebs, and several who vetoed it.[177] More immediately significant was a major land bill, proposed by the tribune L. Flavius with Pompey's backing, the first attempt to tackle that perennial problem since the Rullan bill three years before. As then, the beneficiaries would be both poor citizens in general and Pompey's veterans in particular; and as then, the Senate was suspicious of the authority that would be required to administer it, fearing another of Pompey's special commands. Cicero tried to make it appear harmless to the interests of the rich, but Metellus the consul was so outspoken in his opposition that the people's tribune had him put in prison. Defiant, Metellus called the Senate to meet him there; finally Pompey had to persuade Flavius to let him go. Flavius next threatened to prevent Metellus from going to his province; Metellus called his bluff, and eventually the whole agrarian proposal came to nothing.[178]

The question of Metellus' province was an urgent one. There was a serious military emergency in Gaul, where C. Pomptinus had just put down the revolt of the over-exploited Allobroges. Now came news that the Helvetii had defeated Rome's allies, the Aedui, and were attacking the Roman province. The Senate cancelled the allotted consular provinces; the two consuls were to go to Cisalpine and Transalpine Gaul.[179]

Meanwhile, the arrangements for the provinces to be held by the following year's consuls were causing unusual concern. Caesar was on

[175] Pliny *HN* VII.97f (trans. H. Rackham, slightly adapted); Plut. *Pomp.* 45.2f (adding Media, Colchis, Mesopotamia, Phoenicia, Palestine, Arabia).

[176] Cic. *Att.* I.17.9, 18.3, 18.7, II.1.8; Badian 1972 (A 2) 101–4, 111f (suggesting Crassus had shares in the companies concerned).

[177] Cic. *Att.* I.18.4, 19.5 (C. Herennius).

[178] Cic. *Att.* I.18.6, 19.4, II.1.6 and 8; Dio XXXVII.50.1–4.

[179] Cic. *Att.* I.19.2, 20.5.

his way back from Spain, where he had fought a successful campaign in the far west, and been voted a triumph for it. He was due in Rome in June, in time to stand at the consular elections. But when the Senate, led by Cato, refused to grant him permission to declare his candidacy without crossing the *pomoerium* and losing his *imperium* (necessary for a triumph) prematurely, he gave up the triumph to fight the election. Caesar was very popular ('the wind's in his sails just now', said Cicero), and it was certain that he would be elected. To minimize the damage, therefore, it was proposed in the Senate that the following year's consuls should not go to provinces abroad, but undertake the very necessary job of policing the brigand-infested forests and drove-roads of Italy.[180]

It was probably at this point that Caesar approached first Pompey and then Pompey's old rival Crassus. What all three had in common was an urgent need to overcome the opposition of the senatorial establishment, which, though it now lacked Catulus' clearsightedness, was formidably strengthened by the unbending moral authority of Cato. 'As for our friend Cato', wrote Cicero, who deplored the Senate's dogged opposition to Pompey, in a letter to Atticus, 'I have as warm a regard for him as you. The fact remains that with all his patriotism and integrity he is sometimes a political liability. He speaks in the Senate as though he were living in Plato's Republic instead of Romulus' cesspool.' But Cato turned a blind eye now as the bribes were distributed to ensure that his son-in-law M. Calpurnius Bibulus was elected as Caesar's colleague.[181]

Pompey, yet again, needed a reliable consul. Afranius, it was now clear, was not up to the job;[182] still the ratification of his settlement was being blocked, and still his soldiers had no land. He was, at this time, on close terms with Cicero; clearly he was looking for acceptance and respectability in the eyes of the senatorial establishment. But Cicero could not give him that; he himself was kept at a distance by the 'fish-pond-fanciers' and despaired of the future of the Republic with such men at its head: 'Since Catulus died I have been holding to this optimate road without supporters or companions. As Rhinthon (I think) has it, "Some count for nothing, others nothing care." I shall write to you some other time about the jealousy towards me of our fish-pond-fancying friends . . .'[183] Pompey and Cicero were in the same predicament, excluded from political authority by a clique of nobles. Indeed, it was largely the same clique (now strengthened by Cato) that both of them had attacked ten years before as domineering and corrupt.

180 Suet. *Iul.* 18, Plut. *Caes.* 13.1; Suet. *Iul.* 19.2 ('opera ab optimatibus data'); quotation from Cic. *Att.* II.1.6. Balsdon 1962 (C 168) thought the provinces were given provisionally, till the situation in Gaul should become clear; but there is no parallel for such a holding operation.

181 Suet. *Iul.* 19.1; Cic. *Att.* II.1.8 (trans. Shackleton Bailey).

182 Cic. *Att.* I.18.5 ('quam ignavus et sine animo miles!'), 19.4, 20.5.

183 Cic. *Att.* I.18.6, 20.3 (trans. Shackleton Bailey). For the *piscinarii*, see nn. 24, 38 above.

There should have been a *lustrum* in 60,[184] but the censors failed to achieve it as their predecessors had failed in 65 and 64. Cicero might well be depressed about the prospects for the Republic. He published a collection of his consular speeches in an attempt to remind people of his great deeds, and of a period, as he saw it, of concord and unity.[185] Pompey, on the other hand, allied himself with Caesar and Crassus. Cicero knew what that meant, and declined to join the alliance when invited in December 60. He preferred to fight for the Republic – as the doomed Hector for Troy.[186]

What had happened to the high hopes of the *lustrum* of 69, to the programme of reform through the tribunate? First, the so-called *populares* failed to keep the ideological initiative; the nadir of the popular cause was the moment in 61 when the idea of popular liberty was invoked to frustrate a prosecution so that a patrician playboy might be free to plunder a wealthy province.[187] Secondly, the Sullan oligarchy was tenacious of its power, taking full advantage of Pompey's absence and successfully living down part of its image of avarice and corruption; thanks to Cato, it could almost now be associated with old-fashioned civic virtue. Thirdly, and most fundamentally, the very structure of the Republic itself was strained beyond its capacity for survival. The census of 70–69 doubled the size of the citizen body; the conquests of Pompey doubled the size of Rome's empire. With three new kingdoms to rule as provinces, and the unprecedented glory of Pompey's achievement as a goal for emulous ambition, the prizes of success in the political competition could not be allowed to depend on the free vote of an electorate too big to control by legitimate means. The constant bribery scandals of the sixties show all too clearly that the Republican constitution was fast becoming unworkable.

184 Cic. *Att.* I.18.8, II.1.11. 185 Cic. *Att.* II.1.3; for his depression, cf. I.16.6, 17.8, 18.1f, 18.8.
186 Cic. *Att.* II.3.4, quoting *Iliad* XII.243. 187 See n. 167 above.

CHAPTER 10

CAESAR, POMPEY AND ROME, 59–50 B.C.

T. P. WISEMAN

I. CAESAR AND CLODIUS

It was clear from the moment of their election that the two consuls of 59 B.C. would be at loggerheads. The immediate issue, already foreseen in December, was a land law; Caesar was aiming to do as consul what the tribunes had failed to do in 63 and 60. Bibulus, on the other hand, was determined to resist it on behalf of Cato and the senatorial establishment. The familiar ideology of plebs and *patres* – explicit in Cicero's statement of his position on this occasion[1] – was now to be played out not as a conflict of tribunes and consuls but as a trial of strength between the consuls themselves.

Caesar's attitude to the populace was made clear as soon as he entered office. From now on the Senate's debates (and the proceedings of the people) were to be officially recorded and published, its business made accessible to the general citizen body. Helped, no doubt, by this publicity, Caesar went out of his way to be conciliatory to his opponents in the Senate. He chose Crassus, not Pompey, as the first *consularis* to be asked his opinion (not that the *optimates* would like that much better); he announced that in the alternate months when his colleague held the fasces his own official escort would be merely an orderly (his lictors to follow behind); and he assured the *patres* that he would bring in no legislation that was against their interests.[2]

In particular, they would find that the proposed land law did not contain any of the features they had found so objectionable in Rullus' bill four years earlier.[3] To prove it, he went through the text clause by clause, inviting criticism and offering to delete anything the Senate did not like. The Campanian land was not to be touched; the scheme would bring

Because of the richness of the material for this period, many source references are *exempli gratia.*

[1] Cic. *Att.* II.3.4 (Dec. 60): acquiescence in the land law would bring 'pax cum multitudine', but Cicero's own policy guides him ἀριστοκρατικῶς (see Plut. *Cic.* 22.1, p. 357 above).

[2] Suet. *Iul.* 20.1, and on *acta senatus Aug.* 5, 36.1; Dio XXXVIII.1.1; Suet. *Iul.* 21 (Crassus), 20.1 (*accensus* and lictors).

[3] See Crawford 1989 (C 187) who argues that the bill 'defined the status of almost all, if not all, the land in Italy'.

desolate areas of Italy back into cultivation, and put Roman citizens back on the land instead of encouraging them to riot in the city; the commission administering the distribution was to number twenty men, of whom Caesar as the proposer could not be one; it was to buy property only from willing sellers, and only at the value fixed in the censors' registration; and the money was available, thanks to Pompey's conquests and the heroism of his soldiers, who deserved the right to share in what their labours had made possible. What could be more reasonable than that?

His opponents had no answer, but blocked the bill from instinctive conservatism and fear of the *gratia* Caesar and his board would acquire. The majority distrusted Caesar and admired Cato; when Cato opposed the bill on principle, as an innovation to be resisted because it was an innovation, they followed his lead. Infuriated at Cato's obstructive filibuster, Caesar eventually used his *coercitio* to remove him to prison, but had to back down when so many senators trooped out with him. 'I'd rather be with Cato in prison,' said one, 'than in the senate-house with you.'[4]

The populace had presumably been able to follow all this in the published proceedings of the Senate. The consul had given the *patres* every chance to consider the bill on its merits, and emend it if they chose, but they had refused. Now the people must decide. Caesar called Bibulus to the rostra, and asked him before the citizen body what he thought of the land bill. 'I will have no innovations in my year of office', he replied. Caesar persisted, telling the people the bill would pass if only Bibulus agreed. 'I don't care if you all want it', snapped Bibulus; 'you shan't have it *this* year.' So much for the will of the sovereign people. Caesar followed up this tactical success by calling Pompey, who pleased the crowd with a thoroughgoing endorsement of the bill. Would he help Caesar to get it passed? 'If any dares to raise a sword', he declared impressively, 'I too shall raise my shield.' He meant that he would call up his veterans. Finally, Caesar brought Crassus to the rostra. Crassus, Pompey's lifelong rival, now indicated his approval of these words and his support for the land law. As in their consulship eleven years before, the two men seemed to have laid aside their rivalry for the public good.[5]

Bibulus had three friendly tribunes who might veto the bill, but their colleague P. Vatinius was wholly Caesar's man, and where popular enthusiasm was so strong even a veto could be defeated. So Bibulus (perhaps then, perhaps only after the passage of the bill) played a different card. He announced that on every day when the *comitia* could

[4] Dio XXXVIII.1–3 (3.2 for M. Petreius' remark), Ateius Capito *ap.* Gell. *NA* IV.10.8.
[5] Dio XXXVIII.4–5, Plut. *Crass.* 12.3.

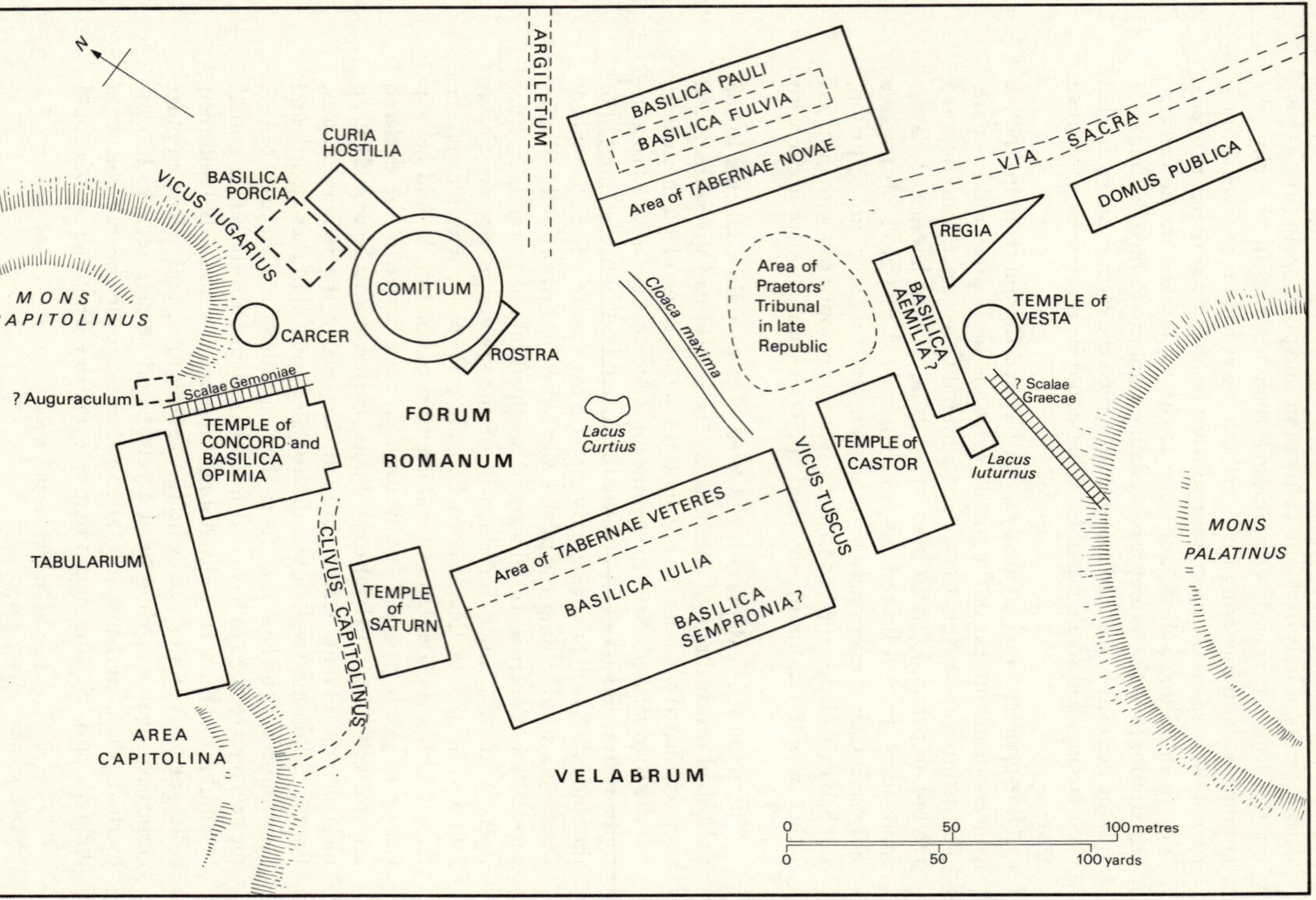

Fig. 2 The centre of Rome in the late Republic

legally meet, he would be watching the sky for omens, thus rendering every assembly technically invalid.[6]

Undeterred, Caesar and Vatinius fixed a day for the *comitia tributa*. The Forum was packed before dawn, and armed men – Pompey's veterans – were on the steps of the temple of Castor. Again it was Cato who led the opposition, this time forcing his way through the crowd as part of the consul Bibulus' escort. Undaunted by the opposition (someone emptied a basket of excrement on him as he passed), Bibulus managed to get up on to the platform with his lictors and his three tribunes to speak against the bill (and perhaps declare unfavourable omens). There was uproar. Bibulus' fasces were smashed, one of the tribunes who tried to veto the proceedings was hurled bodily down the steps, and a riot broke out in which several people were injured. Bibulus' friends got him safely into the temple of Jupiter Stator; Cato tried to hold his ground and make a speech of protest, but was physically removed by Caesar's supporters; when order was restored, in the enforced absence of the opposition, the bill was voted into law.[7]

In the Senate the following day, Bibulus tried to get the law invalidated, but the *patres*, intimidated by a hostile crowd, did nothing. When Bibulus appeared on the rostra, Vatinius ordered him to be imprisoned; the other tribunes, whose bench by the Tabula Valeria was between the rostra and the Tullianum prison, were able to insist on his release, but it was clear that Bibulus would never be allowed to exercise his authority in public again. He retired to his house for the rest of the year, and announced invalidating auspices on each comitial day, though to do so elsewhere than in the assembly seems to have been an innovation of doubtful force. His three tribune friends did the same.[8]

Caesar provocatively demanded from the Senate an oath of obedience to the law, and got it – even, eventually, from Cato and Metellus Celer, who resisted a long time. Celer remembered Metellus Numidicus' refusal to swear to the Lex Appuleia, but both men allowed themselves to be swayed by Cicero's argument that the Republic needed its defenders present and active, not uselessly in exile.[9] The trial of strength had gone totally Caesar's way.

Not long afterwards Metellus Celer died. The command of Transalpine Gaul was therefore vacant, just at the time when the proposed migration of the Helvetii and the installation of Ariovistus' German

[6] Dio XXXVIII.6.1, Cic. *Sest.* 113 for the tribunes.

[7] Dio XXXVIII.6.2–3; App. *BCiv* II.11; Cic. *Vat.* 5; Plut. *Pomp.* 48.1 (Lucullus among Bibulus' supporters); *Cat. Min.* 32.2f.

[8] Dio XXXVIII.6.4–6; Cic. *Vat.* 21 (see Coarelli 1985 (B 277) I 53f and 139 for the topography); at 6.6, Dio refers to a subsequent attempt by Vatinius to imprison Bibulus, this time from his house (cf. Cic. *Vat.* 22). Tribunes: Cic. *Vat.* 16. Legality: Linderski 1965 (F 100) 425–6.

[9] Dio XXXVIII.7.1f, *Plut. Cat. Min.* 22.3–6 (also M. Favonius).

kingdom west of the upper Rhine had made the whole Gallic frontier very unstable.[10] The Senate made out that everything was under control, granting C. Pomptinus a thanksgiving (and thus the expectation of a triumph) for his subjugation of the Allobroges' revolt. Vatinius' ostentatious protest at this gesture – he appeared in black at a huge banquet offered by one of the consular candidates – gave a clear indication of Caesar's thinking about his own proconsular command. No one can have supposed that the present consular 'provinces', the forests and drove-roads of Italy, would remain long unchallenged.[11]

First, however, Caesar had some debts to pay. The Asian society of *publicani* was given back one third of the price they had paid to the treasury for the right to farm the province's taxes (that kept Crassus happy), and the ratification of Pompey's eastern settlement was finally approved. Both measures were passed by popular vote; after his experience with the land law, Caesar took nothing to the Senate for discussion.[12]

Lucullus, with Cato's help, made a last vain attempt to thwart Pompey, but could make no progress against overwhelming popular opposition, and was forced into public humiliation on his knees before Caesar.[13] Cicero too was given a brutal reminder of vulnerability. Vainly defending his ex-colleague C. Antonius against a doubtless richly deserved charge of extortion, he complained about the political situation; in a matter of hours Cicero's deadly enemy P. Clodius had had his long-obstructed 'transition' to the plebs rushed through by Caesar as consul and Pompey as augur, in good time to stand for the tribunate.[14] Now that he and Pompey were on different sides, Cicero had no defence against the unpopularity he had earned with the execution of the plotters in 63. Antonius' condemnation was taken in some quarters as vengeance for Catiline, and greeted with rejoicing; with Clodius now unleashed, Cicero might well fear that he would be next.[15]

After the events of 62–61, Caesar and Pompey had little reason to cherish Clodius. But at the moment their enemies were also his enemies, and his popular attacks on Cicero and 'the tritons of the fish-ponds' (Lucullus and his friends) made him a very useful fellow-traveller. He

[10] Broughton 1948 (C 179) argues that Celer had given up his province and his death, therefore, was irrelevant to Caesar's plans.

[11] Provinces: Suet. *Iul.* 19.2. Metellus: Cic. *Cael.* 59f. Helvetii: Cic. *Att.* I.19.2, Caes, *BGall.* I.2. Ariovistus: Caes. *BGall.* I.31. Pomptinus and Vatinius: Cic. *Vat.* 30, with *Schol. Bob.* 149–50St.

[12] Dio XXXVIII.4.1; App. *BCiv.* II.10. *Publicani*: Cic. *Planc.* 35 (cf. *Att.* I.17.9). Pompey's *acta*: Vell. Pat. II.44.2.

[13] Suet. *Iul.* 20.4, Plut. *Luc.* 42.6.

[14] Cic. *Dom.* 41, *Prov. Cons.* 42, *Sest.* 16, *Att.* VIII.3.3. Antonius may have been on trial for *maiestas*.

[15] Cic. *Flacc.* 95f; for Cicero's *invidia*, cf. *Att.* II.9.1f, 19.4 (contrast I.16.11). Anxiety about Clodius' intentions: *Att.* II.4.2, 5.3, 7.2, 9.3, 15.2 (April); 18.3, 19.1 and 4, 20.2, 21.6 (June–July): 22.1f, 23.3, 24.5 (August?); *QFr* I.2.16 (November?).

was independent and not at all predictable, so to keep him on their side they had given him to understand that he might be offered a very profitable and prestigious mission to Alexandria.[16]

That had come about as the result of the long-disputed recognition of Ptolemy Auletes, now finally decided at a cost to the king of nearly 6,000 talents (140 million sesterces).[17] The money, which would no doubt go to finance the land distribution, had to be fetched from Alexandria by a suitably impressive Roman embassy. But there would also be some embassies going East as a result of the ratification of Pompey's settlement; the patrician Claudii had long had interests in the Greek world, and one of the missions was to king Tigranes of Armenia, at whose court Clodius' brother Appius Claudius had made a bold impression on a mission from Lucullus in 71 (ch. 8*a*, pp. 238–9). Perhaps because they felt Clodius had been given enough with his transfer to the plebs, Caesar and his two allies offered him not the Alexandrian embassy but the Armenian one – an inferior job, as Cicero observed with satisfaction. They also declined to have him on the board of twenty administering the agrarian law.[18] Clodius was stung, and reacted sharply.

Cicero spent early April in his house in Antium on the coast. He was profoundly depressed about the political situation, afraid of the future ('I shall be glad to enjoy even one more summer in my garden on the Palatine'), and vowing gloomily to devote himself wholly to literary study. But his letters show also a persistent hope that the pendulum would swing back, his opponents fall out among themselves, his own policy be vindicated.[19] On 19 April, emerging on to the Via Appia at Tres Tabernae on his way south to Formiae, he ran into one of Clodius' friends, young C. Scribonius Curio, son of a prominent noble:

> Curio asked me whether I had heard the news. I said no. 'Publius', says he, 'is standing for tribune.' 'No, really?' 'Yes, and as Caesar's deadly enemy, and means to undo everything they've done.' 'What about Caesar?' 'Says he had nothing to do with proposing Publius' adoption.'

For ten days or so, away from it all in Formiae, Cicero clung to this vain comfort ('Publius is our only hope!').[20] Then came some hard news which put it totally out of his mind.

Caesar's land law had exempted the Campanian *ager publicus* from distribution, no doubt as a concession to conservative opponents

[16] Cic. *Att.* II.9.1 ('de cynico consulari'); 5.1, 7.3 ('legatio ... illa opima' to Alexandria).

[17] Suet. *Iul.* 54.3, Dio XXXIX.12.1, Cic. *Vat.* 29, *Att.* II.16.2, *Fam.* I.9.7, *Rab. Post.* 6, Caes. *BCiv.* III.107.2.

[18] Cic. *Att.* II.7.2–3 ('subcontumeliose tractatur noster Publius'); Plut. *Luc.* 21 on Appius (perhaps an episode from Archias' epic poem on Lucullus' campaigns).

[19] Cic. *Att.* II.4–12, esp. 7.2–4, 9.1–3 (quotation from 4.7).

[20] Cic. *Att.* II.12.2 (trans. Shackleton Bailey), 15.2; contrast 8.1 ('bene habemus nos, si in his spes est'), and see n. 15 above for Cicero's fear of Clodius' plans about himself.

reluctant to leave the public treasury totally dependent on income from abroad.[21] Now, however, with the opposition reduced to impotence, and after three months' experience of trying to get landowners to sell the commission enough land to distribute elsewhere, the exemption was revoked; a second land law was passed, for the distribution of the *ager Campanus* and the *ager Stellas* nearby to 20,000 citizens with three or more children.[22]

This very controversial measure came at the same time as Pompey's remarriage. His new wife was Caesar's daughter Julia. The combined effect was to confirm Pompey's commitment to Caesar's programme in the eyes of those who had hoped the alliance was merely temporary. Up to now, Pompey had approved of Caesar's measures, but had distanced himself from the means employed to achieve them:

> Very well, my good Sampsiceramus [Cicero liked to refer to Pompey by the somewhat comic name of this oriental potentate], but what are you going to say now? That you have arranged a revenue for us in Mt Antilibanus, and taken away our rents in Campania? Perhaps the answer will be: 'I'll keep you under with Caesar's army.'

The prospects for the Republic did not look good. 'I am entirely of your opinion', wrote Cicero to Atticus, 'Sampsiceramus is out for trouble. We can expect anything. He is confessedly working for absolute power ... They would never have come this far if they were not paving their way to other and disastrous objectives.' Unable to believe that land reform could be politically desirable in its own right, senatorial opinion evidently feared a dictatorship like Sulla's, with opposition held down by terror and massacre.[23]

These fears seemed to be confirmed by the tribune Vatinius, who now passed a law giving Caesar a five-year command in Cisalpine Gaul and Illyricum, with three legions. 'I'll keep you under with Caesar's army'; if necessary, these legions could be stationed only a few days' march from Rome itself. The Senate, which had tried to prevent Caesar from holding a real province at all, now wanted to get him as far away as possible – or did not dare to oppose his will. Transalpine Gaul, with an extra legion, was added to his command by senatorial decree, on the proposal of Pompey. Vatinius himself was named by Caesar as a legate, clearly in order to avoid prosecution when he left office.[24]

21 Dio XXXVIII.1.3 (οἴκοθεν), Cic. *Att.* II.16.1 (*vectigal domesticum*); cf. Cic. *Leg. Agr.* II.80–3 on the Rullan bill.

22 Suet. *Iul.* 20.3, Dio XXXVIII.7.3, Vell. Pat. II.44.4, Brunt 1971 (A 16) 314–8. Cf. Cic. *Att.* II.15.1, which implies a previous shortage of available land.

23 Cic. *Att.* II.16.2, 17.1 (translations by Shackleton Bailey); 18.1, 19.2, 20.3, 21.1, 24.4 (fear of *caedes* etc.); Plut. *Caes.* 14.6–8 (armed soldiers in the Forum, evidently in the context of the *lex Campana*).

24 Suet. *Iul.* 22.1, Dio XXXVIII.8.5, Cic. *Att.* VIII.3.3 (Pompey), *Vat.* 35 (Vatinius).

Caesar also offered Cicero a post as legate; and then, when one of the members of the land commission died, invited him to take the vacant place. He knew that Cicero might be glad of an honourable excuse to avoid Clodius' year as tribune. He knew too that Cicero was resentful of the senatorial establishment, which had so conspicuously refused to give him the honour and recognition he felt his deeds as consul had deserved.[25] So why should he refuse? But Caesar was too late. Earlier in the year Cicero could have been won over (so he confessed, perhaps jokingly, to Atticus) by the offer of Metellus Celer's place in the college of augurs; but he was not going to be beholden to Caesar now that the latter's tactics had brought such universal condemnation from men whose good opinion he valued more. In later years Caesar blamed Cicero's refusal for all that happened afterwards; 'he was so hostile that he wouldn't even accept an honour at my hands.' He could not see that for Cicero in July 59 his hands were those of a potential Sulla.[26]

Pompey was unpopular for the first time in his life, attacked from the stage at the *ludi Apollinares*, savaged by Bibulus in edicts people crowded round to read, abjectly diffident on the rostra where once he had been the people's hero. Cicero was sorry for him, though secretly glad at the collapse of his *gloria*. 'For my part I do not fight what they are doing on account of my friendship with him, and I do not endorse it, for that would be to condemn all that I did in days gone by.' But he was afraid of what Pompey might be provoked to do under the strain of these humiliations.[27]

Caesar too was uneasy about Pompey, seeing him unburden his frustrations to Cicero, of all people. So it suited him very well when a certain L. Vettius gave evidence in the Senate about a group of aristocrats, led by young Curio, who were allegedly plotting to assassinate Pompey. Brought to the rostra by Caesar and Vatinius, Vettius proceeded to incriminate some senior senators as well, his final list including Bibulus, Lucullus and even Cicero as well-wishers to the plot. Cicero was sure the whole thing was a put-up job by Caesar, and certainly it turned out in Caesar's interests, with unresolved suspicions left to poison the political atmosphere between Pompey and the senatorial opposition. For Vettius was strangled in prison before he could be put on trial and his evidence subjected to cross-examination.[28]

[25] Cic. *Att.* II.16.2 ('. . . ingratis animis eorum hominum qui appellantur boni, qui mihi non modo praemiorum sed ne sermonum quidem umquam fructum ullum aut gratiam rettulerunt'), cf. I.18.6, 20.3 (p. 366 above), II.9.3. Caesar's offers: II.18.3, 19.4, Vell. Pat. II.45.2.

[26] Cic. *Att.* II.5.2 (augurate, early April); IX.2a.1 (Caesar's complaint). Condemnation of *regnum*: *Att.* II.13.2 (April), 18.1f (June) 19.2f, 20.3f, 21.1–5 (July), 22.6 (August). See especially 21.1: 'de re publica quid ego tibi subtiliter? tota periit.'

[27] Cic. *Att.* II.17.2 (Cicero's *Schadenfreude*), 19.2 (trans. Shackleton Bailey 1965–70 (B 108)), 19.3 (*ludi*), 21.3 (rostra), 21.4 (edicts), 22.6 (Cicero's fears), 23.2 (Pompey's dilemma).

[28] Cic. *Att.* II.24.2–4, *Vat.* 24–26.

The tensions caused by the Vettius affair exacerbated both the political issues that dominated the second half of the year: the consular elections and the prospects for Clodius' tribunate.

It had been rumoured at first that Pompey and Crassus themselves would stand for election as consuls for 58. That would have blocked the other candidates, of whom five are known: the jurist Ser. Sulpicius Rufus, who had been beaten by Murena for the consulship of 62; Pompey's friend A. Gabinius, the popular tribune of eight years before; Q. Arrius, a *novus homo* whose patient accumulation of political credit was second only to that of his friend Crassus; L. Lentulus Niger, probably one of the three Lentuli who had prosecuted Clodius in 60; and L. Piso Caesoninus, an undistinguished noble with a reputation for old fashioned austerity. Arrius, like Gabinius, advertised his candidacy with a gladiatorial show; he had hoped for the support of the three allies, but it was not forthcoming. Lentulus' prospects were damaged by Vettius' allegation that he knew of the plot to kill Pompey; Piso, on the other hand, emerged unexpectedly as a front runner when Caesar married his daughter. In the event, Pompey's friend A. Gabinius, the popular tribune of 67, and Caesar's new father-in-law L. Piso were the alliance's candidates.[29]

Bibulus had succeeded in getting the elections postponed, and the Senate deliberately did nothing about allocating consular provinces for the successful candidates. When the vote eventually took place in October, Gabinius and Piso were elected. A prosecution for bribery against Gabinius came to nothing: the praetors, no doubt fearing popular reaction, would not allow the prosecutor to make his application. He countered with a violent public speech against Pompey as an 'unofficial dictator', and was lucky to escape with his life.[30]

The result seemed to be good for Cicero. Piso, in spite of the tie with Caesar, looked like a sound conservative; Gabinius was Pompey's man, and Pompey had given his word to protect Cicero from Clodius. Moreover, next year's praetors and tribunes (Clodius apart, of course) were men Cicero felt he could trust.[31] But Clodius himself was dangerously powerful. The Vettius affair had rallied popular feeling behind Pompey and Caesar and against the senatorial opposition, thus restoring the good old plebs–*patres* polarity Clodius relied on for his programme of popular reform and vengeance on the people's enemies. Cicero would pay for the executions of December 63, though whether by a trial before the people or by direct violent action remained to be seen. He himself

[29] Cic. *Att.* II.5.2, 7.3, *Vat.* 25. Piso: Cic. *Sest.* 19f, 21f; Plut. *Caes.* 14.5, Suet. *Iul.* 21 for the marriage (exact date uncertain).

[30] Cic. *Att.* II.20.6 (Bibulus); *Sest.* 18, *Pis.* 12 (provinces); *QFr* I.2.15 (C. Cato's attempt to prosecute).

[31] Cic. *QFr* I.2.16. Pompey's promise: *Att.* II.9.1 ('quae de me pacta sunt', cf. *Sest.* 15), 19.4, 20.2, 21.6, 22.2, 23.3, 24.5.

demanded to stand trial. But why should he be given a chance to defend himself, when Lentulus and Cethegus had not? And in the *comitia centuriata*, where the well-off predominated? For Clodius and the Forum crowd, Cicero was manifestly guilty, awaiting not a trial but summary punishment.[32]

Cicero kept away from the senate-house and the rostra at this time. He concentrated on forensic work – and when his defence speeches touched on political questions, he kept his voice down.[33] He shared with the upper-class jurors alone his misgivings about the power of the ignorant mob and the total loss of the Senate's authority.[34] But he did his own cause no good by defending L. Valerius Flaccus, a man whose prosecutors could confidently raise their voice in indignation beyond the jurors to the citizens standing round the court. Like C. Antonius earlier in the year, Flaccus was notorious for extortion in his province; Pompey, who felt strongly on this subject, had been determined to get them both before a jury.[35]

Flaccus, unlike Antonius, was acquitted – even though, shortly before this, Caesar had passed a new and very comprehensive *lex repetundarum*, which was to remain for centuries the basis of the Roman law of provincial administration. The juxtaposition was eloquent in itself. Cicero could persuade senatorial and equestrian jurors to acquit a corrupt governor; Caesar, the consul with whom the Senate would not co-operate, brought to the assembly the legislation necessary for reform.[36] And Pompey, as in 70 and 67, looked benevolently on as the Roman people attacked the abuse of senatorial authority. (Significantly, equestrian jurors were not made liable for receiving bribes, as magistrates were, under this law.) In that very favourable atmosphere, Clodius entered on his tribunate at the beginning of December.

Like Rullus five years before, Clodius had prepared his legislative programme carefully in advance. He immediately announced four bills to be put to the people at the beginning of January, of which the most important was a thoroughgoing reform of the import of subsidized grain, regulating the whole system from the cornfields of Sicily, Sardinia and Africa, through the shippers and contractors to the warehouses and distribution centres at Rome – and the five-*modius* ration was now to be

32 Cic. *Flacc.* 4f, 96f, *QFr* I.2.16, *Sest.* 40 (*iudicium populi*); n. 15 above. For Clodius' tactical quandary before the Vettius affair, cf. *Att.* II.22.1; for Cicero's view of the Forum crowd as contaminated by slaves, cf. *Att.* I.16.5, II.1.8, 16.1.

33 Cic. *Att.* II.22.3, 23.3, *Flacc.* 66 (contrast *Sull.* 30f, 33).

34 Cic. *Flacc.* 2, 3f, 15 ('nullam enim illi nostri sapientissimi et sanctissimi viri vim contionis esse voluerunt'), 94–6. How much of this was spoken in the Forum, and how much added for the written version?

35 Cic. *Att.* I.12.1 (Antonius), *Flacc.* 14; cf. *Flacc.* 69 (Flaccus' prosecutor appeals to *corona*).

36 App. *BCiv.* II.10, Dio XXXVIII.4.1 – all Caesar's consular business done through the *comitia tributa*. Cic. *Vat.* 29 for the severity of the extortion law.

free to all Roman citizens domiciled in the capital.[37] In addition, the *collegia*, banned by senatorial decree in 64, were to be restored; the use of the auspices to block legislation, especially that by tribunes, was to be rigorously controlled (Bibulus' tactics to be outlawed, in effect); and the censors were to lose their arbitrary power over senatorial membership, a formal investigation and the agreement of both censors being required henceforth before any senator could be expelled. This fourth measure was probably to counter a danger already perceived in 64 – that the opponents of reform would use the censorship to demote active tribunes at the next *lustrum*, thus effectively reactivating the deterrent of Sulla's law (debarring tribunes from further careers) which had been repealed in 75.[38]

Assured of popular support, Clodius could afford to ignore the hostility of his fellow-tribune L. Ninnius Quadratus. The incoming consuls still had no provinces to look forward to, and would need Clodius' help to get good ones; he could be sure they would put up no opposition. As for Cicero, anxiously anticipating his enemy's onslaught on himself, Clodius professed to make a deal with him: no attack on the legislation, no prosecution for getting Lentulus and Cethegus executed.[39] The security of Clodius' position was demonstrated on the last day of the year, when he allowed Bibulus no opportunity to address the people as the consul gave his statutory end-of-term oath, and again on the first day of 58, when his agent Sex. Cloelius celebrated the banned *ludi Compitalicii* in anticipation of the law restoring the *collegia*.[40]

The tribune's tactics worked perfectly. There was no opposition on 1 January, and three days later the four bills were made law. Sex. Cloelius set about administering the corn law, and organized the reconstituted *collegia* with the maximum of provocative publicity, using the temple of Castor as his headquarters.[41]

Clodius' legislation, indeed the very legality of his tribunate, was technically dependent on the validity of Caesar's acts as consul in 59, all of which Bibulus and his friends insisted had been illegal. The opposition concentrated on the greater enemy, hoping that the lesser would fall with him. Two of the new praetors, L. Ahenobarbus and C. Memmius, proposed that the Senate should not recognize Caesar's

[37] Cic. *Dom.* 55 ('omne frumentum privatum et publicum, omnis provincias frumentarias, omnis mancipes, omnis horreorum clavis lege tua tradidisti'); *Pis.* 9, Asc. 8C for the four bills, passed on 4 January after the *trinum nundinum*; for the provinces involved, see Rickman 1979 (G 212) 104–19.

[38] Cic. *Sest.* 55f, *Pis.* 9, Asc. 7–8C; cf. Dio XXXVII.9.4 (64 B.C.), Asc. 66C, 78C (75 B.C.).

[39] Dio XXXVIII.14.1f (Ninnius and Cicero); Cic. *Sest.* 24, *Red. Pop.* 13, *Pis.* 28 (Piso and Gabinius). The deal with Cicero was probably arranged by Atticus, who persuaded him that the restoration of the *collegia* might even be to his advantage (Cic. *Att.* III.15.4, cf. *Sest.* 32).

[40] Dio XXXVIII.12.3 (Bibulus, cf. Metellus Nepos and Cicero in 63); Cic. *Pis.* 8, Asc. 7C (Cloelius). See on the *collegia* and the games Lintott 1968 (A 62) 77–83.

[41] Cic. *Dom.* 25 (*Lex frumentaria*); *Sest.* 34, *Pis.* 11, 23 (Castor temple), cf. *Cael.* 78 for Cloelius.

consular acts. For three days, meeting outside the *pomoerium* so that Caesar could be present, the *patres* debated the question at length. Caesar counter-attacked to good effect, and when the praetors failed to get a majority he left to continue with his recruiting for Gaul. Further attacks on his officers also failed.[42]

Caesar remained close to the city for as long as he could, to see how Clodius' programme would develop. The proximity of the proconsul and his forces would help to intimidate the opposition, but perhaps Caesar and Pompey thought it prudent also to keep an eye on Clodius himself. Though it was in his interests too to insist on the validity of Caesar's *acta*, his popularity was so great that he might be tempted to forgo that advantage if it suited him. He was quite capable (as was shown later that year) of using the *acta* of 59 to blackmail Caesar, Pompey and Crassus – a hostage for their acquiescence, as it were, like the consular provinces for Piso and Gabinius and the memory of December 63 for Cicero. So Caesar waited.

Confident and outrageous, Clodius proceeded to the second stage of his programme, to find the money to pay for the corn law. Just as Caesar had been able to use the king of Alexandria to raise money the year before, so now Clodius made profitable arrangements with the Galatian tetrarch Brogitarus, Deiotarus' son-in-law (see ch. 8*a*, p. 269), who wanted a kingdom of his own based on the Phrygian temple-state of Pessinus, and with certain wealthy citizens of Byzantium, in exile after trial and condemnation in their own city, who were asking for reinstatement backed by Roman authority. Clodius named his price, got the credit documents signed, and brought the appropriate legislation before the sovereign people. Happy to usurp the Senate's traditional role in foreign policy, the assembly passed both laws.[43]

The Ptolemy who was king of Cyprus had not followed his brother's example in 59; he had not paid for Roman recognition of his throne. So now another Lex Clodia was passed, confiscating Cyprus and its royal treasure for the Roman people. The new province would be attached to Cilicia, and the next proconsul of Cilicia would have the immensely profitable task of incorporating it.[44] Who was it to be? Clodius approached the consuls, and a deal was struck.

Two bills were announced on the same day, which would, after the statutory interval, become law simultaneously.[45] One was the long-

[42] Suet. *Iul.* 23.1, Cic. *Sest.* 40, *Schol. Bob.* 130, 146St; Cic. *Vat.* 33f; see Badian 1974 (C 165) 146f, 154–8.

[43] Cic. *Sest.* 56, *Dom.* 129 (*syngraphae*), *Har. Resp.* 28f ('legati te tribuno dividere in aede Castoris tuis operis nummos solebant'), 59. The consuls' law *de insula Delo*, with its reference to 'custodia publici frumenti', probably belongs in this context: see Nicolet *et al.* 1980 (B 212) 98f, cf. 149f for a corrected text of *CIL* I² 2500.

[44] Cic. *Sest.* 57–59, *Dom.* 20, 52f; Badian 1965 (C 162) 115–18 on Cilicia.

[45] Cic. *Sest.* 24f (*foedus*), 53 (*promulgatio*), *Pis.* 21 ('eodem et loci vestigio et temporis').

awaited allocation of the consular provinces, by which Piso and Gabinius received Macedonia and Cilicia respectively; the other was a restatement of the time-honoured principle that no Roman citizen should be put to death without trial, specifying exile ('interdiction from fire and water') as the penalty for a transgressor.[46] The effect of the bill was clearly to prepare the way for the condemnation of Cicero, by making irrelevant his defence that the Senate's emergency decree had given him the legal power summarily to execute Lentulus and the others; the law was the law, whatever the Senate might decide. Cicero was not mentioned by name; technically, Clodius had kept to his agreement not to attack him if he did not oppose his legislation. But the juxtaposition of the two bills carried its own message. The consuls would get their provinces if they left Cicero to his fate.

Though unwell, Piso received Cicero and explained the situation to him. Gabinius had to have a rich province to avoid bankruptcy; he could only get one by co-operating with Clodius; and just as Cicero had helped C. Antonius to a valuable province in 63, so Piso now felt he had to help Gabinius. He was sorry, but the consuls' hands were tied. Pompey had promised to protect Cicero, but now both he and Crassus pleaded helplessness; it was the consuls' business to bring the question to the Senate; Pompey would take action against Clodius if authorized by *senatus consultum*, but could do nothing otherwise. In fact, with the validity of Caesar's acts as consul still under fire, they could not afford to oppose Clodius, who now boasted that the three allies were on his side.[47]

Gabinius summoned the Senate to the temple of Concord, the scene of the momentous decision on 5 December 63. On that day the *equites* had occupied the Clivus Capitolinus; now they assembled on the Capitol again, not in arms but in mourning. The Senate pleaded; the *equites* came in a deputation and pleaded too; Gabinius was unmoved, confident in the knowledge of a hostile crowd outside. On the motion of Cicero's friend the tribune L. Ninnius, the Senate too voted to wear mourning. After the meeting, Gabinius and Clodius ordered the equestrian deputation to appear before the people in the Forum, where they were duly buffeted and insulted. 'You need not think', said the consul, 'that the Senate has any power! As for the *equites*, they are going to pay for that day when they stood on the Clivus with swords in their hands. And those who were afraid then will now be avenged.' Clodius took the same line: Cicero must go, and come back only when the martyrs of 63 B.C. came back from the dead.[48]

[46] Lintott 1967 (C 222) 163 holds with Vell. Pat. II.45.1 that the bill was not intended to create trials but simply banished those guilty.

[47] Cic. *Pis.* 12f (Piso), 77–9 (Pompey and Caesar), *Sest.* 39–41 (Pompey and Crassus).

[48] Cic. *Red. Sen.* 4 ('si revixissent ii qui haec paene delerunt, tum ego redirem'), 12, 32, *Sest.* 26–8, Dio XXXVIII.16.2–4. For the *equites* in 63, Cic. *Att.* II.1.7, *Phil.* II.16.

Cicero himself, meanwhile, was jeered and pelted whenever he appeared in public. He no longer had the protection of Pompey's friendship; Pompey took care to keep out of his way, and the men Cicero called to his advisory *consilium* were Pompey's old enemies, the 'fish-pond-fanciers' Lucullus and Hortensius, and Cato. Bitter things were said about Pompey's betrayal, which were seized on by Cicero's enemies to convince Pompey that his life was in danger. Clodius had succeeded in manoeuvring Cicero into isolation – an enemy of the people, as his brutally simple ideology required.[49] Lucullus, who was used to that role by now and could afford to ignore it, urged Cicero to stay and fight. Cato probably did the same. Hortensius, on the other hand, had already suffered the people's anger for supporting the *equites*' deputation; his advice was for Cicero to withdraw and await a swift and triumphant recall.[50]

What was Caesar's position? He had no love for Cicero's present advisers, and Cicero had refused his own repeated offers of protection. Clodius called a meeting in the Circus Flaminius, outside the *pomoerium*, to question Caesar before he left for Gaul. But the proconsul's careful answer cannot have pleased him: Caesar repeated his known view that the executions had been a mistake, but deplored any attempt to exact vengeance for them by retrospective legislation.[51] He needed Clodius now, but one day he might need Cicero too.

For the time being, however, nobody was to have the benefit of the great orator's golden tongue. Cicero's nerve broke. He took Hortensius' advice and left the city – proof of a guilty conscience, his enemies said. Caesar, knowing that Clodius' popular triumph made his own position secure for the moment, now at last left Rome for a war that urgently demanded his attention.

II. THE CONQUEST OF GAUL

Caesar's huge province – Narbonensian and Cisalpine Gaul, and the Adriatic coast of Illyricum – was threatened from both east and north. Burebista the Dacian had probably already expanded his power across the Danube as far as the Gallic Taurisci, perilously close to the easily

49 Cic. *Dom.* 55; Plut. *Cic.* 30.5 (*πηλῷ καὶ λίθοις βάλλοντες*), 31.2f (Pompey), 31.5 (Lucullus); Cic. *Att.* III.9.2 (Hortensius), 15.2 (Cato); Cic. *Sest.* 41, 67, Dio XXXVIII.17.4 (Pompey's suspicion).

50 Lucullus: Plut. *Cic.* 31.5, Cic. *Dom.* 110 (Clodius and M. Lucullus?); Plut. *Luc.* 43.1 for his retirement from politics. Cato: Cic. Att. III.15.2, *pace* Plut. *Cat. Min.* 35. Hortensius: Cic. *QFr* I.3.8 (also Q. Arrius), *Att.* III.8.4, 9.2, 13.2 (treachery); Dio XXXVIII.16.3f (also C. Curio), cf. *Fam.* VIII.2.1 ('intactus ab sibilo pervenerat Hortensius ad senectutem'). Hope of quick recall: *QFr* I.4.4, *Att.* III.7.2.

51 Dio XXXVIII.17.1f, referring back to his own speech on 5 December 63. For Piso at the Circus Flaminius *contio*, see Cic. *Red. Sen.* 13, 17, *Pis.* 14.

BRITANNIA
TRINOVANTES
Thames
English Channel
MENAPII
SUGAMBRI
EBURONES
UBII
SUEBI
MORINI
NERVII
ATUATUCI
BELGAE
ATREBATES
Sambre
AMBIANI
VIROMANDUI
TREVERI
BELLOVACI
REMI
Seine
Aisne
Meuse
Moselle
Vosges Mts
Rhine
AREMORICAE CIVITATES
PARISII
SUESSIONES
SENONES
Agedincum
CARNUTES
Cenabum
LINGONES
MANDURII
Alesia
VENETI
Quiberon Bay
Loire
SEQUANI
Doubs
Vesontio
Noviodunum
(Nevers)
Avaricum
Saône
AEDUI
Bibracte
BITURIGES
PICTONES
CELTAE
Allier
Jura Mts
HELVETII
Geneva
Gergovia
Gt St Bernard Pass
ALLOBROGES
ARVERNI
Bay of Biscay
Uxellodunum
Dordogne
Cevennes Mts
Rhône
VOCONTII
NITIOBRIGES
GALLIA TRANSALPINA
NARBONENSIS
Garonne
AQUITANI
RUTENI
SALLUVII
Massilia
Narbo
PYRENEES MTS
Land over 1000 metres
0 300 km
0 200 miles
4°W
0°
4°E
8°E
52°N
48°N
44°N
A
B
a
b
c

12 Gaul

passable Julian Alps and the vulnerable north-east corner of Italy. Similarly, the Suebian Ariovistus, invited across the Rhine by the Arverni and Sequani in their rivalry with the Aedui (Rome's allies), had installed an ever-growing body of Germans in lower Alsace, within easy range of the still-disaffected Allobroges in the Roman province.[52] The northern threat had seemed most acute in 61–60, when the defeat of the Aedui by Ariovistus had coincided with restless moves among the Helvetii; they intended to migrate from Switzerland westwards to the Atlantic coast, thus placing a dangerously warlike and powerful people in control of the Garonne valley and the western end of Gallia Narbonensis. But the Helvetian leader had died, and Ariovistus had been bought off by diplomatic gifts and the title of Friend of the Roman People. The disposition of Caesar's legions – three at Aquileia and only one in Narbonensis – showed where the main danger was perceived in early 58.[53]

It was an unwelcome surprise, therefore, when news came that the Helvetian migration had not, after all, been abandoned. They and their allies had burnt their settlements and arranged a muster of over 300,000 men, women and children to begin the great trek on 28 March. It was probably on or about 19 March that Cicero's capitulation left Caesar free to leave Rome. Eight days later he was at Geneva. Buying time with a pretence of considering the request of the Helvetii to pass through Roman territory south of the Rhône, Caesar blocked that route with earthworks, destroyed the Rhône bridge, and ordered new forces to be urgently recruited from the peoples of the Roman province. The Helvetii now succeeded in persuading the Sequani to let their wagon train pass through the Pas de l'Ecluse on the right bank of the Rhône. The borders of the province remained inviolate, but the long-term danger of the migration remained. The Helvetii would have to be stopped somewhere, and against their tens of thousands of fighting men Caesar needed more than just one legion.[54]

The army at Aquileia had been sent for, and Caesar's legates had been busy recruiting in Cisalpine Gaul. To the Transpadanes, the rumble of the Helvetian wagons was surely an ominous sound; old veterans of the war against the Cimbri and Teutones now saw their sons and grandsons enlist for a similar campaign. Leaving T. Labienus in charge at the Rhône, Caesar returned across the Little St Bernard to take command of five more legions – the three from Aquileia, and two made up of

52 Strab. VII.298, 303f (Burebista); Caes. *BGall.* I.31.3–11 (Ariovistus).

53 Cic. *Att.* I.19.2 (March 60); Caes. *BGall.* I.2–4 (Helvetii in 61), 7.2, 10.3 (legions), 35.2, 43.4 (Ariovistus).

54 Caes. *BGall.* I.5–9 (29.2 for the numbers). Dates: Plut. *Caes.* 14.9, 17.4, with Shackleton Bailey 1965–70 (B 108) II 227.

Cisalpine recruits (Latins having probably been accepted into the legions as though they were citizens).

The news from Rome was very satisfactory. Clodius had rearranged the Cyprus business. Ptolemy's kingdom would be taken over, not in 57 by Gabinius as proconsul of Cilicia, but immediately, by a special commissioner with *ad hoc* praetorian powers. The commissioner would be none other than Cato himself, and the Senate had endorsed the choice. A new law on the consular provinces returned Cilicia to praetorian status, and compensated Gabinius with Syria instead, a province where he had fought with Pompey and which offered opportunities for profitable action either against the Parthians or in Egypt. Cato was an honest man, and would bring back every penny of the king's treasure; but his acceptance of an extraordinary command, like those of Pompey in the seventies, legitimized by a law of Clodius, whose tribunate was only valid if Caesar's acts as consul were valid, left the opposition to Caesar and Pompey without a leg to stand on. Caesar wrote warmly to Clodius congratulating him on his *coup*.[55]

Despite opposition from the Alpine tribes, Caesar led his five legions into Transalpina by the most direct route (over Mt Genèvre). He caught up with the Helvetii too late to prevent the main body from crossing the Saône, just above its confluence with the Rhône, and passing into Aeduan territory; however, he defeated their rearguard, the Tigurini, quickly bridged the river himself, and followed. After fifteen days he turned aside towards the main Aeduan centre at Bibracte, to restock his army's grain supplies. Confident, the Helvetii turned in pursuit. Caesar placed all his baggage and equipment on a hilltop, guarded by his new recruits and the auxiliaries, while the four veteran legions waited on the slope for the enemy's attack. The Helvetii were driven back, but regrouped when their allies, the Boii and Tulingi, appeared in force to take the Romans on the flank. Caesar detached the third line from each legion to meet this new threat, and after a long struggle the Romans prevailed on both fronts. The Helvetian camp was captured, their fugitives hunted down, and they and their allies (except the Boii) sent back to rebuild their villages and occupy again the territory they had abandoned.[56]

Caesar now turned against Ariovistus. The excuse was that Ariovistus was demanding yet more land from his hapless allies, the Sequani, and the Aedui to the south-west and the Treveri to the north complained of being plundered by further contingents of Germans whom he had encouraged to follow him into Gaul. When Ariovistus defied his

[55] Cic. *Dom.* 20–23, *Sest.* 60f, Vell. Pat. II.38.6 ('senatus consulto'), 45.4 ('cum iure praetorio'); see Badian 1965 (C 162) 110–13 on Cato's title, 115–18 on Gabinius' provinces.

[56] Caes. *BGall.* I.10–29.

diplomatic threats, Caesar marched his army eastwards into the territory of the Sequani and occupied Vesontio (Besançon). From there he proceeded up the valley of the Doubs and into the territory between the Vosges and the upper Rhine. 'What do you mean,' demanded Ariovistus, 'by coming into lands that belong to me? This part of Gaul is my province, just as the other is yours.' Much good it had done him to become a 'friend of the Roman People' if the Romans were now busy detaching his tributary subjects from him! The parley came to nothing, and Caesar found good reasons to force the Germans to fight. With all six legions in action, he succeeded in breaking their battle-line and pursuing them to the Rhine, killing large numbers.[57]

Caesar had neutralized all the potential threats to the security of the Roman province – at the cost of going beyond it and attacking a 'friend of the Roman People', thus laying himself open to a charge under his own law on the provinces (p. 377) among others. And it was clear that he would not be content with what he had done. For he left his army with Labienus in winter quarters deep in Sequanian territory, 150 kilometres beyond the Rhône frontier; and when he returned to Cisalpine Gaul he sent his recruiting officers out again to raise two more legions.[58]

This time the news from Rome was more alarming. Clodius had gone out of his way to humiliate Pompey over the East by freeing his captive hostage Tigranes, son of the king of Armenia. When Gabinius, always loyal to Pompey, protested at this, he and Pompey were set upon by Clodius' supporters; the consul's fasces were smashed, and Clodius formally declared his property consecrated to the gods.[59] What was worse, Clodius had challenged the validity of Caesar's acts as consul, bringing Bibulus himself to testify before the people.[60] Evidently he was confident enough in his popular support to defy the obvious counter-argument that his own plebeian status was dependent on the validity of Caesar's acts. Who would dare to question the credentials of the man who had given the Roman people free corn? Besides, any attack on the tribunate and its legislation was now also an attack on Cato's Cyprus commission.

Clodius' political tactics, unhampered by concern for principle or consistency, had once again given him effective freedom of action. However, his volte-face had freed Pompey's hands with regard to Cicero; on 1 June the Senate had at last debated the matter of Cicero's return. Its overwhelming vote in favour was vetoed, but the pressure

57 Caes. *BGall.* I.30–54.

58 Caes. *BGall.* I.54.2 (presumably at Vesontio), II.2.1 (mentioned only *after* the news of the Belgic threat).

59 Dio XXXVIII.30.1f, Asc. 47C (Tigranes); Cic. *Dom.* 66, 124, *Pis.* 28.

60 Cic. *Dom.* 40, *Har. Resp.* 48.

had been kept up until 11 August, when a slave of Clodius ostentatiously dropped a dagger in the vestibule of the temple of Castor as Pompey was arriving for a Senate meeting. As always, the threat of assassination sufficed to keep Pompey at home, and Clodius' armed pickets made sure he stayed there.[61]

Was it for this that Pompey had restored the tribunes' powers, and Caesar defied the Senate in the people's name?[62] The Roman populace must be urgently reminded who its true benefactors were. As consul, Caesar had brought the Senate's deliberations directly to the people by the *acta senatus*; so too as proconsul, he would report to them on the way the responsibilities they had entrusted to him were being carried out.

In Caesar's commentary on his first year of campaign, one of the most conspicuous episodes is the panic at Vesontio before the march into Ariovistus' territory. As Caesar tells it, the crisis was caused by the cowardice of the equestrian officers 'who had followed him from Rome to cultivate his friendship' – in pointed contrast with the steadfast loyalty of the Tenth Legion, whom he then mounted as quasi-*equites* for his bodyguard at the parley with the German king. Ariovistus is made to boast of the contacts he has had with Caesar's enemies in Rome; in the subsequent battle, the Roman victory is credited to the quick thinking of Crassus' son. Of Caesar's six senatorial lieutenants – five legates and a quaestor – the only one to be named is T. Labienus, the popular tribune of 63 B.C., who is mentioned on three separate occasions; when he misses a chance to attack the Helvetii, Caesar blames it on the incompetence and cowardice of a certain P. Considius, of the same name (and no doubt the same family) as an old senator who had dared to defy Caesar in 59.[63] Although Caesar was writing no doubt partly for the grateful provincials of Narbonese Gaul (where an epic bard was already at work on the 'Bellum Sequanicum'),[64] it is clear that his main intended audience was the Roman populace, who must have enjoyed listening to these deeds of conquest and vengeance carried out in their name. So too perhaps did the Italians, who provided most of his troops and whose towns he was soon courting with gifts.[65]

The consuls for the coming year would be P. Lentulus Spinther and Q. Metellus Nepos. Lentulus, an enemy of Clodius, had been helped in

[61] Cic. *Sest.* 67–9, *Har. Resp.* 49, *Pis.* 28; Asc. 46–7C, quoting the *acta diurna* ('hominibus armatis praesidiis dispositis a re publica remotus Cn. Pompeius obsessus est').

[62] Dio XXXVIII.30.3 (Pompey and the *trib. pot.*).

[63] Caes. *BGall.* 1.39.2, 40.14f, 42.5f; 44.12 (Ariovistus), 52.7 (P. Crassus). Labienus: 10.3, 21f, 54.3; for Considius (21f), see Cic. *Att.* II.24.4, Plut. *Caes.* 14.8.

[64] Prisc. *Inst.* 1.497H (Varro Atacinus). Gallic Roman citizens mentioned by name: *BGall.* 1.19.3, 23.2, 47.4, 53.5–8. Caesar's care for the *provincia*: 1.8.3, 10.2, 14.3, 28.4, 33.4.

[65] *Populus Romanus*: e.g. *BGall.* 1.13f, 35, 45. Vengeance: 1.7.4, 12.5–7 (L. Cassius, L. Piso). Gifts to Italian towns: Suet. *Iul.* 28.1. There is no evidence for the traditional, but inherently improbable, view that Caesar wrote all seven books of his Gallic *commentarii* together, in 51–50 B.C.

his campaign by Caesar; Nepos, Cicero's enemy since his chaotic tribunate in 62, had broken with Pompey thereafter and opposed Caesar's consulship. That suggested that Caesar and Clodius might be on different sides in the issue that now dominated politics in the city – the question of Cicero's return. One of the tribunes-elect, P. Sestius, had even come to Cisalpine Gaul to enlist Caesar's support on Cicero's behalf.[66] Caesar was cautious: Clodius not only had great support among the Roman populace, support that might still be mobilized after he had gone out of office, but unlike any other popular tribune he could count on the influence of a great patrician family, with all that that meant in patronage and political alliances. His brother Appius was praetor-elect, his other brother Gaius was likely to be successful at the next praetorian elections (for 56); consulships might well follow, and Caesar had to look ahead to the expiry of his five-year command.

Meanwhile, as the proconsul held court in each of the Cisalpine colonies in turn, the messengers doubtless came north with regular news. On 29 October eight tribunes proposed a bill for Cicero's recall; it was vetoed. On 10 December it became clear that the new bench of tribunes was also eight to two in favour of Cicero. On 1 January Metellus Nepos declared himself ready to sacrifice his private animosity to the will of the Senate; a unanimous resolution for Cicero's recall was blocked by a tribune. On 23 January another tribune tried to put a bill to the people for recall, but was prevented by riot and bloodshed (gladiators had been provided by the praetor Ap. Claudius); Q. Cicero, pleading for his brother, was driven from the rostra in fear for his life.[67] Pompey, prudently out of Rome, was touring the country towns of Italy, mobilizing the landowners for a possible vote in the centuriate assembly: *tota Italia*, the new citizen body created by the census of 70–69, might prevail over a city populace still faithful to its patrician demagogue. Before he left to rejoin his legions, Caesar let it be known that he approved of Pompey's initiative.[68]

Labienus' reports during the winter must have told Caesar how the peoples of northern Gaul had reacted to his provocative wintering of the army in the territory of the Sequani. The tribes of the north-west (in Normandy and Brittany) seemed to be acquiescent, but the Belgic peoples north-east of the Seine were mustering their forces to resist. Only the southernmost of them, the Remi, were reluctant. Caesar took his two newly recruited legions to join the six at Vesontio, and then,

[66] Lentulus: Dio XXXIX.6.2 (Clodius), Caes. *BCiv.* I.22.3f. Metellus: Cic. *Att.* II.12.2 (attitude in 59). Sestius: Cic. *Sest.* 71.

[67] Cic. *Att.* III.23, *Sest.* 69–77, *Red. Sen.* 5f, 21f, *Red. Pop.* 11f, *Pis.* 34f; Dio XXXIX.7.2 (gladiators).

[68] Cic. *Prov. Cons.* 43, *Pis.* 80, *Fam.* I.9.9 ('seque quae de mea salute egisset voluntate Caesaris egisse'); *Red. Sen.* 29, *Red. Pop.* 16.

without even the pretence of a defensive motive, marched north into the territory of the Belgae.

The Remi sent an embassy of submission, and told Caesar that the combined forces of the Belgic coalition numbered over 240,000. The Suessiones, Bellovaci and Ambiani were successively invaded and forced to surrender. Beyond them to the north-east, however, the Nervii were defiant. Joined by the Atrebates and Viromandui, they were waiting in ambush in the wooded heights above the Sambre as Caesar's army started to build its camp on the other side of the river. Their headlong assault took the Romans totally by surprise, and it was only by the most desperate improvisation, and heroic work by Labienus and the Tenth Legion, who returned to the rescue after pursuing and defeating the Atrebates, that the Nervii were eventually beaten and their army effectively destroyed.[69]

Caesar now detached a legion under P. Crassus to march south-west and bring into submission the peoples between the Seine and the Loire. With the rest, he continued north-east into the territory of the Atuatuci, who had been on their way to help the Nervii and were now defying the Romans from the heights of their fortress above the Meuse. They surrendered at the sight of the siege-towers, but then tried to break out at dead of night; Caesar therefore enslaved all he found within, 53,000 of them; their sale must have been very profitable.[70]

When in due course reports arrived from young Crassus that the peoples of north-west Gaul had submitted and given hostages, Caesar sent laurelled despatches to Rome. The whole of Gaul, as far as the Rhine and the Ocean, had been brought under Roman control in two seasons' fighting. He put his legions in winter quarters in Belgic territory and along the Loire, with the exception of the Twelfth, which he sent to the Val d'Entremont (the upper Rhône, south-east of Lake Geneva) to secure the Great St Bernard route across the Alps. Then he hurried back to the Narbonese province, to Cisalpina, and eastward to Illyricum.[71]

On the way, he heard that his despatches had been greeted at Rome with immense enthusiasm, that the Senate had voted a fifteen-day thanksgiving (even Pompey had only had ten), and that the proposer of the motion had been – Cicero.[72]

Pompey's appeal to Italy on Cicero's behalf had proved successful. In July, when Rome was always crowded for the *ludi Apollinares* and the elections, the consuls had written to the municipalities summoning all patriotic citizens to the capital. A series of weighty senatorial decrees had

[69] Caes. *BGall.* II.1–28. [70] Caes. *BGall.* II.29–34.

[71] Caes. *BGall.* II.34f, III.7.1 (Illyricum), 8.2–5 (hostages). *Litterae laureatae*: Cic. *Pis.* 39, Pliny *HN* XV.133.

[72] Caes. *BGall.* II.35.4, Cic. *Prov. Cons.* 26f, *Balb.* 61.

been passed while the urban crowd was thus outnumbered, and the loyal Italians were asked to return on 4 August for the vote of the centuriate assembly.[73] They had done so, and with the support of the tribunes P. Sestius and T. Annius Milo, who had raised their own forces to counter Clodius' strong-arm men, the *centuriae* duly voted for Cicero's recall.[74]

On the day the Senate declared in the Capitoline temple that Cicero had saved the state, the immortal gods had seen fit to reduce the price of corn – or perhaps, as cynical persons suggested, the dealers had released enough of their stocks to bring the price down from the crisis level that had driven a hungry crowd to stone the theatre audience at the *ludi Apollinares*.[75] Administering the Lex Clodia frumentaria meant organizing supply and storage as well as distribution, and the man Clodius had put in charge of it – his agent and *scriba* Sex. Cloelius – was perhaps more at home with angry mobs in the streets of the capital than with the wealthy landowners and shippers on whose co-operation the system depended. Cato had not yet brought back the king of Cyprus' treasure; public money was probably short, and they could get better profits selling in other markets. They liked to open their granaries in Rome at the last minute anyway, to get the highest price just before the new harvest, and this time they could manipulate the shortage to help their friend Cicero.[76] Not surprisingly, therefore, when this artificial respite was over and the price crept up again, the crowd had blamed Cicero himself. Encouraged by Clodius' agents, they had stoned Metellus Nepos as he summoned the Senate to the temple of Concord.[77]

Cicero was making a triumphal progress up the Via Appia from Brundisium.[78] He arrived on 4 September to a great welcome, in which the hungry populace took part as well. The Senate was in daily session about the corn shortage. It was a crisis comparable with that of the pirates in 67; perhaps the same solution was called for now? Both plebs and *patres* were divided. Clodius and Pompey, the new champion and the old, competed for the people's allegiance, and Pompey's record of achievement was demonstrably superior. In the Senate, Clodius resumed

[73] Cic. *Sest.* 116–23 (demonstrations at *ludi*), 128–30, *Red. Sen.* 25–7, *Pis.* 34, *Prov. Cons.* 43.

[74] Sestius and Milo: Cic. *Red. Sen.* 19f ('vim vi esse superandam'), *Red. Pop.* 15, *Sest.* 84–92, *Mil.* 94; Cicero's reputation suffered as a result of their tactics (*Att.* IV.2.7, *dedecus*). For the *centuriae* as the whole Roman people, including Italy, as against Clodius' urban supporters, see *Dom.* 89–90 ('homines in campum non tabernis sed municipiis clausis venerant').

[75] Cic. *Dom.* 15 (the two explanations), *Sest.* 129 for the occasion; Asc. 48C (*ludi Apollinares*).

[76] Cic. *Dom.* 11 ('frumentum provinciae frumentariae partim non habebant, partim in alias terras, credo, propter avaritiam venditorum miserant, partim, quo gratius esset tum cum in ipsa fame subvenissent, custodiis suis clausum contenebant, ut sub novum mitterent'); for *sub novum* see Arusianus *Gramm. Lat.* VII.509 Keil, Cic. II *Verr.* 3.214. Sex. Cloelius: Cic. *Dom.* 25f, with Wiseman 1985 (B 127) 39–41. Public money: Cic. *Dom.* 23 ('erepta ex visceribus aerarii'), *QFr* II.6.1 ('inopia pecuniae et annonae caritas', still in April 56). Cicero's friends: e.g. Cic. *Fam.* XIII.75 (C. Avianius Flaccus).

[77] Cic. *Dom.* 11–14 (probably in August, when Metellus had the fasces).

[78] Cic. *Att.* IV.1.4 ('iter ita feci ut undique ad me cum gratulatione legati convenerint').

his aristocratic persona, joining his social equals, Pompey's old enemies, in attacking extraordinary commands.[79]

On 7 September, the first day of the *ludi Romani* in honour of Jupiter Optimus Maximus, the Senate met in his temple. The Capitol was crowded, and those senior senators who opposed Pompey pointedly stayed away. As Cicero told Atticus:

> A crowd flocked first to the theatre and then to the Senate, clamouring at Clodius' instigation that the shortage was my doing . . . Pompey was eager for the commission, and the crowd called on me by name to propose it. I did so in a full-dress speech. In the absence of all the consulars except Messalla and Afranius, because, as they alleged, it was not safe for them to speak, the Senate passed a decree as proposed by me, to the effect that Pompey should be asked to undertake the matter and appropriate legislation be introduced.

On 8 September the *consulares* were present, and tried in vain to block the motion; Clodius dubbed Cicero 'hostis Capitolinus', and taunted him with having gone over to the people.

> The consuls drafted a law giving Pompey control over grain supplies throughout the world for a period of five years. Messius [a tribune] proposed an alternative bill which gives him control over all moneys, and in addition a fleet, an army and authority in the provinces superior to that of their governors.

Although the tribune's proposal, with its ominous reference to *imperium maius*, failed, it spelt out with brutal clarity the realities of Roman imperialism in the fifties B.C.: the empire was for the direct benefit of the Roman people, and its tribute and the armed force necessary to control it might have to be placed directly in the hands of the people's nominee.[80]

That was the atmosphere in which Caesar's despatches came to Rome. It was like the great days of the sixties again – Pompey in command on behalf of the people, whether the Senate liked it or not, and news of glorious conquest coming in from the ends of the earth. The unreliable Clodius, resorting in desperation to tactics of open terrorism (arson and attempted murder), was losing his popular support.[81] So it came about that the Roman people's unprecedented fifteen-day thanksgiving to the

[79] Cic. *Att.* IV.1.5 on Cicero's return ('gradus templorum ab infima plebe completi erant'), 1.6 on support for Pompey among plebs and *boni*. Clodius: *Dom.* 3–31, esp. 4, 18f (parallel with Lex Manilia), 26.

[80] Cic. *Att.* IV.1.6–7 (trans. Shackleton Bailey 1965–70 (B 108)), *Dom.* 4–10, Dio XXXIX.9.2f. 6 September: Cic. *Dom.* 6, 15. *Ludi Romani*: the *fasti Antiates maiores* show the games beginning on either 7 or 8 September; Cicero's reference to a theatre – presumably in the *area Capitolina* – confirms the earlier date.

[81] Cicero: Cic. *Att.* IV.2.5 ('illi, quos ne tu quidem ignoras, qui mihi pinnas inciderant, nolunt easdem renasci'), cf. *Fam.* I.7.7 (July 56). Clodius: *Att.* IV.3.2f ('post has ruinas, incendia, rapinas desertus a suis'); when Sex. Cloelius burnt down the temple of the Nymphs to destroy the corn-supply records, there was great popular hostility at his trial and indignation when the senatorial *iudices* acquitted him (Cic. *QFr* II.5.4, cf. *Cael.* 78).

immortal gods for Caesar's victories was voted by the Senate on the proposal of Cicero, who was indebted to him as well as to Pompey for his recall.

The prospects looked very good for Caesar. As Pompey had conquered from the Caucasus to the Red Sea, so now Caesar had conquered from the Atlantic to the Rhine – and perhaps soon also to the Danube. As he hastened east towards Illyricum, Caesar dictated a much briefer commentary on the second year of his command. This time, the Roman people did not need persuading.[82]

III. EGYPT AND PARTHIA

As in Gaul, so in the eastern Mediterranean, the commands voted by the Roman people had been carried out to good effect. Pompey had organized the Seleucid realm in Syria as a province in 64; after two successive praetorian governors it was now held by Gabinius with a special three-year command under a Lex Clodia.[83] Ptolemy of Cyprus, dispossessed of his kingdom by another Lex Clodia, had poisoned himself in despair; with the people's commissioner (Cato) now completing his account of the royal treasure for transfer to Rome, the island was attached to Lentulus Spinther's province of Cilicia.[84] As for the king of Alexandria, who had paid nearly 6,000 talents in 59 to keep his throne, he had been expelled by his infuriated subjects (ch. 8*c*, p. 319); his daughter Berenice now reigned in his stead, and her agents were in Syria looking for a Seleucid pretender to be her consort. Ptolemy Auletes himself was a guest at Pompey's Alban villa, requesting a Roman army to restore him to the kingdom Rome had guaranteed.[85]

In 57, while Lentulus Spinther was still consul, the Senate voted that he, as proconsul of Cilicia, should restore the king to Alexandria. However, one of the tribunes of 56, Clodius' friend C. Cato, publicized a prophecy found in the Sibylline books (Clodius was one of the *XVviri sacris faciundis* who were allowed to consult them) warning the Romans not to give help to the king of Egypt 'with a multitude'.[86] That suited the conservative majority among the *consulares*: it ruled out any dangerous *ad hoc* military command, whether for Pompey (which is what the king himself wanted), or for the detested Gabinius (whose two legions in Syria were closest to the scene), or even for Lentulus Spinther (whom his

[82] *BGall.* II is only half the length of I. Danube: see n. 52 above.

[83] App. *Syr.* 51 (L. Philippus and Cn. Lentulus Marcellinus, now consuls in 56); for Gabinius' command, see Cic. *Dom.* 23, 55, 80, with Sherwin-White 1984 (D 291) 272.

[84] Plut. *Cat. Min.* 36.1 (death of king), 36.2, 38 (accounts); Vell. Pat. II.45.4f, Strab. XIV.684f.

[85] See n. 17 above; Dio XXXIX.12, 13.1, 57.1, Strab. XVII.796, Cic. *Rab. Post.* 6.

[86] Dio XXXIX.15; Cic. *Fam.* I.1.3, *Pis.* 51 (*senatus consultum* of 57); *QFr* II.2.3, *Fam.* I.4.2 (oracle); *Har. Resp.* 26 (Clodius 'Sibyllinus sacerdos').

peers suspected of harbouring inappropriate personal ambitions).[87]

When the Senate debated the question on 13 January 56 B.C., it was overwhelmingly agreed that no army should be used. P. Servilius Isauricus (cos. 79) was urging that Ptolemy should not be restored at all. M. Bibulus proposed an embassy of three senior senators without *imperium* (excluding Pompey, therefore); Crassus preferred an embassy of three with *imperium*; Q. Hortensius, supported by Cicero and M. Lucullus, wanted Lentulus Spinther to go; L. Volcacius Tullus (cos. 66), supported by L. Afranius and other friends of Pompey, wanted Pompey to go. Bibulus' proposal was defeated; Hortensius' might have been passed, but a tribune friendly to Pompey intervened, and Spinther's opponents, who had no love for Pompey either, took the opportunity to delay any decision. On 2 February C. Cato announced a bill to be put to the people rescinding Lentulus Spinther's command. Another tribune, L. Caninius Gallus, wanted the people to appoint Pompey as ambassador to restore the king. Clodius' supporters were urging that Crassus be sent; Clodius' quarrel with Pompey had perhaps strengthened his ties with Crassus. The consul Marcellinus blocked the tribunes' legislation by putting festivals and thanksgivings on the available comitial days; C. Cato countered by threatening to prevent the elections. Eventually, the Senate voted on Servilius Isauricus' proposal, and resolved not to restore Ptolemy at all; predictably, that was vetoed.[88]

The king had retired to Ephesus to await events, and Rome was glad to be rid of him. Public opinion had been sickened, not only by his blatant bribery but because early in 56 the leader of the embassy which had come to represent the Alexandrians was assassinated in Rome; one of the king's agents, P. Asicius, was tried for the murder, but Cicero, no doubt acting at Pompey's request, got him off.[89]

Pompey's close association with the king was only one of several reasons for his dramatic loss of popularity at this time. Perhaps hopes had been raised too high at the time of the corn-supply crisis; there really was a shortage, and Pompey could not make it disappear in a couple of months as he had once done with the pirate menace. His legates were doing their best, but the price had still not come down. Clodius, now in office again as aedile, was glad to exploit popular dissatisfaction. He was also able to divert the blame for the street violence of 57 B.C. on to his

[87] Cic. *Fam.* I.I.If ('senatus religionis calumniam non religione sed malevolentia et illius regiae largitionis invidia comprobat'), 4.2 ('ut ne quis propter exercitus cupiditatem Alexandream vellet ire'). Pompey: Cic. *Fam.* I.I.4, cf. Plut. *Pomp.* 49.6. Spinther: Cic. *Fam.* I.7.8 ('quem tamen illi esse in principibus facile sunt passi, evolare altius certe noluerunt'), cf. I.I.3 *ad fin.* (unsound on Pompey).

[88] Cic. *Fam.* I.I.3, 2.If, 4.I; *QFr* II.2.3, 3.If, 5.2–5; *Fam.* I.5a.2, 7.4; Plut. *Pomp.* 49.6 (Caninius, cf. Cic. *Fam.* I.7.3); Dio XXXIX.16.If.

[89] Dio XXXIX.13–14, Strab. XVII.796 (for Pompey's involvement); Cic. *Cael.* 18 (Crassus' hostility), 23f, 51, *QFr* II.9.2 on Asicius; Wiseman 1985 (B 127) 60–2.

enemy T. Milo, whom he was now busy prosecuting before the people. Milo was defended by Pompey and Cicero, on whose behalf he had mustered his anti-Clodian forces the year before. But Clodius was confident now in the support both of the urban populace and of the senatorial establishment, perennially hostile to Pompey.

When Pompey spoke for Milo on 7 February, Clodius gave him a rough time:

> Pale with fury, he started a game of question and answer in the middle of the shouting: 'Who's starving the people to death?' 'Pompey' answered the gang. 'Who wants to go to Alexandria?' Answer: 'Pompey'. 'Whom do you want to go?' Answer: 'Crassus' (who was present as a supporter of Milo, wishing him no good).

Two days later, C. Cato attacked Pompey bitterly in the Senate, with the silent approval of Bibulus, Curio and the conservatives. Pompey told Cicero he was sure that Crassus too was supporting both C. Cato and Clodius, and that there was a plot against his own life; he was bringing up men from the country to defend himself.[90]

The news from Gaul was also discouraging. Caesar's legate Ser. Galba had had to abandon his winter camp in the Alps, and the maritime peoples of the north-west were in revolt. Caesar was now asking for ten legates – an unusually large number – and for money to pay the four extra legions he had raised. But Marcellinus' obstruction of tribunician legislation was blocking that, and in any case there was an acute shortage of public money: Cato was not yet back with the Cyprus treasure, and Pompey needed large sums for the corn supply. Serious moves were being made to stop distribution of the Campanian land in order to restore public income from rents, and Pompey seemed ready to accept this.[91] Caesar's old enemies felt confident. Cicero was preparing to press the Campanian question. L. Ahenobarbus had tried as praetor in 58 to get Caesar's command declared invalid; now feeling sure of election as consul, he was threatening that this time he would carry out his intention. Vatinius, on whose law the command depended, had failed to win the aedileship and was now being hounded by an ominously self-confident Cicero. There was even an attempt by one of the tribunes to have Caesar recalled and brought to trial. Nothing came of that, but it showed how violently the pendulum of popular sympathy was swing-

[90] Cic. *QFr* II.3.2–4 (trans. Shackleton Bailey 1980 (B 111)), *Fam.* I.5b.1 ('visus est mihi vehementer perturbatus. Itaque Alexandrina causa ... videtur ab illo plane esse deposita'). Cf. *QFr* II.1.3, 5.3 (Milo and the *boni*), 6.1 (*annonae caritas*).

[91] Gaul: Caes. *BGall.* III.1–9 (and see n. 71 above). *Decem legati, stipendia*: Cic. *QFr* II.5.3 (*monstra*), *Fam.* I.7.10. *Pecuniae inopia: QFr* II.6.1, *Prov. Cons.* 11. Campanian law: *QFr* II.1.1 (tribune P. Rutilius Lupus), 6.1, *Fam.* I.9.8 (Cicero).

ing.[92] Now that the old rivalry of Crassus and Pompey was out in the open again, the triple alliance seemed to be doomed.

Caesar, with more than half his command still to run, was in the strongest position of the three. Already the Via Flaminia had seen ambitious office-seekers on their way to solicit his support – among them Clodius' brother Appius, who would be standing for the consulship next year. Now, in April, Caesar came south to the Italian borders of his province, to confer first with Crassus at Ravenna and then with Pompey at Luca.[93] He offered his disaffected partners a deal: if the elections were delayed until after the campaigning season, when some of Caesar's soldiers could get to Rome and vote, then Ahenobarbus could be kept out and Pompey and Crassus themselves elected; tribunician legislation would then give them commands, if that was what they wanted. Caesar had no wish to monopolize the opportunity of imperial conquest: let his own command be extended at the same time, and they could share the glory and profit equally between them.[94]

Pompey sailed to Sardinia, where he had a serious talk with Quintus Cicero, working as his legate on the corn supply. He told him to remind his brother of a pledge Quintus had given for his behaviour at the time of his recall from exile. Caesar rode north to rejoin his army for the campaign against the Veneti. Clodius ostentatiously praised Pompey at a public meeting, and dropped his prosecution of Milo; Cicero decided not to attack the Campanian land law on 15 May, as he had planned; the threat of contentious tribunes' bills disappeared, and the Senate itself, with Cicero prominent in support, voted Caesar his legates and the pay for his legions.[95]

Cicero was not very proud of his change of course, but he knew whom to blame for it – the 'optimate' group (now centred round Bibulus) who had never really seen him as one of themselves and were on insultingly good terms with their fellow-aristocrat Clodius. In June or July, when an attempt was made to have one or both of Caesar's Gallic provinces assigned under the Lex Sempronia to the consuls about to be elected, Cicero defeated it with a great speech in praise of Caesar and the conquests that were now almost completed. He concluded pointedly:

[92] Suet. *Iul.* 23.1 (with Badian 1974 (C 165) for the date), 24.1; Cic. *Vat.*, *Fam.* I.9.7, *QFr* II.4.1 ('dis hominibusque plaudentibus').

[93] Suet. *Iul.* 23.2 (*petitores*), Cic. *QFr* II.5.4 (Appius); Caes. *BGall.* III.9.1 (shipbuilding on the Loire); Cic. *Fam.* I.9.9, cf. Plut. *Caes.* 21.2, *Pomp.* 51.3, *Crass.* 14.5, App. *BCiv.* II.17.62 for the senatorial well-wishers who thought it worth making the trip to Luca. Crassus was there too, according to the late sources.

[94] Plut. *Caes.* 21.3, *Pomp.* 51.4, *Crass.* 14.5f, App. *BCiv.* II.17.63.

[95] Cic. *Fam.* I.9.8–10, *QFr* II.7.2 (Cicero); *Har. Resp.* 51f (Clodius); *Fam.* I.7.10 ('perpaucis adversantibus omnia quae ne per populum quidem sine seditione se ⟨posse⟩ adsequi arbitrabantur per senatum consecuti sunt'), *Prov. Cons.* 28, *Balb.* 61.

I should like to convince all of you, but I shall not be too disappointed if the senators I fail to convince happen to be those who defied the Senate's authority by defending my enemy [Clodius], or those who will criticize my reconciliation with *their* enemy [Caesar], even though they themselves have not hesitated to be reconciled with one who is their enemy as much as mine.[96]

Cicero wanted Macedonia and Syria, the provinces given to Piso and Gabinius under the Lex Clodia, to be assigned to the next year's consuls, or better still (though he expected this would be vetoed), to the praetors of the present year, thus getting his enemies recalled even sooner. In fact, no tribune defended Piso. Macedonia was made a praetorian province, and Cicero could look forward to taking half his vengeance as early as 55.[97] Syria, however, was too important to be anything but a consular province; Gabinius could complete his three-year command there, and one of the next year's consuls would succeed him in 54.

Gabinius had been paying particular attention to the economic organization of his province. 'Financial deals with tyrants, settlements, robberies, acts of piracy ...'; the details are irretrievable behind the slanderous screen of Cicero's invective. Gabinius had ostentatiously refused to co-operate with the *publicani*, punishing those distinguished equestrians for their deputation on Cicero's behalf in March 58. No doubt that was welcome to the Syrians themselves, as was Gabinius' revival of the tetradrachm coinage with the types of Philippus Philadelphus (the last Seleucid king before Tigranes took over in 83); but in the end the main purpose of all his activity was surely to maximize Syria's contribution to the public income of the Roman treasury.[98]

There had also been serious military work to do, when Alexander, son of the deported Aristobulus, overran much of Judaea in rebellion against his brother Hyrcanus, whom Pompey had left in charge in Jerusalem. Gabinius had marched south in strength, and defeated Alexander in a pitched battle. Judaea then needed to be secured, by the fortification of strategic cities, and the Nabatean Arabs, who had never been properly subdued, demanded his presence as they had demanded that of his praetorian predecessors in 60–58.[99] Good reasons, no doubt, to keep Gabinius and his legions within easy striking distance of Alexandria just at the time Ptolemy Auletes was in Rome asking for an army to reinstate

96 Cic. *Prov. Cons.* 47; *Att.* IV.5.1f ('subturpicula mihi videbatur esse παλινωδία'), *Fam.* I.7.7f, 9.10–18.

97 Cic. *Prov. Cons.* 3–17; cf. 2 ('ad ulciscendi tempora reservabo'), 8 ('nihil dico, patres conscripti, *nunc* in hominem ipsum', anticipating the *In Pisonem*), 17 (expected veto).

98 Cic. *Prov Cons.* 9; Crawford 1985 (B 145) 203–5. *Publicani* (see n. 48 above): Cic. *Prov. Cons.* 10–13, cf. *Pis.* 41, *QFr* II.12.2, III.2.2, with Braund 1983 (C 178). No doubt Gabinius was using the local elites rather than the *publicani* as his partners in exploitation.

99 Joseph. *AJ* XIV.82–90, *BJ* I.160–8, App. *Syr.* 51, cf. Cic. *Prov Cons.* 9, *Sest.* 71; Smallwood 1976 (D 156) 31f. No doubt it was then that Samaria was renamed Gabinia (Cedrenus *Hist. Comp.* 184a).

him. But Gabinius had few friends in the Senate; the command had been given to Lentulus Spinther, and then in any case made nugatory by the Sibyl's prohibition of force.

In May 56 the Senate had refused Gabinius a thanksgiving for the Jewish campaign, and supported the *publicani* in an attack on his fiscal arrangements.[100] And now his province was promised to one of the consuls of 55. But at least Cicero had not been able to persuade the Senate to recall him early, like Piso. He could count on two more campaigning seasons; what could he do with them? First, he had to fight again in Judaea, for Aristobulus conveniently escaped from Rome to renew the rebellion his son had attempted the previous year.[101] Then, secure in the south at last, Gabinius turned his attention north and east.

Phraates of Parthia was dead, murdered by his sons Orodes and Mithridates, who were now fighting each other for the royal power. Mithridates came west, to ask for help from the man who nine years before had so alarmed his father by marching to the Tigris as Pompey's legate. Gabinius was tempted to intervene. Though he had killed enough Jews in the battle against Aristobulus to qualify him for a triumph, he knew it would take an exceptional campaign of conquest to make any impression on the hostile Senate that had rejected his *supplicatio*.[102]

Among Gabinius' advisers was Archelaus, the son of Mithridates of Pontus' renegade general of that name. Pompey's reorganization of the East had made him priest-king of the temple-city of Comana in Cappadocia, but he was ambitious for a greater realm. Claiming to be the son of the great Mithridates himself, he might well be acceptable in Parthia or one of its dependencies, and since his real father had proved a loyal ally to Rome, he would be more reliable than either of the warring sons of Phraates.

It was a bad moment to ask the Senate to approve anything Pompey or his friends might want. The tribune C. Cato, with help from Clodius as aedile, was effectively carrying out the strategy planned by the three allies at Luca – to prevent the consular elections from taking place until some of Caesar's soldiers could come to vote and the consul Marcellinus went out of office. Pompey and Crassus did their best to remain above the conflict, but when challenged by Marcellinus about their intentions had to admit that they would be candidates when the elections were eventually held. Caesar's enemy L. Ahenobarbus was persevering with

[100] Cic. *QFr* II.7.1, *Prov. Cons.* 14f, *Pis.* 41, 45; *Har. Resp.* 1–7, 17 (a slanging-match between Clodius and Cicero). See Shackleton Bailey 1976 (B 109) 70 on 'P. Tullio the Syrian' (i.e. Pantaleo?), supported by Clodius against the *publicani* (*Har. Resp.* 1).

[101] Joseph. *AJ* XIV.92–7, *BJ* I.171–4, Plut. *Ant.* 3.1.

[102] Parthian civil war: Dio XXXIX.56.2, App. *Syr.* 51. Jewish casualties: Joseph. *AJ* XIV.95, cf. Val. Max. II.8.1 (5,000 *una acie* required for triumph).

his own candidacy, strongly supported by his brother-in-law M. Cato (now back from Cyprus), who urged him to resist the tyranny of the three allies and their aim to monopolize the armies and provinces of the Republic.[103]

Not surprisingly, therefore, the Senate rejected Gabinius' proposal about Archelaus. While the proconsul continued his preparations for the Parthian campaign, Archelaus himself seized a new and more splendid opportunity. In Alexandria, Berenice had been disappointed with her Seleucid consort, a vulgar character (nicknamed the Salt-fishmonger) who lasted only a few days before being strangled at the queen's orders. Now her agents approached Archelaus. Gabinius demurred, and put him in irons, but the self-styled son of Mithridates escaped (Gabinius' enemies said the proconsul was bribed to let him go) and took control of the perilous kingdom of Egypt.[104]

For Ptolemy, waiting in Asia Minor, this bad news from one direction coincided with good news from the other; for now his friend Pompey was once more in political control at Rome. When Marcellinus went out of office, the new year, 55 B.C., opened with no magistrates. Elections were set in train under an *interregnum*. Young P. Crassus had come from Gaul, bringing with him substantial numbers of Caesar's soldiers and a glamorous new military reputation of his own. (His campaign in south-west Gaul, to bring the peoples of Aquitania into subjection, gave the promise of a great general in the making.) With this help, and some strong-arm tactics to intimidate Ahenobarbus, Pompey and Crassus duly entered on their second consulship.[105] In the elections for the other magistracies which followed – not without more bloodshed – Vatinius and Milo won praetorships, while M. Cato did not. The allies were firmly in control, and proposed to remain so: 'I dare say it's true', remarked Cicero to Atticus, 'that in the lists in their little notebooks the future consuls take up as many pages as the past ones.'[106]

The elections took place in January; and it must have been immediately afterwards that Pompey sent an urgent confidential message to Ptolemy in Asia Minor, with a letter for him to take to Gabinius. The king and his retinue set off for Syria, hoping to catch the Roman proconsul and his army before they marched east into Mesopotamia.[107]

Pompey and Crassus did their best to revive the atmosphere of their first consulship, fifteen years before. It was for the good of the Republic

[103] Dio XXXIX.27.3–30.4, Plut. *Pomp.* 51.5–52.1, *Crass.* 15.1–3, *Cat. Min.* 41.2f.

[104] Strab. XII.558 (οὐκ ἐπιτρεπούσης δὲ τῆς συγκλήτου), XVII.796, Dio XXXIX.57.

[105] Dio XXXIX.31, Plut. *Cat. Min.* 41.4f, *Crass.* 15.4f, *Pomp.* 52.1f. P. Crassus: Caes. *BGall.* III.20–7, Cic. *Brut.* 282.

[106] Cic. *Att.* IV.8a.2 (trans. Shackleton Bailey (B 108)), cf. *QFr* II.8.3 ('tenent omnia idque ita omnis intellegere volunt'). Cato and Vatinius: Cic. *Fam.* I.9.19, Dio XXXIX.32, Plut. *Cat. Min.* 42, Val. Max. VII.5.6. Milo: Cic. *Mil.* 68.

[107] Dio XXXIX.55.3, 56.3.

that they had allowed their names to go forward for election; now, as in 70, censors would be elected and the tribunes would undertake necessary reforms; a new law on juries, a new bribery law and a new sumptuary law would be introduced.[108] But times had changed since 70 B.C. The very successes of the *populares* had compromised their integrity. It was no longer so much a question of asserting the liberty of the people as of exploiting a hugely expanded empire for its (and their own) benefit – and expanding it still further. Pompey himself had attained a position of unprecedented wealth; he and Crassus, as Hortensius, of all people, ironically pointed out, would hardly be credible as the sponsors of a law to curtail personal expenditure (so that proposal was dropped). And when the tribune C. Trebonius came forward with a bill to give the new consuls five-year commands in Spain and Syria, with unlimited manpower and the right to make peace and war as they pleased, the pretence of Pompey and Crassus that it was no idea of theirs cannot have deceived anyone.[109]

Northern Spain, the territory of the Astures and the Cantabri, was still wholly unconquered. Young P. Crassus knew all about the Cantabri, who had given help to their Gallic neighbours in Aquitania during his recent campaign; in Hispania Citerior, meanwhile, Metellus Nepos was having serious difficulties with a rebellion led by the Vaccaei on the Douro, at the northern limit of his province. Clearly the opportunity existed for a major campaign, to do for Spain what Caesar had done for Gaul, and extend Rome's empire to the whole coast of Ocean from Gibraltar to the Rhine.[110] As for Syria, that offered both Egypt and the Parthians. Gabinius would not have time to do much in Parthia before his command expired at the end of 55; and with Archelaus now in Alexandria the restoration of Ptolemy would certainly need a war, whatever the Sibyl said.

Trebonius faced possible vetoes from two of his colleagues, P. Aquillius Gallus and C. Ateius Capito. When the vote came, Gallus was locked in the senate-house (he had imprudently spent the night there, so as to be on the scene at first light), while Capito, with M. Cato and other opponents of the bill, was forcibly prevented from entering the Forum. There were scuffles, and some bloodshed, but the law was passed; then the consuls put to the vote a bill renewing Caesar's command for five

[108] *Rei publicae causa*: Dio XXXIX.30.1f, Plut. *Pomp.* 51.5, *Crass.* 15.1f. Censors (P. Servilius Isauricus cos. 79, M. Messalla cos. 61): Cic. *Att.* IV.9.1, 11.2, *ILLRP* 496. *Lex iudiciaria*: Cic. *Pis.* 94, *Phil.* I.20, Asc. 17C. *Lex de sodaliciis*: Cic. *Planc.* 36, *Fam.* VIII.2.1. Proposed sumptuary law: Dio XXXIX.37.2.

[109] Dio XXXIX.33.1 (pretence), 37.3f (Hortensius).

[110] Caes. *BGall.* III.23.3–6, 26.6 (P. Crassus), Dio XXXIX.54 (Metellus), cf. 33.2. Caesar himself, meanwhile, had plans to advance beyond the Ocean, and beyond the Rhine.

more years. That too was passed; when his messengers reported it Caesar left Cisalpine Gaul earlier than usual, to begin the next stage of his conquests, in Germany and Britain.[111]

The consuls cast lots for the two provinces. Pompey, still in charge of the city's corn supply, intended to stay at Rome and govern his province through legates. Crassus, on the other hand, with his son the dashing cavalry commander, was eager for the glory and the wealth of conquest that his two political allies had so spectacularly achieved; though now about sixty years of age, he would go and lead a great campaign. In Spain, or in the East? The lot gave him Syria, and he was delighted. Perhaps, as Plutarch suggests, he looked as far as Bactria and India. From the furthest west to the furthest east, from the Atlantic to the Indian Ocean (not forgetting Egypt) the dominions of the Roman people would know no limit.[112]

Meanwhile, the exiled king of Egypt had made contact with Gabinius. He promised 10,000 talents – 240 million sesterces – if the proconsul would turn his legions south to Alexandria. Gabinius' council was divided, with most of his officers against the plan. But the letter the king had brought no doubt promised protection when Gabinius got back to Rome, and perhaps it could be argued that the terms of the Lex Clodia allowed such intervention beyond his province. Besides, there was a military excuse: Archelaus' fleet was harassing the coasts of Palestine and Syria, and such piracy must be stamped out. So the advance into Mesopotamia was abandoned. With a strong force of cavalry sent ahead under Antony, and supplies and auxiliary forces ordered from Antipater in Jerusalem, Gabinius and his legions marched south.[113]

The campaign was swift and brilliantly successful. Antony's advance force, with Jewish help, negotiated the notoriously difficult route through desert and marsh from Gaza to Pelusium. Following up, Gabinius' army defeated the Alexandrians in a pitched battle, which Archelaus did not survive. No doubt he was lucky not to die at the king's hands, as Berenice did. Gabinius installed a garrison of 500 Gallic and German auxiliaries to secure Ptolemy's position, and left him to raise the 10,000 talents by murder and taxation.[114]

Gabinius was in no hurry to report all this to Rome, but the news had reached Puteoli by 22 April 55.[115] Crassus was furious (evidently

111 Dio XXXIX.34–6, Plut. *Cat. Min.* 43, Hirtius *BGall.* VIII.53.1. Caesar: Caes. *BGall.* IV.6.1.

112 Plut. *Crass.* 16.2 and *Comp. Nic. Crass.* 4.4, cf. Cat. 11.1–12; also Nic. Dam. *FGrH* 90F180.95, Cat. 29.12 (Britain as 'ultima occidentis insula'), Cic. *Dom.* 60 (Gabinius, Babylon and the Persae).

113 Cic. *Rab. Post.* 19–21, *Pis.* 48–50; Plut. *Ant.* 3.2, Dio XXXIX.56.3–6. According to Joseph. *AJ* XIV.98, Gabinius had already crossed the Euphrates. Pirates and Lex Clodia: Cic. *Rab. Post.* 20, cf. Dio XXXIX.56.1, 56.6, 59.2.

114 Plut. *Ant.* 3.3–6, Joseph. *AJ* XIV.98f, *BJ* I.175, Dio XXXIX.58, Strab. XII.558, XVII.796.

115 Dio XXXIX.59.1, Cic. *Att.* IV.10.1.

Pompey had not confided in him), but a few days later he changed his tune. It is a reasonable guess that up to that moment Crassus had been keeping both Egypt and Parthia open as options for the great campaign of his proconsulship, and that his irritation at losing one of the possibilities was overcome – perhaps by his son, who had ambitions to emulate Alexander – with the reflection that the other one was both more glorious and politically less invidious.[116]

The rewards of conquest and of the expansion of empire were dramatically displayed at the magnificent games Pompey put on in September, when he dedicated the great theatre complex begun after his triumph in 61. Conspicuous among the statues in its huge portico was one of Pompey himself, as the master of the world, surrounded by the fourteen nations he had conquered.[117] In the summer came news of Caesar's crossing of the Rhine; in the autumn, even more astonishing, of his venture beyond Ocean itself to the island of Britain. A second thanksgiving was voted him, this time for twenty days.[118] By then Crassus had finished his preparations, and was ready to set out to rival the heroic grandeur of his two partners – and attain, if Cicero's account of his motives is to be trusted, even greater wealth.[119]

The two tribunes who had failed to prevent the Lex Trebonia did their best to frustrate it by resisting the consuls' recruiting programme, but to no effect. Their final attempt came as Crassus was actually leaving the city in November. Not even Pompey's presence as he escorted his colleague on his way could counteract the combined effect of their demonstrations – first an announcement of bad omens, then an attempt (frustrated by the other tribunes) to arrest the consul himself, and finally a formal curse by C. Ateius at the city gate. 'They say', wrote Cicero from Tusculum, 'that our friend Crassus left Rome in uniform with rather less éclat than his coeval L. Paulus, also consul for the second time, in days gone by. What a rascal he is!'[120]

A crucial part of the strategy was young P. Crassus and the Gallic cavalry he had led so brilliantly in Aquitania. Caesar could not spare them yet; he was going to follow up his autumn reconnaissance in Britain

116 Cic. *Fam.* I.9.20, with Rawson 1982 (C 247) 543f; cf. Cic. *Brut.* 282 on P. Crassus.

117 Pliny *HN* XXXVI.41, Suet. *Nero* 46.1, with F. Coarelli, *Rend. Pont. Acc.* 44 (1971–2) 110–21. Plut. *Pomp.* 40.5 and 42.4 for the post-triumph context; but it may not have been technically *ex manubiis* (cf. Pliny *HN* VII.97 on the temple of Minerva).

118 Caes. *BGall.* IV.38.5, Tanusius *ap.* Plut. *Caes.* 22.3 (Cato's counter-proprosal that Caesar should be handed over to the Germans for violating the truce). Cf. Cic. *Pis.* 81 (Rhine), Dio XXXIX.53, Plut. *Caes.* 23.2 (Britain); Vell. Pat. II.46.1 ('alterum paene imperio nostro, ac suo, quaerens orbem').

119 Cic. *Fin.* III.75.

120 Cic. *Att.* IV.13.2 (trans. Shackleton Bailey 1965–70 (B 108)): Paulus cos. II 167 and victor over Macedon at Pydna. *Div.* I.29, Dio XXXIX.39 (also for the recruiting), Plut. *Crass.* 16.3–6 (Pompey's presence), Vell. Pat. II.46.3. Cicero had been formally reconciled with Crassus by Pompey (Cic. *Fam.* I.9.20).

with a full-scale campaign there in 54. So Crassus would spend his first season in preparation until his son could join him the following winter with 1,000 horse, when the great expedition could begin in earnest.[121] At least he would have no trouble in the south: Gabinius had come back from Alexandria to face yet another Jewish revolt (under Alexander son of Aristobulus), which he put down bloodily, and had followed his success with a victory over the Nabatean Arabs.[122]

When the elections were eventually held, probably in December 55, L. Ahenobarbus won the consulship, and Cato the praetorship, that Pompey and Crassus had denied them the year before. Ahenobarbus continued his attempts to get Caesar recalled, and with his colleague Ap. Claudius Pulcher attacked Crassus too. But they could not compete with Cicero's eloquence, and no doubt the fourth instalment of Caesar's *Commentaries*, with its exciting narrative of the German and British campaigns, kept popular sympathy with the three dynasts. Cato and his friends made fine defiant speeches, but nothing ever came of them in the end.[123] Caesar was expected to conquer Britain and then return to Rome; both the conquest and the return would have a political effect as powerful as those of Pompey ten years before. One man who expected to benefit was Q. Cicero, now a legate of Caesar's and probably with hopes of higher things. Another was C. Memmius, one of the four evenly matched consular candidates, who in the summer of 54 ruined his chances by first entering into a huge bribery deal with the consuls and one of his competitors, and then revealing the details of it. Whatever moral authority the consuls had was destroyed by the scandal.[124]

In September, in the middle of this affair, Gabinius finally and reluctantly entered Rome. Within a month he was on trial before the *quaestio de maiestate*, no doubt for leaving his province to go to Egypt. Cicero, under intense pressure from Pompey to defend his old enemy, at least did not prosecute him, but gave evidence with studied moderation. The jury yielded to Pompey's prayers, and Gabinius was acquitted to face another trial, this time for extortion.[125] The gods promptly showed their displeasure by making the Tiber inundate the city, causing great

121 Plut. *Crass.* 17.4, Dio XL.21.2, with Rawson 1982 (C 247) 544–7; P. Crassus was still in Rome early in 54 (Cic. *Fam.* V.8.4). For the strategic purpose of the Osrhoene garrisons, see Sherwin-White 1984 (D 291) 283f.

122 Joseph. *AJ* XIV.100–3, *BJ* I.176–8 (10,000 dead in the battle near Mount Tabor); for Gabinius' final settlement of Judaea under Antipater, see Smallwood 1976 (D 156) 35.

123 Cic. *Att.* IV.18.4 on Cato ('id ego puto ut multa eiusdem ad nihilum recasurum'); *Fam.* V.8.1 (Cicero supports Crassus against the consuls), cf. *QFr* II.14.5 on the uneasy political calm; Suet. *Nero* 2.2 (Ahenobarbus).

124 Cic. *Att.* IV.15.7, 17.2f, *QFr* II.15.4, III.1.16, 2.3, 6.3, *Fam.* I.9.2; for the details, see Gruen 1969 (C 208). Memmius and *adventus Caesaris*: *Att.* IV.6.6, *QFr* III.2.3, 6.3. Q. Cicero: see Wiseman, 1987 (A 133) 34–41 on *QFr* II.15.2f, III.6.1.

125 Cic. *QFr* III.1.15, 2.1f, 3.3, 4.2f, 5.5 (cf. 5.4 'ne odium quidem esse liberum').

damage and loss of life. The censors organized large-scale operations to repair the river banks, but they laid down their office without having been able to perform the *lustrum*.[126]

Rome was uneasy. The populace was already in mourning, for the death in childbirth of Caesar's daughter, the wife of Pompey. (Defying the consul Domitius and the Senate, they had her buried in the Campus Martius, where her tomb was now under the flood water.)[127] The electoral scandal was causing nervous talk of a dictatorship, and even the news from Caesar had turned sour: after early successes, he had had to return from Britain for fear of risings in Gaul, and by December there were rumours of a real disaster.[128] If it took place in that atmosphere, Gabinius had no chance at his second trial (but it may have been held later rather than earlier in 53). This time, Cicero gave in to Pompey, and got the worst of both worlds – he defended Gabinius, and Gabinius was condemned.[129]

Meanwhile, young Crassus had brought his father the 1,000 horsemen from Gaul. Artavasdes, king of Armenia, came with 6,000 cavalry of his own to the expeditionary headquarters in Syria; but he took them away again to defend his own kingdom when he learned that Crassus was aiming to march, not north-eastwards through Armenia and down the Araxes valley into Parthian territory from the north, but directly into Mesopotamia by the Euphrates crossing at Zeugma. Orodes, now firmly installed as king, was leading the main Parthian army against Armenia by the Araxes route; his chief general, the Surenas, had his forces in Osrhoene, where Crassus' garrisons, installed the year before, got their first unnerving view of the Parthians' mail-clad cavalry.[130]

In the spring of 53 B.C. the two Crassi, father and son, led the great expedition eastwards. The strategy was to march down the Euphrates to Seleucia, and thus detach the Parthians' nearest dependencies, Mesopotamia and Babylonia. But when the scouts, not far south of the Zeugma crossing, reported the tracks of cavalry in the empty land to the east, Crassus turned in that direction, guided by the Arab ruler of Osrhoene, Abgar.[131]

When the two armies met, not far from the river Balik, the Roman legions were immediately hard pressed by the combined effect of the

126 Cic. *QFr* III.5.8, Dio XXXIX.61; *ILLRP* 496 (censors' works).

127 Dio XXXIX.64, Plut. *Caes.* 23.4, *Pomp.* 53.2–4 (Cic. *QFr* III.1.17 for the date, September 54). See L. Cozza 1983 (B 283) for a possible fragment of her *elogium*: '[statuam . . .] post mortem ponendam cen[suit sepe]lirique eam in Campo Martio iu[ssit]' – sc. *populus Romanus*?

128 Cic. *QFr* II.14.5, III.6.4, 6.6, *Att.* IV.18.3, 19.2 (dictatorship); Caes. *BGall.* V.22.4, Cic. *Fam.* VII.10.2 ('vos istic satis calere audio').

129 Dio XXXIX.63.2–5, Cic. *Rab. Post.* 19, 33, Val. Max. IV.2.4. Date: Lintott 1974 (C 223) 67–8.

130 Plut. *Crass.* 18.2–19.2, Dio XL.16.1f; Sherwin-White 1984 (D 291) 284–7.

131 Plut. *Crass.* 19.3–23.4, Dio XL.17.3–21.1.

Parthian archers and the mailed cavalry. Young Publius, with his 1,000 horse and eight cohorts of legionaries, broke out and pursued the apparently fleeing enemy, but was soon surrounded. The Parthians rode back to the main force with his head stuck on a spear; then Abgar of Osrhoene changed sides and attacked the Romans in the rear; but the legions, despite appalling casualties, doggedly held out till nightfall. The next day the survivors withdrew to Carrhae, from where in due course they escaped piecemeal to the west and north, to Syria, Cilicia and Armenia. Thirty thousand men did not return.[132]

Crassus himself was caught and killed, lured by the false offer of a treaty as his party fled northwards. The Surenas sent his head and hand (with its signet ring) to Orodes in Armenia, but used one of the prisoners to impersonate him in the victorious return to Seleucia. Crassus had plundered the temples of Jerusalem and Syrian Hierapolis to finance his glorious campaign; now Jahweh and Atargatis were avenged, as the pseudo-Crassus, dressed as a woman, rode into the capital of Babylonia in derisive triumph, escorted by lictors whose fasces were hung with money-bags.[133]

IV. *FIN DE SIECLE*

According to one authoritative chronology, later used by Augustus for his consular *fasti*, 53 B.C. was Year 700 from the foundation of Rome. Other versions put the seventh centenary one or two years later,[134] but whatever the exact date, it must have been observed more in anxiety than hope.

The year opened with no consuls in office, and only the tribunes and plebeian aediles among the other magistracies. That had happened two years before, but then it was only a brief and temporary expedient till Pompey and Crassus were elected under an *interregnum*. This time there was no sign of an end to the political deadlock, and the cause of it – the consular election scandal – was a direct threat to the authority of the law.[135] The precedents of the *interregna* in 82 and 77 B.C. were not encouraging, and the demands from Pompey's friends for a dictatorship (Pompey himself was tactfully away from Rome) merely exacerbated the

[132] Plut. *Crass.* 23.4–29.5, Dio XL.21.2–25.5. Casualty figures: Plut. *Crass.* 31.7, App. *BCiv.* II.18, with Sherwin-White 1984 (D 291) 289 n. 49.

[133] Plut. *Crass.* 28.2–32.3, Dio XL.26–7. Jerusalem: Joseph. *AJ* XIV.105–9, *BJ* I.179. Hierapolis: Plut. *Crass.* 17.5f.

[134] *Fasti Capitolini* (ed. Degrassi, *Inscr. Ital.* XIII.1). Cato put the foundation in 752 B.C. (fr. 17P, as interpreted by Dion. Hal. *Ant. Rom.* I.74.2); Polybius (VI.11a.2), Diodorus (VII.5.1), and the *Graeci annales* followed by Lutatius, Cornelius Nepos and Cicero in *De Republica* (II.18, Solin. I.27) put it in 751. Both the latter versions depended on calculation from the supposed date of the fall of Troy.

[135] See n. 124 above; Cic. *QFr* III.2.3 ('magna res in motu est, propterea quod aut hominum aut legum interitus ostenditur'); see also II.15.4 and *Att.* IV.15.8 on *leges* and *iudices*.

sense of crisis.[136] For the first time in five years there was no tale of conquest arriving from Gaul. Caesar had not even come back to Cisalpine Gaul to hold assizes, but fought on in the north to regain control after the Eburones' attack on his winter camps. One of the camps had fallen, with the loss of one whole legion and another five cohorts – say 7,000 men in all.[137] A few months after that disaster came the news of Carrhae.

The messenger from Syria will have found Rome obsessed with games – Favonius' games as plebeian aedile, organized for him by Cato with conscious frugality; the games promised by young Curio in memory of his father, from which Cicero tried vainly to dissuade him; Milo's games, on which he lavished three patrimonies in an attempt to win over the Roman populace for his consular campaign; and now, in July, the *ludi Apollinares*, for which the tribunes schemed to prolong the absence of curule magistrates so that they, and not the urban praetor, should have the glory of presiding over them.[138] No wonder Cicero was in despair for the future of the Republic.[139]

No longer able (since May 56) to carry out the longed-for role of independent senior statesman, Cicero was busy expressing his political creed by other means. He had recently written his *De Oratore*, on the ideal orator-statesman; now he was working hard at his *De Republica*, a treatise 'on the ideal constitution and the ideal citizen', and at its sequel, *De Legibus*.[140] In the mean time, however, the man who for seven years had been in Cicero's eyes the very antithesis of everything his ideal Republic stood for was once again at the centre of affairs.[141]

Clodius was a candidate for the praetorship, with a well-publicized programme of *popularis* legislation ready to be enacted as soon as he was in office. Chief among the proposals was the bill Manilius had failed to carry at the end of 66, allowing freedmen to vote throughout the thirty-five tribes. Clodius' free-corn law had caused a great increase in the rate

136 See n. 128 above; Cic. *QFr* III.7.3, Dio XL.45.5 (Pompey absent, memories of Sulla). Cf. Cic. *Att.* IX.15.2 ('Sulla potuit efficere ab interrege ut dictator diceretur') and *Cael.* 70 ('rei publicae paene extremis temporibus') on 82 and 77 B.C.

137 Caes. *BGall.* V.24–58, esp. 24.4 and 37.6 (losses), 53.3 (Caesar winters with army).

138 Plut. *Cat. Min.* 46.2–5 (Favonius and Cato); Cic. *Fam.* II.3 (Curio), esp. 3.1 ('neque quisquam est quin satietate [sc. ludorum] iam defessus sit'); Cic. *QFr* III.6.6, *Fam.* II.6.3, *Mil.* 95 (Milo); Dio Cass. XL.45.3 (tribunes). For the date of Favonius' tribunate, see J. Geiger, *RSA* 4 (1974) 161–3; for Milo's ambitions, see Lintott 1974 (C 223) 64–8.

139 Cic. *Fam.* II.5.2: 'rem publicam adflictam et oppressam miseris temporibus ac perditis moribus'.

140 Cic. *QFr* II.13.1 (πολιτικά), III.5.1 ('de optimo statu civitatis et de optimo cive'), *Leg.* I.15 ('de optimo rei publicae statu').

141 Cic. *Pis.* 9f, *Sest.* 55, *Prov. Cons.* 46 on Clodius' attitude to the censorship, which was the corner-stone of Cicero's ideal Republic (*Leg.* III.7, 29); *Att.* I.16.1 and 7, 18.2, 19.8, *in Clod. et Cur.* frr. 20–4P for Clodius in 61–60 as the embodiment of *libido*.

of manumission;[142] men freed their slaves, retained their services, and let the state feed them. These new citizens swelled still more the four huge urban tribes in which the freedmen were still confined and their voting impact deliberately minimized. Feelings ran high, with *libertas* invoked on one side and the peril of slaves lording it over their masters on the other.[143]

From among the would-be beneficiaries of his law Clodius reconstituted the organized gangs who had served him so well in 58 and 57. His enemy Milo, with a body of gladiators, was also well equipped for violence. Their rivalry, and the continued crisis over the consular elections, meant that riots and murder persisted throughout the year.[144] Clodius had been thinking of standing at the delayed elections for the year 53 itself, but it was not until July or August that Pompey eventually returned to the city, declined the dictatorship that was offered him, and made sure the long-delayed elections finally took place (M. Messalla and Cn. Domitius Calvinus became consuls). By that time too much of the year had been wasted, so Clodius decided to stand at the elections for 52, to which the new consuls had immediately to turn their attention.[145] He carefully preserved his reconciliation with Pompey, and boasted of Caesar's support. But his enemies were well able to resist, and amid continued bribery and violence the year 53 also ended with no magistrates elected.[146]

Caesar had spent the year restoring Roman control in Belgium after the onslaught on the winter camps, finding time also for a swift march south-westwards to frighten the rebellious Senones and Carnutes. His *Commentaries* probably now brought the Roman people up to date on the campaigns of 54 and 53, disguising as best they could the sudden reversal of fortune after his return from the British expedition. The crisis of the

[142] Dio XXXIX.24.1, cf. App. *BCiv.* II.120, Dion. Hal. *Ant. Rom.* IV.24.5; see Brunt 1971 (A 16) 379–81, and Rickman 1979 (G 212) 174f.

[143] Cic. *Mil.* 33, 87, 89; *de aere alieno Milonis* frr. 17–18P ('illam nefariam libertatem'); Asc. 52C, *Schol. Bob.* 173St ('opinio erat legem ⟨laturum⟩ in praetura ⟨P. Clodi⟩um ⟨de⟩ serv⟨is liberandis⟩'). See esp. Cic. *ap.* Quint. *Inst.* IX.2.54 and *Schol. Bob.* 173St: 'De nostrum omnium – non audeo totum dicere. Videte quid ea vitii lex habitura fuerit, cuius periculosa etiam reprehensio est.'

[144] Asc. 30C: 'saepe inter se Milo et Clodius cum suis factionibus Romae depugnaverant'. Clodius: Cic. *Mil.* 25 ('Collinam novam dilectu perditissimorum civium conscribebat'), cf. *CIL* VI.24627–8 for the likelihood that his agent Sex. Cloelius (*Mil.* 33) was in the *tribus Collina*; *de aere alieno Milonis* fr. 13P, with *Schol. Bob.* 172St ('inmissa seditiosorum manu comitia turbaverat'). Milo: *Schol. Bob.* 169 and 171St for Clodius' allegations. General: Dio XL.45.1; 46.1 (*διὰ τὸν ἐκ τῶν σφαγῶν τάραχον*), 46.3; Asc. 30C, 48C; Cic. *Mil.* 40, *Phil.* II.21 and 49 (attempted murder of Clodius by M. Antonius, winter 52/1).

[145] Dio XL.45.5–46.1, Plut. *Pomp.* 54.2f; Cic. *Mil.* 24, *de aere alieno Milonis* fr. 16P (*Schol. Bob.* 172St), with Badian 1964 (A 2) 150.

[146] Dio XL.46, Asc. 30–1C; cf. Vell. Pat. II.47.3, Cic. *de aere alieno Milonis* fr. 6P for *ambitus*. Clodius, Pompey and Caesar: Cic. *Mil.* 66, 88; cf. *de aere alieno Milonis* frr. 3–4, 9–10P for Cicero's emphasis on Clodius' history of hostility to Pompey.

winter camps was told at dramatic length, but the narrative continued to a climax with Rome's vengeance on the guilty Eburones; and though there was no further conquest to report, Caesar had crossed the Rhine again on a punitive expedition.[147] Pompey was praised as a friend and patriot (for lending Caesar a legion he had recruited in Cisalpine Gaul in 55) and two of the people's heroes, the ex-tribunes T. Labienus and C. Trebonius, were given markedly honorific treatment in the narrative. Q. Cicero's heroic defence of his winter camp was generously reported, but its effect was largely cancelled out by the serious losses his carelessness caused a few months later when the marauding Sugambri attacked his camp at Atuatuca. Conscious, no doubt, of his audience, Caesar gave what credit there could be in that affair to an equestrian officer called C. Trebonius, no doubt related to his legate of the same name.[148]

It was not only the *Commentaries* that kept the Roman people in mind of Caesar. For nearly ten years now surveyors, builders and craftsmen had been at work transforming the public places of the city, as the great men of Rome strove to dominate the Campus Martius and the Forum with the visual evidence of their greatness. But now the plundered wealth of Celtic gods and Gallic chieftains was being poured into the most ambitious programme of all; Caesar's agents were out to put all his rivals architecturally in the shade.[149]

In the Campus, Pompey's great theatre-portico complex loomed over the place where the Roman people elected its magistrates; Caesar planned a monumental voting-enclosure in marble, surrounded by a mile-long colonnade.[150] As for the Forum, ambitious young aristocrats were already at work there. Q. Fabius Maximus, aedile in 57, had restored his ancestor's triumphal arch (the entrance to the Forum piazza from the Via Sacra). L. Paullus, aedile in 56 or 55, was rebuilding one basilica and had let contracts for a second, even more sumptuous, to match it on the other side of the piazza.[151] Whether he could afford it remained to be seen. Caesar's plan to outshine him involved a huge

[147] Caes. *BGall.* v and vi: v.8–23 (Britain), 24–37 (disaster of Cotta and Sabinus), 38–58 (successful defence of other winter camps); vi.2–5 (Senones and Carnutes), 9–10 (Rhine), 11–28 (digression), 32-5 and 43 (Eburones).

[148] Pompey: Caes. *BGall.* vi.1.4. Labienus: v.8.1, 47.4f, 57–8, vi.7–8, 33. Trebonius: v.17, vi.33 (in charge of three legions). Q. Cicero: v.38–52, vi.36–42 (40.4 for C. Trebonius).

[149] Cic. *Att.* iv.16.8 (60m HS), Suet. *Iul.* 26.2 (100m HS), 54.2 (plunder). Agents: Q. Oppius (Cic. *Att.* iv.16.8, *QFr* iii.1.8); and L. Balbus, who evidently wintered at Rome and left to rejoin Caesar each April (*QFr* iii.1.12, *Fam.* vii.18.3).

[150] Pompey: n. 117 above. Saepta and colonnade: Cic. *Att.* iv.16.8 (incorporating also the Villa Publica, for the census).

[151] Fabius: *ILLRP* 392, Cic. *Vat.* 28 ('illis viris clarissimis Paullis Maximis Africanis, quorum gloriam huius virtute renovatam ... iam videmus'). Paullus: Cic. *Att.* iv.16.8, a much-misunderstood passage ('Paulus in medio foro basilicam iam paene texerat isdem antiquis columnis. Illam autem quam locavit facit magnificentissimam. Quid quaeris? Nihil gratius illo monumento, nihil gloriosius.')

extension of the Forum area on the north side, now already well under way. And Caesar may already have been planning his long-term project of a great theatre overlooking the Forum, built up against the slope of the Capitol. If only he could carry it out, it would involve the destruction of the Carcer, scene of the executions of December 63; of L. Opimius' temple of Concord, that reminder of optimate reaction after the killing of C. Gracchus; and perhaps also of the Basilica Porcia, Cato's ancestral monument. All these were symbols of oppression to Clodius and his popular following, as was the senate-house itself, which bore the hated name of Sulla. But Caesar's benefactions stretched beyond Rome, to Italian communities and to cities and dynasts abroad, causing yet more alarm among his opponents.[152]

The new year opened with an *interregnum*, patrician senators being nominated for successive five-day periods until elections could be held. The fourth *interrex* had completed the third day of his office when Clodius' body was brought to Rome at dusk. He had met Milo on the Via Appia near Bovillae; wounded by one of the gladiators in Milo's escort, he was carried into a wayside tavern, then dragged out and finished off at Milo's order.

A huge crowd gathered round Clodius' house, where the blood-stained corpse lay naked in the *atrium*. Distraught, his widow pointed out the wounds. She was a Fulvia, whose name recalled the Fulvii Flacci, father and sons, martyrs to the popular cause sixty-nine years before (though she may not have been of the same family). Next day at first light the crowd reassembled, this time with two tribunes to direct its anger. They ordered the body to be carried, as it was, down the Via Sacra, across the Forum to the rostra. That was where the funeral procession of a great man would halt, for a relative to deliver the *oratio funebris*. Clodius' brothers were away in their provinces; his son was a mere infant. So the tribunes spoke instead, and their harangues over the torn flesh of the people's hero turned the crowd's inarticulate grief into rage against Milo and his senatorial friends.[153]

Sex. Cloelius, Clodius' secretary and faithful lieutenant, was in charge of this *ad hoc* funeral. It was he who ordered the pyre to be built inside the senate-house itself. Benches, tables, tribunals were broken up; the body

[152] Forum extension: Cic. *Att.* IV.16.8. Theatre: Suet. *Iul.* 44.1 ('theatrum summae magnitudinis Tarpeio monti accubans'), not to be confused with the Caesarian project later completed as the Theatre of Marcellus (Dio XLIII.49.2). Concordia: Plut. *C. Gracch.* 17.6. Senate-house: Cic. *Fin.* V.2 (dramatic date 79 B.C.), Pliny *HN* XXXIV.26, Dio XL.49.3. For the topographical data see Coarelli 1985 (B 277) II 80–7 (*saxum Tarpeium*); *ibid.* 45, 59–67, 148f (Basilica Porcia and Carcer). Benefactions elsewhere: Suet. *Iul.* 28.1.

[153] Asc. 31–33C (35C for Clodius' son); the tribunes were Q. Pompeius Rufus and T. Munatius Plancus. Cf. Polyb. VI.53 for the *oratio funebris*; Ap. Claudius (cos. 54) was in Cilicia, C. Claudius (pr. 56) probably not yet home from Asia. For the Fulvii Flacci killed in 121, cf. Cic. *Cat.* I.4, *Phil.* VIII.14, Sall. *Iug.* 16.2, Plut. *C. Gracch.* 16.

was duly placed on the pyre and the torch applied. The whole building went up in flames, and that evening the funeral feast for Clodius was held in the Forum by the smouldering remains of Sulla's senate-house and the adjoining Basilica Porcia.[154]

V. THE RECONQUEST OF GAUL

For the first time in nearly two years, in early 52 Caesar was in his Cisalpine province. The revolts had delayed his triumphant return to Rome, but now that he had stamped them out with proper severity (Acco, the rebellious leader of the Senones, had been flogged to death), Caesar could look forward, after a year or two organizing the new province on a permanent basis, to a glorious triumph, a second consulship, and a place of honour in Roman politics that would eclipse even that of Pompey. The point at which his command would formally run out is notoriously a matter of dispute (1 March 50 or 49? or another date?). As things developed, perhaps it did not matter very much. If he chose to leave his consular candidature for two years, he could have Clodius as his consular colleague.[155] But he could not afford to take any chances. What he needed was a dispensation allowing him to stand for election in absence, and thus to pass straight from his triumph to the consulship, like Marius in 104 and Pompey in 70, without any lapse of *imperium* which would let his enemies destroy him in the courts as they had destroyed Gabinius. He could rely on the assembly to give him this dispensation. But would it be vetoed?

One of the tribunes of 52 was M. Caelius, an able and dangerous young man at present committed to the optimate cause. Caelius was a protégé of Cicero's, and Cicero had come to Ravenna with serious matters to discuss. If he wanted anything from Caesar, he must guarantee Caelius' acquiescence.[156] Caesar also had to talk to the agents of Pompey, about marriages. Pompey had a newly marriageable daughter, whom he had betrothed to Faustus Sulla (no friend to Caesar); Caesar was willing to divorce his own wife and marry her, and Pompey could have his great-niece Octavia (at present married to C. Marcellus).[157]

While these discussions were going on, news came from Rome. First, that Clodius was murdered and the populace was out of hand; Cicero

[154] Cic. *Mil.* 33, 90; Asc. 33, 42C; Dio XL.49.3; for Sex. Cloelius see nn. 40, 41, 81 above.

[155] Caelius in Cic. *Fam.* VIII.8.9 (with Gruen 1974 (C 209) 476) for the option of a candidacy in 50 for 49; cf. n. 124 above for his earlier hopes. Acco: Caes. *BGall.* VI.44.2, cf. Suet. *Nero* 49.2 on 'supplicium more maiorum'.

[156] Cic. *Att.* VII.1.4, cf. *Cael.* 77f for Caelius' politics; Cicero was no doubt still interested in a consulship for Quintus (n. 124 above) or a censorship for himself (cic. *Att.* IV.2.6, October 57).

[157] Suet. *Iul.* 27.1 (cf. 50.1 – Caesar had known Pompeia's mother in the old days); 26.1 for his announcement of a forthcoming banquet and gladiatorial show to remind the populace of Julia.

could count himself lucky he was not in the city. Then, that the Senate had passed the emergency decree, entrusting the safety of Rome – since consular elections were still impossible – to 'the *interrex*, the tribunes of the people, and Cn. Pompeius' (who was a pro-magistrate by virtue of the proconsular authority granted him in 55). The Senate had also ordered levies of troops to be held throughout Italy (Caesar immediately began recruiting in Cisalpine Gaul), and assigned to Sulla's son Faustus the rebuilding of Sulla's senate-house.[158] Pompey was making no secret of the fact that the armed militia he was organizing was for protection against Milo, who, he alleged, was planning to kill him too. Milo was back in Rome, supported by Caelius; of the other tribunes, Q. Pompeius Rufus, T. Munatius Plancus and C. Sallustius Crispus (later the historian) were holding public meetings every day to keep popular indignation on the boil. Predictably, the call was renewed for Pompey to be made dictator. The tribunes preferred that he should be elected consul – with Caesar as his colleague.[159]

News of these events went equally quickly to Gaul. Already alarmed at the fate of Acco, the tribal chiefs conferred in secret and resolved to seize their opportunity. Caesar was safely preoccupied in Italy; his legions were in winter camp far to the north; the winter snows made the Cevennes impassable. The Carnutes moved first, overwhelming Caesar's supply base at Cenabum (Orléans). Then the Arverni in the Massif Central, under the leadership of an energetic young noble called Vercingetorix, quickly organized an anti-Roman alliance of all the Gallic peoples between the Loire and the Garonne. Even the Aedui, Rome's most trusted allies, could not be relied on.[160]

Receiving urgent reports from his legates, Caesar hurried northwards from Ravenna. On the way he got still worse news: one of Vercingetorix' lieutenants had won over the peoples on the border of Gallia Narbonensis, and a hostile force was threatening Narbo itself. Postponing the problem of reaching his legions, Caesar went directly to Narbo to organize the defence of the province. Then he made straight for the heart of the revolt, digging his way through the snowdrifts of the Cevennes to appear unexpectedly in Arvernian territory. With only a small force, it was a very dangerous gamble. Vercingetorix, whose main army was 150 kilometres to the north in the territory of the Bituriges, marched south.

158 Asc. 33–4C, Dio XL.49.3–50.2, Caes. *BGall.* VII.1.1. Mob violence: Asc. 43C, App. *BCiv.* II.22 (random killings of prosperous citizens). Cicero: first attested at Rome in the intercalary month after 23 Feb. (Asc. 34C); for the crowd's hostility, exacerbated by the tribunes, see Cic. *Mil.* 47, Asc, 37–8 and 49–50C.

159 Suet. *Iul.* 26.1, Dio XL.50.3. Milo and Pompey: Asc. 50–2C, cf. 36–8C (slightly later); Pompey had preferred other candidates for the consular elections.

160 Caes. *BGall.* VII.1–5, cf. 8.2f for the snow; VI.44.3 for the winter camps (six legions at Agedincum on the Yonne, two in the Ardennes, two in the Plateau de Langres).

Caesar, pretending to be leaving his camp for only two or three days in search of reinforcements, astonished his escort by heading east, over the mountains again, straight to Vienne in the Rhône valley. From there, with new forces of cavalry, he went north up the valley of the Saône as fast as he could, making for his nearest two legions before Vercingetorix could hear of his ruse, and before the Aedui, whose territory he had to pass, could make up their minds to kill him.[161]

Probably before he left Italy Caesar had known that Pompey had been elected sole consul. That constitutional novelty had been proposed in the Senate by M. Bibulus, with the active support of Cato, who said any government was better than none. Pompey had immediately introduced emergency legislation to bring to justice those responsible for the scandalous bribery and violence of the past few months. The consular 'investigator' elected to preside over the trials *de vi* was L. Domitius Ahenobarbus.[162] Pompey had restored order, but it was Caesar's enemies who would benefit from this new and fateful alliance. Pompey had perhaps already rearranged his matrimonial plans; his bride was to be not Caesar's great-niece but Cornelia, the young widow of P. Crassus who had died at Carrhae. Her highly aristocratic father, Q. Metellus Scipio, had been one of Milo's rivals for the consulship, and was now under prosecution for his part in the violence of the previous winter. Pompey used his influence, and the case was dropped. Not only that, but in July Pompey was to get his new father-in-law elected to the vacant consulship as his colleague.[163]

For the moment, Caesar's enemies were disappointed in their hopes of hearing of his defeat. He managed to reach his army safely, and brought all his legions together at Agedincum. That news turned Vercingetorix north again. It was still winter, and Caesar had no reliable source of supplies. But he could not simply sit and wait, leaving the initiative with Vercingetorix. He led out eight of the ten legions, sacked and plundered Cenabum in vengeance for the Roman citizens who had been killed there, received the surrender of two other strongholds, and headed south to Avaricum (Bourges).

The land of the Bituriges had been devastated. So great was Vercingetorix' authority that he had persuaded his allies to burn their own crops, even their villages, in order to starve the Romans of supplies. Only Avaricum, spared against his better judgement, would be defended, and Vercingetorix encamped his main force not far from the town. Caesar made as if to attack his camp, but thought better of it and concentrated on the siege. It was long and bitterly resisted, but in the end the hungry

161 Caes. *BGall.* VII.7–9 (cf. 65.1 for the Narbo defences).

162 Asc. 36, 38C; Dio XL.50.4f, Plut. *Pomp.* 54.4, *Cat. Min.* 47.3, App. *BCiv.* II.23.

163 Asc. 30–1C, Plut. *Pomp.* 55, App. *BCiv.* II.24f, Dio XL.51.2f.

legions were able to storm the wall. All inside were massacred, men, women and children.

The capture of Avaricum solved Caesar's immediate problem of supplies, but he was as far away as ever from defeating Vercingetorix, whose losses were more than made up by the winning of new allies. All over Gaul, from the Nitiobriges on the Garonne to the Bellovaci on the Oise, his agents found willing listeners. Caesar now divided his forces, sending Labienus north with four legions to the Senones and Parisii while he himself marched south with the other four into Arvernian territory. Both campaigns came to nothing. Labienus brilliantly extricated his army from an unexpectedly dangerous situation on the Seine, but Caesar gambled on a surprise attack against Gergovia (near Clermont-Ferrand) and failed, with the loss of 46 centurions and 700 men. Worse still, the Aedui now came out openly for Vercingetorix, and sacked Caesar's supply base at Noviodunum (Nevers). By desperate forced marches and a hazardous crossing of the Loire, swollen with the winter snows, Caesar managed to get back to the vicinity of Agedincum and link up again with Labienus. His army was reunited, but it was on the defensive, and cut off from the Narbonese province by a solid band of hostile territory from the Bay of Biscay to the Saône.[164]

Vercingetorix took full advantage of the situation. He organized concerted attacks on the whole frontier of Narbonensis, concentrating particularly on the Allobroges, who had rebelled against Rome only ten years before. Caesar would have to march east as well as south, through the territory of the Sequani into that of the Allobroges, if he were to come to the help of the province, and Vercingetorix massed his cavalry forces to stop him. With confident enthusiasm, the Gauls made ready to inflict on Caesar's army the most humiliating defeat.[165]

The news no doubt travelled fast from the nervous colonists of Narbo to the eager gossips of Rome. Caesar's enemies were jubilant. The trials under Pompey's emergency legislation had gone very well. They had suffered only one loss – Milo himself, who could hardly have been successfully defended even if his counsel (Cicero) had stood up better than he did to the extreme hostility of the Forum crowd.[166] On the other hand, Sex. Cloelius and other Clodian supporters were condemned. The *iudices* were men of property: their fear of the populace, and the comforting presence of Pompey's troops, enabled the senatorial conservatives to recover political control. One sign of the times was the

164 Caes. *BGall.* VII.10–62. See especially 43.5 ('ne profectio [from Gergovia] nata ab timore defectionis similis fugae videretur'); 55.9, 56.2, 59.1 (expectation that Caesar would withdraw into Narbonensis).

165 Caes. *BGall.* VII.63–6. Vercingetorix' speech is of course Caesar's invention of τὰ δέοντα.

166 Asc. 40–2, 53–4C; cf. Vell. Pat. II.47.4 on Cato's vote for acquittal.

election of Cicero to the augurship he had long coveted.[167] And now, once again, it seemed that Caesar was finished.

But once again they underestimated him. The defence force Caesar had organized at Narbo in the winter was able to hold off the attacks on the province. And though cut off from reinforcements to the south, he had sent for cavalry from the German tribes across the Rhine, and these were enough to foil Vercingetorix when he launched his onslaught against Caesar's line of march. The Gallic cavalry was defeated; Vercingetorix withdrew the rest of his forces to the stronghold of Alesia in the territory of the Mandubii to the west. Caesar followed, and began preparations for a siege.

Before the Roman siege-works closed around him, Vercingetorix sent out his cavalry with urgent messages to all his allies, asking for a massive relief army from the whole of Gaul. Caesar therefore had to construct two great lines of fortified earthworks – the inner one, seventeen kilometres round, to blockade the fortress itself, the outer one, twenty-two kilometres, to defend the besiegers from the relieving army. He was thus between two huge forces of infantry, inferior in quality to his own but terrifying in sheer weight of numbers: supposedly 80,000 within the siege-works and 240,000 outside. The deciding battle would have to be fought by the legionaries, defending their fortifications against a simultaneous onslaught from both sides.[168]

In Rome, therefore, the news from Gaul was still discouraging for Caesar's friends. While he was trapped at Alesia, the Illyrians were raiding the other end of his province; Tergeste, perilously close to the Roman colony of Aquileia, had actually been sacked.[169]

When the attack at Alesia finally came, despite fierce fighting all round the fortifications, the Gallic army was unable to break through, and eventually turned in flight. Those inside the fortress saw their last chance gone, and surrendered. Vercingetorix' dignified appeal for pardon was rejected; he was put in chains to await Caesar's triumph.[170]

The Senate voted a public thanksgiving of twenty days – the third time this honour had been given to Caesar's victories – and the whole college of tribunes (Caelius included) put to the people a bill giving Caesar permission to stand for the consulship in absence. Cato strongly resisted, but Pompey's support overbore the opposition. In spite of this divergence of attitude to Caesar, Pompey had asked Cato to be one of his

[167] Trials: Asc. 54–6C, ps. Sall. *epist. Caes.* II.3.3, 4.2. Cicero (see n. 26 above): Cic. *Fam.* XV.4.13, *Phil.* II.4 ('me augurem a toto collegio expetitum Cn. Pompeius et Q. Hortensius nominaverunt'); for the date, see Linderski 1972 (C 220) 190–9.

[168] Caes. *BGall.* VII.67–82. Numbers: 71.3, 76.3, 77.8. Contribution of Germans: 67.5, 70.2–7, 80.6.

[169] Hirtius *BGall.* VIII.24.3: perhaps the first incursion into Cisalpine Gaul since the defeat of the Cimbri. [170] Caes. *BGall.* VII.83–9, Dio XL.41.

personal advisers; but Cato said he could advise only for the advantage of the state, not that of any individual.[171]

A further law about magistracies, requiring *professio* in person, obscured the legal situation; after it had been passed Pompey added a note about Caesar's exemption, which could of course have no legal validity.[172] Disingenuous as he often was, Pompey was not necessarily being Machiavellian here; he may not yet have envisaged a break with Caesar, in spite of his new associates.

Cato was a candidate for the consulship of 51, and openly announced his intention of getting Caesar recalled and put on trial. But he failed; in an election conspicuously free from bribery, the successful candidates were M. Marcellus, a formidable orator and no friend of Caesar, and the learned jurist Ser. Sulpicius Rufus. Sulpicius had first tried for the consulship in 63; he was an honest man, hostile to political corruption and perhaps not unsympathetic to the kind of reform Clodius had been urging, though not to Clodius himself. He may have been assisting Pompey's reforming legislation in 52, and inspired his abortive plan for a codification of the law.[173] Sulpicius' election, and the conduct of the poll itself, showed how effective Pompey had been as the 'physician of the state', restoring moral health to the body politic. His colleague Scipio now did his part, introducing legislation to restore the full authority of the censors, restricted by Clodius in 58. Censors would be elected in about eighteen months, and a *lustrum* would confirm Pompey's political settlement as it had done twenty years before.[174]

Of the turbulent consular candidates of the previous two years, those who had not been elected were now in exile.[175] And to prevent such scandals happening again, Pompey had put into law a reform proposed by the Senate a year earlier; after the tenure of praetorship or consulship, five years must elapse – plenty of time for a bribery prosecution – before the ex-magistrate could go to his province. That was the only hope of breaking the nexus of corruption between ambition for office and provincial extortion.[176] However, it was legislation which Pompey did not consider applicable to himself; for another bill granted him an immediate new five-year command in Spain, with the right to remain

[171] Caes. *BCiv.* I.32.3, Cic. *Fam.* VI.6.5, *Att.* VII.1.4, 3.4 (see n. 156 above). *Supplicatio*: Caes. *BGall.* VII.90.8 (see II.35.4, IV.38.5). Cato: Plut. *Cat. Min.* 48.2.

[172] Dio. XL.56.3; Suet. *Caes.* 28.3.

[173] Plut. *Cat. Min.* 49–50, Dio XL.58. Sulpicius: Cic. *Mur.* 47, see p. 353 above; Bauman 1985 (F 179). Codification: Isidore *Etym.* 5.1.5.

[174] Dio XL.57.1. Pompey: Tac. *Ann.* III.28 ('corrigendis moribus'), Cic. *Mil.* 68 (*sanare*), Plut. *Pomp.* 55.3 (ἰατρός), App. *BCiv.* II.28 (θεραπεία).

[175] 54–53: elected, M. Messalla and Cn. Domitius Calvinus; condemned, C. Memmius and M. Scaurus (App. *BCiv.* II.24). 53–52: elected, Q. Metellus Scipio; condemned, T. Milo and P. Plautius Hypsaeus (Val. Max. IX.5.3 for Pompey's studied impartiality).

[176] Dio XL.56.1, cf. 30.1, 46.2.

himself near Rome in command of troops.[177] Finally, when the tribunes went out of office in December, the two who had led the popular uprising after Clodius' death were prosecuted and condemned. For many reasons, the author of *De Republica* was delighted with Pompey's third consulship.[178]

Caesar's weary legions were recovering in widely scattered winter camps, distributed – from Belgium to the borders of Narbonensis – in the hope of discouraging further revolts. Caesar himself was at Bibracte, and it is a reasonable guess that he spent the autumn months composing his long and brilliant account of the campaign against Vercingetorix. With its emphasis on 'the majesty of the Roman people' and the vengeance called for by the deaths of equestrian *negotiatores* (at Cenabum and elsewhere), his vivid narrative of strategy and heroism was surely aimed at the voters of Rome and Italy. Moreover, Labienus featured even more prominently than before; we may suspect that he was being presented as Caesar's prospective consular colleague.[179] But for which year? The war was not over yet, and Caesar would have to move very fast if he hoped to offer himself and his lieutenant for election in 51.

On the last day of December he took the field again, to intimidate first the Bituriges and then the Carnutes. Dividing the labour carefully among the different legions, he then marched north against the Bellovaci, who had declined to commit themselves to Vercingetorix on the grounds that 'they would not take orders from anyone, but would wage war with the Romans on their own account and in their own way'. Which they now did, to good effect. Caesar was disconcerted by the strength of their forces, and sent for three more legions to reinforce the four he had with him. Even so, he was faced with a hard campaign.[180] There would be no consular candidature this year.

Late in May, M. Caelius wrote from Rome to Cicero, who was on his way to Cilicia (Pompey's five-year rule made it necessary for ex-magistrates who had never held a province to be deployed):

As regards Caesar, rumours arrive in plenty about him . . . One says he has lost his cavalry (which I think is certainly a fabrication), another that the Seventh Legion has taken a beating and that Caesar himself is under siege in the country of the Bellovaci, cut off from the rest of his army. But nothing is confirmed as yet, and even these unconfirmed reports are not bandied about generally but

177 Plut. *Pomp.* 55.7, Dio XL.56.2.

178 Cic. *Att.* VII.1.4 ('in illo divino tertio consulatu'); *Fam.* VII.2.2f for his satisfaction at T. Plancus' condemnation. The other condemned tribune was Q. Pompeius Rufus, 'qui fuerat familiarissimus omnium P. Clodio' (Asc. 50C); M. Caelius was the prosecutor (Val. Max. IV.2.7, Dio XL.55.1).

179 Caes. *BGall.* VII.17.3 ('populi Romani maiestas'); 3.1, 17.7, 28.4, 38.9, 42.3 (citizen deaths); 19.4f (Caesar's concern to minimize casualties); 56–62, 86–7 (Labienus).

180 Hirtius *BGall.* VIII.2–16; cf. VII.75.5.

retailed as an open secret among a small coterie – you know who. But Domitius [Ahenobarbus] claps hand to mouth before he speaks.

Caesar's ill-wishers also included the consul M. Marcellus, who had announced that he would raise in the Senate the question of Caesar's supersession. That caused a *frisson* of fear throughout Italy. Would there be a civil war? Marcellus' colleague Sulpicius urged the Senate to take the danger seriously and opposed the plan on legal grounds. Meanwhile, what would Pompey do? Pompey was in Tarentum, and the debate on Marcellus' motion would have to wait till he returned to Rome.[181]

Having finally mastered the Bellovaci, Caesar sent one of his legions back over the Alps into Cisalpina, ostensibly to protect the communities there against the sort of attack Tergeste had suffered the previous year. Marcellus, meanwhile, had raised the political temperature by ordering the flogging of a Transpadane, a decurion at the colony Caesar had founded at Novum Comum under the Lex Vatinia. Since Roman citizens could not legally be flogged, his act called into question the validity of Vatinius' law, and thus of Caesar's command. Pompey, as hereditary patron of the Transpadani, was expected to be no less angry than Caesar himself. Still choosing not to visit his province, Pompey went to inspect his troops at Ariminum, close to the boundary of Cisalpine Gaul.[182]

If he wanted to confer with Caesar, he was disappointed. Caesar was laying waste the lands of the Eburones, effectively wiping out the people who had started the cycle of rebellions by the attack on the winter camps in 54–53. And even that brutal vengeance did not finish the war. The legate C. Caninius Rebilus, in putting down a serious rising among the Pictones, had removed the protection of his legions from the boundaries of Narbonensis. Two bold Gallic leaders had taken advantage of the situation to renew the previous year's threat against the old Roman province. Caninius had pursued them south, but they were now defying him in the fortress of Uxellodunum in the Dordogne. Returning from Belgium with mainly diplomacy on his mind, Caesar found another military crisis that demanded his presence.[183]

In Rome, elections had taken place. Young Curio, who had been so outspoken against the three allies in Caesar's consulship, would be one of the tribunes in 50. The consuls would be C. Marcellus, cousin of Caesar's enemy, and L. Aemilius Paullus. The former was related to Caesar by marriage, the latter owed him a very great favour: Caesar had provided Paullus with the huge sum of 1,500 talents (9 million denarii) to enable

181 Caelius in Cic. *Fam.* VIII.1.2, 1.4 (trans. Shackleton Bailey 1977 (B 110)); Cic. *Att.* V.3.1 ('in oppidis enim summum video timorem'), *Fam.* IV.3.1 (Sulpicius); *Att.* V.7 (Pompey prepared 'ad haec quae timentur propulsanda'), cf. *Fam.* II.8.2. Tarentum: *Att.* V.5.2, 6.1.

182 Hirtius *BGall.* VIII.17–24; Suet. *Iul.* 28.3, Plut. *Caes.* 29.2, Cic. *Att.* V.11.2 ('non minus stomachi nostro ⟨quam⟩ Caesari'); Caelius in Cic. *Fam.* VIII.4.4, Cic. *Att.* V.19.1 (Ariminum).

183 Hirtius *BGall.* VIII.24–39, and VII.7 for Lucterius in 53.

him to complete the rebuilt basilica in the Roman Forum.[184] Caesar had bound other men to him by loans (Cicero among them). If Curio could be won over, and Pompey stayed loyal, there was a good chance that Caesar would be able to use the 'law of the ten tribunes' in a year's time, and go straight from his proconsular army to the consulship. But first he had to stamp out Gallic resistance once and for all.

Caesar hurried to Uxellodunum to take personal charge of the siege, at which a force equivalent to nearly seven legions was now deployed. Eventually, by tunnelling to divert the spring that provided the fortress' water supply, he forced its surrender. Exemplary punishment was inflicted, as a message to the rest of Gaul. Those who had borne arms were allowed to live, with their hands cut off.

With that calculated atrocity Caesar achieved his aim. Gaul was cowed. When Labienus, operating in the far north-east, inflicted a heavy defeat on the Treveri and their German allies, it was the last campaign of the war. After a quick detour into Aquitania, which he had not yet visited in person, Caesar proceeded to Narbo to carry out his judicial duties and receive the congratulations of a grateful province. Then, distributing his legions strategically round the whole country, he rode north to winter in Belgium.[185]

Throughout the year, whether through incompetence or because of Pompey's continued absence, M. Marcellus had kept postponing his threatened senatorial debate on the Gallic provinces. It was finally held at the end of September, in the temple of Apollo, outside the *pomoerium* so that Pompey could attend. By then it had become clear that Pompey was in favour of new proconsuls being allotted to the Gallic provinces the following spring, and thus of Caesar giving up his army and command *before* the consular elections in the summer of 50. And that was what the *patres* decided; the consuls of 50 were to bring the matter to the Senate on 1 March.[186]

Caelius reported to Cicero:

Certain remarks of Cn. Pompeius have been noted, and have greatly raised public confidence. He said that before the Kalends of March he could not in fairness take a decision about Caesar's provinces, but that after this date he would have no hesitation. Asked what would be the position if vetoes were cast at that point, he said that it made no difference whether C. Caesar was going to

184 Curio: Caelius in Cic. *Fam.* VIII.4.2, 10.3; cf. Cic. *Att.* II.18.1, 19.3 (59). Marcellus: Suet. *Iul.* 27.1 (married to Octavia, niece of Caesar's sister). Paullus: Plut. *Caes.* 29.3, *Pomp.* 58.1, App. *BCiv.* II.26. The other basilica ('illa quam locavit', n. 151 above) became in due course the Basilica Iulia, though whether Caesar took it over before 49 is not known.

185 Hirtius *BGall.* VIII.40–7; for the overall strategy, see 1.2f, 24.1, 39.2, 44.1, 49.2.

186 Caelius in Cic. *Fam.* VIII.1.2 (May), 4.4 (July), 9.2 (September), cf. 10.3 on Marcellus' incompetence. Pompey's view: *ibid.* 9.5, 8.4; 1 March had been suggested by Metellus Scipio against the wishes of Caesar's agent L. Balbus.

disobey the Senate or was putting up someone to prevent the Senate from passing a decree. 'And supposing', said another questioner, 'he chooses to be consul *and* keep his army?' To which Pompeius, as gently as you please: 'And supposing my son chooses to take his stick to me?' These utterances of his have produced an impression that Pompeius is having trouble with Caesar.[187]

VI. THE FINAL CRISIS

Early in September 51, a large Parthian force under the command of King Orodes' son Pacorus crossed the Euphrates at Zeugma. Since Carrhae, Rome had neglected the eastern frontier. Syria was still held by Crassus' quaestor C. Cassius with the re-formed survivors of Crassus' army; in Cilicia there were just two under-strength legions; the local populations were ill disposed to Roman rule, and now both provinces had been given to reluctant ex-consuls: Cicero had just arrived in Cilicia, Bibulus was still on his way to Syria.[188]

The first reports reached Rome by mid-November, and caused intense political speculation:

One man is for sending Pompeius out, another says Pompeius ought not to be moved away from Rome. Another school of thought would like to send Caesar with his army, another the consuls.[189]

Pompey was the obvious choice. Pompey himself thought so. 'The Parthians', he wrote reassuringly to Cicero, 'are my business.' Cassius, who did not want to share glory with anyone, sent a series of boastful despatches after successfully defending Antioch, but Cicero's reports (and no doubt those of Bibulus, when he arrived) were much less sanguine. The Parthians were wintering in Cyrrhestike, west of the Euphrates, and would certainly renew their attack in the next campaigning season.[190]

Meanwhile, the new tribunes were about to enter office. Attention was focused on the ambitious Curio, the darling of the urban plebs since his spectacular games, and now married to Clodius' widow. But he was thought to be hostile to Caesar, and it was confidently expected that if anyone vetoed Caesar's supersession on 1 March, Curio would counter-

187 In Cic. *Fam*. VIII.8.9 (trans. Shackleton Bailey 1977 (B 110): 'negotium' meaning 'trouble').

188 Cic. *Fam*. XV.3 (to Cato, 3 Sept.), 1 (dispatch to Senate, 18 Sept.), *Att*. V.18.1–2 (20 Sept.); cf. *Att*. V.15.1 (Cilicia legions), Dio XL.28.1 (Cassius), 28.4 (disaffection), 30.1 (Lex Pompeia); there was also fear of an Armenian invasion of Cappadocia (Cic. *Fam*. XV.3.1). For Cicero's operations in Cilicia see Sherwin-White 1984 (D 291) 290–7.

189 Caelius in Cic. *Fam*. VIII.10.2 (trans. Shackleton Bailey 1977 (B 110)). When Caelius wrote on 17 November, only Cassius and Deiotarus had been heard from, though Cicero had written on 18 September (*Fam*. XV.1), and the king of Commagene even earlier (*Fam*. XV.3.2); forty-six days was reckoned a fast time for a letter from Rome to Cilicia (*Att*. V.19.1).

190 Cic. *Att*. V.21.2, VI.1.14, *Fam*. II.10.2, Dio XL.28–9. Bibulus arrived in October (*Att*. V.20.4).

attack by blocking all provincial allocations.[191] Probably he was hoping to buy conservative acquiescence in the programme of popular legislation he intended to introduce.

His first proposal was a land law. He intended to find land by the dispossession of King Juba of Numidia; he also wanted to use the *ager Campanus* for distribution, no doubt by buying out the existing owners; it may have been for this reason that he was hoping to raise revenue by a tax on slave-owners.[192] In January and February, however, it became clear that he would get nowhere by gentlemanly means. The new consuls, L. Paullus and C. Marcellus, effectively paralysed all political activity, and when the *pontifices* refused to permit the intercalary month (which would have righted the calendar but also given him time for his legislation before the Gallic issue came up on 1 March), Curio abruptly changed his tactics. He brought in two new bills – a Gracchan one about road-building, and a Clodian one about corn distribution – and declared himself an unambiguous *popularis* by supporting Caesar's case in his speeches to the people.[193]

It was later alleged, and it may well be true, that Caesar had bought Curio's allegiance with a huge financial subsidy to pay his debts. Certainly the bill about the *ager Campanus* could have been helpful to Caesar's veterans, and the road bill offered a five-year commission which, failing the Parthian command, might conceivably be used to extend Caesar's immunity when he eventually laid down the proconsulship of Gaul.[194]

When 1 March came, L. Paullus was the presiding consul. He evidently deferred discussion, no doubt with Curio's approval, and gave

[191] Caelius in Cic. *Fam.* VIII.5.2f, cf. Cic. *Att.* VI.2.6. For Curio's attitude in general, cf. Caelius in Cic. *Fam.* VIII.4.2 (August, 'ut spero et volo et ut se fert ipse, bonos et senatum malet'), Cic. *Fam.* II.7, VII.32.3. Hostility to Caesar: Caelius in Cic. *Fam.* VIII.8.10 (Sept.) and 10.3 (Nov.). Popularity: Dio XL.60.2, App. *BCiv.* II.26; cf. Pliny *HN* XXXVI.116–20, Cic. *Fam.* II.3 for the games (late 53 or 52). Fulvia: Cic. *Phil.* II.11, 113.

[192] Caes. *BCiv.* II.25.4, Dio XLI.41.3 (Juba); Caelius in Cic. *Fam.* VIII.10.4 (*ager Campanus*), cf. Cic. *Leg. Agr.* I.14f, II.67 (63), Dio XXXVIII.1.4 (59), with Brunt 1971 (A 16) 316f; Cic. *Att.* VI.1.25, with Lacey 1961 (C 216) 323 n. 67, for the slave tax – not, *pace* Shackleton Bailey 1977 (B 110), part of the later *lex viaria*.

[193] Caelius in Cic. *Fam.* VIII.6.5 ('transfugit ad populum et pro Caesare loqui coepit'). *Lex viaria*: App. *BCiv.* II.27, cf. Plut. *C. Gracch.* 6.3–7.2; the last Roman road to be built had been the Via Aemilia (Scauri) in 115–109 (*Vir. Ill.* 72.7, with Fentress 1984 (B 151). The *lex alimentaria* would have entrusted the corn distribution to the aediles: Sex. Cloelius had done it under the Lex Clodia (Cic. *Dom.* 25) and Pompey in 57–56 (Dio XXXIX.24.1f, cf. Cic. *QFr* II.3.2); but what happened after Pompey's *cura annonae* lapsed? There was a real need for these reforms, as there was for the proposal *de aquis* urged by Caelius as aedile (Frontin. *Aq.* 76); the last aqueduct built had been the Aqua Tepula in 125.

[194] Caelius in Cic. *Fam.* VIII.10.4 ('negant Caesarem laborare'), 6.5 (like Rullus' bill). Bribe: Vell. Pat. II.48.3f, Val. Max. IX.1.6, Suet. *Iul.* 29.1; no contemporary comment, but see Cic. *Att.* VI.3.4 ('huc enim odiosa adferebantur de Curione, de Paulo').

no support when his colleague raised the matter the following month.[195] Caelius reported:

As things stand so far Pompeius seems to be putting his weight along with the Senate in demanding that Caesar leave his province on the Ides of November. Curio is resolved to let that happen only over his dead body, and has given up the rest of his programme ... [Pompeius] regards the idea of Caesar being elected consul before he hands over his province and army with strong disfavour ...

Pompey's suggestion that Caesar should resign his command in mid-November, only forty-six days short of the start of the consular year, was a concession, but it was not enough. There would still be time for the jurors Pompey had hand-picked in 52 to find Caesar guilty of *vis* or *ambitus* for offences committed before he left for Gaul, or perhaps for extortion or *maiestas* when there.[196] Curio, in a series of stormy meetings, urged that if Caesar were to give up his Gallic command, Pompey should also give up his absentee proconsulship of Spain, which still had three years to run.[197]

The only issue on which agreement was possible was the Parthian crisis. The Senate decreed that Pompey and Caesar should give up one legion each to reinforce Syria. Pompey named the legion he had 'lent' to Caesar in 53.[198]

Caesar himself had decided not to seek the consulship in 50. But he came south into Cisalpine Gaul at the time of the elections, to hear that Antony his ex-quaestor had defeated L. Ahenobarbus for the vacancy in the college of augurs caused by the recent death of Hortensius. On the other hand, his ex-legate Ser. Galba had been kept out of the consulship by two men who were likely to be hostile, L. Lentulus Crus and another C. Marcellus, brother of the consul of 51.[199]

Censors too had been elected; Appius Claudius, and Caesar's father-in-law L. Piso. Cicero urged Appius to remember his great ancestor the censor Appius Caecus; despite his own experience of his arrogance and corruption, Cicero claimed to have hopes that Appius might prove to be

195 Caelius in Cic. *Fam.* VIII.11.1 (with Shackleton Bailey *ad loc.*), App. *BCiv.* II.27.

196 Caelius in Cic. *Fam.* VIII.11.3 (trans. Shackleton Bailey 1977 (B 110)). Jurors: Cic. *Att.* VIII.16.2, Vell. Pat. II.76.1, Dio XL.52.1; cf. Caelius in Cic. *Fam.* VIII.1.4, App. *BCiv.* II.25, cf. III.1.4 for Caesar's sympathy with those condemned in 52; Caes. *BCiv.* I.4.3 (*potentes* dominating *iudicia*), Suet. *Iul.* 30.4 ('condemnatus essem').

197 Cic. *Fam.* II.12.1 ('tumultuosae contiones'); Hirtius *BGall.* VIII.52.4, Dio XL.62.3.

198 Hirtius *BGall.* VIII.54.1–3, Caes. *BCiv.* I.32.6, Dio XLI.65; cf. Caelius in Cic. *Fam.* VIII.4.4 (discussion of the 'lent' legion in July 51). *Magnum bellum*: Cic. *Att.* VI.2.6, 3.2, 4.1, 5.3 (April to June), *Fam.* II.11.1. Only issue: App. *BCiv.* II.29.

199 Hirtius *BGall.* VIII.50–1; Caelius in Cic. *Fam.* VIII.14.1 for Antonius ('plane studia ex partium sensu apparuerunt'), cf. 13.2 on senatorial support for Caesar in June.

the moral scourge Rome so desperately needed.[200] In a way, he did, but the effect was disastrous. His vehemence in condemning luxury and vice was mocked for its hypocrisy (Caelius, accused of homosexual behaviour, earned great popularity by turning the charge against Appius himself); and when he emulated the censors of 70–69 with wholesale expulsions from the Senate, his colleague resisted only in the case of Curio, allowing all the others to make their way, full of resentment, to Caesar.[201] Appius, who had recently married one daughter to Pompey's son, and one to Cato's nephew M. Brutus, could only discredit the new alliance of Pompey and the so-called *boni* – whom Caesar and his friends called the *factio*.

Everything conspired to polarize the great issue. Pompey was in Campania, no doubt in connexion with the forces for Syria, when he fell seriously ill. Immediately and spontaneously, the country towns of Italy combined to make supplication to the gods for his recovery; they still saw him as the bulwark of the state, the one hope for peace. When he recovered amid scenes of joy and festivity, Pompey was dangerously encouraged.[202] Then came young Appius, the censor's nephew, bringing the two legions from Gaul; he claimed Caesar's army was disaffected and would desert to Pompey if it came to war.[203] Finally, news arrived that the Parthians had left Syria. Pacorus preferred to fight his father Orodes. The legions would not be needed after all, and could stay in Campania, swelling Pompey's military strength at the expense of Caesar's.[204]

'If neither of the two goes off to the Parthian war,' Caelius had written in August, 'I see great quarrels ahead in which strength and steel will be the arbiters.' Cicero, in Athens on his way home from his province, foresaw 'the greatest struggle that history has ever known'. He was supposedly a friend of both parties; whose side should he be on?[205]

Cicero landed at Brundisium on 24 November, and made his way in a leisurely fashion to his villa at Formiae. His arrival was awaited with keen interest. He was hoping for a triumph; the military activity in Cilicia had been exactly what Caelius had wished for him as he set out, 'just

[200] Cic. *Fam.* III.11.5, cf. 10.3 ('ut et debes et potes'), 10.11, 13.2. The *De Republica* was being widely read at this time: Caelius in Cic. *Fam.* VIII.1.4, cf. Cic. *Att.* VI.1.8, 2.9, 3.3, 6.2, VII.2.4, 3.2.

[201] Caelius in Cic. *Fam.* VIII.14.4 ('persuasum est ei censuram lomentum aut nitrum esse'), 12.3, Cic. *Att.* VI.9.5; Dio XL.63.3–5, Cic. *Att.* VII.3.5 (Caesar's side includes 'omnis damnatos [n. 196 above], omnis ignominia adfectos').

[202] Cic. *Att.* VIII.16.1, IX.5.4, Vell. Pat. II.48.2, Plut. *Pomp.* 57.1–3, App. *BCiv.* II.28. 'In Pompeio spem omnem oti': Cic. *Att.* VI.1.11.

[203] Plut. *Pomp.* 57.4, App. *BCiv.* II.30.

[204] Cic. *Fam.* II.17.1 (18 July); *Att.* VI.6.3, VII.1.2 (providential good fortune). Legions: Hirtius *BGall.* VIII.55, Caes. *BCiv.* I.2.3, 4.5, 9.4.

[205] Caelius in Cic. *Fam.* VIII.14.4, Cic. *Att.* VII.1.2 (trans. Shackleton Bailey 1965–70 (B 108)).

enough to justify a bit of laurel'.[206] More important, however, than the improbable *triumphator* was the conservative statesman, the champion of the rule of law, the author of *De Republica*. Caesar, now at Ravenna, wrote in the friendliest terms, making the most of Cato's niggling opposition to the triumph proposal. Pompey, whom Cicero saw at Cumae and at Formiae, assumed that war was both probable and justifiable, to avoid the political disaster of Caesar's second consulship: 'we will fight in good hope, either of victory or of death as free men.' Cicero's own view was less simple; he did not trust either Pompey or the *factio*.

> Peace is what is wanted. Victory will bring many evils in its train, including the certainty of a despot ... 'Better fight than be a slave,' you say. For what? Proscription if you're beaten and if you win slavery just the same?

Publicly he would support Pompey; privately, he was for peace at any price.[207]

At Rome, meanwhile, Curio's enemies were closing in on him now that the end of his tribunate was approaching. Attacked in a rowdy meeting of the Senate by Appius the censor and the consul C. Marcellus, Curio successfully appealed to majority opinion there, and then followed up his advantage by proposing that both Caesar and Pompey should resign their commands. He was supported by Appius' colleague L. Piso and Antony now tribune-elect. A division was forced. For the motion, 370; against, 22. Curio's main object had presumably been to show how small the *factio* was; he had not specified *when* the great men should resign. While Curio went out to receive the joyful accolades of the crowd in the Forum, Marcellus rounded bitterly on the Senate: they had voted to have Caesar for their master, but *he* would not sit idly listening to speeches while ten legions were marching south across the Alps.

The rumour that Caesar was marching on Rome caused panic and consternation. Marcellus proposed to the Senate that Caesar be declared a public enemy, and that the two legions at Capua be mobilized against him. Curio protested that the rumour was untrue. 'Very well', said Marcellus, 'if the Senate will not allow me to do what is necessary, I will do it on my own authority.' Escorted by his supporters (including, surprisingly, his colleague Paullus), Marcellus proceeded formally to Pompey's Alban villa and instructed him to take command of the two

206 Cic. *Att.* VII.7.5 ('mirifica exspectatio' reported by Atticus), *Fam.* II.10.2, with Wistrand 1979 (C 289) for the full story of Cicero's laurelled lictors.

207 Caesar: Cic. *Att.* VII.1.7, 2.7, 3.11. Pompey: 4.2, 8.4, 9.3f. Cicero: 5.4, 7.7 (trans. Shackleton Bailey 1965–70 (B 108)); cf. 3.4 ('de sua potentia dimicant homines hoc tempore periculo civitatis'), 5.5, 6.2. Patriotism more important than triumph: *Att.* VII.3.2, IX.7.5.

legions, raise whatever other forces might be necessary, and defend the Republic against Caesar. 'I will do so', replied Pompey, 'if all else fails.' Curio, restricted to the city by his office, delivered a series of bitter harangues to the people against the consuls and against Pompey. On 10 December, when his tribunate had expired, he left for Ravenna.[208]

Two of the new tribunes, Antony and Q. Cassius, now took up the attack. On 20 December Antony denounced Pompey's whole career, and complained that the condemnations under the laws he had passed in 52 were a travesty of justice. Curio, meanwhile, had been entrusted by Caesar with an important message to the consuls and the Senate, which he brought post-haste to Rome in time to deliver it on 1 January to the meeting on the Capitol. Lentulus and the other C. Marcellus, the new consuls, were unwilling to accept it, but Antony and Cassius insisted that it should be read. After a long account of the achievements of his career, Caesar proposed that he and Pompey should lay down their commands at the same time and submit to the judgement of the Roman people; if Pompey did not agree, then 'he would come quickly and avenge his country's wrongs and his own'. Lentulus, who was presiding, would not allow a debate on the letter itself but asked for opinions on the political situation in general, and successfully put to the vote Metellus Scipio's proposal that if Caesar did not disband his army by a fixed date (probably that of *professio* for the consular elections) he should be regarded as an enemy of the state. The two tribunes immediately applied their veto.[209]

On 4 January, the day after his fifty-seventh birthday, Cicero returned to Rome. He was alarmed at Caesar's threatening tone, but equally at the intransigence of those whose blind hostility – or jealousy of Caesar's success – was driving the Republic headlong into war. He approved the compromise suggestion that Caesar should keep just Cisalpina and Illyricum, with two legions, until his second consulship; or failing that, just Illyricum, with one legion. Pompey was willing to be persuaded, but Cato, Lentulus and Caesar's other enemies saw to it that the proposal came to nothing.[210]

On 7 January, they succeeded in carrying the emergency decree: 'the consuls, praetors, tribunes of the plebs and proconsuls in the vicinity of the city shall see to it that the Republic suffers no harm'. The strong-points in the city were occupied with soldiers. Two of the tribunes of the

[208] Dio XL.64.1–66.5, App. *BCiv.* II.30–1, cf. Plut. *Pomp.* 58.3–59.1. Cic. *Att.* VII.5.4 ('hoc iter Pompei') suggests that Pompey had left to take command of the two legions by the middle of December; but he was back in the neighbourhood of Rome in early January (Caes. *BCiv.* I.2.1).

[209] Cic. *Att.* VII.8.5 ('querela de damnatis'); Plut. *Pomp.* 59.2, *Caes.* 30.2, App. *BCiv.* II.32 (trans. H. White); Caes. *BCiv.* I.1–2, with Raaflaub 1974 (C 238) 56.

[210] Cic. *Fam.* XVI.11.2 ('ex utraque parte sunt qui pugnare cupiant'), *Att.* IX.11a.2 (to Caesar); Plut. *Pomp.* 59.3–4, *Caes.* 31.1, Suet. *Iul.* 29.2; cf. App. *BCiv.* II.32 (suggested by Caesar himself in December), Vell. Pat. II.49.4, with Woodman 1983 (B 129) 86 for the textual problem.

plebs, Antony and Cassius, were told that their safety could not be guaranteed if they remained in the city. With Curio and Caelius (who had decided Caesar had the better army), they fled indignantly to Caesar.[211]

That was serious, but not unprecedented. Cato no doubt remembered the flight of Metellus Nepos to Pompey in 62; nothing had come of that except a strengthening of the conservative position. Pompey was confident that he himself could raise soldiers in Italy just by stamping his foot. It was therefore a devastating shock when the news came in that Caesar was marching south with the Thirteenth legion.[212]

Caesar's view was that a clique in the Senate had robbed him of six months of his command; Cicero, writing to Atticus in December, implies that the command had already reached its legal term, or at least would reach it very soon. The 'legal question' (*Rechtsfrage*) has generated a vast controversy in modern scholarship, with no clear result achieved. It must have been equally unclear at the time, since there was evidently no one date for the expiry of the command which both sides could accept.[213] But in entering Italy with an army, Caesar made the question irrelevant: whether or not he still held a legally valid command, it was not valid for that.

As against Vercingetorix three years before, Caesar had reacted to the news the tribunes brought with immediate action and a swiftly calculated gamble. 'What's going on?' asked Cicero in despair:[214]

'We hold Cingulum, we've lost Ancona, Labienus has deserted Caesar.' Are we talking about a general of the Roman people? or Hannibal?

211 Caes. *BCiv.* I.5, Cic. *Fam.* XVI.11.2, Dio XLI.3.2f, App. *BCiv.* II.33.

212 Nepos: p. 358–60 above. Pompey's confidence and its sequel: Plut. *Pomp.* 57.5, 60.3–4.

213 Caes. *BCiv.* I.9.2 (message given at Ariminum); Cic. *Att.* VII.7.6, 9.4. The modern controversy begins with Mommsen 1857 (C 229); for good recent discussions. see Gruen 1974 (C 209) 475–6 and Seager 1979 (C 258) 193–5.

214 Cic. *Att.* VII.11.1; for Labienus, Dio XLI.4.2–4.

CHAPTER 11

CAESAR: CIVIL WAR AND DICTATORSHIP

ELIZABETH RAWSON

I. THE CIVIL WAR

We do not know exactly where the Rubicon was; nor are we sure that it was on 10 January that Caesar crossed it (by the sun it was nearly two months earlier). But it is possible that on doing so he did say, quoting a Greek comedy by Menander, 'let the die be cast'.[1]

For the events of the next weeks, we have Caesar's own account, which can occasionally be convicted by Cicero's correspondence (which includes some letters from Caesar and Pompey themselves, as well as from others) of apologetic bias. Dividing his single legion into two parts he marched with five cohorts to Ariminum, and sent Antony, probably immediately,[2] to Arretium to block the route from Rome by the Via Cassia. He himself, on reaching Ancona, held the head of the Via Flaminia. When news of this reached Rome on 17 January, Pompey insisted on abandoning the panic-stricken city, and retired with the consuls and many senators to Campania. Caesar's other troops began to come up, and perhaps even while abortive negotiations were in progress he occupied all Picenum. Several small garrisons went over to him; L. Domitius Ahenobarbus used others, and troops he had raised himself – the equivalent of three legions – to make a stand at the strategic crossroads of Corfinium, refusing as the new proconsul of Gallia Transalpina to obey the pleas of Pompey, the proconsul of the Spains, to join him at Luceria in Apulia. But Domitius was surrounded and forced by his men to surrender. Caesar ostentatiously released all prisoners of senatorial or equestrian rank, not to mention the state funds in Domitius' charge, and recruited the troops (many Domitius' own tenants) whom he then despatched to Sicily.

Pompey withdrew to Brundisium, whither he had already sent some of his men. On 4 March the consuls put to sea from the town with part of the forces, only a few days before Caesar arrived, now with three veteran

[1] Plut. *Caes.* 32.6; *Pomp.* 60.4 (cf. Athen. XIII.559e). Perhaps reported by Asinius Pollio, who (so Plut. *Caes.* 32.7) was with Caesar.

[2] Caes. *BCiv.* I.11 suggests, perhaps apologetically, this took place after negotiations had failed.

and three new legions, to find Pompey still present. But on 17 March, in spite of Caesar's attempts to make the harbour unusable, he escaped the attempted blockade and crossed to Epirus. Caesar tells us that it was bound to take time to collect sufficient shipping from Gaul and the rest of Italy for a pursuit (it was now in fact the depth of winter), though he was able to send troops to Sicily and Sardinia, to ensure the corn supplies of the city of Rome. He returned to the city to regularize his position as far as he could; and then set off for Spain to secure his hold of the West against the Pompeian legions there.

If Caesar's account of these events is not wholly truthful, it is a fascinating propaganda document. It is only unfortunate that we do not know exactly when it was written or published; some suppose that the whole *Bellum Civile* was written in 47, where it breaks off during Caesar's stay at Alexandria, others that part at least dates from the end of 49. Some think publication was posthumous.[3] It is probable that the readership envisaged was a fairly broad one. At all events, Caesar uses detail with familiar brilliance to give the impression, justified or not, that his *res gestae* had made such an impression in Italy that even Auximum, of which Pompey was patron, opened its gates to him, while Cingulum welcomed his forces, though it owed its existence as a *municipium* to Labienus, who had gone over to the Senate immediately after the crossing of the Rubicon. Suetonius reveals that Caesar's agents had been busy, and generous, in Italy as well as Rome and the provinces in the last few years,[4] while Pompey's very influence in Picenum will have raised up enemies to him there. Whether Labienus was one of Pompey's Picene clients, reverting to his first loyalty, as Syme supposed, is uncertain; Cicero acclaimed his Republican principle and others imply personal jealously of his commander.[5]

Caesar makes much of his mercy at Corfinium, of his control of his men and his respect for the property both of the townsfolk and his opponents. It is clear that this did have a great effect on many who had feared he would be Sulla and Catiline rolled into one. He indicates deftly that it is the other side that has links with Sulla and the Sullans.[6] Furthermore it is Caesar who is the defender of the constitution; it is his enemies who are ignoring the rights of tribunes ('even Sulla left their veto'), passing the *senatus consultum ultimum* on inadequate grounds (he

3 Suet. *Iul.* 56.4 reports Pollio as saying that Caesar intended to revise his *Commentaries*, which were distinctly inaccurate; but this probably includes the *BGall.*, certainly published in his lifetime.

4 Suet. *Iul.* 28.1: magnificent public works in Italian towns.

5 Syme 1938 (C 273); Cic. *Att.* esp. VII.12.5, 13.1; Dio XLI.43 says he had become arrogant and quarrelled with Caesar; Hirtius, *BGall.* VIII.52 that he had for some time been tampered with by Caesar's enemies, but Caesar trusted him.

6 Caes. *BCiv.* I.6, noting the presence of Faustus Sulla with his opponents; in a letter of early 49 he said that only Sulla 'whom I shall not imitate' founded a lasting rule on cruelty, Cic. *Att.* IX.7C.

Novum Comum
Brixia
Verona
Cremona
Placentia
Dertona
Genua
Rhegium Lepidum
Mutina
Forum Gallorum
Bononia
Ravenna
Ariminum
Pistoria
Luca
Pisa
Faesulae
Fanum
Sena Gallica
Cales
Ancona
Auximum
Cingulum
Volaterrae
Arretium
Asculum
Ilva
Spoletium
Ameria
Amiternum
Falerii
Capena
Alba Fucens
Corfinium
Tibur
Cosa
Pyrgi
Veii
Roma
Fucinus L.
Praeneste
Ostia
Arpinum
Venafrum
Antium
Interamna
Tarracina
Teanum Sidicinum
Minturnae
Capua
Luceria
Ausculum
Barium
Venusia
Bantia
Cumae
Nola
Puteoli
Neapolis
Pompeii
Paestum
Brundisium
Tarentum
Heraclea
Thurii
Vibo
Aquileia
Tergeste
Patavium
Ateste
VIA POSTUMIA
VIA AEMILIA SCAURI
VIA AEMILIA
VIA AURELIA
VIA CASSIA
VIA CLODIA
VIA FLAMINIA
VIA VALERIA
VIA APPIA
VIA LATINA
VIA ANNIA (?)
CORSICA
SARDINIA
Tyrrhenian Sea
Adriatic Sea
Ionian Sea
Panormus
Messina
Thermae
Rhegium
Lilybaeum
Entella
SICILIA
Heraclea Minoa
Agrigentum
Syracusae
Utica
Carthago
Clupea
Carpis
Curubis
Thapsus
AFRICA
NUMIDIA
Land over 1000 metres
0
300 km
0
200 miles
10°E
15°E
45°N
40°N
35°N
A
B
C
a
b
c
d
e

13 Italy

does not deny the basic legality of the measure as he may have done in 63 B.C.), appointing *privati* to provinces, and so on; all he wants is the consulship for 48 – after the proper ten-year interval.[7] Not that he denies he is fighting primarily to protect his *dignitas*; to safeguard this, to defend the tribunes and free the state from the power of a narrow faction is the order he attaches to his motives.[8] The urban plebs was greatly devoted to its tribunes; the countrymen who made up most of any army will not have cared much about them, or the power of the *factio paucorum*, though Caesar later makes an ex-centurion state that he is fighting for Caesar's *dignitas* 'and our liberty'.[9] The richer classes in Italy also cared little for the squabbles of the *principes*: Sulla's savagery however had been felt by much of the peninsula. Cicero complains that the people he talks to in Campania care for nothing but their 'wretched little estates and fortunes', and now that they have been reassured as to Caesar's intentions love him and fear Pompey, who had been uttering dire threats. The poor, Cicero had already said, were for Caesar.[10]

In addition, many or most people seem to have been unprepared for Pompey's decision to leave Italy.[11] This was probably justified from a military point of view: his troops consisted of the two legions which had been Caesar's and which he insisted could not be trusted, of rusty veterans and of sparse new levies, their men as he said still strange to each other;[12] but he controlled the seas and could expect to raise huge forces in the Orient. 'If Sulla could do it, can't I?' he said of the reconquest of Italy from the East.[13] But Cicero was doubtless right in seeing it as politically and psychologically very damaging to abandon the capital and indeed all Italy, intending to starve and then invade it.[14] Napoleon was to believe that Pompey should have held Rome at any cost. There has even been an attempt to rehabilitate Domitius' policy, but this is unconvincing; Cicero thought him stupid, and in fact he had limited military experience.[15]

Both sides also sought propaganda advantage in negotiation. Whether they sought anything else is hard to say. Naturally Caesar's account is suspect here; and Cicero was not in the confidence of the principals. Caesar's distant kinsman, the younger L. Caesar, seems to have been sent north privately by Pompey before he left Rome – according to Caesar himself Pompey wished to excuse himself for his actions, denying personal animus, and to beg Caesar too to put the state

7 Caes. *BCiv*. I.5, 6, 7. 8 Caes. *BCiv*. I.22. 9 Caes. *BCiv*. III.91.

10 *Att*. VIII.13.2, 3.5.

11 Von Fritz 1942 (C 196). When this was made is uncertain. Cicero knew it was on the cards from the start, but could get no clear information and long thought it would be to Spain if at all.

12 Ap. *Att*. VIII.12A.2 and 3, 12C.2 and 4, 12D.1.

13 *Att*. IX.10.2. 14 *Att*. IX.9.2.

15 Burns 1966 (C 182); *Att*. VIII.1.3, cf. *Brut*. 267 (no rhetorical art).

before his private interests.[16] L. Caesar, and the praetor L. Roscius, who had also come to Caesar, brought back proposals for a compromise: Cicero shows that Caesar offered to let the newly appointed Domitius and Considius take over Transalpine and Cisalpine Gaul, and that he agreed to come to Rome for the elections, if Pompey meanwhile went to Spain; and that the Senate accepted these terms, insisting only that Caesar retire from Italy before Pompey stopped levying or dismissed his troops. Cicero thought Caesar bound to accept; but the latter complains that it was unfair to say he should disarm while his enemies continued to recruit, and he did not suspend operations. Cicero shows the Senate also held that final terms could only be settled by a meeting of the Senate back in Rome. They could then have repudiated the agreement from a far stronger position.[17]

But the real nub of the matter may be this; even if Caesar kept Illyricum – which is not mentioned, but which he had previously asked to retain – till near the elections, even if Pompey was in Spain and Italy demilitarized, so that no court could be intimidated by troops as Milo's had been,[18] even if the *factio* gave a guarantee that they would not allow the threatened prosecution to be mounted at all, was this a promise they could be trusted to keep? In other words could Caesar sincerely give up his old insistence on standing for the consulship in absence? Cicero says that Curio 'laughs at L. Caesar's embassy'; Curio was very frank about his leader, assuring Cicero later that his *clementia* was merely assumed for political ends; and Cicero probably means here that Curio did not think Caesar's proposals for peace were seriously meant either, but designed to gain credit and perhaps time. But the cynical Curio might have been wrong. Cicero came to believe that both the great men wanted war to establish their own supremacy, as did many of their followers on their leaders' behalf; but he too might have been wrong.[19]

Caesar perhaps did hope to detach Pompey from his new allies – something Pompey's zigzag political course hitherto made look possible. The proposals sent back via L. Caesar included one for a personal meeting with Pompey – it was rejected, which may be one of the reasons Caesar broke off negotiations. Later on Caesar sent N. Magius, an officer of Pompey's who had fallen into his hands, to Brundisium to propose a meeting to remove the misunderstandings between them created by their common enemies and restore their old friendship; and Balbus put it about that Caesar only wanted to live in safety with Pompey as the first

[16] Shackleton Bailey 1956 (C 259) and 1965–70 (B 108) IV App. Caes. *BCiv.* I.8, Roscius came from Pompey.

[17] *Att.* VII.14.1, 17.2, VIII.18.2.

[18] This was generally expected, Suet. *Iul.* 30.3.

[19] *Att.* VII.19, X.4.8, cf. Caelius *ap.* X.9A.1; X.4.8, 5.1; VIII.11.2. *Uterque regnare vult.* Atticus agreed, X.1a, when Caesar returned to Rome at least.

men in the state.[20] Pompey sent Magius back for further talks, but it seems refused the interview. Caesar apparently tried again via Libo for one, but Pompey very correctly said he could not negotiate in the absence of the consuls, who had now left Italy. To Caesar, the legitimate authorities seemed simply to be his *inimici*, and he did not try again to negotiate with them; naturally for their part the optimates did not trust Pompey, which was perhaps why he was not granted the overall command which would have made his task so much easier, and which Cato had had the sense to propose.[21]

For the genuineness at least of the attempt to detach Pompey there speaks the fact that Caesar's position was in some ways weak, quite apart from the uncertainty of the outcome in a civil war. True, he had calmed some of the apprehension about his Gallic auxiliaries,[22] and about proscriptions and *tabulae novae*. But his invasion of Italy was high treason, and only a minority of senators had stayed in Rome or returned there after the first panic. He had many nobles on his side, but they tended to be young (families were often split) and/or disreputable; the *principes viri* were elsewhere – a number trying to stand neutral. Perhaps only three consulars – the timid lawyer Ser. Sulpicius, who in fact left Italy later, the elderly and inconspicuous M'. Lepidus and L. Volcacius Tullus – agreed to attend the Senate in Rome; even Caesar's father-in-law L. Piso may have held aloof, though the praetor M. Lepidus (like, probably, his colleague L. Roscius) was there, with several tribunes. Hence strenuous efforts to win over various distinguished men, notably Balbus' original patron the consul Lentulus Crus; the younger Balbus actually tried to go secretly to him in Brundisium.[23] And, of course, Cicero. Cicero was disillusioned with Pompey and the optimates, and hesitated piteously as to whether to go to a neutral area, to stay in Italy, or to follow Pompey overseas, as he finally did from personal loyalty alone. But he never wavered from the conviction that Caesar had morally and constitutionally no leg to stand on: 'What is honour (*dignitas*) without honesty?'; and when the two men met, on Caesar's way back to Rome, Cicero said he would only attend the Senate there if he could propose a decree that Caesar should go to neither Spain nor Greece in arms. 'I don't think he was pleased with me; but I was pleased with myself, which I have not been of late.' He was also shocked by Caesar's dubious entourage and his threats to use their advice if he could get no better.[24]

[20] Caes. *BCiv.* I.26.2ff says Magius did not return (perhaps only not as quickly as expected). But see Cic. *Att.* IX.7 and IX.13A.1, with copies of letters from Caesar.

[21] Plut. *Pomp.* 61, *Cato* 52.

[22] For which e.g. Dio XLI.8.6.

[23] Ser. Sulpicius, Bauman 1985 (F 179). L. Piso, Cic. *Fam.* XIV.14.2, *Att.* VII.13.1, Dio XLI.16.4, Plut. *Caes.* 37.1. Balbus, *Att.* VIII.9A.2, IX.6.1; VIII.15A shows that his uncle, the elder Balbus, also tried in vain to talk to the consul.

[24] *Att.* VII.11.1; IX.18.1–2, cf. 19.1.

Caesar was in Rome for about two weeks. The tribunes Antony and Q. Cassius summoned the Senate to meet outside the *pomoerium*, where Caesar in a self-justifying speech asked for senatorial co-operation; if he did not get it he would do without it. He inspired a decree that an embassy should be sent to Pompey; but not surprisingly, given the threats uttered by Pompey and the optimates against those who had not left with them, no one was willing to serve on it. More embarrassing still was the action of the tribune L. Metellus, who vetoed all proposals, including one giving Caesar the money left in the treasury on the flight from the city, and personally tried to prevent its removal. Caesar crossed the *pomoerium* with a body of troops, which was of course illegal, and threatened the sacrosanct tribune with death. He got the treasure, but naturally the defender of tribunician rights does not mention this contretemps, and he set off for Spain angry at his loss of popularity with the plebs and the time wasted.[25] M. Lepidus was left in charge of Rome.

It was also disturbing that Pompey by messengers, and soon Domitius Ahenobarbus in person, succeeded in persuading the authorities in the famous Greek city of Massilia, directly on Caesar's route, that their own benefactions to and ties with the place should take preference over Caesar's more recent ones; Domitius not only had an inherited *clientela* in the area, but of course claimed to be the new governor of Transalpine Gaul. The Massiliots seized all the shipping and corn in the area. Caesar had little alternative but to besiege the town; he soon had to leave the business to D. Brutus and C. Trebonius, with a few ships and three legions, and the city only surrendered to him, after a brilliant resistance, on his return months later. Massilia's alliance with Rome was supposed to date from the regal period, and there was a long history of co-operation against the barbarians. Though for this reason Caesar did not want the city stormed, and finally while stripping it of its lands and wealth left it its liberty, yet the siege and capture, to judge by Cicero, made a bad impression on Roman – and doubtless on Greek – opinion.[26]

While at Massilia, Caesar says, he sent his legate C. Fabius to seize the passes over the Pyrenees; some have thought he must have done this earlier.[27] He followed with his wonted rapidity. There were three armies in Spain, with Afranius in Citerior, and with Petreius and Varro (the great scholar) in Ulterior. The first two had concentrated their forces in Citerior, where Pompey had support dating from the Sertorian War. They were experienced soldiers, but Caesar's main problems, as so often

[25] Caes. *BCiv.* I.32–3, contrasted with Dio XLI.15–16, App. *BCiv.* II.41. Curio told Cicero that Caesar, spurred on by his followers, was enraged with Metellus, *Att.* X.4.8; X.9A.1.

[26] Caes. *BCiv.* I.34–6, 56–8, II.1–16, 22; Just. *Epit.* 43.3.4; Cic. *Off.* II.28.

[27] Adcock 1932 (C 152) 648; Cic. *Att.* VIII.3.7, rumours at Rome in February of engagements in the Pyrenees.

in Spanish warfare, were with supply and the elements. Reports that he was near defeat decided some laggards in Italy to join Pompey; in Spain there were rumours that Pompey was marching through Africa to his provinces. However, at the beginning of August Afranius and Petreius were forced to surrender near Ilerda, and were spared. Varro, isolated in Ulterior, where Caesar had twice served and had friends, soon capitulated too.[28]

Meanwhile Cato (complaining, according to Caesar, that Pompey had betrayed the Republic by not making better preparations for war) withdrew from Sicily before Curio arrived there for Caesar. Curio went on, according to orders, to Africa, where the governor Attius Varus had a superior force. But it was by the army of king Juba of Numidia – unexpectedly, since the news of Caesar's success at Ilerda had arrived, but Juba had obligations to Pompey and personal grudges against Caesar and Curio – that the Caesarian forces were trapped and Curio, who refused the chance of escape, killed. Caesar, who clearly liked the spirited young noble, is frank about but indulgent to his fatal overconfidence in the *Commentaries*.[29]

In the autumn Caesar returned to Rome, dealing with Massilia and then with a mutiny of his troops in Cisalpine Gaul (which he omits to mention) on the way. Acquiring the consulship for 48, for which he had taken such trouble, was not an entirely straightforward matter. He failed to obtain a ruling that M. Lepidus, though only praetor, could preside over consular elections,[30] so Lepidus proposed a law that Caesar should be made dictator, something for which precedent could be found; and as dictator Caesar presided over his own election to the consulship with P. Servilius Isauricus, respected son of the distinguished man under whom he had served in youth, and someone whose adherence was perhaps something of a *coup*.[31] Caesar passed laws restoring the political rights of the sons of those proscribed by Sulla (these included his first wife's brother P. Cinna), and as expected recalling all those who had been condemned under the compendious procedures introduced by Pompey after Clodius' death, taking the specious ground that they had not had a fair trial. One such was the historian Sallust. These measures enlarged the body of his supporters, but the second at least hardly contributed much respectability. On the other hand, the measures Caesar took to cope with a debt crisis were as we shall see statesmanlike and moderate, though perhaps not quite as moderate as his account suggests. At all events, they displeased debtors, who wanted a cancellation, and a little

[28] Caes. *BCiv.* II.17–20. [29] Caes. *BCiv.* II.36–42.

[30] Cic. *Att.* IX.9.3, cf. 15.2: the augural books were clear that it was illegal.

[31] There were even connexions with Cato, whose niece he had married and with whom he had once co-operated.

later Cicero's friend Caelius Rufus, now praetor, stirred up such unrest that the Senate passed the *senatus consultum ultimum* (Caesar does not record this) and Servilius deposed him. Caelius then raised a Pompeian revolt in south Italy with the aid of Milo, now back from exile; but both were soon killed.[32]

After eleven days Caesar left for Brundisium and the campaign against Pompey, having laid down the dictatorship. Inconclusive naval operations had ended with Pompey's admirals retaining control of the Adriatic, while he himself was busy training his men and the 'Senate' sat at Thessalonica; but politically it was a weakness that elections could not be held for 48.[33] The East had been stripped of troops; the consul Lentulus Crus had raised two legions in Asia (we have his decree exempting Jews who were Roman citizens from service in them).[34] Metellus Scipio was bringing two more from Syria; Pompey's son went on to Egypt. Pompey used his credit to persuade client kings and peoples to send large numbers of auxiliary troops; he even tried to negotiate with Parthia, and was in touch with Burebistas, who had recently welded the Dacians into a great power.[35] Cicero, who was miserable in Pompey's camp, destested what he saw as relying on barbarians against Roman citizens as much as he loathed the threats of the optimates against all who had tried to remain neutral and their greed for the spoils of war and office.[36]

Since Pompey's army was still growing Caesar must strike quickly. But he did not yet have adequate transports, and though he succeeded in getting across with seven legions, the rest of his army was stuck for months with Antony in Brundisium, and Caesar kept in difficulties for provisions, while Bibulus commanded the sea. Another suggestion of a meeting with Pompey came to nothing, perhaps because this time it was Caesar who proposed that the Senate and people at Rome should decide on terms.[37] At last, after Bibulus had succumbed to his exertions, stubborn to the last, Antony got out to join his commander, and manoeuvring ended with Caesar drawing his lines right round Pompey's position outside Dyrrachium – partly for the moral effect on Pompey's eastern allies[38] – though without having enough troops to man them properly. Pompey tried to break out, and finally gained enough success in an engagement for Caesar to retire, telling his friends that if his opponent had been a conqueror he could have conquered Caesar that day.[39]

[32] Caes. *BCiv.* III.20–2.

[33] Dio XLI.43; about 200 senators were present. The magistrates of 49 were prorogued.

[34] Joseph. *AJ* XIV.228ff.

[35] Parthia, Dio XLII.2.5; Burebistas, *SIG*³ 762, 21–36.

[36] Cic. *Att.* IX.10.3, 11.3; XI.6.2 and 6; Plut. *Cic.* 38.

[37] Caes. *BCiv.* III.10.

[38] Caes. *BCiv.* III.43.3, cf. Dolabella, Cic. *Fam.* IX.9.2.

[39] Plut. *Caes.* 39.5.

Caesar now marched east,[40] partly to save one of the legates he had sent into Macedonia and Greece, Domitius Calvinus, whom Metellus Scipio, arrived from Syria, was threatening; he authorized a massacre at Gomphi in Thessaly, which resisted him, but treated generously towns that surrendered. Pompey determined to spare Italy invasion by settling the issue in the East, pursued Caesar to save Metellus; and probably under pressure from his now over-confident optimate allies, who accused him of prolonging the war to extend his command, decided to risk battle rather than harass his tired opponent, as Cato and Cicero are said to have wished (both were left at Dyrrachium).[41] Somewhere near Pharsalus in Thessaly, on 9 August 48 B.C., Pompey was defeated in spite of superior numbers. Domitius Ahenobarbus was among those killed; Pompey fled. Caesar, surveying the field, said 'They would have it. I, Caius Caesar, after all my victories, would have been condemned in the courts if I had not sought the aid of my army.'[42] He burned Pompey's correspondence and let it be known that he would forgive all who asked for mercy. To his pleasure, M. Brutus was one of the first to beg it.[43]

The Pompeian naval squadrons withdrew from Italy, and some surrendered. Cicero, the most senior in rank of those still at Dyrrachium, refused the command of the troops there from Cato and returned to Italy, to find himself stuck in his turn at Brundisium, because Antony, who was soon sent back to Italy to take control, said he could not allow him to return to Rome without Caesar's permission. Cato, with Pompey's sons and others, went to Cyrenaica, hoping to rejoin Pompey. Dio says that Pompey's defeat was so unexpected he had no plans to fall back on.[44] He fled to Lesbos, where he was reunited with his wife, and then made for Egypt, which had sent him aid and where many of the Roman garrison buttressing the regime were his veterans. The Senate in exile had probably recently recognized young Ptolemy XIII and made Pompey his *tutor*.[45] But the king's advisers had him killed as he landed. Cicero claimed tht something like this would have happened wherever Pompey had taken refuge. All he could now say in tribute to his old associate was that he was 'an honest, decent, serious man'.[46]

Caesar was in hot pursuit, though he touched in Asia, where he remitted taxes and was paid extravagant honours. He reached Alexandria with two very depleted legions on 2 October, only three days after Pompey's death, and arrogantly marched into the city with his lictors to establish himself in the palace.[47] Since the Etesian winds would prevent

[40] Plut. *Caes.* 39.6, he felt he should have done so earlier.

[41] Plut. *Pomp.* 67–8, *Cato* 53.3, Cic. *Fam.* VII.3.2.

[42] Suet. *Iul.* 30.4, from Pollio, who claims to be quoting word for word; cf. Plut. *Caes.* 46.1.

[43] Plut. *Caes.* 46.2. Brutus (properly Q. Caepio Brutus), was the son of Caesar's old flame Servilia (born long before that tie is attested, so not Caesar's).

[44] Dio XLII.1–2. [45] Heinen 1966 (D 194). [46] Cic. *Att.* XI.6.5. [47] Dio XLII.7.3.

his leaving at once, he declared that he would arbitrate in the armed struggle between Cleopatra, aged twenty-one, and her husband Ptolemy aged thirteen, the two elder children of Auletes, who had left them as co-rulers and commended them to Rome's protection. He also set about exacting Auletes' still unpaid debts to the so-called triumvirs (which aroused further ill feeling). He soon found himself held up in Alexandria with the ambitious Cleopatra as his mistress, and Ptolemy's ministers, his troops and the Alexandrian populace (which felt it was fighting for Egypt's independence), not to mention a younger sister Arsinoe, as his enemies. A nasty little war dragged on (part of the famous library was among the casualties)[48] until in late March 47 Caesar was reinforced by troops led overland by Mithridates of Pergamum, a Hellenized connexion of the Pontic and Galatian royal families, and including a strong Jewish contingent under the high priest's minister Antipater.[49] The young king was drowned in the subsequent fighting. The *Bellum Alexandrinum*[50] gives the impression that after this Caesar left Egypt almost immediately, though many scholars keep him there till June or even July, and blame him severely for the delay, accepting that he went on a tour up the Nile with Cleopatra.[51] At all events, Cleopatra and a still younger brother were left to rule Egypt, with three legions (under the son of one of Caesar's freedmen) to support them, and the gift of Cyprus to sweeten the pill. Towards the end of June Cleopatra bore a son whom she called Ptolemy Caesar, and the Alexandrians Caesarion; Octavian was jealously to assert that he was not Caesar's child, but Caesar must have believed that he was, if he allowed the name (used in a letter of Cicero's very soon after the Ides of March, shortly before Cleopatra, who had come to Rome in 46, returned to Egypt).[52]

Landing at Antioch in Syria, Caesar heard that all was not well at Rome. But he felt that his most urgent task was to settle the East, and in particular to deal with king Pharnaces of the Cimmerian Bosporus (the Crimea) who had seized the chance to restore the kingdom of his father, the great Mithridates. Pharnaces had invaded Asia Minor and defeated Caesar's legate Domitius Calvinus and the Galatian forces, but was himself immeditely overcome by Caesar at Zela, near which Mithridates had beaten a Roman army. 'Veni, vidi, vici', wrote Caesar; he set up a trophy to overshadow Mithridates', and depreciated Pompey's victory over such foes. At last he could return to Italy.[53]

[48] Fraser 1972 (D 192) I, 334–5, 476.

[49] Joseph. *AJ* XIV.127–36, *BJ* I.187–93.

[50] [Caes.] *BAlex*. 33. This straightforward account has been attributed to Caesar's officer Hirtius, the author of *BGall*. VIII, probably wrongly.

[51] Lord 1936 (D 207); Heinen 1966 (D 194) as App. *BCiv*. II.90.

[52] Heinen 1969 (D 195); Cic. *Att*. XIV.20.2.

[53] Plut. *Caes*. 50.2; Suet. *Iul*. 35.2, 37.2.

Caesar, says Dio, had been ashamed to send a despatch with the news of Pharsalus, which was not believed for a long time.[54] When it was, in September 48, he was made dictator for a year. Antony was nominated as his *magister equitum*, but proved oppressive and inefficient. In 47 Dolabella as tribune renewed the agitation on behalf of debtors. When Antony was in Campania struggling with a mutiny the Senate had recourse again to the *senatus consultum ultimum*, ineffectively since only the plebeian magistrates had been elected, and no one was able to enforce it. Finally Antony restored partial order in Rome, with serious loss of life and so of his remaining popularity. With no news from Alexandria for months, and a great deal from Africa, Italy was on tenter-hooks.[55]

On hearing of Pompey's death Cato had led an epic march through the desert from Cyrenaica to the province of Africa,[56] to join Metellus Scipio, who as a consular was recognized as commander-in-chief of the Republican coalition, though Labienus was probably its military inspiration. It included king Juba, and ultimately disposed of very great forces, though there seems to have been no claim that the Senate was now in Africa. After a period of success, Pompey's naval squadrons were driven from the Adriatic and basing themselves in Africa made descents on Sardinia and Sicily. Contact was made with Spain, where Caesar's governor in Ulterior, Q. Cassius, had united provincials and Roman troops in detestation of him; and Dio says that even an invasion of Italy was planned.[57]

In Rome Caesar made it clear that Antony had lost his confidence, but, surprisingly, that Dolabella had not. He recalled the mutinous troops to their allegiance,[58] had magistrates elected for the rest of 47, and for 46, when he was to be – irregularly – consul again (with Lepidus). He borrowed money for the war, sold up the property of Pompey and those opponents who were dead or unpardoned (exacting, unlike Sulla, the full price from purchasers), and eluded an attempt to delay his departure for Africa by a leading *haruspex*, who prophesied disaster if he set sail before the solstice (he went to Sicily mainly by road, sent a detachment ahead, and himself put out on 25 December – though by the heavens the solstice was still weeks away).[59]

As usual he had inadequate shipping, and this time did not know where he might be able to land. Indeed he had some difficulty in establishing a bridgehead – Appian and Dio represent him as badly mauled by Labienus – and then in provisioning himself by sea. The

[54] Dio XLII.18; cf. Plut. *Caes.* 56.4. [55] Dio XLII.26.

[56] Plut. *Cato* 56.3. Perhaps not as epic as in Lucan *Phars.* IX, but a route rarely attempted by an army. [57] Dio XLII.56.4.

[58] He addressed them as Quirites, i.e. merely citizens, not fellow-soldiers, with marked effect, Suet. *Iul.* 70. [59] Rawson 1978 (C 246) 143.

campaign was to be a difficult one. It is recorded by an anonymous officer who was not in Caesar's confidence and has little strategic grasp, but who conveys vividly the trust his anxious subordinates had in their general's own confidence, as well as the problems caused by the 'amazing' light-armed native troops and the unfamiliar tactics employed by Labienus and the others, which we are told drove Caesar into unaccustomed caution.[60] However, Bocchus of Mauretania and the Roman adventurer in his service, P. Sittius, invaded Numidia to draw off Juba, and propaganda representing Scipio and other Romans as mere tools of a barbarian king, with promises of material benefits to provincials and citizens alike, increased the desertions to Caesar that began to take place; the native Gaetulians' loyalty to the memory of Marius, Caesar's kinsman, was also exploited. Finally Caesar's enemies tried to trap him outside the town of Thapsus, which stood on a spit of land between the sea and a lagoon. Caesar's troops got out of hand and attacked prematurely but with success, under the cry 'Felicitas'. They would give no quarter, even to prominent men. Caesar marched on to Utica, where its citizens refused to resist, as did the numerous Italian *negotiatores* there. Cato, who was in command, after organizing the escape of all senators and others who wished to go, committed suicide, cheating Caesar of a final display of clemency; he held that 'to pardon men as if he were their master' was something Caesar could have no legal right to do.[61] Metellus Scipio, Juba and others perished in different ways, but Labienus and Pompey's two sons managed to establish themselves in Spain. The war was still not over.

A few men, who had been pardoned by Caesar once but renewed the fight, were executed. Arrangements included provincializing part of Juba's kingdom; the rest was given to the Mauretanian kings and Sittius. Fines and confiscations were imposed in the old province. In mid-June 46 Caesar left for Sardinia ('the only one of his new properties he has not yet visited,' wrote Cicero sarcastically);[62] he arrived in Rome in late July 46.

This time he spent rather longer there. At the end of September he celebrated four triumphs, in theory all over foreign enemies (as alone was customary) – Gaul, Egypt, Pharnaces and Juba. Vercingetorix, Cleopatra's sister Arsinoe, and Juba's four-year-old son figured in the processions, and the first-named was then put to death.[63] The citizens received gifts of money and food (some of the soldiers objected, though they themselve got 24,000 sesterces each, the equivalent of a lifetime's pay)[64] and grand games in memory of Caesar's daughter Julia took place.

[60] [Caes.] *BAfr.* 10, 19, 31. [61] Plut. *Cato* 58–70. [62] Cic. *Fam.* IX.7.2.

[63] Val. Max. II.8.7; but App. *BCiv.* II.102 says there were pictures and models of battles against citizens and of Republican generals, except for Pompey (so loved by the plebs).

[64] Suet. *Iul.* 38.1.

But the news from Further Spain was bad and probably towards the end of the year Caesar, who had hoped to deal with the war through his legates,[65] set off once more, leaving Italy under his new *magister equitum*, Lepidus.

By now few veterans were available and Caesar could take only one experienced legion. Though in Rome, and even at Thapsus, he had forgiven most of those who fought for Pompey, he treated those now in arms as plain rebels. It was improper to enslave citizens in civil war, but they could be massacred. Both sides committed atrocities; Caesar's men once adorned their fortifications with severed heads, as the clumsy narrator of the *Bellum Hispaniense* reveals.[66] At first Cn. Pompeius, Pompey's elder son, refused battle, perhaps on Labienus' advice, and Caesar's troops were left to the rigours of a winter campaign, but desertions to his side gained momentum and at last on a fine sunny day Pompeius accepted battle near Munda.[67] He almost prevailed; according to Plutarch Caesar said that for the first time he was fighting not for victory but his life.[68] But a last personal appeal stiffened his men, and in the end they triumphed. Labienus was killed on the field, and Cn. Pompeius some days later in flight. Mopping-up operations took some time, and Caesar remained in Spain till June 45. But, though Sex. Pompeius held out in hiding, and there was a Pompeian outbreak in Syria under one Caecilius Bassus, the civil war was over. Caesar did not publish an estimate of the lives lost in it.[69] Its result had never been a foregone conclusion; Caesar had repeatedly come near defeat, as he and his officers admit, and he had more than once acted very rashly. In spite of their undoubted devotion – not solely due to the fact that he had at some stage doubled their miserable pay[70] – his men had sometimes been mutinous or uncontrollable. But the Fortune he relied on had carried him through.[71]

Caesar spent some time at Narbo Martius in Gaul, and then in northern Italy, entering Rome only at his triumph in October 45. A celebration this time frankly over citizens made a bad impression, while Caesar even let his two legates Fabius and Pedius triumph too, which was quite irregular.

It was already decided that Caesar would go in person again to the East to lead a campaign against the Parthians and so avenge Crassus and

[65] Dio XLIII.28.1.

[66] [Caes.] *BHisp.* 32.

[67] [Caes.] *BHisp.* 29.

[68] Plut. *Caes.* 56. Suet. *Iul.* 36 says he considered suicide, thinking all lost.

[69] Pliny *HN* 7.92; but he probably claimed at his triumphs the 1,192,000 other dead in his wars which Pliny reports.

[70] Suet. *Iul.* 26.5; the context perhaps suggests the late 50s.

[71] See the story of him encouraging the crew of a boat in a storm with the words 'you carry Caesar and his Fortune', Plut. *Caes.* 38.5, App. *BCiv.* II.236.

his son.[72] He may or may not have learnt that they had invaded Syria in support of the Pompeians. His ultimate plans are unknown, but his army was to be huge – sixteen legions – and Suetonius reports that he intended to chastise the Dacians en route, and that he proposed to advance through Armenia Minor and only join battle after gaining experience of the enemy's mode of fighting. To judge by the offices he tied up ahead in Rome, the campaign was expected to last three years. Cicero later said that Caesar would never have returned from it, but it was not necessarily a megalomaniac project doomed to failure; rumours that he intended to return by southern Russia and Gaul are probably false.[73] Six legions and other troops were sent ahead to Macedonia, and Caesar was to leave Rome on 18 March. But his plans were all rendered vain by the conspirators three days earlier, on the Ides of March.

II. THE DICTATORSHIP

1. The empire

It is impossible today to approach Caesar's acts in his last years without some awareness of the different Caesars created by modern scholars. Perhaps it is unnecessary to go back to the idealized Caesar of Mommsen, that is, the man who saw in advance that a monarchy was the necessary cure for Rome's ills, and became a democratic ruler by overthrowing a corrupt and arrogant oligarchy – which was identified by the great liberal scholar with the Prussian Junkers whom he hated.[74] But the Caesar of Eduard Meyer, though perhaps no one now would accept him without reservation, lives on, if often as a model against which to react.[75] Meyer's Caesar fought selfishly for power, which he intended to legitimize by becoming another Alexander, ruling as god and king over a world empire; in fact, thought Meyer, this was a false path, and Augustus returned to the precedent of Pompey, who kept his power within Roman and Republican forms. Many scholars accepted this picture, some adding that Cleopatra had had an important role in converting Caesar to the idea of Hellenistic kingship.[76] Others, especially in Britain before the Second World War, denied that there was contemporary evidence to prove that he wished to be either a king or a god, and argued that the fact that he became dictator for life, *dictator perpetuo*, was enough to explain his assassination; he was a brilliant opportunist, with no long-term plans.[77]

[72] The Parthian War is first mentioned in May 45, Cic. *Att.* XIII.27.1, cf. 31.3, though in June Caesar wrote tht he would stay in Rome, 13.7.

[73] App. *BCiv.* II.110; Suet. *Iul.* 3; Plut. *Caes.* 58.2–5. Malitz 1984 (D 279).

[74] Mommsen 1888 (A 77). [75] Meyer 1918 (C 227).

[76] Gelzer 1921/1960 (C 198), the best and most thorough modern study of Caesar, basically takes this path, but less wholeheartedly in later editions.

[77] Adcock 1932 (C 152); Syme 1939 (A 118) (cf. *id.* 1938 (C 273)), though more concerned with Caesar's partisans than Caesar himself.

More recently there have been attempts, sometimes on the basis of the coins, to show that Caesar did wish to be king, but conceived kingship in Roman terms, harking back to Romulus or even to the kings of Alba Longa, descended like Caesar himself from Aeneas; and that he did wish to be god, but in that too stood largely in the native tradition.[78] A compromise view holds that he was only to bear the title of king outside Rome, to facilitate his expedition against the Parthians.[79] Some think that the explanation of these grandiose plans is that he had succumbed to megalomania and mental decay.[80]

His actual measures, more tangible than his final aims, have also been estimated in different ways. To some, for example, his extension of privileges to new classes is simply an easy and sometimes lucrative method of rewarding adherents. Others have taken his words about 'tranquillity for Italy, peace for the provinces and security for the empire'[81] as showing a conscious intention to abolish the last vestiges of city-state institutions and mentality at Rome and embark on a course that would in the end bring Italians and provincials into full equality with the inhabitants of the capital. And were his other social and administrative measures simply attempts to meet immediate problems and remedy crying abuses, or was there a wider vision that informed all he did?

The material on which we must base a decision is, given the quantity of evidence for the period, surprisingly unsatisfactory. Caesar's own writings come to an end, and various sayings attributed to him may not be genuine.[82] Cicero was so obsessed with Caesar's increasingly cavalier way with Republican forms that he seems never to have tried to understand his measures.[83] The fullest account of the honours that he received comes from the much later historian Dio, whose sources are uncertain and who has been extensively disbelieved.[84] The coin types have been shown conclusively to be a broken reed in establishing Caesar's attitude to kingship and godhead.[85] It is often impossible to tell if a Lex Iulia or a *colonia Iulia* is owed to Caesar or his adopted son Augustus. After Caesar's death Antony passed various measures which he said that Caesar had planned, leaving drafts in his papers, but Antony's assertion was greeted with considerable scepticism.[86] The inscriptional evidence is fragmentary and hard to interpret, and has not

[78] Esp. Alföldi (C 153–4, 158–9), Weinstock 1971 (H 134).

[79] Oppermann 1958 (C 234).

[80] Notably Collins, 1955 (C 186).

[81] Caes. *BCiv.* III.57; cf. esp. Vittinghoff 1952 (A 122).

[82] E.g. those retailed by Ampius Balbus, a violent Pompeian, Suet. *Iul.* 77; and is it true (Cic. *Off.* III.82) that Caesar often quoted Euripides on the attractions of tyrannic power?

[83] And came to believe that Caesar had planned to become master of Rome from the time of his aedileship in 66 (letter *ap.* Suet. *Iul.* 9.2); though *regnum* is a vague word.

[84] The view that he represents the Livian tradition is unfounded; Manuwald 1979 (B 70) shows this for the triumviral and Augustan periods at least.

[85] Kraay 1954 (B 181).

[86] *Att.* XIV.12.1, *Phil.* I.2, 16 etc.

increased substantially of late years. The dates of many measures are also uncertain, and thus it is hard to trace any development of policy. Some things we must reconcile ourselves to not knowing; with others, we must content ourselves with a measure of probability.

We may begin by considering Caesar's attitude to the empire as a whole and the provinces individually. First of all, it must be insisted that 'tranquillity for Italy, peace for the provinces and security for the empire' is not a political programme; it is what Caesar, when trying to negotiate before Pharsalus, tells Metellus Scipio will automatically occur if the war comes to an end. On the other hand, Caesar had spent the last decade out of Rome, and it is very possible that he had imbibed in Gaul a sense of the pettiness of the political squabbles in the capital, and saw things from an imperial perspective. He had in earlier years taken his stand on the old *popularis* plank of clean provincial government, a good base from which to attack the optimates. It is thus not surprising that he, and the authors of the *Corpus Caesarianum*, make much of the extortion and cruelty of Republican leaders in the war. No doubt they exaggerate; for his part, Caesar had acquired immense wealth in Gaul (if mainly from booty, seen as legitimate), and indeed according to some had been extortionate in Spain after his praetorship, owing to his need to pay his debts.[87] But perhaps a reputation for sympathy towards provincials played some part in the desertions to his side which he and his officers assert were so frequent; the *Bellum Africanum* interestingly says that the citizens of Utica favoured him because they had benefited from the Lex Iulia, probably the measure of 59 for the control of senatorial officials.[88]

Not that all Caesar's appointments to provincial governorships were of high quality. The disastrous Q. Cassius, already seen in charge of Further Spain in 48, was drowned with his extorted wealth after his recall.[89] M. Lepidus (in Citerior in 48–47) got home safely with his.[90] Sallust is said to have behaved ill in the new province of Africa Nova, though he was subsequently exonerated by Caesar and himself insists that he never succumbed to *avaritia*.[91] But Caesar began the war with an unsatisfactory lot of subordinates, and to gain better was probably one motive for his *clementia*. In 46 M. Brutus, in spite of the Salamis affair (ch. 15, p. 594) an honourable man, governed Cisalpine Gaul. And Ser. Sulpicius Rufus, lawyer and philhellene, who in Rome had been a cautious reformer, agreed to take Achaea (Greece), gloomy as he was

87 Suet. *Iul.* 54.1.

88 [Caes.] *BAfr.* 87.

89 [Caes.] *BAlex.* 64.

90 Dio XLIII.1.3.

91 Dio XLIII.9.2, Sall. *Cat.* 3.4. But Dio XLIII.47.4 says that in 45 Caesar released some who were about to be found guilty of taking bribes (and so was charged with taking bribes himself).

over the political situation.[92] The younger Servilius Isauricus was in Asia from 46 to 44, and though honorary inscriptions by provincials prove little, there is such a spate of them expressing gratitude to Servilius that he must at least have been energetic.[93] Caesar refused on the other hand to give L. Minucius Basilus a province; we happen to know the man was abominably cruel.[94]

In Greece, Caesar had had contacts since his unsuccessful prosecution, in the 70s, of two senators for extortion. In the late 50s he had given cities there, as in Asia and elsewhere, generous gifts out of his Gallic booty.[95] No wonder that he sent legates from Epirus in 48 to try to detach it from Pompey, though Athens in fact refused to come over and a legate even sold the Megarians as slaves (though primarily as a demonstration, at low prices and to their kin) on account of their resistance.[96] After Pharsalus Caesar returned their freedom to the cities of Thessaly to mark his victory. Soon he put in briefly to Asia. He might have punished the communities which had supported Pompey, though they had had little choice. Instead, he was generous, remitting part of the direct tax and, significantly, allowing the cities themselves, instead of the hated *publicani*, to collect it.[97] From roughly this period date a number of honorary inscriptions from various parts of the Greek world, greeting him as saviour and benefactor.[98] At Ephesus, where he says he arrived just in time to save the temple treasures from a Pompeian legate, the communities of Asia voted to build a monument to him as descendant of Ares, god manifest and saviour of mankind.[99] He gave special honours to certain cities. Ilium, which had received favours from an earlier member of the family, had its freedom and immunity confirmed and lands given it by

[92] Sulpicius' gloom, Cic. *Fam.* IV.3 (with Caesar's respect for his integrity and wisdom); IV.4, he regrets taking the job. Achaea had previously been attached to Macedonia; perhaps Caesar thought it required special temporary attention, rather than permanent separation. Note also Pansa sent to Bithynia in 45; a bouquet to his humanity, *Fam.* XV.17.3, cf. 19.2; respected by Caesar, VI.12.2.

[93] See Magie 1950 (A 67) I 416–17, II 1270–1. Cicero notes *Fam.* XIII.68 that Asia had suffered severely. At Pergamum he 'restored ancient laws and a democracy subject to none' *IGRR* IV 433; (cf. *RDGE* 55, letter to the Pergamenes about the temple of Asclepius). Ephesus worshipped him together with Rome; Aegae was 'saved' by him; Magnesia received benefits, *ibid.* 1178, *IMagnesia* 142. In fact in 61–60 he had joined with Cato in trying to protect 'free' cities against the *publicani*, *Att.* I.19.9, 20.4, II.1.10.

[94] Dio XLIII.47.5, App. *BCiv.* III.98; he gave Basilus money instead. A law of 46 limiting praetorian governors to one year and consular to two was probably as Dio XLIII.25.3 says to prevent the amassing of excessive influence, but may not have been as bad for the provincials as sometimes thought; a Roman governor hardly needed to be an expert on his area. (The Lex Pompeia of 52 was disregarded: Girardet 1987 (C 203).)

[95] Suet. *Iul.* 28.1; W. Ameling, *Herodes Atticus* (Hildesheim, 1983) I 7. His fifty talents to Athens for a new market exactly balanced Pompey's earlier largesse.

[96] Dio XLII.14.3–4.

[97] Embassies, App. *BCiv.* II.89; tax of Asia, Dio XLII.6.3 (but he did levy contributions) App. *BCiv.* V.4. Opinions differ as to whether the *publicani* lost the direct taxes in other provinces; they continued to collect indirect taxes. For generous tax arrangements in Judaea, Joseph. *AJ* XIV.201ff (none in Sabbatical year).

[98] Raubitschek 1954 (B 223); Robert 1955 (B 230).

[99] Caes. *BCiv.* III.105.

the descendant of Trojan Aeneas – or, as Strabo thinks, the admirer of Alexander.[100] Perhaps now he restored its freedom to Pergamum, and was even generous to Mytilene, which had been closely bound to Pompey. Plutarch says he freed Cnidus as a favour to his friend Theopompus.[101] At some point he dedicated a golden Eros at the famous sanctuary of his ancestress Aphrodite at Aphrodisias in Caria; Octavian's patronage of the city was probably inherited.[102]

After Pharsalus Caesar may have believed that the war was almost over, and that he could thus afford to be generous. After Zela, when he was again in Asia, he knew this was not so, and he made up for his earlier leniency, by, according to Dio, extracting vast sums of money from all the states, though violence and cruelty were perhaps not employed.[103] It is difficult to estimate how damaging to the provinces the civil wars were; perhaps very damaging.[104] Almost all areas were involved. They had to produce, often for both sides in turn, not only money, but supplies and manpower, especially cavalry, and sometimes ships; a few wilder areas may have sent willing mercenaries. The economy might be disrupted; merchant shipping was seized for use as transports, and we are told that little grain was harvested in the great corn-exporting province of Africa in 47–46 as the Pompeians had conscripted the farmers.[105] Immunity to enslavement did not extend to foreigners, as the fate of the Megarians shows; and a citizen of Cyzicus records a dream that he had about a friend who had been enslaved while fighting at sea for Caesar at the time of his African campaign.[106]

Caesar did not reward any of the Greek cities of the East with Roman citizenship or with Latin status (which meant that in time the whole ruling class would acquire the citizenship through holding office; and which, since the enfranchisement of the Transpadane Latins, may have seemed like a promise of ultimate enfranchisement for all); they might in fact not have welcomed it. Caesar did however at the end of his life give or intend to give Latin status to all Sicily, which was largely Greek-speaking; Roman and Italian settlement was confined to a few places.[107] But the Greek cities of southern Italy had been enfranchised in 89; while geographers regarded Sicily as originally part of the peninsula.[108] And he

[100] Strab. XIII.594–5. According to Lucan *Phars.* IX.961 Caesar visited it.

[101] Pergamum *SIG*³ 763, *RDGE* 54, 55; Mytilene, *RDGE* 26; Cnidus, Plut. *Caes.* 48. In 45–44 B.C. he enlarged the asylum at the temple of Apollo at Didyma, *OGIS* 473 (with Magie 1950 (A 67) 1271).

[102] Reynolds 1982 (B 226) no. 8.

[103] Dio. XLII.49. He also regulated the affairs of many kings and dynasts.

[104] F. Millar, 'Empire and City, Augustus to Julian', *JRS* 73 (1983) 76–96.

[105] [Caes.] *BAfr.* 20.

[106] *IGRR* IV 135. But M. Stlaccius M.f. was presumably a citizen, and so wrongfully enslaved – a common enough event.

[107] Cic. *Att.* XIV.12.2, Antony wished to upgrade it to citizen status; but even Latinitas was revoked, as many peregrine towns are found later, Pliny *HN* III.88–91.

[108] Strab. I.60 etc.

was generous to individual Greeks, not only to those resident in Italy, as presumably the 500 enrolled at Novum Comum had mostly been, and to the doctors and teachers settling in Rome to whom he gave citizenship in his last years, but also to various figures prominent in the East. We hear, largely by chance, of several cases of such men.[109] It was probably in Caesar's time, not as usually thought in the triumviral period, that the rule enunciated by Cicero, but often ignored, that it was impossible to hold the Roman and another citizenship simultaneously, fell into complete desuetude, and grants began to specify that beneficiaries were still liable to duties and eligible to office in their home towns.[110]

It is in the West that Caesar's grants of privilege were most significant, and are most disputed. In 49, by a Lex Roscia, Caesar gave full citizenship to the Latin colonies beyond the Po, whose cause he had so long championed and which had provided material support and man-power for the Gallic War.[111] This will have meant the end of Pompey's *clientela* here. Although many of the new citizens were Gallic by race, the area had long been considered geographically part of Italy, though in fact Caesar left Cisalpine Gaul as a province, perhaps because he wanted an army close to Italy. In any event, the Lex Roscia provided no real precedent for giving the citizenship in the same year to the Punic city of Gades in Further Spain, an old ally of Rome.[112] Caesar had reformed (and de-Punicized, probably by eradicating child sacrifice) the city's laws when governor of Ulterior in 61–60, and it was the home of his trusted agent Balbus; it had expelled Varro's garrison. What were his motives? It would be easier to say if we knew whether he gave citizenship or Latin rights at the same time to any other towns, or whether Gades was an isolated case.

But after Munda, says Dio, while Caesar confiscated territory from or imposed fines on communities in Further Spain that had supported the Pompeians, those which had been loyal got land and immunity from taxation, or the citizenship, or 'to be considered as colonists' – but had to pay for it. (Caesar even removed the dedications from the temple of Hercules in Gades, so great was his need for money.)[113] In fact we do not

109 Plut. *Caes.* 29.2; Suet. *Iul.* 42.1; Cic. *Fam.* XIII.35; Strab. V.213. Individual grants, Cic. *Phil.* XIII.33, *SIG*³. 761C Plut. *Cic.* 24, Cic. *Fam.* XIII.36; Joseph. *AJ* XIV.137. We do not hear of a law allowing Caesar to enfranchise groups or individuals, but he probably had one passed at some point. Some got the citizenship corruptly via his friends, and so the lists had to be revised, Cic. *Fam.* XIII.36.

110 Rawson 1985 (C 248) 56.

111 Dio XLI.36.3. Perhaps the Lex Roscia relative to Cisalpine Gaul passed on 11 March of some year, mentioned in *Frag. Atest.*, *FIRA* 20 line 14.

112 Dio XLI.41.24.1, Livy *Epit.* CX. Saumagne 1965 (F 138) 71 wrongly argued that Caesar merely gave the town Latin rights and it was made a Roman *municipium* by Augustus, who certainly seems to have been in some way responsible for this title. Caes. *BCiv.* II.21 is unfortunately vague. But [Cic.] *Fam.* X.32.3 (*IVviri* and numerous *equites* in 43 B.C.) is conclusive.

113 Dio XLIII.39.4–5.

know which, if any, native towns were given full citizenship[114] – some think Dio is speaking loosely of grants to individuals; while it is not clear whether, in talking of colonists, he means that the towns became titular Latin colonies, or that some loyal Spaniards were enrolled, in accordance with tradition, as full citizens in the Roman colonies made up of veterans of the legions or civilians from Rome (to which we shall come). By the middle of Augustus' reign there were certainly a fair number of native towns with either citizen or Latin status, especially in the Baetis valley in Further Spain, as Pliny the Elder in particular makes clear;[115] although some of them were insignificant places, and probably little Romanized. But was this the work of Caesar or his successor? Augustus was to become cautious in extending citizenship to *peregrini*; but probably not until after the triumviral period, and indeed he seems to have given Latin rights in Spain later.[116] It has been suggested that all the towns mentioned by Pliny or elsewhere that had 'flowery' titles, made up of the adjective 'Julian' and some virtue or quality, were given either citizenship or Latin status by Caesar, and this might seem likely for Ulia Iulia Fidentia, for example, which had stood by him loyally in 45; but some 'flowery' titles were certainly conferred by Augustus.[117]

The old province of Gallia Transalpina provides similar problems. A number of towns, such as Nemausus (Nîmes) were Latin by the early first century A.D., but we cannot be sure that this was Caesar's work, though the hypothesis seems to have hardened into a dogma. Archaeological evidence suggests that the Romanization of native communities had not advanced far, though there was some Hellenization in the area around Massilia. The legion, known as the Alaudae or Larks, that Caesar had raised from natives in the province was however certainly enfranchised.[118] A few Gallic magnates from the Transalpina had already been given the citizenship, by Pompey or even earlier; Caesar certainly made such grants, and one or two true Gauls from the region were possibly even put into the Senate,[119] as the younger L. Cornelius Balbus of Gades certainly was (Cicero shuddered at the mere thought of his uncle's elevation).[120] But anti-Caesarian invective treated scions of settler

114 Probably Olisipo (Lisbon), according to Vittinghoff 1952 (A 122) 78, but see Brunt 1971 (A 16) 238, who however notes various possible names.

115 Pliny *HN* III.7ff; his sources are mid-Augustan.

116 For discussion see Henderson 1942 (C 212), Vittinghoff 1952 (A 122), Galsterer 1971 (E 15), Hoyos 1979 (E 19).

117 Brunt 1971 (A 16) 250 is cautious, arguing many of the towns had been Pompeian and would not have been favoured by Caesar.

118 Suet. *Iul.* 24.2; cf. Cic. *Phil.* I.20 cf. 13.3, who professes to expect they will get on to the jury lists at Rome.

119 It is difficult to identify individuals. Wiseman 1971 (A 130) 23 suggests T. Carisius, *monetalis* *c.*45, of Avennio (Avignon); but he, like a man from Narbo, may be of settler stock. Cic. *Fam.* IX.15.2 suggests some sort of Transalpine presence at Rome.

120 Suet. *Iul.* 44. Cic. *Att.* XVI.8.2. The elder Balbus was in fact consul in 40, but possibly not in the Senate before that.

families as wild barbarians – Cicero calls L. Decidius Saxa a 'wild Celtiberian', but, though he came from Spain, he was probably of settler stock, since he had a good Italian name and served as an officer in Caesar's army.[121] Jokes about Gauls from the newly conquered province laying aside their trousers for the senator's tunic with broad purple stripe and asking their way to the senate-house are simply jokes;[122] and no Greeks seem to have been put in the Senate. In fact Dio does not mention provincials among the unsuitable persons Caesar was thought to have honoured thus.[123]

Some natives, perhaps often *hybridae* of only partly Roman descent (and so peregrine status) were doubtless, as we noted, included in citizen colonies. After the battle of Thapsus Caesar probably began to settle some of his veterans at colonies at Curubis and Carpis on the African coast.[124] After Munda two and probably more colonies were planted in Provence, certainly Arelate (Arles) for the Sixth legion, Narbo Martius (Narbonne – already a colony) for the Tenth.[125] If there were veterans settled in Spain too, perhaps the Roman colonies at Tarraco and Carthago Nova, on the east coast, which are called *Iulia Victrix*, were for such, and at least planned by Caesar.[126] But he did also settle large numbers of the urban populace of Rome overseas, sometimes at least in places to which he also sent veterans. Hispalis (Seville), certainly founded by him,[127] is called *Iulia Romula*, which perhaps suggests its colonists were largely urban; so clearly were those of Urso, *colonia Genetiva Urbanorum* (if this title is correctly transmitted), for which by luck we have part of the foundation charter, asserting that the settlement was made by Caesar's order but in accordance with a law of Antony.[128]

121 Cic. *Phil.* XI.12, XIII.27. Syme 1937 (C 271).

122 Suet. *Iul.* 76.3, 80.2. 'Gallic' senators might be thoroughly Romanized Cisalpines. The known Cisalpine senators however, such as the poet Helvius Cinna, from Brixia, may be of Italian settler descent.

123 Dio XLIII 47.3 (plain soldiers and sons of freedmen).

124 Curubis, *CIL* I²788 (a freedman *IIvir* before Caesar's death); Carpis, *ILS* 9367. Teutsch 1962 (E 29) 108, 160.

125 Suet. *Tib.* 4 says Caesar's follower Ti. Nero founded colonies 'including Arelate and Narbo' in Gaul; Lepidus perhaps raised a third veteran legion there after Caesar's death, which would imply a third colony. Forum Iulii, perhaps not a colony till after Actium, probably owed its existence as a town to Caesar (attested in 43, Cic. *Fam.* X.15.3). Further urbanization is possible; the native Lutevani Foroneronienses, Pliny *HN* 3.37, perhaps owed their existence as a town (*forum*) to Ti. Nero.

126 Celsa (Iulia Victrix Lepida), up the Ebro, perhaps founded by Lepidus on Caesar's plan, as the name suggests.

127 Isid. *Orig.* 15.1.71 – the Bishop of Seville should have known who founded the town. Henderson 1942 (C 212) however thinks the title Romula points to Augustus. Livy XXXIV. 9 shows Caesar sent some Roman colonists to Emporiae (Ampurias) after Munda, but that the town was not organized formally as a colony at this stage.

128 Pliny *HN* III.12; *FIRA* 21, esp. ch. 104. Note also the prominent role of Caesar's ancestress Venus. The inscription dates from the Flavian period and some changes seem to have been made in the original charter. See Hardy 1912 (B 169) for discussion and translation. A veteran *IIvir*, *CIL* II 1404 (centurion of Legio XXX) may be one of the first magistrates.

The fact that freedmen are permitted to hold office, as they were in most or all of Caesar's other colonies, but not, as far as we know, in Roman towns founded earlier or later, is noteworthy;[129] but there is nothing else at all *popularis* in the constitution – the council is firmly in charge, and the assembly has nothing to do but elect the magistrates.

Caesar's grandest project was the revival of Corinth and Carthage with the titles Laus Iulia and Concordia Iulia, certainly mainly for freedmen and other civilians. They had not got far at his death.[130] And indeed other places were still waiting at this time for their colonists, many of whom were gathered in Rome in anticipation of the journey. A number of colonies were founded abroad in the next few years by all the triumvirs, it is usually supposed often or always in accordance with Caesar's plans.[131] It is not clear how Suetonius reached his figure of 80,000 (perhaps from the city of Rome alone) for those who left Italy to settle abroad.[132]

Of course there was some precedent for Caesar's colonizing activities. A few towns in Spain and elsewhere had been founded for veterans or immigrants even in the second century, and other ex-soldiers had settled down in small groups in the provinces where they had served, or where they had in some cases perhaps even been born of settler families. Informal organizations, *conventus*, of Romans sometimes seem even to have dominated the native towns where they congregated. And Caius Gracchus had proposed colonies overseas for the urban plebs, and Saturninus for veterans. It has been said that Caesar was 'encouraging and organizing on a large scale a natural movement which until his time had been held back by artificial political restraints based on prejudice'. But he dammed it more firmly too, by enacting that no Italian between twenty and forty years of age should spend more than three years abroad unless on military service.[133]

Probably one motive for Caesar's foreign colonization was simply the near-exhaustion of the supply of *ager publicus* in Italy, and a desire to spare the peninsula, and the upper class there that he was courting, too much of the confiscation that had made Sulla so hated. (Senators' estates were probably supposed to be in Italy, though others might own land

[129] *FIRA* 21.CV. Freedmen in office at Curubis, *CIL* I² 788, Carthage and Clupea *CIL* x 6104; freedmen settled in Corinth, Strab. VIII. 381, cf. Crinagoras *Anthol. Graec.* IX.284.

[130] Carthage, Strab. XVII.833, included some veterans, cf. Plut. *Caes.* 57. App. *Lib.* 136 is contradictory, but it seems likely that the colony was planned by Caesar and started soon after his death, though there were later reorganizations and reinforcements. Corinth, veterans and freedmen, Strab. VIII.381, Plut. *Caes.* 57. Coins show it was founded by 44. Dio XLIII.50 says Caesar was especially proud of these two.

[131] Were Lugdunum (Lyons) and Raurica, near Basle, which were founded by Munatius Plancus in 43, planned by Caesar as many think? Grant 1946 (C 204) expands the number of colonies attested by dubious appeal to the coins.

[132] Suet. *Iul.* 42.1.

[133] Levick 1967 (D 275) 4; Suet. *Iul.* 42.1, doubted by Yavetz, 1983 (C 290) 115.

abroad.)[134] It has often been thought, however, that Caesar wanted to Romanize the provinces. But there were also colonies to the Greek East, which was not Romanizable – apart from Corinth, both Lampsacus and Sinope are certainties,[135] others were probably at least projected; in fact the colonies there became gradually Hellenized. In general, colonization was at the expense of the natives, most of whom would lose their land, and sink to mere *incolae*, inhabitants without political rights, of the town where they had been citizens; they would hardly be grateful for the long-term opportunity to become Romanized. In some cases the old colonial function of providing a garrison may have been kept in mind – the charter of Urso gives regulations for mobilization[136] – but an attempt to argue that the eastern foundations were meant as bases for the Parthian War is not convincing.[137] Certainly the new colonies will have been centres of loyalty to Caesar in the provinces; though the formal patron at Urso is to be the actual *deductor*, the inhabitants would be kept aware of what they owed to Caesar himself, whose name was evoked in the very title of the town. But often the actual site must have depended simply on whether there was land available, either as existing *ager publicus*, or ready for confiscation from the disloyal. Caesar promised to cancel the projected colony at Buthrotum in Epirus because Atticus and Cicero made representations on behalf of the Buthrotans, who were simply being punished for not paying their taxes.[138] Occasionally a depopulated area may have been consciously reinforced; and it can hardly be doubted that the revival of Carthage and Corinth by colonists among whom freedmen were prominent would stimulate trade, especially as Caesar intended to cut a canal through the Isthmus of Corinth (though what is mentioned in that context are strategic motives).[139] Parts of the western Mediterranean coast, notably Numidia, entered the Roman monetary system for the first time in these years, but apparently by the accident of heavy coinage in these areas for the payment of armies.[140]

In any event, can a man as intelligent as Caesar have been blind to the far-reaching implications of his actions, whatever his actual motives were in extending privileges among the natives and settling citizens in new colonies, and whatever the exact scale of his innovations? One wonders; the ancients were strikingly averse to long-term political

[134] Rawson, in Finley 1976 (G 67) 90.

[135] Appian *BCiv*. v.137; Strab. xii.546. Perhaps just settlers, not a real colony? New era begins shortly before Caesar's death. He does not seem to have founded new Greek cities, unlike Pompey.

[136] *FIRA* 21 CIII. [Sall.] *Ep*. ii.5.8 says colonies of old and new citizens will increase military resources; for this work see below.

[137] Boegli 1966 (C 176).

[138] Cic. *Att*. xvi.16.

[139] Suet. *Iul*. 44.3, Plut. *Caes*. 58. This is one of the 'final plans' that have been disbelieved, but Plutarch is circumstantial, giving us the name of the man in charge of the project.

[140] Crawford 1985 (B 145) 247–9.

projections. It is particularly frustrating that there is so much dispute over the pamphlet known as Sallust's *Second Letter to Caesar*, ostensibly a letter of advice from the future historian written in 50. Many scholars regard it as a later rhetorical exercise by an unknown author. If, even so, one could be sure that it was based on ideas of the time it would be important, for it urges Caesar to rehabilitate the decadent citizen body by a programme of generous enfranchisements.[141] Such enfranchisements will ease recruiting; new and old citizens are to be settled together in colonies.[142] If such ideas were in the air, it is unlikely that Caesar was acting entirely *ad hoc*. He must also have seen that every citizen living in the provinces made the power of the assemblies at Rome more illogical. But one could still argue that he handed out privileges for badly needed cash, as Dio implies for Spain, and to reward those loyal to himself as generously as he felt Caesar should. If we know anything of his character it is that he carried to extreme lengths the Roman aristocrat's sense of obligation to those who helped him, whoever they might be. Numerous anecdotes illustrate this trait in him.[143] Conversely, disloyalty in recipients of his *beneficia* was unpardonable; he is said to have extended clemency to opponents a second time only if his friends interceded for them, and never to have forgiven mutiny in his troops.[144] Yet it is not clear that he was deeply indebted to Sicily, for example; though there too a practical motive – to encourage those so largely responsible for provisioning Rome – can be found. A firm conclusion is unattainable.

2. *Italy*

Meyer thought Caesar had little *clientela* in Italy; but he is often believed to have possessed, as the heir of Marius and the *populares*, great support especially in Etruria and Samnium, and to have been anxious to see that the whole of Italy was reconciled to Rome and its representatives brought into public life at the capital. The truth, however, seems to be less clear-cut. There was, we saw, little resistance to Caesar in Italy in 49, especially once he had reassured the towns about his intentions as to life and property, and he was able to tell the Massiliots that they should follow the *auctoritas* of all Italy in admitting him.[145] If we may trust Cicero, however, five years later there was rejoicing in the towns at his assassination.[146] What had happened in the interval?

No doubt Caesar had inherited influence in some parts of Italy; and his

[141] [Sall.] *Ep.* II.5.7.

[142] [Sall.] *Ep.* II.5.8. Some think this refers only to the grant to the Transpadanes, but old and new citizens are to go together to colonies, and why should Transpadanes emigrate?

[143] See esp. Suet. *Iul.* 71–2.

[144] Suet. *Iul.* 67.

[145] Caes. *BCiv* I.35, cf. III.12.2, Apollonia will not act 'against the decision of all Italy and the Roman people'; also II.32.2.

[146] Cic. *Att.* XIV.6.2.

defence of a proscribed Samnite in his youth may be significant. We have seen that from Gaul he sent money to adorn Italian towns, and in 49 he complained to men from Corfinium and the neighbouring *municipia* who surrendered to him that by joining his enemies they had forgotten his *beneficia*.[147] But it is a mistake to see Etruria as solid for him (or Picenum for Pompey); Sulla will have left his partisans in control of the towns, and there were senators of Etruscan background in his Senate; later the aristocratic A. Caecina fought for Pompey, though among the proscribed whom Caesar rehabilitated there may have been a number of Etruscans.[148] Unfortunately we do not know where in Italy Caesar's estates lay (as opposed to three holiday villas).[149] His tribe was the Fabia, however, and one may imagine split loyalties among the people of Alba Fucens, which belonged to it too, but was held for a while by Domitius Ahenobarbus (another member of the tribe).[150] Thereafter, if not before, Caesar was the regular patron of Alba as doubtless of many other towns; we know of Vibo in the south and Bovianum in Samnium. From others we have dedicatory inscriptions.[151] It is likely that he tried to extend his Italian *clientela* as much as possible; he could intervene to get a partisan into a local council.[152] It is clear from their names that many of Caesar's officers, and doubtless other ranks too, came from an Italian background; but it is not obvious that, if we knew as much about Pompey's army as we do about Caesar's, we should find the picture very different; recruits were normally countrymen, and parts of old Italy had strong military traditions. None the less, the undoubted devotion of Caesar's men will have affected their friends at home; and centurions at least were often, or might become, men of some local position and influence.

Most of the legionaries themselves did not go home, but some received land in Italy from 47 on, perhaps in accordance with a Lex Iulia.[153] But this of course cut both ways where Caesar's popularity was concerned. Dio makes Caesar tell the mutinous troops in 47 that he would settle them individually on his own estates and land purchased, not confiscated (there was, we recall, little *ager publicus* left in Italy).[154] He

147 Caes. *BCiv.* I.23. 148 Rawson 1978 (C 246).

149 Wiseman 1971 (A 130) 191, 194, 196. 150 *Ibid.* 43.

151 Alba, *ILLRP* 1255, De Visscher 1964 (C 189); Vibo (46 B.C.) and Bovianum Undecimanorum (*ILLRP* 406; the name suggests veterans here), see Bitto 1970 (C 175). *ILLRP* 407, dedication to Caesar from Brundisium. Two inscriptions mention statues set up to Caesar after his death by a Lex Rufrena (*ILLRP* 409, with comm.) usually thought to date from 42, but possibly from early 44, when Dio says Caesar was voted the right to have statues 'in the cities'. A Rufrenus with Lepidus in 43, Cic. *Fam.* X.21.4.

152 *ILLRP* 630: *decurioni [be]neficio dei Caesaris.*

153 The late *Liber coloniarum* names various places where veterans were settled *lege Iulia*, apparently meaning Caesar's, but there is the law of 59 to reckon with.

154 Dio XLII 54.1; cf. App. *BCiv.* II.94; Suet. *Iul.* 38.1; Dio XLIII.47.4 (Caesar auctions *ager publicus*, even consecrated lands, to raise money in 45).

does seem to have tried to avoid the dislocation and hostility caused by Sulla's settlements, drafting the veterans mostly in small groups, perhaps sometimes a cohort at a time, to different places, and leaving the existing municipal framework intact, where Sulla had sometimes at least given the old inhabitants status inferior to that of his colonists. The numbers settled now were perhaps not vast; a maximum of 15,000 has been suggested.[155] But Caesar could not completely avoid offence. Appian makes Brutus say later that there had been confiscations without compensation even from innocent persons;[156] Cicero thought he might lose his property at Tusculum,[157] and while the lands of Arretium and Volaterrae in Etruria had been confiscated by Sulla but never divided, and so were legally *ager publicus* available for distribution, in practice the old inhabitants had continued to occupy them and now complained at being turned out: a friend of Cicero's from Volaterrae, C. Curtius, actually one of Caesar's new senators, was in danger of thus losing his property.[158] Some erosion of Caesar's Etruscan support in this way is likely. Even if a town was spared settlement nearby, it might draw rents from threatened land elsewhere, as Atella did from Cisalpine Gaul; Cicero also tried to intervene on Atella's behalf with one of the senatorial *deductores*, though he dared not do such things often.[159]

Much of the settlement however appears to have been in Campania, where Antony and Octavian in 43 could call on so many Caesarian veterans: notably at Casilinum (for the Eighth legion) and Calatia (for the Seventh); probably also in Samnium, and possibly Picenum.[160] Cicero notes that surveyers were active quite near Rome, at Veii and Capena. We are told that Caesar planned to drain the Pomptine Marshes and the Fucine Lake, which would have given more land for distribution.[161] The allotments were made inalienable for twenty years (a provision repealed after Caesar's death to please the colonists).[162] There is no evidence that civilians were given land in Italy.

There may have been some connexion between the drafting of veterans to existing towns and the probable reorganization of local government in Italy. The literary sources are not interested in this, and the epigraphic ones are puzzling. However, it seems from a passage of

155 Brunt 1971 (A 16) 319; Keppie 1983 (A 56) 50. Dio XLII.54.1, the veterans were scattered so as not to terrorize their neighbours or organize rebellion.

156 App. *BCiv.* III.139–41. Dio XLII.51.2 shows some land of Pompeians was confiscated, see also LIII.47.4, App. *BCiv.* II.140.

157 Cic. *Fam.* IX.17.

158 Cic. *Fam.* XIII.4.5.

159 Cic. *Fam.* XIII.7 – the official had already exempted lands nearby owned by the town of Rhegium Lepidum; cf. *ibid.* 8.

160 Keppie 1983 (A 56) 49ff; he holds the activity near Capua was on Calatian territory, as Capuan territory was exhausted, 57. Cales, Teanum, Minturnae possible sites, 53, 142. Cic. *Fam.* IX.17.

161 Suet. *Iul.* 44.3. The main object of the new road over the Apennines to the Adriatic is not wholly clear, *ibid.*

162 App. *BCiv.* III.7, by Cassius.

Cicero which mentions asking Balbus about its provisions that there was in preparation in 45 a general law regulating, *inter alia* no doubt, eligibility for local office (active *praecones*, heralds or auctioneers, are barred, retired ones not). And Cicero's son and nephew had held office in Arpinum in 46 apparently to reorganize the town.[163] The law may also have extended local self-government to small places hitherto without it (subject for jurisdiction to a *praefectus* sent from Rome or dependent on a bigger neighbour). And parts of Italy organized as *pagi* or cantons were gradually becoming urbanized in the second and first centuries, especially after the Social War: the agrarian law of 59 may have involved Caesar in the process. What is usually known as the Lex Mamilia Roscia Peducaea Alliena Fabia, perhaps a follow-up passed by five tribunes friendly to the 'triumvirs' in 55 B.C., if not to be identified with the Lex Iulia agraria of 59 itself, is a document from which we have extracts, concerned with founding, and delimiting the territories of, urban communities of all kinds.[164] The idea that until Caesar's time local magistrates had no powers of jurisdiction is untenable, but their rights may have needed regulation elsewhere as well as in newly enfranchised Cisalpine Gaul, where there was also the governor's power to be considered (and where what was perhaps a Lex Rubria, Caesarian or a little later in date, in fact excluded the latter by reserving certain actions for the praetor in Rome).[165] We also have a curious inscription from Heraclea, once a Greek city, which may represent sections from recent legislation which the town thought relevant to itself, even though as they stand some are obviously applicable only to Rome (e.g. provisions for cleaning the streets there, and for the corn-distributions).[166] Other sections, however, regulate local registration for the census (usually thought not to be completely new in the first century B.C.) and eligibility to local office – proof of military service is required; grave-diggers, actors, pimps and of course *praecones* are excluded, but apparently not freedmen; on the other hand those who have received a reward for killing a proscribed man are barred, and this might suggest that the document is pre-Caesarian, since not many such men will have been still

163 Cic. *Fam.* VI.18.1, XIII.11.3, *constituendi municipi causa*. *ILS* 5406 records an imperial magistrate at Patavium holding office in accordance with a Lex Iulia, but this might be due to Augustus, or only local in application.

164 *FIRA* 12. Hinrichs 1969 (C 213), dates it to 49, supposing the proposers were praetors that year, but we then have more than the proper number attested, and legislation by a plurality of tribunes is attested, of praetors not.

165 Frederiksen 1965 (B 153); Bruna 1972 (B 138) Laffi 1986 (B 186A), on the Lex Rubria (the Veleia fragment, *FIRA* 19 is probably rightly identified with this law, which it mentions, perhaps also the smaller Ateste fragment, *FIRA* 20). The governor is not mentioned, but Gallia Cisalpina is – the province was abolished in 42.

166 *FIRA* 13. The dating to the period of Caesar's dictatorship is very far from certain, Brunt 1971 (A 16) 519–23.

alive in the late forties.[167] It is hard then to be sure what Caesar did in this field; but he may have thrown himself into work which was already under way and indeed needed doing. Dio says that he prided himself on rebuilding or actually founding many cities in Italy as well as beyond it.[168] The effect of reorganization and settlement must have been to promote uniformity and mix the population, and to create gratitude as well as grievances.

There was other legislation that affected Italy; we are told that one-third of shepherds employed were to be free men, a precaution against the endemic slave unrest on the drove-roads and in the far south.[169] It may also have been intended to cut rural unemployment. We have evidence of widespread indebtedness in Italy (especially in 63); in addition to Caesar's general provisions about debt there were some applying specifically outside Rome, where for example a lower limit was fixed on the year's rent remitted (rents were higher in Rome).[170] And there seems to have been a measure about debt and the ownership of property in Italy, perhaps laying down that senators must invest a proportion of their wealth in Italian land.[171]

It was natural that many of Caesar's new senators (he put the number up to 900) should have come from various parts of Italy; men who had served him, especially in the army, would often have done so. There is no proof that he put many centurions into the Senate, but one is attested,[172] and a number of his officers of equestrian rank were clearly promoted. It has been suggested that members of families on the rebel side in the Social War or noted for resistance to Sulla were also brought in. Asinius Pollio, perhaps the son of a Marsian, as Poppaedius Silo was of a Samnite, leader, and Ventidius from Picenum, who had figured in Pompeius Strabo's triumph in 89, may have owed their seats to Caesar. And Cicero shows that Curtius, the new senator from Etruscan Volaterrae already referred to, had an impeccably anti-Sullan background. But it cannot be proved that Caesar was consciously trying to reconcile and unite Italy by these actions; while we know that some parts of the peninsula, notably the area of the Paeligni, had to wait for Augustus to get their first senator.

We have seen that the veteran settlements may have aroused discontent in some parts of Italy; so no doubt did the exactions on towns made

[167] Brunt 1971 (A 16) 519; Frederiksen 1965 (B 153) 183. It was previously thought to be a Roman *lex satura* (a law combining unrelated provisions) passed by Caesar or perhaps Antony soon after Caesar's death. The fifth clause, about someone authorized to give land to a *municipium fundanum*, whatever that may be (possibly the *municipium* of Fundi) is particularly puzzling, but suggests recent activity. [168] Dio XLIII.50.3.

[169] Suet. *Iul.* 42.1. Perhaps never enforced; Varro's *Rust.* II.10, set in 67 B.C. but written after Caesar's death, assumes shepherds will all be slaves. [170] Suet. *Iul.* 38.2. [171] Tac. *Ann.* VI.16.

[172] Fuficius Fango, Dio XLVIII.22.3, Cic. *Att.* XIV.10.2, and possibly Decidius Saxa from Spain, see n. 121.

to finance the African campaign, and the new permanent taxes.[173] Towards the end of Caesar's life opposition may also have developed on political grounds. The upper classes in the towns may, as Cicero complained, have been most concerned for their own interests, and they may have cared little for the factional squabbles at Rome. But they would not approve of monarchy, especially those in ancient cities which had themselves gone through a development that replaced kings by oligarchies. The Etruscan aristocracy, for example, was quite as proud as the Roman one, and it is worth observing that in his last years Caesar had trouble with *haruspices*, who probably often represented the outlook of this aristocracy. The, or a, *summus haruspex* tried to delay Caesar's departure to Africa in 47, and the famous Spurinna, who bears a noble Etruscan name, prophesied disaster at the time of Caesar's most arrogant actions in early 44.[174] In addition, the sort of Greek education at least as common in much of Italy as in Rome encouraged abhorrence of 'tyranny' and admiration for tyrannicide.

3. Rome

Caesar had great plans for the city of Rome. (In view of these, stories circulating before his death that he wanted to move the capital to Alexandria or Ilium are incredible.)[175] Rome had changed since, in the earlier second century, visiting Macedonians had laughed at its appearance. But it was probably still unimpressive to a Greek eye; marble for instance was not yet much used. Caesar had made preparations as early as 54 for improvements financed from Gallic booty – the Saepta Iulia, a great marble enclosure for voting purposes on the Campus Martius, and the Forum Iulium, to the north of the old Forum, which like the Basilica Iulia facing the original Forum was to provide more space for the lawcourts.[176] These buildings were not finished in Caesar's lifetime,[177] but in 46, on the day after his last triumph, he was able to dedicate the Forum Iulium and the all-marble temple of the ancestress of his family, Venus Genetrix, which dominated it;[178] a statue of himself on horseback stood

[173] Dio XLII.50.2.

[174] Rawson 1978 (C 246).

[175] Suet. *Iul.* 79.3 (Alexandria Troas is hardly the Alexandria meant).

[176] Cic. *Att.* IV.16.3. For the Forum, Coarelli 1985 (B 277).

[177] The Saeptum by Lepidus and Agrippa, Dio LIII.23, App. *BCiv.* II.102, the Forum and Basilica by Augustus, or perhaps rather Octavian, Aug. *RG* 20.3.

[178] Marble, Ovid *Ars Am.* I.81; App. *BCiv.* II.281 says the temple was vowed at Pharsalus, but Weinstock 1971 (H 134) 81 doubts if at this stage Caesar wanted to commemorate victory in civil war and thinks it planned earlier. Some have supposed the Forum with its temple influenced by the sanctuaries of divinized Hellenistic Kings, or even the Kaisareia of Alexandria and Antioch, which is chronologically implausible, Sjöqvist 1954 (B 317).

in front of the building,[179] which contained valuable works of art,[180] so that like many temples it also functioned as a museum. Caesar was also authorized by the Senate to erect a new senate-house, the Curia Iulia, to replace the old one rebuilt by Faustus Sulla (after the funeral of Clodius) but recently again burnt down.[181] The new senate-house was to be at right angles to Caesar's new Forum, while on the site of the old one a temple to Felicitas was planned to rise. Temples to Concordia and to Clementia Caesaris, were also voted. The first two, like the last, commemorated qualities associated with Caesar. As was usual, the builder's name would be prominent on all his buildings; in fact in 46 the Senate decreed that Caesar's name should replace that of Catulus on the Capitoline temple.[182] Thus Caesar imposed his presence on the very heart of Rome, and in every public act of his life the Roman citizen was to be reminded of him.

There was also a project for a substantial enlargement of the city, which as Cicero was told involved diverting the Tiber in order to add part of what is now Trastevere to the Campus Martius; the latter would be built over, and the newly added land take over its functions as an open space. A Greek architect recently arrived in Rome was in charge of the work.[183] Suetonius reports that Caesar proposed to build the biggest temple in the world to Mars on the Campus Martius, and a great theatre at the foot of the Capitol to rival Pompey's.[184] There was a plan to found a public library, such as most Greek cities had; the great scholar Varro accepted the task of collecting as many books in Greek and Latin as possible.[185] As we saw, doctors and teachers of all the liberal arts were encouraged to come to Rome, to make it an educational centre.[186] By his will Caesar left his house and gardens across the Tiber, with all their works of art, to be a public park; such benefactions were on the Greek model.[187] It may be that, even if he was less impressed by the ramshackle

[179] The statue of Caesar's horse with cleft hooves placed here, according to Suet. *Iul.* 61, may not be the equestrian statue which according to Statius *Silv.* I.1.84ff was by Lysippus, originally representing Alexander. The *statua loricata* (in a cuirass) Caesar allowed to be placed in the Forum, Pliny *HN* XXXIV.18, may be different again; within the temple were statues of Caesar and Cleopatra, Dio LI.22.3, App. *BCiv.* II.102.

[180] Two paintings by Timomachus of Byzantium, of Medea and Ajax, Pliny *HN* VII.126, XXXVI.26 and 136, bought by Caesar for eighty talents; six collections of gems, *ibid.* XXXVII.11 (and a corselet adorned with British pearls, IX.116).

[181] Dio XLIV.5, XLV.19, XLVII.19.

[182] Dio XLIII.14, and see XXXVII.44 – not carried out.

[183] Cic. *Att.* XIII.33a (not an Athenian, Shackleton Bailey *ad loc.*, but an enfranchised Greek, some see *gentilis tuus* as referring to the proposing tribune not the architect, *MRR* II.307); 20.1, 35.1. A law *de urbe augenda* seems to have been mooted; it is not clear if it was passed. Having extended the empire, Caesar had the right to extend the *pomoerium*.

[184] Suet. *Iul.* 44.1, and see Dio XLIII.49.2. 'Below the Tarpeian rock' and thus on the edge of the Forum, ruthlessly destroying ancient landmarks.

[185] Suet. *Iul.* 44.2.

[186] Suet. *Iul.* 42.1.

[187] Suet. *Iul.* 83.2. Strab. V.235 thinks it is Roman to concern oneself with roads, sewers and aqueducts.

Ptolemaic monarchy than some scholars have believed, he was dazzled by Alexandria, still the greatest city of the Mediterranean world, and determined to make Rome its equal – to his own greater glory as well as that of his people.[188]

Two remarks of Caesar suggest the cultural competitiveness with the Greeks common in his time: his regret that Terence lacked the *vis*, energy, to make him equal to his model Menander, and his splendid compliment to Cicero, that he had extended the boundaries of the Roman genius.[189] Caesar's dictatorship is probably remarkable for an attempt to harness both Greek and Roman intellectuals to the service of the state. Cicero told friends hoping for pardon that Caesar was favouring talent.[190] The dictator was associated with several lawyers, notably Ofilius and Trebatius, but to some extent also the doyen of the profession, Ser. Sulpicius; his plan for the simplification and codification of the laws will have depended on their aid.[191] He appears to have used an Alexandrian astronomer, Sosigenes, in his reform of the Roman calendar; Sosigenes wrote several treatises in connexion with this task, and a Greek work *On the Stars* was put out under Caesar's own name; this was a calendar on the model of a so-called *parapegma*, tying the rising and setting of stars and constellations to the new civil calendar, with the weather to be expected at each event, and was meant as a practical handbook.[192] There is evidence, admittedly in a late and bad source, that Caesar also charged four Alexandrian 'philosophers' with an empire-wide survey.[193] Caesar is not however recorded as a patron either of poets or of philosophers proper; his brilliant intelligence, which so many of the sources recognize, seems to have been drawn to practical applications; even the grammatical work he wrote in the fifties was meant to regulate and clarify the means of expression.[194] In this he was perhaps ultimately more Roman than Greek; but his respect for Greek skills and willingness to favour and even enfranchise Greeks suggest that one should not see him solely in Roman terms.

Rome was not only to be a cultural and intellectual centre, but a prosperous and well-run city (though whether the regulations stuck up at Heraclea reflect new provisions about the aedile's duty to keep the streets clean is, as we saw, uncertain). The settlement of so many members of the urban populace abroad, with the great public works

188 [Caes.] *BAlex.* 3 admires the skill of the Alexandrian populace.

189 According to Pliny *HN* VII.117.

190 Cic. *Fam.* IV.8.2. *favet ingeniis* (as well as birth and position); and see 6.5 and 6.

191 Suet. *Iul.* 44.2.

192 *Ibid.* 40.1–2; Pliny *HN* XVIII.211, cf. II.39. Plut. *Caes.* 59.2 speaks of a learned committee, Macrob. *Sat.* I.14. 2–3 a scribe, M. Flavius. A sample passage of the *de astris*, *HN* XVIII.237.

193 Iulius Honoratus, *Cosmographia Iulii Caesaris*, *GLM* 21. This is contradictory about dating, and the work may have begun in the 50s.

194 Frags. in *GRF*.

under way or envisaged, may have been meant partly to reduce unemployment, and so doubtless facilitated the cut made in 46 in the numbers receiving free grain, from 320,000 to 150,000; there was an attempt to eliminate connected abuses such as the practice of freeing slaves, retaining their services, but letting the state feed them.[195] A list of those eligible was made with the aid of landlords of *insulae*, and praetors were to fill by lot places falling vacant, to prevent, says Suetonius, assemblies being convened for this purpose, presumably with the risk of disorder.[196] Caesar was also concerned with the actual supply of corn, setting up in 44 two *aediles Ceriales* to be responsible for it, a sound move;[197] and the plans for improved harbour facilities at Ostia, and for a canal from the Tiber to Tarracina,[198] would have eased the import of corn as well as other goods. Caesar also – and this might be seen as markedly anti-*popularis* – abolished all the *collegia* apart from certain ancient ones (Jewish synagogues were also exempted); this was possibly done by a Lex Iulia, which may have laid down the rules allowing the Senate to license 'useful' new associations which obtained under the empire.[199] This measure was designed to prevent disturbances; there was probably also a law *de vi*, against public violence, with the severe penalty of exile, *aquae et ignis interdictio*.[200] If the inadequate police force of Rome was not increased, this was perhaps because troops were now often used in the city to restore order.

Displays of extravagance by the rich were discouraged; these often had a political character, and Caesar may have wished to prevent competition with his own acts of largesse. But sumptuary laws, always ineffective, had a long history at Rome, where social divisions were seen as having moral causes, and the oligarchy was suspicious of individual prominence. Caesar seems to have tried enforcement by means of guards stationed in the market to stop illegal foods being offered for sale, while soldiers or lictors might enter a house and practically snatch the dishes

[195] This abuse is noted in the 50s, Dio XXXIX.24, and still continued in Augustus' time, Dion. Hal. IV.24.5. Dio XLIII.20.4, Caesar threw off the fraudulent.

[196] Suet. *Iul.* 41.3. This *recensus* has sometimes been mistaken for a full census; Nicolet, 1980 (A 82) 195ff suggests that the geographical arrangement (*vicatim*) and use of owners of apartment blocks was a new method of organization, replacing the *collegia* used by Clodius for this purpose. A clause of the *Tab. Herc.* deals with an unidentified class of people who must register with the authorities but do not get corn; as we saw this may not be a Caesarian provision. [Sall.] *Ep.* 1.7.2, 8.6 thinks the plebs corrupted by *largitiones* and free corn, which should go instead to veterans and colonists in the towns.

[197] Dio XLIII.51.3.

[198] Plut. *Caes.* 58.10, Suet. *Claud.* 20.1. Meiggs 1973 (G 156) 53. The coast between Puteoli, where ships from Africa and Sicily would put in, and Ostia at the mouth of the Tiber, was inhospitable. Suetonius might imply Caesar himself gave up the plan as too difficult.

[199] Suet. *Iul.* 42.3; Joseph. *AJ* XIV.215–16. The privileges of the Jews (including exemption from military service, which rules about the Sabbath made difficult) were also proclaimed in the provinces.

[200] Cic. *Phil.* 1.23.8; Lintott 1968 (A 62) 107.

from the table.[201] Though Cicero claims at one point that vegetables, which were not penalized, have become fashionable, the law was rapidly ignored.[202] Women were also forbidden to use litters in Rome, or to wear purple or pearls except on certain days and under certain circumstances; one source suggests the restrictions were primarily aimed against the unmarried and childless, and both the recent losses suffered by the upper class in the civil war and its perpetual tendency not to reproduce itself may be borne in mind. (Dio mentions rewards for large families, perhaps of the poorer classes, but we know no more about this.)[203] There were inevitably new taxes, though the principle that Roman citizens were exempt from direct taxation was not breached. Custom dues at Italian ports may have acted as a tax on luxuries; an impost on columns presumably restrained ostentatious building, and extravagant funerary monuments were penalized.[204] The stepping-up of punishments for various crimes was, says Suetonius, aimed chiefly at the wealthy, who had often been able to retire to a comfortable exile, realizing their property to take with them. Parricides now lost all their property on conviction, and other criminals half.[205] Equity and the treasury benefited. Details of a treason law are disputed, but the penalty involved *interdictio aquae et ignis*.[206]

There was nothing revolutionary about most of these measures; when Cicero in 46 spoke in the Senate in gratitude for the recall of M. Marcellus and in an upsurge of hope for the future it was to ask Caesar to restore the *res publica* by reconstituting the courts, encouraging the birth-rate and repressing vice.[207] He also said credit must be re-established. But he did not approve of Caesar's measures concerning debt, having such a fixation on the sanctity of private property that he even thought direct taxation immoral.[208]

When Caesar reached Rome in 49 he found a special crisis, not solved by the reduced interest rates announced by the tribunes. In the expectation of war and his possible abolition of debt creditors were calling loans in and debtors refusing to pay. Both sides were hoarding coin; land prices had collapsed. Caesar ordered that real and perhaps other property should be valued by assessors at pre-war prices and accepted by the creditors since prices would recover; he revived an old law against hoarding over 60,000 sesterces, so debts could be paid and money lent again. It was against these moderate measures that Caelius agitated for the total cancellation of debts and a year's suspension of rent.

201 Suet. *Iul.* 43.2. Gell. *NA* II.24 does not mention a law or laws of Caesar's own; he was perhaps enforcing existing measures such as the Lex Antia (p. 331).

202 Cic. *Fam.* VII.26; *Att.* XIII.7.1 (June 45).

203 Dio XLIII.25.2.

204 Suet. *Iul.* 43.1; Cic. *Att.* XII.35, 36.1.

205 Suet. *Iul.* 42.3.

206 Cic. *Att.* XII.35.

207 Cic. *Marcell.* 23.

208 Cic. *Off.* II.78ff.

Probably after Caelius' death some concessions to the poor were made; interest accruing since the start of the war was cancelled, likewise a year's rent (up to 2,000 sesterces in Rome). This was still not enough for some. But all Caesar finally did was probably to limit interest rates, and perhaps allow voluntary bankruptcy for the first time, on tolerable terms, so as to encourage payment of debts. These measures did not wholly solve the problem of debt endemic in all classes, and satisfied neither side, but to us they seem remarkably statesmanlike.[209]

However, there is no evidence that either the debt laws, or limitations on the rights of the *publicani*, wholly alienated the rich; Caesar had wealthy supporters throughout, like C. Oppius, probably from a banking family, and C. Matius, who told Cicero he had lost by Caesar's legislation, but who was not shaken in his devotion.[210] Nor was there any real attack on the privileges of the *equites* in the lawcourts; indeed by new legislation the courts were divided between senators and *equites* only, though it is likely that instead of dispossessing the so-called *tribuni aerarii*, who seem to have had the equestrian census, the term *equites* was redefined, in this context at least, to include them. That will have pleased this rather wider class; but it is to be noted that the Senate, though now larger in numbers and broader in composition than before, disposed of half the places. Again, hardly the act of a *popularis*.[211]

But, at bottom, no reform could seem tolerable to the Roman upper class if it was enacted autocratically. When someone mentioned that the constellation Lyra would rise the following day Cicero retorted 'Yes – by edict.' Sallust, writing a few years later out of bitter experience, said that to rule by force, even if it means you can and do reform abuses, is oppressive.[212] We must come at last to the political and constitutional issue.

4. Caesar the dictator

At the start of the war, as we saw, Caesar stressed constitutional propriety, and tried to act on some sort of precedent. Irregularities gradually crept in. Far the fullest account of the privileges and honours that Caesar accepted is Dio's, but it is often thought unreliable, and that it confuses those paid to Caesar and Augustus. But there is no reason not to trust Dio in essentials; not only is the tradition in the other late sources closely related, but where Cicero, or the contemporary coins, can be used as a check, they generally confirm his accuracy, though suggesting a few understandable confusions. Most of the facts could have been verified (if anyone had wanted to do so) from the decrees of the Senate. Dio's interpretation is more debatable; he, and other sources, hold that the

209 Frederiksen 1966 (G 78). 210 Cic. *Fam.* XI.28.2. 211 Suet. *Iul.* 41.2. 212 Sall. *Iug.* 3.2.

senators voted honours without Caesar's impulsion, from flattery, or sometimes to create hostility to him: Caesar could not refuse them all. It is often doubted whether Caesar was so little in control of events; but Dio assures us that he has omitted many honours that Caesar refused, so not everything done in the Senate can have been directly inspired by him.[213]

The real rot set in after Pharsalus, when Caesar was nominated dictator for a year (six months was the traditional limit, though Sulla had not kept to it) and Antony came home as *magister equitum* to take over from the consul; his anomalous position was symbolized by the fact that in Rome he wore the civilian toga – with a sword. Dio says that the Senate also granted Caesar full power to deal with the Pompeians as he wished, and to make peace and war without reference to Senate or people; to take five consulships in succession, hold various privileges of the tribunes and appoint praetorian governors to provinces directly, while the elections, except those for plebeian magistracies, were postponed till his return.[214] As he was in touch by letter from the East until besieged in Alexandria, it is likely that most of this programme met with his approval.[215]

On returning from Asia in 47 he held the postponed elections, and those for 46, and began to increase the number of magistracies, and to replenish the Senate. Dio sees this as reward for adherents, especially since he had borrowed money from them (and made them pay the full price for confiscated property); but there may have been practical reasons as well, though in fact 900 was too large a Senate to be effective, as Augustus found. (An extra post may have been added to each of the great priestly colleges because Caesar himself now belonged to all of them.)[216]

In 46 Caesar was at first consul only, as his second dictatorship had expired in the autumn. After his African victory the Senate voted him annual dictatorships for ten years, the unheard-of position of *curator morum* for three, the right to sit between the consuls in the Senate, preside at all games, and nominate the only candidates for some magistracies; also forty days' *supplicatio*, seventy-two lictors (to mark his three dictatorships) and white horses for his triumphs (supposedly last used by Camillus in the fourth century). A statue of him standing on the globe, with the inscription 'to the unconquered god' was erected, but he subsequently had this erased.[217]

[213] Dio XLII.19.3–4; see XLIV.3.3, 7.2 for interpretation.

[214] Dio XLIV. and see 27.2, 20.3.

[215] Cic. *Att.* XI.6.7, 7.2 mentions letters from Alexandria to Antony; *Phil.* II.62, that Caesar did not authorize Antony's appointment, is implausible invective.

[216] Dio XLII.51.

[217] Dio XLIII.14; Cic. *Fam.* XV.5 and other sources refer to Caesar as *curator morum*, and there is no reason to see this as ironic and to deny Dio's notice.

Dio says that Caesar saw that there was fear and suspicion of him, and so tried to be conciliatory; and that though most of his reforms were put through the Senate, he became unpopular for restoring, even to that body, exiles who had been justly condemned, and for establishing Cleopatra in his suburban property across the Tiber (she had perhaps come in theory to negotiate a treaty with Rome, which she got).[218] None the less, the latter part of 46, extended by the two extra long intercalary months that righted the calendar, was to Cicero a period not without hope. Caesar was amicable, though keeping a careful eye on the political jokes the orator made.[219] And Cicero explained to friends still abroad that, though Caesar was slower to pardon those who had fought in Africa as well as for Pompey, he was becoming more lenient every day, and the lack of a *res publica* was not so much his fault as that of his followers; they had to be rewarded, which could not be done legally.[220] (Perhaps also many would fall victim to courts or censors if these recovered their independence.) Certainly there *was* no *res publica*: 'decrees of the Senate' were concocted at Balbus' house, says Cicero, and his own name put down as witness without his knowledge.[221] But Cicero was active in furthering the return of prominent Pompeians, so that there might be suitable men to run it if the *res publica* ever was restored; and, covering himself by a request from Brutus, he wrote a eulogy of Cato which, as he told Atticus, could not avoid being a political statement.[222] He attended the Senate on occasion, but did not speak until Caesar gave in to senatorial opinion and pardoned M. Marcellus, the hardline consul of 51; then he made a grateful and complimentary oration, praising Caesar's *clementia* and *sapientia* and suggesting that everyone was now so loyal to him that he could safely restore the *res publica*, and thus gain the highest form of glory.[223]

The revival of the war in Spain cut these hopes short. 'I prefer our old and clement master to a new and cruel one', wrote C. Cassius, not yet a conspirator; Cicero agreed in distrusting young Cn. Pompeius, but feared Caesar would this time be harsh in victory.[224] The death of his beloved daughter drove Cicero from Rome for a while and distracted him from politics. But we know that the city was again under a *magister equitum*, Lepidus, and an unparalleled board of prefects directly appointed by the dictator, since elections had not been held for 45. Much power rested with the *equites* Oppius and Balbus, simply as Caesar's confidential agents,[225] and with members of his household. We learn

[218] Dio XLIII.27.3. Other foreign royalties arrived in Rome to get what they could, e.g. (so Cicero *Att.* XIII.2A.2) Ariarathes, brother of the King of Cappadocia. [219] Cic. *Fam.* IX.15.

[220] Cic. *Fam.* VI.10, VI.13, VII.28, cf. IV.4, XII.18. [221] Cic. *Fam.* IX.15.

[222] Cic. *Att.* XII.4.2. [223] Cic. *Marcell.*, esp. 21ff.

[224] Cic. *Fam.* XV.19; *Fam.* VI.1, 2, 4, 6 – the victory of either side will be disastrous.

[225] Usually paired inseparably in Cicero's letters.

from Cicero that Caesar's reaction to his *Cato* had been an *Anticato*, which while scrupulously polite to himself vilified his hero.[226] In May Cicero attempted a letter of advice to Caesar, modelled on Aristotle's to Alexander; there was a good deal of flattery in it, he said, but even so Balbus and Oppius would not pass it, and Cicero felt he simply could not rewrite it to their desires.[227] True, Caesar wrote that he would not go to Parthia 'without settling the state', but he was thinking of his legislation; on another occasion he wrote that he would stay in Rome to see that this was not neglected as the sumptuary law had been.[228] Brutus was still hopeful when he met Caesar on his way home, and wrote to Cicero that Caesar had joined the *boni*; but Cicero commented sourly on his credulity.[229]

When news of Munda was received in April 45, new honours poured from the Senate: fifty days of thanksgiving, the right to triumphal garb at all games (and a laurel wreath, which pleased Caesar as it hid his bald head); the permanent title of *imperator*; a state-owned palace, the title Liberator, a temple of Liberty; the consulship for ten years (apparently turned down);[230] a statue on the Capitol with those of the Kings and L. Brutus; Caesar alone was to command armies and control public finance (perhaps it was on the strength of this grant that he put his own slaves in charge of the mint and taxes).[231] Cicero's letters bear out that his statue was carried with those of the gods in the procession opening all games in the circus, and that another statue was placed in the temple of Quirinus, an honour approaching, but not equivalent to, full divinization.[232] After his return, in the autumn, Caesar resigned the consulship, itself an irregular act, in favour of two adherents; he seems to have been in a touchy mood, and was much irritated when a tribune, Pontius Aquila, failed to rise at his Spanish triumph.[233]

In December Caesar visited Campania, with a large entourage and a guard of 2,000 soldiers. He dined with Cicero, and 'the visit, or billeting' went off well, though conversation was confined to literature.[234] But in January 44 Cicero wrote to a friend in Greece that he now felt shame at

[226] Suet. *Iul.* 56.5, Cic. *Att.* XII.40.1, XIII.46.2. *Top.* 94 calls Caesar's work impudent (it seems to have accused Cato of drunkenness and meanness). Caesar also got Hirtius to write on the same subject, see e.g. *Att.* XII.41.4. But some of his followers admired Cato: [Caes.] *BAfr.* 23.1, 88.5.

[227] Cic. *Att.* XII.40, 51; XIII.27.1, 31.3.

[228] Cic. *Att.* XIII.31.3 'nisi constitutis rebus'; *ibid.* 7.

[229] Cic. *Att.* XIII.40.1. [230] App. *BCiv.* II.107.

[231] Dio XLIII.43–5, indicating this time that some he is mentioning were refused. He also believed Caesar was given the praenomen Imperator as Octavian later was; but it never appears on coins or inscriptions – he was probably simply allowed to keep it as a title after his prospective triumph, Syme 1958 (C 274) 176ff. Slaves in finance, Suet. *Iul.* 76.3; *IIIviri monetales* continued to be appointed. Caesar had in fact coined, perhaps with some sort of authorization, throughout the war. Dio in a rather confused passage XLIII.48 sees the *praefecti* of 45 as forerunners of the imperial *praefecti aerario*.

[232] Cic. *Att.* XIII.44; the people did not applaud the procession. XII.48.1, 12.45.

[233] Suet. *Iul.* 78.2. [234] Cic. *Att.* XIII.52.

living in Rome, and described, as a particular scandal, how on the last day of the year when the death of one of the consuls had been announced, Caesar had illegally turned one sort of assembly into another, and had a friend elected to the supreme post for an afternoon (doubtless so that he could hold the rank of consular). 'The consul's vigilance was extraordinary; in his whole term of office he never closed an eye. You laugh at such things, for you are not on the spot; if you were here to see them, you would weep.'[235]

For some reason we have no more letters till after the Ides of March; perhaps Cicero felt it impossible to write frankly – or his editors tactfully suppressed his outspokenness. The chronology of Caesar's final honours is uncertain; Dio warns us that he is bunching them, and puts them all in the new year, but some may date to the end of 45.[236] Only C. Cassius and a few others voted against any of them. They included the right to triumphal garb and a curule chair for all occasions; the title *parens patriae*, to be put on the coinage; the statue carried in procession was to be kept on a *pulvinar* or couch like those of the gods; other statues were to be placed on the rostra, in all the temples of Rome, and towns of Italy; also, says Appian, in the provinces and allied kingdoms;[237] Caesar's house was to have a pediment like that on a temple. All this he accepted. Next, says Dio, he was made sole censor for life, given tribunician sacrosanctity, and his son, real or adopted, was promised the high priesthood. 'Since he liked this too', he was given a gold chair and the dress of ancient kings, and a bodyguard of senators and *equites*.[238] 'Since he was pleased at this as well', there was more of the same, and finally he was to be worshipped as a god, a temple was to be built to him and his Clemency (possibly just to *Clementia Caesaris*) and Antony was appointed his priest or *flamen*.[239]

The Senate ordered the decrees to be inscribed in gold on silver tablets. At some point the senators went with the consuls in procession to announce their decisions to Caesar. They found him sitting in his new Forum with the architects, and he did not rise. There was outrage, and Caesar seems to have put it about that he had suddenly felt unwell, which was not believed (he had walked home).[240] Perhaps it was also in an attempt to disarm criticism that, somewhere about this time, he issued a general amnesty, restored the statues of Pompey and Sulla on the rostra,[241] and dismissed his Spanish bodyguard, refusing that of senators

[235] Cic. *Fam.* VII.30. Dio XLIII.46, fourteen praetors and forty quaestors, nominally elected but in fact appointed, the swollen numbers being to reward adherents.

[236] Dio XLIV.6.4. [237] App. *BCiv.* II.106. [238] Dio XLV.6.1.

[239] Dio XLIV.6.5–6, App. *BCiv.* II.106. Dio says he was to be worshipped as Jupiter Julius, but has probably made an understandable mistake in translating 'Divus Iulius' from Latin into Greek.

[240] Dio XLIV.8.

[241] The statues had been removed after Pharsalus, Dio XLII.18, XLII. 49. Cicero applauded their return and this may be when he proposed honours for Caesar himself, Plut. *Cic.* 40.4., Suet. *Iul.* 75.4.

and *equites* which had been voted him.[242] But he exacted an oath of loyalty to himself from all the senators, as though he had been a Hellenistic monarch,[243] and tied up the magistracies for the three years he intended to be in the East. From the beginning of 44 his head appeared on the coinage – the first time that of a living man had done so in Rome;[244] and by February 15 he had taken the title of dictator for life.[245] This was the final slamming of the door on Republican hopes.

Here with a vengeance was *regnum*, as the Romans called any overweening power; but Cicero had been describing Caesar as *rex* for some time.[246] The ancients were divided, as modern scholars are, as to whether Caesar wanted to take the actual title of king or whether it was his foes who asserted it to discredit him. His attitude to the word may have been ambiguous. To philosophers the king was the ideally good ruler, and many Romans in the second century had been much impressed by Hellenistic kings. But in a strictly Roman context the name was anathema. It is possible that Caesar felt that the most glorious thing to do would be to have it offered but to turn it down – as Scipio Africanus was said to have done in Spain.[247] Caesar certainly accepted various honours evoking kingship, though it should be remembered that all great Romans regarded themselves as the equals of kings, in a sense really as kings; the power of the consuls was *regia potestas*, inherited from the kings – still more so was that of the dictator, who had the twenty-four lictors split between the consuls at the inception of the Republic; while the dress of a *triumphator* was thought to be that of Etruscan and Roman kings. Thus Caesar may have regarded his triumphal garb, and in particular the gold wreath which the coins of 44 seem to show him wearing, as regal rather than simply triumphal.[248] It is pretty clear that he also rode into Rome early in 44 after celebrating the Latin Festival in what he believed to be the dress (especially the high red boots) of the ancient kings of Alba, from whom he claimed to be descended.[249] It was on this occasion that part of the crowd hailed him as king, to which he

242 Dio XLIV.7.4.

243 Suet. *Iul.* 84.2. Cic. *Div.* II.23 says a majority of senators in 44 were of Caesar's creation, perhaps rightly.

244 Crawford 1974 (B 144) I no. 480.

245 Joseph. *AJ* XIV.211.2. Cic. *Phil.* II 87, *dict. perp.* at the Lupercalia. Alföldi 1953 (C 153); 1962/3 (C 156) tried to prove from the coins that he only took the title in early March, but they cannot be so closely dated. Gasperini 1968, 1971 (B 158), (B 159) argued from an incomplete inscription that the dictatorship was *rei publicae constituendae causa* like Sulla's, but Sordi 1969 (C 264) shows that the inscription refers to Octavian, who was *IIIvir r.p.c.* Caesar's dictatorships, after the first, may have been *rei gerundae causa*.

246 Cic. *Att.* XIII.37.

247 Rawson 1975 (C 245).

248 Kraft 1952 (C 215); cf. Dio XLIV.6.1–3, 11.2, with Dion. Hal. V.35 and Diod. XXXVI.13. The attempt of Alföldi 1953 (C 153) to find a diadem on one of the coins, however, is refuted by Carson 1957 (C 183) and Kraay 1954 (B 181). Cic *Div.* I.119, II.37 shows Caesar in his purple toga and gold chair.

249 Weinstock 1971 (H 134) 324. Dio XLIII.43.2 suggests he wore these boots on various occasions.

answered that he was not Rex – the word was also a Roman *cognomen* – but Caesar.[250] Now or earlier two tribunes, Caesetius and Marullus, had the white ribbon-like diadem that was the Hellenistic mark of kingship torn from a wreath on the statue of Caesar where it had been placed by unknown hands; Caesar was furious, and had them deposed (which angered the plebs) – but according to Suetonius he said it was because they had deprived him of the *gloriam recusandi*, the glory of refusing the title.[251]

Finally, at the ceremony of the Lupercalia, in the Roman Forum, on 15 February, Antony repeatedly tried to crown Caesar – sitting in his golden chair, with his purple toga and gold wreath – with a diadem bound with laurel; he refused it, ordering it to be taken to Jupiter Capitolinus, the only king in Rome, and that it be recorded in the calendar that the consul, at the command of the people, had offered him the diadem, which he had refused. This last act is confirmed by Cicero, who was probably present.[252] This was surely meant to be final, though some scholars persist in believing that Caesar would have accepted if the crowd had been more enthusiastic. Apparently some people at the time did believe this: there was a rumour subsequently that a proposal would be made in the Senate on the Ides of March, in accordance with a Sibylline oracle, that Caesar should bear the title of king outside Italy, since only by a king could the Parthians be vanquished. Cicero is clear that the rumour was false;[253] and it is fairly obvious that in the next year, in which he had frequent occasion to write of Caesar, he did not think, or expect his readers to think, that Caesar had been aiming for the title of king.[254]

Godhead is another matter. Cicero's testimony again makes it plain that within Caesar's own lifetime Antony had been chosen, though not yet inaugurated, *flamen* to Divus Iulius, the God Julius;[255] and it would be odd (and unflattering in its reminder of the honorand's mortality) to select a priest who was to take office only on Caesar's posthumous divinization, as has been suggested; besides, the priest might die first.[256] In Rome, *flamen* was the title of the priests of Jupiter, Mars, Quirinus and some minor deities; though Quirinus was supposed to be the deified Romulus, these were all real gods. Other honours similar to those paid to gods are less crucial.[257] Cicero disapproves of Caesar's divinization, of

[250] Dio XLIV.9.2.

[251] Suet. *Iul.* 79; Nic. Dam. frag. 130.70 (*FGrH* no. 90), App. *BCiv.* II.107. Of course, if he did make these disclaimers, they could have been insincere.

[252] Dio XLIV.11.2, and the other late sources; Cic. *Phil.* II.85–7.

[253] Cic. *Div.* II.110.

[254] Cic. *Off.* III.83 in particular.

[255] Cic. *Phil.* II.43.1.

[256] Gesche 1968 (H 47).

[257] Weinstock 1971 (H 134) attributes wide plans foreshadowing those of Augustus to Caesar; but see North 1975 (H 92).

course, and Augustus was careful to avoid making the upper class worship him in Rome in his life, but Cicero seems to mind *regnum* more. Naturally Caesar had been worshipped in the East; at Ephesus, soon after Pharsalus, the cities of Asia joined in calling him 'the god manifest descended from Ares and Aphrodite, saviour of all human life',[258] though it is unlikely that the sixth-century chronicle of Malalas is right in thinking that the Caesareums at Alexandria and Antioch were instituted by Caesar himself in 47,[259] and an attempt to prove that Caesar intended that the Greek equivalent of *flamines* should be set up in all the provinces has not succeeded.[260] But no one in Rome would worry too much about what the provinces did in this line. Personally Caesar may have been a sceptic in religion, though always aware of its political importance and ready, especially with the cult of Venus, to use it for self-aggrandizement; he may, however, have had faith in Fortuna, and even believed that there was something superhuman in himself.[261]

And so to the murder – that of a *dictator perpetuo*, yes, but one also set apart by numerous extravagant honours and about whom rumours circulated that he wished to be king. The conspirators numbered about sixty, under the lead of C. Cassius and his brother-in-law M. Brutus, both marked out for the position as praetors in office and by family traditions of *libertas*, while the latter, Cato's nephew, had looked like the coming leader of the *boni*.[262] Among the rest were pardoned ex-Pompeians, like the two leaders, and thorough Caesarians, such as D. Brutus and Trebonius, who had actually been consul the previous year; it is by no means necessary that all even in the second class should have been without Republican principle and solely motivated by private grudges. They decided to kill Caesar in full Senate, as Romulus was said to have been killed when he became a tyrant. Though Caesar would take no precautions he knew he was hated, as he told his friend Matius a few days before the Ides, when he saw Cicero waiting in his antechamber – not what a Roman consular, his senior to boot, should do: 'Cicero is easy-going, if anyone is, but I have no doubt he loathes me.'[263] The remark suggests that Caesar did not understand that constitutional

[258] *SIG*³ 760; a number of other Greek inscriptions call Caesar a god in his lifetime: *IG* XII.2.165, 356, 5.557, *MDAI* (A) 1888 61; Raubitschek 1954 (B 223).

[259] Malalas 217.5, 216.17.

[260] Weinstock 1971 (H 134) 401ff, with North 1975 (H 92).

[261] Suet. *Iul.* 59.1 says no religious scruple turned him from or even delayed him in an undertaking (see p. 435 above and in general for the *haruspices* Rawson 1978 (C 246)); cf. Dio XLIII 49.3. The speech Sallust gives him in *Cat.* 51 is sceptical as to the after-life. The *Commentaries*, most unlike Sulla's, make little play with portents etc.

[262] Brutus claimed descent from two early avengers of tyranny, L. Brutus and Servilius Ahala; he was proud of his family history, Nep. *Att.* 8.3, Crawford 1974 (B 144) no. 455. For the Cassii see esp. Cic. *Phil.* II.26, I *Verr.* 30; Crawford 1974 (B 144) no. 452, head of Libertas on coins of Q. Cassius.

[263] Cic. *Att.* XIV.1.2.

principle was still strong in many breasts; for Cicero never really complains of his personal treatment.

To leave Rome on a campaign against Parthia has been seen as an attempt to avoid the issue. Matius was to write a few weeks after the Ides, 'if Caesar with all his genius could not find a way out, who will do so now?'[264] He was aware that his death would be the signal for renewed civil strife.[265] He can hardly have imagined that his position, which was directly based on his personal achievements, could be handed over to an heir. Certainly there seemed no heir to hand in 44. The infant Caesarion, at best foreign and illegitimate, was not even mentioned in the will, written on 13 September 45; Caesar apparently hoped that his wife Calpurnia might still have a child, and provision was made for guardians for it. The chief heir (presumably only if no child was expected) was his sister's eighteen-year-old grandson C. Octavius, who was required to take the testator's name.[266] It is interesting that he had not been adopted in Caesar's lifetime, though he had been marked out for special favour and probably designated *magister equitum*, to enter office when Lepidus went to his province.[267] Caesar must have seen his precocious ability and ambition, for he preferred him over other and older relatives; and a successful Parthian campaign could have been used to promote him to a great position. But Caesar cannot have guessed what he was in fact to achieve. In the end, like Alexander, he left the future to chance.

It may be that Cicero was partly right, and that Caesar with his deep loyalty to his followers felt he could not abandon them to a restored Republic; it is almost certain that he came to feel that he was essential to his own reforms. There is no doubt that he had a total contempt for the shaky structure of the old *res publica* (it may be significant that his formative years included the seventies, when his two prosecutions of patently guilty men got nowhere, and the Senate misbehaved badly.)[268] But fundamentally the ancients understood him better than many moderns. 'What drove Gaius Caesar on to his own and the state's doom? Glory, ambition, and the refusal to set bounds to his own pre-eminence.' So wrote Seneca;[269] and in his own day Cicero, in the *pro Marcello*, showed that he knew that an appeal to Caesar's desire for glory was the only possible way to move him. We find it hard to believe that great men could be dominated by a desire for fame to the exclusion of almost every other consideration. The philosophers indeed attacked the idea; but Caesar had little time for philosophers. Though the evidence is mostly

[264] Cic. *Att.* XIV.1.1. [265] Suet. *Iul.* 86.2. [266] Suet. *Iul.* 83.

[267] Dio XLIII.51.7, confirmed by *Fasti Cap.* under the year 44. Schmitthenner 1952 (C 255) is too sceptical about this; and the *condicio nominis ferendi* (not precise adoption) is well attested. (Antony claimed he had been 'adopted' in an earlier will according to Cic. *Phil.* II.71.)

[268] 'The *res publica* is an image not a reality' sounds authentic, though reported by Ampius Balbus, Suet. *Iul.* 76.3. Early prosecutions, Plut. *Caes.* 4. [269] Sen. *Ep.* 94.65.

not contemporary, it is probable that like so many supremely ambitious Romans he was obsessed with the memory of Alexander.[270] Cicero himself, at least in his earlier years, had been dazzled by the thought of immortal fame; and to a true Roman aristocrat (such as he was not) the claims of personal *dignitas* might well override those of strict legality: Scipio Africanus, to whom Caesar may have looked,[271] was supposed to have flatly refused to stand trial for peculation after his great victories – and got away with it. Yet by tradition the claims of the state were primary. Virtue, the poet Lucilius had said at the end of the second century, consists in placing the interests of our fatherland first, and our own last.[272] Caesar, unlike most conquerors, even among those who have changed the world, was a great man; he probably stood above many of the prejudices of the time, he tried to stand above party, class or race; he certainly stood far above all his associates, none of whom seem to have influenced him, generous as he was to their requests. But Cicero, who was not always fair to him, was right to say, at the beginning of the civil war, that he did not put 'the safety and honour of his country' above his own advantage.[273]

270 Weippert 1972 (C 281) 105ff.

271 See n. 247. Oppius wrote a biography of Scipio, perhaps as Caesarian propaganda (*HRR*).

272 Lucilius 1327–8 Marx.

273 Cic. *Att.* x.4.4 (and the same is true of Pompey).

CHAPTER 12

THE AFTERMATH OF THE IDES

ELIZABETH RAWSON

When Caesar had fallen at the foot of Pompey's statue Brutus lifted his dagger and called aloud on Cicero's name, congratulating him on the recovery of liberty.[1] The nervous old man had not been in the plot, but was a very senior consular and the embodiment of Republican principle; if Brutus hoped, however, for prompt endorsement or even help in keeping the senators in their places he did not get it. They fled in terror, and there was panic in the streets outside. The conspirators, guarded by a body of gladiators previously posted at hand by D. Brutus, made their way instead to the Forum and harangued whomever they could find there, stressing that they had only aimed to kill a tyrant, not to seize anything for themselves.[2] Meeting with no great enthusiasm, they occupied the Capitol, either as a symbolic step, or from fear of the veterans in the city, who were bound themselves to fear for their allotments. And hither Cicero and other senators did come to congratulate them, while young Dolabella appeared in the Forum in the consular insignia which he had been promised when Caesar should have left Rome. Antony, the other consul, had fled to his house;[3] Lepidus, Caesar's *magister equitum*, who had troops close at hand, may have seemed the greater threat.

Though we know more about the next year than any other in Roman history, mainly because Cicero's correspondence is here so rich, the precise course of events in the next few days is hard to reconstruct; there are probably no contemporary letters,[4] and Dio and Appian, our fullest sources, are often contradictory or probably inaccurate. Cicero, however, said later that the spirit of the 'liberators' was as manly as their plans were childish – he had urged that the Senate should be summoned to the Capitol, and power seized. Later at least, he thought Antony should

[1] Cic. *Phil.* II.28, 30; Dio XLIV.20.4 says all the conspirators did so in the Forum. See Horsfall 1974 (C 214) for the events of the day.

[2] Dio XLIV.21.1.

[3] Cic. *Phil.* II.88.

[4] Cic. *Fam.* VI.15, a brief note of congratulation to Minucius Basilus, one of the conspirators, was, some think, sent to him on the Capitol; but the subject is as uncertain as the date.

have been killed too.[5] Instead, the conspirators sent to treat with Antony and Lepidus.

To kill a consul, even one irregularly appointed, would be a poor start to the restored *res publica*; but an immediate declaration by the Senate that Caesar had been a tyrant would have strengthened the hands of the 'liberators'. Brutus, as urban praetor, could have summoned the Senate in the absence of the consul with sufficient legality; but it may have seemed impossible to collect enough senators for decency, and we do not know whether dark was coming on, after which sittings were illegal. And there was hope that Antony might not prove obdurate, while Lepidus was a close connexion of M. Brutus.

Troops, land and money were to be the leitmotiv of the next months, indeed years. During the night, Lepidus' forces occupied the Forum. Probably on the next day, Brutus made another speech to the people on the Capitol,[6] promising that the veterans would keep their rewards and allotments. Antony had perhaps already laid his hands on the treasures and papers in Caesar's house.[7] He consulted with Lepidus and other friends of the dictator. Lepidus is said to have been for violent measures, but Hirtius, Caesar's old officer, who had been designated consul for 43, spoke for reconciliation, and Antony agreed.[8] (As Dio points out, force could have advantaged only Lepidus.) Antony summoned the Senate to meet the following day, the festival of the Liberalia. The temple was surrounded by veterans, probably armed, and Lepidus' troops.

The two estimates of Caesar's killers that were to dominate ancient tradition were probably already being formulated. Either they were sacrilegious parricides, forgetful of private obligations, of the oath of loyalty all senators had sworn, and of Caesar's title of 'Father of the Fatherland', his sacrosanctity and his divine honours; or they were tyrannicides, 'liberators', as Cicero loved to call them who had placed their sacred duty to their country before private ties, demi-gods or even gods.[9] Various proposals were made in the Senate – to honour, thank, or merely spare the conspirators. On the whole, one may note, the Senate, though packed with Caesar's creatures, sympathized with them. Antony pointed out that logically, if Caesar was a tyrant, his body should be thrown into the Tiber and all his measures, his *acta* rescinded; if he was not, his murderers should be punished. But Antony was for an illogical compromise; the assassins should not suffer, but the *acta*, by which as he pointed out so many of those present held their positions, and the

5 Cicero refused any part in the negotiations with Antony, *Phil.* II.89; advised calling the Senate, *Att.* XIV.10.1, XV.11; thought Antony should have been killed, XV.11.

6 Probably the *contio Capitolina* written up for publication, which Cicero thought elegant but chilly, *Att.* XV.1a. Its date is uncertain however; the 15th, or (so Frisch 1946 (C 194)) 17th?

7 Plut. *Ant.* 15.

8 Nic. Dam. *Vita Aug.* 106 (rhetorical elaboration?).

9 Rawson 1986 (C 249).

abolition of which would lead to chaos all over the empire, should stand. Caesar should have a public funeral and his will should be valid.[10] It is not clear how much influence was exercised by Cicero, who recalled the famous Athenian amnesty after the fall of the Thirty Tyrants in 403 B.C., and on whose proposal the vote was taken. But he later said that he had only spoken for a compromise because the cause of the tyrannicides was already lost.[11] Antony, however, gained great credit for what was seen as statesmanlike behaviour. He appeased the veterans' suspicions in a *contio*.[12]

When Antony and Lepidus had sent their sons to the Capitol as hostages, Brutus and Cassius came down to dine with them. A large part of the populace had hitherto been anxious for reconciliation, but when Caesar's will, with its benefactions to the plebs, had been made known, and during the course of the funeral, marked by a probably inflammatory speech by Antony, there was a revulsion of feeling.[13] If Cassius, unlike Brutus, had disapproved of the reading of the will and the public funeral, he showed the shrewdness which, with greater energy and military experience, made some contemporaries admire, or fear, him more than the intellectual and idealistic Brutus.[14] Now, at all events, a tribune, Helvius Cinna – 'Cinna the Poet' – mistaken for the conspirator L. Cornelius Cinna, was lynched,[15] and the homes of the other leaders of the plot almost fired. A cult of Caesar was set up in the Forum where the mob had burned his body, under the influence of one Amatius, or Herophilus, who claimed to be a grandson of Marius.[16] The consuls did not restore order or move to eliminate this demagogue until, by the middle of April, Cassius and Brutus had been forced to flee from Rome, in spite of the bodyguards they had been granted and their attempts to curry favour with the veterans.[17] Antony, who had also been allowed a bodyguard, sped them on their way by getting them exempted from their praetorian duties. Those of the conspirators who had held office in 45 had gone or were about to go to their perhaps newly allotted provinces; even D. Brutus, to the strategically located Cisalpine Gaul to which Caesar may have designated him. The new Gallic province was given to L. Munatius

[10] App. *BCiv.* II.128, Dio XLIV.22.

[11] Cic. *Phil.* I.2, *Att.* XIV.10.1, Vell. Pat. II.58.4. Appian ignores the speech, Dio gives a lengthy version.

[12] App. *BCiv.* II.130, with Botermann 1968 (C 177) 9ff; Plut. *Brut.* 19.

[13] Suet. *Iul.* 84.2. says he only had the decrees honouring Caesar read, and added a few words, but see Cic. *Phil.* II.90 as well as the other late authors.

[14] Plut. *Brut.* 20; Vell. Pat. II.58.2 also says he had wanted to kill Antony. In general, Rawson 1986 (C 249).

[15] Plut. *Brut.* 20. Wiseman 1974 (C 285) 44 rightly accepts this identification of the tribune, mentioned in other sources too, with the poet.

[16] Scardigli 1980 (C 254).

[17] They allowed them to sell their plots, which Caesar had forbidden.

Plancus. Lepidus, bound to Antony by a rapid and irregular appointment as *pontifex maximus*, and a new marriage-alliance, also left for his command in Narbonese Gaul and Nearer Spain, with the task of negotiating peace with Sex. Pompeius, whose strength was reviving in the latter area. Dolabella was also in debt to Antony, who had acquiesced in Dolabella's hastily assumed consulship (though he had originally opposed his election) and arranged for him to have the province of Syria; Antony himself would take Macedonia, no doubt because six of the legions for the Parthian War were waiting there. Perhaps as a result of Antony's actions, though Dolabella had at first seemed hostile to Caesar's memory, he soon gave up this tack. Cleopatra 'fled' home to Egypt.[18]

The legions from Gaul and Spain did not appear in Rome, bent on revenge, as Cicero had feared at one point.[19] But there was one new arrival. On the news of the Ides the young Octavius returned to Italy at his mother's summons from his place with Caesar's army on the far side of the Adriatic (it is not likely that the officers at Apollonia suggested he march the troops to Rome to avenge Caesar[20]), to be met with the news of his adoption in Caesar's will. He was escorted by great crowds, including troops from Brundisium and the new colonies (or so it was later claimed) to Campania and then to Rome; rejecting the cautious advice of his step-father the consular Philippus, he appeared before Antony's brother Gaius, the praetor who had taken over Brutus' duties, to declare formally that he accepted his inheritance.[21]

The policies of the actors in these events are difficult to assess. Antony has been seen as a genuine moderate, who intended to keep to the compromise of the Liberalia, but was driven into extreme and violent courses, either because young Caesar, as he called himself – Octavian is the name modern scholars use to avoid confusion, though he himself dropped this additional name that revealed he was only an adopted son – rapidly threatened to filch the support of those most loyal to Caesar, including the plebs (perhaps chiefly the really poor) and to a large extent the veterans;[22] or because, though Brutus was sincere in wishing the *acta* of Caesar to stand, many Republicans, including Cicero, were outraged at the sight of Caesarian partisans enjoying the property of Pompeians, and – very shortsightedly – anxious to go back on the agreement.[23]

It is certainly true that tension soon developed between Antony and Octavian. The latter promptly applied to the former for the moneys Caesar had left, so that he could pay the legacies to the plebs (300

[18] According to Cic. *Att.* XIV.8.1. [19] Cic. *Att.* XIV.5.1, 6.1.

[20] So, Nic. Dam. *Vita Caes.* 41. But, surely this is later propaganda; aged eighteen and not yet known to be Caesar's heir, he was not a plausible leader.

[21] App. *BCiv.* III.14. [22] Syme 1939 (A 118) 107ff. [23] Wistrand 1981 (C 288).

sesterces apiece). Antony refused to disgorge, perhaps on the grounds that investigation was needed into what was Caesar's and what the state's,[24] and Octavian set about selling his own property to fulfil his obligation, with the aid of the two cousins who had been named heirs to smaller parts of the estate; and probably with the aid also of many of those personally closest to Caesar, who are now found grouped around his adopted son – the inseparable Oppius and Balbus, Matius and others, many of them financiers. (He also succeeded of course as patron to Caesar's confidential freedmen, many of them wealthy.)[25] He thus gained immense popularity.[26] Antony was also obstructive about the confirmation of the young Caesar's adoption, and, at some later point in the summer, frustrated his attempt to capitalize on his popularity by becoming tribune (quite illegal, as he was too young and, whether as Octavius or Iulius, a patrician); and on at least one occasion the consul opposed the young man's placing a golden chair and wreath for Caesar in the auditorium at the games, in accordance with the honorific *senatus consultum* passed the previous year.[27] As Dio notes, the plebs had not forgiven Antony for his harsh repression of them as *magister equitum* in 47;[28] probably they also blamed him for helping suppress the cult of Caesar in the Forum. But Antony perhaps did not take Octavian seriously for some time – Cicero's letters hardly mention him. What Octavian himself was saying is also uncertain; the later sources, perhaps dependent on his autobiography, declare that he was bent on revenge for Caesar, and, they imply, succession to a very great, if not unique, position, and this may well be true. But he had been extremely polite to Cicero when they met in Campania after his arrival in Italy,[29] and was probably cautious in his public utterances – besides, what one said to the plebs could if necessary be discounted.

As for the Republican threat to Antony's other flank, it is not clear that there was any real difference of opinion between Brutus and Cicero at least. It may be that, though Brutus and Cassius had wisely begun by promising to the colonists their land, and to Antony and Lepidus all their

[24] So he claims in a fictitious speech in App. *BCiv.* III.20.

[25] App. *BCiv.* III.94 sees Octavian desiring ratification of the adoption largely to gain patronal rights over Caesar's rich freedmen.

[26] App. *BCiv.* III.21. Alföldi 1976 (C 157) 31 stresses Balbus' role, noting there are stories suggesting he approved autocracy and desired revenge. Note also that Octavian seems to have annexed at Brundisium part of the money being sent east for the Parthian War, App. *BCiv.* III.39, Dio XLV.32, Nic. Dam. *Vita Caes.* 55.

[27] Antony obstructs *lex curiata*, Dio XLV.5.3; tribunate, Plut. *Ant.* 16.2, App. *BCiv.* III.120.2, Suet. *Aug.* 10.2, Dio XLV.6.2–3 (Cinna's place) – Rice Holmes 1928 (C 252) I, 26 puts this in the autumn; chair, perhaps at the delayed *ludi Cereales* and then the *ludi Victoriae Caesaris* – App. *BCiv.* III.28 mentions two occasions, cf. Plut. *Ant.* 16, Nic. Dam. *Vita Caes.* 108, Cic. *Att.* XV.3.2 ('de sella Caesaris bene tribuni', 22 May), with Rice Holmes 1928 (C 252) I, 18.

[28] Dio XLV.6.2.

[29] Cic. *Att.* XIV.12.2 'perhonorifice et peramice', cf. XV.12.2, seems friendly to the 'liberators'.

existing honours, they would not ideally have wished to confirm everything that Caesar had done, let alone what he was said to have been planning to do. Octavian's inheritance was soon entangled in lawsuits initiated by people anxious to recover confiscated property (suits in which Antony is said to have used his influence against the young heir).[30] If Antony did not trust the 'liberators' and their friends, he is not entirely to be blamed; the moderate Hirtius, who probably served as an intermediary, did not do so either.

But, salutary as the attempt to get away from Cicero's and Octavian's invective against Antony may be, and attractive as his bold, generous character might seem, especially to those who had served under him in war, and to some of the now reduced group of his fellow-*nobiles*, it is hard to see him as a devotee of Republican principle. He is said to have claimed at one stage to be Caesar's heir, even his adopted son[31] (his mother was a Julia, as he boasted) and it is likely that his moderation was a temporary expedient, to gain time and strengthen his hand in a bid for great power, though not necessarily in a form identical with that held by Caesar – indeed, he pleased the Senate by proposing the abolition of the office of dictator.[32] Cicero, writing from Campania, shows us that even in April Antony was using his control of Caesar's papers to propose various measures, such as full citizenship for all Sicily (and numerous individuals) and privileges for foreign dynasts. These are said to have been paid for by huge bribes, and must have gained him support and gratitude, though, or indeed because, there was doubt whether such measures had entered Caesar's head.[33] He appears also to have taken control not only of the valuables in Caesar's house, but the money, whatever precisely its purpose, that Caesar had stored in the temple of Ops.[34] Perhaps in early April, certainly before M. Brutus and Cassius left Rome, D. Brutus was writing to them of his deep distrust of Antony, whom he saw as hiding behind protestations about the excited state of the veterans and plebs, and likely soon to have the 'liberators' declared public enemies. He thought it would come to war, with Sex. Pompeius in Spain and Caecilius Bassus in Syria the only hope of the 'liberators' (no wonder Antony was anxious that Lepidus should patch things up with Sextus, though this would also please the Senate).[35]

In late April Antony set off for a tour of the veteran settlements in Campania and Samnium, which Cicero in the *Second Philippic* has

30 App. *BCiv.* III.22.

31 Cic. *Phil.* II.71 (in a will earlier than that adopting Octavian).

32 Cic. *Phil.* II.91. 33 Cic. *Att.* XIV.12.1.

34 Alföldi 1976 (C 157) 77, from confiscated Pompeian property; 700 million sesterces, according to Cic. *Phil.* II.93 and VIII.26.

35 The letter survives as Cic. *Fam.* XI.1. Some suppose it to date from before the compromise of the Liberalia (Syme 1939 (A 118) 97), but see Shackleton Bailey 1977 (B 110).

immortalized as a Bacchic rout, but which had administrative purposes and was also designed to drum up support; he urged the colonists to stand by Caesar's *acta* and drill regularly. His brother Caius, the *de facto praetor urbanus*, and the third brother Lucius, who was tribune, might be expected to see to things in Rome. Veterans – 6,000 says Appian, and soon organized in military fashion – began to congregate in Rome to support measures that Antony had in mind and serve as a bodyguard, more efficient, declares Dio, than the colonists in Rome in the spring had been (these were now mostly settled). Hirtius, whose distress at Antony's behaviour that spring is significant, warned Cicero not to return to Rome for the senatorial meeting at the beginning of June; it was said that no friends of the 'liberators' would be safe from Caesar's soldiers.[36] Indeed Hirtius and his fellow-consul-designate, Pansa, stayed away.

Ignoring the probably very thin Senate, Antony put through the assembly on 2 June – by legislation that was trebly irregular because it was not a *dies comitialis*, due notice had not been given, and violence was used – a bill securing his future by exchanging his province of Macedonia (which his brother Caius would take over after his praetorship) for Cisalpine and Transalpine Gaul, which he was to hold for five years. But he was to have the disposal of the legions now in Macedonia. There had been rumours of something like this since April.[37] Dolabella was won over by getting five years in Syria too. Demands for a commission to investigate Caesar's papers were cut short by another bill; the consuls' decisions as to the dictator's intentions were to be final.[38] Shortly after (in a thunderstorm, so again illegally) a comprehensive agrarian law was proposed by the consuls, to benefit both veterans and plebs; the commissioners were to be headed by L. Antonius (and, improperly, included Antony himself, though he had proposed the bill). To Cicero's rage the plebs at Rome, the military tribunes, and, unkindest cut of all, the business interests centred at the Ianus Medius and the *equites*, all set up statues to Lucius as their patron[39] – perhaps a sign that Antony had support among the better-off citizens, for which there is indeed some other evidence.

But Antony had not yet repudiated the agreement with the 'liberators'. Brutus and Cassius were still hanging about near Rome, and he now persuaded the Senate to give them a function: to organize the corn supply from Asia and Sicily – something which they however regarded

[36] Cic. *Att.* xiv.21.2, xv.5.2–3. Keppie 1983 (A 56) 52. On his tour Antony settled the Eighth Legion at Casilinum.

[37] Vetoing tribunes were also bought off, App. *BCiv.* iii.30. Earlier rumours, Cic. *Att.* xiv.14.4.

[38] The consuls were to have a *consilium*, but perhaps chosen by them, Cic. *Phil.* ii.100.

[39] Cic. *Phil.* vi.12–15. Nicolet 1985 (C 232).

as a humiliating insult, as Cicero shows in a letter to Atticus which gives a vivid picture of a family council, including Brutus' mother, the formidable Servilia, held at Antium south of Rome on 8 June.[40] Perhaps a little later their praetorian provinces were fixed as Crete and Cyrene.[41] It is likely that this was little more than an insult too; it is not probable that Caesar (or the lot) had envisaged quite such minor jobs for the two most important praetors of the year, though Appian's story that the dictator had proposed to give them Macedonia and Syria is probably an attempt to justify their subsequent seizure of these areas.[42] At this point Cicero thought they had no plans at all, though they complained of D. Brutus for 'missing chances'.

Cicero's letter also reveals Brutus' anxiety about the *ludi Apollinares*, now imminent; it was the duty of the urban praetor to preside over these, but Cicero advised against his returning to Rome. They were to be given without his presence but in his name, at considerable expense, in the hope of favourable demonstrations. But C. Antonius advertised them as for the Nones of 'July', not the traditional Quinctilis, to Brutus' distress, and they passed off without much in the way of the hoped-for agitation.[43]

Games were always of political significance at Rome. At the end of July Octavian, who had offered to replace the college in charge, celebrated the *ludi Victoriae Caesaris* (commemorating the victory of Pharsalus) on money borrowed from Matius and other friends of Caesar's.[44] The games coincided with the appearance of a comet. Such things were usually seen as portents of disaster; but this time the people believed, or were told, that here was Caesar's soul translated to the heavens and divinity. Though Octavian is said to have secretly thought it portended greatness for himself,[45] he seized the opportunity and placed a statue of Caesar with a star above his head in the temple of Venus Genetrix.

Octavian was now clearly a real danger to Antony, particularly because he was also attracting the favour of the veterans – though many ex-centurions and higher officers of Caesar stood by Antony throughout. An attempt to retain this favour may explain inconsistencies in Antony's attitude to the 'liberators', whom he now began to attack openly. But then there were rumours that he would make concessions to

40 Cic. *Att.* xv.11.

41 So Plut. *Brut.* 19.1, App. *BCiv.* III.8, but Nic. Dam. *Vita Caes.* 112 gives Cassius Illyricum (perhaps corrupt) and Dio XLIX.41.3 Bithynia, cf. Plut. *Ant.* 54.3, and App. *BCiv.* III.8 for variants.

42 App. *BCiv.* III.8, IV.57, Dio XLVII.21.1. Sternkopf 1912 (C 266); Frisch 1946 (C 194) 102–3.

43 Cic. *Att.* XVI.1, 4.1, 5.1, Plut. *Brut.* 21.2–3. App. *BCiv.* III.28 says members of the plebs bribed by Octavian broke up demonstrations paid for by Brutus' agents and terrorized the audience.

44 Suet. *Aug.* 10.1 'non audentibus facere quibus obtigerat id munus ipse edidit'; see also Obsequens 128, Pliny *HN* II.93, Dio XLV.6.4.

45 Pliny *HN* II.94 (from Augustus' autobiography?).

them when the Senate met on 1 August, giving up Cisalpine Gaul and seeing to it that Cassius and Brutus could return to Rome.[46] Instead, edicts issued by these exasperated the veterans, who now or later forced a temporary reconciliation of Antony and Octavian, a sign of their regard for both Caesar's military and his legal heir, and an act of unexampled enterprise on the part of Roman troops;[47] and Antony himself promulgated an edict accusing the two 'liberators' of preparing for war and tampering with the troops in Macedonia.[48] Brutus and Cassius finally made up their minds to leave Italy – but not for their new provinces; Brutus was soon to be heard of at Athens, where his statue was placed beside those of Athens' own tyrannicides,[49] and Cassius, who left later, was not heard of at all for some time, though there were rumours that he had gone to Alexandria, or to Syria, where his defence of the area after Carrhae had made him popular with the troops. It is not clear when they began to prepare for war; Brutus, at least, perhaps only when hostilities had already broken out in Italy.[50]

Cicero, convinced that nothing could be done against Antony till his consulate ran out, and his own friends, Hirtius and Pansa, took over, also determined to leave for Greece, to visit his son, now a student at Athens, and attend the Olympic games. But in southern Italy he heard that on 1 August an unexpected attack on Antony had been made in the Senate by Caesar's father-in-law L. Piso; and finding also that Brutus and others blamed him for leaving, he turned back to Rome.[51]

We do not know what Piso had said; perhaps that Antony's corruption and violence were unworthy of Caesar's memory. Indeed new legislation, of a *popularis* flavour, introduced by Antony in August and concerned with the composition of the juries, on to which many centurions were put, and allowing appeal from their courts to the people, went directly contrary to Caesar's measures.[52] Piso was, of course, an old enemy of Cicero's (it must have rankled in the latter's breast to see him bold enough to undertake the attack he himself had declined); in spite of the charges in Cicero's invective *In Pisonem* of 56 B.C. he seems to have been a statesmanlike person. Even though no one had dared to follow up Piso's criticisms, his action confirmed that there was distrust of Antony among moderate Caesarians, and it was surely clear that any effective challenge to Antony in Rome must rest largely on these. (Unfortunately

46 Cic. *Phil.* I.8, *Att.* XVI.7.1.

47 App. *BCiv.* III.28ff has two reconciliations, perhaps a doublet.

48 Edicts of all three, Cic. *Phil.* I.8, *Att.* XVI.7.1, 7, *Fam* XI.3.1–3.

49 Plut. *Brut.* 24, Raubitschek 1957 (C 240).

50 Nic. Dam. *Vita Caes.* 135 so of both, but dating departure to October – too late, see Cic. *Phil.* X.8.

51 Cic. *Att.* XVI.7, cf. *Phil.* I.7ff, *Fam.* XII.25.3.

52 Cic. *Phil.* I.8, 19–20; V.12ff; XII.3.5. Hardly a panel specially for centurions, but one with a lesser property qualification, and Antony had some centurions – and new citizens who were Greeks, Cic. *Phil.* V.13 – put on it?

Hirtius was ill all autumn.) This is no doubt why Cicero, on the plea that he was tired from his journey, did not attend the meeting of the Senate on 1 September; for on the agenda were honours for Caesar, which Cicero could hardly support, while to oppose them would offend old Caesarians.[53] Antony was so angry at Cicero's absence that he may have seen the occasion as a trap for him. But next day, in Antony's own absence, Cicero delivered the speech on which his *First Philippic* is based, criticizing the consul with comparative moderation, but cleverly representing his actions as not only unconstitutional, but neither popular with the plebs nor in accord with Caesar's intentions.

Only one consular, P. Servilius, followed this lead, and Cicero dared not return to the Senate, now overawed, he complained, by Antony's bodyguard of Ityraeans – oriental barbarians. But on 19 September Antony's reaction proved to be an onslaught claiming that Cicero had alienated the Pompeians on one hand and on the other instigated the murder of Caesar; it was clearly an attempt to isolate him.[54] This suggests that Cicero seemed a genuine threat; though without close followers, he had much prestige, and was on friendly terms with most of the important figures or groups of the time: many of the 'liberators' of course, but also some of the Caesarians, notably Hirtius, and even his ex-son-in-law Dolabella (who, however, left about this time for Syria).

Cicero retired to his Campanian properties, to work on the great invective against Antony known as the *Second Philippic*,[55] and on the treatises *On Duties* and *On Friendship* which, among other preoccupations, stressed the necessity of putting obligation to the state above personal ties. He was thinking both of the 'liberators', who (he held) had done this, and of Caesarians such as Matius, who had recently written to express his continuing grief for Caesar, and claim that helping Octavian with his games had only reflected this personal loyalty;[56] perhaps also of Octavian, whose private duty to avenge Caesar might seem to many Romans overwhelming. Cicero distrusted the boy, though when Antony, now openly bidding for the favour of the extreme Caesarians (he put up a statue to Caesar 'Parent of his County' and threatened a legate of Cassius as going to join a public enemy) accused Octavian, probably wrongly, of suborning his bodyguard to kill him, Cicero regretted that this had not occurred.[57] The ideals of law and the *res publica* were being corrupted even in the man who seemed to embody them.

Suddenly events began to move. Four of the Macedonian legions had

53 Cic. *Phil.* I.13, II.10.

54 The speech can be partly reconstructed from *Phil.* II, cf. Frisch 1946 (C 194) 130.

55 We do not know when it was published, cf. Cic. *Att.* XV.13.1.

56 Cic. *Fam.* XI.28.

57 Cic. *Fam.* XII.23.2. Octavian may have seen that, as App. *BCiv.* III.39 notes, Antony's death would have left the 'liberators' too powerful for his convenience.

arrived in Brundisium, and Antony went to fetch them, only to find that Octavian's agents, and pamphlets, had been before him, stressing that the consul had neglected his duty to avenge Caesar; and his own offers of money appeared paltry in comparison with their promise of 2,000 sesterces apiece. Meanwhile Octavian himself was in Campania, where by the immediate gift of this sum to each man and the promise of future largesse and, according to Dio, of avenging Caesar, he raised a body of 3,000 veterans to 'protect' him against Antony.[58] He wrote urgently to Cicero, asking for a meeting and advice – should he block Antony's road, join the Macedonian legions or go to Rome? Cicero was in a quandary; he still did not trust Octavian – 'look at his name; look at his age' – but here was a heaven-sent weapon against Antony. He advised the young man, who bombarded him with letters, to go to Rome, but was not brave enough to follow him there at once.[59]

In Rome Octavian addressed the people in a *contio* that disturbed Cicero by its praise of Caesar and the phrase 'so may I attain my father's honours'. But he did not, it seems, threaten the 'liberators', and Oppius assured Cicero that he would even show himself friendly to them.[60] However, on Antony's approach with some of the troops – discipline partly restored by executions and bribes – Octavian was forced to retire, for his men, who were not all armed, were not prepared to fight; they wanted a reconciliation. Octavian made them new offers of money and retired to Etruria, where he had influential friends,[61] continuing to recruit.

Antony brought many of his troops into Rome. Some veterans joined him, but the heavy news arrived that two of the Macedonian legions, the Fourth and the Martia, who were marching up the Adriatic coast, had declared for Octavian[62] (who gave them another 2,000 sesterces, with promises of 20,000 on demobilization, and also captured the army's elephants). Antony summoned an illegal night meeting of the Senate on 28 November (shutting out some hostile tribunes); according to Cicero he gave up his hope of getting it to declare Octavian a *hostis*, but fixed the remaining provinces for the next year (to the advantage of his friends) and deprived Cassius and Brutus of theirs. At Tibur he exacted an oath of loyalty from all the senators who called on him there as well as his troops, whom he paid the now unavoidable 2,000 sesterces. Probably not

[58] The apologetic Nic. Dam. *Vita Caes.* 131 has Octavian move in self-defence after Antony has gone south, cf. App. *BCiv.* III.40. Dio XLV.12.2, reverses the order. Cic. *Att.* XVI.8.2 mentions 3,000 men, Appian 10,000. Linderski 1984 (C 221) for Octavian's traditional form of crisis-levy (*coniuratio*); he could thus claim legality.

[59] Cic. *Att.* XVI.8, 9, 11.6; 10, he bolts in panic to Arpinum.

[60] Cic. *Att.* XVI.15.3.

[61] Friends include members of the great families of the Caecinae (Cic. *Att.* XVI.8.2) and Maecenates (Nic. Dam. *Vita Caes.* 133 – possibly the famous Maecenas' father).

[62] The relative dating of these two events is uncertain: App. *BCiv.* III.45, Cic. *Phil.* XIII.19.

trusting them to fight Octavian, he pressed on to Cisalpine Gaul. But D. Brutus, who had been raising fresh troops and courting popularity with his old ones, apparently with success, perhaps since his first arrival in the province, now barred himself in the town of Mutina and sent to the capital to say that he would keep his command, though he had doubtless only been appointed for a year, and that he put himself at the disposal of the Senate. He had perhaps been encouraged by Cicero, who had arrived in Rome on 9 December and consulted with Pansa, and was now writing to him and other governors to urge them not to hand over to Antony and his friends;[63] he had also received overtures from Octavian, who had followed Antony north.[64]

On 20 December the tribunes summoned the Senate, to discuss protection for the new consuls; perhaps hard on this came D. Brutus' letter. According to Cicero the house filled up when it was known that he would speak.[65] He persuaded the *patres*, in the speech known as the *Third Philippic*, to back D. Brutus by confirming all governors in their provinces, and to honour and reward Octavian and the two legions which had joined him. Though he could not get Antony declared a *hostis*, 'I have laid the basis for a *res publica*', he claimed.[66]

It has been said that such action against the consul was treason. But Cicero held that the Senate was supreme in the state, and that Antony's disregard of it, with his other illegal acts, proved that he was no consul but a tyrant; while the law giving him Cisalpine Gaul was invalid. In defence of Octavian's actions Cicero could have appealed to the principle he had put forward in the *De Republica* in the late fifties, that in a crisis 'no one is a private citizen', and even perhaps his conviction, elaborated in the *De Legibus*, that laws are only laws when they embody what is right, a more subjective doctrine than he realized.[67] As for himself, there can be little doubt that during the next months, when he was in partial control of policy in Rome, he saw himself as the *rector rei publicae*, the guardian and protector of the state, whose position – based on that of the great consulars of the past, who traditionally gave the lead to the Senate – he had sketched in the *De Republica*.[68] Perhaps, too the role of political counsellor to a great general, such as Laelius had been to Scipio Aemilianus, was again in his mind, though Hirtius or Octavian hardly seemed the equal of Pompey, whose Laelius he had once proposed to be.[69] Where Octavian was concerned, Cicero may have thought rather of the brilliant young men, such as P. Crassus and M. Caelius, whose mentor he had been; he should have recalled that all these had ended by throwing off his influence.

[63] Cic. *Fam.* XI.6. (September), 5.7.
[64] Dio XLV.14.
[65] Cic. *Fam.* XI.6a.2.
[66] Cic. *Fam.* XII.25.2.
[67] Cic. *Rep.* II.46, 3.33, *Leg.* I passim.
[68] Cic. *Rep.* Bks V–VI.
[69] Cic. *Fam.* V.7.3, cf. *Att.* II.19.5, 20.5.

On 1 January Pansa opened a debate in the Senate, which lasted several days.[70] It ended with Octavian receiving praetorian *imperium* (which his men had wanted to seize for him)[71] to oppose Antony, and being adlected to the Senate, with the right to speak among the consulars and to stand for the consulship ten years early (which still left him over ten years to wait). The consuls were to start recruiting, and Hirtius was allotted the job of going to the army; he would, of course, outrank Octavian. The Senate undertook to pay the Fourth and Martian legions the 20,000 sesterces promised them, with demobilization after the campaign, and land to be found in Italy; any troops leaving Antony for the consul's army were to get the same terms. Such offers by the Senate were unexampled.

Pansa had called first on Fufius Calenus, his father-in-law, to speak, and perhaps other consulars, before Cicero; the last-named failed to get the *senatus consultum ultimum* (see ch. 3, pp. 84–5) passed and Antony declared a *hostis*, since Piso objected that this was condemning a citizen without trial, while Antony's family staged pathetic demonstrations. Nor was all Antony's legislation declared invalid. Cicero gave a rash pledge of Octavian's loyalty to the state; but where honours for the youth were concerned he found himself outbidden, perhaps surprisingly, by the cautious lawyer Ser. Sulpicius Rufus, and also by P. Servilius, who had betrothed, or was soon to betroth, his daughter to the young Caesar.[72] However, on the proposal of Fufius Calenus, who was perhaps not the mere agent of Antony Cicero calls him, the Senate decided to send an embassy to Antony consisting of Piso, Philippus and Ser. Sulpicius, who was in frail health, to urge him to withdraw from Cisalpine Gaul and to submit to the Senate;[73] if he refused, it would be war. Cicero, addressing the people, made all he could of this ultimatum, and could rejoice that, perhaps as part of a bargain, the agrarian law of June was abolished.[74]

Cicero chafed at the delay the embassy caused in preparations for war, to which he urged the Senate in the *Seventh Philippic*. He rightly thought that Antony might be ready to give up Cisalpine Gaul, if he could keep the Transalpine province, but remembering the power that Caesar had amassed there, felt this would still be intolerable. In fact the embassy, returning early in February without Sulpicius, who had succumbed *en route*, reported that Antony would be content with his full five years in the Transalpina, with six legions, if by their end Cassius and Brutus had also left the provinces they would hold after their consulships, which he

[70] Frisch 1946 (C 194) 168ff, Cic. *Phil.* V.

[71] App. *BCiv.* III.48.

[72] Cic. *ad Brut.* I.12 (and Philippus proposed a statue); Suet. *Aug.* 62, the engagement.

[73] Cic. *Phil.* V.3, 4, 25, 31.

[74] Cic. *Phil.* VI.

thus perhaps accepted.[75] He also claimed rewards for his men equal to those given to Octavian's, and validity for his *acta*. The Senate, after an agitated debate, rejected these demands.[76] It refused to use the word war, but declared a state of emergency and probably passed the *senatus consultum ultimum*; Antony's uncle, L. Caesar, supported by Pansa (Hirtius had now left Rome) prevented him being made a *hostis*. On the declaration of a *tumultus* all citizens had to put on military dress; consulars were exempted, but Cicero wore the *sagum* as an example. Antony's men were told to lay down their arms by the Ides of March. Not long after, all Antony's *acta* were annulled, though Pansa saw to it that those believed to be Caesar's were revalidated;[77] and, significantly, the law barring Pompeians from office was revoked. Massilia recovered the lands Caesar had taken from it – and settled veterans on.

Meanwhile rumours about Cassius' achievements in Syria had been reaching Rome; and soon there came an official letter to the Senate from M. Brutus, who had peacefully taken over Macedonia from his relative Hortensius the retiring proconsul (Brutus had perhaps only moved after hearing of the events of late November in Italy and Antony's removal of his own province). He now controlled most of Macedonia and Greece, and also the greater part of the troops in Illyricum, and was soon to capture C. Antonius, his brother's intended governor of Macedonia. He wrote that he was at the Senate's disposal. Pansa, against the opposition of his father-in-law, who argued that the Caesarian veterans would dislike it, but urged on by Cicero, successfully proposed that Brutus be made proconsul of Macedonia and Illyricum, and asked to stay near Italy. The appointment of C. Antonius had, after all, been revoked by the Senate,[78] and Brutus wrote very properly. Cicero was not to find it so easy to legitimate Cassius.

At the end of February news came that Dolabella, on the way to his province of Syria, had seized and killed the tyrannicide Trebonius, now governor of Asia; according to Cicero's version, after savage torture. Everyone expressed outrage; Fufius Calenus probably had pleasure in proposing that Cicero's ex-son-in-law be declared a *hostis*, though Cicero himself was classing Dolabella with Antony as a monster.[79] It was now known indirectly that Cassius had succeeded in taking control in Syria,

75 Cic. *Phil.* VIII.27, cf. XIII.37. Frisch 1946 (C 194) 197 on the apparent contradiction with VIII.25: possibly he was ready to give up Transalpine Gaul if Cassius and Brutus were not consuls. App. *BCiv.* III.63 says he wanted to punish D. Brutus.

76 Frisch 1946 (C 194) 199–200. *Phil.* IX proposes honours to Ser. Sulpicius assimilating him to an ambassador killed in war.

77 Cic. *Phil.* X.17, cf. XIII.10, 31; 32.

78 On 20 Dec., when the Senate told all governors to keep their provinces, p. 479 above.

79 Cic. *Phil.* XI.1; App. *BCiv.* III.26 with different bias and details.

over both the legions opposing and that supporting the Pompeian adventurer Caecilius Bassus, and that the four legions from Egypt had joined him. Cicero proposed that he be given an extraordinary command in the East, on the excuse of suppressing Dolabella; but Calenus moved that the consuls should do this when the trouble at Mutina was ended (this might encourage them to make peace with Antony) and Pansa, who perhaps would have liked an eastern command, supported him.[80] In fact Cassius' friends and relations, it emerged, did not support Cicero's proposal; the latter's influence was perhaps temporarily weakened.

The campaigning season was approaching, and with it the prospect of fighting in the north, for D. Brutus in Mutina would starve if not relieved. A last attempt at compromise was made by Piso and Calenus, taking up, or putting about, rumours that Antony was ready for concessions. With Pansa's support they got a vote for a new embassy of five consulars (themselves with Cicero, Servilius and L. Caesar), but Cicero soon backed out on the grounds that there was no real evidence Antony had changed his mind, that Hirtius and Octavian were being ignored, morale would be damaged and anyway his own life would not be safe outside Rome.[81] The proposal lapsed.

But others were anxious for an accommodation too; on 20 March letters from Lepidus in Narbonese Gaul and Plancus in northern Gaul (the former at least probably inspired by Antony) arrived urging peace and the preservation of citizen lives. But Cicero was implacably opposed to any agreement that left Antony with an army, and in the *Thirteenth Philippic* he also contemptuously dissected a letter of Antony to Hirtius and Octavian, which urged the reconciliation of all Caesarians in the face of a Pompeian revival, and deplored the use of veterans for purposes other than revenge on Caesar's assassins. Cicero argued that such divisions were dead and done with (but his praise of Sex. Pompeius was hardly tactful); no, all parties were now united against a few criminals who had put themselves outside civilized society.[82] Thus throughout this period he describes Antony as a gladiator, as a *latro*, brigand, or even as a wild beast; his followers are held up to similar obloquy – could the state he handed over to such men? Cicero also wrote to rebuke Plancus, politely, and Lepidus, more sharply – which was perhaps unwise, though at the start of January Cicero had tried to bind the unreliable Lepidus by proposing a gilded equestrian statue of him in the Forum in gratitude for his coming to terms with Sex. Pompeius.[83] Antony had

[80] Cic. *Phil.* XI esp. 16–36; *Fam.* XII.14.4, the consuls to appoint delegates till they could come themselves. See also *Fam* XII.6–7; 12–13; *ad Brut.* II.2.3; II.4.2.

[81] Cic. *Phil.* XII.1–7, 18; Dio XLVI.32.3.

[82] Cic. *Phil.* XIII (Antony's letter in §22–48).

[83] Cic. *Fam..* X.6, 27. Statue, *Phil.* V.40, *ad Brut.* I.15.9 (showing it was pulled down in the summer).

claimed to be in touch with both Plancus and Lepidus, and Cicero knew that of the latter at least this was true. But Plancus wrote to the Senate to apologize for his *démarche*, and blamed his troops, to whom great promises were being made from Antony.[84]

At last Hirtius and Octavian felt able to move against Antony, who fell back towards Mutina. Pansa left his duties in Rome to the loyal but insignificant urban praetor Cornutus, with one legion to protect the city, and pressed north with four of new recruits. On 14 April Antony intercepted them at Forum Gallorum. The inexperienced troops were put to flight and the consul wounded; but Hirtius had detached a strong force to meet the newcomers, which retrieved the situation. Octavian meanwhile had defended his and Hirtius' camp resolutely and all three generals were hailed *imperator*.[85] Seven days later there was a battle near Mutina, from which D. Brutus perhaps made a sortie. Antony was defeated, and decided to retreat with his cavalry and surviving infantry. But in the heavy fighting Hirtius had been killed, and almost simultaneously Pansa died of his wounds at Bononia.[86]

The first news that reached Rome was of Pansa's initial defeat, and there was panic, with rumours that Cicero was planning a *coup*. When calm was restored, and a double victory announced, there was a reaction. Antony was finally declared a *hostis*, as Cicero had so long urged.[87] There were scenes of great enthusiasm for the orator, as he wrote to M. Brutus. Cicero proposed an ovation for Octavian, which was opposed – Octavian himself was to ask for a triumph. Cicero also failed to get Decimus Brutus' name put in the calendar as a permanent memorial of his deeds, but his troops were promised rewards equal to those of the ex-Antonian legions, and when the consuls' disappearance was known, on 27 April, he was put in command of their forces (two senators even proposed that Octavian's troops be transferred to him). The Senate reduced the bounties to be paid to the Fourth and Martian legions, for it was in severe straits for money; but the sum was still large, and a little later the Senate also set up a board to oversee the settlement of the men concerned; against Cicero's advice, it left both Decimus and Octavian off the commission.[88] (In the course of time, this arrived in Cisalpine Gaul and tried to negotiate directly with the troops, bypassing Octavian altogether; the men would have nothing to do with it.) On 27 April too, Cassius' *imperium* was legalized, on the proposal of P. Servilius; and Sex.

84 Cic. *Fam.* x.8.3, 'exercitus magnis saepe promissis sollicitatus'.

85 Vivid account by Hirtius' officer Sulpicius Galba, *Fam.* x.30; cf. App. *BCiv.* III.67. The 15th, Bengtson 1974 (C 172) from the MSS of the letter, but see Shackleton Bailey *ad loc.*

86 App. *BCiv.* III.71, Dio XLVI.38 are our chief sources; Cic. *ad Brut.* I.3.4, Hirtius' death, *Fam.* XI.13.2, D. Brutus reports Pansa's. Bengtson 1974 (C 172) 506 denies the sortie.

87 Cic. *ad Brut.* I.3.4, cf. *Fam.* x.21.4.

88 Cic. *Fam.* XI.21.2, 5 (the commission was not apparently sent to deal with land).

Pompeius, who was now in Massilia, probably building up his powers, was given a naval command.[89] These acts might indeed seem to mark the revival of the Pompeian cause.

Jubilation was premature. The death of the moderate consuls, who formed some sort of buffer between young Caesar and the 'liberators', precipitated disaster. Octavian was refusing to obey Decimus Brutus – and indeed it seems his troops would not have let him do so.[90] Decimus' own forces were in a pitiful way, as he tells Cicero in one of a series of letters of the highest interest; and so Antony got a head start.[91] Antony's legate Ventidius was coming up with three legions raised in the veteran colonies and in his own home area, Picenum. Octavian, it appears, made no attempt to stop them;[92] and Antony, after a hard march to Liguria – according to Plutarch, he was always at his best in adversity – was able to join them. His force was now stronger than that of Decimus Brutus (still in pursuit). And by a feint he soon slipped over the border to Gallia Narbonensis.[93] Lepidus' army there was now the best in the West, with many *evocati* from Caesar's colonies in the province.[94] He had proclaimed his loyalty to the *res publica* in letters, but no one trusted him. He had not punished officers giving aid and comfort to Antony; he now blamed his troops for fraternizing with the newcomers (as they doubtless did), inviting Antony into their camp, and finally 'in their desire for peace' going over to him entirely. Antony from the start of the war had been promising the now usual 2,000 sesterces plus vast benefits on victory. Lepidus followed his men's example; his legate Laterensis fell on his sword.[95]

Plancus still wrote loyally, claiming to have eluded Lepidus' and Antony's advance against him, and D. Brutus was able to join him; but Pollio, coming up from Spain with troops whom he had for some time complained of as unreliable (many of them had served Caesar and some had received Antony's promises) and who had himself been a friend of the dictator, though not, he maintained, of autocracy, threw off the allegiance to the Senate which he had been maintaining under consider-

[89] App. *BCiv.* III.74, Dio XLVI.40.1, Livy *Ep.* 120–1; Cic. *Fam.* XI.19.1.

[90] Botermann 1968 (C 177) 74ff suggests from *Phil.* XI.37 that two of his legions, the Seventh and Eighth, of Campanian *evocati*, had been on strike, unwilling to fight Antony. But they took part in the battles in April.

[91] Cic. *Fam.* XI.13.1 (D. Brutus to Cicero).

[92] App. *BCiv.* III.66 with dubious story of a previous march on Rome to seize Cicero by Ventidius. We do not know his route now; perhaps Octavian could not have stopped him, Bengtson 1974 (C 172) 513. But he is said to have made a point of caring for Antony's wounded.

[93] Plut. *Ant.* 17.2 Shackleton Bailey *ap.* Cic. *Fam.* XI.15.4 denies Antony's threat to Pollentia was a feint.

[94] Cic. *Fam.* X.32. Lepidus' army, Botermann 1968 (C 177) 197ff, seven legions.

[95] Cic. *Fam.* X.8.3, from Plancus; 10.31, from Pollio in the winter, complaining of lack of orders from the Senate and that Lepidus intercepts his mail, cf. 10.32 (June).

able difficulties, and reconciled Plancus (whose troops naturally wanted a share in the rewards going) with Antony. D. Brutus fled, in the desperate hope of reaching Macedonia by land; but he was betrayed by a Gallic chieftain hoping for Antony's favour, and killed.[96]

Cicero was appalled by these successive blows. He begged M. Brutus to bring his troops to Italy, but Brutus – as the Senate had indeed bidden him do when regularizing Cassius' position – had turned east to Thrace and Asia.[97] The prospect of elections for suffect consuls, and for the magistracies of 42, paralysed Rome; Octavian was demanding to stand for the consulship, according to one version finally proposing to do so with Cicero.[98] Plutarch says he later confessed to trying to play on the old man's ambition, but in the surviving letters Cicero opposes Octavian's desire, which he blames on his 'friends'. Octavian was also well aware that Cicero and the Senate were simply using him, and indeed that there was attributed to the former a saying that the young man was to be praised, rewarded and raised up – or removed, as the same word implies.[99] His action, or lack of it, immediately after the relief of Mutina, however, suggests that he was ready for a deal with Antony before senatorial hostility to himself or his troops – later his excuse, and perhaps exaggerated in the apologetic tradition[100] – became apparent.

The men were persuaded that only his consulship would ensure them their rewards. A party of them, led by a centurion, arrived in Rome to demand it.[101] The Senate refused. So, in early August, a Caesar crossed the Rubicon again, this time with eight willing legions. Attempts to negotiate (Octavian concealed an offer by the Senate to pay 10,000 sesterces immediately to the Fourth and Martian legions) and to organize resistance under the praetors failed; for the previously summoned three legions from Africa – they had served under Caesar, and who now was there to command them in the Republic's name? – went over, as did the *legio urbana*. The Senate now offered 10,000 sesterces to all Octavian's men, and the consulship to him. He was camped outside Rome. At the last minute Cicero seems to have made a final attempt at opposition, based on a rumour that the Fourth and Martian legions, whose Republican principle he had so often proclaimed, had mutinied. Finally the senators streamed miserably out to greet Octavian; even Cicero came, though one of the last, as Octavian pointedly observed.[102] The praetor Cornutus killed himself.

96 D. van Berchem 1966 (C 174).

97 Cic. *ad Brut.* I.15.12, 18.1, 5.4 (May 4).

98 App. *BCiv.* III.82, Dio XLVI.42.2; Plut. *Cic.* 45.5–6, Cic. *ad Brut.* I.10.3.

99 Cic. *Fam.* XI.20.1, cf. 21.1 and Vell. Pat. II.62.6. Cicero does not explicitly deny he said this. *Pace* Velleius, Shackleton Bailey doubts if *tollere* alone can mean 'raise up' as well as 'get rid of' (*ap. Fam.* XI.20.1). 100 Suet. *Aug.* 12. 101 App. *BCiv.* III.88.

102 App. *BCiv.* III.92, hostile to Cicero and the Senate.

Octavian had the final ceremonies legalizing his adoption carried out, and was formally, if irregularly, elected consul on 19 August (he was still only nineteen) with Q. Pedius, Caesar's nephew and heir to a part of his estate; the implications were clear. Octavian's adoption was confirmed. The declarations that Antony and Dolabella were *hostes* were repealed; Caesar's assassins – and Sextus Pompeius – were condemned and outlawed *in absentia*.[103] All available moneys were seized; the soldiers all got their 10,000 sesterces on account, and the plebs received Caesar's legacies in full. Very soon Octavian was back in Cisalpine Gaul; here, with stringent security overseen by Lepidus, he met Antony, and to the joy of both armies was reconciled with him. The troops insisted he marry Antony's step-daughter. Years later, at Brundisium, they were still pressing for full reconciliation between the two men they saw as Caesar's heirs.

The confederates now set themselves up as *IIIviri* for the reorganization of the state, *rei publicae constituendae*, for five years (a law was to be passed in Rome). Octavian and Antony were to pursue the war against Caesar's murderers, with twenty legions each. In 59 B.C. the whole empire had perhaps fifteen legions in arms; now there were over sixty,[104] and doubtless auxiliary troops to match. Antony was to keep Cisalpine and Transalpine Gaul, Lepidus Narbonensis and Spain, Octavian, still the junior partner, was to get Africa, Sardinia and Sicily (where he was likely to have trouble with Sex. Pompeius). They were in desperate need of money and land for the troops. And so, after lengthy bargaining as to who should be 'pricked down', they issued an edict declaring, if Appian has correctly recorded the sense,[105] that Caesar's *clementia* had been a failure, appending a list of men to be killed. According to the historians 300 senators and 2,000 *equites* perished, though many of the proscribed escaped, to Macedonia or to Sex. Pompeius in Sicily, in spite of the price (including freedom for slaves) put on their heads. Their property would not be enough to satisfy all demands, so eighteen of the richest towns in Italy, with their territories, were to be given to the soldiers. The peninsula was to be in turmoil for years as a result of what almost amounted to an accidental social revolution. Such was the triumvirs' response to the neutrals' and crypto-Antonians' pleas for peace.

While in Rome Octavian had apparently allowed, or forced, Cicero to retire to his villa at Tusculum in the Alban hills. But Antony made sure that he, with his brother and nephew – and his son, but he was with M. Brutus and survived – were on the fatal list. Cicero tried half-heartedly to

[103] One juror, P. Silicius Corona, voted to absolve; he survived till the proscriptions, App. *BCiv.* III.95, IV.27, Plut. *Brut.* 27.3, Dio XLVI.49.5.

[104] Brunt 1971 (A 16) 449, 473; perhaps 4,000–5,000 in a legion.

[105] App. *BCiv.* IV.8–11 (claiming to give a translation of the Latin).

flee by sea to Macedonia, but on 7 December was caught and killed at his villa at Caieta. He seems in the end to have died bravely.[106]

His role in the final struggle, with which his name is indissolubly linked, has been judged diversely. After November 44 there are no letters to Atticus, who perhaps destroyed from caution any written (but both men were in Rome till near the end). The sources of Dio and Appian are uncertain, and not unbiased.[107] There are however the fourteen *Philippics*, and some fascinating letters to and from M. and D. Brutus and other important figures. It is clear that Cicero was not in unchallenged control at Rome, even after Pansa's departure; he complains bitterly about the other consulars dragging their feet, and though he says he does not distrust the consuls, as many do, he finds them lacking in 'wisdom and energy'.[108] And, as ever, there were those, both in Rome and the provinces, who disliked or distrusted him – he himself speaks of 'envy' reviving against him.[109] But he praises the spirit of the Senate as a whole; indeed after the battle of Mutina it seems to have taken the bit between its teeth and gone further, in an attempt to reassert its supremacy and cut Octavian at least down to size, than Cicero thought wise. But it was soon riven by disagreement and distracting intrigues over the elections. 'The Senate was my tool, and it has fallen to pieces.'[110]

His influence had none the less been great; Antony's letter to Hirtius and Octavian saw him as the impresario or 'manager of gladiators' of the whole war, and M. Brutus blamed him bitterly for raising up Octavian till the youth was as much a tyrant as Antony. As Brutus wrote to Atticus, 'I know that he has always acted with the best of intentions ... But he seems to me to have done some things unskilfully, though the most experienced of men; or from personal ambition, though he did not hesitate to incur the enmity of Antony in all his power for his country's sake.'[111] Brutus it seems was trying to keep open the option of joining Antony against Octavian – he treated Antony's brother Gaius very correctly, a clemency that Cicero deplored;[112] and indeed we are told that Antony wrote to Octavian in the summer threatening to join the 'liberators' if his overtures were rejected. It will be recalled that Lepidus was Brutus' brother-in-law. But could such an alliance have brought long-term peace and constitutional stability to the Republic?

Cicero told Brutus that there had been no alternative to using

106 Frag. of letter from Cic. to Oct. *ap.* Non. 436.22. Death, Plut. *Cic.* 47–9, perhaps ultimately from the slave eyewitnesses, using Tiro's biography and other sources; see Homeyer 1964 (B 45).

107 Appian, Magnino 1984 (B 67) Bk. 3 (introd.): not solely Pollio; Dio, Manuwald 1979 (B 70) (not Livy).

108 Cic. *Fam.* XII.4, X.28, XII.5; *ad Brut.* II.1.1.

109 Cic. *Phil.* VIII.30; XII.50, *Fam.* XII.5.3.

110 Cic. *Fam.* XI.14.1 (to D. Brutus, late May).

111 Cic. *ad Brut.* I.17.1; the authenticity of this letter has been queried, recently by Shackleton Bailey *ad loc.*, but not disproved.

112 Cic. *ad Brut.* I.2a.2 'if we are to be merciful, civil wars will never cease'; Vell. Pat. II.65.1.

Octavian.[113] Had his ill-assorted coalition, however, had any chance of success? The *Philippics* may seem unrealistic; they insist that the people are loyal to the *res publica*, and so is all Italy, with its freshly raised citizen soldiers, who will outweigh the veterans. In fact, if the people cheered Cicero, it was perhaps largely as Octavian's friend; Ventidius and others could recruit for Antony in Italy; and anyway the new levies were largely irrelevant, except as an added expense. A vivid passage of Appian shows the veterans at Forum Gallorum performing terrible and silent execution on each other, to the amazement of the new recruits[114] (the Martian legion was ready to fight Antony, from whom it could expect no mercy; its men were hardly inspired by Republican ardour, as Cicero claims). Furthermore, finance was a crushing problem. Cassius and Brutus were squeezing every drachma from the East – it is likely that they offered their troops the going rate in rewards[115] – and one doubts if the revenues from the West, where all the governors were probably strengthening their armies, were coming in either. Various festivals at Rome had to be suspended. The momentous step was taken of reimposing *tributum*, direct tax on citizens (abolished in 167 B.C.), but the rich were recalcitrant.[116] One may note that in the *De Officiis* Cicero had declared direct taxation an absolute last resort, bound to be resisted.[117] As a result the vital pay (doubled by Caesar, as we saw) and rewards for the troops were delayed or cut down; and the soldiers doubtless recalled the Senate's bad record, even in more normal times, over agrarian legislation. Rewards and honours had also to be distributed to the generals, and these honours, irregular or exaggerated, made a bad basis for the restoration of Republican government; Brutus reproached Cicero for the way he scattered them around, though in fact he was not the worst culprit.[118]

Cicero was aware of these problems, though perhaps not far enough in advance. But it could not be foreseen how formidably single-minded the 'boy' was to prove. The death of the two consuls at once was very bad luck; without it Antony might have been trapped, or seen his forces scattered and unable to join Ventidius. Even after Cicero's death the cause of the 'liberators' might have triumphed; its defeat at Philippi was not a foregone conclusion. For Tacitus that was the end of the Republic, now left defenceless: *nulla iam publica arma*.[119] Yet one doubts if the slide

[113] Cic. *ad Brut.* I.15, a long letter of self-defence.

[114] App. *BCiv.* III.68, possibly rhetoric.

[115] Botermann 1968 (C 177) 94 for Brutus, 104ff for Cassius.

[116] Nicolet 1976 (G 174) 87ff; cf. Cic. *Fam.* XII.30.4; *ad Brut.* I.18.5 (July) refers to a 1 per cent *tributum*, Dio XLVI.31.3 a 4 per cent tax on capital plus 4 obols for every tile on a senator's house. Cic. made armourers work without pay and exacted contributions from Antonians, App. *BCiv.* III.66.

[117] Cic. *Off.* II.74.

[118] In *ad Brut.* I.15.3–9 he defends himself.

[119] Tac. *Ann.* I.2.1 (Sextus Pompeius also proved a formidable nut to crack but Tacitus implies his *arma* were *privata*.)

to disaster could have been reversed; the causes of the Republic's decline went too deep.

In the short term its collapse can be laid at the door of Caesar and 'Caesar's ghost', which many historians have seen ominously active. It was a desire to succeed to at any rate some of his power and splendour, and to base it as he had done on the army, that led the dynasts of 44–43 to oppose the Senate's claims to rule. Octavian at least perhaps also really desired to avenge his death, in a society where family *pietas* and personal *dolor* were proper motives for action, for all Cicero might say about duty to the state. It was loyalty to Caesar (though also desire to be sure of the land he had given them) that made many veterans willing to follow only those who had ties with him, and to press for their reconciliation with each other and for vengeance on his killers.[120] It was Caesar who had set the precedent for vast donatives; and it was the great concentrations of wealth that he had amassed that encouraged Octavian and Antony to make their 'poisoned gifts'. Perhaps also admiration for Caesar and his reforms led some intelligent men to reject the idea of a return to the old regime, with its outdated role for the urban plebs, and its nervous and corrupt Senate unable to keep order in the streets, control the generals or agree on major reforms.

Cicero analysed the *res publica* more profoundly than any other Roman thinker of his time. He understood some of the shortcomings of Sulla's attempted restoration of it; he saw the misbehaviour of the Senate Sulla had left in uncontrolled charge, and that the people could not now be deprived of the tribunate to which they had for so long been strongly attached.[121] But he was too devoted to Roman – and Greek – tradition to see all the problems clearly, at least when he wrote his political treatises in the late fifties. He put his faith in the old ideal of the mixed constitution, viewing the consuls, the Senate and the People with their tribunes as balancing and checking each other in a way they did not now do, if they ever had;[122] rather, their ill-defined powers resulted in continual friction (did tradition, *mos maiorum*, prescribe that a consul should obey the Senate? could the Senate in a crisis override popular rights?). Cicero would also have liked to see strong censors, always in office, decide what the law was and who was breaking it, and this might have helped to control great individuals, and the senators in general.[123] Since we have the *De Republica* and *De Legibus* in incomplete form, we should be careful what we say Cicero failed to understand or find a remedy for. But his comprehension of the social and economic grievances of the poor was certainly deficient, and the liberty to which he was devoted was a narrow aristocratic concept. He does also seem to have

[120] Cic. *Phil.* XIII.35 (Antony in his letter to Hirtius and Octavian).

[121] Cic. *Leg.* III.19ff. [122] Esp. *Rep.* II.41ff. [123] Cic. *Leg.* III.46ff.

been slow to realize the danger from great generals, and was not himself without blame in the matter of *extraordinariae potestates* (had he not supported the Lex Manilia?). But by the end he knew that 'we are the playthings, my dear Brutus, of the whims of the troops and the arrogance of their generals'.[124]

[124] Cic. *ad Brut.* 1.10.3.

CHAPTER 13

THE CONSTITUTION AND PUBLIC CRIMINAL LAW

DUNCAN CLOUD

I. THE ROMAN CONSTITUTION

In what sense can one talk of 'the Roman constitution'? Clearly, Rome had no written constitution of the type introduced into the modern world by the United States in 1787, but did Rome have a constitution in the weaker sense one uses in speaking of the British constitution? The answer must be both 'yes' and 'no'. Bolingbroke in 1734 (*A Dissertation upon Parties*, Letter 10 *ad init.*) offers a working definition: 'By *Constitution*, We mean, whenever We speak with Propriety and Exactness, that Assemblage of Laws, Institutions and Customs, derived from certain fixed Principles of Reason directed to certain fixed Objects of Publick Good that compose the General System, according to which the Community hath agreed to be governed.' Now it is striking how Cicero in dealing with issues which we would label 'constitutional' appeals to an 'Assemblage', to use Bolingbroke's word, with which the latter, and his readers, would have felt immediately at home. For example, when in March 43 the orator wishes to argue that M. Lepidus, the future triumvir currently governing Gallia Narbonensis and Hispania Citerior, cannot do what he likes with his army, he says: 'It is lawful for no man to lead an army against his country, if by lawful we mean (*si licere id dicimus*) that which is allowed by the laws (*legibus*) and by the custom and institutions of our ancestors (*more maiorum institutisque*.)'[1] Sometimes Cicero adds the notion of *ius*, roughly equivalent to 'right' or 'justice'; for instance, he summarizes as follows an attack by L. Aurelius Cotta on the manner in which Clodius had engineered Cicero's exile:

L. Cotta said . . . that nothing in my regard had been carried out rightfully (*iure*), in accordance with the custom of our ancestors or in accordance with the laws: no one can be removed from the body politic without a trial or be the object of a motion or even a judgement involving the loss of civil personality except before the centuriate assembly – Clodius' proceedings had been a case of brute force . . .'[2]

[1] Cic. *Phil.* XII.14.

[2] *Sest.* 73. The translation of 'de civitate tolli' by 'removed from the body politic' is supported by Cicero's usage in *Rosc. Am.* 3, *Clu.* 79, *Sest.* 42 and *Prov. Cons.* 46. I can find no parallel for *de civitate tollere* used in the sense of 'deprive of citizenship', as the Budé and Loeb translators wish.

Another element introduced into what we would regard as constitutional discussions is precedent (*exemplum*): Cicero condemns Gabinius, governor of Syria, for occupying Alexandria although *mos maiorum*, *exempla* and the severest penalties of the law forbade it.[3]

Thus far Cicero seems to be discussing constitutional issues in a thoroughly British manner. But there is one fundamental difference – Cicero does not use the word 'constitution'; Latin lacks any unequivocal equivalent of the word. *Res publica*, sometimes translated 'constitution', is in fact closer to 'state' or 'commonwealth', as the phrases *e re publica*, *contra rem publicam*, indicate; for they mean 'in accordance with/against the interests of the state', not 'constitutionally', 'unconstitutionally'. Of course, there are occasions when it is tempting to translate *iure* or *more maiorum* by 'constitutionally', but we should always remember that *ius* and *mos maiorum* are merely parts of an overarching concept, 'the constitution', which we possess, but the Romans lacked. The Greek words *politeia* and *politeuma* which can mean 'form of government' lend themselves more easily to translation into 'constitution' terminology and it is no doubt precisely because Polybius used these words in his celebrated account of the organization of the Roman state (VI. 11–18) that we find it so natural to talk of the Roman constitution. Nevertheless, if we are to understand the way the *Romans* looked at law and government, we must learn to think like them. This has a couple of consequences.

Firstly, as we have already seen, Cicero when concerned with 'constitutional' issues, usually includes ancestral custom and/or institutions in the list of concepts to be appealed to. But if custom rules, then innovation is *ipso facto* suspect. Thus respectable constitutional change can only be conceptualized in terms of the return to some ancestral norm; when such a norm cannot easily be discerned in the historical record, precedents from the distant Republican past have to be inserted into a suitable context, or context as well as precedent invented. It is noteworthy that the two major 'constitutional' innovations of our period, the Lex Sempronia de capite civis and the *senatus consultum ultimum*, have both been provided with fictitious early Republican pedigrees.[4]

The lack of any unequivocal concept of constitution among the Romans raises a second problem, namely what to include under that head. The offences committed by Gabinius and contemplated by Lepidus, were in fact violations of the Lex Cornelia maiestatis and the Lex Iulia repetundarum; a cluster of offences aimed at preventing magistrates or the Senate from carrying out their duties were dealt with

[3] *Pis.* 50.

[4] For an episode invented to assail the Senate's custom of setting up special courts dealing with capital offences, see Livy IV.50–1 (414–413 B.C.); for a more lively story invented partly to support the custom, see Livy VIII.18 (331 B.C.).

by the *leges de vi*. For a Roman such acts constituted infringements of *ius publicum* (public law) and by the end of our period were handled by a number of permanent criminal courts (*quaestiones perpetuae*). Such offences we shall discuss in the following section entitled *Ius publicum*; in this section we shall deal with certain 'constitutional' institutions or enactments which did not involve recourse to permanent criminal courts. Nearly all of these relate to the citizen's *caput* – a word which in this context can be roughly paraphrased as 'life and civil personality' and the question at issue is the extent to which a citizen's life is sacrosanct.

The literal meaning of the word *caput* is 'head'. The head as the most obviously vital part comes to mean 'life' and then 'civil rights', since a citizen deprived of these ceases to exist as a citizen. *Caput* can even mean 'free status'. This complex of meanings can be attested for the second century[5] and is perhaps of native growth. Loss of *caput* arouses emotion, but emotion of a selective kind. To ascribe to Romans of our period an across-the-board horror at the idea of killing, even killing Roman citizens, would be absurd.

However, what did raise the emotional temperature was treating a citizen as if he were a slave. In virtue of his summary powers of jurisdiction (*coercitio*) a magistrate could have a slave flogged or executed, but he was forbidden to do either to a citizen without due process of law, probably even on active service.[6] This freedom from the arbitrary exercise of power by a magistrate is known as *provocatio ad populum* (appeal to the people). We have been conditioned by Mommsen into thinking of *provocatio* as an appeal to a higher court, in this context the centuriate assembly. This way of looking at *provocatio* is inappropriately legalistic; there is no evidence of any citizen 'appealing' against a flogging or a death-sentence from a magistrate to the *comitia*. The citizen's right to *provocatio* was a challenging reminder to any magistrate tempted to thrash or execute a citizen in summary fashion that such conduct was an affront to the nature of Roman citizenship. Regard for his own *existimatio* coupled with fear of the sympathetic violence of the crowd, the 'people' to whom the threatened citizen appealed, ready, at times, to support the citizen's challenge,[7] were factors that would normally deter the tyrannically inclined magistrate, but if a governor like

[5] For *caput* = 'life', Ter. *An.* 677, probably also Plaut. *Asin.* 132; for *caput* = 'civil personality', Plaut. *Pseud.* 1232; for *caput* = 'free status', Plaut. *Merc.* 153.

[6] Livy X.9.4. In 122 Livius Drusus proposed that the Latins should have *provocatio* against flogging even on military service (Plut. *C. Gracch.* 9): *a fortiori*, Roman citizens already had *provocatio* against capital punishment and flogging on active service. See A. H. M. Jones 1972 (F 89) 23–5 for other evidence. However, as Roman soldiers were frequently decimated in the first century B.C. (see Plut. *Crass.* 10, Suet. *Aug.* 24.2, Dio XLI.35), their right of appeal seems to have had little value by then and was formally abolished by Augustus under the Lex Iulia de vi (Paulus *Sent.* V.26.2).

[7] Livy II.55 provides an imaginative picture of what a tyrannical magistrate might expect from bystanders sympathetic to his victim.

Verres was determined to ignore the crowd and execute a Roman citizen, as Verres did in the case of P. Gavius of Cosa, then nothing could be done to stop him or punish him. All the same, the concept must still have carried emotional weight to justify Cicero's hyperbolical language.[8] However it is unlikely that any *provocatio* legislation was passed during the period covered by this volume; the famous Lex Porcia was sponsored either by the elder Cato in 195 or by P. Porcius Laeca, tribune in 199.[9]

It is not only individuals who can threaten a citizen's *caput*. When C. Gracchus passed his statute *de capite civis* which enacted that no capital sentence could be passed on a citizen without the sanction of the people, his was not yet another *provocatio* law, for his target was not the despotic magistrate, but the special courts set up by the Senate alone without the sanction of the assembly;[10] these had become a controversial institution as soon as one was set up in 132 to punish and execute the supporters of his brother.

This Lex Sempronia, by complicating the processes necessary to establish special courts, may have given a fillip to the growth of the regular criminal courts that form the main subject of this chapter; for these, being set up by a statute of the assembly, did not infringe the Gracchan *lex*. However, according to the standard and plausible interpretation of events, the *optimates* riposted with an appeal to another aspect of *mos*, the tradition that in a state of emergency the consuls must preserve the safety of the state.[11] Indeed, in 133 the Senate had urged the consul P. Mucius Scaevola to defend the state with arms, but he declined and Scipio Nasica took the law into his own hands. In 121, in a similar situation, the consul L. Opimius did respond and the death of C. Gracchus along with many of his followers was the result.

Such an empowering by the Senate of the consuls to protect the state at a time of national emergency is known nowadays as the *senatus consultum ultimum* (hereinafter *scu*). This was probably never a technical term in the Republic and suggests a precise procedural and formulaic structure unsupported by the ancient evidence; there are variations in the wording of the *senatus consultum* and in the number and status of the magistrates invited to act. From 88 onwards named persons are usually designated as *hostes* (public enemies), but by a decision of the Senate distinct from the *scu*. For example, as the Catilinarian conspiracy

[8] In *De Or.* II.199 he calls *provocatio* 'patronam illam civitatis ac vindicem libertatis'.

[9] The scanty evidence points to Cato the censor as author of the law; the language of Livy X.9.4. echoes a fragment of a speech by the elder Cato (Festus p. 266 Lindsay). On the other hand, the celebrated denarius minted *c.* 110 by P. Porcius Laeca (see Crawford 1974 (B 144) 313–14) enhances the claims of his namesake, the tribune of 199, as the statute's author. Perhaps there were two statutes.

[10] See Stockton 1979 (C 137) 117–21 and refs.

[11] See Lintott 1968 (A 62) 159–68; Strachan-Davidson 1912 (F 150) I.240–5.

developed in the course of 63, the *scu* was passed in October, but the decree declaring Catiline and his lieutenant Manlius *hostes* was not passed until the following month. Sometimes a *tumultus*, a state of military emergency, is declared and sometimes a levy of citizens is imposed.[12] Nevertheless, there is a sufficient family likeness between each use of the senatorial decree for *scu* to be a useful shorthand expression. The first instance of the *scu* is in 121 and the last in 43.[13]

It does not get us very far to ask whether the *scu* was 'constitutional' or not. For if we regard *provocatio*, as statutorily defined by the Lex Porcia, as a constitutional right, then Opimius undoubtedly infringed it in 121 by putting to death citizens without a trial and when duly prosecuted in a popular court he ought to have been condemned; instead, he was acquitted.[14] It is more helpful to think of a conflict between two Roman traditions, the right of the citizen to a trial when his *caput* is at stake, and the right of the community to take every step to protect itself from destruction. The latter is the more fundamental of the two rights and that is why the citizen in the field (*militiae*), despite *provocatio*, accepted summary execution from his commander. But as these 'rights' are more in the nature of gut-feelings than constitutional guarantees, then the same act can be regarded as legitimate one year and criminal a few years later, when the feelings have changed, as Cicero was to find to his cost.

Two points are worth making about the *scu*. Firstly, it did not formally give the consuls, or whoever were enjoined to act, powers that they did not have before[15] but gave them rather more than moral support in taking the strongest possible action. It was rather more than moral support in two ways: it was a recognition by the supreme council of state that a state of emergency existed and, by acting in its traditional role as council (*consilium*) to the supreme magistrates, it put extreme pressure on those magistrates to act *de consilii sententia*, in accordance with their council's opinion. For as we shall see, it was generally accepted that persons inviting the advice of a *consilium* would normally take that advice.

The second point is that the *scu* was passed so as to enable the magistrates to *execute* citizens with or without a trial. It is extremely rare for citizens condemned on a capital charge to lose their lives: they lose their civil personalities by being interdicted – in effect, banished – and

[12] In 77, the decree was addressed to the *interrex*, a proconsul and other holders of *imperium* (Sall. *H.* I.77.22M). The decree of 52 (Asc. 34C) was similar. One consul only was addressed in 121 (Cic. *Phil.* V.34). A *tumultus* was decreed in 77 (Sall. *H.*I.69M; III.48.9M), 63 (Dio XXXVII.31.1), 49 (Dio XLI.3.3) and 43 (Cic. *Phil.* VIII.2–3; XIV.2). For the levy in that year see Cic. *Phil.* VIII.32, but there had been one in 63 (Dio XXXVII.33.3 and 40.2; Cic. *Cat.* IV.17). See also refs. in n. 19.

[13] See the list in Greenidge 1971 (F 68) 400–6. The fate of Q. Salvidienus Rufus in 40 (Vell. Pat. II.76.4) may be a further example.

[14] Livy *Epit.* LXI; Cic. *Sest.* 140.

[15] The point is well made by Last *CAH* IX¹ 84–5, cited in Lintott 1968 (A 62) 156–7.

assume the citizenship of some other place,[16] but are not physically killed, a point noted in the speech put into Caesar's mouth by Sallust in the debate on the fate of the Catilinarian conspirators.[17] However, it is much more tolerable to put enemies of the state to death; to declare that a citizen has become a *hostis publicus* is to assimilate him not simply to the citizen of a foreign state, like an interdicted Roman, but to a member of an actively hostile country. The proscriptions of Sulla (82–81) and the triumvirs (43–42) illustrate the point. In those cases legislation or the powers assigned to the triumvirs[18] not merely deprived the proscribed of civil existence and property but declared them *hostes publici* and it was in virtue of this new status as public enemies that they were put to death. No doubt that is why from 88 onwards it was customary for the Senate to add the naming of specified persons as *hostes* to the issuing of the *scu*; herein may lie a reason for Cicero treating the Senate as his *consilium* in the most formal way possible at the debate of 5 December 63; for by this time the naming of *hostes* had become so much the norm that not to name some persons might be regarded as putting them in a less heinous class than persons named. Moreover, this was the first time that an ex-consul was among the potential victims of the *scu* – P. Lentulus Sura had been consul in 71.[19]

We turn next to a small number of developments which have as their common focus the Roman magistracies. Most are connected with Sulla. In 82 Sulla revived the dictatorship in a somewhat different form from the type of dictatorship last seen at Rome in 202; the earlier type had a maximum duration of six months but Sulla's had no time-limit attached to it. On the other hand, if we may trust Appian's intrinsically plausible account,[20] it had this in common with the earlier model, that it was for a purpose, 'to enact such laws as he might deem fittest and to establish a constitution, *epi . . . katastasei tēs politeias*'. Appian's Greek is clearly an attempt to translate the traditional Roman title, *dictator legibus scribundis et rei publicae constituendae*, and since Sulla did in fact enact a large number of laws and set the state in order, Appian is probably right about the nature of Sulla's dictatorship. Sulla came closer than any other legislator, except perhaps Augustus, to producing for Rome a code of criminal law, but he was also active in what we would term constitutional matters. He increased the number of quaestors from eight to twenty, made the quaestorship obligatory for those who wished to proceed to higher office and probably fixed the minimum age for the quaestorship at

[16] Cic. *Caecin.* 100; *Dom.* 78. [17] Sall. *Cat.* 51.22.

[18] In the case of Sulla by the Lex Valeria (Cic. *Rosc. Am.* 125); the triumvirs received their powers from the Lex Titia of 43.

[19] For the specification of Catiline and Manlius as *hostes*, see Sall. *Cat.* 36.2; for Cicero's fastening of *hostis*-status upon P. Cornelius Lentulus Sura, see Cic. *Cat.* IV.11 and 22.

[20] *BCiv.* I.99.

thirty.[21] His purpose in increasing the number of quaestors was to ensure a regular infusion of new blood into the Senate. It is often said that Sulla abolished the censorship but the only evidence for this is the fact that no censors were elected between 82 and 70. It is however a little rash to suppose that Sulla envisaged the total elimination of the censorship. He had used his dictatorship as a kind of super-censorship; he had ensured that the Senate would be regularly replenished but he had devised no mechanisms for expelling those who showed themselves unworthy of the order or for making periodical enrolments of the population; these functions were presumably still to be carried out by the censors. Sulla is also said to have increased the number of praetors from six to eight,[22] supposedly to provide presidents of some status for the permanent criminal courts (*quaestiones perpetuae*) which he had created or reconstituted. He drastically reduced the powers of the tribunes,[23] but though they regained their powers in 70, a decade of impotence contributed to one permanent effect: Sulla's *quaestiones perpetuae* effectively replaced the assemblies as criminal courts. Even though tribunes could once again prosecute on capital charges in the assembly, they seem to have done so seldom.

The final 'constitutional' topic that calls for some comment is *imperium*. The late Republic was faced with two potentially contradictory needs: on the one hand, it needed to adapt to the requirements of an empire institutions which had been framed for the administration of a city state, for adaptation rather than innovation was almost inevitable, given the Roman attitude to *mos* and *instituta maiorum*. On the other hand, it was necessary to find ways of preventing over-mighty magistrates, promagistrates and private citizens from overthrowing the Republican system by some form of *coup*. The first problem was handled in two ways; one was to bestow on individuals *imperium* (the administrative power of higher magistrates) for a specific purpose and over a specific area; for example, M. Antonius in 74 and Pompey in 67 were each given *imperium* covering the whole Mediterranean sea-coast and in Pompey's case for fifty Roman miles inland in order to deal with the pirates. Yet their *imperium* was no greater than that of any individual provincial governor whose *imperium* overlapped with theirs, it merely covered a larger geographical area. Pompey's sole consulship for part of

[21] For the increase in the number of quaestors and its purpose, see Tac. *Ann.* XI.22; for the quaestorship as a compulsory first stage in the *cursus honorum* see App. *BCiv.* I. 100. That Sulla fixed the minimum age for holding the quaestorship at thirty is a plausible inference from Cic. *Phil.* V.46. See, however, Seager in ch. 6 above, p. 201.

[22] The evidence for Sulla increasing the number of praetors from six to eight is circumstantial and ambiguous (see Cloud 1988 (F 37)).

[23] Sulla would seem to have deprived the tribunes of their right to convene meetings of the Senate (though there is no direct statement to this effect in the sources); he restricted their use of *intercessio* (Cic. II *Verr.* I.155) and abolished their right to initiate legislation (Livy *Epit.* LXXXIX, in defence of whom see Keaveney 1982 (C 88) 186–7 n. 3 and Ferrary 1985 (F 52) 440–2).

52 gave one man greater *imperium* than any other magistrate possessed, but at least the consulship was an annual office and Pompey's supreme power could not have been made to last longer than a year without recourse to other statutory instruments.

Much more contentious was the response of Sulla and Caesar to the problem, namely the assumption of the dictatorship itself; for the dictator's *imperium* overrode that of all other magistrates and Sulla's dictatorship was untraditional in that it was not conferred for a fixed period; however, inasmuch as it was conferred for specific and traditional purposes, namely the promulgation of laws and the settling of the state, there was at least the implication that when Sulla had completed these tasks he would lay down his dictatorship, as in fact happened. However, Caesar's last two dictatorships were even more untraditional and thus even more unacceptable than Sulla's by the standard of *mos maiorum*: the third, conferred after the battle of Thapsus in 46, had no specific field and was untraditional in that it was to be for ten years, though probably annually renewable, while the fourth, conferred in 44, went further and was both general in scope and bestowed in perpetuity. It was because this last development gave Caesar the powers of a pre-Republican king and thus, like other measures treated elsewhere in this volume, affronted the whole Republican tradition, that tyrannicide, itself a traditional concept, became a persuasive option.

The late Republic found it impossible to cope with the other problem, the over-mighty magistrate, promagistrate and private citizen. Indeed, the measures described in the previous paragraph tended rather to exacerbate it. Ironically in view of their careers Sulla and Caesar, as we shall see, tried toughening up the statutes regulating the conduct of provincial governors (the *leges maiestatis* and *repetundarum*) and Sulla reaffirmed the old rules regulating the assumption of magistracies.[24] But it was left for Augustus to devise ways of dealing with the problem that were to work quite successfully for a century.

II. *IUS PUBLICUM*

At this point we encounter a difficulty which is the opposite of the one we had to face at the beginning of the chapter: whereas the Romans had no word that exactly corresponds to our 'constitution', we have no word that corresponds to the Roman phrase, *ius publicum*. Cicero uses the

[24] Sulla seems to have confirmed existing regulations defining the minimum ages for holding curule offices (thirty-six for the aedileship, thirty-nine for the praetorship and forty-two for the consulship), as well as enforcing a two-year gap between each office and a ten-year period before anyone could hold the same magistracy a second time (App. *BCiv*. 1.100).

phrase frequently but does not define it.[25] From a passage in one of his rhetorical treatises a number of points are clear:[26] first, public law is contrasted with private law which is in turn virtually equated with civil law. Secondly, its field is defined by the interests, functions and organization of the state. In practice, *ius publicum* includes constitutional, administrative and criminal law. It can even include sacral law.[27] It is thus not equivalent to our statute law, since sacral law was seldom the product of legislation. This presents the British historian with a problem: not only is 'public law' an odd expression in English, since we have no 'droit public' or 'diritto pubblico', but there is no word for an infringement of public law; the Roman jurists, when they eventually felt the need for such a word, used *crimen* (which actually means 'crime' in post-Ciceronian Latin) and its cognates.[28]

The main feature of Roman public law during our period is the establishment of a series of permanent courts (*quaestiones perpetuae*) with a field mainly concerned with crime, though one court was wholly and two others partly concerned with constitutional matters. Anyhow, because the term is applicable to most of their activities, they will be referred to as 'criminal courts' and their field as 'crime', as indeed is the convention in English discussions of the subject. The first of these permanent courts was established in 149, but, since crime did not suddenly come into existence in that year, our first task must be to look briefly at the ways in which the community at Rome dealt with grave offences subsequently handled by the permanent courts.

In 149 there existed five ways of dealing with crime.

1. Jurisdiction arising from patria potestas

The most primitive and arguably the most tenacious was the domestic power of the *pater familias*. From earliest times the male head of the household possessed absolute power in virtue of his *patria potestas* not only over his slaves and freedmen but over all sons and daughters in his *potestas*. These powers antedate law and flow from *mos maiorum*;[29] it is therefore, strictly speaking, improper to speak of the father's domestic 'court' or his 'jurisdiction'. Nevertheless, his procedure when one member of his extended household (*familia*) was suspected of commit-

[25] *Balb.* 34, 64; *Brut.* 222, 267, 269; *Dom.* 33, 34, 128, 136; *Fam.* IV.4.3, IV.14.2, VI.1.5; *Har. Resp.* 14; *Mil.* 70; *Off.* 1.64; *De Or.* 1.201, 256; *Rep.* 1.3; *Vat.* 18.

[26] Cic. *De Or.* 1.201. [27] See esp. *Dom.* 136.

[28] For the practice of the early jurists, see Schulz 1946 (F 268) 72–4. For *crimen* = *crime* cf. *Cod. Theod.* 1.12; D.48.1.1.39.

[29] Dion. Hal. (*Ant. Rom.* II.26) asserts that Romulus assigned powers of life and death (*ius vitae necisque*) to the *pater familias*, while Papinian (*Collatio* IV.8.1) ascribes the conferral of these powers to a statute of the regal period. Clearly, the Romans thought *patria potestas* to be an institution virtually as old as Rome itself. See Lacey 1986 (F 231) and Harris 1986 (F 212).

ting a crime, usually, but by no means invariably, against another member of the household,[30] customarily took the shape of an informal trial. He would normally call in his friends to act as a *consilium* or council and he would normally abide by their advice. However, it needs stressing that, although he was *expected* to do both these things, the ultimate decision was his; he was not absolutely *obliged* to call in a *consilium* or accept their decision, as if it were the final verdict of a jury.

2. *The* IIIviri capitales

Turning next to examples of jurisdiction in the strict sense, we find another institution coexisting with the permanent criminal courts, the *IIIviri capitales*. These minor magistrates, over and above supervising the prisons and executions, exercised over slaves a jurisdiction which could be capital.[31] It is also certain that they exercised some measure of criminal jurisdiction over citizens; Cicero reports a case in which a *IIIvir* handles the initial proceedings against a suspected citizen-murderer.[32] Since, in Cicero's tale, the *IIIvir* is bribed to drop the proceedings, we have no means of telling how much further down the procedural line he could have gone, had he chosen to do so, but another piece of evidence suggests that, in certain circumstances, the *IIIviri* had complete criminal jurisdiction over citizens. Varro tells us that the *IIIviri* took over the role of the parricide quaestors in dealing with crimes (*maleficia*).[33] These parricide quaestors dealt with capital crimes committed by citizen against citizen, particularly with murder – hence their name.[34] It therefore follows that their replacements, the *IIIviri*, had the same sort of jurisdiction over citizens. However, it is most unlikely that such relatively minor magistrates could dispense, over citizens of any consequence, the kind of summary justice implied by the references in Plautus,[35] particularly in view of the Romans' already noted passionate feelings about *caput* and its loss. We seem to be led to the conclusion – which another item of evidence, admittedly from a poor source,

[30] From second and first cent. B.C. incest with stepmother (Val. Max. V.9.1), attempted parricide (Sen. *Clem.* I.15) but extorting money from Macedonians in Val. Max. V.8.2.

[31] In Plaut. *Asin.* 131 the speaker threatens to take the madam of a brothel and her daughter before the *IIIviri* on a capital charge. They were presumably of servile status and the cook jokingly threatened with prosecution before the *IIIviri* in *Aul.* 416 for being *cum telo*, to whit carrying a carving-knife, must have been a slave. Despite Mommsen 1899 (F 119) 180 n. 1 there is no solid evidence that the *IIIviri* had civil jurisdiction; their name suffices to suggest that theirs was a criminal competence.

[32] *Clu.* 38–9.

[33] We know the approximate date of the institution of the *IIIviri* since this is given in Livy *Per.* XI in a context which places it *c.* 290–288.

[34] Both Pomponius (D.1.2.2.23) and Gaius (Lydus *Mag.* 1.26) state explicitly that the *parricidi quaestores* had jurisdiction over citizens; this is implied by Festus, *Parricidi Quaestores* (p. 247 Lindsay).

[35] To the references in n. 31 add *Amph.* 155.

supports[36] – that the *IIIviri* probably had full summary jurisdiction only over lower-class citizens (as well as slaves). If so, a puzzling feature about the permanent courts would be explained, namely that, where we have evidence, even those courts that are concerned with crimes like murder and violence which know no class barriers, are hardly ever found dealing with defendants of low standing and the rare exceptions can be explained in terms of the political significance of the crime alleged.[37] The answer to the puzzle will be that the *quaestiones perpetuae* were not normally concerned with insignificant criminals – it was the business of the *IIIviri* to deal with them.

3. The popular assemblies

Another form of criminal jurisdiction in vigour during the second century was that of the popular assemblies. This role of the assemblies has been a subject of hot controversy over the past fifty years; argument has centred firstly on procedure and the role of the assembly-court, secondly on the range of offences covered by the courts and thirdly on the distinction of roles between the various assemblies. The procedure, if carried out in full, could cause a trial to be protracted over parts of several months.[38] The magistrate would accuse the defendant before three informal public meetings (*contiones*) and then finally before the assembly. There is some reason to think that the three preliminary *contiones* could be dispensed with, if necessary;[39] the evidence also suggests the possibility, though *pace* Mommsen no more than the possibility,[40] that if the full procedure was followed, the third accusation was followed by the magistrate's sentence and an appeal by the defendant to the people (*provocatio ad populum*). Against Mommsen's view is the total absence of any mention of *provocatio* in any account of a historical capital trial or in Cicero's account of the four accusations in the *De Domo*, where he mentions the sentence but no appeal. Indeed, since Cicero refers to the fourth accusation as an accusation and not an appeal, he cannot be thinking of the assembly in Mommsenian terms as a court of second instance, any more than he thinks of the sentence (*iudicium*) as a real sentence. If *provocatio* did link the third and fourth accusations, it must have served as a purely procedural link. It may possibly have

36 Ps. Asconius on *Div. Caec.* 50 (= p. 201 Stangl) which suggests summary jurisdiction over *cives*; and in general see Kunkel 1962 (F 92) 71–9.

37 Political reasons appear to be paramount in cases like that in 52 of M. Saufeius, Milo's henchman, prosecuted *de vi* both in Pompey's special court and in the regular *quaestio* for his part in the fracas at Bovillae which led to Clodius' death.

38 When P. Clodius as curule aedile prosecuted Milo for *vis* in 56 the first *accusatio* took place on 2 February, the fourth on 7 May (Cic. *QFr.* II.3.1–2, 6(5).4.).

39 E.g. the trials of M. Postumius of Pyrgia (212) (Livy XXV.3) and C. Claudius Pulcher (169) (Livy XLIII.16).

40 Mommsen 1899 (F 119) 163–74.

functioned in this way; Cicero in his *De Legibus*, a work which is meant to provide a legal system that looks like the traditional second-century legal system, gives *provocatio* an important, if obscure, role in assembly prosecutions and Livy, reporting a procedure alleged to date from regal times, mentions *provocatio* from magistrates with capital powers called *IIviri perduellionis*. This may do no more than confirm that *provocatio* from capital sentences was a topical subject for discussion in the first century B.C. but it could also suggest that it already had some procedural function.[41] In our period, the magistrate who conducted such prosecutions was most usually a tribune. Prosecutions by aediles and quaestors are also attested.[42]

The vast majority of attested prosecutions before the assembly are for *perduellio*, a word usually translated by 'treason' or 'high treason', but perhaps this translation is too limiting. Livy's story of Horatius[43] shows that Livy's source and Livy himself believed that kin-murder could constitute *perduellio* when the murder threatened the interests of the state, in this case by incurring the wrath of the gods towards the community whose champion Horatius had been. In this they were probably right; no doubt the bulk of prosecutions were concerned with treasonable activities in some shape or form, but in principle, and sometimes in practice, other acts that could be construed as injuring the well-being of the community as a whole provided material for assembly prosecutions.[44]

Mommsen maintained that from 449 onwards the only legitimate forum for capital trials was the centuriate assembly, whereas the two tribal assemblies (*comitia populi tributa* and *concilium plebis*) handled cases where the magistrate demanded a fine.[45] Such a distinction is implied by the Twelve Tables[46] but as the Lex Hortensia of 287 gave the plebiscites passed by the *concilium plebis* the same force as the statutes passed by the centuriate assembly, one would have expected both assemblies to possess thereafter the same jurisdictional as well as law-making powers.

[41] Cic. *Dom.* 45, *Leg.* III.6, 12, 27; Livy I.26, where the procedure described may well have been invented to manufacture a precedent for Caesar's prosecution of C. Rabirius in 63.

[42] For the role of tribunes in assembly prosecution see Giovannini 1983 (F 63). Varro cites a manual on quaestorian prosecutions (*Ling.* VI.90–2) and this proves that quaestors could prosecute in some circumstances, perhaps in connexion with their treasury duties.

[43] Livy I.26, see n. 41.

[44] The best example is a prosecution by the plebeian aediles in 213/12 of several matrons for immorality (*stuprum*) reported by Livy (XXV.2.9), since the authenticity of the information is unimpeachable. A case, certainly late third cent., is reported in Val. Max. VI.1.7 where a curule aedile prosecutes a tribune C. Scantinius Capitolinus for making sodomitical advances to his son, and is doubtless basically authentic, even if Valerius has made an error over Scantinius' magistracy.

[45] Mommsen 1888 (A 77) III.1.357–8 and 1899 (F 119) 168.

[46] Twelve Tables 9.1 (*Bruns*) states that only the *comitiatus maximus* can deal with capital charges against citizens (cf. Cic. *Leg.* III.44 and 11) and the *com. max.* was supposed by Cicero to be the archaic name for the *comitia centuriata*.

Livy's account of the trial of M. Postumius Pyrgensis in 212 apparently displays the *concilium plebis* dealing with a capital charge.[47] Mommsen's dichotomy was at best a convention, not an inflexible rule.

Trials before an assembly, referred to in the modern literature as *iudicia populi*,[48] seem to have continued unabated until the 80s, when they become rare.[49] Four reasons may be suggested for this decline: firstly, Sulla in 81 constituted or reconstituted a set of permanent courts covering a wide range of criminal, constitutional and administrative offences, thus rendering assembly prosecutions unnecessary. It is interesting that the one non-political assembly trial that may have taken place after the 80s involves an offence which was at the same time a flagrant breach of *mos* and one not covered by any statute until the principate of Augustus – bribing a married woman to commit adultery.[50] Secondly, given the existence of alternatives, the extreme cumbersomeness of an assembly trial must have told against it; it was slow – as we have seen, a case in 56 took up parts of four of our months. Moreover, the assemblies had legislative and electoral functions to perform as well; citizens were not paid to attend and employed citizens can hardly have wanted to be perpetually away from work. With the extension of the franchise to most of Italy and the sheer logistical difficulties involved in getting to Rome to vote, it may have been felt that the enlarged assemblies should confine their business to what only they could do: elect magistrates, enact legislation and determine issues of high political significance. A fourth reason for the decline in assembly trials was the limitations placed by Sulla on the powers of tribunes who in the period before 81 most commonly initiated assembly prosecutions.[51] Though these powers were restored in 70, eleven years were long enough to consolidate the role of the new criminal courts as the main organ for handling such trials.

4. *The private criminal action*

There must have been some other way of dealing with non-political crimes, above all murder, committed by citizens in the period before the rise of the permanent criminal courts: the assemblies and the *IIIviri* simply could not have coped. If a slave or humble citizen could be hauled

[47] See Livy XXV.3.

[48] As Lintott points out in 1972 (F 102) 246–9, the ancient evidence for this technical sense of *iudicium populi* is slim, though Cicero may have tried to introduce it at *Brut.* 106.

[49] Cicero points out (*Brut.* 106) that the introduction of the ballot into comitial trials as a result of the Lex Cassia of 137 made more work for defending barristers. This implies that they remained an important part of the legal system after 137.

[50] Val. Max. VI.1.8. It all depends which Q. Metellus Celer prosecuted and whether the prosecutor was tribune or aedile at the time. One was consul in 80, the other in 60. This provides us with possible dates of 90–83 and *c.* 72–64 for the prosecution. The cases noted in n. 44 provided precedents.

[51] See n. 23.

off before a *IIIvir* for carrying an offensive weapon,[52] it is incredible that other citizens could not be prosecuted for murder. Kunkel demonstrated that there had existed since archaic times a form of private criminal action which, if successful, led to the convicted party being handed over to the deceased's closest blood-relative.[53] In primitive Rome he would have undoubtedly been sacrificed to the *manes* of the dead man, but by our period his fate was to become the bondsman of the agnate in much the same way as a recalcitrant debtor became the bondsman (*addictus*) of his creditor.[54] The institution of the murder courts in the late second century will have led to the disappearance of this type of prosecution.[55]

5. *The special courts*

The last type of criminal court to be found in the middle of the second century is the special court or commission, referred to in the modern literature without any clear warrant in the ancient sources as the *quaestio extra ordinem* or *extraordinaria*. This century was in fact its heyday, but examples of its use stretch from the latter part of the Second Punic War down to 43.[56] Its main use was to deal with alleged crimes committed by groups, like the Sila Forest murders of 138 or the multiple poisonings of 184.[57] These special commissions set up by the Senate were regarded by Polybius as particularly concerned with crimes committed in Italy and outside the normal jurisdiction of city magistrates; it is certainly the case that a large number of the recorded instances do concern crimes committed beyond the immediate environs of Rome.[58] At first these commissions were often instituted by the Senate alone without the sanction of a popular assembly and yet without causing any disquiet.[59] However, the use of a *senatus consultum* in 132 to set up a commission to inflict capital punishment on persons convicted of being followers of Tiberius Gracchus raised questions about the propriety of such commissions and, as noted already, his brother Gaius' *lex de capite civis* made it

[52] See n. 31.

[53] Kunkel 1962 (F 92) 40–5, with particular reference to Serv. *ad Ecl.* 4.43.

[54] Kunkel 1962 (F 92) 97–130, esp. 104–5 and n. 386. Livy XXIII.14.2–3 combined with Val. Max. VII.6.1, is persuasive for Kunkel's reconstruction.

[55] Kunkel 1962 (F 92) 98–104. A childhood game, according to Plutarch (*Cat. Min.* 2.6) played by the younger Cato (b. 95), is perhaps the latest possible reference to this type of bondage.

[56] The earliest known examples date from 206 (Livy XXVIII.10.4–5) and 204 (Livy XXIX.36.10–12). The last was the court set up by the Lex Pedia in 43 to punish Caesar's murderers.

[57] See Cic. *Brut.* 85–8 for the Sila Forest murders, Livy XXXIX.41.5–6 for the multiple poisonings of 184.

[58] Besides the examples cited in the previous note, cf. also Livy XL.37.4 and XLIII.2–3. Polybius (VI.13.4) asserts the Senate's right to deal with crimes committed in Italy; I take 'demosia episkepsis' to be referring to investigation by special court.

[59] There is no mention of plebiscite or law setting up the special commission that dealt with the secret cult of the Bacchanals in 186, likewise none in connexion with the various poisoning commissions of 184, 181, 180, 179 and 167 (see Jones 1972 (F 89) 27–8 with refs).

illegal to set up such courts without sanction from the people.[60] By adding this new compulsory hurdle, Gaius made the institution of such special commissions a less attractive option. However, they were still employed occasionally to deal with multiple crime especially when committed outside Rome like the fracas at Bovillae in January 52 which ended in the killing of P. Clodius[61] or to deal with offences not covered by any statute, like the appearance of a male in women's clothing at the all-female religious rites of the Bona Dea in 61.[62] Another point needs to be made about these special courts which would distinguish them from the informal 'courts' of the *pater familias* and from the *consilium* of the provincial governor and link them with the permanent criminal courts that partly superseded them: it looks as if the magistrate was merely a court president and the members of the commission decided the issue by their vote.[63]

III. *QUAESTIONES PERPETUAE*

Of cardinal importance for the early history of the permanent criminal courts (*quaestiones perpetuae*) is a passage in Cicero's *Brutus*:

> [C. Papirius Carbo] was regarded as the finest advocate at that period, and, while he dominated the bar, more courts began to be created. For *quaestiones perpetuae* were established when he was a young man and there were none before – L. Piso, as tribune of the plebs, was the first to carry a law *de pecuniis repetundis* [about provincial extortion] in the consulships of Censorinus and Manilius [= 149] ...[64]

Cicero's *Brutus* is a well-researched work and he has no axe to grind here; we should therefore start from the assumption that what he writes is true. If so, certain consequences follow: first, Piso set up the first *quaestio perpetua* and theories that they existed before 149 must be discarded.[65] Secondly, Piso's court must in some sense have been a *quaestio perpetua*

[60] Cic. *Rab. Perd.* 12, *Cat.* IV.10, *Dom.* 82. This interpretation of the Lex Sempronia, set out by Strachan-Davidson 1912 (F 150) I.239–45, is now generally accepted.

[61] Pompey had other reasons for setting up a special court; he wanted a court immune to bribery and to the rhetoric of barristers with plenty of time to introduce irrelevancies. Hence the stringency exercised in selecting the jurors and limiting speeches; see above all the *argumentum* of Asconius (*Mil.* 35–42C).

[62] Our principal source is Cicero's letters to Atticus (I.12, 13, 14 and 16). Interestingly, the *pontifices* are consulted on the morality of the act and it is only when they have declared it *nefas* (*Att.* I.13.3) that the special commission is set up.

[63] The two deferments are 'de consilii sententia' (Cic. *Brut.* 85); the change of *patronus* from Laelius to Galba 'quod is in dicendo atrocior acriorque esset' (*ibid.* 86) and the latter's playing upon the emotions of the jury, 'multis querelis multaque miseratione adhibita' (*ibid.* 88) make it probable that we are dealing with a jury whose verdict, not that of the presiding magistrate, decided the issue.

[64] Cic. *Brut.* 106.

[65] Thus Fascione 1984 (F 49) 44–51, who dates the first permanent *quaestio ambitus* to 159, cannot be right.

and any theory which assumes that C. Gracchus' *repetundae* court was the first real one is unlikely to be right.[66] Thirdly, other *quaestiones perpetuae* must have been set up while Carbo was a young man – Cicero's phrase 'hoc adulescente' could cover a longer span than the above translation might suggest, since *adulescentia* covers from the late teens to the age of forty, but, all the same, since Carbo was born about 160 and died in 119, it is impossible that only the *repetundae* court existed until towards the end of the century and highly unlikely that only that single *quaestio perpetua* existed before the tribunates of C. Gracchus.[67] Another reason for thinking that a number of permanent courts were in existence at least by about 120 is Cicero's reference to the appearance of professional prosecutors in the immediately post-Gracchan period:[68] defence barristers were useful in an assembly trial, but only magistrates could prosecute in the assembly. Cicero's reference must therefore be to the permanent courts, or *iudicia publica*, to use the conventional phrase for such courts and trials before them,[69] since it was one of their distinguishing features that in virtually every one of them any citizen in good standing could prosecute.[70] The appearance of barristers specializing in prosecution consequently indicates the existence of a number of *iudicia publica* in which they could practise their skills.

The revolutionary element in Piso's new court was that it both had a defined field and was always available for use; the extortion of money by governors of the Spanish provinces had been the subject of special procedures in 171, but this was the first time that a *permanent* court was established to deal with cases as they occurred. In other respects it was a transitional institution. It may well have offered a remedy only to Roman citizens living in the provinces and not to non-Roman provincials.[71] Prosecution in Piso's new court had to be initiated by the *legis actio sacramento* procedure associated with the civil courts[72] and this procedure was only available to Roman citizens. However, in view of the precedent of 171 and the unbroken tradition that *repetundae* legislation was for the benefit of the provincials, it is more plausible to assume, despite the difficulties, that the provincials as well as Roman citizens resident in the provinces were the intended beneficiaries of the statute and that, as in

[66] See Eder 1969 (F 46) 101–19, for the view that the statute was an ingenious device of Piso's with no influence at all on the later *quaestiones perpetuae*.

[67] *Pace* A. H. M. Jones 1972 (F 89) 54–5.

[68] *Brut.* 130: he mentions M. Brutus and L. Caesulenus.

[69] As Jones points out, late Republican Romans also used the phrase *iudicium publicum* of less formal *ad hoc* tribunals (A. H. M. Jones 1972 (F 89)).

[70] Any citizen in good standing could prosecute in a *quaestio perpetua* except in the pre-Gracchan *repetundae* court and Sulla's *quaestio de iniuriis* or whichever *quaestio* heard cases of criminal *iniuria*.

[71] Thus Richardson 1987 (F 130). On 171 see Richardson in ch. 15 below, pp. 577–8.

[72] *Lex de repetundis* on 'Tabula Bembina' (*Bruns*, no. 10; *FIRA* I.7), hereinafter *lex rep.*, 23. For a history of *repetundae* legislation, see Lintott 1981 (F 104).

171, Roman citizens were assigned to represent non-Roman individuals or communities in proceedings at Rome. The most likely candidate for the role of patron (*patronus*) would be the *patronus* whom each community already possessed to represent their interests at Rome. Under the Gracchan *repetundae* law the *legis actio* procedure was dropped and the injured provincial could prosecute in his own right. Furthermore, under Piso's law in the event of conviction the defendant had to do no more than make restitution – there was no penal element in the sentence. We do not know anything for certain about the jury except that it must have been drawn from the senatorial order.[73] It was probably small, as were the later senatorial juries,[74] but it is by no means certain that it consisted merely of the five or so *recuperatores* who operated in some civil actions.[75] Other features first attested in the Gracchan *repetundae* statute,[76] notably provision for retrial (*ampliatio*) in the event of more than a third of the jury voting Non Liquet (Not Proven), and the method of assessing damages (*litis aestimatio*), could well go back to the Lex Calpurnia.

What was it about the situation in 149 that made a novel form of court appear desirable? The full title of the court, *de pecuniis repetundis*, and indeed the penalty, suggest that the court's purpose was to provide a permanent mechanism for enabling provincials, or at any rate Roman citizens resident in the provinces, to get back money or the money equivalent of goods stolen from them by governors and their associates.[77] In the very same year as Piso's statute was passed there was an unsuccessful attempt to set up a special court to prosecute Ser. Sulpicius Galba for massacring or selling into slavery some Lusitanians who had sued for peace. The statute may have been a response, if a rather feeble one, to this situation as well as to complaints about extortion, for, however useless to provincials in the Lusitanians' situation, the legislation did at least serve as a warning to men like Galba that the Senate intended to keep a permanent watch on the conduct of governors. Its feebleness can be gauged from the fact that we know of four acquittals

[73] All our sources for C. Gracchus' judiciary arrangements (except possibly Tac. *Ann.* XII.60) at least imply that he made some change which either eliminated or diluted senatorial participation; Diod. XXXV.25 and Vell. Pat. II.32 state explicitly that senators manned the juries before Gracchus' legislation.

[74] During the immediately post-Sullan period of wholly senatorial juries their size was small; Cic. *Verr.* I.30 implies a *repetundae* court jury of not much more than eight, doubtless an underestimate, but incompatible with a large jury. The jury before which Oppianicus was tried in 74 numbered 32 (Cic. *Clu.* 74). There is no reason to suppose that the Calpurnian juries were any larger.

[75] Recuperatorial juries are posited by some because the praetor who was to be governor of Spain assigned *recuperatores* in 171 when Spanish envoys complained about the rapacity of a number of earlier Roman governors, the closest precedent; but the sources referred to in n. 73 imply no generic differences between pre- and post-Gracchan juries other than the class of person manning them.

[76] *Lex rep.* 47 (*ampliatio*); 58ff. (*litis aestimatio*).

[77] Cic. II *Verr.* 4.17; Livy XLIII.2; Galba and the Lusitanians: Livy *Epit.* and *Oxyr. Epit.* XLIX; Val. Max. VIII.1. *Absol.* 2; Cic. *Brut.* 89, *De Or.* I.227; Liguria in 173: Livy XLII.8–9, 10.9–11.

regarded as scandalous[78] and of only one possible conviction under the law:[79] a community's *patronus* would not necessarily be its most persuasive advocate. But we should beware of assuming that the statute was no more than a cynical device to fob off provincials with an intentionally useless institution, while governors went on fleecing them.[80] The satirist Lucilius appears to have called the statute brutal (*saeva*)[81] and even senators could demonstrate indignation at the malpractices of some of their peers.[82]

Next in the field of *repetundae* legislation comes a Lex Iunia of which we know no more than the name and then a *lex repetundarum* of which substantial fragments have survived on one side of the surviving pieces of the 'Tabula Bembina'. Date and authorship of this statute have been the subject of controversy; Mommsen identified it with a Lex Acilia repetundarum mentioned by Cicero (*Verr.* I.51) and maintained that it was part of C. Gracchus' legislative programme. Despite attempts to give the statute a later date, Mommsen was certainly right to date it to 123 or 122; modern scholars are less confident about ascribing it to M'. Acilius Glabrio and I shall refer to it as the Gracchan *repetundae* statute.[83]

The new statute was altogether much tougher than the Calpurnian *lex*; instead of simple restitution, double the value of the property misappropriated was the penalty. Non-citizens could now sue in their own right; indeed the statute positively encouraged non-citizens to initiate prosecutions by granting them a choice of Roman citizenship or a right to *provocatio*, if they were successful. Procedure was simplified: the *legis actio* procedure, intended for citizens and thus inappropriate for allies and provincials, was therefore dropped and plaintiffs henceforth simply laid information against the defendant before the praetor (*nominis delatio*): laying information before the presiding judge became standard procedure for *quaestio* prosecutions. Jury-membership ceased to be a senatorial prerogative; non-senators provided the panel of 450 from which the 50 jurors required for a trial were to be taken.

Two of the aims of the new extortion law are virtually self-evident. Firstly, Gracchus wished to protect Latins, *socii*, friends and subjects of the Roman people from exploitation by holders of *imperium*, senators and their families; it is clear that if earlier legislation had been intended to

[78] App. *BCiv.* I.22 mentions the acquittals of L. Aurelius Cotta, Livius Salinator and M'. Aquillius; App. *Hisp.* 79 adds Q. Pompeius.

[79] Valerius Maximus (IX.6.10) attests the conviction of L. Cornelius Lentulus Lupus (cos. 156), 'lege Caecilia repetundarum'. Mommsen 1899 (F 119) 708 n. 3, is almost certainly right (*pace* Bauman 1983 (F 178) 205 and n. 369) in regarding this as a mistake for 'lege *Calpurnia*.'

[80] The view of Eder 1969 (F 46) 58–101.

[81] Fr. 573 (Marx).

[82] Cf. the attitude of Senate and natural father to D. Iunius Silanus' conduct towards the provincials of Macedonia as reported in Val. Max. V.8.2.

[83] For the arguments see Stockton 1979 (C 137) 230–5 and Lintott 1981 (F 104) 182–5.

help provincials as well as Roman citizens living in the provinces, it had not worked – delegates from the provinces were loud in complaint over acquittals due to bribery.[84]

A second aim of the statute must have been a diminution in some sense of the Senate's standing. *Repetundae* was a crime which only a senator could commit and the penalty for committing it had been stiffened. Again, by transferring membership of the jury from senators to non-senators, Gracchus was at the very least registering a vote of no confidence in senatorial juries. He may have wished to do no more than give the provincials greater confidence in a fair trial than they could ever have had when defendants were tried by their peers. If so, the diminution of senatorial power might be felt, even by senators, to be counterbalanced by the greater tranquillity to be anticipated in the provinces. It certainly looks as if the Gracchan *repetundae* court and its new jury were not particularly controversial, since, despite the ferocious anti-Gracchan reaction which involved the murder of the tribune and many of his associates, the *lex* was not repealed.

A more radical suggestion is that C. Gracchus intended to establish in the equestrian order an alternative, though lesser, centre of political power and by so doing to diminish the power of the Senate in a more positive sense.[85] This involves consideration of the qualifications for membership of the panel of jurymen for the Gracchan *repetundae* court and consideration of the homogeneity of the equestrian order. The jurymen must have been *equites* in some sense of the word and presumably in one of the two senses of the word current in Cicero's day: (i) persons with a capital of 400,000 sesterces or above; (ii) persons with that capital who belonged to the eighteen centuries of citizens entitled to the public horse.[86] The simplest conclusion is that (ii) were *equites* in the strict, (i) in a looser sense. This would explain why the 'ordo' of *tribuni aerarii* which provided a third of the members of the jury panels under the Lex Aurelia of 70 (the other two-thirds being provided by the Senate and the equestrian order) could be regarded by Cicero sometimes as distinct from and sometimes as part of the equestrian order:[87] the *tribuni aerarii* had the 400,000 sesterces but not the right to the *equus publicus*. This makes it somewhat more likely that the qualification for the Gracchan juror was entitlement to the *equus publicus*.

More important is the question whether or not the Gracchan jurors

[84] App. *BCiv*. I.22.I. [85] See ch. 3 p. 81.

[86] For *eques* = person entitled to the public horse, see esp. Cic. *Phil.* VI.13, VII.16–17; for *eques* = possessor of the financial qualification, see Cic. *Rosc. com* 42 and 48; Hor. *Ep.* I.I.57; see also material in n. 87.

[87] Cicero includes the *tribuni aerarii* in the *equites* at *Font.* 36, *Clu.* 121, *Flacc.* 4 and 96 and elsewhere, but treats them as a separate *ordo* at *Cat.* II.16, IV.15 and elsewhere. See Brunt 1988 (A 19) 210–11.

formed in any sense a homogeneous social or political group, or even contained within their midst a body with interests running counter to those of the senatorial order, supposing that the senatorial order was itself homogeneous. Fortunately, this is a question to which one can produce a reasonably certain answer; the equestrian order in the wider sense was not a homogeneous pressure group. At the top end one can find *equites* like C. Lucilius, and senators like M. Caelius and Cicero himself, with relatives in the other order; there were landed knights and senators who engaged discreetly in commercial activity.[88] Again, it is only between 106 and 70 that control of the courts becomes the subject of political controversy; the literary sources connect dissatisfaction with senatorial juries primarily with their openness to bribery, particularly in *repetundae* cases, while dissatisfaction with equestrian juries is connected with the activities of the *publicani*, men who farmed the provincial taxes on behalf of the government.[89] Clearly, their interests and those of the governor did not necessarily coincide, since the former wished to maximize their profits, while the latter wanted a peaceful province. But to judge from our admittedly scanty source-material this particular clash of interests was almost entirely a feature of the 90s; in the 80s the struggle between Sulla and the Marians and Cinnani and the Mithridatic War put the desire for peace and stability felt by both parties well above any divergence of interests.

Accordingly, the radical theory that C. Gracchus intended the equestrian order to form an alternative political power-group to the Senate is based on a misunderstanding of the nature of the equestrian order. In general, its members as propertied citizens shared the same interests as senators; however, it ought to have been possible for them to adopt a more detached attitude to *repetundae* cases since by definition it was a crime they could not themselves commit. To retroject back to the 120s the situation which arose twenty years later not only attributes to Gracchus an improbable degree of foresight; it also attributes to him a scheme of pointless malice. What could have been the point of rescuing provincials from rapacious governors and their staffs in order to subject them to the more systematic rapacity of the *publicani*? No doubt, the Gracchan *lex repetundarum* did make it possible for the *publicani* to punish governors who tried too vigorously to protect provincials from their extortionate activities, but we should not confuse result with intention.

By this time, other permanent *quaestiones* had come, or were coming,

[88] See Beard and Crawford 1985 (A 6) 47 and n. 19.

[89] For the susceptibility of second-century senatorial juries to bribery see App. *BCiv.* I.22.2 and, for the period between 80 and 70, Gruen 1974 (C 209) 30–4. Dissatisfaction with equestrian juries before the trial of Rutilius as well as after: Vell. Pat. II.13, for after 92, see Cic. *ap.* Asc. *Sc.* 21C, Florus II.5, Livy *Epit.* 70, App. *BCiv.* I.35.7.

into being:[90] a court *inter sicarios*, dealing with professional killers using an offensive weapon, probably also a court concerned with poisoning (*de veneficiis*) and another concerned with electoral corruption (*ambitus*), existed by the late 120s. It has been suggested that Gracchus manned these other courts with a mixture of senators and knights, but it is probable that, like the *repetundae* court, they were now manned wholly by non-senators.[91] Plutarch's view, like another to be found elsewhere in Plutarch and the epitomator of Livy[92] that Gracchus enrolled 300 (Plutarch) or 600 (the epitomator) knights in the Senate and manned the courts from this composite body, is probably an anachronism. If Plutarch's report does reflect authentic tradition, then mixed juries may have marked a transitional stage in the shift from senatorial to equestrian control of the courts (perhaps introduced by the Lex Iunia)[93] or else a project considered by the tribune but subsequently dropped in favour of the more radical scheme embodied in the *lex repetundarum*.

A consequence of the appearance of other *quaestiones* is a decline in the significance of the *repetundae* court; by 81 it was merely one of a group, and, as we shall see, trials for murder were much more frequent. However, for the sake of completeness rather than special significance, we may bring *repetundae* legislation down to the final statute of 59.

The Lex Servilia Caepionis of 106 is sometimes called a *lex repetundarum* but none of the ancient sources treats it as other than a judiciary law. Two sources, probably reflecting an epitome of Livy, state that the consul Q. Servilius Caepio had a bill passed which introduced mixed senatorial and equestrian juries.[94] The other sources either state or imply that Caepio restored the courts to the Senate.[95] Neither view is impossible, but the second view is more likely for two reasons; the epitomators of Livy have a bad reputation as sources for Roman constitutional history and Cicero's references to the intense hatred of the knights for the statute[96] make better sense if Caepio's bill removed the knights altogether from jury-membership; moreover, he quotes from a speech in support of Caepio's bill which refers to the equestrian judges

90 For the dates, see below pp. 514ff.

91 Cic. *Verr.* I.38; Tac. *Ann.* XII.60. Also App. *BCiv.* I.22.2; Diod. XXXV.25; Florus II.1; Vell. Pat. II.6.3, 13.2 and 32.3; by implication, Pliny *HN.* XXXIII.34. Against: Plut. *Comparison of Agis and Cleomenes and the Gracchi*, 2, but the evidence of Cicero backed by Tacitus should be decisive.

92 Livy *Epit.* LX; Plut. *C. Gracch.*, 5.1.

93 Thus Jones 1960 (F 88) 39–42; the alternative is accepted 'without any warm conviction' by Stockton 1979 (C 137) 142, full discussion 138–53, with references.

94 This view is general today; it derives from Cassiod. *Chron.* = Obsequens 41. The latter certainly used an epitome of Livy; the almost identical wording suggests that Cassiodorus used the same Epitome. However, Cic. *Balb.* 54 may imply that Caepio's law was a *lex repetundarum*; see Ferrary 1977 (C 49) 85–91.

95 Tac. *Ann.* XII.60 explicitly; by implication, in addition to the passages noted in the text, Cic. *Clu.* 140, *De Or.* II.199.

96 *Inv. Rhet.* I.92; *De Or.* II.199.

and professional prosecutors together as men whose cruelty can only be slaked by senatorial blood,[97] tactless as well as violent language if knights were still to form half of each jury.

On the other hand, another Lex Servilia, the work of C. Servilius Glaucia, certainly was a judiciary law and a *lex repetundarum*; not only does Asconius, a fairly reliable witness, style it a *lex repetundarum* but Cicero attests that it introduced the compulsory division of *repetundae* trials into two sessions or *actiones*, a device known as *comperendinatio*.[98] If we are right about the first Lex Servilia and it was a judiciary law, not specifically a *lex repetundarum*, then the Lex Servilia that made the receivers of misappropriated moneys as well as the misappropriators themselves guilty of *repetundae* was Glaucia's.[99] There is little doubt, however, that he also revoked Caepio's law and restored equestrian control to all the courts.[100] The date of Glaucia's statute is uncertain since the date of his tribunate is itself problematical; any date between 106 and 100, the date of his praetorship, is conceivable. An earlier rather than a later date is suggested by Cicero's assertion that the equestrian order furnished judges for nearly half a century,[101] i.e. 122–81. The longer the Lex Caepionis remained in force the less true that statement becomes and thus of the favoured dates, 104 and 101, the former is preferable.

There were two more extortion statutes in the late Republic, one introduced by Sulla in 81 and the last by Caesar in 59. It cannot be proved that Sulla made any changes in the law apart from returning the court to senatorial control; his *lex repetundarum* was one of a series of statutes constituting or reconstituting permanent courts and the content need not have been different from that of Glaucia's law. In connexion with Caesar's *lex repetundarum* Cicero mentions a clause which was common to all three laws.[102] However, a reference in Cicero to a trial under the Lex Cornelia in or around 70 suggests that the law had moved in two different ways: P. Septimius Scaevola was accused of wrongs unspecified committed in Apulia and of taking bribes at the trial of Oppianicus in 74. The prosecution tried to increase the penalty from damages to capital.[103] The case shows that *repetundae* now covered judicial corruption as well as misconduct in a province and that it could in certain circumstances be a capital offence.

The word 'capital' (*capitalis*) in Roman public law has a rather peculiar sense; we have already noted that *caput*, the noun from which the adjective is derived, literally 'head', means 'citizen rights' as well as 'life', and in the late Republic a citizen of standing convicted on a capital

[97] *De Or.* I.225. [98] Asc. 21C; Cic. II *Verr.* I.26.

[99] Cic. *Rab. Post.* 8–9. The structure of Cicero's comments also points to the Lex Glauciae.

[100] By implication Cic. *Brut.* 224, *Scaur.* 2.

[101] *Verr.* I.38. For the date of Glaucia's statute see Ferrary 1977 (C 49) 101–5.

[102] See the passage referred to in n. 99 above. [103] *Clu.* 115–16.

charge whether in an assembly-court or in *quaestio perpetua* hardly ever lost his life.[104] He went into exile. A statute or plebiscite passed by the *concilium plebis*, probably annually, prevented such exiles from returning home by interdicting them by name from water and fire (*interdictio aquae et ignis*). Eventually, for perhaps all capital offences, the penalty came to be defined formally as interdiction.[105] Caesar is known to have prescribed interdiction as the penalty for conviction in two other *quaestiones*[106] and it is reasonable to suppose that he did the same for the *quaestio repetundarum* in his statute of 59. In Caesar's hands *repetundae* came to include quasi-constitutional restrictions on a governor's powers, some of these, like forbidding him to make war or enter the kingdom of an ally without authorization from Senate and people, duplicating material in Sulla's treason statute. Caesar's law also limited the governor's powers of requisition and his right to issue free travel passes (*diplomata*). It would also seem to have been more comprehensive in the field of judicial and administrative corruption than any of its predecessors.[107] Caesar's statute was the last of a series that had begun with the Lex Calpurnia of 149 and formed the basis for the treatment of *repetundae* under the Empire.

In two ways the extortion court remained untypical of the *quaestiones perpetuae*. Procedurally it was unusual: the division into two sessions (*actiones*) may have been unique and the *quaestio peculatus* may have been the only other *quaestio* to conclude with a *litis aestimatio* (assessment of damages). Secondly, it may also have been unique until the Augustan age in being a court trying both capital and non-capital offences. In other respects it was characteristic. It came into being to deal with a specific set of problems – the complaints of citizens, and probably also allies and provincials against governors and their officials, particularly in Spain, where their discontent was helping to keep a war going that the Romans seemed unable to win. A second reason for the court became more significant with the passing of time, until many of the new provisions of the Lex Iulia reflect it: the need to regulate the conduct of the governor and his staff. The institution of the *quaestiones* highlights the various ways

104 The only known cases in our period of persons convicted on a capital charge actually being put to death are those of Publicius Malleolus in 101 (*Auct. ad Her.* I.23 and Cic. *Inv. Rhet.* II.149) and apparently Q. Varius Hybrida in 89 (Cic. *Brut.* 305 and *Nat. D.* III.81). The circumstances of Varius' death are mysterious, while Malleolus was convicted of matricide and the death penalty could be inflicted on persons found guilty of *parricidium*.

105 *Pace* Levick 1979 (F 99) in view of Ulpian's explicit statement in *Collatio* XII.5.1 and the passage cited in n. 106 below. Cic. II *Verr.* 2.100 suggests that an annual edict by the tribunes listed by name those exiles who were interdicted.

106 Cic. *Phil.* I.23 refers to statutes of Caesar which order (*iubent*) that a person convicted of *vis*, likewise a person convicted of *maiestas*, be interdicted from water and fire (*aqua et igni interdici*).

107 Cic. *Pis.* is perhaps the best single ancient source (esp. 61, 87 and 90), but Cic. *Flacc.* 13, 21 and 27 contains useful information.

in which *mos maiorum* could no longer cope with the transformation of Rome from small city state to mighty capital with its empire. Some *quaestiones* were set up because of the breakdown of social controls,[108] but this one is the product of a situation for which *mos* provided no guidelines.

In one final respect first-century *repetundae* legislation is characteristic, namely its illogicality. Since *repetundae* is primarily concerned with the misconduct of governors, it is easy to see why the crime should come to include 'constitutional' elements like taking an army outside a province without instructions from Rome, but why should it come to include the corruption of jurors by bribery? The answer must surely lie in the piecemeal institution of the *quaestiones*; for some purposes, there were too many of them. Suppose that a prosecutor wished to arraign a defendant on a number of criminal charges, he had theoretically to prosecute in each of the appropriate courts. This did in fact happen from time to time,[109] but it was tiresome. Prosecutors tackled the problem of multiple charges by introducing matter that was strictly speaking irrelevant to the charge they were actually bringing.[110] Legislators dealt with it by tagging on offences which were quite commonly associated. For example, the *quaestio de repetundis* was particularly open to bribery since the retention of large sums of money or their equivalent in valuables could be at stake. Hence the inclusion of corrupt acquittal as well as corrupt condemnation as an offence under the law.[111] On the other hand, it was only malpractices involving the conviction of an innocent man on a capital charge that came within the scope of the *quaestio de sicariis* (the court which dealt mainly with murder), as was proper, since such malpractices are a form of judicial murder.[112] Similarly, there was an overlap between *repetundae* and *maiestas* (treason). Taking an army out of one's province or making war without instructions from the Roman people and Senate were 'constitutional' offences under both Sulla's treason law and Caesar's extortion law.[113]

Any account of the criminal courts at Rome must be arbitrary, given their capacity for overlap, but it makes sense to deal next with a group of courts which, like the *quaestio repetundarum*, were all concerned with offences committed by senators in their public capacity and were all probably in existence before Sulla's comprehensive criminal legislation

[108] *Vis* legislation is the obvious example; Crassus' statute of 55 punishing the organizers of political clubs is another.

[109] For example, in 52 Milo was condemned first of all for *vis* and then for *ambitus*.

[110] M. Caelius in 56 was prosecuted for *vis*, but two of the alleged offences, involvement in *seditio* at Naples and arranging an attack on an Alexandrian embassy in Puteoli, though certainly examples of *vis*, occurred outside Rome and were thus probably not matter for the court; on the other hand, the murder of Dio and the alleged attempted poisoning of Clodia both took place in Rome, but strictly belonged to the *quaestio de sicariis et veneficiis*!

[111] Cic. *Pis.* 87. [112] Cic. *Clu.* 148. [113] Cic. *Pis.* 50.

of 81. *Peculatus*, the misappropriation of public money, and *sacrilegium*, the stealing of sacred objects from temples, an offence subsumed under *peculatus*, come closest to *repetundae*.[114]

It is certain that Sulla constituted or reconstituted a *quaestio peculatus* in 81.[115] Pompey was prosecuted for *peculatus* in 86, but Plutarch's account is so inexact that one cannot be certain whether it took place in a *iudicium publicum* or *iudicium populi*. The fact that a praetor seems to have presided and that it is unlikely to have been a special commission, makes the former alternative the more likely, and, if so, then we trace the *quaestio peculatus* back as far as 86, though no further.[116] It has not even much of a mythical history: Camillus is prosecuted in the assembly for misappropriating spoils *c.* 390 in circumstances similar to Pompey's in 86, but the word *peculatus* is not used.[117] Our next crime, *ambitus*, has been supplied with a much better pedigree.

Ambitus is untranslatable: roughly speaking, it denotes the making by a candidate for office of the wrong sort of approaches to the electorate, most often involving bribery. However, other forms of intrigue are included. Cicero attests the existence of a *quaestio ambitus* in 66[118] and this must be the *quaestio* envisaged by the Lex Calpurnia of the previous year which increased the penalty from ten years' exclusion from office to perpetual incapacity.[119] There existed a *quaestio ambitus* before the Lex Calpurnia, however; Plutarch reports that Marius was prosecuted for *ambitus* when standing for the praetorship in 116. As usual, the biographer's account demonstrates his indifference to legal niceties, but one thing is decisive for the trial being before a *quaestio perpetua* and not an assembly-court – Marius was acquitted on a tied vote.[120] Such a thing could not happen in an assembly-court where voting was by blocks, either centuries or tribes, and even if the full total voted, the odd numbers involved (193 centuries, 35 tribes) made a tie impossible. A tied vote could, and did, occur in a *quaestio* trial.[121] Precisely when this *quaestio* was established is a matter for conjecture only; the establishment of the first *quaestio de repetundis* in 149 furnishes a *terminus post quem*; the Lex Cornelia Baebia of 181 and the Lex Cornelia Fulvia of 159 attest concern over *ambitus*, though not, *pace* Fascione, the setting up of a permanent

114 So much so that it is not always clear to which of the two crimes a Greek source is referring: e.g. Plut. *Luc.* 1.2. *Klopē* could be either, though probably in this instance *repetundae*.

115 The court existed in 66, see Cic. *Clu.* 147. Cic. *Nat. D.* III.74 is decisive for a Sullan court. The dramatic date of that dialogue is 77–75 and *nova lege* could only refer to the Sullan legislation of 81, especially as the other two references are to the *quaestio de sicariis* and *quaestio testamentaria nummaria*, which we know to have been respectively reconstituted and constituted by Sulla.

116 Plut. *Pomp.* 4.

117 Pliny *HN* XXXIV.13; Plut. *Cam.* 12.1–3; see also Mommsen 1899 (F 119) 765 n. 5.

118 Cic. *Clu.* 147.

119 *Schol. Bob.* on Cic. *Sull.* 17 (p. 78 Stangl).

120 Plut. *Mar.* 5.5.

121 E.g. when M. Servilius was charged with *repetundae* in 51 (Cic. [Cael.] *Fam.* VIII.8.3).

court *de ambitu* in 159.[122] We have noted already that Cicero is quite unequivocal on the existence of a number of permanent criminal courts by *c.* 120. We can go no further than to assert that a *quaestio ambitus* was set up between 149 and 120.

Between the initial statute establishing the court and the Lex Calpurnia of 67 there was probably a Sullan statute. In favour of this view is the fact that in all other cases where we know for certain of pre-Sullan *quaestiones* (e.g. the *quaestio maiestatis*, *quaestio de sicariis*, *quaestio de repetundis*), Sulla reconstituted the *quaestio* in 81 and so we would expect him to have done the same for the *quaestio ambitus*; moreover, there is a reference in the scholia on Cicero *Sull.* 17 to a Lex Cornelia passed in earlier times (*superioribus temporibus*) which banned defendants convicted of *ambitus* from standing for office for ten years.[123] Subsequent legislation attests a continued concern with *ambitus*; the scholia provide evidence that Cicero's own Lex Tullia of 63 increased the penalty to ten years' interdiction from Rome and Italy. In 52 Pompey altered the procedural rules so as to make it easier to secure a conviction; he also probably increased the penalty to interdiction for life.[124] However, these measures may have been temporary, for Pompey may well have simply established a special court concerned with electoral malpractices allegedly committed in 53 and 52; his *quaestio de vi* was undoubtedly a special court.

References to *ambitus* trials in the late Republic are frequent; even the 90s, a decade for which evidence for anything is sparse, yield two or three examples.[125] For the period between the 60s and the 40s a considerable number of cases is attested.[126] We would in any case have inferred from the amount of *ambitus* legislation that there was increasing concern over electoral malpractice.

If we want to probe more deeply into the reasons behind *ambitus* legislation, we need to look at the two items of information in Livy about early *ambitus* statutes; there are two of these, one attached to the year 432 which is manifestly fictional (IV.25.9–14) and the second to 358, a Lex Poetelia which could be genuine (VII.15.12–13). What matters is the

122 Lex Cornelia Baebia: Livy XL.19.11; Lex Cornelia Fulvia: Livy *Epit.* XLVII. Neither passage tells us anything more than that a *lex ambitus* was passed. Fascione 1984 (F 49) 44–56.

123 p. 78 Stangl. The scholiast's point of reference is the Lex Calpurnia of 67, which makes *superioribus temporibus* surprising if he is referring to a Sullan law. Nevertheless, the view that Sulla reconstituted the court is probably correct and Fascione wrong to suppose that the reference is to the Lex Cornelia Fulvia.

124 Asc. *Mil.* 39C.

125 The trial of M. Antonius in 97 (Cic. *De Or.* II.274); the trial of L. Marcius Philippus in 92 (Florus II.5.5.); the trial of P. Sextius, date uncertain, but perhaps *c.* 91 (Cic. *Brut.* 180).

126 The prosecutions of P. Autronius and P. Sulla in 66 were particularly notorious, see Cic. *Sull.* 1, 49–50, 88–90; Sall. *Cat.* 18.2 and elsewhere. The *ambitus* trial of L. Murena in 63 is well documented (Cic. *Mur. passim*). All four consular candidates in 54 were charged with *ambitus* (Cic. *Att.* IV.17.5 and 18.3).

motivation produced by Livy's sources. For that they had to rely on their own imaginations in the absence of more than minimal information, and this is likely to reflect the motivation behind the legislation of their own times. The motivation for the 432 law is the failure of plebeian candidates to get elected to the consular tribunate because of patrician appeals and menaces; this presumably mirrors the complaints of *populares* about the pressures placed upon the electorate by the *optimates* in the second and first centuries B.C. aimed at keeping outsiders out of curule offices. The motivation alleged for the Lex Poetelia is completely different and more suggestive; the statute, so Livy says, was aimed at *novi homines*, men without curule office holders among their ancestors, who were trying to attract the rural voter. It is hard not to connect this motivation with the prosecution of C. Marius in 116, since Marius was the archetypal *novus homo* and, what is more, a man from the country, a *municeps* of Arpinum. One can therefore discern from Livy two motives behind *ambitus* legislation or prosecutions – first, a desire to prevent excesses by traditional candidates, and secondly, to keep outsiders out. Wealth and empire were distorting the workings of *clientela* whereby clients, in return for services rendered, were expected to vote for their patron or their patron's candidate; a client could be tempted to support another *nobilis* or even a *novus homo* if financial incentives were offered; despite the sparseness of the record, there is evidence of increasing liveliness at elections in the second century. This suggests the breaking-down of the system, if indeed it ever operated with the smooth and elegant reciprocity supposed by some scholars;[127] hence, in part, the sudden outbreak of legislation on the subject.

A sub-species of *ambitus* legislation was a statute introduced by Crassus in 55, the Lex Licinia de sodaliciis. This statute was aimed at those who organized associations (*sodalicia*, *sodalitates*) to secure the election of candidates by bribery. Clodius had with considerable success manipulated the *collegia*, trade guilds and religious/social clubs, during his tribunate in 58, but the *sodalitates*, organized on a tribal basis and with recognized heads, clearly provided a simpler medium for organizing bribery. The statute was aimed at the organizers, not the *sodalitates* themselves or their ordinary members. Crassus' statute may also have replaced Cicero's *ambitus* legislation. The penalty was 'capital' in the Roman sense and, as the prosecutor had the major say in the membership of the jury, conviction of defendants ought to have been easier than under the *ambitus* legislation preceding it.[128]

[127] For 185 see Livy XXXIX.32.5–24; for 166 see Obsequens 12. For the workings of *clientela* see Brunt 1988 (A 19) 382–442.

[128] Cic. *Planc.* 36–47, but the whole of the *pro Plancio* is of value for information on this statute. See now Ausbüttel 1982 (F 11).

Maiestas, shorthand for *maiestas populi Romani minuta* or 'diminishing the majesty of the Roman people', is a crime which has affinities both with *repetundae* and the group of crimes against the person with which we shall be concerned next. The affinities with *repetundae* lie not only in the overlap of fields already noted but in the fact that *maiestas* probably applied only to magistrates and senators.[129] But *maiestas* also overlaps with *vis*, since, at least eventually, it came to include sedition which had been a part of *vis* from the beginning. The subject of *maiestas* thus forms a useful bridge between the two main areas of Roman public law – crimes normally restricted to senators and crimes that could be committed by any citizen, though, as has been said, persons prosecuted were usually citizens of some substance.

The early history of *maiestas* raises two serious difficulties. The first is concerned with the relationship between *maiestas* (*minuta*) and *perduellio*. Both these expressions are regularly translated 'treason'; what, then, is the difference between them and why was it necessary to introduce a *quaestio maiestatis* when the primary jurisdictional function of the assembly courts was to handle *perduellio* cases? The second problem is the date of the first permanent *quaestio maiestatis*. Sulla's *quaestio* of 81 was certainly a *quaestio perpetua* but we know of two earlier courts, one set up by a Lex Appuleia of 103 or 101–100 and a second by a Lex Varia of 90; were these special or permanent courts? The first of these courts, set up by the tribune L. Appuleius Saturninus, was probably a permanent court; Valerius Maximus refers to it as a *publica quaestio*. It was still operating when C. Norbanus was prosecuted before it – between 96 and 91.[130] It had an equestrian jury, as did other contemporary permanent courts.[131] These arguments are not overwhelming; special courts could have equestrian juries, special courts could continue their work for longer than a year[132] and Valerius' language may be imprecise. Nevertheless, special *quaestiones* are usually concerned with some specific occurrence and if the *popularis* Saturninus had set up a special *quaestio* for some specific purpose, this could hardly have been to enable *optimates* to attack *populares* like Norbanus! Consequently, his court was more probably a *quaestio perpetua*.

The Lex Varia of 90 (or possibly late 91) is also a puzzle; it is assumed to be a *maiestas* statute because M. Aemilius Scaurus was accused of *proditio* under it[133] but it is a little strange that Cicero uses the word

[129] This was certainly the case under Sulla's *maiestas* law, see Mommsen 1899 (F 119) 710–11; it was probably true for earlier *maiestas* legislation, see Bauman 1967 (F 16) 87–8.

[130] Val. Max. VIII.5.2. for the phrase *publica quaestio* and for the trial of C. Norbanus before it; for the trial of Norbanus under the Lex Appuleia cf. also Cic. *De Or.* II.107.

[131] See Cic. *De Or.* II.199.

[132] Cic. *Brut.* 128 for equestrian juries; Livy XL.19.9–10 for a special *quaestio* being carried over from 182 to 181.

[133] Cic. *ap.* Asc. *Scaur.* 22C. *Corn.* 73C.

proditio and not *maiestas*. The sources agree that it was aimed at those whose assistance and advice were partly responsible for the allies taking up arms against Rome in the Social War.[134] In view of this specificity it is somewhat more probable that the Lex Varia set up a special commission which continued to operate during the Social War,[135] but one cannot exclude the possibility that its purpose was to add a clause on *proditio* to Saturninus' law and extend the purview of his court.

To return to our first, and even tougher, problem: what can have been Saturninus' motive in establishing a *quaestio maiestatis*? Not to create *ex nihilo* a new crime. It is quite likely that diminishing the majesty of the Roman people already constituted a form or part of *perduellio*[136] and in any case the concept *perduellio* which ranged from treason to harming the well-being of the state was already so broad that it could easily embrace *maiestas*. If the answer does not lie in the nature of the crime, it must lie in the nature of the court. Unlike an assembly-court, a *quaestio perpetua* had at this date a jury composed solely of *equites*. Unlike special commissions it was always there. It has been thought that Saturninus was impressed by the success of the Mamilian commission, set up in 109 to prosecute senators who had criminally furthered the anti-Roman activities of Jugurtha, which secured the conviction of at least five senators;[137] when the tribune C. Memmius had tried to do something similar through the *comitia* in 111, he had been baulked by a colleague's veto.[138] But Saturninus cannot have been merely after the blood of incompetent generals like Q. Caepio, partly responsible for the disaster at Arausio in 105, as the precedent of the *quaestio Mamilia* would suggest. The two certain and the other probable trials under his statute are concerned with seditious activities involving a tribune or quaestor[139] and it therefore seems likely that dealing with sedition was at least part of the purpose that Saturninus had in mind, though the fact that his *quaestio* was subsequently used against his fellow *populares* suggests that there was something ambiguous about its terms of reference. It has been acutely suggested that this ambiguity lay in the concept of the *populus Romanus*; Saturninus intended the statute to protect popular leaders like himself who as *populares* embodied the *populus*, but to his optimate opponents the *populus* was the whole community directed by the Senate.[140] Hence the

134 Cic. *ap*. Asc. 135 Cic. *Brut*. 304.

136 Bauman 1967 (F 16) 31 notes these cases antedating the Lex Appuleia where the sources mention a person being charged in an assembly-court with *maiestas*: Claudia in 246, Flamininus' father in 232 and Flamininus in 193.

137 Sall. *Iug*. 40; Cic. *Brut*. 128.

138 Sall. *Iug*. 30–4.

139 See Bauman 1967 (F 16) 45–8: persons tried were Norbanus (tribune), the younger Caepio (quaestor), and possibly Titius and Appuleius Decianus, supporters of Saturninus (tribune).

140 See Ferrary 1983 (C 50) 568–71.

ease with which his statute was exploited for ends which would have appalled him. The imprecision of *imminuta maiestas* was notorious.[141]

We know a little more about Sulla's *lex maiestatis*; like the other Leges Corneliae, it was almost certainly a general law, consolidating elements from earlier legislation[142] and adding (or perhaps only rendering more precise) regulations governing the conduct of a provincial governor, in particular the prohibition against waging war or taking an army out of his province without instructions from the Senate and people, provisions which were also contained in the Lex Iulia de repetundis.[143] It was as imprecise as Saturninus' statute on the exact meaning to be attached to diminishing the majesty of the Roman people,[144] and as, presumably, was the Lex Iulia maiestatis of Caesar,[145] since the ambiguities were duly exploited under the Principate. That law may have done no more than formally abolish the death penalty by substituting interdiction.

To sum up, it is clear that *maiestas* legislation had two main aims, to protect Republican institutions from subversion, since respect for *mos* could no longer be relied upon to do this, and to deter over-mighty governors and commanders in the field from 'unconstitutional' activities. In these aims it was unsuccessful.

We turn now to a group of *quaestiones* dealing with crimes not exclusively or mainly associated with the senatorial order. Sulla brought together under a single statute, the Lex Cornelia de sicariis et veneficiis, two courts that had in the past been separate, one dealing with *veneficia* (poisonings) and the other with *sicarii* (assassins, gangsters). Murder was a popular pastime. However, at least when business was brisk and several courts had to sit simultaneously to deal with cases involving violent death, the old distinctions between the courts seem to have been retained, even after amalgamation.[146]

The genesis and history of the poisoning court, the *quaestio de veneficiis*, present the fewer problems. The earliest specific reference is inscriptional[147] and refers to C. Claudius Pulcher, consul in 92, who had been president of the poisoning court about 98. On the other hand, a series of

141 The whole discussion at the trial of Norbanus as reported by M. Antonius, defence counsel, in Cicero's *De Oratore* (II.107–9), would have been absurd if the statute had defined *imminuta maiestas*.

142 Bauman is almost certainly wrong in his view that it possessed no tralatician elements (1967 (C 50) 68–90). If he were correct, it would be unlike any other of Sulla's consolidating statutes for which we have evidence.

143 Cic. *Pis.* 50.

144 Asconius in his account of Cornelius' trial and in his commentary on Cicero's (lost) speech illustrates the persisting ambiguity of the concept.

145 See Cic. *Phil.* I.21–3 and Bauman 1967 (C 50) 157–8.

146 See Cic. *Clu.* 147 and 148 for the year 66. In view of the frequency of references to slaughter and *perduellio/maiestas*, often in combination, in the *Auctor ad Herennium*, an almost certainly pre-Sullan speakers' handbook, it would be reasonable to suppose that murder, with treason, provided the Roman barrister with most of his bread and butter even before Sulla's *quaestio* legislation.

147 *CIL* VI.1283.

special *quaestiones* from 184 to 152, all concerned with poisoning, illustrate the Roman obsession with poisoning, especially when carried out on a large scale and/or involving the disposal of aristocratic husbands.[148] It is however a fictional case, filling out the record for 331 B.C., that is, as so often, more illuminating than fact.[149] The story involves illustrious victims and a plethora of murderous matrons – 190 either sentenced or carried off by their own lethal potions; it also involves a plague and an expiatory nail hammered into the temple of Jupiter Optimus Maximus. The public dimension of the offence is emphasized by the hammered nail: the poisoning of leading citizens (*primores civitatis*) by their spouses is apt to provoke the wrath of the gods. The case of 152 implicated a mere pair of upper-class husband-slaughterers[150] and it is easy to see why it should have occurred to someone that it would be simpler to have a permanent *quaestio de veneficiis* on hand than to be regularly troubled with the procedural nuisance of setting up a special court. Any date between 149 and 98 is possible for the permanent court's establishment, but the arguments for dating it to before 120 are the same as those for the dating of the first *quaestio ambitus*.

The date and purpose of the first permanent *quaestio de sicariis* are more controversial. We can trace it back to the early 80s or perhaps a little earlier.[151] However, Cicero refers to a praetor, L. Tubulus, presiding over a *quaestio de sicariis* in 142; he was accused of taking bribes and went into exile rather than face trial before a special commission.[152] There is no decisive criterion for determining whether Cicero was referring to a permanent or special court. In favour of the former alternative is the fact that elsewhere Cicero always uses of the permanent court the phrase 'quaestio *inter* sicarios' which he uses of Tubulus' court; in favour of the latter is the fact that never elsewhere does Cicero use of a judge in a permanent court the expression taking bribes 'ob rem iudicandam', (approximately equivalent to 'to give a corrupt verdict'), since in the *quaestio perpetua* it is the jury, not the judge, that determines the verdict. Scholars are divided;[153] the most that can be said is that Cicero states specifically that Tubulus faced trial by a special commission, and thus possibly implies that Tubulus' own court was the regular one.

A similar problem arises over L. Cassius Longinus' presidency of a *quaestio de sicariis*. Asconius tells us that he was more than once *quaesitor* (judge) in a court concerned with the death of a man, while the *Auctor ad*

[148] Livy XXXIX.38.3 (184); *id.* XL.37 and 43.2 (180); *id.* XL.44.6; Livy *Per.* XLVIII (152).

[149] Livy VIII.18.

[150] Livy *Per.* XLVIII; Val. Max. VI.3.8.

[151] Cic. *Inv. Rhet.* II.59–60, even if the case described is fictional, proves the existence of a *quaestio de sicariis* at the time when the book was written (early 80s). Cic. *Rosc. Amer.* 64 shows that the court was operating some years before 80.

[152] Cic. *Fin.* II.54.

[153] E.g. A. H. M. Jones 1972 (F 89) 54 regards it as a special court, Kunkel 1962 (F 92) 45 as a *quaestio perpetua*.

Herennium uses language which makes it probable that he was president of some *quaestio perpetua*, though he does not specify which.[154] If Cassius ever presided over a *quaestio de sicariis*, that must have occurred before 130, the date of his praetorship, since unlike special commissions, the regular criminal courts never had presidents of higher rank than praetor, and the *quaestio de sicariis*, at least subsequently, regularly had presidents of lower rank.

It is important not to translate *quaestio de sicariis* as 'murder-court', for all that such is the normal rendering: in Republican Latin *sicarius* does not mean murderer but a professional killer, a man armed with a *sica* or dagger. There is evidence that carrying an offensive weapon (*telum*) was the first crime mentioned in Sulla's Law.[155] We know of a (pre-Sullan) case where a member of an armed group who had cut off the arm of a Roman knight in an affray thought that he might be prosecuted *inter sicarios*.[156] Also, Sulla's law – and presumably its predecessor – seems to have applied only to offences committed within one Roman mile of the city of Rome, an odd restriction if the statute was primarily concerned with murder.[157] Undeniably, murder was mentioned in the first chapter and at a later date, perhaps by the end of our period,[158] the *lex de sicariis* came to be regarded purely as a murder law, but in view of the evidence it seems likely that it began life as a statute primarily concerned with armed groups operating in Rome, a first attempt to deal with a problem subsequently handled in greater detail by the Lex Plautia de vi and the Lex Licinia de sodaliciis. *Sicarii* are mentioned on several occasions in Cicero's speech on behalf of Roscius of Ameria in connexion with the murder of Roscius' father and the misappropriation of his estates.[159] This suggests that they were not politicized in the same way as the *collegia* or the *sodalitates* which prompted repressive senatorial decrees and Crassus' statute of 55. Again, there is a difference between Clodius' gangs organized for political purposes and the hatchet-men, allegedly employed by Catiline,[160] who might earn their living by working as gladiators or by simple thuggery when not engaged in intimidating

[154] Asc. 45C; *Auct. ad Her.* IV.41.

[155] At all events, it comes first in what purports to be the text of the first chapter (*Collatio* I.3.1).

[156] Cic. *Inv. Rhet.* II.59–60.

[157] *Collatio* I.3.1, which specifies the one mile limit. Another (missing) chapter dealing with murders outside Rome is a possibility; however, it is hard to think of any reason for the distinction nor is there any unequivocal evidence of a citizen being prosecuted *inter sicarios* for crimes committed wholly outside Rome.

[158] This was certainly the case by the middle of the first century A.D. (see Sen. *Ben.* V.14.2 and 6.2, where the use of *homicidium* as a substitute for a phrase involving *sicarii* makes the change certain). But Cicero in a letter written in 44 (*Fam.* XII.3.1) uses *sicarii* more or less as a synonym of *homicidae*.

[159] Section 93 provides the most detailed information about the *sicarii*. but see also 80, 103, 151 and 152.

[160] For *senatus consulta* aimed at *collegia* see Asconius 7 (in 64) and 75C (subsequently); for Catiline's hatchet-men see Cic. *Cat.* II.7 and 22, *Mur.* 49.

electors or political opponents. In other words, the *quaestio* presided over by Tubulus in 142 need not have been concerned with intimidation for political purposes but with persons who made their living by violent crime. That still does not settle the question whether Tubulus' *quaestio* in 142 was regular or special but Cicero in the *Brutus* implies that there was more than one *quaestio perpetua* operating at least by the 130s[161] and a *quaestio de sicariis* is the only court apart from the *quaestio de repetundis* about which we hear in that period.

We know more about the Lex Cornelia de sicariis et veneficiis than about any other Republican criminal statute. We possess two excerpts from it (Cicero, *pro Cluentio* 151 and 154); two speeches (the *pro Roscio Amerino* and the *pro Cluentio*) delivered by Cicero as defence counsel in the court set up by it, and because it forms the basis for jurisprudence on the subject under the Empire, there is a tolerable amount of material in the *Digest* and other law-books.[162] We know that it punished being armed with a view to committing murder or theft, murder itself, arson and procuring the conviction of an innocent party on a capital charge (this last provision being taken over from a Gracchan statute usually referred to as the 'lex ne quis iudicio circumveniretur' or 'circumveniatur').[163] In the sections devoted to poisoning the law punished not only the administrator of the drug but anyone involved, e.g. the manufacturer or the agent's principal.

Two facts lead one to suspect that this court could deal with a somewhat inferior class of defendant than the senators and knights of whom we hear. Firstly, we know that in 66 it took three courts to handle all the cases falling within the scope of this law[164] and it is perhaps unlikely that there were enough homicidally inclined members of the senatorial and equestrian orders to keep three courts in business. Secondly, A. H. M. Jones noted that, unlike all the other courts we know of except the *quaestio de vi*, the *quaestio de sicariis* was normally presided over by an ex-aedile and not a praetor; he reasonably inferred that it must have been a court of lower status.[165] This lower status does not lie in its penalty which was more severe than that for some other courts presided over by praetors, e.g. the *ambitus* court for most of its history, nor in its overall prestige, since Cicero during his praetorship when himself president of the *repetundae* court[166] did not disdain to take on the case of Cluentius. It must therefore presumably have lain in the quality of the defendants.

161 *Brut.* 106.

162 Particularly valuable is *Collatio* 1.3.1 which purports to provide the actual words of the first chapter; linguistic evidence suggests some updating, but upholds in general the validity of the claim. D. 48.8.1 and 3 also contains valuable authentic material; even Paulus *Sent.* v.23 may contain some material that goes back to 81 B.C..

163 Cic. *Clu.* 151. 164 Cic. *Clu.* 147. 165 A. H. M. Jones 1972 (F 89) 58–9. 166 Cic. *Clu.* 147.

Jones' argument would also apply to the *quaestio de vi*. Cicero at the end of his speech for Caelius[167] mentions a *vis* (violence) court set up by a Lex Lutatia, presumably in 78, to deal with sedition. For the rest, all our other, quite numerous, Republican references are to a Lex Plautia or Plotia. The earliest noted example of a prosecution under this law is datable to 63.[168] It must have been passed at some point between 81 and 63; the fact that it duplicates or expands the Lex Cornelia de sicariis of 81 makes this certain. The favoured date nowadays is 70.[169] Its relationship with the mysterious Lex Lutatia is impossible to determine. Q. Lutatius Catulus' statute was no doubt introduced to counter the threat of civil strife posed by the activities of the other consul, M. Aemilius Lepidus, but whether his law set up a special commission which lapsed after the collapse of the insurrection, or a permanent court concerned only with *seditio*, the range of which was subsequently extended by the Lex Plautia, is anyone's guess.

Thanks to Cicero and his ancient commentators, we know a fair amount about the objects of the Lex Plautia. Its targets included those who prevented the Senate from meeting or transacting its business free from intimidation, or who threatened or assaulted magistrates and judges, or who disrupted the courts, or who seized with armed men tactically significant points, or who burnt or wrecked public buildings, or who carried offensive weapons in public, or who purchased or trained gladiators, slaves or others with intent to commit arson or murder or to engage in insurrectionary activities. The law may also have embraced those who stockpiled weapons for mischievous purposes.[170] Chapters 9 and 10 of this volume sufficiently explain the need for such a law; they also document its lack of success.

Pompey's special court *de vi* has already been mentioned. Caesar's *lex de vi*[171] may have done no more than substitute mandatory interdiction for the dead-letter capital penalty.[172]

Two further points about *vis* need brief mention. In the post-Sullan period it is not just the criminal law that takes an interest in *vis*; there is also a considerable amount of activity in the sphere of civil law.[173] The focus is rural rather than urban and its purpose is to protect lawful

167 Cic. *Cael.* 70.

168 The attempted prosecution of Catiline (Sall. *Cat.* 31.4).

169 A Lex Plautia de reditu Lepidanorum and a Lex Plautia agraria are probably to be dated to 70. Though a case can be made for a slightly later date, one is reluctant to postulate yet another unknown Plautius holding a magistracy at a different date.

170 The principal texts are: Cic. *Cael.* 1, *Dom.* 54, *Mil.* 73, *Sest.* 75, 76, 84, 95, *Sull.* 15, 54, *Vat.* 34; Sall. *Cat.* 27.2; [Sall.] *Cic.* 3; Asc. 49C.

171 Cic. *Phil.* 1.23.

172 The Julian laws discussed in D. 48.6 and 7 are Augustan: they (or it) included a section on the right to *provocatio*, but for authorities as late as Livy in Book x (9.4) the standard statute on *provocatio* was the Lex Porcia. Ergo the Digest statute is Augustan, not Caesarian.

173 See Frier 1983 (F 204) and 1985 (F 205) 51–6.

possessors from attacks of one kind of another. This praetorian activity must have been stimulated by the rural unrest consequent upon the settlement of Sulla's veterans on Italian farms. Secondly, the political violence of the 50s is emblematic of the collapse of social controls at Rome. Roman society had always required its members to use an appropriate degree of force in the form of self-help. A role for the people in protecting the innocent and seizing, even punishing, the guilty is part of the exemplary mythology of Roman history.[174] 'Vim vi repellere' – 'to repel force with force' – was regarded as a maxim of conduct self-evidently true.[175] Consequently, if the discipline of *mos maiorum* was to break down anywhere, the delicately balanced attitude to *vis* was likely to be the point where tensions appeared, and this is precisely what happened.

Sulla introduced a new court to deal with the forging of coin and wills. It is easier to provide a context for the criminalizing of false coining; the edict of Marius Gratidianus (86 or 85) and its popularity demonstrate widespread concern at the debasing of the currency.[176] One assumes that it was aimed primarily at dishonest moneyers. Perhaps there was some *cause célèbre* which will account for Sulla rendering criminal the forgery of wills, codicils and signatures. The penalty under his *lex testamentaria nummaria* was interdiction.

Particularly puzzling is the Lex Cornelia de iniuriis. *Iniuria* is the generic title of a number of delicts, chiefly assault and battery, that can be the subject of a civil action. We know that Sulla's statute was concerned with aggravated assault and housebreaking; it may also have dealt with defamation.[177] We can be reasonably sure that it prescribed trial by a *quaestio*.[178] Yet there is no reference to any *quaestio de iniuriis* in the relatively abundant Republican literature and by the time of our legal sources, the second and third centuries A.D., the *quaestio*, if it had ever existed, did so no longer. There are two possibilities, not necessarily exclusive: *iniuria* did not merit a separate *quaestio* but shared one of the others, perhaps the *quaestio de sicariis*,[179] or breaking and entering was a

[174] Livy II.55 and III.56 provide paradigm cases. For a full discussion see Lintott 1968 (A 62) 6–21 and 1972 (F 102) 228–31.

[175] C. Cassius Longinus, a jurist of the first century A.D., actually regarded this maxim as a law of nature, see D. 42.16.1.27.

[176] For the edict of Marius Gratidianus, see Cic. *Off.* III.80; Pliny *HN* XXXIII.132, XXXIV.27; Seager in ch. 6 above, pp. 180–1.

[177] Whether Sulla's statute included it is a moot point: D. 47.10.5.9 (Ulp.) includes defamation in a passage commenting on the Lex Cornelia. On the other hand, D. 47.10.5 *pr.* (Ulp.) suggests that even after juristic interpretation the law applied only to physical *iniuria*.

[178] Ulpian (D. 47.10.5 *pr.*) lists plaintiff's kin none of whom can serve as a *iudex* in an action *ex lege Cornelia*. This kind of list can be paralleled for *quaestio* juries but not for the single *iudex* or very small number of *recuperatores* assigned by the praetor to any particular action for *iniuria*.

[179] The overlap of field makes it a strong contender (see Cic. *Inv. Rhet.* II.59–60). It might also help to explain why there were three courts operating at once in 66.

proletarian crime and thus ignored by literature which is wholly upper-class.[180] As for the few references to defamation in the Republic, they suggest that when one senator defamed another, the matter was dealt with by a kind of verbal duel known as *sponsione provocare*, a form of challenge or wager. Another possible indication of the vulgar character of *iniuria* is the fact that only the injured party or his agent could prosecute under the law.[181] Of course, this rule may not be original; it could have been introduced once the *quaestio* prosecution for *iniuria* had become obsolete, simply in order to bring the procedure into line with that of normal civil actions; but if the rule *is* original, then it demonstrates that Sulla thought of his *quaestio de iniuriis* as being in some respects more like a civil law tribunal than his other *quaestiones* where the defendants were normally persons of consequence. Modern manuals on Roman law state that the penalty was a heavy fine, but there is nothing about the penalty in the legal sources; it may even have been capital.[182]

We know of one more permanent court, a *quaestio* set up by a Lex Papia of 65 to handle cases of disputed citizenship; the similar court established in 95 by the Lex Licinia Mucia was surely *extra ordinem*. A Lex Fabia de plagiariis, passed before 63 but probably post-Sullan, seems to have made some kinds of kidnapping a capital offence. Pompey, perhaps in 55, promoted a *lex de parricidiis* which made some alteration in the law relating to kin-murder.[183]

Judiciary statutes

Sulla is thought to have raised the number of praetors to eight, with a view, it is said, to give each of his *quaestiones* a praetorian president. If this really was his aim, it was soon frustrated, partly by the creation of new courts after his death and partly by the need to keep several courts *de sicariis et veneficiis* going simultaneously; for these courts, and at least sometimes the court *de vi*, have aedilician *quaestio* presidents. He also transferred the courts from the equestrian to the senatorial order, having first enlarged the Senate by adding 300 knights.[184] We have already noted

[180] Assault, on the other hand was, at least under the Empire, a gentlemanly sport; cf. Nero's nocturnal activities (Tac. *Ann.* XIII.25; Suet. *Ner.* 26.1) and Juvenal's upper-class bully-boy (*Sat.* III.278–300).

[181] For *sponsione provocare*, see Crook 1976 (F 199); for the right to prosecute, see Paul *ap.* D. 3.3.42.1 and Ulpian *ap.* D. 47.10.5.6–8.

[182] The overlap of fields between the *lex de sicariis* and *iniuria* was noted in n. 159. It would be paradoxical if X could suffer loss of *caput* for ordinary *iniuria*, whereas Y, found guilty of *iniuria atrox ex lege Cornelia*, was merely liable to a fine.

[183] Lex Papia: Cic. *Balb.* 52, *Att.* IV.18.4, *Arch.* 10, *Off.* III.47; Val. Max. III.4.5; Dio XXXVII.9.5. Lex Licinia: Cic. *Balb.* 48. and, for both laws, Badian 1973 (C 164); Lex Fabia: Cic. *Rab. Perd.* 8 (speech delivered in 63). *Lex de parricidiis*: D. 48.9.1 and 9 *Pr.*-1.

[184] App. *BCiv.* I.100; also Vell. Pat. II.32, Tac, *Ann.* XI.22, Cic. *Verr.* I.37.

that there were complaints about the venality of these senatorial juries: it is also the case that the jurors themselves found their task irksome,[185] doubtless because the smallness of the panels meant a good deal of jury service for each individual member. In 70 L. Aurelius Cotta introduced mixed juries as Drusus seems to have contemplated doing in 91; as we have seen, the Lex Aurelia parcelled out membership of the panels equally between senators, knights and the *tribuni aerarii.*[186] Cotta's judiciary law was not a radical measure but a compromise, and although Caesar, Antony and Augustus all tinkered about with jury membership, the principle of drawing juries from more than one order survived into the Empire.[187]

Vis and murder committed in Italy

There is one glaring lacuna in our knowledge of the punishment of murder and *vis*, namely the regular method of dealing with these crimes when committed in Italy outside the suburbs of Rome. In the provinces the governor's court dealt with such crimes; on occasions, as has been shown, particularly in the second century, special commissions dealt with such crimes in Italy. Defendants like Oppianicus in 74 and Caelius in 56, some of whose crimes had been committed within Rome, were prosecuted in the appropriate *quaestio perpetua* at Rome. But there must have been a large residue of municipal murders whose perpetrators confined their activities to Italy and were not so notorious as to rate a special court. How were they prosecuted? No solution is free from difficulty. One would expect them to have been tried at Rome, since there were limitations even on the civil jurisdiction of municipal magistrates.[188] And whose jurisdiction would have applied to a prima-facie murderer some of whose crimes were committed in Aquinum and others in Arpinum? But against this solution there is not only the plain statement of *Collatio* 1.3.1, limiting the jurisdiction of the *quaestio de sicariis* to within one Roman mile of Rome, but the lack of certain cases of a wholly municipal murderer being tried by the *quaestio de sicariis* and, on the contrary, a tendency to include an implausible charge involving an offence at Rome together with much more plausible charges involving crimes outside the city. A second court dealing with murders

185 Cic. II *Verr.* 1.22; *Cael.* 1.

186 See above, p. 509.

187 Lex Aurelia: Asc. *Pis.* 17C; *Schol. Bob.* 94 Stangl; but by implication Cic. *Att.* 1.16.3. Caesar abolished the panel of *tribuni aerarii* (Suet. *Iul.* 41.2); Antony reintroduced a third panel; they were referred to in most offensive terms by Cicero (*Phil.* 1.20), but were probably the *tribuni aerarii.*

188 The text of the Lex Rubria (*Bruns* no. 16, c. 21) shows magistrates in Cisalpine Gaul obliged to remit to Rome claims for the return of money lent to the value of 15,000 sesterces or more. Nor had they the right of *missio in possessionem*.

committed outside Rome, though unattested in the sources, remains a possibility. But perhaps, after all, capital crimes committed locally by Roman citizens were dealt with in the *municipia*, as, on one interpretation, the Lex Osca Tabulae Bantinae would suggest.[189] Possibly the private criminal action referred to earlier was still available to the kinsfolk of Roman citizens in Italy. Unless some newly discovered municipal charter reveals the truth, any solution to this problem can be little better than guesswork.

An appraisal of the quaestiones perpetuae

It is clear from this account of the *quaestiones perpetuae* that they had two principal functions, the repression of crime, particularly when involving public disorder and committed or organized by persons of standing, and the policing of the activities of magistrates and senators. They did not perform those functions well, but there was some excuse. Rome had managed with a minimum of legal institutions until the second century because custom imposed self-discipline or at any rate a respect for magistrates when discipline broke down. In 186 the consuls acting partly through the aediles and the *IIIviri capitales* were able to round up large numbers of men and women allegedly implicated in the Bacchanalian conspiracy and to execute many of them (Livy XXXIX.14.17–18). The special commission which they headed was not authorized by the people and they had at their disposal a very small number of subordinates to carry out inquiries and effect arrests. Yet their case was accepted after being presented at a public meeting (*contio*); information and, surely, active assistance were forthcoming; the Bacchanalian cult was duly suppressed at Rome and its vicinity. Contrast what happened in 67 when the consul C. Calpurnius Piso endeavoured to support by his authority the acceptance by one tribune of his colleague's veto: he was stoned and his fasces smashed.[190] Small wonder then that the Romans were not at first particularly successful in coping with such a drastic change in attitudes towards legitimate authority.

If one regards criminal courts as machinery for punishing those guilty of specific crimes, then it is easy enough to see where the weaknesses of the *quaestiones perpetuae* lay. First, a system which relies on a member of the public coming forward to prosecute an offender is likely to prove somewhat erratic. This is particularly true of a system which offers the prosecutor only minimal assistance in preparing his case. He will require a strong incentive: personal involvement, possibilities for self-promo-

[189] *Bruns* nos. 8, 8–9 and 14.

[190] Asc. 58C.

tion or the prospect of some financial advantage.[191] In such a situation one can well imagine the discreet or popular criminal evading prosecution altogether.

Secondly, once a defendant was charged, the scales were weighted in his favour. Miscarriages of justice resulting in the conviction of probably innocent men like Rutilius in 92 were rare. Much more often the guilty were acquitted. A striking example occurred in 52. Milo was condemned by Pompey's special court *de vi* for his role in the affray at Bovillae, but the same court acquitted his gang-leader M. Saufeius who had been personally responsible for the death of Clodius.[192] Cicero himself boasted of having pulled the wool over the eyes of the jury in his defence of Cluentius.[193] This was sometimes due to bribery, but bribes could be paid to convict as well as acquit a defendant, as the case of Cluentius shows. More significant was the effect of upper-class Roman codes of behaviour on the quality of advocacy. A Roman was expected to pursue his private and public enmities regardless of his oratorical skills, but a defendant will naturally invite the most eloquent or influential of his friends to support him in court. Thus in 56 P. Sestius was prosecuted *de vi* by a man of straw, M. Tullius Albinovanus, whereas the ex-tribune had for counsel Hortensius and Cicero, the leading advocates of the day, and M. Crassus. Later in the year, M. Caelius was prosecuted *de vi* by a stripling of seventeen pursuing a family vendetta and seconded by two nonentities while Caelius, himself no mean orator, called in Crassus and Cicero to support him.

Thirdly, there were no rules of evidence. We have seen that this state of affairs could be used in the cause of equity, to ensure that villainies were brought into the open, but in the hands of a skilled orator it could be used to arouse irrelevant prejudice. For example, in the *pro Cluentio* Cicero dwelt on the unnatural hatred of her son displayed by Sassia, the woman behind the prosecution of A. Cluentius, and her allegedly murderous past.[194] Even if the story was true, it has little bearing on the charges against Cluentius. Thus the advantage accruing to whoever had the greater rhetorical talent, plaintiff or defence, was compounded.

Finally, as we have already noted, the system of separate courts was clumsy and inconvenient, as was the system of fixed penalties (apart from the element of *litis aestimatio* in *repetundae* and *peculatus* trials). There must have been a temptation to acquit when there were mitigating circum-

[191] The last of these incentives to be discreetly pursued, since the Lex Cincia of 204 forbade the payment of fees to barristers; however, the statute was flouted (Tac. *Ann.* XI.7) and there was always payment by legacy. See also Alexander 1985 (F 3).

[192] Asc. 54–5C. [193] Quint. *Inst.* II.17.21.

[194] Unnatural hatred of son: *Clu.* 17–18, 192–5; murderous past: *Clu.* 11–17.

stances and the alternative, conviction, would result in exile; a third alternative, a verdict of Non Liquet, offered a way round the problem, but such verdicts seem always to have been discouraged and were probably abolished by the Lex Aurelia in 70.[195]

That these weaknesses were eventually at least partly perceived by intelligent Romans is demonstrated not only by the gradual supersession of the *quaestiones*, under the Principate, by the jurisdiction of the *praefectus urbi*, but also by the growth of other forms of criminal jurisdiction, at least one involving at times a magistrate playing an active role in the investigation.[196] Thus the main defects of the *quaestiones* were at least partly remedied. Their most enduring legacy, however, was the legislation that constituted them: these statutes, mainly the work of Sulla, Caesar and Augustus, formed the basis for jurisprudential treatment of the crimes they handled, and continued to be influential wherever Roman Law was influential.

[195] Cicero (*Clu.* 76) speaking in 66 of the trial of Oppianicus in 74 says that some of the jurors 'ex vetere illa disciplina iudiciorum' voted Non Liquet at the earlier trial. This is the last we hear of N.L. and it is therefore likely that it was abolished by the Lex Aurelia in 70. However even the Gracchan *lex repetundarum* discouraged it (*Bruns* no. 10, line 48).

[196] The Princeps himself heard cases, so did the Senate.

CHAPTER 14

THE DEVELOPMENT OF ROMAN PRIVATE LAW

J. A. CROOK

I

Law has several facets, none of which a historical account ought to ignore. It may be seen as a set of rules of behaviour backed by sanctions, an instrument of social engineering, a mechanism for dispute-settlement, or a mode of argument and a way of thinking. It may at a given time be consonant, or be dissonant, with the desires and habits of its society; and it cannot alone give a picture of all the boundaries of behaviour in a society, because there are always social and economic constraints at least as powerful as the law, and in relation to those alone can it be properly understood.

This chapter is about the private law.[1] Conceptual puzzles can be raised about the boundary between that and other categories of law, but for present purposes the plain man's concept of the modern difference between private (what English lawyers call 'civil') and criminal law suffices.[2] The courts that people came into for private litigation were different from those described in the previous chapter, and that can serve as a pragmatic criterion; but there were overlaps and borderline cases. The end-point is, loosely, the death of Cicero; as for the starting-point, discussion will be limited to developments subsequent to the Twelve Tables, and in fact little positive will be said about anything before the end of the Hannibalic War.[3]

Apart from extrapolation backwards from the 'classical' law of the Principate, a procedure which remains essential in spite of its obvious dangers,[4] the evidence for private law in the Republic is mostly not that

[1] For Latin terms not sufficiently defined in their context see Berger 1953 (F 23). 'Jolowicz' refers throughout to Jolowicz and Nicholas 1972 (F 85).

[2] See e.g. Cloud in ch. 13 above, pp. 503–4. One major difference may just be noted: theft stood on the private and not the criminal side of the boundary.

[3] The end-point excludes, arbitrarily, the jurists Trebatius Testa and M. Antistius Labeo, most of whose activity belongs to the triumviral and Augustan period. For developments after the Twelve Tables see, generally, Jolowicz 191–304. The starting-point excludes the 'pontifical period' of jurisprudence: see Schulz 1953 (F 268) 5–32; J. G. Wolf 1985 (F 318) and, most recently, Wieacker 1988 (F 171) 310–40.

[4] For the effort to separate the 'pre-classical' from the 'classical' see especially the works of Watson (F 294; F 295; F 297; F 299; F 300) *passim*.

of technical writings: relatively few things said or written by the Republican jurists survive. One later work requires special mention:[5] a long fragment, preserved in Justinian's *Digest*, of the 'One-Volume Handbook' (*liber singularis enchiridii*) of the jurist Pomponius, written in the middle of the second century A.D.[6] The passage has three sections, of which the first two are about the growth of what we should call the 'sources of the law' and the jurisdictional magistracies, for which we mostly possess much better evidence. The third, however, is a historical list of the great lawyers, and constitutes unique testimony. A few Republican inscriptions are of some importance;[7] otherwise, one must turn to general literature. Plautus and Terence provide dating evidence for some legal institutions;[8] in Cato's and Varro's agricultural writings there are references to standard contracts;[9] Valerius Maximus and the antiquarians Aulus Gellius and Festus contribute definitions and anecdotes; but overwhelmingly the principal source is Cicero, virtually every genre of whose works supplies a contribution.[10]

An important division is between what may be called 'substantive law', i.e. the rules laying down people's rights and duties, and 'adjectival law' (the law of procedure or actions), i.e. how people may go to law so that their rights and duties issue in practical effects. The latter is quite as important as the former, and it is characteristic of Roman Republican law that the substantive law developed mainly through advances in procedure.

The substantive law of Rome did not consist only of statutes (*leges* and *plebiscita*). The sources of law, i.e. what counted as creating legal norms, included also *senatus consulta*[11] and the edicts of the praetors and curule aediles, while some of the most basic rules, e.g. the family law of *patria potestas* and all that went with it, did not rest on any specific enactment but were simply part of *ius*, the immemorial 'structure of Roman legal life'.[12] The Romans did not have a legal code: the Twelve Tables, though much revered, were probably not conceived of as a full code even in their day, and neither they nor anything else were ever regarded as entrenched

[5] Besides, of course, the *Institutes* of Gaius, which offer historical information about the *legis actiones* and sundry statutes.

[6] D. 1.2.2. See Bretone 1971 (F 190) 111–35; Nörr 1976 (F 250) esp. 512ff, Schiller 1978 (F 264) 119.

[7] See the List of select sources, p. 560. The *Tabula Irnitana* is of later date, but permits some reasonable deductions about the late Republic.

[8] Difficult to assess because they may be stating Greek law. For criteria see Watson 1965 (F 294) 46–7; di Salvo 1979 (F 261) 24–8.

[9] See the List of select sources, p. 560.

[10] See the List of select sources, p. 560.

[11] 'Resolutions of the Senate', usually held to have been in principle only advice to magistrates, but see Crifò 1968 (F 40); *contra*, Watson 1974 (F 304) ch. 2.

[12] So Horak 1969 (F 214) 117; we can thus evade the term 'custom' and its disputed role, on which see Nörr 1972 (F 249); Schiller 1978 (F 264) 253ff. On *ius* see Kaser 1973 (F 221) 527.

beyond reach of change.[13] However, the number of private law statutes in the time of the Republic was small (though some were of important scope),[14] and *senatus consulta* were not then used for the private law; so the principal engine of development of the law was the power of the two praetors, *urbanus* and *peregrinus* – and in one special field (the law of sale) the curule aediles. They had no power to make *ius civile*, which was enshrined in the immemorial rules plus the Twelve Tables plus the procedural system known as the *legis actiones*; but the praetors were in charge of the courts and they had *imperium*, executive power, and so, by granting or refusing actions, issuing prohibitions and procedural requirements, granting people possession of assets and stopping others from challenging it, or restoring the legal *status quo* if someone had been tricked, they gradually created new substantive law by way of the remedies. In the phrase of Papinian, *ius praetorium* or *honorarium*, the praetorian law, grew up to 'assist or supplement or correct' the civil law.[15] The stages of the process are much argued,[16] but it is a major development of our period, and certainly by the end of the period the *ius honorarium* counted as a distinct and separate corpus of law,[17] fixed enough to be the object of written commentaries as hitherto only the *ius civile* had been.

A second, not unrelated, major characteristic of the period is the rapid development of jurisprudence. The structure of Roman – as opposed, for example, to Athenian – society was always such as to give necessary place to learned advisers on the law, *iuris prudentes* or *iuris consulti*. In early times the *pontifices* played that role; by the middle Republic, though many *iuris prudentes* were still *pontifices*, the role had become secular. It consisted of *agere*, *cavere* and *respondere*, i.e. respectively, appearing in court for people, drafting legal documents, and giving legal opinions publicly to all comers[18] – that is to say, to the praetors, to the people who judged cases, and to the litigants; and anyone who wished to study the law was allowed to listen. There was in Rome no Bench of professional judges: praetors, and the people who judged cases, and advocates were all, in principle, laymen – neither was jurisprudence itself a profession in the commonly understood modern sense, but rather a hobby of some career

13 *Pace* Ferenczy 1970 (F 50) and Ducos 1984 (F 201) 178–82. See Pugliese 1951 (F 258).

14 Some of the most important are listed in the List of chronological indications, pp. 561–2.

15 D. 1.1.7.1.

16 On *ius honorarium* see, generally, Jolowicz 97–101; Kaser 1984 (F 223); von Lübtow 1983 (F 237). Kelly 1966 (F 225), argues for a 'legislative age' from 200 B.C. to the Lex Aebutia followed by an 'edictal age'; *contra*, Watson 1974 (F 304) ch. 3. Behrends, reviewing Watson (F 304) in *ZSS* 92 (1975) 297–308, puts the *floruit* of the edict from *c.* 100 B.C. onwards, preceded by development via the *bonae fidei iudicia*. Frier 1983 (F 204) argues that the Lex Cornelia of 67 B.C. gradually brought the 'edictal' period to an end, to be followed by the 'juristic' period.

17 'Lex annua', Cic. II *Verr.* 1.109.

18 Though for a denial of this tripartition see Cancelli 1971 (F 194).

members of the governing class, which, if pursued sufficiently far, gave a man's opinion standing when he pronounced what he thought the law was. Praetors were certainly free to compose their edicts without jurisprudential aid, as Verres plainly did; on the other hand, the roles of praetor or *iudex* and jurisprudent could sometimes happen to coincide in the same person. One way and another it is likely that it was the jurisprudents, mainly, who invented the novelties that the praetors put into effect:[19] Roman law was, like English, 'jurists' law'.

The concept of increasing role-differentiation as a society develops applies well to the growing specialization of Roman legal roles. Towards the end of the Republic, jurisprudence and higher career-holding began to part company; equally, *cavere* ceased to be part of the job of the jurisprudents and was left to lesser folk. *Agere*, too, ceased to be part of their role: that was because court pleading became more specialized under the influence of Greek rhetoric and was taken over by quite different people, like Cicero,[20] and because advocacy expanded tremendously with the growth of the *quaestiones*.[21] The legal 'profession' became two 'professions': it is a mistake to forget that advocacy remained an essential component of the legal order.

II

There follows an inevitably rough sketch of the main institutions of the private law as they stood by the end of our period.[22] In Part III an attempt will be made to survey some of the routes by which that state of the law was reached.

1. The law of persons

The law of persons[23] may be considered under the headings *libertas*, *civitas* and *familia*, rooted concepts of Roman society.

Libertas All people were free or they were slaves. It is likely that in earliest Rome slaves were humble servants rather than, as yet, chattels, and that it was the Roman conquests, with their massive imports, that depressed the status of slaves and turned them into chattels; but,

19 See Cic. *Off.* III.65 'a iurisconsultis etiam reticentiae poena est constituta'; *De Or.* I. 200 'domus iuris consulti totius oraculum civitatis'; and generally, Frier 1985 (F 205).

20 For the *causa Curiana*, where one advocate, Q. Scaevola, was 'iuris peritorum eloquentissimus' and the other, L. Crassus, 'eloquentium iuris peritissimus', see n. 128 below. Cicero at *Top.* 51 records the jurist Aquilius Gallus as saying, of a question of fact, 'nihil hoc ad ius: ad Ciceronem'.

21 Cic. *Brut.* 106.

22 The rules will be discussed in the 'institutional' order as found in Gaius' *Institutes*, though neither that nor any other overall system had yet become canonical in the Republican period. See Stein 1983 (F 275).

23 See, generally, Watson 1967 (F 295).

anyhow, by the late Republic, the slave was a paradoxical legal mixture – a *res*, thing, chattel, piece of property, under *dominium*, but also a person, under *potestas*. Slaves were bought and sold, mortgaged, put to labour however dangerous or degrading, or to torture or death, and had no rights or (except in relation to their *dominus*) duties. Yet, already, to kill someone else's slave was not only 'damage to property' but also murder;[24] and, because the slave could play many roles in society that owners wished to avoid, the law had invented mechanisms to utilize him – or her – in such roles. Slaves could be freed by their *domini*,[25] either by lifetime acts (enrolling in the census or freeing *vindicta*, 'by the rod', before a magistrate) or by will.[26] The slave thus freed became a *civis Romanus*, though he was *libertinus*, which meant that he might have duties that were made actionable by the praetor:[27] *obsequium* ('dutifulness') to the manumitter and his *liberi*,[28] *operae* (*opera* is a day's labour) if promised as a *quid pro quo* for liberty, and an automatic right of the manumitter and his *liberi* to a share of the estate if the freedman died without issue.

Civitas Cives Romani, 'Roman citizens', were the 'in-group' to whom alone, unless the Romans themselves chose to bestow it on others, Roman law applied. Most free people in the Roman orbit were still *peregrini*, non-*cives Romani*,[29] though after 49 B.C. all Italians, at least, were *cives Romani*. There were still, in Cicero's time, parts of Roman law from which *peregrini* remained excluded. They did not have *dominium* or *potestas*, could not own Roman land or inherit anything from Romans, nor achieve Roman citizenship by any except a state act: they could not, for example, be adopted by a Roman citizen. That affected the children of mixed marriages, which were not *iustae nuptiae*, fully effective at Roman law: if either parent was peregrine the children were peregrine.[30] But all the Roman law of commerce had become open to peregrines in the Roman courts, and they were subject to the Roman law of delict, or 'tort', sometimes by the legal fiction that they were citizens.

Familia 'Family' is a 'weasel-word': to the Romans, as to us, it could mean different groups, wider or narrower, according to context. But its

24 D. 48.8.1.2, reporting the Lex Cornelia of 81 B.C.

25 See, generally, Fabre 1981 (G 65). Of course, *domini* might require payment.

26 If conditions were imposed, e.g. 'if he shall have submitted correct accounts to my heir', the slave was meanwhile called *statuliber*; there was much Republican discussion about that status, see Watson 1967 (F 295) ch. 17.

27 Watson 1967 (F 295) 227–36.

28 *Liberi* were a person's children, *not* his or her heirs if the heirs were from outside.

29 On Latins, *conubium* and *commercium* see, generally, Jolowicz 58–62.

30 So ruled by a Lex Minicia, of uncertain date but probably at least before the Social War; *contra*, Watson 1967 (F 295) 27 n. 4. Before that, the child of a Roman citizen woman and a peregrine without *conubium* would, by general rule, have been a Roman citizen. See Luraschi 1976 (F 238).

most striking significance, in Roman law, was the 'agnatic' patriline, characterized especially by *patria potestas*, the power held by the eldest male ascendant over all his agnatic descendants as long as he lived.[31] It included the right to put to death.[32] People *in potestate*, e.g. *filii* and *filiae familias*, could own nothing, and what they acquired accrued automatically to the *paterfamilias*. He could arrange the marriages of his children *in potestate* and dissolve them at will. He could, if he chose, release them from his *potestas* by *emancipatio*: the evidence is insufficient to determine whether that was normally done when the children grew up and married; it certainly was not always so, and we hear of *emancipatio* being used as a punishment.[33] In any case, the agnatic structure was not predominant in every sphere. It may have been a residue from a remote age of extended families, but upper-class Romans in the late Republic lived in nuclear, not extended, families.[34] Agnation dominated *potestas* and intestate succession, but in other aspects of family and social life blood-relationships and even marriage-relationships were equally important.[35] As the agnatic bond could be dissolved by *emancipatio* or by a daughter passing into *manus* (which will be explained shortly) upon marriage, so it could be created by adoption, of which there were two forms, *adrogatio* of persons not *in potestate*[36] and *adoptio* of those who were *in potestate*. Only males could adopt: adoption took the adoptee into the *potestas* of the adopter or of his *paterfamilias*.

Even when people became *sui iuris*, i.e. there was no longer anybody with *potestas* over them, they might still have to be subject to *tutela*, guardianship – males had to be so till puberty, females all their lives. The original purpose of *tutela* was protection of family property by (and for) the agnates; but a *paterfamilias* could exclude the agnates by appointing someone quite different to be *tutor* to his children or his wife *in manu*, and by the late Republic *tutela* was perceived as being at least partly for the protection of the vulnerable.[37] The dissonance between *tutela mulierum*

[31] Agnation is descent in the male line: you (male or female) are agnatically related to your father, his father, your brothers and sisters and his brothers and sisters, but not to your mother or her relations nor to your wife or hers, nor, if you are a woman, to your children (unless you have been married with *manus*). It is a relation of law, not blood, and so can be created by adoption or *manus*.

[32] As to whether only upon the vote of a *domesticum consilium*, see Jolowicz 119 and, *contra*, Watson 1975 (F 305) 42–4. In general, see Harris 1986 (F 212) and Y.-P. Thomas 1984 (F 282).

[33] There is also reason to believe that a majority of fathers would have died by the time their sons married: see Saller 1986 (G 220) esp. 15.

[34] In the one or two exceptional cases poverty is stressed as a reason. See, generally, Crook 1967 (F 196); Saller 1986 (G 220).

[35] Thus, in the *domesticum consilium* to consider offences of a wife both families had a right to participate, even when there was *manus*. See also D. 2.8.2.2. and 2.4.4.1–2; *lex repetundarum* (*FIRA* I no. 7) line 20; D. 47.10.5 *pr*. A good deal of Dixon 1985 (G 57) is relevant to this point, and so is Saller 1986 (G 220).

[36] On some criteria for *adrogatio* see (allowing for malice) Cic. *Dom*. 34–8, with Watson 1967 (F 295) 82–8.

[37] So Watson 1967 (F 295) ch. 9.

and the independence of some women in Cicero's age is often noted: the teeth of that *tutela* were being filed away fast, except when it was held by the woman's agnates – *tutores* could be changed at the woman's will, and so on.

The anomaly of grown-up people *in potestate* being unable to own or transact was qualified by the institution of *peculium* (available, actually, to slaves as well as to *filii* and *filiae familias*). At the discretion of the *paterfamilias* or *dominus* they could have a fund which counted as separate to the extent of being dealt with by them as for practical purposes their own. It could comprise any kind of assets – land, slaves, money. No *paterfamilias* or *dominus* was, however, obliged to allow such a fund, and it is uncertain how common it was in the case of the *filii* and *filiae*, for all that we might suppose it to have been the only way in which a married *filius* with his own family could operate a nuclear household or pay for a political career (though most may have been *sui iuris* by then).

The Romans were strictly monogamous and held a high ideal of marriage, but not a sacred one, so marriage could be entered into and dissolved again without legal difficulty. In earlier Rome marriage was usually (to begin with perhaps exclusively) accompanied by *manus*, whereby the woman left her own agnatic patriline and counted as part of that of her husband. It was like an adoption, except that, even in the absence of any formalities, continuous cohabitation automatically created it. But already the Twelve Tables permitted a wife, by 'absence of three nights' each year, to avoid automatic *manus*; and in a marriage where there was not *manus* the wife remained part of her own descent group. (The distinction was one of law, not topography: in both cases equally the husband and wife set up their own neolocal, conjugal domicile and nuclear family.) In the late Republic marriage with *manus* was the less frequent, though it is too bold to claim that we can know by how much the less.[38] As to the often posited relation between what is miscalled 'free' marriage and the alleged emancipation of women in that age,[39] it must be remembered that many women, especially in first marriages, will still have been subject to *patria potestas*.

A woman *sui iuris* with property, if she underwent *manus*, surrendered it to her new agnatic family (though in Cicero's time it counted as dowry, with the relevant consequences if the marriage ended). If there was no *manus* her property remained her own. There was no community of property between husband and wife, and gifts between spouses were null and void. In the property-owning class dowry was the social norm.[40] It

38 *Pace* Watson 1967 (F 295) 19–23. *Manus*-marriages continue to appear in the sources with no hint of being anomalous: Cluentius' mother, Cic. *Clu.* 45; Catullus LXVIII.119–24; *Laudatio 'Turiae'*, *FIRA* III no. 69, lines 13–16.

39 On which see Gratwick 1984 (G 108); Gardner 1986 (F 207) ch. 12.

40 Dowry was, in our period, always a contribution from the bride's side.

was owned by the husband (or his *paterfamilias*) during the marriage; the social expectation was that the husband would contribute to maintain his wife on a scale corresponding to the income of the dowry. As to what should happen to the dowry if the marriage ended, the parties were free to make what bargains their relative social positions enabled them to make, but in the absence of such bargains some rules of law came into play, whose basic purpose was to ensure to the woman a fund to support her.

Succession, the devolution of property, may in earliest Roman times have been purely automatic, but testation was possible already at the time of the Twelve Tables,[41] and long before Cicero the total freedom, so far as the law went, to dispose by will of all his family's assets had become the greatest power of the *paterfamilias*. It was the expected thing that a person should make a will,[42] but intestacy remained important because it came into play not only in the absence of a will but also if a will was for any reason invalid. Intestate succession went by the old automatic rules, which were relentlessly agnatic: first, to *sui heredes*;[43] if none such, to deceased's agnates of the nearest degree only; if none such, to the *gens*.[44] That excluded any children who had gone out of *potestas*, and all cognates, and your husband or wife; and women, who held no *potestas*, had no *sui heredes*, and their children were not agnate to them (unless the mother was *in manu*), and so could not succeed them on intestacy. Now the general sentiment came to be that intestacy kept too many people out, but equally that testation could let too many people in: for example, a *paterfamilias* could legitimately disinherit all his children in favour of a friend or a political boss. So the lifetime of Cicero saw much legal change, via the *ius honorarium*. When anyone claimed an inheritance the praetor granted entry into the assets, *bonorum possessio*, whereupon anybody who believed he had a better claim would have to bring a suit, a *hereditatis petitio*, against the possessor. What praetors began to do was to grant *bonorum possessio* on intestacy according to a list of their own: first, to all the children, whether still *in potestate* or not; if none such, then to all the grades of agnates after the first; if none such, then to cognates; and ultimately even to husbands and wives *inter se*. Such a grant was at first only provisional, *sine re*, i.e. the praetor could not refuse to accept the suit of a challenger under the old civil law rule, if one appeared[45] (though if

[41] See Watson 1975 (F 305) ch. 5; Magdelain 1983 (F 240).

[42] See Crook 1973 (F 198).

[43] Those in the *potestas* or *manus* of the deceased at his death, irrespective of sex, who became *sui iuris* by his death.

[44] The large agnatic kin-group of which the family was only one stem. On the continued existence of gentile succession in Cicero's day see Watson 1971 (F 300) 180–1.

[45] Except that the grant presumably did override the civil claim of the *gens*, or else it would have been pointless.

none did you were home and dry). However, there came a moment when praetors were prepared to give *bonorum possessio cum re*, i.e. would reject the suit of a civil law claimant against their preferred possessor: that important moment does not seem to have come, except in the case of the estates of freedmen, until the very end of our period.[46] In cases, also, where there *was* a will the praetors began to allow *bonorum possessio* to people 'against the will'; and even in the teeth of an express disherison they began in the late Republic to accept the *querela inofficiosi testamenti*, a suit against one or more of the 'named heirs' by a relative claiming to have been unfairly disinherited. That was a great inroad into *patria potestas*.

Legacy was, for the Romans, quite distinct from heirship: the estate accrued to the heir, but came with legacies charged against it. Much juristic discussion was devoted to what ought to be included in a legacy of, say, 'my farm with all equipment' or 'household effects'; but the most difficult question was what the law should do when estates were so burdened with legacies as to leave no assets to the heirs to make it worth their while to accept – for if they did not, all, including the legacies, failed. Rather unsuccessful legislative attempts to deal with that situation culminated in a Lex Falcidia in 40 B.C., assuring to heirs at least a quarter of the assets.

On intestacy, in principle women inherited equally with men, but into testamentary succession an asymmetry was introduced by the Lex Voconia of 169 B.C., preventing people in the top census class from instituting women in their wills. (It was still in force in Augustus' day, but in the late Republic became defeasible by various devices and was nullified when the census ceased to be held.) And then on intestacy, by analogy with the Lex Voconia, the succession of women in the class of 'agnates of the nearest grade' was limited to sisters of the deceased. One procedure that may have begun as an expedient to circumvent the Lex Voconia was *fideicommissum hereditatis*, 'trust of the inheritance', by which the testator left the estate to someone who was entitled to take it, with a request that the taker would in good faith hand it over to someone, e.g. a daughter or a peregrine, who was not. In Cicero's time the trust was still legally unenforceable against the trustee, and some unscrupulous persons were prepared to take the assets and ignore the trust, especially as it could be argued that its purpose was to defeat a statute.[47]

The idea that in the Republic women could not *make* valid wills is common but erroneous: they had to perform a formal act of *capitis deminutio* and have the authority of their *tutor* before they could do so, but there is no reason to think that that posed insuperable difficulties, and

46 See Jolowicz 253–4 and Watson 1971 (F 300) 183.

47 See the cautionary tales, Cic. II *Verr.* I.123–4 and *Fin.* II.55, with Watson 1971 (F 300) 35–9.

women certainly left property, especially mothers to their daughters. Rome was a society in which women had both wealth and the power that came from being able to dispose of it.

2. *The law of property*

The law of property (*res*) comprises the rules about ownership and other rights over immovable and movable things.[48] Roman law had an abstract and total concept of ownership, *dominium ex iure Quiritium*[49] – the corresponding English term is 'title'. Only *cives Romani* had such title. Its abstractness is shown by its complete divorce from *possessio*, legal control: people who were not owners might lawfully possess something, and in certain cases actually retain it as against the owner.[50] Even *possessio* had its abstract side, being not necessarily always the same as having something legitimately at your disposal: a tenant of land, for example, did not even have *possessio* of it, only *detentio* – no *ius in rem* (right in the sphere of property) at all. Title, naturally, could not be conveyed to another by someone who did not have it himself. Conveyance of title also in some cases required a formal act. There was an ancient distinction between *res mancipi* (land, slaves, certain animals, and 'rustic praedial servitudes') and *res nec mancipi* (all other property): title to *res mancipi* could be conveyed only by one of two formal acts, *mancipatio* or *in iure cessio*, whereas title to other property passed by simple handing over, provided there was an agreed legal *causa*, a 'basis', such as sale or gift or dowry. These inhibiting distinctions had great tenacity. They were in part mitigated by the principle of *usucapio*, whereby title was automatically acquired by lawful *possessio* of something uninterruptedly for two years (land) or one year (everything else). The praetors created an important action, *actio Publiciana*, available to somebody who, in the middle of *usucapio*, was deprived of possession (and could not sue for it as owner, because he was not yet owner): it was an action with the fiction that *usucapio* had been completed and title had passed. The *actio Publiciana* is usually thought to have existed by the late Republic, though doubts have been expressed recently.[51]

Especially important to agriculture, and so an ancient branch of the law, were the 'servitudes', by which an owner might surrender a partial right over his property to be enjoyed by whoever owned a neighbouring property. They were such things as rights of way and water or, in an

[48] See, generally, Watson 1968 (F 297).

[49] On Kaser's view that the early Roman concept was different see Jolowicz 142 and the further pages there referred to. For Kaser's revised statement see 1985 (F 224).

[50] The praetor gave the 'possessory interdicts' for the protection of possession as such, independently of ownership; Jolowicz 259–63.

[51] See Watson 1968 (F 297) 104–7; Jolowicz 265 with n. 4; Frier 1983 (F 204) 229 with n. 34.

urban context, the right to unblocked light.[52] Some similar rights did not depend on the existence of a servitude but were available to anybody in the appropriate neighbourly situation, especially the right not to have to receive the neighbour's floodwater and the right to require him to guarantee that the state of his premises would not do harm to your property.

Yet another partial right over the property of another was 'usufruct', the personal right to use and to take the *fructus* (produce) of that of which someone else was owner, for a term of years, often for life. Perhaps, as is commonly suggested, usufruct originated as a provision for widows, the children inheriting but the widow getting the use.

'Real security', the mortgage or pledge, which is yet another right over someone else's thing, was already highly developed by the late Republic, though not mainly, as in modern economies, to make available loan capital for commerce. It had two main forms, *fiducia*, where the creditor took full ownership with a pact to return, and *pignus*, where he took only *possessio*; but the lien (the pledge where the creditor does not hold the object at all but has a right to take possession if the debt is defaulted on) can also be found already in Cato's agricultural contracts, though whether the standard interdict and action for lien of classical law existed so early is a matter of dispute.[53]

3. *The law of obligations*

The Roman lawyers divided *obligationes*[54] into those arising from contract and those arising from delict.

The Roman law of contract bulks large in modern books – perhaps disproportionately large[55] – because of its interest as a comparative subject. In our period its most striking advance was in the following way. The age-old Roman verbal contract, the *stipulatio*, 'Do you promise X?', 'I promise', was brilliantly flexible and applicable to virtually any lawful bargain, but it was unilateral (creating a duty in only one of the parties, the promiser), it required the actual utterance of the formal words and so the simultaneous presence of both parties, and it was *stricti iuris*, which means that if the bargain was sued on and its existence undeniable no plea such as mistake or duress or agreement not to sue, and no counter-claim, could be considered by whoever judged the case unless specifically authorized by the praetor to be pleaded by what was called an *exceptio*. So there came to be invented a number of 'consensual' contracts, the bargain being created simply by agreement between two

52 Servitudes were rights *in rem*, property rights, not just contractual permissions. See, generally, Grosso 1972 (F 210).
53 See Jolowicz 304.
54 See, generally, Watson 1965 (F 294).
55 On the relative infrequency of contract cases in the litigation see Kelly 1976 (F 227) 84.

parties, however phrased and wherever given, which were bilateral (creating rights and duties in both parties) and *bonae fidei*, which means that a *iudex* could, without specific instruction, take all pleas of both sides into account.[56] The consensual contracts were sale, letting, partnership and mandate. Consensual sale, *emptio venditio*, existed by at least the late Republic.[57] So did letting, *locatio conductio*, which covered various economic arrangements that nowadays it seems strange to find under one umbrella, from letting of land and dwellings to acceptance of goods for cleaning and mending and to the hiring of the labour of workmen or servants. The focus of legal discussion in *locatio conductio* was liability of the 'bailee' (the person who had another's goods in his charge) for damage or loss; also, though, liability or otherwise for rent. In *emptio venditio* it was warranty for undisturbed possession of the thing bought and for undisclosed defects in it: how could a buyer obtain redress if he was ejected from what he had bought by its real *dominus*, the man with title, of whom he had never been told? And was it a breach of contract for a seller not to disclose defects?[58] The curule aediles in their edict applied a very stiff rule, that traders in slaves (also, a bit later, cattle) must publish a guarantee against a specific list of defects and be liable to let the purchaser have his money back if any such defect emerged, whether known to the trader or not. The edict applied only to market transactions: it was later generalized, but hardly in our period.[59] Much legal argument was, naturally, generated by what should and should not count as a defect.

Partnership, *societas*, is thought to have begun in early Rome as a relationship between *sui heredes* holding their inheritances in common, and it retained some of the 'between friends' atmosphere of its beginnings.[60] Even by the end of our period it had hardly adjusted itself to a world of arm's-length commerce: the principle of one partner being a direct agent for the others had not developed (except in the case of *argentarii*, bankers), and the principle of limited liability was never to develop, nor that of the company as a legal personality; and the only companies in which you could hold transferable shares were those of the *publicani*.

Mandate[61] was the contract whereby one person specifically instructed another to engage in a legal bargain on his behalf. Actions were created

[56] There were also contracts *re*, such as loan without interest and deposit for safe-keeping, and the contract *litteris* arising through account entries. On *litteris* see Watson 1965 (F 294) ch. 3 with Appendix; Thilo 1980 (F 279) esp. 276–318.

[57] Much earlier, if Cato's agricultural contracts imply consensual *emptio venditio*; but that is disputed. See Jolowicz 288–91; Watson 1965 (F 294) 40–1; Labruna 1971 (F 230).

[58] See Cicero's discussions of this as a moral question, *De Or*. I.178; *Off*. III.55 and 65–7. For the extent of the remedy in the late Republic see Stein 1958 (F 271) 7.

[59] See Jolowicz 293–4.

[60] The attitude is plainly to be seen in Cicero's speeches *Pro Quinctio* and *Pro Roscio Comoedo*.

[61] See, generally, Watson 1961 (F 289).

whereby the one could obtain reimbursement for what he had done and the other damages if anything had been wrongly done. Possibly more important (and strictly not a contract at all – 'quasi-contract') was *negotiorum gestio*, when A did something on B's behalf without specific instructions. It was important when people had to be abroad, in an age of slow communications, and so was the legal basis for the *procurator absentis*, your general agent when you were away.[62] Agency of one free person for another proved a difficult notion for the Romans, and its development hesitant. Slaves were enabled to engage in commercial bargains as agents for their masters by the institution of *peculium*, because the law allowed a master to be sued on liabilities incurred by his slave up to but not beyond the value of the slave's *peculium* (*there* is limited liability!); and by the end of our period the needs of commerce had produced one further step in the shape of the actions (*actio exercitoria* and *institoria*, respectively) available against the principal of someone put in charge of a ship or a business for bargains entered into by that person, whether slave or free.

Commoner, it is usually said, than 'real' security (the pledge and so forth) was 'personal' security, the bringing in of the guarantor or surety. *Sponsor* and *fidepromissor* were such sureties, but they could be accessories only to the *stipulatio*: they 'promised the same', and so could be sued instead of the principal debtor. The institution received regulation from time to time, by legislation rather than by the *ius honorarium*.[63]

The second part of *obligationes* is 'delict' (wrongdoings coming within private and not criminal law: the corresponding English term would be 'tort'). We have to consider three delicts: *furtum* (theft); *iniuria* (assault and personal injury to free persons); and *damnum iniuria datum* (damage to property). In all three, Roman legal progress was tremendous. The first two had a Twelve Tables background, with death or enslavement for the 'manifest thief' (roughly, the taker caught in the act), but long before Cicero's day physical penalties had given way to pecuniary, the 'manifest thief' having to pay fourfold the value of what was stolen, the 'non-manifest thief' only double. By the late Republic, theft had come to be given a much wider definition than we are used to: not just a taking away, but any use of somebody else's thing in a way not authorized by the owner, or even taking your own thing back from someone (e.g. a pledge-creditor) who had legal *possessio* of it. On the other hand, in spite of disagreements the view prevailed that there could not be theft of land.[64]

Iniuria, assault, is remarkable because the praetors, pretty early, created an entire new system of actions based on the plaintiff's estimation

[62] See Jolowicz 298.

[63] Watson 1965 (F 294) 6–9. The *fideiussor*, who could be accessory to any obligation, is said by Watson not to be attested in the Republican period; but the last item of legislation on the subject, which applied to all three kinds of surety, was a Lex Cornelia, and so ought to be Sullan.

[64] D. 41.3.38.

of his damages, and left the old Twelve Tables rules to wither away. The Tables had had special rules against *occentatio* (the 'rough music')[65] and *convicium* (abuse in public) as well as physical assault. Much dispute persists as to when, and how far, these things were subsumed under the various praetorian edicts, and as to how far, by Cicero's day, *iniuria* included what we should call libel and slander generally: Horace, certainly, knew he had to be careful.[66] It was, anyhow, a major creation of the *ius honorarium*.[67]

Damage to property (including slaves) was governed by the Lex Aquilia, a statute that may have been passed as early as 287 B.C. In this case the development, which was massive, was by way of juristic interpretation of the old, laconic statute. The issues argued were especially about responsibility for damage: negligence sufficed, in damage to property, to ground liability, whereas in *furtum* or *iniuria* there had to have been a deliberate act; but the lawyers wrestled painfully with the problems of indirect and remote causes of damage, and the praetors assisted progress by granting *actiones utiles* and *actiones in factum*, which meant, respectively, saying 'Well, under the statute strictly you have no case, but I will allow you an action on the analogy of the statute', or even '. . . on the facts that you allege'.

4. *The law of actions*

Turning to *actiones*, procedure,[68] we must first survey what kinds of court were charged with private law jurisdiction. The men in charge of civil justice were two of the praetors, *praetor urbanus* and *praetor peregrinus* (whose spheres, by Cicero's time, overlapped completely); but they never tried anyone. From very old times Roman civil procedure was twofold. The first stage of an action was before the praetor, *in iure*. It involved appearance of the parties, settlement, by pleadings, of the issue, and referral of that issue in the form of a brief to one or more lay persons, who then, at a second stage, *apud iudicem*, tried the action.[69] These persons who tried the action might constitute three different kinds of court:[70] a single *iudex* or *arbiter*, or a small committee of *recuperatores*,[71] or

[65] See E. P. Thompson, '"Rough music": Le charivari anglais', *Annales* 27 (1972) 285–312. The leading discussion by Fraenkel 1925 (F 54) 185–200 is challenged by Manfredini 1979 (F 242).

[66] Hor. *Sat.* II.1.80–3. Though put with irony, the point is clearly serious.

[67] See Smith 1951 (F 270); Jocelyn 1969 (F 84); Watson 1965 (F 294) ch. 16; Birks 1969 (F 187); Manfredini 1979 (F 242).

[68] For the latest general account see Frezza 1972 (F 203). Greenidge 1971 (F 68) covers both civil and criminal. Kelly 1976 (F 227) and Behrends 1970 (F 19) are interesting but heterodox.

[69] The common assertion that the *iudex* only had to decide facts is erroneous: he judged mixed law and fact.

[70] Ignoring for brevity's sake the *Xviri stlitibus iudicandis*, who took the important *causae liberales*: see Jolowicz 199.

[71] Cicero's *pro Tullio* and *pro Caecina* were before *recuperatores*. See Bongert 1952 (F 189) and Schmidlin 1963 (F 265).

the big jury of the *centumviri*, deciding by majority. There is dispute about the origins and roles of the last two, and whether they had exclusive competence in particular fields. It is at least true to say that the *centumviri* were mostly the forum for major inheritance cases, including the *querela inofficiosi testamenti*: they were chosen three from each *tribus*, surprisingly apparently without reference to property class. *Recuperatores* were picked by lot from the *album iudicum* originally drawn up for the criminal court *de repetundis*, with rights of rejection; so was, or could be, *unus iudex*, but *unus iudex* could be chosen by the litigants themselves, if they were in agreement, entirely at will.[72] Neither praetors nor judges had necessarily any special legal competence; it was open to them, and they were expected, to rely on the consultation of jurists. From proceedings *in iure* a defendant could appeal for intervention by a higher magistrate or the tribunes of the plebs, and if the praetor refused a plaintiff an action he could try his luck before another praetor; but judgement *apud iudicem* was inappellable, and you could not bring the same suit again. All condemnations were *pecuniariae*, for a sum of money, never for the direct recovery of the plaintiff's thing or direct performance of the defendant's contract.[73] The executive arm offered no public force to assist a plaintiff to get his opponent into court, nor to carry out a judgement when given; in fact if a party was not present *in iure* no *iudicium* could be proceeded to. There were, however, sanctions: the person who made no defence was imperilled by the praetor granting to his opponent *bonorum possessio* of all his assets, and the same sanction applied to one against whom judgement had been given but who failed to pay. Also such conduct led to *infamia*, disgrace, with damaging consequences to public office and status. Condemnation in all the delictal actions except that for damage to property, and in numerous others where trust was particularly involved, also resulted in *infamia*.[74]

Great importance is attached by scholars to one development in Roman civil procedure, the 'formulary system'.[75] The earliest form of civil procedure, that of the *legis actiones*, beginning with the *legis actio sacramento*, was characterized by rigorous forms of pleading *in iure*, fixed phrases or *certa verba* to which a plaintiff must adapt his statement of claim. Gaius in his *Institutes* gives a famous account[76] of the frustrations caused by that rigour; whether it hits the nail on the head is doubtful, because any civil law claim could actually be brought as long as a plaintiff was correctly advised about the forms, and new *legis actiones* were added

72 See e.g. for the possibility of a freedman as *iudex* in an *actio furti*, Cic. *Clu.* 120. The freedom is confirmed in chs. 86 and 87 of the *tabula Irnitana*.

73 See Jolowicz 204–5, and, on the crucial function of the *clausula arbitraria* as a way of achieving return of the thing, de Zulueta 1953 (B 130) II, 263–4.

74 See Greenidge 1977 (F 67) and other bibliography in Crook 1967 (F 41) 303 n. 77.

75 See, generally, Jolowicz 199–225.

76 Gai. *Inst.* IV.11 and 30: cf. Watson 1973 (F 303) 389–91.

from time to time: what they did not sufficiently allow for was complex defences, and they were also not open to innovations modifying the *ius civile*. However, Gaius correctly reports the remedy that was found, namely that a statute, the Lex Aebutia, complemented by two (Augustan) Leges Iuliae, introduced a new system of pleading *in iure*, *per formulas conceptas* instead of *per certa verba*; the *formulae* were more flexible and better adaptable to the claims of both sides, and they pushed the old system gradually out. The date of the Lex Aebutia is not known, though scholars mostly put it in the second half of the second century B.C. By Cicero's day, though all the *legis actiones* except that known as *per condictionem* still existed, there were also 'formulas for everything'.[77] The real terms and effects of the Lex Aebutia are also endlessly disputed. If an action with a *formula* was to have equal validity with one under the *legis actio*, it plainly had, as that did, to exclude further litigation once sued on; so perhaps the essence of the Lex Aebutia was to give statutory force to that 'consumptive' effect. In practice the formulary system enabled the praetors to give force to the claims of defendants by granting *exceptiones* in the pleadings before them; it also enabled them to invent new actions of *ius honorarium*: *actiones in factum*, for example, would have been impossible under the *legis actiones*.

A fundamental characteristic of the Roman law of civil procedure (in addition to the absence in principle of the professional except as adviser) is that it was 'adversarial', like the English law: there was a contest,[78] decided on the basis of testimonies and arguments,[79] resulting in a winner and a loser. An adversarial system has at its very heart persuasion and counter-persuasion, so that advocacy was as vital as jurisprudence. Only the advocate was not, as in English law, *amicus curiae*: his duty was solely to do his best for his client by all the arts of persuasion at his command; and since there was no professional judge to sum up and state the law, the court was likely to be much at the mercy of the advocates. That fact tends to be deplored, but it should be remembered that what an adversarial system ensures is an equal chance for both sides to 'do their damnedest'.

5. *Italy and the provinces*

A brief word must be said about the administration of civil justice outside Rome, and, first, in Italy.

Until the legislation of 90/89 B.C. and then of 49 B.C. most of Italy was still peregrine, and the peregrine municipalities had their own judicial

[77] See Jolowicz 218–25; Cic. *QRosc.* 24 'sunt formulae de omnibus rebus constitutae, ne quis aut in genere iniuriae aut in ratione actionis errare possit'. For the *formula* as a triumph of professional jurisprudence, see Wieacker 1988 (F 171) 452–3.

[78] See Y.-P. Thomas 1978 (F 281) 98; Frier 1985 (F 205) 233–4 and 246–50.

[79] Or, which is equally significant, of an oath. The oath proffered by one party to the other, if duly sworn, brought the action instantly to an end in favour of the party who had sworn, D. 12.2.

systems.[80] For some of the municipalities of *cives Romani*, *praefecti* were sent from Rome to provide assizes.[81] Once all the people of Italy had become *cives Romani* their local courts retained a civil jurisdiction, but with an upper limit to the value of the suits they could judge, unless the parties were willing: all else had to go to Rome.[82]

An account of provincial jurisdiction is given in chapter 15 below, so only a few points need to be added on the civil side.[83] How much control did the governor exercise over the legal disputes between Rome's non-citizen provincials? Cicero says there was rejoicing in Cilicia when he announced that he would leave local jurisdictions alone,[84] which seems to imply that such was not always the case, and Verres intervened when he chose; but governors could not possibly have dealt with it all. The normal system emerges from such documents as the *senatus consultum de Asclepiade* and Octavian's letters to Rhosos:[85] there were local courts; the provincials could request a hearing in the governor's court; or arbitrators might be summoned from some outside city. The *tabula Contrebiensis*[86] gives a glimpse of the governor of Spain stepping in – whether on request or not we cannot tell – to a boundary quarrel between small communities with a formulary procedure roughly on the Roman citizen model, in 87 B.C.[87] So far as *cives Romani* were concerned, we learn a lot from Cicero about the constitution of the governor's edict, about the assizes he ran, and about the use of standard formulary procedure with *recuperatores* chosen by lot;[88] but things did not have to be thus, for we also hear of cases where Verres exercised personal *cognitio*, i.e. tried the whole case himself, and though Cicero uses them to denigrate Verres he does not claim that the judgements were null and void. It seems to have been possible, perhaps only for people with 'pull', to obtain transfer of a civil suit to Rome,[89] but judgement given in the provinces was as final as at Rome.[90]

80 See Harris 1972 (F 76).

81 See Girard 1901 (F 208) 295–305; Simshäuser 1973 (F 144) 85–97.

82 Such a limit is referred to in the Lex Rubria and the *frag. Atestinum*, and ch. 84 of the *tabula Irnitana* confirms that it must have varied according to the wealth and importance of the community. See the List of select sources, p. 560.

83 To the sources there quoted add the new fragment of what used to be called the 'Pirate Law', specifying the powers of a provincial governor between the end of his term and his arrival back in Rome; see the List of select sources, p. 560. On the evidence of the Verrines see Mellano 1977 (F 116).

84 Cic. *Att.* VI.1.15. *Pace* A. J. Marshall 1980 (F 111) 656–8, who thinks Cicero is referring to 'xenodikai', the passage cannot mean only that: 'inter se disceptent suis legibus' and 'suis legibus et iudiciis usae' (*Att.* VI.2.4) surely mean the whole of local jurisdiction.

85 *RDGE* no. 22, Greek text, lines 18–20 and no. 58, letter 2, lines 53–6.

86 See the List of select sources, p. 560.

87 The Romans often dealt with local boundary disputes (which had political dimensions), either being called in (see the *sententia Minuciorum* in the List of select sources, p. 560) or *proprio motu*, but here for the first time (to our knowledge) with a procedure based on the formulary system.

88 See Hoffman 1976 (F 213).

89 See A. H. M. Jones 1960 (F 87) 75–7.

90 Though *quaere* as to the finality of judgement by a magisterial *cognitio*.

III

Such, in crude sketch, were the main rules of private law. We turn to the mechanisms of its development and the ideas that propelled the process. As for chronology, an attempt is made at the end of this chapter to tabulate the first appearances of some novelties, but the reader is warned that much is undated and disputed and that the first appearance of an institution in the sources may be much later than its real beginning. It looks as if the time from roughly the Gracchi to Catiline was one of exceptionally rapid change, which included the new edicts restraining intimidation and violence.[91]

The first point to be made about the mechanisms of development is that some changes were made not by the praetors but by statute. Attempts to explain that as a mere matter of chronology (statutes the earlier mode, praetorian interventions the later) are not free from objection,[92] and attempts to explain the statutes as having been used for just one particular kind of legal development, social engineering, do not account satisfactorily for them all.[93] *Damnum* rested on a statute, *iniuria* was wholly praetorian: why? Perhaps, indeed, the Lex Aquilia was passed – and the Lex Poetelia de nexu and Lex Cincia de donis, too – before major praetorian activity began.[94] And statutes were, certainly, used for social engineering:[95] the Lex Cincia may be viewed in that light, the Lex Voconia, the Lex Laetoria protecting minors, the Lex Minicia, and all the sumptuary laws and the laws about the exaction of interest. At a pinch we might add the Lex Cornelia validating the wills of those who died in captivity and the Lex Atilia regulating the appointment of *tutores*, perhaps even the statutes regulating the rules about sureties. But, for example, the Leges Atinia and Scribonia about the rules of *usucapio* do not really fit into that framework. As for the Lex Aebutia, possibly the direct breach it made in the *ius civile* was simply beyond the conceivable range of praetorian intervention.

For the main lines of progress, however, we look to the praetors, and the edict of each of them (*edictum perpetuum*), in which they set forth what actions at law they would grant during their year of office. It must just be noted that, though grant or refusal of an action, *in integrum restitutio*, *missio in bona* and such like[96] were in some cases provided for expressly in

[91] See Frier 1983 (F 204) 221.

[92] See n. 16 above.

[93] Wieacker 1961 (F 309) 61–88, 1988 (F 171) 411–21, and Bleicken 1975 (F 28) 141–5 being no more finally convincing in this respect than Schulz 1936 (F 267) 10.

[94] So de Zulueta *CAH* IX[1], ch. 21, 844.

[95] So Wieacker 1961 (F 309) 66: 'eine Wohlfahrtsgesetzgebung'. Augustus was to use statutes in exactly that way.

[96] For *denegatio actionis* (refusal of an action) see Metro 1972 (F 246) and Ankum 1985 (F 175); for *in integrum restitutio* (restoration of *status quo*) and other 'praetorian remedies' see J. A. C. Thomas 1976 (F 280) 111–17.

the edict, the praetors could, at least under the formulary system, apply them at will. A Lex Cornelia of 67 B.C., 'ut praetores ex edictis suis perpetuis ius dicerent', 'that the praetors should conform their jurisdiction to their annual edicts', may mark a significant stage. It has usually been seen just as a reaction to the vagaries of praetors like Verres, who introduced *ad hoc* novelties in mid-term (to suit his private interests, according to Cicero); but scholars have recently suggested that it prohibited not just *ad hoc* rulings but actual new norms introduced in mid-term, so slowing down what was seen as too rapid a pace of change.[97]

Ius gentium, ius naturale, Greek legal institutions Contact with the wider world took the Romans beyond their *ius civile* to the notion of *ius gentium*,[98] but though that notion could have philosophical implications it was for the Romans a matter of the practice of the courts, being those rules, especially – but not only – commercial and mercantile, that other people applied and it suited the Romans to admit, for application to *cives* as well as *peregrini*. Greek legal philosophers talked about the 'natural law' of all peoples, and the Romans were capable of picking up the jargon; but they retained their pragmatic approach and refused to adopt any institution they did not like into their positive law; so, for example, peregrines had to stay outside the family and succession system. As for slavery, it was convenient to label it a part of the *ius gentium* and insist that everybody had it. How much substantive law the Romans of the Republic borrowed from Greece (as opposed to interpretative and organizational concepts, to which we shall come) remains very disputed. The whole notion, as well as details, of the Twelve Tables is seen by some authorities as Greek; *bona fides* is held derived from *pistis*, *iniuria* from *hybris*, and parts of mercantile law are thought to be borrowings. On the other side it is pointed out that similarity (sometimes exaggerated) does not prove derivation, and that the notion of a common Greek legal system ripe for borrowing is out of favour.

Fiction, transference and analogy We have seen that one way to deal with a peregrine in the Roman courts was by a fiction that he or she was a Roman citizen. That particular fiction is heard of only in the delictal actions for theft and damage, but it illustrates a favourite skill of Roman lawyers, 'deeming' an X to be a Y to get round a procedural difficulty.[99] Further examples are the fiction of completed *usucapio* for the *actio*

[97] See Metro 1972 (F 246); Frier 1983 (F 204), 221–2.

[98] See, generally, Jolowicz 102–7; Schiller 1978 (F 264) 525ff, Wieacker 1988 (F 171) 444.

[99] Gai. *Inst.* IV.34–8. Wieacker 1986 (F 316) shows how this particular legal skill may have developed out of the concerns, and so the thought-patterns, of the *pontifices*.

Publiciana, the fiction that a successor under the praetorian rules was a civil law heir for claiming possession of the assets, and the fiction that something incomprehensible written in a will was 'as if not written'; and a neat new one has turned up in the *tabula Contrebiensis*.[100] Transference is another kind of 'deeming', when a formal act of the law is used to achieve a quite different purpose. Thus, *mancipatio*, the formal conveyance of title to *res mancipi*, was used to achieve *emancipatio*, the freeing of people from *potestas*; and the manumission of slaves was a fictitious 'suit for freedom' on behalf of the slave, to which the *dominus* made no defence. Analogy, thirdly, was a kind of 'deeming', as in the *actiones utiles*, the praetor granting an action as if the case had come squarely under the statute. A final kind was the use of procedures as formalities after their original practical function had been abandoned. *Mancipatio*, for example, had once been an actual sale, before it became a formality to achieve conveyance; and the standard will, the *testamentum per aes et libram*, started as the actual lifetime transfer of an estate to a friend, but finished up as a symbolic transfer having effect only when the testator died.

Bona fides, aequum et bonum, 'equity' These were important notions in the progress of Roman law; they are best understood in a firmly pragmatic way, as practical devices for balancing the certainty and predictability of *strictum ius* (which says 'never mind what may have been intended: what was done has such-and-such legal consequences') with a reasonable flexibility about intention and a general sense of fairness.[101] The whole *ius honorarium* was 'the Roman equity': for example, the *exceptiones* and *replicationes* of the formulary system were an elegant equitable device to enable the parties to bring up, *in iure*, every modification of *strictum ius* that they wanted the *iudex* to take into account. As for *bona fides*, its complex background has been the object of many studies,[102] and it sometimes receives a rather mystical treatment.[103] It is best seen at practical work in the *bonae fidei iudicia*,[104] where all the modifications that in *strictum ius* could only be granted by *exceptio* were conceded by the equally elegant equitable device of writing 'good faith' into the formula for the *iudex*: 'quidquid ob eam rem Numerium Negidium Aulo Agerio dare facere oportet ex fide bona';[105] but its capacity to advance fair

100 See the List of select sources, p. 560.

101 See Schiller 1978 (F 264) 551ff; Wieacker 1988 (F 171) 506–9.

102 See Lombardi 1961 (F 234); Waldstein 1976 (F 287) 66–78.

103 Schulz 1936 (F 267) ch. 11 was too broad; every people tends to think it has a monopoly of good faith.

104 Arising, e.g., from the 'consensual' contracts. See, generally, Wieacker 1963 (F 310).

105 The *formulae* with 'quantam pecuniam ... bonum aequum videbitur' and other variations were essentially the same, *pace* Ciulei 1972 (F 195).

dealing may be observed in another example, that of *usucapio*: it was not originally a necessity for a valid *usucapio* that the possessor should have been in good faith when his possession began (for *usucapio* was *stricti iuris*), but by Cicero's time *bona fides* had won through, and initial good faith *was* required.[106] Furthermore, the whole development of *in integrum restitutio* and of the *exceptio* and *actio* for *dolus malus* rested on the notion that *strictum ius* must not enable people to use the law for unfair ends.

Interpretation[107] We come, finally, to the jurists, who, in framing their *responsa*, had to interpret the law, e.g. to settle whether the words of a statute or a will implied this or that, or whether some set of alleged facts grounded such-and-such a claim or constituted such-and-such an offence, and under whose inspiration the praetors developed the mechanisms that have been described above. They also initiated the biggest-scale branch of technical literature the Romans ever had, by writing about the law. This stage of Roman jurisprudence coincided with the apogee of Greek influence on Roman ideas, and so for Schulz it was the 'Hellenistic Age of Roman Legal Science'. It is true that, labouring under the conviction of Greek cultural superiority, the Romans acquired the urge to turn every subject into an *ars*, a logical system based on partition and division, genus and species.[108] Both Pompey and Julius Caesar had plans to codify the law, and Cicero dreamt of an *ars*;[109] and Q. Mucius, cos. 95 was, according to Pomponius, the first jurist to organize the civil law *generatim*.[110] But it is worth while to distinguish, even if a little artificially, between organization and systematization. Of the latter, some aspects were, for positive law, pretty trivial. It may be doubted, for example, how much it really mattered – especially as the jurists reached no consensus – how many 'kinds' of theft or guardianship there were; and although usufruct and servitudes were eventually, long after our period, conceptualized as two sub-branches of 'rights over someone else's thing', *iura in re aliena*,[111] their positive rules were worked out quite happily long before anyone thought of the logical connexion. Of the organization of the law, on the other hand, one may judge less negatively. Law (English as well as Roman) has gone through phases of purely empirical development followed by phases when the best minds saw that things were in a 'chaos of cases', and sought for general

[106] See Watson 1968 (F 297) 54.

[107] See, generally, Watson 1974 (F 304) ch. 9; Schiller 1978 (F 264) 373–83; Frier 1985 (F 205) 160–8 and 190–4; Wieacker 1988 (F 171) 519–675.

[108] Cic. *De Or.* 1.186–9; *Brut.* 152–3; Watson 1974 (F 304) ch. 15; Rawson 1985 (H 109) ch. 14.

[109] See (with caution) Polay 1965 (F 255) and 1965 (F 256); d'Ippolito 1978 (F 217) 93–8; (again with caution) Bauman 1985 (F 179) 78–83. On Cicero see also von Lübtow 1944 (F 235).

[110] On the originality of Q. Mucius see Frier 1985 (F 205) 160–3.

[111] D. 7.1.1.

principles from which decision might proceed more deductively.[112] Yet, as modern authors remind us, law is not a closed logical system. Analysis of the *rationes decidendi*, the criteria of decision, in the surviving *responsa* of the Republican period – in so far as the jurists stated reasons at all other than just prior authority – shows that they used all the techniques of (common-sense) logical argument according to the problem in hand;[113] but beneath the overt logic of legal reasoning lies, legitimately, a casuistic process of comparison of case with case.[114] Hence, whatever the influence of Greek ideas on the organization of Roman law in our period, it was the individual *responsa* of the jurists that carried the development of positive law, and it is much less clear, from that standpoint, that there was much that was specifically 'Hellenistic' about the increased sophistication of the law.[115]

The assertion of Greek influence on the interpretative thought of the Roman jurists has recently passed through two trends and is currently in a third.[116] The first arose from the observation that the greatest contemporary *ars*, in which all Roman gentlemen were trained, was rhetoric, which offered a sophisticated armoury of generalized topoi and of categories and distinctions, such as the different *staseis* (types of issue) in legal argument (especially '*scriptum* versus *sententia*' ('wording as against intention')). Some of the insights were valuable, but the case for influence on the jurists, as opposed to the advocates, was never strong.[117] For Schulz, who loathed rhetoric, it was Greek dialectic, from Plato and Aristotle, i.e. logical philosophy, the art of definition and division, which supplied the 'Promethean fire' that 'transformed Roman jurisprudence into a systematic science';[118] perhaps enough has been said already to indicate some limitations to the validity of that belief. The third trend looks not to rhetoric nor yet to dialectic but to Greek legal and moral

[112] J. M. Rigg in *Dictionary of National Biography* lxiii, 350 says of Lord Hardwicke, an eighteenth-century Lord Chancellor, that he 'transformed equity from a chaos of precedents into a scientific system'; and the famous aphorism of Justice Holmes 'The life of the law has not been logic: it has been experience' comes from a plea for greater generalization in legal thinking: Oliver Wendell Holmes, jr., *The Common Law* (Boston 1881, repr. (ed. M. de W. Hare) Harvard 1963, repr. 1968), 1. See also Stein 1974 (F 273) 437–41.

[113] See, generally, Horak 1969 (F 214); Schiller 1978 (F 264) 382; Seidl 1966 (F 269) 360 and *passim*.

[114] See Wieacker 1971 (F 314) and 1976 (F 315); Bund 1971 (F 192) 573–9.

[115] For the subtlety of the antique pontifical jurisprudence see Wolf 1985 (F 318) esp. 1: '... durchdachte Zweckschöpfungen einer rationalen Rechtskunde'. See also Wieacker 1986 (F 316) and 1988 (F 171) 310–40.

[116] See, generally, Wieacker 1969 (F 313); Schiller 1978 (F 264) 373ff. Wieacker 1988 (F 171) 347–52, 618–75, gives a more positive picture of Greek influence than is taken in this chapter.

[117] On the key personality, Hermagoras of Temnos, see G. Kennedy, *The Art of Persuasion in Greece* (Princeton, 1963) 303–21. Enthusiastic acceptance: Kunkel 1953 (F 229) 14; dismissal: Watson 1974 (F 304) 194–5, Wesel 1967 (F 308) 137–9, Wieling 1972 (F 317) 56; limits: Bund 1971 (F 192) 578; an Indian summer: Y.-P. Thomas 1978 (F 281); most recently, Wieacker 1988 (F 171) 662–75.

[118] Schulz 1953 (F 268) 62–9; see also Stein 1966 (F 272) 33–48. More negative: Talamanca 1976–7 (F 278) 211ff, esp. 258–61; Wieacker 1988 (F 171) 618–39, esp. 638–9.

philosophy, with which also all Roman gentlemen received some acquaintance, for the guiding force behind the *responsa* of the jurists. The most striking thesis[119] asks us to find not only crucial differences between the brands of Stoicism that influenced the jurists round Scipio Aemilianus and the Gracchi, but a major shift between all that Stoicism and the supposed Carneadean pragmatism of Cicero's contemporaries, beginning with Aquilius Gallus. Its philosophical foundations are under challenge, not least on the ground that Roman interest in philosophy was relatively popular and unspecific. Less controversial are studies that more simply reassert the general importance of Stoicism as an influence on Roman legal thought.[120] At least it may well be admitted that there was an observable shift, whether or not motivated by Greek philosophy, in the principles on which the jurists interpreted the law.[121]

Another current trend in scholarship, overlapping with that just described, is to insist on the involvement of the jurists in the political events and alignments as well as in the ideas of their age.[122] That is welcome to the historian, who finds a wholly autonomous Roman jurisprudence unlikely. Its practitioners forfeit some confidence, however, when they operate with notions of faction and speculative prosopographical combinations such as are no longer current coin, and engage in special pleading to rescue admired figures from insinuations of politically motivated inconsistency.[123] In any case, this treatment illuminates the relation of the jurists to public more than to private law; for the main question to which it is relevant is what part they played in promoting (or even in drafting) the statutes that were passed in their time: no unanimity of view has been reached. Nevertheless, it is valuable to be reminded that the interests of those not inconsiderable men were not narrowly limited to the sphere of private law. They were, down to (say) Sulla's time, career-following members of an intensely political governing class, involved, along with their peers, in all that concerned the *res publica*.

Did they, during Cicero's time, cease to be so, and does that betoken a change in the way law was interpreted? Kunkel's thesis[124] of a class-shift

[119] That of Behrends in numerous papers esp. 1976 (F 180), 1977 (F 181), 1980 (F 21). Criticism by Horak 1978 (F 215) 402–14. The key personalities are Antipater of Tarsus and Blossius of Cumae.

[120] E.g. Bund 1980 (F 193) and, generally, Wieacker 1988 (F 171) 639–61.

[121] See, however, criticism by Bauman 1985 (F 179) 7–12.

[122] See Wieacker 1970 (F 313A); Bretone 1971 (F 190); Schiavone 1976 (F 263); d'Ippolito 1971 (F 216) and 1978 (F 217); Bauman 1983 (F 178) and 1985 (F 179). See also, on Greek political influence, Nicolet 1965 (C 115).

[123] See, e.g., Guarino 1981 (C 70); Bauman 1978 (F 177) and 1983 (F 178) 274. *Contra*, Gruen 1965 (C 67).

[124] Kunkel 1967 (F 228) 50–61. See also Frier 1985 (F 205) 252–60; Rawson 1985 (H 109) 89–90. Criticism by Bauman 1985 (F 179) 10–11; accepted, however, by Wieacker 1988 (F 171) 595–6, 614–15.

in the jurists, from being of senatorial, aristocratic origin to being equestrians and Italian *municipales homines* (with implications as to the kind of law we should expect from them) does not stand up well to recent changes in historical emphasis. In spite of caveats, Kunkel believed, more than would now be acceptable, in the *equites* as a business class with a distinct ideology; and we do not know what he would have made of the point that scholars now emphasize, that the aristocracy itself was not a nobility of blood but had to resubmit itself to competition for office in every generation. Moreover, anybody of non-senatorial origin he put in the 'equestrian' category,[125] which gives a wrong impression, because all these jurists finished up in senatorial careers. *Novi homines* some no doubt were, as were some non-jurists; but there is insufficient reason to attribute to them as such any distinct legal ideology, certainly not a 'business' one. In any case, the thesis could only apply to the very end of our period, for no major jurist remained all his life outside the senatorial order until Ofilius and Trebatius Testa, and no major jurist till that time was a mere *municipalis homo*. Contemporaries imply what the legal shift was really due to: the triumph of specialization, which made jurisprudence and political careers increasingly incompatible.[126]

Pomponius parades the great names, and Cicero puts a little flesh on the bones. Sex. Aelius Paetus 'Catus', cos. 198, a friend of Ennius, wrote the first significant law-book, 'Tripertita'; it listed the clauses of the Twelve Tables and gave each its appropriate *legis actio* and a commentary. The 'founders of the *ius civile*' were M. Iunius Brutus, pr. 142, M'. Manilius, cos. 149, and P. Mucius Scaevola, cos. 133, of whom the last two were 'Ti. Graccho auctores legum'[127] and Manilius also the author of the example-book from which Cato and Varro got their standard forms for agricultural contracts. The most important Mucius Scaevola in the law was, however, Q. Mucius, cos. 95. His books on the law, a treatise on the *ius civile* arranged *generatim* and a book of *horoi* ('distinctions'), were used as the basis for commentaries in the 'classical' age; his edict for the province of Asia was a paradigm; and he took part in the *causa Curiana*, the most celebrated private law case in the Republican age, which was looked back to as a historic moment.[128] Cicero's own friends and contemporaries amongst the jurists were C. Aquilius Gallus, pr. 66, who invented the *actio de dolo* and the *stipulatio Aquiliana*, and Ser.

[125] Cicero would presumably have been so listed if he had counted as a jurist at all in Kunkel's eyes.

[126] Cic. *Att.* I.I.I: 'Aquilius won't be in the race [sc. for the consulship]: he's said 'no' and sworn illness and pleaded his Panjandrumship in the law courts' ('illud suum regnum iudiciale').

[127] Cic. *Acad. Pr.* II.13.

[128] See n. 20 above. The case was formerly hailed as the triumph of equity over *strictum ius*. Cic. *De Or.* I.180; II.140–1; *Brut.* 144–5; *Top.* 44; *Inv.* II.121–3. Huge bibliography: see Wieacker 1967 (F 312); Watson 1971 (F 300) 44, 53–5, 94–6 and 1974 (F 304) 129–30; Wieling 1972 (F 317) 9–15, 65–6; Bauman 1983 (F 178) 344–51.

Sulpicius Rufus, cos. 51,[129] the most formidable systematizer. At the end we come to Julius Caesar's protégés, P. Alfenus Varus, cos. suff. 39[130] (some of whose surviving descriptions of cases have the – for us – precious feature that all the facts are related as well as the *responsum*)[131] and A. Ofilius, who wrote the first substantial commentary on the praetor's edict.[132]

Notwithstanding all the hazards of transmission – the danger of non-representativeness, the possibility of alterations by the later writers in quoting the earlier, the suspicions of interpolation – the best way to look into the minds of these men is to see them at work: there follow six examples.

(i) (Cicero, *De Finibus* I 12, followed by Ulpian in D. 7.1.68 *pr.*) Cicero: 'Shall there be discussion between those pillars of society P. Scaevola and M'. Manilius as to whether the offspring of a slave woman should be counted as "produce"? And shall M. Brutus have a different opinion?' Ulpian: 'It was an old problem whether [human] offspring belonged to the fructuary, but Brutus' view prevailed, that the fructuary had no right to such, for no human being can be the "produce" of a human being.'[133]

(ii) (D. 9.2.27.22) 'If a [slave] woman has been struck by you with your fist, or a mare by some blow of yours, and has miscarried, Brutus says you are liable under the Lex Aquilia as if it was *rumpere*.'[134]

(iii) (D. 24.3.66 *pr.*) 'In respect of things other than money that a husband has by way of dowry, Servius says he is liable to pay for deliberate and for involuntary fault ("dolum malum et culpam"). That is the view of P. Mucius: in the case of Licinia the wife of C. Gracchus he laid down that because things forming her dowry had perished in the sedition in which C. Gracchus was killed, since that sedition had happened as a result of the fault of Gracchus, Licinia was entitled to be reimbursed for them.'[135]

(iv) (D. 32.29.1) 'When a legacy had been phrased thus: "Let Titia my wife have the same share as ['tantamdem partem quantulam'] one heir", if the heirs were heirs to unequal shares, Q. Mucius and Gallus thought

[129] Syme 1981 (F 277) separates the jurist Sulpicius from the orator Sulpicius, though Pomponius evidently thought they were the same: 'in causis orandis primum locum aut pro certo post M. Tullium'. On the jurist see Bauman 1985 (F 179) ch. 1, and, for his 'modernism', Wieacker 1988 (F 171) 603.

[130] Perhaps the man who, with Pollio and Cornelius Gallus, gave Virgil back his farm – if the first and ninth Eclogues contain autobiography.

[131] Alfenus in his *Digesta* is often reporting not his own *responsa* but those of his teacher Servius, and mostly one cannot tell whose is the decision expressed.

[132] See d'Ippolito 1978 (F 217) ch. 5. On Aquilius Gallus, Alfenus Varus and Ofilius see also Bauman 1985 (F 179) ch. 2.

[133] See Kaser 1958 (F 219); Watson 1967–8 (F 296) and 1968 (F 297) 215–16; Behrends 1980 (F 183) 68–79. Some think the reason given is an interpolation, or is at least Ulpian's rather than that of Brutus.

[134] *Rumpere* in the text of the statute probably meant direct physical breaking off of a limb. See Watson 1965 (F 294) 244–5.

[135] See Daube 1963 (F 200); Waldstein 1972 (F 286); Bauman 1978 (F 177) 238–42.

the legacy was of the largest share on the ground that the greater included the less. Servius and Ofilius thought it was of the smallest share, on the ground that since the heir had been charged with making the legacy it was up to him what share he would give.'

(v) (D. 11.3.16 (Alfenus or Servius)) 'A master manumitted his accountant, who was a slave, and afterwards received his accounts, which failed to balance; and he discovered that the accountant had spent the money *chez* a certain little woman ["apud quandam mulierculam"]. The question was, could he have an "action for corruption of a slave" against the woman, in spite of the slave being now a free man? I replied "Yes, and also for theft of the money that the slave had made over to her".'[136]

(vi) (D. 14.1.1.9) 'Ofilius raises the question, if he [an agent] borrowed money to refit the ship and converted the money to his own use, does an action lie against the principal [*exercitor*]? And he says that if he [the agent] received the money on the ground that he was going to spend it on the vessel and then changed his mind the principal is liable, for it is his own fault for employing that agent; but if he [the agent] intended to defraud the creditor from the start the contrary is the case.'[137]

From the above six examples something can be seen of the careful drawing of distinctions, and the readiness to consider both actual and hypothetical cases, that characterize all Republican jurisprudence; also, how little interest any of the jurists had in generalization. But they also illustrate a change in the style of legal thinking.[138] On the one hand is the expansive interpretation of the older jurists of the age, influenced both (as some scholars hold) by a Stoic view of law as the human counterpart of the natural justice of the universe, and also by a paternalistic and patronal attitude to their society, as befitted men of the leading political class. On the other is the positivist thinking of Cicero's contemporaries, a new, more specialist, generation, whether or not influenced by the sceptical Academy, who saw law not as any projection of nature but as an autonomous science that must derive its own rules and exceptions from its own independent axioms. That is to state the contrast much too starkly; but the direction of movement it represents is valid enough.

IV

Evaluation of the private law of the Republic must begin with a consideration of some features that it yet lacked, as well as some that Roman law was destined always to lack.[139]

[136] The words 'and also for theft . . . over to her' are commonly held to be interpolated.

[137] The words 'for it is . . . that agent' are commonly held to be interpolated.

[138] See Watson 1969 (F 298) and 1972 (F 301). For good examples of the legal thinking of the older jurists see Wieacker 1988 (F 171) 572–90.

[139] See Watson 1974 (F 304) 111–12.

Among procedural developments reached only at a later date we may note the absence of civil appeal: until there was a Princeps there could be no hierarchy of courts, since the assembly of the Roman people played no role in civil jurisdiction.[140] Condemnation to direct restitution, as opposed to *condemnatio pecuniaria*, also had to await the growth of the imperial *cognitio* in place of the formulary system; and so, again, did distraint on specific items of property, to replace the crude *bonorum possessio* of a person's whole assets.[141] Virtually no sign yet existed of administrative law:[142] that depended on the growth under Augustus of fiscal demands and a treasury interest in vacant and void inheritances. In the law of persons, Augustus made, by statute, changes in the positions and prospects of slaves and freedmen, and it was with Augustus' invention of *peculium castrense* (comprising anything a *filius familias* received from or in connexion with military service) that the *filius familias* first got a fund that was indisputably his own. The rules of intestate succession were destined to receive further modification in favour of blood relatives. In contract, if you look at a book on the 'classical' law it will be seen to contain sections on 'pacts' and 'innominate contracts', which represent the growth of legal recognition of various sorts of agreement that lay outside the Republican scope of contract, while assignment of debt and remedies for unjust enrichment were two other fields where big developments were yet to come.[143]

It is commonplace to note the limited progress of Roman labour law; and here we move into the things the Romans never developed much or at all. *Locatio conductio* was never unravelled:[144] rules and terms of hiring out one's labour remained a tiny corner of a huge field of socially quite different arrangements, and there emerged no sense of a need to protect labour as the weaker bargaining side. Equally commonplace is the observation that the Romans developed no general theory of contract,[145] but just stopped gaps where they perceived inconvenience. They never got over their difficulty in conceptualizing true agency (though the lawyers of the Principate were fertile in additional stratagems to get an equivalent effect). As we have seen, certain features of law and society made it less necessary: sons *in potestate*, and slaves, were automatically direct agents of their *paterfamilias* or *dominus* in acquiring for him, and *peculium* enabled them to be more or less so in creating obligations

[140] See A. H. M. Jones 1960 (F 87) 77–83.

[141] On distraint replacing *bonorum possessio* see Crook 1967 (F 197) 366–7.

[142] D. 1.2.2.44, where Pomponius appears to say that Ofilius was the first to write a handbook *de legibus vicesimae*, was emended by Huschke: see Lenel, *Palingenesia* I 798 n. 3. Defended, however, by Bauman 1985 (F 179) 83–5.

[143] See, generally, Nicholas 1962 (F 248) 189, 200, 231.

[144] *Pace* Lewis 1973 (F 232). So much for the Roman achievement in systematization!

[145] See Nicholas 1962 (F 248) 165.

binding him. All that is simply an aspect of the fact that the Roman economy remained pre-industrial and pre-capitalist and took slavery for granted. But no less striking than what the Romans did not invent is what they did not abolish: the institutions of *patria potestas* and *tutela*, *dominium* and *possessio*, *res manicipi* and *nec mancipi*, could not be shifted, and had to be ever more ingeniously circumvented: that was the Roman way.

Roman private law is much admired as the one independent creative act of the Roman genius,[146] the late Republic being its apogee of creativity. It presents to posterity especially a paradigm of 'lawyerliness', which is why it retains some interest for those who study law today.[147] An attempt has been made in this chapter to bring out what the 'lawyerliness' consisted of and how much the creativity did and did not achieve. The historian is entitled to cast a cold eye, not to denigrate (for the legal distance the Romans travelled in the 400 years between the Twelve Tables and Cicero, without the stimulus of an industrial and scientific revolution, is tremendous) but to place in context, bearing in mind that, if Roman law is open to criticism, so are all contemporary systems. A commonplace of criticism is that Roman law was the creation of a possessing class, reflecting their interests and enshrining their values. Questions are, for example, asked about how much access to those admired adversarial procedures was available to the man in the street – questions about costs and distances and patronage (*gratia*).[148] It can be seen how contract was assumed to be a bargain between parties of equal 'clout', and what preponderant attention was lavished on property, testament and legacy. The tenant with no *ius in rem*, the slave as chattel: these features show the proprietorial values that applied, just as both the role of the oath in litigation and the importance of *infamia* as a sanction show the societal values. Now, the historian must avoid exaggeration: documentary evidence[149] reveals relatively humble people operating in the obvious expectation that the theoretical system in all its details was available in practice and applied to and against them; and the answers to the questions about costs and so on are not as negative as is sometimes made out. Roman law was not a fraud. But it was, undeniably, conceived as a system 'between gentlemen', amongst whom, indeed, it gave great legal equality.[150]

The law of classical Athens offers a profound contrast. It catered for a much more – if you like, the only truly – populist society; it was

[146] Except by those who think they borrowed most of it from Greece.

[147] See Frier 1985 (F 205) 193.

[148] See especially (if with caution) Kelly 1966 (F 226).

[149] Of the first and second centuries A.D., but that does not invalidate it. There is a mass of relevant material in *FIRA* III.

[150] The theme of Mette 1974 (F 247); see also Watson 1974 (F 304) 60 n. 2; Frier 1985 (F 205) 192.

grounded entirely on statute and people's courts, with no place for edicts or jurists; yet it was evidently capable of generating the legal answers the society thought satisfactory. Wolfgang Kunkel ventured the heretical thought that some Greek ideas about law were 'grander' than anything the Romans ever attained to,[151] but he was talking about Aristotle and the Stoics,[152] and therein lies the fundamental difference: the Greeks talked philosophy of law, the Romans talked jurisprudence.[153]

151 Kunkel 1953 (F 229) 15.

152 He could have had some success even with the positive law: there is a case for thinking that the Hellenistic states had a more sophisticated banking law than did the Roman Republic. See Vigneron 1984 (F 284) especially at the end.

153 See Wieacker 1961 (F 309), essays 1, 'Römertum und röm. Recht' and 3, 'Lex publica'; Galsterer 1980 (F 206). On Greek philosophy of law and its echoes in Roman thinking see Ducos 1984 (F 201).

SELECT NON-JURISTIC SOURCES FOR THE STUDY OF ROMAN PRIVATE LAW OF THE REPUBLIC

Literature:

Cato *Agr.* 144–50
Varro *Rust.* II.2.5–6
Cicero
Orations: *Quinct.*, *QRosc.*, *Tull.*, *Caecin.*
II Verr. 1.103–54; 2 *passim*; 3. 28, 55, 69, 135; 5. 23
Balb. 21–4
Flac. 46–50; 84–9
Letters: *Att.* I.5,6; V.21,6; VI.1,15; VI.2,4; XIII.50,2; XVI.15,2
Fam. III.8,4; VII.12,2; XIII.14,1 and 26,3; XV.16,3
Rhetorical works: *De Or.* I.101; 166–83; 241
Top. passim
Philosophical works:
Acad. II.23–9
Rep. III.8–31
Fin. I.12; II.54–9
Off. III.50–95

Inscriptions:

Lex 'de piratis'	*FIRA* I no. 9 (with *JRS* 64 (1974), 195–220, text at p. 204, lines 31–9)
Lex Antonia de Termessibus	*FIRA* I no. 11
Table of Heraclea, 108ff	*FIRA* I no. 13
Lex Rubria and frag. Atestinum	*FIRA* I nos. 19–20
SC de Asclepiade, lines 17–20	*FIRA* I no. 35
Laudatio 'Turiae'	*FIRA* III no. 69
Sententia Minuciorum	*FIRA* III no. 163
Tabula Contrebiensis	*JRS* 73 (1983) 33–41 and 74 (1984) 45–73
Tabula Irnitana	*JRS* 76 (1986) 147–243

CHRONOLOGICAL INDICATIONS RELATING TO THE DEVELOPMENT OF ROMAN PRIVATE LAW IN THE REPUBLIC

Before 200 B.C.

326 Lex Poetelia (*de nexu*)
? *c.* 287 Lex Aquilia (*de damno*)
by *c.* 241 Lex Plaetoria (*de iurisdictione*)
?210 Lex Atilia (*de tutoribus*)
204 Lex Cincia (*de donis*)

c. 200–150 B.C.

Sex. Aelius, cos. 198, responding on (?consensual) sale, D. 19.1.38.1
?Reference to praetorian *iniuria*, Plaut. *Asin.* 371

c. 200–190 Lex Laetoria (*de minoribus*)

Procedure under Lex Laetoria, Plaut. *Pseud.* 303; *Rud.* 1380–2
Fiducia and *pignus*, Plaut. *Epid.* 697–9
Pact *de fide et fiducia*, *Trinumm.* 117

169 Lex Voconia (*de mulieribus instituendis*)

161: Reference to interdictal procedure, Ter. *Eun.* 319
?Known already to Cato: *actio Serviana* for lien, *Agr.* 149.2; aedilician edict on slaves, D. 21.1.10.1

c. 150–100 B.C.

The *veteres* debating usufruct, Cic. *Fin.* I 12

Lex Aebutia (*de formulis*)

129: Interdict *uti possidetis* (dramatic date of Cic. *Rep.* I 20)
123 and 115: actions on mandate, *Rhet. Her.* II.19; also actions for *iniuria* by Lucilius and Accius
c. 118 (not later): edict of P. Rutilius on burdens imposed on freedmen
111: Procurator, *lex agraria*, *FIRA* I no. 8, line 69; *bonorum emptor*, etc., line 56

c. 100–80 B.C. | Lex Minicia (*de liberis*), at least before the Social War

Q. Mucius cos. 95 knows all the consensual contracts and *commodatum*

87: The *tabula Contrebiensis*, *formulae* in Spain

The Leges Corneliae, including Lex Cornelia de iniuriis

By 81 (date of Cic. *Quinct.*): *bonorum possessio* against *latitantes*.

c. 80–70 B.C.

80 or 79: the *formula Octaviana* on *metus*

?76: the *interdictum Salvianum* for lien

76: edict of M. Lucullus *de vi hominibus armatis*

In the Verrines:

bonorum possessio ab intestato, SINE RE, already old, II *Verr.* 1.114

bonorum possessio secundum tabulas, SINE RE, already 'translaticium', II *Verr.* 1.117

bonorum possessio contra tabulas, CUM RE, against estate of freedman, II *Verr.* 1.125

formula for *vindicatio* with *clausula arbitraria*, II *Verr.* 2.31

By date of the *pro Roscio Comoedo*: '*formulae* for everything'

71: Metellus' interdict *de vi armata*

By 70: *denegatio* of a *iure civili* action, Val. Max. VII 7.5

c. 70–60 B.C.

?67: *actio Publiciana*

Aquilius Gallus' inventions:

exceptio(?) and *actio doli*

stipulatio Aquiliana

?65: *actio Serviana* (but see Cato above)

c. 60–50 B.C.

Ser. Sulpicius commenting on the *actiones exercitoria* and *institoria* and the *actio de peculio*

?56 Lex Scribonia (*de usucapione servitutum*)

The earliest *actiones in factum*

By 52: *querela inofficiosi testamenti*, Val. Max. VII.7.2

post 50 B.C.

The Lex Rubria deals with *damnum infectum*

The *frag. Atestinum* has *actiones famosae*

By 44: The interdict *quorum bonorum*, Cic. *Fam*. VII.21

In Cicero's *Topica*: *actio negotiorum gestorum, actio rei uxoriae*

CHAPTER 15

THE ADMINISTRATION OF THE EMPIRE

JOHN RICHARDSON

The expansion of the power of the city of Rome through the whole of the Mediterranean world during the last three centuries B.C. led to the establishment of Rome as the predominant military and economic force in the region. It also made it necessary to develop ways of administering so large and diverse an area. The patterns which emerged are now usually referred to as the provincial administration of the empire, and there is no doubt that some such collective title is necessary to describe the various methods used by officials of the state to control the communities and individuals with whom they were in contact. It is important at the outset, however, to recognize that 'provincial administration' was not a Roman concept, at least during the period of the Republic, within which the empire took shape.

I. PROVINCES AND *PROVINCIAE*: THE ORIGINS OF THE SYSTEM

Although the English 'province' is obviously derived from the Latin *provincia*, the meaning of the two is by no means identical. A province, whether in a constitutional context, as for example the province of Ulster or of Ontario, or in an ecclesiastical, such as the provinces of Canterbury and York, is an area defined for administrative purposes. The *provincia* on the other hand seems originally to have been a task assigned to a specified Roman magistrate or promagistrate, in the fulfilment of which he would exercise the *imperium* granted to him in virtue of his election or appointment. Although his task might well consist of using that *imperium*, the executive power of the Roman people, in a military command within a particular geographical area, it need not do so. Livy several times describes an Italian tribe as a consul's *provincia*, and during his account of the Second Punic War he refers to the *provinciae* of the fleet and the war against Hannibal in the same way.[1] Similarly the treasury is called the *provincia* of a quaestor, and the *urbana provincia* marked the allocation of the civil jurisdiction within the city. When used by Plautus

[1] Livy III.25.9 ('exercitum ducere'), VI.30.3 ('Volsci'), XXVII.22.2 ('Sallentini'), XLIV.1.3 ('classis'), XXIV.44.1 ('bellum cum Hannibale').

and Terence, writing comedies in the second century,[2] and also in Cicero,[3] the word seems to have a sense rather like the secondary meaning in modern English, of a concern or sphere of influence. When at the beginning of each consular year the Senate assigned *provinciae* to the various magistrates and promagistrates, what they were doing was more like allocating a portfolio than putting people in charge of geographical areas.

The significance of this for the understanding of 'provincial administration' is considerable. The first magistrates to whom *provinciae* were given outside the city of Rome were sent to wage war on her enemies in the surrounding area. In the third and second centuries, when *provinciae* were allotted overseas, the magistrates and pro-magistrates concerned were sent there as military commanders. As the main responsibility of the man whose *provincia* lay in the region named by the Senate was the command of the army stationed there, many of the functions which would be expected of a provincial administrator in the modern sense were his almost by default. However, the decision by the Senate to assign an area as a *provincia* did not constitute a claim to possession of the territory concerned. Although what precisely constituted the annexation of a given territory by the Roman state in the first period of the extension of its power through the Mediterranean world remains disputed,[4] the mere naming of it as a *provincia* certainly did not. Macedonia, for instance, was first assigned as a *provincia* in 211 (to the consul P. Sulpicius Galba), but this act of the Senate, while indicating that they wished the consul to take command of an army there in order to fight against Philip V, did not also imply that they wished the territory to become a part of the Roman empire on a permanent basis. Macedonia continued to be named in this way year by year down to 205, by which time the Peace of Phoinike had brought to an end the First Macedonian War. In the second century it was a consular *provincia* throughout the Second and Third Macedonian Wars. Following the defeat of Perseus in 168, L. Aemilius Paullus, after consultation with a ten-man senatorial commission, issued laws to Macedonia, which provided for the abolition of the kingdom, and its replacement by four allegedly independent states, paying taxation, though at a lower rate from that which they had previously paid to the kings. This might well be considered the consequence of a decision to annex Macedonia, and indeed the later epitomator of Livy's histories summarizes Paullus' work in the language of the imperial period with the words 'Macedonia in provinciae formam redacta'.[5] Yet not only was

[2] Plaut. *Capt.* 156, 158, 474; *Cas.* 103; *Mil. Glor.* 1159; *Pseud.* 148, 158; *Stich.* 689–90; *Trin.* 190. Ter. *Haut.* 516; *Phorm.* 72.

[3] Cic. *Cael.* 26.63; *Fin.* 1.20 (of the patterns of falling atoms).

[4] See, for example Harris 1979 (A 47) reviewed in *History of Political Thought* 1 (1980) 340–2.

[5] Livy *Per.* 45.

14 The Roman world in 50 B.C.

Macedonia already Paullus' *provincia*, and had been since it had been allotted to him by the Senate in the previous year, but once he left the area it ceased to be a *provincia* until the praetor P. Iuventius was sent there to oppose the pretender to the throne of the Macedonian kings, Andriscus, in 149. It is indeed usual to date the annexation of Macedonia from the allotment of the *provincia* to Iuventius' successor, Q. Metellus, in 148, and in later documents this year is taken as the beginning of the provincial era.[6] However, even then there is no sign that what one might think of as typical 'provincial' institutions were set up. The four republics from Paullus' settlement occur in documents of the late Republican and early Imperial periods, and from a passing remark in Livy it seems that Paullus' laws were still in use down to his own time.[7] What happened after 148 was that the Senate regularly named Macedonia as a *provincia* each year, and that, as a result, a Roman commander with Roman forces was always in the region.

This example shows that the naming of an area as a *provincia* did not necessarily result in its immediate annexation. A similarly ambiguous pattern may be seen in the case of the Spanish *provinciae*. In 218 Hispania was named as the *provincia* of the consul P. Cornelius Scipio, but, as with the first allocation of Macedonia, there is no suggestion that this was understood to be a claim to sovereignty over the area. The immediate need was to face the threat of Hannibal, and subsequently the danger that Hannibal might receive reinforcements from the Carthaginian bases in Spain. For a decade after the successful expulsion of the Carthaginians from the peninsula in 206 by Scipio's son, the later Africanus, the Senate seems to have had doubts even about continuing the Roman military presence there. Still less is there any sign of the establishment of 'provincial administration'. Although two additional praetors were elected each year from 196 onwards with the needs of Spain in mind, there was no systematic organization even of relationships with the local communities for nearly thirty years. The few instances of taxation and jurisdiction were purely *ad hoc*, and emerged from the immediate needs of an army, stationed in a strategically important area.[8]

The reason for the examination of these two examples of Spain and Macedonia in some detail is not of course to argue that the Romans never acquired territory at all, still less that they were in any way peaceable or non-aggressive in their relations with other states in the area. The sending of armies and commanders to all parts of the Mediterranean world was a commonplace of Rome's foreign policy at this period, as it had been within Italy in the late fourth and early third centuries B.C. These instances do illustrate, however, that the establishment of institu-

[6] See Larsen, *ESAR* 4.303.

[7] Livy XLV.32.7.

[8] See Richardson 1986 (E 25) esp. chs. 3–5.

tions of provincial administration was not the object of the naming of an area as a *provincia*, at least in the formative years of the third and early second centuries. It was not necessary for there to be a *provincia* in order for such institutions to be established, and, vice versa, a *provincia* could exist in an area for a long time before such institutions were fully developed. This can be seen most clearly by looking at the spheres of responsibility which a provincial governor in the late Republic was usually expected to undertake. They will be examined in more detail later, but for the purpose of examining their origins it will be sufficient to categorize them roughly under three headings: political and military relations, taxation, and jurisdiction.

Political involvement with the communities within the geographical limits of a *provincia* was evidently a major part of the work of a Roman commander in the field. The prosecution of a war involved the establishment and maintenance of alliances, and although this meant different things in different areas, there was always some part to be played by the man on the spot. Such activity obviously required the presence of a magistrate or promagistrate and thus the existence under normal circumstances of a *provincia*. However that did not necessarily imply any permanence. As has been said already, there was considerable uncertainty about the continuity of the Spanish *provinciae*, at least until the decision to send out praetors from 196 B.C. on an annual basis, yet already in 206 the younger P. Scipio had established a settlement for wounded soldiers from among his own forces at Italica (now Santiponce) just north of modern Seville, with a splendid view across the valley of the Guadalquivir. This decision is the more remarkable because, like others taken by commanders in the far-off region of Spain at this time, there seems to have been no consultation of the Senate before it was made, nor indeed, to judge by the fact that Italica appears to have had no official Roman status until the end of the Republican period, did the Senate take very much notice of it once it had been.[9] Such a lack of senatorial involvement was much less common in the eastern Mediterranean, where frequent links between the Senate and the Greek cities and the large-scale reorganizations in the area which followed the wars against the kings of Macedonia and Syria in the first half of the second century led to the practice of sending out commissions of ten senatorial *legati*, to assist the commander in making treaties and determining the relationships between Rome and the various states involved. Yet even in instances such as these, the making of major alterations in the status of the various states in a particular area and the defining of their position

[9] Galsterer 1971 (E 15) 12.

with regard to Rome did not necessarily lead directly to what would now be considered the establishment of a province. The example of Paullus' settlement of affairs in Macedonia and Illyria in 167 has already been mentioned, but the same is true of the arrangements made by Ti. Flamininus in 196 for mainland Greece and at the treaty of Apamaea for Asia Minor in 188, after the defeat of Antiochus IV. A recently discovered set of documents from Entella in western Sicily may record the involvement of a Roman official in the refounding of the city in the middle of the third century B.C., which would again illustrate the way in which such interference with the activity of a non-Roman community might occur long before 'provincialization'.[10]

If the relationship, at least in the third and second centuries, between political involvement with the communities of an area and its becoming a province in a modern sense seems somewhat vague, the same is true of the extraction of revenue by the Roman state. As Cicero pointed out in a well-known passage,[11] forms of taxation varied considerably throughout the empire, and it is clear that in many regions the methods of raising money were simply adapted from those used by previous regimes. The best-known example is the collection of the corn-tithe in Sicily, which was regulated by a code called the Lex Hieronica, after the king of Syracuse, who used it in those parts of eastern Sicily under his control.[12] Moreover, although the presence of a Roman army regularly involved levying cash and supplies from the local population, the collection of such items on a regular and systematic basis, which might be recognized as taxation, often took many years to institute. In Spain there was a levy of grain and money to pay the troops from the Hannibalic War onwards, but regular payments of grain and of silver probably did not begin until the 170s.[13] Even in the rich *provincia* of Asia, to which the Romans sent commanders after the implementation of the will of Attalus III, who died in 133, the taxation seems to have been organized on a local basis until C. Gracchus' famous law of 123.[14] On the other hand monies could be collected from areas which were not even *provinciae*, in which, that is to say, there was no official Roman military or magisterial presence at all. *Stipendium* was exacted as war reparations from Carthage after the First and Second Punic Wars, and a regular *vectigal* was sent from the iron and copper mines of Macedonia after Paullus' arrangements of 167.

10 For these documents and essays on them, see *ASNP* 12 (1982) 771–1,103.

11 Cic. II *Verr.* 3.12–15.

12 See Carcopino 1914 (G 34); Pritchard 1971 (C 120).

13 Richardson 1976 (E 24).

14 Sherwin-White 1977 (D 75) 66–70; on Attalus' bequest, see Braund 1983 (A 13) 21–3.

Even in the case of jurisdiction, which was to play so large a part in the work of provincial governors later on, there was in the second century no inevitable connexion between the undertaking of such functions and the existence of a Roman *provincia*. The Senate might, for example, respond to a request for adjudication of a territorial dispute between two Greek cities in Asia Minor by delegating a praetor to investigate the matter and produce a judgement, even though the cities concerned were not part of his *provincia*, or indeed of that of any Roman magistrate whatsoever.[15] Although in some senses this might be seen as arbitration rather than jurisdiction, the brief provided by senatorial decree for the praetor concerned, on the basis of which he was to decide the question, was clearly modelled closely on the formulae used in the court of the urban praetor, who exercised jurisdiction between Roman citizens on matters of private law. From earlier in the second century there are examples of legal decisions being taken by commanders in areas which were within their *provinciae*, but certainly not yet provinces. In a letter, dated probably to early 190, M'. Acilius Glabrio, who held the *provincia* of Greece as proconsul, wrote to the Delphians, detailing the land which he 'gave' to the god Apollo and to the city, instructing them to ensure that the allocations he had made were not interfered with for the future, and promising assistance should the Thessalians or any one else send embassies to the Senate.[16] Here Glabrio is making legal decisions on his own authority, though no doubt with general senatorial approval, about a matter relating to a city which surely was not at this stage regarded as being within a part of the Roman empire. His action is essentially similar to that recorded on an inscription, dating probably from the following year, which records the decree of L. Aemilius Paullus, assigning land belonging to the people of Hasta, a town in the valley of the Baetis (Guadalquivir), to the slaves (*servei*) of the Hastenses who lived in the 'tower of Lascuta', and granting them their freedom while the People and Senate of Rome see fit.[17] Here again a proconsul makes decisions about legal status and property, apparently without reference to the Senate. The permanence or otherwise of the Roman military presence, which we use as one of the criteria for determining whether a *provincia* is or is not a 'province', apparently made no difference in these two cases.

In legal and fiscal matters, then, as also in questions of relationships with local communities, it is not possible to correlate the activities of a Roman magistrate or promagistrate of the type that subsequently

[15] Sherk, *RDGE* no. 7; for another instance, see *RDGE* no. 14, and in general see A. J. Marshall 1980 (F 111).

[16] *RDGE* no. 37.

[17] *FIRA* 1[2]. no. 51.

constituted what we would call 'provincial administration', with the establishment of a 'province'. It was not even necessary for a *provincia* to exist for this sort of work to be undertaken. This illustrates that the use of 'provinces' was not the only means employed by the Romans to impose control on the various regions of the Mediterranean world in the early stages of their transmarine expansion. Indeed, although there were *provinciae* in the sense of military commands in most of the areas where Roman influence was felt at some stage of the second century, the exercise of such influence through a permanent military presence, and thus the recurrent naming of an area as a *provincia*, seems to have been developed only in the West, at least until the second half of the second century. Sicily and Sardinia-Corsica were assigned to praetors as *provinciae* from 227 onwards, and in Spain Hispania Citerior and Hispania Ulterior became the *provinciae* of praetors with consular *imperium* in and after 196. In the eastern Mediterranean, although *provinciae* were frequently assigned to consuls, and occasionally to praetors, no area was given on a regular annual basis such as might lead to the establishment of a 'province' until the second half of the second century. Only after the defeat of Andriscus, the pretender to the throne of Macedon, by Q. Metellus Macedonicus in 148 was there a regular Roman presence of this kind in the East. Before that the Romans employed other means of ensuring that the Greeks conformed to Roman policy,[18] and even after 148 the rest of the peninsula was controlled by the oversight of the Roman commander in Macedonia.[19] It should be clear from what has already been said that the Senate did not refrain from sending magistrates and promagistrates to the East because of any fear of provincial administration either overstretching available resources or making individuals too powerful by service overseas, as such administration was not part of the purpose of a *provincia* at this date. The difference in Roman approach to the two regions, West and East, was caused rather by the different methods needed to exercise control over them. If this could be achieved satisfactorily without the presence of an army and its commander, there was no need to go to the expense and inconvenience of sending them. A *provincia* was a commission by the Senate to a magistrate or promagistrate for the fulfilment of a particular task, and in this early period the task was, in the case of overseas areas, largely military. It was from such origins that the provinces of the later Republic and Empire developed, and, as will be seen, many of the particular characteristics of the later system derive from the circumstances of these origins.

[18] Derow 1979 (B 26).

[19] See for instance the letter of Q. Fabius to Dyme (*RDGE* no. 43).

II. THE BASIS AND LIMITS OF THE GOVERNOR'S POWER

Because the province was developed from and remained based upon the *provincia*, the power of the provincial governor was always that of a holder of *imperium*, either as a magistrate or as a promagistrate. The magistrates held office as a result of election by the people, which in the case of the consuls and praetors who were sent overseas to *provinciae*, meant the *comitia centuriata*.[20] They held their *imperium* as a consequence of their office. The position of a promagistrate (proconsul or propraetor) was somewhat different. Usually, in the late Republic, he was a man who had previously held either the praetorship or the consulship, and had been allowed to continue to act as though he were still a magistrate after the end of his term of office, by the prorogation of his *imperium* by decree of the Senate. He was no longer, properly speaking, a magistrate, and could not, for instance, exercise his *imperium* within the sacred boundary of the city of Rome; but despite his status as a private citizen he was enabled to command Roman forces and undertake the other work of a magistrate within his *provincia*.[21] Such authority, normally given by a decree of the Senate, was a most useful method of extending the term of a commander in the field beyond the limits of an annual magistracy. This way of providing authority for men not holding a magistracy by means of *imperium pro consule* or *pro praetore* could be used even when the individual concerned did not already hold *imperium* by virtue of his tenure of a magistracy in the previous year. The Roman forces in Spain between 210 and 196 were commanded by a series of men who held *imperium pro consule* given to them by a measure passed either by the *comitia centuriata* or the *comitia tributa*,[22] and in a similar way, Pompey was given command to fight against the rebellious M. Lepidus in 77, and later in the same year received *imperium pro consule* to take an army to Spain to assist in the war against Sertorius.

In such cases, the holder of *imperium* was allotted a *provincia*. In strict logic the *provincia* did not exist until it had been so allotted, although by the late Republic the idea of the *provincia* as a geographical area was so much part of Roman thought that Cicero could write in the year 50 of the *provinciae* being *sine imperio* as a result of the persistent veto of the tribune Curio.[23] It appears from Cicero's speech to the Senate in 56 on the subject of the consular provinces that every consul had to have a *provincia* in

[20] See above, p. 564, and Vol. VII².2, 202–3.

[21] On the private status of the proconsul, see Livy XXXVIII.42.10, and Mommsen 1888 (A 77) I³, 642.

[22] Scipio in 210 (Livy XXVI.18–20); L. Cornelius Lentulus and L. Manlius Acidinus in 206 (Livy XXVIII.38.1); C. Cornelius Cethegus in 201 (Livy XXX.41.4–5); Cn. Cornelius Blasio and L. Stertinius in 199 (Livy XXXI.50.11).

[23] Cic. *Att.* VII.7.5.

order to function at all,[24] and the same could have been said of any holder of *imperium*.

Under normal circumstances the *provinciae* were assigned to magistrates and promagistrates by the Senate. Through the third and for most of the second century this seems to have been done at the first meeting of the Senate in each consular year. The *provinciae* were not assigned to individual magistrates by name, but the areas to be made praetorian and consular commands were specified, and then either divided between the appropriate magistrates by lot (*sortitio*) or by mutual agreement (*comparatio*). This last could be used only by consuls, although there is some evidence that consuls on occasion interfered with the allotment of praetorian *provinciae*, probably by improper and devious means.[25] Only very occasionally did the Senate assign a command *extra sortem* to a particular individual.

Promagistrates were in a different position, no doubt because their *imperium* as well as their *provincia* usually depended upon a decree of the Senate, and consequently their commands were extended or altered simply by such a decree. Of course when a man was made a promagistrate in order to be sent to a previously specified *provincia*, the area was named before the individual concerned; and very occasionally the lot was used to determine which of two promagistrates should take a particular *provincia*,[26] but these exceptions tend to prove the normal rule.

In the last hundred years of the Republic, various changes were made in the ways in which magistrates and promagistrates were assigned to *provinciae*. These were the result of the growing importance of overseas commands from the middle of the second century onwards. In 123 or 122 the tribune C. Gracchus proposed a law which required the Senate to decide upon the consular *provinciae* before the consuls were elected.[27] This had the result that it was impossible for a particular command to be given to a particular consul, since at the time of the decision about *provinciae* the consuls for the following year were still unknown. A more radical way of ensuring that an individual did get a particular command emerged some fifteen years later. In 107 C. Marius, who had been elected consul after an electoral campaign which included severe criticism of Q. Metellus and his conduct of the war against Jugurtha, found himself excluded from the *provincia* of Numidia by a decree of the Senate which continued Metellus in his command. Marius responded to this by having a tribune, T. Manlius Mancinus, propose a law to give the command to

24 Cic. *Prov. Cons.* 37.

25 For instance, Cic. *Fam.* v.2.3–4.

26 In 173, P. Furius Philo and Cn. Servilius Caepio, returning from Hispania Citerior and Ulterior respectively, were required to cast lots to determine which would replace N. Fabius Buteo, the praetor assigned to Citerior, who had died *en route* for his *provincia* (Livy XLII.4.2–3).

27 Cic. *Dom.* 24, and see Lintott, ch. 3 above, 79–80.

Marius instead. Before this time the popular assemblies had been used only rarely in the assignment of *provinciae*. P. Scipio, when consul in 206, had threatened to propose to the people through the tribunes that he should be given Africa when it seemed that the Senate would refuse to assign it to him, but in the event the threat was enough to persuade the Senate to change its mind.[28] In 167 a praetor, M'. Iuventius Thalna, had been about to bring a bill to the people to declare war on the Rhodians, and to choose one of the magistrates of the year to lead a fleet against them. He was only prevented by two tribunes, who were prepared to interpose a veto.[29] The only occasion before 107 when such a move was successful was in 147, when (according to Appian)[30] the tribunes had brought a bill to the people that Africa should be assigned to Scipio Aemilianus *extra sortem*, despite the opposition of his colleague in the consulship, C. Livius Drusus.

After this date, there were a number of occasions in the last decades of the Republic on which such methods were used. Marius again attempted to gain a command by a tribunician law in 88, when P. Sulpicius proposed that he rather than Sulla should be sent against Mithridates, but this was reversed by Sulla after he had marched on Rome.[31] In addition to the famous laws which provided commands for Pompey against the pirates (Lex Gabinia of 67) and Mithridates (Lex Manilia of 66), and for Caesar, Pompey and Crassus in the 50s (Lex Vatinia of 59 and the Leges Licinia Pompeia and Trebonia of 55) there are other examples of consuls receiving their *provinciae* by such means in this period. M'. Acilius Glabrio, consul in 67, obtained Bithynia and Pontus by another law of the tribune A. Gabinius, and Gabinius himself, when consul in 58, and his colleague L. Calpurnius Piso, both received their *provinciae* by means of laws proposed by the tribune P. Clodius. There may well be other cases of which no trace remains in our sources. An inscription which has recently come to light on Cnidus, and of which another copy has long been known from Delphi, contains a tribunician law from the last years of the second century, which includes among its provisions the setting up of a praetorian *provincia* of Cilicia.[32] This piece of legislation, which may have come from the group of *populares* which included Saturninus and Glaucia, illustrates the way in which the normal mechanisms of the Senate might be circumvented.

Despite the occasional creation of proconsular *imperia* for men sent to *provinciae*, the basic model for overseas commands during the Republic was that of the city magistracies, and in particular the praetorship. In

[28] Livy XXVIII.45.1–7. [29] Livy XLV.21.1–8. [30] App. *Pun.* 112.533.

[31] App. *BCiv.* I.63.283, states that Sulla and his colleague, Q. Pompeius Rufus, were then voted their *provinciae* by the people, but this is probably erroneous.

[32] Hassall, Crawford and Reynolds 1974 (B 170).

fact, on several occasions Cicero uses the word *praetor* when he is referring to governors in general.[33] The first move towards the provincial governorship being seen as a separate magistracy was the Lex Pompeia de provinciis of 52.[34] This law, following on a decree of the Senate of the previous year which contained similar provisions,[35] laid down a compulsory interval of five years between the tenure of a magistracy and the taking up of an overseas command. The reason for the law was probably a desire to prevent those who aspired to the magistracies from expending large sums on their electoral campaigns, with the intention of recouping their outlay by exploiting a province: that at least is the context of the senatorial decree of 53. In the event the law was short-lived, for the allocation of *provinciae* was disrupted in 50 by the vetoes of the tribune Curio, and the scheme was subsequently abandoned as a result of the outbreak of the civil war in 49.[36] However, by separating the control of the provinces from the city magistracies, it foreshadowed the pattern which was to emerge as a result of Augustus' reorganization of the command structure of the empire. Even so it was not until the use in the later imperial period of the phrase *praeses provinciae* to describe governors in general that the nomenclature of such officials became separated from that of the city magistracies.[37]

It was no doubt the origins of the province and its governor in the magistracies of the city of Rome, and especially the military magistracies, that led to the inadequacy and inappropriateness of the controls and limitations imposed on governors. A commander in the field could not in practice be under constant supervision from Rome, and moreover the whole tradition of *imperium* from the time of the Kings favoured the independence of action of its holders. Such men were acting for the people of Rome, who had chosen them by election, rather than as servants of the state, and the practical results can be seen in the freedom of decision which they enjoyed and in the length of time it took for any effective means of restricting that freedom to be developed.

Under normal circumstances the only part that the Senate played in the conduct of the affairs of a province was the sending out and equipping of the governor, and, if necessary, the renewal of his *provincia* at the beginning of each year. This was, of course, of major importance to governors, and could well affect their behaviour. It was with this in mind that they took care to inform the Senate about their activities and

33 E.g. Cic. II *Verr.* 3.125, *QFr* I.1.22.

34 Dio XL.56.1. See Marshall 1972 (F 110).

35 Dio XL.46.2.

36 See above ch. 10, p. 419.

37 *Praeses* begins to appear in official contexts at the beginning of the second century A.D. (e.g. Tacitus, *Ann.* VI.41, Trajan *ap.* Pliny *Ep.* X.44), and had become the general term by the beginning of the third (Macer, D. 1.18.1). Already in the first century A.D. generalized phrases such as 'eos ... qui in provincis praessent' (*Tabula Siarensis* col. II(b), line 26, of A.D. 19) were in use.

the state of their territory, at least from the military standpoint. It is noticeable that the letters which Cicero sent to 'the magistrates and the Senate' from Cilicia in 51 were both entirely about military matters, although we know from his other correspondence that he was involved with a far greater range of activities.[38] His assumption appears to have been that it was about his campaigns, and the preparedness of the area to repel any threat of invasion, that the Senate wished to be kept informed. On other occasions commanders wrote to the Senate to inform them of victories or defeats, or to request further supplies of food, equipment or cash in order to continue the military campaigns which they had in hand. For instance the two Scipios in Spain in 215 wrote to ask for money and supplies, as A. Cornelius Mammula, the propraetorian commander in Sardinia, had done the previous year, and as Pompey was to do when fighting Sertorius in Spain in 74.[39] Similarly the younger P. Scipio, the later Africanus, reported back to the Senate about his success in capturing New Carthage in 209, and throughout the early part of the second century, for which we have Livy's account of senatorial proceedings on an annual basis, there was a steady stream of reports coming to the Senate on the military situation both in the long-standing *provinciae* of the West (particularly the two Spains), and from the commanders sent to *provinciae* in the Greek world.

In other areas of the work of the magistrate or promagistrate in his *provincia*, there is surprisingly little sign of senatorial involvement. There are references to the need to determine the boundaries of the area assigned. For instance, the two praetors who were the first to be sent to the two Spanish *provinciae* in 196 were instructed to set the limits of their areas; and the law which set up the praetorian *provincia* of Cilicia at the very end of the second century also ordered the next commander to be sent to Macedonia to adjust the bounds of that *provincia* following the new conquests made by T. Didius.[40] The same law also instructs this official to see to it that the public revenues from this area should be collected, as seems best to him, and he is ordered to spend at least sixty days of each year of his tenure of the *provincia* in these parts. Such precise instructions are unusual, and may be the result of the desire of the author of this law, who was in any case dealing with business more commonly handled by the Senate, to exercise greater control than usual over magistrates and promagistrates. Even so there is very little on the inscription as we have it imposing limits on what the various governors

[38] Cic. *Fam.* xv.1 and 2.

[39] Spain: Livy xxiii.48.4 – 49.4. Sardinia: Livy xxiii.21.4. Pompey: Sall. *H.* fr. 2.98; Plut. *Pomp.* 20.1.

[40] Spain: Livy xxxii.28.11. Macedonia: Hassall, Crawford and Reynolds 1974 (B 170) 204, Cnidus col. iv, lines 25–31 (the newly conquered Caenic Chersonese was to be incorporated into his *provincia*).

who are appointed or referred to are permitted to do while in their *provinciae*. This is particularly striking because the law does forbid a governor to leave his *provincia* either with or without an army, and goes on to describe what the praetors to whom Asia and Macedonia were assigned may do after they have left those areas, particularly with respect to legal matters.[41]

As might be expected, it seems that only rather generalized instructions would be given to a governor on his assignment to a *provincia*, and that while he was there, it was mostly military matters which concerned the Senate. Once he had left his area of command, his *imperium* was no longer automatically operative, and he needed more explicit authority to act in the capacities in which he had acted while in his *provincia*. Similarly it was virtually impossible either by ordinary administrative means or through the courts to prevent a governor misbehaving, or to punish him if he did, while he was in his *provincia* and in possession of his *imperium*. Theoretically a governor could have his *imperium* removed, but in practice so severe a measure was used only in exceptional circumstances. In 136 M. Aemilius Porcina, the proconsul in Hispania Citerior, not only attacked the tribe of the Vaccaei in direct contravention of an order brought to him by a messenger from the Senate, but subsequently suffered a disastrous defeat, and as a result was deprived of his *imperium*.[42] Even in this case it is unlikely that Porcina would have been treated so harshly had not his misdemeanour occurred at the same time as the Senate was debating the repudiation of the treaty of Mancinus.[43] Normally, though a governor might slaughter and enslave the inhabitants of his *provincia*, as Ser. Sulpicius Galba did the Lusitanians in 150, or exploit them ruthlessly, as Cicero alleged Verres had done in the 70s, no action would be taken against him during his tenure.

Once he had returned to Rome, however, the situation was different. Already by the year 171 it was possible for provincial communities to bring complaints against provincial governors, although the procedure seems to be diplomatic rather than to involve the lawcourts. In that year, embassies were received in Rome, objecting to the greed and arrogance of three of the men who had been sent out to the two Spanish *provinciae* over the past six years. The Senate arranged for the hearing of their suit by boards of *recuperatores*, appointed specially for the purpose, and for the selection by the ambassadors of four distinguished Romans to represent them. In the event, despite it being said that they were clearly guilty of the illegal seizure of money, all three accused seem to have escaped scot-free. One was acquitted after a prolonged hearing, and the

[41] Cnidus col. III, lines 32–9; col. IV, lines 32–9.

[42] App. *Hisp.* 81.351 – 83.358.

[43] See Lintott, ch. 2 above, p. 21, and Vol. VIII², 135.

other two removed themselves from Roman jurisdiction by withdrawing to Tibur and Praeneste.[44] However, although the outcome was unsatisfactory, and there were allegations that the praetor who had been put in charge of the matter colluded with the accused, the Senate had at least shown that it was prepared to listen to such accusations from the provincials.

In the latter half of the second century, the means by which such complaints were dealt with were regularized. In 149 a tribune of the plebs, L. Calpurnius Piso Frugi, introduced a law to set up a permanent court, the *quaestio de repetundis*, to hear cases against magistrates or promagistrates accused of the illegal seizure of money. Almost nothing is known about the detail of this law, but certainly by the time C. Gracchus had proposed his legislation on the same topic in 123, it was possible for a provincial to bring a case in Rome against a provincial governor on this charge.[45] Indeed this became the main and the only formal means by which non-Romans could obtain satisfaction for wrongs done to them by Roman officials, so that Cicero described the *quaestio de repetundis* as the defence of the allies against such depredations.[46] Sulla seems to have expanded the scope of the law, and Caesar in his consulship in 59 enlarged it still further. Cicero's references to Caesar's Lex Julia, in the letters he wrote while governor in Cilicia in 51, show that this at least acted as a check on certain forms of exploitation. However, as a protection of the provincials, this court had certain obvious weaknesses. As already mentioned, it could only be used after the governor returned to Rome, and even then only by such provincials as were able to undertake the considerable expense of mounting a prosecution in Rome itself. In practice only those who had the resources of considerable wealth and, more important still, friends in high places in Rome, were likely to succeed, and such people might in any case have found less formal ways of using their influence to inhibit the actions of a governor against them at an earlier stage. Even if a prosecution was successful, there was no guarantee that the plaintiff would receive any of his money back, despite the careful provisions which, for instance, C. Gracchus included in his law to this end.[47] It was still possible, as it had been in 171, for the accused to withdraw beyond the reach of Roman jurisdiction, and C. Verres, whom Cicero prosecuted in 70 on behalf of the Sicilians, was still enjoying his ill-gotten gains in Massilia in 43 when Marcus Antonius had him proscribed in order to acquire his wealth.[48]

[44] Livy XLIII.2.1–2.

[45] On the history of the *quaestio de repetundis*, see Balsdon 1938 (F 12) and Lintott 1981 (F 104). On Gracchus' law Sherwin-White 1982 (C 133).

[46] Cic. *Div. Caec.* 17–18.

[47] *Lex rep.* (*FIRA* I^2 no. 7) lines 57ff.

[48] Pliny *HN* XXXIV.3.6; Lactantius *Div. Inst.* II.4.37.

The other law which, by the late Republic, might be used against a governor for acts done while in his *provincia*, was Sulla's Lex Cornelia de maiestate. From Cicero's remarks about this law, it is clear that it prohibited a commander from leaving, or leading an army out, of his *provincia*, conducting a war on his own account, or attacking a foreign kingdom without explicit instructions from the Senate or People of Rome.[49] As has already been seen from the law which set up the *provincia* of Cilicia in about 100, some of these provisions had already appeared before Sulla's time, and Cicero also attests this.[50] Besides regulations about particular areas, such as those about Macedonia and Asia, there is also mention in this law of a more general statute, a Lex Porcia, which seems to have laid down similar rules. It seems clear that in this, as in other parts of his legislation, Sulla was codifying earlier attempts to define the limits of a governor's actions. It is noteworthy that, when he does so, it is by means of a charge of demeaning the majesty of the Roman people, by misuse of the *imperium* which the governor exercises on behalf of the Roman people. This emphasizes again that the *provinciae* are seen in relation to the magistrate or promagistrate to whom they are assigned, and that those officials are seen as holders of the military power of the whole state. The particular misuses which we know to have been prohibited by these various laws all relate to the military function of the governor, and, more significantly, are described not in terms of the 'provinces' or of some idea of provincial administration, but of appropriate, or (more properly) inappropriate actions taken by a holder of *imperium*.

It is perhaps surprising to discover that even in the last century of the Republic, when Roman officials were being sent out to areas all round the Mediterranean, there was no mechanism by which the Senate might prevent the misgovernment of those areas by the men it had despatched. This might seem more remarkable still when it is remembered that the laws which provided penalties for those particular forms of misbehaviour which *were* recognized depended for their implementation, like all other parts of the Roman law, on prosecutions undertaken by private individuals. This can really only be placed in a true perspective when the origins of what became the administration of the empire are kept in mind. A magistrate or promagistrate in an overseas *provincia* was not originally or (in the Republican period, at least) primarily administering an area of Roman territory, but commanding Roman forces in a foreign land. It was important that he should not exacerbate the situation there unnecessarily by pillaging the local inhabitants, and that he should not turn the forces of the state into a private army by going outside the limits

[49] See Bauman 1967 (F 16) 68–87.

[50] Cic. *Pis.* 50.

assigned to his command by the Senate. Within those very broad boundaries, he had the freedom that was essential to any commander to exercise the power of the Senate and people of Rome as he saw fit: that indeed was what *imperium* meant.

III. THE GOVERNOR AT WORK

It was through the sending of Roman armies to areas outside Italy that the overseas *provinciae* came into existence, and their gradual transformation into a territorial empire was the result of such commands becoming permanent in certain parts of the Mediterranean world. It was through the acquisition of various responsibilities, which grew from the presence of Roman forces and their commander there, that the institutions which might be described as 'provincial administration' began to appear. To see how this happened, it is easiest to examine the activities of the men who went out to the provinces of the empire in the middle of the first century B.C., and the resources which were available to them.

1. The governor and his staff

The personnel who were present with the governor can be divided into three groups, on the basis of the manner in which they were chosen.

First, some of the governor's staff were assigned to him by the Senate. Of these, the quaestor was exceptional in being himself a magistrate of the Roman people, and holding office by virtue of his election. Consequently, like other executive magistrates, he needed a *provincia* in which to function, and at least in the late second and first centuries, such *provinciae* were usually distributed by lot, following a decree of the Senate, although, as with the other magistracies, it could also be done through a direct senatorial decree.[51] The main responsibilities of the quaestor were financial, and he had to account to the treasury at Rome at the end of his period of office for the monies he had received and the expenditure he had made. After the passing of the Lex Julia de repetundis in 59 he was required to leave copies of his accounts in the two main cities of the *provincia*.[52] Cicero criticizes Verres for the jejune accounts he submitted after his period as quaestor with Cn. Carbo, during the latter's consulship in 84.[53] They were no doubt quite unsatisfactory as a representation of the movement of the funds for which Verres was responsible, but they do show the extent of the task which a quaestor undertook. Verres records payments for the wages and

[51] Ulpian, D.1.13.1.2, dates the usual pattern to 138 or 137 B.C. though undoubtedly the lot was used earlier.

[52] Cic. *Fam.* v.20.2.

[53] Cic. II *Verr.* 1.36.

provisioning of the consul's army, as well as the expenses of his staff. This was a major undertaking for a man at the outset of his political career, which no doubt partly accounts for the almost paternal relationship which was supposed to exist between a senior magistrate or promagistrate and the quaestor attached to him.[54] No doubt the quaestor would to a great extent depend upon the financial expertise of his own staff of *apparitores*, who will be further discussed below, together with the similar officials attached to the governor himself.

In addition to the quaestor, the governor also took with him a number of senior men, usually of senatorial rank, as *legati*. These were also assigned to him by the Senate, though there is considerable evidence to show that the governor was consulted about who were to be his legates, and often he would take members of his own family and other friends and associates.[55] Cicero in 51 included his brother, Q. Cicero, among his *legati*, as well as C. Pomptinus, M. Anneius and a certain L. Tullius. Of these all but the last are known to have been men of military reputation, and certainly all four were used by Cicero in military capacities.[56] This indeed would seem to be the main function of the *legati*, and their position and authority derived entirely from that of the governor himself.

The other people accompanying the governor were not allotted to him by the Senate in the way that the quaestor and the *legati* were. He had for instance a number of *apparitores*. This is really a general term for a varied group of individuals who performed functions directly related to the work of the magistrates and promagistrates to whom they were assigned.[57] In Rome such men were organized into colleges, known as *decuriae*, which by the time of Augustus had a structure and hierarchy of considerable complexity, and already in the Republic had an official position and certain privileges.[58] Among them were the lictors and other attendants on the magistrates, and also the *scribae*, who served the quaestors by keeping accounts and other records. Although there is no epigraphic record of *scribae* attached to the consuls or praetors, they are found on the staff of provincial governors, and Cicero had with him in Cilicia a *scriba* named Tullius, who was probably a freedman from his own household.[59] This example suggests that, although in the early Empire the *scribae* of the quaestors were assigned by lot, it was possible in the late Republic for governors to select the men they wanted; this is confirmed by a scathing account by Cicero of the *scriba* who served

54 Cf. the relationship between M. Antonius and C. Norbanus in *c.* 95 B.C., Cic. *De Or.* II.198.

55 On the *legati*, see Schleussner 1978 (A 106) 101–240.

56 Cic. *Fam.* XV.4.8.

57 See in general A. H. M. Jones 1949 (G 130) and Purcell 1983 (G 199).

58 As in the Lex Cornelia de XX quaestoribus (*FIRA* I² no. 10).

59 Purcell 1983 (G 199) 128; Cic. *Fam.* V.20.1, with Shackleton Bailey's note 1977 (B 110).

Verres as legate, praetor and propraetor.[60] Such men were important because they did belong to what was in some sense a professional body, but it is clear that even they had no specialist knowledge of the areas to which they went when on the staff of a provincial governor or his quaestor, but went out from Rome, just as did the other members of the goveror's staff. They probably differed from the rest of the entourage in being of a lower social class, since although *scribae* could be of equestrian status, they were not likely to be members of that part of the *equites* which was closest to the senatorial order, and from which senators were drawn.[61]

The other group chosen by the governor without reference to the Senate was the *cohors amicorum*, a collection of associates of the governor, who had no official status at all, but received allowances from the Senate for their expenses while in the *provincia*. They not only gained valuable experience for themselves and enjoyed the opportunities of foreign travel, but also performed an important function, in that they acted, together with the quaestor and the *legati*, as the governor's *consilium*. It was a part of the normal functioning of any Roman official, especially in the juridical sphere, for decisions to be taken only after consultation with others, even in cases where there was no doubt that the person making the decision himself had the necessary authority to decide.[62] Cicero accuses Verres of 'hearing a charge when there was no accuser, reaching a verdict without a *consilium*, pronouncing condemnation without hearing a defence',[63] which illustrates the moral necessity of such consultation for the proper conduct of affairs. Even the consuls in Rome, hearing a dispute between the inhabitants of the Boeotian town of Oropus and representatives of a group of *publicani* about the status of a piece of sacred land, consulted a *consilium* before recommending the form of senatorial decree that should be issued. Similarly Cn. Pompeius Strabo, giving citizenship to a group of Spanish cavalrymen while on campaign as consul in Picenum in 89, lists his *consilium*.[64] Such lists reveal that these *consilia* included men of very different ages, several of whom had close connexions with the magistrate or promagistrate involved. Pompeius for instance included his son, who was of course the great Pompey, along with thirty-two other young men and twenty-two of higher status. The number of members of this *consilium* may have been unusually large, but such a pattern confirms the indications in the sources of the composition of the group of friends (*comites* or *amici*) who accompanied a provincial governor. The poet Catullus, for instance,

[60] Pliny *Ep.* 4.12; Cic. II *Verr.* 3.187.

[61] On equestrian *scribae* in the imperial period, see E. Kornemann, *RE* IIA 853.62.

[62] J. Crook, *Consilium Principis* (Cambridge, 1955) ch. 1.

[63] Cic. II *Verr.* 5.23.

[64] *FIRA* I². no. 36 (Oropus); *ILS* 8888 (Pompeius).

almost certainly still in his twenties at the time, went out to Bithynia in 57 with C. Memmius, who had held the praetorship in the previous year.[65]

The *amici*, along with the quaestor and the *legati*, were given allowances by the *aerarium* for their living expenses, and this sum was included in the monies paid over to the quaestor at the beginning of his period of office. Cicero's entourage clearly expected him to divide between them the million sesterces of surplus that he had left from this amount at the end of his time in Cilicia, but, as he explains in his letter to Atticus, not only was this against his conscience, but he had to account for the money to the treasury.[66] The sums involved could be large, both for these allowances and for the money given to the governor himself for his own use, called *vasarium*. Cicero claims that L. Piso took 18 million sesterces as his *vasarium* when he was appointed to Macedonia as proconsul in 58 (a sum equivalent to a very substantial private fortune), and that he left it on interest in Rome.[67] Whether or not this is true, it does seem that the *vasarium*, unlike the other allowances, was not accounted for by the governor at the end of his tenure.

One other arrangement made by the Senate for the provisioning of the governor and his staff is known in some detail. Before he left for his *provincia*, the governor was given an amount of money for the purchase of grain for himself and those on his staff, and a price was fixed by the Senate at which this grain was to be bought. He could then compel farmers there to sell that quantity of grain (known as *frumentum in cellam* or *frumentum aestumatum*) to him at that fixed price. Although this scheme was no doubt instituted to protect the representatives of the Roman people from exploitation by the provincials, it was, like all attempts to fix a price other than the ordinary sale-price for a commodity, open to abuse. If the fixed price was higher than the current price, the governor could pocket the difference, while if it was lower, farmers might try to bribe him to buy the grain from someone other than themselves. Even if the fixed price and the current price were at about the same level, an unscrupulous governor might require the delivery of the grain to some distant part of the *provincia* at the expense of the farmer, and thus put pressure on him to bribe his way out of the situation. Cicero certainly accused Verres of all these manoeuvres, and he was by no means the first to have tried this sort of extortion.[68]

In addition to these groups of people round the governor, whose

65 Catullus 10 and 28. See further Marquardt and Wissowa 1881–5 (A 69) I² 531–3.

66 Cic. *Att.* VII.1.6.

67 Cic. *Pis.* 86. Compare the fortune of the younger Pliny, probably about 16 million sesterces (R. Duncan-Jones, *The Economy of the Roman Empire* (2nd edn, Cambridge 1982) ch. 1).

68 Cic. II *Verr.* 3.188 ff. Similar problems had been encountered in Spain before 171 (Livy XLIII.2.12), and were still to be found in Britain when Agricola arrived there in A.D. 78 (Tac. *Agr.* 19.4).

presence was officially recognized, at least to the extent that financial provision was made by the treasury at Rome for their food, there were also people attached directly to the household of the governor. Cicero's brother, Quintus, when governor of Asia from 61 to 58 after his praetorship, had with him his slave Statius, whom he manumitted during his tenure of the *provincia*, despite Cicero's advice. This man evidently had great influence with Quintus, so much so that Cicero actually reprimanded his brother for listening to him more than was proper, and complained that he had been asked by several people to write letters of recommendation for them to Statius.[69] It was inevitable that a governor, with comparatively little administrative assistance, should turn to those who undertook similar tasks for him in the management of his own domestic affairs, but it is not surprising to discover that this often caused comment and resentment.

2. *The publicani*

Besides the governor and his staff, one other set of people in the *provincia* acting on behalf of the Roman people were the representatives of the *societates publicanorum*.[70] These institutions, made up of a number of stockholders, and in many ways similar to modern joint-stock companies, undertook work for the Republic which required any major capital investment. This included the building of the Roman aqueducts, the supplying of the army and the collection of certain taxes and dues. It is particularly in this latter connexion that the governor was most likely to have dealings with them, though it must be remembered that, if he was in a *provincia* which involved a great deal of military activity, their supply function might also bring him into contact with them.

Two forms of taxation in particular were entrusted to the *publicani*. Throughout the empire customs dues were collected by them, and in those eastern provinces which paid a tithe of their agricultural produce, that too was gathered by the *societates*. More will be said below about Roman fiscal practice, but certain consequences of the presence of the *publicani* are of more general significance in understanding the work of the governor.

Because the contracts for the collection of taxes were made between the censors in Rome and the publican company which made the most successful tender on a five-year basis, the representatives of the company would be in the *provincia* for at least five years at a time. This is no doubt part of the reason for the use of the funds of the *publicani* as a local bank,

[69] Cic. *Att.* II.19.1; *QFr.* I.2.1–3.

[70] On the *publicani*, see Badian 1972 (A 4) esp. ch. 4; Nicolet (G 175), esp. pp. 70–82, and in ch. 16 below, pp. 635–7.

on which the governor could draw. Verres, for instance, was authorized to draw money for the purchase of grain from the *publicani* in Sicily.[71] Such an arrangement is perhaps not surprising in that the money that they had collected was the tax which in any case belonged to the Roman people. It may also be that a governor on leaving his *provincia* sometimes left any surplus money in their possession, and, if this was so, it illustrates the superiority of the facilities available to the *publicani* for the care of large amounts of coinage.[72] In other respects also they were certainly better served. Cicero mentions the *tabellarii* of the *publicani* who seem to have operated a regular service, carrying letters from Cilicia to Rome, which he himself used for some of his correspondence.[73] Otherwise he used friends or slaves of his own as couriers, since there was no provision of this kind by the state.

The role of the *publicani* in a particular area varied a great deal, depending on the form of taxation that was employed there, and the nature of the provincial communities. The size and importance of the *societates* would itself vary, as it would appear that in principle a new grouping was formed for each state contract. The larger *societates*, including those which collected taxes, had certain legal privileges, including the recognition of a corporate existence which, unlike that of purely private commercial associations, survived the death of individual members of the group. No doubt there was in fact a degree of continuity among partners from contract to contract, but these companies were privately owned, and not a centrally organized bureaucracy. The use to which a particular governor put the services of the *publicani* in his *provincia* would be bound to depend upon the particular people who were there, and on his relations with them. Inevitably this put him under considerable pressure not to offend them. When Cicero wrote to his brother Quintus about the governing of Quintus' *provincia* of Asia in 60 or 59, he stressed the difficulties of dealing with the *publicani*,[74] and although the problems to which he was referring were mainly political, the dependence of the governor upon the *societates* for assistance in the day-to-day matters of administration cannot have made the position easier.

IV. TAXATION

Of the non-military occupations of a provincial governor in the first century B.C., two were of particular importance. These were the

[71] Cic. II *Verr.* 3.165ff.

[72] Cicero states that he intended to take sureties at Laodicea for all the public money in his possession (*Fam.* II.17.4). Badian 1972 (A 4) 77–8, takes this as a reference to security for a deposit made with the *publicani*, though Shackleton Bailey 1977 (B 110) believes it to be insurance against loss in transit.

[73] Cic. *Att.* V.15.3, V.16.1.

[74] Cic. *QFr.* I.1.32–3.

responsibility, either direct or indirect, for the collection of the various taxes payable within his area, and the exercise of jurisdiction.

Taxation took a wide variety of forms throughout the empire. Cicero, in a famous passage in the *Verrines*,[75] explains that there were two forms of tax in the *provinciae*: a fixed amount, called *stipendium*; and those taxes which were dealt with by the censors at Rome. The first kind he describes as having been imposed as the price of victory on the defeated, and instances the Spaniards and the majority of the Carthaginians as paying it; while in the second category he mentions the tithe in Asia, which was arranged by a law of C. Gracchus. He then adds a third sort, different from either of the others, the tithe on grain, as practised in Sicily, which like the Asian tax, was a variable amount, but the collection of which was left in the hands of Sicilian rather than Roman tax-collectors.

Cicero distinguishes between different taxes on the basis of the methods used to collect them, but in fact the different types of taxation also had quite different origins. The *stipendium* at an early stage had two forms, which both contributed elements to make up the pattern of the 'fixed tax' to which Cicero refers. Large-scale reparations were exacted from, for instance, the Carthaginians after the First and Second Punic Wars, as a punishment and a means of redress, but these were not taxation in the ordinary sense of the word since they were fixed amounts which had to be paid once for all.[76] In Spain the situation was quite different, in that there the *stipendium* seems originally to have been money raised, largely from Rome's somewhat unreliable allies, to pay the wages of the troops stationed there.[77] Pay for soldiers was in fact the first meaning of the word *stipendium*. Both these forms of exaction, reparations and army pay, eventually became regularized into fixed annual payments. In the case of Carthage, after the destruction of the city in 146, a head-tax and a land-tax were imposed, and it appears from an inscription of 111 that this taxation was called *stipendium*. The same inscription shows that those who paid this *stipendium* were entered by name on a public register.[78] The means of collecting *stipendium* no doubt varied widely from area to area. In Spain, for instance, during the Hannibalic War, the *stipendium* which was levied to pay the troops was collected from the tribal chieftains,[79] and the use of local communities must have been common. In Spain and elsewhere the Romans seem to have introduced *stipendium* themselves, but in some places it was developed from taxes taken over from previous regimes. When L.

[75] Cic. II *Verr.* 3.12.

[76] Livy XXI.1.5, 40.5, 41.9; XXX.37.5; XXXII.2.1; XXXIII.46.8–9; XXXVI.4.7.

[77] See Richardson 1976 (E 24) 147–9.

[78] App. *Pun.* 135.641; lex agr. (*FIRA* I² no. 8) lines 77–82.

[79] Livy XXVIII.25.6ff, 34.11.

Aemilius Paullus reorganized Macedonia after the battle of Pydna in 168, he instituted a *stipendium* which was half that paid to the kings, and this certainly suggests that the form of tax was modelled on that already in force.[80]

This tendency of the Romans to base their taxation in the empire on what they found when they arrived is even more noticeable in the case of those taxes which were levied by others on behalf of the state, following an auction of the right to collect, held every five years by the censors in Rome, or, as happened with the Sicilian tithe, annually by the governor.[81] In such cases also the provincial cities played a large part. Whereas with the fixed *stipendium* the money appears to have been paid directly to the Roman officials in the *provincia*, these taxes (in Cicero's second and third categories), which were all percentage levies of various types, were collected by *publicani* based in Rome (or in the case of Sicily, by Sicilians). The exact amount that such taxes would raise could not be estimated precisely, and that is no doubt part of the reason why such taxes were sold off to private collectors, who in effect underwrote the revenue to be gained by the censors. The *publicani* had bought by auction the right to levy the amounts due, and usually made their own agreements with the local cities about the collection at local level. Frequently the form of taxation was the same as had existed previously, as for instance with the Sicilian tithe. Another form of taxation found in Sicily and elsewhere was the *scriptura*. This was based on the number of grazing animals owned, and appears to have been a complement to tithes on grain. It was also collected by *publicani*.

A similar adaptation of previous patterns can be seen in the customs dues (*portoria*), which were also collected by *publicani*, and were based on those previously in force in the various parts of the Mediterranean in which the Romans had now established *provinciae*. This can be seen from the fact that the customs boundaries were not identical with the boundaries of the *provinciae*, and indeed it was a matter of dispute between merchants and *publicani* whether a cargo landing twice within one provincial area had to pay *portorium* once or twice.[82]

This variety and lack of overall system suggests that the Romans did not see their empire as a fiscal unit. They were no doubt keen to extract as much money as came readily to hand, and one of the arguments which Cicero used to urge the sending of Pompey to the East in 67 was the importance of the revenues from the provinces there, especially from Asia.[83] It is also true that the taxation which the Romans took from the East was immensely important for the patterns of trade and of the

[80] Livy XLV.29.4. Macedonia was not a permanent *provincia* at this time.

[81] See Carcopino 1914 (G 34), 77–107.

[82] S. De Laet 1949 (G 141) esp. ch. 5.

[83] Cic. *Leg. Man.* 6.14–16.

economy in the whole Mediterranean region.[84] This does not show, however, that the Romans achieved this effect intentionally, nor even that they established themselves in various areas because they could gain substantial revenues from them. Cicero, in the passage just cited, states that Asia was the only *provincia* which did more than pay for the cost of defending it, and although this may well have been an exaggeration to win an argument in the assembly, it must have seemed credible to at least some of his hearers. On the other hand there was undoubtedly an income to the state from taxation, which grew as the empire itself grew, especially after Pompey's conquest and reorganization of the East. Through the last century of the Republic, in the same period in which the *provincia* was beginning to be seen as a province in the modern sense, this seems to have become a larger part of the Roman understanding of the benefits of their empire.

It is also important to realize that the taxes described so far did not exhaust the financial demands which provincial communities might be expected to meet. The costs of billeting Roman forces might well be high, and it is significant that this was limited by the Lex Julia de repetundis in 59; before that law, exemption from such expenses had been a reward to especially favoured allies. Other semi-official demands came from senators and magistrates in Rome. In his consulship in 63, Cicero attempted to abolish the practice of senators being voted the right to go to provinces on private business, and succeeded in restricting the time allowed for such 'embassies' (*liberae legationes*) to one year. This limit was probably repeated in the Lex Julia. Cicero also commended his brother Quintus for forbidding the voting by provincial communities in Asia of contributions to the aediles' games in Rome (*vectigal aedilicium*), much to the anger of certain members of the Roman establishment.[85] In addition, governors might demand payments, allegedly on a voluntary basis, as a mark of favour from the cities in their *provincia*: this too was restricted by the Lex Julia.[86] Finally we must take into account the wholly illegal sums extorted by the governors and their staff and by the *publicani*. Cicero's accusations against Verres may be exaggerated, but there is no doubt that such extortion occurred. A provincial governorship was part of a political career, and political careers in the late Republic were expensive. In 53 the Senate passed a decree which required a five-year interval between the holding of a magistracy and being assigned to a *provincia*.[87] The reason for this, and for Pompey's law of the following year which contained the same provision, was the

[84] Crawford 1977 (G 46); Hopkins 1980 (G 124); Nicolet in ch. 16 below, esp. pp. 637–40.

[85] *Liberae legationes*: Cic. *Leg.* III.5, *Att.* XV.11.4. *Vectigal aedilicium*: Cic. *QFr.* I.1.26.

[86] On the Lex Julia, see Cic. *Pis.* 90. For freedom from billeting as a reward, see the Lex Antonia de Termessibus (*FIRA* I² no. 11) col. II. lines 6–17.

[87] Dio XL.46.2.

extraordinarily large amounts of money being spent on electoral bribery in the late 50s, in the expectation that a spell in a rich *provincia* would make it possible to recoup the loss without delay.

V. JURISDICTION

In many *provinciae* the greater part of the governor's time was probably taken up with the law courts. This is somewhat surprising, since the law which a Roman magistrate was empowered to enforce was the Roman *ius civile*, and this, as its name implies, provided rights and remedies for Roman citizens; but if he had dealt only with cases involving Roman citizens, the governor would have had much less to do than we know was in fact the case.[88] When it came to non-citizens (the bulk of the provincial population) a Roman governor could, within certain limits, make his own arrangements.

It is by no means clear what the legal basis of that part of the governor's jurisdiction was. It has mostly been believed that there was for each area a special statute, the *lex provinciae*, which determined the extent of the governor's powers, including his jurisdiction.[89] It is true that in some *provinciae* there was some measure of this kind in existence, usually called a *lex*, though probably not passed by the assemblies in Rome, but rather a decree of a commander (sometimes advised by a group of ten senators), subsequently ratified by the Senate. In Sicily, the Lex Rupilia specified the circumstances in which the governor could hear cases which were brought to him by non-Roman inhabitants of his area.[90] Many *provinciae*, however, give no indication of ever having had a *lex provinciae*, and even in the case of Sicily the Lex Rupilia dates only from 132, when the consul P. Rupilius put an end to the slave-wars which had been ravaging the island. There must have been cases brought to the governor before 132, and there is no reason to believe that he was unable to hear them because of the lack of a *lex provinciae*. Indeed such *leges* were probably imposed, not to enable the governor to exercise jurisdiction, but to limit the types of cases he could hear, and thus to prevent provincials from bringing him into too many of their local disputes. As can be seen from the case of Verres, a skilful use of the power to assign judges or to hear cases could give a governor great power over those in his *provincia*.

The *lex provinciae* (if such existed for his area) might therefore limit a governor's scope. By the first century he was also limited by his own statement of intent, issued in the form of an edict at the beginning of his

[88] For the judicial activity of governors, see Marshall 1966 (F 109).

[89] Stevenson 1939 (F 149) 68 and 82–4; Hoyos 1973 (F 79).

[90] Cic. II *Verr.* 2.32; Mellano 1977 (F 116).

tenure, which gave the grounds for such actions as he was prepared to hear. This was inevitably modelled on the edict of the urban praetor in Rome, and thus related to the basic forms of the *ius civile*, but the precise shape could be varied by each incoming governor.[91] Cicero added to that of his predecessor, Appius Claudius Pulcher, and he also drew substantially from the edict of Q. Mucius Scaevola, promulgated when the latter was governor of Asia in the 90s, which was regarded as a classic of the form.[92]

Something of the practice of a governor in a western *provincia* at the beginning of the first century can be seen in an inscription recently discovered in northern Spain. This records the settlement of a water dispute between two Spanish communities, on the judgement of a third community. The court was set up by the governor of Hispania Citerior in 87, and, despite the fact that neither of the parties to the matter nor the judges are Roman, the whole case is set out with considerable sophistication in the language of the formulae used in the court of the urban praetor.[93] Such phrases as 'si parret ... si non parret ...' and such concepts as the use of a fiction in the presentation of a case were the everyday practice of the legal profession in Rome, but can have meant little to the inhabitants of the Ebro valley. The governor has used the forms of the *ius civile*, not because he was required to do so, but because this was the natural way for a man schooled in the patterns of Roman law to express the essence of a case brought to him. Indeed the main difference between the position of a magistrate in the courts in Rome and a governor in his *provincia* was precisely that the latter was not in Rome, and therefore not under the eye of other lawyers. Cicero remarks to his brother Quintus that not much in the way of knowledge is needed for cases in the *provinciae*, just consistency and firmness, so as to resist the suspicion of partiality.[94]

Such cases could take up a great deal of time, especially once an area had been organized into districts (called *conventus*) for the purposes of jurisdiction. It was then necessary for a governor to travel round his *provincia* to hear cases in those areas. He could to some extent delegate this responsibility to others on his staff, in particular his quaestor and legates; and in Sicily, which was unusual in having two quaestors assigned to it, one, based at Lilybaeum in the extreme west of the island, spent most of his time exercising jurisdiction. However, as has been seen, the juridical authority of the governor was vested to a considerable extent in his own person, rather than in any systematic body of

[91] On the provincial edict, see Greenidge 1901 (F 68) 119–29 and Marshall 1964 (F 108).

[92] Cic. *Fam.* III.8.4; *Att.* VI.1.5.

[93] Richardson 1983 (B 227); Birks, Rodger and Richardson 1984 (B 133).

[94] Cic. *QFr.* I.1.20.

provincial law, so that it is not surprising that much the greater part of the work was done by the governor himself.[95] By the time of Augustus, the governor of Tarraconensis in northern and eastern Spain spent the whole of the winter with such cases, and even Caesar, in the midst of his campaigns in Gaul, crossed the Alps at the end of each campaigning season, in order to hear cases in Illyricum and Cisalpine Gaul.[96]

It is not difficult to see why such calls on the governor arose. Demands for jurisdiction were made of the Senate by peoples and kings in the orbit of Roman power throughout the second century, and in those cases for which documentary evidence survives, they can be seen to have been met by a similar combination of diplomacy and use of the *ius civile* as appears later in the practice of the governors.[97] In both instances, the reason for the approach made by the non-Roman parties to the disputes was the unarguable fact that Rome was the supreme power in the Mediterranean world. If need be, Roman might could be no doubt exercised to enforce decisions taken by a Roman official, or by a judge appointed by such an official. It is improbable however that that was stated explicitly as the reason for invoking Roman jurisdiction. The mere fact of her supremacy imposed both an expectation and an obligation which Rome was quite prepared to fulfil, whether through the Senate or through the judicial activity of her magistrates and promagistrates. Here, as in other cases, the exercise of such authority led inevitably to its extension.

VI. THE *PROVINCIAE* AND THE PROVINCIALS

Just as the *provincia* was not at first seen as a territorial or administrative unit, so too the inhabitants of the *provinciae* were not regarded as a single category. From the legal point of view, such people were either Roman citizens (*cives*) or non-citizens (*peregrini*), and remained so whether they were within the area of a *provincia* or not. At the level of international relations, the latter might be described as being allies, or 'within the control, under the sway, in the power or within the friendship of' the Roman people,[98] and again such status did not depend upon the existence or otherwise of a *provincia*. The same irregular pattern can be seen in the variations of status given to communities. It has been asserted that such communities which did not hold the Roman citizenship were either states with a treaty (*civitates foederatae*) or free states (*civitates liberae*) or else states 'paying the *stipendium*' i.e. regular taxation to Rome,

[95] Greenidge 1901 (F 68) 129–32; Marshall 1966 (F 109) 231.

[96] Tarraconesis: Strab. III.4.20. Caesar: Caes. *BGall.* I.54.3; V.I.5; V.2.I; VI.44.3.

[97] E.g. the arbitration between Magnesia and Priene (*FIRA* III no. 162). See above n. 16.

[98] Lex rep. (*FIRA* I² no. 7) line I.

(*civitates stipendiariae*).[99] This is true in the sense that each of these types of community might exist within the bounds of any *provincia*, but is misleading if it suggests that such a division was part of a provincial system. All these variations of status existed both within and outside the permanent *provinciae*, particularly in Greece, and belong not to a system of provincial administration, but of diplomatic relations between states.[100]

That is not to say that the status of a particular community did not affect the way a governor dealt with it. If a city had some form of guarantee that it could use and observe its own laws, interference with its legal or political activities by a governor might well bring objections from its citizens, and such cities were likely to have friends in the Senate at Rome. Moreover, certain protection against interference with the affairs of *civitates liberae* was given by senatorial decree and by Caesar's Lex Iulia de repetundis in 59.[101] In the ordinary course of events, however, both these specially privileged communities and others without such privileges were able to conduct their own affairs. The governor's tasks, military, juridical and fiscal, usually meant that he treated the communities within his *provincia* as self-governing entities, which indeed they were.

The position of individuals within the empire, and their relations with the governor were, like those of the communities, largely dependent upon their own connexions with Rome. There were a number of Roman citizens living outside Italy by the late Republic, some on the staff of the *societates publicanorum*, some engaged in various forms of business, some, like Cicero's correspondent, M'. Curius, combining commercial activity with a desire to keep away from Rome in the difficult and dangerous period of the war between Caesar and Pompey.[102] In addition there were individuals from among the native population who had been granted citizenship for services to Rome, such as the band of Spanish cavalrymen enfranchised by Cn. Pompeius Strabo in 89.[103] Such people obviously had to be handled with care, not only because of their legal rights as citizens, but because of their contacts with men of influence in Rome. The same was true of some non-Roman provincials. The trial of Verres took place partly because one of the people Verres had harmed as governor of Sicily was a certain Sthenius of Thermae, who included among his Roman patrons past and present both Marius and Pompey. The correspondence of Cicero includes a number of letters commending individual provincials and whole communities to the attention of

[99] E.g. Stevenson 1939 (F 149) 81–2.

[100] For the origins of these terms, see Sherwin-White 1973 (F 141) ch. 6.

[101] Cic. *Prov. Cons.* 7.

[102] Cic. *Fam.* VII.28–31. In general, see Wilson 1966 (A 128).

[103] *ILS* 8888.

Roman governors and other officials overseas.[104] As Roman power grew throughout the Mediterranean, so the links between important Romans and those who held positions of power and responsibility within the cities and communities of the rest of the ancient world became closer and more complex.

VII. *PROVINCIAE*, PROVINCES AND EMPIRE: THE BEGINNINGS OF A CHANGE IN PERCEPTIONS

The *provincia* at the beginning of the second century was still fundamentally part of the system of military magistracies which was the basis of the Roman constitution, and this background does much to explain the apparent limitation of 'provincial administration' as it is found in the last two centuries B.C.

For the governor of an overseas *provincia* the time spent away from Rome was an essential but not always welcome part of a political career. He had reached that position by election to a magistracy, and, as soon as he returned to Rome, he was involved once again in the political life of the city. Although Cicero's appointment to take charge of Cilicia was not typical, and came much later in his career than was usual, his complaints about his absence from Rome are likely to have been echoed by others. He writes to his correspondent, Caelius Rufus, from a military encampment within his *provincia*: 'The city, the city, my dear Rufus! Hold fast to it and live in its light! All service abroad, as I decided from my youth, is mean and sordid for anyone who can make a name for himself by working in Rome.'[105]

Such an attitude is hardly surprising, given the lack of interest shown by the political establishment at Rome in what was going on in the rest of the empire. In a speech delivered some three years before he himself went out to Cilicia, Cicero complained that there was so much going on in the capital that no one knew what was happening overseas, and illustrated this with an amusing story about his own return as a young man from a period of service as quaestor at Lilybaeum in Sicily. He had been full of his achievements while in the island, and was piqued to discover that the first person he met did not even know where he had been.[106]

It was inevitable, when there was such a lack of interest in the events in the overseas *provinciae* and while the link between the position of governor and the city magistracies was so strong, that the welfare of the provincials would not be uppermost in the minds of those sent out from

[104] Sthenius: Cic. II *Verr.* 2.113. Examples of Cicero's commendations: individual provincials – *Fam.* XIII.19; XIII.20; XIII.25; XIII.26; XIII.37; communities – XIII.38a (Lacedaemonians); XIII.48 (Paphians on Cyprus).

[105] Cic. *Fam.* II.12.2.

[106] Cic. *Planc.* 64–5.

Rome. Cicero says that Verres boasted openly that he did not intend to keep all the profits of his time in Sicily for himself, but that he had divided his period into three, one for himself, one for his patrons and those who would defend him at his trial, and one (the most lucrative third) for bribing the jury.[107] Not all Roman officials will have been as predatory as Cicero represents Verres as being, but the Greek historian, Appian, writing about events in the second century B.C. with the hindsight of some 300 years, comments that there were some who sought from their governorships reputation, gain or the glory of a triumph, but not the advantage of the Roman state.[108] The emphasis on individual attainment that was so much part of the creed of the Roman noble meant that such attitudes were not at all unusual.

This in turn explains why provincial governors in the first century found themselves open to pressures of various kinds from people, both in Rome and the provinces, who might be of importance to their political advancement. As is well known, Cicero had to cope not only with demands from his friend Caelius Rufus, who was aedile while Cicero was in Cilicia, for panthers for his aedilician games, but also a request for military support from an agent of M. Brutus, to enable him to collect a debt owed by the local senate of the city of Salamis on Cyprus.[109] Further investigation revealed to Cicero that the circumstances of the loan itself were irregular, to say nothing of the proposed method of securing its repayment. In addition to approaches from the city of Rome itself, powerful *publicani* and important personages in the province might well have an effect on the governor's subsequent career that left him exposed to the possibility of undue influence from such sources. Cicero admitted that Verres was far from unique in his misbehaviour in his *provincia*; the unusual thing about him, according to his accuser, was that he was already corrupt before he went.[110]

Because the provinces of the Roman empire grew out of the *provinciae* of magistrates and pro-magistrates, what we call 'provincial administration' was still by Cicero's time virtually identical with what the governor did. For this reason, and because what the governor did was determined in part by the particular situation in his area, there was little consistency between one *provincia* and another. The only general guidelines which applied to all *provinciae* were to be found in such laws as Sulla's Lex Cornelia de maiestate and Caesar's Lex Julia de repetundis. These laws were not sets of instructions on administration, emanating from some Roman equivalent of the Colonial Office, but parts of the criminal law, specifying criminal charges which could be brought

107 Cic. I *Verr.* 40. 108 App. *Hisp.* 80.349.

109 Panthers: Cic. *Fam.* VIII.4.5, VIII.9.3, VIII.8.10, VIII.6.5, II.11.2. Brutus: Cic. *Att.* V.21.10–13, VI.1.3–7. 110 Cic. II *Verr.* 2.39.

against individual holders of *imperium*. Moreover in the event of a charge being brought under such a law, the accusation came from a private individual, as in all Roman criminal law. The state as such was not involved with the implementation of these safeguards. The whole business of provincial administration was apparently the responsibility of the individual governor, and checks were placed upon him by means of the due process of law.

This might lead to the conclusion that even by the late Republic, the empire did not exist at all in the Roman mind, other than as a series of separate military commands. Such a conclusion, though it contains part of the truth, does not take account of the changes in attitude to the empire which took place during the last two centuries B.C., and which began to transform the *provinciae* into the provinces of an empire. The feeling that the well-being of the provincials was the responsibility of the governor received perhaps its finest expression in Virgil's famous lines: 'Remember, Roman, that your skill is to rule the nations through your power (*imperium*), to give a settled order to peace, to spare the conquered and in war to defeat the proud.'[111]

No doubt the poet of Augustan Rome wished to give the impression that, despite the horrors of the civil wars, the destiny of the Roman people was a noble one, but similar views can be found from the Republican period also. Cicero's letter to his brother Quintus, which is a tract on how a provincial governor should behave, includes this summary of what Quintus' attitude should be, after two years in the province of Asia: 'Put all your heart and mind to that line of thought you have followed so far, that you love those whom the Senate and people of Rome have committed to your trust and authority, and protect them and desire their greatest happiness.'[112]

Obviously both these authors are presenting an idealized picture of relations between Rome and the inhabitants of the provinces, but it is notable that such an ideal has at its centre a sense of responsibility that is almost paternalistic in nature. The same feeling can be found in the complaints heard from time to time in the late Republic of the bad behaviour of provincial governors. Those individuals who were accused by Cicero before the *quaestio de repetundis* should not be taken as typical, and in any case the accounts which Cicero gives of them are clearly not without bias. However, when addressing the people on the subject of the Lex Manilia, which was to give the command against Mithridates to Pompey in 66, he states that it is hard to describe how much the Romans are hated by foreign nations because of the lust and injustice of those men who have been sent out to them as holders of *imperium*.[113] Once again

[111] Virgil *Aen.* VI.851–3. [112] Cic. *QFr.* I.I.27. [113] Cic. *Leg. Man.* 65.

there is a clear presupposition that the proper relationship is one of just and responsible government.

This blend of paternalism and self-interest is seen with particular clarity in the letters which Cicero wrote from Cilicia during his year there from July 51. Despite his frequent assertions of his dislike of his task, not only to his friends Caelius and Atticus, but also to Appius Claudius Pulcher,[114] whom he succeeded as governor, he was aware of the responsibilities that his position gave him, and to some extent at least seems to have enjoyed them. He wrote to Atticus, after his victory over a stronghold belonging to the perpetually troublesome mountain peoples on the boundary between Cilicia and Syria, that nothing in his whole life had given him so much pleasure as the integrity which his governorship had called upon him to display. His military skill, his handling of the delicate and unstable situation in the allied kingdoms on his frontiers, and above all the self-conscious rectitude of his dealings with the inhabitants of his own area clearly gave him a delight which went beyond the acquisition of a good reputation.[115] Moreover, he was able to claim that his scrupulousness, which extended not only to refusing even those allowances from the provincials which were permitted by law, but insisting that his entourage did the same, had brought positive benefits to the Romans at a critical moment. When war threatened from the Parthians in Syria, he could report to Cato in Rome that his moderation had secured the support of the provincial communities.[116]

It is almost impossible to discover what the provincials actually felt about the Roman presence. Cicero lamented the miserable state of Cilicia when he arrived there, and attributed the problems of the people to the ravages of Appius Claudius, yet at least some cities would have sent embassies to Rome commending Appius' governorship, and it is possible that one was intending to erect a temple in his honour.[117] Between Cicero's complaints and the public honours decreed by the Cilicians themselves, it is hard to know how far the provincials felt they had benefited from Appius' proconsulship and how far convention and subservience combined to ensure that genuine resentments were hidden by a parade of official gratitude. Even in Cicero's own account of what he clearly intended to be an exemplary tenure of his *provincia*, there are indications that Roman attitudes irritated and offended the Greeks. Even before his arrival in his own area, he writes to Atticus that the behaviour of his staff while in Athens, their daily rudeness, stupidity and arrogance in word and deed, considerably upset Cicero himself.[118] Equally,

[114] Caelius: see above n. 105. Atticus: *Att.* v.10.3. Appius Claudius: *Fam.* III.2.1.

[115] *Att.* v.20.6. [116] *Fam.* xv.3.2.

[117] Cicero's complaints: *Att.* v.16. Embassies: *Fam.* III.10.6. Temple(?): *Fam.* III.7.2–3.

[118] *Att.* v.10.3.

Cicero's well-intentioned interventions into the internal affairs of the cities in his area, whether he was castigating the corrupt administration of the local magistrates or ensuring that the richer citizens gave grain to the poorer during a famine, will have displeased those who prided themselves on their civic independence.[119] In contrast to Appius, he actively prohibited the provincials from expressing their gratitude to him in other than verbal form, a move which was doubtless intended to save the cities expense, but which also removed one of the few freedoms which they had left under Roman control.[120] There is no doubt, from the tone of his letters, that Cicero believed that he knew what was best for those committed to his charge, and that he saw it as his duty to act accordingly.

The place in Rome where the development of this attitude is perhaps most evident is in the courts which tried cases *de repetundis*. Although the system left much to be desired as a mechanism for the control of misgovernment, it did at least exist, and could be used to prosecute former governors. The most remarkable feature of this procedure was that, by the time of C. Gracchus' law at least, a court in Rome was available in which an action could be brought by a non-Roman against a man who had been elected to one of the highest offices of the Roman state. In effect, the accuser was being treated for the purpose of the law as though he were a Roman citizen. Whereas, early in the second century, complaints of this sort could only be reported to the Senate, which could then decide, if it so wished, to institute some form of investigation, by the end of the century the matter could be dealt with in a court of law. What had been a matter of foreign policy had become the business of the courts.

Such an attitude was, of course, not merely the result of Roman good will. It was increasingly necessary, as the empire grew, to seek the support of at least that section of the provincial population which had most influence locally.[121] Moreover, the acquisition of such advantages was not without cost to the provincials themselves. In effect they ceased to be members of foreign states with control over their own affairs in return for a degree of paternalistic attention from the dominant power in the Mediterranean world. Even such states as were granted the guaranteed use of their own laws held that right only by the grace and favour of the Roman people.[122]

It might seem that an attitude such as that described above is somewhat insubstantial compared with the military might of the armies

[119] Corruption: *Att.* VI.2.5. Famine: *Att.* V.21.8. [120] *Att.* V.21.7.

[121] Class and other divisions could result in pro- and anti-Roman factions, as at the time of Mithridates' conquest of western Asia Minor: see Hind in ch. 5 above, pp. 148–9.

[122] E.g. Lex Antonia de Termessibus (*FIRA* I² no. 11) col. I, lines 5–10.

of Rome. Its significance, however, can scarcely be overestimated. It was the belief of the Romans that they had some responsibility for those they controlled which was to turn the military power of Rome into the Roman empire, just as it turned the military *provinciae* into imperial provinces. The development of the world-state that the emperors ruled began with this change in the nature of the work of the provincial governor during the Republican period.

CHAPTER 16

ECONOMY AND SOCIETY, 133–43 B.C.

C. NICOLET

If we define 'economy', un-theoretically, as the production, exchange and consumption of goods (not only material goods but also what are called 'services'), a study of all these three elements throughout the whole Mediterranean world, even for the period covered in this volume, would vastly exceed the dimensions of the present chapter. Some limitations will therefore be applied. First, a spatial limitation: we shall look at the history mainly from the standpoint of Italy and its political centre, Rome.[1] Secondly, a limitation in time: the economy of Roman Italy already had a long history behind it in 133 B.C., but we shall take for granted and only briefly allude to that earlier structure and development, and lay all the stress on the changes that occurred in our period, which were considerable and have become better known as a result of modern research. A third limit will be in terms of orientation. It is the most delicate point to explain, although the most interesting. One cannot study the ancient (or any other) economy without relating it to the kind of society and the political structure within which its developments took place. In ancient society men were not only producers or consumers, rentiers or wage-earners: they were also free or slave, Romans or 'allies';[2] they had a social status derived not just from their place in the economy but, mostly, from the role, hereditary or otherwise, assigned to them by the way the community was organized. Strongly emphasized in law, with its privileges and its exclusions, status was more civic than economic (though naturally certain economic facts, such as property, might be part of its definition). But status, in turn, affected the economy, directly: the control by the state of access to real property is a good example, or the exclusion of certain status groups – the upper 'orders' – from certain economic activities, or the way in which the availability of slave labour varied as a function of Rome's conquests. So a particular effort will be made in this chapter, in describing and analysing the facts

[1] The economy of the area as a whole was not yet a unity: eastern Asia Minor, Syria, Gaul and Egypt only became integrated during the first century B.C.

[2] i.e., in Italy, subjects, down at least to 89 B.C.

and changes of the Roman economy, to signal wherever appropriate the interaction between economy and status.[3]

One further preliminary word is necessary, on a characteristic of our period. The century from the Gracchi to Julius Caesar was one of almost continuous upheaval, of successive 'crises' or 'revolutions': the agrarian crisis of 133–121, the military *coups* and civil wars of 103–100, 88–80, 78, 73–71, 63, 49–44, the uprising of Italy in 90–88, the slave-wars of 136, 106, 73 (and again in 47 and 36). Now in every one of these events, the sources strongly emphasize the social dimension: 'rich' and 'poor', 'nobles' (*sic*) or 'best people' (*optimates*) against the 'plebs' or the 'people' or the 'lower classes'. The political history, even at its most purely narrative level, is rooted all the time (as one might, indeed, expect) in the social and structural context. But besides that, to a greater extent than earlier, this age of 'revolutions' experienced specifically *economic* crises:[4] the crisis of food supply in Rome in 124–123 (recurring periodically at least down to Augustus); financial crises threatening circulation and credit in 89–88, 66–63, 48–47; crises of public finance linked to warfare and setbacks in the march of conquest; pure coinage crises, from the unevenness in the quantities of coinage minted to the manipulations of the denominations and their relative value in 88, 82, 63–61, 45–44. One can even speak of crises – or rather, perhaps, successes – in certain fields of economic activity like the expansion of Italian viticulture or of construction (related, *inter alia*, to urbanization), which archaeology has recently cast new light on, corroborating and illustrating the literary evidence. We shall not try to conclude from all this that the economy played a more predominant role in our period than earlier, but the fact that it is more in evidence and better known plainly justifies an attempt to set down its story.

I. CONTEXT: GEOGRAPHY AND DEMOGRAPHY

Economies are responses to the needs of people for goods – material goods and services. So the number of people there are, not absolutely but relatively to the resources of a territory, is a fundamental datum. But in dealing with antiquity the concept of a territory is more tricky than it would be nowadays, because there was no such thing as a unitary territorial state: 'Roman Italy' is, before 89 B.C., a misleading term. Cisalpine Gaul, north of the line Pisa–Rimini, would have, formally, to

[3] This is not to engage in any search for the will-o'-the-wisp of a specific 'ancient economy': such interactions are not unique to any one period of history and could equally well be observed in 'modern' economies.

[4] How far that impression may be the result merely of the hazards of source-survival is a preliminary and basic question.

be excluded: it was a province, even after 89.[5] Yet although it had, unlike the rest of the peninsula, a partly Gallic population, it had been colonized very early by Romans and Italians, and underwent a remarkable demographic and economic development alongside the rest of Italy. It was the earliest receptacle of Italian emigration. It requires, therefore, to be considered together with the rest. On the other hand, even peninsular Italy in the narrow sense was, down to about 90–60 B.C., only relatively unified politically, and displays an even more marked human and economic diversity. It was a big federation – technically an 'alliance' – of some dozens of *populi*, themselves divided into some hundreds of more or less autonomous 'cities', which were only under Roman hegemony for military and, to a lesser degree, fiscal purposes. And the diversity of political structures of the cities, some more and some less closely tied to Rome, corresponds to a diversity of juridical statuses, of the cities and of the individuals within them, which had a powerful influence on economic relationships: this or that right of ownership of real property; freedom or otherwise of change of domicile; possibility or not of economic relationships between each other or with Rome (*commercium*).

In the territory of ancient Italy, then, neither people nor peoples were fully free or fully equal, and their mere numbers are not the only determinant of their demography or their production and exchange. And political, fiscal, military inequalities not only affected economic relationships; they determined movements of population.

First, movements in space. Rome, the dominant city, possessed or annexed distant territories in amongst the allies, and filled them – the process took generations, but it was directed and controlled – with organized groups or with individuals installed in agricultural settlements (the *coloniae*), many of which became a focus for new urban settlements. Rome controlled part of the land of Italy, confiscated by right of conquest; and access to ownership or enjoyment of that land was to be a principal battleground of economic and political conflict. Shifts of population in Italy were never entirely spontaneous, at least before about 89–75 B.C., and even after that the ruling authority, for political as much as socio-economic reasons, did its best to control or direct them, for example by the 'colonizations' of Sulla and Julius Caesar and Augustus.

Secondly, internal movements. Ancient cities, for obvious military and fiscal reasons, were very conscious of their 'wealth of men' and very jealous to maintain it (within limits that we shall observe). They sought periodically to count it with exactitude: censuses run all through their history and are often central to their institutions. The censuses reflect

[5] Not administratively annexed to Italy till the creation of the Augustan *regiones*, perhaps *c.* 7 B.C.

two contradictory anxieties: the dread of manpower shortage (military above all) and lack of resources in the face of potential rivals, and the opposite dread of being swamped by outsiders, of free or slave origin, who might threaten the economic, social or political balance of the community. We could no doubt write a much better demography of antiquity if only we had all the statistical records they must have accumulated in their archives. And yet even if we did have all the demographic figures of the ancients they would still be misleading. For they are always affected by the segmentation of their societies into different juridical statuses: their degree of accuracy was very different according to whether they were dealing with full Roman citizens or with Latins or allies, or with free as against non-free.[6]

The vital importance, as well as the great difficulty, of these questions is shown by the changes that occurred several times in our period in the organization of the censuses in Rome and Italy. At first, a census certainly implied the physical presence of the citizen at the political centre of his city and his personal appearance before the authorities. It is probable[7] that from the third century onwards, for many Roman citizens *sine suffragio*, the census took place locally, and so also for the inhabitants of the *coloniae Latinae*; the overall figures[8] were sent to Rome and centralized there. Whether that is so or not, after the Social War[9] the whole population of Italy was counted locally: the ancient personal procedure persisted – down to Julius Caesar, anyhow – just for the inhabitants of Rome.

I. *Population figures*

For trying to evaluate the population of Italy and its evolution all we have is thirty-nine sets of Roman census figures (i.e. of *capita civium*) between 508 B.C. and A.D. 14; that is about 38 per cent of all there were, and ought to be enough for seeing how it evolved.[10] But for our period the gaps are due not just to the accidents of survival but to the evident collapse of the administrative machinery consequent upon the political and economic difficulties of the first century B.C. Also the interpretation of the figures we do have, sometimes dubiously transmitted, has been the object of many an argument. The standard view is now that before 28 B.C. the only people listed, with one or two exceptions, were adult males; they were included right down to the poorest (with varying degrees of

[6] To say nothing of the large margin of error due to the inadequacies of communication and transport and of the administration itself.

[7] Humbert 1978 (F 80) 310ff.

[8] Which might well be inadequate, since they were arrived at according to the local rules.

[9] The evidence is in the Table of Heraclea, to be dated between 75 and 45 B.C.

[10] See the table opposite.

ROMAN CENSUS FIGURES

508 B.C.	130,000	Dionys. v. 20.
503	120,000	Hieronym. Ol. 69. 1.
498	150,700	Dionys. v. 75.
493	110,000	Dionys. vi. 96.
474	103,000	Dionys. ix. 36.
465	104,714	Livy iii. 3.
459	117,319	Livy iii. 24; Eutrop. i. 16.
393/2	152,573	Pliny, *HN* xxxiii. 16.
340/39	165,000	Euseb. Ol. 110. 1 (cf. Beloch (1886) A 8, 340 n. 9).
c. 323	150,000	Oros. v. 22. 2; Eutrop. v.9; the MSS figure in Livy ix. 19 (250,000) should be amended; likewise that in Plut. 326c (130,000). Cf. Beloch (1886) A 8, 341.
294/3	262,321	Livy x. 47; for variants see Beloch (1886) A 8, 343.
289/8(?)	272,000	*Per.* Liv. xi.
280/79	287,222	*Ibid.* xiii.
276/5	271,224	*Ibid.* xiv.
265/4	292,234 (or 292, 334. *Per.* Liv. xvi gives 382,233)	Eutrop. ii. 18, and Greek translation.
252/1	297,797	*Per.* Liv. xviii.
247/6	241,712	*Ibid.* xix.
241/0	260,000	Hieronym. Ol. 134.1 (Euseb. Armen. Ol. 134. 3, gives 250,000, cf. Beloch (1886) A 8, 344 n. 2).
234/3	270,713	*Per.* Liv. xx.
209/8	137,108 (perhaps rather 237,108)	Livy xxvii. 36; so too in the *Perioche*.
204/3	214,000	Livy xxix. 37 and *Per.*
194/3	143,704 (perhaps rather 243,704)	Livy xxxv. 9.
189/8	258,318 (258,310. *Per.* Liv. xxxviii)	Livy xxxviii. 36.
179/8	258,794	*Per.* Liv. xli.
174/3	269,015 (267,231. *Per.* Liv. xlii)	Livy xlii. 10.
169/8	312,805	*Per.* Liv. xlv.
164/3	337,022 (Plut. *Paul.* 38 gives 337,452)	*Ibid.* xlvi.
159/8	328,316	*Ibid.* xlvii.
154/3	324,000	*Ibid.* xlviii.
147/6	322,000	Euseb. Armen. Ol. 158. 3.
142/1	327,442	*Per.* Liv. liv.
136/5	317,933	*Ibid.* lvi.
131/0	318,823	*Ibid.* lix.
125/4	394,736 (?294,336)	*Ibid.* lx.
115/4	394,336 (?)	*Ibid.* lxiii.
86/5	463,000 (or, if amended, 963,000)	Hieronym. Ol. 173. 4.
70/69	910,000	Phlegon (Jacoby no. 257) F. 12. 6. *Per.* Liv. xcviii gives 900,000.
28	4,063,000	*Res Gestae* 8. 2.
8	4,233,000	*Ibid.* 8. 3.
A.D. 14	4,937,000	*Ibid.* 8. 4. The *Fasti Ostienses* give 4,100,900 (Ehrenberg and Jones, *Documents Illustrating Reigns of Aug. and Tib.* 40).

Table from P. A. Brunt, *Italian Manpower 225* B.C. – A.D. *14* (1971 (A 16)) pp. 13–14.

accuracy), but women and children were excluded. In 28 and 8 B.C. and A.D. 14, on the other hand, the figures are only explicable on the assumption that the whole citizen population was included (again with varying margins of error). That basic difference means that we cannot talk in terms of a long-term natural population increase (i.e. through births). We have always, also, to take into account the granting of citizenship to people – individuals or groups – who did not have it before: the increase between 115/4 and 70/69, for example, from 395,000 to 910,000 can only be explained in that way. But even when the whole free population of Italy had been subsumed under Roman citizenship (which was not before the 60s B.C.) the figures only give us a very partial sense of the whole population: how many women and children were there, and, above all, how many slaves, so essential to the economy? One can only make cautious hypotheses.

Then again, for the first half of our period (133 to 70–60 B.C.) what proportion of the population of Italy was non-Roman? All we possess are remote and imperfect testimonies concerning, essentially, the contingents the 'allies' were supposed or able to provide for the Roman levy. From figures for 225 B.C., for example,[11] we can perhaps conclude that the total of all Roman citizens was of the order of 923,000, the Latins and allies together up to 1,829,000.[12] That proportion, 1 to 2, will have maintained itself till the end of the second century: it corresponds roughly to the proportion of Italian contingents in the Roman army, which was at times 60 per cent. But whole regions of Italy – the southernmost part – remain out of account. Nevertheless, a free population of Italy in *c.* 225 B.C. of 3 million is in line with reasonable probability. By the time of Augustus, Italy (and by then it included the Cisalpina) must have had nearly 4½ million free inhabitants.

The crucial problem of slave numbers remains.[13] We have only very indirect means of judging their numbers. There are figures for war-prisoners imported in the second and first centuries: 150,000 from Epirus in 167, a million Gauls, maybe, in 58–52.[14] We hear of the importance of the market at Delos – mainly for export to Italy – at the end of the second and beginning of the first century, and of the political problem over integrating freed slaves in the census lists that raged from 177 to 57 B.C. at least, which is clear proof that their numbers must have been considerable. Brunt[15] cautiously allows 3 million slaves under

[11] Polyb. II.24; Diod. XXV.13; Pliny, *HN* III.138; Livy *Per.* 20.

[12] Corresponding to corrected figures for male adults of 300,000 and 575,600.

[13] So, less crucial, does that as to free non-Romans from overseas.

[14] Epirus: Polyb. XXX.14; Livy XLV.34.5–6. Gaul: Plut. *Caes.* 15; App. *Celt.* 2.

[15] Brunt 1971 (A 16) 124–5.

Augustus, in a total population of 7½ million, perhaps even that an overestimate. There are a few things we know for certain. First, the number of slaves was certainly much more important at the end of the second century B.C. than at its beginning, and still more important in the first century. Secondly, if the 'Slave Wars' can be taken as an index of their numbers – as well as their employment in agriculture and the worsening of their lot – then the apogee was the wars in Sicily and Campania in 136–132, in Sicily in 106 and in southern Italy in 73–70; but they were still a potential or even critical factor in the civil wars in 63, 47 and especially 46–36 with Sextus Pompeius. Thirdly, the rise in the number of slaves in Italy in our period is due principally to enforced immigration. That had effects on economic consumption, not because slaves consumed more than they produced (for most slaves are, by definition, at the bottom of the economic pecking order) but because, not being free to choose what to work at, slaves can be used in sectors not necessarily producing what they personally consume at all, such as pasturage, vine and olive growing and services of various kinds, and may thus in the long run contribute to an overall deficit of food resources. Finally, slavery was perhaps a more transitory condition than we tend to think, and the grant of freedom a normal expectation for a high proportion of slaves, maybe up to a third. Now at Rome a freed slave became a Roman citizen; so the citizen population of Italy, or certainly of Rome, included at any time a significant proportion of former slaves and their families.[16]

To have any significance these hypothetical global figures must be seen in the context of the Mediterranean population as a whole. According to Diodorus and Josephus[17] Egypt, the 'most-populated country', had 7 to 7½ million inhabitants, not counting Alexandria. Recent calculations[18] have given for the three Gauls plus Narbonensis a total of the order of 5 million. Nothing certain can be said, notwithstanding Beloch's heroic efforts[19] in the last century, about Spain, Africa or Asia Minor. But it does look as if Italy was one of the most densely populated zones of the Mediterranean world, perhaps – considering its area – the most of all after Egypt.[20] That was certainly one of the reasons for Rome's conquests, but also, by virtue of the enforced immigration of slaves, one of the consequences of those conquests.

[16] Perhaps 200,000 such in Rome between 58 and 45 B.C. (which swelled the number of recipients of public grain) out of a total population of 600,000 to 800,000.

[17] Diod. I.31; Joseph. *BJ* II.16.4.

[18] J. Harmand, *Les Celtes au second âge du fer* (Paris, 1970), 61–5.

[19] Beloch 1886 (G 13).

[20] Which was a world of its own, an 'India of the Mediterranean', as Strabo suggests, XV.1.13.690C.

2. *Distribution and movements of population*

Is there a global pattern to be found? It looks as if, over two centuries, the overall population of Italy, slaves included, increased by about 50 per cent. That is an average of ¼ per cent per annum, and is very small. If we could measure the immigration accurately we could deduce how much was due to natural rise; but we have to content ourselves with a pointer or two. The period was marked, especially from 90 to 28 B.C., by external wars and internal civil strife that involved the call-up of numbers as great as or even greater than in the Second Punic War.[21] But were the losses as significant demographically as in that war? Can one trust Velleius' figure[22] of 300,000 dead in the Social War? That is uncertain. It is, however, probable that those conflicts had at least the effect – when one thinks how long some of the mobilizations lasted – of putting a brake on any *expansion* that might have occurred. The testimonies to, and complaints of, depopulation from 133 to 18 B.C., from Ti. Gracchus, from Julius Caesar, from Augustus, even allowing for the fact that they were only talking about Roman citizens and perhaps only the upper classes, are too persistent not to represent some reality, as seen at least by contemporaries. But what did it amount to? We hardly know anything about their demographic behaviour, either general or of particular status-groups; we have no certain measure of the rate of nuptiality or natural fecundity or mortality. The decline in *capita civium* from 164 to 136 B.C., from 337,000 to 317,000, less than 1,000 per annum, would represent 6 per cent of the population, if it was absolute. But between 136 and 115 the figure bounces back to 395,000, a rise of 24 per cent, which cannot conceivably be a natural rise: it must have been due either to the enfranchisement of peregrines or a massive liberation of slaves (which has left no trace) or, more likely, to differences or changes in the compilation of the census – and no doubt to the Gracchan agrarian assignments.

Unfortunately, nothing in these figures tells us anything about the fecundity of the groups concerned. Ti. Gracchus' fear was that poor citizens could not bring up their children; he did not say they were no longer having any.[23] Nevertheless, it is possible that that was tending to happen: but it would be a diminution in the number of future citizens, not present adults, otherwise where did the new citizens of 115 come from? Are we to suppose that the rather lower figures of the second century included only the *adsidui*, those who had at least some property, the best future soldiers? But the poor were not in principle excluded from

[21] 25 per cent of *iuniores* under arms *c.* 42 B.C., Brunt 1971 (A 16) 512.
[22] Vell. Pat. II.15.
[23] App. *BCiv.* I.30 and 40; Plut. *Ti. Gracch.* 8; Rich 1983 (C 121) 300ff.

the census: and the decline – a very small one – in the number of the rich would hardly have been so disturbing to the political establishment. Be that as it may, we have to remember that although there was a set of census grades within the overall totals we do not have the detailed figures for each grade: we are almost entirely ignorant of the real distribution of individual fortunes or how they changed.[24]

We are perhaps not quite as ignorant as to the division of the population by regions, and more generally between town and country. The 'depopulation' of the Italian countryside, so frequently referred to in the sources for our period,[25] perhaps only affected certain regions and certain social classes (the free peasants, in fact). But the evidence of archaeology, of which much has been made recently, cannot wholly overturn so unanimous a tradition. We must stress the growing importance of urbanization in Italy in this period. Doubtless the majority of important colonial foundations date from the end of the third and beginning of the second century, and they were, to begin with, too restricted to contain within their walls the whole of the new *coloni*.[26] But most of those centres, as well as the older towns, indigenous and otherwise, expanded considerably in the second century (not only in the first, as used to be supposed). According to Beloch, after Pliny,[27] there were 434 'cities' (not all important, of course) in Augustan Italy, which would give an urban population of at least 3 million out of the total of 7–8 million, i.e. of the order of 40 per cent. That is a considerable proportion: it is also the proportion characteristic of the Hellenistic world.[28] Evidence is not lacking of the rural exodus into the towns, Rome principally but also other minor towns like Fregellae. A huge increase in the size of Rome is attested in the second century,[29] but the rural influx was greatest in the first, when the *leges frumentariae* had their full effect;[30] the number of beneficiaries of the public grain was 320,000 between 57 and 46 B.C.[31] Archaeology confirms the impression: recent studies dealing with the Cisalpina, as well as the cities of central and southern Italy,[32] show the transformation after the Social War, with urban planning, public edifices and walls. It is hard to believe that that did not carry with it demographic – and so economic – consequences.[33]

Lastly, can one find, for Italy in our period, evidence of a trend of

[24] But see below as to agriculture.

[25] From Cic. *Att.* I.19.4 to Livy VI.12.5 at least for Latium; Plut. *Ti. Gracch.* 8 for the Etruscan seaboard; App. *BCiv.* I.7.

[26] Tozzi 1974 (G 246), Frederiksen 1976 (G 79).

[27] Beloch 1880 (A 7) 360, following Pliny *HN* III.

[28] Beloch 1909 (G 14) 424–34.

[29] Frontinus gives two new aqueducts built in 144 and 125, VII.1.2.

[30] Sall. *Cat.* 37.7; *App. BCiv.* II.506.

[31] Suet. *Iul.* 41.5.

[32] Gabba 1972 (G 86).

[33] Gabba 1976 (G 88).

overseas emigration? We have already spoken of enforced immigration, that of slaves, their numbers considerable but their mortality perhaps greater than that of the free population and their nuptiality and fecundity certainly less. But some proportion of that group merges, through the grant of freedom, with the citizen population in a generation or so.[34] Conversely, Rome and allied Italy saw during the same period substantial emigration. First to the Cisalpina, as we have seen: the 'Romanization' of the Celtic region of the Po is a major phenomenon of the period.[35] Also to places abroad: in Spain, Narbonensis, Sicily, Africa, numerous Roman communities are attested in the second and first centuries. Elsewhere – in Greece and Asia Minor particularly – many 'businessmen' were settled (but also some people owning land): 80,000 are supposed to have been massacred by Mithridates in 88 B.C. Partly officially encouraged by the despatch of colonies or the settlement of individuals on confiscated land, partly spontaneous, this emigration was obviously linked to Rome's conquests. Brunt estimates the total number of Roman citizens outside Italy as 370,000 in 69 B.C., 450,000 in 49 and $1\frac{1}{4}$ million in 28.

To sum up. From 133 to 43 B.C. the *total* population of Italy, it is highly probable, grew with regularity, enough to maintain the victorious wars in Africa, Greece and Asia and Gaul, notwithstanding the huge internal military upheavals. There was no collapse, there were no dramatic famines[36] or plagues, and there was substantial emigration. Italy in the broad sense was probably at that time the most important high-density zone in the Mediterranean, the biggest agglomeration in the world, the centre of power and, presently, exchange. Moreover – and this was essential in a world where no man was complete except as a citizen of somewhere – Italy was the one massive unitary block in a fragmented world, its entire free population being Roman citizens from about 60 B.C. onwards. This positive assessment doubtless hides crises and disparities and internal shifts that we can dimly perceive in general but cannot describe in particular; but the basic pattern is as stated. The image of a dramatic 'depopulation' of Italy must be discarded.[37]

[34] More cannot be said: the phenomenon was already one of dispute at the end of the second century and even more in the first.

[35] See the figures already given. Naturally, the inhabitants of the Cisalpina under Augustus include the indigenous population, now Roman citizens.

[36] Only recurrent 'food-crises' in Rome, which is not the same thing.

[37] And growth continued in the first century A.D. Of the 5,984,000 *cives* of Claudius' census in A.D. 48, a million more than in A.D. 14, not all can have been freedmen and enfranchised peregrines, and many must have been domiciled in Italy. Tac. *Ann.* XI.25.

II. ITALIAN AGRICULTURE

It is all the more impossible to give a full account of Italian agriculture in a short chapter, in that the tendency of recent research has been to insist on diversities, not only geographical but social and economic, because different products, even different 'modes of production', could succeed one another over time in the same place or coexist in different places at the same time. The sources are also diverse, being of three kinds. First there is technical literature, that of the agronomists, spread over several centuries from Cato, *c.* 180–150, to Varro *c.* 57–37 and Columella, *c.* A.D. 50, and of the writers of 'Natural History' (for example Pliny the Elder, *c.* A.D. 60, on plants and trees). Their examples, figures, and recommendations have to be handled very critically, but we have now, at least, some good aids to doing that.[38] Under the same heading should be put the treatises, containing theory and practice, of the 'Gromatici', which are vital evidence for such things as the juridical and fiscal status of land and the procedures for establishing landed estates and shaping landscapes. The second main kind of source derives from the particular statements of the historians, or of contemporaries, about economic questions; in their case, too, prudence is called for in view of the discontinuities of such evidence as well as various sorts of *parti pris*. Thirdly, in the wake of the pioneers, Beloch, Pais, Fraccaro, but especially since the Second World War, we have the ever-intensifying results of archaeology: broad-scale reconnaissance of settlements and cultivation patterns, and ever more detailed research into the objects of production – wine and oil, anyhow – and the routes of exchange, through study of the spread of pottery. All this has contributed an infinity of new elements to the pattern, though often difficult to interpret and still more to generalize upon.

1. Geographical diversity

A re-reading of Nissen, E. C. Semple, Cary, or encyclopaedic surveys like Almagia–Miglioni, will simply confirm the ecstatic assertions of the ancients – Varro, Strabo, Vitruvius, Virgil, Pliny – as to the diversity, yet always moderateness, of the climate of Italy, the multiplicity of her resources, the equal capacity of her land for all forms of agriculture, not excluding animal husbandry. However imperfect, before Agrippa and Augustus,[39] their ethnographic and statistical information, their mensuration and their cartography, the Romans, masters of their space in every

[38] Such as the works of White 1967 (G 257), Capogrossi Colognesi 1969/1976 (G 30), Martin 1971 (B 73), and good recent editions of Varro, Cato and Pliny.

[39] Everything changed with Augustus.

sense, and consumers of an ever widening range of goods, knew all about these diversities and complementarities. It is clear that in our period Italy, only just beginning to be unified politically under Rome's hegemony, was not a unity agriculturally. The geographical horizon of Cato in the second century does not extend beyond Latium and Campania, whereas that of Varro a century later encompasses the whole peninsula, including the Cisalpina (which geographically is not even part of the Mediterranean system).

The peninsula exhibits great regional disparities, of relief, climate and soil. But in broad terms the climatic conditions (relative dryness, with Mediterranean rainfall pattern) determined an agriculture essentially of cereals and arboriculture (vine and olive), with irrigation necessary for the cultivation of grasses and legumes. Equally primary, however, was the opposition between highlands – the central mountain chain, the plateaux and hill-slopes – which alone retain in summer enough vegetable cover for pasturage, and the coastal plains, cultivable all the year round but also capable of serving as winter pasture. A forest cover certainly much thicker than today, even in southern parts like Bruttium (the Sila Forest), provided a necessary complement for the pasture of certain livestock, particularly pigs, in addition to timber.[40] In detail, however, every region contained internal contrasts in the agriculture it supported, especially the hilly parts on the one hand and the valleys or intensely cultivated river basins, Val di Chiana in Etruria, Foligno–Spoleto depression in Umbria, Val di Diano in Lucania, on the other.

A trait common to all Italy is the importance of drainage in the coastal plains, and also up to a point in the plain of the Po, which was being populated and Romanized in the second century. Greeks and Etruscans introduced very early, in the eighth and seventh centuries, in their respective areas, sophisticated drainage techniques without which those regions are too insalubrious for any agricultural development at all. One historical problem is whether the depopulation and decay of certain areas in our period (Latium from the fourth century, the coastal plain of Etruria from the second, the Pomptine Marshes, etc.) were in part related to the abandonment of drainage systems.

The variety of landscapes within the broad regions explains why, in spite of the changes in the overall pattern that our period underwent, Italy was still the 'land cultivated like a garden', as Varro called it,[41] and remained very prosperous, even though it abandoned some kinds of product to the overseas provinces and took readily to the importing of some kinds of product (paying for them, indeed, by taxing the said provinces). It is only in a very general sense that one can talk about the

[40] Toynbee 1965 (A 121) II p. 595–8.

[41] *Rust.* I.3; 6.

'abandonment' of the cultivation of some items and the 'substitution' of others; because in fact at the local level polyculture remained the rule and subsistence economy quite certainly predominated.

However, in the first century B.C. it is possible to pick out some broad areas of relative specialization: Campania, very rich,[42] with arable, vines and olives; the plain of the Po, with arable, sheep and pigs; the highlands of Samnium and the Sabellian lands, with pasturage and transhumance; the Etruscan and Sabine plains and coasts with arable and vines; the exclusively pastoral zones of Lucania and Bruttium. And at the end of our period a new speculative agriculture, *pastio villatica*, is practised in certain areas determined by urban geography (because producing luxury products for the urban market): southern Latium, Campania and the lands actually round the cities. The only marked contrast to this unity-in-diversity of Italy was the annexation of the plain of the Po (involving no economic or political discontinuity); for its climate and topography were quite different: more unvaryingly humid and misty, but above all vast and flat, and thus open, after forest clearing and the expulsion or containment of the Celtic inhabitants, to large-scale *occupatio* and the organization of enormous centuriated areas, for the benefit of Roman and Italian immigrants.

To the physical diversity we must not neglect to add a diversity of indigenous patterns of life and traditional social structures, surviving conquest by Rome, right down to our period: agro-pastoral communities in Liguria and the Sabellian lands and Samnium; Gallic tribal systems with dispersed habitation in the Cisalpina; semi-free peasantry in Etruria even down to the beginning of the first century, and so on.

2. *Diversity of agricultural products*

That, too, is attested by the geographers and agronomists and natural historians; and not to be neglected is the evidence afforded by detailed studies of diet,[43] which show on the one hand the growing importance of imported items, but also the taking on board of almost all those items by the agriculture of Italy itself. From quite early on, even in the diet of the country people, more isolated than the inhabitants of Rome, a great diversity is observable: vegetables, fruits of all kinds, spices, poultry: one need look no further than the pseudo-Virgilian *Moretum*. But, those important complements apart, the ancient Italian was a consumer of cereals, olives, vegetables, pork and salt fish, and a drinker of wine; and cooking, as well as lighting and medicine, relied on olive oil. That is what was decisive for the destiny of Italian agriculture.

[42] Dion. Hal. *Ant. Rom.* 1.37.

[43] André 1981 (G 3).

3. *Techniques*

Agriculture was essentially manual, utilizing human and animal labour. Other sources of energy known to antiquity (which means, really, the water-mill) only emerged much after our period. Tools were those developed in the Iron Age – and destined to continue to the present day: notable, however, was the predominance of the sickle over the scythe for harvesting grain. The Italian plough of our period was still, at best, wheel-less[44] and without mould-board, though its metal share may well have been just as efficient on light soils. The only agricultural machinery were the grape- and olive-presses described by Cato, which could be quite powerful pieces of mechanism. One must not underestimate the technical satisfactoriness of such an agriculture. Provided, always, that there was a sufficiency of labour it could prove well adapted to soil and climate, whether for clearing and preparation of ground or for ploughing, tilling, harvesting and storing. (More seriously *dis*advantageous were the bottle-necks of land transport.) The traditional practices were improved, from the second century onwards, by the lessons of agricultural science derived from the Greeks: selection and improvement of species, grafting and hybridization, introduction of new species of grains, fruits and vines, manuring. Rotation was known, but not triennial rotation: fallow every other year remained the rule. On the other hand certain traditional intercultivations flourished, such as two tree-crops together (vine on poplar in Campania – the Italian vine is high-grown, with consequences for investment costs) or grain between olive-rows, with sheep pastured between the trees after the harvest.

4. *The major items of production*

In our period there were four major items of production (for the market or otherwise) existing in Italy; and the second and first centuries B.C. were a period when the respective developments of these items brought about changes, sometimes rapid and considerable, which contributed, along with more purely economic and political factors, to give to the history of Italian agriculture its touch of excitement and even drama.

(a) The first item is cereals. The lowest level of production, and the commonest, was part of that 'peasant' or 'subsistence' economy that recent work has stressed:[45] cereals, originally barley, then wheat, with millet as a back-up, as the staple foodstuff, eaten in the form of porridge, *puls*. So they are found as part of every type of agricultural enterprise, giving no doubt very modest returns (three or four times the seed sown,

[44] Except, by the beginning of the Principate, north of the Alps.
[45] Frayn 1979 (G 75) and Evans 1981 (G 64).

on average). If the property or unit of management was too small, the peasant's survival can only be explained by positing supplementary resources – garden, common pasture, hiring out of the peasant's own labour. Cereal production had also always to feed the cities, which was a basic problem in the ancient Mediterranean. Hence its presence in areas, such as the Roman 'Campagna', not suited to it, and hence the shortages and famines recorded at Rome from the fifth century onwards, when corn had to come from Etruria, Campania or Sicily.

In the third and second centuries we can observe considerable changes (which, for once, can be seen more clearly in general than in detail). First an increase in demand, due to urbanization (the growth of Rome from the third century, accentuated in the second) and to the requirements of the armies. Then changes in the eating habits of the rich and the city dwellers: bread supplanting porridge and demanding proportionally more corn.[46] In the second century the import of grain rises – sporadically, and for the public distributions, but certainly involving a private-enterprise market. The grain is from Sicily, Greece, Sardinia, Spain, Africa; conquest and political factors play a role, and soon (especially after 123 B.C.) part of the regular import of grain to Rome comes in as tax. Does all that point to a 'crisis' or a big shift in the products of Italian agriculture? No, for the imports concern only the urban market (though that may, it is true, mean 40 per cent of the population), and cereals go on being needed to feed the work-force even in areas given over to other items of production. So they probably continued to be grown everywhere, except in a few areas where we can document for certain the abandonment of land or its conversion into vine or olive growing. If the Roman 'Campagna' ceased to be cereal-growing, along with some parts of southern Italy (the coast of the Gulf of Taranto), Campania, for all its vineyards, remained a 'granary' at least down to 63 B.C. and the really determining fact is that Italy did not produce *enough*: that was the real reason for the growing importance of a large-scale commerce in grain from a distance (concurrently with the supplies that came in as tax), and it was the imports that created an equilibrium, however fragile and punctuated by 'grain crises' in 154, 124, 115, culminating, maybe, in 66 and 57 B.C. Commercial importation, it was, on the grand scale, always highly speculative, making huge profits in time of shortage but always liable to undercutting by state intervention. What we never hear of in our sources, though, is a total decline in Italian cereal production, nor of a collapse of internal prices nor even of a competition with external prices.

(b) The second main item is arboriculture, i.e. fruit orchards of every

46 Pliny *HN* XVIII.107–8, Plaut. *Asin.* 200.

sort but especially, of course, the olive and the vine. Both had ancient roots in Italy: both were imported, probably from Greece, at an early period. But – climatic constraints apart, which excluded the olive from the Cisalpina – their development, a tremendous feature of our period, is the result of new outlets for production and new structures of management. Significantly, of some six different estates discussed by Cato in his thoroughly practical treatise, the two best known and most important, of 100 and 240 *iugera* respectively, are a vineyard and an olive-plantation. They involve, allowing for the area necessarily taken up with feeding the labour-force, substantial initial capital outlay: deferred harvest, quincunx planting, labour intensiveness. Italy in Cato's and Varro's time produced oil of high reputation, but by the end of the Republic the huge production of Spain and Africa was beginning to supply Rome and the rest of Italy.

More disputed – and more interesting – are the vicissitudes of Italian wine production; and one is beginning to know them much better, thanks above all to the systematic study of amphora stamps, though the results only go to confirm what an unprejudiced reading of the texts ought to have shown anyhow.

Local vineyards, producing, more or less everywhere, wines of no particular quality and so no export potential; that was no doubt the situation in the fourth and third centuries. The cities, especially Rome, could offer a clientèle with plenty of well-off people, but they imported their wine from Greece.[47] From the beginning of the second century all that changes. The Italians begin to produce their own quality wines, and in quantity, so that their traces are found at great distance. First on the Adriatic coast from Picenum to the Po delta, then in Apulia. About the middle of the century progress accelerates: first, a memorable novelty, the appearance of the Italian *vins de cru* that we meet in the literature, all concentrated, in our period, in south Italy and Campania (Falernian); then, an increase in consumption at Rome and in other cities, due to changes in food-habits (bread) and the enrichment of the governing class and even, however relatively, the plebs, who were getting grain at subsidized prices. Rome thus became the commercial outlet for both mass-produced wines, from Latium and a bit further, and quality wines, Campanian and Apulian. Consumption has been estimated, for the end of the first century B.C., at more than a million hectolitres per annum, much more than in eighteenth-century Paris.[48] Yet more striking is the growth of an export trade that became massive – hundreds of thousands of hectolitres per annum – at first, maybe, to satisfy the demands of the

[47] Attested from the middle of the second century, Macrob. *Sat.* III.16.14, down to Horace and even later, and confirmed by Rhodian amphorae that turn up here and there.

[48] Tchernia 1969 (G 237).

armies and of Roman *émigrés* in Spain and Gaul; but presently we find attested a huge stream of export, both eastwards, centring on the market of Delos, and westwards into mid-Gaul (Aquitania and the Rhône valley).[49] The product originated in the vineyards of Campania and the coast of Etruria; the end-points, often the mining districts of Gaul, are proof that the consumers were not only the Roman armies, as has sometimes been held.[50] The emergence of Italy between the beginning of the second and the end of the first century B.C. as a major centre of consumption, production and *also* export of wine is a historical fact of the first order; and 'crisis', in fact, only came, relatively, in the first and second centuries A.D., with the rise of the vineyards of Spain and Gaul.

(c) The third item is animal husbandry. The Roman agronomists, perhaps unconscious inheritors of proto-historic conflicts between pastoralists and agriculturalists, are at times unforthcoming about it; the question of the 'decline' of agriculture in the face of pasturage touches a sensitive nerve in old dreads of famine.[51] That does not prevent them, however, from Cato to Pliny,[52] from declaring stock-raising the most profitable of farming enterprises. Questions about its development bring us to numerous well-known problems: the size of estates (problem of *latifundia*); the status of land (problem of *ager publicus*); the type of labour involved.

We must certainly begin by distinguishing two types of animal husbandry. The first is omnipresent in every mode of agricultural production, intensive but secondary. Cattle are reared for traction, for hides, for meat, not for milk or manure; sheep are reared for their wool, the staple of Roman clothing. We should note (however disputed) the importance of the goat, and also that of the big-scale rearing of equines – horses, mules, etc. – for transport, private and public but especially military. We should further note[53] that in most Roman colonial foundations, which doubtless acted as a kind of model of land use, the very small size of the plots allotted for cultivation can only be explained by the existence of common and public pastures, usually on the fringes, in the swampy or hilly areas.

Secondly, however, in various parts of Italy, from the beginning of the second century onwards, there emerges a different type of animal husbandry altogether, grand-scale transhumance, linking the winter

[49] According to Tchernia, more than 100,000 hectolitres per annum throughout a century, just for Gaul alone.

[50] A discovery, and an excavation, remarkable but certainly not unique, is that of the villa at Settefinestre, of the first half of the first century B.C., whose amphorae, doubtless belonging to the owners of the estate, Cicero's Sestii, illustrate the relationship between production and commercialization. Manacorda 1978 (B 309); Rathbone 1981 (G 207); Carandini 1985 (B 267).

[51] Varro *Rust.* II Praef., Columella, *Praef.* 4–5.

[52] Cic. *Off.* II.89; Pliny *HN* XVIII.29.

[53] With Tibiletti 1955 (G 242) and Gabba 1978 (G 90).

pastures of the coastal plains with summer grazing in the high pastures of the central Apennines.[54] From that time at least exist the *calles*, the reserved transhumance tracks, under the charge of the *publicani* who levied the *scriptura*. We are dealing here with hundreds of thousands of animals on the move, accompanied by armies of herdsmen; that led to repeated conflicts with the farmers beside whose lands the *calles* passed.[55]

It is certain that many of the extensive stock-raising enterprises began on lands that were *occupati* out of *ager publicus* by methods or in virtue of privileges that met with opposition, even if the squatters were also using *ager publicus* they had rented, e.g. in the mountains. So it is not surprising that the 'agrarian question' revolves partly round this extensive stock-raising.[56] However, it must not be forgotten that long-distance transhumance is attested in Italy from proto-historic times.[57] Be that as it may, and whatever the resistance encountered, large-scale animal husbandry proliferated at the end of the Republic.[58]

Along with the exploitation of pasture went, in a sense, that of forest. For example, it was by virtue of its forests as pasture for pigs that the Cisalpina was able to keep all Italy supplied with pork products down to the first century.[59] Ancient forests – and Italy was one of the major sources, along with the northern Balkans – supplied not only wood for heating, for shipbuilding and for building construction in general (and one notes what an important feature that was of Rome from the third to the first century B.C.), but also resources subsidiary to stock-raising and especially resin and pitch; and timber was also absolutely bound up with the development of viticulture.[60]

(d) Lastly, the most specialized item: the new speculative agriculture which only developed in the first century B.C. in relation to urban markets, especially Rome, i.e. 'villas' and even simple smallholdings given over either to very specialized animal raising – poultry, luxury table birds, nanny-goats for milking (the *pastio villatica* of Varro) – or to luxury market gardening – flowers, fruit and vegetables. It is, significantly, for these sorts of enterprise that Varro quotes the highest profit figures.

5. *The structures of agriculture and their evolution*

By 'structures' we are to understand the dimensions and nature both of the properties and of the units of management. We have to study the

54 Varro *Rust.* II.1.16. 55 Varro *Rust.* II.10.1–11, Cic. *Clu.* 161.

56 See the *elogium* from Polla, *CIL* I² 638 = *ILLRP* 454.

57 Radmilli 1974 (G 205) 20, and Gabba and Pasquinucci 1979 (G 95) 87f.

58 Domitius Ahenobarbus enrolled his herdsmen in his fleet, Caes. *BCiv.* I.57; and C. Caecilius Isidorus, under Augustus, owned 7,200 cattle and 257,000 sheep, Pliny *HN* XXXIII.134.

59 Polyb. II.15.2, Strab. V.1.12. 60 Meiggs 1982 (G 157); Giardina 1981 (G 103).

relationship of two main forms of management: direct management, with various sub-forms, on the one hand, and letting to tenants, whether at a rent or sharecropping, on the other. Other questions are posed by the status of the work-force – slaves (of various kinds) or free wage-earners (also of various statuses). Finally we shall touch on the obvious interaction, in our period, between civic and political questions, such as use of *ager publicus*, agrarian legislation, colonization of various sorts, and the impact of civil war, and the economic problems of agriculture.

The changes in the main sectors of production, sketched above, were accompanied – the tradition is unanimous, and even if archaeology may modify it somewhat it would be idle to deny it altogether – by profound changes in the structures of agriculture (though let us recall once more its great diversity). The first fact, on the global scale incontestable, is the increase in the number, area and value of 'large estates', already in the second century but especially in the first, after the Social War and Sulla. Although the word *latifundium* only turns up under the Empire, the thing, or something like it, is certainly attested in numerous sources.[61] But what is the level at which one ought to begin talking of 'large estates'? 400 *iugera*, as in a passage in the Gromatici?[62] Or the 500 *iugera* plus 250 per child plus 1,800 – according to Tibiletti's figures – for the number of animals to be pastured, making 625 hectares or 1,545 acres, given by the second-century agrarian legislation? Certainly those are already substantial figures: the estates described by Cato are of 100 and 240 *iugera* (though doubtless the owner would have had other pieces of property given over to other crops); and the individual plots attested when Roman or Latin colonies were founded or lands assigned were always notably smaller, even in the Cisalpina.[63] But we know, particularly from prosopography,[64] that most senatorial and even equestrian landed fortunes in our period must have been much larger still. Q. Roscius of Ameria, round about 80 B.C., had thirteen estates in the Tiber valley worth 6 million sesterces; and he is presented as a man with a modest fortune. Already at the end of the second century P. Crassus Mucianus possessed perhaps 100,000 *iugera*,[65] and the scale is still changing in the first century, with the fortunes of M. Crassus, Lucullus, Pompey[66] and numerous others. Nothing illuminates better these immense concentrations of landed property than Caecilius Isidorus, already cited, and L. Domitius Ahenobarbus, who in 49 was in a position to promise several *thousands* of his soldiers plots of land from 4 to 10

[61] White 1967 (G 257).
[62] 'Gromatici' p. 157 Lachm.; Evans 1980 (G 63) 24, but the sense dubious.
[63] 140 *iugera* at Aquileia in 181 B.C., for the *equites*, is an exception.
[64] Shatzman 1975 (A 112), Nicolet 1974 (A 80) 285–313, Rawson 1976 (G 209).
[65] His fortune exceeded 10 million denarii, Cic. *Rep.* III.17.
[66] 200 million sesterces just in land.

hectares and to man a fleet out of his 'tenants, freedmen and slave herdsmen'.[67] If one adds that the Roman upper class, senators and many *equites*, possessed also extensive lands in the provinces,[68] it can be seen that the emergence of huge landed patrimonies, and the accentuation of the trend in the first century B.C., ought not to be doubted.

To know whence that arose, or measure it in economic terms, is another matter. To read the agronomists, one would not think that the profit from land, even in the sectors and at the epochs of expansion, such as the fine wines in the second century, could have fostered a significant enlargement of estates, for a return of 6 or 7 per cent on capital would not have done it. Political history provides the answer: it was imperialism, whether military or peaceful, that caused the movement to take off. First, *ager publicus*, i.e. usually land confiscated from defeated enemies, which built up gradually in the fourth and third centuries, but with a big surge in south Italy after the Hannibalic War. That was where the customary squatting took place (*occupatus ager*), excessive or even blatantly illegal, which the various agrarian laws tried to hold down to 500 *iugera* (in practice much more); and that was the land that authors of agrarian bills like Rullus in 63 were accused of 'speculating' on. Next, the direct results of conquest, or civil war, for the Roman political class: the most fabulous fortunes in the first century were made by successful generals, by friends of the powerful like Chrysogonus in times of proscription, and so on. The Roman landed magnates were, in fact, the product of power. Finally, in some cases, large or even very large properties could be the proceeds, invested in land, of commercial and financial enterprise, sometimes of a kind to keep quiet about, like the slave trade. We know one or two cases,[69] but many must lurk unattested.[70]

Now concentration of ownership even into enormous units does not necessarily carry with it unity of management. It is actually certain that the very big Roman proprietors, like Pliny later on, even at the municipal or equestrian level, preferred, through prudence or predilection, multiple separate *fundi* to one enormous management unit: we know some cases, from Pompey to Atticus and Varro himself. So it is highly probable that the same patrimony would consist of a number of smaller units of very different types.[71]

But a central problem is still what happened to small and medium properties in Italy. It used to be the standard view that such properties

[67] See n. 58 above.

[68] Like Varro's friends the stock-raisers of Epirus, *Rust.* II Praef. 7 and Cic. *Att.* 1.5.7. Cf., however, Wiseman, pp. 328–9 and Rawson, pp. 446–7, above.

[69] Fulcinius in Cic. *Caec.* 11; Cic. *Off.* 1.151.

[70] See however the recent studies of Praeneste, e.g. Bodei Giglioni 1977 (G 17).

[71] By 'types' here we mean types of management, discussed immediately below.

declined considerably from the beginning of the second century, at least in many areas, to the advantage either of the great 'villa' with a slave labour-force or of the agro-pastoral *latifundium*. It is clear that one should not speak of total disappearance (though that is done, too often and too hastily), if only in the light of the official counter-measures that were taken, by colonization and agrarian assignation; clear, also, that within the same geographical area the big domain and the big slave-run villa could coexist with an earlier traditional agriculture of small peasants. However, we must not allow the pendulum to swing back too far and, in particular, make archaeology say what it cannot say. The fact that one can find traces of dispersed rural habitation in such-and-such an area at such-and-such an epoch (supposing them datable at all) gives us very little precise information about the real scale of operations, and *nothing whatever* about the type of management: these dwellings may have housed tenant-farmers, sharecroppers, even 'living-out' slaves. Equally, the reasoning, logical enough, that consists of estimating the size of the *non-servile* work-force implied for the functioning of the slave-run villa of Catonian-Varronian type is certainly valid in demographic terms, but it does not enable us to be precise about exactly what this subsidiary work-force consisted of; it might have been neighbouring small landowners hiring out their labour; neighbours hiring out their slaves; free non-owners or non-tenants hiring out their labour; groups of workers, free or slave, hired out by an entrepreneur supplying seasonal labour; tenants or sharecroppers of the owner of the villa; and so on. All this, indeed, counsels prudence; but in these pages we shall accept,[72] broadly, the testimony of the literature: small citizen – and no doubt Latin and allied – properties did decline sharply from the second century, for a variety of reasons. First the Hannibalic War, which killed and ruined farmers; then the pressures of recruitment for service overseas, making a hole every year in the free population of the countryside; again, the squeeze of the rich neighbour who could afford to buy at a high price or might profit by the absence of the family head to seize bits of land illegally; finally, simple abandonment and departure into the town in search of work or subsistence. For one thing is certain: whatever the subsidiary resources provided by the 'peasant economy' or the rights of common pasture in the territories of the *coloniae*, the fate of the small peasant in the second and first centuries was bound to be precarious, except in a few special cases, and the exodus to the towns, the armies, or overseas frequent enough for the state to have tried repeatedly in different ways to halt it; but the tiny size of the plots usually envisaged for distribution often only put off the evil day.[73]

72 With Gabba and *contra* Frederiksen, Garnsey, Rathbone, Evans.

73 App. *BCiv.* 1.7 and 30 and 40; Plut. *Ti. Gracch.* 8, Sall. *Iug.* 41.

One must not think only in terms of land*owners*. Tenancy at a rent and sharecropping[74] were widespread. Unfortunately we cannot draw up either a geographical or a chronological table; but Cato, and more often Varro and Columella, mention contracts of tenancy and discuss (from the landowner's point of view) the respective advantages of these systems: everything depended on the size and the location and the type of enterprise. There could even exist a class of 'gentlemen tenants',[75] but others were quite small fry: those who obeyed the summonses of Pompey and Domitius Ahenobarbus can only have been more or less clients. There were even *coloni* who were 'out-dwelling' slaves.[76]

And so we come, of course, to the most famous of all the changes in Italian agriculture: the slave-based enterprise, whether a mixed farm practising polyculture or a specialized villa with vines and a semi-industrial organization, or a huge stock-raising ranch. It would not be right to look simply at the *ager Cosanus*[77] and declare that that evidence shows that this type of villa only appears in the first century B.C.; that would make nonsense of the whole of Cato and the second- and first-century agronomists like the Sasernas. Villas, and extensive stock-raising with armies of herdsmen, must have begun to develop from the second century,[78] and one must therefore relate them to the enormous round-up of humanity that that century saw, with the Delos slave-market at its apogee, and to the slave revolts in Sicily and Italy from 136 to 73 B.C. So it is quite certain that, at one particular time and in certain particular areas and at a particular level there did come into being a new and characteristic 'mode of production'.[79] That said, to ask whether the slave 'mode of production' was cause or effect of the conquests is to pose a false question: many factors, demographic and economic, played their part, the existence of Rome as a market, for example. Where it existed, though, it certainly in its turn created new factors, very disturbing ones. It introduced a large non-Italian element into the population of Italy; it broke the vital traditional links between ownership of the soil and the life, rights and duties of the *civis Romanus*; it interposed between the owner and his work-force, for all the paternalism of a Varro or a Columella,[80] a whole hierarchy of supervisory grades, both costly to employ and leading at times to ruinous rebellions. Fragile, therefore, in the long run, in spite of apparent advantages, the slave 'mode of production' is certainly a fact of importance for our purposes; but its

[74] The generic name is *locatio conductio*, and the word *colonus*, at least in the first century B.C., means either. [75] Like the *colonus* in Cic. *Clu.* 175.

[76] Alfenus Varus, D.15.3.16; 40.7.14; Labeo, D.33.7.12.3.

[77] The *villa maritima* of the Sestii, devoted to vines.

[78] Gabba 1977 (G 89); 1982 (G 92); 1979 (G 95).

[79] Which is not to deny, of course, that slavery in general is a wider phenomenon and lasted much longer. [80] Colum. *Rust.* 1.8.20.

importance was by no means purely economic, as Columella's misleading calculations might lead one to imagine,[81] for every aspect of agriculture was always bound up with civics and politics and mythologies, which is why the political and ideological battles that raged around it in the Roman experience were so bitterly waged.

6. *The 'agrarian question'*

Of those famous battles there is no place for a detailed account here.[82] It remains to draw attention to a fact or two often misunderstood or neglected.

(a) Land-distributions, whether colonial or viritane, involved only *ager publicus*, which formally remained such (even if the rights of the *populus* over it seem to have been tacitly abandoned in 133 for certain pieces of land). Not until the civil wars of 83–80 and 44–36 B.C. do we get the distribution of what had been private land; and even of that the origins often lay in *occupatio*. The principle of private property remained inviolate, and agrarian legislation actually reinforced it.

(b) The whole colonizing movement, culminating in the early second century, consisted in planting nuclei of small-to-medium private ownership in agrarian zones: it was a rural movement,[83] even if in the long run it created a new urban geography for Italy.

(c) Not enough study has been given to exactly how colonization worked. In the case of the military colonies, i.e. colonies of veterans, we know roughly who were the beneficiaries, but the criteria for recruitment for the viritane assignments, both before and after the Gracchi, are infinitely less well known,[84] and equally so the real procedures for installing people on their plots of land, the costs, and so on.

(d) Even when there was *divisio et assignatio* the presiding magistrates had an absolute right to plots of land 'kept aside', for themselves and their associates.[85] A probable source of some big landed concentrations.

(e) Not enough study has been given, either, to the legal rules and practical procedures of how people were granted contracts 'let' by the censors for handling the public revenues, nor to how people got access to *occupatio*, the right to squat on and farm *ager publicus*,[86] which pre-Gracchan legislation and the Lex Sempronia purported to set limits to. Where were such contracts entered into? How? On what terms? A proper study of those questions ought to shed some extra light on the

[81] *Ibid.* I.7–8. [82] They are dealt with in several chapters in Part I.

[83] Tibiletti 1955 (G 242) Tozzi 1974 (G 246).

[84] For an exception, Suet. *Iul.* 20.3, in 59 B.C.

[85] 'Gromatici' pp. 133 and 157 Lachm.

[86] A kind of 'emphyteusis'? (Buckland, *Text Book of Roman Law*[3] (London, 1963) 275: 'land ... granted in perpetuity for a long term at a rent fixed in kind'.)

concentration of big squatters' holdings and on the nature of the conflicts aroused by the Gracchan laws.

(f) If there had not been an accumulation of 'big estates' – above 120 hectares at least, and in fact much bigger – there would *not have been* a socio-political problem in 133 B.C.; equally so, if there had still been *ager publicus* not yet taken up and available for distribution.[87] The stock of at least Italian land was evidently exhausted by 133.

(g) The texts, by referring to the activities of the agrarian commission in 129 and again in 123–119, and the archaeological data of centuriations and *cippi*, prove that the Lex Sempronia must have been functioning at least down to 111. To try to put a figure on its results, in people and in acreage, is another question. The Brunt–Nicolet estimate,[88] that if you count the number of beneficiaries at 75,000 you get an area redistributed of 562,500 hectares or well over $1\frac{1}{4}$ million acres, is not implausible: it is equivalent to a square of side 75 kilometres.

(h) Then there is the question, not much studied as such, of the real scope of the imposts that agricultural exploitation of *ager publicus* was subject to. (They might take the form of tax or rent or licence fees.) The one *as* per *iugerum* on *ager trientabularius* ceded to creditors of the Republic in 202 was nominal, purely a licence fee. But in other cases *ager publicus* ceded to its existing holders or to new holders brought revenue to the Roman state. How much? And even before that, there was some charge for *occupatio*, apparently standard.[89] Now such imposts, on various categories of land, reduced, *pro tanto*, the income from that land of the owner or possessor. Were they seen as fiscal in character – hence their disappearance after 167 – or as a contribution to *annona* – hence their reappearance from 123?[90] In any case, it does not seem as if this aspect of things, though important politically, had any strictly economic impact: no source ever, for Italy, speaks of economic consequences of taxation (on this or that type of enterprise, for example).

(i) Lastly, what do we know in general about the market in land in our period? We can be sure that it was dependent on some strictly economic considerations, quality of the soil, climate, closeness or otherwise to routes of transport, and so on. But, as almost always, it was also dependent on a whole range of other factors, especially the shifts of politics. First of all, the social value of land in a society based on *census*, where status actually in part depends on the possession of real estate: one notices that land was forever being demanded as security in a whole range of contracts, public and private. Secondly, the fact that a

[87] As at the beginning of the second century, with colonies being depopulated.
[88] Brunt 1971 (A 16) 75–80; Nicolet 1978 (A 83) 132–3.
[89] A tenth or a fifth of the fruits? App. *BCiv.* 1.27 and 75–6.
[90] The question needs looking at again. See Nicolet 1976 (G 174) 79–86.

considerable fraction of the land was *ager publicus*, and so had an ambiguous status, whether advantageous or otherwise: that fact was bound to affect the mobility as well as the value of landed property. Even more plainly, great quantities of confiscated property came on to the market, for reasons not at all economic but political, at times of proscription or civil war (83–80, 48–47, 44–43 B.C.), with consequences, noted in our sources, for prices. Some of the consequences were natural, some the results of skulduggery of various kinds: the usual initial effect was a slump.

The influx of coin, on the other hand, from conquest, from enlarged emissions, and so on, had the opposite effect of pushing prices up. And there were more subtle factors to upset the laws of the market: a threat of civil war, as in 63 B.C., or an agrarian bill, might raise or lower the value of some particular bit of land. A detailed history of these fluctuations within a given area is not altogether out of reach. It makes difficult the assertion of any general tendency; but one will not be likely to be wrong to assert that real estate went on being, for Roman society in our period, an investment for both long-term security and social prestige.

III. INDUSTRY AND MANUFACTURE

We have seen the extent and richness of Italy's arable land, its vineyards and olive-groves and its pastures. Many of the products of this land (to which should be added stone) were important also for industrial production:[91] wool, for example, for clothing, or wood for buildings, ships, heating and lighting,[92] stone for building and sculpture, clay, again for building, and for pottery. Italy is well supplied all over with such items, and we should begin by recalling that in antiquity a good – perhaps a major – part of industrial production was widely diffused, turning up more or less everywhere and based on primary materials, including minerals, that were present everywhere, if only in minute quantities. One cannot write the history of production at that purely local level. However, antiquity did go through successive industrial revolutions. They occurred, first, when the demand for some product in some centre of consumption outran the local supplies and necessitated the importation of ever greater quantities from ever further away: in that situation, according to the soil, the ease of transport, the availability of labour, there would arise privileged 'zones of production', a geography of primary products with their markets and the centres where they were converted into secondary products. Secondly, industrial revolutions occurred in respect of the scarce resources that did not occur at all (or

[91] In the sense proper to antiquity, of course.

[92] And we have already noted (p. 616) the importance of resin and pitch.

only negligibly) in a given region. First and foremost, mines and metals: from proto-historic times on, the history of long-distance contacts in the Mediterranean has been mainly determined by the search for metals (gold, silver, copper, tin and, to a lesser degree, iron), the whereabouts of which is conditioned by the facts of geology, though mines, too, have a history of change: discovered, exploited, exhausted, sometimes resumed. From the production of iron tools, indispensable for every sort of work (including warfare), to the working of bronze for ordinary or luxury use, metallurgy was an intensively practised activity, both widespread and concentrated, a fact which must be constantly borne in mind. And when monetized economies appeared and spread, with their three metals, gold, silver and bronze, access to those metals became a first-order problem for governments: it may well be that metal production and metallurgy determined, especially in our period, the most striking changes.

Now from this point of view, Italy as a whole is in an anomalous situation, having virtually no gold or silver.[93] Italy was considered rich in copper and iron in the Greek archaic and classical periods, in Magna Graecia and Etruria; but except for the iron mines of Elba,[94] which maintained a significant activity even at the end of the first century B.C., most of those mines were exhausted or closed during our period. The same is true of those that began to be exploited less early, in the Cisalpina and the Alps in the second century; they were initially the object of a sort of 'rush' of private enterprise,[95] and were subsequently exploited by *publicani*;[96] but they were soon either closed by authority[97] or abandoned because they were less productive than those of Gaul and Spain.[98] The major centres of production were, anyway, elsewhere: in the East and the Balkans,[99] but above all, of course, Spain, whose mining areas were exploited in turn by Carthage and Rome from the beginning of the second century to the end of the first century B.C. And at the extreme end of our period Gaul and Britain begin to come into the pattern.

The disappearance of extractive industry did not stop the continuation of secondary metal industry, based on the importation of the metal in ingots: it went on all over Italy, being well attested around Arretium in the Second Punic War[100] and also in the famous passage where Cato gives the places of production – and even in some cases the names of the craftsmen – of the agricultural implements he says are needful: Rome, Cales, Venafrum, Pompeii, Capua, Nola, Suessa, Casinum.[101] The

[93] Except in the Alpine region.

[94] Diod. v.13; Strab. v.2.6.

[95] Strab. IV.6.12, from Polybius.

[96] Strab. IV.6.7; Pliny *HN* XXXIII.78.

[97] Pliny *HN* III.138.

[98] Strab. V.1.12.

[99] Laurium was still active in 136–133, and the iron and silver mines of Macedonia still essential in 167 and 158.

[100] Livy XXVIII.45.13.

[101] Cato *Agr.* 135.

importance of a metal industry is corroborated by the mention of armament production in Italy in 100 and 90 B.C.[102]

Let us, as in the case of agriculture, briefly note the extremely traditional, empirical and small-scale character of the industrial techniques, resting essentially on human and animal power, but at the same time (as in the case of agriculture) not underestimate the efficacity, often noted by ancients as well as moderns, and indeed the spectacular success, of some of the achievements: advanced mining techniques, especially in Spain; mastery of bronze founding or of goldsmith's craft; employment of some machinery, wooden or metal, like pumps for draining mines and washing ore;[103] other advanced hydraulics;[104] technical progress in amphora construction, especially with regard to the ratio of weight to content. There has been too much emphasis on the 'technical bottlenecks' of antiquity, in the field of transport, for example; study of the literature of technology and material culture permits some correction of these over-hasty views. However, it is mainly in the organization of labour and diversification of use of the labour-force that those changes in the nature and scale of production occurred which interest us: the case of building techniques perhaps gives the key.[105]

Let us rapidly review a few major sectors.

(a) Of the wood, textile and leather industries we have none but indirect and fleeting testimony: a 'portico of the wood-merchants' at the port of Rome in 192 B.C.;[106] Strabo saying that the wool of the plain of the Po and of Liguria 'clothes all Italy';[107] Sicily equipping the Roman army in 90 B.C.;[108] Rome itself an important textile centre in *c.* 150 and in *c.* 53 B.C.[109]

(b) We are a great deal better informed about the mines of Italy and Spain, with famous descriptions from Polybius, Diodorus, Strabo and Pliny. The big exploitation was in Spain, beginning with the area round New Carthage (argentiferous lead) from the beginning of the second century.[110] Polybius is already talking of 40,000 workers[111] in that region in Carthaginian times; and he says that the revenue 'to the Romans' (i.e. from *c.* 200 to 150 B.C.) was 25,000 drachmae a day.[112] Archaeological study of the mines and of the ingots found *in situ* or in wrecks[113] shows that exploitation of the mines of the centre and south-west only really began at the end of the second century B.C. and culminated about the end

102 Cic. *Rab. Post.* 20; *Pis.* 87.
103 Healy 1978 (G 115) fig. 28.
104 E.g. Roman aqueducts in Frontin. *Aq.*, *passim*.
105 Torelli 1980 (G 244); Coarelli 1977 (G 42).
106 Livy XXXV.41.10.
107 Strab. V.1.12.
108 Cic. II *Verr.* 2.5.
109 Cato, *Agr.* 135, Cic. *Rab. Post.* 40.
110 The gold mines of Lusitania and the north west were not reached till the time of Augustus.
111 *ap.* Strab. III.2.10. Perhaps not all mine-workers, though.
112 The drachma may be equated with the denarius.
113 Of 250 ingots found, 200 are Republican in date.

of the first. An important fact about it is that the exploitation was the work of immigrants from Italy[114] and Rome, whatever the fiscal or concessionary regime that governed it.[115] Italy, therefore, for metal for coinage and industry, was largly an importer; yet, whether directly or otherwise, Italy owned the mines by right of conquest, so they were a source of wealth, not an item of expense.

(c) A third sector of great importance is building construction and public works. It is linked to the growth of the cities, especially Rome, from the early second century, and the general urbanization of Italy at the end of the second century and during the first.[116] That necessarily gave rise to a huge demand for housing; and, if most houses were of poor construction, the continual collapses and fires gave opportunity for even more building activity, sometimes in the hands of speculators like M. Crassus, who employed great numbers of workmen, slave and free.[117] And the growth of cities and of mass demand was accompanied by increased demand for luxury residences, the *aedes* and rural *villae* of the aristocracy, influenced by Hellenistic fashion.[118] The 'building mania' of senators and *equites*, even of *nouveaux riches* like Sulla's soldiers and centurions, who, having received rural allotments, wanted to live in town and 'build', is well attested in the sources.[119] It is evident that all that activity involved transport to Rome on a vast scale, and the growth of specialized enterprises and of large gangs of workmen, slave or free. And to private construction we must add public building, which flourished all through the second and first centuries. There was perhaps a 'bulge' in 194–174, with the fitting out of the port of Rome and the big warehouses, another in 144–136 with the *Aqua Marcia*, and a series of encroachments on the Campus Martius, first in 110–106 and then in the 60s with the great benefactions of the political bosses, Scaurus, Pompey, Julius Caesar and others. The few figures for expenditure given in the sources,[120] including the cost of the *Aqua Marcia* at 45 million denarii, confirmed by calculations of the size of coin emissions,[121] suffice to show the importance of the sums involved, which went on to irrigate vast sectors of economic life. We guess – rather than really know – how this world of enterprise worked: companies taking up, from the state, contracts to do the work, more or less like the *publicani*; architects; middlemen with capital to lend and forming associations to do it (or to borrow); agents for hire of labour, free or slave; and finally, we may be sure, a mass of small craftsman *institores*, free or slave, making their living

[114] Diod. v.36.3. [115] See further below, p. 635.

[116] Vitr. II.8.17; Cic. *Leg. Agr.* II.96; Frontin. *Aq.* I.7.

[117] Plut. *Crass.* 2.5. [118] Coarelli 1976 (G 41).

[119] Cic. *Cat.* II.20; cases have been listed, at least for senators: Shatzman 1975 (A 112).

[120] Livy XL.46.16 and 51.2–7; XLIV.16.9–11.

[121] Although military expenses were the main factor in that.

from the whole whirligig of enterprise. The origins of the funds that went into these works are interesting to study in detail; often public monies of the Roman treasury, when it was gorged with the acquisitions of conquest; sometimes costs passed on to property-owners who benefited, as for the maintenance of the streets of Rome (from at least 75 B.C.) and of certain public roads; but often also private funds furnished by magistrates wishing to gain popularity by good works, or generals spending their *manubiae*, or just private individuals who had had a stroke of luck, like the oil-merchant who dedicated the temple of Hercules Victor in the Forum Boarium.[122]

(d) The ceramic industry (in the broad sense: tiles, bricks, amphorae, as well as cups and plates) is only just beginning, thanks to archaeology, to receive the attention it deserves. Amongst the numerous Italian centres of production Rome itself begins to emerge in a preponderant role. The staggering accumulation of sherds of the Monte Testaccio,[123] corroborated by the thousands of tons of sherds dredged from the Saône,[124] confirms the quantitative importance of the production of wine and oil amphorae for long-distance transport.[125] We now know that it was Italian amphorae – first from the Adriatic coast and Apulia, later from Campania and the coast of Etruria – that accompanied the Italian wines that went to Spain, Gaul, and even the East, Delos for example. Whether they were actually produced by the owners of the vineyards, by nearby producers, or by urban manufacturers does not matter: the overall profit must have been considerable. Even more so for luxury wares ('Campanian', Roman, Arretine finally in the age of Augustus), produced in large quantities for an export market determined, perhaps, more by the tastes of *émigré* Italians, civil and military, than of the locals. Here, too, recent research may now enable us to discern the organization of the trade and its labour-force.[126]

IV. COMMERCE AND MONEY

Italian argriculture and industry, then, underwent, in the second and first centuries B.C., *pari passu* with Rome's conquests, considerable change and expansion. Those changes and that expansion cannot be understood except in relation to the methods and channels of exchange that made them possible. Rome had certainly been a centre of production and exchange much earlier than used to be generally allowed – from the end of the fourth century; nevertheless 'commerce' and 'finance',

122 On the building programme as a kind of 'manna' for the people, see Plut. *C. Gracch.* 6–7.

123 Dating from the Principate, it is true.

124 Tchernia 1969 (G 237).

125 And *dolia* for storage of cereals.

126 Pucci 1973 (G 198); Delplace 1978 (G 55).

whatever their specific modalities and characteristics, were, from the middle of the second century, along with conquest itself, the very hallmark by which outsiders recognized Romans and Italians. Merchants and businessmen from abroad coming to Rome to look after their public and private interests; Roman bankers, businessmen, *publicani*, turning up in Spain, Narbonensis, Illyria, at Delos or in Asia (soon even in Egypt): these are the sign of the change in the scale and radius of commerce as well as, doubtless, its volume. And these quantitative changes, linked to world conquest, were accompanied by deep qualitative ones as well. For the first time the processes of exchange were beginning to unify all across the then world, and to even out under the effect of a common currency, a common tax system and a common legal order: that process was only just beginning, of course, in our period, and was destined to take centuries to develop and undergo many a vicissitude; all the more interesting is it to discern some of the vital factors in the process at their very inception.

1. The technical underpinning

All commercial development presupposes an adequate technical basis, material (transport, roads, wagon teams, ports, ships, etc.) and non-material (money, accounting, commercial law, etc.). In all these spheres Italy – and Rome – is to be placed firmly in the context of Greek and Hellenistic practice; for it was the Greeks who had brought such techniques to a high pitch of efficiency in the eastern Mediterranean by the middle of the second century B.C. So let us assert, once for all: the ships, harbours, coinage, financial and juridical structures of the Romans were not fundamentally different from those of the Greeks, but just a variant. When insistence is presently laid on differences they will be differences of detail, though it is just those detailed differences that are significant. We may therefore be very brief in recalling some general points.

The Roman road system was regarded under the Empire as the very hallmark of the *pax Romana*.[127] It was already there in essence in the second century B.C., in Italy down to the south and Brundisium and up to the plain of the Po, and in the provinces the *via Domitia* in Gaul and the *via Egnatia* from Dyrrachium to the Hebrus. That the roads contributed to bring regions out of isolation and accelerate contacts may well be true; but they remained essentially strategic and official.[128] Land transport used pack animals more than wagons, because the defective technique of harnessing was one of the biggest obstacles to development in the

[127] Pliny *HN* XXVII.3. [128] Cic. *Prov. Cons.* 31.

ancient economy: land transport remained, in fact, slow and costly, and so was reserved mainly for military operations, and the commerce of the age rested almost entirely on maritime transport – which accorded in any case with the nature of Mediterranean geography. There was little technical progress in this regard during our period. The Romans never went through the megalomaniac stage in shipbuilding like the Hellenistic monarchs. However, as we are beginning to learn, commercial vessels were actually bigger on average and better built and more manoeuvrable than used to be thought, as can be seen from the extension of the routes: along the Tyrrhenian coast, the coasts of Gaul and Spain, between Brundisium and Dyrrachium, Delos and Asia, Rhodes and Egypt, there was now a sailing programme that transcended mere land-hugging. (True, they were still obeying the rule of the winter close season, and the big convoys – the 'Alexandrian fleet'[129] – are a later development.) Evidence accumulates in the wrecks located by underwater archaeology:[130] their number rises notably in the second and first centuries B.C.[131] A hundred or two hundred trips a year will have been needed to carry the 50,000–100,000 hectolitres of Italian wine that went to Gaul between 150 and 50 B.C.[132] Equally, the carriage of the corn – whether tax-corn or free-market corn – imported in growing quantities to Rome and Puteoli from 123 B.C. at least, first from Sicily, Sardinia and Spain,[133] subsequently from Africa, Asia, and finally Egypt, involved sizeable merchant fleets, regulated by government for the first time in 57 under Pompey's *cura annonae* and then supported and ultimately organized more and more closely.

We shall return below to the economic organization, properly speaking, of this maritime traffic: for the moment let us just note that the political policy of states, especially Rome, helped to furnish for it two major and indispensable technical supports: new harbours, and freedom of navigation.

As to the first, the salient fact is the big development of the port of Rome, on the Tiber, at the foot of the Capitol, Palatine and Aventine, from early in the second century B.C. but especially between 193 and 174; by the end it extended more than 2 kilometres, and on both banks. The size of the warehouses like the *Porticus Aemilia* (487 × 60 metres) is significant – equally so the first Roman *horrea*, the *Horrea Galbana* or *Sulpicia*, *Horrea Sempronia* for example. The port of Rome is of course linked to that of Ostia: the latter, in the second and first centuries B.C., was still a river port: ships up to 3,000 amphorae could get in there,[134] and even perhaps up to Rome. But probably the silting that made the

[129] Suet. *Aug.* 98.2.

[130] Developed mainly in the western Mediterranean.

[131] Parker 1984 (G 187).

[132] Tchernia 1969 (G 237) 70.

[133] Cic. *Leg. Man.* 30.

[134] Dion. Hal. *Ant. Rom.* III.44.

crossing of the bar hazardous had begun to menace Ostia already by the end of the century.[135] In the rest of Italy there were two profound changes in our period: the decline of Tarentum and Naples to the advantage of Brundisium and, especially, Puteoli. The former was the road terminus and sea crossing-point for Dyrrachium and the *Via Egnatia*, 'invented' by Rome,[136] the latter had a *colonia* settled in 194 and customs installed in 199. Polybius, Lucilius and Diodorus are witness[137] to Puteoli being the 'premier port of Italy', a 'baby Delos'; and its connexions with Tyre and Alexandria are already attested for the second century – also with Spain and Sicily.[138] Puteoli profited from the decline of Delos after 88 B.C., especially for the slave trade and the grain trade: this latter seems to have been the most characteristic interest of the Puteolans in Cicero's time.[139]

The problem of 'freedom of the seas' met with a less clear-cut response. For piracy was not only endemic in our period, at least in certain areas like Illyria, Crete and Cilicia – a hindrance to normal commerce and combated, as far as international conflicts allowed, by the interested powers, notably Rhodes.[140] It happened also to be at times the principal supplier of a commodity much in demand – slaves, and was consequently sometimes tolerated, within limits, certainly so at times of conflict or of rising demand. Only in about 100 B.C., and then more firmly in 74–66, did Rome decide to intervene against the Cretan pirates and then the Cilicians, the latter in the huge, successful campaign entrusted to Pompey; they did so only when insecurity had become intolerable and had reached the very coast of Latium. Even after that, the war against Sextus Pompeius, 41–36 B.C., could be represented by Octavian as a 'pirate war'. Full freedom of the seas was only assured from Augustus onwards: slaves then came from elsewhere, Gaul and the Danube regions.

2. *Money*

But of all the technical underpinnings of commerce, from the sixth century B.C. at least, the most important was, of course, money.[141]

135 Strab. III.5.231–2. 136 Zonar. VIII.7.3.

137 Polyb. III.91.4; Lucilius III.123; Diod. V.13.2.

138 Spain: Strab. III.2.6, 144C; Sicily: Cic. II *Verr.* 5.154.

139 The *Avianii*, Cic. *Acad.* II.80.

140 Which 'gave its laws to the sea', as they still said in the time of the Antonines, D.14.2.9, Volusius Maecianus.

141 The ancient world, certainly from Aristotle on, knew quite well the immense role the invention of money played in the passage from barter to sale, by giving a measure of value. Although money was metal, and so had a market value of its own, its coining by states turned it into a guaranteed conventional measure to express the exchange value of things other than itself. Arist. *Pol.* 1257a.34; Paul in D.18.1.1 (with Nicolet 1984 (G 177) 105ff).

Rome's monetary system was a late arrival; it was definitively reorganized in 212/11 B.C. with the introduction of the silver denarius reckoned at 10 bronze *asses*, and it remained fundmentally bimetallic (apart from a few brief strikings of gold, in 212/11 and under Sulla) down to Julius Caesar. Its detailed history – the successive weight reductions of the *as*, the weight and fineness of the denarius, the occasional emission of silver sesterces (always in times of war), is very varied and complex and cannot be gone into here.[142] We can do no more than bring out a few strictly economic features, while admitting that this is a field more for hypotheses than for certitudes.

Like most of the peoples of Italy, the Romans began with a bronze coinage: it is in units of bronze that the census classes were expressed and the earliest taxes perhaps paid. The Romans only adopted, and then themselves coined, silver money about the time of Pyrrhus, to pay military expenses in the south of Italy (i.e. in the Greek world). Only *c.* 212/11 was the silver piece, the denarius, more or less equivalent to a drachma, put into relationship with the bronze system; after which, while the denarius remained remarkably stable in weight and fineness (except in some temporary crises such as, perhaps, in 91–85) the bronze coins went down and down and ended as small change for everyday use: the unit of measure, the *as*, which still weighed a pound as late as 218 B.C., finished by weighing only half a ounce, *c.* 91 B.C. The more important transactions, official payments and balances, were all done in silver, denarii mainly but *victoriati* (half-denarii at the end of the Republic) and *sestertii* (quarter-denarii) in certain regions like the Cisalpina or special situations such as wars. Even then, it should be noted that to pay in cash the price of an upper-class house, say 4 million sesterces (normal in the first century B.C.) would have involved moving four tonnes of silver. Hence the role of gold in bars, in the reserves of the *aerarium* or of private individuals, as a means of coping with really large payments.[143]

Our period is marked by two very large-scale phenomena. The first is the spread of the Roman denarius all over the Mediterranean world, above all in Greece and Asia, but even outside the frontiers, in Dacia, for example.[144] The spread was slow at first, but picked up speed at the beginning of the first century. The Roman unit of accounting, the *sestertius*, also tended to be used everywhere. Doubtless, independent local issues survived all over the place, even in Italy, where it was a privilege of some cities; but many such issues were aligned to the Roman metrological values, while others, minted by Roman governors, like the *cistophori* of Asia and the coins of Macedon, were also obviously linked to

[142] See Crawford 1974 (B 144).

[143] Cic. *Clu.* 179; *Rab. Post.* 47; *Phil.* III.10; *Att.* XII.6.1.

[144] Linked to the slave-trade, about 67–50 B.C.?

the fiscal and monetary system of Rome. Also it is very possible that as the Romans came to dominate great areas they at first used the local coinages for their own purposes – those of the Spanish cities, Massilia, Athens, Rhodes, and so on.[145] There remained, still, some areas outside the system, Syria and Egypt, and, even within the empire, some provinces, Sicily, Greece and Asia: money-changing went on being essential for long-distance commerce. But the monetary unification of the Mediterranean was coming into being, and part, at least, of the circulation of coin, that which concerned fiscal relations and the official expenditure of the state, was more and more standardized.

The second major phenomenon, stark and incontestable, is the growth in the sheer quantity of Roman coins in circulation. The methods we employ to estimate that are, it must be allowed, uncertain: we study the number of dies per issue; but how many coins does that represent? Or we try to work from estimates of total annual state expenditure. Nevertheless, the general tendency is certain: the Roman coinage of some years was greater by itself than, for example, the whole of the 'second style' Athenian coinage from *c.* 170 to 70 B.C.,[146] and although there was a cessation of striking from 167 to 157, due doubtless to the influx of booty to the *aerarium*, from *c.* 140–130 down to *c.* 90 B.C. the amounts struck annually increased more than five times[147] and settled down, for thirty years, at a very high level. This continued injection of new coined money cannot have failed to have economic consequences; but there remain a lot of things not yet understood. The striking of coins was evidently linked to the purposes of the *aerarium*, and evidently served to meet with new coinage the expenses of the state, which were primarily military (though not exclusively so: from 123 and then from 58 we must take into account the supplying of grain, first subsidized and then gratis, and we must not forget public works). But did the state always pay out in new coin? And what exactly came *into* the *aerarium*? The replies to those questions are by no means evident, either for the product of the regular taxation (what coinage was it paid in?), or for booty, or for the product of the mines of Macedon or Spain (did they send metal to Rome in ingots, or was a monetary equivalent paid in?). We do know for certain that individuals could be in account with the *aerarium*, but only on the basis of taxes or public works, for the state never borrowed nor lent. Could individuals be in account with the mint? There was certainly no private striking of coinage: but could you deposit money with the mint?[148] Could you offer it ingots? That is very doubtful, though you could certainly get it to change bronze for silver at the official rate. What

[145] Such is the hypothesis of Crawford.

[146] Crawford 1985 (B 145).

[147] Hopkins 1980 (G 124) 109.

[148] Cic. *Att.* VIII.7.3 and XV.15.1; not very explicit.

can, anyhow, be taken as certain is that, even if the issues of coin decided on by government were mainly intended to meet state expenses, and the decisions were made in concert with the *aerarium*, the money very quickly got into general circulation and irrigated and animated the entire economy.

It has been doubted, quite rightly, whether the Roman government ever had an exact concept of the 'monetary needs of the economy', and whether coinage was ever *intended* for anything but the meeting of the state's expenditure. Nevertheless, decisions – or non-decisions – about weights and fineness, or the offical tariff of silver and bronze, could have enormous effects on commerce and on economic and social life in general. All those problems might converge at times of monetary crisis, which sometimes coincided with political crises, as in 92–86 B.C.: we get the creation of the semiuncial *as*, the Lex Livia of 91 concerning the alloying of metals,[149] the edict of Marius Gratidianus, which probably settled the fluctuating silver–bronze tariff;[150] all those things posed a threat, at least in Rome, to the stability of very big financial deals. It is also certain that the problem of debt, about which there will be more to say, had specifically monetary aspects: the fact that rich landed proprietors might be in debt shows that there was a shortage of liquid funds to go round. Since, however, there was a general increase in the amount of coinage struck, yet, as far as one can tell, no spectacular inflation at the end of the second century and during the first, it seems to follow that production and exchange must have grown more or less *pari passu* during the period, though we do not know the history of prices well enough to be altogether sure.

At any rate, the manipulation of money certainly became an important phenomenon in economy and society during our period – linked, of course, to the development of financial interests in general. It is towards the end of the second century that the *tesserae nummulariae* appear: seals, dated and named, recording the verification by professionals (slaves) of the contents of sacks of coin belonging to individuals or companies. They are evidence that such people or groups owned, or had charge of, big sums of money; and the names can be related to those of Italian businessmen at Delos and in the East and to monetary officials and *publicani* and big landed proprietors.[151] At the same time we begin to encounter evidence of the different kinds of professionals involved with money:[152] money-changers, *nummularii*, at Praeneste and of course at Rome, bankers proper, the *argentarii*, who took deposits and lent money,

149 If that is what it was, Pliny *HN* XXXIII.132.

150 Crawford 1968 (C 45); Seager in ch. 6 above, pp. 180–1.

151 Herzog 1919 (G 119) and 1937 (G 120); Andreau 1987 (G 6).

152 Elaborately distinguished by Andreau 1987 (G 6).

auctioneers (sales at auction being common), who were prosperous enough to be a source of short-term credit for small-scale businesses. But the most characteristic feature of the whole society is the existence of a big turn-round of money amongst the upper classes, Senate and *equites* at Rome and the curial class in the *municipia*. More or less everybody was borrowing, lending, pledging, buying and selling real estate; and the size of the sums involved rose in line with the growth of private fortunes. There is need of a detailed analysis of the purposes of these transactions: in the case of the upper classes, no doubt most of them were to help maintain a standard of living fraught with innumerable social obligations and demanding an ostentatious lifestyle – slaves, houses, political funds, benefactions. But we shall see, before we have finished, that some strictly economic goals could also be the object of these financial dealings.

Was there such a thing as 'Roman banking' in our period, and, if so, what role did it play? It was limited, to begin with, by technical inadequacies and by the strait-jacket of legal rules. Transfers of credit existed: you could pay a third party through your banker or through a personal friend with whom you held a deposit or who would give you credit. The transfer of specie about the Mediterranean could be avoided by making a *permutatio*, a written draft, but that fell short of being a bill of exchange.[153] The transfer of book-debts, *novatio* and *delegatio*, was costly, because of its slowness, and complicated.[154] Consequently, there was nothing like a real 'money market' (although, of course, if a number of big lenders failed, as they did in 85 and 66 and might have done in 63, the peril could spread and endanger 'the whole Forum').[155] We hear, indeed, of 'bankers': at Delos, Syracuse, Rhegium, Volaterrae, Puteoli, Rome. But their economic role is unclear. The lenders of money amongst the governing class, like Considius or Atticus[156] no doubt had as customers not only noble senators but tradesmen and artisans too: but in what proportion? What characterizes Rome is individual rather than corporate financial activity: the legal rules, indeed, imposed it. There were no big banking *societates*, as far as we know, and there was no state bank.[157] But that was offset by the existence of the upper-class financiers: in spite of the disapproval visited by law and society upon gain, *quaestus*, and still more upon lending at interest, it looks as if[158] the Roman governing class, for all that their property was in land and their supposed role military and civic, was also a financial class – bankers and money-lenders

[153] And there were no settlement days or banker's commissions.
[154] Cic. *Att.* XII.3; 12; 46.
[155] Cic. *Leg. Man.* 17–20.
[156] Whose probity was highly regarded: that of his uncle Q. Caecilius less so.
[157] Such as some Greek states did have.
[158] It is not *quite* certain.

and slave-dealers, distinguished only by the veil of hypocrisy from the mercantile aristocracies of Carthage or of Venice.

3. Economic structures of commerce and industry

The Romans, like the Greeks, had partnership, *societas*, the grouping of persons for a gainful purpose.[159] Its rules were gradually fixed by the private law; they remained formalistic and limiting. The *societas* was limited in time, being dissolved automatically by the death of a partner (unless the whole partnership was formally renewed); and limited liability had not been invented, so every partner was liable in full up to the limit of all he possessed. The law also fixed certain rights of partners, for example, a remarkable novelty of the time of Ser. Sulpicius Rufus, that there could be unequal shares of profit and loss for the sake of a partner whose contribution lay not in supplying but in doing something.[160] Many of the partnerships of which we hear, even for the mines in Spain, consisted of only two or three partners, often linked by family or *clientela* (freedmen, co-freedmen, etc.), which naturally limited their financial scale. However, there were two notable exceptions.

(a) First, partnerships for maritime commerce. Some were involved in the ownership or renting and the exploitation of ships; others, technically more interesting, were concerned with bottomry (*traiecticia pecunia*, *faenus nauticum*), a curious contract, half sleeping-partnership and half insurance. A plurality of persons could insure a single cargo, or split their stake between several vessels. Cato, we know, was engaging in a bottomry contract already *c.* 160 B.C.[161] Senators and *equites* could own ships.[162] They normally entrusted the management to an *exercitor*, though there was nothing to stop the owner doing it himself. But the partnerships for the purchase and equipping of ships and purchase of cargo were still, in the Republican age, governed by the limiting rules, personal and short-term, of the ordinary commercial *societas*.

(b) The second great exception was the *societates publicanorum*, the most considerable financial organizations known to the Roman world and perhaps to the whole of antiquity. Their activities and their status depended, of course, primarily on their relation to public finance, to the system of taxation; but their – by definition – semi-private character had economic implications. First, the sums involved were very large indeed: the capital that had to be assembled in advance either to furnish security (for the *publicani* had to contract to pay the government in advance the

159 More or less any lawful purpose, e.g. running an elementary school, D.17.2.71 *pr*.

160 D.17.2.30; Gaius III.149; *C.J.* 3.25.

161 Plut. *Cat. Mai.* 21.

162 The Sestii of Cosa; Domitius Ahenobarbus (perhaps); Rabirius Postumus. On the Lex Claudia, see D'Arms 1981 (G 50) 31–9.

tax they were going to collect) or, in the case of public works or military supplies, to be granted the licence to undertake the contract, was quite beyond the scale of individual fortunes. Hence, from early on, the grouping into partnerships: in 215 B.C. there were nineteen people in five partnerships for supplying the armies in Spain.[163] Originally, the partnerships of the *publicani* were probably of the ordinary legal kind, but about the end of the second century B.C. some of them – for the *vectigalia* and the mines – changed in character and scale, on the initiative of the state. The change of character was that they became 'anonymous', carrying only the title of their object ('customs of Sicily', 'mines of Hispalis', '*decuma* of Asia', and so on), thus having a collective existence separate from that of the individual partners, and that they became 'permanent', i.e. for the duration of their contract with the state, so that the death of a partner did not dissolve them. It is probable that one could have *partes*, transmissible shares, in them[164] more easily than in ordinary partnerships. Secondly, change of scale: their organization was complex and sophisticated; they were like a state in miniature, 'ad speciem rei publicae', with a common chest, a representative in dealings with the state (*manceps*, *actor*), presidents (*magistri*) and provincial managers (*promagistri*), a General Meeting,[165] slaves, employees, troops, buildings at Rome[166] and in the provinces, boats, postmen, and so on. It is true that between one censorial *lustrum* and the next these *societates* might close, reopen, merge;[167] but mostly they just went on.[168] Now, however rich may have been the *equites* who were normally the shareholders and directors of these firms, when it came to guaranteeing to the state, for five years, the estimated tax revenue of an entire province such as Asia or Bithynia, the resources needed were immense, and must have involved calling, whether legitimately or clandestinely, upon the fortunes of very many other people – landed proprietors, merchants, senators even (through men of straw). And it would have been useless to call upon them unless the expected profits, however narrowly limited by the state, had been worth having. In addition, the *publicani*, as firms but also as individuals, engaged in other types of financial and commercial activity on the side: deposit banking for private clients (including provincial governors); slave-dealing; trade in luxury items;[169] advancing to local communities, at usurious rates, the money they were going to have to pay in tax (very typical, that); farming local taxes, and so on. (The abstention of Atticus from such activities is exceptional.) It can – unless subsequent research should show otherwise – be taken as the case that financial activities of the above kind, semi-public and linked to the fruits

[163] Livy XXIII.49.1.
[164] Whether negotiable is a moot point.
[165] Cic. II *Verr.* 2.173.
[166] Vitr. VI.5.2.
[167] Cic. *Fam.* XIII.9.
[168] Cic. *Leg. Man.* 18.
[169] Rabirius Postumus in Egypt in 54 B.C.

of conquest, mobilized a large fraction of the resources of the Roman governing class, because of the high profits and because of the scale of operations, which was more or less the whole budget of the Roman Republic. Much more was to be got out of this than out of ordinary commercial or industrial activity (not but what they engaged in that, too). But we must not forget the effects of legal and social bias: no senator (and perhaps no *eques* not resident in Rome) could be a *publicanus*, nor could any freedman,[170] so naturally the one class went into landed property and the other into commercial and manufacturing enterprises. Nevertheless, the only 'big business houses' the ancient world knew were – and it is symbolic – the state revenue collectors.

4. *Summing-up*

Let us finally attempt to encapsulate the changes that the Roman conquest of the Mediterranean produced in commerce and the transfer of resources (for a balance of payments it cannot be called).

The first incontestable fact is the establishment of a whole new map of production, consumption and exchange, by means of the rapid integration of zones hitherto politically distinct (Africa, for example, and Gaul, first Narbonensis and then the rest), and by the creation of organic links between Italy and the Aegean and Asia and, finally, Egypt. That process coincided with a vital new fact: round about 116 B.C. Eudoxus of Cyzicus, a Greek captain in the service of the Ptolemies, discovered the route to India and perhaps the monsoon.[171] And in the north also new routes opened: the conquest of Gaul brought in the tin of Britain, and from Aquileia went up, to the Alpine regions rich in iron (Noricum), the wine and pottery of Italy.

Within the Mediterranean basin itself new routes and new axes emerged. Puteoli and Rome on the west coast of Italy and Brundisium on the east coast welcomed goods, and people, from Greece, Asia, the East, Egypt. Most of the old ports of call changed: Carthage and Corinth were brutally eliminated in 146 B.C., for political and economic reasons together, as Cicero stated clearly;[172] Rhodes, not destroyed or systematically ruined in 167, *pace* Polybius,[173] was nevertheless subjected to the severe rivalry of Delos. Delos, though Athenian again from 167, was declared a free port, and between, say, 130 and 88 B.C. enjoyed a phase of unheard-of prosperity, attested by literary texts,[174] archaeology and epigraphy alike. It was an entrepôt and turntable, where people from every point of the compass settled and organized themselves into powerful guilds: especially Italians and Romans[175] but also, e.g., Syrians,

[170] Cic. *Planc.* 23; Tac. *Ann.* IV.6.3. [171] Strab. II.3.4,99C. [172] Cic. *Leg. Agr.* II.87.
[173] Polyb. XXX.31. [174] Strab. XIV.5.2. [175] Not only Italian *Greeks*.

Phoenicians, Alexandrians. Above all, it was a centre of the slave trade on a scale that astonished even contemporaries. Delos is not the only Aegean port where we hear of that kind of concentration of business activities: the same can be said of Chios, of Ephesus, of Thasos. But Delos, until its destruction in 88 (followed by the mere ghost of a restoration *c.* 58–50) was the queen of them all, certainly for slaves,[176] and its veritable aristocracy of bankers and merchants from all over the world had fruitful connexions, business and political, with the cities of Italy. The growth of these new commercial axes depended on the displacement of people, preceding or accompanying the products. Roman and Italian merchants, bankers, businessmen spread all over the Mediterranean – to the advantage, of course, of Roman power. The displacement was hardly ever on a large enough scale to constitute a whole new population anywhere, save in the Cisalpina, in Narbonensis and in Spain, but it was a powerful diaspora, the more so because it was a diaspora of the ruling race: New Carthage, Narbo, Cirta, Utica in the west; Dyrrachium, Patrae, Thessalonica, Mytilene, Ephesus, Alexandria even,[177] in the east. The 'Italians' on Delos were often from Rome or old Latium; but Campanians from Puteoli and Nuceria were also powerful business figures, like the Annii or the famous P. Sittius. Like the English in the eighteenth and nineteenth centuries, Roman entrepreneurs followed or preceded the armies.

We have described the principal objects of commerce: Italy the conqueror imported from everywhere, especially luxury goods, more and more costly, from further and further away: Greek wines, spices, Alexandrian glassware, eastern fabrics, works of art (this latter a big item in money terms). But in the second and first centuries B.C. Italy imported above all two specific products. The first was slaves, captured in war or bought from *venaliciarii*, from all over the place, Asia Minor, Bithynia, Cappadocia, Syria, the Balkans, and finally Gaul. And the second, especially from 123 B.C., was grain – the tax grain, i.e. not paid for, but also free market grain, to meet a demand that it was one of government's most important tasks to keep regularly supplied. The quantities involved, which rose as Italian agriculture went over to vines and stock-raising, were huge, e.g. about 1½ million hectolitres a year merely for the *frumentatio* in the years 58–45 B.C.[178] The centre of this import market for grain seems to have been Rome itself[179] and Puteoli: it was to merchants of Puteoli, amongst others, that Pompey turned in 57 when he was entrusted with the *annona*. Italy did also export, as we have seen: wine in

176 The 'agora of the Italians' was perhaps one of those *stataria*, slave markets, erected often as benefactions, in Asia and elsewhere, by Romans.

177 *ILS* 7273.

178 60 *modii* (= 4.8 hectolitres) × 320,000 beneficiaries.

179 Furius Flaccus, member of the *collegium* of the *Capitolini* and *Mercuriales*, Cic. *QFr.* II.5.3.

large quantities, to Spain and Gaul, and (as we are beginning to learn) to Delos and the East; pottery and oil to Delos and Greece.

But what were the overall terms of the exchange? Given that we have nothing like customs statistics to go on[180] we cannot draw up a detailed balance; but the basic global fact we know well enough: the balance of exchange was *un*-equal, because it was largely determined by military and political conquest and there is, by definition, a deliberate inequality between the ruling race (in this case all Italy, by before the end of our period) and its subjects. Fiscal and financial inequality: it was the provinces – taken as a whole and notwithstanding, of course, a host of exemptions and special cases – that bore almost alone the burden of taxation. Taxation began as, and was in principle, a tax in kind on agricultural wealth, but it was transformed into a prestation in money, though only slowly: the change had still not entirely happened in Sicily under Verres, nor in the 'frumentary' provinces as a whole even in 58–57. It goes without saying that a fiscal bite of that size out of the production of grain had an influence on the 'free market'. The same is true of the supply of metal for the coinage: it was not commercial balance nor payment that fed the Roman mint, but the fact that Rome imposed the taxes. True, in a period of peace and order, that very system could carry with it a certain economic equilibrium, for the provincial economies would have to acquire currency by economic activity in order to pay their required taxes.[181] But in our period such a mechanism was not at work: we are still in the age of stark conquest, accentuated by wars, foreign and civil, and by the uncontrolled exactions of Roman magnates. Greece and Asia were, between 90 and 31 B.C., subjected to a fiscal and monetary squeeze that could not but distort the normal mechanisms of production and exchange: the indebtedness of Greece, and especially Asia, during the first half of the first century B.C., unilaterally imposed by Rome, was an absolute economic cataclysm, as the sources attest: 120,000 talents, i.e. 720 million denarii at compound interest, in 70 B.C.[182] Consequently, as we also know for certain, the provincials had to borrow at usurious rates from their very creditors, the *publicani* and bankers of Rome, until they were bankrupt or Rome itself called a moratorium (as occasionally happened). It was these operations rather than economic operations in the usual sense, with land or commerce or industry that attracted the Roman capitalists, who were actually, therefore, a kind of rentiers of the power-structure rather than true men of commerce. Of course, one must not underestimate true economic

180 Italian *portoria* did exist down to 60 B.C. and again from 45, at least on certain 'foreign goods', Suet. *Iul.* 43.1.

181 That is perhaps how it worked under the Empire, Hopkins 1980 (G 124).

182 Plut. *Luc.* 20.

production-and-exchange and the role played in it by the Roman governing and commercial class; but in our period, on balance, it was an economics of spoliation that prevailed. Consider just two figures, arbitrary but significant: the 1½ million hectolitres of corn distributed in the year 57 B.C. would, at a market price of three sesterces a *modius*, come to 57,600,000 sesterces or near enough 15 million denarii; yet that is hardly 2 per cent of the sum Asia owed in taxation in 70 B.C.

The provincials, the *peregrini*, were not deceived: the pillage of the world by the Romans from 146 B.C. to the end of the civil wars is a massive economic fact, testified as much by Sallust as by Posidonius or Agatharchides of Cnidus,[183] and illustrated by the 'lust for gold' of the notorious Crassus. Given this brutal and quite un-'economic' manner of enriching themselves, it is difficult to discern anything like an economic policy of the Roman state in our period. No more commercial treaties (as with Carthage in an older day); belated efforts, only, to stamp out piracy and ensure freedom of the seas; absence of any customs policy except as a way of raising revenue; only, of course, the perpetual seizure of any advantage or concession in the Roman favour.

When foreign produce like Greek wine or perfume was taxed or penalized, that was only in the context of traditional sumptuary legislation: such measures did, of course, have some – unplanned – economic effects of a secondary sort, but they were not really economic in character but civic and moralizing and political (and although they were re-enacted from time to time, the last time by Julius Caesar, their effectiveness was in any case almost nil). There was, then, no Roman economic protectionism. The only text that gets, too often, invoked for this, Cicero, *De Republica* III.16 about the ban on planting vineyards imposed on the 'Transalpines', surely does not apply to Gaul, nor to our period; and the allegedly similar ban by Domitian two centuries later[184] only proves the perpetual Roman fear of a shortage in the grain supply.

It is only at that elementary level that the 'economic policy' of a state like Rome is to be found: to secure subsistence, to facilitate access to necessary products (what is 'necessary' varying according to class), and to maintain that degree of general security, and by the least possible intervention, that suits the ruling race.[185]

V. ECONOMY AND SOCIETY

Such being the economic basis, what were its effects upon social structures and relationships? The subject would need a chapter to itself:

[183] Sall. *H.* IV.60M, letter of Mithridates; Diod. III.47.8. [184] Suet. *Dom.* 7.2.

[185] A broader vision, adumbrated perhaps by Cicero, only really emerges with Augustus, Nicolet 1988 (G 179) chs. 2 and 3.

here we can only fix attention, summarily, on a couple of aspects that characterize the Roman world as a whole, and our particular period.

First, what is traditionally called the 'Problem of Debt' (though it actually covers a complex range of phenomena). It appears very early in the Roman annalistic tradition, always linked to violent political and social conflicts. In those early days it perhaps had a structural aspect, enslavement and self-enslavement for debt being closely related to the nature of the work-force on the land. But by the second century B.C. it had already taken on more 'modern' and more strictly economic aspects, i.e. the borrowing of money, in all its forms. We must try to make some distinctions. There was, as we have seen, (a) rural indebtedness, involving the small subsistence owners or tenants – an essential part of the story of 'agricultural crisis', and with two sets of consequences, either new forms of dependence between the landowner and his *coloni*, or the flight from the land with its attendant concentration of large estates. There was, secondly, (b) urban indebtedness. Usury, *faenus*, is too common a theme, from at least the time of the elder Cato down to Julius Caesar and Augustus, and as much in political oratory as in private documents, for us to doubt that it was built into the structure of the society. And it has long been observed that the problem of debt impinged – at certain moments, anyhow, e.g. in 66–63 and 47 B.C. – upon the governing class itself, the rich, who possessed lands and were creditors but who also had debts, contracted usually for non-economic ends, standard of living, building, politics and so on. Was that due to a lack of liquid cash in the economy? Was it due to the normal income from rural and urban real estate being too low? Or to inflation in the price of things they were eager for, like works of art and exotic luxuries? Detailed studies are needed in this regard. What we can say is that usury did not profit merely a specialized class: the great *faeneratores* belonged, themselves, to the very same social groups (with some individual variations of behaviour, as between, for example, Atticus and M. Crassus, which were a matter of personal moral choice). However, if the movement of money in this way had only affected this limited upper range of people it would not have had the cataclysmic consequences that it did have on two or three occasions: in 92–88, when it provoked monetary legislation, riots against the judiciary, and new debt regulations; in 66–63, accompanying the political traumas of the *bellum Catilinae*; in 48–47 when it more or less led to civil war. So, certainly, other social groups and categories besides the aristocracy were involved; at the lowest level, for example, the very humble urban plebeians who got into debt in at least one way, over the rents of their tenements and workshops, so that Julius Caesar in 47 had to impose a moratorium and then a system of control. And above them were the small-scale businessmen – artisans, shopkeepers, entrepreneurs in a small way, who needed working funds. Now we have already seen the role (more widespread than is usually thought) of short-term credit, through auctioneers, in modest current commercial operations: when political upheavals occurred, with wars, postponement of sailings, and so on, the indebtedness of this class, too, which archaeology and epigraphy are showing to have been numerous and diverse, could be traumatic. Hence the, at first sight, paradoxical link between these modest and easily ruined urban debtors and some of the big-scale debtors, who used them to further their own ambitions. Thus, from Marius Gratidianus to L. Antonius, tribune in 44 B.C., via Catiline and Caelius Rufus in 48, the economic crises merged with politics.[186] But with this kind of credit (or usury) who were the creditors? We see them massacring a praetor in 89,[187] opposing Caelius in 48,[188] honouring L. Antonius in 44:[189] they are the 'money men' installed in the Forum, 'in Iano medio', grouped into guilds of a sort. They are not the big capitalists; they are not *argentarii* in the proper sense; nor are they agents of the great magnates who are, the while, lending and borrowing whole fortunes as between each other. They do not seem to be on the same status level as the Romans in the provinces who lend money, again on a quite different scale, to the provincial cities and communities. Were they a class in their own right? It is to them alone that Cicero attributes the 'science of acquiring and placing money' in the *De Officiis*.[190] Not that we need doubt that Cato, Crassus, Atticus, P. Sittius, Pompey and Brutus possessed that same science in equal measure!

For the question whether Roman society was a 'society of orders' or a 'society of classes', whether, that is, it functioned fundamentally in civic or in economic structures, is a false dichotomy: like virtually every society, it operated on several registers. The official social hierarchy was defined by legal statuses and founded in principle on the individual's capacity for public roles: it was, therefore, by definition a 'society of orders', and the aristocracy was a functional aristocracy (patriciate, *nobilitas*, Senate, *equites*). But simultaneously it was a property hierarchy, because the 'orders' were also based on a scale of required wealth. There were, of old and down at least to 218 B.C., certain incompatibilities, which banned the functional aristocracy from 'chrematistic' activities – except agriculture. But the interdiction, more ethical than legal, did not affect everything: not, for example, commerce in agricultural products, nor the letting of land or housing. It also tended to lapse into desuetude and have to be renewed, seldom with much effect. One can, therefore –

[186] An endemic and structural phenomenon down to at least 33 B.C., after which the overwhelming power and riches of the Princeps brought about other solutions.

[187] Livy *Per.* 74, App. *BCiv.* I.54.

[188] Caesar, *BCiv.* III.21.

[189] Nicolet 1985 (C 232).

[190] Cic. *Off.* II.87.

and people have done so recently – find plenty of cases, especially from the first century B.C., of senators acting as traders (often selling their own produce, but not always so), entrepreneurs in building or pottery production, or proprietors of *horrea*, which brought in very large sums. Even the 'principes viri', the Crassi and Pompeys and Domitii, were not above making money in this way, like the duc d'Orléans, whom Louis XVI called the 'boutiquier du Palais-Royal': the owners of big Italian vineyards, of huge flocks in Apulia or Epirus, of ships at Alexandria or mines in Spain, could well be counted as men of commerce. But if they were also senators, magistrates, generals, it was not economic enterprise that pushed them into that but on the contrary the desire to take their role in the only official social hierarchy there was. Of course, they could often use the 'pull', or the legitimate powers, of their status as, for example, senators for the advancement of their commercial interests (by such things as the *libera legatio*, in principle not allowed), but their status did not depend on those commercial interests. It was not, in our period, a matter of mere title, but corresponded to the exercise of actual military, political and social functions, so that the economic activities did not tend to eliminate the old society of orders but fitted into it, while the society of orders[191] in its turn adapted itself to the new economic parameters: it was never eliminated during the whole of Rome's history.

[191] Which Augustus actually reactivated.

CHAPTER 17

THE CITY OF ROME AND THE *PLEBS URBANA* IN THE LATE REPUBLIC

NICHOLAS PURCELL

For *people* are the City, not the houses or the
porticoes or the fora empty of men
(Dio LVI.5.3)

It is said that Caligula's exasperated wish was that the people of Rome had only a single neck. That they had a single – and very strongly felt – collective identity is, by contrast, our historical problem. Urban populations at all periods suffer from being treated corporately – as the *demos*, the many, the mob, the multitude, the masses: under such concepts a sneer lies close below the surface, and the dehumanizing effect of the collective designation has never lost its political point. The difficulty is particularly acute in the case of ancient Rome. The population in question was very large (though for reasons that we shall see, quantification poses serious problems, not just of evidence). Secondly, the Roman elite had every reason to develop the vocabulary of disdain, and has processed almost all the information we possess. Thirdly, there were indeed ways in which the *plebs Romana* was in reality a corporate entity, and really did cohere as a collectivity, so even when the dismissive perceptions of ancient aristocrats have been allowed for, our analysis still has to penetrate an institutional façade before it can depict and explain the differentiations within the Roman populace.

Our subject-matter in this chapter is the resident population of the city of Rome; but there are two other collectivities that need to be distinguished. The first, the *plebs urbana*, was a subset of the urban population; it comprised the Roman citizens resident in the city who were not members of the senatorial or equestrian census-categories: it excluded slaves and foreigners (*peregrini*). The second, the *populus Romanus*, was the sum of all Roman citizens of whatever status everywhere.

The *populus Romanus* and the *plebs urbana* were in early Roman history very nearly co-extensive, but as Rome was involved in increasingly far-flung theatres of activity and new citizens outside Rome were included within the body politic, they became widely separated. The *populus*

Romanus had had from an early date an important practical and theoretical standing in the Roman state, producing what could be regarded as a spectacular example of a mixed constitution.[1] Since the political function of the body of ordinary Romans could usually take place only at Rome, and since logistics often made attending Rome regularly to use the vote inconvenient or impossible, the constitutional role of the *populus* to an important extent devolved on the *plebs urbana* and gave it its considerable self-awareness and sense of cohesion. The broadening of the *populus Romanus*, which cannot be discussed in detail here, was thus paralleled by an evolution of the *plebs urbana* as such into a significant constitutional, social and political entity. It is the later stages of this development, from the second century B.C. until the sole ascendancy of Augustus, that will concern us in this chapter.

The constitutional origins of the position of the *populus Romanus*, and so of the plebs, were reflected in some of the more important features of its organization. One is the concept, profitably stressed in recent discussions of the subject, of 'registeredness', a system of recording, docketing and assessing the precise place, in a hierarchy of means and status, of all citizens. The registered individual citizen was the basic unit of the *plebs urbana*, and the precision of the registration, the product of the census, was something which the Romans themselves perceived as unusual among states. Secondly, the citizen acted as a member of various assemblies, principally the legislative assembly of the *tribus* (formerly territorial divisions), and the elective assembly based on the (basically military) organization of the *centuriae*. Although the individual citizen's position in either was, for various reasons, hardly influential in a democratic sense, the precise management of both assemblies was a matter of intense political controversy. Already in the third century B.C. a major adjustment to the centuriate assembly had given more influence in it to the plebs; but the membership of the *tribus* never ceased to cause problems when it came to incorporating new citizens.[2]

Alongside the political assemblies a prominent place must be assigned to the *contiones*, public meetings at which the citizenry was addressed by the magistrates, and the gatherings of citizens for religious observances or the military muster. Collective behaviour of various kinds was an

[1] Place of the plebs in the Roman constitution: Millar 1984 (A 75); Millar 1986 (C 113); controversial observations in Finley 1983 (A 32) 56–8, 89. Mixed constitution: von Fritz 1954 (A 36). See also Hoffman–Siber 1957 (G 122); Prugni 1987 (G 197); K. A. Raaflaub, ed., *Social Struggles in Archaic Rome: New Perspectives on the Struggle of the Orders* (Berkeley, 1986) 1–51.

[2] Basic account of the citizen within the constitution: Nicolet 1980 (A 82) esp. ch. 7. Working of the assemblies: Taylor 1966 (F 157). Reform of the *comitia centuriata* in third century: Grieve 1985 (F 70). Numbers voting: MacMullen 1980 (G 150). Tribes: Taylor 1952–4 (G 236); Taylor 1960 (F 156); Nicolet 1985 (C 232).

integral part of the experience of citizen life at Rome, and there is observable a gradual transition from the assemblies which were part of the machinery of state to less structured manifestations of the general will. Only in relatively recent years has serious attention been given to the informal politics of the Roman 'mob', but it is a subject which closely reflects the double nature of the life of the city: on the one hand this political activity was a regular aspect of the behaviour of the *plebs urbana* in the strict sense – the Roman citizens in the capital; on the other it was the characteristic of a rather different social phenomenon, the city population as a whole, with its (by the late Republic) very large numbers of slaves and foreigners.[3]

The barrier between the citizen and the non-citizen, between the *plebs urbana* and the rest of the city population, was partly blurred and obscured by the ambiguity of status of the newly enfranchised, both the manumitted slave and the favoured foreigner; this ambiguous category and its behaviour are central to the understanding of the life of the city in the late Republic. Cicero makes the point for us, disjoining the urban populace, tainted by servility and poverty, from the respectable political concept of the *populus Romanus*: 'or do you really suppose that the Roman People is that body composed of those who are contracted for a wage? of slaves, hirelings, criminals and paupers?'[4]

The other defining barrier around the *plebs urbana*, separating it from all the other low-status citizens in the *populus Romanus*, potentially a geographically based distinction, was made equally unclear by the difficulty of defining the city of Rome spatially. Boundaries such as the walls or the limits of the *ager Romanus*, the old territory, on one view, of the Roman city state, had little social reality: the Romans themselves were impelled to evolve a concept of the city as 'built-up area', *continentia aedificia*, during the period dealt with here, because of the difficulty of defining either the population as a social group, or the city, in terms of boundaries.[5]

So no account will be neatly bounded; an 'archaeological' view of the city and its inhabitants will fall short through lack of understanding of the institutional ingredients which had repercussions even on the foreigner and the slave; while the historian of ideas and rights risks failing to appreciate the urban circumstances, social and physical, which differentiated Rome from the *coloniae* and overseas communities. The account that follows attempts to combine the two, but there will inevitably be ragged edges. No one who works on this subject can fail to

[3] First serious account of the informal politics of the plebs: Brunt 1974 (G 23). Significant further steps: Lintott 1968 (A 62); Veyne 1976 (G 250) 201–61; Vanderbroeck 1987 (C 279).

[4] Cic. *Dom.* 89.

[5] *Continentia aedificia*: Nicolet 1985 (C 232) 831–2.

echo the heartfelt remarks about the near impossibility of producing a synthetic account of it made by the scholar who has done most over the last twenty-five years to explain the position of the plebs.[6]

The evidence for the numbers, origin and composition of the urban plebs, for its activities, problems and historical significance, and for how all those things changed with time, is elusive and fragmentary and has defied synthesis. The major difficulty is that the best evidence on particular questions is limited now to one small part and now to another of the 500-year period during which Rome was by far the largest city in the Mediterranean. Thus, our best evidence for *collegia* comes from late antiquity, for *insulae* from the middle Empire, for informal popular politics from the Julio-Claudian period: despite the works of Cicero, or because of his prejudices, the late Republic is the period for which we are not best informed about virtually any important aspect of the history of the *plebs urbana*. However, it is clear that the years from the Hannibalic War to Actium saw all the most important stages in the formation of the physical setting of the city of Rome and the society which occupied it, and there is, fortunately, enough genuinely Republican material to provide the rudiments of an account. Not all aspects of the subject are, in any case, dealt with in this chapter: religion and the informal politics of the City are discussed in ch. 15 of Volume x, the major question of Rome's relationship to the economy of Italy and the Mediterranean in ch. 16 above. While this division makes the edges of what follows still more ragged, that remains preferable to a false synthesis which would obscure the probable changes of five centuries of very various history.

Rather than aiming at such a synthesis, the present account seeks to propound a model for the place of the city of Rome within a wider social context which can help to explain the salient characteristics of its place in Roman history in general. Earlier accounts advanced political impotence, overcrowding, appalling conditions, food crises, elite manipulation, as reasons for the turmoil of the life of the ordinary inhabitants of Rome. Here it is our aim to show how all these things were aspects of one basic underlying phenomenon. Put simply, the case is that the immeasurable success of the Roman elite generated a continuous growth and regrowth of the social organisms of the city and their economic aspects, within which the tensions of readjustment and incorporation, the insecurities about belonging, and the struggle of people for social locations to achieve survival and prosperity, generated the particular crises and instabilities which appear in the historical record and the numerous similar events which do not. Rome's problems were the problems of success.[7]

[6] Yavetz 1958 (G 261); Yavetz 1988 (G 262) spanning the transition from the Republic to the early Principate. For the opinion quoted see G 262 viif and 130–1.

[7] See ch. 16 above, *passim*.

I

The *plebs urbana* was a very large body. The populace of the city altogether was, by the standards of the ancient world, enormous, and during the period under consideration the city of Rome came to be home to the largest single social organism, the largest urban community, in the Mediterranean world. The fact is often stated, but the search for exact quantification (which is doomed) has oddly distracted researchers from the qualitative implications. As geographers know well, when a city stands at the head of a rank-size hierarchy it is common for it to be grossly larger than all the other members of the hierarchy: but they have also attempted, as ancient historians have usually not, to explain, in terms of social mobility and economic behaviour, why that should be so. The sheer size of Rome is much discussed, without much attempt to say how its size changed from 150 B.C. to A.D. 350, or why; and the much more interesting fact that the largest of cities is also likely to have constituted one of the most complex of societies has also received little attention. Accurate figures, even if they were available, would be of relatively little interest; speculation about the actual size of the population is rather vain.[8]

Of the supposed available statistics the only helpful one, interesting also from other points of view, is the number of adult males receiving donatives: 320,000 for the corn dole in 46 B.C., 150,000 immediately after and 200,000 in 2 B.C.; and 320,000 receiving cash from Augustus in A.D. 5.[9] The 53 per cent variation should at once make one cautious about what these figures represent, and it is very likely that the people counted here are simply those who could be expected to frequent the centre of the city on a fairly regular basis. Caesar and Augustus attempted to make *domicilium* (residence at Rome) the basis of eligibility by establishing lists arranged by the constituent topographical subdivisions of the city, the *vici*, and a fixed quota of the entitled, with vacancies filled by a lottery procedure, *subsortitio*. If that worked at all (and the enormous problems of registration should not be underestimated) the quotas of 150,000 and 200,000 may be a rough guide to adult males with *domicilium* at Rome, which would give a citizen population of about 500,000. There are, however, two problems. First, the quotas may represent the level from which great reductions were being sought, and, second, we know neither the boundary of the area conceived of as *domicilium Romae*, nor what degree of absenteeism was tolerated before the right to claim that *domicilium* was lost. Could a bailiff at Saxa Rubra with an adult son

[8] Best account: Brunt 1971 (A 16) 376–83; see also Hermansen 1978 (G 118).

[9] *Res Gestae* 15.4; 15.2.

engaged for eight months of the year in the perfume-business at Puteoli legitimately collect two portions of corn in the time of Caesar?

In any case, it is not clear that in the period before 46 either *domicilium* or *origo* (place of birth) made any difference to eligibility for the corn dole. What was required was more general participation in the life of the metropolis. Nor was need the criterion; the corn was provided to the accessible part of the *populus Romanus* of all levels, not only to the plebs. There was no status-test, let alone a means test. Far from being a guide for us to the 'real' population of the city, the phenomenon of the *frumentatio* was one of the main ingredients in the creation, independently of the social realities, of a privileged and extensive status, at the heart of the citizen-body as a whole, focused on the city of Rome. C. Gracchus was the originator of the *frumentationes*, and it is only natural that the process should have begun in an age when the city was in other ways too becoming capital of empire rather than conquering city state. The old Roman corn supply had been basically utilitarian; from 123 B.C. the supplying of a need was ingeniously made simultaneously into the symbol of a status for a portion of the populace and for the city which housed it.[10]

A second approach, estimating the population from the habitable area within the city core, is made very shaky by our uncertainty as to where people lived for how long.[11] Even if we thought that the sacred boundary, the *pomoerium*, defined the area of *domicilium Romae*, we would still not know what the average duration of such *domicilium* was within individuals' lifetimes. Altogether, the concept 'population of the city of Rome' is slippery and unhelpful. It is time to recognize that the urban population was probably not a huddle, however huge, of lifelong urbanites, inhabitants of a Rome around which a tight boundary could be drawn. We must not impose a notional Aurelianic Wall on the Republican city, separating the urban and rural, dividing an imagined core of teeming *insulae* from an agrarian desert on the periphery. We cannot assume that all those who *used* Rome lived there, or that all those who lived there did so throughout their lives. It is futile to try to count totals in the city of Rome as if the stability from generation to generation of a mediaeval town prevailed there. Our figures, such as they are, refer to things that happened *at* Rome; they are not the vital statistics *of* Rome. So the 'urban population' is the people at Rome at any particular time. Rome must be assessed, as it was experienced, from day to day. We must include the Praenestine in the market, the Galatian at his patron's, the

[10] Corn supply: Rickman 1979 (G 212) (eligibility pp. 175–85). See also Garnsey 1988 (G 100) 167–270.

[11] Population density: von Gerkan 1940 (G 102); Castagnoli 1980 (G 37); Packer 1967 (G 184).

freedman of the visiting Volsinian magistrate, the Bruttian soldier in the process of joining up – as well as people who had perhaps really lived in the same building in the Subura for thirty years. We need not work with the assumption that the last category was ever in a majority. It is significant that the ancient sources do not emphasize any such group: their own subdivisions are not based on places of regular domicile. The atmosphere of the mediaeval town, with its burgher dynasties, is not that of the ancient city, above all not that of the greatest metropolis.

A principal reason for that fact is the demography of large pre-industrial cities. They act, largely through being disease pools and centres of unhygienic conditions, as net consumers of population. London, it has been estimated, needed an influx of 2,700 per annum to maintain its population of some 200,000 in the early seventeenth century; yet it grew rapidly in size, since so great was the pull of the metropolis that one in five Englishmen of that period had at some time been a Londoner.[12] In ancient Rome conditions were no better, as recent research has made clear.[13] The explanation lies in the disease associated with urban life, of which an early example is at hand in the terrible mortality of the pestilence of 175–174 B.C.[14] But all pre-industrial cities have shared that feature: the privileges of Rome were such that some aspects of urban conditions were better there – without the beneficial effects of river and aqueducts it is likely that Rome could not have survived. Conditions, horrific by twentieth-century standards, must still be seen against an even worse background. It was the sudden disasters of collapse, fire, flood and epidemic, rather than the low level of amenities from day to day, that made Rome more than usually dangerous demographically. Rome cannot have experienced demographic stability, and that it remained so huge an agglomeration for so long can be regarded as entailing a constant movement towards it on a large scale. That immigration has left many traces in the literary sources.

We should begin by considering the movement to Rome of the free-born. It is worth remembering that the Romans believed that their city had first originated as an amalgam of the stateless, the outcast and the desperate (the tradition of the Asylum is an ancient one):[15] that foundation myth tells us a great deal about the society which propagated it, when we reflect how potentially discreditable it is by the standards of a world in which autochthony, being there from time immemorial, was the *summum bonum*. Of non-Romans, in historical times too it was the Latins who could be incorporated most easily both by right and by

12 R. Finlay, *Population and Metropolis, the Demography of London, 1580–1650* (Cambridge, 1981).

13 Conditions: Scobie 1986 (G 223). Demographic calculations for Rome in the Principate: Frier 1982 (G 83); see also *CAH* Vol. XI².

14 Livy XLI.21.6.

15 Livy I.8.5–6.

culture in the Roman polity, and we hear of a striking episode in the years 187–172 B.C. when the authorities of the Latin cities complained to the Senate of the decline in their numbers caused by emigration to Rome. In 187 the figure quoted is 12,000, from a catchment area of only some 500 or 800 square kilometres. Livy implies both that the Senate's measures against the movements were ineffective, but also that the process did not in fact involve citizens of Ardea or Lanuvium in turning their backs on their home towns, but rather just shifting the centre of their activities to Rome as they forged chains of family and professional ties right across the region.[16] It is important for our understanding of the *regio Romana* (the neighbourhood of Rome) in the age of Cicero to observe how the half-century after the Hannibalic War made Rome home for many Praenestines, Veientines or Tusculans, and forever changed the social geography of west central Italy.

Throughout the second century the peoples of Italy were in flux. Rome sent her own subjects far afield in military expeditions and planned settlements. Romans and Italians began to be widely diffused throughout the Mediterranean world.[17] Resettlement was a policy with the use of which the Romans became increasingly familiar; of disloyal allies after the Hannibalic War, of Ligurians in 180 B.C., of Samnites in the years before 177.[18] Conversely, the power of Rome grew in the East and many more Greeks came to the city in various ways.[19] We cannot doubt that the number of *peregrini* and *Latini* in the city was often very large, but we can only see its impact when measures were taken against the disagreeable results – above all against the practice of usurping the rights of citizens, especially the vote. Rome's early institutions had developed an effective resilience in the face of the arrival of relatively small numbers of newcomers, and the registration of citizens itself has been set in this context: 'the institution of the census presupposes a small territorial state and a citizen body with shared moral and political values and a developed civic loyalty, and not unduly socially differentiated'.[20] But the arrival of various aliens in huge numbers inevitably threatened to destabilize the Roman state. Measures like those of Pennus (126 B.C.), Fannius (122) and Crassus and Scaevola (95), who expelled aliens from the city, probably

[16] Livy XXXIX.3.4–6 (note esp. 6, 'iam tum multitudine alienigenarum urbem onerante', which shows the wider context of the Latin migration); XLI.8.6–12 and 9.9–12; XLII.10.3. Later immigration: Hübner 1875 (G 125) the evidence of names in '-anus'. *Ius migrandi*, to *ager Romanus* if not to Rome: Brunt 1965 (C 31); Brunt 1971 (A 16) 70 and 380–1; Brunt 1988 (A 19) 240–5; Hopkins 1978 (A 53) 64–74. Movement of Romans of the rural tribes to Rome: Lintott 1968 (A 62) 86.

[17] Wilson 1966 (A 128).

[18] Livy XXVI.16 (not carried out); XL.38.1; XL.91.34.

[19] Salmon 1982 (A 102) 118–19. For the sequel in the Principate, G. La Piana, *Foreign Groups in Rome during the First Centuries of the Empire* (Cambridge, MA, 1927), and *CAH* Vol. XI².

[20] Gabba 1984 (G 93) 193.

only on a temporary basis, or took steps to ensure that they did not usurp rights in the city which were not their due, proved, not surprisingly, quite unequal to the problem.[21] They suggest, anyhow, that the pressure of newcomers was particularly intense at certain seasons, and this is confirmed by laws of the middle of the second century (the Leges Aelia et Fufia) that controlled the flux of even Roman citizens towards Rome when legislation was in progress.

Serious as this situation had been, it was nothing to the chaos that followed the enfranchisement of the Italians after the Social War. The movement of the new citizens to Rome might have been less precipitous had it not been for the increasing political rewards of life in the capital; as Sallust observed, 'the prime of Italian manhood, which had previously been prepared to put up with a meagre existence in the countryside through wage-labour, was lured by the hand-outs made by the state and by individuals, and came to prefer the leisured and civilized existence of the Urbs to their thankless toil'.[22] The concept of *urbanum otium* to which Sallust alludes is one to which we shall return in section IV, below. It is from the period of the crisis of the Republic that the clearest testimonies to the swelling of the population of the city come, and it is not too daring to assert that it was between 89 B.C. and 31 B.C. that the rate of arrival of new would-be inhabitants of the city was steepest, probably by a long way. Appian, probably quoting a Republican source, takes a sterner line than Sallust: 'the orchestration [his word, *choregoumenon*, puts the corn dole in the context of spectacular entertainments] of the *annona* at Rome and Rome only attracts to it the workless, mendicant and miscreant population of Italy'.[23] For Varro, as for Livy, commenting on the Latin problem of the early second century, it is the *patres familias* who count, sneaking in to live in the city and employ their hands not with the pruning-hook and the plough but with the applause of theatre and circus.[24] Varro is clear that the state's policy with regard to the maintenance of the city was instrumental in the process, and Augustus thought the same.[25] Their view was too simple, but it remains true that it was the escalating munificence of the imperial elite which created the conditions in which Rome could grow and, in growing, none the less survive.

But more people came to Rome than were entitled to the perquisites of the citizen status. Many tried for that too, of course, in some cases successfully, both at Rome and in the Italian *municipia*, and a severe law of 65 B.C., the Lex Papia, attempted to control the practice.[26] More significantly for our theme, it also attempted an explusion from Rome of all those resident there who were not of Italian origin.[27] The unmistak-

[21] See above, ch. 3 pp. 76, 102; ch. 4 p. 110. [22] Sall. *Cat.* 37.7. [23] App. *BCiv.* II.120.
[24] Varro *Rust.* II. *praef.* 3. [25] Suet. *Aug.* 42.3. [26] Cic. *Arch.* 10; *Balb.* 52.
[27] Dio XXXVII.9.5.

able xenophobia of the measure puts it in the company of those various expulsions of ideologically suspect groups which long characterized Roman policy and reflect a lasting insecurity about the tenacity of the Roman character; but also, concerned with far more than the maintenance of electoral propriety, the Lex Papia is eloquent evidence for the scale of non-Italian presence at Rome.

Furthermore, although the movement of the free-born in and out of Rome must not be underestimated, it is less conspicuous in the ancient literary evidence than the accumulation of population through the institution of slavery. A high proportion of the enslaved victims of Rome's foreign successes from the Hannibalic War onwards was deployed in the furtherance of the comfortable lifestyles of the urban elites of Italy and especially of Rome. Something of the role of those members of the *familiae urbanae* may be seen in Roman comedy, which suggests at least how the urban slave had a place of his own in the economic and social framework of the life of the city streets: the *domus* were not slave-prisons. The inscriptions of the late Republic, and still more those of the early Imperial period, show us a little of slave-ownership on a small scale by families far below the elite in means.[28] While quantification is not possible, it is probable that more slaves served in those numerous smaller *familiae* than in the huge but rarer ménages of the elite.

Free-born elite opinion was hostile to the taint of servility not only in the current slave but in the freed slave (*libertinus*) and the child of the freed slave (and even, sometimes, yet further generations). Roman masters freed very large numbers of slaves, and the number of *libertini* who received the Roman citizenship in this way in the late Republic is likely to have reached many thousands a year. We can trace a series of measures modifying their status and the deployment of their political rights from the Hannibalic War on, and it is not too bold a conclusion that freedman numbers increased to some extent in line with the boom in the slave trade. The difficulty of reaching agreement on how the *libertini* should be incorporated in the political system made them a marginal and debatable group in the life of Rome, though their numbers and the strong ties which bound them to their patrons gave them considerable importance. With slaves and foreigners they came to constitute a subdivision of the city populace (overlapping, through the citizen status of the formally free *libertinus*, with the *plebs urbana*) whose effect on Rome in the late Republic was profound.[29] The disdain felt for the servile was compounded with mistrust of the foreign. The new slaves were mainly from beyond Italy, and politicians in the second half of the second

[28] Plut. *Mar.* 44, a slave of a poor client.

[29] Treggiari 1969 (G 247) 6–52; on *libertini* as a term for all the newly enfranchised, Cels-Saint-Hilaire 1985 (G 38). Numbers: Harper 1972 (G 113).

century were already inclined to silence in political debate 'those to whom Italy is only a stepmother'.[30]

In this way Rome became a 'city formed from the concourse of the peoples of the world',[31] and there is little doubt that that is how the population of the city was maintained. We should, however, be cautious about overstating, as did the ancient critics, the alienness of the *libertini*. Whatever their origin, they were in a position to become rapidly acculturated by the society of the city, and even to play a role in transmitting its *mores*. In the inscriptions, it is true, an overwhelming proportion of freedmen seem to be Greek; but refinements on earlier studies of the phenomenon suggest that Greek names were in many cases cultural rather than ethnic, and the relation of free and freed in the families of the city was rather more complex than was once thought.[32] Nor is it clear to what extent the simply Hellenic was seen as automatically alien. However, inscriptions and literary texts alike assist our picture of discontinuity in the history of the urban population; the slave- and freedman-phenomenon at Rome is a case history in the problem of incorporating the essential, but unwelcome, new arrival.

Not that they only moved *in* to Rome. Just as the economic and political concerns of their *patroni* will have brought to Rome at some point in their lives a very high proportion of the 2 million or so freedmen in the Roman world at any time, so they also often moved away again. Thus in 35 B.C. a slave *unguentarius* (perfume-dealer) from the Sacra Via, dependent of a well-known Campanian family, set up an inscription on the island of Ithaca:[33] he is a typical member of the 'population of Rome', reminding us that that phrase is only a label of convenience for an agglomeration which changed from day to day.[34] Static models for the social history of the city should be replaced by one which has a place for the mobility of the individual, the fluidity and mutability of social groups and the transience of family and household structures there.

Movement away from Rome took place from time to time on a large scale. It is not surprising that the Romans themselves reacted with consternation to the discovery that their city was becoming populous on a scale otherwise unheard of; and not with the abundant citizen manpower in which any ancient state would take pride, but with people whose relationship to the citizen body was either dubious or clearly inferior. Used as they were to disposing of large groups by resettlement, and possessing – as the Latin citizen expulsion discussed above shows –

[30] Val. Max. VI.2.3; the same description of the plebs, plus its mercenary side: Petron. *Sat.* 122.

[31] *Comment. Pet.* 54.

[32] Tenney Frank 1915–16 (G 73); Taylor 1961 (B 248). More recent approach: Huttunen 1974 (G 127); Solin 1982 (G 228). Acculturation of the upwardly-mobile: Jongman 1988 (G 133) ch. 6.

[33] *ILLRP* 826.

[34] Pensioning off of freedmen: Rawson 1976 (G 209) 93–4.

an adequate degree of registration to make selection possible, they naturally undertook planned 'drainings-off' (the phrase is Cicero's, of Rullus' proposed settlements in 63 B.C.)[35] of the accumulated population of the city. Colonies of Romans and Latins, linked in purpose to recruitment, were the main precedent, and it was generous but prudent to allow freedmen to take part in them. Philip V of Macedon at least thought that the use of freedmen in that way was the secret of Rome's astonishing *euandria*, her resources of population,[36] and new evidence of the third-century *colonia* at Paestum shows that he was not wholly mistaken.[37] But it is hard to assess the numbers of freedmen involved in the colonies of the middle Republic, and the overall numbers sent out were quite modest at that time. The sources of slaves, moreover, were then closer to home, so that the freedmen involved may have seemed less alien than was perhaps normal in the late Republic.

In the last decades of the Republic the problem and the solution were alike on a much larger scale. Sulla's foundation of Urbana in Campania may be the prototype; Rullus in 63 was planning the settlement of numerous *egentes* from the city in the *ager Campanus*.[38] But Julius Caesar did most in practice to promote the resettlement of the urban freedman. His foundation for such colonists at Corinth, in particular, seems to have been chosen specially because of the commercial associations of the ancient city,[39] a rare recognition of the plebeian ethos which we shall discuss below. But freedmen were included also in Caesar's African colonies and elsewhere, and the charter of his foundation at Urso in Spain shows that in those settlements they were not subject to the usual constitutional disabilities. From the early Empire, but strongly Republican in tradition, we may compare the measures of A.D. 6,[40] when famine led Augustus to expel, probably temporarily, slaves and foreigners except for teachers and doctors, and the coincidence of the Pannonian revolt impelled him to recruit freedmen into the regular army. In A.D. 19 Tiberius responded to tension in the city by removing 4,000 Jewish freedmen to Sardinia in a kind of colonial deduction.[41] Throughout the late Republic, in fact, we see the Roman ambivalence towards the lowest stratum of the free population: they are despised but useful, the objects of insult and consideration at the same time. We must certainly not be misled by the obligatory sneers of the literary sources into taking a wholly negative view of Roman attitudes to the freedmen *en masse*, for all the numerous disadvantages under which they stood.

Neither must we overlook the mobility of individuals, again in aggregate probably much more important than that brought about by

35 Cic. *Leg. Agr.* II.70. 36 *SIG* 543.31–4. 37 Pedley 1990 (E 21A) ch. 7.
38 Brunt 1971 (A 16) 312–13. 39 Strab. VIII.6.23.
40 Suet. *Aug.* 42.3; Oros. VII.3.6. 41 Tac. *Ann.* II.85.

these spectacular measures. The Ithaca slave mentioned above was far from unique. Freedmen in particular were mobile, serving their patrons' needs, and some of the free-born too travelled quite widely. Epitaphs from all over the Mediterranean world commemorate people who were, at some time in their lives, part of the *plebs urbana*.[42] But commoner by far than moving to the ends of the empire was to move a little way out into the densely populated and comfortable periphery, either to the inner suburban zones or to the dormitory towns and resorts of Latium, Campania and Etruria. Such movements took place also of course on a seasonal basis, as those who could fled the scorching summer, taking with them dependents and employees, or as the opportunities for seasonal labour in the fields or at the ports presented themselves. The process will have been easier for those who were free-born, and this may be reflected in the relative paucity of funeral epitaphs relating to the *plebs ingenua*: their burials are to be sought at Nomentum and Setia, at Gabii and Lavinium. From the freedman world comes a classic example: Geganius Clesippus, an *apparitor* of Roman magistrates whose connexion with an old patrician family is casually attested, left Rome on his last journey to be buried in a grand tomb at Ulubrae overlooking the Pomptine Marshes.[43] The close ties between Rome and its region are apparent in the tombs of many others of his milieu too.

So the close interdependence of Rome and its region and the degree of mobility from one to the other are a key to resolving the old problem of the balance of free and freed in the city.[44] The problem arose from the balance in the thousands of Romans known to us from epitaphs – which means that it was in any case really about the composition of the *plebs* under the Empire, since Republican inscriptions are much less common. The proportion of those who were certainly freedmen to those who were certainly *ingenui* was remarkably high, and the conclusion, to which we have alluded, about the correlation between Greek *cognomina* and servile background made the apparent imbalance still more marked. Now that the *cogomina* are receiving detailed study, and the family relationships of the tombstones, as well as the mere names on them, are being considered, more of the free-born seem to be represented in this body of evidence, but the main factor is the mobility of *ingenui*, which took them for burial away from the urban nucleus, and so out of the purview of the sixth volume of the *Corpus Inscriptionum Latinarum*, whose confines have done more than even Aurelian's Wall to promote a mistakenly isolationist picture of the social life of Rome.

[42] Musicus, the imperial slave from Gaul who died in Rome under Tiberius and was mourned by his entourage of sixteen other slaves: *ILS* 1514 and *CAH* Vol. XI².

[43] *ILLRP* 696, and see Purcell 1983 (G 199) 140–1; Bodel 1989 (G 18).

[44] See above, n. 32.

It must remain a formal possibility, for all that, that there was in the late Republic a group of free-born Romans 'largely too poor to erect even the simplest epitaphs', a steadily dwindling group of families of 'Romani di Roma', poor, honest, proud, immemorial inhabitants of the city, struggling to preserve Romulean decency and, generation by generation, outnumbered and outclassed in means by the servile rabble. That view is largely founded on a passage of Tacitus which divides the *populus* into a 'sound section closely tied to the great families' and 'the filthy plebs habituated to circus and theatres';[45] the first group is glossed as including the clients and freedmen of those who had suffered death or exile for political reasons, and the second as being associated closely with the 'worst kind of slave and profligate'. Discussion of this passage properly belongs in a later volume, but simply quoting it should serve to show how hard it is to relate to anything in the epigraphic evidence. In particular, Tacitus is saying nothing about the means of any of these plebeians except the profligates, and his view of poverty is in any case hopelessly distorted by social distance. Nor is he putting all freedmen on one side: he would have agreed with Cicero that there could be, strange phrase, 'libertini optimates'.[46] Tacitus' remark is in fact ethical, not demographic, and more informative about the residual influence of the 'great families' at the end of their Julio-Claudian eminence than about the nature of the society of the populace.

In fact such a stratum of poor *ingenui* is not likely to have been a perennial aspect of the life of Rome. Economic poverty at Rome was not a state that an individual is likely to have endured for long, let alone a family: it was, if at all extreme, usually rapidly fatal. Ancient concepts of poverty, of being an *egens*, tend to reflect this; they are either status-based, like the analysis of Tacitus, or refer to the result of sudden calamity rather than to the prolonged state of economic poverty.[47] It is the social mobility of urban society that makes the long survival in Rome of families of poor *ingenui* unlikely. Stability was abnormal; the most needy went to the wall, and survival entailed betterment. Each 'generation' of freedmen was the parent of the next generation of the *plebs ingenua*. Families that survived several generations had excellent chances of considerably bettering their social position; that very often meant leaving Rome, and, as we saw, its epigraphic record. And that social mobility was the product of the privilege of Rome, the opportunities created by the enormous outpouring of every kind of resource there. Thus was created a state of social flux in which the families that survived underwent rapid fluctuations of fortune and status. And that is what the

[45] Tac. *Hist.* 1.4. [46] Cic. *Sest.* 97, and see Treggiari 1969 (G 247) 33.

[47] Poverty at Rome: Whittaker 1989 (G 260). Poverty as sudden calamity: MacMullen 1971 (G 149).

epigraphic record, fragmentary though it is, shows us faithfully: it is a picture of a complex society moving fast, a snapshot of a population in motion in every sense.[48] There are no great anomalous gaps: the hypothesis of the ancient but poverty-stricken burgher families of the *plebs ingenua* must yield to Occam's razor.

So the movements which we have been describing bound the city closely to what was around it; the study of the motive power that generated those exchanges of people must account for what was singular about the city in relation to its nearer and further periphery. The theme of the privilege of the city will be discussed most fully in section IV below; first it will be useful to consider some basic aspects of the setting of Rome and its social and economic consequences.

The ancient city was always intimately connected to its agricultural base; the physically highly urban forms of the town must not persuade us that it was firmly separated from the country. The characteristic activities of the town were concerned with the redistribution of the food produced by the country, and with the intensification of that production in various ways. The city demanded, and assisted the exploitation of, the nutritional resources of the area with which it was associated. The production of agricultural equipment is typical of the simplest level of that relationship: it is not strange that the elder Cato recommended the farmers of west central Italy to turn to Rome for some of their more specialized hardware.[49]

But the link soon passes beyond simple foodstuffs and their production into the area of more elaborate and luxurious products of agriculture and pastoralism – wine for pleasure as well as for nutrition, finer cereals instead of pulses and coarse grains, exotic fruits, oil for light and cleaning, and the range of secondary products including wool, leather and flax. The production of those and their processing and redistribution is another example of the co-operation and interdependence of the town and the countryside, and those activities were characteristic of the pre-industrial Mediterranean city. Rome itself was the most developed case of the interweaving of agricultural intensification and urban growth, drawing, as it came to, on the whole Mediterranean basin as well as transforming the economy of peninsular Italy.[50] So the relationship of Rome with its economic hinterland generated a characteristic range of service, processing, redistributive activities in the city, those associated above all with the retail unit known as the *taberna*. As Origen put it in a

[48] *ILS* 1926 provides a classic example of such upward social mobility seen across the ramifications of a family of the Augustan age.

[49] Cato *Agr.* 135.

[50] Nicolet in ch. 16 above, *passim*; Garnsey 1980 (G 98) 44, 'a continuum existed between agricultural and industrial employment'. Visual depictions of crafts on tombstones: Zimmer 1982 (G 266).

later period, it was through the contact of children with 'the typical base filth, woolworkers, cobblers, launderers'[51] that, according to its opponents, Christianity spread. Working with wool, leather, astringents and dyes, metal, clay, timber and straw, oil, wine, grain and fresh produce was not an accident of city life, an opportunity available to those who found themselves in a city, as a secondary thing; it was city life itself, the behaviour without which the city would not have been, except as a symbolic meeting-place of the elite.

Such retail activity, *kapēleia*, was normal in the Greek city too, and was early regarded as sordid on grounds of a simple economic logic: retail can only support the retailer through the addition of an arbitrary sum to the original 'real' price of a commodity, and that addition is essentially a lie, and dishonest by nature. Cicero passes on the idea in a Roman context: agriculture is respectable, but the workshop can contain no one of good character: 'neque quicquam ingenuum habere potest officina'.[52] Craftsmen were not good raw material for military excellence.[53] Also, the associations of the *taberna* were the very antithesis of elegance and civilization.[54] The notion that the redistributive labour of the retailer was a service deserving a wage seems not to have occurred to the thinkers of antiquity: a wage was, in any case, itself a source of shame, not a neutral social value at all.

The *taberna* was the setting of a whole range of activities of a retail-related kind, like service-industry and the sale of cooked food, not simply shopkeeping as we know it. Its centrality to the whole life of the Italian city and to the structure of urban populations in our period justifies making it the principal subject of the next section.

II

> Camillus found doors wide open, shops doing business with all their contents out on display. Each artisan was intent on his own work. He could hear the learning-games of the children, voice raised against voice. He saw that the streets were full of people, women and children wandering at will to do whatever they needed.[55]

The picture of happy Tusculum, unafraid of siege, is so conventional that it may be applied to any Roman town, but more particularly to Rome itself. In it, what is most specially characteristic of the Roman city landscape is the shop, the *taberna*. Rome was a city of shops, its people a nation of shopkeepers.

The great importance of the *taberna* has indeed been observed, but it

[51] Origen *Contra Celsum* 3.55. [52] Cic. *Off.* I.150–1; Treggiari 1969 (G 247) 89.
[53] Livy VIII.20.4. [54] Pliny *HN* XXXIII.49. [55] Livy VI.25.9.

has generally been thought of as a casual and contingent phenomenon, whereas it is actually an outward aspect of, and the key to understanding, the social structure of the city. Economically, of course, the prominence of the *taberna* need only mean that a large proportion of the population (and we include women as well as men in this statement; some of the Minturnae *collegia* are of women) was involved in the redistribution of the products of primary activities, above all of agriculture.[56] But *kapēleia* in the earlier Greek world was shopkeeping without the shops: it denoted an activity which could take place anywhere and was inherently mobile. Temporary booths were its usual setting, such as characterized the Athenian agora in the fifth and fourth centuries B.C.[57] The arrival of the *taberna*, the permanent, usually rectangular, module in which storage and negotiation took place besides the private life of the *tabernarius*, and its systematic arrangement within the city, are significant developments in ancient urban architecture. Its origin may lie in the buildings for specially important or valuable economic activities, like the Athenian mint, which began to appear in Greek cities at the end of the fifth century. The fringes of *tabernae* added to public buildings – Hellenistic *stoai* and the predecessors of the first basilicas at Rome – are a prototype, and the development in southern Italy of the specialized foodstuff bazaar, the *macellum*, which, through Campania and Rome, was diffused widely in the later Roman world, parallels the process closely at a slightly later date.[58] Somewhere in the ancestry of the concept a place must also be allotted to the notoriously luxurious market street of Capua in the third century B.C., the Seplasia, famous above all for its scent-makers.[59] The origins and spread of the type should be closely associated with the growth in the volume and variety of high-value luxury articles in Mediterranean trade over the period from the sixth to the third centuries: at Rome the *taberna*, however despised, never quite lost its association with high-value commodities – the Sacra Via was for long a market street of luxury *tabernae*, perhaps not so unlike the Seplasia – and the *tabernae* of the money-changer, the jeweller or the luxury clothier or perfumier remained important in the associations of the retail world for the Romans.[60] The arrival of the luxury *taberna* was accomplished at Rome by the age of the Hannibalic War, as recent work on the Forum has emphasized: Livy describes a fire between the Tiber and the Forum

56 *Tabernae*: Loane 1938 (G 147); Staccioli 1959 (B 318); Yavetz 1970 (G 263) 144–6. Women: Kampen 1981 (G 136). See also Skydsgaard 1976 (G 226).

57 Demosthenes 18 (*On the Crown*) 169.

58 Stoas: Coulton 1976 (B 282) 9–11; 85–8. They too began in the late fifth century B.C. See also Coarelli 1985 (B 277) 146; De Ruyt 1985 (B 285).

59 Asc. *Pis.* 10C.

60 Lipinsky 1961 (G 146); Panciera 1970 (B 214).

Boarium in 192 B.C. in which 'all the shops with wares of great value' were destroyed.[61]

From those beginnings the world of the *taberna* expanded dramatically. The evidence of commonplaces like Livy's Tusculum and the testimony of the archaeological record – the thousands of *tabernae* apparent on the Flavian and Severan Marble Plans of Rome and in the streets of Pompeii and Ostia and elsewhere – is unambiguous. Closely associated with the *taberna*, moreover, was a variant which needs some mention – the *officina*. This type was associated in the Romans' mind with craft or artisans' work – production, in other words, or what we might cautiously call 'industry'. The Greek term is *ergastērion*, and from the extraordinary impression produced on him by the sheer multiplicity of Rome's *tabernae* and *officinae* we find an author of the second century A.D. praising Rome as 'the common *ergastērion* of the whole world'.[62] This is the craftsmen's activity which we noted in Cato's *De Agricultura*, typical of the ancient Mediterranean town.

The steady expansion of the trade of the Mediterranean and the gradual enrichment of Italian society no doubt had an effect on the proliferation of the 'luxury-*taberna*' type here sketched, but neither process will quite explain how the *taberna* itself, as a specific form, became so universal as to be the hallmark of Roman urbanism.[63] On the one hand we have the fundamental activities of the ancient city, and on the other a tradition of utilitarian building associated with the protection of the most rarefied of those activities, the collection and redistribution among the higher elite of the requirements of the status-giving life of luxury. Nothing made it inevitable that the tanning or dyeing of the one should take place in the physical setting of the other, or that there should be any very intimate social relationship between the practitioners of the more mundane urban activities and those who carried on the equivalent pursuits at the more luxurious level.

By the last days of the Republic, however, the *tabernarii* had become almost synonymous with the urban population. Their closing of the *tabernae* and boycotting of the tribunals of the Forum in the chaos of the 40s B.C. was a formal protest to the triumvirs, a sign that the city was no longer functioning.[64] The view of the elite was not sympathetic;[65] it represented the *tabernarii* as the dregs of Rome. Cicero, in a passage which does much to confirm the insignificance of an alleged

[61] Livy XXXV.40; Coarelli 1977 (G 42). At that period the state, mainly through the censors, involved itself in the provision of premises for such activities: a novel mood, which did not last into the age of anxiety about plebeian activities, but was resumed in the Principate.

[62] Aristides *To Rome* 11.

[63] Boethius 1960 (B 264) chs. 2 and 4.

[64] App. *BCiv.* V.18.

[65] Yavetz 1970 (G 263) 144–6.

right-thinking, stalwart but needy, traditional *plebs ingenua* at Rome, blames the lack of support he experienced when he was driven into exile on the malice of the *populus Romanus* mustered in the city by his opponents: 'a populace which could only be gathered because the shops were ordered closed'. The genuine Roman people, to whom dominion of the world had properly been given, and who would have supported Cicero, would have been assembled not through the closure of the *tabernae* but through the emptying of the municipalities.[66] Examples of the same hostility to the *tabernarii* could easily be multiplied. Cicero himself provides the key to the elite's ambivalence about *tabernae*. A famous letter to Atticus[67] reveals how he owned a complex of *tabernae* at Puteoli which were in danger of collapse, but on which he need not fear making a loss because a local agent – himself a man of considerable substance in the town – would manage the redevelopment with sufficient care and acumen. It was the initiative of the Roman upper class which produced the proliferation of the *taberna*.

The inconsistency between the disgust of the orator and the enthusiasm of the investor was resolved through the institution of the freed slave. The Romans, as we saw, inherited from the Greeks their disdain for the range of urban activities which we have described as native to the urbanism of the ancient Mediterranean. Wages, profit, fees and salaries were all despised. Pliny the Elder remarks that the cultivation of madder and soapwort as dye plants for the cloth-business is extraordinarily profitable, as we would expect in the vicinity of a city like Rome – and therefore is something of which all are ignorant except for the 'filthy multitude':[68] Varro likewise claimed (despite the association of the fish-pond with the luxury villa) that commercial pisciculture was practised *apud plebem*.[69] The stock figure of the honest artisan was not familiar in ancient Rome: being hired to do a day's work made you a villain, as in the passage from Cicero's *De Domo*. Such pursuits had the taint of the servile, and they had in fact in the early days of the city been done by the slaves of individual households. The last three centuries B.C. saw the progressive emancipation of the urban producer from that household framework, no doubt above all because the scale of Rome's urban catchment area and the size of her population and the rate of interest of her wealthy all rose so dramatically; but he was not emancipated from the stigma.

So it was particularly through the institution of manumission that the involvement of the elite, actors in the play of power and landed wealth, with the backdrop of the *taberna* and its activities was maintained (though the role of other free *clientes* should not be overlooked). The history of the Roman *libertinus* is the history of the *plebs urbana* and the

[66] Cic. *Dom.* 89–90. [67] Cic. *Att.* XIV.9.1.
[68] Pliny *HN* XIX.47. [69] Varro *Rust.* III.17.

history of the city, socially, economically and culturally. The growth of the relative independence of freedmen is the central chapter in the story of the emancipation of the life of the city from the households of the elite, taking the former slave by successive stages (of which the action of the praetor Rutilius in about 118 B.C. in reducing the formal obligations (*operae*) of freedman to patron is an example)[70] to the degree of independence vividly shown in the first century A.D. by the business archive of a Puteoli firm found in the 'Agro Murecine' near Pompeii, in which we see freedmen taking responsibility for trading transactions of very high value.[71] It was not simply that by manumission the patron disembarrassed himself of an ageing slave and gained the purchase price of a new one. The new, ever more informal, economic relationships offered much wider possibilities for various sorts of gain (a possible example is the freedman of a consular family, perhaps of a consul of 106 B.C., operating as a *margaritarius* (pearl-dealer) on the Sacra Via in the Forum:[72] the capital involved for a *taberna* in this locality must have been the patron's rather than the client's in the first instance). It is a curious paradox that by allowing and encouraging the gradual emancipation of the freedman from formal ties with the manumittor, the slave-owning class of Rome (and we must not identify them with the freeborn high elite, since even many freedmen owned many slaves) actually came to gain far more than they had lost. The less acceptable result was inevitably that freedmen could and did aspire to ever higher status; and although the state was prepared to pass measures reducing their burdens, it actively discouraged their upward social mobility.[73] That inconsistency, characteristic of the late Republic, did much to aggravate social instability.

Throughout the Republic and early Empire the characteristic freedman, part of the world of the *tabernarii*, preserved both the stigma of the servile associations of his employment and with it the minutely subdivided tasks characteristic of slave households. The division of labour was therefore intense at Rome, where 160 kinds of jobs are attested by the haphazard epigraphic evidence, as opposed to 100 or so in the far better known cities of late mediaeval western Europe: not primarily an economic phenomenon, but a reflection of the social origins of the *taberna*-world.[74] So the Romans themselves recognized that there had

[70] D.38.2.1.1 (Ulpian); Watson 1967 (F 295) 228.

[71] Bove 1979 (B 135).

[72] *ILLRP* 797; Hopkins 1978 (A 53) 115–31; Garnsey 1980 (G 98) and 1981 (G 99) for the relationship between free and slave artisan labour; D'Arms 1984 (G 51).

[73] Treggiari 1969 (G 247); Fabre 1981 (G 65); Waldstein 1986 (F 288).

[74] Division of labour: Hopkins 1978 (G 123); Treggiari 1980 (G 248); E. Patlagean, *Pauvreté économique et pauvreté sociale à Byzance* (The Hague, 1976); Park 1975 (G 186); Maxey 1975 (G 155). Much of the evidence is from the Imperial age, but extrapolation back to the Republic is justified by

only been barbers operating at Rome since the beginning of the third century B.C., and traced the moment, approximately, when the baking of bread became a trade rather than a domestic service.[75] Here again we are witnessing not just the dislocation of a servile occupation from its original setting, but the creation of a wider market for the produce. From roughly the age of the Hannibalic War a change took place in the dietary regime of the urban plebs which has been seen as a revolution; as well as the diffusion of higher quality bread it involved the much more widespread drinking of wine, and we may add the intensification of the agriculture of the urban periphery, creating a growing zone of market gardens.[76]

The importance of this change for the life of the plebs was more than a matter of mere consumption (though it must be seen as one of the improvements in the background standard of living discussed in sections III–IV below). The economy of wine production, with its seasonal demand for labour, offered many opportunities to the casual labourer; as quantity came to be more in demand than quality, the smallest property became a suitable site for the growing of at least one vine. The *tabernarii* could grow their own stock; the *taberna* was a constituent unit of a new agriculture, not just of the new retail and production network: indeed it is in many ways almost a term for a kind of relationship between labour and production more or less concerned with agriculture. So with the market gardens too, the people who hired them or owned them and who sold the produce in the *tabernae* of the *macella* and other retail points, lived very like those whom they fed but who were involved in crafts or services for more of their time. It is therefore not surprising to find a steady expansion of the intensive horticulture which brought the huge profits to Pliny's dye-plant growers, from the second century B.C. through to the early Imperial period; nor that once again the really wealthy were in on the act. Cicero wrote to his freedman Tiro:

> Put Parhedrus up to making his own bid for the tenancy of the garden – that's the way to get the market gardener himself moving. That criminal Helico used to hand over a thousand in cash and what did he get? A plot without sheltered beds, built drain, a proper boundary-wall, or a shed. Are we going to let the man laugh at our handing out so much on the improvements? Make it hot for him as I am with Motho: I'm getting every last petal out of these flower-arrangements.[77]

Garlands for the festivals and ceremonies integral to plebeian life at Rome were produced and marketed through the smallholding *taberna*

evidence for trades at Capua (Frederiksen 1984 (A 35) ch. 13), Minturnae (Johnson 1935 (B 298)) and Praeneste (*ILLRP* 101–10). The view here builds on the suggestions of Skydsgaard 1976 (G 226). See also Jongman 1988 (G 133) 184–6.

[75] Barbers: Pliny *HN* VII.211, cf. Varro *Rust.* II.11.10. Bakers: Pliny *HN* XIII.107.

[76] Wine: Tchernia 1986 (G 238). Market gardening: Carandini 1988 (G 33), who, however, overemphasizes the elite. See also Nicolet in ch. 16 above, p. 616.

[77] Cic. *Fam.* XVI.18.

network; freedman moved against freedman in a great everlasting wrangle whose motive power often came in the end, as here, from the most important men in Rome.

Predictably, also, the new alimentary habits found their distinctive location in the physical setting of the *tabernae*. As the eating of baker's bread and the drinking of wine became an ever more important ingredient in the ordinary existence of the people of the city of Rome, this alimentary revolution took place in the world of the *taberna*,[78] which became the basic source of daily staples; 'bread and wine from the barman, straight out of the jar'.[79] *Tabernae* included cookshops, wine bars, places of resort, to such an extent that those were the functions associated with the very word *taberna* when it passed into the post-classical languages. Those lowly functions too in the end lined the pockets of the elite.

It is scarcely surprising that freed slaves stood thus between the servile but lucrative activities of the ancient city and the high standards of the nobility which depended upon them, and, given the paradoxes on which we have remarked, that their position was extremely ambiguous. On the one hand the language of disgust as we have quoted it from Cicero and Pliny: on the other the concession from Cicero himself that there are 'good types amongst the freedmen' (*optimates libertini*), and the almost affectionate persona of the 'busy freedman' the *navus libertinus*,[80] patronizing but not hostile. A certain amused sanction for the weakness of the *tabernarius* milieu is found; the commonest Greek cognomen by far among the freedmen of Rome is Philargyrus, 'lollylover'.[81] The behaviour of the freedmen themselves was ambiguous; they can be found taking a perverse pride in the shamefulness of their activities, advertising them vividly on tombstones like that of the great contract-baker Eurysaces, or, outside Rome, that of Caprilius Timotheus who grew rich on exchanging wine for slaves, clearly without shame.[82]

Timotheus reminds us that the world of the *taberna* was not unique to Rome. Not only do we find it even earlier in Campania (where the first examples of the '*taberna*-tombstones' occur), but it is the hallmark of this set of economic and social relations wherever they are found in the Mediterranean. On the way to Ithaca where the *unguentarius* set up his stone[83] was the flourishing line of ports of the Epirot coast; the Republican inscriptions of towns like Buthrotum closely resemble those of Rome.[84] And these are all on their way to the economic centres of the

[78] Kleberg 1957 (G 137). [79] Cic. *Pis.* 67.

[80] Cic. *Sest.* 97; *Comment. Pet.* 29. [81] Solin 1982 (G 228) 755.

[82] Eurysaces: *ILLRP* 805. Timotheus: Duchène 1980 (B 149).

[83] See above, n. 33.

[84] Epirus: Purcell 1987 (G 201); Buthrotum: Cabanes 1986 (B 139) 151, with cults of Stata Mater and the Lares Vici.

East; Corinth in its new Caesarian freedman incarnation at the end of the Republic, and, earlier, Delos. In the West too, at New Carthage or Narbo, the same atmosphere can be detected.[85] But all this was at its most intense in Rome; without Rome, indeed, many of the other communities would have lacked a prototype and the central links in the economic chains to which they belonged could not have functioned. It was, moreover, at Rome that the life of the *taberna* and the *officina*, the cookshops and the stews, made possible a climate of public agitation central to the informal politics of the time; it was a defining characteristic of Rome to have developed to such an extent a distinctive and elaborate social behaviour of low-status people, what one might call a 'low life'.[86]

The ancient writers who comment with distaste on the socially extended immorality are not unaware that it derives in the end from Rome's supereminent position, that it is a symbol, if a repugnant one, of the status of the city that has conquered the world. First, the whole city can be seen as a great household, an enormous cluster of operations devoted to the maintenance of the luxury of the elite: the luxury-*taberna* belongs in this context. Secondly, arising from this, the *tabernae* and their produce are there to further the typically aristocratic activity of benefaction. Without the existence of *macellum* and *officinae*, how would the Roman magnate stage the lavish triumphal *epulum* (banquet), or equip the spectacular aedilician games? Thirdly, arising in turn from this, just as the functions of retail and production, when emancipated from the household, like their practitioners, take on a life of their own, so the diffusion of the *taberna*-world and its benefits outwards and downwards from the service of the elite comes to be a kind of unplanned general benefaction or 'liturgy' of the all-owning, all-spending wealthy to the privileged city-community where they belong. The provision of quite good wine, of good cheap bread, of the social life of the cookshops, of the services of barbers, cobblers, dyeshops, fullers, cheap-clothes-shops and so on is part of the general advantage of being a Roman of the capital.

Thus the proliferation of the *taberna* was organically connected with other aspects of the life of the city; with the provision of subsidized or free grain (which promoted the system in its turn by encouraging the growth of manumission),[87] the multiplication of spectacles and entertainments and the escalation in their cost; and the spectacular investment in the beautification of the city with more and more audacious and opulent architectural projects. But it is perhaps in the close parallel with

[85] Geography of these socio-economic phenomena: Fabre 1981 (G 65) maps. Reflected also in the distribution of the *tesserae nummulariae*, *ILLRP* 987–1063, see Nicolet in ch. 16 above, p. 633.

[86] For the informal politics see Vol. x², ch. 15.

[87] Dion. Hal. *Ant. Rom.* IV.24.5; Dio XXXIX.24.1.

the changes in housing of the living (and to some extent of the dead) that most interest lies. In the development of the multi-storey apartment block, the *insula*, as in the spread of the *taberna*, we see systematic management for profit of phenomena which were growing naturally as the city grew, and it is perhaps better to regard *insula* and *taberna* (and the strip-house which combined elements of both and was to have so long a history in Italy) as parallel and interwoven urbanistic tendencies rather than allot primacy. The ordered rows of systematically laid out *tabernae* are not so basic or immemorial a phenomenon: both *taberna* and *insula* share a common origin in the chaotic labyrinths of huts and shanties which characterized the city in the middle Republic but were only a memory in Varro's day: Festus writes that 'an *adtibernalis* is a dweller in one of a set of *tabernae*. That this was the oldest kind of dwelling at Rome may be deduced from the foreign peoples who to this day dwell in *aedificia tabulata* [buildings of planks]. This is why the structures in military camps even when they are made of leather are still called *tabernacula*.'[88] The *taberna* remained a dwelling as well as a place of employment.[89]

In *insula* as well as *taberna* the plebeian was integrated fully and in a complex way into the social structure of the whole city; for the *insula* was an expensive and artificial construction, and the tenant was expected to pay rent, often substantial.[90] We are wrong to regard the flats in the *insulae* as intolerable slums. They were intended to be an extension of the relative solidity and comfort of the houses of the independently wealthy, and were indeed often contiguous with them. That they were often disastrously jerry-built or in terrible condition did not, probably, make them less pleasant than the dwellings of the rural poor; and at least they had the advantage of the urban location with all the privileges of status and benefaction which that entailed. It is certain that by the Empire, at least, such blocks were by no means the preserve of the poorest. Neither should they be seen as a new way of housing people who had previously lived otherwise: just as the *tabernae* were the location of new activities by a new social group, not the scene of freedmen doing jobs which had once been done by a now dispossessed free poor, so the *insulae* were the dwelling-places of the new social strata and corresponded to nothing in the Rome that went before. In the world of the dead the advent of the tomb-reliefs and the funerary self-expression which goes with them provides a parallel.[91] It is noteworthy that all these phenomena developed side by side in the last years of the Republic: the reliefs and

[88] Festus p. 11L. See Boethius 1960 (B 264) ch. 4 and Vol. x², ch. 15.

[89] Varro *Ling.* v.160; Hor. *Odes* I.4.

[90] Frier 1980 (G 82) 39–47; Frier 1977 (G 81); Hermansen 1978 (G 118).

[91] Zanker 1975 (B 262); Purcell 1987 (G 202).

tombstones which reveal the *taberna*-world to us spread from Campania in the age of Cicero, and it is at that period that we begin to hear of major investment in the *taberna* and the *insula*.[92]

The whole system of interlocking concerns, retail, patronage, profit, rent, gift, trade, the worlds of house, work, recreation and death, binding everyone in Rome, elite and dependent – *honestiores* and *humiliores*, in a sense, already in the age of Scipio Aemilianus – constituted an integrated society in which everyone had a place. There was a very great range of status and prestige in these places, in these social niches; a continuum stretching from the senator to the slave.[93] Only the interdependence we have been describing could have been capable of producing so cohesive a system, in which there were no classes in any of the usual senses of the term, no major independent and alienated groups. Being unused to such a society, scholars have looked (in vain) for signs of a heavily stratified system at Rome; hence the major problems in interpreting the plebs: its poorer sections do not behave as a lower class, it is impossible to talk of a middle class, and the often postulated group of ancestral Roman plebeians of slender means is, as we saw, a myth.

What cement binds this system? What kinds of cohesion are there in the relationships we have put forward? The tie of ownership and ex-ownership, with all the duties and obligations provided under the law of slavery and manumission, is the most important of those mentioned thus far;[94] but there are two other central aspects of the relationship. One is at heart economic; the other can be described as essentially political.

The relations of superior to inferior at Rome during this period were never simply those of social obligation: the economic aspect was no less important. Such relationships, whether between free-born and free-born, free-born and freed or even free-born and slave, fundamentally depended on the lubrication of money. This is why the *taberna* and the *insula* were of such significance; they were the physical expression of a range of essentially economic relationships. The simplest of them is of course payment for services rendered, either through wages or, more often through contract payments. The Juvenalian picture of an idle populace interested in nothing but *panem et circenses* (bread and spectacles) is a most unreliable basis for a reconstruction of the life of the Roman plebs at any period: the multitude wanted and needed to buy food and it was a concern of the state to provide them with the opportunity to do so.[95] The world of the *tabernae* reflects this; the poor of Rome worked for their

[92] Frier 1980 (G 82) 121–6. Note the implication of Diod. XXXI.18.2 that high-rent apartments were already to be found in the middle of the second century B.C.

[93] Purcell 1983 (G 199).

[94] Treggiari 1969 (G 247) 68–91.

[95] Tac. *Hist.* IV.38; Suet. *Vesp.* 18; Brunt 1980 (G 26); Le Gall 1971 (G 145).

daily sustenance and earned most of it; the generosity of the state and the great was not intended to fulfil any practical need, and only served to lighten the burden of the need to earn, not to remove it. So, in a great variety of employments, the men and women of the city earned a proportion of the money accumulated by the political elite from the empire. 'You've had eight different job opportunities: you've been a barman, you've been a baker; you've tried farming, you've worked in the mint, you've been a salesman, now you're a pot seller – one more job will make 69!'[96] That list reminds us once again that one feature of the world of the *taberna* and *officina* was production. It is only on the extreme, literal interpretation of the demand for *panem et circenses* that the view that Rome was a Great Wen, an all-consuming parasite, is based, and that view sits uneasily with the image of Rome the 'common workshop of the world'. The inhabitants of Rome produced very substantial quantities of finished goods, and the fact that the economic and social conditions of their employment could not be much more different from the manufacturing activities that began in Europe in the early modern period should not obscure the fact that, within the economy of west central Italy at least, Rome did not consume wholly without return.[97]

Not that we intend to overemphasize the technically productive aspects of the employment of the *plebs libertina*. As would be expected, given their basically servile origins, many were devoted to what we could label 'service employments'. The *familiae urbanae* of the great and their libertine peripheries, forming a distinctive section of the plebs, if not a major subdivision, should be remembered in this context: in the late Republic they were in the process of gathering size and importance as the heads of the great political *domus* gained power and status in the increasingly exclusive political game. The process culminated in the enormous *familiae* of the grandees of the Augustan period (and, beyond the period which is primarily our concern here, in the *familia Caesaris* itself).[98] The *operae* which were, at least in theory, owed by many a freed person to his or her *patronus* or *patrona* kept the domestic connexion alive and could substantially reduce the independence of the former slave. That limited freedom made the freedman an excellent agent of the patron, reliable and answerable for his actions but not so closely associated with the patron as to infect him with the taint of ignoble

96 Graffito, *NSA* 1958, 128 no. 268 (slightly adapted in translation), from the *Praedia Iuliae Felicis* (II, VII, 10) at Pompeii.

97 The idea of Rome as the 'Consumption City' goes back to A. Sombart and Max Weber: see Finley 1973 (A 31) ch. 5; Hopkins 1978 (G 123); P. Garnsey and R. P. Saller, *The Roman Empire, Economy, Society and Culture* (Berkeley, 1987) 58–9. The alternative view of Rome as part of a much more complex economy, locally within west central Italy and in the world at large, is discussed at greater length in *CAH* Vol. XI².

98 See Roddaz and Fabre 1982 (G 214).

employment. Hence the involvement of the freedman in business, trade and finance, not restricted of course to the city of Rome but distributed Mediterranean-wide according to the geography of the economic interests of the Roman elite. Here again the years after the Rutilian reform of *c.* 118 B.C. were the formative period.[99]

For various reasons the authority of the *patronus* might be limited, or non-existent; in some circumstances a freedman might have no patron, or cease to have one.[100] So the economic activities of freedmen were to some extent conducted for their own benefit, and not all the Roman world of work had its impetus in the greed of the elite, important motive force though that was. At the humblest level it is clear that there was an extensive labour market at Rome: people were available for hire as general labourers, and *diurnae operae* were a feature of daily life. Being generally available for such labour, *conducticius*, was recognized as one of the most demeaning options for the free: that reflects its commonness.[101]

Of all the activities of such labourers, the one most easily overlooked by us who live in the post-industrial world is probably porterage: fetching and carrying at a moment's notice, the very pulse-rate of a huge conurbation like Rome, above all one where most streets were too narrow or steep for vehicles (and from the late Republic it was only at night that those were allowed in the city).[102] Porterage, and the running of boats on the river, were activities actually generated by the city and part of its day-to-day existence.

Again, the physical maintenance of the fabric of the city was a never-ending process, one of the characteristic activities of the ancient town; self-regeneration was part of its nature. So the various professions associated with building were of enormous importance.[103] The dependence of the city's population on that sort of job can probably be retrojected, from the times when it is best attested, a considerable way back into the Republic. It is noteworthy that the contractor for work on Q. Cicero's Palatine house could not make satisfactory progress with the work because of the distracting effect of Clodius' politics.[104] There was always some kind of building to do; but two kinds need particular comment. First, the great public buildings sponsored by the upper classes did most to occupy very large numbers; no figures survive from the ancient city, but the modest restoration of a limited section of the ancient aqueduct system of Rome in the sixteenth century, renamed as the Acqua Felice, occupied 2,000 men for three years, rising at times to

99 Garnsey 1981 (G 99); Fabre 1981 (G 65) esp. maps 1–3; D'Arms 1984 (G 51).

100 Garnsey 1981 (G 99).

101 Treggiari 1980 (G 248).

102 Table of Heraclea, *Bruns* 18, lines 56–61 (*FIRA* I no. 13).

103 See Nicolet in ch. 16 above, pp. 626–7.

104 Cic. *QFr.* II.2.2.

4,000.[105] Fluctuations in the availability of these jobs have been blamed by some scholars for outbreaks of discontent, and it is remarkable, in fact, how regular the provision of this sort of work actually seems to have been.[106] Secondly, the increase in the two distinctive forms of private building, the great *domus* and *suburbana* of the wealthy and the investment-architecture of the *taberna* and the *insula*, provided another link in the network of the life of the city by keeping employment up in times when public building was not booming. The increasing solidity and structural uniformity of those buildings, public or private, underneath their ornamental veneer, is a sign of the coherence of the labour force on which they depended; not by any means entirely slaves, but rather the ordinary city populations of Italy.[107] The characteristic architecture of urban Italy from the age of the Gracchi to the baked-brick revolution of the time of Nero is strongly symptomatic of contemporary urban society, and was produced directly by the economic forces which animated that society.

The association of builders, *collegium fabrorum*, was one of those which the Romans believed to be of immemorial antiquity, and which during the last years of the Republic stood the best chance of immunity from the legislation with which the nervous authorities sought to curb the power of such associations.[108] It is the clearest example of how the characteristic associations of the city populace originated in the basic conditions of the functioning of the city. But in general the ancient *collegia* of Rome are not easy to see in the historical record of the late Republic, though we may guess that they took on new roles and acquired a new meaning with the general evolution of the life of the city during the second century and particularly in its last decade. What we can see more clearly is the parallel emergence of less formal associations of the economically active, predominantly freedman, plebs. As in the case of tomb-reliefs and architectural forms, it is in Campania that those new developments are first visible, and we are probably right to deduce that they originated there. In the organizations of freedman *magistri* at Capua and the more professionally organized and slightly later equivalent at Minturnae[109] we

[105] J. Delumeau, *Vie économique et sociale de Rome dans la seconde moitié du XVIe siècle* (Paris, 1959).

[106] Coarelli 1977 (G 42); M. K. Thornton, 'Julio-Claudian building programs', *Historia* 35 (1986) 28–44; and see Nicolet in ch. 16 above, pp. 626–7.

[107] Torelli 1980 (G 244), maintaining that alongside the characteristic agricultural changes in the late Republic these new approaches to building are part of a general and highly significant shift in production relations.

[108] Nervousness: Asc. *Pis.* 6–7C. The heyday of the *collegium fabrorum* was, however, in the Principate: Pearse 1980 (B 217) and discussion in *CAH* Vol. XI². For the Republic: Gabba 1984 (G 93).

[109] *ILLRP* 724–46, with parallels at Praeneste. Frederiksen 1984 (A 35) ch. 13; for Minturnae: Johnson 1935 (B 298). Nuanced view of the position of these organizations between public and private: Flambard 1983 (G 69).

see the beginnings of the rise of new social forms to match the new urban conditions, assisted in the case of Capua by the absence, since the Hannibalic War, of traditional political institutions which might have blighted the efflorescence of new types of behaviour. This behaviour is, in fact, strikingly parapolitical: the freedmen are organized on quasi-political lines and act in imitation of the elite, dedicating public buildings under the protection of the traditional gods of the community. Less traditional is their social openness and potentially subversive character; in Capua their euergetism, if not illegal, was certainly a bold gesture of defiance on the part of the old rival of Rome, now *urbs trunca*; and at Minturnae the boards of *magistri* included slaves and, in several cases, women (the *taberna*-world was no male domain).[110] During the first century similar institutions appear in other Italian towns, such as Pompeii,[111], linked to *vici* and their focal crossroads, the *compita*; at Sena Gallica the workmen, *opifices*, formed a recognizable sub-group of the town's population.[112] They were often devoted to prominent local cults (at Tusculum to Castor and Pollux),[113] especially to Mars and Mercury, and their religious organization was carried over into their direct heir, the formal and stereotyped institution of the *collegia Augustalium*.[114]

Similarly at Rome the ancient associations of Capitolini and Mercuriales and Luperci fulfilled something of the same role; the Mercuriales at least were certainly connected with business.[115] The *apparitor* Clesippus, whom we have encountered, was *magister Capitolinus* and *magister Lupercus*.[116] We should not play down their status; Cicero alludes to the shameful fawning of a Roman *eques* whom the combined Capitolini and Mercuriales expelled in the crisis of the corn supply of 56 B.C.:[117] to him at least membership was significant. Despite such allusions our knowledge is frustratingly incomplete: but it is clear that it was on the activities and ever-shifting aims of those associations, as manifested in established festivals like the Compitalia, which were subverted by the new behaviour, that much of the characteristic political violence of the late Republic centred.[118]

These groups appear in our evidence because they were politically important. The way has been long, but we are now in a position to discuss the other means by which the plebs 'earned' the favour shown it by the elite political faction. Not that it would be proper to separate the activities of the populace sharply into 'economic' and 'political': the dichotomy is simply an investigative convenience. There were many

[110] Women's employments: Kampen 1981 (G 136) 130–7.

[111] *ILLRP* 763. [112] *ILLRP* 776. [113] *ILLRP* 59. [114] Ostrow 1985 (B 213).

[115] Livy II.27, cf. Mommsen at *CIL* I² 1004.

[116] *ILLRP* 696. [117] Cic. *QFr.* II.6 (5).

[118] *Capitolini*: Coarelli 1984 (C 184). *Compitalia*: Flambard 1981 (G 68); Lintott 1968 (A 62) 80ff.

points of overlap and cross-fertilization between the two worlds, and the creation, partly accidental, partly intentional, of the half-dependent, economically active, Roman populace was both an economic phenomenon and a part of the evolution of Roman politics. Work, membership of the *taberna*-world, was one of the ways in which a person aspired to a social niche. Employment was a form of social inclusion.[119] The relationships of the *taberna* and the *insula*, of the tomb-relief and the *collegium*, of the *familia* and the neighbourhood, had their final counterpart in the *comitia*, the *contio* and the riot.

III

In a famous passage of the *Commentariolum Petitionis*, the purported letter of advice directed at Cicero by his brother to help him in his election campaign of 64 B.C., the author describes the complex organizations which make up the *plebs urbana*, and on which depend the hopes of the candidate seeking election.[120] What we know of those social bodies does not suggest that their existence and political behaviour were necessarily immemorial, despite the fact that we hear of many of them in a literary tradition that is ultimately antiquarian and therefore concerned especially with arcane usages and inexplicable rites. Cases like the famous *equus October*, the observances of the *Septimontium* and the layout of the shrines of the *Argei* may seem to have ancient traditions behind them, but even in such cases we must not make the assumption that 'peculiar' equals old,[121] for in both religion and politics innovation was natural. With the social changes which we have described the neighbourhoods of the city changed shape, size, composition and relative importance. There were numerous old units, *vici*, *pagi*, *montes*, of different sizes and shapes, which, like the ancient *collegia*,[122] offered new advantages to politicians at the end of the Republic, e.g. to Clodius or, on a larger scale, Augustus, both astute at building new institutional forms on traditional foundations. The *curiae*, for example, a very ancient division of the plebs, survived as entities in the Augustan age: their members did not understand what they were, but they provided some sense of belonging.[123]

[119] Patlagean (see n. 74).

[120] *Comment. Pet.* 30. The work is likelier to be a learned exercise than a genuine letter, but is probably based on good late Republican sources: Henderson 1950 (B 44); David *et al.* 1973 (B 25).

[121] North 1976 (H 93) and ch. 19 below.

[122] Flambard 1981 (G 68) stresses, against Waltzing 1895–1900 (G 254) that the *vici*, like the *pagi* and *montes*, were essentially collegiate. See also Crook 1986 (B 20) on *pagani* and *montani* and their association with new arrangements for the urban infrastructure as it came under increasing strain: they saw to some aspects of the distribution of channelled water.

[123] Ov. *Fast.* II.527–32.

Some of the *montes* and *pagi*, whether or not they were the linear descendants of the first pre-urban hilltop village communities of Rome, can be seen taking on new life in the first century B.C., administering their property, enjoying benefactions and setting up inscriptions like autonomous political bodies.[124] They are indeed the 'public meetings, almost Councils' ('conventicula, quasi concilia'), of Cicero's speech *De Domo*,[125] and have a prominent place in the subdivided polity of the advice in the *Commentariolum Petitionis*.

A subdivided polity was the natural consequence of the social and eonomic conditions we have described. The transience of the Roman urban population made of its subdivisions similarly temporary associations which formed and dissolved relatively frequently, changing their character and importance. But the associations of the more or less accidentally juxtaposed individuals had a vital part to play in conferring a social – and political – identity on the flowing population ('lieux de passage, d'intégration progressive à la cité officielle').[126] More than mere 'friendly societies', they provided structures of belonging which were the only means of protection against the insecurity of life in the anonymous crowds of the perilous urban environment.

The associative tendency is thus more significant than the classification of the forms it took, which could not but be highly labile. Hence the new life of the probably immemorial *montes* and *pagi*. The *vici*, another subdivision ('parts of the urban continuum defined by district or communications for the sake of convenience', Festus called them),[127] seem first to have acquired political prominence during the troubles of the 80s B.C. – too much prominence, since it was found necessary to repress their principal form of self-expression, the 'crossroad games' (*ludi compitalicii*), during the 60s. It was as vehicles for corporate activity of this kind that the *vici* were important, and we should not see them as 'wards' like the parish-based divisions of mediaeval western cities, or as the transplanted rural villages whose immiscible identities created the cellular fabric of the Islamic metropolis.[128] They were closer in character to the less topographically identifiable associations, the *collegia*, which bound together those who shared a cult or a craft, many of which arose naturally out of the economy of the *taberna* as did the *vici*, *pagi* and *montes* out of the physical form of the city. They naturally served as the means of expression of discontent, but their purpose was to provide labels for the ever-changing social groups, as we can see in the passion with which they fought the repression which would dissolve their cohesion – such as the authorities' attempts to destroy the worship of Isis which was central

[124] *ILLRP* 698–9. [125] Cic. *Dom.* 74.

[126] Flambard 1981 (G 68) 166; and see n. 118 above. [127] Festus 502L.

[128] Frederiksen 1976 (G 79) for the various meanings of *vicus*.

to the existence of the Capitolini.[129] The zeal for new associations can be seen in the cult of Stata Mater, which was created for a statue left untouched in a devastating fire in the early first century B.C.; a *vicus* was named for the cult, a potent reflection of one of the perennial anxieties of the life of the city.[130] The confidence implied in the *Commentariolum* was inappropriate; such organs were of populace, not plebs, and they were not pawns of the elite political chessboard.

In this flux *plebs* and elite are mixed inseparably. Although some sites at Rome for aristocratic houses were much more sought after than others, places of political significance like Sacra Via or Forum, or of natural amenity like Tiber bank or hilltop, that did not create urban zoning according to wealth. The wealthy were always surrounded by the lower in status; indeed by the lowest, since they could not but live alongside their numerous slaves, and their part in the tight social net described in section II also meant that they had frequent contact with the *taberna*-world. The rich houses were fringed with such properties to let. Topographical juxtaposition thus gave the houses of the elite a place in the social subdivisions of the city, expressed also through the relationships of their inhabitants. The contiguity of the rich with the low in status is crucial to understanding the vertical structures of patronage and economic and social interest that bound them together, and the political behaviour that resulted.[131]

The character of the subdivisions of the *plebs* resulted in part from their connexions with a range of patrons: in a *collegium* the connexion might be mainly economic; in a *vicus*, property or topographical context; in some cases the link was manumission, as with Sulla and the younger, fitter slaves of his victims, the 10,000 'Cornelii', whom he freed, 'so many that they actually made a *collegium*',[132] or with the great households of the Augustan age. However based, the relationship was not simply passive or static. The political activities of the plebeians, in *comitia*, *contio* or riot, were integral to the way the city worked, and were always, like all aspects of the life of the urban population, motivated by the demands for allegiance by those higher up the edifice of patronage. Violent intervention in public events usually had a political point, just as the public display itself did; witness the neat response of the *plebs* to the snub to Lucullus by Q. Caecilius, his equestrian client, in leaving him out of his will: they smashed up his funeral.[133] Politicians who suffered from the collective action of the urban populace would raise the spectre of the collapse of all public order – freedmen were often blamed for fire-raising and general disorder – but in practice Roman urban society showed a remarkable stability; the violence of Roman politics owed more to the

[129] Coarelli 1984 (C 184). [130] Festus 317L. [131] Veyne 1979 (G 251) 273–4.
[132] Asc. *Corn.* 75C. [133] Val. Max. VII.8.5.

politicians than to any popular ideology of class-hatred.[134] However, in the turbulent conditions of the late Republic the instability of the groupings and the ease with which they were manipulated greatly increased, hence Augustus' careful attempt to crystallize the framework of the popular organizations to a greater extent, giving them eras, magistrates, patrons, a legal role, in an attempt to fix the flux somewhat and calm its political destructiveness.

This threatening potential was already observable when Appius Claudius Pulcher confronted Scipio Aemilianus over the election to the censorship of 142 in the Forum in the midst of a throng of 'men of low birth and former slaves, familiar with the Forum and quite capable of getting together a mob and having their way on any subject whatsoever thanks to its din and determination'.[135] Pulcher's attack, invoking the horror of the shade of Aemilianus' father at the indignity of relying on the support of 'Aemilius the *praeco* [huckster] and Licinius Philonicus the *publicanus* [contractor]', depends on the relative novelty of such behaviour. Not that such people were the lowest of the low in either status or means: this is a nice case of distortion of the long perspective of diminishing plebeian statuses from the viewpoint of the higher aristocracy. But it is the mob that they could control which is truly significant here: the ever-growing population of Rome, with new political consequences for everyone. It is no coincidence that that is the time when, after a long interval, 'we find evidence of increased readiness by the tribunes to adopt a popular role'.[136] Part of the cause for that no doubt lay in the injustices of recruitment and the domestic and overseas miseries of the poor: but the potential power of the newly growing populace and its links with the elite were the main cause. The two types of explanation are closely connected in any case, as we shall see.

In the same period the formal roles played by the *populus* in Roman politics were removed from the constraints of space in the old circular *comitium* in front of the senate-house. From 145 the passing of legislation, from after 142 the regular election of magistrates, and from the time of C. Gracchus *contiones* were all moved to less restricted venues – legislation and the *contiones* to the main body of the Forum, which was now an architectural setting of some grandeur, thanks to the censors of the early part of the century – and the election of magistrates to the Campus Martius.[137] The simple need to accommodate greater numbers was the obvious pretext for those changes, but it is hard not to see in them an appreciation, on the part of popular politicians, of the potential for a new kind of democracy. Such innovations transformed the formal power of

[134] Hahn 1975 (G 112); Lintott 1968 (A 62) esp. ch. 12; Brunt 1974 (G 23); Vanderbroeck 1987 (C 279).
[135] Plut. *Paull.* 38.4; see also *Praec. reip. ger.* 14 (*Moralia* 810B).
[136] Brunt 1971 (A 17) 65.
[137] Coarelli 1985 (B 277) 11–21.

the swelling population and gave a great stimulus to that growth of its informal power which Pulcher had perceived.

The new complexity of the organization of the *plebs* resisted the maintenance of social control along the lines which had characterized the middle Republic, and a new relationship was slow to develop. The impossibility of relying on the older forms of *coercitio* was clear by the end of the second century, and the forms which were to replace it were only then nascent.[138] In the gap the plebs became, and remained into the Empire (as chapter 16 of Volume x will show), a political force of a new kind. For all the parallels drawn, at this time and later, by politically acute historians and historically minded politicians, this was a very different kind of popular politics from that which succeeded in the Struggle of the Orders.[139] Rome was no longer a city state. The numbers involved reflected that: the walk-out of the plebs as a protest, successful in Rome's early history, was hardly an option in the age of the Gracchi. The economic and social world described in section II had come into being, more intricate and mutable than anything in the fifth and fourth centuries. The controversies of the second half of the second century are described in detail in other chapters. Tiberius and Gaius Gracchus, Servilius Glaucia and Appuleius Saturninus certainly took advantage of the new social situation to attempt a readjustment of the constitution of Rome definitely in favour of the democratic element. The proposed changes concerned the most basic institutions of the Roman state. The mood was rather different from that of the half-century which followed the Social War, and although the popular politicians of the second century served as precedents for those of the age of Cicero and Caesar, and the populace acquired aspirations and self-confidence which formed the necessary foundation for its later self-assertiveness, we should distinguish the two epochs. By the early Empire, if not by the Augustan period, it was held that it was *after* the Social War that the aristocracy had withered while the plebs gained in power – as was allegedly portended by the relative health of the patrician and plebeian myrtle-bushes in front of the temple of Quirinus.[140]

The first dramatic quickening of popular vigour is to be seen in the civil troubles of the 80s. That period saw the forcible incorporation of the new Italian citizens, and no doubt a vast increase in the scale of movement to and from Rome, which meant a serious intensification of the new social patterns. A story like that of Marius Gratidianus illustrates the savagery of public violence on the part of the dynasts,

138 Nippel 1988 (A 85); Lintott 1968 (A 62) ch. 7.

139 *Pace* Ungern-Sternberg 1986 (F 164) though he brings out many real continuities between the earlier struggle and later popular politics.

140 Pliny *HN* xv.120–1; Richard 1986 (B 97); Lintott 1987 (A 65) 50–1.

which brought to a bloody end the man 'than whom no one has ever been dearer to the plebs'.[141] The plebs had responded spectacularly to his measures for the control of debt, which had become an impossible burden in the aftermath of the Social War and of Rome's eastern difficulties – a sign of strain in the economic aspect of the life of the populace. The voting tribes undertook the dedication of statues to him in every *vicus* – it is the first time we hear of such action by the *tribus*, or of the political importance of the *vici* of the city;[142] and the statues were the objects of worship with libations, incense, and candles, as had previously been those of the Gracchi and the places where they fell. The terrible example made in public of this popular hero by the victorious Sulla, like the brutality of the more famous Marii, father and son, belongs in the context of the popular spectacle and the institutionalization of violence. A gruesome public exhibition was the form of punishment which suited the practitioners of popular politics, and it was the result of the culture of the populace, not an imposition from above.[143]

The politics of the *plebs urbana* were in part its own. It was not a slate on which the schemers of the Senate wrote whatever they wanted. The culture and social forms of the many were not the product of skilled formation by the aristocrats: they were agents too. If Cicero, Sallust and Plutarch were reluctant to allow that, we must not share their error. At the base of the popular culture lay the shared insecurity of marginality: the urban population was united by the precariousness of belonging.

The plebs suffered from various disadvantageous aspects of the circumstances which had allowed its formation. First, its simple aggregation, especially in a topographically convoluted place like Rome, made it vulnerable to flood, fire, disease and food-shortage.[144] Secondly, the social structures of the world of the *taberna* and *insula* as they evolved through the second century brought their own problems: the system depended on money, and money brought debt as a major disaster. Whenever there was a crisis of credit or a debasement of the coinage the repercussions on urban Roman society were terrible: they can be explored in the time of Gratidianus and the age of Cicero and observed in the agitation of the late 20s B.C. and on into the latter part of the reign of Tiberius.[145] Simply being part of the city cost money. Rent was one of the more obvious cases: as we observed before, the dwellers in the

[141] Cic. *Off.* III.80. [142] Pliny *HN* XXXIV.27.

[143] Brutality of Roman public life: Wiseman 1985 (B 127) 5–10; Lintott 1968 (A 62) ch. 3; cf. M. Foucault, *Discipline and Punish: The Birth of the Prison*, trans. A. Sheridan (Harmondsworth, 1977) 32–69. On the proscriptions: Hinard 1985 (A 52) esp. 40–51.

[144] Flood: Le Gall 1953 (G 144) 27–35; fire, collapse, disease: Scobie 1986 (G 223); food-shortage: Garnsey 1988 (G 100); Virlouvet 1985 (G 252).

[145] Debt: Frederiksen 1966 (G 78); C. Rodewald, *Money in the Age of Tiberius* (Manchester, 1976); Yavetz 1970 (G 263). See also Nicolet in ch. 16 above, pp. 641–2.

speculative *insula* were, by definition, not destitute (though they might pay rent only a day at a time), but they might become desperate. In 7 B.C. it was believed that debtors had started a serious fire on the calculation that their debts might be remitted because of the scale of their losses.[146] The indebtedness did not entail their being destitute – until the debt was called in. Direct oppression of a terrifying kind was usually the result of insolvency; the urban plebeian was, no doubt, as often the victim as the agent of violence. The perils of loss of status and loss of all means were very real: poverty at Rome was seen more as a disaster which struck suddenly than as a continuing state – like the hope of sudden gain, part of the day-to-day existence of the society. Beyond disabling penury lay the danger of enslavement, no doubt effectively reducing the numbers of destitute.[147] The precariousness and the risks were direct consequences of the system which kept the plebs together and linked it to the elite which was the principal source of finance from outside the zone of the city.

Living in a threatening environment in a system in which your personal status was always under threat, alongside many thousands of others competing for the only possibilities of survival and improvement – to this the natural response was the elaboration of more or less permanent groups to provide security of a sort and pool resources and opportunities. That underlies the changing political role of the populace from the Social War onwards. We can see it clearly in Cicero's alarm at the escalation of violence in popular politics.[148]

Cicero's speeches present us with a consistent portrait of the threat. He conjures up a Rome in which every way in which the populace can combine or act collectively will be seized on and turned to the destruction of all that is right. The tribes are suspect: Clodius 'called up the tribes, put himself in command, enrolled a whole new *tribus Collina* by recruiting all the lowest citizens'[149] (significantly it was legal to offer favours to one's *own* tribe, but not to others). The word 'recruiting' suggests the corruption of military service and the fear of the plebeian turned soldier which lasted well into the Empire; the paramilitary language is a feature of this kind of invective.[150] The fear of the economic solidarity of the *tabernarii* and those who live by daily labour, those who are united by a particular trade, is another recurrent theme, as when Cicero sketches Catiline's client 'the *agent provocateur* of the *tabernarii*', the

[146] Dio. LV.8.6.

[147] Debt-enslavement was not legal in the late Republic; but the free frequently found themselves in slave-prisons, *ergastula*, if they could not establish their free status, and that was a serious risk at Rome, especially in times of civil disturbance. Voluntary entry into slavery as a means of self-improvement: Crook 1967 (F 41) 59–60.

[148] Flambard 1977 (C 193); Brunt 1974 (G 23).

[149] Cic. *Mil.* 87.

[150] Cic. *Sest.* 34.

lapidator.[151] The hurling of stones and the threat of arson are the two great – highly appropriate – weapons of the distinctively urban mob.[152] The relations which bound the patron to his slaves and former slaves could also be perverted: 'at his home laws were being drawn up which would make us the property of our slaves'; 'he made our slaves his freedmen'.[153]

Even the charismatic public appearances on which the elite relied could be subverted by simple imitation, or by more or less comic heckling and interpolations. A popular hero who claimed to be the son of the younger Marius returned from death had the temerity to speak to Caesar's audience at a great *epulum* in his suburban *horti*, without the dictator realizing at first – Caesar was standing between the columns of a portico, and his rival was entertaining the company from the invisible vantage-point of the next intercolumnation.[154]

In this last case we see at its clearest the rivalry for control of the social structures that had arisen out of plebeian insecurity. Despite Cicero's constant outrage, that rivalry was, of course, shared by all Roman politicians. As the insecurity on which the associations and organisms of Roman city life were founded became more and more intense, the possibilities for exploiting it expanded and the rewards grew. Caesar defeated the false Marius, and put into practice much of what Clodius had been unable to;[155] Augustus did more, with new tribal organizations, new festivals, new paramilitary organizations for *collegia*, new parapolitical offices at all levels of city life. But behind the whole process, from the middle Republic, when the distinctive social and economic structures of Rome were forming, through the period of strain and crisis, to the Imperial system, lie the rewards for which the insecure plebeians were striving and the baits with which the elite entrapped them. As Cicero put it,[156] Rome was a kind of perverted democracy where the allegiance of groups of the foolish and ignoble could be won by the provision of leisure and comfort, where political decisions could be expected of cobblers and girdlemakers after they had been stuffed at public banquets. The reality or otherwise behind this picture of enticement forms the subject of the last section.

IV

In 309 B.C. the *dictator* Papirius Cursor gave the gilded shields of the Samnites over whom he triumphed to the owners of the *tabernae*

[151] Cic. *Dom.* 13. [152] Lintott 1968 (A 62) 6–10. [153] Cic. *Mil.* 87 and 89.

[154] Val. Max. IX.14.5. The false Marius: Scardigli 1980 (C 254); Rini 1983 (G 213); and see the discussion of the informal politics of the spectacles in Vol. X², ch. 15.

[155] Dio. XL.60.4 on Caesar's relations with other people's freedmen.

[156] Cic. *Flac.* 15–17.

argentariae in the Forum. Livy tells us that from then on began the practice of decorating the centre of the city on special occasions:[157] it is clear that the trophies were to be brought out to contribute to future festivities. The practice that started then is a significant step towards the developed system by which the plebs was involved in the public success of the great in the city as an agent, as an integral part of what was going forward. The *triumphator* gave the grateful plebeians the means to commemorate his greatness: that simple formula is the secret of the relationship between the elite and the people of the city. It is far more common than the concerned popular welfare measure, and it was responsible for keeping the process which we know as Rome in steady movement: without it the next generation would never have arrived from elsewhere and the present one would have done well to flee. Too much concentration on what we would have hated in ancient Rome, noise, squalor, stench, lack of privacy, danger, disease, prevents us from appreciating the calculus of goods the Romans might have used, in which rewards we find nearly incomprehensible, the range of perceived benefits summed up in the phrase 'urbanum otium', acted to balance degradation, misery and fear.[158] Instead of producing more studies of the obvious urban problems, we need to pay attention to the nature of the gains in status and other benefits, and to how the concentrated benefaction of the rulers of the Mediterranean to some extent succeeded in 'aristocratizing' the populace in Rome.[159]

The ideology of benefaction was not, of course, unique to Rome. Other cities too had long gained from the wish of their notables to make clear how splendid, noble and fortunate they were by spending their resources in bettering the lot of the generality of their fellow-citizens. The betterment took the form, naturally enough, of moving up the scale of material goods towards the high lifestyle of the very wealthy, and success was measured by how high on that scale were the community's shared facilities. By the Imperial period we find that Rome is the outstanding example of this tendency. It remains to inquire how it became so.

Behind the inquiry lies the Romans' own perception that from the war against Pyrrhus onwards the material comfort and extravagance of life in the city grew steadily.[160] There were various landmarks along the way. It is important to notice that the perception applies to the whole city: some notoriously debauched individuals feature in the narration, but it is the *widespread* corruption of luxury that we are told about. Thanks to Pliny

[157] Livy IX.40.16.
[158] On the latter: Ramage 1983 (G 206); Scobie 1986 (G 223).
[159] Veyne 1990 (G 250) 201–61.
[160] The Romans' own attitudes to this process and its moral consequences: Levick 1982 (A 61).

the Elder in particular we have quite a store of the conventional dates at which items of the standard equipment of Roman high living were thought to have arrived – good food and wine, baths, building materials, clothing, habits, spectacles and amenities. The progression – a phenomenon of Roman self-awareness – fits very closely the evolution of the relations between ex-slave and freeborn that has been sketched here.

Although Etruscans, Greeks and Orientals all had, in the tradition, elements of high living to offer the wealthy, the place where all three met, Campania, had a particularly important role in diffusing luxury towards Rome. How it grew up there it is not our present purpose to inquire, but it does seem as if the natural resources of the region came to generate a very dense population and a most phenomenal wealth. Capua's luxury was a byword and was the more extraordinary for being, as at Sybaris before, diffused widely throughout society. So it is in Campania that the amenities of the more expansive style of Hellenistic architecture reach the West, that public baths develop in the natural hot springs of the coast, that the solution of the amphitheatre is devised for the problem of admitting the people to the exclusive excitements of the rich, that an economy develops to service all this, and that some political awareness grows with it on the part of many of the ordinary populace.[161]

The games of the amphitheatre are a good example. According to our records, the first occasion on which gladiators were presented as a piece of aristocratic display whose provision added to the prestige of both donor and audience was the funeral of D. Iunius Brutus Pera in 264 B.C. when three pairs were displayed. In 216 it was twenty-two pairs; in 200, twenty-five; in 183, sixty; in 174 B.C. seventy-four; though there were other occasions in the year when the entertainment could be found on a much smaller scale.[162] The escalation of display is apparent, but the pace modest; the plebeians of the age of the Gracchi knew that their entertainment was a privilege of relatively recent origin. The first quarter of the first century sees the open cultivation of this activity by the most influential men of the state: Sulla in particular, with his *ludi Victoriae Sullanae*, made the giving of great public entertainments axiomatic for a *princeps*.

Sulla was of course also known for his connexion with the men and women who created and played in the increasingly diverse theatrical life of the city, which had been developed alongside the social position of its audience.[163] In 155 B.C. it had been thought useful to house the spectacle in a permanent theatre of stone, like those of many other Italian towns: architecture and the interests of the plebs were again linked. But the consul and *pontifex maximus* Scipio Nasica had the building demo-

[161] Frederiksen 1984 (A 35) ch. 14; Gros 1978 (G 109).
[162] Livy XLI.28.10.
[163] Weber 1983 (G 256) chs. 6 and 8; Garton 1964 (C 61).

lished – not the last time that that nobleman found it necessary to take an uncompromising stand against the wishes of the plebs. There were further setbacks, but the various branches of theatrical life flourished despite them and grew into an integral part of the daily life and method of self-expression of the plebs, as well as one of the corner-stones of their new political activity. The spread of 'theatre politics' via the economy of the Mediterranean among the commercial classes of southern Italy, and its setting within the freedman world and the new urban society of the city, made it a phenomenon highly characteristic of the period.[164]

The background to the rise in popularity of the gladiatorial spectacles should be sought in the place in urban Roman society of the *ludi* in general. The *ludi* underwent a development parallel in many ways to the growth of the distinctive social patterns examined in this chapter. They were grounded firmly in the corporate religiosity of the city population, and were acts of divine worship demanding large-scale participation by the inhabitants of Rome, decorating their homes and neighbourhoods, and performing a multitude of individual observances while sharing in the group activities of the games themselves. So the 'crossroad games' and the various recreations of the plebs, at the festival of Anna Perenna, for example,[165] were the occasions underlying the grander celebrations paid for by the state and its officials. Those appear first to have acquired a place in the display of the aristocracy during the third century, and some have seen a division between the high-class displays, at the *ludi Megalenses* from 204, and a plebeian-oriented response, with the regularization of the *ludi Plebeii* (at the expense of the plebeian aediles) and, possibly in direct response to the *Megalenses*, the *ludi Cereales*, which likewise had plebeian associations. The violence of Clodius' disruption of the *Megalenses* may have had something to do with this kind of tension. It is clear enough at least that the last quarter of the second century saw a great escalation in the importance of the *ludi* at Rome, which continued over the next generation. At one level the religious observance bound Rome to the gods in years of crisis; at another the begnnings of the vast growth in the scale of Roman urban society and its instabilities made inevitable the creation of new forms of expression of solidarity and incorporation, especially in the face of critical military peril from outside. It is significant that the next period of expansion of the numbers of days devoted to the *ludi* and creation of new ones, which initiates the much more unrestrained inflation of the holiday-phenomenon under the Empire, is the age of Sulla. By the time of Caesar's death the Roman populace enjoyed fifty-nine days of the great *ludi* every year.[166] A statement from the first century A.D. sums up the process, succinctly

[164] Wiseman 1985 (B 128). [165] Ov. *Fast.* V.523–42.

[166] Development and character of the *ludi*: Scullard 1981 (H 117); Rawson 1981 (G 210).

describing the extension of privilege to the plebs: on feast days 'the right to luxury is given to the people at large', 'ius luxuriae publice datum est'.[167]

The physical setting was improved at the same time. The censors of 204 systematized the approaches to the open space in the great valley on the south side of the city, the Circus Maximus, the traditional location for many of the old festival games: in 196 L. Stertinius dedicated a monumental arch there to commemorate his activities in Spain.[168] That was a natural development, for there the *monumenta* of victorious generals had been built for a century, and the transition to the beautification of the setting of the spectacles was easy. By the end of the 190s the seating of spectators had received legislative attention: in 174 the censors contracted for major works connected with the games; elaborate beast-hunts appeared there from 169.[169] The political importance of the games a century later emerges clearly in the provision by the great of the age of Cicero of places for their clients in whatever buildings overlooked the now crowded valley;[170] but we must remember that resistance to the new ways somewhat retarded the development (compare the ancient ruling of the Senate against beast-shows, which had to be overthrown by tribunician legislation).[171] And just as, in the end, the first permanent theatres and amphitheatres of Rome were the work of Pompey and the Augustan age, so the monumental shaping of the Circus Maximus like a gigantic hairpin is due above all to the work of Caesar, right at the end of the Republic.

Nor did the elite have a monopoly of the giving of *ludi*. The inscriptions show us the arranging of *ludi* by the officials of the humble organizations examined above – and, characteristically, it is in Campania, with the *magistri* of Capua, that we find the earliest dated example, from 108 B.C.;[172] and not much later from Rome comes the record of the '*magistri Herculis* first to be appointed after a vote of the *pagus*' holding games likewise.[173] New officials, democratic organization and the spread of the *ludi* are all to be seen together in this document. The *ludi* in question are more probably the games of the stage, *ludi scaenici* (as the Minturnae evidence makes plain): it was not until the Augustan age, when we find freedmen giving gladiatorial *munera* in the towns of Italy, that the low in status could aspire to give so prestigious an entertainment as that. But in *ludi scaenici* too the city population found much to admire; in the second century B.C. at Amiternum the slave of one Cloelius described himself as 'the sweet mime-artist who time and again provided

167 Sen. *Ep.* 18.1.
168 Livy XXXIII.27.4.
169 Development of the Circus Maximus: Humphrey 1986 (G 126) 60–75.
170 Cic. *Mur.* 73.
171 Pliny *HN* VIII.64.
172 *ILLRP* 727.
173 *ILLRP* 701.

the fun of delectable light entertainment for the *populus*',[174] and later a henchman of Clodius of the same name furthered his patron's political activities through management of the compitalicial games. The *dissignator* Decumus, who has also sometimes been seen as a dependant of Clodius, established a troupe of singers in Greek, who had their own officials and patron and managed a common burial place in the suburbs of the city.[175] The elaboration of the organizations of the plebs, their intimate link with the world of public entertainment, and the long chains of dependence leading up to the elite can be traced in such accidentally surviving records.[176]

In the passage from his defence of Murena quoted above,[177] about the immorality of buying up whole *tabernae* alongside the Circus to provide a good view for the *tribules* whose votes are required in return, Cicero draws a close and revealing parallel – that of the free meal, to which he actually devotes more attention, and whose centrality to the whole political system of Rome by 63 B.C., could hardly be more lucidly expounded than it is in that speech. That practice too has a history recorded in well-known anecdotes, and we can scarcely be surprised to find that it conducts us once again to that epoch of change, the late second century, when the Stoic Tubero offended the plebs by his austerity in his share of the funeral banquet for Aemilianus (129 B.C.) to such an extent that he failed subsequently to be elected praetor. As Cicero says, the Roman people hated private luxury but revelled in public display;[178] or as a later telling of the story puts it: 'the City felt that it was not just the limited number of guests at that dinner but itself in all its entirety that had been lying on the rough hides; and got its own back for this embarrassment of the meal on election day'.[179] So there was still room for austerity in 129, and numbers were still small. It was over the next century that the escalation took place, producing the corrupt democracy of Cicero's sneer,[180] at the mercy of over-fed and foolish cobblers and belt-makers. The common meal, resembling the *ludi* of which it often formed part, and sharing their religious overtones, was one of the great expressions of the community life of the plebs. The various local and social organizations provided them: Varro comments on how the ever more numerous dinners of the *collegia* raised prices in the provision market,[181] and we are reminded of the direct economic link between those forms of behaviour and the economic character of the city: the *epulum* would not have been possible without the *taberna*. But the greatest of such occasions were the triumphal banquets of conquering generals. Popular rumour had it that the great Aemilius Paullus had the

[174] *ILLRP* 804. [175] *ILLRP* 771. [176] Frézouls 1983 (G 80).
[177] See n. 170. [178] Cic. *Mur.* 76, cf. *Flac.* 28.
[179] Val. Max. VII.5.1. [180] Cic. *Flac.* 15–17. [181] Varro *Rust.* III.2.

maxim that 'the organization of a feast and the giving of games were the business of the man who knew how to win wars'.[182] Those of Julius Caesar, which raised the threshold of competition and started chains of imitation in other towns of Italy and the provinces, were particularly significant. From Caesar's time, just as the gladiatorial display is given more often by people of lower status, so too the wine and sweetcake party becomes a common feature of municipal life.[183]

Such feasts, along with the various other signs of *magnificentia* to which the plebs expected to be treated, supplied the *raison d'être* for the new public architecture of the late Republic. Vitruvius specified great halls and spacious colonnades for the house of the statesman because of the numbers of visitors it was his job to receive,[184] and the public architecture of the city developed in the same way. With the temples that were the traditional *monumentum* of the successful aristocrat there came increasingly to be associated places in which the general public might benefit further from his felicity. The porticoes of the temples themselves became wider, and the temples were placed in precincts. In the surrounding colonnades could be admired the works of art which were either the spoils of victory or the product of the general's later expenditure. The architecture became more and more luxuriant, and was used to share with the people not just the statues and paintings which had been the private delight of foreign potentates but rare plants and animals too, signs of the power of their donors even over nature.[185]

In the development of such buildings from the middle of the second century onwards (the first of the series is the Porticus Octavia of 168 B.C.) we can see much of the growing interdependence between elite 'actors' and the audience of the city. But in that case also the plebeians can be found as agents, as when they write their own texts, bearing demands for land for the needy, on *porticus*, *muri* and *monumenta* – i.e. among the written and visual messages of the elite.[186] Pompey's major buildings of 55 B.C. (probably following Sulla) are a turning-point – the temple he placed at the top of the *cavea* of the great theatre with which he dared to break the ancient prohibition against making such buildings permanent; and the vast *porticus* with densely planted gardens and famous paintings, such as the Cadmus and Europa of Antiphilus, that stretched out behind the stage-building. Pompey thus trumped even the fantastic extrava-

[182] Polyb. XXX.14, see also Livy XLV.32.11.

[183] Banquets for the people: Toller 1889 (G 243); Mrozek 1972 (G 169); Purcell 1985 (G 200). An early second-century distribution of what must have closely resembled vermouth, *mulsum rutatum*: Pliny *HN* XIX.45. See also Val. Max. II.4.2 for an *epulum* in 183 B.C.

[184] Vitr. VI.5.2.

[185] Exotic displays put on in these elaborate settings: Rawson 1976 (G 209).

[186] Plut. *Gracch*. 8.

gance of Scaurus' aedilate of 58 which has also been seen as a turning-point in the game of luxury benefactions and popular politics.[187] The close relationship between spectacles and the other forms of munificence is very apparent.

It was in buildings like this that the great public banquets took place, though they also had their private equivalent. Anticipating the advice of Vitruvius, the great men of the late Republic developed the *porticus* architecture in their own urban and suburban palaces. Julius Caesar's famous *Horti* in Transtiberim could even be made into a public precinct like those of the Campus Martius in his will.[188] This was the setting of the incident of the False Marius, and shows us not just how much such an agitator could dare, but also what it was that *Caesar* was doing, and how it fitted the architecture of the Gardens.

Much of the luxury of the late Republic was aimed at a public reception. The way of life of the great was part of the process of 'aristocratizing the citizen' which we have already identified. Doubly so, for not only was it meant to benefit the populace but it also kept in existence the *officina* and the *taberna*, which were so essential to the society of the city. And it was not just by calling into being the *taberna*-world that the beneficence and display of the successful elite was more than merely the conferment of favours on a passive population of inferior recipients; for those inferiors came by a painful process to have their own active role and their own ideology of what they wanted: *commoda*, perquisites.[189] *Commoda* is a key term in the thought-world of the Roman cities. It stands at the centre of a system of values which promoted the identity of otherwise unstable social groups. Those values had their clear physical expression too, in the relative uniformity of the architectural taste, decorative repertoire and building methods of the late Republic.[190] Across west central Italy the terraced buildings of the great sanctuaries and the portico-architecture of villa and *forum* spread rapidly and homogeneously. The tastes of the Roman elite have rightly been linked with this; better, it has been explained as an aspect of a social system. Best of all is it to see that it was not the practice of the great slave-owning *familia*, or the predominance of the wealth-bringing *latifundium*, which brought the development about, but the unique and precarious relationship of the elites with the teeming and ever-changing populations of the cities, above all Rome. That is the sense in which the singular and

[187] Scaurus: Pliny *HN* VIII.96. Generally, Millar 1984 (A 75); Coarelli 1983 (G 43A), exploring the connexions between house, theatre and temple as the setting for politically oriented public festivals.

[188] Cic. *Phil.* II.109; Dio XLIV.35.

[189] *Commoda*: Nicolet 1985 (C 232).

[190] Ward-Perkins 1977 (G 255); Gros 1978 (G 109); Boethius 1960 (B 264) ch. 2; Torelli 1980 (G 244).

arresting physical developments of the time must be seen as secondary, and in which we can say truly that 'the city is not buildings, but people' – the *plebs urbana*, and, wider, the multifarious human population experiencing the extraordinary life of Rome.

CHAPTER 18

THE INTELLECTUAL DEVELOPMENTS OF THE CICERONIAN AGE

MIRIAM GRIFFIN

In considering the level and nature of intellectual activity in Roman society, we are bound to be discussing, in the main, the culture of the Roman and Italian upper classes.[1] Our evidence is such that it is easier to gauge their knowledge of Greek than the general level of literacy. We can note that second-century Roman legislators already assumed that their laws would be read throughout the peninsula and required that they be publicly displayed in a place where they could be easily seen; we can point to the graffiti at Pompeii which show that, in the first century A.D., in a prosperous town, a substantial proportion of the population could read and possibly write, though not to a very high standard.[2] But such evidence tells us little about the numbers and kinds of people who could and would read sophisticated Latin prose and verse. There the most important factor must be the availability of education. One point, however, is worth making at the outset: that is, the importance of oral culture. Not only was drama, one of the earliest forms of Latin literature, accessible without reading, but so was oratory, which was not only the key to understanding public life but an intellectual and artistic product that reached its peak of sophistication and polish in this period. Political and forensic speeches in the Forum were a form of popular entertainment like dramatic performances, and Cicero attests the sensitivity of an ordinary audience to the arrangement of words and the use of metre or prose rhythm.[3] Other forms of literature too were regularly recited: indeed the serious study of Latin literature had started in the middle of the second century when scholars started to prepare the works of Naevius and Ennius for recitation.[4]

[1] See Rawson 1985(H 109) which surveys all the material except for Cicero's own works. Still valuable is Kroll 1933(H 70) chs. 8,11.

[2] E.g. Tarentum fragment (Lintott 1982 (B 191) 131 (clause 14), cf. *FIRA* I, 9, lines 25–6; Harris 1983 (H 58).

[3] *De Or.* III.195–6, 198; *Orat.* 173.

[4] Suet. *Gram.* 2. Varro defined *grammatica* as the study of poets, historians and orators with the aim of being able to read (aloud), explain, correct the text and evaluate it (*GRF* nos. 235–6).

I. EDUCATION

Cicero, making a contrast with Greek education, notes with approval that Roman education was not publicly regulated or uniform.[5] After their establishment, perhaps in the middle of the third century, fee-paying primary schools must have become a regular feature of life in Rome, though, apart from allusions in Plautine comedy, we have little direct evidence.[6] Many continued to learn their letters and the rudiments of arithmetic at home or, with other children, at the home of a neighbour who had a suitably trained slave, such as Cato's Chilo.[7] Secondary education on the Greek model developed rapidly in the latter part of the second century. After the visit of the celebrated scholar Crates of Mallos, the study of language and literature in Greek and Latin (*grammatica*) became so popular that by the early first century there were more than twenty schools in Rome offering instruction.[8] The institutionalization of rhetoric, the secondary stage of education, is firmly attested for the same period by a censorial edict of 92 B.C. attacking the new schools of Latin rhetoric as inferior to the Greek ones set up by 'our ancestors': a senatorial decree of 161 B.C. directed against philosophers and *rhetores* had made no mention of schools.[9] Yet a more domestic setting was often preferred by the upper classes. Thus Cicero and his brother were taught along with their cousins and others, including Atticus, in the house of the consular orator L. Licinius Crassus, and in the next generation we find Cicero supervising the instruction of his son and nephew by trained grammarians and rhetoricians.[10]

For further training in rhetoric and law, both essential to a public career, a more informal kind of apprenticeship was customary: so Cicero and others listened to Q. Mucius Scaevola the augur giving legal opinions to those who consulted him, and heard and imitated the great orators of the day.[11] In Cicero's youth it was becoming the custom to go abroad as part of one's education, in order to hear Greek philosophers and rhetoricians.[12] But already in the preceding century, Romans on public duty in the East had started to avail themselves of this kind of edification and entertainment,[13] while the aristocratic household in

[5] *Rep.* IV.3. [6] Bonner 1977 (H 16) 34ff. [7] Plut. *Cat. Mai.* 20.3. [8] Suet. *Gram.* 2–3.4.

[9] Suet. *Gram.* 25.1; Gell. *NA* XV.11, see also Cic. *De Or.* II.133 (dramatic date 91 B.C.): 'istorum magistrorum ad quos liberos nostros mittimus'.

[10] Cic. *De Or.* II.2; Nep. *Att.* I.1; Cic. *QFr.* II.4, 2; II.13 (12),2; III.3, 4; *Att.* VI.1, 12, cf. Suet. *Gram.* 7.2 for M. Antonius Gnipho who first taught in the home of Julius Caesar.

[11] *Brut.* 306; 304–5.

[12] *Brut.* 315–6; *Fin.* V.1ff; *Acad.* I.12 (Varro and Brutus); Suet. *Iul.* 4.1 (Caesar). See also Cic. *Off.* I.1; *Fam.* XVI.21 (Cicero's son).

[13] Cic. *De Or.* III.74–5; I.45 (L. Licinius Crassus, cos. 95 B.C.); I.82 (M. Antonius, cos. 100 B.C.); III.68 (Metellus Numidicus, cos. 109 B.C.). In the next generation: *Acad.* II.11 (Lucullus); Strab. XI.1,6; Pliny *HN* VII.112; Plut. *Pomp.* 42.4; 75.3–4 (Pompey); Cic. *Brut.* 250 (M. Claudius Marcellus in exile).

Rome and the magisterial entourage abroad were acquiring Greek intellectuals with whom scholarly interests, if any, could be pursued.[14]

The predominantly domestic and uninstitutionalized nature of Roman education must have meant that the population at large enjoyed only a very limited number of the opportunities open to the rich, especially as girls were mostly taught at home. But to the general parallelism of social class and educational opportunities there was one important exception, at least in Rome: slaves and freedmen were not at the bottom of the educational ladder. Greek-speaking captives, already educated, did much of the teaching and trained other slaves at their master's house to increase their value. Some, manumitted for their talents, opened schools. Education could be an instrument of social mobility for such men and, occasionally, for the free poor, like Horace's teacher Orbilius, who had received some training in youth before being left a destitute orphan, and then acquired fame if not fortune through teaching.[15] This was partly a measure of the contempt felt by Romans for purely intellectual professions: as the Elder Seneca remarks of the first Roman knight to teach rhetoric at Rome in the Augustan period, 'Before his time, the teaching of the most noble of subjects was restricted to freedmen and, according to the distasteful custom that prevailed, it was disgraceful to teach what it was honourable to learn.'[16] But the importance of captives from Greek-speaking areas to Roman education was also due to its content, which, in the second and first centuries, became, at all levels, thoroughly Greek.

Children would often learn to speak Greek first at home from Greek slaves, *paedagogi*, who could give elementary instruction and might accompany the child to primary school. *Grammatica* had started with a Latin version of Homer's *Odyssey* made by a bilingual freedman, and Greek poetry remained the principal ingredient, Latin works being added as teachers edited them and applied Greek techniques of analysis to them.[17] The teaching of rhetoric was conducted entirely in Greek until the first decade of the first century, when Plotius Gallus tried to set up a school of Latin rhetoric. Whereas, seventy years earlier, the Senate had distrusted the Greek *rhetores*, now in 92 the censors, one of them the accomplished orator L. Crassus, insisted on the superiority of instruction in Greek. Cicero was deterred from trying the new school on educational grounds by 'highly trained men' (probably Crassus himself). There have been attempts to find political motives, because Plotius was a close friend of Marius, but there is no reason to disbelieve Cicero, who would have been old enough to grasp the issues at the time. The new

[14] See the list in Balsdon 1979 (A 5) 54ff.

[15] E.g. Plut. *Cat. Mai.* 20.3; Plut. *Crass.* 2, 6; Nep. *Att.* 13.3; Suet. *Gram.* 9. Bonner 1977 (H 16) 37ff, 58ff; Treggiari 1969 (G 247) 110ff; Forbes 1955 (H 39).

[16] Sen. *Controv.* II, pref. 5; cf. Cic. *Off.* 1.151.

[17] Suet. *Gram.* 1–2.

school did not impart the traditional Greek technical instruction but offered a short cut in practical exercises backed by a minimum of theory. Cicero hints that it would thus have made rhetorical training more accessible and perhaps given opportunities for success in public life to an increased number: it is notable that in this period there was pressure from the Italian upper classes for the franchise and the chance of political participation. In this rather broad social sense the edict can be regarded as political.[18]

Crassus is represented in a Ciceronian dialogue set in 91 B.C. as hoping that a proper Latin rhetorical training would eventually develop. His older contemporary, the orator M. Antonius, had produced a volume giving the fruits of his own experience, and by 80, Cicero had written a systematic treatise *De Inventione* based on Greek rhetorical works.[19] Cicero's dream, which he also ascribed to Crassus, was that a broad education would result, in which not only Greek rhetorical theory, but the study of history and philosophy as well, would be combined with Roman experience. This remained an ideal still advanced by Quintilian and Tacitus, but in fact, as all three writers make clear, rhetorical training in both Latin and Greek became increasingly narrow and technical. Cicero was going back to an ideal held by Isocrates and the sophists before him, but the tradition had long lapsed in Greece itself. The exercises which he himself practised in youth became the principal ingredient. Cicero himself tried to impose on his son and nephew a more theoretical training than their Greek *rhetor* espoused, but his zeal for declaiming on abstract philosophical themes was not popular with them or their contemporaries.[20] It was not surprising. Cicero himself ascribes the popularity of rhetorical training at Rome to its practical benefits, namely reputation, wealth and influence. He also notes that specialization was well established in the Greek intellectual tradition by the time it was imported into Rome.[21]

II. SOCIAL SETTING

Like Roman education, Roman intellectual life was not served, until the collapse of the Republic, by publicly supported institutions such as the libraries of the Hellenistic kingdoms. As dictator, Caesar planned to build the first public library in Rome, enlisting the eminent scholar M. Terentius Varro, who had written a treatise *De Bibliothecis*, as its first

[18] Suet. *Gram.* 25–6; Cic. *De Or.* III.93–4 where Crassus defends the edict; Tac. *Dial.* 35; Cic. *Arch.* 20 (Marius); Bonner 1977 (H 16) 71ff.; Rawson 1985 (H 109) 49–50.

[19] Cic. *De Or.* I.94; 206; 208; *Brut.* 163. Rawson 1978 (H 107) dates the first Roman efforts to organize a work on formal Greek principles as an *ars* to the period of *De Inventione*.

[20] Cic. *Inv. Rhet.* I.1ff.; *De Or.* I.22; III.131; *QFr.* III.3, 4.

[21] *De Or.* I.22; III.131–6.

librarian. But the project may have been impeded by the burning in 47 of the Alexandrian library from which some of the Greek books might have come, and nothing seems to have been done by the time of Caesar's death three years later.[22]

In the mean time, however, Roman commanders had been bringing back Greek libraries from the East, looted or purchased with their booty. Thus the library of king Perseus of Macedon was acquired by the sons of Aemilius Paullus, and Lucullus' library, rich in Greek books, came from his Pontic spoils, while Pompey was to take the medical treatises owned by Mithridates.[23]

But the most romantic acquisition was made by Sulla when he seized the library of Apellicon of Teos, who had become enmeshed with the enemy cause in Athens. That collection included the library of Aristotle. To those facts, related by the contemporary philosopher Posidonius, Strabo and Plutarch add further details: the library, containing the books of Aristotle and Theophrastus, had come by chance into the hands of ignorant people who buried it in the ground to protect it from agents of the king of Pergamum; the books were badly damaged and inexpertly emended by Apellicon; until Sulla brought them to Rome and Tyrannio worked on them, the Peripatetics had been without the technical works of Aristotle and his successor; Tyrannio now supplied copies to Andronicus of Rhodes, who published the books and compiled indices.[24] Though there is room for doubt whether the works in question had really been unknown in Greece, and whether that was the reason for the becalmed state of the Peripatetic School, there is every reason to believe that the books made a great impact, and that an important role was played by Tyrannio, with whom Strabo, one of our sources, had studied. He is known from Cicero's letters as an outstanding scholar and teacher who helped to organize Cicero's library at Antium.[25]

The collections of Sulla and Lucullus now made it possible for Greek scholars to do serious work at Rome – though, even earlier, Polybius had first met Scipio, a son of Aemilius Paullus, when the historian came to borrow some books from Perseus' library. Lucullus' library had colonnades and study-rooms where such Greeks in Rome congregated. Tyrannio, already an accomplished grammarian when captured, had been manumitted by Murena, an act which his commander Lucullus regarded as showing the scholar inadequate respect, since it implied that

22 Suet. *Iul.* 44.2. Asinius Pollio built a public library in 39 B.C. in his *atrium libertatis* (Pliny *HN* VII.115; Ov. *Tr.* III.1.71–2) and Augustus followed suit (Suet. *Aug.* 29.3).

23 Plut. *Aem.* 28; Isid. *Orig.* VI.5.1; Plut. *Luc.* 42; Cic. *Fin.* III.7; Pliny *HN* XXV.7.

24 Ath. V.214d (= Posidonius ed. Edelstein–Kidd 1988 (B 32) F253.145ff); Strab. XIII.608–9C; Plut. *Sull.* 26.

25 Strab. XII.548C; Cic. *Att.* IV.4a.1. On the Peripatos and Andronicus of Rhodes, see e.g. Donini 1982 (H 33) 81ff.

he had been a slave. He could clearly have returned to the East but preferred to become rich and esteemed at Rome. Similarly the great student of medicine, Asclepiades, refused to leave Rome for the court of Mithridates despite the king's medical library.[26]

In Cicero's day, he and his friends were building up their own smaller collections. With the book trade in an embryonic condition, there was need of trained slave copyists not only to duplicate new works but to supply existing gaps.[27] Some of the problems are vividly described by Cicero, to whom his brother Quintus turned for help in expanding his library. Latin books on sale were corrupt and unreliable; to acquire good Greek ones required the advice of a trained person, and Tyrannio this time was too busy.[28] The situation clearly provided an incentive to scholars to prepare authoritative texts. Cicero also mentions the possibility of exchanging books, swapping duplicates or borrowing to make copies. Keeping such a library up to date was a perennial problem. For his own use, he had to send to Athens for a work of Posidonius, despite the excellent collection of Stoic texts in Lucullus' library to which he had access.[29]

How essential books were to the idea of civilized leisure in this period is shown by Cicero's remark that, when Tyrannio had arranged his library, he felt his house had acquired a soul.[30] It was clearly necessary and regular to call on friends and borrow from them, especially as men like Cicero had their collections of books split up, with libraries in each villa as well as in their town houses.[31] The result was that intellectual life was of necessity social in nature, as we see it in the *Topica* where Cicero and Trebatius each pursue their own interests in Cicero's library at Tusculum, or in *De Finibus* where Cicero comes upon Cato, at Lucullus' villa not far away, surrounded by Stoic tomes.[32]

Cicero's letters in fact confirm what his dialogues depict, that study, being a leisure activity for the governing classes, was associated with the country and with villas. In certain areas, such as Tusculum, Antium and the Bay of Naples, such villas were thickly clustered. At Tusculum for example we hear of villas owned by Cicero, Hortensius, Lucullus and Varro, just as in the previous generation Q. Mucius Scaevola, L. Licinius Crassus and M. Aemilius Scaurus had spent their holidays in close

26 Polyb. XXXI.23.4; Plut. *Luc.* 42; 19.7 (Tyrannio); Asclepiades: Pliny *HN* XXV.6; XXVI.12.

27 Cicero's *librarii*: *Att.* XII.14.13; XIII.21a.1; Atticus': *Att.* XIII.13.1; XIII.21a.1; XII.40.1; Nep. *Att.* 13.3. On others see Rawson 1985 (H 109) 43–4.

28 Cic. *QFr.* III.4.5; III.5,6.

29 *Att.* XVI.11.4; *Fin.* III.7.

30 *Att.* IV.8.2.

31 Cicero had libraries at Tusculum (*Div.* II.8; *Top.* 1), Antium (*Att.* II.6.1; IV.4a, 1), and Astura (XII.13.1) at least, and he was given by a grateful client one that had belonged to the grammarian Ser. Clodius (Suet. *Gram.* 3; *Att.* I.20.7; II.1.12).

32 *Top.* 1; *Fin.* III.7.

proximity to each other.[33] Whereas a rural setting is an exception in Plato's dialogues, it is the rule for Cicero.[34]

Villa life was not, of course, simple rustic life. On the contrary, what we see displayed in Cicero's dialogues and letters is a highly sophisticated life of social etiquette and manners. We hear of dining with Roman friends or members of the local aristocracy, where shop-talk is banned in favour of literary conversation or recitation.[35] A certain formality obtains. Compliments are sent and calls made; apologies are expected for casual visits and formal invitations to stay are necessary;[36] politeness is shown to their elders by the young;[37] controversy is carried on with the utmost courtesy and charm.[38]

To some extent we are dealing with an ideal that the over-sensitive Cicero could only try to realize. Unwelcome guests did just drop in on him; the young Brutus and Calvus were sometimes tactless and harsh in their criticisms, and Cicero, if provoked, could write in a similar vein.[39] But Cicero normally preferred urbanity[40] and in this Caesar sympathized and agreed with him: they were effusive in praising each other's works on Cato, though one was eulogistic, the other vituperative.[41]

Social relations with Greek attendants or companions must have varied according to their status and accomplishments, from the near equality with Roman aristocrats enjoyed by Panaetius and Posidonius, who held high office in Rhodes, to the semi-independent status of Philodemus who may have been provided by L. Calpurnius Piso with his own cottage in Herculaneum,[42] right down to the humiliating position of the Peripatetic Alexander who travelled everywhere with Crassus, receiving a cloak for his journey and returning it when he came home.[43] Cicero regularly portrays Greeks like these as having a solemn attitude to intellectual matters, verging on *ineptiae* ('owlishness'), unlike

[33] *De Or.* II.60 (leisure); II.10 (*rus* and *otium*); *Fat.* 28 (Hortensius); *Acad.* II.148 (Lucullus); *Fam.* IX.2.1 (Varro); *De Or.* I.265 (Scaevola); I.24 (Crassus); I.214 (Scaurus). See now Linderski 1988 (G 145A).

[34] The *Phaedrus* is exceptional in this respect, as is the *Laws* whose rural setting is specifically mentioned as paralleled in that of *De Legibus* (I.15). Gell. *NA.* I.2.1 owes more to Cicero than to Plato.

[35] Cic. *De Or.* I.27 (*humanitas*), cf. *Att.* XIII.52.2, of the awkward visit of Caesar the dictator: 'homines visi sumus'). Cicero gives rules for conversation in *Off.* I.132ff. Recitation: Nep. *Att.* 14.1.

[36] *De Or.* II.13–14; II.27, cf. *Att.* IV.10.2; XIII.9.1.

[37] *De Or.* I.163; II.3, see also Plut. *Cic.* 45; *Ad Brut.* 26.5 (Octavian rather exaggerated the role).

[38] *De Or.* I.262; *Acad.* II.61; *Off.* I.136–7; *Fam.* VII.18; XV.21.4.

[39] *Att.* XIII.33a,1; Tac. *Dial.* 18.4; 26, see also *Att.* VI.1.7; *Fam.* VII.27.

[40] *Fam.* V.1 and 2 show how Cicero replied to the pompous Q. Metellus Celer.

[41] Cic. *Att.* XIII.40, 1; XIII.46, 2; XIII.50, 1, and see Suet. *Iul.* 73 for Caesar's way with young Calvus and Catullus. Varro could write a satire called *Tricaranus* (three-headed monster) in 59 (App. *BCiv.* II.9) and still be on close terms with Caesar and Pompey.

[42] Strab. XIV.655C; Philodemus: *Anth. Pal.* XI.144 (see Gow–Page 1968 (B 43) no. 23 and Nisbet ed. 1961 (B 77) App. 3 and 4; but cf. Rawson 1985 (H 109) 23.

[43] Plut. *Crass.* 3.

the Roman gentlemen amateurs who know that intellectual subjects must be broached only when the place, time and company are appropriate.[44]

The social nature of intellectual activity is revealed again when we consider the custom of dedication which had arisen in the Hellenistic period. Dedications of works by Greek intellectuals to Romans are attested from the second century on. They could be a mark of homage, a sign of ambition or an expression of genuine and shared interests.[45] When Roman writers imitated the habit, they were often addressing their social equals. Though the element of honour was present, as Varro's eagerness to receive a Ciceronian work makes clear, the choice of dedicatee was often intellectually appropriate: Atticus received historical works from Cornelius Nepos and Varro, while Cicero received works on the Latin language from Caesar and from Varro, to whom in turn he dedicated a work on Academic philosophy.[46] Sometimes we can see that a closer connexion is involved: Atticus was inspired by Cicero's *De Republica* to write his chronological summary, which in turn inspired Cicero's *Brutus*; Brutus dedicated his work *On Virtue* to Cicero, who says that it spurred him on to write philosophy in Latin, as his own works may have stimulated Varro.[47] In Cicero's letters we can see the importance of Atticus as a catalyst, pressing Cicero to compose a work on geography, encouraging him to write his eulogy of Cato, urging him to make Varro a speaker in, and the recipient of, a work of philosophy. It has been plausibly suggested that Atticus had the same sort of influence on his friend Cornelius Nepos.[48]

With Caesar's dictatorship these social customs were threatened with deformation. Whereas Cicero in 46 had seemed no more worried about offending Caesar with his *Cato* than about displeasing Varro with the *Academica*,[49] in 45, when he was dissuaded by Caesar's 'friends' from sending him a letter of advice, Cicero felt that he was now dealing with a tyrant who expected flattery and, if disappointed, would retaliate in more than words.[50]

III. HELLENIZATION

What were the intellectual products of this society? One general characteristic has emerged in what has already been said about educa-

[44] E.g. *De Or.* I.103; 111; II.18.

[45] Ambaglio 1983 (H 2) 7ff.

[46] Atticus was the dedicatee of Nepos' *De Excellentibus Ducibus* and Varro's *De Vita Populi Romani*; Cicero of Caesar's *De Analogia* and most of *De Lingua Latina*. Varro finally received, and was made a speaker in, Cicero's *Academica*.

[47] *Brut.* 19; 11; 16 (with Douglas' note 1966 (B 29) *ad loc.* for the problems); *Fin.* I.8; *Acad.* I.3; 12.

[48] *Att.* II.6.1; XII.4.2; IV.16.2; XIII.12. See Geiger 1985 (B 42) 98ff.

[49] Caesar: *Att.* XII.4.2, though, in retrospect, Cicero says he was afraid of retaliation, *Att.* XIII.28.3; Varro: *Att.* XIII.22.1; 24.2; 25.3.

[50] *Att.* XII.51.2; XIII.2: 'humanitatem omnem exuimus', see n. 35 above; XIII.27.1; XIII.28.3.

tion, travel, libraries and the presence of Greeks in Roman households: in the first century B.C. the process of Hellenization intensified. To some extent this can be connected with the progress of Roman imperialism, for eastern wars, diplomatic activity and the acquisition of new provinces led to more Romans visiting Greek-speaking lands on official business and to more captives and refugees coming to Rome. The battle of Pydna resulted in the first great influx; the next came in the wake of the Mithridatic Wars. In the First War during the 80s, Philo of Larissa, the head of the Academy, came as a refugee from Athens, the Stoic philosopher Posidonius and possibly the rhetorician Apollonius Molo were sent as envoys from Rhodes, and Alexander Polyhistor entered Rome as a war captive.[51] In the First and Third Wars, Lucullus, first as quaestor, then as commander, kept the poet Archias and the Academic philosopher Antiochus of Ascalon in his entourage. When Lucullus returned home in the 60s, Rome gained not only a library, a globe and statues, including one by Sthenis, but the grammarian Tyrannio of Amisus and the poet Parthenius of Nicaea, both captives who were to make a considerable impact on Roman cultural life.[52] When Pompey returned after the final defeat of Mithridates, he was accompanied by the historian and politician Theophanes of Mytilene.

These new contacts with Greek intellectuals, eager to ingratiate themselves with the new masters of the world for the sake of their communities and themselves, resulted in flattering accounts in Greek of Roman achievements. Archias wrote up the campaigns of Lucullus in verse; Theophanes, perhaps also Posidonius, did the same for Pompey in prose.[53] But we must not exaggerate their influence on Roman policy[54] nor even their contribution to the Hellenization of Rome, which had now acquired its own momentum through the effects of Greek education and the presence of Greeks in the household.

In its showy, even frivolous, aspects, Greek culture could be an instrument of aristocratic competition. Those in public life particularly could attract popular interest by displaying Greek painting and sculpture, erecting great public buildings in the Greek manner and staging performances and competitions of a Greek type. Yet to speak of pretension and exhibitionism is not enough to explain the zeal of the Roman upper class to acquire Greek culture, especially in its less visual

[51] Cic. *Brut.* 306; Plut. *Mar.* 45.4; Cic. *Brut.* 305.

[52] Cic. *Arch.* 11; Antiochus: *Acad.* II.4; 11; 61; Plut. *Luc.* 42, 3–4; globe: Strab. XII. 546C; statues: *ibid*; Plut. *Luc.* 23.4; library and Tyrannio: n. 26; Suda s.v. Parthenius.

[53] Archias: Cic. *Arch.* 21; *Att.* I.16.15; Theophanes: *Arch.*24; Plut. *Pomp.* 42. Theophanes' influence on Pompey is probably exaggerated by Strabo XIII.617–18C: see Crawford 1978 (H 29) 203–4; cf. Anderson 1963 (H 3) 35–41. Posidonius: for the problematic evidence of Strab. XI.492C, see Malitz 1983 (B 69) 70–4.

[54] Gruen 1984 (A 43) II e.g. 271; Ferrary 1988 (A 30) 223ff.

and public aspects.[55] What, after all, gave those things their prestige, if not some genuine appreciation of their value? And that appreciation must have been powerful enough to overcome the negative attitudes that continued, albeit in a more subtle form than they had taken in the generation of the Elder Cato. Greek culture was now definitely the culture of a conquered people, and many thought it shameful to learn from foreigners the arts that, they suspected, had contributed to Greek defeat.[56] Hence to be too Hellenized could bring ridicule, as T. Albucius learned to his cost. He studied in Athens in youth and became a convert to Epicureanism and to Greek language and culture generally, to such an extent that Q. Mucius Scaevola, the augur, when he visited Athens on his way out to govern Asia in about 119 B.C., had his entire retinue, lictors and all, salute Albucius ironically in Greek – although Scaevola himself had studied with the Greek philosopher Panaetius, while the poet Lucilius, who immortalized the incident in satiric verse, shows in other verses a comfortable familiarity with Greek literature and learning.[57] It did not pay to seem too serious about such matters, and indeed various types of concealment were practised. Of the two leading orators in the early first century, Cicero tells us that M. Antonius pretended to be ignorant of Greek learning, whereas L. Licinius Crassus pretended to despise it in comparison with Roman achievements. Cicero still employed both techniques.[58]

The fact that Roman education in the late Republic was based on Greek language and literature still leaves room for doubt as to how well even the most literate could speak Greek or understand difficult literary texts, for the accomplishments of leading Romans in those respects were laced with pretence in both directions. In formal diplomacy, then as now, officials preferred to use their own language to avoid misunderstanding and uphold national pride.[59] On the other hand, there may be an element of Greek wishful thinking, if not flattery, in Plutarch's remarks on the prowess of his Roman heroes in his own language.[60] But there is no reason to doubt that Apollonius was impressed by Cicero's ability to declaim in Greek, and Cicero and Atticus were not the only ones to compose works of literature in the language.

[55] A distinction Cicero hints at in *Balb.* 14–15.

[56] Cicero's grandfather maintained that the more Greek a Roman knew the more wicked he was (*De Or.* II.26). *Cael.* 40 for the idea that the Greeks wrote about virtues they could not attain; *QFr.* I.1.16 for the contemptible character of contemporary Greeks attributed to long servitude.

[57] Cic. *Fin.* I.8–9; *Brut.* 131; *De Or.* I.75 (Scaevola and Panaetius). On Lucilius' culture, see Gratwick 1982 (H 52) 167ff.

[58] *De Or.* II.4, cf. II Verr. 4.5 (display of ignorance); *Mur.* 63; *Arch.*2 (patronizing apologies for discussion of these matters).

[59] See Horsfall 1979 (H 61) 79ff. Diplomacy: Val. Max. II.2.2. Aemilius Paullus spoke Latin and used Roman interpreters on these occasions (Livy XLV.29.3), though he could address Perseus in Greek (Polyb. XXIX.20; Livy XLV.8.5).

[60] E.g. *Luc.* 1.2; *Brut.* 2.3; *Flam.* 5.6 (the Greek of his extant letter is flawed: *RDGE* 199); *Cic.* 4.4.

If Fabius Pictor and his second-century successors wrote history in Greek because there was then no tradition of Latin historiography to follow, later writers composed in the language either to show off their skill or when they wished to reach all or part of the large readership, comprising the whole Mediterranean basin, for which Greek was the *lingua franca*. Thus Rutilius Rufus, when living in Asia Minor, wrote a history in Greek down to his own time, and Lucullus composed a history of the Marsic War in Greek (into which he claimed to have introduced barbarisms deliberately to prove the author's nationality).[61] Cicero and Atticus both wrote accounts of Cicero's consulship with which Cicero hoped to impress the cities of Greece.[62] Ultimately, however, history in Greek was to be left to Greeks; it was philosophy that Romans were ultimately to expound in Greek, despite the efforts of Brutus, Cicero and Seneca to forge a technical philosophical vocabulary in Latin.[63]

Writing in Greek, however, was not the solution for any but the most recherché subjects. It would clearly not do for drama and oratory, which were meant for the public at large, and it would not serve the potentially large middle-brow readership for other kinds of literature, people who had neither sufficient education nor travelling experience to read Greek fluently and hence regularly. That was the audience for whom Cornelius Nepos was to write and whom even Cicero claimed to have reached with his works on philosophy and rhetoric.[64]

The original solution had been translation, or rather, by our standards, adaptation. Livius Andronicus had made Homer accessible in this way, and practical works on agriculture and medicine were even later to be produced in Latin versions.[65] But a Roman public wanted Roman subject matter. Even the early dramatists had not merely put their Greek models into Latin: they had introduced Roman customs and ideas, though they avoided causing offence by presenting the often frivolous and immoral conduct in a Greek setting. Cicero sometimes spoke of them as translators, but he knew that they preserved the effect, not the words, of the Greek originals, so that even those who could read the Greek enjoyed the Latin versions as well. Roman pride was also

[61] Cic. *Arch.* 23; Ath. IV.168; Plut. *Luc.* 1.2; Cic. *Att.* I.19.10: Lucullus was thinking of the conventional apology used by Romans writing in Greek, which Cato had ridiculed in the case of the historian Postumius Albinus (Polyb. XXXIX.1.1–2 with Walbank's commentary *ad loc.*).

[62] Cic. *Att.* II.1.1–2; Nep. *Att.* 18.6, see below, pp. 712–13.

[63] On Brutus, see below, p. 719. A work *Περὶ καθήκοντος* by him is mentioned by Seneca, *Ep.* 95.45 but Priscian 199.8–9 cites in Latin from a work *De Officiis*.

[64] Nep. pref. 2; *Pelop.* 1; Cic. *Off.* I.1 where he claims to have fulfilled the hopes expressed in *Acad.* I.10; *Fin.* I.10. On this public see Horsfall 1979 (H 61); Geiger 1985 (B 42) 70–1.

[65] Agriculture: a translation of Mago's Punic treatise was commissioned by the Senate after the destruction of Carthage in 146 B.C. (Pliny *HN* XVIII.3.22–3; Columella *Rust.* I.1.13). Varro preferred to use (*Rust.* I.1.10) the Greek translation dedicated to a 'Sextilius praetor', perhaps the man attested in Africa in 88 B.C. (*MRR* II.41,43). Medicine: Pompey had Pompeius Lenaeus translate medical books from Mithridates' library (Pliny *HN* XXV.7).

involved: it may have been Varro who christened Ennius the Roman Homer;[66] Quintilian's comparison of Greek and Latin authors, genre by genre, is a later product of this desire, not only to emulate Greek culture, but to equal, if not surpass it. Cicero knew his compatriots had a long way to go before the Roman people ceased to depend on Greek writers. He himself admits that when he set up Antonius and Crassus as ideals in *De Oratore* and praised Roman oratory in the *Brutus*, he was really trying to encourage Latin speakers, and that although it was better not to use a foreign model, Demosthenes still came closest to the ideal. And it was Demosthenes whom Cicero really set out to rival.[67]

The Romans were educated by the Greeks and their literature. They learned to increase the resources of Latin, to employ sophisticated prose rhythms and poetic metres, and to organize both their thoughts and their literary compositions. They learned to render Greek ideas precisely in both languages and they entered into intellectual controversies current in the Greek world. How great the debt was will emerge when we come to consider the various types of intellectual activity. It is also important to remember how great was the effort involved. As Cicero's Crassus says in explaining his attitude to the new *Latini rhetores*, 'The importation of the ancient and pre-eminent wisdom of the Greeks as part of our national habits and practices requires men of advanced learning, of whom so far we have had none in this sphere.'[68]

Direct importation, that is, translation from the Greek, was employed, not only as an end in itself, but as a form of training: it stretched the resources of Latin. Cicero did a lot of such work in youth, as did his brother Quintus, Julius Caesar, and, earlier, Julius Caesar Strabo.[69] Even later in life Cicero translated verses for citation in his philosophical works, and many other Latin works contained passages of translation.[70] The difficulty and novelty of the Roman achievement in this area should not be underestimated. As the Greeks rarely translated works from other languages for their own use, there were no treatises on the subject to guide Roman writers. The Greeks themselves, as Cicero points out, coined new words to cover new concepts, and philosophers struggled to create a technical language, but Latin translators had to grasp the difference in character of two languages and preserve the genius of their own while developing its full potential.[71]

[66] Cic. *Fin.* I.4 on verbatim translations: but *Acad.* I.10 probably represents what Cicero really thought. On the nature of these Latin adaptations of Athenian drama, see Jocelyn 1967 (B 48) 23–8.

[67] *Brut.* 138ff.; *Orat.* 22–3; 132–3.

[68] Cic. *De Or.* III.95.

[69] *De Or.* I.155, and see *Brut.* 310; Quint. X. 5,2. D.M. Jones 1959 (H 67); Horsfall 1979 (H 61) 83–4.

[70] Cic. *Tusc.* II.26 (verse); *Fin* I.7 (passages in philosophical works): cf. Livy's use of Polybius.

[71] See above, n. 65 on translation by Cassius Dionysius of Mago; Cic. *Fin.* III.3–4; *Acad.* I.24–5, cf. Sedley 1973 (B 107) 21ff.

IV. SCHOLARSHIP AND SCIENCE

Increased exposure to Greek culture and contact with Greek intellectuals helped to erode upper-class inhibitions about studying and writing on subjects not directly connected with Roman public life or traditional practical training. In those areas most closely related to formal education, scholarship and science, the outstanding figure is Marcus Terentius Varro, who was regarded, at the time and later, as the most learned Roman of his age.[72] An older contemporary of Cicero, whom he resembled in social background and political sympathies, Varro too had an active political career, but was able to settle down calmly after Caesar's victory to a life of retirement, producing in the next twenty years voluminous works on the Latin language and its literature, on Roman antiquities, and on philosophy. Invited by Caesar to run the first public library, he was eventually the only living man to be honoured with a bust in the library of Pollio.[73] His uneasy relationship with Cicero probably sprang from their different priorities: Varro attached less importance to politics and to stylistic polish.[74] As a result, many more works of Cicero remain for us. Yet Varro's books had great influence on the learned poetry and romantic history of the Augustan age and then on later antiquarians and the Church Fathers. It was appropriate that Cicero did not outlive the Republic: Varro survived, perhaps until 27 B.C., and his vision of Rome was adopted by Augustus as the spirit of the new regime.

The two extant works of Varro show some of his leading characteristics, though the more accessible, *De Re Rustica*, published in 37 B.C. when he was in his eightieth year, is probably not typical of his weightier works in its use of dialogue form to enliven a technical discussion of agriculture. Aside from the heavy-handed humour with which Varro first chooses speakers with agricultural names and then carefully underlines the fact, the most typical feature is his concern with organizing the subject-matter along the lines of an *ars* or *τέχνη* in the Greek fashion. There is an emphasis on definition, on classification of topics into orderly subdivisions and on the two functions of profit and pleasure.[75] Despite Varro's claim to be providing his wife and countrymen with a reference work on practical farming, the material is neither detailed nor technical enough for the working farmer, or indeed for the capital investors like himself who composed his audience, though the

[72] Cic. *Acad.* I, fr. 36 Reid = Aug. *De civ. D.* VI.2; Dion. Hal. *Ant. Rom.* II.21.2; Quint. X.1.95; Apul. *Apol.* 42; Dahlmann 1935 (B 22) and 1973 (B 23).

[73] Pliny *HN* VII.115.

[74] Kumaniecki 1962 (H 72).

[75] *Rust.* I.2.9; II.4.1; the work is dedicated to his wife, probably because she was called Fundania. I.1,11; I.3–4.1; I.5,1, see also Cassiod. ap. Keil *Grammatici Latini* VII (1880), 213. On the names and on the literary qualities of the work, Linderski 1988 (G 145A) 112ff.

information, as far as it goes, seems to be reliable. Instead this is more of a theoretical work, where analysis is often pursued for its own sake, as elsewhere in Varro. Here, albeit with a touch of self-parody, 81 subdivisions of the subject of pasturage are listed as a minimum; in *De Philosophia* 288 possible philosophical sects are distinguished.[76] Division into four is particularly favoured, a scheme that Varro felt to be natural and rooted in the cosmos, but which he took over from the Greeks and traced back to the Pythagorean analysis of things into antithetic pairs.[77]

Equally typical of Varro's other works is the emphasis on citing authorities, here particularly inappropriate in a supposedly improvised discussion, and a certain carelessness both in matters of literary presentation and in the adaptation to context of his source-material. The carelessness is not surprising in view of the haste with which Varro composed: he claimed to have written 490 volumes by the age of seventy-seven and went on writing, working on several things simultaneously, until the day of his death.[78] But it is also a result of the methods of compilation used by ancient scholars: as the papyrus roll makes finding references difficult, excerpting was crucial and verification of words and context avoided.[79]

It is natural for us to regret most the loss of works in which Varro could use his own experience, just as we find what he says about his own estates and about contemporary methods the most valuable parts of *De Re Rustica*. Varro wrote two works for the instruction of his friend Pompey, one on senatorial procedure, when Pompey entered the Senate in 70 B.C. as consul without having held any of the lower offices, and one on naval matters: Varro served as Pompey's legate both in Spain in the 70s and in 67 in the campaigns against the pirates for which he was awarded the naval crown.[80] Yet what made him a final authority for later generations was his application of Greek systematic methods to every type of subject-matter, and particularly to past and present Roman life.

In the *De Re Rustica*, Varro was talking about Italian agriculture in particular. Book I includes a eulogy of Italy; in Book II Varro celebrates the old rural way of life and castigates Greek refinements in Roman villas (and the Greek names for them) as a sign that the salubrious habits of the

[76] *Rust.* II.1.12; 25–8; Aug. *De civ. D.* XIX.1–3: fragments of *De Philosophia* have been edited by Langenberg (1959 (B 62)). See however Spurr 1986 (G 230) x–xiii for the argument that Varro's schematization is not incompatible with practical realism.

[77] *Rust.* I.5.3; *Ling.* V.12; IX.31; V.11 (Pythagoras). The division was basic to both *Antiquitates* (below, p. 706), according to Augustine, *De civ. D.* VI.3 = *Antiquitates Rerum Divinarum* I fr.4 (Cardauns); elsewhere in Varro (Gell. *NA* XIV.7; XIII.11.3).

[78] Gell. *NA* III.10.17; Val. Max. VII.3.

[79] Skydsgaard 1968 (B 113) ch. 7.

[80] Procedure: Gell. *NA* XIV.7.2: Pompey needed to know 'quid facere dicereque deberet cum senatum consuleret'; *Ephemeris navalis*: Dahlmann 1935 (B 22) 1252–3; service with Pompey: *Rust.* II, pref.6; Pliny *HN* VII.115; XVI.7.

past are being abandoned. Though he follows Dicaearchus' *Life of Greece* in describing the successive, then coexisting, stages of gathering, pasturage and agriculture, and ascribes dignity to pasturage, which merits a whole book, he none the less berates his countrymen for returning farm land to pastoral use. He is thinking not only of Rome's increased dependence on grain imports, but of the decline of traditional Roman virtues. The Roman dilemma could not be made clearer: if the Greeks provided the intellectual framework for understanding the historical development and current practice of Italian farming, they also provided the refinements that were destroying traditional Italian life.[81]

One curious feature of *De Re Rustica* is the persistent use of etymology as an explanatory instrument. In the context of agriculture, this is mere embellishment, but it was a more fundamental tool for Varro's antiquarian scholarship. In fact the study of the Latin language, to which his other extant work is devoted, was a life-long passion. In addition to the twenty-five books of *De Lingua Latina*, of which six survive in poor condition, Varro is known to have written at least nine works on the subject over a period of fifty years.[82] He was interested not only in the literary language but in that of common speech, both for its own sake and because it was the key to cultural, religious and social history.[83]

In *De Lingua Latina*, written in the 40s,[84] Varro, after an introductory volume, deals at length with three subjects: how words were imposed on things (etymology); how different forms of words arise (derivation and inflection), and how words are combined logically to make sentences (syntax) (VIII.1). The books that survive are the last three of the six on etymology, which deal with its practical application, and the first three of the six on derivation and inflection, which concern theory. The division of treatment into theory and application was applied to all three subjects.

Given the loss of the opening books it is difficult to recover what theory Varro adopted to explain the origin of language, perhaps his mysterious 'fourth level' of the science of etymology (V.7–9). There are, however, some hints that he favoured a 'natural' theory of language (VI.3), adopting a Stoic idea according to which the one thousand or so elemental words (*primigenia*) reflected the nature of the things they denoted (VI.37); he perhaps acknowledged also the fashionable Pythagoreanism of his day in the notion of an original imposition of words by wise men (VIII.7).

This issue went back to the *νόμος/φύσις* (convention vs. nature)

81 *Rust.* I.2.3–8; II, pref, 2–4; II.1.3–6.

82 An early work *De Antiquitate Litterarum* is dedicated to L. Accius who died *c.* 84 B.C.; the *Disciplinae*, written in 34–33 B.C., contained a book on *grammatica* (Pliny *HN* XXIX.65,9).

83 *Ling.* V.8–9.

84 Cicero had been promised the dedication of the work in 47 (Att. XIII.12.3) for which he was still waiting in the summer of 45 (*Fam.* IX.8).

controversy of the fifth century B.C. Plato in the *Cratylus* discusses whether words denote objects, actions and qualities according to convention or nature, and the question had never ceased to stimulate debate. Varro's contemporary, the poet Lucretius, presents, in an imaginative reconstruction of primitive human life, the view of Epicurus on the origins of language, whereby each group of men named things as a natural and instinctive reaction to its particular environment. He omits, however, Epicurus' later refinement which granted a role to convention in rationalizing language at a later stage. Another contemporary, Nigidius Figulus, seems to have had views based, like Varro's, on Stoicism with a possible dash of Pythagoreanism.[85]

In Books VIII–X Varro enters into the complexities of a Hellenistic controversy over the morphology of language, which he discusses and illustrates as it applies to Latin. According to him the followers of the Pergamene grammarians led by Crates of Mallos defended, under Stoic influence, linguistic irregularity ('anomaly') as justified by common usage reflecting the natural growth of language. The adherents of the Alexandrian school believed that language in common use should be corrected in the direction of regularity, and that words should be derived and inflected in strict observance of the principle of 'analogy'. The controversy was still generating great excitement in this period. Not only freedmen grammarians like Caesar's teacher Antonius Gnipho and Staberius Eros were concerned with it, but Caesar himself, while travelling over the Alps in 54 B.C., wrote a defence of the analogist position held by his old instructor. Cicero too alludes to the controversy in works written about the same time as *De Lingua Latina*.[86]

Varro points out the value of some arguments on both sides of the anomalist–analogy dispute.[87] He concludes that there is a *natural* regularity or analogy which is exhibited in the inflected forms of a language (VIII.23). This should be followed by speakers of the language as a body and by individuals except where common custom has established an aberrant form (X.74), though poets can influence usage in the direction of analogy (IX.17). In deriving words from other words, however, individuals can follow their own wishes (X.53), though even those derived forms are subject to some 'natural' (in Varro's sense) restrictions (IX.37). Varro claims to be setting out the first principles governing the derivation and inflection of words as no one before him had done (X.1),

[85] See Sedley 1973 (B 107) for Epicurus' final and refined view, represented by D.L. X.75 (cf. Lucr. V. 1041ff), and for the philosopher's earlier change from a purely conventionalist to a primarily naturalist position. On Nigidius Figulus see pp. 708–710 and n. 110.

[86] Gnipho: Suet. *Gramm.* 7 mentions a work *De Latino Sermone* and a tradition that he studied in Alexandria: Quint. I.6.23 illustrates his analogist views; Staberius Eros: Priscian 385.1, see also Quint. I.6.3. Caesar: Suet. *Iul.* 56.5; Cicero: *Or.* 155ff.; *Brut.* 258–9.

[87] *Ling.* X.1; IX.1–3; 113–14; Taylor 1975 (H 123).

that is, he sees his own contribution to the subject as systematization, not invention.

In writing on Latin literature and Latin poets, Varro was principally following his teacher L. Aelius Stilo who, at the turn of the first century B.C., had been the first to lift 'grammatical' studies above the practical needs of teaching. Cicero, who had heard him lecture, commends Aelius for his grasp of Greek and Latin literature, of older Roman writers and of Roman antiquities. Varro appealed to Aelius' authority in stating that if the Muses wanted to speak Latin they would speak like Plautus, but he was prepared to correct his master's mistakes in etymology. In establishing the canon of authentic Plautine plays, Varro disagreed with his other main predecessor Accius, and, though not concerned with textual criticism in our sense, suggested that certain other plays might be genuine 'because of the texture and the humour displayed'.[88]

The triumph of Varronian systematization was the *Disciplinae* in which, out of the Greek tradition of a general education, the ἐγκύκλιος παιδεία, he created a specifically Roman product, the encyclopaedia or summary of basic knowledge. Following the Greeks, the Romans of the first century B.C. had come to view *grammatica*, rhetoric and dialectic, arithmetic, geometry, astronomy and music as studies befitting a free citizen (*artes liberales*), which could also prepare him for the study of philosophy. Now Varro offered a canon of nine subjects, by adding to these seven liberal arts the practical ones of medicine and architecture. The mediaeval *trivium*, consisting of the three preparatory subjects, grammar, dialectic and rhetoric, and the *quadrivium*, consisting of the mathematical subjects, were therefore the legacy of Varro as modified by St Augustine, who rejected the two practical subjects.[89] Of those, medicine, theoretical and practical, returned to the hands of the Greeks, but architecture, to judge by the one Latin treatise to survive, retained the clear stamp of Varro. Vitruvius, a practical architect appointed by Augustus to look after the repair of military machines, wrote, as an old man, ten books *De Architectura* in which he insists on the importance for architects of a training in the liberal arts, gives a long list of authorities (mainly Greek but including Varro), and criticizes some earlier writers for their unsystematic presentation: he himself promises to compose an *ars* covering the entire subject, with different subjects handled in different books.[90]

Varro's contribution to science was that of a compiler. It is appropriate to invoke the dictum of Cicero that the Romans, unlike the Greeks,

88 Cic. *Brut.* 205; Quint. X.1.99; Gell. *NA* I.18.1; 3; III.3; above n. 82. See Winterbottom 1982 (H 136).

89 Hadot 1984 (H 57) doubts Varro's later influence and the existence of this canon of seven subjects before Porphyry in the third century A.D., but see the review by Rawson 1987 (H 110).

90 Pliny *HN* XXIX.17; Vitr. VII, pref.10; pref.4; IV, pref.1.

had never held geometry or mathematics in high esteem but were only interested in their practical applications, surveying and calculation. Yet it is also important to note that Greek science itself had lost much of its creative impetus in the latter part of the second and the first century B.C. The Greeks themselves were largely concerned with the production of handbooks based on earlier discoveries and often written by literary polymaths rather than working scientists. Even the third-century B.C. poem of Aratus on astronomy, which was translated by Cicero and enjoyed such a vogue among Latin poets, had been written 'without any knowledge of astronomy but with a certain poetic talent'.[91]

It was in his antiquarian works that Varro most fully displayed the application of Greek techniques to the loving investigation of Roman institutions and traditions. The two most important were the monumental *Antiquitates Rerum Humanarum* and *Antiquitates Rerum Divinarum*, of which the second and later was dedicated to Caesar as *pontifex maximus*, possibly at the time when he was also dictator. The order of composition reflects the fact that Varro dealt with Roman religion as a human creation, which he felt should be preserved (whether or not it conformed to philosophical truth). To that end he provided practical information on the particular powers of particular gods.[92] Of the benefit those works conferred on Rome, Cicero wrote in 45:

> When we were wandering and straying like visitors in our own city, your books brought us home and enabled us to realize at last who and where we were. You have revealed the age of our fatherland, its systems of chronology, its rules governing religious rites and priests, its civil and military institutions, the location of its districts and sites, and the names, the types, the functions and the causes of everything divine and human.[93]

These words also direct us to self-identification as the common theme that underlies the various Roman responses, positive and negative, to Greek culture in this period. From the Greeks the Romans acquired both the analytic tools and the basis of comparison necessary to understand themselves.

This function of Varro's works is made explicit in a curious work called *Hebdomades*, the first illustrated Roman book.[94] In fifteen volumes,

[91] See Stahl 1962 (H 119) chs. 3–5; Cicero on mathematics: *Tusc.* I.5, cf. *Att.* II.4.1 for Cicero's own troubles in understanding mathematical geography; Cicero on Aratus: *Nat. D.* II.104ff (Cicero's translation); *Rep.* I.22 'non astrologiae scientia, sed poetica quadam facultate'.

[92] On the date of the later work, see Cardauns 1976 (B 11) II, 132–3 and 1978 (B 12) 80ff; Jocelyn 1982–3 (H 65) 148ff. Grafton and Swerdlow 1985 (H 51) 460, n. 26 suggest that the earlier work may have described the Julian calendar reform, which perhaps strengthens the case for a date during the dictatorship. Varro's rationale: *Antiquitates Rerum Divinarum* I fr.5 (Cardauns) = Aug., *De civ. D.* VI.4; I fr. 12 = *De civ. D.* IV.31; I fr.3 = *De civ. D.* IV.22; Beard in ch. 19 below, pp. 758–9.

[93] *Acad.* I.9.

[94] Pliny *HN* XXXV.11; Symmachus, *Epp.* I.2.2; I.4.1,2; Auson. *Mos.* 305–7.

published in 39 B.C., he provided portraits and accompanying epigrams for 700 Greeks and Romans in different categories of achievement: intellectual, political and religious. In this alignment of Greeks and Romans lay the inspiration for the parallel books *De Viris Illustribus* of Cornelius Nepos and for Plutarch's *Lives*. In writing about foreign and Roman generals, Nepos states explicitly that the purpose of the double series is to enable readers to judge which generals were superior, though his preface reveals also a less partisan purpose, of making men aware that conduct must be judged by the standards of the society in question.[95]

V. PYTHAGOREANISM

In the first book of the *Hebdomades*, Varro spoke of the importance of the number seven in the organization of the heavenly bodies, in the birth and growth of human beings and in historical tradition, adding that he himself had entered the twelfth hebdomad of his age and written seventy hebdomads of books.[96] This concern with the link between nature and number, shown here and elsewhere by Varro, is clearly connected with the revival of interest in Pythagoras whose studies in astronomy and acoustics had led to the development of a superstitious numerology. Varro, in fact, is said to have been buried in the 'Pythagorean way' in leaves of myrtle, olive and black poplar.[97]

Cicero affords a glimpse of the attention paid to Pythagoras in his day. He insists that the Pythagorean communities of southern Italy in the sixth to fourth centuries must have had an influence on institutions of the early Roman state, and, indeed, Pliny the Elder tells us that there was a statue of the sage in the Roman *comitium* in the fourth century.[98] In 181 B.C. an archaeological find revealed the 'Books of Numa', the Greek volumes which were identified in the earliest historical accounts, less than fifty years later, as Pythagorean philosophy. The identification was based on the tradition that Numa was a pupil of Pythagoras: Cicero and his sophisticated friends, Atticus, Varro and Nepos, rightly rejected it on chronological grounds.[99]But Cicero still emphasized the earliness of Pythagorean influence: he liked the idea that Roman interest in Greek philosophy went back to an early period and an Italian source.[100]

95 *Hann.* 13.4; pref. 3. Though Varro was probably already at work on *Hebdomades* in 44 (Cic. *Att.* XVI.11.3 with Shackleton Bailey 1965–70 (B 108) *ad loc.*) and some of the later Nepos lives can be dated between 35 and 32 B.C., Varro's priority is regarded as uncertain by Geiger 1985 (B 42) 81.

96 Gell, *NA* III.10.1. 97 Pliny *HN* XXXV.160.

98 Cic. *Tusc.* IV.2ff; Pliny *HN* XXXIV.26. Some confirmatory evidence for Cicero's claim is adduced by Jocelyn 1976–7 (H 64).

99 Livy XL.29.3–14; Pliny *HN* XIII.84ff; Polyb. VI.59.2 whom Cicero and his friends were probably following (cf. *Rep.* II.27).

100 *De Or.* II.154; *Rep.* II.28, cf. *Tusc.* IV.5: philosophical interest of long standing in Rome.

This Pythagorean revival was not, however, a specifically Roman development. Here as in other areas, Roman intellectuals were participating in a more general movement. For example, Cicero's notion, shared by Varro, that the dogmatic teachings of Plato were traceable to his contacts with Pythagoreans in the West reminds us that Posidonius had traced to Pythagoras Plato's theories on the soul and the passions. At this period also Alexander Polyhistor wrote a book on Pythagorean precepts and included the Pythagoreans in his *History of the Philosophical Schools*.[101] Moreover, various texts, some composed in the Doric dialect of Italy and Sicily, purporting to emanate from ancient Pythagorean writers, are now thought to have been composed in the second and first centuries B.C., probably by the middle of the first century.[102]

With this thirst for Pythagorean doctrine went a fascination with Plato's *Timaeus*, for which Posidonius had provided an exegesis and which was to become a key dialogue for the Middle Platonists. Cicero translated part of the work, and his introduction, written in 45, survives. In it he pays tribute to the recently deceased Nigidius Figulus, the scholar whom a later antiquarian was to set beside Varro, regarding them as the two pillars of learning in the age of Cicero and Caesar.[103] Cicero says of him that he was born to revive the *disciplina* of the Pythagoreans and was a man versed in all the liberal arts, but particularly concerned with the 'secrets of nature', by which Cicero means science or natural philosophy.[104] Cicero's description of Nigidius, a senatorial ally in the Catilinarian conspiracy and later a fellow-supporter of Pompey in the civil war, fits well with his attested works on the gods, on the nature of man, on animals and on the wind, especially as Pythagoras was associated with natural science in this period. But by writers under the Empire Nigidius is sometimes depicted as an astrologer and prophet,[105] and he is known to have written on astrology, dreams and divination. It is possible that Nigidius, though writing as a scholar, expressed belief in at least some of these methods of predicting the future which gave him the reputation of an occultist, just as the practice of necromancy is alleged of Appius Claudius who, dedicating a work to his fellow-augur Cicero, expressed some belief in divination. These interests of prominent contemporaries remind us that Cicero's attack on all forms of divination as superstition may not be pure rhetoric, and that the robust rationalism

[101] Cic. *Rep.* I.15–16; *Fin.* V.87; Varro in Aug. *De civ. D.* VIII.3: Posidonius, Edelstein–Kidd 1988 (B 32) T95, cf. Cic. *Tusc.* IV.10; I.39; Alexander, *FGrH* no. 273, frs. 94,93. See Burkert 1965 (H 22); Rawson 1985 (H 109) 291–3 for possible Roman influence on Greek interests in this area.

[102] Thesleff 1961 (H 125); essays by Burkert 1971 (H 23) and Thesleff 1971 (H 127); Dillon 1977 (H 31) 117ff.

[103] Edelstein–Kidd 1988 (B 32); Gell. *NA* XIX.14.1.

[104] *Tim.* 1, and see *Acad.* I.15;19 for natural science as unveiling mysteries.

[105] Cicero: *De Or.* I.42, cf. *Rep.* I.16; *Tusc.* V.10; later writers: Suet. *Aug.* 94.5, cf. Lucan I.639.

be expounds in *De Divinatione* was pitched against something more widespread than theoretical Stoicism.[106]

Whether or not such interests were connected with Pythagoreanism is disputed. Cicero, attacking Caesar's associate Vatinius, says that he claimed to be a Pythagorean and justified his barbaric customs by using the name of a most learned man, and the latter is reasonably identified as Nigidius by a later scholiast, who adds that enemies spoke of a shady cabal (*factio*), though its members claimed to be followers of Pythagoras.[107] Cicero drops hints about Vatinius' interest in haruspicy, while elsewhere he regards Pythagoras as a leading authority on divination and dreams.[108] Finally, in his thirty-volume grammatical work, Nigidius exhibited an interest in etymology and stated firmly that names were imposed on things by nature, not convention. The particular example preserved resembles an argument ascribed to the Stoic Chrysippus, but the view is also consonant with the idea attributed to Pythagoras by Cicero that, as in Plato's *Cratylus*, a primordial sage named things correctly to represent their nature.[109]

In view of the interest in Pythagoras in Rome and elsewhere that we have mentioned, it is hard to see what Cicero means when he says that, in his view, Nigidius renewed Pythagorean teaching, even if we allow for the exaggeration of a compliment. It has been suggested that Nigidius actually founded a society of some kind or that he initiated the move, taken up by Eudorus of Alexandria, to turn Pythagoreanism into a serious philosophy again.[110] In any case this Neo-Pythagoreanism, though espoused by charismatic individuals, did not become a separate philosophical sect comparable to the four major schools, for which Marcus Aurelius was to establish professorial chairs. In the first century A.D. in Rome it contributed elements, such as vegetarianism and the nightly examination of conscience, to the (roughly Stoic) doctrine of the 'Sextii';[111] otherwise it became an important ingredient in the new

106 Appius: Cic. *Leg.* II.32; *Tusc.* I.37; *Div.* I.132. Cicero's attack: *Div.* II.148: That this passage had a real target remains true even if it was not meant to express Cicero's personal views, as is maintained by M. Schofield 1986 (H 116).

107 Thesleff 1965 (H 126) 44ff is sceptical of Nigidius' Pythagoreanism. Cic. *Vat.* 14; *Schol. Bob. ad loc.* The *Invective against Sallust*, purporting to be by Cicero, mentions the *sodalicium* of Nigidius.

108 *Div.* I.5; 62; II.119; I.102.

109 Gell. *NA* X.4; Cic. *Tusc.* I.62. For the view of Chrysippus, see von Arnim, *Stoicorum Veterum Fragmenta*, II, fr. 895, on which see Dillon 1977 (H 31) 181.

110 The first suggestion is that of Thesleff 1961 (H 125) 52; the second of Dillon 1977 (H 31) 117–19.

111 In the 60s A.D. Seneca (*QNat.* VII.32.2) speaks of the Pythagorean school as having no *praeceptor* and of the Sextii as a separate sect, while noting practices of theirs (*Ep.* 108.17–18; *Ira* III.36.1) that were thought of as Pythagorean (Ov. *Met.* XV.60ff: Cic. *Sen.* 38). For charismatic individuals thought of as Pythagorean in the second half of the second century A.D.: C. P. Jones, *Culture and Society in Lucian* (Cambridge, MA, 1986) 30, 135.

Platonism. By the Antonine period, Nigidius himself was hardly read; his scholarship was not as closely related to Roman life as Varro's, and it was more abstrusely written.[112]

VI. THE NEW POETRY

The basis of the Greek style of education was poetry. At Rome epic declined after Ennius, and tragedy and comedy were largely replaced by the humbler mime. Although some aristocrats in Terence's day were suspected of writing poetic drama which they would not avow, by the end of the second century the consular Q. Catulus was only one of several to compose, quite openly, Latin epigrams in the current Greek mode.[113]

Though Cicero himself advertised the glories of his consulship in poetry as well as prose, his social peers seem to have written verse mostly for amusement in particularly tedious moments. Thus Caesar composed a poem on his journey from Rome to Spain, and Quintus Cicero, when serving on Caesar's staff in Gaul, wrote four tragedies in sixteen days. The youthful Varro, however, composed Menippean satires in a combination of prose and verse, which he seems to have thought of as a kind of popular philosophy.[114]

In the next generation, possibly under the influence of Parthenius, a recherché type of Greek poetry became fashionable, as Catullus and those whom Cicero calls the 'neoteroi', the 'new poets', sought inspiration from Callimachus and Euphorion. Though this is no place to discuss literary fashions as such,[115] it is worth noting their connexion with general intellectual developments. This 'neoteric' poetry was learned poetry, written for an elite and requiring knowledge not only of Greek literature and scholarship but of Greek science, notably astronomy, such as was available in Aratus' poem. Even Lucretius, an apparently isolated figure, is a product of his time in his exhibition of Greek learning, including Aratean astronomy, his interest (shared by Posidonius and Varro) in the history of civilization, his determination to conquer a new province for Latin literature, and his poetic inventiveness and sophistication, comparable to that of his 'neoteric' contemporaries.[116]

[112] Gell. *NA* XIX.14.2–3.

[113] Cic. *Brut.* 132; Gell. *NA* XIX.9–10.

[114] Caesar's *Iter*: Suet. *Iul.* 56.5; Quintus: Cic. *QFr.* III.5(6).7; Varro: Cic. *Acad.* II.18.7.

[115] On which see now Clausen 1982 (H 26).

[116] Dalzell 1982 (B 24) 210; Grimal 1978 (H 54), though the links Grimal sees with contemporary politics are not convincing.

VII. HISTORY AND RELATED STUDIES

In two celebrated passages, written at the mid-point of the first century B.C., Cicero laments the absence of a Latin equivalent to the great historians of Greece.[117] Though his principal criticisms of Latin historiography down to his time were about style, he also reveals, here and elsewhere, much about the conception of the historian's task in his own day.

Cicero assumes that the choice of subject for the historian lies between recounting contemporary events or starting *de Romulo et Remo*. The earliest Roman annalists, who were senators, had started from the beginning of Rome's history; but, from the last third of the second century B.C., that type of history was left to lesser men, and senators turned to writing the history of a period they had lived through or monographs on particular subjects.[118] (An exception was Licinius Macer who, in the 70s, went back to the beginning in order to impart a *popularis* bias to the history of early times and celebrate the deeds of his ancestors.)

At the turn of the century L. Coelius Antipater wrote a history of the Hannibalic War, and Sempronius Asellio wrote up the events of his own troubled times, in which he had played an active part.[119] The most illustrious historian in this tradition was L. Cornelius Sisenna, one of Sulla's most trusted adherents, who told the story of the Social War and the civil wars from Sulla's standpoint. Though Sallust was to pay him the compliment of starting his history where Sisenna's finished, Cicero regarded him only as less bad than the others. Among other things, he disliked his idiosyncratic style, full of neologisms and unusual word forms, for Sisenna's adherence to 'analogy' was not accompanied, as it was in Caesar's case, by severe self-restraint: he wanted to correct and reform common linguistic usage.[120]

Cicero's correspondent L. Lucceius, possibly in order to give a more balanced account, wrote on the same subject.[121] Cicero's letter to Lucceius urging him to compose a monograph on Cicero's role in the Catilinarian crisis and its aftermath fills out our evidence for what he and his contemporaries felt about the writing of history. Cicero expected

[117] *De Or.* II.51ff; *Leg.* I.5ff. In the latter he represents himself as turning down a request by his brother and his friend Atticus to write history himself.

[118] Publication of the *annales maximi* is adduced as the reason for this change by Badian 1966 (H 4); Ogilvie 1965 (B 79) 7ff; Rawson 1985 (H 109) 218, prefers to stress the influence of contemporary events and of Polybius.

[119] Cic. *De Or.* II.54; Gell. *NA* II.13.

[120] Sall. *Iug.* 95.3; Cic. *Leg.* I.7; *Brut.* 228; 260–1. On his writing see Badian 1966 (H 4) 25–6; Rawson 1979 (H 108).

[121] *Fam.* V.12, 1–2. This work may be covered by Cicero's allusion in *Leg* I.7, written *c.* 52, to those whose work had not yet been published, for when Cicero wrote the letter in 55 he had seen some of it but it was not finished.

Roman historians and their readers to be aware of the Greek historical tradition, as is shown by the precedents he cites to Lucceius and his strictures elsewhere on Sisenna for reading only Clitarchus. The great work of Polybius will have brought that tradition closer to the Romans. Cicero assumed that Lucceius (and the others he intended to read his letter – his 'very pretty piece'[122]) would agree with him that history should be written primarily by and for men in public life, and that it must explain events in terms of accident and human intent, exploring the motives and characters of the participants so as to furnish political models and moral lessons.

Sempronius Asellio had already made most of those points, and Cicero makes them again through Asellio's contemporary M. Antonius in *De Oratore*. Cicero's Antonius, however, like Lucceius and Cicero himself, is clearly more concerned with style and with enlivening qualities than Asellio or Polybius had been.[123] Yet Cicero does not even deign to mention the later annalists, Claudius Quadrigarius and Valerius Antias, who attached great importance to entertainment, for they achieved it by wild exaggeration and invention.[124] Cicero distinguishes sharply between the licence permitted to poets and the truth required of historians: facts, not fiction, in reporting, and fairness, not bias, in giving judgement, with the emphasis on the latter. Polybius had stressed impartiality, and Cicero regards this as the foundation on which the elaborate structure of history must be built.[125] It is clear that Lucceius claimed to do this in the prologue to one of his compositions, and that Cicero, when he urged him to glorify his own deeds even at the expense of the *leges historiae*, was only putting up a pretence of modesty: he clearly expected everyone to feel that of his own merits there *could* be no exaggeration.

Cicero at least avoided violating his own rule about impartiality and did not publish his account of his own exploits in Latin prose (only one in verse). (The vituperative *De Consiliis Suis* was written for Atticus' private perusal and only published posthumously.) He did, however, provide Lucceius, who had agreed to Cicero's request, with *commentarii*, i.e. a bare narrative outline of facts without embellishment.[126] A similar outline in Greek had been sent to Posidonius in 60 in the hope that he would help to ensure Cicero's reputation. When the notable historian

122 *Att.* IV.6.4. 123 *Fam.* V.12.4; *De Or.* II.62–3; Gell. *NA* V.18.7.

124 Badian 1966 (H 4) 18–22. On Valerius' mendacity, Livy XXVI.49; Ogilvie 1965 (B 79) 12–16.

125 *Leg.* I.3–5; Polyb. I.14; Cic. *De Or.* II.62.

126 *De Consulatu Suo* in Greek prose: *Att.* I.20.6; *De Temporibus Meis* in Latin verse: *Att* IV.8a, 3; *Fam.* I.9.23 shows that he considered posthumous publication even for the poem – see Shackleton Bailey 1977 (B 110) *ad locc. De Consiliis Suis*: *Att.* II.6.2; *Att.* II.8,1; Rawson 1982 (B 94). The Latin *commentarii*: *Att.* IV.6.4; IV.11.2, also *Fam.* V.12,10; those planned in 60 (*Att.* I.19.10) are not heard of again.

evaded the task with the compliment that the excellence of Cicero's work had only deterred him from attempting it, Cicero had the outline circulated in Greece. He himself and others had made the same point about the daunting brilliance of Caesar's *commentarii* on his exploits in Gaul, which were ostensibly written as raw material for historians.[127]

These two skilled performers had found a subtle solution to the problem confronting the ambitious politicians of the period, who naturally wished to glorify their own exploits and stamp their own interpretation on events in which they had taken part. Indeed, the political turmoil of the late Republic did not produce the classic history, contemporary or annalistic, that Cicero contemplated: Sallust and Livy were to fulfil that task after his death and not as he had imagined.[128] Instead there developed, on the one hand, literature that reflected the dominance of powerful individuals, and, on the other, scholarship that celebrated what was being destroyed.

Cicero's *commentarii* were probably on the scale of the *Liber de Consulatu et de Rebus Gestis Suis* of Q. Lutatius Catulus (cos. 102 B.C.), but the works *De Vita Sua* of M. Aemilius Scaurus (cos. 115), P. Rutilius Rufus and Sulla the dictator were more substantial. Though the two earlier authors were already ignored by the reading public a generation later, the works of Rutilius and Sulla were very influential: Rutilius reached Plutarch via Posidonius.[129] Their bias, well attested in the case of the virtuous Rutilius who blackened Marius and Pompey's father, was, in the case of Sulla, to leave a permanent mark on the Romans' interpretation of their history. Even after Cicero's scruples, Varro did not hesitate to write three books of autobiography: he lived through the triumviral period and had a lot to tell.[130]

At about the same time there arose out of this autobiographical tradition and the Peripatetic tradition of literary biography, with some inspiration from Varro's *Hebdomades* and the eulogies and invectives prompted by the younger Cato's death in 46 B.C., the biographies of statesmen, generals and kings which Cornelius Nepos included in his *De Viris Illustribus*.[131]

Why Cicero did not write his history can only be surmised. He himself notes that a great deal of time would be required: the pains he took to be

[127] *Att.* II.1.2 cf. I.19.10, see above, p. 699; *Brut.* 262 with Douglas 1966 (B 29) *ad loc.*, Hirtius *BGall.* VIII, pref. 4–5.

[128] Syme 1964 (B 116) ch. 5; Rawson 1972 (H 104) 42–3.

[129] Cic. *Brut.* 112; 132.

[130] *De Vita Sua*: *HRR* II, XXXVIIII–XXXX: some of the details about Varro's career in Pliny the Elder (e.g. *HN* VII.115; XVI.7) may derive from this work.

[131] The thesis of Geiger 1985 (B 42) that political biography was an innovation of Cornelius Nepos (p. 61) requires him to maintain, implausibly, that the work of Munatius Rufus on the younger Cato (Plut. *Cat. Min.* 25.1; 37) was not a biography, but a memoir which stopped at the outbreak of civil war.

accurate about the settings and participants in his dialogues suggest his high standards of historical research, while his consultation of Varro and Atticus shows that he would have accepted the labour imposed by the new antiquarianism.[132] We can trace the first serious enthusiasm for uncovering the history of Rome's institutions, customs and language to the days of Cicero's youth when M. Junius Congus Gracchanus dedicated a work on the powers of magistrates to Atticus' erudite father. In *De Oratore* Cicero attributes to Crassus enthusiasm for these *Aeliana studia*, which are furthered by the study of ancient Roman law: Cicero himself had studied with Aelius Stilo. Just as it is reasonable to connect those interests with the political crisis that the Gracchi set in motion by challenging the established order, so it is tempting to trace the second wave of antiquarianism in Cicero's maturity to the new crisis provoked by the tactics of the 'First Triumvirate'.[133]

Fundamental for history was the establishment of accurate chronology. By 54 Nepos had produced a list of events from the earliest times to his own day in three books. Atticus improved on it and contracted the material into one book, starting with the foundation of Rome. Cicero, to whom this *liber annalis* was dedicated, praised it for making oratory easier and works like the *Brutus* possible. Cicero seems to have used both works, though he preferred the one by Atticus: Varro may later have improved on both.[134] Atticus also prepared, at the request of their descendants, genealogies of several great families, giving filiations and listing magistracies with precise dates.[135]His Roman emphasis was again apparent in his picture album, inspired by Varro's *Hebdomades* but celebrating only the magistracies and achievements of great Romans.[136]

The *Chronica* of Nepos was the first work of Roman historiography not concerned with exclusively Roman and Italian history. It was based on the verse chronicle of Apollodorus, a second-century Athenian scholar, and synchronisms of Greek and Roman history were an important feature, which looked forward to the universal histories of the Augustan age.[137] Polybius had been the first to see that the Roman Empire had to be treated in a history embracing the whole of the known world, but his example was not imitated in the Republic except by Posidonius, who continued his history from 146 into the 80s B.C. This work, though excellent in its breadth of interest, ethnographical insight,

[132] *Leg.* I.8; Sumner 1973 (B 115) 161ff; Rawson 1972 (H 104), who notes the increase in Cicero's knowledge between *De Oratore* and *Brutus*.

[133] Cic. *Leg.* III.49; Nep. *Att.*1; *De Or.* I.256; 193; *Brut.* 207. See Rawson 1972 (H 104).

[134] Nepos: Gell. *NA* XVII.21.3; Atticus: Nep. *Att.* 18.2; Cic. *Att.* XII.23.2; *Orat.* 120; *Brut.* 14–16; Varro: Gell. *NA* XVII.21.23 mentions *chronici* which Peter (*HRR* II.24, XXXVIII) identifies with his *Annalium* III.

[135] Nep. *Att.* 18.3. [136] Nep. *Att.* 18.5–6; see above, pp. 706–7.

[137] Geiger 1985 (B 42) 68–72; Momigliano 1984 (H 86).

and understanding of mass psychology, imbued Roman political history with the uncritical ancestor-worship of his Roman sources and the particular political bias of Rutilius Rufus. If already known by 60, the history may be what encouraged Cicero to ask for a eulogy from the same hand, but Cicero never mentions the work itself.[138]

Plutarch says that Cicero intended to blend Greek material into his Roman history, but the closest he ever actually came to historical subject-matter was in the *De Republica* and the *Brutus*. The introduction to *De Oratore* III, however, may give us some idea of what his historical narrative would have been like.[139] The loyal Cornelius Nepos, though writing after Sallust and perhaps in the very year of his death, says that only Cicero could have given Latin literature a history worthy of the Greeks. He adds that it was Cicero's eloquence that gave polish to Roman oratory and refinement to philosophy in Latin, both of which were crude and primitive before.[140]

VIII. CICERO'S THEORETICAL WORKS

The works to which Nepos refers last belong to the end of Cicero's life. They show us how he thought his talents could be best employed to serve his country and his own reputation, once his role in politics was diminished, as it was in the 50s, or obliterated, as in the 40s until Caesar's assassination.

'Non hominis nomen sed eloquentiae' was Quintilian's tribute to Cicero. Cicero's own notorious description to Atticus of some of his writings as 'mere transcripts, requiring less work; I just contribute the words, which I have in plenty', though not to be taken literally, shows that he thought of himself primarily as a man of words.[141] His unrivalled control of Latin was acknowledged by his contemporaries in their dedication to him of linguistic works: it was probably in the *De Analogia* that Caesar wrote 'You have won greater laurels than the triumphal wreath, for it is a greater achievement to have extended the frontiers of the Roman genius than those of Rome's empire.'[142]

Cicero's concentration on the concept of the ideal orator in all his mature rhetorical works, as well as the broad hint at the end of the *Brutus*, shows that he knew he was unsurpassed in oratory and could impart

[138] Posidonius' history: Malitz 1983 (B 69). Posidonius died in the 50s and the work could have been written late in his life.

[139] Plut. *Cic.* 41; Rawson 1972 (H 104) 43–4.

[140] Nep. fr. 3.

[141] Quint. X.1.112; *Att.* XII.52.3. It is not clear to which of the philosophical works that Cicero was writing in June 45 the remark refers. A comparison is being made either with other works of his own or with the work of Varro.

[142] Pliny *HN* VII.117. See also the flattering citation from the work (here mentioned under the Latin title *De Ratione Latine Loquendi*) in Cicero's *Brutus* 253–5.

something valuable from his experience. He counts these works among his philosophical writings, for Aristotle and Theophrastus had laid down precepts for oratory, while Cicero's ideal was the philosophical rhetoric of Aristotle and Isocrates. The dialogue form itself was borrowed from Plato and Aristotle.[143] Moreover, Cicero was at pains to insist that the works were not technical treatises, and though he thought they would be useful to the young, he presented himself as a critic not a teacher. He had in mind here not only that an *ars* would not be literature and would suggest the Greek professional rather than the Roman gentleman scholar, but also his belief that the Hellenistic rhetors up to his own day took too limited a view of their subject.[144] Therefore he tried to camouflage his treatment of the main topics in such manuals and also covered subjects not usually included, such as prose rhythm and the abstract philosophical themes for declamation known as *θέσεις*.[145]

His contact with the scholarly concerns of his time is shown already in *De Oratore*, written in 55, where he exhibits considerable knowledge both of Greek cultural history and of Roman education and intellectual interests at the dramatic date of the dialogue, 91 B.C. Then, in the *Brutus*, Cicero uses the new chronological tools to create a new form, the historical survey in the shape of a dialogue. Nepos' series of lives of intellectuals in the Greek manner is part of the same phenomenon,[146] which was not confined to contemporary Rome: the Greek Academic philosophers who taught Cicero were, after all, interested in the history of philosophical doctrines, and that interest is reflected in Cicero's history of philosophy in *De Oratore* III.60ff.

The rhetorical works constitute a contribution to the old debate of rhetoric and philosophy specifically mentioned here. Though the dramatic date of *De Oratore* did not allow Cicero to stray chronologically beyond the controversy in Athens that Crassus and Antonius had heard and the innovation of the philosopher Philo in treating not only *θέσεις* but the more concrete *controversiae*,[147] the issue was not dead when Cicero was writing. Only six years previously Posidonius had delivered a lecture before Pompey at Rhodes in which he attacked, in the name of philosophy, the claim made for rhetoric by the influential second-century rhetorician Hermagoras that such general questions of a

[143] *Div.* II.4; *Fam.* I.9.23: 'Aristoteliam et Isocratiam rationem oratoriam'. In *De Or.* I.28 and the final prophecy about Hortensius, there are clear allusions to Plato's *Phaedrus*, while the subject matter owes much to the *Gorgias* (cf. III.128–9). Cicero thinks of the form of *De Oratore* as Aristotelian dialogue (*Fam.* I.9.23) and the *Brutus* is even more in that tradition as Cicero is the main speaker (*Att.* XIII.19.4).

[144] *De Or.* I.111; 165; II.10; *Orat.* 117; 112; 123; 43. For the young: *De Or.* II.4 cf. *Fam.* I.9.23; Roman amateurs: *De Or.* I.115; 138; Greek rhetors: III.70.

[145] *De Or.* III.188; 108–9. See Barwick 1963 (H 6).

[146] The *Brutus*: Douglas 1966 (B 29) xxii–xxiii; Nepos: Fantham 1981 (B 34) 7–17; Geiger 1985 (B 42) 23.

[147] *De Or.* I.47; 75; 83ff; III.10; *Tusc.* II.9.

philosophical nature belonged to the province of the orator. This claim Cicero had ridiculed over twenty years earlier but now sought to assert for the ideal oratorical education he proposed.[148]

A newer Roman controversy comes to the fore in the *Brutus* and *Orator*, composed in 46. Some of the younger orators, in reaction against Hortensius and Cicero, began to espouse a more austere style, deeming themselves Atticists, champions of the pure oratory of classical Athens, and opponents of the verbose and flowery 'Asianic' style that had developed in the Greek diaspora.[149] The leader of the movement seems to have been C. Licinius Calvus and, as with the new poetry in which Calvus was also involved, the reaction took the form of emulating Greek writers not previously important in Rome, in this case the orator Lysias. Cicero responded by improving his knowledge of Lysias and then pointing out that the greatest 'Attic' orator had in fact been Demosthenes, who represented a further development in rhetorical history and was the master of all three styles of oratory (Grand, Middle, and Plain), not just one.[150] Cicero implies that the Atticist movement, which developed in the late 50s, had lost its force by 45 B.C., because its proponents, hostile to his own command of the full resources of oratory which they were unable to master, had ignored the fact that oratory is a popular art.[151]

After *De Oratore*, but while he was still in some sense 'at the helm of the state', Cicero composed *De Republica* and started the *De Legibus*, which he never completed. As in *De Oratore*, the inspiration of Plato is explicit but his ideas are transformed: Cicero is giving the Roman answer to Plato, setting up a Roman ideal grounded in ancestral wisdom.[152] Just as Cicero's ideal orator was a Roman statesman, versed in all subjects but only to the extent that is practically necessary, so his ideal state was not a theoretical construction but the Roman state, analysed here as the mixed constitution of Greek theory and restored to its idealized past condition, as it could in fact be if run by men of high principle and appropriate education like Cicero's ideal orator.[153]

148 Plut. *Pomp.* 42.5: on the various sources and interpretations of this incident, see Malitz 1983 (B 69) 25–7; Posidonius' speech was later published. Cic. *Inv.* I.6.8; *De Or.* III.106–7; 120; *Orat.* 125. On Cicero's originality here, see Grube 1965 (H 55) 174–5.

149 *Brut.* 50; 67–8; 325 and Douglas 1966 (B 29) xiiff. For Brutus' possible sympathy with the Atticist movement, see Douglas 1966 (B 29) xiii–xiv.

150 *Brut.* 284ff; 35; 185; *Orat.* 23ff; 75; 234. On Cicero's increase in knowledge of Greek oratory between *De Oratore* and these later works, Douglas 1966 (B 29) xiv–xvi and 1973 (H 35) 103–6.

151 *Tusc.* II.3.

152 *Rep.* I.65; II.3; 22; 51; IV.4–5; *Leg.* II.14. Cicero's remark (*Rep.* I.16) about Plato ascribing his own ideas to Socrates warns us not to take too seriously his account of the learning and interests of his 'Scipionic circle'.

153 Possibility of restoration is hinted at in *Rep.* V.2 and *Leg.* III.29. Cicero clearly envisages more than one *rector rei publicae* at a time (*Rep.* II.67, and see *De Or.* I.211); importance of education: *Leg.* III.29. See Coleman 1964 (H 27) 13–14 on the relation of the *rector* of *De Republica* to *De Or.* III.63 and Cicero's conception of his own qualities at *Rep.* I.6; 13; *Leg.* III.14 *ad fin.*

The intellectual interests of his age are everywhere apparent. For the history of the Roman monarchy and early Republic he made critical use of the Roman annalists and Varro's researches, and for *De Legibus* he consulted old senatorial decrees and used etymology to reconstruct social customs.[154] The skeletal law code he presents, starting with a definition of law and and exploration of its nature and then working systematically through divine, religious and secular law, reminds one of the project ascribed to Crassus in *De Oratore* of reducing Roman *ius civile* to an *ars* in the Greek sense. But here Cicero is putting Roman law itself, regarded as the most appropriate intellectual activity for Roman statesmen, into a larger framework of human nature and natural justice, derived from philosophy. Finally, *De Republica*, particularly the *Somnium Scipionis* corresponding to Plato's Pythagorean Myth of Er, abounds in the fashionable numerology and astronomy associated with Pythagoras' name.[155]

In the period of his enforced leisure under the dictatorship, Cicero composed what he regarded as his most serious works, those treating the philosophical doctrines of the Hellenistic schools.[156] Though philosophy was a life-long interest and there were emotional reasons, such as the death of his daughter in 45, for his choice,[157] the sheer difficulty of expounding philosophy in Latin must have made it an attractive challenge. It was not absolutely virgin territory. The Epicureans had been first, Amafinius, Rabirius, Catius and others who, by their own confession, wrote without technical language and without the definitions and divisions of a proper *ars*. Cicero says that they also had no pretensions to literary skill and thus appealed only to the converted and the poorly educated.[158] Though Cicero remarks that such a simple type of exposition was only possible for such a simple philosophy, Cassius complains about *rustici Stoici* as well.[159]

Cicero may have read Lucretius' work, but a poet naturally approaches exposition in a different way and is not as free to invent and explain technical terms. Cicero does not seem to have learned much from

[154] Rawson 1972 (H 104) 36–8. Use of Varro: Cic. *Att.* IV.14,1, but see Shackleton Bailey 1965–1970 (B 108) *ad loc.*

[155] *Leg.* II.18ff; *De Or.* I.190; *Fin.* I.12; *Leg.* I.16–17. Pythagoreanism: see Coleman 1964 (H 27).

[156] *Div.* II.1–7; *Orat.* 148.

[157] *Nat.D.* I.9; *Div.* II.3 which brings out the relevance of the death of Cato, the Stoic *par excellence*, in 46 B.C. Earlier in that year, when Cato was leading the Republican forces in Africa, Cicero had composed the *Paradoxa Stoicorum* with him in mind (1ff).

[158] *Acad.* I.5; *Fin.* III.40; *Tusc.* I.6; II.7. Not mentioned is Atticus' Epicurean friend L. Saufeius (Nep. *Att.* 12.3; Cic. *Att.* VII.1; IV.6) who was a writer on philosophical themes (*Att.* I.3.1) in Latin(?): see Rawson 1985 (H 109) 9.

[159] *Fam.* XV.19.1. Shackleton Bailey 1977 (B 110) *ad loc.*, while admitting that the context suggests writers in Latin, believes these were Greek writers, but *Tusc.* IV.6 only says there were few in Latin. Rawson 1985 (B 109) 49 and 284–5 adduces the Stoics ridiculed by Horace.

him.[160] More important was the example of Brutus, whose *De Virtute* preceded Cicero's ethical works and whom Quintilian places second to Cicero.[161] Yet his judgement on Brutus, 'You can tell that he means what he says', suggests a passionate style of exposition not suitable to Cicero's balanced presentation of philosophical views or to his discussion of Greek terms and the problems of translation. If modern scholars often regret that Cicero, in his determination to be readable, was not consistent in the translations he adopted, for Seneca and Quintilian he was already the ultimate authority on philosophical vocabulary, while for St Augustine he was the originator and perfector of Latin philosophy.[162]

One of the attractions for Cicero of writing about philosophy must have been the fact that Varro had so far eschewed the task. Indeed, in the second edition of the *Academica*, which Cicero had rewritten so as to include Varro as an interlocutor, Cicero represents him as objecting to the idea of writing philosophy in Latin on the ground that for those who cannot face it in Greek it will be too difficult in Latin, requiring, as it is bound to, the creation of new terms (I.5–6). He is then made to disprove his own contention by expounding the philosophical system he favours, employing new words and justifying them (I.24). Cicero's Varro points to the philosophy included in his Menippean satires, funeral orations and the prefaces to his *Antiquitates* (I.8), but it was only after Cicero's *Academica* that Varro himself produced serious philosophical works, including a *Liber de Philosophia* in which, after taking to extremes the Carneadean notion of classifying different possible systems by different conceptions of the ultimate aim, he came down in favour of the 'Old Academy' of Antiochus of Ascalon. He also wrote *logistorici*, dialogues with double titles on particular philosophical topics of more general and practical interest, rather in the manner of Cicero's *Cato de Senectute* or *Laelius de Amicitia*.

In philosophy it was Cicero who was the encyclopaedist. Within two years he had treated all three branches into which the post-Aristotelian schools regularly divided the subject: logic represented by the *Academica*, ethics mapped out in *De Finibus*, and physics to which he devoted *De Natura Deorum*. The last two subjects were then pursued in works on specific practical questions in which Cicero's own views were made more explicit, the last being *De Officiis* in which he recommends his philosophical writings to his son, as contributing even more to the development of the Latin language than to the subject-matter of philosophy (I.1–2). He goes on to name the Stoics, Academics and Peripatetics as respectable guides for conduct and says he is following the Stoics here, not as a mere

[160] *QFr.* II.9.3. [161] Cic. *Fin.* I.8; Quint. I.I.123; see also n. 63, above.

[162] Aug. *Contra Acad.* I.8; Sen. *Ep.* 58.6; Quint. II.14.4; Plut. *Cic.* 40. Seneca, however, still complains about the jejuneness of Latin, despite Cicero, *Fin.* I.10; *Nat.D.* I.8.

translator but using his own judgement in selecting from his sources, as is his usual custom (I.5–6).

Based on this passage and others like them, a view of Cicero's philosophical writing and philosophical understanding has long prevailed which, crudely summarized, is that Cicero was able to produce these works at high speed by simply reproducing arguments he found in works by Greek philosophers, adapting them to his setting and speakers and embellishing them with Roman examples and digressions; he was not concerned with philosophical consistency but followed, in an eclectic fashion, the views of different schools on different subjects; he had no use for the more technical aspects of Hellenistic philosophy; while Greeks continued to write and argue about such aspects, Cicero and his countrymen were only interested in ethics of a practical sort. This conception, developed in the nineteenth century, is now being seriously revised. It is worth looking at the different points separately.

Cicero makes no secret of his use of Greek sources. In fact, Pliny the Elder, while noting the habit of even the most respectable modern writers of simply transcribing older writers verbatim without acknowledgement, singles out Cicero for his honesty: 'In *De Republica* he declares himself an acolyte of Plato, in his *Consolation* a follower of Crantor and in *De Officiis* of Panaetius.'[163] Elsewhere Cicero was not so explicit, but in the *Academica*, for example, he intimates that he had to hand two books of Philo of Larissa and a reply by Antiochus of Ascalon.[164] On the other hand, he says that the work of Posidonius, to which he had recourse when Panaetius failed him in *De Officiis*, was only a brief summary and that he had to rely considerably on his own invention.[165] He was particularly proud of the *Academica* and thought it acute in argument and surpassing anything in Greek of its kind. And in *De Finibus* he draws a parallel between his works as they relate to their Greek sources and the works of later Stoics like Panaetius and Posidonius writing on the same subjects as Chrysippus but in a different way. Yet he assumed that only Romans would, and should, read the philosophy that he and Brutus wrote.[166]

The issue is complex, involving such difficult questions as what we mean by translation, what intellectual activity is involved in rendering abstract concepts in another language, and, finally, what counts as being

[163] *HN* pref. 22–3. Cf. *Off.* II.60; III.7; *Att.* XVI.11.2.

[164] *Acad.* II.11–12. Antiochus' work was called *Sosus*. On these works and the use Cicero made of them, see Glucker 1978 (H 48) esp. ch. 1 and Excursus II and Barnes 1989 (H 5).

[165] *Att.* XVI.11.4; *Off.* III.8; 34 cf. I.159. He may only have seen the summary of the work of Posidonius made by Athenodorus Calvus (*Att.* XVI.11.4).

[166] In *Att.* XIII.19.5 Cicero claims that the revised *Academica* combined the *acumen* of Antiochus with the *nitor* of his own (clearly superior) style; *Att.* XIII.18; 13.1; *Fin.* I.6 where Cicero's parallel relates to other philosophical sects as well.

a philosopher. There is force in recent arguments that Cicero, given his excellent memory, could use his broad philosophical training and his wide reading, which the letters show often went beyond what was necessary for the particular work in hand, to select and organize appropriate arguments into an account of the doctrines of Greek philosophers, adding personal criticisms and illustrations – which is all he claimed to do. That is not the work of an original philosopher in the highest sense, but it involves not just repeating the issues but really understanding them.[167] That is an activity which, reasonably enough, qualifies one to be called a philosopher in most academic institutions.

IX. CICERO AND ROMAN PHILOSOPHY

Cicero has often been described as an 'eclectic'. He accepted, for example, the Stoics' view of ethics and of divine providence but rejected their epistemology and, apparently, their views on fate. He was ideally suited to his role of encyclopaedist because he had been exposed in youth to teachers of all the main philosophical schools.[168] Others of his contemporaries, like Atticus and Brutus, also made the rounds when in Athens; some, like Cato, had 'domestic chaplains' of different doctrinal persuasions.[169] Even in the generation before, we hear of Aurelius Opillus, the learned slave manumitted by his Epicurean master, who taught 'philosophy' (unspecified) and later followed the Stoic Rutilius Rufus into exile.[170] That example already reminds us that we are not dealing only with an attitude of the upper-class dilettante Roman consumer. Greek philosophy itself in this period has often been characterized as 'eclectic', and the proliferation of commentaries, works of exegesis and histories of philosophical sects points to scholarly interest in studying different doctrines.[171] The disruption caused by the Mithridatic Wars, which put an end to the Academy and Lyceum as physical institutions and dispersed philosophers from Athens to rival intellectual centres, discouraged organized school controversy.[172]

The term 'eclecticism', however, is used in more than one sense. Usually it signifies the assembling of doctrines from various schools on the basis of personal preference without any explicit or proper rationale. In this sense, it is currently being rejected as a characterization of

[167] Boyancé 1936, 1970 (H 17); Douglas 1973 (H 35); Barnes 1985 (B 4).

[168] Diodotus the Stoic lived and died in his house (*Brut.* 309); he heard Philo of Larissa in Rome in 88 (*Brut.* 306); Antiochus of Ascalon at Athens (*Brut.* 316; *Fin.* v.1; *Tusc.* v.22; Plut. *Cic.* 4); Phaedrus and Zeno, Epicureans, at Athens in 79 and 78 (*Fam.* XIII.1.2; *Fin.*I.16) and Posidonius at Rhodes (Plut. *Cic.* 4; *Nat.D.* I.6).

[169] Cic. *Fin.* v.1; Plut. *Brut.* 24; *Cat. Min.* 65.5, and see Plut. *Brut.* 12.3.

[170] Suet. *Gram.* 6.

[171] Donini 1982 (H 33) 36–9; Tarrant 1985 (H 122) 127–8.

[172] Glucker 1978 (H 48); J. P. Lynch, *Aristotle's School: A Study of a Greek Educational Institution.* (Berkeley, 1972).

thinking in the late Republic, because it is too pejorative and does not reflect the way philosophers of the period viewed what they were doing.[173]

Cicero was behaving as a consistent adherent of the 'New Academy', not only when he suspended judgement like a Sceptic, but when he adopted doctrines from different schools because, after argument on both sides, he judged them, at least on this occasion, to be probable. That, after all, was the point on which Carneades himself had come closest to definite doctrine, and his teacher Philo had emphasized the probable as a reasonable basis for action.[174] Antiochus of Ascalon, however, who tried to steer the Academy in an even more dogmatic direction, had a completely different rationale for intermingling theories of Plato, Aristotle and the Stoa. He and his adherents had a theory about the history of philosophy according to which Plato abandoned the approach of his teacher Socrates, which was to question all opinions and affirm nothing himself, and handed down a coherent body of doctrine. This philosophy, though modified by Aristotle and changed in terminology by the Stoics, had remained essentially the same, until Arcesilas and Carneades denied the possibility of certain knowledge. Antiochus presented his amalgam as the teaching of the 'Old Academy',[175] and it is possible that a similar view of the history of philosophy, whereby the Stoa was an improved version of the Academy, was held by Panaetius, who went back to Plato and Aristotle on important points. He was followed in his respect for the views of those philosophers by Posidonius.[176]

Epicureanism too, though the most conservative of the philosophical sects, was being modified to answer objections. Thus Philodemus, who came to Italy in the 70s and was closely attached to L. Calpurnius Piso, seems to have qualified Epicurus' idea that poetry distorted language and was therefore inimical to truth. Following the lead of his teacher Zeno of Sidon, he seems to have ascribed to Epicurus, in the teeth of opposition from Epicureans outside Athens, the view that sophistic rhetoric was a *τέχνη* i.e. that there is an art of pure style that can be taught. The popularity of Epicureanism in the upper classes in Cicero's

[173] When used of philosophers by ancient writers, however, 'eclectic' meant a member of a separate and identifiable philosophical sect adhering to specific tenets, adopted from a number of existing sects but presumably made to cohere in some way (D.L. I.21 and see Galen XIV.684K; XIX.353K). On the various ancient and modern uses (without reference to Cicero), see Donini 1988 (H 34).

[174] *Inv. Rhet.* II.10; *Tusc.* I.17; II.5; V.82; *Acad.* II.8; *Off.* II.7–8; III.20; 33.

[175] Cic. *Acad.* I.15–18; *Fin.* V.93–5. Our ignorance of Plato's oral teaching and the works of his successor Polemon may have made his distortion seem greater than it was: Dillon 1977 (H 31) 11; 57–8; Donini 1982 (H 33) 74.

[176] Panaetius: fr. 57 van Straaten, p. 17; Cic. *Fin.* IV.79; *Tusc.* I.79; see Glucker 1978 (H 48) 28ff. Posidonius: Edelstein–Kidd F150a, 151, 157.

time is well attested and may owe something to Philodemus' personal contacts and to his interest in poetry and rhetoric, subjects not associated with the school before Zeno of Sidon. Even while ridiculing Philodemus' patron Piso, Cicero is complimentary about the philosopher's elegant verse, of which samples survive in the *Greek Anthology*. It is true that his views, in so far as they can be recovered from the charred remains of the Herculaneum papyri, could not have appealed to a Varro or a Cicero, since he denied any moral content to poetry (which he regarded as a legitimate form of entertainment) or to oratory, and even denied the status of a teachable art to political and forensic oratory.[177] None the less, Zeno and Philodemus applied Epicurean attitudes to areas of current intellectual interest at Rome, such as the relation of philosophy to rhetoric, the classification of different types of style, and the criteria for judging poetry.

Some Roman Epicureans, like Piso, could have been intrigued by these developments, though Lucretius shows no clear awareness of the philosophical polemics or changes current in his school. His contemporaries seem to have thought of him more as a poet than as a philosopher, yet his poem was apparently kept with Greek Epicurean texts in the library of Piso's villa at Herculaneum.[178] It may not be fanciful to think that, on the subject of poetry so close to his heart, he does implicitly answer Philodemus. For while stressing the importance of the pleasure to be derived from poetry in general (V.1450–1) and from his own (I.28; IV.1–25), Lucretius suggests that, for the Epicurean goal of pleasure to be fully achieved, that knowledge of the universe that he seeks to impart is also necessary. In the *De Rerum Natura*, then, he eludes Philodemus' distinction between the correct use of poetry to entertain and the improper use of it to instruct.[179]

That brings us to a very difficult general question: were the Romans really aware of the deepest and most technical aspects of contemporary Greek philosophy? Cicero shows not only L. Crassus but his own contemporaries insisting on their amateur status, but wearing one's learning lightly does not mean one is ignorant. Cicero admits that, in the first edition of the *Academica*, his speakers, Catulus, Lucullus and Hortensius, were out of their depth; but that work contained more

177 Cic. *Fin.* I.71–2; *Pis.* 28; 68–70; Grube 1965 (H 55) 193ff; Rawson 1985 (H 109) 23–4; 59–60; 280–1.

178 Furley 1978 (H 43). Cic. *QFr.* II.10,3; Nep. *Att.* 12.4 (who links him with Catullus as later Velleius Paterculus II.36.2), but cf. Vitr. IX pref. 17 who is interested in the poem as a product of *sapientia*. Kleve, 'Lucretius in Herculaneum', *Cronache Ercolanesi* 19 (1989) 5–27 claims to identify lines of Lucretius Books I, III, IV and V on badly preserved papyri and suggests that the poem inspired Philodemus' defence of epideictic oratory.

179 For the relation of his verse to his Epicureanism, see e.g. Dalzell, 1982 (B 24) 216 and Kenney 1977 (B 53) 11.

difficult material than most of his other works, and Cicero contrasts their lack of expertise with the undoubted suitability for the dialogue of Cato, Brutus and Varro. Moreover, though he had insisted on the real learning of his original interlocutors in prologues which took in Plutarch, he did actually rewrite the work so as to use Varro and himself instead.[180]

Cicero clearly did not expect his readers to believe that the discussions he reports actually took place. They knew the *mos dialogorum*.[181] But can we similarly dismiss the claim made by his Crassus to have disputed with philosophers at Athens about the boundaries of rhetoric and philosophy, or the report of his Lucullus that two Romans first reported to Antiochus at Alexandria the revolutionary content of lectures that Philo delivered at Rome in the 80s, and how the Elder Catulus objected to Philo's new theories?[182] Cicero himself clearly understood the intricacies of the conflict between Philo and Antiochus and presented in the *Academica* his own point of view, which was more sceptical than that of Philo's 'Roman books'.[183] His concern with a debate that took place in his youth does not mean that he was out of touch with current developments, for the Academy seems to have been in the doldrums since the death of Antiochus in the early 60s: many of Antiochus' adherents defected, while Cicero himself represents the sceptical camp as deserted, even in Greece.[184]

That ethics made a particular appeal to the practical and moral sense of the Romans can hardly be denied, but natural philosophy is strongly represented by Lucretius and Catius, who wrote *de rerum natura*,[185] by Nigidius Figulus, and by Cicero, who not only translated Aratus and part of the *Timaeus*, but was clearly fascinated by the questions of fate and divination. On those subjects he not only wrote dialogues but liked showing off his knowledge in writing to Varro.[186] If he shrank from treating geography, it is as well to remember that Posidonius was

[180] M. Pupius Piso (cos. 61) is made to say at *Fin.* v.8 that he never thought he would be holding forth 'ut philosophus'. *Att.* XIII.12.3; 19.5; 18.1; 16.1. Plutarch deceived: Plut. *Luc.* 42.4.

[181] *Fam.* IX.8.1. See also the hints given at *De Or.* I.97; II.13; II.22; *Rep.*I.15.

[182] *De Or.* I.57; *Acad.* II.12; 11. The two Romans brought a copy of Philo's lectures written down ('the Roman books') to Alexandria.

[183] *Acad.* II.64ff. According to Glucker 1978 (H 48) 413ff Cicero was following a subsequent work of Philo; according to Tarrant 1985 (H 122) 42–3, Cicero tempered Philo's view in the 'Roman books' with his own common sense.

[184] *Acad.* II.11 (dramatic date 63–61 B.C.); *Nat.D.* I.6 (cf. 11). Aenesidemus probably dedicated his *Pyrrhonian Logoi* to Cicero's friend (*Lig.* 21) L. Aelius Tubero, an Academic of the same – namely sceptical – tendency (αἵρεσις) as himself (Phot. *Bibl.* 212, 169b33), in the early decades of the first century B.C.: Tarrant 1985 (H 122) 60; 140 n. 4; Barnes 1989 (H 5) Appendix C.

[185] Quint. X.1.24. Cicero compares Lucretius' poem favourably in 54 B.C. (*QFr.* II.10.3) with the *Empedoclea* of Sallustius, which suggests that Sallustius' poem also dealt with physics and was perhaps based on Empedocles' περὶ φύσεως: see Rawson 1985 (H 109) 285.

[186] *Fam.* IX.4.1 (46 B.C.). It is no longer confidently believed that Cicero followed one Greek source in *De Fato*, see Boyancé 1936, 1970 (H 17) and Barnes 1985 (B 4).

unusual among Greek philosophers in this period for the range of his scientific interests.[187]

It would not be pertinent here to consider how far the similarity between Roman philosophical interests in this period and that of the Greek schools was due to Greek efforts to please their Roman masters,[188] but it is worth returning briefly to the question raised earlier of the actual importance of their intellectual interests to members of the Roman elite.

There were a few Romans who devoted themselves entirely to study in this period, but Cicero was probably not alone in thinking that only exceptional academic talent could justify such a course for those who had access to a public career.[189] On the whole, the standard picture of the Romans as uninterested in theory for its own sake can stand. It was the Greek Sosigenes who wrote the astronomical treatises and did the calculations on which Caesar's reformed calendar was based, and Cicero's Crassus says that those engaged in public life can acquire the necessary knowledge of philosophy and other studies quickly and without strenuous effort.[190] Indeed Cicero often speaks as if he favoured the Academy and Peripatos because, as opposed to the Stoa and the Garden, their training was good for one's oratory,[191] and he regarded the Roman constitution, which had evolved in practice, as superior to those thought up by single law-givers, and Roman tradition and experience in government as superior to Greek book-learning in general.[192]

Greek writers were prone to suggest that Greek culture had a beneficial effect on Roman political and moral conduct. Thus Posidonius said of P. Scipio Nasica (cos. 111 B.C.) that 'in practising his philosophy in his life and not just his words, he maintained the tradition of his family and his heritage of virtue'.[193] Though there is an element of wishful thinking in that, Romans such as Cicero, Cato and Varro did claim to live their philosophical beliefs, while his friend and biographer vouches for the role of philosophical precepts in Atticus' freedom from anger.[194] The belief that philosophy influences conduct had a darker side too, as is

[187] See above, p. 706. None of the Middle Platonists (Dillon 1977 (H 31) 49) nor Philodemus (Rawson 1985 (H 109) 295) seems to have been interested in the scientific end of natural philosophy. But Strabo, pupil of Posidonius and continuator of his history, criticizes Roman writers of geography for merely translating from the Greek (III.166C).

[188] An affirmative answer is given to this question by Williams 1978 (H 135) 116–18; and by Momigliano 1975 (H 85) 65–6; 121–2; and a predominantly negative answer by Rawson 1985 (H 109) 54–65.

[189] Pompey's uncle Sextus Pompeius devoted himself to geometry; others to dialectic and law (Cic. *Off.* I.19) or to Stoic philosophy (*De Or.* I.67; III.87).

[190] Pliny *HN* XVIII.210; Rawson 1985 (H 109) 112; Cic. *De Or.* III.86–8.

[191] *De Or.* III.80; 64ff; *Brut.* 120; 332, see also Quint. XII.2.25–9.

[192] *Rep.* II.2.

[193] *FGrH* no.87, fr.112 = Diod. XXXIV/V.33, cf. Plut. *Cat.Mai.* 23; *Cic.* 4.2 suggesting that Cicero even contemplated devoting his life to philosophy – no hint of this in *Brut.* 314–16.

[194] Cic. *Nat.D.* I.7; *Acad.* I.7 (of Varro, presumably not misrepresenting this living and difficult man); *Fam.* XV.4, 16 (Cato); Atticus: Nep. *Att.* 17.3, cf. Cic. *Att.* XVI.11.3 and XV.2.4.

shown by the hostility to Greek doctrine as a corrupting influence which could divert the young from traditional pursuits, seduce them away from public life, or inculcate doctrines that were too impractical to be applied there. Thus philosophers were expelled from Rome in 161 B.C. and the embassy of 155 B.C. met with considerable hostility. A grammarian in the late Republic was thought to be unsuited to keeping a public school because he was an Epicurean (he had to retire and write history), and the conviction of Rutilius Rufus was rightly taken to show that the Stoic belief in unemotional oratory could be damaging, for Rutilius pleaded his own case in that style and lost it.[195]

There is, however, support in the ancient evidence for the popular modern view that there was a complete dichotomy between the notions the upper-class Roman imbibed from the Greeks and his standards of Roman conduct, interest in things intellectual being just a fashionable pose. So men who claimed to be Epicureans are found pursuing public careers, and Cicero can make the *pontifex* C. Aurelius Cotta declare his belief in traditional Roman religion while admitting that none of the proofs for the nature and existence of the gods satisfy his standards as an Academic philosopher.[196] There is also ample support for the idea that the Romans were casual to the point of frivolity about intellectual matters. We have noted the insistence on amateur status and avoidance of Greek *ineptiae*. Cicero recounts how the new governor of Asia stopped in Athens *en route*, rounded up all the philosophers and urged them to settle their differences employing him as arbitrator.[197] Sophisticated Roman Epicureans looked down on the solemn orthodoxy of their Greek teachers. The gourmet Papirius Paetus, when his tame philosopher Dion tried to initiate a philosophical discussion by asking him to pose a question, said there was one question which had been troubling him all day: who would invite him to dinner?[198]

Unconvincing attempts to make firm connexions between intellectual concerns and political activity have only confused the issue. Thus Cassius' conversion to Epicureanism has been connected with his role in the assassination of Caesar, though it took place four years before and is associated, in his letters to Cicero, with an emphasis on peace and a willingness to tolerate an old and clement master.[199] And Varro's

[195] Plut. *Cat. Mai.* 23; Suet. *Gram.* 8; Cic. *Brut.* 113ff; *De Or.* I.227ff, cf. D.L. VII.122.

[196] Epicureans: Cic. *Tusc.* V.108; *Fin.* II.76; Cotta: *Nat.D* III.6–7.

[197] Above, pp. 695–6. Cic. *Leg.*I.53: the point here is that Cicero and others thought this was a joke, whether or not they were right: Badian 1976 (D 4) 126, n. 46 adduces possible political implications.

[198] Cic. *Nat.D.* II.74; Atticus (see below, n. 204) is made to mock Epicurean orthodoxy in Cic. *Leg.* I.21; III.1 cf. Cicero's teasing in *Att.* VII.2.4. Paetus: *Fam.* IX.26.3: the word 'baro' used here, though not restricted to Epicureans (see *Fin.* II.76), is common in this context (e.g. *Att.*V.11.6).

[199] Momigliano 1941, 1960 (H 84) 151ff. Cic. *Fam.* XVI.3 (with Shackleton Bailey 1977 (B 110) vol. II. 378, s.v. 'nuper'); XV.15.1; 19.2 and 4.

Antiquitates have been seen as directly linked with commitment to Caesar the dictator and his programme of moral and religious reform.[200] Yet Cicero's *De Republica* and *De Legibus*, conceived in the 50s, already show a concern for preserving and strengthening traditional institutions, while the project Caesar ultimately adopted of reducing the *ius civile* to order had been adumbrated in *De Oratore* in 54, was discussed further by Cicero in a lost treatise, and was perhaps carried out by Servius Sulpicius Rufus before 46.[201] We are probably dealing with similar preoccupations in intelligent men concerned with the political disruption around them.

It is more profitable to concentrate on the subtler contributions made by intellectual developments to Roman life, namely, the provision of tools of thought and expression. We have already noted the way the Romans used their new knowledge and skill to define their own identity. We can see Pythagorean numerology and Greek techniques of analysis deeply ingrained in Varro's thinking on any subject; we can observe the effect of Caesar's interest in analogy on his prose style.[202] Cicero may have been unusual in feeling that the connexion between philosophy and conduct was so tight that it was wrong to commit oneself to Greek doctrines that were incompatible with one's belief in traditional Roman morality;[203] but the connexion can be seen in Atticus' choice of Epicureanism, which clearly suited his detached and placid personality,[204] and Cicero's selection of a creed that reflected his own open-mindedness and love of debate.[205] When we see Cicero analysing possible courses of action in politics 'by the Socratic method', or borrowing a Greek treatise on concord on the eve of the civil war, or debating in Greek and Latin a series of philosophical θέσεις on tyranny, we can see that philosophy had entered his marrow.[206] But his correspondence also reveals that his friends, too, told philosophical jokes and resorted naturally to the same methods of analysis in trying to reach or justify their decisions.[207]

[200] Horsfall 1972 (H 60) admits that, even if both *Antiquitates* were written under the dictatorship, the work must largely have been done earlier. Even I fr.20 (Cardauns) of *Rerum Divinarum*, if it alludes to Caesar's claim to divine descent, is not entirely flattering: 'etiamsi falsum sit' (see Cardauns' commentary, 1976 (B 11) 149). For scepticism towards Horsfall's arguments see Jocelyn 1982/3 (H 65): he favours the fifties for the composition of the work, but see n. 92 above.

[201] Suet. *Iul.* 44; Cic. *De Or.* I.190; Gell. *NA* I.22.7; Quint. XII.3.10; Cic. *Brut.* 152–3.

[202] Above, pp. 701–3; Ogilvie 1982 (B 80) 283–4.

[203] *Fin.* II.67–8.

[204] Atticus' Epicureanism is well attested: Cic. *Leg.* I.21;54; III.1; *Att.* IV.6.1, cf. *Fin.* I.16 of his youth. Cicero does not use him as an Epicurean spokesman, perhaps because the ironic Atticus would have disliked being shown expounding a system (and see n. 198). On Nepos' failure to mention his Epicureanism, see Griffin 1989 (H 53) 18.

[205] Cicero praises personal assessment and critical judgement over blind acceptance of authority in his first work (*Inv. Rhet.* II.4.5) and his last (*Off.* II.8).

[206] *Att.* II.3.3 (60 B.C.); *Att.* VIII.11.7 (49); *Att.* IX.4 (49).

[207] E.g. Varro: *Fam.* IX.4; Fabius Gallus: *Fam.* VII.26; Trebatius: *Fam.* VII.12; Cassius: *Fam.* XV.16; Ser. Sulpicius: *Fam.* V.19; Appius Claudius Pulcher: *Fam.* III.7.5; 8.5; Cato: *Fam.* XV.4 and 5.

At the end of the Republic, the Romans had the sophisticated intellectual equipment with which to formulate theories and express differences of opinion about religion and history, morals and politics. Yet these skills had not saved the Greeks from foreign rule, and they could not save Rome from civil war and autocracy.

CHAPTER 19

RELIGION

MARY BEARD

I. THE CONSTANTS

Roman religion had its centre in politics, military activity and public life. The gods of the Roman state, in co-operation with its political leaders, ensured Rome's safety, prosperity and victory in war; while, on the part of men, the proper fulfilment of ritual and cult obligations ensured the gods' continuing support of the city. Religion was not principally concerned with private morality, ethics or the conduct of the individual Roman citizen.

The support of the gods for the fortunes of Rome was direct and active. They did not merely offer remote sanction to the conduct of Rome's political and military leaders; they intervened directly on Rome's behalf. Sometimes this intervention occurred, on the pattern of Greek divine epiphanies, in the midst of battle – as when, according to legend, Castor and Pollux came to the Romans' aid at the battle of Lake Regillus in 499 B.C.[1] On other occasions the gods were seen to be active in the internal politics of the state. So Cicero claimed in his letters to Atticus that they had been involved in the suppression of the Catilinarian conspiracy, and, in the midst of Roman assemblies, a clap of thunder or other ill omen might be taken as a direct sign of divine displeasure at the proposal under discussion.[2]

When the state fared badly, it was assumed that the gods had withheld their support. The major axioms of state religion were reversible: just as the safety of Rome depended on the co-operation of the gods, which in turn depended on the proper fulfilment of ritual, so it followed that Rome's failures stemmed ultimately from lapses, conscious or unconscious, in the performance of cult obligations. The strength of this logic was reinforced by a series of exemplary anecdotes, such as the story of Publius Claudius Pulcher, during a naval campaign in the First Punic

[1] Cic. *Nat.D.* II.6; Livy II.20.12.

[2] Catilinarian: Cic. *Att.* I.16.6 (a reference perhaps to the divine sign of a leaping flame, encouraging Cicero in his resolve against the conspirators, at the ritual of the Bona Dea being celebrated in his house, Plut. *Cic.* 19.3–4; 20.1–2). Ill omens: Obsequens 46; Plut. *Cat.Min.* 42.4 (though beware of Plutarch's automatic assumption that the omen was fabricated).

War; exasperated that the oracular chickens kept on his ship would not produce a favourable omen for engaging battle, he cast them overboard to their deaths; as a consequence the Romans suffered a disastrous defeat.[3] The same logic may also be seen to have operated in a notorious form of Roman ritual punishment. The six Vestal Virgins kept permanently alight the flame at the sacred hearth of the city in the temple of Vesta in the Forum; they were vowed to chastity, any breach of this vow being punished by their burial alive. In 216 B.C. and 114–113 B.C. Vestals were put to death on charges of unchastity. We cannot now assess the truth behind the allegations, but we can detect a significant pattern: on both occasions on which the priestesses suffered this punishment the state was threatened with a military crisis – in 216 B.C., defeats in the Second Punic War, in 114–113 B.C., the northern threat of the Cimbri and Teutones, combined with the annihilation of C. Porcius Cato's army in Thrace. The proper conduct of the Vestals was vital for the safety of Rome; when that safety was in doubt, so also was the proper conduct of the Vestals.[4]

The political and military leaders of Rome not only co-operated directly with the gods, they also handled the various axes of communication between the human and divine sphere. In a speech addressed to one of the major colleges of priests, the *pontifices*, Cicero makes it clear that he sees no distinction of personnel between the 'religious' and 'secular' authorities in the city:

> Among the many divinely inspired expedients of government established by our ancestors, there is none more striking than that whereby they expressed their intention that the worship of the gods and the vital interests of the state should be entrusted to the same individuals, to the end that the citizens of the highest distinction and the brightest fame might achieve the welfare of religion by a wise administration of the state and of the state by a sage interpretation of religion.[5]

The religious affairs of the state were in the hands of the same men who directed her politics.

The principal religious authority was the Senate. Although often considered by modern scholars as an entirely political body, the Senate had a crucial religious role as focus of mediation between men and gods: it controlled, for example, men's approaches to the gods, authorizing or proscribing new forms of cult, and it ordained which of the anomalous events reported to it each year (rains of blood, for example, or sweating statues) men should regard as true signs from the gods (*prodigia*). The

[3] Cic. *Nat.D.* II.7; Suet. *Tib.* 2.2.

[4] 216 B.C.: Livy XXII.57.2–3; 114–113 B.C.: Livy *Per.* 63; Asc. *Mil.* 45–6C. See Cornell 1981 (F 38) 28; Fraschetti 1981 (H 41).

[5] Cic. *Dom.* 1 (trans. Loeb).

active religious power of the Senate outweighed that of any other body.[6]

The priestly groups of Rome must be seen in relation to the Senate, as repositories not so much of religious power as of religious knowledge and expertise. In particular the three major colleges of priests, the *pontifices*, *augures* and *XVviri sacris faciundis* (earlier the *decemviri sacris faciundis*), gave advice to the Senate on their respective areas of specialism – the *XVviri*, for example, being consulted over the recommendations of the oracular Sibylline books which they had in their care. These and the other minor groups of priests also fulfilled particular roles in the ritual of the state – the *VIIviri epulonum* organizing banquets for the gods, the Salian priests performing ritual dances through the streets of Rome in March and October (the beginning and end of the campaigning season in primitive Rome). Yet despite such specialist roles, most Roman priests were not full-time professional specialists. They were male members of the Roman elite, who held priestly office (usually for life, after entry into the priesthood) alongside a series of magistracies. Amongst the few exceptions to this rule, most notable were the (female) Vestal Virgins and the *flamen Dialis*, a priest of Jupiter of ancient foundation, whose life was bounded with such strict taboos (a prohibition, for example, against being away from his bed for more than three consecutive nights) that political office was in practice impossible. But even some holders of the office of *flamen Dialis* tried to assert their right also to a political career, or, at least, their traditional (but often forgotten) privilege of a seat in the Senate; so strong was the assumption that the public life of a Roman aristocrat had both a political and a religious dimension.[7]

The religious sphere at Rome cannot easily be distinguished from the political; the overlap between the two areas went far beyond the overlap of personnel and the simple identity of priests and politicians. Political action was, by and large, physically located in a religious context. Not only did the Senate always meet in a *templum* – that is, a piece of 'augurated ground', specially marked out as in direct relationship with the gods; but in public meetings in the Forum, the magistrate addressed the people from a platform (the rostra) also defined as a *templum*. In addressing the Roman citizens, in urging this or that course of political action, the magistrate was operating within publicly defined religious space.[8]

6 Beard 1989 (H 10).

7 For priesthoods in general, see Beard 1989 (H 10); Gordon 1989 (H 50); Scheid 1984 (F 139); Szemler 1972 (F 154) 21–46. Sibylline books: below p. 764. Prohibitions surrounding the *flamen Dialis*: Gell. *NA* X.15. Seat in the Senate: C. Valerius Flaccus in 209 B.C. (Livy XXVII.8.7–10), who later held both the aedileship and the praetorship (Livy XXXI.50.7; XXXIX 45.2 and 4).

8 The rostra explicitly called *templum*, Cic. *In Vatinium* 18; 24; *Sest.* 75; Livy VIII.14.12. For the complicated process of creating a *templum* and for the different kinds of *templum*, Linderski 1986 (F 101) 2256–96.

The political focus of Roman religion did not exclude individual devotion or private cult in the context of the home, the family or social peers. In fact, it is a common feature of polytheistic religious systems, such as Rome's, that they allow particular devotion by individuals or groups – women, soldiers, slaves, paupers – to particular cults or deities; for privileged attention to one part of the system or one aspect of the religious range is not perceived as a rejection of the whole system within which such choices are possible. So, for example, there is considerable evidence for private worship in the terracotta models of parts of the human body (hands, feet, eyes and so forth) discovered in great numbers in excavations at Rome and in Italian countryside shrines – votives once offered, we must assume, by the sick to god or goddess in the hope of cure;[9] the houses of Pompeii, likewise, show us the material traces of family shrines to the household gods (*lararia*);[10] while in Rome itself, literary sources clearly attest the particular popularity of, say, the cult of Ceres among the lower social orders of the city.[11] The importance of such devotions necessarily varied from individual to individual: for some, maybe, a personal commitment to one particular deity might have amounted to an implicit rejection of the official pantheon; for others it was, no doubt, just one form of worship among many. Overall, for most of our period, there is little evidence that the existence of such choices within the religious system threatened the efficacy of the system's central axioms.[12]

This profusion of individual and group commitment is important for our understanding of the full, variegated character of Roman religion; in particular, its ability to generate all kinds of individual religious interpretations and, we may guess, to fulfil all kinds of individual religious needs. But its significance for our understanding of the central focus of the Roman religious system must not be exaggerated. Two principal factors should be borne in mind. First, Roman religion, as a system, was ideologically committed to the public, not the private, sphere; wherever possible, what we regard as the most private forms of devotion were drawn into the public domain and were understood as part of public, social religious observance. This is vividly illustrated by the Roman practice of making a public display of private sacrifice to the gods: on the occasion of, at least, the most important private dedications, the individual went in procession through the city on his way to sacrifice, preceded by a man holding a placard (*titulus*) displaying the reason for

[9] See, for example, *Mysteries of Diana* 1983 (H 89); Pensabene *et al.* 1980 (B 313); Gatti lo Guzzo 1978 (B 293).

[10] Boyce 1937 (B 137). For the evidence of private religion from the Italian colony in Delos, Bulard 1926 (H 21); Bruneau 1970 (H 19) 585–620.

[11] Le Bonniec 1938 (H 73) 342–78.

[12] But see below, pp. 761–2, for the perception of such a threat in the case of the Bacchic cult of the early second century B.C.

the sacrifice. Thus what might have been 'merely' private devotion became part of public, city life.[13]

The second factor which serves to limit the general significance of private worship concerns the status of personal belief. The modern Judaeo-Christian tradition ascribes crucial importance to the personal commitment of the believer to his or her god; in a world where many choose to reject religion altogether, it is personal faith that marks out the religious adherent. This stress on individual belief has led modern scholars to overestimate the importance of those areas of religious life where they could imagine personal commitment to be most prominent – the individual vow and sacrifice or the private shrine. But the religious world of pagan antiquity was quite different from the modern world of doubt and uncertainty. For all but a very few at Rome, towards the very end of our period, the gods – and the ordering of the world which they represented – simply and self-evidently existed. The individual might make different choices and develop different interpretations within the religious system as a whole, but the main axioms that I have outlined were simply part of 'how the world was'. It is in that light, not in terms of faith and belief, that we must understand those axioms.

The close interrelationship of Roman religion and Roman politics might suggest that Roman state cult can best be understood in terms of a modern 'establishment religion', a religion used, at least in part, to justify or prop up the established political order. Such a conflation of the modern and ancient worlds would be seriously mistaken. It is impossible to overstress that Roman religion is for us an alien religious system. This alienness goes beyond the simple unfamiliarity of Roman religious practices, rules and assumptions; it impinges also on our understanding of the intellectual and social space occupied by 'religion' at Rome and its boundaries with other areas of Roman experience.

In some cases, the unfamiliarity (and even incomprehensibility) of Roman religious rituals is immediately apparent. In 228, 216 and 114/13 B.C., for example, the Romans practised a form of human sacrifice, burying alive two Gauls, male and female, and likewise two Greeks. This ritual is poorly understood. Attempts have been made to link it with the punishment of unchaste Vestals, to which on two occasions (216 and 114/13 B.C.) it is closely related in time; or again the choice of victims has suggested a connexion with Rome's activities in the outside world. But no consistent pattern of circumstances can be traced through all three instances nor has any satisfactory link been demonstrated between Gauls and Greeks, either in Roman perceptions or in Roman military activity.[14]

[13] Veyne 1983 (H 131).

[14] 228: Plut. *Marc.* 3.3–4. 217: Livy XXII.57.2–6; 114/13: Plut. *Quaest. Rom.* 83. For different attempts at interpretation, Cichorius 1922 (H 25); Bémont 1960 (H 12); Fraschetti 1981 (H 40); Briquel 1981 (H 18); Eckstein 1982 (H 37).

The ritual remains most of all a clear indication of the foreignness of a system that modern writing has often too closely assimilated to the familiar, while at the same time throwing light on Roman reactions to a practice that seemed alien even to some Romans themselves. Livy, for example, in describing the burials of 216, defined them as 'minime Romano sacro' – 'an entirely un-Roman ritual'.[15] This is no certain indication of a (literal) foreign origin for the practice, but rather a sign that the boundaries of what was properly 'Roman' in religion were negotiable.

The more fundamental cultural alienness of Roman religion lies in the degree to which it was undifferentiated from the political sphere. In modern world religions there is frequently considerable influence, in both directions, between religion and politics; but they remain separable and usually separate (if interacting) spheres of activity. In Rome, by contrast, we are not simply dealing with a close interaction between religion and politics; religion, as in many traditional societies, was a deeply embedded element within public life, hardly differentiated as a separate sphere of activity or intellectual interest until the very end of the Republic. This lack of differentiation presents a terminological and conceptual problem for modern analysis. By using our own language we necessarily (and often awkwardly) translate Roman cultural forms into our own terms; we make modern sense of ancient religion at the cost of blurring or redefining ancient categories. We talk, for example, of the Senate being a body with both religious and political responsibilities; for a Roman of the Republic, the Senate would have evoked a complex amalgam of associations, of which both politics and religion (in our terms) would have been a part. These translations are, of course, inevitable; but they demand explicit recognition.

II. SOURCES OF EVIDENCE AND THE PROBLEMS OF COMPARISON

Roman religion in the late Republic must be understood against the background of the long-established religious traditions of the city of Rome; but within that traditional context those elements must be identified which form the distinctive religious character of the period. Problems of evidence and of comparison between one period and another make this programme more difficult than it might at first sight appear. On the one hand, the stark differences between the quality and quantity of surviving evidence for religion in the Ciceronian age and that for periods both earlier and later confound easy analysis; there is, in fact,

[15] Livy XXII.57.6.

a common tendency to overestimate the distinctiveness (and particularly the disruption) of religion in the late Republic, simply because the source material for the Ciceronian age is so different from that of the immediately adjacent periods. On the other hand, demonstrations of apparent continuity in the religion of the late Republic can also be misleading; for it cannot be assumed, simply because religious practices were maintained from earlier periods, that they were maintained with the same symbolic force and with the same significance in the religious system as a whole. Both these problems may be clarified by a brief consideration of the general character of the surviving evidence for religion from the middle Republic to the Augustan period and by the analysis of one particularly disputed example of continuity – the foundation and restoration of temples in the first century B.C.

The age of Cicero is the first period of Roman history in which it is possible to analyse the operation of religion from relatively abundant contemporary literature – largely the writings of Cicero himself, but also the works of Sallust, Caesar, late Republican poets and the surviving portions of Varro's encyclopaedic output. For all earlier periods a modern historical account must rely largely on Livy and other Roman historians of later centuries, who offer a retrospective view of the earlier stages (including the religious developments) of their city's history. Whether 'accurate' or not on the details of religious history, these later Roman writers necessarily present a perspective very different from Cicero and his contemporaries. Livy, for example, with the benefit of hindsight, orders and structures the course of events, which to a contemporary observer might well have appeared unpredictable and even chaotic. The choice of priests, the reporting of prodigies and the actions taken in their expiation take their place within the regular annalistic framework of Livy's history; while religious crises such as the suppression of the Bacchanalia in 186 B.C.[16] are described from the vantage-point of one who knows their outcome and has already assessed their importance. The contrast with the evidence of Cicero, in particular, is striking. Cicero is the contemporary observer, for whom the regularities of religious and political life are barely remarkable; his interest lies in religious anomaly or crisis, as lived through, undigested and unreflected, of immediate preoccupying importance, though maybe of little long-term significance. The image of late Republican religion gained from this material is one of fluidity and disorganization, if not chaos; but only at the risk of gross oversimplification can that image be directly compared with the retrospective view of Livy on the early and middle Republic.

Difficulties remain, even when late Republican evidence can be

[16] Below, pp. 761–2.

compared with strictly contemporary material from periods both earlier and later; for any straightforward comparison is marred not only by differences in the quantity of contemporary evidence between one period and the next, but also by important differences in the character of that contemporary evidence. This is clearly true of the inadequately documented middle Republic, where the Graeco-Roman fantasy world of Plautus and Terence presents obvious (but still unfathomable) difficulties for any study of explicitly 'Roman' religion; but also, almost equally so, of the triumviral and Augustan ages. Despite their abundance, none of the Augustan sources includes anything like the day-to-day reportage found in Cicero. Those most concerned with religion (parts of Augustus' *Res Gestae*, for example, or some of the *Odes* of Horace) offer a self-conscious, and sometimes propagandist, statement of the piety of the age – a piety that, within the traditional axioms of Roman religion, was necessarily seen to go hand in hand with the Augustan political and religious restoration. Just as in Livy's retrospective view of early Roman history (also written from an Augustan standpoint), the concerns of the moment, the uncertainties, the contested decisions, so prominent in the main late Republican source, are invisible.

The case of the foundation and repair of temples in the city of Rome provides a clear instance of the difficulties of setting the religious character of the late Republic against that of other periods. At first sight, care and concern for the religious buildings of the city during the last decades of the Republic compare unfavourably with that demonstrated both earlier and later. On the one hand, the regular series of temple building and dedications documented up to the middle of the second century B.C. through the surviving text of Livy is absent from the record of the first half of the first century B.C. The writing of Cicero, for example, includes mention of only the occasional temple repair or of particular crises in temple upkeep, such as Verres' supposedly fraudulent restoration of the temple of Castor or the accidental destruction of the temple of the Nymphs in riots in 57.[17] On the other hand, several classic passages of Augustan literature lay stress not only on the new foundations and restoration of temples under Augustus (according to the *Res Gestae*, eighty-two temples were restored in Augustus' sixth consulship), but also on the neglect of the previous generation that made that restoration necessary: 'You will expiate the sins of your ancestors, though you do not deserve to, citizen of Rome, until you have rebuilt the temples and the ruined shrines of the gods and the images fouled with black smoke.'[18]

It is easy to understand how, on the basis of this material, the late

[17] Cic. II *Verr.* 1.129–154; *Mil.* 73; *Paradoxa Stoicorum* 31.

[18] Hor. *Odes* III.6.1–4 (trans. Gordon Williams); Augustus, *Res Gestae* 20.4. See further Price, *CAH* x², ch. 16.

Republic came to be seen by modern scholars as a low point in the history of respect and care for the religious buildings of the city of Rome and, at the same time, a low point in the history of Roman religious observance in general; but closer examination of the evidence shows how misleading that view is. The testimony of Livy, with its regular inclusion of temple foundations, is not directly comparable with the Ciceronian evidence for the first century B.C., where temple building and repairs intrude only when they are out of the ordinary or in some way relevant to Cicero's immediate oratorical purpose.[19] Likewise, the parade of piety in Augustan literature – with its obvious exaggerations and its strategic construction of a convenient foil in the supposed impiety of the late Republican era – cannot be taken as reliable evidence for the religious climate of the Ciceronian age. In fact, a full survey of the scattered references in contemporary and later writers to temple construction in the middle of the first century B.C., together with the archaeological evidence for the period, offers a picture quite different from the conventional one: while temples, like the other buildings of the city, suffered in the violence and unrest of the late Republic, they continued to be newly founded and to be repaired after damage by human hand or the forces of nature.

Particularly important were the first-century foundations of Pompey. A temple of Hercules ('Pompeianus') and one of Minerva are associated with his name, as well as the temple of Venus Victrix in Pompey's great building complex on the Campus Martius. The religious significance of this shrine of Venus has often been undervalued by both modern and some ancient writers, because of its close association with a 'secular' theatre; but, in fact, its plan fits into a tradition of so-called 'theatre-temples', well attested in other areas of Italy. Other leading men also were associated with new foundations and repairs. A temple of Diana Planciana (perhaps of the 50s B.C.) can probably be linked to the Plancii; and Cicero himself was engaged in embellishing the temple of Tellus in 54 B.C. The temple of Jupiter Capitolinus, too, was restored after a fire in 83 B.C. There is no sign of tardiness in carrying out that work: it was formally rededicated in 69 B.C. and had already been in a good enough condition to house some Sibylline oracles in 76 B.C.[20]

19 *Contra* Coarelli 1976 (G 41) who assumes that after 70 B.C. (with the start of the Ciceronian corpus) documentation on building activity is again comparable with the period covered by Livy's history.

20 Pompey's foundations: Pliny *HN* XXXIV.8.57; Vitr. *De Arch.* III.3.5; Pliny *HN* VII.26.97; Gell. *NA* X.1.6–7; Pliny *HN* VIII.7.20; Tert. *De Spect.* X.5–6; see also Hanson 1959 (H 56). Diana Planciana: Panciera 1970/1 (B 215) arguing for a foundation in the 50s B.C., questioned by C.P. Jones 1976 (H 66). Jupiter Capitolinus: *Lugli* XVII.126–48 – esp. Livy *Per.* XCVIII and Lactant. *De Ira* 22.6; there is no reason to suppose, with Nock, *CAH* X[1], 468, that the dispute about the temple's restoration and upkeep in 62 – Suet. *Iul.* 15 – implies that the repairs were still unfinished. Tellus: Cic. *QFr.* III.1.14. For archaeological evidence of restoration, see temple A of the Largo Argentina (temple of Juturna), considerably refaced in the middle years of the first century B.C.: Coarelli *et al.* 1981 (B 274) 16–18 (early 50s to the third quarter of the first century B.C.); Jacopi 1968/9 (B 297).

It must remain uncertain, however, how far this continuity in the foundation and repair of the fabric of the religious buildings of Rome reflects a continuity of religious attitude. We cannot know what Romans 'felt' at any period when they decided to use their wealth to erect a temple to a particular deity; far less how they felt when entering, walking past or simply gazing upon the religious buildings of their city. But it seems inconceivable in the rapidly changing world of the late Republic, in the 'political' upheavals affecting the city, that the symbolic significance of the 'religious' environment of Rome (whatever its physical continuity) should have remained the same. A comparison with the changes in ideology underlying one apparently conservative Roman ritual well illustrates the possible degree of discontinuity. The festival of the Parilia, held in April each year, was, as far as we know, celebrated in broadly the same way throughout the Republic – with its prayers to the obscure deity Pales and its bonfires through which the participants in the festival are said to have leapt.[21] By contrast, its principal religious 'meaning' changed markedly. What seems in the early history of Rome to have been a festival primarily concerned with the well-being of the community's flocks, came in the urban society of the late Republic to be associated (equally, if not more so) with a celebration of the birthday of the city of Rome and, under Caesar, with the celebrations in commemoration of his victory at Munda.[22] Superficial continuity (whether in the conservatism of ritual forms or a maintained commitment to the upkeep of temples) can mask deep differences and developments of religious ideology in a changing world.

This chapter aims to determine, as far as possible, the particular characteristics of Roman religion between 146 and 44 B.C. and set them against the long-established traditional religious rules of Rome. It is not intended as a narrative history of religious events of the period, nor as a full coverage of the religious traditions in Rome's expanding territory in Italy and overseas, but as an exploration of the elements of continuity and change that together formed the distinctive pattern of religion in the late Republic. This exploration involves more than delineating a simple spectrum between the poles of 'continuity' and 'change'. It involves also an understanding of how continuity of religious attitude was, paradoxically, upheld by adaptations and changes in religious form and, conversely, how conservative and superficially unchanging religious practices could incorporate in time significant developments in underlying ideology and evocation. The major theme of the chapter is the active and complex interrelationship between the elements of continuity and change.

[21] Ov. *Fast.* IV.735–82.

[22] Beard 1987 (H 9); Price, *CAH* X², ch. 16.

III. POLITICAL AND RELIGIOUS DISRUPTION

The disruption of political and social life at Rome in the late Republic necessarily brought with it the disruption of religion. In a society in which religion was deeply embedded in public life as a whole, changes and upheavals in the political sphere could not help affecting the religious sphere also. These effects took many forms; but the most marked and controversial disturbances occurred when the unprecedented developments of political life in the late Republic threw up problems for which the traditional religious rules had no answer. This is illustrated by the events of 59 B.C., when the consul Bibulus tried to block his colleague Caesar's legislation by the declaration of ill omens.

As consul in 59, Caesar introduced in the popular assembly controversial legislation (including the bill for redistribution of Campanian land), bitterly opposed by his colleague M. Calpurnius Bibulus. At the beginning of the year, it seems, Bibulus offered religious objection to Caesar's proposals in the traditional way, according to the process known as *obnuntiatio*:[23] he appeared in the Forum and declared to the presiding magistrate that he had seen evil omens, preventing the progress of legislation. As the year went on, however, civil disturbances increased and Bibulus became the object of such violent assaults that he took refuge in his house and merely issued messages that he was watching the sky for omens. The assemblies went ahead despite such objections and the legislation was passed: it was later attacked on the ground that it flouted religious law, but was never repealed.[24]

This incident has been seen as an illustration of the ruleless chaos into which the traditional religious system had fallen by the first century B.C.: the absolute domination of religious concerns by factional political interests; blatant disregard for religious obligations where they conflicted with secular ambitions; heedless flouting of religious rules once taken seriously. Attractive at first sight, such an interpretation is, however, a serious oversimplification, for underlying the story, and others like it, can be seen continuing attempts to apply the traditional religious rules, but in a situation of unprecedented problems, for which the rules provided no self-evident solution.

The force of Bibulus' objections to Caesar's legislation was problematic because it raised new issues of interpretation, unparalleled in earlier

[23] The assumption is supported by a rather muddled passage of Suetonius (*Iul.* 20.1). For debate on the laws regulating the practice of *obnuntiatio* (Leges Aelia et Fufia) and Clodius' reform of them in 58 B.C., see Weinstock 1937 (F 170); Balsdon 1957 (F 13); Sumner 1963 (F 152); Astin 1964 (F 7); Weinrib 1970 (H 133); Mitchell 1986 (H 83).

[24] Cic. *Att.* II.16.2; 19.2; 20.4; 21.3–5 with Taylor 1951 (C 277) and Shackleton Bailey 1965 (C 261). Attacks on the religious status of the legislation, Cic. *Dom.* 39–41; *Har.Resp.* 48; *Prov.Cons.* 45–6. See also Wiseman in ch. 10 above pp. 369–71.

religious practice. He claimed through much of his consulship to be watching the heavens, but did not carry out the correct procedure for the declaration of ill omens. His actions could be understood in two ways. On the one hand, it might be (and no doubt was) argued that, once Bibulus had incarcerated himself at home and simply gave notice of 'watching the sky' by message, his objections had no validity; for ill omens constituted proper obstruction to political business only if announced in person at the assembly concerned.[25] On the other hand, it could be claimed that, since violence made it impossible for Bibulus to attend the assemblies and since there must have been *some* religious force in his objections, even if they were not procedurally correct in every detail, his watching of the heavens should have nullified Caesar's legislation.[26] Resolution of these two opposing views was not easy. The established conventions of religious practice in this area had taken shape over a period when the prolonged urban violence of the late Republic could not have been foreseen; and, particularly within the atmosphere of disunity and conflict among the governing elite, it was difficult to reach agreement on how the conventions should be applied in this case. There is no suggestion in our surviving sources that the potential religious import of Bibulus' actions was ignored; on the contrary, precisely because of the religious uncertainty, the validity of Caesar's legislation proved controversial. The disruption of the religious system lay in the impossibility of that uncertainty being resolved according to the traditional rules in unprecedented circumstances.

Other incidents in the late Republic reveal similar problems; disruption often stemmed from difficulties in applying the traditional religious rules. This was clearly the case in 62–61 B.C. in the *cause célèbre* which followed the invasion of the ceremonies of the Bona Dea, traditionally restricted to women, by a man believed to have been P. Clodius Pulcher (tribune 58 B.C.). The sacrilege was followed by the apparently correct action of the Senate in asking the appropriate priestly college to investigate the sacrilege and then instructing the consuls to frame a bill to institute a formal trial. Yet it is also clear that the religious system was under stress. This stress is evident not so much in the act of sacrilege itself (for, no doubt, there had always been such isolated, high-spirited attacks on the sober conventions of religion), nor in the eventual acquittal of Clodius (for, despite the effusions of Cicero, who attributed the outcome to the graft and corruption of Clodius' friends, we cannot in

[25] Linderski 1965 (F 100) 425–6; Lintott 1968 (A 62) 144–5. Mitchell 1986 (H 83) while broadly working along the same lines, suggests that it was only after Clodius' legislation of 58 B.C. that personal announcement of ill omens became an explicit requirement.

[26] Even some who accepted the contents of Caesar's legislation felt that it should be resubmitted with proper observance of the auspices. Cic. *Prov.Cons.* 46.

fact be certain that the young man was guilty); but rather in the problems that arose in formulating the details of the judicial action – the disagreements not only as to whether there should be a formal trial at all, but also, later, as to the precise composition of the jury.[27] There was, we may deduce, no established procedure for dealing with this particular religious crime. As in the case of Bibulus' attempted religious obstruction, in a situation where the governing elite were deeply divided, when there was no clearly defined pattern of action to follow, it proved hard to find consensus on the correct establishment and implementation of a new procedure.

The disruption of religion in the late Republic should not, however, be overemphasized. It is important to recognize how religion was necessarily implicated in the general disturbances and changes in Roman public life during the period; but, at the same time, it should not be assumed that all aspects of what appear to modern observers as religious manipulation, abuse or disregard are symptoms of a particular decline, rather than entirely traditional elements in the religious life of Rome. The handling of oracles is a case in point. In 56 B.C., for example, a Sibylline oracle was produced which stated that no army should be used to restore the king of Egypt – an apposite intervention in the political battles of the time, when several prominent politicians were competing to lead an expedition to restore to the throne the deposed Ptolemy Auletes. Cicero had no doubt that the oracle was a blatant forgery (*ficta religio*), invented to prevent Pompey obtaining a further major military command.[28] It might seem easy to conclude that fraudulence of this kind was another distinctive part of the disruption of religion in the late Republic; in fact, this conclusion would be mistaken. Although we possess no reliable information on the frequency of oracular fraud in the earlier history of Rome, comparative studies of other traditional religions show that such fabrication is almost universal in oracular systems. Wherever oracles form a major element in a religious system, forgery and accusations of forgery are also regularly present; they are not indications that the system is failing.[29] So it is ethnocentric of the modern observer to suppose that such practices prove the failure or disruption of religion at any period of Rome's history. The dividing line between

[27] See especially Cic. *Att.* 1.13.3; 14.1–5; 16.1–6. Such legal problems have led many modern scholars to treat the issue as simply 'political': Moreau 1982 (C 230); Latte 1960 (A 60) 285. See Wiseman in ch. 9 above, pp. 361–3.

[28] Cic. *Fam.* 1.4.2. But Pompey was probably not the sole target of the oracle; see Fenestella Fr. 21 (*HRR*), who claims that C. Cato (who produced the oracle) was also raising opposition to Lentulus Spinther, proconsul of Cilicia, and so also anxious to intervene. In general, Cic. *Fam.* 1.1–7.

[29] See, for example, E. E. Evans-Pritchard, *Witchcraft, Oracles and Magic among the Azande* (Oxford, 1937) 359–74.

'proper' and 'improper' religious conduct and usage varies from society to society. One culture's 'abuses' are another culture's 'traditions'.

IV. NEGLECT AND ADAPTATION

A prominent feature of religion in the late Republic is the dying out of certain traditional religious practices and the apparent neglect of elements of cult once central to the religious system. This aspect of the period is often stressed by modern writers, who have sometimes (as in the case of the alleged neglect of the city's temples) been too ready to see the age of Cicero as the nadir of Roman religious piety. But ancient authors also commented on the lapse of particular pieces of religious observance. Cicero himself, for example, lamented the decline of augural skill in his own day; while other authors noted that from 87 B.C. for almost seventy years the ancient priesthood of Jupiter (the office of the *flamen Dialis*) was left unfilled.[30]

Neglect is a multifaceted phenomenon and the nostalgia of ancient writers hard to assess. Some laments for past piety were tendentious – it being as tempting in the ancient world as in the modern to assume without much justification that one's forebears behaved more scrupulously than oneself. Other laments, however, reflect real changes in religious practice, which (at their most acute) may be related, once again, to the unsettled conditions of public life in general. Disturbances in the city created a situation in which it was impossible to do what had always previously been done.

The non-appointment of the *flamen Dialis* throughout the last forty years of the Republic, and beyond, provides a clear instance of neglect stemming from disturbance. Various factors were no doubt involved in this lapse. In part, for example, it may have resulted from a new-found, or increased, unwillingness amongst the Roman elite to countenance the burdensome taboos of that particular office. But the confusion of the Sullan period was, at the very least, an important catalyst to the suspension of the priesthood. During the dominance of Cinna and Marius, in 87 or early 86 B.C., the young Julius Caesar was designated as *flamen Dialis*, in succession to L. Cornelius Merula, who had committed suicide after the Marian take-over of the city. But before Caesar had been formally inaugurated into the office, Rome had fallen once more to Sulla, who annulled all the enactments and appointments made by his enemies.[31] It is impossible now to reconstruct how the Roman elite would have viewed the vacant flaminate or Caesar's status in relation to

[30] Augury: Cic. *Leg.* II.33; *Div.* I.25 (speaking in the character of Quintus Cicero); *Nat.D.* II.9 (in the character of Balbus). *Flamen Dialis*: Tac. *Ann.* III.58; Dio LIV.36.1.

[31] Taylor 1941 (C 140) 113–16; Leone 1976 (H 76).

the priestly office that he had arguably already filled. It is clear only that Sulla's action in dismissing Caesar, in the confusion of the period of civil war, represented the first step in the temporary suspension of the priesthood: the office remained vacant until an appointment was made by Augustus in 11 B.C., while the rituals associated with it were carried out over that period by the college of *pontifices*.[32]

Other instances of neglect have a more positive aspect. Roman religion adapted with changes in social and political life and, in particular, with Rome's expansion into empire. It was not, nor could it be, the same in the late Republic as it had been three or four centuries before. New elements were introduced; other elements, as always, died away. Losses as well as gains were part of Rome's living and adapting religion.

The geographical expansion of Roman imperial power underlies several of the most striking losses and adaptations in the Roman religious system. Various rituals that originated when Rome was fighting her neighbours and expanding within the Italian peninsula were no longer appropriate when Rome's expansion was far overseas. The ritual of the Fetial priests on declaration of war is perhaps the clearest instance of such a change. Traditional Fetial practice was to proceed to the border of Rome's territory with her enemy and to hurl into the enemy land a ritual spear, as first symbolic mark of the coming war. When Rome's enemies were no longer her neighbours, however, but were often hundreds of kilometres away outside Italy, the ritual was clearly no longer appropriate and was retained only in vestigial form: a piece of land in Rome itself, near the temple of Bellona, was, by a legal fiction, designated enemy ground and into that the Fetials cast their spear.[33]

A rather more complex change is evident in the ritual of *evocatio*. Tradition here was that the Roman commander should press home his advantage in war by offering to the patron deity of the enemy a better temple and better worship in Rome, if he or she were to desert their erstwhile favourites and come over to the Roman side. The best recorded instance of this practice concerned the goddess Juno, patron of Veii, who deserted the Veians for the Romans in 396 (thus ensuring Rome's victory)[34] and was thereafter worshipped at Rome with a famous temple on the Aventine Hill. It has been thought by modern scholars that this practice (with its apparently crude notions of the bribery of the deity) died out entirely by the late Republic; for no temples in Rome later

[32] Tac. *Ann.* III.58 makes it clear that ostensible neglect of the office did not entail neglect of the rituals associated with it.

[33] The precise chronology of the changes, disuse and revivals of the Fetial rituals is unclear. See Rich 1976 (A 95) 56–8; 106; 127.

[34] Livy V.21.2–4 (with a version of the formula of evocation); 22.4–7.

than that of Vortumnus (founded 264 B.C.) are thought to owe their origin to the ritual of evocation, and ancient claims that Scipio practised *evocatio* at the capture of Carthage in 146 B.C. have been viewed with scepticism. But an inscription discovered in Asia Minor suggests that the practice did not die out, for it records the evocation of the patron deity of Isaura Vetus in 75 B.C. and the erection of a new, Roman, temple for the god near his old home, in the newly conquered territory.[35] Further evidence is scanty; but this one inscription makes it plausible enough to argue that right up to the late Republic new temples continued to be founded in the Roman provinces as a result of evocation, even if it no longer happened in Rome itself. The logic underlying this adaptation is fairly clear. Whereas in the early Republic offering a rival deity a *Roman* home meant precisely offering a temple in the city of Rome itself, by at least the second century B.C., the geographical definition of what was 'Roman' had so expanded that the enemy deity could quite properly be offered a home in Roman territory outside Rome. What appears from the perspective of the city of Rome to be the dying out of a practice is thus better understood as a change in its geographical location.

Ancient regrets about the disuse of the auspices can also be related to Rome's imperial development – at least in the case of the so-called 'military auspices', the formal confirmation by the general before engagement of battle that the gods were favourable to the Roman cause. In the early and middle Republic, when Rome's wars were fought nearby and the internal government of the city was a relatively light burden, military commanders were normally magistrates campaigning during their year of office. As magistrates, they fought 'under their own auspices' and so had the right to determine the will of the gods on behalf of the Roman people. By the late Republic, when the government of the city had become more complex and time consuming and, by and large, Rome's wars were many months distant, the major magistrates remained at home for at least part of their year of office and often undertook military commands later, as promagistrates. In so far as they were not then, in the strictest sense, magistrates and had no official right to consult the gods on Rome's behalf, they could not, as previously, take the military auspices before battle.[36] In this case, the apparent neglect of a religious practice in fact stems from a continuing scrupulous regard for the traditional religious rules.

Several traditional religious practices lapsed during the period of the late Republic. The causes of those lapses varied, as did also contemporary perceptions of their significance. Some people were no doubt

[35] Hall 1972 (B 168); Le Gall 1976 (H 74); for Carthage the evidence is reviewed by Rawson 1973 (H 105) 168–72.

[36] This point is made by Cicero himself, *Div.* II.76–7.

wantonly indifferent; others, rigidly traditional, lamented any change. For the modern observer two, rather different, aspects of the lapses are important: neglect of religious practice was certainly in part a consequence of the confusion and disturbance of the late Republic; but it was also part of the necessary process by which the religious system adapted to the changing circumstances of the community within which it was embedded. The process of losses and gains had always been so, and, until the end of paganism, always would be. Paradoxically some neglect was traditional, being essential for the continuance of a religion which could still make sense within a changed society.

V. COMPETITION, OPPOSITION AND THE RELIGION OF THE *POPULARES*

As part of Roman public life, religion had always been a part of the political struggles and disagreements in the city. Disputes that were, in our terms, concerned with political power and control, were in Rome necessarily associated with rival claims to religious expertise and to privileged access to the gods. That, at least, was the view of the Romans themselves, who perceived the political struggles of the early Republic partly in terms of struggles against patrician monopoly of religious knowledge and of access to the divine. Livy, for example, gives a vivid account of the passing of the Lex Ogulnia in 300 B.C., the last major event in the so-called 'Struggle of the Orders', which gave the plebeians the right finally to hold places in the pontifical and augural colleges. The patricians, according to Livy, saw such a law as a contamination of religious rites and so liable to bring disaster on the state; the plebeians regarded it as the necessary culmination of the inroads they had already made into magisterial and military office-holding.[37] Full political involvement in the governing of Rome demanded also full involvement in man's relations with the gods. It would make no sense in Roman terms to claim rights to political power without also claiming rights to religious authority and expertise.

The struggles of the late Republic and the ever-intensifying competition between both individuals and groups provide even clearer testimony of the inevitable religious dimension within political controversy at Rome. Not only were individual political arguments (on particular decisions or the particular conduct of leading public figures) often framed in terms of the will of the gods or of divine approval manifest for this or that course of action; but also, as political debate became (at least in part) ranged around the opposition between *optimates*

[37] Livy x.6.1–9.2.

and *populares*, so there were, from the side of the *populares*, increasing attacks on what seemed the optimate stranglehold on priestly office and attempts to locate religious, along with political, power in the hands of the people as a whole. Sallust, for example, puts into the mouth of C. Memmius (trib. 111 B.C.) a virulent attack on the dominance of the nobles, who 'walk in grandeur before the eyes [of the people], some flaunting their priesthoods and consulships, others their triumphs, just as if these were honours and not stolen goods'.[38] The juxtaposition of priesthoods and consulships here is not fortuitous. Those who resented what they saw as the illicit monopoly of power by a narrow group of nobles would necessarily assert the people's right of control over both religious and political office, over dealings with the gods as well as with men.

A clear instance of the successful assertion of popular control over religion is found in the legislation governing the choice of priests for the major priestly colleges, especially the Lex Domitia of 104 B.C. The traditional means of recruitment to most of the colleges was co-option: on the death of a serving priest his colleagues in the college themselves selected a replacement. This process was first formally challenged (as far as we know) in 145 B.C., when C. Licinius Crassus introduced a bill to transfer the selection to a system of popular election. The bill was defeated, but a similar proposal introduced in 104 by Cn. Domitius Ahenobarbus (cos. 96) succeeded: the priests of the four major colleges (*pontifices*, *augures*, *XVviri* and *VIIviri*) retained the right to nominate candidates for their priesthoods, but the choice between the candidates nominated was put into the hands of a special popular assembly, formed out of seventeen of the thirty-five Roman voting tribes – a method of election used since the third century for the choice of the *pontifex maximus*. The priests themselves no longer had complete control of membership of their colleges.[39]

The surviving ancient sources offer various interpretations of this measure. Suetonius stresses the personal motives of Domitius: having himself failed to be co-opted into the pontifical college, he proceeded out of pique to reform the method of entry.[40] We cannot now judge the truth of such allegations; all kinds of personal and narrowly political motives may have played a part. We can, however, see how such reforms of priestly selection fit into a consistent pattern of political and religious opposition to the dominance of the traditional elite and assertion of

[38] Sall. *Jug.* 31.10.

[39] C. Licinius Crassus: Cic. *Amic.* 96. Cn. Domitius Ahenobarbus: *Leg.Agr.* II.18–19; Suet. *Ner.* 2.1.

[40] Suet. *Ner.* 2.1; in a similar vein, Asc. *in Scaurian.* 21C ascribes Domitius' prosecution of M. Aemilius Scaurus for religious negligence to his pique at not being co-opted augur. See Rawson 1974 (H 106); Scheid 1981 (H 112) 124–5; 168–71.

popular control over the full range of state offices. The first proposer of such legislation, for example, C. Licinius Crassus, was also reported to have offered a symbolic challenge to the authority of the Senate by being the first, when speaking on the rostra, to turn to address the people in the Forum, rather than the elite gathered in the Comitium outside the senate-house.[41] And the later history of the legislation on the selection of priests confirms its significance as part of wider conflicts at Rome: the Lex Domitia was repealed by Sulla in his reassertion of traditional senatorial control, and later re-enacted in 63 B.C. by the tribune Labienus, a well-known radical and friend of Caesar.[42] Support of the popular cause had come to involve support for popular control of man's relations with the gods.

A similar challenge to traditional religious authority is found in the events of 114–113, when a number of Vestals were declared guilty of unchastity and put to death. In 114 the daughter of a Roman equestrian had been struck dead by lightning, while riding on horseback – a prodigy interpreted by the Etruscan *haruspices* as an indication of a scandal involving virgins and knights. As a result, in December 114, according to traditional practice, three Vestal Virgins were tried for unchastity before the pontifical college, though only one was found guilty and sentenced to burial alive. In reaction to the acquittal of the other two Vestals, Sextus Peducaeus, tribune in 113 B.C., carried a bill through the popular assembly to institute a new trial – this time with equestrian jurors and a specially appointed prosecutor, the consular L. Cassius Longinus. The new trial resulted in the conviction and subsequent execution of all three Vestals.[43] The traditional competence of the *pontifices* to preserve correct relations with the gods had been called into question, while the power of the people themselves to override the priestly college and control the behaviour of public religious officials had been asserted.

On other occasions rival claims by individual politicians to privileged access to the gods provided the focus of political debate; a man could demonstrate the correctness of his political stance by demonstrating that he, rather than his political opponent, was acting in accordance with divine will. This was clearly the case in 56 B.C., when Cicero and Clodius engaged in public debate on the proper interpretation of a prodigy. A mysterious rumbling had been heard in territory outside Rome and *haruspices* had been called in to interpret the prodigious occurrence. In a lengthy response they alluded to the causes of divine anger, of which the prodigy was a sign: the pollution of games (*ludi*); the profanation of

41 Cic. *Amic.* 96. 42 Dio XXXVII.37.1–2.

43 See n. 4 above. The implications for popular control of religion are drawn by Rawson 1974 (H 106) 207–8.

sacred places; the killing of orators; neglected oaths; ancient and secret rituals performed improperly.[44] Yet much remained unclear and unspecific. In the ensuing debate on the precise significance of the response both Clodius and Cicero offered further, opposing, explanations: Clodius, in a public meeting, claimed that 'the profanation of sacred places' was a reference to Cicero's destruction of the shrine of Liberty which he, Clodius, had erected on the site of the orator's house during his exile; Cicero, on the other hand, in a speech to the Senate which still survives, related 'the pollution of games' to Clodius' action in disrupting the Megalesian Games (held in honour of Cybele) and claimed that the 'ancient and secret rituals performed improperly' were the rituals of the Bona Dea, reputedly invaded by Clodius some years earlier.[45] This debate is more than a simple series of opportunistic appeals to a conveniently vague haruspical response; more than a crafty exploitation of religious forms at the (political) expense of a rival. Both Cicero and Clodius, by claiming as correct their own, admittedly partisan, interpretation of the prodigy, were attempting to establish their own position as privileged interpreters of the will of the gods. Divine allegiance was important for the Roman politician. In the turbulent politics of the mid-50s, it was no doubt increasingly unclear where that allegiance lay. Connexions with the gods, and the alienation of the divine from one's rivals, had to be constantly paraded and reiterated.

A striking consensus of religious ideology underlay these apparently deep divisions over the control of religion and the access to divine favour. Both sides in political debate, *populares* as well as *optimates*, seem to have publicly accepted the traditional framework for understanding the gods' relations with man. The difference between political rivals lay rather in their different views of how and by whom access to the gods was to be controlled. There is no evidence that a radical political stance ever involved a fundamental challenge to traditional views of the operation of the divine in the world. There were, to be sure, individual cults and individual deities that were invested, for various reasons, with a particular popular resonance. The temple of Ceres, for example, had from the early Republic special 'plebeian' associations: it acted as the headquarters of plebeian magistrates; it housed a treasury which received the property of all those convicted of violating the sacrosanctity of a tribune of the people; it was the centre of distribution of corn to the poor.[46] Likewise the cult of the Lares Compitales at local shrines throughout the regions (*vici*) of the city of Rome was a focus of worship and social life, particularly for the slaves and poor; while Clodius'

[44] Cic. *Har.Resp.*, with the 'reconstructed' text of the haruspical pronouncement in Wissowa 1912 (H 137) 545, n. 4.

[45] Cic. *Har.Resp.* 9; 22–9; 37–9. For the exaggeration of Cicero's claims, Lenaghan 1969 (B 65) 114–17; Wiseman 1974 (C 285) 159–69.

[46] Le Bonniec 1938 (H 73) 342–78.

dedication of a shrine to Libertas on the site of Cicero's house was no doubt intended to have particular appeal to those who felt that Cicero and his like seriously restricted the liberty of the people.[47] But these individual focuses of popular enthusiasm brought with them no radical rethinking of the overall relations between gods and men. They were simply a consequence of the availability of a range of individual choices, as is traditional within polytheistic systems.

The opposition between Clodius and Cicero in the closing years of the Republic well illustrates the nature of this broad religious consensus. The battles between the two rivals are, of course, known almost entirely (whether directly or indirectly) from the side of Cicero, who constantly characterized Clodius as 'the enemy of the gods' – accusing him not only of sacrilege against the Bona Dea, but also of destruction of the auspices and the magistrates' traditional right to obstruct legislation by the declaration of ill omens (*obnuntiatio*). The literal truth of such allegations remains, at the very least, doubtful. More important is the fact that Clodius appears to have returned in kind what were, after all, quite traditional accusations of divine disfavour. As is clear from Cicero's defence in *De Haruspicum Responso*, Clodius did not disregard or simply ridicule Cicero's religious rhetoric; he did not stand outside the system and laugh at its conventions. He turned the tables, and within the same religious framework as his opponent, he claimed the allegiance of the gods for himself and their enmity for Cicero. It was similar with other radical politicians: Saturninus, for example, protected his contentious legislation by demanding an oath of observance (*sanctio*) sworn by the central civic deities of Jupiter and the Penates;[48] and Catiline kept a silver eagle in a shrine in his house, as if taking over for his illegal uprising the symbolic protection of the eagle traditionally kept in the official shrine of a legionary camp.[49] The basic pattern of the gods' co-operation with the political leaders of Rome seems to have been accepted by all; the only question was: which political leaders?

VI. POLITICAL DOMINANCE AND DEIFICATION: THE DIVINE STATUS OF CAESAR AND ITS ANTECEDENTS

The honours granted to Julius Caesar immediately before his assassination and just after suggest that he had attained the status of a god: already

[47] See Allen 1944 (C 160); Gallini 1962 (H 45) 267–9. For the popular character of the Compitalia, the associations surrounding the cults of the local Lares and the relations between those associations and 'professional' *collegia*, Accame 1942 (F 1); Lintott 1968 (A 62) 77–83; Flambard 1977 (C 193); Purcell in ch. 17 above, pp. 674–5.

[48] Riccobono, *FIRA* I.6.3 (the Lex Latina Tabulae Bantinae); for arguments that it is a law of Saturninus, see Hinrichs 1970 (B 172) 473–86. Cf. Riccobono, *FIRA* I.9, c. 13 and Hassall, Crawford and Reynolds 1974 (B 170) 205 lines 13–15; 216.

[49] Cic. *Cat.* I.24. Note the additional symbolic association that this eagle had been one of the legionary standards on Marius' campaigns against the Cimbri and Teutones, Sall. *Cat.* 59.3.

during his lifetime he had been given the right to have a priest (*flamen*) of his cult and to display various symbols of divinity (a pediment on his house, as if it were a temple, and a place for his image in formal processions of the gods) and from shortly after his death he was endowed with other marks of divine status – altars, sacrifices, a temple and a formal decree of deification.[50] These honours, particularly those granted during his lifetime, have been the focus of much debate: what (it has often been asked) would have been the correct, Roman, answer before the Ides of March 44 B.C. to the question 'Is Caesar a god, or is he not?'[51] Unresolved disagreement on this issue, combined with the apparent ambiguity of the ancient sources, is sufficient to suggest that the question is inappropriately framed. The important and uncontestable fact is that before his death Caesar was in various specific aspects assimilated to the gods.

This assimilation of Caesar to the gods can be understood in different ways, both as a new, or foreign, element within the political and religious horizons of the Roman elite, and as one with strong traditional roots in Roman conceptions of deity and of the relations between political leaders and the gods. On the one hand, particular inspiration for various of Caesar's divine symbols may have been taken from the Greek East and the cult of the Hellenistic kings. It is certainly the case, for example, that the public celebrations of Caesar's birthday and the renaming of a calendar month and a voting tribe in his honour had clear precedents in the honours paid to certain Hellenistic monarchs.[52] On the other hand, some aspects of Caesar's divine status are comprehensible as the development of existing trends within traditional Roman thought and practice. The boundary between gods and men was never as rigidly defined in Roman paganism as in the modern Judaeo-Christian tradition: Roman mythology could incorporate men, such as Romulus, who became gods; the Roman ritual of triumph involved the impersonation of a god by the successful general; in the Roman cult of the dead, past members of the community (or of the individual family) shared in some degree of divinity. There was no simple polarity, but a continuous spectrum, between the human and the divine.[53] Throughout the late

[50] Cic. *Phil.* II.110; Suet. *Iul.* 76.1; Dio XLVII.18–19.

[51] The classic study is Weinstock 1971 (H 134) (with North 1975 (H 92)). See also, with different answers to the questions, Taylor 1931 (H 124) 58–77; Adcock 1932 (C 152) 718–35; Vogt 1953 (H 132); Taeger 1960 (H 121) II, 3–88; Ehrenberg 1964 (C 192); Gesche 1968 (H 47). Full bibliography: Dobesch 1966 (C 190).

[52] Dio XLIV.4.4 (with Weinstock 1971 (H 134) 206–9); XLIV.5.2 (with Weinstock 152–62).

[53] For the traditions of Romulus and Caesar's assimilation of them, Weinstock 1971 (H 134) 175–99; the triumph: Weinstock 60–79 (and n. 54, below). Some have seen also the traditions of Etruscan–Roman kingship in the honours paid to Caesar; for example, Kraft 1952/3 (C 215). For a different approach to 'Latin' traditions of deification, see Schilling 1980 (H 115).

Republic, the status of the successful politician veered increasingly towards the divine. Caesar represented only the culmination of this trend.

Rome's political and military leaders had always enjoyed close relations with the gods. The underlying logic of much of the political display and debate discussed in earlier sections of this chapter was that magistrates and gods worked in co-operation to ensure the well-being of Rome; that the success of the state depended on the common purpose of its human and divine leaders. The logic could also be reversed: successful action, whether political or military, necessarily brought men into close association with the divine. This association was most clearly apparent in the traditional ceremony of triumph, when the successful general processed through the city to offer thanks on the Capitol, dressed in the garb of Jupiter Optimus Maximus: his face was painted red, just like the cult statue of the god; he wore the god's purple cloak and crown, and carried his golden sceptre. The general's victories had been won through his co-operation with the gods and, in celebration of these victories, just for a day he stepped into a god's shoes.[54]

Changes in the pattern of political office-holding, however, brought changes in patterns of association with the gods. The essentially temporary identification of man and god implied by the triumphal ceremony was appropriate to the likewise temporary periods of formal political power enjoyed by the elite in the early and middle Republic. The duration of office-holding was limited and so too was the potential for any long-term association with the divine. The late Republic, by contrast, set a new pattern of political dominance. As the great dynasts of the age increasingly managed, by the repetition and extension of offices and by series of special commands, to exercise power for long periods, in some cases almost continuously, so they came to claim long-term association or identification with the gods. Sometimes adopting the symbolism of the triumph, sometimes using other marks of proximity to the divine, they displayed themselves, or were treated by others, as favourites of the gods, in part gods themselves. In a world where political action was conceived in terms of the action of both gods and men, and where the boundaries between the human and divine sphere were in any case not rigidly defined, this development is not hard to understand.

Already by the late third or early second century B.C. there are clear signs of the divine elevation of powerful political and military figures. Scipio Africanus, for example, displayed close connexions with the gods. The legend of his divine origin, as son of Jupiter, was no doubt inflated

[54] Versnel 1970 (H 130) who demonstrates both divine and regal associations in the traditional ceremony.

after his death; but it seems certain that during his lifetime he made a point of parading his association with Jupiter, letting it be known that he communicated privately with the god in his Capitoline temple before taking any important new action.[55] A little later Aemilius Paullus, after his victory at Pydna in 168, was granted not only a triumph, but the right to wear triumphal dress at all Circus games.[56] That was an important symbolic break with the very temporary honorific status conferred by the traditional triumphal ceremony: Paullus, appearing at games in the dress of Jupiter Optimus Maximus, was allowed to extend, even to regularize, his identification with the god. It was to be an honour granted again to Pompey in 63 B.C. and later, with even further extensions, to Caesar: the dictator was allowed to wear such costume on all public occasions.[57]

The leading figures of the post-Gracchan era paraded, or were popularly invested with, even clearer marks of assimilation with the gods. The political dominance of Marius, for example, seven times consul and triumphant victor over Jugurtha and over the Germans, was matched by his religious elevation. Not only did he go so far as to enter the Senate in his triumphal dress – a display of religious and political dominance amongst his peers from which he was forced to draw back; but after his victory over the northern invaders he was promised by the grateful people offerings of food and libations of wine along with the gods (*hama tois theois*).[58] Such a – no doubt temporary and informal – outburst of popular support for a favoured political leader was not unprecedented; the Gracchi had received some kind of cult after their death at the places where they had been killed.[59] But Marius seems to have set a pattern for the cult of the living. Twenty years later the praetor Marius Gratidianus issued an immensely popular edict reasserting the traditional value of the Roman denarius and was rewarded by the people with 'statues erected in every street, before which incense and candles were burned'. It is significant that Cicero connects Gratidianus' elevation by the people with his independent action in issuing the edict in his own name, without reference to his colleagues.[60] Divine status, it seems, went hand in hand with political dominance, or claims to such dominance.

Association with the gods could also be displayed through connexions with individual deities other than the triumphal Jupiter. Venus, in particular, ancestor of the family of Aeneas (and so, by extension, of the

55 See Walbank 1967 (B 122). 56 *De Vir. Ill.* 56.5.

57 Pompey: Dio XXXVII.21.4; Vell. Pat. II.40.4 (stating that he only used the honour once); Cic. *Att.* I.18.6. Caesar: Dio XLIII.43.1; App. *BCiv.* II.106.442.

58 Plut. *Mar.* 27.9; Val. Max. VIII.15.7. 59 Plut. *C. Gracch.* 18.2.

60 Cic. *Off.* III.80, with Pliny *HN* XXXIII.132 (who connects the honours simply with the popularity of the measure); Seager in ch. 6 above, pp. 180–1.

Romans as a whole), became prominent in the careers of several dynasts of the first century B.C.; and, at least between Pompey and Caesar, there seems to have been an element of conscious competition in displaying the closest possible connexion with the deity.

At the beginning of the century Sulla claimed the protection of Venus in Italy and of Aphrodite (conventionally seen as the Greek 'equivalent' of the Italian goddess) in the East. This association was paraded not only on the coins minted by the dictator, in his temple-foundation and his famous dedication of an axe at Aphrodite's major sanctuary at Aphrodisias in Asia Minor, following the goddess' appearance to him in a dream; but Sulla's titles also incorporated his claims to her divine favour. In the Greek world he was officially styled Lucius Cornelius Sulla 'Epaphroditus'; in the West he took the extra cognomen 'Felix', a title which indicated good fortune brought by the gods, in this case almost certainly by Venus.[61] Pompey followed suit. Although in many respects more traditional, at least in Rome, in his display of divine connexions, he too made much of his closeness to Venus, as is clear from coins issued by his supporters and the dedications of his own lavish building schemes: the enormous complex of theatre and temple, for example, dedicated in 55 B.C., was centred on a shrine of Venus Victrix (Venus the Victorious), through whose aid, one was to assume, Pompey had won his victories; and a later dedication in the same building project was of a shrine to Felicitas, an echo of Sulla's title 'Felix'. It is as if he was taking over from the memory of Sulla the particular patronage of Venus, the divine ancestress of the Roman race.[62]

Caesar, of course, could outbid both Sulla and Pompey. Venus was for him more than a patron goddess; she was the ancestor of the family of Aeneas, from which his own family of the Iulii claimed direct descent. Caesar is known to have stressed this very point already in 68 B.C. in his funeral oration for his aunt Julia, when he celebrated her divine ancestry in the goddess Venus. And later during his dictatorship, when he embarked on the grand development of a new and lavish forum, in no doubt conscious rivalry with the building schemes of Pompey, he chose to dedicate the central temple to Venus Genetrix (Venus the ancestress). The significance of this would not have been lost on many: while Pompey and others could claim the support of Venus as forebear of the

[61] Plut. *Sull.* 19.9; 34.4–5; App. *BCiv.* 1.97.451–5 – with Schilling 1954 (H 114) 272–95. For a discordant view (that Sulla's associations were with the Greek Aphrodite, rather than the Roman Venus) and a bibliography of earlier work, Balsdon 1951 (C 18).

[62] Coins: Crawford 1974 (B 144) 424.1; 426.3. Temple of Venus Victrix: see n. 20, above. Shrine of Felicitas: *F.Allif.* in *Inscr. Ital.*, II.177–84, 12 Aug. – with Weinstock 1971 (H 134) 93 and 114. Plut. *Pomp* 14. 6 records a dispute with Sulla over Pompey's right to triumph in 81 B.C.: Pompey wished to ride into Rome on a chariot drawn by four elephants (a vehicle associated with Venus), which perhaps indicates that the symbolic patronage of Venus was already an issue between the two men.

Roman race as a whole, Caesar could and did parade her as the particular ancestor of his own family.[63]

Rome's expansion, especially in the eastern Mediterranean, brought with it another context in which the leading figures of Rome were assimilated to the gods. Following broadly in the pattern of cult offered to the Hellenistic kings, at least from the second century B.C., various forms of divine honours were granted by eastern cities to individual Roman generals and governors. From the point of view of the cities themselves this may be understood as a strategy by which they incorporated the new, Roman dominance with which they were now confronted into a system of honours and power with which they were already familiar.[64] From the point of view of the Romans thus honoured the granting of this divine status represented both a confirmation of the traditional Roman association between political domination and the divine and also an opportunity, if they so wished, to explore more lavish and explicit forms of cult away from the gaze of their Roman peers. Many examples could be cited: the establishment of a priest, sacrifices and hymns of praise to Flamininus at Chalcis; games in honour of Q. Mucius Scaevola in Asia; temples voted to Cicero (though refused by him) on more than one occasion in the East.[65] But by far the most striking array of divine honours were those offered to Pompey during his major commands in the East: statues, cult, dedications, the renaming of months in his honour, maybe even temples. Although in Rome itself Pompey, with a traditionalist image, sought no further elevation of divine honours, as conquering hero in the East he was granted as much divine status as Caesar was later to attain in the capital. Caesar, in other words, finally brought to Rome a level of deification that his erstwhile rival had already achieved outside Italy.[66]

We cannot know in any individual case the motives of either the giver or recipient of divine honours. It would be naive to suppose that some leading Romans did not positively enjoy the prospect of being treated like gods, that they did not perceive it as a useful political advantage over their rivals and that they did not plan or deliberately solicit further extensions of the honours. It would be likewise naive to imagine that those offering divine honours did not on some occasions calculate that

[63] Funeral speech: Suet. *Iul.* 6. New Forum and its connotations: Weinstock 1971 (H 134) 80–90. Note the explicit recognition of symbolic rivalry in Plut. *Pomp.* 68.2–3 (Pompey's fears before Pharsalus that his dream of spoils on the temple of Venus Victrix was in fact a good omen for Caesar whose ancestor Venus was).

[64] Price 1984 (H 103) 234–48.

[65] Plut. *Flam.* 16.7; *IOlympia* 327; Cic. *QFr.* I.1.26; *Att.* V.21.7 (though note the lavish honours to various members of the family of Cicero at Samos, Dörner and Gruber 1953 (H 32)).

[66] For example *IGRR* IV.49–55; *IG* XII.2, 59 line 18 (with Robert 1969 (D 289) 49 n. 8); *SIG* 749 A and B; for the (debatable) evidence for a temple, App. *BCiv.* II.86.361; Dio LXIX.11.1. Pompeian precedents for Caesar's divine honours: Weinstock 1971 (H 134).

the offer would redound to their own benefit: there were advantages to be won if it was your community (rather than the town a few miles down the road) that presented the Roman governor with a series of sacrifices and a grandiose temple. Yet underlying these disparate (and for us irrecoverable) motives, there is a consistent logic of Roman political action and religion: the exercise of political power involved close association with the gods. Only in the context of that traditional Roman logic can the elevation of any of the major political figures in the late Republic be understood.

VII. THE DIFFERENTIATION OF RELIGION

1. *Scepticism, expertise and magic*

The developments of Roman religion in the late Republic must also be seen as part of the intellectual and cultural developments of the period. So far in this chapter most emphasis has been placed on the integration of religion with political life and on the religious changes that followed directly on political changes in the second and first centuries B.C. But religion is also part of the world of ideas and of the mind. The changes in patterns of thought in the late Republic, and new ways of perceiving and classifying human experience, provide another important context for understanding religious developments. They were not unrelated to the material, economic or political life of Rome; but taken on their own (simply for the sake of clarity) they provide another means of illuminating the developments within what is necessarily a complex amalgam.

One of the most striking processes of change in the late Republic was the process of 'structural differentiation'. As Roman society became more complex, many areas of activity that had previously remained undefined or, at least, widely diffused through traditional social and family groups, developed for the first time a separate identity, with their own specific rules, relatively autonomous from other activities and institutions. Rhetoric, for example, became a specialized skill, professionally taught, not an accomplishment picked up at home or by practice in the Forum; likewise the institutions of criminal and civil law witnessed the development of legal experts, men who had made themselves knowledgeable in the law and carefully distinguished their skill from that of advocates and orators.[67] The precise stages and causes of those developments are complex to reconstruct, and it is hard to evaluate the relative weight that should be placed upon Rome's internal developments as against the effects of her growing contact with the already

[67] Rhetoric: Hopkins 1978 (A 53) 76–80; Rawson 1985 (H 109) 143–55. Law: ch. 14 above, p. 534.

highly differentiated world of some of the Greek states. The consequences are nevertheless clear: by the end of the Republic a range of new, specialized activities existed, and with those activities went new, specialized areas of discourse and intellectual expertise.

The differentiation of religion was part of that process. Traditionally, religion was deeply embedded in the political institutions of Rome: the political elite were at the same time those who controlled man's relations with the gods; the Senate was the central *locus* of both 'religious' and 'political' power. In many respects that remained as true at the end of the Republic as it had been two or three centuries earlier. But at the same time we can trace, over at least the last century B.C., the beginning of the isolation of religion as an autonomous area of human activity, with its own rules and specialized discourse. This process can be seen most clearly in three particular aspects: the development of a discourse of scepticism about traditional religious practice; the emergence of religious experts and enthusiasts; and the development of more rigidly defined boundaries between different types of religious experience – between the licit and illicit, between religion and magic.

The earliest surviving works fully to develop arguments sceptical of the established traditions of Roman religion are the philosophical treatises of Cicero. The second book of his dialogue *On Divination*, in particular, written during 44 and 43 B.C., incorporates an extended attack on the validity of Roman augury, the significance of portents and the agreed interpretation of oracles. All manner of ridicule is poured on the gullible, who believe, for example, that cocks crowing before a battle may portend victory for one particular side, or that the absence of a heart from the entrails of a sacrificial animal indicates forthcoming disaster. The 'rational' philosopher argues that the crowing of cocks is too common an occurrence to be significant of anything and that it is simply a physical impossibility for an animal ever to have lived without a heart. No element of Roman divination escapes such ruthlessly 'logical' scrutiny.[68]

The presentation of such arguments does not necessarily indicate that a deeply sceptical mentality was common amongst the Roman upper class. Even in the case of *On Divination*, the sceptical second book is preceded and balanced by a first book which presents the arguments, in terms of Greek Stoic philosophy, *in favour* of divination; and the views of Cicero himself for and against the practice can hardly be judged with certainty. The central significance of such intellectualizing treatises on Roman religion lies rather in the fact that a sceptical argument about traditional religious practice could at this time be mounted. Religion was

[68] See, for example, Cic. *Div.* II.36–7; 56.

being defined as an area of interest in its own right; and as such it became the subject of critical scrutiny.[69]

This degree of differentiation of religion developed in Rome first in the Ciceronian age. It was associated not only with the growing complexity of Roman society, which provided the general context for the various processes of structural differentiation, but also with increasing Roman familiarity with Greek philosophy. Contact with the philosophical traditions of the Greek world did, of course, stretch back considerably further than the middle of the first century B.C. As early as the beginning of the second century Ennius produced a Latin translation of Euhemerus' work on the human origins of the gods; and through the second and early first centuries there is ample evidence for the exposition in Latin of Greek philosophical doctrines.[70] But, as far as we can tell from such evidence as survives, it was not until the age of Cicero and his contemporaries that Greek theory was so integrated with Roman practice that it played a part in defining and differentiating new areas of recognizably Roman (rather than translated Greek) discourse. Even the famous Mucius Scaevola (cos. 95), whose remarks on state religion as quoted by St Augustine appear to foreshadow the philosophical sophistication of Cicero, provides no convincing early example of the later trend: Augustine, in a recent scholar's view, was quoting the words not of the 'real' Scaevola but of Scaevola as a character in a dialogue of Cicero's contemporary, Varro. Intellectual discourse on religion was a new phenomenon of the very latest phase of the Republic.[71]

The increasing differentiation of religion was also characterized by its definition as an area of antiquarian inquiry and by the emergence of religious enthusiasts or self-styled experts; it was not restricted to the development of negative or sceptical discourse on religion. Cicero's dialogue *On Divination* reveals something of many different strands involved in the process of differentiation, with its Greek philosophical arguments deployed both to attack and to uphold the traditions of Roman state religion; and other, more fragmentary, material highlights even more sharply the growth of religious expertise and religious curiosity that contributed to the distinctive character of religion in the late Republic.

[69] Beard 1986 (H 8); Schofield 1986 (H 116). For stress on the scepticism of the work, Linderski 1982 (H 78); Momigliano 1987 (H 87).

[70] Roman philosophical experts: Spurius Mummius (middle of the second century B.C.): Cic. *Brut.* 94; P. Rutilius Rufus (cos. 105 B.C.): *Brut.* 114; *De Or.* I.227; T. Albucius (praetor *c.* 105 B.C.): *Brut.* 131. For Latin treatises, note the work of Amafinius (?early first century B.C.): *Tusc.* IV.6; Rabirius: *Acad.Post.* I.5; Catius; *Fam.* XV.16.1; 19.1.

[71] Beard 1986 (H 8) 36–41. Mucius Scaevola: Augustine, *De civ.D.* IV.27, with Cardauns 1960 (B 10). Others accept the quoted views as the views of the 'real' Scaevola; see Rawson 1985 (H 109) 299–300.

The most comprehensive and best known of the antiquarian treatises on Roman religion was Varro's encyclopaedia in sixteen books on the gods and religious institutions of the city (*Antiquitates Rerum Divinarum*). Though it does not survive complete, enough is preserved (largely quoted by St Augustine in his *City of God*) for us to have some idea of its structure and content. It was partly a work of classification, dividing its subject into five principal sections (priesthoods, holy places, festivals, rites and gods) and offering within those sections yet finer distinctions on types of deity and institutions: shrines (*sacella*), for example, were treated separately from temples (*aedes sacrae*); gods concerned with man himself (such as those presiding over his birth or marriage) were placed in a separate category from those concerned with food or clothing. But the *Antiquitates* was also (and perhaps more so) a work of compilation, assembling often recondite information on traditional Roman religion: the reason for the particular type of head-dress worn by the *flamen Dialis*; the significance of the festival of the Lupercalia; the precise difference in responsibility between the god Liber and the goddess Ceres.[72] Other works of this explanatory, antiquarian type are known, although they do not now survive even to the same extent as Varro's, nor did they originally reach such copious lengths. Granius Flaccus, for example, dedicated to Caesar a work (*De Indigitamentis*) on the formulae used by the *pontifices* in addressing the city's gods; and at about the same time one Veranius wrote several studies on the rituals of the augurs and of the pontifical college. Looking outside Rome, Aulus Caecina, another contemporary of Cicero and Caesar, and a man with distinguished Etruscan forebears, produced a Latin version of the Etruscan science of thunderbolts and their religious interpretation.[73]

These works are a phenomenon of the latest phase of the Republic. Not that there had been no writing associated with Roman religion before that time; the pontifical and augural colleges had long kept records of ritual prescriptions and various aspects of religious law.[74] The late Republican works were, however, different from traditional writing of that kind; for they were not part of internal priestly discourse *within* religion, but commentaries *on* religion from an external standpoint. Unlike the so-called 'priestly books', they existed apart from traditional religious practice, defining religion as a subject of scholarly interest. The causes of the development are complex. Varro himself explains his antiquarian project as a necessary attempt to rescue from oblivion the

[72] Cardauns 1976 (B 11). For antiquarian information, see, for example, frr. 51; 76; 260. See also Griffin in ch. 18 above, p. 706.

[73] Granius and Veranius: *GRF* 429–35. Caecina: Rawson 1985 (H 109) 304–5.

[74] Regell 1878 (B 95); *idem* 1882 (B 95); Preibisch 1874 (B 89); *idem* 1878 (B 89); Rohde 1936 (H 111); Norden 1939 (H 91). For an analysis of the role of writing in Roman religion, Gordon 1989 (H 50); Beard 1991 (H 10A).

most ancient strands of Roman religious tradition, offering a somewhat baroque comparison with Aeneas' rescue of his household gods from the flames of burning Troy.[75] But we should not conclude from this that antiquarianism was simply a response to neglect of religion in the late Republic: it is after all always possible to perceive at any period that ancient knowledge is in danger of disappearing. Much more important is the fact that Varro's justification of his endeavour, and the works themselves, indicate that religion could now be independently defined, as an autonomous subject – whether in need of rescue or not.

Some of the writers of antiquarian treatises on Roman or Etruscan religion fall also into the category of religious enthusiasts, men for whom religion in various forms came to be an object of personal concern. Appius Claudius Pulcher (cos. 54 B.C.) provides an example. He was not only a passionate defender of the practice and principles of augury – so enthusiastic that he earned among his contemporaries the nickname 'Pisidian', after the people of Pisidia, renowned for their devotion to augury; he also endowed buildings at Eleusis and made a point of going to consult the Delphic oracle.[76] Nigidius Figulus (praetor 58 B.C.) likewise, although more famous for his devotion to magic and astrology, was known also for his enthusiastic commitment to traditional divination, both Roman and Etruscan.[77] Men such as these have been seen by modern scholars as deeply conservative, representatives of the long-standing traditions of Roman religion, against whom the more radical religious sceptics were reacting. That is hardly convincing: both the enthusiasts and the sceptics were new phenomena of a time when religion, in addition to being a part of the political and social life of the community, first became an independent subject towards which it was possible to define a personal attitude. Enthusiasm and scepticism were different sides of the same coin.

The interest of Nigidius Figulus in 'magic' provides an example of another area of differentiation of religion in the late Republic: that is, the development of increasingly precise boundaries between types of religious activity, between true religion and its illicit variants. In part, this differentiation was a reflection of a growing diversity of religious practices and an increasingly wide range of options in man's relation with the gods; but to an equal, if not greater, extent, it was a consequence of more subtle forms of categorization and definition. Many of the practices of what was defined as magic in the late Republic had no doubt

[75] Fr. 2a Cardauns 1976 (B 11).

[76] Augury: Cic. *Div.* 1.105. Delphic oracle: Val. Max. 1.8.10. Eleusis: *ILLRP* 401; Cic. *Att.* VI.1.26; 6.2.

[77] Two attested works are entitled *De augurio privato* and *De extis*; see frr. 80 and 81 (Swoboda). For magic and astrology, see Rawson 1985 (H 109) 309–12.

always formed part of religious activity at Rome; what was new was the designation of magic as a separate category.[78]

The historical development of the concept of magic at Rome is clear enough in its broad outlines. In terms of modern western understanding, there is ample evidence for magical practice and its prohibition in the early and middle Republic. Cato's treatise on agriculture includes a clear example of (in our terms) a magical charm for the healing of sprains and fractures and the fifth-century Twelve Tables contain the famous clause that 'no one should enchant another man's crops'.[79] In contemporary Roman terms, however, such recommendations and prohibitions were not perceived as falling into any particular category of 'the magical'. Cato, it seems, saw the healing charm no differently from the 'scientific' remedies suggested in his work and the legal prohibition on enchanting crops was almost certainly directed against the results of the action – that is damage to property – rather than against the method by which that damage was brought about. Not until the late Republic, and then only tentatively, was magic defined as a particular and perverted form of religion.

The clearest and earliest theory of magic preserved at Rome is that offered by Pliny the Elder (A.D. 23/4–79) in his *Natural History* (especially Books 28 and 30). He presents a coherent account of the 'origins' of magical practice (starting in Persia and spreading through Greece and Italy) and defines magic in relation to science and religion. He refers, for example, to the bestial quality of magic (men sacrificing men, or drinking human blood) and to its characteristic use of spells, charms and incantations. In general magic is seen as opposed to the normal rules of human behaviour and the traditions of Roman religion.[80] No late Republican author provides such a developed analysis of magic; but we can at least see a foreshadowing of various elements of Pliny's theoretical account in some writing of the middle of the first century B.C. Catullus, for example, abuses his favourite target Gellius with the suggestion that a magician (*magus*) will be the result of Gellius' incestuous relationship with his mother and alludes, at the same time, to the Persian origin of magical practices.[81] Cicero, likewise abusing his opponent Vatinius, charges him with the kind of bestial activities characterized by Pliny as 'magical': under the cloak of so-called 'Pythagoreanism', Vatinius indulged in calling up spirits from the underworld and sacrificing young human victims to the gods below.[82] It seems clear that the definition of

[78] R. Garosi, *Magia: Studi di storia delle religioni in memoria di Raffaela Garosi*, ed. P. Xella (Rome, 1976); North 1980 (H 95); for full bibliography, Le Glay 1976 (H 75).

[79] Cato *Agr.* 160; Sen. *QNat.* IV.7.2; Pliny *HN* XXVIII.4.17–18.

[80] For example Pliny *HN* XXVIII.2.4–5; 4.19–21; XXX.4.13, with Köves-Zulauf 1978 (H 69) 256–66.

[81] Catull. 90.

[82] Cic. *In Vatinium* 14.

magic as something outside the boundaries of traditional Roman religion was already taking place.

Many factors contributed to the development of a category of magic. Foreign influences no doubt played some part. In particular, the convenient view that the 'origin' of magic lay somehow outside the civilized world (in barbarian Persia) may well have derived from Greek definitions of magic and Greek polemic against the Persians.[83] But in general, as with the other themes discussed in this section, the underlying context for the increasing differentiation (in this case between proper and improper uses of religion) lay in the growing complexity of Roman society and the definition of religion for the first time as an autonomous area of human activity.

2. *The emergence of religious groups*

A further aspect of the differentiation of religion in the late Republic was the development of 'religious groups' – associations founded for a specifically religious purpose and often focused on one particular deity or group of deities. The practice of religion within groups big or small was not new at Rome: private religious cult had traditionally taken place in the context of the family; Roman *collegia*, whether functioning as trade guilds, burial clubs or political organizations, had often incorporated a 'religious' dimension and a particular patron deity. What was new about the religious groups of the late Republic was that their central and defining purpose was religious.

Such groups could easily be perceived as a threat to the traditional forms of religion at Rome, to the largely undifferentiated amalgam of religion and politics and, more specifically, to the control of man's relations with the gods vested in the political elite of the city. Not only were many of them centred on explicitly 'foreign' deities such as Dionysus or Isis, but their very existence suggested an alternative *locus* of religious power in the state – alternative, that is, to the Senate and the traditional political leaders. This element of opposition, implicit in the new religious associations, largely explains the periodic attempts to abolish their cults, expel their adherents or, at least, control their practices.

The best-documented example of the emergence of a religious group and its subsequent repression is found in the history of the Bacchic cult in Italy in the early second century B.C. and in the strict regulation of its future activities by decree of the Senate in 186 B.C. By good fortune, we have not only Livy's account of the discovery of this cult by the Roman

[83] Pliny *HN* xxx.2.3–11, with Garosi, *Magia* (above, n.78) 30–1.

authorities but also a copy of the *senatus consultum*, inscribed on bronze, giving full details of the restrictions imposed upon it and its practitioners. Together these documents allow us a relatively full understanding of the nature of the Bacchic groups and the crisis they caused at Rome.[84] The history of religious groups in the later second and first century B.C. and the causes of their occasional repression can only be analysed in terms of a model derived from this one well-documented incident.

Livy gives a racy account of the origin of this particular form of the Bacchic cult in Italy and of its disclosure to the Senate. He talks of the introduction of 'orgiastic rites' from Greece, first into Etruria, then to Rome itself; and with those rites the spread of crime and debauchery of every kind – perjury, promiscuity and murder.[85] Yet despite such flagrant crimes, it was not (according to Livy's story) until one young potential initiate was induced by his mistress and his aunt to turn all his information over to the consul Postumius that the Roman authorities became fully aware of what had been going on. The Senate then moved to suppress the cult, destroying the existing places of Bacchic worship and requiring senatorial permission, under rigorous conditions, for any form of cult to continue.

The crisis caused by the Bacchists was rather more than the simple spread of lust and crime that Livy's account, at first sight, seems to imply. While the lurid details preserved in the historian reflect, no doubt, the senatorial justification for control of the cult, careful analysis of Livy's story together with the surviving decree of the Senate suggests a more complex underlying problem. The crucial fact that emerges from both sources is that the Senate did not attempt to suppress the cult entirely – the obvious response to the criminal activity stressed by Livy. Instead it framed a decree which aimed to remove its independent group identity; destroying its cult centres; restricting the numbers of those who could take part in any rite; forbidding their holding of funds in common; abolishing the hierarchy of office-holding within the cult. The ruling suggests an awareness on the part of at least some senators that the danger of the cult lay in its function as an alternative religious and social group outside the control of the traditional religious and political authorities of the state. A differentiated religious group, demanding the symbolic commitment of initiation, offered its adherents a new focus of loyalty and an independent sense of belonging; it was this that the Senate attempted to regulate.[86]

Similar tensions between new specifically religious groups and the

[84] *ILLRP* 51; Livy XXXIX.8–19. See Gallini 1970 (H 46) 11–96; Turcan 1972 (H 128); North 1979 (H 94). Archaeological evidence for the character and destruction of Bacchic shrines: Paillier 1976 (H 98) 739–42 and 1983 (H 100).

[85] Livy XXXIX.8.5–8.

[86] Gallini 1970 (H 46) 86–90; North 1979 (H 94) 90–8.

traditional forms of religious and political authority underlay the later attempts by the Roman authorities to control the cult of Isis and the practice of astrology. Neither case is as fully documented as the crisis over the worship of Bacchus, and, indeed, almost nothing can be said about the particular circumstances that led to the expulsion of the 'Chaldaei' (astrologers) from Rome in 139 B.C. or to the repeated destruction of Isiac shrines in (probably) 59, 58, 53, 50 and 48.[87] But the nature of the problem in general terms may easily be deduced. The cult of Isis, with its independent priesthood and its focus on devotion in a personal and caring deity could represent (like the Bacchic cult) a potentially dangerous alternative society, out of the control of the traditional political elite.[88] Likewise astrology, with its specialized form of religious knowledge in the hands of a set of experts outside the traditional priestly groups of the city, necessarily constituted a separate, and perhaps rival, *locus* of religious power. Although it did not offer a social alternative in the sense of group membership, it represented another form of religious differentiation which threatened the undifferentiated politico-religious amalgam of traditional Roman practice.

In all these matters the attitudes of the Roman Senate and senators were complex. It would be oversimplifying to suggest that the Senate was straightforwardly opposed to what *we* perceive as the differentiation of religion. Senators themselves were, after all, caught up in that process and provide (as was seen in the last section) some of the classic examples of differentiation, in terms of the development of a specifically religious discourse or religious enthusiasm. It would also be oversimplifying to suggest that there was only one reason for senatorial repression of new cults or religious practices. There were no doubt just as many senators who genuinely feared the crimes spread by the Bacchists or objected to the absurdity of astrology as those who sensed the danger in the development of independent religious groups or the definition of new forms of religious knowledge. Nevertheless, the underlying logic of the periodic regulation or repression of new cults and religious groups in the late Republic lies primarily in the clash between traditional and differentiated forms of religious organization and experience.

VIII. ROMAN RELIGION AND THE OUTSIDE WORLD

The major factor that determined the changing character of religion in the late Republic was Roman imperial expansion. Almost every section

[87] Astrologers: Val. Max. I.3.3; Livy *Per.* LIV; Cramer 1951 (H 28) 14–17, with n. 78 above. Shrines of Isis: Varro, *ap.* Tert. *Ad. Nat.* I.10.17–18; Dio XL.47.3–4; XLII.26.2; Val.Max. I.3.4; Malaise 1972 (H 80) 362–77.

[88] The potential of the cult of Isis to develop into an independent focus of loyalty is illustrated by the account of it in Apul. *Met.* – e.g. XI.21–5.

of this chapter has touched on the religious consequences of the growth of Rome's empire: the dying out of the traditional Fetial ritual for declaration of war; religious honours paid to Rome's conquering generals in the Greek East; the effect of growing contact with Greek intellectual currents on the development of religious discourse at Rome. This final section will consider three further aspects of religious change in the context of Rome's expanding empire: the importation of 'foreign' cults to Rome; Rome's export of its own traditional religious forms to the outside world; and the development of foreign perspectives on Roman religion, as outsiders, particularly Greeks, began to scrutinize the religious practices of their conqueror.

In the last century of the Republic foreign deities and cults came to Rome in considerable numbers. The novelty should not be overrated: Roman religion, like most polytheistic systems, had always imported and incorporated elements from the outside. Gods as central in the Roman pantheon as Apollo and Castor and Pollux were early fifth-century imports from the Greek world;[89] and the Sibylline oracles, preserved on the Capitol, according to Roman legend, from the reign of the last king Tarquin, were written in Greek and certainly owed their origin to a non-Roman source.[90] The new feature of the imports of the late Republic was not so much their number (if anything, smaller than in the third century), but the fact that they came from further afield and were not so fully incorporated in the traditional religious forms of the city.

The point of transition was reached as far back as 205 when, following consultation of the Sibylline oracles, the Senate decided to bring to Rome the cult of Cybele and even the cult image of the goddess – a large black stone – from her temple at Pessinus in Asia Minor.[91] In certain respects that action can be seen as just one of a series of new cult foundations in the second half of the third century, stimulated by the Romans' need for divine support in the crises of the Second Punic War. But in other respects the importation of Cybele (or 'Magna Mater', 'The Great Mother', as she was commonly known) differed from those that had gone before. Not only was she a deity from outside the central areas of the Graeco-Roman world – an indication of how far Rome's influence and knowledge now spread. But also, despite the official initiative that lay behind the establishment of the cult in Rome, the Senate did not permit Roman citizens full involvement in its orgiastic rites. The cult of

[89] Castor and Pollux: Livy II.20.12; Weinstock 1960 (B 257) 112.14; Castagnoli 1959 (B 268); *idem* 1975 (B 269). Apollo: Livy IV.25.3–4; Gagé 1955 (H 44) 19–68; Simon 1978 (H 118).

[90] Gell. *NA* I.19; Dion. Hal. *Ant.Rom.* IV.62. For the role of the Sibylline books in innovation, North 1976 (H 93) 9, and, generally, Parke 1988 (A 89).

[91] Livy XXIX.10.4–11.8; 14.5–14.

Cybele remained a recognizably 'foreign' element within religious life at Rome.[92]

The pattern of imports through the last years of the Republic broadly followed that of Cybele. The new cults – Isis and Sarapis, for example, or Mithras, who was possibly introduced to Italy before the end of the Republic – had their origin in more distant countries (Egypt and Persia) and, although to some degree already Hellenized by the time of their entry into Italy, kept a foreign identity, undomesticated within traditional Roman cult.[93] In part this change is to be connected with the tendency towards the differentiation of religious groups discussed in the last section, but in part it also relates to Rome's greater and greater territorial expansion. Even traditional Roman polytheism, expansive as it was, could not simply incorporate the yet more alien religious forms that the Romans encountered abroad or met in their increasingly cosmopolitan city. 'Religion at Rome' began in the late Republic to be something rather different from 'Roman religion'.

The religious interaction between Rome and the outside world operated also in the opposite direction. Just as the cultures of Rome's empire and beyond brought new elements into the city of Rome, so in turn Roman power influenced the religion of Rome's territories in Italy and overseas. In this sense, by the late Republic, recognizably 'Roman' religion could be found elsewhere than in Rome itself.

The clearest instance of the direct export of Roman religious forms can be seen in the establishment and regulation of religious practice in the Roman citizen colonies founded for the settlement of military veterans and the poor in Italy and sometimes (at least from the Gracchan period) in provincial territory. Not only were they founded, as was traditional with new Roman settlements, according to a religious ritual believed to mirror that used by Romulus in the foundation of Rome, but also their religious organization was modelled directly on that of the mother-city. This is well illustrated by the surviving charter of foundation for Julius Caesar's colony at Urso in southern Spain. Several clauses lay down regulations for the selection and service of the priests of the community – *pontifices* and *augures*:

And the said pontiffs and augurs who shall be members of the several colleges, and also their children, shall have exemption from military service and compulsory public service solemnly guaranteed, in such wise as a pontiff in

[92] The 'foreign' elements are most clearly illustrated by the visual evidence for the cult; see Vermaseren 1977 (H 129) esp. Pls. 44; 64–8. For official ambivalence towards full Roman involvement in the cult and the reported prohibition against Roman citizens becoming castrated priests of Cybele see Bömer 1964 (H 14).

[93] Survey and discussion of the early development of Mithraism: Gordon 1977/8 (B 166); Beck 1984 (H 11) 2002–115, with Plut. *Pomp.* 24.7. Egyptian cults: Malaise 1972 (H 80); Dunand 1980 (H 36); Coarelli 1984 (C 184).

Rome has or shall have the same, and all their military service shall be accounted as discharged. Respecting the auspices and matters appertaining to the same, jurisdiction shall belong to the augurs. And the said pontiffs and augurs shall have the right and power to use the *toga praetexta* at all games publicly celebrated by magistrates, and at public sacrifices of the Colonia Genetiva Iulia[94] performed by themselves, and the said pontiffs and augurs shall have the right and power to sit among the decurions to witness the games and gladiatorial combats.[95]

We should note particularly here the explicit reference in the colonial charter to the religious practice of Rome itself. It was not a question of vague, haphazard similarities between the religion of a colony and the religion of the mother-city. The export of a community, whether to Italy or further afield, involved the systematic and conscious replication of the religious forms of the city of Rome.

Moreover, the spread of Roman power led provincial communities, whether directly encouraged by Rome or not, to adopt various symbolic forms in explicit recognition of Roman dominance or even drawn from Roman religion itself. The best-known development, from the early second century on, was the spread through the Greek world of cults centred on a deified personification of Rome – 'Dea Roma' – or such variants as 'The People of the Romans' or 'Rome and the Roman Benefactors'. A few communities in the East dedicated temples to Rome – notably Smyrna, from as early as 195 B.C., Alabanda in Caria and Miletus. Many more had priests of the goddess Rome, festivals and sacrifices. A particularly vivid second-century inscription from Miletus, for example, details the sacrifices to be performed to 'Roma' and 'The People of the Romans' – not only were there special occasions when priests or magistrates were to make such offerings, but the regular political turning-points of city life (such as the entry into office of new magistrates) were also to be marked by such sacrifices to the deification of Rome and its people.[96] No similar cult of Roma is known from Rome itself until the reign of Hadrian,[97] so we are not here dealing with Greek emulation of contemporary Roman practice: the cults are rather, like the deification of individual Roman governors or generals, part of a process by which eastern cities incorporated Roman power into their own religious, cultural and symbolic world – a religious representation of Rome developed side by side with Roman dominance.

Other developments, by contrast, show the cities of the Greek world adopting elements of traditional Roman symbolism or even parading

[94] That is, Urso.

[95] *FIRA* I.21.66 (p. 181); trans. Hardy 1912 (B 169) 29.

[96] Smyrna: Tac. *Ann.* IV.56. Alabanda: Livy XLIII.6.5. Miletus: Sokolowski 1969 (B 245) 49. In general, see Mellor 1975 (H 82); Fayer 1976 (H 38); Price 1984 (H 103).

[97] Mellor 1975 (H 82) 201; J. Beaujeu, *La religion romaine à l'apogée de l'empire* (Paris, 1955) 128–36.

allegiance to Rome in the religious centre of Rome itself. An inscription from the island of Chios provides a particularly clear, if exceptional, illustration of Roman symbolism in a Greek context. It records the establishment, probably in the early second century B.C., of a procession, sacrifice and games in honour of Roma; but alongside these fairly standard elements, it also records the dedication to Roma of a sculpture of Romulus and Remus suckled by the wolf – a classic scene of Roman myth used in a Greek cultic context.[98] In the city of Rome itself a series of inscriptions from the Capitoline hill recording dedications by various eastern communities in gratitude for Roman benefactions or assistance shows the other facet of Greek assimilation of Roman religious forms. The original texts (of which some are now preserved only in reinscriptions of the Sullan era or Renaissance manuscript copies) dated from the early second to the middle of the first century B.C. and included a dedication by the Lycians of a statue of Roma to Jupiter Capitolinus and the Roman People and likewise a dedication by Mithridates Philopator (middle of the second century B.C.) and by Ariobarzanes of Cappadocia (early first century B.C.) presumably also to the Capitoline god.[99] The principal significance of these texts, as of the Chiot dedication, lies in the evidence they provide for the gradual 'Romanization' of the religion of the cities of the Greek world. As Roman power spread, so also Roman religious forms began to have a meaning further and further afield and the cult places of the city of Rome itself became seen by the eastern communities as an appropriate area for their own religious dedications.

Rome's imperial expansion influenced religious thought as much as religious practice. In earlier sections we have already noted the effects of growing contact with Greek philosophy on the intellectual approaches of the Romans to their own religious system. Such contact had, of course, another aspect: Greek intellectuals, as they became perforce more familiar with the Roman world, began to formulate for the first time their own views on Roman religion and cult practice. Greek writing from the second century B.C. onwards includes several such analyses of the character of traditional religion at Rome – important as contemporary evidence, but as the evidence of outsiders rather than of native practitioners.

The earliest surviving and best-known Republican account of Roman religion from the pen of a Greek is that by Polybius. A native of Achaea, he was resident in Rome (at first as a hostage, later of his own free will) for much of the period from 170 to his death in the last years of the

98 *Bull. ép.* 1980, 353; Moretti 1980 (H 88); Derow and Forrest 1982 (B 148) with arguments for a date around 190–188 B.C.

99 The Republican texts, *ILLRP* 174–81. Full publication and discussion by Degrassi 1951–2 (H 30). For a review of the controversy over the date and type of monument from which these texts came, see Mellor 1975 (H 82) 203–6.

second century; and during this time he wrote his history of Rome's rise to power in the Mediterranean. It included a discussion of Roman political institutions and briefly (at least in the surviving text) of Roman religion. The analysis is pointed and distinctive. The Romans are acknowledged to be superior to other nations in the nature of their religious convictions, which have entered public and private life to a degree unparalleled elsewhere; but, as if to undercut this apparent devotion, the motivation for such a prominence of religion is reckoned to be the need of the Roman elite to control the masses. Adopting a philosophical position attested in Greece since at least the fifth century B.C. and with an even longer history since, he argues that 'as every multitude is fickle, full of lawless desires, unreasoned passion and violent anger, the multitude must be held in by invisible terrors and suchlike pageantry'.[100] Roman religion, for Polybius, came close to being the 'opiate of the people'.

This analysis is both less and more important than it has been conventionally held to be by modern scholars. It is less important, because it is not (as it has often been taken to be) an 'objective' analysis of the strength of Roman religious practice. It cannot be used as the final tool with which to undermine the religious 'sincerity' of the Roman elite, for it is, after all, the individual, sense-making, perspective of one man, and one whose intellectual roots lay in a religious and cultural environment quite alien from that of Rome. Its importance lies rather in the further evidence it gives of the increasing complexity of Roman religious thought in the late Republic. More people had more views on Roman religion, from more different perspectives, than ever before. And those views, necessarily, increasingly interacted: few senators, for example, whether they accepted it or not, could have read Polybius' account of their traditional religious practice without being in some way affected and having to think out attitudes previously unthought. If religion is, at one level, the sum of possible religious attitudes, Roman religion in the late Republic was quite simply getting bigger.

[100] Polyb. VI.56.6–15, with Walbank 1957–69 (B 121) 741–3; Pédech 1965 (H 101); Dörrie 1974 (B 28).

EPILOGUE

THE FALL OF THE ROMAN REPUBLIC

J. A. CROOK, ANDREW LINTOTT AND ELIZABETH RAWSON

At the beginning of this volume readers were offered a brief survey of opinions down the ages about the causes of the fall of the Republic; now, with the facts before them, they will have formed opinions of their own. However, they may still, reasonably, expect the editors of the volume to state theirs: how should this tumultuous period be summed up,[1] and, especially, are there any integrating concepts to link the political and military narrative of the first part with the subsequent chapters about law and society, economics, religion and ideas?

Some parallel may here be perceived to the debates about the fall of the Roman Empire. In that case the simplistic question, 'did it decline or was it assassinated?', though requiring to be reformulated and answered with considerable subtlety, remains not a bad starting-point. So: did the political order that we know as the Roman Republic decline, or was it assassinated? Did it contain the dialectic of its own collapse, or could it, but for the ambitions of certain dynasts (above all, Pompey and Caesar, Antony and Octavian), have survived the changes taking place in Roman society?

Both the experience of another twenty centuries and the refinements of modern historical explanation make it out of the question for us to be content with the standard answer given by the Romans themselves, that the political order was destroyed by moral decline resulting from wealth, greed and luxury.[2] Change was occurring in moral conceptions, as in everything else, but that is true of all periods and is not necessarily a symptom of morbidity in the body politic. Nor is it easily open to us now to say that what fell was in any case only a corrupt and unlamented oligarchy. Recent analyses of the Republican constitution have laid stress on its genuinely democratic aspects:[3] it is nowadays insisted that Polybius drew a true picture after all, and that Rome did have a 'mixed

[1] For such a summing-up, on a larger scale than is here attempted, see Brunt 1988 (A 19) ch. 1.

[2] There are examples enough in history of wealth and materialism accompanying not decline but advance of a society.

[3] Thus Nicolet 1974 (A 81) and 1976 (A 82) *passim*; Millar 1984 (A 75) and 1986 (C 113); Lintott 1987 (A 65); Brunt 1988 (A 19) chs. 1 and 6–9.

constitution', and the governing class, being dependent in each generation upon the electorate, could not treat the *res publica* as their private game. In so far as such analyses are right, we cannot ascribe the fall of the Republic merely to the fortuitously disastrous outcome of a political poker-match amongst the *principes viri*, any more than to a downturn in some Dow-Jones index of morality, but must turn to the identification of structural faults. To the very extent that the Republic displayed genuine elements of liberty and democracy, we have to ask what it was about the institutions that were supposed to guarantee those values that made them vulnerable to the political challenges at home and abroad created by the growth of wealth and power, and the conceptual challenges caused by the cracking of the narrow framework of Roman perceptions.

The ancient history-writers themselves, as we have seen, recognized two dominant motifs in the later Republic. Florus' Epitome of Roman history illustrates this most simply: one book of foreign conquests, one book of civil strife. So, also, Appian followed his monographs on the Roman subjection of foreign powers by his five books of *Civil Wars*. The implied succession is actually somewhat un-historical. Though Roman expansion slowed after the dramatic advances of the middle Republic, it did not cease altogether in the fifty years before the Social War. Almost ten years of civil and quasi-civil war did then cause an intermission, but following that setback the last twenty years of the Republic saw striking new conquests, which remained largely untouched by the new civil wars of the forties.

Now Rome's success abroad brought wealth, both to the state and to individuals, whether commanders and soldiers or financiers and businessmen. It opened new opportunities for trade, and for the acquisition of real estate abroad, to both Romans and Italians. At the same time it was the natural form of self-fulfilment for perhaps the most military-minded society in antiquity: it satisfied the desire for *gloria* which was the supreme value of the aristocracy.

Yet the conquests fuelled the strife, and empire made new and burdensome demands. If the armies were victorious, wealth accrued, first as booty and later as regular tribute. But it became increasingly hard to maintain citizen manpower for the number of legions needed: there was a growing imbalance between activities and resources. The traditional source of legionaries was the country population, not that of the town, and the land came under competing pressures, from the rich seeking safe investment for the new capital that was largely the spoils of empire, and the peasantry fighting to retain their traditional landholdings, as was essential if the reservoir of conscript manpower was to be maintained. That is why agrarian laws were a particular focus of conflict; and some of the *principes viri* decided that it conduced to their own political standing as well as the good of the *res publica* for them to support agrarian programmes. And when spare land was all taken up, what then? It is not justified to claim that the primary cause of the civil wars was the hunger of peasant conscripts for land; nevertheless, attempts to satisfy the demand were regularly the cause of political crises, and finally, during the civil wars with which our narrative ends, serving armies did begin explicitly to bargain for land for themselves. And in Italy, short of purchase, Paul could only be paid by robbing Peter.

Besides being an opportunity, the expansion of empire was a strain and a temptation for the *principes viri*. Their ambitions grew to match the widening horizons of Roman power: both Pompey and Caesar were lured by the ghost of Alexander the Great. New commands of long-term duration, conferred by the assembly of the people or by the Senate, and often covering wide and distant regions, encouraged and even entailed independent initiatives on the part of their holders, making them impatient of consultation with the home government when immediate and decisive action seemed necessary. The habits so acquired inclined them to take short cuts in the political sphere at home, in order to achieve what they regarded as legitimate aims. We should not deduce from their manipulation of violence and corruption that they necessarily wanted to become dictators.

Deep divisions certainly existed in Roman society between slave and free, rich and poor, citizen and non-citizen; but none of them was a direct cause of the fall of the Republic. The slave revolts that occurred during our period, though traumatic in their time, did not shake Roman society in the long term, nor did the rural revolt that was part of the tale of the Catilinarian conspiracy. The conflict between Rome and the Italian *socii* came within an ace of destroying Rome, but did not do so; it did, however, by resulting in the incorporation of the *socii*, contribute an important indirect factor to the fall of the Republic. The change was slow: it took another generation for the Italians to achieve parity with the Romans in a unified Roman state. But an evolution had been started which had at least one fundamental consequence, that the *populus Romanus* was an altogether larger and wider body than before, and the city population of Rome could no longer claim to count as its principal and decisive element. On the one hand, to the new, wider citizen body not all the preoccupations of the older, narrower *populus Romanus* were of much interest; and, on the other, the city population, consisting very heavily of the class of freed slaves, socially despised by the upper class, began to form a political entity (not constitutionally, of course) in its own right, once again with the support of interested politicians.

During the late Republic the rural and the urban poor (but especially and most significantly the latter) were stimulated by the *populares* to assert themselves and back measures conducive to their welfare by cheers, by votes, and in the end by force. That culminated in the anarchy of the fifties, when violence, compounded by bribery, made the city of Rome at times unmanageable, and basic constitutional functions, such as elections, could not be performed. Ancient democracies and oligarchies all (with the one exception of Athens for a period) suffered from the structural defect that major conflicts of policy could only take the form of *stasis*, civil strife. The Romans, moreover, accepted the use of force (in the form of self-help, for example, and sometimes symbolic rather than actual) as part of the structure of their law and politics, so that the barrier between normal political conflict and *vis* was flimsy. On the other hand, notwithstanding the acceptance of force, Rome had been a society with a strong traditional discipline, obedient to the *auctoritas* of the *principes viri*; but if the *principes* themselves were at odds and ready to support violence in the Forum and the assembly, such traditional mechanisms could no longer work.[4]

It should not be concluded from the violence that the whole Roman body politic was rotten and the story of the late Republic no more than a power-struggle between a handful of self-seeking political bosses. In the great conflicts over *repetundae*, the agrarian laws, the franchise and the extensions of *imperium* we should be prepared to allow that serious men were applying their minds and efforts to the problems of their times. And that there was conflict between radicals and conservatives, that there were passions and prosecutions, demonstrations, vetoes and filibusters, shows that Roman public life was healthy, not ailing. Like politicians at all periods of history, the *principes* of the late Republic were moved by personal ambition; but that does not require us to deny them public spirit or political ideals. Saturninus and Clodius will have had a political vision, a *species rei publicae*, even if it was one in which they themselves bulked large; and that applies equally to their optimate opponents who sought to preserve order and the *status quo* in the face of popular agitation. Even Sulla, the portent of catastrophe, virtuously retired from his dictatorship.

Sulla had attempted a diagnosis of Rome's structural weaknesses, identifying them as the excessive power of over-mighty individuals as against the Senate and the excessive power of the tribunes to stir up opposition (seen, of course, as *stasis*, in the absence of any concept of the *value* of an opposition). The diagnosis, at least as to the former point, was correct, but the remedies inadequate, for reasons that Sulla's own career made plain to ambitious successors: the army would have had, somehow, to be de-politicized. As for the tribunate, its treatment by Sulla

[4] See the (in some ways contrasting) views of Lintott 1968 (A 62) and Nippel 1988 (A 85).

highlights a yet more general weakness: the inability of the Romans (as, indeed, of the people of antiquity in general) to conceive political improvement as anything but putting the clock back – reverting to some better state supposed to have existed in the past. Change was occurring rapidly in every branch of Roman life; it needed to be lived with and not wished away, to be adapted to and not just proscribed. Whether the Republic could have modified its political institutions and remained the Republic we can never really say; but it did not try radically enough.

The last century of the Republic, though an age of change, was anything but an age of decline. Most emphatically repudiated in these pages has been the stereotype (believed in by many Romans themselves) in which the alleged decline was measured in terms of the decay of respect for the traditional religion. Both as to the facts and as to their interpretation that can now be seen to have been mistaken. Change there certainly was, and tension between older and newer concepts – structurally related, indeed, to the new tensions in politics. And although that was not decline, it was certainly a factor making for instability.

As to the economic, cultural and intellectual fields, our period was one of rapid advance and achievement. The increasing wealth of the political class, largely acquired from empire, stimulated economic demand and cultural pretensions. The increase in the slave population and the economic pressures on the peasantry in parts of Italy fuelled grave social conflicts, though, as was said above, they were not direct factors in the fall of the Republic. More directly culpable of a part in that fall, perhaps, was the other serious economic problem of the era, that of indebtedness, which afflicted all orders of society, though in different ways. In particular the cycle of borrowing and lending on the security of land, amongst the governing class, for the maintenance of a high lifestyle conducive to prestige with the electorate and the funding of political manipulation, not only led to the sacrifice of political independence but was a powerful destabilizer in times of political crisis.

On the other hand, *ambitio*, the traditional competitiveness of the upper class, while greater and greater resources made it ever more potentially destructive, had also its positive side, in the patronage by the *principes viri* of arts, philosophy, thought and letters. In the cultural sphere, wherever we look we see rapid responses to the challenge of acquaintance with Greek achievements; and in the last twenty years or so of the Republic the Romans began to feel that they could rival their mentors in sophistication in some fields. Readers of Cicero, Catullus, Sallust and Lucretius may agree with them, and will remember that the famous 'Augustan' writers, except Ovid, were formed before the 'Augustan' age ever began, and that there were salons of patronage before, and other than, that of Maecenas.

Another fruit of both empire and *ambitio* was public architecture; and Rome learnt about urban amenity and grandeur not just from Greece directly but in part, at least, through the mediation of the Italian *socii*, whose rising prosperity during those years produced monumental centres of new elaboration, with forum-complexes and stone theatres and amphitheatres.

It is a familiar historical phenomenon that the arts and sciences often flourish most in troubled times. The same was true, at Rome, of the law. The criminal law was expanded from very slender beginnings in an effort – only partially successful – to uphold social order at a time of perceived disintegration; and the civil law underwent its most creative phase ever, in response both to social demands and to those of internal logic and cohesion.

But the effect of all the cultural developments (including the greater professionalism of the law) upon people in the late Republic was unsettling. The assault on *mos maiorum*, from all directions, was too rapid, and too many landmarks and handholds were swept away.[5] Scholars have more than once suggested that Augustus was not the architect or even the culminator of the 'Roman Revolution'; on the contrary, once he had achieved sole power he stopped it. He applied the brake to a society that had been racing frenetically in new directions; and the Principate brought stability to Rome once more at the cost of the slowing down and eventual stagnation of ideas and experiments.

Nevertheless, men's perceptions did change with, or were changed by, the Principate, and necessarily so. For in the wider world of which Rome had, by conquest and with a view to exploitation, made herself the mistress, most people did not think like antique Romans, and maintenance of the old Republican polity would have been a nonsense. The more emphasis we choose to place upon the degree of liberty and equality that characterized – for free-born *cives Romani* only – the traditional, face-to-face Republican political order, the more plainly that can be seen to be true. It may be banal so to conclude, but *some* sea-change of the Roman Republic, as Scipio Aemilianus had known it and Cicero revered it, was as inevitable as anything in history can be, though the venerability of its institutions ensured that they would be used to clothe the new order that succeeded it. Whether that particular *sort* of new order was equally inevitable is altogether too hard a question.

A final question that can be more easily (if not so very easily) answered

[5] Cicero wrote in a bewildered way to Atticus after Caesar's murder: 'We have recovered *libertas* but not got back the *res publica* along with it.' What he had hoped for was 'business as usual': in 43 B.C., not long before Octavian's first march on Rome, he was preparing for the praetorian elections just as he would have done before the civil wars: *Fam.* X.25.2; XI.16.2 and 17.

is what was gained and lost with the fall of the Republic. The liberty and equality of the Republican era, such as they were, were lost, to be sure;[6] and as to the 'rule of law', Cicero's fears expressed in a letter to Papirius Paetus in 46 B.C. well reflect not only his current unease about Julius Caesar but the fears that lurked among the aristocracy under the Principate even in its tranquil periods under 'good emperors': 'Everything becomes uncertain when the rule of law is abandoned, and there is no guaranteeing the future of anything that depends on someone else's will, not to say whim.'[7] At first sight that comment scarcely seems applicable to the Augustan system: the rule of law returned – indeed, that was one secret of Augustus' success – and the doctrine that the emperor was *legibus solutus*, dispensed from the laws, was canonized only at the end of long further developments. Nevertheless, the rule of law was only there because, and in so far as, the ruler as a matter of practice determined it should be, and that arbitrariness stood revealed at times of crisis.

On the other hand, we may view a little cynically the cries of woe about the loss of liberty and equality and the rule of law uttered by men whose notion of those virtues was the perpetuation of the traditional dominance of their own kind: the humbler free-born probably had a better economic and social deal under the emperors, and so had the class of freed slaves, the former *socii* came into their own, and the provincial upper class in due time joined the ranks of the imperial governing elite. For some of the changes most characteristic of the last century of the Republic created the basis for an imperial world-order, even though the Republican system was unable to handle so changed a world. The enfranchisement of Italy and the spread of Roman citizens – and Roman citizenship – into the provinces provided the emperors, as time went on, with a vastly enlarged governing class to call on, and by the end of the Republic Rome had discovered that empire demanded government. The incipient long-term professionalism of the armies[8] made it relatively easy for Augustus to create the kind of force appropriate to a vast territorial empire; and the new commands and tenures of the *principes viri* that resulted from the problems of the late Republic provided a paradigm for the commands and tenures of the new *principes*, the emperors, and their *collegae imperii*.[9] Finally, perhaps most important of all, the first steps were taken in our period (they were of necessity so taken) towards the integration of city-governments, in Italy and the West, into a structure of

[6] Brutus and Cassius to Antony in May and August 44 B.C.: 'We have sought nothing but a shared liberty . . . we desire you to be a great and renowned man in a free *res publica*; we challenge you to no feud, but we value our liberty more than your friendship' (*Fam.* XI.2.2 and 3.4).

[7] *Fam.* IX.16.3.

[8] Smith 1958 (A 114A) *passim*.

[9] See the fragment of Augustus' *laudatio* of Agrippa, *PKöln* I. 10.

municipal and central government, which was to be of ever wider application.[10] The Roman Empire did not have to be invented out of nothing: many of the changes described in this volume prepared the way for it.

And yet, to return in the end to politics and policy and the making of decisions about the goals of society and the means of reaching them, the most significant thing in the long run about the transition from Republic to Principate is the restriction of possibilities, the disappearance of political alternatives – or, to put it another way, the reduction of the independent points of decision-making to, ultimately, just one. In the *Dialogus* attributed to the historian Tacitus that point is made with high irony:[11] 'What need is there for long speeches in the Senate, when the Top People come swiftly to agreement? What need for endless harangues at public meetings, now that policy is settled not by the inexperienced masses but by a supremely wise man, and one alone?' That irony can serve as epilogue to our volume.

[10] For a convenient survey (though its principal thesis remains controversial) see Galsterer 1987 (F 60).

[11] *Dial.* 41.4 and, for the irony, Heldmann 1982 (H 59) 280–5.

STEMMATA

THE HASMONEAN DYNASTY

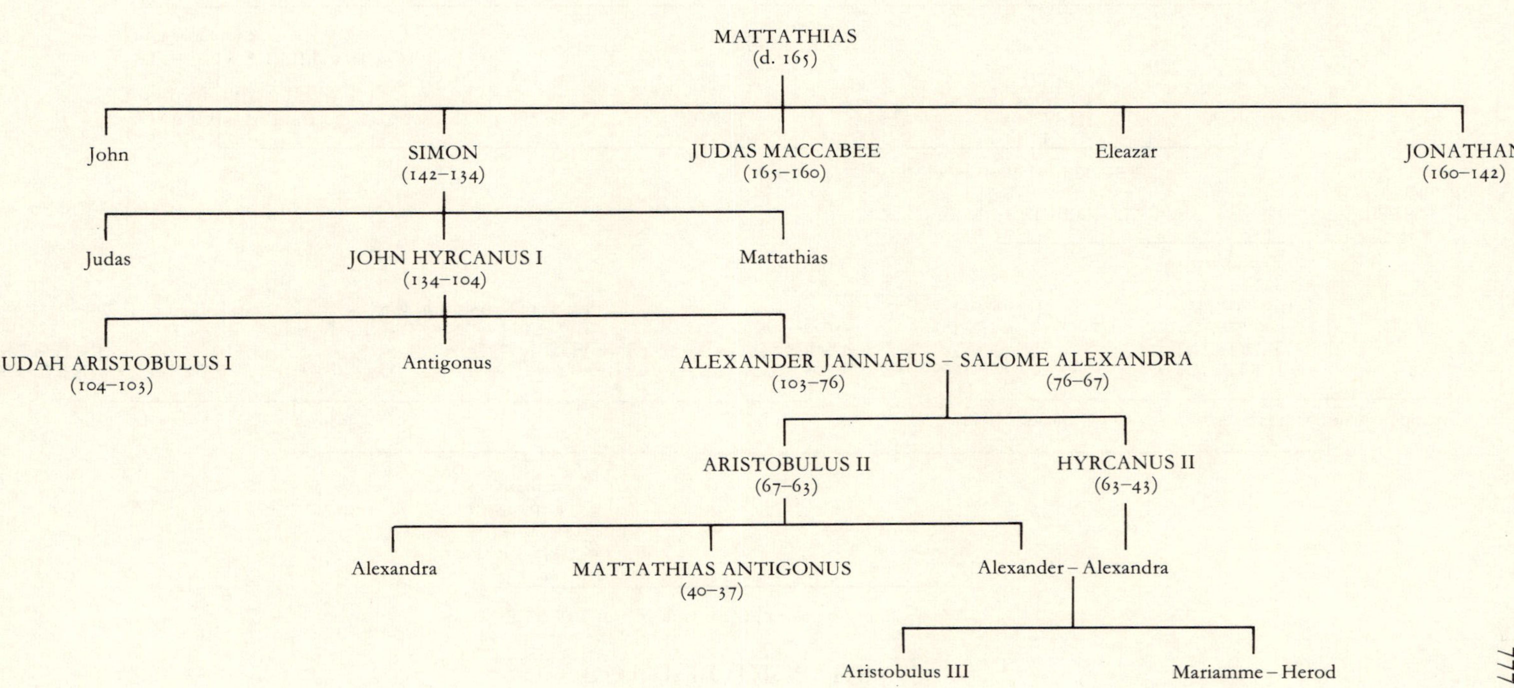

THE PTOLEMIES

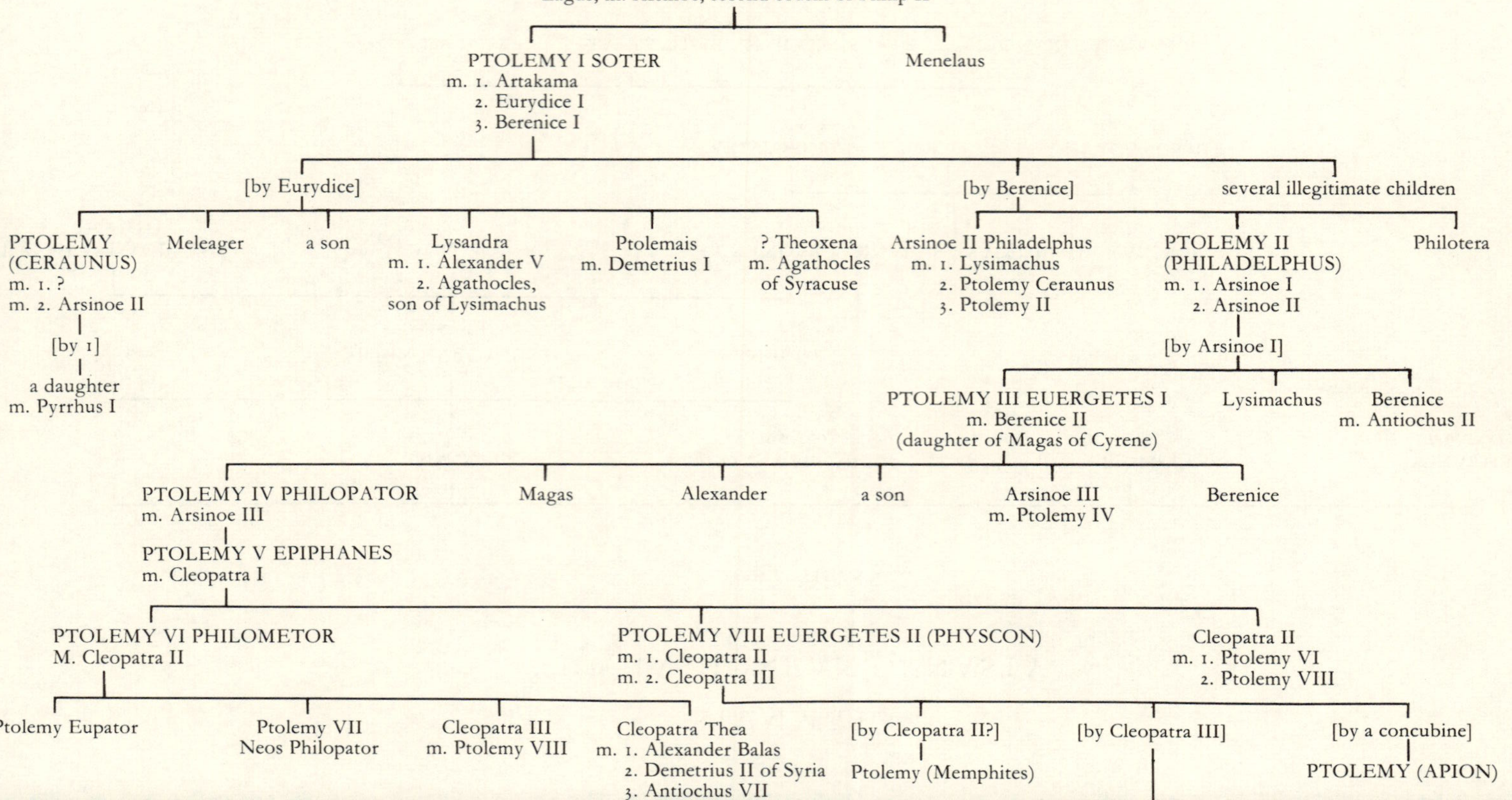

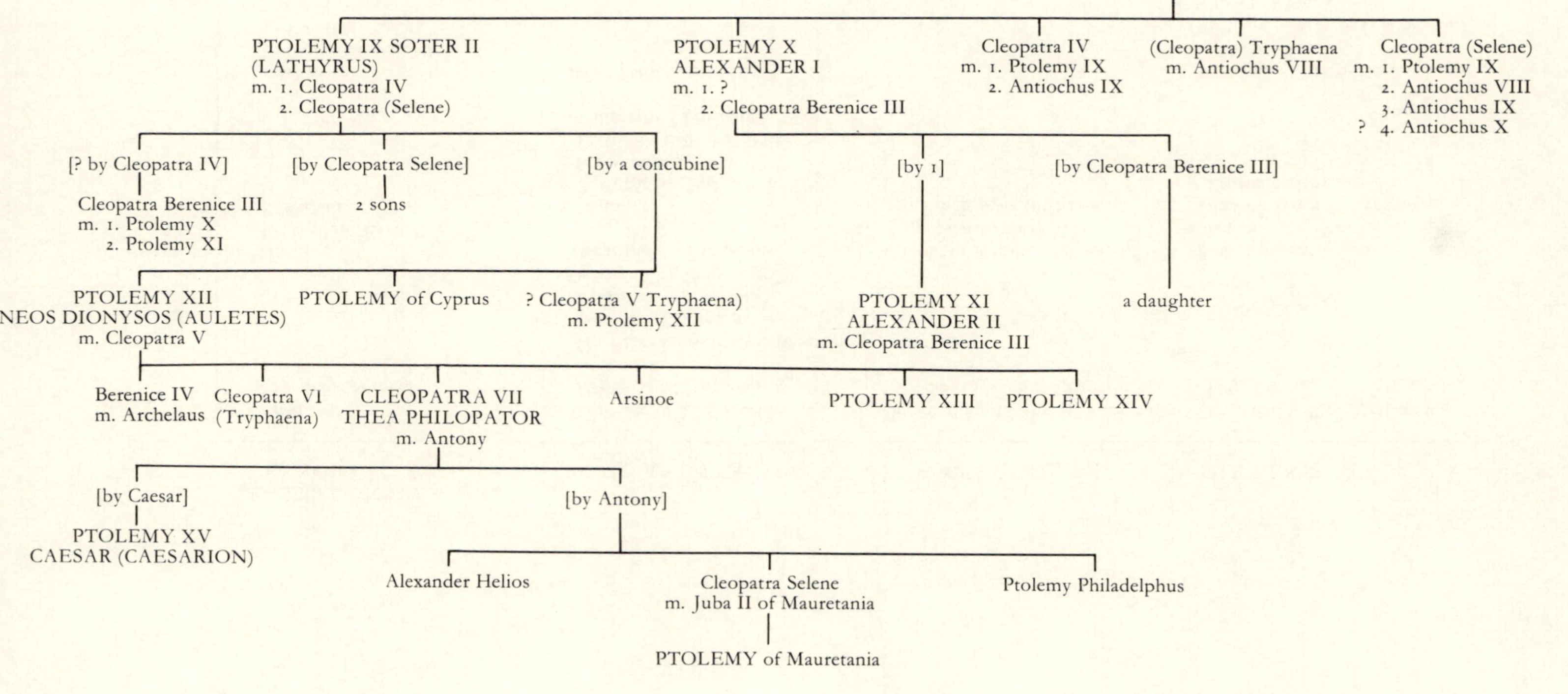
PTOLEMY IX SOTER II
(LATHYRUS)
m. 1. Cleopatra IV
2. Cleopatra (Selene)
PTOLEMY X
ALEXANDER I
m. 1. ?
2. Cleopatra Berenice III
Cleopatra IV
m. 1. Ptolemy IX
2. Antiochus IX
(Cleopatra) Tryphaena
m. Antiochus VIII
Cleopatra (Selene)
m. 1. Ptolemy IX
2. Antiochus VIII
3. Antiochus IX
? 4. Antiochus X
[? by Cleopatra IV]
[by Cleopatra Selene]
[by a concubine]
[by 1]
[by Cleopatra Berenice III]
Cleopatra Berenice III
m. 1. Ptolemy X
2. Ptolemy XI
2 sons
PTOLEMY XII
NEOS DIONYSOS (AULETES)
m. Cleopatra V
PTOLEMY of Cyprus
? Cleopatra V Tryphaena)
m. Ptolemy XII
PTOLEMY XI
ALEXANDER II
m. Cleopatra Berenice III
a daughter
Berenice IV
m. Archelaus
Cleopatra VI
(Tryphaena)
CLEOPATRA VII
THEA PHILOPATOR
m. Antony
Arsinoe
PTOLEMY XIII
PTOLEMY XIV
[by Caesar]
[by Antony]
PTOLEMY XV
CAESAR (CAESARION)
Alexander Helios
Cleopatra Selene
m. Juba II of Mauretania
Ptolemy Philadelphus
PTOLEMY of Mauretania

CHRONOLOGICAL TABLE

	FASTI: CONSULS AND CENSORS	ROME AND ITALY	THE WEST	THE EAST
133	Consuls: P. Mucius Scaevola L. Calpurnius Piso Frugi	Tribunate of Ti. Gracchus His agrarian laws and commission. His proposal to use the funds of the Attalid kingdom. Deposition of Octavius. Death of Gracchus.	Destruction of Numantia: the end of Scipio's wars in Spain. The First Sicilian Slave War in progress.	Death and will of Attalus of Pergamum.
132	Consuls: P. Popillius Laenas P. Rupilius	The tribunal of Popillius. Triumphs: P. Cornelius Scipio Aemilianus for Numantia. D. Iunius Brutus over the Callaeci and Lusitanians (? or 133).	Victory of Rupilius and end of First Sicilian Slave War. The *Lex Rupilia* for Sicily.	Revolt of Aristonicus in Asia begins. Dynastic quarrels weaken Ptolemaic Egypt.
131	Consuls: P. Licinius Crassus Mucianus L. Valerius Flaccus Censors 131–130: Q. Caecilius Metellus Macedonicus cos. 143	*Lex Papiria tabellaria.* His speech 'de prole augenda'		P. Licinius Crassus defeated and killed in Asia. Ptolemy Euergetes II (Physcon) flees to Cyprus.

130	Consuls: L. Cornelius Lentulus (? died in office) M. Perperna Suffect: Ap. Claudius Pulcher			M. Perperna besieges and captures Aristonicus at Stratonicea: Aristonicus executed at Rome. Return of Ptolemy Physcon to Memphis.
129	Consuls: C. Sempronius Tuditanus M'. Aquillius	Death of Scipio Aemilianus. Triumph: C. Sempronius Tuditanus over the Iapydes, 1 Oct.		Death of M. Perperna: M'. Aquillius proceeds with the organization of *provincia Asia* (to 126).
128	Consuls: Cn. Octavius T. Annius Rufus			
127	Consuls: L. Cassius Longinus Ravilla L. Cornelius Cinna			
126	Consuls: M. Aemilius Lepidus L. Aurelius Orestes	*Lex Iunia (Penni) de peregrinis.* Triumph: M'. Aquillius for Asia, November.	Campaigns of Aurelius Orestes in Sardinia. Gallic wars begin: appeal from Massilia against the Salluvii.	
125	Consuls: M. Plautius Hypsaeus M. Fulvius Flaccus Censors 125–124: Cn. Servilius Caepio, cos. 141 L. Cassius Longinus Ravilla, cos. 127	Fulvius Flaccus' abortive *rogatio* to grant citizenship and *provocatio.* Revolt of Fregellae. 394,736 citizens on the census.	Ligurian campaigns 125–124.	
124	Consuls: C. Cassius Longinus C. Sextius Calvinus			Reconciliation in the Egyptian dynasty.

	FASTI: CONSULS AND CENSORS	ROME AND ITALY	THE WEST	THE EAST
123	Consuls: Q. Caecilius Metellus (Baliaricus) T. Quinctius Flamininus	First tribunate of C. Gracchus. 123–122 Principal measures of Gracchus: *lex de capite civium* *agraria* *frumentaria* *de provincia Asia* *ne quis iudicio circumveniretur* *de provinciis consularibus* *de repetundis* *Rogatio de civitate* *Lex Rubria de Africa* (or 122) Triumph: M. Fulvius Flaccus over Ligurians etc.	Balearic campaigns: foundation of Palma and Pollentia by Metellus.	
122	Consuls: Cn. Domitius Ahenobarbus C. Fannius	Second tribunate of C. Gracchus. Continuation of his legislation. Triumphs: C. Sextius Calvinus over Ligurians. L. Aurelius Orestes for Sardinia, Dec.	Allobrogic and Arvernian wars, 122–120. Foundation of Aquae Sextiae.	
121	Consuls: L. Opimius Q. Fabius Maximus (Allobrogicus)	*scu* and death of C. Gracchus. Triumph: Q. Caecilius Metellus for the Balearic Islands.		*c.* 121 Assassination of Mithridates V of Pontus.
120	Consuls: P. Manilius C. Papirius Carbo Censors: Q. Caecilius Metellus Baliaricus, cos. 123 L. Calpurnius Piso Frugi, cos. 133	Triumphs in uncertain years 120–117: Q. Fabius Maximus over the Allobroges and king of the Arverni. Cn. Domitius Ahenobarbus over the Arverni.	Province of Transalpine Gaul (Narbonensis) created.	

119	Consuls: L. Caecilius Metellus (Delmaticus) L. Aurelius Cotta	C. Marius tribune: his law on electoral procedure. *Lex ?Thoria agraria*, ending the work of the land-commission.	Wars in Macedonia and Thrace for many years.	
118	Consuls: M. Porcius Cato Q. Marcius Rex		Colony of Narbo Martius founded.	28 April the royal Ptolemaic amnesty decree.
117	Consuls: L. Caecilius Metellus Diadematus Q. Mucius Scaevola 'the Augur'	Triumphs: L. Caecilius Metellus Delmaticus over the Dalmatians. Q. Marcius Rex over the Ligures Stoeni, December.	Dalmatian and Ligurian campaigns.	
116	Consuls: C. Licinius Geta Q. Fabius Maximus Eburnus		The Jugurthine problem begins: commission of *legati* sent.	June: death of Ptolemy Physcon 116–107 rule of Cleopatra II and Ptolemy Soter. Ptolemy Alexander in Cyprus. Ptolemy Apion in Cyrene.
115	Consuls: M. Aemilius Scaurus M. Caecilius Metellus Censors 115–114: L. Caecilius Metellus Diadematus cos. 117 Cn. Domitius Ahenobarbus, cos. 122	Triumph: M. Aemilius Scaurus over the Carni. 32 senators removed and stage performances banned. 394,336 citizens on the census.		
114	Consuls: M'. Acilius Balbus C. Porcius Cato	*Lex Peducaea* to prosecute Vestals.	114–111 Spanish Wars.	
113	Consuls: C. Caecilius Metellus Caprarius Cn. Papirius Carbo		113–101 Cimbric Wars. Defeat of Papirius Carbo at Noreia by the Cimbri.	*c.* 113 Mithridates VI seizes power at Sinope and begins to acquire his Black Sea empire (or 115).
112	Consuls: M. Livius Drusus L. Calpurnius Piso Caesoninus		The massacre at Cirta.	

	FASTI: CONSULS AND CENSORS	ROME AND ITALY	THE WEST	THE EAST
111	Consuls: P. Cornelius Scipio Nasica Serapio L. Calpurnius Bestia	*lex agraria.* Tribunician activity over the conduct of the Jugurthine war begins. Triumphs: M. Caecilius Metellus for Sardinia. C. Caecilius Metellus for Thrace, on the same day.	111–105 Jugurthine War. Jugurtha surrenders to Bestia and journeys to Rome. His murder of Massiva.	
110	Consuls: M. Minucius Rufus Sp. Postumius Albinus	Triumph: M. Livius Drusus over the Scordisci and Macedonians, May.	Surrender of Albinus' army to Jugurtha.	
109	Consuls: Q. Caecilius Metellus (Numidicus) M. (Iunius) Silanus Censors: M. Aemilius Scaurus, cos. 115 M. Livius Drusus, cos. 112	The censor Drusus died, and Scaurus was made to resign.	Metellus takes command against Jugurtha. Roman reverses in Gaul. The Via Aemilia built.	
108	Consuls: Ser. Sulpicius Galba ?L. Hortensius (condemned) Suffect: M. Aurelius Scaurus Censors: Q. Fabius Maximus Eburnus, cos. 116 C. Licinius Geta, cos. 116	The *quaestio Mamilia* over conduct in the Jugurthine War.		*c.* 108–107 Partition of Paphlagonia by Mithridates and Nicomedes.
107	Consuls: L. Cassius Longinus C. Marius	*Lex Caelia tabellaria.* Triumph: Q. Servilius Caepio over Further Spain, October.	Marius takes command against Jugurtha. Cassius Longinus defeated by Gauls at Tolosa.	107, Oct., to 101 Cleopatra III rules Egypt jointly with Ptolemy Alexander. Ptolemy Soter rules in Cyprus.

Year	Magistrates	Rome	Wars and external affairs	Other events
106	Consuls: Q. Servilius Caepio C. Atilius Serranus	*Lex Servilia de repetundis.* Triumphs: Q. Caecilius Metellus Numidicus over the Numidians and King Jugurtha. M. Minucius Rufus over the Scordisci and Thracians, August.	Caepio takes Tolosa; he also takes the 'gold of Tolosa'.	
105	Consuls: P. Rutilius Rufus Cn. Mallius Maximus		Capture of Jugurtha. Defeat of Caepio and Mallius by the Cimbri at Arausio.	
104	Consuls: C. Marius II C. Flavius Fimbria	Triumph: C. Marius over the Numidians and King Jugurtha, 1 Jan. *Lex Cassia de senatu.* *Lex Domitia de sacerdotiis.*	Marius' Cimbric campaigns, 104–101. The Second Sicilian Slave War, 104–101.	
103	Consuls: C. Marius III L. Aurelius Orestes	First tribunate of Saturninus. Assignment of land in Africa to Marius' veterans. *Lex Appuleia de maiestate* (or 100).	Lusitanian War, 103–102.	
102	Consuls: C. Marius IV Q. Lutatius Catulus Censors 102–101: Q. Caecilius Metellus Numidicus, cos. 109 C. Caecilius Metellus Caprarius, cos. 113		Victory over the Teutones at Aquae Sextiae.	M. Antonius' campaigns against the Cilician pirates. T. Didius' campaigns in Thrace.
101	Consuls: C. Marius V M'. Aquillius	*Lex Servilia (Glauciae) de repetundis* (or 104). The 'piracy law'. Triumphs: C. Marius over the Cimbri and Teutones. Q. Catulus over the Cimbri.	Victory over the Cimbri at Vercellae.	Death of Cleopatra III of Egypt.

	FASTI: CONSULS AND CENSORS	ROME AND ITALY	THE WEST	THE EAST
100	Consuls: C. Marius VI L. Valerius Flaccus	Second tribunate of Saturninus. *leges frumentaria, de coloniis deducendis, de agro Gallico.* *scu* and lynching of Glaucia and Saturninus. ? Triumphs: M. Antonius over the pirates. T. Didius for Macedonia.		
99	Consuls: M. Antonius A. Postumius Albinus			
98	Consuls: Q. Caecilius Metellus Nepos T. Didius	*Lex Caecilia Didia.* Triumph: L. Cornelius Dolabella over Further Spain and Lusitania, Jan.	98–93 Celtiberian Wars.	
97	Consuls: Cn. Cornelius Lentulus P. Licinius Crassus Censors 97–96: L. Valerius Flaccus, cos. 100 M. Antonius, cos. 99			
96	Consuls: Cn. Domitius Ahenobarbus C. Cassius Longinus			Tigranes I king of Armenia. Ptolemy Apion leaves Cyrene to Rome. Ptolemy Alexander leaves Egypt to Rome. Between 97/6 and 93/2: Sulla as proconsul of Cilicia overawes Mithridates into withdrawing from Cappadocia and meets Parthian envoys at the Euphrates.

95	Consuls: L. Licinius Crassus Q. Mucius Scaevola	*Lex Licinia Mucia.*	
94	Consuls: C. Coelius Caldus L. Domitius Ahenobarbus		Death of Nicomedes Euergetes of Bithynia.
93	Consuls: C. Valerius Flaccus M. Herennius	Triumphs: T. Didius (II) for Spain over the Celtiberi, 10 June. P. Licinius Crassus over the Lusitanians, 12 June.	
92	Consuls: C. Claudius Pulcher M. Perperna Censors: Cn. Domitius Ahenobarbus, cos. 96 L. Licinius Crassus, cos. 95	Censorial edict suppressing Latin rhetors.	
91	Consuls: L. Marcius Philippus Sex. Iulius Caesar	Tribunate of M. Livius Drusus. His proposals: agrarian law; *lex frumentaria*; addition of *equites* to Senate and reconstitution of juries (passed but annulled); citizenship for the allies. Assassination of Drusus. The Social War begins: massacre at Asculum.	Tigranes takes Cappadocia and Mithridates takes Bithynia. M'. Aquillius takes commissioners to restore *status quo*: they incite raids on Pontus.
90	Consuls: L. Iulius Caesar P. Rutilius Lupus (killed in action, but no suffect)	The *quaestio Varia.* 11 June: battle of Marius and Rutilius against Vettius Scato. *Lex Iulia de civitate danda.*	
89	Consuls: Cn. Pompeius Strabo L. Porcius Cato (killed in action) Censors 89–88: P. Licinius Crassus, cos. 97 L. Iulius Caesar, cos. 90	Victories of Pompeius Strabo, Sulla, etc. in the Social War. Lynching of A. Sempronius Asellio. *Lex Plautia Papiria.* *Lex Pompeia de Transpadanis.* Triumph: Cn. Pompeius Strabo over Asculum, 27 Dec.	Beginning of the First Mithridatic War.

	FASTI: CONSULS AND CENSORS	ROME AND ITALY	THE WEST	THE EAST
88	Consuls: L. Cornelius Sulla (Felix) Q. Pompeius Rufus	The tribunician bills of P. Sulpicius, esp. to divide the new citizens among all the tribes and to give the Mithridatic command to Marius. Sulla seizes Rome. ?Some *Leges Corneliae*. Marius flees to Africa. Triumph: P. Servilius Vatia, Sept. (for an unknown command).		Massacre of Romans in Asia. Defection of Athens. Siege of Rhodes. Archelaus in Greece: seizure of Delos. Ptolemy Alexander ejected by the Alexandrians: Ptolemy Soter II (Lathyrus) takes his place.
87	Consuls: Cn. Octavius (killed in office) L. Cornelius Cinna (declared a *hostis*) Suffect for Cinna: L. Cornelius Merula	Sulla leaves for the East. Cinna's bill to put the new citizens in all the tribes. The 'Bellum Octavianum'. The siege and taking of Rome.		Sulla in Greece: siege of Athens and Piraeus.
86	Consuls: L. Cornelius Cinna II C. Marius VII (died 13 Jan.) Suffect: L. Valerius Flaccus Censors 86–85: L. Marcius Philippus, cos. 91 M. Perperna, cos. 92	The financial edict of M. Marius Gratidianus (or 85). Flaccus appointed to supersede Sulla. 463,000 citizens on the census.		Fall of Athens. Battles of Chaeronea and Orchomenus. Flaccus murdered by Fimbria in Asia. Negotiations of Sulla and Archelaus.
85	Consuls: L. Cornelius Cinna III Cn. Papirius Carbo			Fimbria's campaigns in Asia. Treaty of Dardanus (not ratified at Rome). Sulla at Ephesus organizing Asia.

84	Consuls: Cn. Papirius Carbo II L. Cornelius Cinna IV (killed: no suffect)	Distribution of the new citizens among all the tribes ordered by *senatus consultum*.		
83	Consuls: L. Cornelius Scipio Asiaticus C. Norbanus	Spring: Sulla lands in Italy. The praetor Sertorius flees to Spain.		The 'Second Mithridatic War': L. Murena's campaigns against Mithridates, 83–82.
82	Consuls: C. Marius (junior) Cn. Papirius Carbo III Interrex: L. Valerius Flaccus, cos. 100 Dictator: L. Cornelius Sulla Felix. cos. 88 Master of Horse: L. Valerius Flaccus	Battle of Sacriportus: massacre of Samnites. Siege of Praeneste. Battle of the Colline Gate, 1 Nov. Proscriptions. Fall of Praeneste. Both consuls killed in the war.	Pompey recovers Sicily for Sulla, and kills Carbo.	
81	Dictator: L. Cornelius Sulla Felix Master of Horse: L. Valerius Flaccus Consuls: M. Tullius Decula Cn. Cornelius Dolabella	Triumphs: L. Cornelius Sulla Felix over Mithridates, Jan. Cn. Pompeius Magnus, March. L. Licinius Murena over Mithridates. L. Valerius Flaccus over the Celtiberi and Gauls. Sulla's principal measures: Admission of *equites* to Senate. Curbing of *tribunicia potestas*. Systematization of the *quaestiones perpetuae*. Laws about *maiestas*. Rules concerning magistracies.	Pompey recovers Africa for Sulla, and kills Domitius Ahenobarbus.	Death of Ptolemy Lathyrus; Sulla sends Ptolemy Alexander II to Egypt.
80	Consuls: L. Cornelius Sulla Felix II Q. Caecilius Metellus Pius	Fall of Nola. Trial of Roscius of Ameria.		Ptolemy XII (Auletes) takes the throne of Egypt.

	FASTI: CONSULS AND CENSORS	ROME AND ITALY	THE WEST	THE EAST
79	Consuls: P. Servilius Vatia (Isauricus) Ap. Claudius Pulcher	Fall of Aesernia and Volaterrae. Triumph: Cn. Pompeius Magnus (II) for Africa, March.	Metellus Pius and M. Domitius Calvinus, with the two Spanish provinces, against Sertorius. Calvinus defeated and killed.	
78	Consuls: M. Aemilius Lepidus Q. Lutatius Catulus No consular elections.	Death and state funeral of Sulla. Insurrection begun by the consul Lepidus. Triumph: Cn. Cornelius Dolabella for Macedonia (or 77).		Campaigns of P. Servilius Vatia in 'Cilicia', 78–75. Mithridates tries to get the Peace of Dardanus ratified.
77	Interrex: Ap. Claudius Pulcher, cos. 79 Consuls: D. Iunius Brutus Mam. Aemilius Lepidus Livianus	Special *imperium* for Pompey: he and Catulus put down the insurrection of Lepidus, and Pompey kills M. Iunius Brutus. Pompey given command in Spain with a special *imperium*.	Sertorius in control of Spain; joined by M. Perperna. Pompey on the way to Spain suppresses revolt in Transalpine Gaul.	
76	Consuls: Cn. Octavius C. Scribonius Curio	Tribunician agitation of Sicinius for restoration of full powers of the tribunate. Edict of the praetor M. Lucullus *de vi hominibus armatis*.	Sack of Lauro by Sertorius. Metellus defeats Hirtuleius at Italica.	
75	Consuls: L. Octavius C. Aurelius Cotta	*Lex Aurelia Cottae* restoring the right of tribunes to stand for further office.	Battle of Segovia: deaths of the Hirtuleii. Battles of Sucro and Segontia. Negotiations betweeen Sertorius and Mithridates (or spring 74).	Cyrene annexed by Rome. Nicomedes of Bithynia leaves his kingdom to Rome (or early 74).
74	Consuls: L. Licinius Lucullus M. Aurelius Cotta	Tribunician agitation of L. Quinctius. Trial of Oppianicus. Lucullus and Cotta given Mithridatic commands and M. Antonius the pirate command.	Pompey and Metellus begin to turn the tide in Spain.	M. Antonius' campaigns against the pirates

		Triumph: P. Servilius Vatia (Isauricus) over the Isaurians.		
73	Consuls: M. Terentius Varro Lucullus C. Cassius Longinus	Tribunician agitation of C. Licinius Macer. *Lex Terentia Cassia* on grain supply. Beginning of the Revolt of Spartacus.	73–71 Verres governor of Sicily.	The 'Third Mithridatic War' begins. Relief of Cyzicus by L. Lucullus and Battle of the Rhyndacus.
72	Consuls: L. Gellius Publicola Cn. Cornelius Lentulus Clodianus	*Lex Gellia Cornelia* (*de civitate*). Both consuls defeated by Spartacus. M. Licinius Crassus given the command against Spartacus. ?Triumph: C. Scribonius Curio over the Dardanians.	Assassination of Sertorius; M. Perperna put to death by Pompey.	Victories of Lucullus in Pontus.
71	Consuls: P. Cornelius Lentulus Sura Cn. Aufidius Orestes	Defeat and death of Spartacus. Ovation: M. Licinius Crassus over Spartacus. Triumphs: M. Terentius Varro Lucullus over the Bessi. Q. Caecilius Metellus Pius for Spain (i.e. Sertorius). Cn. Pompeius Magnus (III) for Spain (i.e. Sertorius).		Mithridates flees to Armenia and is held there by Tigranes. Sinope and Amisus taken.
70	Consuls: Cn. Pompeius Magnus M. Licinius Crassus Censors 70–69: Cn. Cornelius Lentulus Clodianus, cos. 72 L. Gellius Publicola, cos. 72	*Lex Pompeia Licinia* finally restoring all powers of tribunate. *Lex Aurelia (Cottae) iudiciaria.* ?*Lex Plautia de vi.* Trial of Verres. The censors expel 64 senators. 910,000 citizens on the census.		Lucullus' measures for the relief of the province of Asia. Tigranes declines to surrender Mithridates.

	FASTI: CONSULS AND CENSORS	ROME AND ITALY	THE WEST	THE EAST
69	Consuls: Q. Hortensius Hortalus Q. Caecilius Metellus (Creticus)	Triumphs: ? L. Afranius. M. Pupius Piso Frugi for Spain.		Lucullus' invasion of S. Armenia. October: Battle of Tigranocerta.
68	Consuls: L. Caecilius Metellus (died in office) Q. Marcius Rex Suffect (but died before taking office): . . . Vatia No further suffect.			Campaign of Lucullus in N. Armenia. Capture of Nisibis. Mithridates returns to Pontus. Campaign of Q. Metellus in Crete against the pirates.
67	Consuls: C. Calpurnius Piso M'. Acilius Glabrio	Tribunate of C. Cornelius: proposals on *ambitus*, on loans to foreign states, on *privilegia*, and *Lex Cornelia* making praetors follow their *edictum perpetuum*. Tribunate of A. Gabinius: *Lex Gabinia* granting *imperium* to Pompey against the pirates. Tribunate of L. Roscius Otho: *Lex Roscia theatralis*.		Supersession of Lucullus. Mithridates defeats Romans at Zela. Tigranes recovers Cappadocia. Pompey's campaign against the pirates.
66	Consuls: M'. Aemilius Lepidus L. Volcatius Tullus	*Lex Manilia* of the tribune C. Manilius, giving Pompey command against Mithridates. (The 'First Catilinarian Conspiracy') Consuls designate, P. Cornelius Sulla and P. Autronius Paetus, declared non-elected for bribery.		Pompey's agreement with Parthia. Pompey defeats Mithridates and takes surrender of Armenia.
65	Consuls: L. Aurelius Cotta L. Manlius Torquatus Censors: Q. Lutatius Catulus, cos. 78	*Lex Papia de peregrinis* (or 64). Trials of C. Manilius (condemned) and C. Cornelius (acquitted). Catiline acquitted *de repetundis*.		Mithridates flees to the Crimea. Pompey's campaign in the Caucasus.

	M. Licinius Crassus, cos. 70 (the censors abdicated without completing the census)	Proposal of Crassus for the annexation of Egypt, and his 'Transpadane manifesto'.		
64	Consuls: L. Iulius Caesar C. Marcius Figulus Censors: L. Aurelius Cotta, cos. 65 and an unknown (they abdicated)	*Senatus consultum de collegiis.*		Pompey in Syria, and annexation of Syria by Rome.
63	Consuls: M. Tullius Cicero C. Antonius Hibrida	*Rogatio Servilia* (the 'Rullan Bill'). Trial of Rabirius. *Lex Tullia de ambitu.* Julius Caesar made *pontifex maximus.* Triumph: L. Licinius Lucullus for Pontus and Armenia. October: the Catilinarian Conspiracy: *scu.*		October: fall of Jerusalem to Pompey. Death of Mithridates.
62	Consuls: D. Iunius Silanus L. Licinius Murena	*Lex Iunia Licinia* requiring deposit of bills in the *aerarium.* Death of Catiline. Triumph: Q. Caecilius Metellus Creticus for Crete (i.e. the pirates).	62–61 Campaigns of C. Pomptinus against the Allobroges in Transalpine Gaul.	Pompey's 'Eastern Settlement'. December: Pompey returns to Rome.
61	Consuls: M. Pupius Piso Frugi Calpurnianus M. Valerius Messalla Niger Censors: L. Iulius Caesar, cos. 64 and an unknown	Trial of P. Clodius for sacrilege. Triumph: Cn. Pompeius Magnus (IV) over pirates, Mithridates and Tigranes, Sept. L. Flavius' agrarian proposals.	61–60 Campaigns of Julius Caesar in Western Spain.	
60	Consuls: Q. Caecilius Metellus Celer L. Afranius	The 'First Triumvirate' of Pompey, Crassus and Caesar.	The Aedui defeated by Ariovistus. 60–59 the Helvetii menace Gaul.	

	FASTI: CONSULS AND CENSORS	ROME AND ITALY	THE WEST	THE EAST
	Consuls: C. Iulius Caesar M. Calpurnius Bibulus	*Leges Iuliae de actis senatus, agrariae, de repetundis.* Ratification of Pompey's eastern settlement and remission of Asiatic tax contracts.		Recognition of Ptolemy XII (Auletes) as 'socius et amicus populi Romani'.
58		*Lex Vatinia* giving Gallic command to Julius Caesar. Transfer of P. Clodius to plebs. Death of Metellus Celer.		
57	Consuls: L. Calpurnius Piso Caesoninus A. Gabinius	Tribunate of P. Clodius; laws *de capite civium*, *de collegiis*, *frumentaria*, etc. Flight of Cicero. Caesar to Gaul, Cato to Cyprus.	Caesar against the Helvetii and Ariovistus.	Flight of Ptolemy Auletes to Rome (or 57). Cato organizes Cyprus.
	Consuls: P. Cornelius Lentulus Spinther Q. Caecilius Metellus Nepos	P. Lentulus given command to restore Ptolemy XII, but it is blocked.	Caesar against the Belgae and the Nervii.	Gabinius' proconsulate of Syria: Jewish campaign.
56		Return of Cicero. Grain crisis: Pompey receives *cura annonae*. 15-day *supplicatio* for Caesar's victories in Gaul.		
55	Consuls: Cn. Cornelius Lentulus Marcellinus L. Marcius Philippus	April: the 'Conference of Luca'. Tribunes block the consular elections so as to ensure a second consulship for Pompey and Crassus.	Caesar against the Veneti and Morini.	Gabinius' second Jewish campaign.
	Interrex: M. Valerius Messalla Niger Consuls: Cn. Pompeius Magnus II M. Licinius Crassus II Censors 55–54: M. Valerius Messalla Niger, cos. 61	*Lex Trebonia*: commands for Pompey and Crassus; *Lex Pompeia Licinia*: extension of Caesar's command. *Lex Licinia de sodaliciis.* *Lex Pompeia de iudicibus.*	Caesar against the Usipetes and Tencteri, and then in Britain.	Gabinius restores Ptolemy Auletes to Egypt. Gabinius' third Jewish and Nabatean campaigns.

	P. Servilius Vatia Isauricus, cos. 79	?*Lex Mamilia Roscia*, etc. Dedication of Pompey's theatre. 20-day *supplicatio* for Caesar's victories. November: Crassus leaves for Syria.		
54	Consuls: L. Domitius Ahenobarbus Ap. Claudius Pulcher	Death of Julia. Triumph: C. Pomptinus over the Allobroges. Electoral scandal implicates the consuls: no consular elections this year.	Caesar's second campaign in Britain. Caesar on the defensive in Gaul: losses against the Eburones.	
53	Interreges: known are M. Valerius Messalla Niger, cos. 61 Q. Caecilius Metellus Pius Scipio Nasica Consuls (from July): Cn. Domitius Calvinus M. Valerius Messalla Rufus	Rioting under Clodius and Milo. Numerous sets of *ludi*. Only when Pompey returned to Rome were elections held. But again no magistrates were elected for 52.	Winter: the great Gallic alliance under Vercingetorix.	Defeat and death of Crassus at Carrhae.
52	Interreges: known are M. Aemilius Lepidus M. Valerius Messalla Niger, cos. 61 Ser. Sulpicius Consuls: Cn. Pompeius Magnus III (at first *solus*) Q. Caecilius Metellus Pius Scipio Nasica (from August)	Rioting: in Jan. the 'Battle of Bovillae' and death of Clodius. Firing of the *curia* and *scu*. Pompey's legislation including *leges de vi* and *de provinciis*. The 'Law of the ten tribunes'. 20-day *supplicatio* for Caesar's victory at Alesia.	Battle of Gergovia. Capture of Alesia.	

	FASTI: CONSULS AND CENSORS	ROME AND ITALY	THE WEST	THE EAST
51	Consuls: Ser. Sulpicius Rufus M. Claudius Marcellus	Beginning of the 'Rechtsfrage' – the question of the supersession of Julius Caesar. Triumph: P. Cornelius Lentulus Spinther for Cilicia.	Caesar against the Bellovaci. Capture of Uxellodunum.	Death of Ptolemy XII (Auletes): the Egyptian throne now inherited by Ptolemy XIII and Cleopatra VII. Parthian invasion of Syria: an anxiety to Cicero in his province (Cilicia).
50	Consuls: L. Aemilius Lepidus Paullus C. Claudius (C.f.M.n.) Marcellus Censors 50–49: Ap. Claudius Pulcher, cos. 54 L. Calpurnius Piso Caesoninus, cos. 58	Tribunate of C. Scribonius Curio: his proposals and his support for Caesar. November: the consul Marcellus urges Pompey to 'save the State'. Numerous expulsions from the Senate, including Sallust.		
49	Consuls: C. Claudius (M.f.M.n.) Marcellus L. Cornelius Lentulus Crus Dictator (11 days): C. Iulius Caesar, cos. 59	7 Jan. *scu.* 10 Jan. the Rubicon. The consuls, and Pompey, leave Italy. Caesar first to Spain, then returns as Dictator and presides over his own election as consul. Measures for relief of debt and return of exiles. Then Caesar sets off for Epirus.	Siege of Massilia. Battle of Ilerda. Juba's army traps Curio in Africa.	
48	Consuls: C. Iulius Caesar II P. Servilius Isauricus Dictator (October, for a year): C. Iulius Caesar II Master of Horse: M. Antonius		August: Battle of Pharsalus. Pompey flees to Egypt. Cato marches from Cyrene to Africa. October: Caesar to Egypt.	Murder of Pompey. The 'Bellum Alexandrinum' and Caesar's liaison with Cleopatra.

47	Consuls (from September): Q. Fufius Calenus P. Vatinius	September: Caesar returns to Italy. Moratorium on debts. ?Triumph: M. Aemilius Lepidus for Hither Spain. 25 December: Caesar sets out for Africa.		Caesar to Pontus: victory at Zela over Pharnaces of the Crimea. Birth of Caesarion.
46	(THE 'INTERCALARY YEAR') Consuls: C. Iulius Caesar III M. Aemilius Lepidus Dictator (April, for 10 years): C. Iulius Caesar III Master of Horse: M. Aemilius Lepidus, cos.	July: Caesar returns to Rome. His principal measures 46–44: calendar reform; juries returned to half senators and half *equites*; abolition of *collegia*; *interdictio* for *vis* and *maiestas*; reduction of recipients of public corn to 150,000; enlargement of Senate; a third of labour on estates to be free men; citizenship for the Transpadanes; colonial foundations. Triumph: C. Iulius Caesar for Gaul, Egypt, Pontus and Africa, Sept. Dedication of the Forum Iulium. Caesar departs for Spain.	Battle of Thapsus (Feb.).	
45	Consuls: C. Iulius Caesar IV (*solus*, till October) Suffects: Q. Fabius Maximus (died 31 Dec.) C. Trebonius C. Caninius Rebilus (31 Dec., suffect for Fabius Maximus) Dictator (from April): C. Iulius Caesar IV Master of Horse: M. Aemilius Lepidus, cos. 46	Caesar returns from Spain. 50-day *supplicatio* for Munda. Triumphs: C. Iulius Caesar for Spain. Q. Fabius Maximus for Spain. Q. Pedius for Spain.	Battle of Munda (March).	Parthian invasion of Syria.

	FASTI: CONSULS AND CENSORS	ROME AND ITALY	THE WEST	THE EAST
44	Consuls: C. Iulius Caesar V (to 15 March) M. Antonius Suffect: P. Cornelius Dolabella	15 Feb. Refusal of the diadem.		
	Dictator: C. Iulius Caesar V (and *perpetuus*) Master of Horse: M. Aemilius Lepidus	15 March. Assassination of Caesar. Legislation by Antony. Brutus and Cassius leave for the East.	Emergence of Sextus Pompeius.	Trebonius executed by Dolabella in Asia. Brutus seizes Macedonia.
43		Arrival of C. Octavius, who makes formal acceptance of Caesar's inheritance. Antony departs to Gaul.	Antony besieges D. Brutus in Mutina.	
	Consuls: C. Vibius Pansa Caetronianus A. Hirtius (both died in action) Suffect: C. Iulius Caesar ('Octavian') to November Q. Pedius (died in office) C. Carrinas P. Ventidius Bassus	Triumphs: L. Munatius Plancus for Gaul. M. Aemilius Lepidus for Spain. C. Iulius Caesar ('Octavian') marches on Rome and gets himself made consul, 19 Aug.	Defeat of Antony at Forum Gallorum and Mutina. Death of the consuls in action. Antony joins Lepidus in Transalpine Gaul.	Cassius seizes Syria.
	Triumviri rei publicae constituendae (from November): M. Aemilius Lepidus, cos. 46 M. Antonius, cos. 44 C. Iulius Caesar ('Octavian'), cos.	Proscriptions: 7 Dec. the murder of Cicero.		

BIBLIOGRAPHY

Abbreviations

A&A	*Antike und Abendland*
AAntHung	*Acta Antiqua Academiae Scientiarum Hungaricae*
AAPal	*Atti dell'accademia di scienze, lettere e arti di Palermo*
AAWM	*Abhandlungen der Akademie der Wissenschaften in Mainz, geistes- und sozialwissenschaftliche Klasse*
ABAW	*Abhandlungen der bayerischen Akademie der Wissenschaften, philos.-hist. Klasse*
ABSA	*Annual of the British School at Athens*
AC	*L'antiquité classique*
ACD	*Acta Classica Universitatis Scientiarum Debrecensis*
AClass	*Acta Classica. Proceedings of the Classical Association of South Africa*
AD	Ἀρχαιολογικὸν Δελτίον
AE	*L'année épigraphique*
AEA	*Archivo español de arqueologia*
AFLC	*Annali della facoltà di lettere e filosofia della Università di Cagliari*
AG	*Archivio giuridico*
AHB	*The Ancient History Bulletin*
AHR	*American Historical Review*
AIIN	*Annali dell'istituto italiano di numismatica*
AIRF	*Acta Instituti Romani Finlandiae*
AJA	*American Journal of Archaeology*
AJAH	*American Journal of Ancient History*
AJPh	*American Journal of Philology*
AMA	*Antičnyj Mir i Arkheologija*
AMSI	*Atti e memorie della società istriana di archeologia e storia patria*
AncSoc	*Ancient Society*
Annales (ESC)	*Annales (Économies, Sociétés, Civilisations)*
ANRW	*Aufstieg und Niedergang der römischen Welt*, ed. H. Temporini and W. Haase. Berlin and New York, 1972–
ANSMusN	*The American Numismatic Society Museum Notes*
APhD	*Archives de philosophie du droit*
ArchOrient	*Archiv Orientálni*
ARID	*Analecta Romana Instituti Danici*
ArchClass	*Archeologia Classica*

AS	*Anatolian Studies*
ASAW	*Abhandlungen der sächsischen Akademie der Wissenschaften zu Leipzig*
ASNP	*Annali della scuola normale superiore di Pisa, Classe di lettere e filosofia*
ASPap	*American Studies in Papyrology*
BAR	*British Archaeological Reports*
BASO	*Bulletin of the American Schools of Oriental Research*
BCAR	*Bullettino della commissione archeologica comunale di Roma*
BCH	*Bulletin de correspondance hellénique*
BEFAR	*Bibliothèque des écoles françaises d'Athènes et de Rome*
BGU	*Aegyptische Urkunden aus den Museen zu Berlin. Griechische Urkunden*. Berlin, 1895–
BIAO	*Bulletin de l'institut français d'archéologie orientale*
BICS	*Bulletin of the Institute of Classical Studies of the University of London*
BIDR	*Bullettino dell'istituto di diritto romano*
Les Bourgeoisies	*Les 'Bourgeoisies' municipales italiennes aux IIe et Ier siècles avant J.-C.* (Colloque internat. *CNRS* 609, Naples 7–10 déc. 1981). Paris, 1983
BRL	*Bulletin of the John Rylands Library, Manchester*
Bruns	C. G. Bruns, ed., *Fontes Iuris Romani Antiqui*, edn 7 by O. Gradenwitz, Tübingen, 1909
Bull. ép.	J. and L. Robert, *Bulletin épigraphique* (in *REG*)
CAH	*The Cambridge Ancient History*
CE	*Chronique d'Egypte*
Du Châtiment	*Du châtiment dans la cité. Supplices corporels et peine de mort dans le monde antique* (Table ronde, Rome 9–11 nov. 1982) (Coll. éc. fr. de Rome 79). Rome, 1984
CHCL	*The Cambridge History of Classical Literature:* I: *Greek Literature*, ed. P. E. Easterling and B. M. W. Knox. Cambridge, 1985. II: *Latin Literature*, ed. E. J. Kenney and W. V. Clausen. Cambridge, 1982
CIJ	*Corpus Inscriptionum Judaicarum*
CIL	*Corpus Inscriptionum Latinarum*
C&M	*Classica et Mediaevalia*
COrdPtol	*Corpus des ordonnances des Ptolémées*, ed. M. Th. Lenger. Brussels, 1964; 2nd corr. edn 1980
CPh	*Classical Philology*
CQ	*Classical Quarterly*
CR	*Classical Review*
CRAI	*Comptes rendus de l'académie des inscriptions et belles-lettres*
CronErc	*Cronache ercolanesi*
CS	*Critica storica*
CSCA	*California Studies in Classical Antiquity*
DArch	*Dialoghi di archeologia*
Le délit religieux	*Le délit religieux dans la cité antique* (Table ronde, Rome 6–7 avril 1978) (Coll. éc. fr. de Rome 48). Rome, 1981

Delo e l'Italia
Delo e l'Italia, edd. F. Coarelli, D. Musti and H. Solin (Opusc. Inst. Rom. Finlandiae II). Rome, 1982

Les dévaluations
Les dévaluations à Rome, I (Colloquio, Roma 1975) Rome, 1978; II (Colloquio, Gdansk 1978) Rome, 1980

DHA *Dialogues d'histoire ancienne*

EEThess *'Επιστημονικὴ 'Επετηρὶς τῆς φιλοσοφικῆς Σχολῆς τοῦ Πανεπιστημίου Θεσσαλονίκης*

EMC *Échos du monde classique*

Entretiens Hardt
Entretiens sur l'antiquité classique. Fondation Hardt. Vandoeuvres-Geneva, 1952–

ESAR *An Economic Survey of Ancient Rome*, ed. Tenney Frank. 6 vols. Baltimore, 1933–40

FGrH F. Jacoby, *Fragmente der griechischen Historiker*. Berlin and Leiden, 1923–

FIRA S. Riccobono *et al., Fontes Iuris Romani Anteiustiniani*. 3 vols. Florence, 1940–3

FPL W. Morel and C. Buechner, *Fragmenta Poetarum Latinorum*. Leipzig, 1982

GIF *Giornale italiano di filologia*

Girard–Senn P.F. Girard and H. Senn, *Les lois des Romains* (Textes de droit romain I, 7th edn revised by various persons). Paris and Naples, 1977

GLM *Geographi Latini Minores*, ed. A. Riese. Heilbron, 1878

G&R *Greece & Rome*

GRBS *Greek, Roman and Byzantine Studies*

Greenidge–Clay
A. H. J. Greenidge and A. M. Clay, *Sources for Roman History 133–70 B.C.* 2nd edn revised by E. W. Gray. Oxford, 1960. Further corrected and augmented 1986

GRF *Grammaticae Romanae Fragmenta*, ed. H. Funaioli (Vol. I only). Leipzig, 1907

HebrUCA *Hebrew Union College Annual*

Hellenismus *Hellenismus in Mittelitalien*, ed. P. Zanker (Kolloq. Göttingen 5–7 juni 1974) (Abh. Göttingen 97). Göttingen, 1976

HRR H. W. G. Peter, *Historicorum Romanorum Reliquiae*. 2 vols. Leipzig, 1906–14

HSPh *Harvard Studies in Classical Philology*

HThR *Harvard Theological Review*

IA *Iranica Antiqua*

IDélos F. Durrbach and others, *Inscriptions de Délos*. Paris, 1926–50

IEJ *Israel Exploration Journal*

IFay E. Bernard, *Recueil des inscriptions grecques du Fayoum*. 3 vols. Leiden, 1975–81

IG *Inscriptiones Graecae*

IGBulg G. Mihailov, *Inscriptiones Graecae in Bulgaria repertae*. Sofia, 1958–

IGRR R. Cagnat and others, *Inscriptiones Graecae ad res Romanas pertinentes* I, III, IV. Paris, 1906–27

ILLRP A. Degrassi, *Inscriptiones Latinae Liberae Rei Publicae*, 2 vols. 2nd edn Florence, 1963–5

ILS H. Dessau, *Inscriptiones Latinae Selectae*. 3 vols. Berlin, 1892–1916

IMagnesia O. Kern, *Die Inschriften von Magnesia am Maeander*. Berlin, 1900

L'impero romano *L'impero romano e le strutture economiche e sociali delle provincie* (Bibl. di Athenaeum 4), ed. M. H. Crawford, Como, 1986

Inscr. Ital. *Inscriptiones Italiae* XIII, *Fasti et Elogia*, ed. A. Degrassi. 3 vols. Rome, 1937–63

IOlympia W. Dittenberger and K. Purgold, *Die Inschriften von Olympia*. Berlin, 1896

IOSPE B. Latyschev, *Inscriptiones Antiquae Orae Septentrionalis Ponti Euxini Graecae et Latinae*. 2nd edn St Petersburg, 1916

IPriene F. Hiller v. Gaertringen, *Die Inschriften von Priene*. Berlin, 1906

JBM *Jahrbuch des bernischen historischen Museums*

JDAI *Jahrbuch des deutschen archäologischen Instituts*

JEA *Journal of Egyptian Archaeology*

JFA *Journal of Field Archaeology*

JHS *Journal of Hellenic Studies*

JJSt *Journal of Jewish Studies*

JMS *Journal of Mithraic Studies*

JNG *Jahrbuch für Numismatik und Geldgeschichte*

JRH *Journal of Religious History*

JRS *Journal of Roman Studies*

JS *Journal des Savants*

JVEG *Jaarbericht van het Voor-Aziatisch-Egyptisch Genootschap ex Oriente Lux*

LCM *Liverpool Classical Monthly*

LEC *Les études classiques*

LSJ H. G. Liddell and R. Scott, *A Greek–English Lexicon*, 9th edn revised by H. S. Jones. Oxford, 1940

Lugli G. Lugli, *Fontes ad Topographiam veteris Urbis Romae pertinentes*. Rome, 1952

MAAR *Memoirs of the American Academy in Rome*

MDAI (A) (D) (I) (M) (R) *Mitteilungen des deutschen archäologischen Instituts (Athens, Damascus, Istanbul, Madrid, Rome)*

MEFRA *Mélanges d'archéologie et d'histoire de l'école française de Rome*

Mél. Heurgon *L'Italie préromaine et la Rome républicaine. Mélanges offerts à Jacques Heurgon*. 2 vols. Rome, 1976

MH *Museum Helveticum*

Misurare la terra *Misurare la Terra: Centuriazioni e coloni nel mondo romano*. 5 vols. Modena, 1983–8

MRR T. R. S. Broughton and M. L. Patterson, *The Magistrates of the Roman Republic*. 3 vols. I, II New York, 1951; III Atlanta, 1986

MünchBeitrPapyr *Münchener Beiträge zur Papyrusforschung und antiken Rechtsgeschichte*

NAWG *Nachrichten der Akademie der Wissenschaften in Göttingen, Philol.-Hist. Klasse*

NC *Numismatic Chronicle*

NE *Numismatika i Epigraphica*

NJNW *Neue Jahrbücher für Wissenschaft und Jugendbildung*

Non-slave Labour *Non-slave Labour in the Greco-Roman World*, ed. P. Garnsey (Camb. Phil. Soc. Suppl. 6). Cambridge, 1980

NRS *Nuova Rivista Storica*

NSA *Notízie degli Scavi dí antichità*

NZ *Numismatische Zeitschrift*

OGIS W. Dittenberger, *Orientis Graecae Inscriptiones Selectae*. 2 vols. Leipzig, 1903–5

Des Ordres *Des ordres à Rome*, sous la direction de C. Nicolet (Publ. de la Sorbonne. Sér. hist. ancienne et mediévale 13), Paris, 1984

ORF H. Malcovati, *Oratorum Romanorum Fragmenta*. 2 vols. 4th edn Turin, 1976–9

ORom *Opuscula Romana (Acta Inst. Rom. Regni Suediae)*

Pagan Priests *Pagan Priests: Religion and Power in the Ancient World*, ed. M. Beard and J. A. North. London, 1989

PalEQ *Palestine Exploration Quarterly*

Palingenesia O. Lenel, *Palingenesia Iuris Civilis*. Leipzig, 1889; repr. with supplement, Graz, 1960

PapBrux *Papyrologica Bruxellensia*, Brussels, 1962–

PapColon *Papyrologica Coloniensia*, Cologne and Opladen, 1964–

PapLugdBat *Papyrologica Lugduno-Batava*, Publications of the Institute of Papyrology of Leiden

PAPhS *Proceedings of the American Philosophical Society*

P Berl dem *Demotische Papyrus aus den Kgl. Museen zu Berlin*, ed. W. Spiegelberg. Leipzig and Berlin, 1902

PBSR *Papers of the British School at Rome*

PCPhS *Proceedings of the Cambridge Philological Society*

Philosophia Togata *Philosophia Togata: Essays in Philosophy and Roman Society*, ed. M. Griffin and J. Barnes. Oxford, 1989

Phoenix *The Phoenix*

PLeid *Papyri graeci Musei antiquarii publici Lugduni-Batavi*, ed. C. Leemans. 2 vols. 1843, 1885 (= *P. Lugd. Bat.*)

PLond *Greek Papyri in the British Museum*, ed. F. G. Kenyon. 5 vols. 1893–1917

Points de vue *Points de vue sur la fiscalité antique*, ed. H. van Effenterre. Paris, 1979

PP — *La parola del passato*
P&P — *Past and Present*
PRyldem — *Catalogue of the Demotic Papyri in the John Rylands Library, Manchester*, ed. F.Ll. Griffith. 1909
PTebt — *The Tebtunis Papyri*, ed. B. P. Grenfell, A. S. Hunt and E. J. Goodspeed. Parts 1–3 London, 1902–38
PSI — *Pubblicazioni della società italiana per la ricerca dei papyri greci e latini in Egitto*. Florence, 1912–
PYale — *Yale Papyri in the Beinecke Rare Book and Manuscript Library*, ed. J. F. Oates and others. 2 vols. New Haven and Toronto, 1967 and 1981
Quaderno 221 — *Problemi attuali di scienza e di cultura* (Colloquio italo-francese: La filosofia greca e il diritto romano, Roma 14–17 apr. 1973) (Quaderno Lincei 221). 2 vols. Rome, 1976–7
RA — *Revue archéologique*
RAL — *Rendiconti della classe di scienze morali, storiche e filologiche dell' Accademia dei Lincei*
RAN — *Revue archéologique de Narbonne*
RBA — *Revue Belge d'archéologie et d'histoire de l'art*
RBi — *Revue biblique*
RD — *Revue historique de droit français et étranger*
RDGE — R. K. Sherk, *Roman Documents from the Greek East*, Baltimore, 1969
RE — A. Pauly, G. Wissowa and W. Kroll, *Real-Encyclopädie der classischen Altertumswissenschaft*
REA — *Revue des études anciennes*
REG — *Revue des études grecques*
REgypt — *Revue d'égyptologie*
REJ — *Revue des études juives*
REL — *Revue des études latines*
RFIC — *Rivista di filologia e di istruzione classica*
RHD — *Revue d'histoire du droit* (= *Tijdschrift voor Rechtsgeschiedenis*)
RhM — *Rheinisches Museum*
RHR — *Revue de l'histoire des religions*
RIA — *Rivista dell'istituto nazionale di archeologia e storia dell'arte*
RIDA — *Revue internationale des droits de l'antiquité*
RIL — *Rendiconti dell'istituto Lombardo, Classe di lettere, scienze morali e storiche*
La Rivoluzione Romana — *La rivoluzione romana: Inchiesta tra gli antichisti* (Biblioteca di Labeo VI). Naples, 1982
RN — *Revue numismatique*
Roma e l'Italia — *Incontro di studiosi 'Roma e l'Italia fra i Gracchi e Silla'* (Pontignano 18–21 sett. 1969) (DArch 4/5 1970–1, 163–562)
Rotondi — G. Rotondi, *Leges publicae populi Romani* (Estratto dalla

Enciclopedia Giuridica Italiana). Milan, 1912; repr. Hildesheim, 1962

RPAA *Rendiconti della pontificia accademia di archeologia*

RPh *Revue de philologie*

RPhilos *Revue philosophique de la France et de l'étranger*

RSA *Rivista storica dell'antichità*

RSC *Rivista di studi classici*

RSI *Rivista storica italiana*

RSO *Rivista degli studi orientali*

SA *Sovietskaja Archeolgija*

Sammelbuch F. Preisigke and F. Bilabel, *Sammelbuch griechischer Urkunden aus Ägypten*. 1915–

SAWW *Sitzungsberichte der österreichischen Akademie der Wissenschaft in Wien*

SBAW *Sitzungsberichte der bayerischen Akademie der Wissenschaften, philos.-hist. Klasse*

SCO *Studi classici e orientali*

SDHI *Studia et Documenta Historiae et Iuris*

SE *Studi etruschi*

Seaborne Commerce
The Seaborne Commerce of Ancient Rome: Studies in Archaeology and History, ed. J. H. D'Arms and E. C. Kopff (MAAR 36). Rome, 1980

Seager, *Crisis*
The Crisis of the Roman Republic: Studies in Political and Social History, selected and introduced by R. Seager. Cambridge, 1969

SEG *Supplementum Epigraphicum Graecum*

SGE *Soobščenija Gosudarstvennogo Ermitaža*

SIFC *Studi italiani di filologia classica*

SIG W. Dittenberger, *Sylloge Inscriptionum Graecarum*. 4 vols. 3rd edn Leipzig, 1915–24

SMSR *Studi e materiali di storia delle religioni*

SO *Symbolae Osloenses*

Società Romana
Società romana e produzione schiavistica, edd. A. Giardina and A. Schiavone (Acta of the Colloquium, Pisa 1979), 3 vols. Bari, 1981

TAPhA *Transactions and Proceedings of the American Philological Association*

Tecnologia *Tecnologia, economia e società nel mondo romano* (Atti del convegno, Como 27–9 sett. 1979). Como, 1980

Trade *Trade in the Ancient Economy*, edd. P. Garnsey, K. Hopkins and C. R. Whittaker. London, 1983

Tskhaltubo I
Problemy Grecheskoi Kolonizatsii Severnogo i Vostochnogo Prichernomorya (Materialy I Vsyesoyuznogo Symposiuma po Drevnyei Istorii Prichernomorya, Tskhaltubo 1977). Tbilisi, 1979

Tskhaltubo II
Demographicheskaya Situatsia v Prichernomorya v period Velikoi Grecheskoi Kolonizatsii (Materialy II Vsyesoyuznogo Symposiuma po Drevnyei Istorii Prichernomorya, Tskhaltubo 1979). Tbilisi, 1981

Tskhaltubo III
Prichernomorye v Epokhu Ellinizma (Materialy III Vsyesoyuznogo Symposiuma po Drevnyei Istorii Prichernomorya, Tskhaltubo 1982). Tbilisi, 1985

UPZ U. Wilcken, *Urkunden der Ptolemäerzeit*, Parts 1 and 2, Berlin and Leipzig, 1922–35

VDI *Vestnik Drevnei Istorii*

WChrest L. Mitteis and U. Wilcken, *Grundzüge und Chrestomathie der Papyruskunde* I. Part 2 (*Chrestomathie*)

WJA *Würzburger Jahrbücher für die Altertumswissenschaft*

WS *Wiener Studien*

ZPE *Zeitschrift für Papyrologie und Epigraphik*

ZSS *Zeitschrift der Savigny-Stiftung für Rechtsgeschichte* (romanistische Abteilung)

BIBLIOGRAPHY

A. GENERAL STUDIES

1. Badian, E. *Foreign Clientelae (264–70 B.C.)*. Oxford, 1958
2. Badian, E. *Studies in Greek and Roman History*. Oxford, 1964
3. Badian, E. *Roman Imperialism in the Late Republic*. Oxford, 1968
4. Badian, E. *Publicans and Sinners*. Ithaca, 1972
5. Balsdon, J. P. V. D. *Romans and Aliens*. London, 1979
6. Beard, M. and Crawford, M. H. *Rome in the Late Republic*. London, 1985
7. Beloch, K. J. *Der italische Bund unter Roms Hegemonie. Staatsrechtliche und statistische Forschungen*. Leipzig, 1880
8. Beloch, K. J. *Die Bevölkerung der griechisch-römischen Welt*. Leipzig, 1886
9. Beloch, K. J. *Römische Geschichte bis zum Beginn der punischen Kriege*. Berlin and Leipzig, 1926
10. Bernhardt, R. *Polis und römische Herrschaft in der späten Republik*. Berlin, 1985
11. Bickerman, E. J. *Chronology of the Ancient World*. London, 1968, revd 1980
12. Bloch, G. and Carcopino, J. *Histoire romaine II, La république romaine de 133 avant J.-C. à la mort de César, 1re Partie, Des Gracques à Sulla*. Paris, 1930
13. Braund, D. C. 'Royal wills and Rome', *PBSR* 51 (1983) 16–57
14. Braund, D. C. *Rome and the Friendly King. The Character of Client Kingship*. London and New York, 1984
15. Brisson, J.-P. (ed.) *Problèmes de la guerre à Rome*. Paris and The Hague, 1969
16. Brunt, P. A. *Italian Manpower 225 B.C.–A.D.14*. Oxford, 1971
17. Brunt, P. A. *Social Conflicts in the Roman Republic*. London, 1971
18. Brunt, P. A. '*Laus imperii*', *Imperialism in the Ancient World*, ed. P. D. A. Garnsey and C. R. Whittaker, Cambridge, 1978, 159–91 (=A20 288–323)
19. Brunt, P. A. *The Fall of the Roman Republic and Related Essays*. Oxford, 1988
20. Brunt, P. A. *Roman Imperial Themes*. Oxford, 1990
21. Cary, M. *The Geographical Background of Greek and Roman History*. Oxford, 1949
22. Ciaceri, E. *Processi politici e relazioni internazionali*. Rome, 1918
23. Ciaceri, E. *Cicerone e i suoi tempi*. 2 vols. Milan, 1939–41

24. Cimma, M. R. *Reges socii et amici populi romani*. Milan, 1976
25. Crawford, M. H. *The Roman Republic*. London, 1978
26. Degrassi, A. *Scritti vari di antichità*. 4 vols. Venice and Trieste, 1967
27. Dilke, O. A. W. *Greek and Roman Maps*. London, 1985
28. Earl, D. C. *The Moral and Political Tradition of Rome*. London, 1967
29. Ferrary, J.-L. 'Le idee politiche a Roma nell'epoca repubblicana', *Storia delle idee politiche, economiche e sociali 1*, ed. L. Firpo, Turin 1982, 723–804
30. Ferrary, J.-L. *Philhellénisme et impérialisme*. Rome, 1988
31. Finley, M. I. *The Ancient Economy*. London, 1973, 2nd edn 1984
32. Finley, M. I. *Politics in the Ancient World*. Cambridge, 1983
33. Fraccaro, P. *Opuscula*. 4 vols. Pavia, 1956–7
34. Frank, T. *An Economic History of Rome to the End of the Republic*. Baltimore, 1920
35. Frederiksen, M. *Campania*, ed. with additions by N. Purcell. London (British School at Rome), 1984
36. von Fritz, K. *The Theory of the Mixed Constitution in Antiquity*. New York, 1954
37. Fuchs, H. *Der geistige Widerstand gegen Rom in der antiken Welt*. Berlin, 1938
38. Galsterer, H. *Herrschaft und Verwaltung im republikanischen Italien. Die Beziehungen Roms zu den italischen Gemeinden vom Latinerfrieden 338 v. Chr. bis zum Bundesgenossenkrieg 91 v. Chr.* (Münchener Beitr. 68). Munich, 1976
39. Garlan, Y. *War in the Ancient World: A Social History*, transl. by J. Lloyd. London, 1975
40. Gelzer, M. *Die Nobilität der römischen Republik*. Berlin, 1912, transl. by R. Seager as *The Roman Nobility*. Oxford, 1975
41. Gelzer, M. *Kleine Schriften*, ed. H. Strasburger and Ch. Meier. 3 vols. Wiesbaden, 1962–4
42. Griffin, M. T. *Seneca. A Philosopher in Politics*. Oxford, 1976
43. Gruen, E. S. *The Hellenistic World and the Coming of Rome*. 2 vols. Berkeley, 1984
44. Hahn, L. *Rom und der Romanismus im griechisch-römischen Osten*. Leipzig, 1906
45. Harmand, J. *L'armée et le soldat à Rome de 107 à 50 avant notre ère*. Paris, 1967
46. Harris, W. V. *Rome in Etruria and Umbria*. Oxford, 1971
47. Harris, W. V. *War and Imperialism in Republican Rome 327–70 B.C.* Oxford, 1979
48. Heichelheim, F. M. *Wirtschaftsgeschichte des Altertums*. Leiden, 1938. Italian edn with introd. by M. Mazza, Bari, 1972
49. Hellegouarc'h, J. *Le vocabulaire des relations et des partis politiques sous la République*. Paris, 1963. 2nd edn 1972
50. *Hellenismus in Mittelitalien*. See Abbreviations under *Hellenismus*
51. Hill, H. *The Roman Middle Class in the Republican Period*. Oxford, 1952
52. Hinard, F. *Les proscriptions de la Rome républicaine* (Coll. éc. fr. de Rome 93). Rome, 1985
53. Hopkins, K. *Conquerors and Slaves*. Cambridge, 1978
54. Hopkins, K. and Burton, G. *Death and Renewal*. Cambridge, 1983

55. Jones, A. H. M. *The Greek City*. Oxford, 1940
56. Keppie, L. *Colonisation and Veteran Settlement in Italy 47–14 B.C.* London, 1983
57. Keppie, L. *The Making of the Roman Army. From Republic to Empire*. London, 1984
58. Kromayer, J. *Antike Schlachtfelder in Griechenland* II. Berlin, 1907
59. Kromayer, J. and Veith, G. *Heerwesen und Kriegführung der Griechen und Römer* (Handb. d. Altertumsw. IV 3.2). Munich, 1928
60. Latte, K. *Römische Religionsgeschichte* (Handb. d. Altertumsw. V 4). Munich, 1960.
61. Levick, B. M. 'Morals, politics, and the fall of the Roman Republic', *G&R* 29 (1982) 53–62
62. Lintott, A. W. *Violence in Republican Rome*. Oxford, 1968
63. Lintott, A. W. 'Imperial expansion and moral decline in the Roman Republic', *Historia* 21 (1972) 626–38
64. Lintott, A. W. 'What was the *imperium Romanum*?', *G&R* 28 (1981) 53–67
65. Lintott, A. W. 'Democracy in the middle Republic', *ZSS* 104 (1987) 34–52
66. Lintott, A. W. 'Electoral bribery in the Roman Republic', *JRS* 80 (1990)
67. Magie, D. *Roman Rule in Asia Minor*. 2 vols. Princeton, 1950
68. Manni, E. *Fasti ellenistici e romani, 323–31 a.C.* (*Kokalos* Suppl. 1). Palermo, 1961
69. Marquardt, J. and Wissowa, G. *Römische Staatsverwaltung* (Handb. d. röm. Alterthümer 4–6). 2nd edn, 3 vols. Leipzig, 1881–5
70. Marsden, E. W. *Greek and Roman Artillery. Historical Development*. Oxford, 1969; *Technical Treatises*, Oxford, 1971
71. de Martino, F. *Storia della costituzione romana*. 2nd edn, 5 vols. Naples, 1972–5
72. Meier, Ch. *Res Publica Amissa. Eine Studie zu Verfassung und Geschichte der späten römischen Republik*. Wiesbaden, 1966
73. *Mélanges Heurgon*. See Abbreviations under *Mél. Heurgon*.
74. Michels, A. K. *The Calendar of the Roman Republic*. Princeton, 1967
75. Millar, F. G. B. 'The political character of the classical Roman Republic, 200–151 B.C.', *JRS* 74 (1984) 1–19
76. Mommsen, Th. *Römische Geschichte*. 1854–6. 8th edn, 4 vols., Berlin 1888–94. Transl. by W. P. Dickson as *The History of Rome*, 5 vols. London, 1894, and by C. A. Alexandre as *Histoire Romaine*, repr. with introd. by C. Nicolet, 2 vols., Paris, 1985
77. Mommsen, Th. *Römisches Staatsrecht*. Vols I and II 3rd edn, Leipzig, 1887; Vol. III Leipzig, 1888
78. *Gesammelte Schriften von Theodor Mommsen*. 8 vols. Berlin, 1905–13
79. Münzer, F. *Römische Adelsparteien und Adelsfamilien*. Stuttgart, 1920
80. Nicolet, C. *L'ordre équestre à l'époque républicaine (313–43 av. J.-C.)* (*BEFAR* 207). 2 vols. Paris, 1966 and 1974
81. Nicolet, C. 'Polybe et les institutions romaines', *Entretiens Hardt* 20 (1974) 209–65

82. Nicolet, C. *Le métier de citoyen dans la Rome républicaine*. 2nd edn Paris, 1976. Translated by P. S. Falla as *The World of the Citizen in Republican Rome*. London, 1980

83. Nicolet, C. *Rome et la conquête du monde méditerranéen 264–27 avant J.-C.* I *Les structures de l'Italie romaine* (*Nouvelle Clio* 8); II *Genèse d'un empire* (*Nouvelle Clio* 8 bis). Paris, 1977 and 1978

84. Nicolet, C. 'Centralisation d'état et problèmes des archives dans le monde gréco-romain', *Culture et idéologie dans la genèse de l'état moderne, Actes du colloque de Rome 15–17 oct. 1984* (Coll. éc. fr. de Rome 82), Rome, 1985, 9–24

85. Nippel, W. *Aufruhr und Polizei in der römischen Republik*. Stuttgart, 1988

86. North, J. A. 'The development of Roman imperialism', *JRS* 71 (1981) 1–9

87. North, J. A. 'Democratic politics in Republican Rome', *P&P* 126 (1990) 3–21

88. Ormerod, H. A. *Piracy in the Ancient World*. Liverpool, 1924

89. Parke, H. W. *Sibyls and Sibylline Prophecy in Classical Antiquity*, ed. B. C. McGing. London and New York, 1988

90. Perelli, L. *Il movimento popolare nell'ultimo secolo della repubblica*. Turin, 1982

91. Platner, S. B. and Ashby, T. *A Topographical Dictionary of Ancient Rome*. Oxford, 1929

92. von Pöhlmann, R. *Geschichte der sozialen Frage und des Sozialismus in der antiken Welt*. 2 vols. Munich, 1912

93. Préaux, C. *Le monde hellénistique*. 2 vols. Paris, 1978

94. Ramsay, W. M. *The Historical Geography of Asia Minor*. London, 1890

94A. Rawson, E. D. *Roman Culture and Society*. Oxford, 1991

95. Rich, J. W. *Declaring War in the Roman Republic in the Period of Transmarine Expansion* (Coll. Latomus 149). Brussels, 1976

96. *La rivoluzione romana*. See Abbreviations.

97. Rostovtzeff, M. *The Social and Economic History of the Roman Empire*. 1926. 2nd edn, 2 vols. Oxford 1957

98. Rostovtzeff, M. *The Social and Economic History of the Hellenistic World*. 3 vols. Oxford, 1941

99. Rouland, N. *Pouvoir politique et dépendance personnelle dans l'antiquité romaine*. (Coll. Latomus 166). Brussels, 1979

100. de Ste Croix, G. E. M. *The Class Struggle in the Ancient Greek World from the Archaic Age to the Arab Conquests*. London, 1981

101. Salmon, E. T. *Samnium and the Samnites*. Cambridge, 1967

102. Salmon, E. T. *The Making of Roman Italy*. London, 1982

103. De Sanctis, G. *Per la scienza dell'antichità*. Turin, 1909

104. De Sanctis, G. *Problemi di storia antica*. Bari, 1932

105. Sands, P. C. *The Client Princes of the Roman Empire under the Republic*. Cambridge, 1908

106. Schleussner, B. *Die Legaten der römischen Republik*. Munich, 1978

107. Schneider, H. *Die Entstehung der römischen Militärdiktatur. Krise und Niedergang einer antiken* Republik. Cologne, 1971

108. Scullard, H. H. *From the Gracchi to Nero*. 5th edn 1982, repr. London and New York, 1988
109. Seager, R. '*Factio*: some observations', *JRS* 62 (1972) 53–8
110. Seager, R. *Crisis*. See Abbreviations
111. Semple, E. C. *The Geography of the Mediterranean Region in relation to Ancient History*. London, 1932
112. Shatzman, I. *Senatorial Wealth and Roman Politics* (Coll. Latomus 142). Brussels, 1975
113. Sherwin-White, A. N. *The Roman Citizenship*. 2nd edn, Oxford, 1973
114. Smith, R. E. *The Failure of the Roman Republic*. Cambridge, 1955
114A. Smith, R. E. *Service in the Post-Marian Roman Army*. Manchester, 1958
115. Stranger, P. P. *Untersuchungen zu den Namen der römischen Provinzen*. Diss. Tübingen, 1955
116. Strasburger, H. 'Optimates', *RE* 18.1 (1939) 773–98
117. Suolahti, J. *The Junior Officers of the Roman Army in the Republican Period*. Helsinki, 1955
118. Syme, R. *The Roman Revolution*. 1939. 2nd edn Oxford, 1952
119. Syme, R. *Roman Papers*. Vols. I–II ed. E. Badian, vols. III–V ed. A. R. Birley. Oxford, 1979–88, vols. VI–VII ed. A. R. Birley, Oxford, 1991
120. Taylor, L. R. *Party Politics in the Age of Caesar*. Berkeley, 1949
121. Toynbee, A. J. *Hannibal's Legacy*. 2 vols. OUP London, 1965
122. Vittinghoff, F. *Römische Kolonisation und Bürgerrechtspolitik unter Caesar und Augustus* (*AAWM* 1951, 14). Wiesbaden, 1952
123. Vogt, J. *Ancient Slavery and the Ideal of Man*, transl. by T. E. V. Wiedemann, Oxford, 1974
124. Walbank, F. W. *Selected Papers*. Cambridge, 1985
125. Weber, M. *Storia economica e sociale dell'antichità* (pref. by A. Momigliano). Rome, 1981
126. Wheeler, R. E. M. *Rome beyond the Imperial Frontiers*. London, 1954
127. Will, E. *Histoire politique du monde hellénistique (323–30 av. J.-C.)* (*Annales de l'Est* 32). 2nd edn 2 vols. Nancy, 1979 and 1982
128. Wilson, A. J. N. *Emigration from Italy in the Republican Age of Rome*. Manchester, 1966
129. Wirszubski, C. *Libertas as a Political Idea at Rome during the Late Republic and Early Principate*. Cambridge, 1950
130. Wiseman, T. P. *New Men in the Roman Senate*. Oxford, 1971
131. Wiseman, T. P. 'The definition of "eques Romanus" in the late Republic and early Empire', *Historia* 19 (1970) 67–83
132. Wiseman, T. P., ed. *Roman Political Life 90 B.C.–A.D. 69*. Exeter, 1985
133. Wiseman, T. P. *Roman Studies Literary and Historical*, Liverpool, 1987

B. SOURCES

a. LITERARY SOURCES

1. Austin, R. G. *M. Tulli Ciceronis Pro M. Caelio Oratio*. 3rd edn Oxford, 1960

2. Badian, E. 'Where was Sisenna?', *Athenaeum* 42 (1964) 422–31
3. Badian, E. 'An unrecognised date in Cicero's text?', *Mnemai: Classical Studies in Memory of Karl K. Hulley*, ed. H. D. Evjan, Chico, CA, 1984, 97–101
4. Barnes, J. 'Cicero's *De Fato* and a Greek source', *Histoire et structure: à la mémoire de Victor Goldschmidt*, Paris, 1985, 229–39
5. Barwick, K. *Caesars Bellum Civile. Tendenz, Abfassungszeit und Stil* (*ASAW* 99.1). Berlin, 1951
6. Bloch, H. 'The structure of Sallust's *Historiae*. The evidence of the Fleury manuscript', *Studies in Honor of A. M. Albareda*, ed. S. Prete, New York, 1961, 61–76
7. Buchheit, V. 'Ciceros Kritik an Sulla in der Rede für Roscius aus Ameria', *Historia* 24 (1975) 570–91
8. Buchheit, V. 'Chrysogonus als Tyrann in Ciceros Rede für Roscius aus Ameria', *Chiron* 5 (1975) 193–211
9. Calboli, G. *M. Porci Catonis Oratio pro Rhodiensibus*. Bologna, 1978
10. Cardauns, B. *Varros Logistoricus über die Götterverehrung* (Diss. Köln). Würzburg, 1960
11. Cardauns, B. *M. Terentius Varro, Antiquitates Rerum Divinarum*. 2 vols. Wiesbaden, 1976
12. Cardauns, B. 'Varro und die Religion. Zur Theologie, Wirkungsgeschichte und Leistung der "Antiquitates Rerum Divinarum"', *ANRW* II.16.1 (1978) 80–103
13. Carter, J. M. *Sallust: Fragments of the Histories* (*Lactor* 6). London, 1970, repr. 1978
14. Castagnoli, F. 'L'insula nei cataloghi regionari di Roma', *RFIC* 104 (1976) 45–52
15. Castiglioni, L. 'Motivi antiromani nella tradizione storica antica', *RIL* 61 (1928) 625–39
16. Cichorius, C. *Untersuchungen zu Lucilius*. Berlin, 1908, repr. 1964
17. Clark, A. C. *Pro T. Annio Milone ad Iudices Oratio*. Oxford, 1895
18. Collart, J. *Varron grammairien latin*. Paris, 1954
19. della Corte, F. *Varrone: il terzo gran lume romano*. 2nd edn Florence, 1970
20. Crook, J. A. 'Lex "Rivalicia" (*FIRA* I, no.5)', *Athenaeum* 64 (1986) 45–53
21. Cuff, P. J. 'Prolegomena to a critical edition of Appian B. C. I', *Historia* 16 (1967) 177–88
22. Dahlmann, H. 'Terentius' (84), *RE Suppl.* 6 (1935) 1172–277
23. Dahlmann, H. 'Varroniana', *ANRW* I.3 (1973) 3–25
24. Dalzell, A. 'Lucretius', *CHCL* II (1982) 207–29
25. David, J. M. *et al.*, 'Le commentariolum petitionis de Q. Cicéron', *ANRW* I.3 (1973) 239–77
26. Derow, P. S. 'Polybius, Rome and the East', *JRS* 69 (1979) 1–15
27. Dilke, O. A. W. *The Roman Land Surveyors. An Introduction to the Agrimensores*. Newton Abbott, 1971. (Also *ANRW* II.1 (1974) 564–92)
28. Dörrie, H. 'Polybios über "pietas", "religio" und "fides" (zu Buch 6, Kap. 56)', *Mélanges de philosophie, de litt. et d'hist. ancienne offerts à Pierre*

Boyancé (Coll. éc. fr. de Rome 22), Rome, 1974, 251–72
29. Douglas, A. E. *M. Tulli Ciceronis Brutus*. Oxford, 1966
30. Douglas, A. E. *Cicero* (Greece and Rome New Surveys in the Classics 2). Oxford, 1968, repr. with addenda 1978
31. Earl, D. C. *The Political Thought of Sallust*. Cambridge, 1961
32. Edelstein, L. and Kidd, I. G. *Posidonius*. I Cambridge, 1972, II (2 vols.) Cambridge 1988
33. Ensslin, W. 'Appian und die Liviustradition zum ersten Bürgerkrieg', *Klio* 20 (1926) 415–65
34. Fantham, E. 'The synchronistic chapter of Gellius (*NA* 17.21) and some aspects of Roman chronology and cultural history between 60 and 50 B.C.', *LCM* 6 (1981) 7–17
35. Ferrary, J.-L. 'L'archéologie du *De Re Publica* (2.2,4–37,63): Cicéron entre Polybe et Platon', *JRS* 74 (1984) 87–98
36. Forni, G. *Valore storico e fonti di Pompeio Trogo* I. Urbino, 1958
37. Frier, B. W. *Libri annales pontificorum maximorum. The Origins of the Annalistic Tradition* (Pap. and Monog. Amer. Ac. Rome 27). Rome, 1979
38. Gabba, E. *Appiano e la storia delle guerre civili*. Florence, 1956
39. Gabba, E. 'Note sulla polemica anticiceroniana di Asinio Pollione', *RSI* 69 (1957) 317–39
40. Gabba, E. *Appiani Bellorum Civilium Liber I*. 1958, 2nd edn Florence, 1967
41. Gabba, E. 'Studi su Dionigi di Alicarnasso III. La proposta di legge agraria di Spurio Cassio', *Athenaeum* 42 (1964) 29–41
42. Geiger, J. *Cornelius Nepos and Ancient Political Biography*. Stuttgart, 1985
43. Gow, A. S. F. and Page, D. L. *The Greek Anthology* II. *The Garden of Philip*. 2 vols. Cambridge, 1968
44. Henderson, M. I. '*De commentariolo petitionis*', *JRS* 40 (1950) 8–21
45. Homeyer, H. *Die antiken Berichte über den Tod Ciceros und ihre Quellen*. Baden-Baden, 1964
46. How, W. W. *Cicero, Select Letters* II, *Commentary*. Oxford, 1925
47. Janke, M. *Historische Untersuchungen zu Memnon von Herakleia*. Diss. Würzburg, 1963
48. Jocelyn, H. D. *The Tragedies of Ennius*. Cambridge, 1967
49. Jonkers, E. J. *Social and Economic Commentary on Cicero's De Imperio Cn. Pompei*. Leiden, 1959
50. Jonkers, E. J. *Social and Economic Commentary on Cicero's De Lege Agraria Orationes Tres*. Leiden, 1963
51. Keaveney, A. 'Four puzzling passages in Appian', *GIF* 33 (1981) 247–50
52. Keaveney, A. and Strachan, J. C. G. 'L. Catilina legatus: Sallust, *Histories* I.46M', *CQ* (1981) 363–6
53. Kenney, E. J. *Lucretius* (Greece and Rome New Surveys in the Classics 11). Oxford, 1977
54. Kinsey, T. E. 'The dates of the *pro Roscio Amerino* and *pro Quinctio*', *Mnemosyne* 20 (1967) 61–7
55. Kinsey, T. E. *M. Tullii Ciceronis pro Quinctio Oratio*. Sydney, 1971
56. Kinsey, T. E. 'Cicero's case against Magnus, Capito and Chrysogonus in

the *Pro Sex. Roscio Amerino* and its use for the historian', *AC* 49 (1980) 173–90

57. Kinsey, T. E. 'The political insignificance of Cicero's *pro Roscio*', *LCM* 7 (1982) 39–40
58. Koestermann, E. *C. Sallustius Crispus. Bellum Jugurthinum*. Heidelberg, 1971
59. Kornemann, E. *Zur Geschichte der Gracchenzeit. Quellenkritische und chronologische Untersuchungen* (Klio Beih. 1). Leipzig, 1903
60. Kumaniecki, K. 'Les discours égarés de Cicéron "pro C. Cornelio"', *Med. Kon. Vlaam. Acad. Belg.* 32 (1970) 3–36
61. Laffranque, M. 'Poseidonios historien. Un épisode significatif de la première guerre de Mithridate', *Pallas* 11 (1962) 103–9
62. Langenberg, G. *M. Terenti Varronis Liber De Philosophia. Ausgabe und Erklärung der Fragmente*. Cologne, 1959
63. La Penna, A. *Sallustio e la rivoluzione romana*. Milan, 1969
64. Larsen, J. A. O. 'Consilium in Livy XLV.118.6–7', *CPh* 44 (1949) 73–90
65. Lenaghan, J. O. *A Commentary on Cicero's Oration De Haruspicum Responso*. The Hague, 1969
66. McGushin, P. *C. Sallustius Crispus. Bellum Catilinae. A Commentary* (*Mnemosyne* Suppl. 45). Leiden, 1977
67. Magnino, D. *Appiani Bellorum Civilium Liber Tertius*. Florence, 1984
68. Malitz, J. *Ambitio mala. Studien zur politischen Biographie des Sallust*. Bonn, 1975
69. Malitz, J. *Die Historien des Poseidonios* (Zetemata 74). Munich, 1983
70. Manuwald, B. *Cassius Dio und Augustus. Philologische Untersuchungen zu den Büchern 45–56 des dionischen Geschichtswerkes* (Palingenesia 14). Wiesbaden, 1979
71. Marsden, E. W. *Greek and Roman Artillery. Technical Treatises*. Oxford, 1971
72. Marshall, B. A. *A Commentary on Asconius*. Columbia, Missouri, 1985
73. Martin, R. *Recherches sur les agronomes latins*. Paris, 1971
74. Nagle, D. B. 'An allied view of the Social War', *AJA* 77 (1973) 367–78
75. Nardo, D. *Il Commentariolum Petitionis: la propaganda elettorale nella ars di Quinto Cicerone*. Padua, 1970
76. Nisbet, R. G. *M. Tulli Ciceronis de Domo Sua ad Pontifices Oratio*. Oxford, 1939
77. Nisbet, R. G. M. *M. Tulli Ciceronis in L. Calpurnium Pisonem Oratio*. Oxford, 1961
78. Nisbet, R. G. M. 'The *Commentariolum Petitionis*', *JRS* 51 (1961) 84–7
79. Ogilvie, R. M. *A Commentary on Livy Books 1–5*. Oxford, 1965
80. Ogilvie, R. M. 'Caesar', *CHCL* II (1982) 281–5
81. Ogilvie, R. M. and Pelling, C. B. R. 'Titi Livi Lib. XCI', *PCPhS* 30 (1984) 116–25
82. Paterson, J. '*Transalpinae gentes*: Cicero, *De Re Publica* 3.16', *CQ* 28 (1978) 452–8
83. Paul, G. M. *A Historical Commentary on Sallust's Bellum Jugurthinum*. Liverpool, 1984

84. Pelling, C. B. R. 'Plutarch and Roman politics', *Past Perspectives*, ed. I. S. Moxon *et al.*, Cambridge, 1986, 159–87
85. Philippson, R. 'Tullius' (29), 'Die philosophischen Schriften', *RE* 7A (1939) 1104–92
86. Phillips, E. J. 'Cicero, ad Atticum I 2', *Philologus* 114 (1970) 291–4
87. Pocock, L. G. *A Commentary on Cicero in Vatinium*. London, 1926
88. Powell, J. G. F. *Cicero, Cato Maior de senectute*. Cambridge, 1988
89. Preibisch, P. *Two Studies on the Roman Pontifices*. New York, 1975 (repr. of *Quaestiones de libris pontificiis*, Bratislava, 1874 and *Fragmenta librorum pontificiorum*, Tilsit, 1878)
90. Rambaud, M. *Cicéron et l'histoire romaine*. Paris, 1953
91. Rambaud, M. *L'art de la déformation historique dans les Commentaires de César*. 2nd edn Paris, 1966
92. Ramsey, J. T. *Sallust's Bellum Catilinae*. Chico, CA, 1984
93. Rawson, E. 'The literary sources for the pre-Marian army' *PBSR* 39 (1971) 13–31 (= A 94A, 34–57)
94. Rawson, E. 'History, historiography, and Cicero's *expositio consiliorum suorum*', *LCM* 7 (1982) 121–4 (= A 94A, 408–15)
95. Regell, P. *Roman Augury and Etruscan Divination*. New York, 1975 (repr. of *De augurum publicorum libris*, Bratislava, 1878 and *Fragmenta auguralia*, Hirschberg, 1882)
96. Reid, J. S. *M. Tulli Ciceronis Academica*. London, 1885
97. Richard, J. C. 'Pline et les myrtes du temple de Quirinus', *Latomus* 45 (1986) 783–96
98. Richardson, J. S. 'Polybius' view of the Roman empire', *PBSR* 47 (1979) 1–11
99. van Rinsveld, B. 'Cicéron, *de re publica* III, 9, 15–16', *Latomus* 40 (1981) 280–91
100. Rostovtzeff, M. I. *Strabon kak istochnik dlya istorii Bospora*. Kharkov, 1914
101. Rubinsohn, Z. 'A note on Plutarch, Crassus X.1', *Historia* 19 (1970) 624–7
102. Schmidt, O. E. *Der Briefwechsel des M. Tullius Cicero von seinem Prokonsulat in Cilicien bis zu Caesars Ermordung*. Leipzig, 1893
103. Seager, R. 'Two urban praetors in Valerius Maximus', *CR* 84 (1970) 11
104. Seager, R. 'Valerius Maximus VII 7.7: addendum', *CR* 86 (1972) 314
105. Seager, R. '"Populares" in Livy and the Livian tradition', *CQ* 71 (1977) 377–90
106. Seager, R. 'The political significance of Cicero's *pro Roscio*', *LCM* 7 (1982) 10–12
107. Sedley, D. 'Epicurus, *On Nature* Book XXVIII', *CronErc* 3 (1973) 5–83
108. Shackleton Bailey, D. R. *Cicero's Letters to Atticus*. 7 vols. Cambridge, 1965–70
109. Shackleton Bailey, D. R. *Two Studies in Roman Nomenclature*. New York, 1976
110. Shackleton Bailey, D. R. *Cicero, Epistulae ad Familiares*. 2 vols. Cambridge, 1977
111. Shackleton Bailey, D. R. *Cicero, Ad Quintum Fratrem et M. Brutum*.

Cambridge, 1980

112. Sherwin-White, A. N. *The Letters of Pliny*. Oxford, 1966
113. Skydsgaard, J. E. *Varro the Scholar: Studies in the first Book of Varro's De Re Rustica*. Copenhagen, 1968
114. Strasburger, H. 'Poseidonios on problems of the Roman empire', *JRS* 55 (1965) 40–53
115. Sumner, G. V. *The Orators in Cicero's Brutus: Prosopography and Chronology*. Toronto, 1973
116. Syme, R. *Sallust*. Berkeley, 1964
117. Twyman, B. L. 'The date of Sulla's abdication and the chronology of the first book of Appian's *Civil Wars*', *Athenaeum* 54 (1976) 271–95
118. Tyrrell, W. B. *A Legal and Historical Commentary to Cicero's Pro C. Rabirio Perduellionis Reo*. Amsterdam, 1978
119. Valgiglio, E. *Plutarco, Vita di Silla*. 2nd edn Turin, 1960
120. Vretska, K. *C. Sallustius Crispus de Catilinae Coniuratione*. 2 vols. Heidelberg, 1976
121. Walbank, F. W. *A Historical Commentary on Polybius*. 3 vols. Oxford, 1957–69
122. Walbank, F. W. 'The Scipionic legend', *PCPhS* 13 (1967) 54–69 (= *Selected Papers* 120–37)
123. Walbank, F. W. *Polybius*. Berkeley, 1972
124. Walser, G. *Der Briefwechsel des L. Munatius Plancus mit Cicero*. Basle, 1957
125. Walton, F. R. 'A neglected historical text', *Historia* 14 (1965) 236–51
126. Wiseman, T. P. *Clio's Cosmetics*. Leicester, 1979
127. Wiseman, T. P. *Catullus and his World*. Cambridge, 1985
128. Wiseman, T. P. 'Who was Crassicius Pansa?', *TAPhA* 115 (1985) 187–96
129. Woodman, A. J. *Velleius Paterculus: the Caesarian and Augustan Narratives (2.41–93)*. Cambridge, 1983
130. de Zulueta, F. *The Institutes of Gaius*. 2 vols. Oxford, 1946 and 1953

b. EPIGRAPHY AND NUMISMATICS

131. Anderson, J. G. C., Cumont, F. and Grégoire, H. *Recueil des inscriptions grecques et latines du Pont et de l'Arménie* (*Studia Pontica* III). Brussels, 1910
132. Bagnall, R. S. and Derow, P. *Greek Historical Documents: The Hellenistic Period*. Chico, CA, 1981
133. Birks, P., Rodger, A. and Richardson, J. S. 'Further aspects of the *Tabula Contrebiensis*', *JRS* 74 (1984) 45–73
134. Boehringer, C. *Zur Chronologie mittelhellenistischer Münzserien, 220–160 v. Chr.* Berlin, 1972
135. Bove, L. *Documenti processuali dalle Tabulae Pompeianae di Murécine*. Naples, 1979
136. Bove, L. *Documenti di operazioni finanziarie dall'archivio dei Sulpici*. Naples, 1984
137. Boyce, G. K. *Corpus of the Lararia of Pompeii* (*MAAR* 14). Rome, 1937
138. Bruna, F. J. *Lex Rubria: Caesars Regelung für die richterlichen Kompetenzen der Munizipalmagistrate in Gallia Cisalpina. Text, Übersetzung und*

Kommentar. Leiden, 1972

139. Cabanes, P. 'Nouvelles inscriptions d'Albanie méridionale (Bouthrotos et Apollonia)', *ZPE* 63 (1986) 137–55
140. Calabi Limentani, I. *Epigrafia latina*. Venice and Milan, 1968
141. Camodeca, G. 'Per una riedizione dell'archivio puteolano dei Sulpici', *Puteoli* 6 (1982) 3–53; 7–8 (1984) 3–25; 9–10 (1985–6) 3–40
142. Coarelli, F. 'Su alcuni proconsoli di Asia tra la fine del II e gli inizi del I secolo a.C. e sulla politica di Mario in oriente', *Tituli* 4 (= *Atti del colloquio internazionale AIEGL su epigrafia e ordine senatorio* 1, Rome, 1982), 435–51
143. Cormack, J. M. R. 'The gymnasiarchal law of Beroea', *Ancient Macedonia* II (*Papers of the 2nd International Symposium, Thessalonike, 10–12 Aug. 1973*), Thessalonica, 1977, 139–49
144. Crawford, M. H. *Roman Republican Coinage*. 2 vols. Cambridge, 1974
145. Crawford, M. H. *Coinage and Money under the Roman Republic*. London, 1985
146. Crawford, M. H. and Wiseman, T. P. 'The coinage of the age of Sulla', *NC* 4 (1964) 141–58
147. Dakaris, S. 'I Romaiki politiki stin Ipeiro', *Nikopolis* 1 (*Proc. of the 1st Internat. Symposium on Nikopolis, 23–9 Sept. 1984*), Preveza, 1987, 11–21
148. Derow, P. S. and Forrest, W. G. 'An inscription from Chios', *ABSA* 77 (1982) 79–92
149. Duchène, H. 'Sur la stèle d'Aulus Caprilius Timotheos, sômatemporos', *BCH* 110 (1980) 513–30
150. Engelmann, H. and Knibbe, D. 'Das Zollgesetz der Provinz Asia, eine neue Inschrift aus Ephesos', *EA* 14 (1989) 1–206
151. Fentress, E. '*Via Aurelia, Via Aemilia*', *PBSR* 52 (1984) 72–6
152. Frederiksen, M. 'The Lex Rubria, reconsiderations', *JRS* 54 (1964) 252–77
153. Frederiksen, M. 'The Republican municipal laws: errors and drafts', *JRS* 55 (1965) 183–98
154. Galsterer, H. 'Die lex Osca Tabulae Bantinae – eine Bestandaufnahme', *Chiron* 1 (1971) 191–214
155. Galsterer-Kroll, B. 'Untersuchungen zu den Beinamen der Städte des Imperium Romanum', *Epigraphische Studien* 9 (1972) 44–145
156. Garnsey, P., Gallant, T. and Rathbone, D. 'Thessaly and the grain supply of Rome during the second century B.C.', *JRS* 74 (1984) 30–44
157. Gascou, J. 'Inscriptions de Tébessa', *MEFRA* 81 (1969) 537–99
158. Gasperini, L. 'Su alcuni epigrafi di Taranto romano', *Misc. greca e romana* II, Rome, 1968, 379–97
159. Gasperini, L. 'Ancora sul frammento cesariano di Taranto', *Epigraphica* 33 (1971) 48–59
160. Gilyevich, A. M. 'Chersonesus and the Pontic state of Mithridates VI according to numismatic data' (Russ.), *Tskhaltubo* III, 608–17
161. Giovannini, A. *Rome et la circulation monétaire en Grèce au IIe siècle avant J.-C.* Basle, 1978
162. Golenko, K. V. 'Bronze coins of the cities of Pontus and Paphlagonia in the time of Mithridates VI from the finds on the Bosporus' (Russ.), *Klio*

46 (1965) 307–22
163. Golenko, K. V. 'Anonymous Pontic copper' (Russ.) *VDI* 1969.1 (107) 130–54
164. Golenko, K. V. 'Pontus und Paphlagonien', *Chiron* 3 (1973) 467–99
165. Golenko, K. V. and Karyszkovski, P. J. 'The gold coinage of King Pharnaces of the Bosporus', *NC* 12 (1972) 25–38
166. Gordon, R. L. 'The date and significance of CIMRM 593 (British Museum, Townley Collection)', *JMS* 2 (1977/8) 148–74
167. Grebenkin, V. N. and Zaginailo, A. G. 'On the question of coin circulation in the state of Pontus at the time of Mithridates Eupator (Russ.), *Tskhaltubo* III, 22–4
168. Hall, A. S. 'New light on the capture of Isaura Vetus by P. Servilius Vatia', *Akten des VI internat. Kongresses für gr. und lat. Epigraphik* (*Vestigia* 17), Munich, 1972, 568–71
169. Hardy, E. G. *Roman Laws and Charters*. Oxford, 1912
170. Hassall, M., Crawford, M. H. and Reynolds, J. 'Rome and the eastern provinces at the end of the second century B.C.', *JRS* 64 (1974) 195–220
171. Head, B. V. *Historia Numorum*. 2nd edn Oxford, 1911
172. Hinrichs, F. T. 'Die lateinische Tafel von Bantia und die "Lex de Piratis"', *Hermes* 98 (1970) 473–502
173. Holleaux, M. 'Décret de Chéronée relatif à la première guerre de Mithradates', *Etudes d'épigraphie et d'histoire grecques* I, Paris, 1938, 143–59
174. Holleaux, M. 'Le décret de Bargylia en l'honneur de Poseidonios', *Etudes d'épigraphie et d'histoire grecques* II, Paris, 1938, 179–98
175. Imhoof-Blumer, F. 'Die Kupferprägung des mithridatischen Reiches und andere Münzen des Pontus und Paphlagoniens, *NZ* 5 (1912) 169–84
176. Johannsen, K. *Die lex agraria des Jahres 111 v. Chr.* Diss. Munich, 1971
177. Jones, H. S. 'A Roman law concerning piracy', *JRS* 16 (1926) 155–73
178. Karyshkovsky, P. O. 'Monetary circulation at Olbia at the end of the second century and in the first half of the first century B.C.' (Russ.) *NE* 5 (1965) 62–74
179. Knapp, R. C. 'The date and purpose of the Iberian denarii', *NC* (1977) 1–18
180. Koukouli-Chrysanthaki, Ch. 'Politarchs in a new inscription from Amphipolis', *Ancient Macedonian Studies in honor of Charles F. Edson* (*Inst. for Balkan Studies* 158), Thessalonica, 1981, 229–41
181. Kraay, C. M. 'Caesar's *quattuorviri* of 44 B.C. The arrangement of their issues', *NC* 14 (1954) 18–31
182. Kraay, C. M. and Hirmer, M. *Greek Coins*. London, 1966
183. Kleiner, F. S. 'The 1926 Piraeus hoard and Athenian bronze coinage *c.*86 B.C.', AD 28 (1973) 169–86
184. Kleiner, G. 'Pontische Reichsmünzen', *MDAI(I)* 6 (1955) 1–21
185. Krahmer, G. 'Eine Ehrung für Mithradates Eupator in Pergamon', *JDAI* 40 (1925) 183
186 Laffi, U. 'La *lex Aelia Furfensis*', *La Cultura Italica* (*Atti del Convegno della Società Italiana di Glottologia, Pisa 19–20 dic. 1977*), Pisa, 1978, 121–48
186A. Laffi, U. 'La Lex Rubria de Gallia Gisalpina', *Athenaeum* 64 (1986) 5–44

187. La Regina, A. 'Le iscrizioni osche di Pietrabbondante e la questione di Bovianum Vetus', *RhM* 109 (1966) 280–6
188. Lewis, D. M. 'The chronology of the Athenian new style coinage', *NC* 2 (1962) 275
189. Lintott, A. W. 'Notes on the Roman law inscribed at Delphi and Cnidos', *ZPE* 20 (1976) 65–82
190. Lintott, A. W. 'The *quaestiones de sicariis et veneficis* and the Latin *lex Bantina*', *Hermes* 106 (1978) 125–38
191. Lintott, A. W. 'The Roman judiciary law from Tarentum', *ZPE* 45 (1982) 127–38
192. Lintott, A. W. 'The so-called Tabula Bembina and the Humanists', *Athenaeum* 61 (1983) 201–14
193. Lopez Melero, R., Sanchez Abal, J. L. and Garcia Jimenez, S. 'El bronce de Alcantara: una *deditio* del 104 a.C.', *Gerion* 2 (1984) 265–323
194. Luce, T. J. 'Political propaganda on Roman republican coins: *circa* 92–82 B.C.', *AJA* 72 (1968) 25–39
195. Mackay, P. 'Macedonian tetradrachms of 148–147 B.C.', *ANSMusN* 14 (1968) 15–40
196. Mackay, P. 'The coinage of the Macedonian republics 168–146 B.C.', *Ancient Macedonia* 1 (*Papers of the 1st International Symposium, Thessalonike 1968*), Thessalonica, 1970, 256–64
197. Manganaro, G. 'Città di Sicilia e santuarii panellenici nel III e II secolo a.C.', *Historia* 13 (1964) 414–39
198. Mattingly, H. B. 'The two Republican laws of the *Tabula Bembina*', *JRS* 59 (1969) 129–43
199. Mattingly, H. B. 'Some third magistrates in the Athenian new style coinage', *JHS* 91 (1971) 85–93
200. Mattingly, H. B. 'The date of the "de agro Pergameno"', *AJPh* 93 (1972) 412–23
201. Mattingly, H. B. 'L. Julius Caesar, governor of Macedonia', *Chiron* 9 (1979) 147–67
202. Mellor, R. 'The dedications on the Capitoline hill', *Chiron* 8 (1978) 319–30
203. Mørkholm, O. 'Some Cappadocian problems', *NC* 2 (1962) 407–11
204. Mørkholm, O. 'Some Cappadocian die-links', *NC* 4 (1964) 21–5
205. Mørkholm, O. 'The coinage of Ariarathes VIII and IX of Cappadocia', *Essays in Greek Coinage Presented to Stanley Robinson*, ed. C. M. Kraay and G. K. Jenkins, Oxford, 1968, 241–58
206. Mørkholm, O. 'The classification of Cappadocian coins', *NC* 9 (1969) 21–31
207. Mørkholm, O. 'Ptolemaic coins and chronology: the dated silver coinage of Alexandria', *ANSMusN* 20 (1975) 7–24
208. Mørkholm, O. 'The Cappadocians again', *NC* 19 (1979) 242–6
209. Mørkholm, O. 'The Parthian coinage of Seleucia on Tigris *c*.90–55 B.C.', *NC* 20 (1980) 38–47
210. Nenci, G. 'Considerazioni sui decreti di Entella', *ASNP* 12 (1982) 1069–86

211. Newell, E. T. *Royal Greek Portrait Coins*. New York, 1937
212. Nicolet, C. *et al*. *Insula Sacra. La loi Gabinia-Calpurnia de Délos* (Coll. éc. fr. Rome 45). Rome, 1980
213. Ostrow, S. 'Augustales along the Bay of Naples', *Historia* 34 (1985) 64–101
214. Panciera, S. 'Tra topografia e epigrafia II', *ArchClass* 22 (1970) 138
215. Panciera, S. 'Nuovi documenti epigrafici per la topografia di Roma antica', *RPAA* 43 (1970/1) 109–34
216. Pani, M. 'Su un nuovo cippo graccano dauno', *RIL* 111 (1977) 389–400
217. Pearse, J. L. D. 'Three *Alba* of the *Collegium Fabrorum Tignariorum* of Rome', *BCAR* 85 (1980) 164–96
218. Pfeiler, H. 'Die frühesten Porträts des Mithridates Eupator und die Bronzeprägung seiner Vorgänger', *Schweizer Münzblätter* 18.7 (1968) 78–80
219. Plassart, A. 'Décrets de Thespies', *Mélanges d'arch. et d'hist. offerts à Ch. Picard, RA* 29–32 (1949) 825–32
220. Price, M. J. 'The new-style coinage of Athens', *NC* 4 (1964) 27–36
221. Price, M. J. 'Mithridates VI Eupator Dionysos and the coinages of the Black Sea', *NC* 8 (1968) 1–12
222. Quoniam, P. 'A propos d'une inscription de Thuburnica', *CRAI* (1950) 332–6
223. Raubitschek, A. E. 'Epigraphical notes on Julius Caesar', *JRS* 44 (1954) 65–75
224. Reinach, T. *Numismatique ancienne: trois royaumes d'Asie Mineure*. Paris, 1888
225. Reinach, T. 'A stele from Abonouteichos', *NC* 5 (1905) 113–19
226. Reynolds, J. *Aphrodisias and Rome* (*JRS* Monograph 1). London, 1982
227. Richardson, J. S. 'The *Tabula Contrebiensis*: Roman law in Spain in the early first century B.C.', *JRS* 73 (1983) 33–41
228. Robert, J. and Robert, L. *Claros* I. *Décrets hellénistiques* I. Paris, 1989
229. Robert, L. *Etudes anatoliennes. Recherches sur les inscriptions grecques de l'Asie mineure*. Paris, 1937
230. Robert, L. 'Inscriptions de Phocée', *Hellenica* 10, Paris, 1955, 257–61
231. Robert, L. 'Recherches épigraphiques', *REA* 62 (1960) 276–361
232. Robert, L. 'Deux tétradrachmes de Mithridate V Evergète, roi du Pont', *JS* July/Sept. 1978, 151–63
233. Robinson, D. M. 'Greek and Latin inscriptions from Sinope and environs', *AJA* 9 (1905) 294–333
234. Robinson, E. S. G. 'Cistophori in the name of king Eumenes', *NC* 14 (1954) 1–8
235. Rolland, H. 'Deux nouvelles inscriptions celtiques', *CRAI* (1955) 91–9
236. Rowland, R. J. 'Numismatic propaganda under Cinna', *TAPhA* 97 (1966) 407–19
237. Seltman, C. *Greek Coins*. London, 1933. 2nd edn 1955
238. Seyrig, M. 'Le trésor monétaire de Nisibe', *RN* 17 (1955) 85–128
239. Sherk, R. K. *Rome and the Greek East to the Death of Augustus* (Documents in translation). Cambridge, 1984

240. Sherwin-White, A. N. 'The date of the *lex repetundarum* and its consequences', *JRS* 62 (1972) 83–99
241. Simonetta, B. 'Notes on the coinage of the Cappadocian kings', *NC* 1 (1961) 9–50
242. Simonetta, B. 'Remarks on some Cappadocian problems', *NC* 4 (1964) 83–92
243. Simonetta, B. *The Coins of the Cappadocian Kings*. Fribourg, 1977
244. Sokolowski, F. *Lois sacrées de l'Asie mineure*. Paris, 1955
245. Sokolowski, F. *Lois sacrées des cités grecques*. Paris, 1969
246. Sumner, G. V. 'The piracy law from Delphi and the law of the Cnidos inscription', *GRBS* 19 (1978) 211–25
247. Sydenham, E. A. *The Coinage of the Roman Republic*. London, 1952
248. Taylor, L. R. 'Freedmen and freeborn in the epitaphs of imperial Rome', *AJPh* 82 (1961) 113–32
249. Thompson, M. *The New Style Silver Coinage of Athens*. New York, 1961
250. Torelli, M. R. 'Una nuova iscrizione di Silla da Larino', *Athenaeum* 51 (1973) 336–54
251. Vetter, E. *Handbuch der italischen Dialekten*. Heidelberg, 1953
252. Vinogradov, Y. G., Molyev, E. A. and Tolstikov, V. P. 'New epigraphical sources on the history of the Mithridatic period' (Russ.), *Tskhaltubo* III, 589–600
253. Waddington, W. H., Babelon, E. and Reinach, T. *Recueil général des monnaies grecques d'Asie Mineure* I.1, *Pont et Paphlagonie*. 2nd edn Paris, 1925
254. Walbank, F. W. '*Via illa nostra militaris*: some thoughts on the Via Egnatia', *Althistorische Studien Hermann Bengtson zum 70. Geburtstag dargebracht*, ed. H. Heine *et al.* (Historia Einzelschr. 11), Wiesbaden, 1983, 131–47 (= A 124, 193–209)
255. Walker, A. S. 'Four AES coin hoards in the collection of the American School of Classical Studies at Athens', *Hesperia* 47 (1978) 40–9
256. Walker, D. R. *The Metrology of the Roman Silver Coinage. Part 1: From Augustus to Domitian* (*BAR Suppl. Ser.* 5). Oxford, 1976
257. Weinstock, S. 'Two archaic inscriptions from Latium', *JRS* 50 (1960) 112–18
258. Welles, C. B. *Royal Correspondence in the Hellenistic Period*. New Haven, 1934
259. Wiseman, T. P. '*Viae Anniae*', *PBSR* 32 (1964) 21–37
260. Wiseman, T. P. '*Viae Anniae* again', *PBSR* 37 (1969) 82–91
261. Yailenko, V. P. 'New epigraphical data on Mithridates Eupator and Pharnaces' (Russ.), *Tskhaltubo* III, 617–24
262. Zanker, P. 'Grabreliefs römischer Freigelassener', *JDAI* 90 (1975) 267–315

C. ARCHAEOLOGY

263. Barker, G., Lloyd, J. and Webley, D. 'A classical landscape in Molise', *PBSR* 46 (1978) 35–51

264. Boethius, A. *The Golden House of Nero: Some Aspects of Roman Architecture* (Jerome Lectures, ser. 5). Ann Arbor, 1960
265. Bruneau, P. and Ducat, J. *Guide de Délos*. Paris, 1965
266. Callender, M. H. *Roman Amphorae*. London, 1965
267. Carandini, A. *Settefinestre: una villa schiavistica nell'Etruria romana*. 3 vols. Modena, 1985
268. Castagnoli, F. 'Dedica arcaica lavinate a Castore e Polluce', *SMSR* 30 (1959) 109–17
269. Castagnoli, F. *et al. Lavinium* II (Ist. di topografia antica dell'Univ. di Roma). Rome, 1975
270. Celuzza, M. and Regoli, E. 'La Valle d'Oro nel territorio di Cosa', *DArch* 4 (1982) 31–62
271 Chouquer, G. *et al. Structures agraires en Italie centro-méridionale: Cadastres et paysages ruraux* (Coll. éc. fr. de Rome 100). Rome, 1987
272. Coarelli, F. 'Il complesso pompeiano di Campo Marzio e la sua decorazione scultorea', *RPAA* 44 (1971–2) 99–122
273. Coarelli, F., ed. *Studi su Praeneste* (Reprints di archeologia e di storia antica). Perugia, 1978
274. Coarelli, F. *et al. L'area sacra di Largo Argentina* (Studi e materiali dei musei e monumenti comunali di Roma x). Rome, 1981
275. Coarelli, F. *Fregellae. La storia e gli scavi*. Rome, 1981
276. Coarelli, F. 'L' "agora des italiens" a Delo: il mercato degli schiavi?', *Delo e l'Italia* 119–45
277. Coarelli, F. *Il foro romano II: periodo repubblicano e augusteo*. Rome, 1985
278. Coarelli, F. *Fregellae 2. Il santuario di Esculapio*. Rome, 1986
279. Coarelli, F. *I santuari del Lazio in età repubblicana*. Rome, 1987
280. Cotton, M. A. *The Late Republican Villa at Posto, Francolise. Report of an Excavation by the Institute of Fine Arts, New York and the British School at Rome* (British School at Rome Suppl. Pub.). London, 1979
281. Cotton, M. A. and Metraux, G. P. R. *The San Rocco Villa at Francolise*. London, 1985
282. Coulton, J. J. *The Architectural Development of the Greek Stoa*. Oxford, 1976
283. Cozza, L. 'Le tegole di marmo del Pantheon', *Città e architettura nella Roma imperiale* (*ARID* Suppl. x), ed. K. de Fine Licht, Odense, 1983, 109–18
284. Crawford, M. H., Keppie, L., Patterson, J. and Vercnocke, M. L. 'Excavations at Fregellae 1978–84. An interim report on the work of the British team', *PBSR* 52 (1984) 21–35; 53 (1985) 72–96; 54 (1986) 40–68
285. De Ruyt, C. *Macellum: marché alimentaire des Romains*. Louvain, 1985
286. Domergue, C. 'Les lingots de plomb romains du Musée Archéologique de Carthagène et du Musée Naval de Madrid', *AEA* 39 (1966) 41–72
287. Domergue, C., Laubenheimer-Leenhardt, F. and Liou, B. 'Les lingots de plomb de L. Carullius Hispallus', *RAN* 7 (1974) 119–37
288. Dyson, S. A. 'Settlement patterns in the *Ager Cosanus*: the Wesleyan University Survey 1974–6', *JFA* 5 (1978) 251–8
289. Ervin, M. 'The sanctuary of Aglauros on the south slope of the

Acropolis and its destruction in the first Mithridatic war', *Arch. Pontou* 22 (1958) 129–66

290. Fasolo, F. and Giulini, G. *Il santuario della Fortuna Primigenia a Palestrina.* 2 vols. Rome, 1875

291. Flambard, J.-M. '*Tabernae* républicaines dans la zone du Forum de Bolsena', *MEFRA* 96 (1984) 207–59

292. Frederiksen, M. 'The contribution of archaeology to the agrarian problem in the Gracchan period', *Roma e l'Italia*, 330–67

293. Gatti lo Guzzo, L. *Il deposito votivo dall'Esquilino detto di Minerva Medica* (Studi e materiali di etruscologia e antichità italiche 17). Rome, 1978

294. Gertsiger, D. S. 'A plastic vase from Panticapaeum (on the iconography of Mithridates Eupator)' (Russ.) *Tskhaltubo* III, 13–14

295. Hackens, T. and Lévy, E. 'Trésor hellénistique trouvé à Délos en 1964', *BCH* 89 (1965) 503–66

296. Heurgon, J. 'L'Ombrie à l'époque des Gracques et de Sylla', *Problemi di storia e archeologia dell'Umbria* (*Atti I Convegno di Studi Umbri, 1963*), Perugia, 1964, 113–31

297. Jacopi, I. 'Area sacra dell'Argentina: considerazioni sulla terza fase del Tempio A', *BCAR* 81 (1968/9) 115–25

298. Johnson, J. *Excavations at Minturnae* II.1.Philadelphia, 1935

299. Jones, G. D. B. 'Capena and the *Ager Capenas*', *PBSR* 30 (1962) 116–207; 31 (1963) 100–58

300. Jones, G. D. B. 'The Roman mines at Rio Tinto', *JRS* 70 (1980) 146–65

301. Jones, G. D. B. 'Il tavoliere romano: l'agricoltura romana attraverso l'aerofotografia e lo scavo', *ArchClass* 32 (1980) 81–146

302. Kahane, A., Murray Threipland, L. and Ward-Perkins, J. 'The *Ager Veientanus*, north and east of Veii', *PBSR* 36 (1968) 1–218

303. Laffi, U. 'Storia di Ascoli Piceno nell'età antica', *Asculum* I (see the following item), xviii–xxi

304. Laffi, U. and Pasquinucci, M. *Asculum*. 4 vols. Pisa, 1975–81

305. Lamboglia, N. *Per una classificazione preliminare della ceramica campana.* Bordighera (Ist. di Studi Liguri), 1952

306. La Regina, A. 'I territori sabellici e sannitici', *DArch* 4–5 (1970–1) 443–59

307. La Regina, A. *Sannio. Pentri e Frentani dal VI al I sec. a.C.* Rome, 1980

308. Liverani, P. 'L'*ager Veientanus* in età repubblicana', *PBSR* 52 (1984) 36–48

309. Manacorda, D. 'The *ager Cosanus* and the production of the amphorae of Sestius. New evidence and a reassessment', *JRS* 68 (1978) 122–31

310 Mertens, J. *Alba Fucens.* 2 vols. Rome and Brussels, 1969

311. Painter, K., (ed.) *Roman Villas in Italy. Recent Excavations and Research* (British Museum Occasional Papers 24). London, 1980

312. Palmer, R. E. A. 'The neighborhood of Sullan Bellona at the Colline Gate', *MEFRA* 87 (1975) 653–65

313. Pensabene, P. *et al. Terracotte votive dal Tevere* (Studi miscellanei 25). Rome, 1980

314. Polverini, L., Parise, F., Agostini, S. and Pasquinucci, M. *Firmum*

Picenum I. Pisa, 1987

315. Quilici, L. and Quilici Gigli, S. 'Ville dell'Agro Cosano con fronte a torrette', *RIA* 3.1 (1970) 11–64
316. Schulten, A. *Numantia*. 4 vols. Munich, 1927–31
317. Sjöqvist, E. 'Kaisareion', *ORom* 1 (1954) 86–108
318. Staccioli, R. A. 'Le tabernae a Roma attraverso la Forma Urbis', *RAL* 8.14 (1959) 56–66
319. Thompson, D. B. 'The garden of Hephaestus', *Hesperia* 6 (1937) 396–425
320. Thompson, H. A. 'Two centuries of Hellenistic pottery', *Hesperia* 3 (1934) 311–480
321. Thompson, H. A. 'Buildings on the west side of the Agora', *Hesperia* 6 (1937) 1–226
322. Todua, T. 'Forts of Mithridates VI Eupator in Colchis' (Russ.), *VDI* 1988.1 (184) 139–46
323. Ward-Perkins, B., Mills, N., Gadd, D. and Delano Smith, C. 'Luni and the *Ager Lunensis*: the rise and fall of a Roman town and its territory', *PBSR* 54 (1986) 81–146
324. Young, R. S. 'An industrial district of ancient Athens', *Hesperia* 20 (1951) 135–288

C. POLITICAL HISTORY

a. 146–70 B.C.

1. Alexander, M. C. 'Hortensius' speech in defense of Verres', *Phoenix* 30 (1976) 46–53
2. Astin, A. E. *Scipio Aemilianus*. Oxford, 1967
3. Aymard, A. 'L'organisation de Macédoine en 167', *CPh* 45 (1950) 96–107
4. Badian, E. '*Lex Acilia Repetundarum*', *AJPh* 75 (1954) 374–84
5. Badian, E. 'The date of Pompey's first triumph', *Hermes* 83 (1955) 107–18
6. Badian, E. 'Caepio and Norbanus', *Historia* 6 (1957) 318–46 (= A 2, 34–70)
7. Badian, E. 'Servilius and Pompey's first triumph', *Hermes* 89 (1961) 254–6
8. Badian, E. 'Forschungsbericht. From the Gracchi to Sulla (1940–59)', *Historia* 11 (1962) 197–245 (= Seager, *Crisis*, 3–51)
9. Badian, E. 'Waiting for Sulla', *JRS* 52 (1962) 47–61 (= A 2, 206–34)
10. Badian, E. 'The *lex Thoria*: a reconsideration', *Studi in onore di Biondo Biondi* I, Milan, 1963, 187–96 (= A 2, 235–41)
11. Badian, E. 'Sulla's augurate', *Arethusa* 1 (1968) 26–46
12. Badian, E. '*Quaestiones Variae*', *Historia* 18 (1969) 447–91
13. Badian, E. *Lucius Sulla the Deadly Reformer* (7th Todd Memorial Lecture). Sydney, 1970
14. Badian, E. 'Additional notes on Roman magistrates', *Athenaeum* 48 (1970) 3–14
15. Badian, E. 'Roman politics and the Italians (133–91 B.C.)', *Roma e l'Italia*, 373–409

16. Badian, E. 'Tiberius Gracchus and the beginning of the Roman Revolution', *ANRW* I.1 (1972) 668–731
17. Badian, E. 'The death of Saturninus. Studies in chronology and prosopography', *Chiron* 14 (1984) 101–47
18. Balsdon, J. P. V. D. 'Sulla Felix', *JRS* 41 (1951) 1–10
19. Barnes, T. D. 'A Marian colony', *CR* 21 (1971) 332
20. Bates, R. L. 'Rex in senatu', *PAPhS* 130.3 (1986) 272–3
21. Bauman, R. A. 'The *hostis* declarations of 88 and 87 B.C.', *Athenaeum* 51 (1973) 270–93
22. Bell, M. J. V. 'Tactical reform in the Roman Republican army', *Historia* 14 (1965) 404–22
23. Bellen, H. 'Sullas Brief an den Interrex L. Valerius Flaccus', *Historia* 24 (1975) 555–69
24. Bennett, H. *Cinna and his Times*. Menasha, 1923
25. Bernstein, A. H. *Tiberius Sempronius Gracchus*. Ithaca, 1978
26. Berve, H. 'Sertorius', *Hermes* 64 (1929) 199–227
27. Boren, H. C. 'The urban side of the Gracchan economic crisis', *AHR* 63 (1957–8) 890–902 (= Seager, *Crisis*, 54–66)
28. Bruhns, H. 'Ein politischer Kompromiss im Jahre 70: die *lex Aurelia iudiciaria*', *Chiron* 10 (1976) 263–72
29. Brunt, P. A. 'The *equites* in the late Republic', *Proc. 2nd Int. Conf. of Ec. Hist.*, 1962, 117–49 (= Seager, *Crisis*, 83–115), revd. in A 19, 144–93
30. Brunt, P. A. 'The army and the land in the Roman Revolution', *JRS* 52 (1962) 64–86, revd. in A 19, 240–75
31. Brunt, P. A. 'Italian aims at the time of the Social War', *JRS* 55 (1965) 90–109, revd. in A 19, 93–143
32. Brunt, P. A. '*Amicitia* in the late Roman Republic', *PCPhS* 2 (1965) 1–20 (= Seager, *Crisis*, 199–218), revd. in A 19, 351–81
33. Brunt, P. A. 'Patronage and politics in the "Verrines"', *Chiron* 10 (1980) 273–89
34. Brunt, P. A. '*Nobilitas* and *Novitas*', *JRS* 72 (1982) 1–17
35. Bulst, C. M. 'Cinnanum tempus', *Historia* 13 (1964) 307–37
36. Carcopino, J. *Autour des Gracques*. Paris, 1928
37. Carcopino, J. *Sylla ou la monarchie manquée*. Paris, 1947
38. Cardinali, G. *Studi Graccani*. Rome, 1912
39. Carney, T. F. 'The flight and exile of Marius', *G&R* 8 (1961) 98–121
40. Carney, T. F. 'The death of Sulla', *AClass* 4 (1961) 64–79
41. Carney, T. F. *A Biography of Caius Marius* (*Proceedings of the African Classical Associations* Suppl. 1). 1962
42. Cary, M. 'Sulla and Cisalpine Gaul', *CR* 34 (1920) 103–4
43. Coarelli, F. 'Le *tyrannoctone* du Capitole et la mort de Tiberius Gracchus', *MEFRA* 81 (1969) 137–60
44. Corbellini, G. 'La presunta guerra tra Mario e Cinna e l'episodio dei Bardiei', *Aevum* 50 (1976) 154–6
45. Crawford, M. H. 'The edict of M. Marius Gratidianus', *PCPhS* 194 (1968) 1–4
46. von Domaszewski, A. *Bellum Marsicum* (*SAWW* 201.1). Vienna, 1924

47. Earl, D. C. *Tiberius Gracchus – A Study in Politics* (Coll. Latomus 66). Brussels, 1963
48. Ericsson, H. 'Sulla felix', *Eranos* 41 (1943) 77–89
49. Ferrary, J.-L. 'Recherches sur la législation de Saturninus et de Glaucia', *MEFRA* 89 (1977) 619–60; 91 (1979) 85–134
50. Ferrary, J.-L. 'Les origines de la loi de majesté à Rome', *CRAI* 1983, 556–72
51. Fraccaro, P. *Studi sull'età dei Gracchi*. Città di Castello, 1914
52. Frank, T. 'On some financial legislation of the Sullan period', *AJPh* 54 (1933) 54–8
53. Frier, B. W. 'Sulla's propaganda: the collapse of the Cinnan Republic', *AJPh* 92 (1971) 585–604
54. Gabba, E. 'Politica e cultura in Roma agli inizi del I secolo a.C.', *Athenaeum* 31 (1953) 259–72
55. Gabba, E. *Esercito e società nella tarda Repubblica romana*. Florence, 1973. Transl. by P. J. Cuff as *Republican Rome: The Army and the Allies*, Oxford, 1976
56. Gabba, E. 'Mario e Silla', *ANRW* I.1 (1972) 764–805
57. Gabba, E. 'Motivazioni economiche nell'opposizione alla legge agraria di Tib. Sempronio Gracco', *Polis and Imperium, Studies in honour of Edward Togo Salmon*, ed. J. A. S. Evans, Toronto, 1974, 129–38
58. Gabba, E. 'La rifondazione di Salapia', *Athenaeum* 61 (1983) 514–16
59. Gabba, E. 'Un episodio oscuro della storia di Mediolanum', *RIL* 118 (1984) 99–103
60. Garnsey, P. and Rathbone, D. 'The background to the grain law of Gaius Gracchus', *JRS* 75 (1985) 20–5
61. Garton, C. 'Sulla and the theatre', *Phoenix* 18 (1964) 137–50
62. Gelzer, M. 'Cn. Pompeius Strabo und der Aufstieg seines Sohnes Magnus', *Abh. Preuss. Akad. Wiss.* 14, 1941 (= A 41, II, 106–38)
63. Gelzer, M. 'Hat Sertorius in seinem Vertrag mit Mithradates die Provinz Asia abgetreten?', *Phil. Wochenschr.* 52 (1932) 185–92 (= A 41, II, 139–45)
64. Gillis, D. 'Quintus Sertorius', *RIL* 103 (1969) 711–27
65. Göhler, J. *Rom und Italien. Die römische Bundesgenossenpolitik von den Anfängen bis zum Bundesgenossenkrieg* (Breslauer Historische Forschungen 13). Breslau, 1939, repr. Aalen, 1974
66. Gruen, E. S. 'The lex Varia', *JRS* 55 (1965) 59–73
67. Gruen, E. S. 'The political allegiance of P. Mucius Scaevola', *Athenaeum* 43 (1965) 321–32
68. Gruen, E. S. *Roman Politics and the Criminal Courts, 149–78 B.C.* Cambridge, MA, 1968
69. Gruen, E. S. 'Pompey, Metellus Pius, and the trials of 70–69 B.C.', *AJPh* 92 (1971) 1–16
70. Guarino, A. *La coerenza di Publio Mucio*. Naples, 1981
71. Hackl, U. *Senat und Magistratur in Rom von der Mitte des 2. Jahrhunderts v. Chr. bis zur Diktatur Sullas*. Kallmünz, 1982
72. Hall, U. 'Notes on M. Fulvius Flaccus', *Athenaeum* 55 (1977) 280–8
73. Hantos, T. *Res publica constituta: die Verfassung des Diktators Sulla* (Hermes

Einzelschr. 50). Stuttgart, 1988

74. Haug, I. 'Der römische Bundesgenossenkrieg 91–88 v. Chr. bei Titus Livius', *WJA* 2 (1947) 100–39
75. Hayne, L. 'M. Lepidus (cos. 78): a re-appraisal', *Historia* 21 (1972) 661–8
76. Henderson, M. I. 'The establishment of the equester ordo', *JRS* 53 (1963) 61–72 (= Seager, *Crisis* 69–80)
77. Heurgon, J. 'The date of Vegoia's prophecy', *JRS* 49 (1959) 41–5
78. Hill, H. 'Sulla's new senators in 81 B.C.', *CQ* 26 (1932) 170–7
79. Katz, B. R. 'The first fruits of Sulla's march', *AClass* 44 (1975) 100–25
80. Katz, B. R. 'The siege of Rome in 87 B.C.', *CP* 71 (1976) 328–36
81. Katz, B. R. 'Studies on the period of Cinna and Sulla', *AClass* 45 (1976) 497–549
82. Katz, B. R. 'Caesar Strabo's struggle for the consulship – and more', *RhM* 120 (1977) 45–63
83. Katz, B. R. 'The selection of L. Cornelius Merula', *RhM* 122 (1979) 162–6
84. Keaveney, A. 'Pompeius Strabo's second consulship', *CQ* 28 (1978) 240–1
85. Keaveney, A. 'Sulla, Sulpicius and Caesar Strabo', *Latomus* 38 (1979) 451–60
86. Keaveney, A. 'Deux dates contestées de la carrière de Sylla', *LEC* 48 (1980) 149–59
87. Keaveney, A. *Sulla, the last Republican*. London, 1982
88. Keaveney, A. 'Young Pompey: 106–79 B.C.', *AClass* 51 (1982) 111–39
89. Keaveney, A. 'Sulla and Italy', *CS* 19 (1982) 499–544
90. Keaveney, A. 'Sulla augur: coins and curiate law', *AJAH* 7 (1982) 150–71
91. Keaveney, A. 'What happened in 88?', *Eirene* 20 (1983) 53–86
92. Keaveney, A. 'Studies in the *dominatio Sullae*', *Klio* 65 (1983) 185–208
93. Keaveney, A. 'Who were the Sullani?', *Klio* 66 (1984) 114–50
94. Keaveney, A. *Rome and the Unification of Italy*. London, 1987
95. Keaveney, A. and Madden, J. A. 'Phthiriasis and its victims', *SO* 57 (1982) 87–99
96. Laffi, U. 'Il mito di Silla', *Athenaeum* 45 (1967) 177–213; 255–77
97. Levick, B. M. 'Sulla's march on Rome in 88 B.C.', *Historia* 31 (1982) 503–8
98. Lewis, R. G. 'A problem in the siege of Praeneste', *PBSR* 39 (1971) 32–9
99. Lintott, A. W. 'The tribunate of P. Sulpicius Rufus', *CQ* 21 (1971) 442–53
100. Lintott, A. W. 'The offices of C. Flavius Fimbria in 86–5 B.C.', *Historia* 20 (1971) 696–701
101. Luce, T. J. 'Marius and the Mithridatic command', *Historia* 19 (1970) 161–94
102. Luraschi, G. 'Sulle "leges de civitate" (Iulia, Calpurnia, Plautia Papiria)', *SDHI* 44 (1978) 321–70
103. McDermott, W. C. 'Lex de tribunicia potestate (70 B.C.)', *CPh* 72 (1977) 49–52

104. Marino, R. E. 'Aspetti della politica interna di Silla', *AAPal* 33 (1973–4) 361–529
105. Maróti, E. 'On the problems of M. Antonius Creticus' *imperium infinitum*', *AAntHung* 19 (1971) 252–72
106. Marshall, B. A. 'Crassus' ovation in 71 B.C.', *Historia* 21 (1972) 669–73
107. Marshall, B. A. 'The *lex Plotia agraria*', *Antichthon* 6 (1972) 43–52
108. Marshall, B. A. 'Crassus and the command against Spartacus', *Athenaeum* 51 (1973) 109–21
109. Marshall, B. A. 'Q. Cicero, Hortensius and the lex Aurelia', *RhM* 118 (1975) 136–52
110. Marshall, B. A. 'Catilina and the execution of M. Marius Gratidianus', *CQ* 79 (1985) 124–33
111. Mattingly, H. B. 'The *consilium* of Cn. Pompeius Strabo', *Athenaeum* 53 (1975) 262–6
112. Meyer, H. D. 'Die Organisation der Italiker im Bundesgenossenkrieg', *Historia* 7 (1958) 74–9
113. Millar, F. G. B. 'Politics, persuasion and the people before the Social War (150–90 B.C.)', *JRS* 76 (1986) 1–11
114. Mitchell, T. N. 'The *volte-face* of P. Sulpicius Rufus in 88 B.C.', *CPh* 70 (1975) 197–204
115. Nicolet, C. 'L'inspiration de Tiberius Gracchus', *REA* 67 (1965) 142–58
116. Nicolet, C., (ed.), *Demokratia et Aristokratia. A propos de Caius Gracchus: mots grecs et réalités romaines.* Paris, 1983
117. Passerini, A. 'Caio Mario come uomo politico', *Athenaeum* 12 (1934) 10–44; 109–143; 257–97; 348–80 (= *Studi su Caio Mario*, Milan, 1971)
118. Porrà, F. 'La legge Varia del 90 e quella Sulpicia dell'88 a.C.: il problema degli esuli', *AFLC* 36 (1973) 13–28
119. Pozzi, E. 'Studi sulla guerra civile Sillana', *Atti r. accademia delle scienze di Torino* 49 (1913/14) 641–79
120. Pritchard, R. T. 'Verres and the Sicilian farmers', *Historia* 20 (1971) 224–38
121. Rich, J. W. 'The supposed Roman manpower shortage of the later second century B.C.', *Historia* 32 (1983) 287–331
122. Richard, J.-C. '*Qualis pater, talis filius*', *RPh* 46 (1972) 43–55
123. Richardson, J. S. 'The ownership of Roman land: Tiberius Gracchus and the Italians', *JRS* 70 (1980) 1–11
124. Rose, H. J. 'The "Oath of Philippus" and the Di Indigetes', *HThR* 30 (1937) 165–81
125. Rossi, R. F. 'Sulla lotta politica in Roma dopo la morte di Silla', *PP* 20 (1965) 133–52
126. Salmon, E. T. 'Notes on the Social War', *TAPhA* 87 (1958) 159–84
127. Salmon, E. T. 'The causes of the Social War', *Phoenix* 16 (1962) 112–13
128. Salmon, E. T. 'Sulla redux', *Athenaeum* 42 (1964) 60–79
129. de Sanctis, G. *La guerra sociale* (*Opera inedita a cura di L. Polverini*). Florence, 1976
130. Scardigli, B. 'Sertorio: problemi cronologici', *Athenaeum* 49 (1971) 229–70

131. Schneider, H. 'Die politische Rolle der plebs urbana während der Tribunate des L. Appuleius Saturninus', *AncSoc* 13/14 (1982/3) 193–221
131A. Schulten, A. *Sertorius*. Leipzig, 1926
132. Sherwin-White, A. N. 'Violence in Roman politics', *JRS* 46 (1956) 1–9 (= Seager, *Crisis*, 151–9)
133. Sherwin-White, A. N. 'The *lex repetundarum* and the political ideas of Gaius Gracchus', *JRS* 72 (1982) 18–31
134. Smith, R. E. 'The *lex Plotia agraria* and Pompey's Spanish veterans', *CQ* 51 (1957) 82–5
135. Smith, R. E. 'Pompey's conduct in 80 and 77 B.C.', *Phoenix* 14 (1960) 1–13
136. Stockton, D. L. 'The first consulship of Pompey', *Historia* 22 (1973) 205–18
137. Stockton, D. L. *The Gracchi*. Oxford, 1979
138. Sumner, G. V. 'The Pompeii in their families', *AJAH* 2 (1977) 8–25
139. Sumner, G. V. 'Sulla's career in the 90s', *Athenaeum* 56 (1978) 395–6
140. Taylor, L. R. 'Caesar's early career', *CPh* 36 (1941) 113–32
141. Taylor, L. R. 'Forerunners of the Gracchi', *JRS* 52 (1962) 19–27
142. Tibiletti, G. 'Il possesso dell'*ager publicus* e le norme *de modo agrorum* sino ai Gracchi', *Athenaeum* 26 (1948) 173–236; 27 (1949) 3–41
143. Tibiletti, G. 'Ricerche di storia agraria romana', *Athenaeum* 28 (1950) 183–266
144. Treves, P. 'Sertorio', *Athenaeum* 10 (1932) 127–46
145. Tuplin, C. 'Coelius or Cloelius?', *Chiron* 9 (1979) 137–45
146. Turcan, R. 'Encore la prophétie de Végoia', *Mél. Heurgon* II, 1009–19
147. Twyman, B. L. 'The Metelli, Pompeius and prosopography', *ANRW* I.1 (1972) 816–74
148. Twyman, B. L. 'The date of Pompeius Magnus' first triumph', *Studies in Latin Literature and Roman History* I, ed. C. Deroux (Coll. Latomus 164), Brussels, 1979, 175–208
149. Ward, A. M. 'Cicero and Pompey in 75 and 70 B.C.', *Latomus* 29 (1970) 58–71
150. Ward, A. M. 'The early relationships between Cicero and Pompey until 80 B.C.', *Phoenix* 24 (1970) 119–29
151. Ward, A. M. 'Caesar and the pirates II', *AJAH* 2 (1977) 26–36

b. 70–43 B.C.

152. Adcock, F. E. 'Caesar's dictatorship', *CAH* IX (1932) 691–740
153. Alföldi, A. *Studien über Caesars Monarchie* (Bull. Soc. des Lettres de Lund 1952/3 I). Lund, 1953
154. Alföldi, A. 'Caesars Tragödie im Spiegel der Münzprägung des Jahres 44 v. Chr.', *Schweizer Münzblätter* 4 (1953) 1–11
155. Alföldi, A. 'Der Machtverheissende Traum des Sulla', *JBM* 41/2 (1961/2) 275–88 (= C 158, 3–16)
156. Alföldi, A. 'Der Mettius-Denar mit Caesar dict. quart.', *Schweizer Münzblätter* 13/14 (1962/3) 29–33 (= C 158, 17–33)

157. Alföldi, A. *Oktavians Aufstieg zur Macht* (Antiquitas Reihe *1*). Bonn, 1976
158. Alföldi, A. *Caesariana. Gesammelte Aufsätze zur Geschichte Caesars und seiner Zeit*, ed. E. Alföldi–Rosenbaum. Bonn, 1984
159. Alföldi, A. *Caesar in 44 v. Chr. 1: Studien zu Caesars Monarchie und ihren Wurzeln*, ed. H. Wolff. Bonn, 1985
160. Allen, W., jr. 'Cicero's house and *libertas*', *TAPhA* 75 (1944) 1–9
161. Allen, W., jr., 'Cicero's provincial governorship in 63 B.C.', *TAPhA* 83 (1952) 233–41
162. Badian, E. 'M. Porcius Cato and the annexation and early administration of Cyprus', *JRS* 55 (1965) 110–21
163. Badian, E. 'Notes on *provincia Gallia* in the late Republic', *Mélanges d'archéologie et d'histoire offerts à André Piganiol*, ed. R. Chevallier, Paris, 1966, 901–18
164. Badian, E. 'Marius' villas: the evidence of the slave and the knave', *JRS* 63 (1973) 121–32
165. Badian, E. 'The attempt to try Caesar', *Polis and Imperium: Studies in honour of Edward Togo Salmon*, ed. J. A. S. Evans, Toronto, 1974, 145–66
166. Badian, E. 'The case of the cowardly tribune', *AHB* 3 (1989) 78–84
167. Balsdon, J. P. V. D. 'Consular provinces under the late Republic', *JRS* 29 (1939) 57–73
168. Balsdon, J. P. V. D. 'Roman history, 65–50 B.C.: five problems', *JRS* 52 (1962) 134–41
169. Balsdon, J. P. V. D. *Julius Caesar and Rome*. London, 1967
170. Bengtson, H. *Zur Geschichte des Brutus*. Munich, 1970
171. Bengtson, H. 'Die letzten Monate der römischen Senatsherrschaft', *ANRW* I.1 (1972) 967–81 (= *Kleine Schriften zur alten Geschichte*, Munich, 1974, 532–48)
172. Bengtson, H. 'Untersuchungen zum mutinensischen Krieg', *Kleine Schriften zur alten Geschichte*, Munich, 1974, 479–531
173. Benner, H. *Die Politik des P. Clodius Pulcher* (Historia Einzelschr. 50). Stuttgart, 1987
174. van Berchem, D. 'La fuite de Decimus Brutus', *Mélanges d'arch., d'épigraphie et d'hist. offerts à J. Carcopino*, Paris, 1966, 941–53
175. Bitto, I. 'La concessione del patronato nella politica di Cesare', *Epigraphica* 31 (1970) 79–83
176. Boegli, H. *Studien zu den Koloniegründungen Caesars*. Diss. Basle, 1966
177. Botermann, H. *Die Soldaten und die römische Politik in der Zeit von Caesars Tod bis zur Begründung des zweiten Triumvirats* (Zetemata 46). Munich, 1968
178. Braund, D. C. 'Gabinius, Caesar, and the *publicani* of Judaea', *Klio* 65 (1983) 241–4
179. Broughton, T. R. S. 'More notes on Roman magistrates', *TAPhA* 79 (1948) 63–78
180. Bruhns, H. *Cäsar und die römische Oberschicht, 49–44 v. Chr.* (Hypomnemata 53). Göttingen, 1978
181. Burckhardt, L. A. *Politische Strategien der Optimaten in der späten römischen Republik* (Historia Einzelschr. 57). Stuttgart, 1988
182. Burns, A. 'Pompey's strategy and Domitius' stand at Corfinium',

Historia 15 (1966) 74–95

183. Carson, R. A. G. 'Caesar and the monarchy', *G&R* 4 (1957) 46–53.

183A. *Cesare nel bimillenario della morte. Edizioni Radio Italiana*, 1956.

184. Coarelli, F. 'Iside Capitolina, Clodio e i mercanti di schiavi', *Alessandria e il mondo ellenistico-romano. Studi in onore di Achille Adriani*, ed. N. Bonacasa and A. Di Vita (Studi e materiali Ist. arch. Univ. Palermo 4–6) III, Rome, 1984, 461–75

185. Cobban, J. *Senate and Provinces 78–49* B.C. Cambridge, 1935

186. Collins, J. H. 'Caesar and the corruption of power', *Historia* 4 (1955) 445–65

187. Crawford, M. H. 'The lex Iulia agraria', *Athenaeum* 67 (1989) 179–90

188. Dahlmann, H. 'Clementia Caesaris', *Neue Jahrbücher für Wissenschaft und Jugendbildung* 10 (1934) 17–26 (= Wege der Forschung 43, Darmstadt, 1967, 32–47)

189. De Visscher, F. 'Jules César patron d'Alba Fucens', *AC* 33 (1964) 98–107

190. Dobesch, G. *Caesars Apotheose zu Lebzeiten und sein Ringen um den Königstitel*. Vienna, 1966

191. Eckhardt, K. 'Die armenischen Feldzüge des Lucullus', *Klio* 9 (1909) 400–12; 10 (1910) 73–115 and 192–231

192. Ehrenberg, V. 'Caesar's final aims', *HSPh* 68 (1964) 149–61

193. Flambard, J.-M. 'Clodius, les collèges, la plèbe et les esclaves. Recherches sur la politique populaire au milieu du Ier siècle', *MEFRA* 89 (1977) 115–56

194. Frisch, H. *Cicero's Fight for the Republic*. Copenhagen, 1946

195. von Fritz, K. 'The mission of L. Caesar and L. Roscius in January 49 B.C.', *TAPhA* 72 (1941) 125–42

196. von Fritz, K. 'Pompey's policy before and after the outbreak of the Civil War of 49 B.C.', *TAPhA* 73 (1942) 145–80

197. Geiger, J. 'M. Favonius: three notes', *RSA* 4 (1974) 161–70

198. Gelzer, M. *Caesar der Politiker und Staatsmann*. Stuttgart and Berlin, 1921. 6th edn, Wiesbaden, 1960, transl. by P. Needham, Oxford, 1969

199. Gelzer, M. 'Das erste Konsulat des Pompeius und die Übertragung der grossen Imperien', *Abh. Preuss. Akad. Wiss.* 1943, 1 (= A 41 II, 146–89)

200. Gelzer, M. *Pompeius*. Munich, 1949. 2nd edn, 1959

201. Gesche, H. 'Hat Caesar den Oktavian zum *magister equitum* designiert?', *Historia* 22 (1973) 468–78

202. Gesche, H. *Caesar*. Darmstadt, 1976

203. Girardet, K. 'Die Lex Iulia de provinciis: Vorgeschichte, Inhalt, Wirkungen', *RhM* 130 (1987) 291–330

204. Grant, M. *From Imperium to Auctoritas*. Cambridge, 1946

205. *Greece and Rome* IV no.1, March 1957. *Julius Caesar 44 B.C.–A.D. 1957*, Bimillenary Number

206. Greenhalgh, P. *Pompey, the Roman Alexander*. London, 1980

207. Griffin, M. 'The tribune C. Cornelius', *JRS* 63 (1973) 196–213

208. Gruen, E. S. 'The consular elections for 53 B.C.', *Hommages à Marcel Renard*, ed. J. Bibauw (Coll. Latomus 102) II, Brussels, 1969, 311–21

209. Gruen, E. S. *The Last Generation of the Roman Republic*. Berkeley and Los Angeles, 1974
210. Hardy, E. G. *Some Problems in Roman History. Ten Essays bearing on the Administrative and Legislative Work of Julius Caesar*. Oxford, 1924
211. Hardy, E. G. *The Catilinarian Conspiracy in its Context: a Re-Study of the Evidence*. Oxford, 1924
212. Henderson, M. I., 'Julius Caesar and Latium in Spain', *JRS* 32 (1942) 1–13
213. Hinrichs, F. T. 'Das legale Landversprechen im Bellum Civile', *Historia* 18 (1969) 521–44
214. Horsfall, N. 'The Ides of March: some new problems', *G&R* 21 (1974) 191–9
215. Kraft, K. 'Der goldene Kranz Caesars und der Kampf um die Entlarvung des "Tyrannen"', *JNG* 3/4 (1952/3) 7–98
216. Lacey, W. K. 'The tribunate of Curio', *Historia* 10 (1961) 318–29
217. Lacey, W. K. *Cicero and the End of the Roman Republic*. London, Sydney, Auckland and Toronto, 1978
218. Leach, J. *Pompey the Great*. London, 1978
219. Linderski, J. 'Cicero and Sallust on Vargunteius', *Historia* 12 (1963) 511–12
220. Linderski, J. 'The aedileship of Favonius, Curio the Younger and Cicero's election to the augurate', *HSPh* 76 (1972) 181–200
221. Linderski, J. 'Rome, Aphrodisias and the *Res Gestae*: the *Genera Militiae* and the status of Octavian', *JRS* 74 (1984) 74–80
222. Lintott, A. W. 'P. Clodius Pulcher – *Felix Catilina*?', *G&R* 14 (1967) 157–69
223. Lintott, A. W. 'Cicero and Milo', *JRS* 64 (1974) 62–78
224. Lintott, A. W. 'Cicero on praetors who failed to abide by their edicts', *CQ* 27 (1977) 184–6
225. McDonald, W. 'Clodius and the Lex Aelia Fufia', *JRS* 19 (1929) 164–79
226. Marshall, B. A. *Crassus*. Amsterdam, 1976
227. Meyer, E. *Caesars Monarchie und das Prinzipat des Pompeius. Innere Geschichte Roms von 66 bis 44 v. Chr.* 1918. 3rd edn, Stuttgart and Berlin, 1922
228. Mitchell, T. N. *Cicero: The Ascending Years*. London, 1979
229. Mommsen, Th. *Die Rechtsfrage zwischen Caesar und dem Senat*. Breslau, 1857 (=A 78, 92–145)
230. Moreau, P. *Clodiana religio: un procès politique en 61 av. J.-C.* Paris, 1982
231. Münzer, F. 'Aus dem Verwandtenkreis Caesars und Oktavians', *Hermes* 71 (1936) 222–30
232. Nicolet, C. 'Plèbe et tribus: les statues de Lucius Antonius et le testament d'Auguste', *MEFRA* 97 (1985) 799–832
233. van Ooteghem, J. *Pompée le grand, bâtisseur d'empire*. Brussels, 1954
234. Oppermann, H. *Caesar, Wegbereiter Europas*. Göttingen, 1958. 2nd edn, 1963
235. Pelling, C. G. R. 'Plutarch and Catiline', *Hermes* 113 (1985) 311–29
236. Phillips, E. J. 'Cicero and the prosecution of C. Manilius', *Latomus* 29

(1970) 595–607

237. Phillips, E. J. 'The prosecution of C. Rabirius in 63 B.C.', *Klio* 56 (1974) 87–101

238. Raaflaub, K. *Dignitatis Contentio. Studien zur Motivation und politischem Taktik im Bürgerkrieg zwischen Caesar und Pompeius* (Vestigia 20). Munich, 1974

239. Ramsey, J. T. 'The prosecution of C. Manilius in 66 B.C. and Cicero's *pro Manilio*', *Phoenix* 34 (1980) 323–36

240. Raubitschek, A. E. 'Brutus in Athens', *Phoenix* 11 (1957) 1–11

241. Raubitschek, A. E. 'The Brutus statue in Athens', *Atti III cong. internat. epigr. gr. e lat.*, Rome, 1959, 15–21

242. Rawson, B. *The Politics of Friendship: Pompey and Cicero*. Sydney, 1978

243. Rawson, E. D. 'The eastern clientelae of Clodius and the Claudii', *Historia* 22 (1973) 219–39 (= A 94A, 102–24)

244. Rawson, E. D. *Cicero. A Portrait*. London, 1975

245. Rawson, E. D. 'Caesar's heritage: Hellenistic kings and their Roman equals', *JRS* 65 (1975) 148–59 (= A 94A, 169–88)

246. Rawson, E. D. 'Caesar, Etruria and the Disciplina Etrusca', *JRS* 68 (1978) 132–52 (= A 94A, 289–323)

247. Rawson, E. D. 'Crassorum funera', *Latomus* 41 (1982) 540–9 (= A 94A, 416–26)

248. Rawson, E. D. 'Cicero and the Areopagus', *Athenaeum* 63 (1985) 44–67 (= A 94A, 444–67)

249. Rawson, E. D. 'Cassius and Brutus: the memory of the Liberators', *Past Perspectives: Studies in Greek and Roman Historical Writing*, ed. I. Moxon *et al.*, Cambridge, 1986, 101–19 (= A 94A, 488–507)

250. Rawson, E. D. '*Discrimina ordinum*: the *Lex Iulia Theatralis*', *PBSR* 55 (1987) 83–114 (= A 94A, 508–45)

251. Rice Holmes, T. *The Roman Republic*. 2 vols. Oxford, 1923

252. Rice Holmes, T. *The Architect of the Roman Empire*. 2 vols. Oxford, 1928–31

253. Sandford, E. M. 'The career of Aulus Gabinius', *TAPhA* 70 (1939) 64–92

254. Scardigli, B. 'Il falso Mario', *SIFC* 52 (1980) 207–21

255. Schmitthenner, W. 'Oktavian und das Testament Cäsars' (Zetemata 4). Munich, 1952, revd. 1973

256. Seager, R. 'The first Catilinarian conspiracy', *Historia* 13 (1964) 338–47

257. Seager, R. 'The tribunate of Cornelius: some ramifications', *Hommages à Marcel Renard*, ed. J. Bibauw (Coll. Latomus 102) II, Brussels, 1969, 680–6

258. Seager, R. *Pompey, A Political Biography*. Oxford, 1979

259. Shackleton Bailey, D. R. '*Expectatio Corfiniensis*', *JRS* 46 (1956) 57–64

260. Shackleton Bailey, D. R. 'The credentials of L. Caesar and L. Roscius', *JRS* 50 (1960) 80–3

261. Shackleton Bailey, D. R. 'Points concerning Caesar's legislation in 59 B.C.', in B 108, I, 406–8

262. Shackleton Bailey, D. R. *Cicero*. London, 1971

263. Smith, R. E. *Cicero the Statesman.* Cambridge, 1966

264. Sordi, M. 'Ottaviano patrono di Taranto nel 43 a.C.', *Epigraphica* 41 (1969) 79–83

265. Sternkopf, W. '*Lex Antonia agraria*', *Hermes* 47 (1912) 146–51

266. Sternkopf, W. 'Die Verteilung der römischen Provinzen vor dem mutinensischen Krieg', *Hermes* 47 (1912) 321–401

267. Stockton, D. *Cicero. A Political Biography.* Oxford, 1971

268. Sumner, G. V. 'Manius or Mamercus?', *JRS* 54 (1964) 41–8

269. Sumner, G. V. 'Cicero, Pompeius and Rullus', *TAPhA* 97 (1966) 569–82

270. Sumner, G. V. 'A note on Julius Caesar's great-grandfather', *CPh* 71 (1976) 341–4

271. Syme, R. 'Who was Decidius Saxa?', *JRS* 27 (1937) 127–37 (=A 119 I, 31–41).

272. Syme, R. 'Caesar, the Senate and Italy', *PBSR* 14 (1938) 1–32 (=A 119, I, 88–119)

273. Syme, R. 'The allegiance of Labienus', *JRS* 28 (1938) 113–28 (=A 119, I, 62–75)

274. Syme, R. 'Imperator Caesar: a study in nomenclature', *Historia* 7 (1958) 172–88 (=A 119, I, 360–77)

275. Syme, R. 'Ten tribunes', *JRS* 53 (1963) 55–60 (=A 119, II, 557–65)

276. Syme, R. 'Senators, tribes and towns', *Historia* 13 (1964) 105–25 (=A 119, II, 582–604)

277. Taylor, L. R. 'On the chronology of Caesar's first consulship', *AJPh* 72 (1951) 254–68

278. Treu, M. 'Zur Clementia Caesaris', *MH* 5 (1948) 197–217

279. Vanderbroeck, P. J. J. *Popular Leadership and Collective Behavior in the Late Roman Republic.* Amsterdam, 1987

280. Ward, A. M. *Marcus Crassus and the Late Roman Republic.* Columbia, MO, 1977

281. Weippert, O. *Alexander-Imitatio und römische Politik in republikanischer Zeit* (Diss. Würzburg, 1970). Augsburg, 1972

282. Wirszubski, C. 'Cicero's *cum dignitate otium*: a reconsideration', *JRS* 44 (1954) 1–13 (=Seager, *Crisis*, 183–95)

283. Wiseman, T. P. 'The ambitions of Quintus Cicero', *JRS* 56 (1966) 108–15, repr. in A 133, 34–41

284. Wiseman, T. P. 'Two friends of Clodius in Cicero's letters', *CQ* 18 (1968) 297–302

285. Wiseman, T. P. *Cinna the Poet and other Roman Essays.* Leicester, 1974

286. Wiseman, T. P. *Catullus and his World: a Reappraisal.* Cambridge, 1985

287. Wistrand, E. 'The date of Curio's African campaign', *Eranos* 61 (1963) 38–44

288. Wistrand, E. *The Policy of Brutus the Tyrannicide.* Gothenburg, 1981

289. Wistrand, M. *Cicero Imperator. Studies in Cicero's Correspondence 51–47 B.C.* Gothenburg, 1979

290. Yavetz, Z. *Caesar in der öffentlichen Meinung.* Düsseldorf, 1979, transl. as *Julius Caesar and his Public Image*, London, 1983

D. THE EAST

a. MITHRIDATICA

1. Anderson, J. G. C. 'Pompey's campaign against Mithridates', *JRS* 12 (1922) 99–105
2. Badian, E. 'Q. Mucius Scaevola and the province of Asia', *Athenaeum* 34 (1956) 104–23
3. Badian, E. 'Sulla's Cilician command', *Athenaeum* 37 (1959) 279–303 (= A 2, 157–78)
4. Badian, E. 'Rome, Athens and Mithridates', *Assimilation et résistance à la culture gréco-romaine dans le monde ancien. Travaux du VI. congrès internat. de la FIEC, Madrid, Sept. 1974*, ed. D. M. Pippidi, Bucharest, 1976, 501–22 (= *AJAH* 1 (1976) 105–28)
5. Blavatskaya, T. V. *Zapadnopontiiskiye Goroda v VII–I Vyekakh do nashei Ery* (*West Pontic Cities in the Seventh to First Centuries* B.C.). Moscow, 1952
6. Brashinsky, J. B. 'The economic links of Sinope in the fourth to second centuries B.C.' (Russ.), *Antichny Gorod*, Moscow, 1963, 132–44
7. Castagna, M. *Mitridate VI Eupatore re del Ponto*. Portici, 1938
8. Chapot, V. *La province romaine proconsulaire d'Asie depuis ses origines jusqu'à la fin du Haut-Empire*. Paris, 1904
9. Danov, C. M. *Zapadnyat Bryag na Chernomorye v Drevnostata* (*The West Coast of the Black Sea in Antiquity*). Sofia, 1947
10. Deininger, J. *Der politische Widerstand gegen Rom in Griechenland 217–86 v. Chr.* Berlin and New York, 1971
11. Desideri, P. 'Posidonio e la guerra mitridatica', *Athenaeum* 51 (1973) 3–29 and 238–69
12. Diehl, E. 'Pharnakes', *RE* 19 (1938) 1849–53
13. Dow, S. 'A leader of the anti-Roman party in Athens in 88 B.C.', *CPh* 37 (1947) 311–14
14. Dundua, G. F. and Lordkipanidze, G. A. 'Georgia and Mithridates VI' (Russ.), *Tskhaltubo* III, 601–8
15. Fletcher, W. G. 'The Pontic cities of Pompey the Great', *TAPhA* 70 (1939) 17–29
16. Geyer, F. 'Mithridates' (1 and 3–15), *RE* 15 (1932) 2157–206
17. Glew, D. G. 'The selling of the king: a note on Mithridates Eupator's propaganda in 88 B.C., *Hermes* 105 (1977) 253–6
18. Glew, D. G. 'Mithridates Eupator and Rome: a study of the background of the first Mithridatic war', *Athenaeum* 55 (1977) 380–405
19. Glew, D. G. 'Between the wars: Mithridates Eupator and Rome, 85–73 B.C.', *Chiron* 11 (1981) 109–20
20. Gozalishvili, G. V. *Mit'ridat Pontiisky* (Georgian, with Russian summary). Tbilisi, 1965
21. Gross, W. H. 'Die Mithridates-Kapelle auf Delos', *A&A* 4 (1954) 105–17
22. Habicht, C. 'Zur Geschichte Athens in der Zeit Mithridates' VI', *Chiron* 6 (1976) 127–42

23. Hammond, N. G. L. 'The two battles of Chaeronea, 338 and 86 B.C.', *Klio* 31 (1938) 186–201
24. Havas, L. 'Mithridate et son plan d'attaque contre l'Italie', *ACD* 4 (1968) 13–25
25. Karyshkovsky, P. O. 'On the title of Mithridates Eupator' (Russ.), *Tskhaltubo* III, 572–81
26. Kleiner, G. 'Bildnis und Gestalt des Mithridates', *JDAI* 68 (1953) 73–95
27. Kolobova, K. M. 'Pharnaces I of Pontus' (Russ.), *VDI* 1949.3 (29) 27–35
28. Leskov, A. M. *Gorny Krim v Pyervom Tysyacheletii do n. E.* (*Mountain Crimea in the first Millennium B.C.*). Kiev, 1965
29. Levi, E. I. *Ol'via-Gorod Epokhi Ellinizma* (*The City of Olbia in the Age of Hellenism*). Leningrad, 1985
30. Lintott, A. W. 'Mithridatica', *Historia* 25 (1976) 489–91
31. Lomouri, N. Y. *K Istorii Pontiiskogo Tsarstva* (*On the History of the Pontic Kingdom*). Tbilisi, 1979
32. McGing, B. C. 'Appian, Manius Aquillius and Phrygia', *GRBS* 21 (1980) 35–42
33. McGing, B. C. 'The date of the outbreak of the third Mithridatic war', *Phoenix* 38 (1984) 12–18
34. McGing, B. C. 'The kings of Pontus: some problems of identity and date', *RhM* 129 (1986) 248–59
35. McGing, B. C. *The Foreign Policy of Mithridates Eupator, King of Pontus.* Leiden, 1986
36. Marshall, A. J. 'Pompey's organisation of Bithynia-Pontus: two neglected texts', *JRS* 58 (1968) 103–7
37. Maximova, M. I. *Antichnye Goroda Yugo-Vostochnogo Prichernomorya* (*Ancient Cities of the South-East Black Sea*). Moscow and Leningrad, 1956
38. Meyer, E. *Geschichte des Königreichs Pontos.* Berlin, 1878
39. Minns, E. H. *Scythians and Greeks in South Russia.* Cambridge, 1913
40. Molyev, E. A. 'The establishment of the power of Mithridates Eupator on the Bosporus' (Russ.), *AMA* 2 (1974) 60–72
41. Molyev, E. A. *Mitridat Eupator.* Saratov, 1976
42. Molyev, E. A. 'Armenia Minor and Mithridates Eupator' (Russ.), *Problemy Antichnoi Istorii i Kultury* I, Yerevan, 1979, 185–9
42A. Molyev, E. A. 'On the question of the origin of the Pontic Mithridatids' (Russ.), *VDI* 1983.4, 131–8
43. Molyev, E. A. 'Mithridates Ktistes, ruler of Pontus' (Russ.), *Tskhaltubo* III, 581–8
44. Möll, A. 'Der Überseehandel von Pontos', *Akten 1. hist.–geogr. Kolloqu. Stuttgart, 8–9 Dec. 1980, Geographia Historica* (1984)
45. Munro, J. A. 'Roads in Pontus, royal and Roman', *JHS* 21 (1901) 52–66
46. Neverov, O. Y. 'Mithridates as Dionysus' (Russ.), *SGE* 37 (1973) 41–5
47. Neverov, O. Y. 'Mithridates and Alexander, on the iconography of Mithridates VI' (Russ.) *SA* 1971.2, 86–95
48. Niese, B. 'Die Erwerbung der Küsten des Pontos durch Mithridates VI' (Straboniana 6), *RhM* 42 (1887) 559–74

49. Olshausen, E. 'Mithridates VI und Rom', *ANRW* I.1 (1972) 806–15
50. Olshausen, E. 'Zum Hellenisierungsprozess am pontischen Königshof', *AncSoc* 5 (1974) 153–64
51. Olshausen, E. and Biller, J. *Historisch-geographische Aspekte der Geschichte des pontischen und armenischen Reiches* I. Wiesbaden, 1984
52. Ormerod, H. A. 'Mithridatic advance in Asia Minor and Greece', *CAH* IX (1932) 238–60
53. Perl, G. 'The eras of the Bithynian, Pontic and Bosporan kingdoms' (Russ.), *VDI* 1969.3 (109) 39–69 (= 'Zur Chronologie der Königreiche Bithynia, Pontos und Bosporos', *Studien zur Geschichte und Philosophie des Altertums*, ed. J. Harmatta, Amsterdam 1968, 299–330)
54. Raditsa, L. 'Mithridates' view of the Peace of Dardanus in Sallust's *Letter of Mithridates*', *Helikon* 9–10 (1969–70) 632–5
55. Reinach, T. *Mithridate Eupator, roi du Pont*. Paris, 1890
56. Robinson, D. M. *Ancient Sinope*. Baltimore, 1906
57. Rostovtzeff, M. I. 'Mithradates of Pontus and Olbia' (Russ.), *Izvestia Arkheologicheskoi Kommissii Rossii* 23 (1907) 21–7
58. Rostovtzeff, M. I. 'Pontus, Bithynia and the Bosporus', *ABSA* 22 (1916–18) 1–22
59. Rostovtzeff, M. I. *Iranians and Greeks in South Russia*. Oxford, 1922
60. Rostovtzeff, M. I. *Skythien und der Bospor*. Berlin, 1931
61. Rostovtzeff, M. I. 'Pontus and its neighbours: the first Mithridatic War', *CAH* IX (1932) 211–38
62. Salomone Gaggero, E. 'La propaganda antiromana di Mitridate VI Eupatore in Asia minore e in Grecia', *Contributi di storia antica in onore di Albino Garzetti*, Genoa, 1977, 89–123
63. Salomone Gaggero, E. 'Relations politiques et militaires de Mithridate VI Eupator avec les populations et les cités de Thrace et avec les colonies grecques de la Mer Noire occidentale', *Pulpudeva, semaines philippopolitaines de l'histoire et de la culture thrace, Plovdiv 4–19 oct. 1976* II, ed. A. Fol, Sofia, 1978, 294–305
64. Saprykin, S. Y. 'Heraclea, Chersonesus and Pharnaces I of Pontus' (Russ.), *VDI* 1979.3 (149) 43–59
65. Sarikakis, T. C. 'Les vêpres ephésiennes de l'an 88 av. J.-C.', *EThess* 15 (1976) 253–64
66. Savelya, O. 'On the relations between Greeks and barbarians in the south-western Crimea' (Russ.), *Tskhaltubo* I, 166–76
67. Schultz, P. M. 'Late Scythian culture and its variants on the Dnieper and in the Crimea' (Russ.), *Problemy Skiphskoi Arkheologii* (*Problems of Scythian Archaeology*), Moscow, 1971, 127–36
68. Sheglov, A. N. 'The Tauri and the Greek colonies in Taurica' (Russ.) *Tskhaltubo* II, 204–18
69. Shelov, D. B. 'Tyras and Mithridates Eupator' (Russ.), *VDI* 1962.2 (80) 95–102
70. Shelov, D. B. 'Concerning the ancient literary tradition of the Mithridatic wars (Posidonius and Cicero)' (Russ.), *Istoria i Kultura antichnogo Mira*, Moscow, 1977, 197–201

71. Shelov, D. B. 'Colchis in the system of the Pontic empire of Mithridates VI' (Russ.), *VDI* 1980.3 (153) 28–43
71A. Shelov, D. B. 'Le royaume pontique de Mitridate Eupator', *Journal des Savants* 1982, 3–4, 243–66
71B. Shelov, D. B. 'The cities of the north Black Sea area and Mithridates Eupator' (Russ.), *VDI* 1983.2, 41–52
72. Shelov, D. B. 'The Pontic state of Mithridates Eupator' (Russ.), *Tskhaltubo* III, 551–72
73. Shelov, D. B. 'The ancient idea of a unified Pontic state' (Russ.), *VDI* 1986.1 (176) 36–42
74. Sherwin-White, A. N. 'Rome, Pamphylia and Cilicia', *JRS* 66 (1976) 1–9
75. Sherwin-White, A. N. 'The Roman involvement in Anatolia 167–88 B.C.', *JRS* 67 (1977) 62–75
76. Sherwin-White, A. N. 'Ariobarzanes, Mithridates and Sulla', *CQ* 27 (1977) 173–83
77. Sherwin-White, A. N. 'The opening of the Mithridatic war', *Φιλίας Χάριν, Miscellanea di studi classici in onore di Eugenio Manni*, ed. M. J. Fontana, M. T. Piraino and F. P. Rizzo, VI, Rome, 1980, 1979–95
77A. Solomonnik, E. I. 'On the Scythian state and its relations with the North Black Sea Region', *Arkheologia i Istoria Bospora* I (Russ.), ed. Gaidukevich, V. F., 1952, 103–29
77B. Todua, T. *Kolkhida v Sostavye Pontiiskogo Tsarstva*. Tbilisi, 1990
78. Vinogradov, Y. G. 'Discussion on chronology of Mithridates' early career, 120–111 B.C.' (Russ.), *Tskhaltubo* III, 624–5
78A. Vinogradov, Y. G. *Politicheskaya Istoria Ol'viiskogo Polisa VII–I Vyekov do n.E.* Moscow, 1989
79. Vitucci, G. *Il regno di Bitinia*. Rome, 1953
80. Vysotskaya, T. *Pozdniye Skiphy v Yugozapadnom Krimu* (*Late Scyths in the South-West Crimea*). Kiev, 1972
81. Vysotskaya, T. *Skiphskiye Gorodischa* (*Scythian Sites*). Simferopol, 1975
82. Weimert, H. *Wirtschaft als landschaftsgebundenes Phänomen: die antike Landschaft Pontos'. Eine Fallstudie*. Frankfurt, 1984
83. Widengren, G. 'La légende royale de l'Iran antique', *Hommages à Georges Dumézil* (Coll. Latomus 45), Brussels, 1960, 230–1
84. Wilhelm, A. 'König Mithridates Eupator und Olbia', *Klio* 29 (1933) 50–9
85. Winfield, D. 'The northern routes across Anatolia', *AS* 27 (1977) 151–66
86. Winter, F. 'Mithridates VI Eupator', *JDAI* 9 (1894) 245–54

b. THE JEWS

87. Abel, F. M. *Les livres des Maccabées*. Paris, 1949
88. Abel, F. M. *Histoire de la Palestine depuis la conquête d'Alexandre jusqu'à l'invasion arabe* I. Paris, 1952
89. Alon, G. 'Did the Jewish people and its sages cause the Hasmoneans to be forgotten?', *Studies in Jewish History in the Times of the Second Temple and Talmud*, transl. by I. Abrahams, Jerusalem, 1977, 1–17
90. Ariel, D. T. 'A survey of coin finds in Jerusalem', *Liber Annuus, Studium*

Biblicum Franciscanum 32 (1982) 273–307
91. Avigad, N. 'The rock-carved façades of the Jerusalem Necropolis', *IEJ* 1 (1950–1) 96–106
92. Avigad, N. 'A bulla of Jonathan the High Priest', *IEJ* 25 (1975) 8–12, and 'A bulla of King Jonathan', *ibid.* 245–6
93. Avigad, N. *Discovering Jerusalem.* Oxford, 1984
94. Bar-Adon, P. 'Another settlement of the Judaean desert sect at 'En el-Ghuweir on the shores of the Dead Sea', *BASO* 277 (1977) 1–22
95. Barag, D. and Qedar, Sh. 'The beginning of Hasmonean coinage', *Israel Numismatic Journal* 4 (1980) 8–21
96. Bartlett, J. *Jericho.* London, 1982
97. Beall, T. S. *Josephus' Description of the Essenes Illustrated by the Dead Sea Scrolls* (*SNTS* Monogr. ser. 58). Cambridge, 1988
98. Benoit, P. 'L'inscription grecque du tombeau de Jason', *IEJ* 17 (1967) 112–13
99. Bickerman, E. *From Ezra to the Last of the Maccabees.* New York, 1962
100. Bickerman, E. *The Jews in the Greek Age.* Cambridge, MA, 1988
101. Bowsher, J. M. C. 'Architecture and religion in the Decapolis', *PalEQ* Jan.–June 1987, 62–9
102. Burr, V. 'Rom und Judäa im 1. Jahrhundert', *ANRW* 1.1 (1972) 875–86
103. Charlesworth, J. H. *The Old Testament Pseudepigrapha.* 2 vols. London, 1985
104. Collins, J. J. 'The epic of Theodotus and the Hellenism of the Hasmoneans', *HThR* 73 (1980) 91–104
105. Collins, J. J. *Between Athens and Jerusalem. Jewish Identity in the Hellenistic Diaspora.* New York, 1983
106. Cross, F. M. *The Ancient Library of Qumran and Modern Biblical Studies.* Revd. New York, 1961
107. Davies, P. R. 'Hasidim in the Maccabean period', *JJSt* 28 (1977) 127–40
108. Davies, P. R. 'The ideology of the Temple in the Damascus document', *JJSt* 33 (1982) 287–302
109. Davies, P. R. *Qumran.* Guildford, 1982
110. Delcor, M. 'Le temple d'Onias en Egypte', *RBi* 75 (1968) 188–205
111. De Vaux, R. *Ancient Israel, its Life and Institutions.* 2nd edn, London, 1965
112. De Vaux, R. *Archaeology and the Dead Sea Scrolls.* Revd. Oxford, 1973
113. Dever, W. G. *Gezer IV. The 1969–71 Seasons.* Jerusalem, 1986
114. Efron, J. *Studies on the Hasmonean Period.* Leiden, 1987
115. Egger, R. *Josephus und die Samaritaner* (Novum Test. et Orbis Antiquus 4). Göttingen, 1986
116. Foerster, G. 'Architectural fragments from Jason's tomb reconsidered', *IEJ* 28 (1978) 152–6
117. Gafni, I. 'Josephus and I Maccabees', in *Josephus, the Bible and History*, ed. L. H. Feldman and G. Hata, Detroit, 1989, 147–72
118. Giovannini, A. and Müller, H. 'Die Beziehungen zwischen Rom und den Juden im 2. Jh. v. Chr.', *MH* 28 (1971) 156–71
119. Goldstein, J. A. *1 Maccabees.* New York, 1976
120. Goodman, M. *The Ruling Class of Judaea.* Cambridge, 1987

121. Habicht, Chr. *2 Makkabäerbuch (Jüdische Schriften aus hellenistisch–römischer Zeit* 1:3). Gütersloh, 1976
122. Hayward, R. 'The Jewish temple at Leontopolis: a reconsideration', *JJSt* 33 (1982) 429–43
123. Hengel, M. *Judaism and Hellenism*, transl. by J. Bowden. 2 vols. London, 1974
124. Hengel, M., Charlesworth, J. H. and Mendels, D. 'The polemical character of "On Kingship" in the Temple Scroll: an attempt at dating "11Q Temple"', *JJSt* 37 (1986) 18–38
125. Kasher, A. 'Gaza during the Greco-Roman era', *Jerusalem Cathedra* 2 (1982) 63–78
126. Kasher, A. *Jews, Idumaeans and ancient Arabs* (Texte und Studien zum antiken Judentum 18). Tübingen, 1988
127. Knibb, M. A. *The Qumran Community*. Cambridge, 1987
128. Lane, E. N. 'Sabazius and the Jews in Valerius Maximus: a re-examination', *JRS* 69 (1979) 34–8
129. Laperrousaz, E.-M. *Qumran. L'établissement essénien des bords de la Mer Morte. Histoire et archéologie du site*. Paris, 1976
130. Levine, L. I. 'The Hasmonean conquest of Strato's Tower', *IEJ* 24 (1974) 62–9
131. Lichtenstein, H. 'Die Fastenrolle. Eine Untersuchung zur jüdisch-hellenistischen Geschichte', *HebrUCA* 8–9 (1931–2) 257–351
132. Lohse, E. *Die Texte aus Qumran hebraisch und deutsch*. 2nd edn, Munich, 1971
133. Macalister, R. A. S. *The Excavation of Gezer, 1902–1905 and 1907–1909* I. London, 1911
134. Mendels. O. *The Land of Israel as a Political Concept in Hasmonean Literature* (Texte und Studien zum antiken Judentum 15). Tübingen, 1987
135. Meshorer, Y. *Ancient Jewish Coinage*. 2 vols. New York, 1982
136. Momigliano, A. 'The date of the first book of Maccabees', *Mél. Heurgon* II, 657–61 (= *Sesto contributo alla storia degli studi classici e del mondo antico* II, 561–6).
137. Moore, G. F. 'Fate and free will in the Jewish philosophies according to Josephus', *HThR* 22 (1929) 371–89
138. Netzer, E. 'The Hasmonean and Herodian winter palaces at Jericho', *IEJ* 25 (1975) 89–100
139. Neusner, J. 'The fellowship (haburah) in the second Jewish commonwealth', *HThR* 53 (1960) 125–42
140. Neusner, J. *The Idea of Purity in Ancient Judaism*. Leiden, 1973
141. Nickelsburg, G. W. E. *Jewish Literature between the Bible and the Mishnah*. London, 1981
142. Puech, E. 'Inscriptions funéraires palestiniennes: tombeau de Jason et ossuaires', *RBi* 90 (1983) 481–533
143. Purvis, J. O. 'The Samaritans and Judaism', *Early Judaism and its Modern Interpreters*, ed. R. A. Kraft and G. W. E. Nickelsburg, Philadelphia, 1986, 81–98
144. Qimron, E. and Strugnell. J. 'An unpublished Halakhic letter from

Qumran', *Biblical Archaeology Today*, ed. J. Amitai (*Proc. of the 1984 Internat. Congr. on Biblical Archaeology*), Jerusalem, 1985, 400–7

145. Raban, A. 'The city walls of Strato's Tower', *BASO* 268 (1987) 71–88
146. Rahmani, L. Y. 'Jason's tomb', *IEJ* 17 (1967) 61–100
147. Rajak, T. 'Roman intervention in a Seleucid siege of Jerusalem?', *GRBS* 22 (1981) 65–81
148. Rappaport, U. 'La Judée et Rome pendant le règne d'Alexandre Janée', *REJ* 127 (1968) 329–45
149. Rappaport, U. 'Les Iduméens en Egypte', *RPh* 43 (1977) 73–82
150. Rappaport, U. 'The emergence of the Hasmonean coinage', *Association for Jewish Studies Review* 1 (1976) 171–86
151. Reich, R. and Geva, H. 'Archaeological evidence of the Jewish population of Hasmonean Gezer', *IEJ* 31 (1981) 48–52
152. Schalit, A., (ed.) *The World History of the Jewish People*. VI, *The Hellenistic Age*. London, 1976
153. Schürer, E. *The History of the Jewish People in the Age of Jesus Christ*. Transl. and rev. by G. Vermes, F. Millar, M. Goodman and M. Black. Vols. I, II, III.1, III.2. Edinburgh, 1973–87
154. Seger, J. D. 'The search for Maccabean Gezer', *Biblical Archaeologist* 39 (1971) 142–4
155. Sievers, J. 'The role of women in the Hasmonean dynasty', *Josephus, the Bible and History*, ed. L. H. Feldman and G. Hata, Detroit, 1989, 132–46
156. Smallwood, E. M. *The Jews under Roman Rule from Pompey to Diocletian*. Leiden, 1976
157. Stern, E. 'The excavations at Tel Dor', *The Land of Israel: Cross-Roads of Civilization*, ed. E. Lipinski, Louvain, 1985, 169–92
158. Stern, M. *Greek and Latin Authors on Jews and Judaism* I. Jerusalem, 1974
159. Stern, M. 'Judaea and her neighbours in the days of Alexander Jannaeus', *Jerusalem Cathedra* 1 (1981) 22–46
160. Stone, M. E. *Scriptures, Sects and Visions. A Profile of Judaism from Ezra to the Jewish Revolts*. London, 1982
161. Stone, M. E. *Jewish Writings of the Second Temple Period* (Compendia Rerum Iudaicarum ad Novum Testamentum 2.2). Assen and Philadelphia, 1984
162. Tcherikover, V. *Hellenistic Civilization and the Jews*. Jerusalem, 1966
163. Tsafrir, Y. 'The location of the Seleucid Akra at Jerusalem', *RBi* 82 (1975) 501–21
164. Vermes, G. 'The Essenes and history', *JJSt* 32 (1981) 18–31
165. Vermes, G. *The Dead Sea Scrolls: Qumran in Perspective*. 2nd edn, London, 1982
166. Vermes, G. *The Dead Sea Scrolls in English*. 3rd edn, London, 1987
167. Vermes, G. and Goodman, M. D. *The Essenes according to the Classical Sources*. Sheffield, 1987
168. Wacholder, B. Z. 'Josephus and Nicolaus of Damascus', *Josephus, the Bible and History*, ed. L. H. Feldman and G. Hata, Detroit, 1989, 147–72

C. EGYPT

169. Badian, E. 'The testament of Ptolemy Alexander', *RhM* 110 (1967) 178–92
169A. Bagnall, R. S. 'Stolos the admiral', *Phoenix* 26 (1972) 358–68
169B. Bagnall, R. S. *The Administration of the Ptolemaic Possessions outside Egypt* (Columbia Studies in the Classical Tradition 4). Leiden, 1976
170. Bingen, J. 'Les epistratèges de Thébaïde sous les derniers Ptolémées', *CE* 45 (1970) 369–78
171. Bingen, J. 'Présence grecque en milieu rural ptolémaique', *Problèmes de la terre en Grece ancienne*, ed. M. I. Finley, Paris, 1973, 215–22
172. Bingen, J. 'Kerkéosiris et ses Grecs au IIe siècle avant notre ère', *Actes du XVe congrès internat. de papyrologie* IV (Papyrologica Bruxellensia 19), Brussels, 1978, 87–94
173. Bingen, J. 'Les cavaliers catoeques de l'Heracléopolite au I[e] siècle', *Studia Hellenistica* 27 (1983) 1–11
174. Bingen, J. 'Les tensions structurelles de la société ptolémaïque', *Atti del XVII congresso internaz. di papirologia* III, Naples, 1984, 921–37
175. Bloedow, E. *Beiträge zur Geschichte des Ptolemaios XII*. Diss. Würzburg, 1963
176. Bonnet, H. *Reallexikon der ägyptischen Religionsgeschichte*. Berlin, 1952
177. Boswinkel, E. and Pestman, P. W. *Les archives privées de Dionysios, fils de Kephalas* (*PapLugdBat.* 22). Leiden, 1982
178. Cauville, S. and Devauchelle, D. 'Le temple d'Edfou: étapes de la construction; nouvelles données historiques', *REgypt* 35 (1984) 31–55
179. Clarysse, W. 'Greeks and Egyptians in the Ptolemaic army and administration', *Aegyptus* 65 (1985) 57–66
180. *Cleopatra's Egypt. Age of the Ptolemies*, ed. R. S. Bianchi *et al.* Brooklyn Museum, New York, 1988
181. Crawford, D. J. *Kerkeosiris: an Egyptian Village in the Ptolemaic Period.* Cambridge, 1971
182. Crawford, D. J., Quaegebeur, J. and Clarysse, W. *Studies on Ptolemaic Memphis* (Studia Hellenistica 24). Louvain, 1980
183. van 't Dack, E. 'La date de *C.Ord.Ptol.* 80–83 = *BGU* VI 1212 et le séjour de Cléopatre VII à Rome', *AncSoc* 1 (1970) 53–67
184. van 't Dack, E. *Reizen, expedities en emigratie uit Italië naar Ptolemaeïsch Egypte* (*Meded. koninkl. Acad. Wetensch., Lett. en schone Kunsten, Kl. der Letteren* 42,4). Brussels, 1980
185. van 't Dack, E. 'L'armée romaine d'Egypte de 55 à 30 av.J.-C.', *Das römisch–byzantinische Ägypten. Akten des internat. Symposions 26–30 Sept. 1978 in Trier*, Mainz, 1983, 19–29
186. van 't Dack, E. 'Les relations entre l'Egypte ptolémaïque et l' Italie, un aperçu des personnages revenant ou venant d'Alexandrie ou d'Egypte en Italie', *Egypt and the Hellenistic World. Proc. of the Internat. Colloquium Louvain 24–6 May 1982* (Studia Hellenistica 27), Louvain, 1983, 383–406
186A. van 't Dack E. *Ptolemaica Selecta. Etudes sur l'armée et l'administration lagides* (Studia Hellenistica 29) Louvain, 1988

187. Derchain, P. 'Miettes', *REgypt* 26 (1974) 7–20
188. Donadoni, S. 'Una testata di decreto Tolemaico', *Alessandria e il mondo ellenistico-romano. Studi in onore di Achille Adriani*, ed. N. Bonacasa and A. Di Vita (Studi e Materiali Ist. arch. Univ. Palermo 4–6) I, Rome, 1983, 162–4
189. Dunand, F. 'Droit d'asile et refuge dans les temples en Egypte lagide', *Hommages à la mémoire de Serge Sauneron* II, ed. J. Vercoutter, Cairo, 1979, 77–97
190. Fraser, P. M. 'Inscriptions from Ptolemaic Egypt', *Berytus* 13 (1959–60) 123–61
191. Fraser, P. M. 'A *prostagma* of Ptolemy Auletes from Lake Edku', *JEA* 56 (1970) 179–82
192. Fraser, P. M. *Ptolemaic Alexandria*. 3 vols. Oxford, 1972
193. Gara, A. 'Limiti strutturali dell'economia monetaria nell'Egitto tardo-tolemaico', *Studi Ellenistici* I, ed. B. Virgilio, Pisa, 1984, 107–34
194. Heinen, H. *Rom und Aegypten von 51 bis 47 v.Chr.* Diss. Tübingen, 1966
195. Heinen, H. 'Cäsar und Kaisarion', *Historia* 18 (1969) 181–203
196. Heinen, H. 'Die Tryphè des Ptolemaios VIII Euergetes II', *Althistorische Studien Hermann Bengtson zum 70. Geburtstag dargebracht von Kollegen und Schülern*, ed. H. Heinen (Historia Einzelschriften 40), Wiesbaden, 1983, 116–30
197. Johnson, J. H. 'Is the Demotic Chronicle an anti-Greek tract?' *Grammatika Demotika. Festschrift für Erich Lüddeckens zum 15. Juni 1983*, ed. H.-J. Thissen and K.-T. Zauzich, Würzburg, 1984, 107–24
198. Kaplony-Heckel, U. 'Ein neuer demotischer Brief aus Gebelen', *Festschr. zum 150-jährigen Bestehen des Berliner ägyptischen Museums* (Staatl. Museen zu Berlin, Mitt. aus d. ägyptischen Sammlung 8), Berlin, 1974, 287–301
199. Koenen, L. '*ΘΕΟΙΣΙΝ ΕΧΘΡΟΣ*. Ein einheimischer Gegenkönig in Ägypten (132/1[a])', *CE* 34 (1959) 103–19
200. Koenen, L. 'Die Prophezeiehungen des "Töpfers"', *ZPE* 2 (1968) 178–209
201. Koenen, L. 'The prophecies of a potter: a prophecy of world renewal becomes an apocalypse', *Proc. of the XIIth Int. Congress of Papyrology, Ann Arbor, 13–17 August, 1968* (Am. Stud. Pap. 7), Toronto, 1970, 249–54
202. Koenen, L. 'Bemerkungen zum Text des Töpferorakels und zu dem Akaziensymbol', *ZPE* 13 (1974) 313–19
203. Kyrieleis, H. *Bildnisse der Ptolemäer* (Deutsches arch. Institut, Arch. Forschungen 2). Berlin, 1975
204. Lewis, N. 'Dryton's wives: two or three?, *CE* 57 (1982) 317–21
205. Lewis, N. *Greeks in Ptolemaic Egypt*. Oxford, 1986
206. Lloyd, A. B. 'Nationalist propaganda in Ptolemaic Egypt', *Historia* 31 (1982) 33–55
207. Lord, L. E. 'The date of Julius Caesar's departure from Egypt', *Classical Studies presented to F. Capps on his 70th Birthday*, Princeton, 1936, 223–32
208. Lüddeckens, E. *Ägyptische Eheverträge* (Ägyptologische Abhandlungen 1) Wiesbaden, 1960
209. Maehler, H. 'Egypt under the last Ptolemies', *BICS* 30 (1983) 1–16.

210. Meeks, D. *Le grand texte des donations au temple d'Edfou.* Cairo, 1972
211. De Meulenaere, H. 'Les stratèges indigènes du nome tentyrite à la fin de l'époque ptolémaique et au début de l'occupation romaine', *RSO* 34 (1959) 1–25
212. De Meulenaere, H. 'Prosopographica Ptolemaica: le règne conjoint de Ptolémée XII Aulète et de Cléopatre VII', *CE* 42 (1967) 300–5
213. Mond, R. and Myers, O. H. *The Bucheum.* 3 vols. London, 1934
214. Musti, D. 'I successori di Tolemeo Evergete II', *PP* 15 (1960) 432–46
215. Olshausen, E. *Rom und Ägypten von 116 bis 51 v.Chr.* Diss. Erlangen, 1963
216. Otto, W. and Bengtson, H. *Zur Geschichte des Niederganges des Ptolemäerreiches. Ein Beitrag zur Regierungszeit des 8. und des 9. Ptolemäers* (*ABAW* 17). Munich, 1938
217. Peremans, W. 'Les révolutions égyptiennes sous les Lagides', *Das ptolemäische Ägypten. Akten des internat. Symposions 27–29 September 1976 in Berlin*, Mainz, 1978, 39–50
218. Pestman, P. W. 'Les archives privées de Pathyris à l'époque ptolémaique. La famille de Peteharsemtheus, fils de Panebkhounis', *PapLugdBat.* 14 (1965) 47–105
219. Pestman, P. W. *Chronologie égyptienne d'après les textes démotiques 332 av. J.-C.–453 ap. J.-C.* (*Pap.Lugd.Bat.* 15). Leiden, 1967
220. Pestman, P. W. *Textes grecs, démotiques et bilingues.* (*Pap.Lugd.Bat.* 19). Leiden, 1978
221. Porter, B. and Moss, R. L. B. *Topographical Bibliography of Ancient Egyptian Hieroglyphic Texts, Reliefs and Paintings.* Oxford, 1927– . 2nd edn, with E. W. Burney and J. Málek, 1960–
222. Préaux, C. 'Esquisse d'une histoire des révolutions égyptiennes sous les Lagides', *CE* 22 (1936) 522–52
223. Préaux, C. 'La signification de l'époque d'Evergète II', *Actes du Ve congrès internat. de papyrologie, Oxford 30 août – 3 septembre 1937*, Brussels, 1938, 345–54
224. Préaux, C. *L'économie royale des Lagides.* Brussels, 1939
225. Quaegebeur, J. 'The genealogy of the Memphite high priest family in the Hellenistic period', *Studia Hellenistica* 24 (1980) 43–82
226. Reekmans, T. 'The Ptolemaic copper inflation', *Studia Hellenistica* 7 (1951) 61–118
227. Reymond, E. A. E. *From the Records of a Priestly Family from Memphis* I (Ägyptologische Abhandlungen 38). Wiesbaden, 1981
228. Roccati, A. 'Nuove epigrafi greche e latine da File', *Hommages à M. J. Vermaseren*, ed. M. B. Boer and T. A. Edridge, III, Leiden, 1978, 988–96
229. Samuel, A. E. *Ptolemaic Chronology* (*MünchBeitrPapyr* 43). Munich, 1962
230. Samuel, A. E. 'Year 27 = 30 and 88 B.C.', *CE* 40 (1965) 376–400
231. Shatzman, I. 'The Egyptian question in Roman politics (59–54 B.C.)', *Latomus* 30 (1971) 363–9
232. Shore, A. F. 'Votive objects from Dendera in the Graeco-Roman period', *Orbis Aegyptiorum Speculum. Glimpses of Ancient Egypt. Studies in Honour of H. W. Fairman*, ed. J. Ruffle, G. A. Gaballa and K. A. Kitchen, Warminster, 1979, 138–60

233. Skeat, T. C. *The Reigns of the Ptolemies* (*MünchBeitrPapyr* 39). Munich, 1954
234. Tait, W. J. *Papyri from Tebtunis in Egyptian and in Greek*. London, 1977
235. Tarn, W. W. 'The Bucheum stelae: a note', *JRS* 26 (1936) 187–9
236. Thissen, H. J. 'Zur Familie des Strategen Monkores', *ZPE* 27 (1977) 181–91
237. Thomas, J. D. *The Epistrategos in Ptolemaic and Roman Egypt*. II. *The Ptolemaic Epistrategos* (*PapColon* 6). Opladen, 1975
238. Thompson (Crawford) D. J. 'Nile grain transport under the Ptolemies', *Trade* 64–75 and 190–2
239. Thompson (Crawford) D. J. 'The Idumaeans of Memphis and the Ptolemaic *politeumata*', *Atti del XVII congresso internaz. di papirologia*, Naples, 1984, 1069–75
240. Thompson, D. J. *Memphis under the Ptolemies*. Princeton, 1988
241. Traunecker, C. 'Essai sur l'histoire de la XXIX[e] dynastie', *BIAO* 79 (1979) 395–436
242. Volkmann, H. 'Ptolemaios' (24–37), *RE* 23.2 (1959) 1702–61
243. Walbank, F. W. 'Egypt in Polybius', *Orbis Aegyptiorum Speculum. Glimpses of Ancient Egypt. Studies in Honour of H. W. Fairman*, ed. J. Ruffle, G. A. Gaballa and K. A. Kitchen, Warminster, 1979, 180–9
244. Winkler, H. *Rom und Aegypten im 2. Jahrhundert v.Chr.* Diss. Leipzig, 1983
245. Winnicki, J. K. 'Ein ptolemäischer Offizier in Thebais', *Eos* 60 (1972) 343–53
246. Winter, E. 'Der Herrscherkult in den ägyptischen Ptolemäertempeln', *Das ptolemäische Ägypten. Akten des internat. Symposions 27–29 September 1976 in Berlin*, Mainz, 1978, 147–60
247. de Wit, C. 'Inscriptions dédicatoires du temple d'Edfou', *CE* 36 (1961) 56–97, 277–320
248. Yoyotte, J. 'Bakhthis: religion égyptienne et culture grecque à Edfou', *Religions en Egypte hellénistique et romaine. Colloque de Strasbourg 16–18 mai 1967*, Paris, 1969, 127–41
249. Zauzich, K.-T. 'Zwei übersehene Erwähnungen historischer Ereignisse der Ptolemäerzeit in demotischen Urkunden', *Enchoria* 7 (1977) 193

d. OTHER EASTERN MATTERS

250. Accame, S. *Il dominio romano in Grecia dalla guerra acaica ad Augusto*. Rome, 1946
251. Bellinger, A. R. *The End of the Seleucids*. Trans. Connecticut Acad. 38, 1949
252. Bivar, A. D. H. 'The political history of Iran under the Arsacids', *Cambridge History of Iran* III.1. Cambridge, 1983, 21–99
253. Bowersock, G. *Augustus and the Greek World*. Oxford, 1965
254. Brunt, P. A. 'Sulla and the Asian Publicans', *Latomus* 15 (1956) 17–25 (= A 20, 1–8)
255. Burstein, S. M. *Outpost of Hellenism: The Emergence of Heraclea on the Black Sea*. Berkeley, 1976

256. Burstein, S. M. 'The aftermath of the Peace of Apamea: Rome and the Pontic War', *AJAH* 5 (1980) 1–11
257. Calder, W. M. and Bean, G. E. *A Classical Map of Asia Minor*. London, 1958
258. Candiloro, E. 'Politica e cultura in Atene da Pidna alla guerra mitridatica', *SCO* 14 (1965) 134–76
259. Debevoise, N. C. *A Political History of Parthia*. Chicago, 1938, repr. 1968
260. *Delo e l'Italia*. See Abbreviations
261. Dilleman, J. 'Les premiers rapports des Romains avec les Parthes', *ArchOrient* 3 (1931) 215–56
262. Dillemann, L. *Haute Mésopotamie orientale et pays adjacents* (Inst. fr. d'arch. de Beyrouth, Bibl. arch. et hist. 72). Paris, 1962
263. Dobbins, K. W. 'The successors of Mithridates II of Parthia', *NC* 15 (1975) 19–45
264. Downey, G. 'The occupation of Syria by the Romans', *TAPhA* 82 (1951) 149–63
265. Drew-Bear, T. 'Deux décrets hellénistiques d'Asie Mineure', *BCH* 96 (1972) 443–71
266. Ferguson, W. S. *Hellenistic Athens*. London, 1911
267. Fraser, P. M. and Bean, G. E. *The Rhodian Peraea and Islands*. Oxford, 1954
268. Grousset, R. *Histoire de l'Arménie des origines à 1071*. Paris, 1947
269. Habicht, C. 'Über die Kriege zwischen Pergamon und Bithynien', *Hermes* 84 (1956) 90–110
270. Hatzfeld, J. *Les trafiquants italiens dans l'orient hellénique*. Paris, 1919
271. Hoben, W. *Untersuchungen zur Stellung kleinasiatischer Dynasten der ausgehenden Republik*. Mainz, 1969
272. Jones, A. H. M. *The Cities of the Eastern Roman Provinces*. Oxford, 1937
273. Jones, C. P. 'Diodoros Pasparos and the Nikephoria of Pergamum', *Chiron* 4 (1974) 183–205
274. Jonkers, E. J. 'Waren der Aufstand des Aristonicus und die mithridatischen Kriege Klassenkämpfe?', *JVEG* 18 (1964)
275. Levick, B. *Roman Colonies in Southern Asia Minor*. Oxford, 1967
276. Liebmann-Frankfort, T. *La frontière orientale dans la politique extérieure de la République romaine*. Brussels, 1968
277. Liebmann-Frankfort, T. 'La provincia Cilicia et son intégration dans l'empire romain', *Hommages à M. Renard*, ed. J. Bibauw (*Coll. Latomus* 102) II, Brussels, 1969, 447–57
278. Lynch, H. F. B. *Armenia, Travels and Studies*. 2 vols. London, 1901
279. Malitz, J. 'Caesars Partherkrieg', *Historia* 33 (1984) 21–59
280. Manandrian, H. A. *The Trade and Cities of Armenia in Relation to the Ancient World Trade*. Lisbon, 1965
281. Mancinetti Santamaria, G. 'Filostrato di Ascalone, banchiere in Delo', *Delo e l'Italia* 78–89
282. Marshall, B. A. 'The date of Q. Mucius Scaevola's governorship of Asia', *Athenaeum* 54 (1976) 117–30
283. Mattingly, H. B. 'M. Antonius, C. Verres and the sack of Delos by the pirates', *Φιλίας Χάριν*, *Miscellanea di studi classici in onore di Eugenio Manni*,

ed. M. J. Fontana, M. T. Piraino and F. P. Rizzo, IV, Rome, 1979, 1491–515

284. Mattingly, H. B. 'Rome's earliest relations with Byzantium, Heraclea Pontica and Callatis', *Ancient Bulgaria* I, ed. A. Poulter, Nottingham, 1983, 239–52

285. Ormerod, H. A. 'The distribution of Pompey's forces in the campaign of 67 B.C.', *Liverpool Ann. Arch. Anth.* 10 (1923) 46–51

286. Raschke, M. G. 'New studies in Roman commerce with the East', *ANRW* II.9.2 (1978) 604–1361

287. Reynolds, J. 'Cyrenaica, Pompey and Cn. Cornelius Lentulus Marcellinus', *JRS* 52 (1962) 97–103

288. Rizzo, F. *Le fonti per la storia della conquista pompeiana della Siria* (*Kokalos* Suppl. 2). Palermo, 1963

289. Robert, L. 'Théophane de Mytilène à Constantinople', *CRAI* (1969) 42–64

290. Seibert, J. *Historische Beiträge zu den dynastischen Verbindungen in hellenistischer Zeit.* Wiesbaden, 1967

291. Sherwin-White, A. N. *Roman Foreign Policy in the East.* London, 1984

292. Sherwin-White, S. M. *Ancient Cos.* Göttingen, 1978

293. Solin, H. 'Appunti sull'onomastica romana a Delo', *Delo e l'Italia*, 101–17

294. Syme, R. 'Observations on the province of Cilicia', *Anatolian Studies presented to William Hepburn Buckler*, ed. W. Calder and J. Keil, Manchester, 1939, 299–32 (= A 119, I 120–48)

295. Warmington, E. H. *Commerce between the Roman Empire and India.* Cambridge, 1928

296. Wellesley, K. 'The extent of the territory added to the Roman empire by Pompey', *RhM* 96 (1953) 293–318

297. Wilson, D. R. *The Historical Geography of Bithynia, Paphlagonia and Pontus in the Greek and Roman Periods.* Diss. Oxford, 1960

298. Wolski, J. 'Iran und Rom', *ANRW* II.9.1 (1976) 191–214

299. Wolski, J. 'L'Arménie dans la politique du haut-empire parthe', *IA* 15 (1980) 252–67

300. Ziegler, K. H. *Die Beziehungen zwischen Rom und dem Partherreich.* Wiesbaden, 1984

E. THE WEST

1. Birot, P. and Gabert, P. *La péninsule ibérique et l'Italie.* Paris, 1964

2. Broughton, T. R. S. *The Romanisation of Africa Proconsularis.* Baltimore, 1929

3. Chevallier, R. 'Essai de chronologie des centuriations romaines de Tunisie', *MEFRA* 70 (1958) 61–128

4. Chevallier, R. *La romanisation de la celtique du Pô.* I. *Les données géographiques. Géographie, archéologie et histoire en Cisalpine.* Paris, 1980

5. Chevallier, R. *La romanisation de la celtique du Pô. Essai d'histoire provinciale* (*BEFAR* 249). Rome, 1983

6. Clemente, G. *I romani nella Gallia meridionale.* Bologna, 1974

7. Corsaro, M. 'La presenza romana a Entella: una nota su Tiberio Claudio di Anzio', *ASNP* 12 (1982) 917–44

8. Dilke, O. A. W. 'Divided loyalties in eastern Sicily under Verres', *Ciceroniana* 4 (1980) 43–51

9. Domergue, C. *Les mines de la péninsule ibérique à l'époque romaine.* Thèse Paris, 1977

10. Domergue, C. *La mine antique d'Aljustrel (Portugal) et les tables de bronze de Vipasca.* Paris, 1983

11. Ebel, C. *Transalpine Gaul. The Emergence of a Roman Province.* Leiden, 1976

12. Ewins, U. 'The enfranchisement of Cisalpine Gaul', *PBSR* 23 (1955) 73–98

13. Gabba, E. 'Sui senati delle città siciliane nell'età' di Verre', *Athenaeum* 47 (1959) 304–20

14. Gabba, E. 'La Sicilia romana', *L'impero romano e le strutture economiche e sociali delle provincie* (Bibl. di Athenaeum 4), ed. M. H. Crawford, Como, 1986, 71–86

15. Galsterer, H. *Untersuchungen zum römischen Städtewesen auf der iberischen Halbinsel.* Berlin, 1971

16. Galsterer-Kroll, B. 'Zum *ius Latii* in den keltischen Provinzen des Imperium Romanum', *Chiron* 3 (1973) 277–306

17. Gonzalez, J. 'Tabula Siarensis, fortunales Siarenses et municipia civium Romanorum', *ZPE* 55 (1984) 55–100

18. Grispo, R. 'Della Mellaria a Calagurra', *NRS* 36 (1952) 189–225

19. Hoyos, B. D. 'Pliny the Elder's titled Baetican towns: obscurities, errors and origins', *Historia* 28 (1979) 439–70

20. Keay, S. J. *Roman Spain.* London, 1988

21. Knapp, R. C. *Aspects of the Roman Experience in Iberia, 206–100 B.C.* Valladolid, 1977

21A. Pedley, J. G. *Paestum.* London, 1990

22. Piganiol, A., (ed.) *Atlas des centuriations romaines de Tunisie.* Paris, 1954

23. Rice Holmes, T. *Caesar's Conquest of Gaul.* 2nd edn, Oxford, 1911

24. Richardson, J. S. 'The Spanish mines and the development of provincial taxation in the second century B.C.', *JRS* 66 (1976) 139–52

25. Richardson, J. S. *Hispaniae. Spain and the Development of Roman Imperialism, 218–82 B.C.* Cambridge, 1986

26. Rivet, A. L. *Gallia Narbonensis. Southern Gaul in Roman Times.* London, 1988

27. Roldán Hervas, J. M. 'Da Numancia a Sertorio: problemas de la romanización de Hispania en la encrucijada de las guerras civiles', *Studien zur antiken Sozialgeschichte. Festschrift Friedrich Vittinghoff*, ed. W. Eck, H. Galsterer and H. Wolff (Kölner hist. Abh. 28), Cologne, 1980, 157–78

28. Sancho Rocher, L. 'Los conventus iuridici en la Hispania romana', *Caesaraugusta* 45–6 (1978) 171–94

29. Teutsch, L. *Das Städtewesen in Nordafrika in der Zeit von C. Gracchus bis zum Tode des Kaisers Augustus.* Berlin, 1962

30. Verbrugghe, G. P. 'Sicily 210–70 B.C. Livy, Cicero and Diodorus', *TAPhA* 103 (1972) 535–59

31. Verbrugghe, G. P. 'Slave rebellion or Sicily in revolt?', *Kokalos* 20 (1974) 46–60
32. Wightman, E. M. *Gallia Belgica*. London, 1985

F. THE LAW

a. PUBLIC LAW AND CRIMINAL LAW

1. Accame, S. 'La legislazione romana intorno ai collegi nel I. secolo a.C.', *Bull. del Mus. dell'Impero romano* 1942, 134–48
2. Adcock, F. *Roman Political Ideas and Practice*. (Jerome Lectures, 6th series). Michigan and Toronto, 1959
3. Alexander, M. C. 'Praemia in the Quaestiones of the late Republic', *CPh* 80 (1985) 20–32
4. Alexander, M. C. 'Repetition of prosecutions, and the scope of prosecutions, in the standing courts of the late Republic', *CSCA* 13 (1982) 141–66
5. Allison, J. E. and Cloud, J. D. 'The Lex Iulia Maiestatis', *Latomus* 21 (1962) 711–31
6. Astin, A. E. 'The Lex Annalis before Sulla', *Latomus* 16 (1957) 588–613
7. Astin, A. E. 'Leges Aelia et Fufia', *Latomus* 23 (1964) 421–45
8. Astin, A. E. 'Censorship in the late Republic', *Historia* 34 (1985) 175–90
9. Astin, A. E. 'Cicero and the censorship', *CPh* 80 (1985) 233–9
10. Astin, A. E. '*Regimen morum*', *JRS* 78 (1988) 14–34
11. Ausbüttel, F. M. *Untersuchungen zu den Vereinen im Westen des römischen Reiches* (Frankfurter althist. Studien 11). Kallmünz, 1982
12. Balsdon, J. P. V. D. 'The history of the extortion court at Rome, 123–70 B.C.', *PBSR* 14 (1938) 98–114 (= Seager, *Crisis*, 132–50)
13. Balsdon, J. P. V. D. 'Three Ciceronian problems. 1. Clodius' "repeal" of the Lex Aelia Fufia', *JRS* 47 (1957) 15–17
14. Balsdon, J. P. V. D. '*Auctoritas, dignitas, otium*', *CQ* 10 (1960) 43–50
15. Baltrusch, E. *Regimen Morum* (Vestigia 41). Munich, 1986
16. Bauman, R. A. *The Crimen Maiestatis in the Roman Republic and Augustan Principate*. Johannesburg, 1967
17. Bauman, R. A. 'Il "sovversivismo" di Emilio Lepido' (in English), *Labeo* 24 (1978) 60–74
18. Bauman, R. A. 'La crisi del "diritto"', *La rivoluzione romana*, 208–16
19. Behrends, O. *Die römische Geschworenenverfassung*. Göttingen, 1970
20. Behrends, O. rev. of Watson, *Law Making*, *ZSS* 92 (1975) 297–308
21. Behrends, O. 'Tiberius Gracchus und die Juristen seiner Zeit', *Das Profil des Juristen in der europäischen Tradition, Symposium aus Anlass des 70. Geburtstages von Franz Wieacker*, ed. K. Luig and D. Liebs, Ebelsbach, 1980, 25–121
22. Behrends, O. 'Staatsrecht und Philosophie in der ausgehenden Republik', *ZSS* 100 (1983) 458–84
23. Berger, A. *Encyclopedic Dictionary of Roman Law* (*TAPhS* 43.2). Philadelphia, 1953

24. Bleicken, J. *Das Volkstribunat der klassischen Republik*. Munich, 1955
25. Bleicken, J. 'Kollisionen zwischen Sacrum und Publicum', *Hermes* 85 (1957) 446–80
26. Bleicken, J. *Staatliche Ordnung und Freiheit in der römischen Republik* (Frankfurter althist. Studien 6). Frankfurt, 1972
27. Bleicken, J. 'In provinciali solo dominium populi Romani est vel Caesaris. Zur Kolonisationspolitik der ausgehenden Republik und frühen Kaiserzeit', *Chiron* 4 (1974) 359–414
28. Bleicken, J. *Lex Publica. Gesetz und Recht in der römischen Republik*. Berlin and New York, 1975
29. Bonnefond-Coudry, M. *Le sénat de la république romaine de la guerre d'Hannibal à Auguste* (Col. éc. fr. de Rome 273). Rome, 1989
30. Botsford, G. W. *The Roman Assemblies from their Origin to the End of the Republic*. New York, 1909, repr, 1968
31. Brasiello, U. 'Sulla ricostruzione dei crimini in diritto romano: cenni sulla evoluzione dell'omicidio', *SDHI* 42 (1976) 246–64
32. Burton, G. P. 'Proconsuls, assizes, and the administration of justice under the empire', *JRS* 65 (1975) 92–106
33. Cancelli, F. 'A proposito di tresviri capitales', *Studi in onore di P. de Francisci* III, Milan, 1956, 17–35
34. *Du Châtiment*. See Abbreviations
35. Classen, C. J. 'Bemerkungen zu Ciceros Äusserungen über die Gesetze', *RhM* 122 (1979) 278–302
36. Cloud, J. D. 'The primary purpose of the lex Cornelia de sicariis', *ZSS* 86 (1969) 258–86
37. Cloud, J. D. 'Sulla and the praetorship', *LCM* 13 (1988) 69–73
38. Cornell, T. J. 'Some observations on the "crimen incesti"', *Le délit religieux*, 27–37
39. Crawford, M. H. '*Foedus* and *sponsio*', *PBSR* 41 (1973) 1–7
40. Crifò, G. 'Attività normativa del senato in età repubblicana', *BIDR* 10 (1968) 31–121
41. Crook, J. A. *Law and Life of Rome*. London, 1967
42. Crook, J. A. 'Lex Cornelia "de falsis"', *Athenaeum* 65 (1987) 163–71
43. Dahlheim, W. *Gewalt und Herrschaft: das provinziale Herrschaftssystem der römischen Republik*. Berlin and New York, 1977
44. Daube, D. *Forms of Roman Legislation*. Oxford, 1956
45. *Le délit religieux*. See Abbreviations
46. Eder, W. *Das vorsullanische Repetundenverfahren*, Berlin, 1969
47. Ewins, U. '*Ne quis iudicio circumveniatur*', *JRS* 50 (1960) 94–107
48. Fascione, L. '*Aliquem iudicio circumvenire* e *ob iudicandum pecuniam accipere*', *AG* (1975) 29–52
49. Fascione, L. *Crimen e quaestio ambitus nell'età repubblicana*. Milan, 1984
50. Ferenczy, E. 'Die "Grundgesetze" der römischen Republik', *Sein und Werden im Recht, Festgabe für Ulrich von Lübtow zum 70. Geburtstag*, ed. W. G. Becker and L. Schnorr von Carolsfeld, Berlin, 1970, 267–80
51. Ferrary, J.-L. 'Cicéron et la loi judiciare de Cotta', *MEFRA* 87 (1975) 321–48
52. Ferrary, J.-L. 'La lex Antonia de Termessibus', *Athenaeum* 73 (1985)

419–57

53. Fraccaro, P. 'I "decem stipendia" e le "leges annales" repubblicane', *Opuscula* II, Pavia, 1957, 207–34
54. Fraenkel, E., rev. of Beckmann, *Zauberei und Recht in Roms Frühzeit*, *Gnomon* 1 (1925) 185–200
55. von Fritz, K. *Schriften zur griechischen und römischen Verfassungsgeschichte und Verfassungstheorie*. Berlin, 1976
56. Fuks, A. and Geiger, J. 'The "lex iudiciaria" of M. Livius Drusus', *Studi in onore di Edoardo Volterra* II, Milan, 1971, 422–7
57. Gabba, E. 'Osservazioni sulla legge giudiziaria di M. Livio Druso', in C 55, 369–82
58. Gabba, E. 'M. Livius Drusus and Sulla's reforms', in C 55, 131–41
59. Galsterer, H. 'Roman law in the provinces: some problems of transmission', *L'impero romano*. (see Abbreviations), 13–28
60. Galsterer, H. 'La loi municipale des romains: chimère ou réalité?', *RD* 65 (1987) 181–203
61. Gaudemet, J. *Les gouvernants à Rome* (Antiqua 31). Rome, 1985
62. Giovannini, A. *Consulare Imperium* (Schweizerische Beitr. zur Altertumswiss. 16). Basle, 1983
63. Giovannini, A. 'Volkstribunat und Volksgericht', *Chiron* 13 (1983) 544–606
64. Gnoli, F. 'Sulla paternità e sulla datazione della "lex Iulia peculatus"', *SDHI* 38 (1972) 328–38
65. Gnoli, F. 'Cic. *nat deor*. 3.74 e l'origine della quaestio perpetua peculatus', *RIL* 109 (1975) 331–41
66. Gnoli, F. *Ricerche sul crimen peculatus*. Milan, 1979
67. Greenidge, A. H. J. *Infamia. Its Place in Roman Public and Private Law*. Oxford, 1894, repr. Aalen, 1977
68. Greenidge, A. H. J. *The Legal Procedure of Cicero's Time*. London, 1901, repr. New York, 1971
69. Grierson, P. 'The Roman law of counterfeiting', *Essays in Roman Coinage Presented to Harold Mattingly*, ed. R. A. G. Carson and C. H. V. Sutherland, Oxford, 1956, 240–61
70. Grieve, L. J. 'The reform of the comitia centuriata', *Historia* 34 (1985) 278–309
71. Griffin, M. T. 'The "leges iudiciariae" of the pre-Sullan era', *CQ* 23 (1973) 108–26
72. Guarino, A. 'Senatus consultum ultimum', *Sein und Werden im Recht, Festgabe für Ulrich von Lübtow zum 70. Geburtstag*, ed. W. G. Becker and L. Schnorr von Carolsfeld, Berlin, 1970, 281–94
73. Guarino, A. *Storia del diritto romano*. 8th edn, Naples, 1990, ch. 2, 'Il diritto romano preclassico'
74. Hall, U. 'Voting procedure in Roman assemblies', *Historia* 13 (1964) 267–306
75. Hands, A. R. 'Livius Drusus and the courts', *Phoenix* 26 (1972) 268–74
76. Harris, W. V. 'Was Roman law imposed on the Italian allies?', *Historia* 21 (1972) 639–45
77. Henderson, M. I. 'The process de repetundis', *JRS* 41 (1951) 71–88

78. Homo, L. *Les institutions politiques romaines. De la cité à état.* Paris, 1927. Transl. by M. R. Dobie as *Roman Political Institutions, from City to State*, London and New York, 1929
79. Hoyos, B. D. 'Lex provinciae and governor's edict', *Antichthon* 7 (1973) 47–53
80. Humbert, M. *'Municipium' et 'civitas sine suffragio'. L'organisation de la conquête jusqu'à la guerre sociale* (Coll. éc. fr. de Rome 36). Rome, 1978
81. Humbert, M. 'Le tribunat de la plèbe et le tribunal du peuple: remarques sur l'histoire de la *provocatio ad populum*', *MEFRA* 100 (1988) 431–503
82. Jashemski, W. F. *The Origins and History of the Proconsular and Propraetorian Imperium to 27 B.C.* Chicago, 1950
83. Jameson, S. 'Pompey's *imperium* in 67: some constitutional fictions', *Historia* 19 (1970) 539–60
84. Jocelyn, H. D. 'The poet Cn. Naevius, P. Cornelius Scipio and Q. Caecilius Metellus', *Antichthon* 3 (1969) 32–47
85. Jolowicz, H. F. and Nicholas, B. *Historical Introduction to the Study of Roman Law.* 3rd edn, Cambridge, 1972
86. Jones, A. H. M. 'Civitates immunes et liberae', *Anatolian Studies presented to William Hepburn Buckler*, ed. W. Calder and J. Keil, Manchester, 1939, 103–18
87. Jones, A. H. M. *Studies in Roman Government and Law.* Oxford, 1960
88. Jones, A. H. M. 'De legibus Iunia et Acilia repetundarum', *PCPhS* 6 (1960) 39–42
89. Jones, A. H. M. *The Criminal Courts of the Roman Republic and Principate.* Oxford, 1972
90. Kloft, H. *Prorogation und ausserordentliche Imperien 326–81 v.Chr. Untersuchungen zur Verfassung der römischen Republik* (Beiträge zur kl. Philologie 84). Meisenheim, 1977
91. Kubitschek, J. W. *Imperium Romanum tributim discriptum.* Prague, 1889, repr. Rome, 1972
92. Kunkel, W. *Untersuchungen zur Entwicklung des römischen Kriminalverfahrens in vorsullanischer Zeit* (*SBAW* 56). Munich, 1962
93. Kunkel, W. 'Quaestio', *RE* 24 (1963) 720–69 (= F 96, 33–110)
94. Kunkel, W. 'Das Konsilium im Hausgericht', *ZSS* 83 (1966) 219–51 (= F 96, 117–49)
95. Kunkel, W. *An Introduction to Roman Legal and Constitutional History.* 2nd edn, transl. by J. M. Kelly, Oxford, 1973
96. Kunkel, W. *Kleine Schriften.* Weimar, 1974
97. Lambertini, R. *Plagium.* Bologna, 1986
98. La Rosa, F. 'Note sui tresviri capitales', *Labeo* 3 (1957) 231–45
99. Levick, B. 'Poena legis maiestatis', *Historia* 28 (1979) 358–79
100. Linderski, J. 'Constitutional aspects of the consular elections in 59 B.C.', *Historia* 14 (1965) 423–42
101. Linderski, J. 'The augural law', *ANRW* II 16.3 (1986) 2146–312
102. Lintott, A. W. '*Provocatio* from the struggle of the orders to the Principate', *ANRW* I.2 (1972) 226–67
103. Lintott, A. W. 'The *quaestiones de sicariis et veneficis* and the Latin *lex Bantina*', *Hermes* 106 (1978) 125–38

104. Lintott, A. W. 'The *leges de repetundis* and associate measures under the Republic', *ZSS* 98 (1981) 162–212
105. Luraschi, G. *Foedus Ius Latii Civitas, Aspetti costituzionali della romanizzazione in Transpadana* (Publ. Univ. Pavia, Studi scienz. giurid. e soc. 29). Padua, 1979
106. MacCormack, G. 'Criminal liability for fire in early and classical Roman law', *Index* 3 (1972) 382–96
107. Magdelain, A. *La loi à Rome. Histoire d'un concept.* Paris, 1978
108. Marshall, A. J. 'The structure of Cicero's edict', *AJPh* 85 (1964) 185–91
109. Marshall, A. J. 'Governors on the move', *Phoenix* 20 (1966) 231–46
110. Marshall, A. J. 'The lex Pompeia de provinciis (52 B.C.) and Cicero's imperium in 51–50 B.C. Constitutional aspects. *ANRW* I.1 (1972) 887–921
111. Marshall, A. J. 'The survival and development of international jurisdiction in the Greek world', *ANRW* II.13 (1980) 626–61
112. Mattingly, H. B. 'The extortion law of the Tabula Bembina', *JRS* 60 (1970) 154–68
113. Mattingly, H. B. 'The extortion law of Servilius Glaucia', *CQ* 25 (1975) 255–63
114. Mattingly, H. B. 'The character of the lex Acilia Glabrionis', *Hermes* 107 (1979) 478–88
115. Mattingly, H. B. 'A new look at the Lex repetundarum Bembina', *Philologus* 131 (1987) 71–81
116. Mellano, L. D. *Sui rapporti tra governatore provinciale e giudici locali alla luce delle Verrine.* Milan, 1977
117. Miners, N. J. 'The lex Sempronia ne quis iudicio circumveniatur', *CQ* 8 (1958) 241–3
118. Mitchell, T. N. 'Cicero and the senatus consultum ultimum', *Historia* 20 (1971) 47–61
119. Mommsen, Th. *Römisches Strafrecht.* Leipzig, 1899
120. Nardi, E. *L'otre dei parricidi e le bestie incluse.* Milan, 1980
121. Niccolini, G. *Il tribunato della plebe.* Milan, 1932
122. Niccolini, G. *Il fasti dei tribuni della plebe.* Milan, 1934
123. Nicholls, J. J. 'The reform of the *comitia centuriata*', *AJPh* 77 (1956) 225–54
124. Nicolet, C. 'Les lois judiciaires et les tribunaux de concussion', *ANRW* I.2 (1972) 197–214
125. Nippel, W. *Mischverfassungstheorie und Verfassungsrealität in Antike und Früher Neuzeit* (Geschichte und Gesellschaft, Bochumer hist. Studien 21). Stuttgart, 1980
126. O'Neal, W. J. 'Composition of the juries de repetundis from the lex Calpurnia to Sulla', *RSC* 26 (1978) 359–62
127. Oost, S. I. 'The date of the lex Iulia de repetundis', *AJPh* 77 (1956) 19–28
128. Pieri, G. *L'histoire de cens jusqu'à la fin de la république romaine* (Publ. de l'inst. de droit romain de l'univ. de Paris 25). Paris, 1968
129. Quaderno 221. See Abbreviations
130. Richardson, J. S. 'The purpose of the lex Calpurnia de repetundis', *JRS* 77 (1987) 1–12

131. Rilinger, R. *Der Einfluss des Wahlleiters bei den römischen Konsulwahlen von 366 bis 50 v.Chr.* (Vestigia 24). Munich, 1976
132. Rödl, B. *Das senatus consultum ultimum und der Tod der Gracchen.* Bonn, 1968
133. Rudolf, H. *Die städtische Organisation des ältesten römischen Gebietes und die Wirkung der cäsarischen Munizipalgesetzgebung.* Diss, Leipzig, 1932
134. Rudolph, H. *Stadt und Staat im römischen Italien.* Göttingen, 1985
135. Salerno, F. 'Collegia adversus rem publicam?' *Index* 13 (1985) 541–56
136. Santalucia, B. 'La legislazione Sillana in materia di falso nummario', *Iura* 30 (1979) 1–33
137. Santalucia, B. *Diritto e processo penale nell'antica Roma.* Milan, 1989
138. Saumagne, C. *Le droit latin et les cités romaines sous l'Empire. Essais critiques* (Pubs. de l'inst. de droit romain de l'Univ. de Paris 22). Paris, 1965
139. Scheid, J. 'Le prêtre et le magistrat. Réflexions sur les sacerdoces et le droit public à la fin de la République', *Des Ordres*, 243–80
140. Seager, R. 'Lex Varia de maiestate', *Historia* 16 (1967) 37–43
141. Sherwin-White, A. N. *The Roman Citizenship.* Oxford, 1939, repr. with addenda, 1973
142. Sherwin-White, A. N. 'The extortion procedure again', *JRS* 32 (1942) 43–55
143. Sherwin-White, A. N. 'Poena legis repetundarum', *PBSR* 17 (1949) 5–25
144. Simshäuser, W. *Iuridici und Munizipalgerichtsbarkeit in Italien* (*MünchBeitr Papyr* 61). Munich, 1973, ch. 2, 'Zur Entstehung der Munizipalgerichtsbarkeit in Italien'
145. Staveley, E. S. 'The reform of the comitia centuriata', *AJPh* 74 (1953) 1–33
146. Staveley, E. S. 'The constitution of the Roman Republic', *Historia* 5 (1956) 74–122
147. Staveley, E. S. 'Cicero on the comitia centuriata', *Historia* 11 (1962) 299–314
148. Staveley, E. S. *Greek and Roman Voting and Elections*, London and Southampton, 1972, Part II, 'Rome'
149. Stevenson, G. H. *Roman Provincial Administration.* Oxford, 1939
150. Strachan-Davidson, J. L. *Problems of the Roman Criminal Law.* 2 vols. Oxford, 1912
151. Sumner, G. V. 'Cicero on the comitia centuriata. *De re publica* II. 22.39–40', *AJPh* 81 (1960) 136–56
152. Sumner, G. V. 'Lex Aelia, lex Fufia', *AJPh* 94 (1963) 337–58
153. Sumner, G. V. 'Cicero and the *comitia centuriata*', *Historia* 13 (1964) 125–8
154. Szemler, G. J. *The Priests of the Roman Republic: a Study of Interactions between Priesthoods and Magistracies* (Coll. Latomus 127). Brussels, 1972
155. Taylor, L. R. 'The centuriate assembly before and after the reform', *AJPh* 78 (1957) 337–54
156. Taylor, L. R. *The Voting Districts of the Roman Republic* (*MAAR* 20). Rome, 1960
157. Taylor, L. R. *Roman Voting Assemblies.* Ann Arbor, 1966
158. Thomas, J. A. C. 'The development of Roman criminal law', *Law Quarterly Review* 79 (1963) 224–37

159. Thomas, Y.-P. 'Parricidium I', *MEFRA* 93 (1981) 643–715
160. Tibiletti, G. 'Le leggi *de iudiciis repetundarum* fino alla guerra sociale', *Studi offerti dai discepoli a P. Fraccaro per il suo LXX genetliaco, Athenaeum* 31 (1953), 5–100
161. Tibiletti, G. 'The *comitia* during the decline of the Roman Republic', *SDHI* 25 (1959) 94–127
162. Tyrrell, W. B. 'The duumviri in the trials of Horatius, Manlius and Rabirius', *ZSS* 91 (1974) 106–25
163. von Ungern-Sternberg, J. *Untersuchungen zum spätrepublikanischen Notstandsrecht: senatus consultum ultimum und hostis-Erklärung* (Vestigia 11). Munich, 1970
164. von Ungern-Sternberg, J. 'The end of the conflict of the orders', *Social Struggles in Archaic Rome. New Perspectives on the Conflict of the Orders*, ed. K. A. Raaflaub, Berkeley, 1986, 353–77
165. Venturini, C. *Studi sul 'crimen repetundarum' nell'età repubblicana.* Milan, 1979
166. Volk, A. *Die Verfolgung der Körperverletzung im frühen römischen Recht* (Forschungen zum röm. Recht 35). Vienna, 1984
167. Volterra, E. *Bibliografia di diritto agrario romano.* Florence, 1951
168. Weinrib, E. J. 'The prosecution of Roman magistrates', *Phoenix* 22 (1968) 32–56
169. Weinrib, E. J. 'The judiciary law of M. Livius Drusus', *Historia* 19 (1978) 414–43
170. Weinstock, S. 'Clodius and the lex Aelia Fufia', *JRS* 27 (1937) 215–22
171. Wieacker, F. *Römische Rechtsgeschichte* I, *Einleitung, Quellenkunde, Frühzeit und Republik* (Handbuch der Altertumswissenschaft x.3. 1, 1). Munich, 1988
172. Willems, P. *Le sénat de la république romaine.* 2 vols, I Louvain, Paris and Berlin, 1878, repr, 1885, II Louvain, 1883
173. Wiseman, T. P. 'The census in the first century B.C.', *JRS* 59 (1969) 59–75
174. Zumpt, A. W. *Das Criminalrecht der römischen Republik.* 2 vols. Berlin, 1865–9

b. PRIVATE LAW

175. Ankum, H. 'Denegatio actionis', *ZSS* 102 (1985) 453–69
176. Archi, G. G. *Problemi in tema di falso nel diritto romano.* Pavia, 1941
177. Bauman, R. A. 'Five pronouncements by P. Mucius Scaevola', *RIDA* 25 (1978) 223–45
178. Bauman, R. A. *Lawyers in Roman Republican Politics. A Study of the Roman Jurists in their Political Setting, 316–82 B.C.* (*MünchBeitrPapyr* 75). Munich, 1983
179. Bauman, R. A. *Lawyers in Roman Transitional Politics. A Study of the Roman Jurists in their Political Setting in the Late Republic and Triumvirate* (*Münch BeitrPapyr* 79). Munich, 1985
180. Behrends, O. *Die Wissenschaftslehre im Zivilrecht des Q. Mucius Scaevola Pontifex* (*NAWG* 1976, no. 7)

181. Behrends, O. 'Les "veteres" et la nouvelle jurisprudence à la fin de la République', *RD* 55 (1977) 7–33
182. Behrends, O. 'Institutionelles und prinzipielles Denken im römischen Privatrecht', *ZSS* 95 (1978) 187–231
183. Behrends, O. *Prinzipat und Sklavenrecht*. Göttingen, 1980
184. Behrends, O. *Die Fraus Legis*. Göttingen, 1982
185. Behrends, O. 'Le due giurisprudenze romane e le forme delle loro argomentazioni', *Index* 12 (1983–4) 189–225
186. Birks, P. 'From legis actio to formula', *The Irish Jurist* 4 (1969) 356–67
187. Birks, P. 'The early history of iniuria', *RHD* 37 (1969) 163–208
188. Bona, F. 'Sulla fonte di Cicerone de oratore I 56, 239–40 e sulla cronologia dei "decem libelli" di P. Mucio Scevola', *SDHI* 39 (1973) 425–80
189. Bongert, Y. 'Recherches sur les récupérateurs', in his *Varia. Etudes de droit romain*, Paris, 1952, 99–266
190. Bretone, M. *Tecniche e ideologie dei giuristi romani*. Naples, 1971
191. Bund, E. 'Die Fiktion "pro non scripto habetur" als Beispiel fiktionsbewirkter Interpretation', *Sein und Werden im Recht, Festgabe für Ulrich von Lübtow zum 70. Geburtstag*, ed. W. G. Becker and L. Schnorr von Carolsfeld, Berlin, 1970, 352–80
192. Bund, E. 'Zur Argumentation der römischen Juristen', *Studi in onore di Edoardo Volterra* I, Rome, 1971, 571–87
193. Bund, E. 'Rahmenerwägungen zu einem Nachweis stoischer Gedanken in der römischen Jurisprudenz', *De Iustitia et Iure, Festgabe für Ulrich von Lübtow zum 80. Geburtstag*, ed. M. Harder and G. Thielmann, Berlin, 1980, 127–45
194. Cancelli, F. 'Per una revisione del "cavere" dei giureconsulti repubblicani', *Studi in onore di Edoardo Volterra* V, Rome, 1971, 611–45
195. Ciulei, G. *L'équité chez Cicéron*. Amsterdam, 1972
196. Crook, J. A. 'Patria potestas', *CQ* 17 (1967) 113–22
197. Crook, J. A. 'A study in decoction', *Latomus* 26 (1967) 363–76
198. Crook, J. A. 'Intestacy in Roman society', *PCPhS* 19 (1973) 38–44
199. Crook, J. A. 'Sponsione provocare: its place in Roman litigation', *JRS* 66 (1976) 132–8
200. Daube, D. 'Licinnia's dowry', *Studi in onore di Biondo Biondi* I, Milan, 1963, 199–212
201. Ducos, M. *Les romains et la loi: recherches sur les rapports de la philosophie grecque et de la tradition romaine à la fin de la République*. Paris, 1984
202. Ebert, U. *Die Geschichte des Edikts de hominibus armatis coactisue* (Heidelberger rechtsw. Abh. 23). Heidelberg, 1968
203. Frezza, P. 'Storia del processo civile in Roma fino alla età di Augusto', *ANRW* I.2 (1972) 163–96
204. Frier, B. W. 'Urban praetors and rural violence. The legal background of Cicero's *pro Caecina*', *TAPhA* 113 (1983) 221–41
205. Frier, B. W. *The Rise of the Roman Jurist. Studies in Cicero's pro Caecina*. Princeton, 1985
206. Galsterer, H. 'Diritto e scienza giuridica in Grecia e Roma', *CS* 17 (1980) 185–98

207. Gardner, J. F. *Women in Roman Law and Society*. London and Sydney, 1986
208. Girard, P. F. *Histoire de l'organisation judiciaire des romains* I, *Les six premiers siècles de Rome* (all published). Paris, 1901
209. Grosso, G. 'Publio Mucio Scevola tra il diritto e la politica', *AG* 175 (1968) 204–11
210. Grosso, G. 'Schemi giuridici e società dall'epoca arcaica di Roma alla giurisprudenza classica: lo sviluppo e la elaborazione dei diritti limitati sulle cose', *ANRW* 1.2 (1972) 134–62
211. Guarino, A. *Diritto privato romano*. 6th edn, Naples, 1981
212. Harris, W. V. 'The Roman father's power of life and death', *Studies in Roman Law in Memory of A. Arthur Schiller*, ed. R. S. Bagnall and W. V. Harris, Leiden, 1986, 81–95
213. Hoffman, R. J. 'Civil law procedures in the provinces of the late Roman Republic', *The Irish Jurist* 11 (1976) 355–74
214. Horak, F. *Rationes decidendi. Entscheidungsbegründungen bei den älteren römischen Juristen bis Labeo* I. Aalen, 1969
215. Horak, F. Rev. of Behrends, *Wissenschaftslehre* and Schiavone, *Nascita della giurisprudenza*, *ZSS* 95 (1978) 402–21
216. d'Ippolito, F. 'Sextus Aelius "Catus"', *Labeo* 17 (1971) 271–83
217. d'Ippolito, F. *I giuristi e la città, ricerche sulla giurisprudenza romana della repubblica*. Naples, 1978
218. Jolowicz, H. F. 'The judex and the arbitral principle', *Mélanges F. De Visscher* I, *RIDA* 3 (1949) 477–92
219. Kaser, M. 'Partus ancillae', *ZSS* 75 (1958) 156–200
220. Kaser, M. *Das römische Zivilprozessrecht* (Handb. d. Altertumswissensch. x.3.4). Munich, 1966
221. Kaser, M. 'Die Beziehung von *lex* und *ius* und die XII Tafeln', *Studi in memoria di Guido Donatuti* II, Milan, 1973, 523–46
222. Kaser, M. *Über Verbotsgesetze und verbotswidrige Geschäfte im römischen Recht (SAWW* 312). Vienna, 1977
223. Kaser, M. '"Ius honorarium" und "ius civile"', *ZSS* 101 (1984) 1–114
224. Kaser,M. 'Über "relatives Eigentum" im altrömischen Recht', *ZSS* 102 (1985) 1–39
225. Kelly, J. M. 'The growth-pattern of the praetor's edict', *The Irish Jurist* 1 (1966) 341–55
226. Kelly, J. M. *Roman Litigation*. Oxford, 1966
227. Kelly, J. M. *Studies in the Civil Judicature of the Roman Republic*. Oxford, 1976
228. Kunkel, W. *Herkunft und soziale Stellung der römischen Juristen* (Forschungen zum röm. Recht 4). Weimar, 1952, rev. Graz, Vienna and Cologne, 1967
229. Kunkel, W. 'Legal thought in Greece and Rome', *Juridical Review* 65 (1953) 1–16
230. Labruna, L. 'Plauto, Manilio, Catone: premesse allo studio dell' "emptio consensuale"', *Studi in onore di Edoardo Volterra* V, Rome, 1971, 23–50
231. Lacey, W. K. 'Patria potestas', *The Family in Ancient Rome*, ed. B. Rawson, London, 1986, 121–44

232. Lewis, A. D. E. 'The trichotomy in locatio conductio', *The Irish Jurist* 8 (1973) 164–77
233. Lindsay, R. J. M. 'Defamation and the law under Sulla', *CPh* 44 (1949) 240–3
234. Lombardi, L. *Dalla 'fides' alla 'bona fides'*. Milan, 1961
235. von Lübtow, U. 'Cicero und die Methode der römischen Jurisprudenz', *Festschr. für Leopold Wenger zu seinem 70. Geburtstag dargebracht von Freunden, Fachgenossen und Schülern* I, Munich, 1944, 224–35
236. von Lübtow, U. 'Die Ursprungsgeschichte der exceptio doli und der actio de dolo malo', *Eranion Maridakis* I, Athens, 1963, 183–201
237. von Lübtow, U. 'Die Aufgaben des römischen Praetors', *Studi in onore di Arnaldo Biscardi* IV, Milan, 1983, 349–412
238. Luraschi, G. 'Sulla data e sui destinatari della "lex Minicia de liberis"', *SDHI* 42 (1976) 431–43
239. Magdelain, A. *Le consensualisme dans l'édit du preteur* (Publ. de l'inst. de droit romain de l'Univ. de Paris 18). Paris, 1958
240. Magdelain, A. 'Les mots *legare* et *heres* dans la loi des XII Tables', *Hommages à Robert Schilling*, ed. H. Zehnacker and G. Hentz, Paris, 1983, 159–73
241. Manfredini, A. D. *Contributo allo studio dell'iniuria in età repubblicana*. Milan, 1977
242. Manfredini, A. D. *La diffamazione verbale nel diritto romano* I, *Età repubblicana*. Milan, 1979
243. Marshall, A. J. 'The case of Valeria: an inheritance dispute in Roman Asia', *CQ* 25 (1975) 82–7
244. Martini, R. *Ricerche in tema di editto provinciale*. Milan, 1969
245. Metro, A. 'La lex Cornelia de iurisdictione alla luce di Dio Cass. 36.40.1–2', *Iura* 20 (1969) 500–24
246. Metro, A. *La denegatio actionis*. Milan, 1972
247. Mette, H. J. *Das römische Zivilrecht zu Beginn des Jahres 46 vor Christus*. Heidelberg, 1974
248. Nicholas, B. *An Introduction to Roman Law*. Oxford, 1962
249. Nörr, D. *Divisio und Partitio. Bemerkungen zur römischen Rechtsquellenlehre und zur antiken Wissenschaftstheorie*. Berlin, 1972
250. Nörr D. 'Pomponius, oder zum Geschichtsverständtnis der römischen Juristen', *ANRW* II.15 (1976) 497–604
251. Nörr, D. *Causa Mortis. Auf den Spuren einer Redewendung* (*MünchBeitr Papyr* 80). Munich, 1986
252. Partsch, J. *Die Schriftform im römischen Provinzialprozesse*. Breslau, 1905
253. Plescia, J. 'The development of Iniuria', *Labeo* (1977) 271–89
254. Polak, J. M. 'The Roman conception of the inviolability of the house', *Symbolae ad Jus et Historiam Antiquitatis pertinentes Julio Christiano van Oven dedicatae*, ed. M. David, B. A. van Groningen and E. M. Meijers, Leiden, 1946, 251–68
255. Polay, E. 'Der Kodifikationsplan des Pompeius', *AAntHung* 13 (1965) 85–95
256. Polay, E. 'Der Kodifizierungsplan des Julius Caesar', *Iura* 16 (1965) 27–51

257. Prichard, A. M. 'The origins of the "legis actio per condictionem"', *Synteleia Vincenzo Arangio-Ruiz*, ed. A. Guarino and L. Labruna, I, Naples, 1964, 261–8
258. Pugliese, G. 'Intorno al supposto divieto di modificare legislativamente il *ius civile*', *Atti del congresso internaz. di diritto romano e di storia del diritto, Verona 27-28-29-IX-1948,* II, Milan, 1951, 61–84
259. de Robertis, F. M. *Storia delle corporazioni e del regime associativo nel mondo romano*. Bari, 1971
260. Sacconi, G. 'Appunti sulla lex Aebutia', *AG* 197 (1979) 63–93
261. di Salvo, S. '*Lex Laetoria*'. *Minore età e crisi sociale tra il III e il II a.C.* Camerino, 1979
262. Sargenti, M. 'Studi sulla "restitutio in integrum"', *BIDR* 8 (1966) 194–298
263. Schiavone, A. *Nascita della giurisprudenza: cultura aristocratica e pensiero giuridico nella Roma tardo-repubblicana*. Rome and Bari, 1976
264. Schiller, A. Arthur, *Roman Law. Mechanisms of Development*. The Hague, Paris and New York, 1978
265. Schmidlin, B. *Das Rekuperatorenverfahren. Eine Studie zum römischen Prozess*. Friburg, Switzerland, 1963
266. Schmidlin, B. 'Horoi, pithana und regulae', *ANRW* II.15 (1976) 101–30
267. Schulz, F. *Principles of Roman Law*. Oxford, 1936
268. Schulz, F. *Roman Legal Science*. Oxford, 1946, repr. 1953
269. Seidl, E. 'Prolegomena zu einer Methodenlehre der Römer', *Aktuelle Fragen aus modernem Recht und Rechtsgeschichte, Gedächtnisschrift für Rudolf Schmidt*, ed. E. Seidl, Berlin, 1966
270. Smith, R. E. 'The law of libel at Rome', *CQ* 45 (1951) 169–79
271. Stein, P. G. *Fault in the Formation of Contract in Roman Law and Scots Law*. Edinburgh, 1958
272. Stein, P. G. *Regulae Iuris: From Juristic Rules to Legal Maxims*. Edinburgh, 1966
273. Stein, P. G. 'Logic and experience in Roman and Common Law', *Boston University Law Review* 59 (1974) 437–51
274. Stein, P. G. 'The place of Servius Sulpicius Rufus in the development of Roman legal science', *Festschrift für Franz Wieacker zum 70. Geburtstag*, ed. O. Behrends *et al.*, Göttingen, 1978, 175–84
275. Stein, P. G. 'The development of the institutional system', *Studies in Justinian's Institutes in Memory of J. A. C. Thomas*, ed. P. G. Stein and A. D. E. Lewis, London, 1983, 151–63
276. Sturm, F. *Stipulatio Aquiliana: Textgestalt und Tragweite der aquilianischen Ausgleichsquittung im klassischen römischen Recht* (*MünchBeitrPapyr* 59). Munich, 1972
277. Syme, R. 'A great orator mislaid', *CQ* 31 (1981) 421–7 (=A 119, III, 1414–22)
278. Talamanca, M. 'Lo schema "genus–species" nelle sistematiche dei giuristi romani', Quaderno 221 II, 1–319, esp. 211ff
279. Thilo, R. M. *Der codex accepti et expensi im römischen Recht. Ein Beitrag zur Lehre von der Litteralobligation* (Göttinger Studien zur Rechtsgeschichte 13). Göttingen, 1980

280. Thomas, J. A. C. *Textbook of Roman Law*. Amsterdam, New York and Oxford, 1976
281. Thomas, Y.-P. 'Le droit entre les mots et les choses. Rhétorique et jurisprudence à Rome', *APhD* 23 (1978) 93–114
282. Thomas, Y.-P. 'Vitae necisque potestas', *Du Châtiment* 499–548
283. Turpin, C. C. 'Bonae fidei iudicia', *Cambridge Law Journal* 1965, 260–70
284. Vigneron, R. 'Résistance du droit romain aux influences hellénistiques: le cas du dépot irrégulier', *RIDA* 31 (1984) 307–24
285. Volk, A. 'Zum Verfahren der "actio legis Corneliae de iniuriis"', *Sodalitas: Scritti in onore di A. Guarino*, II, Naples, 1984/5, 561–613
286. Waldstein, W. 'Zum Fall der "dos Licinniae"', *Index* 3 (1972) 343–61
287. Waldstein, W. 'Entscheidungsgrundlagen der klassischen römischen juristen', *ANRW* II.15 (1976) 3–100
288. Waldstein, W. *Operae libertorum: Untersuchungen zur Dienstpflicht freigelassener Sklaven* (Forschungen zur antiken Sklaverei 19). Stuttgart, 1986
289. Watson, A. *Contract of Mandate in Roman Law*. Oxford, 1961
290. Watson, A. 'Actio Serviana', *SDHI* 27 (1961) 356–63
291. Watson, A. 'Consensual societas between Romans and the introduction of formulae', *RIDA* 9 (1962) 431–6
292. Watson, A. 'Some cases of distortion by the past in classical Roman law', *RHD* 31 (1963) 68–91
293. Watson, A. 'The origins of consensual sale: a hypothesis', *RHD* 32 (1964) 245–54
294. Watson, A. *The Law of Obligations in the Later Roman Republic*. Oxford, 1965
295. Watson, A. *The Law of Persons in the Later Roman Republic*. Oxford, 1967
296. Watson, A. 'Morality, slavery and the jurists in the later Roman Republic', *Tulane Law Review* 42 (1967–8) 289–303
297. Watson, A. *The Law of Property in the Later Roman Republic*. Oxford, 1968
298. Watson, A. 'Narrow, rigid and literal interpretation in the later Roman Republic', *RHD* 37 (1969) 351–68
299. Watson, A. *Roman Private Law around 200 B.C.* Edinburgh, 1971
300. Watson, A. *The Law of Succession in the Later Roman Republic*. Oxford, 1971
301. Watson, A. 'Limits of juristic decision in the later Roman Republic', *ANRW* I.2 (1972) 215–25
302. Watson, A. '"Ius Aelianum" and "Tripertita"', *Labeo* 19 (1973) 26–30
303. Watson, A. 'The law of actions and the development of substantive law in the early Roman Republic', *Law Quarterly Review* 89 (1973) 387–92
304. Watson, A. *Law Making in the Later Roman Republic*. Oxford, 1974
305. Watson, A. *Rome of the Twelve Tables. Persons and Property*. Princeton, 1975
306. Wenger, L. *Die Quellen des römischen Rechts*, Vienna, 1953, 473–88, 'Die republikanische Jurisprudenz'
307. Wesel, U. 'Über den Zusammenhang der lex Furia, Voconia und Falcidia', *ZSS* 81 (1964) 308–16

308. Wesel, U. *Rhetorische Statuslehre und Gesetzesauslegung der römischen Juristen*. Cologne, 1967
309. Wieacker, F. *Vom römischen Recht. Zehn Versuche*. 2nd edn, Stuttgart, 1961
310. Wieacker, F. 'Zum Ursprung der bonae fidei iudicia', *ZSS* 80 (1963) 1–41
311. Wieacker, F. 'Die XII Tafeln in ihrem Jahrhundert', *Entretiens Hardt* 13 (1967) 291–362
312. Wieacker, F. 'The Causa Curiana and contemporary Roman jurisprudence', *The Irish Jurist* 2 (1967) 151–64
313. Wieacker, F. 'Über das Verhältnis der römischen Fachjurisprudenz zur griechisch-hellenistischen Theorie', *Iura* 20 (1969) 448–77
313A. Wieacker, F. 'Die römischen Juristen in der politischen Gesellschaft des zweiten vorchristlichen Jahrhunderts', *Sei und Werden im Recht, Festgabe für Ulrich von Lübtow zum 70. Geburtstag*, ed. W. G. Becker and L. Schnorr von Carolsfeld, Berlin 1970, 183–214
314. Wieacker, F. Rev. of Horak, *Rationes Decidendi*, *ZSS* 88 (1971) 339–55
315. Wieacker, F. 'Zur Rolle des Arguments in der römischen Jurisprudenz', *Festchr. für Max Kaser zum 70. Geburtstag am 21. April* 1976, ed. D. Medicus and H. H. Seiler, Munich, 1976, 3–27
316. Wieacker, F. 'Altrömische Priesterjurisprudenz', *Iuris Professio, Festgabe für Max Kaser zum 80. Geburtstag*, ed. H.-P. Benohr *et al.*, Vienna, Cologne and Graz, 1986, 347–70
317. Wieling, H. J. *Testamentsauslegung im römischen Recht* (*MünchBeitrPapyr* 62). Munich, 1972
318. Wolf, J. G. 'Zur legis actio sacramento in rem', *Römisches Recht in der europäischen Tradition, Symposion aus Anlass des 75. Geburtstages von Franz Wieacker*, ed. O. Behrends *et al*, Edelsbach, 1985, 1–39
319. Yaron, R. 'Vitae necisque potestas', *RHD* 30 (1962) 243–51

G. ECONOMY AND SOCIETY

1. Abbott, F. F. *The Common People of Ancient Rome*. London, 1912
2. Almagia, R. and Miglioni, E. *Le regioni d'Italia*. 18 vols. Turin, 1961–5
3. André J. *L'alimentation et la cuisine à Rome*. 2nd edn, Paris, 1981
4. Andreau, J. *Les affaires de Monsieur Jucundus* (Coll. éc. fr. de Rome 19). Rome, 1974
5. Andreau, J. 'Histoire des métiers bancaires et évolution économique', *Opus* 3 (1984) 99–114
6. Andreau, J. *La vie financière dans le monde romain: les métiers de manieurs d'argent (IVe siècle av. J.-C. – IIIe siècle ap. J.-C.) (BEFAR* 265). Rome, 1987
7. Andreau, J. 'M. I. Finley, la banque antique et l'économie moderne', *ASNP* 7 (1977) 1129–52
8. *Atlante aerofotografico delle sedi umane in Italia*. Florence, 1964–70
9. Bagnall, S. and Bogaert, R. 'Orders for payment from a banker's archive, papyri in the collection of Florida State University', *AncSoc* 6 (1975) 79–108

10. Bandelli, G. 'Per una storia agraria di Aquilea repubblicana', *Atti del Museo di Trieste* 13 (1983/4) 93–111
11. Barker, G. and Hodges, R. (ed.), *Archaeology and Italian Society* (*BAR* Internat. ser. 102). Oxford, 1981
12. Barrow, R. H. *Slavery in the Roman Empire*. London, 1928
13. Beloch, K. J. *Die Bevölkerung der griechisch-römischen Welt*. Leipzig, 1886
14. Beloch, K. J. 'La popolazione della Gallia al tempo di Cesare'; 'Per la storia della popolazione nell'antichità'; 'La popolazione dell' antichità', coll. (with essays by E. Ciccotti, A. Holm, O. Seeck and E. Kornemann) by V. Pareto in *Biblioteca di Studi Economichi* IV, Milan, 1909
15. Besnier, M. 'L'interdiction du travail des mines en Italie sous la République', *RA* 10 (1919) 31–50
16. Bodei Giglioni, G. *Lavori pubblici e occupazione nell'antichità classica*. Bologna, 1974
17. Bodei Giglioni, G. 'Pecunia fanatica. L'incidenza economica dei templi laziali', *RSI* 89 (1977) 33–76, repr. in B 273, 185–207
18. Bodel, J. 'Trimalchio and the candelabrum', *CPh* 84 (1989) 224–31
19. Bogaert, R. *Les origines antiques de la banque de dépôt*. Leiden, 1966
20. Bogaert, R. *Banques et banquiers dans les cités grecques*. Leiden, 1968
21. *Les bourgeoisies*. See Abbreviations
22. Brunt, P. A. 'The fiscus and its development', *JRS* 56 (1966) 75–91 (= A 20, 134–62)
23. Brunt, P. A. 'The Roman mob', *P&P* 35 (1966) 3–27, repr. in *Studies in Ancient Society*, ed. M. I. Finley, London, 1974, 74–102
24. Brunt, P. A. rev. of F. P. White, *Roman Farming*, *JRS* 62 (1972) 153–8
25. Brunt, P. A. 'Two great Roman landowners', *Latomus* 34 (1975) 619–35
26. Brunt, P. A. 'Free labour and public works at Rome', *JRS* 70 (1980) 81–100
27. Brunt, P. A. 'The revenues of Rome', *JRS* 71 (1981) 161–72, repr. with additions, A 20, 324–46
28. Burford, A. M. 'Heavy transport in classical antiquity', *Economic Hist. Review* 13 (1960–1) 1–18
29. Burford, A. M. *Craftsmen in Greek and Roman Society*. London, 1972
30. Capogrossi Colognesi, L. *La struttura della proprietà e la formazione dei iura praediorum nell'età repubblicana*. 2 vols. Milan, 1969 and 1976
31. Capogrossi Colognesi, L. *La terra in Roma antica* I. Rome, 1981
32. Capogrossi Colognesi, L. *L'agricoltura romana*. Bari, 1982
33. Carandini, A. 'Hortensia. Orti e frutteti intorno a Roma', *Misurare la terra* 5, 66–74
34. Carcopino, J. *La loi de Hiéron et les Romains*. Paris, 1914
35. Cassola, F. 'Romani e Italici in oriente', *Roma e l'Italia*, 305–22
36. Casson, L. *Ships and Seamanship in the Ancient World*. Princeton, 1971
37. Castagnoli, F. 'Installazioni portuali a Roma', *Seaborne Commerce* 35–42
38. Cels-Saint-Hilaire, J. 'Les *libertini*: des mots et des choses', *DHA* 11 (1985) 331–79
39. Chevallier, R. *Roman Roads*, transl. by N. H. Field. London, 1976
40. Clemente, G. 'Le leggi sul lusso e la società romana tra III e II sec. a.C.',

Società romana III, 1–14
41. Coarelli, F. 'Architettura e arti figurative in Roma, 150–50 a.C.', *Hellenismus*, 21–51
42. Coarelli, F. 'Public building in Rome between the second Punic War and Sulla', *PBSR* 45 (1977) 1–23
43. Coarelli, F. 'I santuari del Lazio e della Campania tra i Gracchi e le guerre civili', *Les Bourgeoisies*, 217–40
43A. Coarelli, F. 'Architettura sacra e architettura privata nella tarda repubblica', *Architecture et société de l'archaisme grec à la fin de la république romaine*, 1983, 191–217
44. Colini, A. M. 'Il porto fluviale del foro boario a Roma', *Seaborne Commerce*, 43–53
45. Cori, B. *The Italian Settlement System*. Warsaw, 1979
46. Crawford, M. H. 'Rome and the Greek world: economic relationships', *Economic Hist. Review* 30 (1977) 42–52
47. Crawford, M. H. 'Economia imperiale e commercio estero', *Tecnologia*, 207–17
48. Crawford, M. H. *La moneta in Grecia e a Roma*. Bari, 1982
49. D'Achiardi, G. 'L'industria metallurgica a Populonia', *SE* 3 (1929) 397–404
50. D'Arms, J. H. *Commerce and Social Standing in Ancient Rome*. Cambridge, MA and London, 1981
51. D'Arms, J. H., rev. of Fabre, *Libertus*, *CPh* 79 (1984) 170–4
52. D'Arms, J. H. and Kopff, E., (ed.) *The Seaborne Commerce of Ancient Rome* (*MAAR* 36). Rome, 1980 (also in Abbreviations)
53. David, J.-M. 'Promotion civique et droit à la parole: L. Licinius Crassus, les accusateurs et les rhéteurs latins', *MEFRA* 91 (1979) 135–81
54. David, J.-M. 'Les orateurs des municipes à Rome: intégration, réticences et snobismes', *Les Bourgeoisies*, 309–23
55. Delplace, C. 'Les potiers dans la société et l'économie de l'Italie et de la Gaule au Ier siècle av. et au Ier siècle ap. J.-C.', *Ktema* 3 (1978) 55–76
56. *Les dévaluations*. See Abbreviations
57. Dixon, S. 'The marriage alliance in the Roman elite', *Journal of Family History* 10 (1985) 353–78
58. Dumont, J. C. *Servus. Rome et l'esclavage sous la République*. Rome, 1988
59. Dupont, F. *La vie quotidienne du citoyen romain sous la république, 509–27 av. J.C.*, Paris, 1989
60. Durand, J. D. 'Mortality estimates from Roman tombstone inscriptions', *American Journal of Sociology* 65 (1959/60) 364–73
61. Dureau de la Malle, M. *Economie politique des Romains*. 2 vols. Paris, 1840, repr. New York, 1971
62. Etienne, R. 'Les rations alimentaires des esclaves de la familia rustica d'après Caton', *Index* 10 (1981) 66–78
63. Evans, J. K. 'Plebs rustica', *AJAH* 5 (1980) 19–47; 134–73
64. Evans, J. K. 'Wheat production and its social consequences in the Roman world', *CQ* 31 (1981) 428–42
65. Fabre, G. *Libertus: recherches sur les rapports patron-affranchi à la fin de la*

République romaine (Coll. éc. fr. de Rome 50). Paris, 1981
66. Fallu, E. 'Les règles de la comptabilité à Rome à la fin de la republique', *Points de vue*, 97–112
67. Finley, M. I. (ed.) *Studies in Roman Property*, Cambridge, 1976
68. Flambard, J. M. 'Collegia compitalicia: phénomène associatif, cadres territoriaux et cadres civiques dans le monde romain à l'époque républicaine', *Ktema* 6 (1981) 143–66
69. Flambard, J. M. 'Les collèges et les élites locales à l'époque républicaine d'après l'exemple de Capoue', *Les Bourgeoisies*, 75–89
70. Forbes, R. J, *Studies in Ancient Technology*. 2nd edn, 9 vols. Leiden, 1964–72
71. Forni, G. 'Problemi di ergologia virgiliana', *Misurare la terra* 2, 154
72. Fowler, W. Warde *Social Life at Rome in the Age of Cicero*. London, 1909
73. Frank, T. 'Race mixture in the Roman empire', *AHR* 21 (1915–16) 689–708
74. Fraschetti, A. 'Per una prosopografia dello sfruttamento: romani e italici in Sicilia (212–44 a.C.)', *Società romana* I, 51–61
75. Frayn, J. M. *Subsistence Farming in Roman Italy*. London, 1979
76. Frederiksen, M. 'Puteoli', *RE* 23.2 (1959) 2036–60, revd. in his *Campania*, 319–58
77. Frederiksen, M. 'Theory, evidence, and the ancient economy' (review of M. I. Finley, *The Ancient Economy*), *JRS* 65 (1975) 164–71
78. Frederiksen, M. 'Caesar, Cicero, and the problem of debt', *JRS* 56 (1966) 128–41
79. Frederiksen, M. 'Changes in the patterns of settlement', *Hellenismus* II, 341–55
80. Frézouls, E. 'Le théâtre romain et la culture urbaine', *La città antica come fatto di cultura, Atti del convegno Como/Bellagio 1979*, Como, 1983, 105–30
81. Frier, B. 'The rental market in early imperial Rome', *JRS* 67 (1977) 27–37
82. Frier, B. *Landlord and Tenant in Imperial Rome*. Princeton, 1980
83. Frier, B. 'Roman life expectancy: Ulpian's evidence', *HSPh* 86 (1982) 213–51
84. Früchtl, A. *Die Geldgeschäfte bei Cicero*. Erlangen, 1912
85. Fussel, G. E. and Kenny, A. 'Equipement d'une ferme romaine', *Annales (ESC)* 21 (1966) 306–23
86. Gabba, E. 'Urbanizzazione e rinnovamenti urbanistici nell'Italia centro-meridionale del I. sec. a.C.', *SCO* 21 (1972) 73–112
87. Gabba, E. 'Mercati e fiere nell'Italia romana' (with append. by F. Coarelli), *SCO* 24 (1975) 141–66
88. Gabba, E. 'Considerazioni politiche ed economiche sullo sviluppo urbano in Italia nei secoli II e I a.C.', *Hellenismus* II, 315–26
89. Gabba, E. 'Considerazioni sulla decadenza della piccola proprietà contadina nell'Italia centro-meridionale del II. sec. a.C.', *Ktema* 2 (1977) 269–84
90. Gabba, E. 'Per la tradizione dell'*heredium* romuleo', *RIL* 112 (1978) 250–8
91. Gabba, E. 'Strutture sociali e politica romana in Italia nel II sec. a.C'. *Les Bourgeoisies*

92. Gabba, E. 'Per la storia della società romana tardo-repubblicana', *Opus* I (1982) 373–88

93. Gabba, E. 'The *collegia* of Numa: problems of method and political ideas', *JRS* 74 (1984) 81–6

94. Gabba, E. 'Per un'interpretazione storica della centuriazione romana', *Athenaeum* 63 (1985) 265–84

95. Gabba, E. and Pasquinucci, M. *Strutture agrarie e allevamento transumante nell'Italia romana (III–I sec. a.C.)*. Pisa, 1979

96. Galsterer, H. 'Urbanisation und Municipalisation', *Hellenismus* II, 327–33

97. Garnsey, P. 'Where did Italian peasants live?', *PCPhS* 25 (1979) 1–25

98. Garnsey, P. 'Non-slave labour in the Roman World', *Non-slave Labour* 34–47

99. Garnsey, P. 'Independent freedmen and the economy of Roman Italy under the Principate', *Klio* 63 (1981) 359–72

100. Garnsey, P. *Famine and Food-Supply in the Graeco-Roman World*. Cambridge, 1988

101. Garnsey, P., Hopkins, K. and Whittaker, C. R. (eds.) *Trade in the Ancient Economy*. London, 1983 (also in Abbreviations)

102. von Gerkan, A. 'Die Einwohnerzahl Roms in der Kaiserzeit', *RhM* 55 (1940) 149–95

103. Giardina, A. 'Allevamento e economia della selva', *Società romana* I, 87–114

104. Giardina, A. and Schiavone, A., ed. *Società romana e produzione schiavistica*. I. *L'Italia: insediamenti e forme economiche*; II. *Merci, mercati e scambi*; III. *Modelli etici, diritto e trasformazioni sociali* (*Atti del colloquio Pisa, 1979*) Bari, 1981. (Discussion, *Opus* I (1982) 371–439 and D. Rathbone G 208 below. Also in Abbreviations

105. Girri, G. *La taberna nel quadro urbanistico e sociale di Ostia*. Milan, 1956

106. Giuffrè, V. 'Mutuo', *Enciclopedia del Diritto* XXVII, Milan, 1977, 411–44

107. Glautier, M. W. E. 'A study in the development of accounting in Roman times', *RIDA* 19 (1972) 311–43

108. Gratwick, A. S. 'Free or not so free? Wives and daughters in the late Roman Republic', *Marriage and Property*, ed. E. M. Craik, Aberdeen, 1984, 30–53

109. Gros, P. *Architecture et société à Rome et en Italie centro-méridionale aux deux derniers siècles de la République* (Coll. Latomus 156). Brussels, 1978

110. Gummerus, H. 'Industrie und Handel', *RE* 9.2 (1916) 1381–535

111. Habermann, W. 'Ostia, Getreidehandelshafen Roms', *Münstersche Beiträge zur antiken Handelsgeschichte* 1.1 (1982) 35–59

112. Hahn, I. 'Der Klassenkampf der plebs urbana in den letzten Jahrzehnten der römischen Republik', *Die Rolle der Volksmassen*, ed. J. Herrmann, Berlin, 1975, 121–46

113. Harper, J. 'Slaves and freedmen in imperial Rome', *AJPh* 93 (1972) 341–2

114. Havas, L. 'The *plebs Romana* in the late 60s B.C.', *ACD* 15 (1979) 23–33

115. Healy, J. F. *Mining and Metallurgy in the Greek and Roman World*. London, 1978

116. Heitland, W. E. *Agricola. A Study of Agriculture and Rustic Life in the Greco-Roman World from the Point of View of Labour*. Cambridge, 1921
117. Helen, T. 'Organisation of Roman brick production', *AIRF* 9 (1975) 1–21
118. Hermansen, G. 'The population of imperial Rome: the Regionaries', *Historia* 27 (1978) 129–68
119. Herzog, R. '*Tesserae nummulariae*', *Abh. der giessener Hochschulgesellschaft 1* (1919) 1–42
120. Herzog, R. 'Nummularius', *RE* 17 (1937) 1415–55
121. Hinrichs, F. *Die Geschichte der gromatischen Institutionen*. Wiesbaden, 1974
122. Hoffmann, W. and Siber, H. 'Plebs', *RE* 21.1 (1957) 73–187
123. Hopkins, K. 'Economic growth and towns in classical antiquity', *Towns in Society*, ed. P. Abrams and E. A. Wrigley, Cambridge, 1978, 35–78
124. Hopkins, K. 'Taxes and trade in the Roman Empire', *JRS* 70 (1980) 101–25
125. Hübner, E. '*Quaestiones onomatologicae Latinae* I, *nomina* in *-anus*', *Ephemeris Epigraphica* II (1875) 25–92
126. Humphrey, J. *Roman Circuses*. Berkeley and Los Angeles, 1986
127. Huttunen, P. *The Social Strata in the City of Rome*. Oulu, 1974.
128. *L'impero romano*. See Abbreviations
129. Jacota, M. 'La condition de l'esclave agricole', *Etudes offertes à J. Macqueron*, Aix-en-Provence, 1970, 375–83
130. Jones, A. H. M. 'The Roman civil service (clerical and sub-clerical grades)', *JRS* 39 (1949) 38–55 (=F 87, 151–75)
131. Jones, A. H. M. *The Roman Economy. Studies in Ancient Economic and Administrative History*, posth., ed. P. A. Brunt, Oxford, 1974
132. Jones, R. F. J. and Bird, D. J. 'Roman gold mining in north-west Spain II: workings on the Rio Duerna', *JRS* 62 (1972) 59–74
133. Jongman, W. *The Economy and Society of Pompeii*. Amsterdam, 1988
134. Jouanique, P. 'Le *codex accepti et expensi* chez Cicéron. Etude d' histoire de la comptabilité', *RD* 46 (1968) 5–31
135. Kahrstedt, U. 'Ager publicus und Selbstverwaltung in Lukanien und Bruttium', *Historia* 8 (1959) 174–206
136. Kampen, N. *Image and Status: Roman Working Women in Ostia*. Berlin, 1981
137. Kleberg, T. *Hôtels, restaurants et cabarets dans l'antiquité romaine*. Uppsala, 1957
138. Kniep, F. *Societas Publicanorum* I (all pubd.). Jena, 1896
139. Kolendo, J. *La traité agronomique des Sasernae*. Warsaw, 1973
140. Kolendo, J. *L'agricoltura nell'Italia romana* (with pref. by A. Carandini). Rome, 1980
141. De Laet, S. J. *Portorium, étude sur l'organisation douanière chez les Romains*. Bruges, 1949
142. Laffranque, M. 'Poseidonios, Eudoxe de Cyzique et la circumnavigation de l'Afrique', *RPhilos* 153 (1963) 199–222
143. Landels, J. G. *Engineering in the Ancient World*. London, 1978
144. Le Gall, J. *Le Tibre, fleuve de Rome, dans l'antiquité*. Paris, 1953

145. Le Gall, J. 'Rome, ville de fainéants?', *REL* 49 (1971) 266–77
145A. Linderski, J. 'Garden parlours: nobles and birds', in R. I. Curtis (ed.), *Studia Pompeiana et Classica in honour of Wilhelmina F. Jaskemski* II, 202ff. New York, 1988
146. Lipinsky, A. 'Orafi e argentieri', *L'urbe* XXIV (1961) 3–14; 3 (1961) 3–13
147. Loane, H. J. *Industry and Commerce of the City of Rome*. Baltimore, 1938
148. Lo Cascio, E. 'Obaerarii: la nozione della dipendenza in Varrone', *Index* 11 (1982) 265–84
149. MacMullen, R. 'Social history in astrology', *AncSoc* 2 (1971) 105–16
150. MacMullen, R. 'How many Romans voted?', *Athenaeum* 58 (1980) 454–7
151. Mancinetti Santamaria, G. 'La concessione della cittadinanza a Greci ed orientali nel II e I sec. a.C', *Les Bourgeoisies* 125–36
152. Marshall, A. J. 'Roman women and the provinces', *AncSoc* 6 (1975) 109–27
153. de Martino, F. *Storia economica di Roma antica* (Il pensiero storico 75). 2 vols. Florence, 1979
154. de Martino, F. 'Produzione di cereali in Roma nell'età arcaica', *PP* 34 (1979) 241–55
155. Maxey, M. *Occupations of the Lower Classes in Roman Society*. Chicago, 1938, repr. New York, 1975
156. Meiggs, R. *Roman Ostia*. Oxford, 1960, 2nd edn, 1973
157. Meiggs, R. *Trees and Timber in the Ancient Mediterranean World*. Oxford, 1982
158. Melillo, G., ed. *Due saggi intorno ai concetti economici di valore nell'antichità classica, 1886, 1889, H. v. Scheel e G. Alessio* (Antiqua 13). Naples, 1981
159. Minto, A. 'L'antica industria mineraria in Etruria', *SE* 8 (1934) 291–309
160. *Misurare la terra*. See Abbreviations
161. Moeller, W. O. *The Wool-Trade of Ancient Pompeii*. Leiden, 1976
162. Molin, M. 'Quelques considérations sur le chariot des vendanges de Langres (Haute-Marne)', *Gallia* 42 (1984) 97–114
163. Morel, J. P. 'Céramiques d'Italie et céramiques hellénistiques', *Hellenismus*, 471–501
164. Morel, J. P. 'La laine de Tarente', *Ktema* 3 (1978) 93–110
165. Morel, J. P. 'Aspects de l'artisanat dans la Grande Grèce romaine' *La Magna Grecia* (*Atti del XV. convegno di studi sulla Magna Grecia nell'età romana, Taranto, 1975*), Naples, 1980, 263–324
166. Morel, J. P. 'Les producteurs de biens artisanaux en Italie à la fin de la République', *Les Bourgeoisies*, 21–39
167. Morgan, M. G. 'The introduction of the Aqua Marcia into Rome, 144–40 B.C.', *Philologus* 122 (1978) 25–58
168. Moritz, L. A. *Grain-Mills and Flour in Classical Antiquity*. Oxford, 1958
169. Mrozek, S. '*Crustulum* et *mulsum* dans les villes italiennes', *Athenaeum* 50 (1972) 294–300
170. Nagle, D. B. 'Toward a sociology of south-eastern Etruria', *Athenaeum* 57 (1979) 411–47
171. de Neeve, P. W. *Colonus*. Amsterdam, 1984
172. Nicolet, C. 'Les variations des prix et la "théorie quantitative de la

monnaie" à Rome de Cicéron à Pline l'ancien', *Annales(ESC)* 26 (1971) 1203–27

173. Nicolet, C. 'Polybius VI.17.4 and the composition of the *societates publicanorum*', *The Irish Jurist* 6 (1971) 163–76

174. Nicolet, C. *Tributum. Recherches sur la fiscalité directe sous la République romaine* (Antiquitas Reihe I 24). Bonn, 1976

175. Nicolet, C. 'Deux remarques sur l'organisation des sociétés de publicains à la fin de la République romaine', *Points de vue*, 69–95

176. Nicolet, C. 'Economie, société et institutions au IIe siècle av. J.-C.', *Ann(ESC)* 35 (1980) 871–94

177. Nicolet, C. 'Pline, Paul et la théorie de la monnaie', *Athenaeum* 62 (1984) 105–35

178. Nicolet, C. 'Il pensiero economico dei Romani', *Storia della idee politiche, economiche e sociali* I, ed. L. Firpo, Turin, 1982, 877–960 (=G 179, ch. 2)

179. Nicolet, C. *Rendre à César: Economie et sociéé dans la Rome antique*. Paris, 1988, of which Ch. 1, 'Economie et société', is the present ch. XVI before translation and Ch. 2, 'La pensée économique des Romains', is no. 178 above before translation

180. Nissen, H. *Italische Landeskunde*. 2 vols. Berlin, 1883–1902

181. *Non-slave labour*. See Abbreviations

182. Oliver, E. H. *Roman Economic Conditions to the Close of the Republic*. Toronto, 1907

183. *Des ordres à Rome*, sous la direction de Claude Nicolet (Publications de la Sorbonne, Sér. hist. ancienne et mediévale 13). Paris, 1984 (also in Abbreviations)

184. Packer, J. E. 'Housing and population in imperial Rome and Ostia', *JRS* 57 (1967) 80–95

185. Panella, C. 'I commerci di Roma e di Ostia in età imperiale', *Misurare la terra* V, 180–89

186. Park, M. E. *The Plebs in Cicero's Day, a Study of their Provenance and of their Employment*. Cambridge, MA, 1918, repr. New York, 1975

187. Parker, A. J. 'Shipwrecks and ancient trade in the Mediterranean', *Archaeological Review from Cambridge* 3.2 (1984) 99–113

188. Paterson, J. 'Salvation from the sea: amphorae and trade in the Roman west', *JRS* 72 (1982) 146–57

189. Perelli, L. 'La chiusura delle miniere macedoni dopo Pidna', *RFIC* 103 (1975) 403–12

190. Persson, A. W. *Staat und Manufaktur im römischen Reiche*. Lund, 1923

191. Pleket, H. W. rev. of *Trade*, *Gnomon* 57 (1985) 148–54

192. *Points de vue*. See Abbreviations

193. Pomey, P. and Tchernia, A. 'Il tonnellagio massimo delle navi mercantili romane', *Puteoli* 4/5 (1981) 29–59

194. Potter, T. W. *The Changing Landscape of South Etruria*. London, 1979

195. Pritchard, R. T. 'Land tenure in Sicily in the 1st century B.C.', *Historia* 18 (1969) 545–56

196. *Producción y comercio del aceite en la Antigüedad* (*1st Internat. Congr.*). Madrid, 1980

197. Prugni, G. '*Quirites*', *Athenaeum* 65 (1987) 121–61
198. Pucci, G. 'La produzione della ceramica aretina', *DArch* 7 (1973) 255–93
199. Purcell, N. 'The *apparitores*, a study in social mobility', *PBSR* 51 (1983) 125–73
200. Purcell, N. 'Wine and wealth in ancient Italy', *JRS* 75 (1985) 1–19
201. Purcell, N. 'The Nicopolitan synoecism and Roman urban policy', *Nikopolis* 1 (*Proceedings of the 1st Internat. Symposium on Nikopolis, 23–9 Sept. 1984*), ed. E. Chrysos, Preveza, 1987, 71–90
202. Purcell, N. 'Tomb and suburb', *Römische Gräberstrassen: Selbstdarstellung, Status, Standard*, ed. H. von Hesberg and P. Zanker, Munich, 1987, 25–41
203. Radke, G. 'Viae publicae Romanae', *RE* Suppl. 13 (1973) 1417–686
204. Radke, G. 'Wollgebilde an den Compitalia', *WJA* 9 (1983) 173–8
205. Radmilli, A. M. *Popoli e civiltà dell'Italia antica* I. Rome, 1974
206. Ramage, E. S. 'Urban problems in ancient Rome' *Aspects of Greek and Roman Urbanism, Essays on the Classical City*, ed. R. T. Marchese (*BAR* Internat. ser. 188), Oxford, 1983
207. Rathbone, D. W. 'The development of agriculture in the *Ager Cosanus* during the Roman Republic', *JRS* 71 (1981) 10–23
208. Rathbone, D. W. rev. of *Società Romana*, *JRS* 73 (1983) 160–68
209. Rawson, E. D. 'The Ciceronian aristocracy and its properties', *Studies in Roman Property*, ed. M. I. Finley, Cambridge, 1976, 85–102 (= A 94A, 204–22)
210. Rawson, E. D. 'Chariot-racing in the Roman Republic', *PBSR* 49 (1981) 1–16 (= A 94A, 389–407)
211. Rickman, G. *Roman Granaries and Store Buildings*. Cambridge, 1971
212. Rickman, G. *The Corn Supply of Ancient Rome*. Oxford, 1979
213. Rini, A. 'La plebe urbana a Roma dalla morte di Cesare alla sacrosancta potestas di Ottaviano', *Epigrafia e territorio, politica e società: temi di antichità romane*, ed. M. Pani, Bari, 1983, 161–90
214. Roddaz, J.-M. and Fabre, G. 'Recherches sur la *familia* de M. Agrippa', *Athenaeum* 60 (1982) 84–112
215. *Roma e l'Italia*. See Abbreviations
216. Rougé, J. *Recherches sur l'organisation du commerce maritime en Méditerranée sous l'empire romain*. Paris, 1966
217. Rougé, J. 'Prêt et société maritime dans le monde romain', *Seaborne Commerce*, 291–304
218. Royer, J. P. 'Le problème des dettes à la fin de la République romaine', *RD* 45 (1967) 191–240; 407–50
219. de Ste Croix, G. E. M. 'Greek and Roman Accounting', *Studies in the History of Accounting*, ed. A. C. Littleton and B. S. Yamey, London, 1956, 14–74
220. Saller, R. P. '*Patria potestas* and the stereotype of the Roman family', *Continuity and Change* 1 (1986) 7–22
221. Salvioli, G. *Il capitalismo antico. Storia dell'economia romana*. Bari, 1929. 2nd edn by A. Giardina, Bari, 1982
222. Schneider, H. C. *Altstrassenforschung*. Darmstadt, 1982
223. Scobie, A. 'Slums, sanitation and mortality in the Roman world', *Klio* 68

(1986) 399–443
224. Sereni, E. *Paesaggio agrario italiano*. Bari, 1961
225. Sirago, V. A. 'La personalità di C. Vestorio', *Puteoli* 3 (1979) 3–16
226. Skydsgaard, J. E. 'The disintegration of the Roman labour market and the theory of clientela', *Studia Romana in honorem P. Krarup septuagenarii*, ed. K. Ascami *et al.*, Odense, 1976, 44–8
227. Skydsgaard, J. E. 'Non-slave labour in rural Italy during the late Republic', *Non-Slave Labour*, 65–72
228. Solin, H. *Die griechischen Personennamen in Rom: ein Namenbuch (Auctarium ad CIL)*. 3 vols. Berlin and New York, 1982
229. Spurr, S. 'The cultivation of millet in Roman Italy', *PBSR* 51 (1983) 1–15
230. Spurr, S. *Arable Cultivation in Roman Italy*. London, 1986
231. Stambaugh, J. E. *The Ancient Roman City*. Baltimore, 1988
232. *Stato e moneta fra la tarda repubblica e il primo impero. Incontro di studio, Roma, 19 aprile 1982. AIIN* 29 (1982)
233. Steffensen, F. 'Fiscus in der späten römischen Republik', *C&M* 28 (1967) 254–85
234. Steinby, M. 'L'edilizia come industria pubblica e privata', *ARID* Suppl. x (1983) 219–21
235. Tanzer, H. H. *The Common People of Pompeii*. Baltimore, 1939
236. Taylor, L. R. 'The four urban tribes and the four regions of Rome', *RPAA* 27 (1952–4) 225–38
237. Tchernia, A. 'Les fouilles sousmarines de Planier (Bouches-du-Rhône'), *CRAI* 1969, 292–309
238. Tchernia, A. *Le vin de l'Italie romaine. Essai d'histoire économique d'après les amphores* (*BEFAR* 261). Rome, 1986
239. *Tecnologia, economia e società nel mondo romano* (*Atti del convegno, Como 27–9 sett. 1979*). Como, 1980 (also in Abbreviations)
240. Thebért, Y. 'Economie, société et politique aux deux derniers siècles de la République romaine', *Annales (ESC)* 48 (1980) 871–911
241. Thiel, J. H. *Eudoxus of Cyzicus. A Chapter in the History of the Sea-Route to India and the Route round the Cape in Ancient Times* (Historische Studies van de R. U. te Utrecht 23). Groningen, 1966
242. Tibiletti, G. 'Lo sviluppo del latifondo', *Atti del X. congresso internat. per le scienze storiche* II, Rome, 1955, 237–92
243. Toller, O. J. *De spectaculis cenis distributionibus in municipiis Romanis Orientis imperatorum aetate exhibitis*. Altenburg, 1889
244. Torelli, M. 'Innovazioni nelle tecniche edilizie romane tra il I. sec. a.C. e il I. sec. d.C.', *Tecnologia*, 139–62
245. Tozzi, G. *Economisti greci e romani*. Milan, 1961
246. Tozzi, P. *Saggi di topografia storica*. Florence, 1974
247. Treggiari, S. *Roman Freedmen during the Late Republic*. Oxford, 1969
248. Treggiari, S. 'Urban labour in Rome: mercennarii et tabernarii', *Non-Slave Labour*, 48–64
249. Vélissaropoulos, J. *Les nauclères grecs. Recherches sur les institutions maritimes en Grèce et dans l'Orient hellénisé*. Geneva and Paris, 1980

250. Veyne, P. *Le pain et le cirque. Sociologie historique d'un pluralisme politique.* Paris, 1976, in part transl. by B. Pearce as *Bread and Circuses*, London, 1990
251. Veyne, P. 'Mythe et réalité de l'autarcie à Rome', *REA* 81 (1979) 261–80
252. Virlouvet, C. *Famines et émeutes des origines de la République à la mort de Néron* (Coll. éc. fr. de Rome 87). Rome, 1985
253. Wallace-Hadrill, A., ed., *Patronage in Ancient Society*. London and New York, 1989
254. Waltzing, J.-P. *Etudes historiques sur les corporations professionnelles chez les Romains.* 4 vols. Louvain, 1895–1900
255. Ward-Perkins, J. B. *Roman Architecture.* New York, 1977
256. Weber, C. W. *Panem et circenses. Massenunterhaltung als Politik im antiken Rom.* Düsseldorf, 1983
257. White, K. D. 'Latifundia', *BICS* 14 (1967) 62–79
258. White, K. D. *A Bibliography of Roman Agriculture.* Reading, 1970
259. White, K. D. *Roman Farming.* London, 1970
260. Whittaker, C. R. 'Il povero', *L'uomo romano*, ed. A. Giardina, Rome, 1989, 299–333
261. Yavetz, Z. 'The living conditions of the plebs in Republican Rome', *Latomus* 17 (1958) 500–17 (= Seager, *Crisis*, 162–79)
262. Yavetz, Z. *Plebs and Princeps.* Oxford, 1969. 2nd edn, 1988
263. Yavetz, Z. 'Fluctuations monétaires et condition de la plèbe à la fin de la République', *Recherches sur les structures sociales dans l'antiquité classique, Caen, 25–6 avril 1969*, introd. de C. Nicolet, Paris, 1970, 133–57
264. Yeo, C. A. 'Land and sea transportation in imperial Italy', *TAPhA* 77 (1946) 221–44
265. Zehnacker, H. *Moneta. Recherches sur l'organisation et l'art des émissions monétaires de la République romaine (287–31 av. J.-C.)* (*BEFAR* 222). 2 vols. Rome, 1973
266. Zimmer, G. *Römische Berufsdarstellungen.* Berlin, 1982

H. RELIGION AND IDEAS

1. Alföldi, A. 'Zum Gottesgnadentum des Sulla', *Chiron* 6 (1976) 143–58
2. Ambaglio, D. 'La dedica delle opere letterarie antiche fino all'età dei Flavi', *Saggi di letteratura e storiografia antiche*, ed. D. Ambaglio *et al.* (Bibl. di Athenaeum 2). Como, 1983
3. Anderson, W. S. *Pompey, his Friends, and the Literature of the First Century B.C.* (Univ. of Calif. Pubs. in Class. Philol. 19.1). Berkeley, 1963
4. Badian, E. 'The early historians', *Latin Historians*, ed. T. A. Dorey, London, 1966, 1–38
5. Barnes, J. 'Antiochus of Ascalon', *Philosophia Togata*, 51–96
6. Barwick, K. *Das rednerische Bildungsideal Ciceros* (*ASAW* 54.3). Berlin, 1963
7. Basanoff, V. *Evocatio: étude d'un rituel militaire romain.* Paris, 1947
8. Beard, M. 'Cicero and divination: the formation of a Latin discourse',

JRS 76 (1986) 33–46

9. Beard, M. 'A complex of times: no more sheep on Romulus' birthday', *PCPhS* 33 (1987) 1–15

10. Beard, M. 'Priesthood in the Roman Republic', *Pagan Priests*, 19–48

10A. Beard, M. 'Writing and religion: *Ancient Literacy* and the function of the written word in Roman religion', in *Literacy in the Roman World*, ed. S. Humphrey, Ann Arbor, 1991, 35–58

11. Beck, R. 'Mithraism since Franz Cumont', *ANRW* II.17.4 (1984) 2002–115

12. Bémont, C. 'Les enterrés vivants du Forum Boarium. Essai d'interprétation', *MEFRA* 72 (1960) 133–46

13. Bömer, F. *Untersuchungen über die Religion der Sklaven in Griechenland und Rom.* I *Die wichtigsten Kulte und Religionen in Rom und im lateinischen Westen.* Mainz, 1957. 2nd edn revd. by P. Herz (Forsch. zur antiken Sklaverei 14.1), Wiesbaden, 1981

14. Bömer, F. 'Kybele in Rom', *MDAI(R)* 71 (1964) 130–51

15. Boissier, G. *Cicéron et ses amis. Etude sur la société romaine du temps de César.* 11th edn, Paris, 1899

16. Bonner, S. F. *Education in Ancient Rome from the Elder Cato to the Younger Pliny.* London, 1977

17. Boyancé, P. 'Les méthodes de l'histoire littéraire: Cicéron et son oeuvre philosophique', *REL* 14 (1936) 288–309 (= *Etudes sur l'humanisme cicéronien*, Brussels, 1970, 199–221)

18. Briquel, D. 'Rituel d'ensévelissement au Forum Boarium', *REL* 59 (1981) 30–7

19. Bruneau, P. *Recherches sur les cultes de Délos à l'époque hellénistique et à l'époque impériale* (*BEFAR* 217). Paris, 1970

20. Brunt, P. 'Philosophy and religion in the later Republic', *Philosophia Togata*, 174–98

21. Bulard, M. *La religion domestique dans la colonie italienne de Délos d'après les peintures murales et les autels historiés* (*BEFAR* 131). Paris, 1926

22. Burkert, W. 'Cicero als Platoniker und Skeptiker', *Gymnasium* 72 (1965) 175–200

23. Burkert, W. 'Zur geistesgeschichtlichen Einordnung einiger Pseudopythagorica', *Entretiens Hardt* 18 (1971) 23–55

24. della Casa, A. *Nigidio Figulo* (Nuovi saggi 42). Rome, 1962

25. Cichorius, C. 'Staatliche Menschenopfer', *Römische Studien*, Leipzig, 1922, 7–20

26. Clausen, W. V. 'The new direction in poetry', *CHCL* II (1982) 178–206

27. Coleman, R. 'The dream of Scipio', *PCPhSA* 10 (1964) 1–14

28. Cramer, F. H. 'Expulsion of astrologers from ancient Rome', *C&M* 12 (1951) 9–50

29. Crawford, M. H. 'Greek intellectuals and the Roman aristocracy', *Imperialism in the Ancient World*, ed. P. D. A. Garnsey and C. R. Whittaker, Cambridge, 1978, 193–207

30. Degrassi, A. 'Le dediche di popoli e re asiatici al popolo romano e a

Giove Capitolino', *BCAR* 74 (1951–2) 19–47 (=A 26, I, 415–44)

31. Dillon, J. *The Middle Platonists*. London, 1977
32. Dörner, F. K. and Gruben, G. 'Die Exedra der Ciceronen', *MDAI(A)* 68 (1953) 63–76
33. Donini, P. *Le scuole l'anima l'impero: la filosofia antica da Antioco a Plotino*. Turin, 1982
34. Donini, P. 'The history of the concept of electicism', *The Question of 'Eclecticism', Studies in Later Greek Philosophy*, ed. J. M. Dillon and A. A. Long, Berkeley, Los Angeles and London, 1988, 15–33
35. Douglas, A. E. 'The intellectual background of Cicero's Rhetorica: a study in method', *ANRW* I.3 (1973) 95–138
36. Dunand, F. 'Cultes égyptiens hors d'Egypte. Essai d'analyse des conditions de leur diffusion', *Religions, pouvoirs, rapports sociaux* (Ann. litt. Univ. Besançon 237), Paris, 1980, 71–148
37. Eckstein, A. M. 'Human sacrifice and fear of military disaster in Republican Rome', *AJAH* 7 (1982) 69–95
38. Fayer, C. *Il culto della dea Roma* (Coll. di saggi e ricerche 9). Pescara, 1976
39. Forbes, C. A. 'The education and training of slaves in antiquity', *TAPhA* 86 (1955) 321–60
40. Fraschetti, A. 'Le sepolture rituali del Foro Boario', *Le délit religieux*, 51–115
41. Fraschetti, A. 'La sepoltura delle Vestali e la città, *Du Châtiment*, 97–129
42. Frier, B. W. 'Augural symbolism in Sulla's invasion of 83', *ANSMusN* 13 (1967) 111–18
43. Furley, D. J. 'Lucretius the Epicurean', *Entretiens Hardt* 24 (1978) 1–37
44. Gagé, J. *Apollon romain* (*BEFAR* 182). Paris, 1955
45. Gallini, C. 'Politica religiosa di Clodio', *SMSR* 33 (1962) 257–72
46. Gallini, C. *Protesta e integrazione nella Roma antica* (Bibl. di cultura moderna 698). Bari, 1970
47. Gesche, H. *Die Vergottung Caesars* (Frankfurter althist. Studien 1). Frankfurt, 1968
48. Glucker, J. *Antiochus and the Late Academy*. Göttingen, 1978
49. Glucker, J. 'Cicero's philosophical affiliations', *The Question of 'Eclecticism'. Studies in Later Greek Philosophy*, ed. J. M. Dillon and A. A. Long, Berkeley, Los Angeles and London, 1988, 34–69
50. Gordon, R. L. 'From Republic to Principate: priesthood, religion and ideology', *Pagan Priests*, 179–98
51. Grafton, A. T. and Swerdlow, N. M. 'Technical chronology and astrological history in Varro, Censorinus and others', *CQ* 35 (1985) 454–65
52. Gratwick, A. S. 'The satires of Ennius and Lucilius', *CHCL* II (1982) 156–71
53. Griffin, M. 'Philosophy, politics and politicians at Rome', *Philosophia Togata*, 1–37
54. Grimal, P. 'Le poème de Lucrèce en son temps', *Entretiens Hardt* 24 (1978) 233–70

55. Grube, G. M. A. *The Greek and Roman Critics*. London, 1965
56. Hanson, J. A. *Roman Theater Temples*. Princeton, 1959
57. Hadot, I. *Arts libéraux et philosophie dans la pensée antique*. Paris, 1984
58. Harris, W. V. 'Literacy and epigraphy I', *ZPE* 52 (1983) 87–111
59. Heldmann, K. *Antike Theorien über Entwicklung und Verfall der Redekunst* (Zetemata 77). Munich, 1982
60. Horsfall, N. 'Varro and Caesar: three chronological problems', *BICS* 19 (1972) 120–8
61. Horsfall, N. 'Doctus sermones utriusque linguae?', *EMC* 22 (1979) 85–95
62. Horsfall, N. 'Prose and mime', *CHCL* II (1982) 286–94
63. Jocelyn, H. D. 'The Roman nobility and the religion of the Roman state', *JRH* 4 (1966) 89–104
64. Jocelyn, H. D. 'The ruling class of the Roman Republic and Greek philosophers', *BRL* 59 (1976/7) 323–66
65. Jocelyn, H. D. 'Varro's *Antiquitates rerum diuinarum* and religious affairs in the late Roman Republic', *BRL* 65 (1982/3) 148–205
66. Jones, C. P. 'The Plancii of Perge and Diana Planciana', *HSPh* 80 (1976)
67. Jones, D. M. 'Cicero as a translator', *BICS* 6 (1959) 22–34
68. Keaveney, A. 'Sulla and the gods', *Studies in Latin Literature and Roman History* III, ed. C. Deroux (Coll. Latomus 180), Brussels, 1983, 44–79
69. Köves-Zulauf, T. 'Plinius d. Ä. und die römische Religion', *ANRW* II.16.1 (1978) 187–288
70. Kroll, W. *Die Kultur der ciceronischen Zeit*. Leipzig, 1933
71. Kroll, W. 'Tullius' (29): 'Die rhetorischen Schriften', *RE* 7A (1939) 1091–103
72. Kumaniecki, K. 'Cicerone e Varrone. Storia di una conoscenza', *Athenaeum* 40 (1962) 221–43
73. Le Bonniec, H. *Le culte de Cérès à Rome des origines à la fin de la République* (Et. et commentaires 27). Paris, 1938
74. Le Gall, J. 'Evocatio', *Mél. Heurgon* I 519–24
75. Le Glay, M. 'Magie et sorcellerie à Rome au dernier siècle de la République', *Mél. Heurgon* I 525–50
76. Leone, M. 'Il problema del flaminato de Cesare', *Φιλίας Χάριν, Miscellanea di studi classici in onore di Eugenio Manni*, ed. M. J. Fontana, M. T. Piraino and F. P. Rizzo, I, Rome, 1976, 193–212
77. Liebeschuetz, J. H. W. G. *Continuity and Change in Roman Religion*. Oxford, 1979
78. Linderski, J. 'Cicero and Roman divination' *PP* 36 (1982) 12–38
79. MacBain, B. *Prodigy and Expiation: a Study in Religion and Politics in Republican Rome* (Coll. Latomus 177). Brussels, 1982
80. Malaise, M. *Les conditions de pénétration et de diffusion des cultes égyptiens en Italie* (Etudes préliminaires aux religions orientales dans l'empire romain 22). Leiden, 1972
81. Marshall, A. J. 'Library resources and creative writing at Rome', *Phoenix* 30 (1976) 252–64
82. Mellor, R. *ΘΕΑ ΡΩΜΗ. The Worship of the Goddess Roma in the Greek*

World (Hypomnemata 42). Göttingen, 1975
83. Mitchell, T. N. 'The *leges Clodiae* and *obnuntiatio*', *CQ* 36 (1986) 172–6
84. Momigliano, A. 'Epicureans in revolt', *JRS* 31 (1941) 151–7 (= *Secondo contributo alla storia degli studi classici*, Rome, 1960, 379–88)
85. Momigliano, A. *Alien Wisdom. The Limits of Hellenization.* Cambridge, 1975
86. Momigliano, A. 'The origins of universal history', Univ. of London Creighton Lecture, *ASNP* 12 (1982) 533–60 (= *Settimo contributo alla storia degli studi classici*, Rome, 1984, 77–103)
87. Momigliano, A. 'The theological efforts of the Roman upper classes in the first century B.C.', *CPh* 79 (1984) 199–211 (= *Ottavo contributo alla storia degli studi classici*, Rome, 1987, 261–77)
88. Moretti, L. 'Chio e la lupa Capitolina', *RFIC* 108 (1980) 33–54
89. *Mysteries of Diana. The antiquities from Nemi in Nottingham museums.* Castle Museum, Nottingham, 1983
90. Nock, A. D. 'Religious developments from the close of the Republic to the reign of Nero', *CAH* x, 1st edn, 1934, 465–511
91. Norden, E. *Aus altrömischen Priesterbüchern. Die Spruchformel der Augurn auf der Burg* (*Skr. utgivna av Kongl. Humanistiska Vetenskabssamfundet i Lund* 29). Lund and Leipzig, 1939
92. North, J. A. 'Praesens divus', rev. of Weinstock, *Divus Iulius*, *JRS* 65 (1975) 171–7
93. North, J. A. 'Conservatism and change in Roman religion', *PBSR* 44 (1976) 1–12
94. North, J. A. 'Religious toleration in Republican Rome', *PCPhS* 25 (1979) 85–103
95. North, J. A. 'Novelty and choice in Roman religion', *JRS* 70 (1980) 186–91
96. North, J. A. 'Diviners and divination at Rome', *Pagan Priests*, 51–71
97. *Pagan Priests.* See Abbreviations
98. Paillier, J.-M. '"Raptos a diis homines dici . . ." (Tite-Live 39.13): les Bacchanales et la possession par les nymphes', *Mél. Heurgon* II, 731–42
99. Paillier, J.-M. 'La spirale de l'interprétation: les Bacchanales', *Annales (ESC)* 37 (1982) 929–52
100. Paillier, J.-M. 'Les pots cassés des Bacchanales', *MEFRA* 95 (1983) 7–54
101. Pédech, P. 'Les idées religieuses de Polybe. Etude sur la religion gréco-romaine au second siècle av. J.-C.', *RHR* 167–8 (1965) 35–68
102. *Philosophia Togata.* See Abbreviations
103. Price, S. R. F. *Rituals and Power: the Roman Imperial Cult in Asia Minor.* Cambridge, 1984
104. Rawson, E. 'Cicero the historian and Cicero the antiquarian', *JRS* 62 (1972) 33–45 (= A 94A, 58–79)
105. Rawson, E. 'Scipio, Laelius, Furius and the ancestral religion', *JRS* 63 (1973) 161–74 (= A 94A, 80–101)
106. Rawson, E. 'Religion and politics in the late second century at Rome', *Phoenix* 28 (1974) 193–212 (= A 94A, 149–68)

107. Rawson, E. 'The introduction of logical organisation in Roman prose literature', *PBSR* 46 (1978) 12–34 (= A 94A, 324–51)
108. Rawson, E. 'L. Cornelius Sisenna and the early first century B.C.', *CQ* 29 (1979) 327–46 (= A 94A, 363–88)
109. Rawson, E. *Intellectual Life in the Late Roman Republic*. London, 1985
110. Rawson, E, rev. of Hadot, *Arts libéraux*, *JRS* 77 (1987) 214–15
111. Rohde, G. *Die Kultsatzungen der römischen Pontifices* (*Religionsgeschichtliche Versuche und Vorarbeiten* 25). Berlin, 1936
112. Scheid, J. 'Le délit religieux dans la Rome tard-républicaine', *Le délit religieux*, 117–71
113. Scheid, J. *Religion et piété à Rome*. Paris, 1985
114. Schilling, R. *La religion romaine de Vénus* (*BEFAR* 178). Paris, 1954
115. Schilling, R. 'La déification à Rome. Tradition latine et interférences grecques', *REL* 58 (1980) 137–52
116. Schofield, M. 'Cicero for and against divination', *JRS* 76 (1986) 47–65
117. Scullard, H. H. *Festivals and Ceremonies of the Roman Republic*. London, 1981
118. Simon, E. 'Apollo in Rom', *JDAI* 93 (1978) 202–27
119. Stahl, W. H. *Roman Science: Origins, Development, and Influence to the Later Middle Ages*. Madison, WI, 1962
120. Süss, W. *Cicero: eine Einführung in seine philosophischen Schriften*. Mainz, 1966
121. Taeger, F. *Charisma. Studien zur Geschichte des antiken Herrscherkultes*. 2 vols. Stuttgart, 1957 and 1960
122. Tarrant, H. *Scepticism or Platonism? The Philosophy of the Fourth Academy*. Cambridge, 1985
123. Taylor, D. J. *Declinatio: a Study of the Linguistic Theory of Marcus Terentius Varro*. Amsterdam, 1975
124. Taylor, L. R. *The Divinity of the Roman Emperor* (Amer. Philological Ass. Philological Monographs 1). Middletown, CT, 1931
125. Thesleff, H. *An Introduction to the Pythagorean Writings of the Hellenistic Period*. Abo, 1961
126. Thesleff, H., rev. of della Casa, *Nigidio Figulo*, *Gnomon* 37 (1965) 44–8
127. Thesleff, H. 'On the problems of the Doric Pseudo-Pythagorica. An alternative theory of date and purpose', *Entretiens Hardt* 18 (1971) 57–102
128. Turcan, R. 'Religion et politique dans l'affaire des Bacchanales', rev. of Gallini, *Protesta*, *RHR* 181 (1972) 3–28
129. Vermaseren, M. *Cybele and Attis: the Myth and the Cult*. London, 1977
130. Versnel, H. S. *Triumphus. An Inquiry into the Origin, Development and Meaning of the Roman Triumph*. Leiden, 1970
131. Veyne, P. '"Titulus praelatus": offrande, sollénisation et publicité dans les ex-voto gréco-romains', *RA* (1983) 281–300
132. Vogt, J. 'Zum Herrscherkult bei Julius Caesar', *Studies presented to D. M. Robinson*, ed. G. E. Mylonas and D. Raymond, II, St Louis, 1953, 1138–46
133. Weinrib, E. J. 'Obnuntiatio: two problems', *ZSS* 87 (1970) 395–425

134. Weinstock, S. *Divus Julius*. Oxford, 1971
135. Williams, G. W. *Change and Decline: Roman Literature in the Early Empire*. Berkeley, 1978
136. Winterbottom, M. 'Literary criticism', *CHCL* II (1982) 33–50
137. Wissowa, G. *Religion und Kultus der Römer*. 2nd edn (Handb. der Altertumswissensch. v.4). Munich, 1912
138. Zeller, E. *Die Philosophie der Griechen in ihrer geschichtlichen Entwicklung*. 5th edn, Leipzig, 1923

INDEX

References in italics are to maps (by map number) and illustrations (by page number).

Arrangement of material within entries is predominantly chronological, though some material of a topical nature is alphabetically ordered; all dates are B.C. *unless otherwise defined.*

Footnotes are referred to only where the subject is not mentioned in the corresponding page of text.

Abgar, ruler of Osrhoene 402, 403
Accius, L. 561, 705
Acco, chief of Senones 408, 409
Acerrae *2 Aa*, *3(ii) Bc*, 120, 121
Achaea, province of *9 Ac*, *14 Bb*; Roman conquest and settlement 17, 31, 32, 33, 571; law allowing colonies 99; and Mithridates VI 151; Sulpicius Rufus' command 440–1; *see also* Greece
Achaei (Causcasian tribe) 140
Achillas (Egyptian regent) 321
Acilius Glabrio, M'. (*cos.* 191) 570
Acilius Glabrio, M'. (*cos.* 67) 792; divorces Aemilia 196; command in east 244, 249, 250, 332–3, 336, 338, 574; replaced by Pompey 339
Acilius Glabrio, M'. (*trib.* 123) 508
actiones: *de dolo* 554; *exercitoria* 543; *in factum* 563; *institoria* 543; *Publiciana* 540, 549–50, 562; *Serviana* 562; *utiles* 550; see also *legis actiones*
actions, law of 532–3, 538–9, 544–6, 548–9; see also *ius* (*honorarium*)
Ad Herennium (treatise) 9, 120, 520n, 521–2, 561
Adana *9 Cc*, 266
addiction 354, 504
Adherbal, king of Numidia 29, 89
Adiabene *9 Ec*; Armenian occupation 238, 241, 242; Parthian occupation 253; Roman control 255, 259; Parthian reoccupation 263
administration: local 267, 450–2, 455, 775–6; see also *municipia*; provinces
adoption 51, 535, 536
Adora *10 Ac*, 291
Adramyttium 148
adrogatio (adoption) 536
adscripti in allied communities 126
advocacy 534, 546, 755
Aeclanum *3(ii) Cb*, 125
aediles Ceriales 456
aediles, curule 43; games 588, 594; and private law 532, 533, 542; and public law 55, 502, 523, 526, 528
aediles, plebeian 41, 683
Aedui *1 Bb*, *12 Bb*, 24, 365; and Ariovistus 383, 384, 793; and Vercingetorix' revolt 409, 410, 411
Aegae 441n
Aelius Paetus 'Catus', Sex. (*cos.* 198) 554
Aelius Stilo, L. 705, 714
Aelius Tubero, L. 724n
Aemilia (daughter of M. Scaurus) 196
Aemilius Lepidus, M. (*cos.* 78) 790; governor in Sicily 206; champions dispossessed in Sullan colonies 204–5, 207, 208; profits from proscriptions 206; elected consul 207; quarrel with Catulus 207, 208, 524; revolt 208–10, 790; forces in Spain after defeat 209, 217, 790; amnesty for supporters 227; and tribunate 211
Aemilius Lepidus, M'. (*cos.* 66) 337, 792
Aemilius Lepidus, M. (*cos.* 46, *triumvir*): *praetor urbanus* 429, 430, 431; governor of Hispania Ulterior 440; consulship 435, 797; Caesar's *magister equitum* 437, 460, 797, 798; and death of Caesar 468, 469; *pontifex maximus* 471; alliance with Antony 471, 798; command in Gaul 445n, 471, 482–3, 484, 491, 492, 798; in Second Triumvirate 486, 798; relationship to Brutus 487
Aemilius Lepidus Livianus, Mam. (*cos.* 77) 198, 206–7, 210, 328, 343, 790
Aemilius Lepidus Paullus, L. (*cos.* 50) 406, 415, 418, 796
Aemilius Lepidus Porcina, M. (*cos.* 137) 61, 67, 77, 577
Aemilius Paullus Macedonicus, L. (*cos.* 182,

168) 22, 570, 685–6, 698n, 752; and Macedonia 55, 565, 693
Aemilius Scaurus, M. (*cos.* 115) 783, 784; and Jugurtha 89; injured in *seditio Norbana* 93; and Lex Licinia Mucia 111; trial for *proditio* 518–19; connexion with Metelli 88, 167; *De Vita Sua* 713; villa 694
Aemilius Scaurus, M. (*praetor* 56) 51, 261, 262, 626, 687
Aesernia *3(ii) Ba*, 120, 121, 125, 195, 790
Aetolia *9 Ac*, 153
Afella *see under* Lucretius
Afranius, L. (*cos.* 60): praetor in Spain 228; Pompey's legate in east 263; consulship 364, 366, 793; and restoration of Ptolemy Auletes 392; in Civil War 430, 431
Africa: Egyptian trade with Horn of 17, 20; locust plagues (125) 58, 76; *see also individual states and* Africa, province of
Africa, province of *1 Cd*, *2 Ae*, *13 Ae*, *14 Bb*; 2nd cent. events and administration 17, 27–31; Scipio Aemilianus' command 91, 574; Roman and Italian settlers 17, 20, 27–8, 30, 31, 83–4, 85, 608; land division 5, 27–8, 31, 85, 87, 89; C. Gracchus' attempt to found colony 5, 56, 83–4, 85; and Jugurtha, *see* War, Jugurthine; settlement of Marius' veterans 95, 110, 785; Marius exiled in 171, 788; Metellus Pius in 177, 180, 187; in civil war of 83–81 191, 195, 196, 789; Catiline's extortion 335, 340, 345; Civil War campaign 431, 435–6, 442, 452–3, 796–7; Caesar's veteran colonies 445, 655; agriculture 613, 614, 629
Agatharchides of Cnidus 640
Agedincum *12 Bb*, 410
agency, legal concept of 543, 557, 569–70
ager Campanus 55; proposals for distribution 56, 57, 65, 73, (63) 350, 655, (50s) 368, 373–4, 393, 394, 418
ager Cosanus 56, 57, 620
ager Falernus 57
ager Gallicus 3(i) Ca-Da, 65, 73, 347
ager Leontinus 25
ager publicus, *see* agrarian issue *and individual areas under ager*
ager Stellas 350, 374
Agis IV, king of Sparta 66
agnation 536, 538
agrarian issue 4–5, 8, 53–9, 600, 621–3, 770–1, 773; *ager publicus* shortage 446, 449, 450, 622; and allies 62–3, 64, 74, 75–6, 85, 86–7, 99, 104, 107, 109–10, 112, 127; archaeological evidence 3, 56–7, 68; and army manpower 770; *cippi* 622; condition of *ager publicus* 53–7; excessive holdings by wealthy 52, 54, 56, 60, 62, 204, 618, 622; expulsion of peasants 8, 12, 54, 57; inheritance of allotments 63; large estates, *latifundia*, *see under* agriculture; leasing of land by censors 25, 28, 34, 64, 87; *occupatio* 611, 616, 618, 621–2; pasture-land 65, 87; and population movements 601; public and private land distinguished 74, 87; rents 78, 83, 87; sale of allotments 63, 83, 86–7, (in Africa) 85, 87, 89; size of land holdings 54, 55, 56, 63, 64–5, 74, 78, 87; and social conditions in Italy 57–9; *trientabula* 54
LEGISLATION AND MEASURES: Lex Flaminia (232) 52, 65, 66, 99; law limiting holdings (before 167) 54, 55; Laelius' 60; Ti. Gracchus' 48, 62–3, 64–7, 87, 104, 107, 606, 622, 780; proposed use of revenues of Asia to fund 33, 68, 73, 780; land commission 62, 67–8, 73–4, 75–6, 85, 87; C. Gracchus' 28, 63, 67–8, 78, 83, 85, 107, 606, 622, 780; Lex Rubria (121) 28, 83–4; Livius Drusus' (122) 83; law (111) 5, 28, 31, 32, 63, 74, 85, 86–7, 98, 99, 561, 784; Saturninus' (104, 100) 5, 95, 97–8, 98–9, 102, 109–10, 749; Lex Thoria 87, 783; Livius Drusus' (91) 112–13, 787; *Rogatio Servilia* (Rullan bill, 63) 349–50, 352, 353, 793; Flavius' (60) 365, 793; Lex Iulia agraria (59) 368–9, 371, 373, 375, 451, 739, 793; Curio's 418; Lex Mamilia Roscia Peducaea Alliena Fabia 451; agrarian law (44) 474, 480; Second Triumvirate's confiscations 486; *see also* Africa, province of (land division); centuriation; land; veterans
agriculture 609–23; contracts 532, 554, 560; drainage 610; geographical diversity 609–11; Greek science 612, 699; ideal of farmer citizen 8, 41; investment 54, 56, 60, 106–7, 328–9, 618, 637, 642, 770; large estates, *latifundia* 54, 55, 56, 57, 106–7, 204, 615, 616, 617–18, 619, 620–1, 622; and law of property 540–1; machinery 56, 612; major items of production 612–16; market gardening 664; mixed 56; public revenue 622; rents 617, 620, 622; rotation 612; seasonal labour 656, 664; sharecropping 617, 620; slave production 27, 54, 617, 619, 620–1; speculative 611, 616; structures of 616–21; subsistence 611, 612; taxation 622; techniques 612; tools 56, 612, 624, 658; villas 56, 611, 615n, 616, 619, 620; writings on 54, 55, 56, 609, 615, (*see also under* Porcius Cato, M. (*cos.* 195); Terentius Varro, M.); *see also individual crops, countries and regions and* animal husbandry; arboriculture; pasture; smallholders; wine production
Agrigentum *1 Cd*, *2 Be*, *13 Be*, 25

Ahenobarbus *see under* Domitius
Akbar, king of Osrhoene 264
Akko (Ptolemais) 295
Alabanda *9 Bc*, 766
Alaudae (Larks, Gallic legion) 444
Alba, kings of 463
Alba Fucens *2 Bc*, *3(i) Dc*, *13 Bc*, 120, 121, 449
Alba Pompeia *2 Ab*, 209
Albani (Caucasian tribe) *9 Eb*, 253, 255, 256, 257, 269
Albinovanus, P. 194
Albinus *see under* Postumius
Albucius, T. (*praetor c.*105) 698, 757n
Alcimus (Jewish high priest) 280–1, 300
Aleria *1 Cc*, *2 Ac*, 204
Alesia *12 Bb*, 412, 795
Alexander, Peripatetic 695
Alexander, son of Aristobulus II (Jewish prince) 272, 273, 395, 401, 794
Alexander I, king of Egypt 271
Alexander III the Great, king of Macedon 130, 294, 322, 442, 467, 771
Alexander Balas 281, 282, 288
Alexander Jannaeus (Yannai), king of Judaea 291; coinage 298–9; and religion 302, 306–7; style of rule 297, 298; wars 293–6
Alexander Polyhistor 697, 708
Alexandra Salome, queen of Judaea 261, 307–8, 777
Alexandria, Egypt *1 Ee*, *9 Bd*, *11 Aa*, *14 Cb*; and Ptolemy VIII Euergetes II 310, 311; and late Ptolemaic succession 318, 788; and Ptolemy Auletes *see under* Ptolemy XII; opposition to Rome after Auletes' restoration 320; Alexandrian War 321, 433–4, 693, 796; capture by Octavian 321 Julius Caesar's attitude to 433–4, 453; Caesarea 465; Greeks 311, 325; Jews 279, 297; grammarians 704; library 434, 693; trade with Italy 630, 638
Alexandrium *9 Cd*, *10 Bb*, 261, 296
Alfenus Varus, P. (*cos. suff.* 39) 555, 556, 620n
allies, Roman: enslavement 26, 43, 507, 577; coinage 3; expulsions from Rome 76, 83, 106; in Roman army 21, 38, 62, 75, 95, 99, 109, 604; *see also names of individual allies and census*; Italy; Latins; *repetundae*; treaties
Allobroges *1 Bb-Cb*, *12 Bb*; Roman campaigns (122–120) 24, 782; embassy to Rome 355–6; revolt 347, 358, 365, 372, 793; and Ariovistus 383; and Vercingetorix 411
Amafinius 718
Amanus mountains *9 Cc*, 269
Amasia *5 Da*, *9 Cb*, 130, 135, 136–7, 267
Amastris *4 Ab*, *5 Ca*, *9 Cb*, 131, 133, 136, 267
Amathus *10 Bb*, 294, 296
Amatius (demagogue) 470
Ambiani *12 Ba*, 388
ambitio (pursuit of popular favour) 45, 773
ambition; ancient theories on 6, 7–8, 40
ambitus (electoral bribery): *quaestio ambitus* 511, 517; *see also* elections (bribery)
Ambrones 24, 95, 96
Ameria, Pontus 137
Ameria, Umbria *3(i) Cb*, *13 Bc*, 198
Amida *9 Dc*, 240
Amisus *4 Bb*, *5 Da*, *9 Cb*, 131, 133, 135, 136; in Third Mithridatic War 237, 238, 245, 246, 262, 791; Pompey's settlement (62) 267
Amiternum *3(i) Dc*, *13 Bc*, 684
Amon 326
Amphipolis *9 Ab*, 153
amphitheatres 682, 684, 774
amphorae 614, 625, 627
Anaitis, cult of 137
Ananias (Egyptian Jewish general) 296
Ancharius, Q. 178
Ancona *2 Bb*, *3(i) Da*, *13 Bb*, 184, 186, 424
Andriscus (Macedonian pretender) 31, 567, 571
Andronicus of Rhodes 693–4
animal husbandry 55, 615–16, 618n, 628; large estates 56, 615, 618n, 620, 638; regional specialization 27, 55, 610, 611; transhumance 56, 611, 615–16
Anisa 268
Anna Perenna, festival of 683
annalists 1, 4, 67, 68, 711; *see also* Calpurnius Piso, L.
Anneius, M. (legate in Cilicia, 51) 581
Annii (Campanian businessmen) 638
Annius, T. (*praetor c.*132) 73
Annius, T. (*quaestor* 119) 32
Annius Chilo, Q. 356
Annius Luscus, C. (*praetor* 81) 206
Annius Luscus, T. (*cos.* 153) 67
Annius Milo, T. (*trib.* 57): and Cicero's recall 389; Clodius' prosecution of 2, 392–3, 394, 501n; praetorship 397; consular campaign (53) 404; gang warfare against Clodius 405, 795; and murder of Clodius 407; Pompey's fear of 409; condemned *de vi* 411, 505, 529
Antemnae 195
Anthedon *10 Ac*, 294
Antigonus Monophthalmus, king of Macedon 130
Antioch, Syria *9 Cc*, *14 Cb*, 417, 465
Antiochus (son of Cleopatra Selene) 318
Antiochus, king of Commagene 259, 265
Antiochus III the Great, king of Syria 258
Antiochus IV Epiphanes, king of Syria 274–5, 280, 292, 303, 310
Antiochus V, king of Syria 300
Antiochus VI, king of Syria 282

Antiochus VII Sidetes, king of Syria 262, 278, 284, 285, 286, 289–90
Antiochus IX Cyzicenus, king of Syria 291, 306
Antiochus X Eusebes, king of Syria 262
Antiochus XIII Philadelphos, king of Syria 241, 259
Antiochus of Ascalon 697, 719, 720, 721n, 722, 724
Antipater, king of Armenia Minor 139
Antipater of Derbe 269
Antipater of Idumaea 273, 308, 320, 399, 434
antiquarianism 706, 714, 757–9
Antistia (wife of Pompey) 196
Antistius, P. 166, 181, 192
Antium (Anzio) *2 Bc*, *3(ii) Aa*, *7 Bc*, *13 Bc*, 177, 694
Antius Briso, M. (*trib.* 137) 61, 66–7
Antius Restio, C. 331
Antonius, C. (*praetor* 44) 471, 474, 475, 481, 487
Antonius, L. (*trib.* 44) 474, 642
Antonius, M. (*cos.* 99) 786; war against pirates 96–7, 101, 249, 497, 785, 786; trial for *ambitus* 516n; and Norbanus 581n; death 178; intellectual interests 690n, 692, 698
Antonius, M. (*praetor* 74) 213, 790
Antonius, M. (*cos.* 44, *triumvir*): with Gabinius in Egypt 320, 399; augur 419; tribune; denounces Pompey 421–2; on Caesar's march to Rome 424; summons Senate 430; leaves for east 432; *magister equitum* in Italy 433, 435, 459, 472, 796; *flamen* to Divus Iulius 462, 464; consulship 797; in aftermath of Caesar's death 468, 469–70, 471–2, 473; legislation 439, 473, 474–5, 476, 480, 527, 797; courts Caesar's veterans 473–4, 475, 476, 747; and 'liberators' 474–5, 475–6; temporary reconciliation with Octavian 476; Piso attacks 476; Cicero's enmity 477, 479, 480, 481, 482; declared *hostis* 483, 486; hostilities against Octavian 477–86, 797–8; reconciled with Octavian in Second Triumvirate 482, 486, 487, 798; proscription of Cicero 486–7, (and of Verres) 578; and Cleopatra 321; Sallust's portrayal 34–5
Antonius Balbus, Q. 191
Antonius Gnipho, M. 690n, 704
Antonius Hybrida, C. (*cos.* 63) 210, 225, 348–9, 351, 363, 372, 793
Aorsi *9 Ea*, 258
Apamea, Phrygia *5 Bb*, *9 Bc*, *14 Cb*, 147n, 232, 236, 265; Peace of 135, 229, 569
Apellicon of Teos 150, 693
Aphrodisias *1 Ed*, *5 Bb*, *9 Bc*, *14 Cb*, 34, 146, 162, 163, 442, 753
Aphrodite, cult of 753; *see also* Venus
Apis, cult of 317
Apocrypha 279
Apollo, cult of 20, 764
Apollodorus; verse chronicle 714
Apollonia, Thrace *1 Dc*, *4 Ab*, *14 Bb*, 139, 148
Apollonius Molo 697, 698
apparitores 581–2, 656, 672
appeal, judicial 69, 352, 476; absence of civil 557
Appian 2, 3, 487, 770; sources 4, 9, 54–5
Appuleius Decianus 519n
Appuleius Saturninus, L. (*trib.* 103, 100) 4, 95–6, 97–102, 103, 785, 786; accuses Pontic embassy of bribery 97, 142; agrarian law 5, 95, 97–8, 98–9, 102, 109–10, 749, 786; and corn supply 83, 98, 786; *lex de maiestate* 518; death 101; Rabirius tried for lynching 352, 357, 502n; and Metellus Numidicus 102; political programme 677, 772; and settlement of veterans 30, 95, 98–9, 102, 109–10, 446, 786; sources' attitudes to 9; violence 85, 101, 103, 142
Apuleius (Spanish bandit chief) 22
Apulia *2 Bc*; land redistribution 73; in Social War 115, 119, 120, 125; under Sulla 203; rural distress 347, 354; slave revolt 354; in Civil War 424; viticulture 614, 627
Aquae Sextiae (Aix) *1 Bc*, 24, 96, 782, 785
aqueducts 584, 625n, 626, 650
Aquileia *1 Cc*, *2 Ba*, *13 Ba*, 23
Aquilius Gallus, C. (*praetor* 66, jurist) 534n, 553, 554, 555–6, 562
Aquillius, M'. (*cos.* 129) 34, 35, 508n, 781
Aquillius, M'. (*cos.* 101) 785; suppresses Sicilian slave revolt 26, 96; in east 35, 79, 132, 143, 145, 146–7, 781, 787; alleged corruption 77, 132
Aquillius Gallus, P. (*trib.* 55) 398, 400
Aquitania *12 Ac*; defeat of L. Cassius 24, 93; Pompey settles Sertorius' men in 221; Caesar's campaigns 397, 398, 416; Roman wine exported to 615
Arabs 241, 254; *see also* Nabataeans
Aratus 706, 710, 724
Arausio (Orange) *1 Bc*, 24, 36, 37, 93, 785
arboriculture 25, 610, 612, 613–15
Arcathias, prince of Pontus 153, 154
Arcesilas (philosopher) 722
archaeology 3, 5–6; on agriculture 3, 56–7, 609; on Delos 637; on economic expansion 600; on Italian cities 76, 106; on Jews 280; on land holdings 56–7, 619, 622; on population distribution 607; on Romanization of native communities in Gaul 444; on Settefinestre villa 615n;

archaeology (*cont.*)
shipwrecks 56, 625, 629; on Spanish mines 625–6; on *tabernae* 661; on temples in Rome 737
Archelaus (Mithridates VI's general): in First Mithridatic War 145, 147, 151, 153, 154, 155, 156–7, 158, 788; and treaty of Dardanus 161, 163, 788; Sulla grants land to 32–3; prompts Murena's expedition 163
Archelaus, king of Comana and of Egypt 267, 272, 319, 320, 396–7, 399
arches, monumental *see under* Rome
Archias (poet) 697
Archimedian screw 21
architecture: Greek influence 106, 682; Hasmonean 297–8; impost on columns 457; Italian 106, 682, 687, 774; Varro's writings 705; *see also* amphitheatres; arches; houses; public works; temples; theatres; tombs; *and under* Iulius Caesar, C.; Pompeius Magnus, Cn.; Rome
Arelate (Arles) *14 Aa*, 445
Aretus of Petra 259
Arevaci *8 Ba*, 21
Argei, shrines of 673
Argos *1 Dd*, 32
Ariarathes V Eusebes Philopator, king of Cappadocia 268
Ariarathes VI Epiphanes, king of Cappadocia 131, 132, 141
Ariarathes VIII Philometor, king of Cappadocia 141
Ariarathes IX, king of Cappadocia 141, 144
Ariarathes, prince of Cappadocia 460n
Aricia *3(i) Cc*, *3(ii) Aa*, *7 Bb*, 177
Ariminum (Rimini) *1 Cc*, *2 Bb*, *3(i) Ca*, *13 Bb*, *14 Ba*, 176, 190, 191, 193, 194, 424
Ariobarzanes, king of Cappadocia 142, 767; *see also under* Cappadocia
Ariobarzanes, king of Pontus 131
Ariobarzanes of Cius 130
Ariovistus (Suebian leader) 371–2, 383, 384–5, 386, 793, 794
Aristeas, Letter of 279, 297
Aristion (Athenian politician) 150–1, 153, 154, 157, 158
Aristobulus I (Jewish high priest) 291, 293, 297
Aristobulus II (claimant to Jewish high priesthood) 260, 261, 272–3
Aristobulus (son of Alexander Salome of Egypt) 307–8, 396
aristocracy *see* upper classes
Aristogeiton, sculptured head from Capitol 72
Aristonicus (Eumenes III, Pergamene pretender) 34, 35, 132
Aristotle 693, 715
Armenia Maior *5 Eb*, *9 Db-Eb*, *14 Cb*, 135; Tigranes' accession 142, 238, 786; alliance with Pontus 142; invades Cappadocia 143, 787; conquests 135, 238, 263, 266; in Third Mithridatic War 237, 238–9, 791; Lucullus' invasion 239–44, 328, 792; enters Cappadocia 244, 249, 792; submits to Pompey 252, 253, 792; and Parthians 253, 263, 264; withdrawal from Syria 259; Gabinius' advance to southern 263; Pompey's settlement 265, 269; Clodius offered embassy to 373; and Crassus' Parthian expedition 402
Armenia Minor *4 Cb*, *5 Eb*, *9 Db*, 133; Pontic hegemony 131, 137, 139; in Third Mithridatic War 237, 238; given to Deiotarus 269
arms and armour: chariots, Pontic 145, 156; mail-clad cavalry, (Armenian) 241, (Parthian) 402, 403; Roman 37, 38; *see also* siege engines
army, Roman 36–9; allied troops 21, 38, 62, 75, 95, 99, 109, 604; cavalry *see separate entry*; in Civil Wars 442, 486, (bounties) 478, 480, 483, 484, 485, 486, 488, 489, (growth) 486, (land allocations) 470, 471, 473–4, 475, 476, 478, 617, 621, 623, 771; *classis* 41; coin issues for 631, 632; costs to provincials 586, 588; equipment 37, 38, 615; freedmen in Augustan 655; light-armed troops 21, 38, 39; limits on legal use of 491, 579; Marius' reforms 37–8, 39; policing of Rome 456; political power based on 10, 11, 14, 489, 490; property qualification 36, 37, 39; *provocatio* 493; recruitment 36–7, 39, 57–8, 60, 62, 63, 91–2, 95, 602, 619, 770; in Social War 119–20; summary executions 222, 493n, 495; tactical organization 37–9; *see also* supply, military; veterans
Arpinum *2 Bc*, *3(ii) Ba*, *13 Bc*, 66, 86, 90, 451
Arretium (Arezzo) *2 Bb*, *3(i) Ba*, *13 Bb*, 204, 424, 450, 624, 627
Arrius, Q. 222, 376
ars (scholarly systematization) 551, 701, 718
Arsinoe (Egyptian princess) 321, 434, 436
art collections 454, 638, 686
Artanes, ruler of Sophene 238
Artavasdes, king of Armenia 402
Artaxata *9 Eb*, 238, 242, 252, 253, 255, 263
Artaxias, king of Armenia 238
Artoces, king of Iberians 256
Arverni *1 Bb-c*, *12 Bb*, 24, 383, 409, 411, 782
Ascalon *10 Ab*, 288
Asclepiades 694
Asculum *2 Bb*, *3(i) Db*, *13 Bb*, 76, 114; in Social War 115, 122, 124, 165, 181, 787
Asellio *see under* Sempronius

Ashdod (Azotus) *10 Ab*, 288
Asia, province of *1 Ed*, *5 Ab-Bb*, *9 Bc*, *14 Cb*; willed to Rome 33–4, 68, 135, 233; Aristonicus' revolt 34, 35, 132, 780, 781; Roman settlement and administration 17, 20, 34–5, 77, 79, 132, 569, 754, 781; Ti. Gracchus' proposal for use of revenues 33, 68, 73, 780; Scaevola's governorship 554, 590, 754; Mithridates' occupation 20, 144–9, 158, 172; Sulla's settlement 162, 258–9, 788; in Third Mithridatic War 213, 219, 234, 788; Lucullus' settlement 239, 244–8, 788, 791; Pompey's settlement *see under* Pompeius Magnus, Cn.; renegotiation of tax contracts (59) 365, 372, 793; effect of Civil War 442; Caesar's treatment 433, 441–2
corn exports to Rome 629; money system 631, 632; taxation and revenues, (Aquillius') 34–5, 569, (Gracchan) 68, 73, 79, 569, 586, (Mithridatic wars) 147, 172, 245, 246–7, (Sulla's) 162, (Lucullus') 247, (Pompey's) 251, 269–70, (Caesar remits) 433, 441–2, (indebtedness to Rome) 639–40
Asicius, P. (agent of Ptolemy Auletes) 392
Asinius Pollio, C. (*cos.* 40) 3, 452, 484–5, 693n, 701
Aspis 258
assassins, see *sicarii*
assault, see *iniuria*
assemblies, Roman citizen 41, 43–5; assign commands 91, 148, 244, 248, 271, 573–4; decline in use 646; intimidation 86; judicial functions 61, 69, 77, 80, 84, 93, 352, 476, 494, 501–3, 504–5, 515; legislative powers 41, 43, 474, 502; Marius' support in 573–4; *populares*' use 11, 67, 69, 74–5, 103, 369, 372, 379, 474; religious sanctions 99–100, 729; sovereignty 67, 98, 103; Sulla and 190, 193, 203; tribal 44, 502, 645, (see also *comitia tributa*; *concilium plebis*); voting procedures 61, 75, 86, 93, 190; see also *comitia centuriata*; *comitia tributa*; *concilium plebis*
assidui (owners of property) 36, 57–8
astrology 708, 763
astronomy 455, 706, 710, 718, 725
Astura, Cicero's villa at 694n
Astures *8 Aa-Ba*, 398
Ateius Capito, C. (*trib.* 55) 398, 400
Atella *3(ii) Bc*, 450
Ateste *13 Bb*; *fragmentum Atestinum* 547n, 560, 563
Athenaeus 150
Athenion (Sicilian slave leader) 26
Athens *1 Dd*, *6 Cb*, *9 Ac*, *14 Bb*; Delos returned to 20, 637; free city 33; under Aristion 150–1, 153, 154, 157, 158; in First Mithridatic War 149, 150–1, 153–4, 157, 246, 697, 721, 788; Sulla's stay in 162; loyalty to Pompey (48) 441
Academy 154, 556, 697, 716, 721, 722, 725; Acropolis 153, 154; coinage 632, 660; Heptachalcum 154; intellectual life 476, 556, 697, 716, 721, 722, 725, (*see also individual philosophers*); law 558–9; Long Walls 153; Lyceum 154, 721; Odeum 154, 315
Athribis *11 Aa*, 318
Atrebates *12 Ba*, 388
Atropatene *9 Ec-Fc*, 238, 253, 263, 269
Attalus II, king of Pergamum 132
Attalus III, king of Pergamum 33–4, 68, 73, 135, 233, 780
Attica, tetradrachms 33
Atticus *see under* Pomponius
Attius Varus, P. (*propraetor* of Africa, 49) 431
Atuatuca 406
Atuatuci *12 Ba*, 388
auctioneers 451, 634
auctions, credit 642
Auctor ad Herennium 9, 120, 520n, 521–2, 561
Aufidus, river *3(ii) Da*, 125
augurs and augury 198, 205, 731, 742, 745, 759; elections 185, 746; in Urso 765–6
Augustine, St 705, 719, 757, 758
Augustus, Emperor *see* Octavius, C.
Aurelius Cotta, C. (*cos.* 75) 167, 198, 210, 211, 213, 790
Aurelius Cotta, L. (*cos.* 119) 88, 783
Aurelius Cotta, L. (*cos.* 65) 340, 342, 491, 726, 792, 793; Lex Aurelia on mixed juries 225–6, 227, 509, 527, 530, 791
Aurelius Cotta, M. (*cos.* 74) 212, 790; command against Mithridates 213, 234, 235, 237, 245, 246
Aurelius Opillus 721
Ausculum *3(ii) Da*, *13 Cc*, 125
auspices 744, 749
Autronius Paetus, P. 340, 342, 350, 351, 356, 360, 516n
auxilium, tribunes' power of 41
Auximum *3(i) Da*, *13 Bb*, 425
Avaricum (Bourges) *12 Bb*, 410–11
Azotus (Ashdod) *10 Ab*, 288

Babylon, Talmud of 280
Bacchanalian cult 504n, 528, 735, 761–2
Bacchides (Seleucid general) 281
Bactria 257–8
Badian, E. 13
Baebius (*trib.* 103) 95, 96
Bagradas valley *2 Ae*, 28, 30
Baiae 331, 333
bakers 664, 665

Balbus *see under* Antonius; Cornelius; Thorius
Balearic Islands *1 Bc-d*, *8 Db*, 99, 781
ballot, secret 45, 52, 60, 61, 93, 503n
banking 272, 542, 559n, 633, 634–5, 638; in provinces 584–5, 636, 639; *see also* money-changers; money-lenders
bankruptcy, voluntary 458
banquets, public 203, 205, 225, 685–6, 687
Bantia *2 Cc*, *3(ii) Db*, *13 Cc*; Tabula Bantina 96, 98, 749n
Barba (Lucullus' legate) 236
barbers 664
Bardyaei (Marius' bodyguard) 178, 179
basilicas *see under* Rome
baths, public 682
Belgae *12 Ba*, 387–8, 794
Bellienus, L. 348n
Bellovaci *12 Ba*, 388, 414, 795
Bellum Africanum 440
Bellum Alexandrinum 434
Bellum Hispaniense 437
'Bellum Octavianum' 174, 788
benefactions to Roman plebs 652, 666, 680–8
beneficia 50
Beneventum *2 Bc*, *3(ii) Bc*, 121
Berenice IV, queen of Egypt 272, 319, 320, 391, 779; consorts 391, 397; death 320, 399
Beroia *9 Dc*; battle of 262
Bestia, L. (*trib.* 62) 357
Bestia *see also under* Calpurnius
Beth Zur *10 Ab*, 288, 289
Bible 279, 297
Bibracte *12 Bb*, 384, 414
Bibulus *see under* Calpurnius
Bigga Island 318
Bilbilis *8 Ca*, 217, 219
birth rate 457, 606, 780
Bithynia *1 Ec*, *4 Ab*, *5 Ba*, *9 Bb*, *14 Ca-b*
under Nicomedes I 131, 132; under Prusias 16; under Nicomedes II 34; under Nicomedes III 35, 140, 141, 142, 784, 787
under Nicomedes IV 142–3, 144, 145, 146, 160, 787; in Treaty of Dardanus 158, 161, 229; death of Nicomedes, bequest of kingdom to Rome 213, 233, 790
as Roman province *14 Ca-b*; in Third Mithridatic War 213, 219, 234, 235, 249, 332–3, 338, 574; Pompey's settlement 266–7, 268, 270, 329; Catullus in 582–3; Pansa's governorship 441n
Bithynium *5 Ca*, 145
Bituitus, chief of Arverni 24
Bituriges *12 Ab-Bb*, 409, 410, 414
Bizerta *2 Ad*, 27–8
Blasio *see under* Cornelius
Blossius, C., of Cumae 73
Bocchus, king of Mauretania 30, 95, 436
Boeotia *6 Bb*, 32, 33, 151, 153, 154–9, 236
Boii 384
Bona Dea *see* Goddess, Good
bona fides 549, 550–1
bondslavery 504
books 694, 702; oracular, (of Numa) 707, (*see also* Sibylline books); priestly 758
booty 54, 107, 181, 453, 632
Bosporus, Cimmerian *see* Crimea
bottomry 635
boundaries: Judaean markers 289; land-, markers of 68, 73, 85; provincial 576, 587; religious 750–1, 759–61; of Rome 646, (see also *pomoerium*)
Bovianum *3(ii) Ca*, 124, 125, 449
Bovillae *7 Bb*, 407, 795
bread 613, 614, 664, 665
breviaria 130
bribery 52; *collegia* disbanded to counter 346; C. Cornelius' proposals to restrict 335–6; electoral, *see under* elections; by foreign states 97, 132, 141–2, 392, 473, (Jugurtha) 29, 30, 88, 89; judicial 60, 213–14, 224, 330, 332, 340–1, 365, 377, 509, 510, 512, 514, 527; laws against 8, 59, 60, 94, 336–7, 353, 358, 364, 515, 516–17, 793; Marius and 91, 97; of married woman, to commit adultery 503; of provincial governors over corn 583
brigandage 204, 260, 366
Britain *12 Aa*, *14 Aa*; Caesar's campaigns 399, 400–1, 402, 794–5; governor's grain supply 583n; mines 624, 637
Brogitarus, tetrarch of Galatia 379
bronze founding 625
Brundisium (Brindisi) *1 Dc*, *2 Cc*, *13 Cc*, *14 Bb*, 187, 630, 637; in Civil War 424–5, 428, 432, 433, 471, 478
Brunt, P. A. 14, 54
Brutobriga 22
Bruttium *2 Cd*, 198, 204, 610, 611
Bruttius Sura, Q. 151, 163
Brutus *see under* Iunius
Buchis, cult at Hermonthis 317, 321
building 59, 626–7; contracts 626; finance 626, 627, 641, 643; in Italy 106; private 671; *see also* houses; port facilities; public works; roads; warehouses; *and under* Rome
Bulla Regia *1 Cd*, *2 Ae*, 30
bullae of Alexander Jannaeus 299
Burebistas, king of the Dacians 381, 383, 432
businessmen, Roman and Italian: agricultural investment 618; debt 641–2; and equestrian order 107–8; Italian allies 107–8, 151; Marius supported by 89, 91; mobility 628, 633, 638; overseas 24–5, 30, 31, 151, 436, 592, 608; sphere of operation 258; *see also* commerce; *publicani*; trade

Buthrotum *14 Bb*, 447; inscription 665
Byzantium (Istanbul) *1 Ec*, *4 Ab*, *5 Ba*, *9 Bb*, 145, 160, 379

Cabira *5 Da*, *9 Db*, 237, 238, 243, 246
Cabiri, temple of, Samothrace 163
Caecilii Metelli 87–8, 166–7, 206, 226–7
Caecilius, Q. (client of Lucullus) 675
Caecilius Bassus, Q. 437, 473, 482
Caecilius Isidorus, C. 616n, 617
Caecilius Metellus, C. (*fl.*83) 197
Caecilius Metellus, L. (*cos.* 68) 227, 792
Caecilius Metellus, M. (*praetor* 69) 227
Caecilius Metellus, Q. (*aedile*, late 2nd cent.) 58, 60
Caecilius Metellus Balearicus, Q. (*cos.* 123) 22, 781, 782
Caecilius Metellus Calvus, L. (*cos.* 142) 88, 311
Caecilius Metellus Caprarius, C. (*cos.* 113) 96, 783, 784, 785
Caecilius Metellus Celer, Q. (*cos.* 60) 793; tribunate 503n; command in Cisalpine Gaul 354; defeats Catiline 360; consulship 364, 365; and Lex Iulia agraria 371; death 371, 794; pomposity 695n
Caecilius Metellus Creticus, L. (*trib.* 49) 430
Caecilius Metellus Creticus, Q. (*cos.* 69) 792; candidate for praetorship (75) 211; subjection of Crete 249, 250, 251, 331, 338–9, 792; and peasants' revolt 354; and Clodius' trial 361; triumph 342, 354, 793; and Verres 227
Caecilius Metellus Macedonicus, Q. (*cos.* 143) 68, 74, 88, 567, 571, 780
Caecilius Metellus Nepos, Q. (*cos.* 57) 794; tribunate (62) 357, 358–9, 359–60; consulship 386–7; stoned over corn crisis 389, 390; command in Spain 398; in Civil War 422
Caecilius Metellus Numidicus, Q. (*cos.* 109) 9, 784, 785; in Jugurthine War 30, 89, 91, 573–4, 784, 785; conflict with tribunes 96, 102, 371; exile 100; restoration 101; intellectual interests 690n
Caecilius Metellus Pius, Q. (*cos.* 80) 789; in Social War 120, 125, 176; and Cinna's government 177, 179; withdraws to Africa 177, 180, 187; supports Sulla in civil war 187, 191–2, 193, 194; consulship 200, 205, 789; war against Sertorius 206, 210, 211, 212, 215, 217, 218, 219, 790; triumph 223, 791; interdict *de vi armata* 562; and trial of C. Cornelius 343; death 353
Caecilius Metellus Scipio, Q. (*formerly* P. Cornelius Scipio Nasica) (*cos.* 52) 410, 422, 432, 433, 435, 436, 795
Caecilius Niger, Q. 227
Caecilius Rufus, L. (*trib.* 62) 350, 351
Caecina, A. 449, 758
Caelius Rufus, M. (*praetor* 49): prosecution *de vi* (56) 527, 529; tribunate 408, 409, 412; aedileship 594; charge of homosexuality 419; in Civil War 422, 432, 457; and Cicero 408, 414, 416–17, 420, 479, 529, 593, 594; debt 642
Caenic Chersonese 32, 97
Caeparius, M., of Tarracina 356, 357
Caepio *see under* Servilius
Caesar *see under* Iulius
Caesarion 321, 434, 466, 796
Caesetius (Roman tribe) 464
Calabria *2 Cc*, 60–1, 203
Calagurris *8 Ca*, 217, 219, 220
Calatia *3(ii) Bb*, 189, 450
calendar 418, 455, 460, 725, 750
Cales *3(ii) Ba*, *13 Bb*, 450n, 624
calles (drove-roads) 87, 366, 452, 616
Callimachus (garrison commander at Amisus) 245
Calpurnia (Caesar's wife) 466
Calpurnius Bestia, L. (*cos.* 111) 29, 89, 784
Calpurnius Bibulus, M. (*cos.* 59) 793; aedileship (65) 344; consulship 366, 371, 375, 376, 378, (obstruction of Caesar's legislation) 368, 369, 371, 739–40; testifies against validity of Caesar's *acta* 385; and restoration of Ptolemy Auletes 392; centre of 'optimate' group in Senate 394; proposes sole consulship of Pompey 410; governor of Syria 320, 417; in Civil War 432
Calpurnius Piso, C. (*cos.* 67) 792; evades charge of bribery 332; consulship 215, 333–4, 335, 336–7, 338, 528; charged with extortion 347, 351
Calpurnius Piso, Cn. 342, 343
Calpurnius Piso Caesoninus, L. (*cos.* 58) 794; Caesar marries daughter 376; command in Macedonia 380, 574, 583; Cicero's attack on 395, 583; censorship 419, 421, 796; in Civil War 429, 476, 480, 482; intellectual interests 695, 722, 723
Calpurnius Piso Frugi, L. (*cos.* 133) 7, 59, 79, 505–6, 578, 780, 782
Calpurnius Piso Frugi, L. (*procos.* 111) 21
Calvinus *see under* Domitius
Cambysene 257
Camertes *3(i) Cb*, 109
Camillus, M. Furius 515
Campagna, Roman 613
Campania *2 Bc*; slave revolts (136–132) 605; in Social War 115, 119, 120–1; Sulla's treatment of 203; and in Civil War 427; mutiny (47) 435; Caesar's veteran settlements 450, 473–4; Caesar visits 461

Campania (*cont.*)
agriculture 611, 612, 613; commerce 627, 638, 665, 682; local associations 671–2, 684; migration from Rome to 656; tomb-reliefs 668; wine production 614, 615, 627; see also *ager Campanus*
Campi Raudii (Vercellae) 96
canals: Corinth, plans for 447; Rhône 24; Tiber–Tarracina 456
Caninius Gallus, L. (*trib.* 57) 392
Caninius Rebilus, C. (*cos.suff.* 45) 415, 462, 797
Cannae *3(ii) Da*, 125
Cannicus (member of Spartacus' rebellion) 223
Cantabri *8 Ba*, 398
cantons, see *pagi*
Canusium *3(ii) Da*, 121, 125
canvassing, electoral 44, 49, 60
Capena *3(i) Cc*, *7 Aa*, *13 Bc*, 450
capitalism, growth of 54, 87; *see also* agriculture (investment)
capite censi 36, 39, 57, 92, 95
capitis deminutio 539
Capitolini 672, 674–5
Cappadocia, kingdom of *1 Fd*, *5 Db*, *9 Cc-Dc*, 14 Cb, 133; 3rd–2nd-cent. history 16, 96, 131, 132; Mithridates VI occupies 141, 142–3, 786
under Ariobarzanes: accession of Ariobarzanes 142; Armenia annexes 143, 787; Ariobarzanes restored 143, 144; Pontus expels Ariobarzanes 144; in Sertorius' pact with Mithridates 219; Peace of Dardanus calls for Pontic withdrawal 158, 161, 229; Murena's intervention 229; Mithridates evacuates 232; routes through 232, 233; in Third Mithridatic War 237, 240, 244, 249, 792; Pompey's settlement 262, 265, 268–9, 269–70; treaty with Rome under Caesar 460n
Cappadocia, Pontic 130, 133
'Cappadocian Faction' 151, 159, 160, 162
Caprilius Timotheus (wine and slave dealer) 665
Capua *1 Cc*, *2 Bc*, *3(ii) Bc*, *13 Bc*; road to Rhegium 73; C. Gracchus' scheme for colony at 78; in Social War 119, 120, 121; in civil war 169, 189, 190; Spartacus' revolt 221; peasant revolt 354
industry and commerce 624, 660, 664n, 682; organizations of freedmen 671–2
caput (legal concept) 493–4, 500, 512–13
Caraca 217
Carbo *see under* Papirius
Caria *1 Ed*, *5 Bc*, 34, 144, 146, 147, 162
Carisius, T. 444n
Carmel 294
Carneades of Cyrene 722
Carnutes *12 Ab*, 405, 409, 414
Carpis *13 Ae*, 445
Carrhae *9 Dc*, *14 Cb*, 263; battle of 402–3, 476
Carrinas, C. 191, 192, 193, 194, 195
Carteia *1 Ad*, *8 Bc*, 22
Carthage *1 Cd*, *2 Ae*, *13 Ae*, *14 Bb*; constitution 41, 43; exploits Spanish mines 624; destruction 17, 27, 48, 637, 744, (as beginning of decline of Republic) 7, 26, 40, 48, 77; reparations 569, 586; land division 27, 28, 43; attempts to revive, (C. Gracchus) 28, 78, 82, 83, 85, 99, (Caesar's) 446, 447
Carthago Nova (Cartagena) *1 Bd*, *8 Cc*, *14 Ab*, 21, 445, 576, 625, 638, 666
Casilinum *3(ii) Bc*, 189, 450
Casinum *3(ii) Ba*, 624
Cassander, son of Antipater, of Macedon 130
Cassius Dio 2, 3, 10, 263
Cassius Dionysius of Utica 699n, 700n
Cassius Longinus, C. (*cos.* 96) 145, 146, 177, 786
Cassius Longinus, C. (*cos.* 73) 214, 222, 791
Cassius Longinus, C. (*trib.* 49, tyrannicide): Crassus' quaestor in Syria 417, 476; opposes Caesar's final honours 462; and murder of Caesar 465; in Italy after death of Caesar 470, 472–3, 474–5, 476; leaves Italy 476, 797; deprived of province 478; establishes position in Syria 481–2, 483, 798; outlawed 486
ability 470; on Caesar's style of rule 460, 726; finances 488; intellectual interests 718, 726–7
Cassius Longinus, C. (*cos. suff.* A.D. 30, jurist) 525n
Cassius Longinus Ravilla, L. (*cos.* 127) 521–2, 747, 781
Cassius Longinus, L. (*cos.* 107) 24, 37, 88, 93, 784
Cassius Longinus, L. (*trib.* 105) 93
Cassius Longinus, L. (*praetor* 64) 356
Cassius Longinus, Q. (*trib.* 49) 421, 422, 430, 435, 440
Cassius Vecellinus, Sp. (*cos.* 493) 72
Castor and Pollux, cult of 729, 764
Castus (member of Spartacus' rebellion) 223
Catalonia 218
Catiline *see* Catilinarian conspiracy *and under* Sergius
Catilinarian conspiracy 48, 354–8, 494–5, 641, 708, 729, 749, 771; reaction to execution of conspirators 357–8, 358–9, 362, 364, 372, 376–7, 300–1, 407, 495; *see also* Sergius Catilina, L.
Catius, T. 718, 724, 757n
Cato *see under* Porcius
cattle 542, 615
Catullus *see under* Valerius

Catulus *see under* Lutatius
Cauca *8 Ba*, 219
Caucasus mountains *9 Eb*; Pompey's campaigns in 255–8, 792; *see also* Albani; Iberi
Caudine Forks 61
Caudium *3(ii) Bc*, 189
Caunus *5 Bc*, 148
causa Curiana 534n, 554
causa Iuniana 234
Causinius Schola 363
cavalry: Armenian 241; Parthian 402, 403; Pontic 155; review of (*transvectio equitum*) 225; Roman 29, 30, 33, 38, 75, (from Spain) 21, 125–6, 582, 592
Celsa *8 Ca*, 445n
Celtiberia *1 Ac*, *8 Bb-Ca*, 21, 22, 61–2, 218, 219, 786, 787
Celts *12 Ab-Bb*, 22–3, 254; *see also individual tribes and* Gauls
Cenabum (Orléans) *12 Bb*, 409, 410, 414
Cendebaeus (Seleucid general) 289
Censorinus *see under* Marcius
censors 43; and *ager publicus* 25, 28, 32, 33, 63, 64, 87; ban stage performances 783; Caesar as sole 462; Cicero's wish for permanent 489; Clodius limits powers 378, 413; and equestrian rolls 90; and jury lists 332; and Latin rhetoric 690, 691, 787; Pompey appoints in east 268; Pompey and Metellus Scipio restore powers 413; and public contracts 584, 586, 587, 621–2; repair banks of Tiber 402; and senatorial rolls 46, 327, 378, 413, 419–20, 783, 791, 796; Sulla's attitude to 201, 497; tax-farming 584, 586, 587, (see also *publicani*); *see also* census; *lustra*; *and individual censors*
census 43, 600, 602–5, 645, 655; *ager publicus* to be declared 63; and allies 111, 225, 451, 601–2, 651; classes 631; figures 600, 602–5; local registration in Italy 451; numbers 57, 74, 180, 225, 600, 602–5, 780, 781, 783, 788, 791; organization 57, 74, 602, 606
centumviri 545
centuriation (land-division) 27–8, 87, 99, 611, 622
centurions 452, 475, 476, 626
Cerasus *5 Ea*, 131, 136
cereals *see* corn
Ceres, cult of 732, 748
Cethegus *see under* Cornelius
Chaeremon of Nysa 146
Chaeronea *6 Aa*, *9 Ac*, 151; battle of 154–5, 156–7, 236, 788
Chalcedon *9 Bb*, 160; naval battle of 234, 235, 244
Chalcis *6 Ca*, 32, 153, 157, 754
Chaldaei (astrologers) 763
Chaldaei (tribe) *9 Db*, 238
Charondas of Catane 268
Chelidon (C. Verres' mistress) 335
Chersonese, Caenic 32, 97
Chersonesos, Crimea *4 Ba*, *9 Ca*, 131, 139, 254
Chiliocomum 136
Chilo (Cato's slave) 690
Chios *1 Ed*, *5 Ab*, *14 Bb*; inscription 17, 767; and Mithridates 147, 159, 162, 246; Roman religious influence 767; Roman settlers, *c.* 200 17; trade 638
Chnoum, cult at Elephantine 317
Chonouphis (mummifier, of Saqqara, Egypt) 325
Chrestus, prince of Pontus 133
Christianity, spread of 659
chronology, historical 403; Atticus' 696, 714
Chrysippus 709, 720
Chrysogonus *see under* Cornelius
Cicero *see under* Tullius
Cilicia *1 Fd*, *5 Cc*, *9 Cc*, *14 Cb*; becomes praetorian province 35–6, 97, 135, 574, (*see also* 'pirate law'); M. Antonius' command (102) 96–7, 785; Tigranes annexes lowland 238, 263; Servilius Vatia's campaigns 210, 212–13, 232–3, 249, 790; Roman operations (75–74) 96–7, 211, 212–13; M. Antonius' command (74) 213, 233, 249, 497, 790; Lucullus' command 233, 234, 331; Marcius Rex's command 248–9, 331; Pompey's command *see under* Pompeius Magnus, Cn.; Pompey's settlement 264–5, 265–6, 269, 270; Cyprus added to 319; Gabinius' governorship 380; Ap. Claudius Pulcher's governorship 590, 596; Cicero's proconsulship *see under* Tullius Cicero, M.
Greek cities 266, 269; highland tribes 265, 266, 269, 596; mercenaries in Judaea 297; *see also* pirates
Cimbri: wars (114–111) 730, 783, 784–5; defeat Silanus 93–4; defeat Romans at Arausio (105) 24, 36, 37, 93, 785; invade Cisalpine Gaul, defeated at Vercellae 96, 785; Marius' campaigns (104–101) 24, 39, 95, 97, 109, 166, 328, 785; Mithridates and 140, 143
Cimiane 267
Cimiata 130
Cimmerian Bosporus *see* Crimea
cinctus Gabinus 72
Cingulum *3(i) Db*, *13 Bb*, 425
Cinna *see under* Cornelius; Helvius
cippi 622
Cirta *1 Bd*, *14 Ab*, 28, 30, 108, 638, 783
citizenship, Roman: for allies on battlefield 109, 125–6, 582, 592; assemblies' role in granting 45; Augustus' grants 444; Caesar's grants after Civil War 442, 443–4; dual,

citizenship (*cont.*)
Roman and other 443; effect of increased numbers 328, 329, 331–2, 367, 535, 547, 604, 771; ideal of farmer citizen 8, 41; Italian allies and (abortive proposals for) 69, 75, 76, 78, 102, 105–6, 112, 113, 781, (aim of Social War) 114, 122–3, 126, (granted) 66, 109, 122–3, 126, 176, (Sulla and) 191, 203, 204, (distribution of new citizens amongst Roman tribes) 165, 167–9, 172, 174, 175, 180, 182–3, 185, 186, 190, 203, 645, 677, 788, 789; Latin allies and 75–6, 81, 82–3, 102, 105–6, 126; and law of persons 535; Lex Licinia Mucia (95) 102, 110, 526, 651–2, 787; Lex Papia (65) on usurpation 344–5, 526, 652–3, 792; Lex Plautia Papiria (89) 126, 128, 787; in Marius' colonies 99, 110; in provinces 591, 592; *provocatio* 493–4; for Sicily 473; Spain 22, 125–6, 215, 444, 582, 592; for successful *repetundae* prosecutors 508; Transpadane Gaul 126, 344, 415, 442, 443, 797; usurpation, prevention of 102, 110, 344–5, 526, 651–2, 652–3, 792, 797; *see also* census
Cius *5 Ba*, 130, 131
civitates foederatae 591
civitates liberae 591, 592
civitates stipendiariae 591–2
Clanis, river *3(i) Ba-b*, 193
classes, census 57, 631
classis (body of infantry) 41
Claudii 47, 387
Claudiopolis 145
Claudius, Ap. (military tribune, 87) 176
Claudius, Ap. (nephew of consul of 54) 420
Claudius, C. 387
Claudius Asellus, Ti. 60
Claudius Glaber, C. 221
Claudius Marcellus, C. (*cos.* 50) 408, 415, 418, 796
Claudius Marcellus, C. (*cos.* 49) 419, 421, 424, 796
Claudius Marcellus, M. (*cos.* 166, 155, 152) 22
Claudius Marcellus, M. (*cos.* 51) 413, 415, 416, 450, 795, 690n
Claudius Nero, Ti. (*praetor* 42 *or* 41) 445n
Claudius Pulcher, Ap. (*cos.* 185) 45
Claudius Pulcher, Ap. (*cos.* 143) 51, 60, 65, 67, 676
Claudius Pulcher, Ap. (*cos.* 79) 174, 179, 180, 206, 210, 790
Claudius Pulcher, Ap. (*cos.* 54, *censor* 49): envoy to Tigranes of Armenia 238–9; opposes Cicero's recall 387; consulship 394, 401, 795; governor of Cilicia 590, 596; censorship 419–20, 421, 796; and philosophy 727n; religious enthusiast 759
Claudius Pulcher, C. (*cos.* 177) 501n
Claudius Pulcher, C. (*cos.* 92) 520, 787
Claudius Pulcher, P. (*cos.* 249) 729–30
Claudius Quadrigarius, Q. (annalist) 712
Clazomenae *5 Ab*, *9 Bc*, 163, 248
Cleochares (garrison commander of Sinope) 245
Cleomenes III, king of Sparta 66
Cleon (leader of Sicilian slave revolt) 25, 26
Cleopatra, queen of Armenia 142
Cleopatra II, queen of Egypt 310, 311, 313–14, 315, 779, 783
Cleopatra III, queen of Egypt 295–6, 311, 314, 315–16, 779, 784–5
Cleopatra VII Thea Philopator, queen of Egypt 320–1, 434; rule with Ptolemy XIII 272, 320–1, 795; rule with Ptolemy XIV 321; and Alexandrian War 434; liaison with Caesar 321, 438, 795; in Rome 321, 322, 434, 460; returns to Egypt 471; liaison with Mark Antony 321; death 321; debasement of coinage 322
Cleopatra Berenice III, queen of Egypt 315, 318, 326, 779
Cleopatra Tryphaena 319, 779
Clepius, T. 125
cleruchs in Egypt 313, 314, 324
clientela, *see* patronage
climate: Egypt 322, 323; Italy 610
Clodius, P. (*trib.* 58): rivalry with Lucullus 243, 341; supports Philip's claim to Seleucid throne 259; and Catiline's trial 345; trial for sacrilege 361–3, 367, 505, 740–1, 748, 793; allocation of province 363, 364; transition to plebs 365, 372, 794; and tribunician elections 372–3; threat to Cicero 372, 375, 376–7, 380–1, 491, 748, (religious rivalry) 679–80, 747–8, 749; tribunate 376, 377–81, 794; free corn distribution 319, 377–8, 385, 404–5, 794; restores *collegia* 378, 517; limits power of censors 378, 413; and allocation of consular provinces 379–80, 574; and annexation of Cyprus 319, 379–80, 384; quarrel with Pompey 385, 386; challenges validity of Caesar's *acta* 379, 385; and Cicero's return 387; and corn crisis 389–90; *XVvir sacris faciundis* 391; and restoration of Ptolemy Auletes 392; rapprochement with Crassus 392, 393; aedileship (56) 392–3, 396; trial of Milo 2, 392–3, 394, 501n; candidate for praetorship (53) 404; and tribal allocation of freedmen 404–5; gang war against Milo 405, 795; death 407, 408, 505, 795; funeral 407–8, 795; supporters condemned by *quaestio de vi* (52) 409, 410, 411, 501n, 505, 516, 529, 795
appeals to ancient tradition 673; disrupts

ludi Megalenses 683, 748; political vision 772; use of plebeian associations 673; use of violence 85, 385, 386, 390, 522
Clodius, Ser. (grammarian) 694n
Cloelius, Sex. 378, 389, 407, 411
Clonius, P. (slave-owner in Sicily) 26
clothing manufacture 623
clubs (*sodalitates*) 51, 517, 522
Cluentius, L. 124
Cluentius Habitus, A., prosecution of Oppianicus 213–14, 225, 507n, 512, 527, 530n, 790, (Cicero's speech) 214, 234, 523, 529
Clunia *8 Ba*, 218, 220
Clupea *13 Ae*, 446n
Clusium (Chiusi) *3(i) Cb*, 193, 194, 204
Cnidus *5 Ac*, *9 Bc*, *14 Cb*, 160, 442; inscription of law of 101–100 5, 17, 32, 35, 97–8, 547n, 560
Coelius Antipater, C. 191
Coelius Antipater, L. 711–13
Coelius Caldus, C. (*cos.* 94) 93, 787
coercitio, magistrates' 493
cohabitation 537
coinage 3, 631–3; access to metals for 624, 629; army expenses paid by issuing 631, 632; Attic 33; Caesar's 439, 458, 461, 463; Cinna and Carbo's 186; crises 600; Egyptian 311, 322, 632; forgery; Sullan law 525; Greek 33; history of 631–3; hoarding 457; Italian 118, 631; Judaean, Hasmonean 280, 284, 286–7, 298–9; legislation marked by 45, 46, 98, 102; local issues 631, 632; Macedonia 33, 631; Marius Gratidianus' edict 180–1, 525, 633, 677–8, 752, 788; Numidian 447; on agreement of Caudine Forks 61; Pontic 132, 140, 149; quantity in circulation 632–3; revaluation of denarius (*c.*140 B.C.) 58; on settlement of Gaul 25, 102; Spanish 4, 21, 632; Sulla's 183, 753; Syrian 395; Tyrian 286; *see also* money system
Colchis *4 Cb*, *9 Db*, 133; under rule of Pontus 129, 139, 140; revolt (80s) 163; Pompey invades 256; Pompey's settlement 265
Colenda 21
collegia (district and trade associations) 51, 671–2, 674; Augustus' 672, 680; Clodius and 378, 517; dinners 685; economic connexions within 675; evidence for 647; freedmen 675; Italian traders on Delos 20; at Minturnae 660, 672; politicization 522, 672; public works 672; religious role 761; suppressions and restorations 346, 378, 456, 671, 680, 793, 797; women in 660, 672
Colline Gate *7 Ab*; battle of 118, 194–5, 205, 789
colonies: Scipio Africanus' 22, 218, 568; C. Gracchus' schemes 5, 28, 56, 78, 82, 83–4, 85, 446; Livius Drusus' proposals 83; Narbo Martius 6, 24, 86, 99, 783; Marius' *see under* veterans; Saturninus and 99, 102, 446; Sullan 172, 203–4, 204–5, 208, 347, 601, 655, (*see also under* veterans); plans for (63) 350; Pompey founds Nicopolis 252, 267; Caesar's 415, 445–8, 449–50, 471, 473–4, 489, 601, 655, 796; Augustus' 601
agriculture 615, 617, 621; assemblies' role 45; on site of Carthage 5, 28, 78, 82, 83, 85; Cisalpine Gaul 108, 126; citizenship grants in 99, 100; constitutions 446; freedmen in Roman 654–5; in Italy 53, 78, 85, 189, 607, 621, (Sulla's) 203–4, 204–5, 208; native residents 444, 447; Roman religion 765–6; size of land allotments 56, 617, 619; *see also under* Latins; veterans
Colopene *9 Cb*, 267
Colophon *5 Ab*, 148, 159
Columella 609, 620, 621
Comana *5 Da*, 137, 238, 267, 396
comedy 65, 653
comet (44) 475
Cominius, P., and brother 339
comitia centuriata 43–4, 645; and capital trials 45, 502; and Cicero's recall 389; election of magistrates 572; *equites* in 90; new citizens in 332, 337, 389; Sulpicius proposes restructuring 353; property qualifications 57, 65, 80; Sulla's reforms 172, 190; voting procedures 44, 80, 172, 190
comitia tributa 371, 502, 572, 645
comitiatus maximus 502n
Commagene *9 Cc-Dc*, 259, 265
commentarii 712–13; *see also under* Cornelius Sulla, L.; Iulius Caesar, C.; Tullius Cicero, M.
Commentariolum Petitionis 673, 674, 675
commerce 627–30; economic structures 635–7; *equites* 7, 31, 91, 107–8, 635, 637; investment of profits 54, 618; Italian allies and 106–7, 151; law of 535; motives for Jugurthine War 31; Narbo Martius and 6, 86; senators evade ban 329, 599, 635, 642–3, 662–3, 664, 669–70; technical underpinning 628–30; *see also* businessmen; trade
commercium, Latin right of 64, 601
communications, speed of 543
companies, see *societates*
comperendinatio (legal procedure) 94
compita (crossroads) 672, 685
Compitalia (festival) 338, 672, 685, 749n
concilium plebis 41, 44, 502, 513
condictio 546
connexions, political 51, 60, 88, 166–7, 228; *see also* factions, family; patronage

Connocorix (commander of Heraclea) 237
Consabura 217
consensus: political 48, 50, 772; religious 741, 748–9
Considius, P. 386, 428, 634
consilia (groups of advisers) 500, 536n, 582
Constantine, Africa 28
constitution, Roman 40–53, 491–8; Augustus as stopping change 774; inadequate to demands of empire 497, 513–14, 774; innovation justified by ancient pedigree 492, 673; integration of Italy and provinces 775–6; *mos maiorum institutaque* (custom) as standard 491, 492, 497, 513–14, 725, 774; Polybius on 6, 40, 66, 329, 769–70; popular element 41, 43–5, 45–6, 49, 52, 75, 645; sovereignty of people 67, 72, 78, 86, 98, 103; *see also* law, public *and individual institutions*
constitutions, non-Roman: Amisus 136; Italian allies' 109, 118; Sinope 136
consulship 43; allocation of provinces 43, 47, 79–80, 166; eligibility 105, 201, (waived) 46, 223, 461; electoral procedure 43–4, 205; family succession 45, 46–7, 87–8, 211; iteration 61, 68, 90, 91, 95, 97, 105, 180; plebeians 46–7; power as *regia potestas* 463
contiones 44, 501, 645, 676; allies' participation 106, 112
contracts 541–3, 557, 558, 561, 668; agricultural 532, 554, 620; building 626; land used as security 62; *stipulatio* 541; *see also under* censors; *publicani*
Contrebia *1 Bc*, *8 Ca*; Tabula Contrebensis 22–3, 547, 550, 560, 561
conventus: jurisdictional districts 590; organizations of Romans in colonies 446
convicium (abuse in public) 544
Coracesium *9 Cc*; naval battle of 250
Corduba (Cordoba) *8 Bc*, 22
Corfinium *2 Bc*, *3(i) Dc*, *13 Bc*, *14 Ba*, 118, 121, 124, 424, 425, 449
Corinth *1 Dd*, *6 Ab*, *14 Bb*; destruction 17, 32, 637; land division 5, 87, 99; Caesar plans colony 446, 447, 655; *tabernae* 666
corn: *aediles Ceriales* 456; coin issues to purchase 632; crises in supply 60, 62, 76–7, 211, 613, (57–55) 389, 390, 392, 393, 394, 399; Curio's bill (50) 418; distribution at Rome, (free) 319, 377–8, 385, 404–5, 456, 607, 614, 648–9, 794, (subsidized) 52, 58–9, 203, 208, 225, 329, 359, 614, 649, 652, 666, 748; Egyptian 322–3; free market 638, 639; Gracchan measures 58–9, 78–9, 83, 649; Italian production 610, 611, 612–13, 658; Marius and 86; Numidian 28, 76, 77; pirates interrupt supply 249, 331, 334–5; Pompey's control 389–90, 392, 393, 399, 629, 638; price 58–9; provincial governors' supply 583; Puteoli and trade 630; Saturninus and 83, 98; tax paid in 569, 613, 638, 639, (Sicilian tithe) 569, 586, 587, 639
Cornelia (mother of Gracchi) 77
Cornelia (Cinna's daughter, wife of Caesar) 198
Cornelia (wife of P. Crassus and of Pompey) 410, 433
Cornelius (Catilinarian *eques*) 355
Cornelius, C. (*trib.* 67) 228, 332, 333, 335–6, 347, 792; trial 339, 343–4, 792
Cornelius Balbus, L. (the elder, *cos.*40) 215, 428–9, 443, 444n, 472; influence on government 451, 460, 461
Cornelius Balbus, L. (the younger) 429, 444
Cornelius Blasio, Cn. 572n
Cornelius Cethegus, C. 356, 357, 572n
Cornelius Cethegus, P. 187, 213
Cornelius Chrysogonus, L. 198, 206, 618
Cornelius Cinna, L. (*cos.* 87, 86, 85, 84) 173–87, 788; consul (87) 173–4; and distribution of new citizens amongst all tribes 174, 186, 788; seizes power in Rome 174–7, 178–9, 185, 219, 788; domination of (86–84) 173, 179–85, 201; actions against Sulla 157, 160, 182, 184; assassination 184, 186; assessment 184–5; coinage 186
Cornelius Cinna, L. (*praetor* 44) 210, 470
Cornelius Cinna, P. 431
Cornelius Dolabella, Cn. (*d.* 100) 101
Cornelius Dolabella, Cn. (*cos.* 81) 200, 210, 789, 790
Cornelius Dolabella, P. (*cos.suff.* 44) 797; tribunate 435; consulship, Syrian command 468, 471, 474; *hostis* declaration 481, 797, (repealed) 486; and Cicero 477, 481
Cornelius Lentulus, L. (*cos.* 199) 572n
Cornelius Lentulus Clodianus, Cn. (*cos.* 72) 215, 222, 225, 791
Cornelius Lentulus Crus, L. (*cos.* 49) 419, 422, 424, 429, 432, 796
Cornelius Lentulus Marcellinus, C. (*cos.* 56) 392, 393, 794
Cornelius Lentulus Marcellinus, P. 319
Cornelius Lentulus Niger, L. 376
Cornelius Lentulus Spinther, P. (*cos.* 57) 272, 320, 386–7, 391–2, 396, 741n, 794
Cornelius Lentulus Sura, P. (*cos.* 71) 791; purged from Senate 225, 327; return to public life 344; and Catilinarian conspiracy 354, 356; execution 357, 496
Cornelius Mammula, A. 576
Cornelius Merula, L. (*cos. suff.* 87) 175, 176, 177–8, 788
Cornelius Merula, L. (*flamen Dialis*) 742

Cornelius Nepos 2, 696, 699, 715; *Chronica* 714; *De Viris Illustribus* 707, 713, 716
Cornelius Scipio, P. (*cos.* 218) 567
Cornelius Scipio Aemilianus Africanus Numantinus, P. (*cos.* 147, 134); given African command by plebiscite 91, 574; defeat and settlement of Carthage 27, 43, 744; first consulship by special dispensation 46; censorship 60, 676; and elections of 142 51; embassy to Egypt 311; and Lex Cassia 61, 66–7; second consulship, dispensation by plebiscite 61; Numantine campaign 21, 22, 29, 36, 37, 39, 61–2, 73, 91, 576, 780; and Ti. Gracchus 8, 51, 73; and redistribution of land 73, 74, 104; death 74, 685, 781
and Greek political thought 53; on moral decline and extravagance 8, 59, 60; meets Polybius 693–4; popular support 65, 676; speeches 4, 8, 60; wife of 74
Cornelius Scipio Africanus, P. (*cos.* 205, 194) 22, 91; *imperium pro consule* in Spain 572n; popular support for command in Africa 91, 574; Spanish campaign 463, 567, 576; settles veterans at Italica 22, 568; stresses own *dignitas* 467, 751–2
Cornelius Scipio Asiaticus, L. (*cos.* 83) 187, 189–90, 190, 191, 198, 789
Cornelius Scipio Nasica Serapio, P. (*cos.* 138) 7, 60, 68, 69, 72, 73, 682–3
Cornelius Scipio Nasica Serapio, P. (*cos.* 111) 88, 725, 784
Cornelius Sisenna, L. (*praetor* 78) 4, 227, 711–13
Cornelius Sulla, L. (*cos.* 88, 80, *dictator* 82–1) 165–207; Marius' legate in Numidia 30, 95, 262; governor of Cilicia 142, 262, 786; in Social War 120, 121, 124–5, 787; elected consul (88) 125, 165–6, 788; and distribution of new citizens amongst tribes 168, 172; rivalry with Marius over Mithridatic command 167, 168, 169, 170, 574, 788; march on Rome 169–71, 180, 187, 574, 788; exiles Marians 171; restored to command 172; constitutional legislation 172–3, 180, 190; takes up command in east 148, 151, 153, 173–4, 317, 318, 788; Cinna fails in attempt to prosecute 173–4; campaigns in Greece 39, 153–4, 154–9, 246, 788; attempts to replace in command 157, 160, 161, 179, 181, 788; negotiations with Archelaus 32–3, 158, 160–1, 163, 181–2, 788; settlement of Asia 162, 258–9, 788; and Parthians 262; stops in Athens 162; contacts with Senate 183–4, 185–6; assumes *agnomen* 'Felix' 163–4, 199; civil war 187–97, 219, 789; and Second Mithridatic War 212, 232; dictatorship 197–207, 496, 498, 772, 789, (constitutional legislation) 200, 201–2, 203, 329–30, 489, 497, 562, (resigns) 205, 772; consulship (80) 200, 205, 206, 789; death 207, 790
and Caesar 198, 431, 452, 742–3; and censorship 201, 497; coinage 183, 753; *commentarii* 4, 164, 179, 713; and constitution 170, 172, 190, 200–1, 226; and *cursus honorum* 200, 201, 205, 223, 496–7, 498, 526, 789; cult of Venus 753; diplomatic ability 30, 189; and Etruria 449; and freedmen's tribes 203, 337; and Italian allies 168, 172, 191, 203–4; and juries 512, 526–7; legislation *see* law (*leges* (Corneliae)); library 693; *ludi Victoriae Sullanae* 205, 682, 683; and Marius Gratidianus 677–8; marriages 166–7, 206; political alliances 166–7, 223; and Pompey 196–7, 223; proscriptions and political killings 9–10, 171, 185, 190, 192, 196, 197–8, 200, 206, 348, 352–3, 431, 496, 789; and provinces 498, 594; *quaestiones perpetuae* 202, 497, 499, 503, 515, 516, 789; and religion 162, 170, 172, 173, 183, 189, 753; and Senate 170–1, 172, 180, 181, 183–4, 185–6, 190, 195, 199, 200–1, 202, 226, 407, 526, 772, 789; sources on 9–10, 164; titles 163–4, 183, 199, 753; treatment of prisoners 195, 196, 197; and tribunate 170, 172, 201, 329–30, 497, 503, 772, 789; veteran colonies 203–4, 204–5, 208, 347, 450, 524–5, 601, 626, 655
Cornelius Sulla, Faustus 341, 408, 409, 454
Cornelius Sulla, P. (*d.*45) 340, 342, 350, 351, 363, 516n, 792
Cornutus (*praetor urbanus* 43) 483, 485
corruption: ancient theories 11–12, 48–9; C. Gracchus' measures 80; in provinces 22, 26, 335, 363–4, (*see also* Verres, C.); senators 77, 225, 330, 331, 335, 363–4; *see also* bribery
Corsica *1 Cc*, *2 Ab-c*, *13 Ab-c*, *14 Ba-b*, 99, 204, 571
Corupedium 130
Cos *1 Ed*, *5 Ac*, 146, 147, 160, 315–16, 318
Cosa *3(i) Bc*, *13 Ac*; battle of 209; see also *ager Cosanus*
Cosconius, C. (*praetor* 89) 125, 210
Cosconius, M. (*praetor* 135) 32
Cossinius, L. 221
Cossyra *2 Ae*, 196
Cotta *see under* Aurelius
Cotyora *5 Ea*, 131
Council of the Hellenes of Asia 247
countryside: depopulation 57, 204, 606, 607, 608, 610, 641; intellectual life 694–5; plebs' opposition to urban plebs 106, 110; political influence 44; *see also* agrarian issue;

countryside (*cont.*)
agriculture; peasants' revolt
couriers 585
courts, see *quaestiones*
craftsmen 626–7, 661
Crantor 720
Crassus *see under* Licinius
Crates of Mallos 690, 704
credit: auctions 642; crises 600
Cremona *2 Aa*, *13 Ab*, 23
Crete *1 Ed*, *9 Ac-Bc*, *14 Bb-Cb*, 630; M. Antonius defeated by pirates (71/70) 249; Q. Metellus' command 249, 250, 251, 331, 338–9, 792
Crimea (Cimmerian Bosphorus) *4 Ba*; Mithridates and 129, 139, 163, 229, 238, 245, 253, 254, 792; under Pharnaces II 434, 797; in Pompey's settlement 265, 269
crimen 499
crisis of Republic; ancient theories on 1, 6–10, 40, 769–76
Crixus (member of Spartacus' rebellion) 221, 222
Crocodilopolis *11 Aa*, 313
crossroads, see *compitales*
crucifixion 307
Curia *see* Rome (senate-house)
curiae (division of plebs) 673
Curiatius, C. (*trib.* 138) 60
Curio *see under* Scribonius
Curius (Spanish bandit chief) 22
Curius, M'. 534n, 554, 592
Curius, Q. 355
cursus honorum 200, 201, 205, 223, 496–7, 498, 526, 789
Curtius, C. (senator, from Volaterrae) 450, 452
Curubis *13 Ae*, 445, 446n
custom, see *mos maiorum institutaque*
customs dues (*portoria*) 22, 24, 35, 79, 187, 584, 587, 639n, 640
Cybele, cult of 137, 764–5
Cybistra *9 Cc*, 265
Cynaras (brigand in Phoenicia) 259–60
Cyprus *1 Fd*, *9 Cc*, *14 Cb*; Ptolemy VIII Euergetes II and 16, 310, 311, 313, 780; Ptolemy IX Soter II in 315, 316; Ptolemy X Alexander I and 315, 316; bequeathed to Rome 316; supplies ships to Roman fleet (88) 158; Ptolemy of Cyprus' rule 260, 318; annexation by Rome 319, 329, 379–80, 384, 391, 794; Caesar restores to Egypt 321
Cyrene, Cyrenaica *1 De*, *9 Ad*, *14 Bb*; Ptolemaic rule 16, 310, 316; bequeathed to Rome 316, 786; Rome annexes 319, 329, 790; in Civil War 433, 435, 796
Cyrrhestike 417
Cyrus, river *9 Eb*, 255, 257
Cyzicus *1 Ec*, *5 Ba*, *9 Bb*, *14 Cb*; requests Roman protection 32; in Mithridatic Wars 160, 234, 235, 236, 244, 791; enslavements in Civil War 442

Dabod 318
Dacia *1 Db*, 432, 438, 631
Dalmatia 783
damage, law on 543, 544, 549
damages, assessment of legal 507, 513, 529, 543–4
Damascus *9 Cd*, 260
Damasippus *see under* Iunius
damnum, law of 548, 561; *d. infectum* 563; *d. iniuria datum* 543, 544
Damophilus (landowner in Sicily) 25
dances: Asiatic 7–8; ritual 731
Dardanus *5 Aa*; Treaty of 158, 160–1, 163, 181–2, 229, 788; Rome refuses to ratify 212, 232, 788
Darius III, king of Persia 130
Dasteira 252
Dazimonitis *5 Da*, 136
dead, cult of 750
Dead Sea Scrolls 278–9, 299, 301–3
debt 773; and agrarian issue 62, 641; bondage 354, 504; book-debts 634; Caesar's measures 431–2, 457–8, 796; crises 435, 641; in Egypt 314, 323, 434; in Italy 452; law on 557; monetary aspects 633; moratoria and remissions (Egypt) 314, (Mithridates') 147, 159, (Roman) 33, 79, 172, 180, 247, 639, 796; plebs 435, 641; in provinces 33, 247, 270, 347, 593, 639–40; Rullan bill on 349–51; smallholders 346–7, 352, 353, 452, 641; social effects 641–2; upper classes 62, 168, 344, 347–8, 350, 355, 440, 634, 641, 642, 773
Decapolis 296
Decidius Saxa, L. 445, 452n
decimation 222, 493n
Decius Subulo, P. (*trib.* 120) 84
decline of Republic 769–76; gains and losses by 774–6; Roman theories 1, 6–10, 40, 769
Decumus (*dissignator*) 685
defamation, see *iniuria*
Deiotarus, king of Galatia 265, 269, 270
Deir el Medina 318
delatio, nominis 508
delict, law of 535, 543–4, 545
Delos *1 Ed*, *9 Ac*, *14 Bb*; 'agora of the Italians' 20, 638n; Athenian domination 20, 637; banking 634, 638; decline 630; in First Mithridatic War 20, 147, 150–1, 788; free port 20, 637–8; Heroön 147n; inscription 637; Italian businessmen 20, 628, 633; pirates sack (69) 331; pottery and oil trade

639; prosperity (130–88) 630, 637–8; Rhodian rivalry 637; slave trade 20, 604, 620, 638; *tabernae* 666; wine trade 615, 627, 639
Delphi *1 Dd*, *6 Aa*, *14 Bb*, 25, 154, 570, 759; inscription of law of 101–100 5, 17, 32, 35, 97–8, 560, 574, 576–7, 579
Demetrias *9 Ab*, 151
Demetrius I Nicator, king of Syria 17, 262, 281, 282
Demetrius II, king of Syria 283, 285
Demetrius III Eukairos, king of Syria 262, 296, 297, 303, 307
democracy, Greek 78, 86, 98
Dendera *11 Bb*, 318
detentio (title to property) 540, 558
Dianium *8 Cb*, 219
Diaspora, Jewish 275, 297; *see also under* Egypt
Dicaearchus 703
dictatorship: Pompey declines 405, 409; *see also under* Cornelius Sulla, L.; Iulius Caesar, C.
Didius, T. (*cos.* 98) 786; Thracian campaign 32, 36, 97, 576, 786; Spanish campaigns 21, 22, 787
Didyma, temple of Apollo 442n
diet 611, 613, 614, 664, 665
Dio Cassius 2, 3, 10
Diodorus Pasparos of Pergamum 247
Diodorus Siculus 7, 21, 81, 113, 278, 289
Diodotus the Stoic 721n
Dion 726
Dionysiac Artists, Guild of 32, 33
Dionysius of Halicarnassus 4–5
Dionysus, cult of 761
Diophanes (rhetor) 73
Diophantus (Pontic general) 139
Dioscurias *4 Cb*, *9 Db*, 253
diplomacy 252, 253, 568–9, 571, 592, 698
display, aristocratic 456–7, 634, 641, 683, 685, 773
divinatio, prosecutors selected by 93, 94
divination 708–9, 756–7, 759
divinity *see* godhead; gods
Dolabella *see under* Cornelius
dolus malus 551, 555
domicilium (residence at Rome) 648
dominium, legal 535, 540, 558
Domitian, Emperor 640
Domitius, C. 114
Domitius, Cn. (*trib.* 104) 93
Domitius Ahenobarbus, Cn. (*cos.* 122) 24, 33, 782, 783
Domitius Ahenobarbus, Cn. (*cos.* 96) 114, 196, 219, 746, 786, 787
Domitius Ahenobarbus, L. (*cos.* 94) 192, 787
Domitius Ahenobarbus, L. (*cos.* 54): quaestor 338n; opposition to Caesar 378–9, 393, 401; consular candidacy (56) 394, 396–7; consulship (54) 401, 402, 795; in emergency of 52 410; enmity to Caesar 414; defeated in elections for augurate 419; in Civil War 424, 427, 428, 430; death 433
estates and wealth 616n, 617–18, 635n; patronage 430, 449
Domitius Calvinus, Cn. (*cos.* 53) 405, 433, 434, 795
Domitius Calvinus, M. (*procos.* 80) 215, 790
Dor (Dora) *10 Aa*, 294, 296
Dorylaus 157
dowries 62, 537–8, 555
drainage 610, 625
drama 684–5, 689, 699, 710; *see also* comedy *and individual authors*
drove-roads (*calles*) 87, 366, 452, 616
Drusus *see under* Livius
Dryton (Egyptian soldier) 324
IIviri perduellionis 502
Dyme *1 Dd*, 33, 266
Dyrrachium (Durazzo) *1 Dc*, *2 Cc*, *14 Bb*, 31, 189, 432, 638

Eburones *12 Ba*, 404, 406, 415, 795
eclecticism, philosophical 721, 727
eclipse of moon (63) 352
economy 599–643, 773; agrarian problem and 53–9; geographical and demographic context 600–8; money 106, 627–40; and society 599–600, 640–3; structures of commerce and industry 635–7; *see also* agriculture; commerce; finance; industry; trade; workforce
Edfu *11 Bc*; temple of Horus 310, 317, 325; inscriptions 315, 316
edicts: aediles' 532, 542; praetors' 335, 532, 534, 544, 548–9, 792; provincial governors' 547, 554, 589–90
Edom *see* Idumaea
education 690–2, 705; Greek influence 23, 453, 476, 690, 691, 697, 698
Egnatius, Cn. 31
Egypt *1 Ee-Fe*, *9 Be-Ce*, *11*, *14 Cb*, 310–26; wars against Antiochus IV 310; under Ptolemy VII Neos Philopator 310; under Ptolemy VIII Euergetes II *see separate entry*; succession to Euergetes II 275, 295, 314–17, 783; bequeathed to Rome 316, 318, 345, 786; and Mithridatic Wars 143, 153, 317–18; succession to Ptolemy Alexander I 318; under Ptolemy Auletes *see separate entry and under* Roman involvement *below*; under Berenice 272, 319, 320, 391, 397, 399; under Cleopatra VII *see separate entry*; Alexandrian War 321, 433–4, 796; Roman annexation 321

Egypt (*cont.*)
ECONOMY AND SOCIETY: administration 323, 324–5; agriculture 313, 314, 322–3, 629; army 323–4, 326; cleruchs 313, 314, 324; coinage 311, 322, 632; debt 314, 323, 434; Egyptian culture 313, 317, 318–19, 321, 324–5; Idumaeans 293; Jews 295, 296, 297, 299–300, 306, 320; mummifiers 324, 325; population 605; religion 318–19, 321, 323, 324, 325–6, 765; taxation 399; trade with Horn of Africa 17, 20
ROMAN INVOLVEMENT: intervention in war against Antiochus IV 310; and Euergetes II 311, 316; embassy (140/39) 311; bequeathed to Rome 316; annexation proposed 271, 319, 329, 345–6, 792; Lucullus seeks ships for Sulla 153, 317–18; recognition of Ptolemy Auletes 373; Auletes flees to Rome 271–2, 319, 794; command to restore Auletes allocated, but blocked 272, 320, 391–2, 395–6, 794; Gabinius restores Auletes 320, 397, 399–400, 794; Auletes' taxation to pay debt to Rome 399; Ptolemy XIII recognized by Senate in exile 433; Pompey killed in 321, 433, 796; Caesar's involvement 319, 320, 321, 322, 433–4, 436, 796; treaty 460; Octavian's annexation 321; businessmen in 628
see also Cyprus; Cyrene; Ptolemies; *and individual rulers and places*
Elatea, plain of 156
Elba (Ilva) *13 Ab*, 624
Eleasa *10 Ab*; battle of 281
elections 45–6; bribery and corruption 45, 46, 59, 330, 332, 336–7, 340–1, 346, 353, 355–6, 364, 367, 511, 515, 516n, 517, 772; canvassing 44, 49, 60; of consuls 43–4, 45–6, 51, 60, 205; delayed 396, 397, 403, 405, 459, 772, 790, 794, 795; disruption 336, 340, 346, 772; expansion of electorate 328, 329, 331–2, 337; Lex Gabinia (139) 45, 60; personal connexions and 51; of priests 59, 94, 352, 746; secret ballot 45, 52, 60
Elephantine *11 Bc*, 317
Eleusis *6 Bb*, 153; Mysteries 162, 759
embassies 16–17; 'philosophic' 726; private (*liberae legationes*) 588, 643
emergencies (*tumultus*) 36, 72, 84–5, 95, 494, 495; (52) 409, (*see also under* Pompeius Magnus, Cn.); (49) 422, 431; (43) 481
empire, expansion of 770; and chattel slavery 534–5; and constitution 497; and religion 743, 763–8; wealth from 54, 55–6, 332, 770, 773; *see also* provinces
Emporiae *1 Bc*, *8 Da*, 24, 445n
emptio venditio (consensual sale) 542
encyclopaedia, Varro's *Disciplinae* 705
enemy of state see *hostis*
Ennius 689, 700, 757
Entella *13 Bd*, *14 Bb*, 569
entertainments, public 666
Entremont (Gallic Celtic citadel) 24
Ephesus *1 Ed*, *5 Ab*, *9 Bc*, *14 Cb*; in Roman settlement of Asia 34; in First Mithridatic War 144, 148, 159; settlement after war 162; Ptolemy Auletes in 319–20, 392
cult of Caesar 441, 465; inscription on taxation 35n; trade 638
Epicureanism 704, 718, 722–3, 726–7
Epidaurus 154
epigrams, Greek style 710
epigraphy *see* inscriptions
Epiphania *9 Cc*, 266
Epirus *1 Dd*, *9 Ab*, 55, 604, 618n, 796
epitaphs 65, 325, 656, 657–8
Eporedia (Ivrea) *2 Aa*, 99
equestrian order 90–2; Caesar promotes members to senate 452; censors control membership 90; in *comitia centuriata* 43, 90; commercial interests 7, 31, 91, 107–8, 635, 637; definition 46, 90, 509; Diodorus Siculus on 7; and Gracchi 102; Marius and 86, 90–2, 168; Meier on 14; new citizens 332; political influence 43, 46, 80, 89, 90; property qualification 46, 90; and Senate 4, 90–2, 111–12, 200–1, 202, 365, 510; senators' sons 90, 197; Sullan proscriptions 198; theatre seating 332, 352; *see also* juries (legislation on composition)
Equitius, L. 96, 97, 101
equity, legal notion of 550–1
equus October 673
eras, chronological: Jewish 283; Pontic 130, 149
Erythrae *5 Ab*, 159
Essenes 275, 300, 308; Qumran sect 278–9, 299, 300, 301–4
Esther, Book of 279
ethics 719, 729
Etruria *2 Ab*; and Livius Drusus' laws 112–13; in Social War 115, 122, 123, 124; in civil war 191, 193; Sulla's treatment of 203, 208, 449; and Lepidus' rising 209; peasants' revolt 347, 353, 354, 358; and Caesar 448, 449, 450, 453; Octavian's support in 478
agriculture and land holdings 55, 57, 610, 613, 615, 627; kingly regalia 463; metal resources 624; social structure 113, 611
etymology 703, 709
Euboea *6 Ba-Ca*, *9 Ac*, 32, 151; *see also* Chalcis
Eudorus of Alexandria 709
Eudoxus of Cyzicus 637
Eumenes, ruler of Amastris 131
Eumenes II, king of Pergamum 131
Eunus (Sicilian slave leader) 25, 26

Eupatoria *5 Da*, 238
Eupolemus (Jewish historian) 279
Eurysaces (baker), tomb of 665
Eusebius 315
Eutropius 155
evocati (time-served soldiers) 92
evocatio (religious ritual) 743–4
exceptio (legal procedure) 541, 550, 551, 562
exemplum (legal precedent) 491, 492
exile 456, 457, 495–6, 512–13, 561, 797
expiation, public 521
expulsions from Rome: astrologers 763; foreigners 76, 83, 102, 106, 110, 290, 526, 651–2, 652–3, 655; philosophers 726
extortion, see *repetundae*
Ezekiel (tragedian) 279

Fabius, C. (Caesar's legate) 430, 437
Fabius Buteo, M. (*d.*173) 573n
Fabius Gallus 727n
Fabius Hadrianus, C. (governor of Africa) 187, 191
Fabius Hadrianus, M. (Lucullus' legate) 243
Fabius Hispaniensis, L. 22
Fabius Maximus, Q. (*cos. suff.* 45) 406, 462, 797
Fabius Maximus Aemilianus, Q. (*cos.* 145) 21
Fabius Maximus Allobrogicus, Q. (*cos.* 121) 24, 32, 33, 782
Fabius Pictor, Q. 699
Fabius Quintilianus, M. 692, 700, 715, 719
Fabrateria Nova *3(ii) Ba*, 105
Fabricius Luscinus, C. (*cos.* 282, 278) 91
factio 48, 87
factions, family 13, 14, 50–1, 87–8, 102; *see also* connexions
faenus (usury) 641; *f. nauticum* (bottomry) 635
Faesulae (Fiesole) *2 Ab*, *3(i) Ba*, *13 Ab*, 204, 208, 354
Falerio *3(i) Db*, 120
Falernian region 57, 614
family: law 499–500, 535–40, (see also *patria potestas*); and political alliances 13, 14, 50–1, 87–8, 102; religious cult in 761; succession to magistracies 45, 46–7, 211
famines 60, 76
Fannius, C. (*cos.* 122) 55, 82, 83, 651–2, 782
Fanum *2 Bb*, *3(i) Da*, *13 Bb*, 73
farmer citizen, ideal of 8, 41
Faventia *2 Bb*, 193, 194
Favonius, M. (*aedile* 53) 404
feasts, public 203, 205, 225, 685–6, 687
feriae imperativae 169
festivals 488, 664–5, 680, 766; *see also* Compitalia; games; Liberalia; Lupercalia; Panathenaia; Parilia
Festus *see under* Pompeius
Fetial priests 743, 764
fideicommissum hereditatis (trust of inheritance) 539
Fidentia *2 Ab*, 194
fidepromissor (personal security) 543
fides (financial confidence) 89
fiducia (pledge) 541, 561
Fimbria *see under* Flavius
finance: in Asia, after Mithridatic Wars 246–7, 273; building 626, 627, 641; Caesar's control as dictator 461; confidence 89; crises 148, 172, 180–1, 600; denarius–*as* exchange rate 180–1; policy-making bodies 45; Pompey and 258; provincial 580–1, 583, 588, 639–40; in war 488, 600; *see also* banking; money-changers; money-lenders; money system; reparations; taxation
fires, urban 626, 650, 660–1
Firmum *3(i) Db*, 120, 122
fish: farming 662; preserved 7, 611
Flaccus *see under* Valerius
flamen of Caesar 462, 750
flamen Dialis 198, 731, 742–3, 758
Flamininus *see under* Quinctius
Flaminius, C. (*trib.* 232, *cos.* 223, 217) 6–7, 52
Flavius, L. (*trib.* 60) 365, 793
Flavius Fimbria, C. 160, 161–2, 163, 179, 181–2, 243, 788
flax 658
fleet, Pontic: timber supply 136; in First Mithridatic War 145, 149, 157, 158, 159; fleet rebuilt 233; in Third Mithridatic War 235, 236, 237
fleet, Rhodian 149
fleet, Roman 36, 124, 136, 212, 248; in First Mithridatic War 145, 146, 147, 158, 159, 160–1, 162, 181–2; in Third Mithridatic War 234, 235, 237, 245, 254, 256; in Civil War 427, 432, 433, 435; Sex. Pompeius' command against Antony 483–4; *see also under* piracy
floods 541; Tiber 401–2, 650
Florus 1, 7, 8, 9, 770
foodstuffs: crises in supply 600, 608, 613 (*see also under* corn); imports 610–11, 614; luxury 7, 203, 660; urban demand 58, 613; *see also* agriculture; corn; *macella*; supply, military
foreign affairs, conduct of 16–17, 45, 379, 568–9, 570; restrictions on governors 491, 579; senatorial commissions 22, 27, 29, 34; *see also* diplomacy; embassies
foreigners (*peregrini*) 602, 620, 646, 652–4; legal status 64, 535, 546–7, 549; *see also* expulsions
forests 610, 616
forgery 525
Formiae *2 Bc, 3(ii) Ab*, 66
formula Octaviana 562
Forum Gallorum *13 Ab*, 483, 488, 798

Forum Iulii (Fréjus) *14 Aa*, 445n
forum-complexes 774
fragmentum Atestinum 547n, 560, 563
free cities and states 20, 25, 27, 28, 33, 591, 592, 637–8
freedmen: agents for senators 329, 662–3, 664, 669–70; in army 655; Bardyaei 178, 179; in *collegia* 675; in colonies 446, 447, 451, 654–5; commercial activities 637; edict of P. Rutilius on 561; education 691; elite's disdain for 653, 646; Greek *cognomina* 654, 656; incorporation into tribes 44, 203, 337, 338, 404–5, 604, 653; Italian allies 203; legal status 499, 535, 557, 561; in local office 451; massacre under Marius and Cinna 179; mobility 654–5, 656, (social) 663; numbers 605, 653; and patrons 663, 668, 669–70, 680; under Principate 655, 775; in service employments 669; tombs 665; urban 653–6, 662–5, 771; voting rights
Fregellae *2 Bc*, *3(ii) Ba*; migrations to 105, 115, 607; revolt 5–6, 76, 77, 105, 781
Frentani *3(i) Gc*, 115
Frontinus *see under* Iulius
frumentum in cellam, *frumentum aestumatum* 583
Fucine Lake *3(i) Dc*, *13 Bc*, 121, 124, 450
Fuficius Fango 452n
Fufidius *or* Fursidius 197
Fufidius, L. (governor of Hispania Ulterior) 206, 215
Fufius, Q. (*trib.* 61) 362, 363
Fufius Calenus, Q. (*cos.* 47) 480, 481, 482, 796
Fulcinius (landowner) 618n
Fulvia (wife of Clodius and of Curio) 407, 417
Fulvius Flaccus, M. (*cos.* 125) 24, 28, 68, 84, 781, 782; and allies' civil rights 75, 76, 82, 781
Fundi *2 Bc*, *3(ii) Ba*, 66
funerals 203, 207, 457
Furius (Varinius' legate) 221
Furius, P., of Faesulae 356
Furius, P. (*trib.* 99) 101
Furius Camillus, M. 515
Furius Flaccus 638n
Furius Philo, P., command in Spain 573n
Furius Philus, L. (*cos.* 136) 61
furniture, luxury 7
Fursidius *or* Fufidius 197

Gabinius, A. (*trib.* 139) 60
Gabinius, A. (*cos.* 58) 794; in First Mithridatic War 156; tribunate (67) 244, 249, 332–5, 574, 792; Pompey's legate in east 263, 339; prosecution for bribery abandoned 376; consulship 376, 380, 384, 385; command in Syria 271, 272–3, 384, 391, 395, 396, 574; Judaean campaigns 272–3, 294, 395–6, 401, 794; Nabataean campaigns 273, 395, 401, 794; and Parthia 271, 272, 396–7; reinstates Ptolemy Auletes 320, 322, 395–6, 397, 399–400, 491, 492, 794; trials and bankruptcy 273, 320, 401–2; and Sthenius of Himera 215
Gabinius, P. 356
Gadara *10 Ba*, 296
Gades (Cadiz) *1 Ad*, *8 Ac*, 443
Gaetulians 30, 436
Galaistes (Egyptian officer) 311
Galatia *1 Fc*, *4 Bb*, *5 Cb*, *9 Cb*, *14 Cb*, 132, 133, 141, 143, 159; in Mithridatic Wars 229, 232, 237, 250; Pompey's settlement 269, 270; tetrarchs 265, 269, 270; under Brogitarus 379; defeated by Pharnaces II 434
Galba *see under* Sulpicius
Galilee *10 Aa-Ba*, 273, 292, 295
Galilei (north Syrian people) 262
Gamala *10 Ba*, 296
gambling 203
games 475, 683–5, 686; aedilician 588, 594; Caesar's, in Julia's memory 436; of (53) 404, 795; Pompey's 225, 400; privileges for leading citizens 358, 459, 461, 463, 752
ludi: *Apollinares* 353, 375, 389, 404, 475; *Cereales* 683; *Compitalicii* 378, 674, 683, 685; *Megalenses* 344, 683, 748; *Plebeii* 683; *scaenici* 684–5; *Victoriae Caesaris* 475; *Victoriae Sullanae* 205, 682, 683
Garganus, Mount *3(ii) Da*, 222
Gauda, king of Numidia 30
Gaul *12*
Cisalpine *14 Aa*; 2nd-cent. Roman expansion 23, 108; Cimbri defeated at Vercellae 96, 785; colony founded at Eporedia 99; Lex Appuleia (100) 99, 102, 110; and Lex Licinia Mucia 111; in Social War 115, 119, 121; settlement of Transpadane 126–7; in civil war 175, 176, 191, 194; Sulla's province (80) 206; and Lepidus' rising 208, 209; Lucullus assigned (74) 213, 234; Spartacus' rebellion and 222; citizenship for Transpadane 126, 344, 345, 415, 442, 443, 444, 797; Caesar's command 374, 381, 383, 431, 591; M. Brutus as governor (46) 440; D. Brutus' command, siege of Mutina 470, 479, 482, 483, 798; demography and economy 600–1, 607, 608, 611, 624, 638; Pompey's *clientela* 415, 443
Transalpine *12*, *14 Aa*; 374; defence of Massilia 23–4, 781; foundation of Narbo Martius 6, 24, 86, 99, 782; Germanic invasions (109–105) 24, 37, 93, 99, 785; Marius' campaigns *see* Cimbri; Lepidus' province 208; Pompey's campaign (77–76) 217; revolt of Allobroges 347, 358, 365,

372, 793; Helvetii attack 365; Caesar's campaigns *see* Wars, Gallic; Caesar's settlement 444–57; cavalry in Roman army 38; mines 624; numbers enslaved in wars 604; Roman and Italian migration to 608, 628, 638; trade 23, 24–5, (wine) 615, 627, 639; *see also individual tribes and places*
Gaulanitis (Golan) *10 Ba*, 294
Gauls *1 Cc*, *12*, 22–3, 733; of Galatia 131, 133; in Macedonia 32; in Roman army 38, 121, 175, 179
Gavius, P., of Cosa 494
Gaza *9 Cd*, 261, 288, 294, 296
Gazara (Gezer) *10 Ac*, 286, 288–9, 290
Gazioura *5 Da*, 243
Geganius Clesippus (*apparitor*) 656, 672
Gellius, A. 532
Gellius Publicola, L. (*cos.* 72) 215, 222, 225, 791
Gelzer, M. 12–13, 14
genealogy 714
gentes 46–7, 538
Genua (Genoa) *1 Cc*, *2 Ab*, *13 Ab*, 23
geography 724–5
geometry 725n
Gerasa *10 Bb*, 296
Gergovia *12 Bb*, 411, 795
Gerizim, Mount *10 Ab*, 291
Getae *1 Eb*, *4 Aa*, 133
Gezer (Gazara) *10 Ab*, 286, 288–9, 290
Glabrio *see under* Acilius
gladiatiors 387, 405, 682, 686; *see also* Spartacus
glassware, Alexandrian 638
Glaucia *see under* Servilius
globe, terrestrial 697
glory, pursuit of 62, 65, 329, 466–7, 594, 770
Goddess, Good (Bona Dea), rites of 361, 729n; Clodius' alleged sacrilege 361–3, 367, 505, 740–1, 748, 793
godhead, Caesar and 439, 462, 464–5, 749–55, 764
gods: foreign 290, 761, 764–5; intervention in events 729; leading politicians' identification with 751–4; personifications of Rome 766; *see also* godhead *and individual gods*
Golan (Gaularitis) 294
gold: Athenian, taken in siege 154; ingots, as currency 631; Pompey acquires Mithridates' 258; of Tolosa 24, 93, 99, 785; working of 625
Gomphi *14 Bb*, 433
Gordius, regent of Cappadocia 141, 142, 143
Gordyene *9 Ec*, 238, 241, 253, 255, 263, 264
government, local 267, 450–2, 455
governors *see under* provinces
Gracchuris *8 Ca*, 22
Gracchus *see under* Sempronius
graffiti 62, 316, 689
grain *see* corn
grammarians 455, 703–5
grammatica (study of language and literature) 690, 691
Gran Sasso 124
granaries 79, 629
Granicus, river *5 Aa*, 236
Granius Flaccus, *De Indigitamentis* 758
gratia 50, 331; *see also* obligation
grazing *see* pasture
Greece *6*; Greeks in human sacrifice in Rome 733; Roman annexation and settlement 17, 32–3, 107, 569, 570, 571; in First Mithridatic War 149, 150–1, 788; Sulla and 179, 210; Caesar and 210, 440–1, 441–3, 455; Brutus' control 481
CULTURE AND LEARNING 23, 651, 654, 695–6, 696–700, 706, 726, 773; architecture 106, 697; coinage 33; education 23, 453, 476, 690, 691, 697, 698; language 23, 699, 764; law 549, 551, 552–3, 556; libraries 162, 693; literature translated into Latin 699, 700, 706, 708, 724, 757; in Massilia 23, 444; in Numidia 29; philosophy 721, 723–4, 726, 757, 764; political thought 49, 53, 78, 86, 98; poetry 710; religion 767; rhetoric 534; Roman attitudes offend 596; systematic methods 551, 701, 702, 718; in Sicily 25; and tyranny 453
ECONOMY: agricultural science 612; commerce; technical base 628; debts to Rome 639–40; drainage techniques 610; money system 33, 631, 632; slaves and freedmen in Rome 654, 665, 691, 697; trade 608, 613, 614, 638, 639
greed 6, 7–8, 26, 40, 769
Gromatici (land-surveyors) 609, 617
Gruen, E. 14
Grumentum *3(ii) Dc*, 120
guardianship, see *tutela*
guilds: Delos 637; Egypt 324; money-lenders 642; see also *collegia*
Gutta (a Capuan) 193

Hadrian, Emperor 22
Halaesa *2 Bd*, 25
halakhah (Jewish legal observance) 303
Hannibal 564, 567
Harsiesis (Egyptian leader in Thebaid) 313
haruspices 344, 435, 453
hasidim ('Pious' Jews) 275, 300, 308
Hasmoneans *see under* Jews
Hassaia, epitaphs 325
Hasta *8 Bc*, *14 Ab*, 22, 570

Helvetii *12 Bb*, 24, 365, 371–2, 383, 384, 793, 794
Heniochi 140
Henna (Enna) *2 Bd*, 25, 26
Heraclea, Lucania *2 Cc*, *3(ii) Ec*, *13 Cc*, 123; Table of 451, 455, 456n, 560, 602n
Heraclea, Pontus *4 Ab*, *5 Ca*, *9 Cd*, 133, 139, 140; in Mithridatic Wars 159, 236, 237, 244–5, 246
Heraclea Minoa, Sicily *2 Bd*, *13 Bd*, 26
Heracleopolis *11 Ab*, 313, 322, 323
Herakles Kallinikos, temple at Philadelphia, Egypt 325
heralds (*praecones*) 451
Herculaneum *3(ii) Bc*, 120, 125, 695, 723
Hercules, cult of 20, 225, 325
Herennium, *Auctor ad* 9, 120, 520n, 521–2, 561
Herennius, C. (*trib.* 87) 173, 218
Herius Asinius (general of Marrucini) 121
Hermagoras (rhetorician) 716
Hermonthis (Armant) *11 Bc*, 313, 318; Buchis bull 317, 321
Herod the Great, king of Judaea 274
Herodotus 135, 258
Herophilus (demagogue) 470
hever (Jewish people) 287, 299
Hiarbas, king of Numidia 30, 196, 219
Hiempsal I, king of Numidia 29, 196
Hiera Nesos 323
Hierapolis, Syria *9 Dc*, 403
Hiero II of Syracuse 25
Hiero of Laodicea 248
Hirpini *3(ii) Ca-b*, 115, 118, 124, 125
Hirtius, A. (*cos.* 43) 469, 473, 474, 477, 798; command against Antony 480, 482, 483, 487; death 483, 488, 798
Hirtuleius, L. (Sertorius' legate) 215, 217, 218, 790
Hispalis (Seville) *8 Bc*, *14 Ab*, 445
historiography, ancient 1–10, 65, 164, 699, 711–15; *see also* annalists; chronology; *and individual historians*
historiography, modern 10–15; *see also individual historians*
Hittites 137
hoards, coin- 457
Homer 699
Horace (Q. Horatius Flaccus) 736
horses, public 75, 90
Hortensius, L. (*cos.* 108) 91, 784
Hortensius, L. (Sulla's legate) 155–6
Hortensius Hortalus, Q. (*cos.* 69) 792; in Sullan period 202, 206, 207; forensic speeches 181, 210, 211, 226–7, 339, 340, 343, 352, 529; advises Cicero 381; and restoration of Ptolemy Auletes 392; death 419; villa 694; wealth 331, 398
Hostilius Mancinus, C. (*cos.* 137) 21, 61
Hostilius Tubulus (*praetor* 141) 80
hostis, designation as 494–5, 496; Sullan era 171, 174–5, 179, 209
housebreaking 525–6
houses 626; Gezer 288; letting of 642; strip-houses 667; see also *insulae*; villas; *and under* Rome
hydraulics 625
hygiene, public 650
Hypaepa 159
Hyrcania, Palestine *9 Fc*, *10 Bb*, 257, 296
Hyrcanus I, John, high priest of Judaea 286–7, 289–90, 291–3, 297, 305–6, 777
Hyrcanus II, high priest of Judaea 260, 261, 273, 307–8, 395, 777

Iapygia 125, 781
Iasus *5 Ab*, 163
Iberia, Caucasus *9 Eb*, 143, 253, 255, 256, 257, 269
Iconium *9 Cc*, 232, 233
Idumaea *10 Ac*, 273, 291, 292–3, 294
Ilerda *8 Ca*, *14 Aa*, 217, 219, 431, 796
Iliturgi *8 Bc*, 22
Ilium *5 Ab*, *14 Cb*, 147, 160, 162, 441–2, 453
Illyricum *1 Dc*, *2 Ca-b*, *14 Ba*, 210, 481, 628; Caesar's command 374, 381, 383, 388, 412, 591
imperator, Caesar's title of 461
imperium 85; praetorian 533; pro-magistrates' 572; prorogation 10, 14, 43, 61, 572, 751, 771; provincial governors' 564–5, 572, 577, 579–80; specific nature 497–8
in iure proceedings 544, 545, 546
in iure cessio (transfer of title) 540
incolae (natives in colonies) 444, 447
indemnities *see* reparations
India 257–8, 323, 637
Indigetes *8 Ca-Da*, 217
industry 58, 623–7; economic structures of 635–7; *tabernae* and *officinae* 659, 661, 666, 669
infamia 545, 558
inheritance *see* succession
iniuria, quaestio de iniuriis 525–6, 543–4, 548, 549, 561, 562
inquisitio (search for legal evidence) 94
inscriptions 3, 5, 689; on Caesar's dictatorship 439–40, 441; on Guild of Dionysiac Artists 32; on freedmen 654; on jurisdiction in provinces 22–3, 570, 590; of laws, presuming literacy 689; on local government 451, 455, 456n; on local Italian courts 547n; on migration to southern Gaul 25; on Mithridates IV of Pontus, from Capitol 132; on Pompey's settlement of east

268; on private law 532, 560; of *senatus consulta* 48; on Sicilian slave revolt 27, 73–4; on slave ownership 653; *see also* epitaphs; graffiti; milestones; 'pirate law'; Tabula Bembina; *and under* Ateste; Bantia; Buthrotum; Chios; Contrebia; Delos; Edfu; Ephesus; Heraclea; Olympia; Tarentum; Val di Diano
insulae (housing) 647, 667, 668, 671
insurance, bottomry 635
intellectual developments 689–728; Hellenization *see* Greece (culture and learning); measure of importance 725–8; oral culture 689; and political activity 726–7; religion; foreign perspectives on 767–8; Roman self-identification 706, 727; social setting 692–6; speed of change 773; *see also* education; Greece (culture and learning); grammarians; *grammatica*; historiography; philosophy; poetry; scholarship; science; *and individual authors*
intercalcary months 418, 460
intercessio (tribunician right) 41
interdictio aquae et ignis (interdiction, exile) 456, 457, 495–6, 513, 561, 797
interdictum (legal injunction on possessions) 55; *i. Salvianum* (lien) 562
interest: fixing of rates 45, 172, 247; laws on 548, 634–5; legal and social disapproval 634–5; rates in wartime 338, 457, 458
interregna 199, 397, 403, 405, 409
intestacy 538, 539, 557, 562
Invective against Sallust (attr. Cicero) 709n
investment *see under* agriculture
Ionia 144, 146, 159, 163; *see also individual cities*
Iran 257–8, 262, 285, 290; *see also* Persia
Iranian peoples in Pontus 136, 137, 267
iron resources 135, 624
Isaura Vetus *9 Cc*, 744
Isauria 232–3, 236, 269, 329
Isis, cult of 674–5, 761, 763, 765; Eseremphthis, at Philadelphia 325, 326
Italica (Corfinium) 118
Italica, Spain *8 Bc*, *14 Ab*, 22, 218, 568
Italy and Italians *2*, *3*, *7*, *13*; agriculture 106–7; architecture 600, 687, 774; C. Gracchus and 75, 77–8, 81, 82–3, 85; under Caesar 386, 439, 448–53, 462; censuses 225, 601–2; in Civil War 424–5, 433, 437, 448; coinage 118, 631; colonies 53, 78, 85, 189, 203–4, 204–5, 208, (*see also under* veterans); commerce 106, 107–8; *commercium* 601; constitutions 109, 118; debt 452; equestrian order 332; expulsions from Rome 76, 83, 106; geographical diversity 609–11; Jews 290, 456, 655; jurisdiction 504, 527–8, 546–7, 601, 602; local government 267, 450–2, 775–6; migration to Rome 106, 112, 652; monetization of economy 106; oratory 109; political structure 600–1, 608; and political life in Rome 106, 112; population 600, 602–5, (movements) 601–2; prosperity 106, 107; and provinces 107–8, 328–9, 332; *provocatio* 75, 76, 81, 508, 781; religion 113; *repetundae* prosecutions 105, 109; resentment of Rome after Social War 165; solidarity 109; Sulla's treatment 198, 203–4; taxation 104, 107, 452–3; treaties 64, 104, 114; *tributum* 107; upper classes 89, 104, 105, 106–7, 109, 113, 328, 332, 453, 692; urbanization 451, 600; voting rights 82–3, (*see also under* citizenship); *see also individual cities and peoples and* agrarian issue; citizenship, Roman; Latins; War, Social
Ithaca 654
Itineraries 233
Ituraeans 293, 477
iudices 544, 545
iudicia publica see *quaestiones perpetuae*
Iulius Caesar, C. (*cos.* 59, 48, 46, 45, 44, *dictator* 49, 48, 46–44): education 690n; *flamen Dialis* designate 178, 198, 742–3; proscription under Sulla 198; in Cilicia 210, 213; returns to Rome 210; prosecutes Dolabella and C. Antonius 210; aedileship 344; funeral oration for Julia 344, 753; president of *quaestio de sicariis* 348; and Rullan bill 349; prosecutes C. Piso 351; and trial of Rabirius 103, 352; *pontifex maximus* 353, 361, 793; and Catilinarian conspiracy 48, 357; praetorship (62) 358, 360; acquittal by *quaestio de vi* 360; and trial of Clodius 361; divorces Pompeia 361; campaigns in western Spain 365–6, 440, 443–4, 793; alliance with Pompey and Crassus 366, 367, 374, 793; consulship (59) 204, 368–77, 793–4; legislation *see* law (*leges* (Iuliae)); Bibulus' obstruction 368, 369, 371, 739–40; attitude to Clodius 372–3; and Ptolemy Auletes 271, 319, 322; five year command in Gauls and Illyricum 91, 374, 574, 794; marries Calpurnia 376; legality of *acta* contested 378–9, 380, 384, 385, 739, 740; departs for province (58) 381, 383–4, 794; Gallic campaigns *see* Wars, Gallic; and Cicero's recall 387, 391; validity of command questioned 393, 394–5; deal with Pompey and Crassus at Luca 272, 394, 397, 398–9, 794; command renewed for five years 398–9, 794; German campaigns 400, 794; British campaigns 400–1, 402, 794–5; Ahenobarbus' attacks on 401; death of Julia 402; setbacks in Gaul (54–53) 402, 404, 405–6, 795; *Rechtsfrage* 408, 416–17, 418–19,

Iulius Caesar, C. (*cont.*)
423, 795; changed relationship with Pompey 408, 410; campaigns against Vercingetorix 409–12, 795; stands for consulship in absence 408, 412, 416, 795; final Gallic campaigns (51–50) 414, 415, 416, 795; validity of *acta* queried 415; breach with Pompey 419, 420, 421; letter to Senate 183, 422; march on Rome 421, 422–3, 424, 425, 448, 796; negotiations with Pompey 427–9; in Rome 425, 429–30; siege of Massilia 430, 431; campaign in Spain 425, 430–1, 796; puts down mutiny in Cisalpine Gaul 431; dictatorship and consulship 431–2, 641, 796; campaign in east, victory at Pharsalus 321, 433, 435, 442, 459, 796; in Egypt 319, 320, 321, 322, 433–4, 436, 796; defeats Pharnaces at Zela 434; dictatorship for year 435, 459, 796; consulship (46) 435, 459, 797; African campaign 435–6, 452–3, 796–7; triumphs and games in memory of Julia 436–7; campaigns in Spain 425, 430–1, 435, 436, 437, 443, 460, 461, 478, 797; plans expedition against Parthians 437–8, 439, 447, 466; dictatorship (46–44) 438–67, 498, 696, 797, 798; resigns consulship (45) 461, 797; will 454, 466, 470, 471–2, 486, 687; death 465, 468, 797; aftermath of murder 468–90, 504n; funeral 470; cult set up in Forum 470, 472; Senate votes honours 477

aims and measures as dictator 458–67; admiration for Alexander 442, 467, 771; anti-Sullan stance 198, 201, 204, 210, 348, 452; and assembly 91, 372, 374; bribery 270, 353; building projects 406–7, 449, 453–5, 626, 684; calendar reform 455, 725, 750; and Cicero *see under* Tullius Cicero, M.; citizenship grants 442, 443–4; *clementia* 424, 425, 428, 433, 440, 442, 448, 460, 486; and Clodius 372–3, 379, 381; coinage 439, 458, 461, 463; colonies 415, 445–8, 449–50, 471, 489, 601, 655; and debt crisis 431–2, 457–8, 798; debts 344, 440; *dignitas* 427; Domitius Ahenobarbus' attacks on 378–9, 393, 401, 414; donatives and public benefactions 251, 344, 489, 640, 685–6, 738, (*see also* will *above*); and equestrian order 452; empire under 438–48; and 'False Marius' 680, 687; glory as motive 466–7; godhead 439, 462, 464–5, 749–55, 764; and Greeks 210, 440–1, 441–3, 455; and *haruspices* 435, 453; house and gardens 454, 680, 687, 750; and intellectual life 454, 455, 675, 690n, 692–3, 696, 701; Italy under 439, 448–53; and kingship 12, 438, 439, 463–4, 465, 498, 750; and law 527, 591, (plans codification) 455, 551, 727; and library for Rome 692–3, 701; local government reorganization 450–2; manipulation of consulship 408, 412, 416, 461; as Marius' successor 344, 448; military basis of power 489; modern scholars on 12; and obligation 391, 408, 415–16, 448; opportunism 438; oratory 344, 753; priesthoods 459, 706; and *publicani* 441n; religious views 437, 465, 735; rent controls 641; rights and privileges 458–67, 752; Rome under 406–7, 453–8; and Senate 202, 452, 466; on *senatus consultum ultimum* 85; statues 453–4, 462; support 386, 387, 429, 431, 440, 444, (in Italy) 448–9, 450, 489 (Transpadane Gaul) 344, 345; and tribunate 91, 201, 227, 425, 427, 430, 462, 574; triumphs 366, 436, 437, 459, 461; and Venus/Aphrodite cult 442, 445n, 453–4, 465, 753–4; wealth 440

WRITINGS: *Anticato* 461, 695, 713; *Bellum Civile* 424, 425, 427, 430; *Commentaries* 2, 109, 386, 391, 401, 405–6, 414, 431, 713; *De Analogia* 715, 727; poetry 710; prose style 713, 727; translations from Greek 700

Iulius Caesar, C. (Octavian) *see under* Octavius
Iulius Caesar, L. (Caesar's father) 95
Iulius Caesar, L. (*cos.* 90) 120, 121, 123, 178, 787
Iulius Caesar, L. (*cos.* 64) 345, 352, 427–8, 481, 482, 793
Iulius Caesar, Sex. (*quaestor* 47) 122
Iulius Frontinus, Sex. (*cos. suff.* A.D. 73) 38–9
Iulius Vopiscus Caesar Strabo, C. (*aedile* 90) 165–6, 168, 178, 700
Iunius, C. (president of court trying Oppianicus, 74) 214
Iunius Brutus, D. (*cos.* 77) 210, 790
Iunius Brutus, M. (*praetor* 142, jurist) 554, 555
Iunius Brutus, M. (*praetor* 88) 196
Iunius Brutus, M. (trib.83) 189, 208, 209
Iunius Brutus, M. (*praetor* 44): family connections 420; asks for mercy after Pharsalus 433; governor of Cisalpine Gaul 440; on Caesar's intentions 461; murder of Caesar 465, 468; in Italy after death of Caesar 469, 470, 471, 472–3, 474–5, 476; and Caesar's *acta* 469, 471, 472–3; in Greece and east 476, 478, 481, 485, 797; outlawed in absentia 486; considers joining Antony 487

and Cicero 487, 593, 696; *De Virtute* 696, 719; finances 488, 593; intellectual interests 690n, 695, 699, 721

Iunius Brutus Albinus, D.: besieges Massilia 430; and murder of Caesar 465, 468; command in Cisalpine Gaul 470; distrust of Antony 473, 475, 479; besieged in Mutina

470, 479, 482, 483, 798; joins Plancus 484; death 485; correspondence with Cicero 487
Iunius Brutus Callaicus, D. (*cos.* 138) 22, 60, 780
Iunius Brutus Damasippus, L. (*praetor* 82) 191, 192
Iunius Brutus Pera, D. (*d.* 264) 682
Iunius Congus Gracchanus, M. 714
Iunius Pennus, M. (*trib.* 126) 76, 651–2
Iunius Silanus, D. (*fl.*207) 54, 508n
Iunius Silanus, D. (*cos.* 62) 353, 793
Iunius Silanus, M. (*cos.* 109) 24, 37, 77, 93–4, 784
Iunonia (proposed colony at Carthage) 78, 99
iuris consulti, *iuris prudentes*, *see* jurisprudence
ius (right, justice) 491, 492, 532; *civile, see* law, private; *gentium* 549; *honorarium* 533, 538–9, 540, 544, 546, 548–9, 550; *imaginum* 336; *in rem* 540, 558; *naturale* 549; *praetorium* see *honorarium* above; *publicum, see* law, public; *strictum* 543, 550; see also *in iure* proceedings
iustitium (ban on public business) 169
Iuventius, P. (*praetor* 149) 567
Iuventius Thalna, M'. (*praetor* 167) 574

Jamnia *10 Ab*, 289
Jason (Jewish high priest) 298, 306
Jericho *9 Cd*, *10 Bb*, 273
Jerusalem *1 Fe*, *9 Cd*, *10 Cd*; Jonathan occupies 281–2, 284; Antiochus VII's treatment 289; Pompey's occupation 252, 261, 275, 308; Crassus plunders Temple 403
Akra 282, 283, 284; Diaspora Jews' view of 297; Jason, tomb of 298; Hellenizers 282, 283, 284, 298; *synhedrion* 273; Talmud of 280; Temple 147, 275, 285
Jews and Judaea *9 Cd*, *10*, *14 Cb*, 274–309; Ptolemaic taxation 282; war against Antiochus IV Epiphanes 274–5; under Judas Maccabaeus 275, 280–1, 300; Hellenizing crisis 299–300, 302; under Jonathan 281–3, 284, 288, 290; under Simon 277, 283–6, 287, 288–9, 290, 296; under John Hyrcanus 286–7, 289–90, 291–3, 297, 305–6; independence from Seleucids 283, 290; under Aristobulus 291, 293, 297; under Alexander Jannaeus 291, 293–6, 297, 298–9, 302, 306–7; under Salome Alexandra 291, 296, 297, 307; war of succession between Aristobulus and Hyrcanus 262–3, 274, 307–8, 395–6, 401, 794; Pompey's conquest 252, 260–1, 274, 275, 308, 793; Pompey's settlement 261, 270, 294, 296, 793; Gabinius' campaigns 272–3, 294, 395–6, 401, 794; support Romans in Egypt 399, 434; under Herod the Great 274; Tiberius and Jewish freedmen in Rome 655; Vespasian suppresses revolt 299–300
apocalyptic writers 300; archaeology 280; attitudes to Rome 272–3; coinage 280, 284, 286–7, 298–9; Diaspora 275, 297, (*see also under* Egypt); era 283; *hasidim* 275, 300, 308; Hasmoneans' style of sovereignty 274, 285, 286–7, 296–9, 305–7; Hellenizers, (2nd cent.) 275, 281, 282, 283, 284, 299–300, 302, (1st cent.) 298; high priesthood 273, 282, 297, 306–7; in Italy 290, 456, 655; Law 275, 279, 303, 306; Messianism 308; pilgrimage 297; popular mandate for leaders 281, 285, 287, 299; privileges under Rome 432, 456n; Rabbinic literature 279–80; religious divisions 274, 275, 278, 299–309; religious reaction to Hasmonean rule 274, 305–7; Roman alliance 275, 282, 290; Roman expulsion of Jews from city (139) 290; Second Temple Judaism 280, 300; sources 277–80; *synhedria* 273; taxation 270, 273; Temple cult 275; territorial expansion 274, 275, 277, 282, 287–96; Torah 275; wars of independence against Seleucids 274–5, 283, 284, 287–90, 306; *see also individual rulers and under* Egypt
Jonathan (Jewish high priest) 281–3, 284, 288, 290, 298, 302
Joppa *9 Cd, 10 Ab*, 260, 261, 288, 289–90
Josephus, Flavius 277–8, 280–1, 286, 300
Juba, king of Numidia 418, 431, 435, 436, 796
Jubilees, Book of 279, 292
Judaea, Judaism *see* Jews
Judas Maccabaeus (rebel leader) 275, 280, 281, 290
Jugurtha, king of Numidia: in Scipio's force against Celtiberi 62; disputes with brothers 17, 783; accused of bribery 29, 30, 88, 89, 519; *see also* War, Jugurthine
Julia (Caesar's daughter, Pompey's wife) 374, 402, 436, 795
Jupiter, cult of 751–2; Capitoline 113, (*see also under* Rome)
juries: bribery 60, 213–14, 224, 330, 332, 340–1, 377, 509, 510, 514, 527; censors select non-senatorial 332; *centumviri* for private actions 545; equestrian privileges 377, 458; legislation on composition, (Gracchan) 69, 80, 81, 508, 509–10, (Lex Servilia Caepionis) 93, 511–12, (Lex Servilia) 94, 96, 102, 512, (Livius Drusus') 111, (Sullan) 202, 512, 526–7, (Lex Aurelia Cottae) 215, 225–6, 227, 509, 527, (Caesar's) 377, 458, 527, 797, (Antony's) 476, 527; *quaestiones perpetuae* 96, 511, (see also under *repetundae*); *quaestio Variana* 114–15;

juries (*cont.*)
  recuperatores 507; for sacrilege 362, 363, 741; special courts 505
jurisdiction, Roman external 570, 591; in Italy 504, 527–8, 546–7, 601, 602; in provinces 567, 570, 582, 589–91, 628
jurisprudence 532, 533–4, 545, 551–6, 753
justice *see* law
Justin, *Epitome of Pompeius Trogus* 130, 133, 315, 316
Justinian; *Digest* 523, 532

Karnak *11 Bb*, 318
Kerkenna Island (Cercina) *2 Ae*, 30
Kerkeosiris *11 Aa*, 313, 314
kidnapping 526
kingship 358; Caesar and 12, 438, 439, 463–4, 465, 498, 750
Kom Ombo *11 Bc*, 318

Labienus, T. (*trib.* 63) 103, 352, 747; in Gallic War 383, 385, 386, 388, 406, 411, 414, 416; in Civil War 423, 425, 435, 436, 437
labour: day- 670; division of 663; law 557; seasonal 656, 664
Lacetani *8 Ca*, 217
Lacobriga *8 Ac*, 217
Laelius, C. (*cos.* 140) 51, 53, 59, 60, 61
Laelius, D. (Pompey's legate) 218, 228
Lafrenius, T. (praetor of Piceni) 120–1, 122
Lamponius, M. (praetor of Lucani) 120, 125, 193, 195
Lampsacus *9 Bb*, 235, 236, 447
land: division in Africa 5, 27–8, 31, 85, 87, 89; fiscal and juridical status 543, 609; letting of 642; market in 457, 459, 622–3; *occupatio* 611, 616, 618, 621–2; *peregrini* not to own Roman 535; private 621; reclamation 450; senators not to own abroad 329, 446–7; social value 622, 623; *see also* agrarian issue; centuriation
language: anomaly/analogy controversy 704, 711, 727; Greek 23, 699, 764; poetic 722; *see also* Latin language
Lanuvium *3(ii) Aa, 7 Bb*, 177, 332
Laodice (wife of Mithridates II of Pontus) 131
Laodice (daughter of Mithridates III of Pontus) 132
Laodice (wife of Mithridates V of Pontus) 132, 133
Laodice (daughter of Mithridates V of Pontus) 132, 141, 142
Laodicea-on-Lycus *5 Bb*, 34, 146, 248
Lares Compitales, cult of 20, 748
Larinum *3(ii) Ca*, 125, 198
Laterensis, M. (Lepidus' legate) 484
latifundia, see under agriculture
Latin language 455, 703–5; Cicero's control 715; literary resources 700, 711; philosophical terminology 699, 718, 719; rhetoric 690, 691–2, 715, 787
Latins: agriculture and land holdings 56, 64, 610, 611; in army 384, 493n; colonies, (new foundations) 22, 126, (overseas) 442, 444, (revolt of Fregellae) 5–6, 76, 77, 105, (in Social War) 115, 119, 120, 123, 126; migration to Rome 83, 650–1, 656; numbers 604; rights 64, 82–3, 493n; and Roman citizenship 75–6, 82–3, 102, 105–6, 126, (Transpadane colonies) 126, 344, 415, 442, 443, 444, 797; under Sulla 203
Latopolis *11 Bc*, 317
Laudatio 'Turiae' 560
Laurium silver mines 624n
Lauro *8 Cb*, 218, 228, 790
law, 774; administrative 499, 557; constitutional *see* law, public; education in 690; experts 532, 533–4, 545, 556, 753; *ius civile, see* law, private; *ius publicum, see* law, public; Greek 23, 549, 552–3, 556, 558–9; legal personality 79, 542; sacral 499
  leges: Acilia *repetundarum* 93, 508; Aebutia *de formulis* 546, 548, 561; Aelia et Fufia (*c.*150) 100, 652; *agraria* (111) 5, 28, 31, 32, 63, 74, 85, 86–7, 98, 99, 561, 784; *agraria* (44) 474; *de ambitu* (61) 364; of Antius Restio, sumptuary (69) 331; Antonia *de Termessibus* (?71) 560; Appuleia *agraria* (104, 100) 5, 95, 97–8, 98–9, 102, 109–10, 749, 786; Appuleia *de maiestate* (103 or 101–100) 102, 110, 371, 518, 785; Aquilia *de damno* 544, 548, 555, 561; Atilia *de tutoribus* 548, 561; Atinia *de tribunis plebis in senatum legendis* (before 102) 46; Atinia *de usucapione* 548; Aufeia 35; Aurelia Cottae *iudiciaria* (70) 225–6, 227, 509, 527, 530, 791; Aurelia Cottae on tribunician power (75) 211, 790; Caecilia Didia (98) 102, 786; Caelia *tabellaria* (107) 45, 784; Calpurnia *de ambitu* (67) 336–7, 515; Calpurnia *de repetundis* (149) 81, 505–8, 578; Cassia *de senatu* (104) 785; Cassia *tabellaria* (137) 45, 46, 61, 66–7, 503n; Cincia *de donis* (204) 529n, 548, 561; Corneliae (81) 201–4, 562, 789; Cornelia *annalis* (81) 201, 205, 223, 496–7, 498, 526, 789; Cornelia *de iniuriis* (81) 525–6, 562; Cornelia *de maiestate* (81) 202, 234, 492, 498, 518, 520, 579, 594, 709, 789; Cornelia on praetors' edicts (67) 549, 792; Cornelia *repetundarum* (81) 202, 498, 512, 578, 709; Cornelia *de sicariis et veneficiis* (81) 80, 348, 520, 523; Cornelia on sureties 543n; Cornelia *testamentaria nummaria* 525, 548; Cornelia *de XX quaestoribus* (81) 201, 581n, 789; Cornelia

Baebia (181) 515; Cornelia Fulvia (159) 515; Didia (143) 59, 60; Domitia *de sacerdotiis* (104) 203, 746, 747, 785; Fabia *de plagiariis* 526; Falcidia (40) 539; Fannia *sumptuaria* (161) 59; Flaminia *agraria* (232) 52, 65, 66, 99; Fufia (*c.* 150) 100; Gabinia *tabellaria* (139) 45, 46, 60; Gabinia (67) 249, 250, 251, 333, 574, 792; Gellia Cornelia *de civitate* (72) 791; Hieronica 569; Hortensia (287) 41, 502; *de iudiciis* (61/60) 365; Iulia *de actis senatus* (59) 368, 793; Iulia *agraria* (59) 368–9, 371, 373, 375, 451, 739, 793; Iulia *de civitate danda* (90) 123, 128, 787; Iulia *maiestatis* (59) 498, 513; Iulia *de repetundis* (59) 98, 377, 385, 492, 512, 513–14, 520, 578, 580, 588, 592, 594–5, 793; Iulia *sumptuaria* 456–7; Iulia *de vi* (59) 513, 524; Iulia *de vi* (Augustan) 493n; Iunia *repetundarum* 508, 511; Iunia Licinia (62) 793; Iunia Penni *de peregrinis* (126) 76, 781; Laetoria *de minoribus* 548, 561; Latina Tabulae Bantinae 749n; Licinia *sumptuaria* (131 or later) 77, 203; Licinia *de sodaliciis* (55) 517, 522, 794; Licinia Mucia (95) 102, 110, 526, 651–2, 787; Licinia Pompeia (55) 574; Livia (146) 27; Livia *agraria* (91) 112–13, 787; Livia on alloying of metals (91) 633; Livia on citizenship (91) 112, 113, 787; Lutatia *de vi* (78?) 524; Mamilia *de coniuratione Iugurthina* 90, 784; Mamilia Roscia Peducaea Alliena Fabia 451, 794; Manilia (66) 249, 250, 251, 339, 490, 574, 792; Minicia *de liberis* (before 90) 535n, 548, 562; Ogulnia (300) 745; Orchia *sumptuaria* (182) 59; Osca Tabulae Bantinae 109, 528; Papia *de peregrinis* (65 or 64) 344–5, 526, 652–3, 792; Papiria *tabellaria* (131) 45, 780; Pedia (43) 504n; Peducaea (114) 86, 783; 'pirate' 5, 17, 32, 35, 97–8, 108, 547n, 560, 574, 576–7, 579, 785; Plaetoria *de iurisdictione* 561; Plautia *or* Plotia *de vi* (?70) 522, 524, 791; Plautia Papiria (89) 126, 128, 787; Poetelia *de ambitu* 358, 516–17; Poetelia *de nexu* (326) 548, 561; Pompeia 'on cities of Bithynia and Pontus' 267–8; Pompeia *de iudicibus* (55) 794; Pompeia *de parricidiis* 526; Pompeia *de provinciis* (52) 413, 441, 575, 795; Pompeia *de Transpadanis* (89) 126–7, 787; Pompeia *de vi* (52) 409, 410, 501n, 516, 529, 795; Pompeia Licinia (70) 791; Pompeia Licinia (55) 398–9, 794; Porciae 46; Porcia (101/100) 98, 579; Porcia *de provocatione* (199) 46, 494; *provinciae* 589; Roscia *theatralis* (67) 332, 352, 792; Roscia *de civitate Transpadanorum* (49) 442, 443; Rubria *de Gallia Cisalpina* (123 *or* 122) 28, 83–4, 85, 95, 449n, 451, 527n, 547n, 560, 563; Rufrena 449n; Rupilia *de iure Siculorum* (131) 589, 780; Scribonia *de usucapione servitutum* (?56) 548, 563; Sempronia *agraria* (133) 62–8, 73, 87, 622, 782; Sempronia *de capite civium* (123) 77–8, 80, 84, 492, 494, 505, 782; Sempronia *ne quis iudicio circumveniretur/circumveniatur* 523, 782; Sempronia *de repetundis* (?122) 5, 51–2, 75, 78, 81–2, 89, 90, 506, 507, 508–10, 511, 530n, 578, 597, 782; Sempronia *de provinciis consularibus* 79–80, 394, 573, 782; Servilia *de repetundis* (106–100) 94, 96, 102, 512, 785; Servilia Caepionis (106) 93, 511–12, 785; *tabellaria* (119) 86; Terentia Cassia (73) 791; of the ten tribunes (52) 412, 416, 795; Thoria *agraria* (119) 87, 783; Titia *de IIIviris reipublicae constituendae* (43) 496n; Trebonia *de provinciis consularibus* (55) 398, 574, 794; Tullia *de ambitu* (63) 353, 516, 793; Valeria (82) 496n; Varia *de maiestate* (90) 114–15, 120, 165, 167, 518–19, 787; Vatinia (59) 393, 415, 574, 794; Voconia *de mulieribus instituendis* (169) 539, 548, 561

see also law, private; law, public; legislation

law, private 531–63, 774; *actiones*, see separate entry; actions, law of 532–3, 638–9, 544–6, 548–9, (see also *ius* (*honorarium*)); advocacy 534, 546; appeal not available 557; Caesar's plans to codify 455, 551, 727; changes 550, 548, (*see also* actions, law of); chronology 548, 561–3; commercial law 535; contracts *see separate entry*; criminal actions under 503–4, 524–5, 528, 579; damages 543–7; definition 531; delict 535, 543–4, 545; development 548–56, 561–3; equity, notion of 550–1; fictions 535, 540, 549–50, 590; formulary system 545–6, 547, 550, 557, 570; Greek influence 552–3, 556; initiation of actions 506, 595; interpretation 551–6; in Italy 528, 546–7; jurists 532, 533–4, 545, 551–6, 753; labour law 557; *legis actiones see separate entry*; and lower classes 548, 558; obligations, law of 541–4, 557–8; partnerships 635–7; *patria potestas* 532, 536–7, 557–8; and *peregrini* 535, 549; persons, law of 534–40, 557; pragmatism 549, 550, 553, 556; procedure 532, 544–6; property law 540–1, 549–50, 558; in provinces 22–3, 547, 561, 589, 590, 595; sale, law of 533, 542, 561; and social engineering 548; sources on 531–2, 560; sources of law 532; status at end of Republic 534–47; Stoic influence 556; *vis*, private prosecutions of 524–5, 528; see also *actiones*; contracts; *ius* (*honorarium*); jurisprudence; *legis actiones*; succession; *and individual crimes and procedures*

law, public (*ius publicum*) 493, 498–505, 774; administrative law 499, 557; appeal 69, 352, 476; assemblies' functions 61, 69, 77, 80, 84, 93, 352, 476, 494, 501–3, 504–5, 515; constitutional law 499; evidence 529; fictions 743; Greek influence 549, 558–9; institutions before *quaestiones perpetuae* 499–505; interdiction as penalty 495–6, 512–13; laying of charge 506, 508; and lower classes 500n, 501, 523; multiple charges 514; multiple defendants 504, 505; Non Liquet verdicts 529–30; *patria potestas* 499–500; Pompey and Crassus' reforms 224, 225–6, 227; private criminal actions 503–4, 524–5, 528, 579; in provinces 527; *quaestiones perpetuae see separate entry*; secret ballot 52, 61, 93, 503n; special courts, see *quaestio extra ordinem*; sovereignty 41, 775; tribunes' right to initiate trial 41, 329, 330n; *IIIviri capitales* 500–1, 528; see also *ambitus*; *caput*; *iniuria*; juries; jurisdiction, Roman external; *maiestas*; *peculatus*; *provocatio*; punishments; *quaestio extra ordinem*; *quaestiones perpetuae*; *repetundae*; *sicarii*; sumptuary laws; *veneficii*; *vis*
lead resources 135, 625
leather industry 615, 625, 658
Lebadea *6 Aa*; oracle of Trophonius 189
Lebanon 288
legacies 539, 555–6
legates, provincial 581, 582, 590
legationes, *liberae* 588, 643
legis actiones 508, 533, 545–6; *sacramento* 506, 528–9, 545
legislation: assemblies' role 41, 43, 474, 502; coinage marks 45, 46, 98, 102; *contiones*' role 44; magistrates' role 43, 100; religious obstruction, *see under* religion; tribunes' right to introduce 41, 201, 329–30; *see also* law (*leges*)
leisure, *urbanum otium* 652, 681
Lemnos *5 Ab*, *9 Ab*, 236
Lenaeus *see under* Pompeius
Lentulus *see under* Cornelius
Leonnippus (garrison commander of Sinope) 245
Leontini *2Bd*, 25
Leontocephalae *5 Bb*, 146
Leontopolis *11 Aa*, 297, 299–300
Lepidus *see under* Aemilius
Lesbos *5 Ab*, *14 Cb*, 146–7, 159, 433
letting: consensual 542, 557, 620; of land 642
liability, legal 635
libel 544
Liberalia 469
libertas 534–5; shrine erected by Clodius on site of Cicero's house 748, 749
Libo *see under* Scribonius
libraries 692–4, 697; Alexandria 434, 693; Athens 162; Mithridates' 693, 694, 699n; private Roman 694, 697, 723; public at Rome 454, 692–3, 701
Liburnia *1 Dc*, *2 Bb-Cb*, 184
licence fees 622
Licinia (C. Gracchus' wife) 555
Licinianus 208
Licinii, political tradition 47
Licinius, Sex. (*trib.* 138) 60
Licinius *or* Lucilius, Sex. (*trib.* 87) 179
Licinius Crassus, C. (*trib.* 145) 59, 746–7
Licinius Crassus, L. (*cos.* 95) 787; and foundation of Narbo Martius 24, 86; and Caepio's proposal on juries 93; expulsion of aliens from Rome 102, 651–2; and *causa Curiana* 534n, 554; death 113; intellectual interests 690, 691, 694, 698
Licinius Crassus, P. (*cos.* 97) 177, 178, 786, 787
Licinius Crassus, P. (*d.* 53): in Gallic Wars 386, 388, 397, 398, 400–1; Parthian campaign 399, 400, 402–3; and Cicero 479
Licinius Crassus Dives, M. (*cos.* 70, 55, *triumvir*): in Spain 180; in civil war 187, 193, 195, 198, 223; and revolt of Spartacus 222–3, 790; first consulship 223–8, 239, 791; restores tribunician powers 224–5, 227; reconciliation with Pompey 228; censor 792; proposes annexation of Egypt 271, 319, 345–6, 792; and Rullan bill 349; and Catilinarian conspiracy 354; opposes ratification of Pompey's settlement of east 364; and re-negotiation of Asian tax contract 365, 372; alliance with Caesar and Pompey 366, 367, 368, 369, 374, 793; and Clodius 380, 392, 393; and restoration of Ptolemy Auletes 392, 398, 399–400; defends Caelius and Sestius 529; deal with Caesar and Pompey at Luca 272, 394, 794; second consulship with Pompey (55) 394, 396, 397, 398–9, 517, 794; Ahenobarbus' attacks on 401; Syrian command 91, 264, 398–9, 400, 402–3, 574, 794, 795
political style 345; public benefaction 225; rivalry with Pompey 223, 225, 228, 272, 364, 392, 393, 394; wealth and financial activities 59, 198, 225, 398, 400, 617, 626, 640, 641, 643
Licinius Crassus Mucianus, P. (*cos.* 131) 34, 59, 65, 68, 73, 617, 780
Licinius Lucullus, L. (*praetor* 103) 26
Licinius Lucullus, L. (*cos.* 74) 790; in First Mithridatic War 147, 151, 153, 158, 160, 181–2, 317–18; and settlement after war 162; and Sulla's march on Rome 170; consulship 212, 213, 233, 234, 236, 790; in

Third Mithridatic War 235, 236, 239–44, 791–2; re-organization of Asia 239, 244–8, 791; invades Armenia 239–44, 266, 328, 792; contacts with Parthia 240, 241–2, 243, 252, 263; negotiations with Antiochus of Commagene 259; replaced in command 244, 248, 250, 251, 331, 332–3, 339, 341, 792; triumph 341–2, 351, 358; opposes ratification of Pompey's settlement of east 361, 364; public humiliation before Caesar 372; opposition to Pompey 375, 381; and restoration of Ptolemy Auletes 392

and Clodius 243, 341; intellectual interests 4, 690n, 693, 694, 697, 699, 724; wealth and luxury 331, 333, 617, 675

Licinius Lucullus, M. (*later* M. Terentius Varro Lucullus, *q.v.*) 562

Licinius Macer, C. (*trib.* 73, *praetor* 68) 214, 331, 340, 345, 790; history of Rome 330, 346–7, 711

Licinius Macer Calvus, C. (82–47) 363, 695, 717

Licinius Murena, L., (*propraetor* 84) 136, 156, 163, 212, 229, 232, 789

Licinius Murena, L. (*cos.* 62) 347, 353, 355–6, 359, 516n, 693–4, 793

Licinius Nerva, P. (*praetor* 105) 26

Licinius Stolo, C. 55, 68

lictors 200, 205, 459, 581

lien (security) 541, 561, 562

Ligurians *1 Cc*, *2 Ab*; resettlement (180) 651; resubjection of Monaco-Antibes to Massilia (155/4) 23; Roman subjection (125/4) 24, 781, 782; campaigns (117) 783; settlement after Social War 126; Metellus Pius and 187; and Lepidus' rising 209; social structures 611

Lilybaeum *2 Bd*, *13 Bd*, *14 Bb*, 26, 196, 590, 593

literacy 689

literature: dedications 696; Greek language 699, 764; patronage of 773; recitation 689, 695; *see also individual authors and genres and* Latin language; translation

litis aestimatio (assessment of damages) 507, 513, 529, 543–4

Livius, T. (Livy) 1–2

Livius Andronicus, L. 699

Livius Drusus, C. (*cos.* 147) 574

Livius Drusus, M. (*cos.* 112) 32, 83, 783, 784

Livius Drusus, M. (*trib.* 91) 52, 102, 118, 167, 787; tribunate 111–13, 493n, 527, 787; murder 112, 113–14, 165, 787

Livius Salinator, M. (*cos.* 219) 508n

loans, maritime 17, 20

local government 267, 450–2, 455, 775–6; see also *municipia*

locatio conductio (consensual letting) 542, 557, 620n

lodges, see *collegia*

logic 719

Lollius Palicanus, M. (*trib.* 71) 215, 228, 336, 337

lower classes: justice 500n, 501, 523, 558; land holdings 54, 57; rise through education 691; political consciousness 14–15, 368, 376, 646, 647, 682; under Principate 775; rights and protections 40, 41; *see also* freedmen; peasants' revolt; plebeians; plebs, urban; slaves; smallholders

Luca (Lucca) *3(i) Aa*, *13 Ab*, *14 Ba*; conference (56) 394, 397, 398–9, 794

Lucan 7, 8, 10, 76

Lucania *2 Bc-Cc*, *3(ii) Db-Eb*; land redistribution (132) 73; in Social War 115, 118, 120, 123, 125, 126; in civil war 193, 204; agriculture 204, 610, 611; *see also* Val di Diano

Lucceius, L. 4, 711–12

Luceria *2 Bc*, *3(ii) Ca*, *13 Bc*, 73, 424

Lucilius, C. (satirist) 467, 508, 561, 698

Lucilius *or* Licinius, Sex. (*trib.* 87) 179

Lucretius Afella, Q. 166, 192, 194, 195, 200

Lucretius Carus, T. (poet) 704, 710, 718–19, 732, 724

Lucullus *see under* Licinius; Terentius

Lugdunum (Lyons) 446n

Lugdunum Convenarum 221

Lupercalia 464, 758

Luperci 672

Luscius, L. (Sullan assassin) 348n

Lusitania *1 Ac*, *8 Ab*, 58, 780, 785, 786, 787; campaigns of 150s 21, 577; Sertorius in 217, 218

lustra 327–9, 344, 345–6, 367, 402, 413

Lutatius Catulus, Q. (*cos.* 102) 178, 195, 328, 785; intellectal interests 710, 713, 724

Lutatius Catulus, Q. (*cos.* 78): in Sullan period 197, 202; consulate 206–7, 208, 209, 211, 524, 790; puts down Lepidus' rising 209, 790; and temple of Jupiter Capitolinus 327, 358; leadership of Senate 328; opposes commands for Pompey 334, 339; and trial of C. Cornelius 343; opposes Caesar 344; and Catiline's trial 345; censorship 319, 345–6, 792; defeated by Caesar in pontifical election 353; and Catilinarian conspiracy 355; Caesar accuses of embezzlement 358; and Clodius' trial for sacrilege 361, 363; and *quaestio de vi* 524

Lutevani Foroneronienses 445n

luxury, denunciations of 6, 7–8, 59, 73, 419, 769

luxury goods 56, 59, 638, 660–1, 663, 666, 681–2

Lycaonia *5 Cb*, *9 Cc*; Roman control 35, 96,

Lycaonia (*cont.*)
97, 135; in Mithridatic Wars 145, 232–3, 236, 265, 329
Lycia *1 Ed*, *9 Bc* 34, 767; in Mithridatic Wars 144, 146, 147, 149, 162
Lysias (viceroy of Judaea) 280–1
Lysimachus (companion of Alexander) 130

Ma, cult of 137, 170, 189
Macalister, R. A. S. 288
Maccabees, Books of 277, 280–1, 283–4, 287, 306
Macedonia *1 Dc*, *9 Ab*, *14 Bb*; Third Macedonian War 36, 693; four independent republics 31, 565, 567; Andriscus' revolt 31, 567, 571; Roman annexation 17, 31, 567, 571; wars (from 119) 32, 36, 37, 97, 576, 783, 784, 785; law of 101–100 on administration 97, 99; Mithridates VI and 149, 153; Ap. Claudius' campaign 210, 211; Piso's governorship 380, 574, 583; praetorian province (56) 395; Antony's province 471; Brutus' power in 481, 797 coinage 33, 631; commanders' misconduct 508n, 583; Greece governed from 571; mines 624n, 632; *vectigal* 569
macella (food bazaars) 660, 664, 666
Macer *see under* Licinius
Machaerus *10 Bc*, 296
Machares, son and viceroy of Mithridates VI 238, 253
machinery: agricultural 56, 612; siege 150
Mactar *2 Ae*, 28
Maelius, Sp. 72, 357
magic 756, 759–61
magistrates 43, 496–8; Augustus' regulation 498; auspices 744; Caesar increases numbers 459; *coercitio* 493; *consilia* 582; deposition 67; family succession 45, 46–7, 211; *imperium* 85, 497–8, 572; *ius publicum* controls 497, 498, 520, 528; land holdings 621; Latin, acquire Roman citizenship 105, 126; and legislation 43, 100; limits on re-election 68, 201; new men 91; plebeians 46; presiding 45, 46, 82, 100; and private law 545; property qualification 41, 46; prorogation 10, 14, 43, 61, 572, 751, 771; prosecution of incompetent 61, 94, 95–6; and provincial administration 16, 17, 43, 201–2; Sulla's legislation on 201–2, 496–7, 498; and warfare 43; see also *cursus honorum*; elections; provinces; *and individual magistracies*
Magius, M. (officer in Pompey's army) 428, 429
Magna Mater, cult of 764–5
Magnesia, Thessaly *9 Ab*, 151, 153
Magnesia-on-the-Maeander *5 Ab*, 144, 147, 162, 441n
Mago (Carthaginian agriculturalist) 54, 699n, 700n
maiestas, *quaestio maiestatis* 95–6, 518–20; legislation (Saturninus') 102, 110, 371, 518, (Varius') 114–15, 120, 518–19, (Sulla's) 202, 234, 492, 579, 594, 789, (Caesar's) 513n, 797; and *perduellio* 518, 519–20; and provincial governors 520, 579; *repetundae* overlaps with 514, 518, 520
Malalas, chronicle of 465
Mallius Maximus, Cn. (*cos.* 105) 24, 37, 93, 95, 785
Mallus *9 Cc*, 266
Mamilius Limetanus, C. (*trib.* 110); *quaestio Mamilia* 89, 519
Mammius, C. (*trib.* 111) 746
Mammula *see under* Cornelius
mancipatio (conveyance) 540, 550
mandate 561; consensual 542
Mandubii *12 Bb*, 412
Manilius, C. (*trib.* 66) 250, 337, 338, 342–3, 345, 792; *see also* law (*leges* (Manilia))
Manilius, M'. (*cos.* 149) 554, 555
Manlius, C. (rebel leader) 354, 360, 495
Manlius, Cn. (*praetor* 72) 222
Manlius, L. (governor of Transalpine Gaul, 78) 217
Manlius Acidinus, L. (commander in Spain, 210) 572n
Manlius Capitolinus, M. 72
Manlius Mancinus, T. (*trib.* 107) 573–4
Manlius Torquatus, L. (*cos.* 65) 340, 342, 345, 792
Manlius Vulso, Cn. (*cos.* 189) 7
Marcellinus *see under* Cornelius
Marcellus *see under* Claudius
Marcius Censorinus, C. 178, 193, 194, 195
Marcius Figulus, C. (*cos.* 64) 345, 793
Marcius Philippus, L. (*cos.* 91) 95, 112, 113, 180, 516n, 787, 788
Marcius Philippus, L. (*cos.* 56) 471, 480, 794
Marcius Rex, Q. (*cos. suff.* 68) 792; command against pirates 244, 248–9, 250, 259, 331, 339; triumph delayed 342, 354
Marcus Aurelius, Emperor 709
Marissa *10 Ab*, 291, 292, 293
Marius, C. (*cos.* 107, 104–100, 86), 784–6; origins 90–1; military career 62, 91; tribune of plebs 86, 91, 783; first consulship (107) 44, 90, 91, 784; command against Jugurtha 30, 35, 36, 89, 91–2, 95, 166, 573–4, 784, 785; second consulship (104) 95, 785; Cimbric War 24, 39, 95, 96, 97, 109, 166, 328, 785; consular election for (100) 97; and Saturninus and Glaucia 98, 99, 100, 101, 103, 109–10; travels in Asia 142; in Social War 120, 121, 124, 787; rivalry with Sulla over Mithridatic command 167, 168, 169,

170, 574, 788; defends Rome against Sulla 171; exiled 171; takes Rome with Cinna 175–7, 178–9, 788; death 179
accumulation of power 166, 201; army reforms 37–8, 39; Bardyaei (bodyguard) 178, 179; bribery allegations 91, 97, 515, 517; cult of 752; and Italian allies 99, 109, 110, 175, 219; patron of Sthenius of Thermae 592; political support 89, 90–2, 168, 219; probity 91; reputation after death 199, 200, 328, 344, 436, 448, 713; sources on 4, 10; veteran settlements 30, 92, 95, 98, 99, 100, 109–10, 344, 785
Marius, C. (*cos.* 82) 191, 192, 194, 195, 198, 789
Marius Egnatius the Samnite 120, 121, 125
Marius Gratidianus, M. (*praetor* 86) 173, 174, 176, 642; edict on coinage 180–1, 525, 633, 677–8, 752, 788; murder 195, 348, 678
market gardening 664
markets, regulation of 456–7
marriage law 535, 536, 537–8
Marrucini *3(i) Ec*, 115, 124
Mars, cult of 672
Marsi *3(i) Dc*, *3(ii) Ba* 114, 115, 121–2, 124, 187
Martino, F. de 14
Marullus (Roman tribune) 464
Masada *10 Bc*, 296
Massilia (Marseilles) *1 Bc*, *12 Bc*, *14 Aa*; Roman defence against Gauls 23–4, 781; Sullan proscribed flee to 198; Caesar's siege of 430, 431, 481, 796; Verres in 578; coinage 632; Greek culture 23, 444; trade 20
Massiva, son of Gulussa 29, 784
Mastarnabal, son of Massinissa of Numidia 29
Mater, Magna 137, 764–5
Mater, Stata 675
Matius, C. 458, 465, 466, 472, 475, 477
Matrinius, T., of Spoletium 110
Mattathias (Jewish leader) 280
Mauretania *1 Ad*, *14 Ab*, 30, 95, 436
Mazaca *5 Db*, *9 Cc*, 135, 268
Medamud 318
Medeba *10 Bb*, 291, 292
Media *9 Ec-Fc*, 143, 262; *see also* Atropatene
medicine 693, 694, 699, 705
Medinet Habu 318
Megalopolis (Sivas), Armenia *9 Cb*, 244, 267
Megara *6 Bb*, 153, 441, 442
Megillath Taanith 280
Meier, Christian 13–14
Melitaea *9 Ab*, 157
Memmius, C. (*trib.* 111) 85, 86, 88–9, 101, 519
Memmius, C. (*praetor* 58) 338, 341, 378–9, 401, 582–3
Memmius, C. (Pompey's brother-in-law) 196, 218, 228
Memnon, history of Heraclea Pontica 130, 139, 143, 155, 181, 242, 244
Memphis *11 Aa*, 310, 313, 317, 319, 326, 781
Memphites (Ptolemy Memphites) 310, 313
Mēn Pharnacou, cult of 137
Menander (comic poet) 424, 455
mercenary soldiers 297, 324, 442
Mercuriales 672
Mercury, cult of 20, 672
Merula *see under* Cornelius
Mesopotamia *9 Dc-Ed*, 238, 240, 253, 255, 259, 264, 402–3
Messalla *see under* Valerius
Messianism, Jewish 308
metal resources 21, 135, 624, 625–6, 639; *see also individual metals*
metal working 624–5
Metella (Sulla's wife) 166–7, 179, 203, 205
Metellinum *8 Bb*, 217
Metellus *see under* Caecilius
Metrophanes (Pontic general) 151
Metropolis 159
Meyer, Eduard 12, 438
Michmash 281
Micipsa, king of Numidia 27, 28, 76, 77
middle ages, education 705
Midrashim (Jewish exegetical texts) 280
migration: businessmen 628, 633, 638; freedmen 654–5, 656; to Fregellae 105, 115, 607; of Helvetii 371–2, 383, 384; overseas 607–8, 626, 627; from Rome 654–5, 656; to Rome 44, 650–3; to Venusia 115; *see also* colonies; settlers
milestones 31, 73–4
Miletus *9 Bc*, 248, 766
militarism, Roman 10, 24, 62, 489, 490
Milo *see under* Annius
Milonius, C. 174, 176
Minatius Magius of Aeclanum 124
minors, protection of 548, 561
Minturnae *2 Bc*, *3(ii) Ab*, *13 Bc*, 55, 450n; *collegia* 660, 664n, 671–2, 684
Minucius Basilus, L. 441
Minucius Felix (naval commander) 145
Minucius Rufus, M. (*trib.* 121) 84
Minucius Rufus, M. (*cos.* 110) 32, 784, 785
Minucius Thermus, Q. (*trib.* 62) 359
Minucius Thermus, subdues Mytilene 163
miqvaot (Jewish ritual bathing pools) 288
Mishnah 280, 304
Misthion 232
Mithras, cult of 765
Mithridates, king of Armenia 131
Mithridates I, king of Parthia 262, 285
Mithridates II Megas, king of Parthia 143, 149, 238, 262
Mithridates III, king of Parthia 396
Mithridates I Ktistes, king of Pontus 130–1

Mithridates II, king of Pontus 131
Mithridates III, king of Pontus 131
Mithridates IV Philopator Philadelphus, king of Pontus 132, 767
Mithridates V Euergetes, king of Pontus 132, 782; *see also under* Pontus
Mithridates VI Eupator, king of Pontus 129–64; birth 132; as fugitive in interior 129, 133; rule, *see under* Pontus; deposition and death 254–5, 261–2, 328, 349, 793
atrocities 20, 35, 129, 130, 144–5, 148–9; coinage 140, 149; emulates Alexander 140, 145–6; and Greeks of Pontus 137; library 693, 694, 699n; magnanimity 145–6, 147; portraits 140; sources on 130; *syntrophoi* 137; *see also* Wars, Mithridatic *and under* Pontus
Mithridates of Cius 130
Mithridates of Pergamum 434
Moab 291, 292, 294
mobility, social 657–8, 663, 691
Modiin *10 Ab*, 298
Mommsen, Th. 11–12, 13, 49, 438; on *ius publicum* 493, 501, 502, 503, 508
money-changers 632, 633, 660
money-lenders 17, 20, 147, 270, 272, 634–5, 642
money system 106, 180–1, 630–5; *see also* coinage
Montlaurès 24
monuments to dead 27, 73–4, 203, 457; *see also* epitaphs; tombs
morality 7–8, 40, 68, 73, 725, 727, 729; *see also* greed; luxury
mortgages 541
mos maiorum institutaque (custom) 491, 492, 497, 499, 717, 773; inadequacy 513–14, 528, 774
Mother, Great 137, 764–5
Mucia Tertia (Pompey's wife) 206, 361, 364
Mucius Orestinus, Q. (*trib.* 64) 346n
Mucius Scaevola, P. (*cos.* 133) 65, 69, 72–3, 80, 494, 554, 780
Mucius Scaevola, Q. ('augur', *cos.*117) 171, 690, 698, 783
Mucius Scaevola, Q. (*pontifex maximus*, *cos.*95) 787; expels aliens from Rome 102, 110, 526, 651–2; governor of Asia 754, (edict) 554, 590; Fimbria's attempt to assassinate 179; death 192; jurist 534n, 551, 554, 555–6; on state religion 757
Mulvian Bridge *7 Ab*; battle of 209
mummifiers, Egyptian 324, 325
Mummius (Crassus' legate) 222
Mummius (*trib.* 133) 69
Mummius, Sp. 311, 757n
Mummius Achaicus, L. (*cos.* 146) 32, 107
Munatius Plancus, L. 470–1, 798
Munatius Plancus, T. (*trib.* 52) 407, 409, 413–14, 482–3, 484–5
Munatius Rufus 713n
Munda *8 Bc*, *14 Ab*; battle of 437, 443, 461, 738
municipia 109, 113, 127–8, 204, 547
Münzer, F. 12, 13, 50–1, 52
murder 527–8; of kin 526; political 171, 178, 185, 190, 192, 197, (*see also* proscription); private actions for, in Italy 528; see also *sicarii*; *vis*
Murena *see under* Licinius
music: Asiatic 7–8; 'rough' (*occentatio*) 544
Musicus (imperial slave) 656n
Muthul, battle of river 39
Mutina (Modena) *2 Ab*, *13 Ab*, *14 Ba*, 209; siege of 479, 482, 483, 798
Myra *9 Bc*, 316
Myrlea *5 Ba*, 130
Mysia *1 Ec*, *5 Ab-Bb*, 34, 146
myth, Roman foundation 650
Mytilene *5 Ab*, 144, 145, 146–7, 163, 442, 638

Nabataeans *9 De*; assistance to Jonathan 288; Jewish wars against 292, 296; Pompey's campaign 254, 259, 260, 261, 262; Scaurus' campaign 262; Pompey's settlement 269; continuing unrest 271; Gabinius' campaigns 273, 395, 401, 794; tombs at Petra 298
Nabis, king of Sparta 66
Naevius, Cn. (poet) 689
Naevius, Sex. (businessman) 25
Namier, L. 11, 52
Narbo Martius (Narbonne) *1 Bc*, *12 Bc*, *14 Aa*, 217, 409, 437, 445; commerce 6, 86, 638, 666; foundation 6, 24, 86, 99, 783
navigation, freedom of 629, 630, 640
Neapolis (Naples) *3(ii) Bc*, *13 Bc*, 123, 193, 630, 694
Nechthyris (Egyptian officer) 317
negotiorum gestio (agency) 543
neighbours, rights of 540–1
Nemausus (Nîmes) 444
Neoptolemus (Pontic general) 145
Nero *see under* Claudius
Nerva *see under* Licinius
Nervii *12 Ba*, 388, 794
new men 91, 348–9, 517, 554
nexum (Latin right) 64
Nicaea *9 Bb*, 236
Nicolaus of Damascus 278
Nicomedes I, king of Bithynia 131, 132
Nicomedes II, king of Bithynia 34
Nicomedes III, king of Bithynia 35, 140, 141, 142, 787
Nicomedes IV, king of Bithynia *see under* Bithynia

Nicomedia *1 Ec*, *5 Ba*, *9 Bb*, 160, 236
Nicopolis, Armenia Minor *9 Db*, 252, 267
Nigidius Figulus, P. (*praetor* 58) 704, 708, 709, 710, 724, 759
Ninnius *or* Nunnius, A. (*d.* 101) 97
Ninnius Quadratus, L. (*trib.* 58) 378, 380
Nisibis *9 Dc*, 242, 253, 792
Nola *3(ii) Bc*, *13 Bc*; in Social War 115, 120, 124; siege continues after war 169, 174, 789; besiegers support Cinna's march on Rome 175, 179, 185; in Sullan civil war 195; Sullan colony 204; metal working 624
nominis delatio (laying of accusation) 508
νόμος/φύσις controversy 703–4, 709
Nonius Sufenas, Sex. 173
Norba *2 Bc*, *7 Bc*, 195
Norbanus, C. (*cos.* 83): tribunate, *seditio Norbana* 93; *maiestas* prosecution 96, 102, 518, 519n, 520n; in civil war 187, 189, 190, 193, 194; proscription 198; suicide 194; and M. Antonius 581n
Noreia 783
Norica 37
Noricum *2 Ba*, *14 Ba*, 637
novatio (transfer of debts) 634
Noviodunum (Nevers) *12 Bb*, 411
Novum Comum (Como) *13 Aa*, *14 Ba*, 415, 443
Nuceria *3(ii) Bc*, 115, 120, 638
Numa: Books of 707; Treasures of 148
Numantia *1 Ac*, *8 Ba*; Scipio's campaign 21, 22, 29, 36, 37, 39, 61–2, 73, 91, 576, 780
numerology 707, 718, 727
Numidia *1 Bd*, *2 Ae*, *13 Ae*, *14 Ab*; acquires territory after defeat of Carthage 27, 43; war against Rome *see* War, Jugurthine; and Roman Civil War 418, 431, 435, 436
  coinage 447; Roman diplomacy 17, 262, 783; Roman and Italian settlers 28; support to Roman army, (forces) 29, 38, 62, 119, 121, (supplies) 28, 76, 77; *see also* Jugurtha; War, Jugurthine
Numitorius Pullus, Q. 76, 105
Nunnius *or* Ninnius, A. (*d.* 101) 97
Nymphaion *9 Ca*, 254

oaths 100, 113, 173, 558
obligation: Antony's use 471; Caesar and 415–16, 448; Cicero and civic 467, 477; freedman's to patron 663; law of 541–4, 557–8; monetary dealings and social 634; *peculium* and 557–8; ritual and cult 729–30
obstruction of legislation (*obnuntatio*) *see under* religion
occentatio ('rough music') 544
occupatio 611, 616, 618, 621–2
Octavia (Caesar's great-niece) 408
Octavius, C. (C. Iulius Caesar, Augustus): Caesar's heir 466, 471, 798, (pays out legacies) 472, 473; and Antony 471–2, 476; *ludi Victoriae Caesaris* (44) 475; hostilities against Antony 84, 477–86, 487; marches on Rome 485; *consul suffectus* (43) xiii, 485–6, 798; *triumvir* 486, 798; war against Sex. Pompeius 630; occupies Alexandria 321
  Principate: citizenship grants in Spain 444; colonies in Italy 601; and constitutional change 673, 774; cult of 465; on depopulation of Italy 606; expels slaves and foreigners from Rome 655; library 693n; magistracies regulated under 498; Meyer on motives 438; and popular organizations 676, 680; provincial administration 98, 575; *Res Gestae* 736; and Senate 452, 459; and tribes 680; and Varro 701
  and Cicero 477, 478, 479, 487–8; and Caesarion 434; bounties to troops 478, 480, 483, 484, 485, 486, 488; funded by Caesar's friends 472, 475, 477; letters to Rhosos 547; personal duty to avenge Caesar 477, 489; and Senate 487; veterans' support 475, 476
Octavius, Cn. (*cos.* 87) 173, 174, 175, 176, 178, 788
Octavius, Cn. (*cos.* 76) 211, 790
Octavius, L. (*cos.* 75) 211, 213, 790
Octavius, M. (*trib.*133) 4, 66–7, 69, 77, 96
Octavius, M. Cn. f., repeals Gracchan corn law 83
Odessus *4 Ab*, 131
Oenomaus (gladiator, rebel) 221
Ofella *see* Lucretius Afella
officinae (workshops) 661, 666, 669
Ofilius, A. (jurist) 455, 554, 555, 556
Olbia *4 Aa*, 139
oligarchy 32, 33, 41
olive production 136, 610, 611, 614, 639, 658; olive-mill 56, 612
Olympia *1 Dd*, 154; inscription 33
Olympus, Lycia *9 Bc*, 232
omens: and assembly business 99–100, 102, 185, 729, 739–40; and refounding of Carthage 83; Sulla's good 170, 189; *see also* thunder
Onias, high priest of Judaea 283; line of 282, 295, 296, 297, 299–300
Opimius, L. (*cos.* 121) 782; destruction of Fregellae 76; elected consul 83; defeats Gracchus 84; execution of Gracchus' followers 84–5, 494, 495; and Jugurthine War 89; political standing 9, 88
Opimius, Q. (*cos.* 154) 23
Opimius, Q. (*trib.* 75) 211
Oppianicus, Statius Albius 198; prosecution

Oppianicus (*cont.*)
  by Cluentius 213–14, 225, 507n, 512, 527, 530n, 790, (Cicero's speech) 214, 234, 523, 529
Oppius, C. (Caesar's friend) 458, 460, 461, 472, 478
Oppius, Q. (*prob. praetor* 89) 145, 146
optimates and *populares* 48, 49–50, 52–3, 745–9; modern scholarship on 11, 12–13, 14; *see also individual issues and politicians*
oracles: Delphic 759; fraud 741; of Trophonius, at Lebadea 189; *see also* Sibylline Books
oral culture 689
Orange *see* Arausio
oratory: aristocrats' call on forensic 529; Atticist/Asianic controversy 717; Caesar 344, 753; Cicero's ideal of 205–6, 715; development of Latin 534, 690, 691–2, 699, 787; Epicurean 722; Greek influence 534, 717; Italian allies' 109; Philodemus on 723; as popular entertainment 689, 717; specialization 534, 753; Stoic 726; treatises on 1, (see also *Ad Herennium*)
Orbilius Pupillus, L. 691
Orbius (Roman prefect in Delos) 151
Orchomenus *6 Ba*, 32; battle of 39, 154–5, 157–8, 236, 788
Orders, Struggle of the 41, 46–7, 745
Origen 658–9
Orobazus (Parthian envoy) 262
Orodes II, king of Parthia 396, 402, 403, 420
Oroises, chief of Albanians 256, 257
Orondeis people 232
Orophernes (Cappadocian pretender) 16
Oropus *6 Cb*, 33, 582
Orosius, Paulus 155, 197–8, 264
Osca, Spain *8 Ca*, 21, 217, 219, 220
Osrhoene *9 Dc*, 264, 266, 402
Ostia *2 Bc*, *3(i) Cc*, *7 Ab*, *13 Bc*, 176, 456, 629–30, 661
Otryae 235
ownership, concept of 540

Pacorus, prince of Parthia 417, 420
pactiones (tax collection system) 270
paedagogi 691
Paeligni *3(i) Dc*, 76, 105, 115, 118, 120, 452
Paestum *13 Bc*, 655
pagi: Italian cantons 451; Roman urban 673–6, 684
painting, Greek 697
Paionians *9 Ab*, 254
Palicanus *see under* Lollius
Pallantia *8 Ba*, 219
Palma *8 Db*, 22
Pamphylia *5 Bc-Cc*, *9 Bc-Cc*, 35, 97, 144, 146, 147, 158–9, 232
Panaetius (philosopher) 695, 698, 720, 722
Panathenaia 29
Pansa *see under* Vibius
Panticapaeum *4 Ba*, 139
Paos (Egyptian military leader) 313
Paphlagonia *4 Bb*, *5 Ca*, *9 Cb*, 130, 131, 132, 133, 141, 142, 784; in Mithridatic Wars 144, 158, 161, 229, 234
Papinian (Aemilius Papinianus) (jurist) 533
Papirius Carbo, C. (*cos.* 120) 65, 68, 74–5, 85, 86, 782
Papirius Carbo, C. (*trib.*89) 126
Papirius Carbo, Cn. (*cos.* 113) 783
Papirius Carbo, Cn. (*cos.* 85, 84, 82) 37, 176, 181, 186; consulships 180, 182, 184, 201, 788, 789; war against Sulla 182, 184, 185, 190–1, 191–2, 193, 194, 196; proscription 198; death 196, 789
Papirius Carbo, Cn. (quaestor in Sicily) 580–1
Papirius Carbo Arvina, C. (*d.* 82) 192
Papirius Cursor, L. (*dictator* 309) 9, 680
Papirius Paetus (gourmet) 726
Papius, C. (*trib.* 65) 344–5; *see also* law (*leges* (Papia))
Papius Mutilus, C. (Samnite leader) 118–19, 120, 121, 125
Pappa *9 Cc*, 232
papyri: on Egyptian agriculture 313, 314, 322, 323; on Idumaeans in Egypt 293; of Philodemus, from Herculaneum 723; on Ptolemy Euergetes II's reign 311; roll, difficulty of checking references 702; on voyage to Horn of Africa, *c.*200–150 17, 20
Parapotamii *6 Aa*, 156
Parilia 738
Parisii *12 Ab-Bb*, 411
parricide 457, 500
Parthenius of Nicaea 697, 710
Parthia *9 Fd*, *14 Cb*, 262–5; build-up of power under Mithridates I and Phraates II 36, 262, 285, 290; under Mithridates II the Great 143, 238, 262–3; Sulla's contact with Orobazus 262, 786
  under Phraates III 263–5; negotiations with Lucullus 240, 241–2, 243, 252, 263; dealings with Pompey 252, 253, 259, 260, 263–5, 792; expansion into Armenian territory 253, 263, 264; succession to Phraates III, Gabinius' intervention 271, 272, 396–7
  under Orodes II: Crassus defeated at Carrhae 402–3; invasion of Syria (51) 417, 419, 420, 596; Pompey negotiates with 432; invasion of Syria (45) 478, 797; Caesar plans expedition against 437–8, 439, 447, 464, 466; in early Principate 257
  Euphrates boundary issue 263–4; methods of warfare 264, 402, 403

partnership law 542, 635–7; see also *societates*
pastio villatica 611, 616
pasture 55, 65, 87, 610, 611, 613, 615
Patara *5 Bc*, 147, 150
Patavium (Padova) *2 Ba*, *13 Ba*, 451n
Pathyris *11 Bc*, 315, 317, 324
Patrae (Patras) *14 Bb*, 638
patria potestas 499–500, 532, 536–7, 538, 539, 557–8
patronage: and Civil War 425; cultural 773; freedman–patron relationship 663, 668, 669–70, 680; and politics 13, 45–6, 50, 51–2, 517; and provinces 196, 215, 221, 507, 508, 592; urban setting 675
Patronis *6 Aa*, 155
Paullus *see under* Aemilius
Pausanias 150, 315
pearl-dealer 663
peasants' revolt (63) 352, 354, 358, 359–60, 771
peculatus, quaestio de peculatu 341, 515, 529
peculium (fund held by person *in potestate*) 537, 543, 557–8, 563; *p. castrense* 557
Pedius, Q. (*cos. suff.* 43) 437, 797, 798
Peducaeus, Sex. (*trib.* 113) 747
Pegae (Antipatris), Judaea *10 Ab*, 290
Pella, Macedonia *2 Dc*, *14 Bb*, 31
Pella, Palestine *10 Bb*, 293, 296
Pelopidas (Pontic envoy) 139, 143, 144
Pelusium *9 Cd*, *11 Ba*, *14 Cb*, 321
Pennus *see under* Iunius
Peraea, Judaean 273, 294
Peraea, Rhodian *5 Bc*, 162
perduellio (treason) 352, 502, 518, 519–20
peregrini, see foreigners
perfumery 654, 660
Pergamum *1 Ed*, *5 Ab*, *9 Bb*, *14 Cb*; under Attalids 34, 131; Attalus III's bequest to Rome 33–4, 68, 135, 233, 780; Scipio Nasica's embassy 73; Aristonicus' revolt 35, 37, 132, 780, 781; Roman annexation 135; in First Mithridatic War 146, 148, 149, 159; Caesar's benefactions 441n, 442; Diodorus Pasparos of 247; grammarians 704; *see also* Asia
Peripatetic philosophers 693–4, 713, 725
permutatio (financial draft) 634
Perperna, M. (*cos.* 130) 26, 34, 781
Perperna, M. (*cos.* 92) 180, 181, 787, 788
Perperna, P. (legate in Social War) 120
Perperna Vento, M. (*praetor* 82) 196, 209, 217, 218, 219–20, 790, 791
Perseus, king of Macedon, library 693
Persia: religion 760, 761, 765; *see also* Iran
persons, law of 534–40, 557
pesher (biblical interpretations) 279
Pessinus *9 Cb*, 379, 764–5
Peteharsemtheus son of Panebkhounis 324
Petelia *2 Cd*, 223
Petesis (mummifier of Saqqara, Egypt) 325
Petra *9 Ce*, 298
Petreius, M. (*propraetor* 63) 360, 430, 431
Phaedrus (Epicurean) 721n
Phanagorea *9 Ca*, 136, 254
Pharasmenes, prince of Pontus *see* Pharnaces II
Pharisees 275, 279, 300–1, 304–5, 308; and Hasmonean rulers 305–6, 307; Josephus' commitment 278; Qumran texts' possible reference to 302–3
Pharnaces I, king of Pontus 131–2, 136
Pharnaces II, king of Cimmerian Bosporus 136; coup against Mithridates 254; Pompey's settlement 262, 265, 269; defeated by Caesar 434, 436, 797
Pharnacia *4 Cb*, *5 Da*, 135, 136
Pharsalus *14 Bb*; battle of 321, 433, 435, 442, 796
Phaselis *9 Bc*, 232
Phasis *4 Cb*, 254, 257
Phazimonitis *5 Da*, 136
Philadelphia, Palestine *9 Cd*, 261
Philae, Egypt *11 Bc*, 316, 318
Philio (head of Athenian Academy) 150
Philip (claimant to throne of Syria) 259, 262
Philip V, king of Macedon 655
Philippi *14 Bb*, 153; battle of 488
Philippus *see under* Marcius
Philo Judaeus 304
Philo of Larissa 697, 716, 720, 721n, 722, 724
Philoboeotus, battle of 156
Philodemus (Epicurean) 695, 722, 723
Philopoemen (*episcopus* at Ephesus) 148
philosophy 718–28; and conduct 725, 727; eclecticism 721, 727; expulsions from Rome 726; Greek 721, 723–4, 726, 757, 764, 767, (political thought) 49, 53, 78, 86, 98; Greek language used by Romans 699; Latin technical vocabulary 699, 718, 719; natural 724–5; patronage of 773; and religion 767; *see also individual philosophers and schools*
Phocis *6 Aa*, 32, 33, 155
Phoenicia *9 Cd*, 158
photography, aerial 5, 27–8
Phraates I *see under* Parthia
Phraates II *see under* Parthia
Phraates III, king of Parthia 396
Phrygia *1 Ec-d*, *5 Ab-Cb*, *9 Bb-c*; acquisition by Pontus 34, 131, 132; Rome re-annexes 35, 79, 137; Pontic occupation in First Mithridatic War 144, 146; Gauls of *see* Galatia; Phrygia Epicteta 133; Phrygia Maior 34, 131, 132, 133, 137
physics 719
Picenum *2 Bb-c*; and Social War 114, 115, 118,

Picenum (*cont.*)
120, 582; in civil war of 80s 187, 190–1, 203; Spartacus' rebellion and 222; rural distress 347; peasant revolt 354; in Civil War 424, 425; Pompey's patronage 425, 449; Caesar's veteran colonies 450; support for Antony 484
Pictones *12 Ab*, 415
Pietrabbondante *2 Bc*, 76
pignus (pledge) 541, 561
pig husbandry 610
pilgrimage, Jewish 297
Pinna *3(i) Ec*, 115, 124
Piraeus *6 Cb*, 151, 153–4, 788
'pirate law' 5, 17, 32, 35, 97–8, 108, 547n, 560, 574, 576–7, 579, 785
pirates 17, 497, 630, 640; M. Antonius' command (102) 96–7, 785; Servilius Vatia's command 210, 212–13, 232–3, 249, 790; M. Antonius' command (74) 213, 233, 249, 497, 790; Caesar captured by 213; assist Mithridates 213, 233; growth after First Mithridatic War 163; and Spartacus' rebellion 222; in province of Cilicia 232; Metellus' campaign *see under* Crete; Marcius Rex commissioned against 248–9, 331; Pompey's command *see under* Pompeius Magnus, Cn.; Gabinius' fear 320; and corn supply 212, 331, 334–5; Levantine 260
Pisidia *5 Bb-Cb*, 232–3, 236, 297
Piso *see under* Calpurnius; Pupius
Pistoria (Pistoia) *3(i) Aa*, *13 Ab*, 360
Pitane *5 Ab*, 181–2
pitch 60–1, 616
Pitholaus (Judaean rebel) 273
plague (175–174), Rome 650
plagues, African locust 28, 58, 76
Plancus *see under* Munatius
Plato 695, 709–10, 715, 716n, 717, 720, 722, 724; *Cratylus* 704, 709; *Gorgias* 716n; *Phaedrus* 716n; *Timaeus* 708, 724
Platon (*epistrategos* of Thebaid, Egypt) 317
Platonism 709–10; Middle 708, 725n
Plautius *or* Plotius (*trib.* 70) 227
Plautius Silvanus, M. (*trib.* 89) 115, 126
Plautus 564–5, 690, 705, 736; on law 500, 532, 561
plebeians 48; admission to priesthoods 745; admission to Senate and curule magistracies 41, 46–7; Clodius' transition to 365, 372, 394; on juries 115; rights and protections 40, 41; *see also* lower classes; plebs, urban
plebs, urban 644–88; Antony and 472, 474; benefactions 652, 666, 680–8, (*see also under* Iulius Caesar, C.); *collegia* 671–2; colonies 172, 350, 445, 446, 455–6; common meals 685; constitutional role 645; *contiones* 645, 676; cult of Ceres 732, 748; debt 435, 641; enmity towards rural plebs 106, 110; flux in population 649–50; freeborn poor 657–8, 662, 668; freedmen 653–6, 662–5, 771; and Ti. Gracchus 69; identification 644–7, 771; industries 659; insecurity 647, 674; Octavian and 471–2, 486; organizations 671–6; political consciousness 14–15, 646, 647, 682; privileges of life in Rome 614, 657; and Saturninus 99, 100, 103; size 648–50; sources 644, 647; and Sulla 170, 171, 173, 187; upper classes and 675, 679; violence 771–2; xenophobia 106, 168; *see also* corn (distributions)
pledges, legal 541
Pliny the Elder 323, 444, 609, 662, 681–2, 707, 720, 760
Pliny the Younger 268
Plotius *or* Plautius (*trib.* 70) 227
Plotius Gallus 690, 691–2
plough 612
Plutarch 2, 3, 707, 713, 724
Po valley *2 Ab-Bb*, 107, 610, 611
Poediculi 125
poetry: Epicurean view 722, 723; neoteric 710, 717; on religion 735
poisoning, see *veneficii*
Polemon of Athens 722n
police work 43, 456
politeia/*politeuma* (Gk) 491, 492
politeumata, Cappadocian 268
political structure of Italy 600–1, 608
politics: cost of participation 575, 588–9, 641, 773; Greek philosophy and 49, 53, 78, 86, 98; opposition not valued 772; patronage in 50, 51–2; party-sentiment 14, 51; political awareness 1, 14–15, 368, 376, 646, 647, 682; Republic and Principate compared 776; wealth and power 43–4, 49, 59, 80, 89; *see also* connexions, political; constitution; religion (political nature)
Pollentia *8 Db*, 22, 781
Pollio *see under* Asinius
Polybius 1, 6–7, 8, 10–11, 712, 714; life 311, 693–4; on Roman constitution 40, 66, 329, 491, 492, 769–70
pomoerium 101, 205, 366, 649
Pompaedius *see under* Poppaedius
Pompaelo *8 Ca*, 221
Pompeia (wife of Caesar) 361
Pompeii *3(ii) Bc*, *13 Bc*; family shrines 732; freedmen's organizations 672; graffiti 689; metal working 624; *Praedia Iuliae Felicis* 669n; in Social War 115, 124–5; Sulla's treatment of 204; *tabernae* 661
Pompeius, Cn. (elder son of Pompey) 432, 433, 436, 437, 460
Pompeius, Q. (*cos.* 141) 21, 32, 51, 60, 61, 68, 508n

Pompeius, Sex. (governor of Macedonia, 119) 37
Pompeius, Sex. (Pompey's uncle) 725n
Pompeius, Sex. (Pompey's son): goes to Cyrenaica after Pharsalus 433; in Spain 436, 437; revival of strength 471, 473, 797; Cicero praises 482; naval command against Antony 483–4; outlawed by Octavian 486; war of Second Triumvirate against 486, 605, 630
Pompeius Festus, Sex. 532, 674
Pompeius Lenaeus 699n
Pompeius Magnus, Cn. (Pompey, *cos.*70, 55, 52, *triumvir*) 208–28, 791, 794; on father's *consilium* 582; acquitted on charge of embezzlement 181, 515; and death of Cinna 184; in civil war 187, 190–1, 192, 193, 194, 196; Sulla's favour 196, 223; command in Sicily and Africa 196, 789; triumph and cognomen Magnus 197, 789; marries Mucia 206; supports Lepidus for consulship 207; and Sulla's funeral 207; command against Lepidus' rising 209, 572, 790; command against Sertorius 210, 211, 212, 217–18, 219, 220, 221, 572, 576, 790, 791; and Spartacus' rebellion 222, 223; first consulship (70) 223–8, 239; triumph 223, 224; and trial of Verres 215; relations with Crassus 223, 225, 228; restores tribunician power 214, 224–5, 227, 228, 330, 338, 791; reconciliation with Crassus 228; command against pirates 91, 221, 243, 244, 249, 250, 260, 266, 333–5, 337, 338–9, 497, 574, 630, 792; secures command against Mithridates 249, 250, 251, 339, 490, 574, 792; command in east 248–70, 587, 792–3; size of forces 250–1; invasion of Pontus 251–2, 792; submission of Armenia 253, 792; campaigns in Caucasus 255–8, 792; annexation of Syria 259–60, 264–5, 274, 793; campaign in Judaea 252, 260–1, 274, 275, 308, 793, (founds and refounds cities) 294, 296; campaign in Nabatene 260, 261, 262; dealings with Parthia 252, 253, 259, 260, 263–5, 792; diplomacy 252, 253; pattern of conquest 257; public revenues increased by 349, 365; settlement of east 253, 258–9, 261, 262, 264–5, 265–70, 391, 588, 793; Rullan bill fails to secure land for veterans 350; honours 358; not given command against Catiline 359–60; return from east 358–9, 360–1, 362; alienates Metelli 361, 364; plans for Senate's ratification of eastern settlement 361; and Clodius' trial for sacrilege 362; Cato declines offer of marriage to niece 362; Senate blocks ratification of eastern settlement and grants of land for veterans 364, 365, 366; triumph 364–5, 793; alliance with Caesar and Crassus 366, 367, 368,369, 374, 793; opposition of Sullan clique 366, 367; Lex Iulia agraria benefits veterans 369, 371; Senate ratifies eastern settlement 372; augur (59) 372; and Clodius 372–3; marriage to Julia 374; popularity wanes 375, 392; Vettius' allegations of plot against 375, 376; and Clodius 376, 380, 381, 385, 386; and Cicero's return 385–6, 387, 388–9, 394; five-year control of corn supply 389–90, 392, 393, 399, 629, 638, 794; and Ptolemy Auletes 319, 320, 322, 391, 392, 741; defends Milo 393; deal with Caesar and Crassus at Luca 272, 394, 794; stands for consulship 394, 396; consulship with Crassus (55) 397, 398–9, 400, 401, 794; initiates Gabinius' reinstatement of Ptolemy Auletes (55) 397; allocated command in Spain 398–9, 574, 794; supports Gabinius on return 401; death of Julia 402; declines dictatorship 405; lends legion to Caesar 406; and emergency on death of Clodius 409, (special *quaestio de vi*) 409, 410, 411, 501n, 505, 516, 529, 795; declines dictatorship 409; consulship (52) 409, 410, 497–8, 795; alienation from Caesar 408, 410; supports law of the ten tribunes 412; rapprochement with Cato 412–13; reforming legislation 410, 413, 414, 431, 516, 526, 588–9; command in Spain renewed for five years 413, 419; and question of supercession of Caesar in Gaul 416–17, 418–19; ambition for Parthian command 417; alliance with Ap. Claudius 420; illness 420; breach with Caesar 420, 421, 422; leaves Italy on outbreak of Civil War 424–5, 427, 433, 796; negotiations with Caesar 427–9; Massiliots support 430; raises troops in east 432; defeat at Pharsalus 433, 796; flees to Egypt, killed 321, 433, 796
agricultural estates 618; and Alexander the Great 771; building projects in Rome 400, 406, 626, 684, 686–7, 737, 753, 794; and Cicero 414, 420–1, 424, 433; contemporary sources' attitudes to 10; and Crassus 223, 225, 228, 272, 369, 394; honesty in public finance 258, 330; honours and privileges 752, 754; intellectual interests 690n, 693, 697, 699n, 716–17; and law reform 224, 225–6, 227, 551; modern scholars on 12, 438; political connexions 196, 206, 221, 228, (*clientelae*), in Massilia 430, in Picenum 425, 449, in Sicily 196, 592, in Spain 221, 228, in Transpadane Gaul 415, 443, 444, (and Metelli) 206, 361, 364, 410; popularity 330, 335, 364, 375, 401; public persona 330, 334; and Varro 702;

Pompeius Magnus (*cont.*)
and Venus 753; wealth 617
Pompeius Rufus, Q. (*cos.* 88) 125, 788; election to consulship 165; connexion with Sulla 166; and Sulpicius' legislation 167, 168, 169; stripped of consulship 169; supports Sulla's march on Rome 170; restored 172; death 173
Pompeius Rufus, Q. (*praetor* 63) 354
Pompeius Rufus, Q. (*trib.* 52) 407, 409, 413–14
Pompeius Strabo, Cn. (*cos.* 89) 787; in Social War 120, 122, 124, 125–6, 181, 452, 787, 788; enfranchises group of Spanish cavalry 582, 592; and Lex Pompeia 126–7; attempts to stand for re-election 166; remains in command in Italy (87) 173; and Cinna's attack on Rome 175–7; death 177; son, Pompey, acquitted of charges of embezzlement by father 181
consilium 582; Rutilius Rufus denigrates 713
Pompeius Trogus, epitome of *see* Justin
Pompey *see* Pompeius Magnus, Cn.
Pomponius, Cn. (*trib.* 90) 115
Pomponius, Sex. 532, 554
Pomponius Atticus, T.: and Cicero 696, 487; diplomacy 349, 447; education 690, 721; estates 618; financial operations 634, 636, 641; literary works dedicated to 696; philosophy 725, 727; writings 696, 698, 699, 712n, 714
Pomptine Marshes *7 Bc*, 450, 610
Pomptinus, C. (*praetor* 63) 365, 372, 581, 793, 795
pontifex maximus 86, 353, 471, 706, 746
pontifices 731, 743, 745, 746; in Urso 765–6
Pontius Aquila, L. (*trib.* 45) 461
Pontius Telesinus, C. (Samnite commander) 118, 193
Pontus *1 Fc*, *4*, *9 Cb*
under early rulers 130–2
under Mithridates V Euergetes: capital 136; docility towards Rome 34, 35, 132, 133, 135; opposes Aristonicus in Pergamum 34, 132; territorial gains 34, 131, 132, 141, 229; intervention in Cappadocia 132, 141; assassination of Mithridates 132, 782; succession 132–3; Romans re-annexe Phrygia on death 35, 79, 137
under Mithridates VI 129–64, 783; early conquests 36, 137, 139–40, 783; change in relationship with Rome 140–3; occupies Paphlagonia, Galatia and Cappadocia 141, 784; dealings with Rome over occupied lands, withdrawal 97, 141–3, 786; supports Armenian invasion of Bithynia 142–3; invasion of Cappadocia 144; first war against Rome *see* Wars, Mithridatic (First); new era (88–85) 149; Rome refuses to ratify Treaty of Dardanus 212, 232, 788, 790; Sulla seeks aid in civil war 219; second war against Rome 136, 163, 212, 229, 232; renewed threat to Rome 211, 212–13; negotiations with Sertorius 213, 217, 219, 220, 233, 790; invasion of Bithynia 213; advance forces in Paphlagonia 234; third war against Rome *see* Wars, Mithridatic (Third); Pompey's reorganization in province of Bithynia and Pontus 258–9, 266, 267–8, 270, 793
under Pharnaces II 136; coup against Mithridates 254; Pompey's settlement 262, 265, 269; defeated by Caesar 434, 436, 796
KINGDOM 129, 133–7; coinage 132, 140, 149; era of 130, 149; Greek cities 133, 136, 137, 139, 229, (in Third Mithridatic War) 238, 244–8, (Pompey's settlement) 259, 266–7, 267–8, 269; Iranian culture 136, 137, 267; routes 139, 232–3
Popillii Laenates 45
Popillius Laenas, C. (*cos.* 172) 318
Popillius Laenas, C. (*cos.* 132) 73, 77, 78, 80, 85, 93, 780
Popillius Laenas (naval commander against Mithridates) 145
Poppaedius Silo, Q. (Marsian leader) 118–19, 121, 125, 452
populares 49–50, 52–3, 327–67; bypass Senate 11, 49, 59; perception of *populus Romanus* 519; pursuit of own interests 52–3; and religion 745–9; *see also* assemblies; *optimates* and *populares, and individual politicians*
population 57, 600, 602–8; depopulation, apparent 57, 204, 606, 607, 608, 610, 641; distribution and movements 601–2, 606–8; figures 600, 602–5, (*see also under* census); Mediterranean regional 605; policies to increase 63, 74, 780
populus Romanus 519, 644–7
Porcius Cato, C. (*cos.* 114) 32, 37, 65, 730, 783
Porcius Cato, C. (*trib.* 56) 391, 392, 393, 396, 741
Porcius Cato, L. (*cos.* 89) 124, 787
Porcius Cato, M. (*cos.* 195, *censor* 184) 22, 46, 494, 635; on morals 7, 59, 75; writings on agriculture 54, 55, 56, 609, 610, 614, 617, 620, 760, (on contract law) 532, 541, 554, 560, 561, 620, (on tool production) 624, 658
Porcius Cato Uticensis, M. (*praetor* 54): recovers Sulla's supporters' profits 348; actions against *ambitus* 353, 355; prosecutes Murena 355; supports execution of Catilinarians 48, 357; extends corn

distribution 359; opposition to Pompey 359–60, 362, 364, 429; and Asian tax contract 365, 441n; and Caesar's consulship 366, 369, 371; attempts to prosecute Gabinius 376; advises Cicero over Clodius' attack 381; commissioner in Cyprus 319, 384, 391, 794; and elections for 55 397; and triumvirs' commands 398; praetorship 401; supports sole consulship of Pompey 410; opposes 'law of the ten tribunes' (52) 412; rapprochement with Pompey 412–13; alliance with Ap. Claudius 420; demands Caesar lay down command 422; in Civil War 431, 433, 435, 796; suicide 436

Cicero's eulogy and Caesar's reply 366, 460–1, 695, 696, 713; frugality 404; moral authority 366, 367; and philosophy 721, 725, 727n; and *popularis* cause 52; ridicules Postumius Albinus 699n; sources' attitudes to 9

Porcius Laeca, P. (*trib.* 199) 494
port facilities 456, 629–30, 656
portents 344, 352, 730; *see also* omens
porterage 670
portoria, see customs dues
Posidonius 1, 2; and Cicero 694, 712–13, 720, 721n; on crisis of Republic 7, 26; geography 724–5; historiography 714–15; relationships with Roman aristocracy 695; in Rhodes 697, 716–17; use of Rutilius Rufus 713, 715
possessio (legal control) 204, 540, 558, 561; *bonorum* 538, 539, 562, (as legal penalty) 457, 545, 557
Postumii 45
Postumius (soothsayer) 170, 189
Postumius Albinus, A. (*cos.* 151) 699n
Postumius Albinus, A. (*cos.* 99) 29
Postumius Albinus, L. (*cos.* 173) 55
Postumius Albinus, Sp. (*cos.* 110) 29, 89, 784
Postumius Pyrgensis, M. 501n, 503
potestas 535; see also *patria potestas*
Potheinus (Egyptian regent) 321
'Potter's Oracle, The' 313
pottery: amphorae 23, 136, 614, 625; black-glaze Campanian ware 23; Italian exports 23, 637, 639; luxury wares 627; senatorial wealth from 643
poverty: concepts of 9, 657; /wealth nexus 7, 8–9, 26, 27
Praecia (mistress of P. Cethegus) 213
praecones (heralds or auctioneers) 451
praefectus urbi, jurisdiction of 530
Praeneste (Palestrina) *3(i) Cc, 7 Bb, 13 Bc*, 106, 174, 204, 633, 664n; in civil war 190, 192, 193, 194, 195–6, 789
Praesenteius, P. 120
praetors 43, 47; and development of law 532, 533, 534, 538–9, 540, 544, 546, 548–9, 550; edicts 335, 532, 534, 544, 548–9, 792; eligibility 201; financial measures (86–85) 180–1; number increased 20, 497, 526; *peregrinus* 533, 544; provincial commands 329, 572, 574–5; Sulla's legislation 201, 497, 526; *urbanus* 508, 533, 544, 570
precedent, constitutional 491, 492; see also *mos maiorum*
prefects, board of, in Rome 460
presses, grape- and olive- 56, 612
prices 58–9, 203, 457, 623, 633
Priene *9 Bc, 14 Cb*, 35, 247
priesthoods 731; Caesar's 178, 198, 353, 459, 706, 742–3; legal expertise 533–4; of Rome, in provinces 766; selection 59, 94, 203, 352, 746; *see also* augurs; *XVviri*; Fetial priests; *flamen; pontifex maximus; pontifices*; Vestal Virgins
proditio, trial for 518–19
promagistrates 572, 573, 744
propaganda 284, 294, 436
property 540; basis of social hierarchy 72, 353, 510, 642; damage to 543, 544; landed 64, 599, 637, 770; Latin right of *nexum* or *commercium* 64, 601; law of 540–1, 549–50, 558; married woman's 537; public and private 63, 621; qualifications, (for *comitia centuriata*) 57, 65, 80, (for equestrian order) 46, 90, (for magistracies) 41, 46, (for military service) 36, 37, 39; *res mancipi/nec mancipi* 540, 558
prorogation of office 10, 14, 43, 61, 572, 751, 771
proscriptions: Second Triumvirate 486–7, 496, 578; and land market 618, 623; *see also under* Cornelius Sulla, L.
prosecutors, professional 93, 94, 506
prostitution, Pontic temple 137
Protopachium 146
provinces 6, 16–39, 564–98; administration 16, 17, 22, 43, 201–2, 564–98; agricultural investment 328–9; allocation to magistrates 43, 47, 79–80, 329, 394, 573–4, 588, 782; change in Roman attitude to 593–8; concept, (as task) 564–5, (geographical) 572; control of governors 97–8, 201–2, 575–80, (*see also* 'pirate law'; *repetundae*); governors' edicts 547, 554, 589–90; governors' *imperium* 564–5, 572, 577, 579–80; governors' staff 580–4; justice 22–3, 248; law *see* 'pirate law' *and under* jurisdiction; law, private; military costs 568, 588; misconduct of senators 22, 77, 214–15, 224, 225–7, 335–6, 413, 575–80, (see also *repetundae*); origins 564–71; Roman protection extended to allies in 108; status

provinces (*cont.*)
of provincials 591–3; wealth derived from 54, 55–6, 107–8, 332, 618, 639–40, 770, 773; *see also individual provinces and under* debt; finance; patronage; *publicani*; taxation; *repetundae*
provocatio 13, 41, 46, 52, 85, 493–4; C. Gracchus and 77–8, 81; in criminal procedure 501–2; for Italian allies 75, 76, 81, 508, 781; waived in public interest 495
Prusa *9 Bb*, 236, 268
Prusias II, king of Bithynia 16, 132
Psalms of Solomon 279, 308
Psenptais, high priest of Memphis 319
Pseudepigrapha 279
Ptolemais (Akko) *10 Aa*, 295
Ptolemies 36, 282, 310–21, 326; dynastic cult 321, 323, 324, 326; *see also individual members of dynasty*
Ptolemy II Philadelphus 297, 778
Ptolemy VI Philometor 778; death 310
Ptolemy VII Neos Philopator 310, 778
Ptolemy VIII Euergetes II (Physcon) 16, 310–11, 313–14, 778, 780, 781; succession to 314–17
Ptolemy IX Soter II (Lathyrus) 779; rule in Cyprus 315, 316, 784; reign in Egypt 316–18, 322, 783, 788, 789; and Jews 291, 295
Ptolemy X Alexander I 315, 779, 783, 784, 788; bequeaths kingdom to Rome 316, 318, 345, 786; and native Egyptian cults 317, 326
Ptolemy XI Alexander II 318, 779, 789
Ptolemy XII Neos Dionysos (Auletes) 779; rule in Egypt 318–19, 789, 793–5; Roman recognition 373, 793; flight to Rome 271–2, 319, 324, 391, 392, 397, 794; Roman refusal to reinstate 391–2, 395–6, 398, 741, 794; Gabinius reinstates 320, 322, 395–6, 397, 399–400, 491, 492, 794; will 320–1 bribery 392; coinage 322; debts to Romans 322, 373, 399, 434; and native cults 318–19
Ptolemy XIII 320–1, 433, 434, 779, 794
Ptolemy XIV 321, 434, 779
Ptolemy son of Abubus (Aboub) 285–6
Ptolemy Apion 316, 778, 783, 786
Ptolemy Caesar (Caesarion) 321, 434, 466, 796
Ptolemy of Cyprus 260, 318, 319, 379, 391, 779
Ptolemy Memphites 310, 313, 778
public works 626–7, 666, 686–7, 774; *collegia* and 672; Greek influence 697; issue of coinage to pay for 632; Italian allies' 106; numbers employed 670; *see also* roads
publicani (contractors) 79, 584–5; army supply 584, 636; Asian tax contract 365, 372, 793; banking 584–5, 636; Caesar limits rights 441, 458; Calabrian 60–1; in Cisalpina 624; and drove-roads 616; in east 35, 270, 273; Gabinius and Syrian 395, 396; and jury issue 510; loans to provincials 639; and provincial governors 584–5, 593; *societates* (companies) 79, 542, 584, 585, 635–7; tax collection 584, 585, 587, 636; *tesserae nummulariae* 633
Publicius Malleolus 513n
Publicola *see under* Gellius
Pulcher *see under* Claudius
pumps, drainage 625
punishments: fixed penalties 529; of slaves 493; *see also* exile; *possessio (bonorum)*
Pupius Piso Frugi Calpurnianus, M. (*cos.* 61) 360, 361, 362, 363, 364, 793
purification, ritual, see *lustra*
Puteoli (Pozzuoli) *3(ii) Ac*, *13 Bc*, 634, 638, 662; port 629, 630, 637; Sulla's villa 206, 207
Pydna *14 Bb*; battle of 697
Pylaemenes, king of Inner Paphlagonia 132, 147
Pyrrhus, war against 631
Pythagoreanism 702, 703, 704, 707–10, 727, 760
Pythodorus of Tralles 248

quadrivium, medieval 705
quaestio Mamilia 89, 519
quaestio Variana 114–15, 165, 167, 519
quaestiones extra ordinem or *extraordinariae* 494, 504–5, 506, 521, 527; Pompey's (52) 409, 410, 501n, 505, 516, 529, 795
quaestiones perpetuae 69, 80, 202, 499, 505–30; appraisal 528–30; assembly sanctions 80, 494; institution 497, 499, 503, 515, 516, 578, 789; and oratory 534; *praefectus urbi* assumes functions under Principate 530; tribunes' powers reduced by 497, 503; *see also* juries, and under *ambitus*; *iniuria*; *maiestas*; *peculatus*; *repetundae*; *sicarii*; *veneficii*; *vis*
quaestors 43; conduct capital trials 502; number increased 328, 496–7; *parricidi quaestores* 500; in provinces 580–1, 582, 590; in Sicily 590, 593; Sullan reforms 201, 496–7
Quinctius (Lucullus' besieger in Social War) 194
Quinctius (*praetor* 68) 239–40
Quinctius, C. (Cicero's client) 25
Quinctius, L. (*trib.* 74) 213–14, 223, 234, 248, 331, 790
Quinctius Flamininus, T. (*cos.* 198) 569, 754
XVviri sacris faciundis 391, 731, 746
Xviri 199

Quintilian 692, 700, 715, 719
Qumran sect *10 Bb*, 278–9, 300, 301–4; texts 278–9, 299, 301–3

Rabbinic literature 279–80
Rabirius (philosopher) 718, 757n
Rabirius, C. (murderer of Saturninus) 352, 357, 502n, 793
Rabirius Postumus, C. 272, 320, 322, 635n
Rammii (Thessalian family) 17
Raphia *10 Ac*, *11 Ba*, 294
Raurica 446n
Ravenna *2 Bb*, *13 Bb*, 193
Rechtsfrage 408, 416–17, 418–19, 423, 795
recitation 689, 695
recuperatores 507, 544, 545, 547, 577–8, 597
Regillus, battle of Lake 729
Reginus, L. (trib.104) 93
regnum, *see* kingship
religion, Roman 729–68; abuse, apparent 741–2; alienness 733–4; antiquarians on 757–9; belief 733; change 738, 773; *collegia* and 761; comparison between periods 734–8; consensus 741, 748–9; dedications 732, 753, 767; disruption 739–42; effect of empire 743, 763–8; and ethics 729; *evocatio* 743–4; experts and enthusiasts 756, 757–9; foreign cults in Rome 290, 761, 764–5; foreign perspectives on 767–8; groups 761–3; household cults 732, 761; individual devotion 732, 733; institutions 729–34; Italian allies and Roman cults 113; Latin cults 82; *ludi* grounded in 683; and magic 756, 759–61; and morality 729; neglect and adaptation 742–5; obstruction of legislation 89, 99–100, 102, 371, 378, 739, 749, (Bibulus') 368, 369, 371, 739–40, (Marcellinus') 392, 393; and philosophy 767; political nature 45, 706, 729, 730–1, 733, 734, 756, 761–2; and political upheavals 739–42, 745–9, 761–3, 773; in provinces 765–7; scepticism 465, 756–7; sources 734–8; specialization 755–63; Sulla and 162, 170, 173, 183, 189, 753; traditional forms 729–34; and triumphs 750, 751, 752; and warfare 729–30, 743, 764; *see also* Bacchanalian cult; Goddess, Good; godhead; gods; omens; oracles; portents; priesthoods; sacrifice; temples
religions, non-Roman: foreign cults in Rome 290, 761, 764–5; *see also under* Egypt; Greece; Jews
Remi *12 Ba*, 387, 388
rents 457, 458, 617, 620, 622, 641
reparations 32–3, 35, 158, 161, 162–3, 246, 569, 586
repetundae, *quaestio de repetundis* 77, 505–14, 588–9, 597; allies 77, 79, 81, 109, 355; cases (138–123) 43, 60, 77; *comperendinatio* 94; C. Cornelius' proposals (67) 335–6; damages 513, 529; early 2nd-cent. processes 506, 597; evidence 94; governors limited by 492, 513, 520; Gracchan statute 5, 51–2, 75, 78, 81–2, 89, 90, 506, 507, 508–10, 511, 530n, 578, 597, 782; and judicial corruption 512, 514; juries 81–2, 93, 94, 102, 507, 508, 509, 511–12, 545; laws *see* law (*leges* (Acilia; Calpurnia; Cornelia; Iulia; Iunia; Sempronia; Servilia; Servilia Caepionis)); *maiestas* overlaps with 514, 518, 520; non-Roman citizens sue in own right 506–7, 508; procedure of court 94, 513; *quaestio perpetua* established 578; *recuperatores* 597; special court (171) 506; Sulla and 512, 578; *see also under* Verres, C. *and other individuals accused*
Republic, causes of decline 489–90, 769–76
res mancipi/nec mancipi 540, 558
res publica 491
retail trades 59, 658, 659–66, 667
Rhegium (Reggio) *1 Dd*, *2 Cd*, *13 Cd*, 73, 634
Rhegium Lepidum *13 Ab*, 450n
rhetoric *see* oratory
Rhodes *1 Ed*, *5 Ac*, *9 Bc*, *14 Cb*; in First Mithridatic War 145, 146, 147, 149–50, 159, 160, 697, 788; in settlement after war 162; in civil war 194
  coinage 632; Delos' rivalry with 637; pirate wars 97, 630; Pompey in 716–17; Posidonius' office 695, 697; wine exports 614n
Rhône valley *1 Bc*, *12 Bc*, 24, 37, 615
Rhosos, Octavian's letters to 547
Rhyndacus, river *5 Bb*, *9 Bb*; battles on 160, 235–6, 791
rights: civil, see *caput*; Latin, *see under* Latins; popular 49, 52
roads 628–9; in Asia 34; Curio's bill (50) 418; Empriae to Rhône 24; C. Gracchus and building of 78; King's Highway 292; repair 331, 344, 627; Rhegium to Capua 73; in Social War 119, 121
  viae: Aemilia *2 Ab*, *13 Bb*, 784; Appia *2 Bc-Cc*, *3(ii) Da-Eb*, *7 Bb-c*, *13 Cc-Cc*, 121, 177, 189, 223, 344; Cassia *2 Bb*, *3(i) Cb*, *7 Aa*, *13 Bb-c*, 193; Clodia *2 Ab-Bc*, *3(i) Cc*, *7 Aa*, *13 Bc*, 193; Domitia 23, 628; Egnatia 31, 628, 630; Labicana *7 Bb*, 192; Latina *2 Bc*, *3(ii) Aa*, *7 Bb*, *13 Bc*, 189, 192; Postumia *2 Aa-Ba*, *13 Ba*, 23; Praenestina *7 Bb*, 192, 194; Valeria *2 Bc*, *3(i) Cc-Dc*, *7 Ba*, *13 Bc*, 121
Rogatio Servilia ('Rullan bill') 349–51, 618, 655, 793

Rome *1 Cc*, *3(i) Cc*, *3(ii) Aa*, *7 Ab*, *370*

CITY LIFE 644–88; benefits of 652, 657, 666, 667, 681; boundaries 646, (see also *pomoerium*); building 626, 670–1; emigration from 654–5, 656; expulsions of non-Romans *see separate entry*; financiers 633, 634; fires 626, 650, 660–1; floods 401–2, 650; flux in population 649–50, 654, 657–8, 674; food supply 58, 60, 79, 600, 629, 638, 658 (*see also* corn); foundation 403, 738, (myth) 650; growth 607; and hinterland 656, 658; housing 650, 667, 671, (see also *insulae*); hygiene 650; immigration 44, 650–3; industries 58, 624, 625, 627, 658, 661, 669; leisure; *urbanum otium* 652; library, first public 454, 692–3, 701; luxury goods 627, 666; as market 620; social mobility 657–8; personifications, deified 766; plague (175–174) 650; policing 43, 456; retailing 658, 659–66, 667; slaves 653; social integration 668; street maintenance 627; suburbs 656; *tabernae* 654, 658, 659–66, 667; theatre 652, 652, 682–3, 684; *urbana provincia* 565; *vici* 648; water supply 626, 650, 670–1, 673n; xenophobia 106, 168, 652–3, 653–4

BUILDINGS AND LOCATIONS *370*; amphitheatre 684; aqueducts 626, 650, (Acqua Felice) 670–1, (*Aqua Marcia*) 626; arch of Q. Fabius Maximus 406; arch of L. Stertinius 684; *area Capitolina* 72; Basilica Aemilia *370*, 415; Basilica Iulia *370*, 453; Basilica Opimia *370*; Basilica Pauli *370*; Basilica Porcia *370*, 407, 408; Caesar's building works 406–7, 449, 453–5, 626, 684; *Campus Martius 7 Ab*, 626, 676; Capitol 132, 189, 203, 344, 356–7, 468; Carcer *370*, 407; Circus Maximus 684; Colline Gate *see separate entry*; Comitium 44, 59, 676; Flavian and Severan Marble Plans of 661; Forum Iulium 406–7, 453, 753, 757; Forum Romanum 44, 69, *370*, 470, 472, 676; Horrea Galbana 629; Horrea Sempronia 629; houses 650, 667, 671, (Caesar's) 454, 462, 750, (M. Cicero's) 363, (Q. Cicero's) 670; Janiculum *7 Ab*, 209; Monte Testaccio 627; Mulvian Bridge *see separate entry*; *pomoerium* 101, 205, 366, 649; Pompey's building projects 400, 406, 626, 684, 686–7, 737, 753, 794; Pons Sublicius 84; port of 626, 629, 637; Porticus Aemilia 629; Porticus Octavia 686; rostra *370*, 731; Saepta Iulia (voting-enclosure) 406, 453; senate-house *370*, 407–8, 409, 454, 795

temples 736–8, 742; Apollo 416; Bellona 195, 352; Castor *370*, 371, 378, 386, 736; Ceres 185, 748; Clementia Caesaris, planned 454, 462; Concord *370*, 380, 407; Concordia, planned 454; Diana, Aventine 84; Diana Planciana 737; Felicitas, planned 454; Fides 69; Hercules Pompeianus 737; Hercules Victor, Forum Boarium 627; Juno, Aventine 743; Jupiter Capitolinus 327, 454, 737, 752; Jupiter Optimus Maximus 358, 390, 521; Jupiter Stator 355, 371; Largo Argentina A 737n; Luna 185; Minerva, Pompey's 737; Nymphs 736; Ops 473; Quirinus 677; Saturn *370*; Tellus 171, 737; Venus Erycina 194; Venus Genetrix 453–4, 475, 753; Venus Victrix, Pompey's 737; Vortumnus 744

theatres 407, 454, 682–3, 684; Via Sacra 654, 660, 663; warehouses 79, 626

Romulus 750–1, 767

Roscii of Ameria 198; Sex. Roscius 205–6, 226, 789; Q. Roscius 617

Roscius Fabatus, L. (*praetor* 49) 428, 429

Roscius Otho, L. (*trib.* 67) 332, 334, 352, 792

Rostovtzeff, M. 54, 56

Rubicon, crossing of 424, 485

Rubrius (*trib.* 133) 69

Rubrius (*trib.* 123/122) 78; *see also* law (*leges* (Rubria))

Rufus *see under* Minucius; Rutilius; Sulpicius

'Rullan bill' 349–51, 618, 655, 793

Rullus *see under* Servilius

Rupilius, P. (*cos.* 132) 26, 589, 780

Rutilius, P. (*praetor c.*118) 561, 663

Rutilius Lupus, P. (*cos.* 90) 120, 121, 787

Rutilius Rufus, P. (*cos.* 105) 785; conviction *de repetundis* and exile 81–2, 103, 529, 721, 726; intellectual interests 715, 721, 757n; writings 100, 145, 699, 713

Sabellian lands 611

Sacastan 262

sacrifice: human 733–4; at *lustrum* 327; private 732–3; to Rome, in provinces 766

sacrilege *see under* Clodius, P.

sacrilegium (theft from temples) 515

Sacriportus *7 Bb*; battle of 192, 789

Sadducees 275, 300, 305–6, 308

Saguntum *1 Bc*, *8 Cb*, 218

Salamis, Cyprus *1 Fd*, *9 Cc*, *14 Cb*, 593

Salapia *3(ii) Da*, 125

sale, law of 533, 542, 561

Salernum (Salerno) *3(ii) Cb*, 120

Salian priests 731

Sallust (C. Sallustius Crispus, *praetor* 47): political career 409, 431, 440, 796; *Catilina* 8, 9, 351, 496; *Histories* 2, 4, 9, 11, 711; *Jugurtha* 8, 28–9, 30, 38, 39, 88; *Second Letter to Caesar* 448; on Caesar's autocracy 458; on *factio* 11, 48, 87; on moral decline 7, 9, 10, 40, 48–9; on *optimates*/*populares* struggle 13, 14; on wealth/poverty nexus 8

Salluvii *12 Bc*, 24, 781

Salome Alexandra, queen of Judaea 291, 296, 297, 307, 777
salt industry in Priene 35
Salvidienus Rufus, Q. 495n
Salvius (Sicilian slave leader) 26
Samaria *10 Ab*, 282, 288, 291–2, 294
sambuca (siege machine) 150
Samnium and Samnites *2 Bc*, *3(ii) Ba-Ca*; agreement of Caudine Forks (321) 61; resettlement 651; migration to Fregellae 76, 105, 607; in Social War 115, 118, 125, 126; in civil war 176, 191, 192, 193–4, 195, 196, 219, 789; Caesar and 448–9, 450, 473–4; Antony courts support of veterans 473–4 agriculture 611; land holdings 56, 57, 73, 204
Samoga (Samega) *10 Bb*, 291
Samos *5 Ab*, *9 Bc*, 163
Samosata 265
Samothrace *5 Aa*, 163
Sampsiceramus of Emesa 259
sanctio (oath) 749
Saône, river *12 Bb*, 627
Saqqara *11 Aa*, 325
Sarapis, cult of 765
sarcophagus of Alexander the Great 322
Sardinia *1 Cc-d*, *2 Ac-d*, *13 Ac-d*, *14 Bb*; 3rd-cent. Roman military presence 571, 576; Ti. Gracchus' campaign (177) 55; Aurelius Orestes' campaigns 781; C. Gracchus' quaestorship 28, 76, 77; in Sullan civil war 191; Lepidus dies in 209; Perperna escapes to 217; in Civil War 394, 425, 435, 436; Tiberius settles Jewish freedmen in 655; corn exports to Rome 425, 613, 629
Sardis *5 Bb*, 159
Sarmatians *1 Eb-Fb*, *9 Ba*, 129, 146
Sasernae, on large villa estates 620
Saticula *3(ii) Bc*, 189
satires, Menippean, Varro's 710, 719
Satureius, P. (*trib.*133) 72
Saturnia *3(i) Bb*, 193
Saturninus *see under* Appuleius
Saufeius, M., 101, 501n, 529
Saumacus (rebel leader of Panticapaeum) 139
Scaevola *see under* Mucius; Septimius
Scantinius Capitolinus, C. (*trib.*) 502n
Scaurus *see under* Aemilius
Sceptics 724
scholarship 701–7; systematic methods 551, 701, 702, 705, 718, 719, 727, 758
Sciathus *9 Ab*, 151
sciences 21, 705–6, 708, 710; *see also* astronomy
Scipio *see under* Cornelius
Scordisci *1 Db-c*, *2 Ca*, *9 Aa*, 32, 140, 254, 784, 785
scribae 581–2
Scribonius Curio, C. (*cos.* 76) 210, 211, 227, 404, 790; in First Mithridatic War 154, 157, 161
Scribonius Curio, C. (*trib.* 50) 373, 375, 404; tribunate 415, 417–19, 420, 421, 572, 575, 796; in Civil War 422, 428, 431, 796
Scribonius Libo, L. (*cos.* 34) 429
scriptura (Sicilian tax) 587
sculpture: Aristogeiton, from slope of Capitol 72; of Caesar 453–4, 462; gilt equestrian, Sulla's 199; Greek 697; of Jupiter, for Capitol 344, 356–7; Lucullus brings from east 697
Scyllacium *2 Cd*, 78
Scyllaeum, promontory of *2 Cd*, 222
Scythians 129, 133, 139, 254
Scythopolis *10 Bb*, 292, 295
seals: of Alexander Jannaeus 299; *tesserae nummulariae* 633
security, legal 541, 543, 622
sedition, charge of 518, 519
Segesta *2 Bd*, 26
Segobriga *8 Bb*, 217, 219
Segontia *8 Bb*, 217, 218, 790
Segovia *8 Bb*, 218, 790
Selene (Seleucid princess) 259
Seleucus I, king of Syria 131
Seleucus II, king of Syria 131
Seleucus (garrison commander of Sinope) 245
self-help; use of force 525, 772
Sempronius Asellio, A. (*praetor* 89) 642, 787
Sempronius Asellio, P. (*trib.* 133, historian) 1, 66, 711–13
Sempronius Gracchus, C. (*trib.* 123–122) 77–86; in Celtiberian wars 62; quaestor in Sardinia 28, 76, 77; tribunate 77–86, 781–2; re-election (122) 82, 782; fails to be re-elected (121) 83; death 28, 84, 494, 495, 782 and agrarian issue 28, 63, 67–8, 78, 83, 85, 107, 606, 622, 780; and allies' rights 75, 77–8, 81, 82–3; and allocation of provinces 79–80, 394, 573, 782; Asia, organization of 35, 79, 569, 586; use of assemblies 74–5; assessment 85–6; and balance of power 9, 80, 86, 90; biography of Ti. Gracchus 4, 8, 9, 54–5; colonization schemes 5, 28, 56, 78, 82, 83–4, 85, 446; and corn supply 58–9, 78–9, 83, 649; and corruption 79, 80; cult of 752; and debt repayment 79; and equestrian order 80, 90; legislation *see* law (*leges* (Semproniae)); and Lex Rubria 28, 83–4; and Lex Aufeia 35; and military enlistment 37; and Octavius 77; political innovation 40, 677; and *provocatio* 77–8, 81; road building 78; sources on 4, 7, 9; and Spain 79; suspected of murdering Scipio Aemilianus 74; wife's dowry 555
Sempronius Gracchus, Ti. (*cos.* 177, 163) 20–1, 22, 55

Sempronius Gracchus, Ti. (*trib.* 133) 62–77, 780; quaestor in Spain 61; and revenues of Pergamum 33, 68, 73, 780; agrarian proposal 48, 62–3, 64–7, 87, 104, 107, 606, 622, 780; on land commission 67, 780; stands for re-election as tribune (132) 48, 68–9, 72; death 69, 72–3, 780; trial of followers 494, 504–5
C. Gracchus' biography 4, 8, 9, 54–5; cult after death 752; and Greek political thought 53; political connexions 51, 61; political innovation 40, 677; popular support 46; on slave workforce 54, 55, 57–8, 606; and Spain 61; speeches 4, 8, 63–4; use of force 85
Sempronius Tuditanus, C. (*cos.* 129) 781
Sena Gallica *3(i) Da*, *13 Bb*, 193, 672
Senate 46–8; *acta* published 368; and Antony 474, 478, 480–1; army challenges claim to rule 489, 771; *auctoritas* 48, 49, 377; Caesar's enlargement 444, 452, 459, 797; in Civil War (in Rome), 428, 429, 430, (in exile) 432, 433, (in aftermath of Caesar's murder) 468–9, 469–70, 471, 480–1, 487, 489; censors determine membership 46, 327, 378, 413, 419–20, 783, 791, 796; Cicero's belief in rule of 337, 353, 479, 489; and Clodius 362, 378, 394; collective dominance 48, 50, 72, 183, 337, 353, 479, 489; consensus 48, 50, 772; disavowal of treaties 4, 29, 61; and foreign affairs; commissions 22, 27, 29, 34; and Gracchi 67, 69, 80, 81, 84–5, 86, 509; Lex Plautia against intimidation of 524; Livius Drusus and 111–12; militarism 62; and Octavian 480, 485, 487; optimate group's control 338, 358–9, 364, 366, 367, 375, 393, 394–5, 411; plebeians admitted 46; political alliances within 50–2; and Pompey 358–9, 364, 366, 367, 393, (Pompey's reforms) 409, 410, 413; *populares* bypass 11, 49, 59; and provincial administration 568, 573, 575–6, 577, 580–1, 588; religious role 730–1, 734, 756, 761–2; and special courts 494, 504–5; and Sulla *see under* Cornelius Sulla, L.; Varro's handbook on procedure 224, 702; *virtus* 49–50; *see also* magistrates; senatorial order; *senatus consulta*
senate house *see under* Rome
senatorial order: commercial activities 329, 599, 634, 635, 642–3, 662–3, 664, 669–70; and equestrian order 4, 80, 90–2, 111, 200–1, 202, (*see also* juries (legislation)); land ownership abroad not allowed 329, 446–7; limit on debts 168; *see also* Senate; upper classes
senatus consulta 48; *de Asclepiade* 547, 560; *de collegiis* (64) 346; on C. Gracchus' leaving Rome when tribune 83; on release of enslaved allies 26; rewarding Greek sea-captains 32; sources of law 532; *ultima* 84–5, 492, 494–6, (100) 101, 786, (83) 189, (78) 209, (63) 354, 494–5, 793, (52) 795, (49) 425, 427, 432, 796, (47) 435, (43) 174, 480, 481
Seneca the Elder 10, 466, 691, 699, 709n, 719
Senones *12 Bb*, 405, 408, 409, 411
sententia Minuciorum 547n, 560
Sentius, C. (governor of Macedonia) 149
VIIviri epulonum 731, 746
Septimius Scaevola, P. 512
Septimius Severus, Emperor 9–10
Septimontium 673
Sequani *12 Bb*, 383, 384, 387
Sergius Catilina, L.: in Sullan period 195, 205; extortion in Africa 335, 340, 345, 792; consular candidacy not allowed 340; and trial of Manilius; alleged preliminary conspiracy 2, 342, 343, 792; consular candidacy (64) 348–9, 353; acquitted by *quaestio de sicariis* 349, 524n; Catilinarian conspiracy 354–8, 495, 749; command of peasants' revolt 355, 358, 359, 360; death 360; debt 348, 642; *see also* Catilinarian conspiracy
Sertorius, Q. 220–1; and Social War 120; supports Marius and Cinna 173, 174, 175, 176, 179; in civil war 190, 191; proscription 198; establishes power in Spain 191, 204, 206, 209, 789, 790, (Roman-style administration) 215, 217, 220; Senate's campaigns against 209, 210, 215–21, 790; pact with Mithridates 213, 217, 219, 220, 233, 790; assassination 219–20, 791
service industries 669; see also *tabernae*
Servilius (Pompey's naval legate) 256
Servilius, Q. (or C., *d.* 91) 114
Servilius Caepio, Cn. (commander in Spain, 173) 573n
Servilius Caepio, Q. (*cos.* 140) 60
Servilius Caepio, Q. (*cos.* 106) 784, 785; Lex Servilia Caepionis on juries 93, 511–12; Gallic campaign 24, 37, 93, 785; prosecution 93, 95, 96, 102, 519; and Metelli 88
Servilius Caepio, Q. (*quaestor* 100) 98, 102, 121, 519n
Servilius Glaucia, C. (*trib.* 101) 4, 9, 97, 101, 103, 677; *lex de repetundis* 94, 96, 102, 512, 785; law of 101/100 on praetorian provinces *see* 'pirate law'
Servilius Globulus, P. (*trib.* 67) 333
Servilius Rullus, P. (*trib.* 63) 349–51, 618, 655, 793
Servilius Vatia Isauricus, P. (*cos.* 79) 173, 206, 339, 392, 790, 794; command against pirates 210, 212–13, 232–3, 249, 790, 791

Servilius Vatia Isauricus, P. (*cos.* 48) 431, 432, 441, 796; after Caesar's death 477, 480, 482, 483
servitudes (rights to property) 540, 551
Servius Tullius, king of Rome 37
Sestii of Cosa 615n, 635n
Sestius, P. (*trib.* 57) 387, 389, 529
Settefinestre 615n
settlers abroad, Roman and Italian 17, 20, 22, 25, 27–8, 30, 31, 35, 85; *see also* colonies; veterans
Sextii (philosophical group) 709
Sextius, P., trial for *ambitus* 516n
Sextius Calvinus, C. (*cos.* 124) 24, 781, 782
Sextius Lateranus, L. (*trib.* 376–367) 68
sharecropping 617, 620
shares, company 636
Shechem *10 Ab*, 291, 292, 297
sheep farming 452, 615
shipping 629–30; bottomry 635; construction 135, 136, 616, 623, 629; Egyptian contractors 322–3; fraud 89; freedom of navigation 629, 630, 640; loans 17, 20; partnerships 635; wrecks 56, 625, 629; *see also under* fleet
shrines 758; family 732
Sibylline Books 203, 328, 344, 464, 737, 764; and Ptolemy Auletes 272, 320, 391, 396; *XVviri sacris faciundis* consult 391, 731
sicarii, quaestio de sicariis 348, 349, 507n, 511, 520, 521–3; covers unjust conviction 514; extent of jurisdiction 522–3, 527; *quaestio de sicariis et veneficiis* 526
Sicily *1 Cd*, *2 Bd-e*, *13 Bd-e*, *14 Bb*; Roman military presence established 571; 2nd-cent. events and administration 17, 25–7; slave revolts 25–7, 55, 620, (138/7–132) 25–7, 58, 61, 73, 605, 780, (104–101) 26, 94, 96, 785; law of 100 allows for colonies 99; situation of Romans and Italian allies in 108; in Social War 119; in civil war of 80s 195, 196, 789; Lepidus' governorship 206; Verres' governorship *see under* Verres, C.; Pompey's settlement 221; Spartacus' rebellion and 222; in Civil War 425, 431, 435
agriculture 25, 27, 425, 613, 629; jurisdiction 589; migration to 608; money system 632; pirates 249; privileges 442, 448, 473; quaestors 590; taxation 639, (corn-tithe) 569, 586, 587, 639; textiles 625; trade with Puteoli 630
Sicinius, Cn. or L. (*trib.* 76) 211, 790
Side 233
Sidi-bou-Ali *2 Ae*, 27–8
siege engines 150, 153, 154
Signia *3(ii) Aa*, 192
Sila Silva *2 Cd*, 60–1, 504, 610
Silanus *see under* Iunius
silver: Athenian 154; Pontic 135, 258; price rise 59; tableware 56, 59; Spanish 21, 625
Simeon ben Shetah 306, 307
Simon (Jewish high priest) 277, 282, 283–6, 288–9, 290, 298; death 285–6, 287, 296
Sinope *1 Fc*, *4 Bb*, *5 Da*, *9 Cb*, *14 Ca*, 131, 132, 133, 135, 136, 137, 139; in Third Mithridatic war 236, 238, 245, 246, 791; Pompey's settlement (62) 267; Caesar's colony 447
Sinora 252
Sisenna *see under* Cornelius
Sittius, P. (adventurer) 436, 638
slander 544
slaves: aedilician edict on 561; agents for masters 543; agricultural 27, 54, 617, 619, 620–1; allies enslaved 26, 35; armed bands 210; bond- 504; Caesar limits proportion in workforce 797; book copyists 694; captives enslaved 55, 162, 292, 388, 442, 599, 604, 653; chattel status 534–5, 558; domestic 653, 662, 697; and education 690, 691; and food supply 605; freedom 57, (civil war leaders offer) 171, 174, 175, 177, 179, (Mithridates grants) 159, (for slaves of proscribed) 203, 486, (*see also* manumission *below*); Greek culture 691, 697; growth in population 55, 602, 604–5, 773; industrial and craft 662, 664; legal status 499, 500, 534–5, 544, 555, 557, 558; manumission 404–5, 456, 535, 550, 556; Mommsen on 12; *peculium* 537, 543; and political and social life 646; provincials enslaved 43, 507, 577; punishment 493, 500; relationship with master 668; revolts 55, 354, 452, 600, 605, 620, 771, (*see also* Spartacus *and under* Sicily); in Spanish silver-mines 21; tax on slave-owners proposed (50) 418; Ti. Gracchus on 54, 55; trade 20, 25, 59, 258, 618, (Delos) 604, 620, 630, 638, (law on) 542,(pirates supply) 630, (*publicani* and) 636, (Puteoli) 630; *see also* freedmen
smallholders 56–7, 65, 74, 618–20; distress 346–7, 352, 353, 641
Smyrna *5 Ab*, 145, 159, 766
societates (companies) of businessmen 79, 270, 542, 584, 585, 635–7
society 599–643; class consciousness 14–15; effect of economy on 640–3; integration 668; Italian social conditions 57–9; of orders 642–3; social engineering 548; social setting of intellectual life 692–6; social status 599–600, 602, 622; traditional structures in regions 611; value of land 622, 623; *see also individual classes*
Socrates Chrestus (claimant to throne of Bithynia) 143

sodalicia, sodalitates (clubs) 51, 517, 522
Soknebtunis (Egyptian god) 313
Soli *9 Cc*, 266
Sophene *9 Dc*, 238, 240, 241, 253
Sosates 279
Sosigenes (astronomer) 455, 725
Souchos (Egyptian god) 313
sources 1–15; on agriculture 609, 615; on domination of Cinna 179; on Jews 277–80; on Mithridates 130; on private law 531–2, 560; on religion 734–8; on urban plebs 644, 647; *see also individual authors and* archaeology; coinage; inscriptions; papyri
Spain: Roman acquisition 20, 567, 568; early Roman and Italian settlers 17, 20, 22; Ti. Gracchus' governorship 20–1, 22, 61; Viriathic War 21, 22, 37, 61; Numantine War *see* Numantia; wars (114–111) 783; M. Crassus takes refuge in 180, 187; Sulla's enemies hold 195, 204, 209; campaigns against Sertorius 191, 204, 206, 209, 210, 211, 212, 215–21, 572, 576, 789–91; Pompey's settlement 221, 228; M. Antonius' operations against pirates 249; Cn. Piso's command (65) 342; Caesar's campaign in west 365–6, 440, 443, 793; Pompey's command 398–9, 413, 419; Caesar's war against Pompeians 425, 430–1, 435, 436, 437, 443, 460, 461, 478, 797; Q. Cassius' unpopularity 435, 440; Caesar's settlement 443–4, 445; Sex. Pompeius' revival 471, 473
administration 22; agriculture 613, 614, 615, 629; citizenship grants 22, 125–6, 215, 444, 582, 592; coinage 4, 21, 632; extortion 506, 577–8, 583n; forces in Roman army 21, 38, 119, 125–6, 582, 592; Gracchi and 20–1, 22, 61, 79; inscriptions 22–3, 570, 590; law 22–3, 547, 567, 590; mines 21, 624, 625–6, 632, 635; praetors with consular *imperium* 571, 572; Roman and Italian settlers 17, 20, 22, 608, 615, 628, 638; Roman military problems 36–7, 39; Rome disavows treaties 4, 21, 61, 577; taxation 21–2, 567, 569, 586; trade with Italy 613, 615, 627, 629, 630, 639; veteran colonies 22, 568
Sparta *1 Dd*, 32, 66, 151, 282–3
Spartacus' insurrection 221–3, 605, 791
special courts, see *quaestiones extra ordinem*
specialization: labour 663; law 554, 556; religion 755–63
Spoletium (Spoleto) *3(i) Cb*, *13 Bb*, 192, 193
sponsio (legal wager) 67, 73, 526
sponsor (personal security) 543
Spurinna (astrologer) 453
Staberius Eros (grammarian) 704
Stabiae *3(ii) Cb*, 120, 125
Stata Mater, cult of 675
Statilius, L. (Catilinarian conspirator) 356
Statius (slave to Q. Cicero) 584
steel, Chalybian 135
Stertinius, L. (*praetor* 197–196) 572n, 684
Sthenis (sculptor) 697
Sthenius of Himera (Thermae) 196, 215, 592
stipendium 569, 586–7, 591–2
stipulatio (verbal contract) 543; *s. Aquiliana* 554
stock-rearing *see* animal husbandry
Stoicism 694, 703, 704, 709, 722, 726; Cicero and 721, 725, 756; and law 553, 556
Strabo (historian and geographer) 136, 238, 267, 278
Strabo *see also under* Iulius; Pompeius
Strasburger, H. 13
Stratonicea *5 Bc*, 147, 162, 781
Strato's Tower (Caesarea) *10 Ab*, 294, 296
strictum ius 543, 550
Struggle of the Orders 41, 46–7, 745
stuprum 502n
succession, law of 535, 536, 538–40, 545, 555–6, 558; to *ager publicus* 63; intestacy 538, 539, 557, 562
Suessa *3(ii) Ab*, 190, 388, 624
Suetonius Tranquillus, C. 425, 438, 446, 454, 457, 464
Sugambri *12 Ba*, 406
Sulla *see under* Cornelius
Sulpicius, P. (*trib.* 89) 9, 166, 788; and distribution of new citizens through all tribes 167–9, 182, 337, 788; and Sulla's command against Mithridates 168, 169, 170, 574, 788; death 171
Sulpicius Galba, P. (*cos.* 211) 565
Sulpicius Galba, Ser. (*cos.* 144) 43, 507, 577
Sulpicius Galba, Ser. (Caesar's legate) 393, 419
Sulpicius Rufus, Ser. (*cos.* 51) 795; political career 353, 376, 413, 415, 429, 440–1, 455, 480; jurist 554–5, 556, 563, 635, 727; and philosophy 727n
sumptuary laws 59, 60, 331, 548, 640; *see also* law (*leges* (Didia; Fannia; Iulia; Licinia; Orchia))
supplicationes, *see* thanksgivings
supply, military 613, 615; from Asia 73, 442; in Civil War 442; in Mithridatic Wars 153, 154, 155; in Numantine campaign 73; Numidians supply in Sardinia 28, 76, 77; profits from 54; in provinces 569, 576; *publicani* and 584, 636; textiles 625
Surenas (Parthian general) 402, 403
sureties, law on 548
Surrentum (Sorrento) *3(ii) Bb*, 120
Sybaris 682
Syme, Sir Ronald 13
synhedria (Jewish regional councils) 273

Syracuse *1 Cd*, *2 Be*, *13 Be*, *14 Bb*, 25, 634

Syria *1 Fd*, *9 Cc-Dc*, *14 Cb*; 3rd–2nd-cent. relations with Pontus 131, 132; under Demetrius I 17, 262; wars against Parthia 260, 262; Mithridates of Pontus approaches 143; supports Rome in First Mithridatic War 153; and Peace of Apamea 229; Armenian occupation of northern 238, 259, 263; under Antiochus XIII Philadelphos 241; Antiochus' rivalry with Philip II 259; Pompey's annexation 259–60, 264–5, 266, 270, 274, 391; allocation to M. Piso and Clodius 363, (revoked) 364; Gabinius' command 271, 272–3, 384, 391, 395, 574; Crassus' command 398–9, 400, 402–3; Bibulus allocated 417; Parthian invasions (51) 417, 419, 420, 596, (45) 478, 797; Caecilius Bassus in 437, 473; Dolabella's command 474; Cassius establishes power in 481–2

coinage 395, 632; and Jews 274–5, 283, 289, 290; Seleucid insecurity 17, 36, 275, 282, 290; *see also individual rulers*

Tabae *5 Bb*, 147, 162

tabellarii (couriers) 585

tabernae 658, 659–66, 667, 668, 669

Tables, Twelve 532; on capital jurisdiction 45; on constitution 41, 502; on delict 543, 544; drawn up by *Xviri* 199; Greek influence 549; and magic 760; on marriage 537; on testation 538

Tabulae: Bantina 96, 98, 749n; Bembina 5, 63, 75, 508–10; Contrebensis 22–3, 547, 550, 560, 561; Heracleana 451, 455, 456n, 560, 602n; Irnitana 547n, 560

Tacitus 10, 240, 488, 657, 692, 776

Talaura 244, 258

Talmudic literature 280, 299, 305, 306, 307

Tarcondimontus, dynast of Amanus 269

Tarentum (Taranto) *1 Dc*, *2 Cc*, *3(ii) Eb*, *13 Cc*, 78, 630; bronze inscription of law 51–2, 94, 98

Tarpeian Rock 179

Tarraco *8 Cb*, *14 Ab*, 219, 445, 591

Tarsus *1 Fd*, *5 Dc*, 135

Tauri *1 Eb-Fb*, *4 Ba*, 139

Taurisci *1 Cb*, 381

Tauromenium (Taormina) *2 Bd*, 26

taxation: on agriculture 622; assemblies' role 45; Caesar's, in Italy 452–3, 457, 488; Cicero on direct 457, 488; on columns 457; in corn 569, 586, 587, 613, 638, 639; Curio proposes, on slave-owners 418; in east 251, 269–70, 273, 586, (*see also under* Asia); in Egypt 399; farming of 22, 35, 54, 79, 90, 91, 251, (*see also* publicani); Greece 32; Italian allies 104, 107; on land 609; Massilia 24; metals for coinage acquired by 639; *pactiones* 270; provincial 32, 34–5, 567, 569, 576, 585–9, 639–40; *see also* customs dues; *stipendium*; *vectigal*; *and under* Asia; Sicily; Spain

Taylor, L.R. 13

Teanum Sidicinum *3(ii) Ab*, *13 Bc*, 121, 189, 450n

technology: Archimedean screw 21; metal-working 625; mining 625; olive- or grape-press 56, 612; siege engines 150, 153, 154

Tectosagi 269

Telesinus 194, 195

Telmessus *5 Bc*, 147, 149

temples: art displayed in 686; dedicated to Rome, in east 766; foundation and repair in Rome 736–8; founded by *evocatio* 744; Italian allies' 106; public use 686; shrines distinguished from 758; *see also under individual places and* Jews

templum (consecrated space) 731

tenants' rights to property 540, 558

Tenedos *9 Bb*; naval battle of 237

Tenney, Frank 54

Terence (P. Terentius Afer) 455, 532, 561, 565, 736

Terentius Varro, M.: education 690n; Pompey's legate 702; in Civil War 430, 431, 443; and Caesar's plans for public library 454, 692–3, 701

and Atticus 696; chronology 714; and Cicero 696, 701, 703n, 706, 719; on Ennius 700; estates 618; and philosophy 704, 707, 708, 719, 725, 727n; and Pompey 224, 228, 695n, 702; on religion 706, 735; systematic methods 701, 702, 705, 719, 727, 758; on *IIIviri capitales* 500; villa at Tusculum 694

WRITINGS: *Antiquitates* 702n, 706, 719, 726–7, 758; autobiography 713; *Disciplianae* 705; *Hebdomades* 706–7, 713; *De Lingua Latina* 703–5; *Menippean Satires* 330, 710, 719; *De Philosophia* 702, 719; *De Re Rustica* 55, 609, 610, 662, 699n, 701, 702–3, (on contracts) 532, 554, 560, 620; on senatorial procedure 224, 702; *Tricaranus* (satire) 695n

Terentius Varro Lucullus, M. (*cos.* 73; *formerly* M. Licinius Lucullus) 791; in Sullan period 194; *praetor peregrinus* 210, 562; consulship 214; and Spartacus' rebellion 222, 223; trial and acquittal 341; and trial of C. Cornelius 343; and trial of Clodius 361

Tergeste (Trieste) *13 Ba*, 412

Termessus *5 Bc*, 147

termini (boundary stones) 73

tesserae nummulariae 633

Teutones 24, 95, 96, 730, 785

textile industry 65, 625
thanksgivings (*supplicationes*), Caesar's 390–1, 400, 412, 459, 461,794, 795, 797
Thapsus *13 Ae*, *14 Bb*, 436, 797
Thasos *9 Ab*, 638
Theadelphia *11 Aa*, 325, 326
theatres 737, 774, 783; Lex Roscia theatralis 332, 352, 792; *see also under* Rome
Thebaid, Egypt *11 Ab-Bb*, 313, 316–17, 318, 322, 325
Thebes, Greece *6 Bb*, 32, 153, 157
theft 543, 549
Themiscyra, plain of 136
Theodorus, ruler of Amathus 294, 296
Theodosia *4 Ba*, *9 Ca*, 254
Theophanes of Mytilene 697
Theophrastus 693, 715
Theopompus (friend of Caesar) 442
Thespiae *6 Bb*, 151
Thessalonica *1 Dc*, *14 Bb*, 31, 432, 638
Thessaly *1 Dd*, *9 Ab*, 17, 33; grain 58, 60, 153; in First Mithridatic War 153, 155, 158; in Civil War 441
Thoranius, C. (Varinius' quaestor) 221
Thorius, Sp. (*trib.*) 63
Thorius Balbus, L. 217
Thracians *1 Dc-Ec*, *14 Ba*, 129, 133, 297; Roman campaigns 32, 36, 37, 97, 149, 730
Thuburnica *2 Ae*, 30
Thucydides 9, 48
Thugga *2 Ae*, 28
thunder as omen 99, 344, 474, 729, 758
Thurii *2 Cd*, *3(ii) Ec*, 222
Thurium, Mt *6 Aa*, 155
Tibareni *9 Db*, 238, 265
Tiberius, Emperor 655
Tibur (Tivoli) *3(i) Cc*, *7 Bb*, *13 Bc*, 174, 478
Tifata, Mount 189
Tigranes I, 'The Great', king of Armenia Maior *see under* Armenia
Tigranes the younger, prince of Armenia 385
Tigranocerta *9 Dc*, 240, 241, 246, 253, 266, 792
Tigurini 93, 384
Timagenes of Alexandria 278
timber resources 135–6, 153, 610, 616, 625
tin, British 637
Tinteris 323
Tisaeum 154
tithes, agricultural: Asia 584, 586; Sicily 569, 586, 587, 639
Titius, Sex. (*trib.* 99) 101–2, 519n
title, legal (ownership) 540
Tium *4 Ab*, *5 Ca*, 131, 133
toga picta 358
Tolenus, river *3(i) Dc*; battle of 121
Tolistobogii 269
Tolosa (Toulouse) *1 Bc*; gold of 24, 93, 99, 785
tombs: Italian 457, 665, 667, 668, (Eurysaces') 665, (Geganius Clesippus') 656, (Sulla's) 207; Near Eastern 298; Pontic royal 136
Tomisa *9 Dc*, 240, 244, 265
Torah 275, 279
Torquatus *see under* Manlius
tort *see* delict
Tosefta 280
Toynbee, A. 54
traction animals 612, 615, 628
trade: Delos as centre 20, 615, 620; effect of Roman conquest of Mediterranean 608, 637–40, 770; exports from Italy 639–40; freedmen conduct in colonies 447; retail 59, 658, 659–66, 667; and taxation 22, 587–8; pirates endanger 249; *see also individual commodities and under individual countries*
tradition, see *mos maiorum*
traiecticia pecunia (bottomry) 635
Trajan, Emperor 22
Tralles *5 Ab*, *9 Bc*, 148, 159, 248
transhumance 56, 615–16
transit-dues *see* customs dues
translation into Latin: from Greek 699, 700, 706, 708, 724, 757; of Mago's agricultural writings 54
transport 612, 625, 626; *see also* roads; shipping; traction
transvectio equitum (review of cavalry) 225
Trapezus *4 Cb*, *5 Ea*, *9 Db*, 131, 135, 136
treason 96, 457, 502; see also *maiestas*; *perduellio*
treasure: Egyptian royal 147, 315–16; of Delos 151; of Numa 148; Roman seizure in east 154, 251, 258, 269; of Tolosa 24, 93, 99, 785
treaties, Roman: assemblies' role 45; Italian allies' 64, 104, 114; with Jugurtha 29; Pompey empowered to make 250; Roman disavowal 4, 21, 29, 61; Sicilian 25; states with (*civitates foederatae*) 591; *see also under* Latins
Trebatius (Samnite leader) 125
Trebatius Testa, C. (jurist) 455, 554, 727n
Trebellius, L. (*trib.* 67) 334
Trebonius, C. (equestrian officer in Caesar's army in Gaul) 406
Trebonius, C. (*cos. suff.* 45) 398, 406, 430, 465, 481, 797
Tremellius Scrofa, Cn. 223
trenches, 'royal' or 'Phoenician' 27, 28
Treveri *12 Ba*, 384, 416
Triarius *see under* Valerius
tribal assembly, see *comitia tributa*
tribes: in assemblies 44; Augustus' organization 680; Italian allies' inclusion 645, (in minority) 123, 127, 165, 172, (proposals for distribution throughout all

tribes) 167–9, 172, 175, 180, 182–3, 185, 337, 788, (Senate approves) 186, 190, 203, 789, (*see also* freedmen (voting rights)); and political influence 51; *sodalitates* organized on basis of 517

tribunate of plebs: successes (146–134) 59, 60; public demonstration at funeral of popular tribune (138) 60, 65; Ti. Gracchus' tribunate *see under* Gracchus; Octavius' deposition 66–7, 69; Ti. Gracchus' attempt at re-election, death 68–9, 72; Carbo's proposal for unlimited re-election fails 68, 75; C. Gracchus' tribunate 77–86, 781–2; Marius' tribunate 86, 91, 783; *populares* tribunes and Jugurthine War 88–9; attacks on aristocracy (107–100) 92–103; Glaucia's and Saturninus' tribunates *see* Appuleius Saturninus, L.; Servilius Glaucia, C.; L. Equitius' tribunate 101; M. Livius Drusus and allied question 111–13; Sulpicius' tribunate, *see* Sulpicius, P.; Sulla curtails powers 170, 172, 201, 329–30, 497, 503, 772, 789; issue of power (77–71) 208, 210–11, 213–14, 215, 336, 790, 791; Pompey and Crassus restore powers 214, 224–5, 227, 228, 330, 338, 791; triumvirs' exploitation of 227, 228; exercise of restored power 329–38; Gabinius' tribunate 244, 249, 332–5, 574, 792; oppose severe bribery law 346; Rullan bill 349–51; repeal of Sullan legislation (63) 352–3; and return of Pompey 358–9; and Lex Iulia agraria 369, 371; Clodius' 372–3, 376, 377–81, 794; and Cicero's return 384, 387, 389; preside over *ludi Apollinares* (53) 404; law of ten tribunes (52) 412, 416, 795; Caesar and 91, 201, 227, 425, 427, 430, 462, 574

bound by people's will 67, 334; Cicero on 343–4, 346, 489; convening of Senate 43, 47; establishment 41; ex-tribunes admitted to Senate 46; intervention in private actions 545; legislation 41, 201, 329–30; moral initiative lost in 60s 343, 367; prosecution, right of 41, 329, 330n, 502; readiness to adopt popular role 676; re-election 68, 75, 82; sacrosanctity 41, 67, 748; tribunes divided against each other 333, 334; veto 29, 41, 201; violence 103, 168–9, 334, 343

tribuni aerarii 46; and equestrian order 90, 509; on juries 225–6, 332, 458, 527

tribute 22, 24, 31, 32, 35, 107, 269, 270

tributum (tax) 488

trientabula (form of *ager publicus*) 54

triumphs 781–98 *passim*; banquets 685–6; donatives to soldiers 92; religious aspects 750, 751, 752; triumphal dress 358, 463, 752

triumvirs: First Triumvirate (60) 366, 367, 793; Second Triumvirate (43) 486; *IIIviri agris iudicandis adsignandis* 67–8; *IIIviri capitales* 500–1, 528

trivium (mediaeval education) 705

Trocmi 269

Trophonius, oracle at Lebadea 189

trophies: Caesar's and Mithridates', at Zela 434; Pompey's, in Pyrenees 221

trust of inheritance 539

Tryphon, Diodotus (pretender to Seleucid throne) 282, 283, 288

Tubero, Q. 53, 685

Tubulus, L. (*praetor* 142) 521, 523

Tuder *3(i) Cb*, 193

Tulingi 384

Tullius (Cicero's *scriba*) 581

Tullius, L. (Cicero's legate) 581

Tullius Albinovanus, M. 529

Tullius Cicero, M. (*cos.* 63): education 714, 716; in Social War 124; quaestor at Lilybaeum 593; exposure of Verres 225–6, 227, 327, 330n, 337; praetorship 337; popularity in Rome 337; supports Lex Manilia 339, 348, 364, 490; prosecutes C. Licinius Macer 340; and proposed prosecution of Faustus Sulla 341; defence of Manilius 342, 343; defends C. Cornelius 343–4, 346, 348; and Catiline's trial 345; opposes proposals to annexe Egypt 319, 346; move towards Senate 346; consulship 348–9, 350–1, 352, 353, 793; defeats *Rogatio Servilia* 319, 350–1; defends C. Piso 351; enables Lucullus to hold triumph 351; defends Rabirius 352, 357; Lex Tullia de ambitu 353; defends Murena 355–6; and Catilinarian conspiracy 354, 355, 356, 357–8, 729; unpopular for execution of conspirators 357–8, 364, 372, 495; and Pompey's return 358, 361, 362, 364, 365; and Clodius' trial for sacrilege 363; and Flavius' land bill 365; declines invitation to join First Triumvirate 367; and Lex Iulia agraria 368, 371; loses Pompey's protection 372, 381; Clodius' attacks on 372; under Caesar's consulship 373, 374, 375; and Vettius' allegations 375; Clodius attacks 375, 376–7, 380–1, 491, 747–8, 749; defends Flaccus 377; exile 100, 381, 383, 748; recall 385–6, 387, 388–9, 391, 394; and corn crisis 389, 390; and restoration of Ptolemy Auletes 392, 491; defends P. Asicius 392; defends Milo (56) 393; and distribution of *ager Campanus* 393, 394; transfers allegiance to Caesar 394–5; supports triumvirs 401, 491–2; and Gabinius' trials 273, 401, 402; and Curio's games 404; writings (56–53) 404; defends Caelius and Sestius 529; agrees

Tullius Cicero, M. (*cont.*)
to control Caelius for Caesar 408; defends Milo (52) 411; augurship 411–12; approves Pompey's consulship 414; Caesar binds to him by loan 416; governor of Cilicia 417, 420, 422, 547, 576, 581, 590, 593, (finance) 269, 270, (and highland tribes) 265, 266, 269, 596; and breach between Caesar and Pompey 420–1, 427, 428, 429, 432; on siege of Massilia 430; with Pompey on Pharsalus campaign 432, 433; under Caesar's dictatorship 447, 451, 455, 460, 461–2, 464, 465–6; death of daughter 460, 718; in aftermath of Caesar's death 468, 469, 470, 471, 476, 477, 479, 481, 482, 485, (and Octavian) 472, 477, 478, 479, 485, 487–8, (enmity towards Antony) 468–9, 477, 479, 480, 482, 483; proscription and death 486–7, 701, 788
and astronomy 718; and Atticus 696, 714; and Balbus 444, 451; and Caelius 408, 414, 416–17, 420, 479, 529, 593, 594; and Caesar (rejects help against Clodius) 375, 381, (Caesar and Cicero's return from exile) 387, 391, (in period of triumvirate) 394–5, 408, 416, 420, 439, (and Caesar's dictatorship) 447, 448, 455, 457, 458, 460, 461–2, 464–5, 465–6, 466–7, (intellectual contacts) 461, 695, 696, 713; on causes of decline of Republic 489–90; and Clodius 372, 375, 376–7, 380–1, 491, 679–80, 747–8, 749; conservatism 53, 420, 491; on education 690, 692; Greek language 698, 699, 720; historiography 711–12, 713–14; houses 363–4, 694; and Latin language 691, 692, 699, 700, 704, 715, 718, 719; libraries 693–4; on obligation to state 467, 477; on oratory 700, 715, 717; patronage of provincials 592–3; philosophy 696, 707, 708, 718–28, 756, (eclecticism) 721–2, 727, (education in) 714, 716, (and conduct) 727; and Posidonius 712–13; prejudices against plebs 647; on provincial government 585, 595, 596–7; and Q. Cicero 581, 584, 585, 595; and religion 730, 735, 737, 747–8, 749, 760; Republican allegiance 346, 367, 404, 422, 423, 461–2, 479, 487, 489–90, 701, 727; role in final stages of Republic 479, 487, 488, 489–90; and Senate's authority 49, 337, 346, 353, 377, 477, 479, 487, 489, 727; senatorial establishment excludes 348–9, 366, 375, 394–5; and tribunate 343–4, 346; urbanity 695; and Varro 696, 701, 703n, 706, 719
WRITINGS 2–3, 715–21; *Academica* 696, 719, 720, 723–4; *De Amicitia* 477; *Brutus* 93, 505, 696, 700, 714, 715, 716, 717; *Pro Caelio* 524, 529; *Cato* 366, 460, 461, 695, 696, 713; *Pro Cluentio* 214, 234, 523, 529; *Commentarii* 712–13; *De Consiliis Suis* 712; *Consolation* 720; *De Consulatu Suo* 699, 712n; *Pro Cornelio* 343–4, 346, 348; correspondence 2, 51, (with Atticus) 487, (with D. Brutus) 487, (with M. Brutus) 487–8; *De Divinatione* 708–9, 756–7; *De Domo* 501; *De Finibus* 719, 720; *Pro Flacco* 130; *De Haruspicum Responsio* 749; *Invective against Sallust* (attr.) 709n; *de Inventione* 692; *Pro Lege Manilia* 130, 251, 339, 348, 364, 490, 587, 588, 595; *De Legibus* 404, 479, 489, 502, 717–18, 727; *Pro Murena* 130, 254–5; *De Natura Deorum* 719; *De Officiis* 477, 489, 719, 720; *Orator* 717; *De Oratore* 700, 712, 714, 715, 716–17, 727; *Philippics* 487, 488, (*First*) 477, (*Second*) 473–4, 477, (*Third*) 479, (*Seventh*) 480, (*Twelfth*) 190, 491, (*Thirteenth*) 482; *In Pisonem* 476; poetry 724; *De Republica* 37, 75, 479, 489, 696, 715, 717–18, 720, 727; *Pro Roscio Amerino* 522, 523; *Pro Sestio* 529; *Topica* 694; translations from Greek 700, 706, 708, 724; *In Vatinium* 709; *Verrines* 494, 586

Tullius Cicero, M. (junior) 690, 692
Tullius Cicero, Q. (*praetor* 62): education 690; pleads against M. Cicero's exile 387; in Sicily 394; in Gallic War 401, 406; in Cilicia 581; governor of Asia 584, 585, 588, 595; house 670; library 694; writings 700, 710
Tullius Cicero, Q. (junior) 476, 486, 690, 692
Tullius Decula, M. (*cos.* 81) 200, 789
tumultus, *see* emergencies
turris Lascutana 22
Tusculum *7 Bb*, 659, 661, 672, 694
tutela (guardianship) 536–7, 539, 548, 558, 561
Tyana *5 Db*, 135
Tyrannio of Amisus (grammarian) 693–4, 697
tyranny: Gracchi accused of 68, 69, 72, 84; *see also* kingship
Tyre *9 Cd, 14 Cb*, 286, 294, 630

Uchi Maius *2 Ae*, 30
Ulubrae *3(ii) Aa*, 656
Umbrenus, P. (Gallic businessman) 356
Umbria *2 Bb*; and Livius Drusus' laws 112–13; in Social War 115, 122, 123, 124; Sulla's treatment of 203; agriculture 610; society 113
upper classes: building activities 626, 641; competitive nature 6, 8, 329, 697; commercial activities 329, 599, 634, 635, 637, 642–3, 662–3, 664, 669–70; *dignitas* 467; early Republic 41; family traditions 46–7; Gracchan reforms and 75, 80; Greek culture 697; ideology of 49; investment in land 106–7, 328–9, 618, 637, 642, 770;

intellectual interests, depth of 725–8; Italian 89, 104, 105, 106–7, 109, 328, 453, 692, (Etruscan and Umbrian) 113, 453; judicial dominance 80, 529; losses in Civil War 457; manipulation of assemblies 45; and urban plebs 675, 679; wealth, and political influence 59; *see also* display; glory; obligation; *optimates*; Senate; *and under* debt
Urbana *3(ii) Ac*, 204, 655
urbana provincia (Rome) 565
urbanization 127, 451, 600, 607; and building construction industry 626; and decline of smallholders 619; debt causes 641; and food supply 613
urbanum otium (leisure) 681
Urso (Colonia Genetiva Urbanorum, *mod.* Osuna) *8 Bc*, *14 Ab*, 445, 447, 655, 765–6
usucapio (acquisition by possession) 540, 548, 549–50, 551
usufruct (property right) 541, 551, 561
usury 330, 634–5, 641; loans abroad 333, 347, 355, 636, 639
Utica *2 Ae*, *13 Ae*, *14 Bb*, 27, 191, 436, 440, 638
Uxama *8 Ba*, 220
Uxellodunum *12 Ab*, 415, 416, 795

Vaccaei *1 Ac*, *8 Ba*, 21, 398, 577
Val di Diano *3(ii) Db*, 610; inscription 27, 73–4
Valentia *8 Cb*, 22, 218, 220
Valeria (Sulla's wife) 206
Valerius (officer of Ostia garrison) 176
Valerius Antias (annalist) 712
Valerius Catullus, C. (poet) 582–3, 695n, 710, 760
Valerius Flaccus, C. (*flamen Dialis* 209) 731n
Valerius Flaccus, C. (brother of *cos. suff.* 86) 22–3, 184
Valerius Flaccus, L. (*cos.* 100) 97, 181, 183, 199, 786, 789
Valerius Flaccus, L. (*cos. suff.* 86) 157, 160, 180, 181, 788
Valerius Flaccus, L. (*praetor* 63) 377
Valerius Maximus (historian) 532
Valerius Messalla Niger, M. (*cos.* 61) 361, 362, 793, 794; *interrex* (53) 405, 795
Valerius Triarius, C. (Lucullus' legate) 236, 237, 243, 245
Vargunteius, L. (Catilinarian) 340, 354, 355, 356, 360
Varii brothers (Roman slave-owners in Sicily) 26
Varinius, P. (*praetor* 73) 221
Varius Hybrida, Q. (*trib.* 90) 22, 114, 115, 513n
Varro *see under* Terentius
Varus *see under* Alfenus; Attius
vasarium (provincial governor's fund) 583
Vatinius, P. (*cos.* 46): and Lex Iulia agraria 369, 371; and Pomptinus' thanksgiving 372; Lex Vatinia 374; Caesar's legate 374; Cicero attacks 393, 709, 760; praetorship 397
vectigal (tax) 569, 636; *v. aedilicium* 588
Veii *7 Aa*, *13 Bc*, 450, 743
Velia *1 Cd*, *2 Bc*, *3(ii) Cc*, 20
Velleius Paterculus, C. 118, 123, 150, 201, 606
Venafrum *3(ii) Ba*, *13 Bc*, 120, 624
veneficii, *quaestio de venefiis* 504, 511, 520–1; *quaestio de sicariis et veneficiis* 526
Veneti *2 Aa-Ba*, *12 Ab*, 109, 394, 794
Ventidius, P., in Social War 120–1
Ventidius Bassus, P. (*cos. suff.* 43) 452, 484, 488, 798
Venus, cult of 752–4; Caesar and 442, 445n, 453–4, 465, 753–4
Venusia *2 Cc*, *3(ii) Db*, *13 Cc*, 115, 121, 125
Veranius; on religious rites 758
Vercellae *2 Aa*, 96, 785
Vercingetorix, chief of Arverni 409–12, 436, 795
Vergilius *or* Verginius, M. (*trib.* 87) 173–4
Verres, C. (*praetor* 74): joins Sulla 187; urban praetorship 335, 736; governor of Sicily 214, 222, 318, 791, (finance) 580–1, 583, 585, 588, (jurisdiction) 494, 534, 547, 582, 589, (*scriba*) 581–2; prosecution 214–15, 225–7, 327, 330n, 337, 577, 592, 594, 791; in Massilia, proscribed 578
Vesontio (Besançon) *12 Bb*, 385, 386
Vespasian, Emperor 299–300
Vestal Virgins 198, 361, 731; unchastity 86, 730, 733, 747, 783
Vestini *3(i) Dc-Ec*, 115, 124
Vesuvius, Mount *3(ii) Bc*, 221
veterans 621, 771; 2nd-cent. colonies 20, 22, 25, 446, 568; Marius' colonies 30, 92, 95, 98, 99, 100, 109–10, 344, 785; Saturninus' settlement 30, 95, 98–9, 102, 109–10, 446, 786; distress of smallholders, 60s 346–7; Sullan colonies 203–4, 204–5, 208, 347, 450, 524–5, 601, 626, 655; settlement of Pompey's 227, 350, 364, 365, 366, 369, 371; Lex Iulia agraria and 369, 371; Caesar's colonies 445, 449–50, 473–4, 489, 655; reaction to Caesar's death 468, 469, 470; support courted in war 470, 471, 473–4, 475, 476, 478, 771; settlement by Second Triumvirate 486; executions at Forum Gallorum 488
Vettius (Roman slave-owner in Sicily) 26
Vettius, L. (informer) 375, 376

Vettius Scato, P. (praetor of Paeligni) 120, 121, 124, 787
Veturius Calvinus, Ti. (*cos.* 321) 61
viae, *see under* roads
Vibius Pansa Caetronianus, C. (*cos.* 43) 441n, 474; consulship 479, 480, 481, 482, 798; death 483, 488
Vibo *13 Cd*, 449
vicus (administrative unit) 648, 672, 673–6, 748
Vidacilius, C. (Asculan commander) 120–1, 124, 125
villas 331, 333, 626, 694–5; estates 56, 611, 615n, 616, 619, 620
violence, public 14, 770; Catulus' law 208; Cicero on escalation 679–80; over corn crisis 389, 390, 736; and elections 336, 346, 772; and freedmen's associations 346, 672; gangs 522–3, 524, 405; legitimate self-help 525, 772; politicians incite 675–6, 771–2; religious rules inadequate to cope with 739–40; tribunes' use 85, 101, 103, 142, 168–9, 333, 334, 343, 385, 386, 390, 405; Saturninus' use 85, 101, 103, 142; see also *vis*
Virgil 595, 609; pseudo-, *Moretum* 611
Viriathus (Spanish leader) 21, 22, 37, 61
Viromandui *12 Ba*, 388
vis (force): constitutional offences 492–3; interdiction as penalty 513n, 797; in Italy 527–8; Lex Plautia 522; *maiestatis* 518; M. Lucullus' edict (70) 790; private prosecutions 524–5, 528; *quaestio de vi* 355, 360, 456, 524–5, 526, (Pompey's special court of 52) 409, 410, 501n, 516, 529; self-help 525, 772
Vitruvius Pollio 609, 705
Vocontii *12 Bb-c*, 24
Volaterrae (Volterra) *2 Ab*, *3(i) Aa*, *Ab*, 195, 204, 450, 634, 790
Volcacius Tullus, L. (*cos.* 66) 337, 340, 392, 429, 792
Volturcius, T., of Croton 356
Volturnus, river *3(ii) Bb*, 121, 189
votive offerings 732

Wadi Qelt, Hasmonean winter palace 298
wager, legal (*sponsio*) 67, 73, 526
war and warfare: citizenship granted on battlefield 109, 125–6, 582, 592; civil 10, 12, 14, 600; demographic effect 606; finance 488, 600; magistrates' leadership 43; power of declaring 45, 250; and religion 729–30, 731, 743–4, 764; wealth from 54, 55–6, 632; *see also* army; fleet; interest; reparations; slaves (captives) *and individual wars*
War, Alexandrian (48) 321, 433–4, 693, 796
war, civil (80s) 7, 9–10, 126, 187–97, 788–9; effect on war against Mithridates 119, 148, 161
War, Civil (49–43) 424–38; Caesar's march on Rome 424–5, 427, 796; Pompey and consuls leave Italy 427, 796; negotiations between Caesar and Pompey 427–9; Caesar in Rome 425, 429–30; siege of Massilia 430, 431; campaigns in Spain 425, 430–1, 796; mutiny in Cisalpine Gaul 431; Caesar's dictatorship and election as consul 431–2, 796; naval engagements in Adriatic 432; campaign in east, Caesar's victory at Pharsalus 321, 433, 435, 442, 459, 796; campaigns in Egypt 433–4; Caesar defeats Pharnaces at Zela 434; disorder in Rome and Campania 435; campaigns in Africa 431, 435–6, 442, 452–3, 796–7; Caesar in Rome for triumphs 436–7; campaign in Spain 437, 460, 461; Caecilius Bassus' outbreak in Syria 437; wars after murder of Caesar 8, 468–90
  armies (bounties) 478, 480, 483, 484, 485, 486, 488, 489, (growth and political power) 486, (land allocations) 470, 471, 473–4, 475, 476, 478, 617, 621, 623, 771
War, Jugurthine 29–31, 39, 95, 140, 784–5; defence of Cirta 108, 783; Marius' involvement 30, 35, 36, 91–2, 95, 166, 573–4, 784, 785; Metellus and 89, 95, 573–4; political crisis at Rome 29, 87, 88–9, 784; Roman tactics 30, 31, 36, 37, 39
War, Social 104–28, 600, 771, 787–8; events leading up to 104–15; outbreak 115, 787; rebel organization 118–19; rebel and Roman forces 119–20, 121; campaigns 120–6, 165; settlement after 123–4, 126–8, 165; trials under Lex Varia for incitement 114–15, 120, 165, 167, 519, 787
  effect on Mithridatic War 143, 144, 148; number of dead 606; Roman financial crisis after 172; Sisenna's history 711; unifies interests of senatorial and equestrian orders 226
War, Third Macedonian 36
warehouses 626, 629, 643
Wars, Gallic 794–5; Caesar gathers forces 383–4; campaigns (58–57) 383, 384–5, 386, 387–8, 390, 391, 794; campaigns (56) 393, 394, (P. Crassus' in Aquitania) 397, 398, 794; Cicero prevents Caesar's supersession 394–5; Caesar's command renewed for five years 398–9, 794; German campaigns 399, 400, 794; British campaigns 399, 400–1, 794–5; setbacks (54–53) 402, 404, 405–6, 795; revolt under Vercingetorix 409–12, 795; final campaigns (51–50) 414, 415, 416, 795; Caesar's public works funded by booty 453

Wars, Mithridatic
First: outbreak 139, 144, 788; Mithridates' conquest of Asia 144–9, 172, 788; Sulla secures command 166, 167, 168, 169, 170, 574, 788; siege of Rhodes 149–50, 788; extends into Greece 149, 150–1, 788; Sulla takes up command 173, 174, 788; sieges of Athens and Piraeus 153–4, 721, 788; battles in Boeotia 154–9, 236, 788; reaction against Mithridates in Asia 159–61; Flaccus appointed to supersede Sulla, murdered and replaced by Fimbria 157, 160, 181, 788; Fimbria blockades Mithridates in Pitane 160, 181–2, 788; Treaty of Dardanus 158, 160–1, 163, 181–2, 229, 788; settlement of Asia (85–84) 162–3, 246, 788; Sulla as victor 163–4, 200; effect of Roman domestic wars 122, 143, 144, 148, 219; Greek migration to Rome 697
Second 136, 163, 212, 229, 232, 789
Third 233–70, 791–3: campaigns in Bithynia 233–6; Roman naval victories 236; campaigns in Pontus 236, 237–9, 244–6, 791; Mithridates held by Tigranes 238, 239, 791; Roman invasion of Armenia 239–44, 266, 328, 792; Mithridates assistance to Tigranes 135, 241; Lucullus' contact with Parthia 240, 241–2, 243, 252, 263; Lucullus' withdrawal from Armenia 243–4; Lucullus' settlement of Asia 246–8, 791; Lucullus replaced 244, 248, 250, 251, 331, 332–3, 339, 341, 792; Mithridates recovers whole of Pontus 244, 249, 792; Tigranes enters Cappadocia 244, 792; Acilius Glabrio's command 244, 249, 250, 332–3, 336, 338, 574; Pompey's command *see under* Pompeius Magnus, Cn.; Mithridates' withdrawal, deposition and death 252–3, 254–5, 261–2, 792, 793; Pompey's settlement 253, 258–9, 261, 262, 264–5, 265–70, 391, 588, 793; Greek migration to Rome 697; plunder 331
Wars, Punic, First 729–30; Second 20, 23, 25, 37, 38, 54, 55, 730; Third 132, 619
water supply 626, 650, 670–1, 673n
wealth: agricultural investment 54, 56, 60, 106–7, 328–9, 618, 637, 642, 770; Asia 247–8; blamed for decline of Republic 7, 8–9, 769; Caesar and 440, 456–7, 458; of empire 54, 55–6, 332, 770, 773; and political power 43–4, 49, 59, 80, 89; /poverty nexus 7, 8–9, 26, 27; women's 540
weaponry *see* arms; siege engines
weaving 625
widows 541
wills: bequests of kingdoms to Rome *see under* Bithynia; Cyprus; Cyrene; Egypt; Pergamum; Caesar's 454, 466, 470, 471–2, 486, 687; law 525, 538–9, 539–40, 548, 550, 563, (on contested) 539, 545, 563
wine production and trade 600, 611, 612, 620, 658; Campania 615; consumption 611, 614, 664, 665; Gaul 615; grape-presses 56, 612; Greek 614, 638; Italian exports 56, 614–15, 627, 629, 637, 638–9; seasonal labour 664; Spain 615
women: education 691; in *collegia* 660, 672; marriage 537; and *patria potestas* 537; succession 538, 539–40; *tutela* 536–7, 539; wealth 540
wool production 615, 623, 625, 658
workforce 625, 663; *see also* slaves
workshops *see officinae*
wrecks 56, 625, 629

xenophobia, Roman 104, 168, 652–3, 653–4; *see also* expulsions from Rome
Xenophon, *Anabasis* 135

Zacynthus *9 Ac*, 157
Zadok (Jewish priest), line of 299, 305
Zarbenios of Gordyene 239, 241
Zariadris (Armenian general) 238
Zela *5 Db*, *9 Cb*, *14 Cb*, 135, 137, 267; battles of (67) 243, 249, 250, 792, (47) 434, 442, 796
Zeno Cotylas, dynast of Philadelphia 286
Zeno of Sidon 721n, 722, 723
Zenobius (Pontic general) 159
Zenocoetes (Pamphylian ruler) 232
Zenodorus (Syrian brigand) 260
Zeus Stratios, cult at Amasia 137
Zigana Pass 135
Zizos (Arab dynast) 259
Zoilus, ruler of Strato's Tower and Dor 294, 296
Zosimus (wealthy citizen of Priene) 247
Zygi 140